# Shooter's Bible

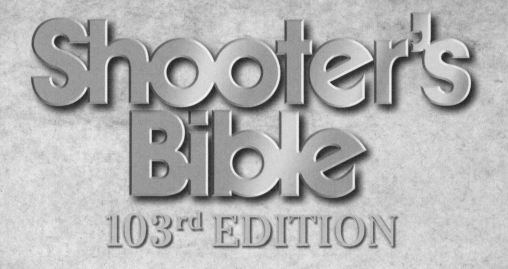

# Shooter's Bible
## 103rd EDITION

SKYHORSE PUBLISHING

Skyhorse Publishing books may be purchased in bulk at special discounts for sales promotion, corporate gifts, fundraising, or educational purposes. Special editions can also be created to specifications. For details, contact the Special Sales Department, Skyhorse Publishing, 307 West 36th Street, 11th Floor, New York, NY 10018 or info@skyhorsepublishing.com.

Skyhorse® and Skyhorse Publishing® are registered trademarks of Skyhorse Publishing, Inc.®, a Delaware corporation.

www.skyhorsepublishing.com

10 9 8 7 6 5 4 3 2

ISBN-13: 978-1-61608-367-0
ISSN: 0080-9365

Printed in Canada

# CONTENTS

# INTRODUCTION

For those of you who bought this latest edition of the *Shooter's Bible*, and who buy one every year without hesitation, we thank you for your continuing loyalty. And for those of you first-time buyers who just purchased this 103rd edition, we thank you, and welcome you to the most complete and up-to-date shooting reference book available.

The *Shooter's Bible* has a long and storied past. The first numbered edition of the *Shooter's Bible* was published in 1925; it's been published annually, and in some cases bi-annually, ever since. More than seven million copies have been sold in that time, and it continues to be the ultimate reference book for millions of people who want information on new guns, ammunition, optics, and accessories, as well as up-to-date prices and specs for thousands of firearms.

2011 marks the third year that the *Shooter's Bible* has been published by Skyhorse Publishing. With new dedicated staff members now on board, and with an extensive (and ever-growing) new database to work from, we are now able to track down every product, check every spec and price throughout the book, and make sure all of the photos are clear, precise, and correct.

In this edition, we have taken all of the new products that appeared in last year's 102nd edition and incorporated them into the main section of the book. All guns, ammunition, optics, and accessories that are no longer in production have been removed. All prices have been double-checked and updated. We have also made a serious effort to find any guns that may have inadvertently been omitted from last year's edition and added them to this new volume. If you know of any guns, optics, ammunition, or accessories that are not in this book and should be, please email us at sb@skyhorsepublishing.com and let us know.

SKYHORSE SENIOR EDITOR JAY CASSELL USED A NEW REMINGTON VERSA MAX TO TAKE THIS MERRIAM'S GOBBLER NEAR CHEYENNE, OKLAHOMA. THE MODEL HE USED CAME IN REALTREE AP, AND FEATURED A SOFT-TOUCH FINISH, SUPER-SOFT RECOIL PAD, AND EXTRA-FULL CHOKE.

This year, the 2011 New Products section covers a total of 218 guns, bullets, optics, and more. Assembled by head researcher Kristin Kulsavage, this full-color section has photos, specs, and descriptions of the latest new rifles, shotguns, handguns, muzzleloaders, bullets, shotshells, riflescopes, sights, and accessories, including new handloading equipment.

Not only that, but, as a bonus, we are running three feature-length stories that should be of interest to all. The first, "Guns 2011," takes a close and detailed look at many of the new rifles (including air rifles), shotguns, and handguns that have entered the market in the past year. As you'll see, AR-style sporting rifles are still hot, carving out a larger and larger section of the firearms pie. In shotguns, youth guns and tactical models headline the field, though innovative traditional-style shotguns (see the Remington Versa Max) continue to attract a large following. In the handgun arena, the 100th anniversary of the 1911 has seen many companies coming out with their own version of the venerable pistol. Browning even has a .22 LR version. And, as you'll see, revolvers haven't been ignored, by a long shot.

The other two features, right after the New Products sections, are by Dr. Wayne van Zwoll, a firearms expert who has written innumerable books on the subject (more on that to come).

The first feature, "One Shot Only," explores a type of rifle that many shooters avoid . . . the single shot. Van Zwoll carefully traces the history of the single shot, from the Sharps Models 1869 and 1874, a gun popular with the plains buffalo hunters, up to the modern Ruger No. 1. A solid case can also be made for the single shot, just as it can be made for using a blackpowder rifle. "There's no substitute for one well-directed bullet," the author concludes. "Carry a single-shot rifle for a season, and you may come to think of additional cartridges as simply extra weight." That's something well worth considering.

The second piece, "Fastest Bolt Rifles of All," explores the workings of some of the fastest bolt-action rifles over the years, from the Mauser 1898 to the Mannlicher-Schoenauer Model 1903, to the Blaser R93 and R8. Helpful tips on how to shoot faster with bolt actions are included.

The Skyhorse staff is justifiably proud of this completely updated and carefully fact-checked 103rd edition. And as you read through it, keep this in mind: This isn't all! Earlier this year, Skyhorse published the *Shooter's Bible Guide to Rifle Ballistics*, also by Wayne van Zwoll. A book designed for hunters and shooters who want to know more about the behavior of bullets in flight, the *Guide to Rifle Ballistics* sifts out the best loads for big game, and examines the trend toward lead-free bullets. If you want to learn not only why bullets behave like they do, but how to aim so they go where you want them to, then this book is for you.

A second *Shooter's Bible* guidebook, titled the *Shooter's Bible Guide to Cartridges*, by Todd Woodard, is designed to specifically teach gun users how to select the right cartridge for every one of their shooting needs. Written in an accessible and engaging style, the *Guide to Cartridges* is loaded with color photographs, clear and detailed diagrams, and easy-to-read charts with cartridge data. If you want to know about all things cartridge, then this is the book for you.

Yet a third guidebook also just came off the presses. Titled the *Shooter's Bible Guide to AR-15s*, by Doug Howlett, this is the most comprehensive source on AR-style guns to date. In this complete book, you can peruse the products of all AR manufacturers, learn about the evolution of the AR from its early days in the military to its adaptation for law enforcement and civilian uses, and gain important knowledge on the parts and function of the rifle. There's even a chapter on how to customize and accessorize your own AR.

Future *Shooter's Bible* guidebooks include guides to knives, sporting optics, combat handguns, and whitetail strategies. If you're a *Shooter's Bible* fan, times couldn't be better.

— **Jay Cassell**
*Senior Editor*
Skyhorse Publishing

# Shooter's Bible

# GUNS 2011

For 2011, firearms manufacturers are taking a wait-and-see attitude. No one wants to ramp up production of new models until they see solid proof that a tepid economy is beginning to pick up a little steam. As a result, most new products this year are model extensions, especially in personal defense. The one bona fide hot spot has been spurred by the 100th anniversary of John Browning's classic 1911. To cash in on this event, a number of manufacturers will be issuing commemorative models. That should generate the kind of excitement that will drive customers into your store.

## RIFLES 2011

Some years seem to have a strong theme regarding new rifle product introductions. This isn't one of years. Nonetheless, manufactures have come up with an interesting grab bag of products. The AR-style modern sporting rifle is still hot item, and this year sees a number of new models, including piston-driven operating systems. Rimfires are also prevalent, as are wallet-friendly combo rifle/scope packages. Southpaws and junior shooters haven't been ignored-a number of new products are directed specifically toward that market. Lastly, classic lever guns and calibers seem to be making a comeback as well.

## BROWNING ARMS

Browning's new offerings in their 2011 rifle line-up should appeal to two of the most overlooked shooter groups-southpaws and juniors. Southpaws will see true left-handed models in Browning's popular

X-Bolt line in the X-Bolt Medallion Left-Hand, X-Bolt Hunter Left-Hand and X-Bolt Micro Hunter Left-Hand. These new models will incorporate all the standard features of the X-Bolt line, including the Feather Trigger System, X-Lock scopemounting system, detachable rotary magazine and Inflex Technology recoil pad. The new left-hand models will be available in the most popular long-and short-action calibers. SRP: $800 to $1,040.

Smaller-framed shooters will be interested in the new Micro Midas X-Blot. This product line features a 20-inch barrel, 12.5-inch length of pull, low-luster blue finish, receivers that are drilled and tapped for optics and a satin-finished walnut stock sporting an Inflex Technology recoil pad. It will be offered in .22-250 Rem., .243 Win., 7mm-08 Rem. And .308 Win. SRP: $799.99.

Smaller-statured rimfire shooters will also want to look at the new BL-22 Micro Midas lever-action. It features a 16.25-inch barrel and a 12-inch length of pull. The walnut stock and forearm are gloss-finished and the trim little rimfire weighs 4.75 pounds. SRP: $479. **(801-876-2711; browning.com)**

## CZ-USA

A new bolt-action model, upgrades to an existing line, several new rimfire models and an upper-end air rifle highlight CZ-USA's newest rifles for 2011. CZ's newest bolt-action is the Model 557 Sporter, chambered initially in .30-06 Springfield, which has been designed to provide the same performance as the CZ 550, but at a reduced price. It retains the forged receiver, integral scope-mount dovetails and hammer-forged barrel of CZ 550, but incorporates a short extractor and plunger-style ejector. The two-position receiver-mounted safety has been upgraded to allow the bolt to be operated in the safe position. The trigger is fully user-adjustable for pull weight, creep and over-travel, but does not have the set function of the

**MICRO MIDAS X-BOLT**

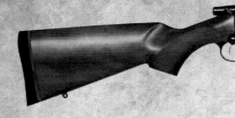

**CZ 557 SPORTER**

CZ SST trigger system. The CZ 557 sports a checkered American-patterned hardwood stock, features a 20.6-inch barrel and is finished in matte blue steel. Empty weight is 7.8 pounds.

The CZ 550 action sees the addition of two new models with American-style Kevlar stocks that incorporate a full-length bedding block. The Carbine version will be available with a 20.6-inch barrel in 9.3x62 ($1,058) and .30-06 Springfield ($999). Weight is 7 pounds. A Medium version will be available in 7mm Rem. Mag. with a 23.6-inch barrel ($1,058). It weighs 8 pounds. Both models feature back-up iron sights in addition to the integral scope-mount base system.

On the rimfire front, the CZ 512 semi-auto is an entirely new addition to the CZ line-up. It features a modular design that is easy to maintain and requires only a coin as a field-stripping tool. It is constructed with an aluminum-alloy upper receiver that secures the barrel and bolt assembly, and a fiber-glass-reinforced polymer lower half that contains the trigger mechanism and detachable magazine.

The CZ 512 shares the same magazines and scope rings as the CZ 455, and features adjustable sights in addition to the standard 11mm dovetail for optics mounting. The blue-finished CZ 512 will be available in .22LR ($449) and .22 WMR ($479).

The bolt-action CZ 455 will now be available in a switch-barrel combo set ($531), allowing shooters to shift between .22LR and .17 HMR. The necessary tools and magazines to shift between the two calibers are included.

The CZ 455 also will now be available in CZ's Lux configuration, which features a 20.6-inch barrel, adjustable iron sights and a Lux-style stock that is optimized for use with iron sights. It will be offered in .22LR ($420) and .22 WMR ($448).

Lastly, air-rifle enthusiasts will want to look at the new CZ 200 S. Caliber Combo. This high-power precision air rifle is based upon CZ's 10 Meter Olympic competition model. The increased velocity of the 200 S (up to 800 fps with its .177-caliber pellet) makes it an excellent choice for pest control, competition or training/practice. The gun features a two-stage adjustable trigger and a red laminated competition stock optimized for three-position shooting. It is shipped with a 4x32 scope (capable of parallax adjustments down to 10 yards) and rings, and adapters for filling and discharging the 2900 psi gas cylinder are included. Accessories—including diopter aperture rear iron sights, a manual pump, 5- and 10-shot magazines and spare gas cylinders—are available from CZ. SRP: $429. **(913-321-1811; cz-usa.com)**

## HECKLER & KOCH

After more than two years of development work, H&K is debuting its production version of its new gas-piston MR556A1 rifle. The new rifle is inspired and influenced by the HK416 selective-fire rifle in use by military and law-enforcement personnel, and is considered by many to be a leading candidate in a possible competition to replace the U.S. military's current M4 carbine.

**H&K MR556 A1**

According to H&K, the 5.56mm MR556A1 is a major improvement over conventional MSR rifles and carbines. It uses an H&K proprietary gas-piston operating system that employs a piston and a solid operating push rod in place of the gun tube normally found in MSR-style firearms. This operating system virtually eliminates malfunctions that are common to direct-impingement action, since hot carbon fouling and propellant gases do not enter the receiver area. This is the same feature found on the HK416.

In addition, the new MR556A1 uses many of the assemblies and accessories originally developed for the HK416. These include the H&K free-floating four-quadrant rail system that allows the use of all current accessories, sights, lights and lasers used on MSR-style rifles to be fitted to the MR556A1. The H&K rail system can be installed and removed without tools, and returns to zero when reinstalled. In addition, the MR556A1 upper receiver (which will also be available as the Upper Receiver Kit) is fully interchangeable with other quality-made MSR-style firearms. **(706-568-1906; hk-usa.com)**

## MOSSBERG

The popularity of the MSR-style rifles has prompted more than a few makers to bring out .22LR versions, and this year Mossberg enters that market with the Tactical .22. Chambered for .22LR, it features an 18-inch barrel as well as the option of a six-position adjustable stock or a fixed A2-style stock. The rifle also sports a quad Picatinny rail and includes a Picatinny carry-handle mount. SRP: $276. **(203-230-5300; Mossberg.com)**

## NOSLER

Introduced into the upper-level bolt-action rifle market in 2010, the Nosler Model 48 Trophy Grade rifle features a Nosler Model 48 action, free-floating 24-inch barrel and a 3-pound Basix trigger. Exterior surfaces are protected by a magnesium-colored Cerakote finish; interior action parts are coated with MicroSlick. The action is glass-bedded into an internal aluminum chassis on a Bell & Carlson composite stock. Nosler guarantees MOA accuracy

**MOSSBERG TACTICAL .22**

**NOSLER M48 TROPHY GRADE**

when mated with Nosler Trophy Grade ammunition. For 2011, Nosler will expand the caliber offerings with the addition of the .243 Win., .257 Roberts, 7mm-08 Rem., .280 Ackley Improved, .338 Win. Mag. and the .35 Whelen. SRP: $1,795.

The Nosler Custom Model 48 Sporter Rifle takes the basic gun one step further by incorporating the same metal-coating features with a hand-lapped 24-inch stainless-steel barrel and a hand-laid Kevlar stock with a pillar-bedded action and Teflon coating on the stock. In addition, some models will be available in both a right- and left-hand action. Nosler guarantees .75 MOA (with Nosler Trophy Grade ammunition). For 2011, this rifle will be available in .22-50 Rem., .257 Roberts +P, 6.5-284 Norma (right- and left-hand actions), .270 Win. (right- and left-hand actions), .280 Ackley Improved (light contour barrel), .280 Ackley Improved (standard barrel, right- and left-hand actions) and .30-06., .300 Win. Mag., .338 Win. Mag. and .35 Whelen (all in right- and left-hand actions). SRP: $2,995, right-hand action; $3,195, left-hand action **(800-285-3701; nosler.com)**

## ROCK RIVER ARMS

Piston-operated modern sporting rifles (MSRs) are big news this year, and Rock River Arms adds to the mix with their PDS Carbine, which uses a piston-driven operating system that has been in development for more than two years. The new PDS Carbine is available in a 5.56mm NATO chamber that also handles commercial .223 Rem. Cartridges. It features a 16-inch chrome-moly barrel with a 1-in-9 twist rate that has been proven to accurately handle bullet weights between 40 and 75 grains. The muzzle is threaded for 1/2-28 threads to accept popular muzzle accessories, and is supplied with a A2 flash hider.

The PDS Carbine has a full-length upper rail from the rear of the receiver to the regulator housing, to allow the mounting of optics, lights or lasers. The side-folding RRA six-position Tactical CAR stock provides an overall length of 37.75 inches in the extended position and folds to a compact 26 inches. The buttstock features a storage compartment that can house extra batteries for optical sights. An injection-molded ribbed handguard and a Hogue rubber pistol grip provide secure holds. Folding, ambidextrous, non-reciprocating charging handles can be used independently or together to charge the gun. The trigger assembly is Rock River's well-respected two-stage model. The gas regulator is adjustable in two positions to handle differing pressure loads. The empty weight of the PSD Carbine is 7.4 pounds, and it is shipped with one magazine (but accepts all standard AR-15-style magazines). SRP: $1,685.

The 5.56mm AR-style rifle has become one of the most popular rifles in America, but the original design was actually clambered for the NATO 7.62mmn (.308 Win.), using a larger receiver and called the AR-10. The U.S. military decided it wanted a smaller cartridge, and thus the AR-15 was born. The original AR-10 (7.62mm version) languished for a while, but now it's back, and has proved popular with those who appreciate the form and function of the AR-15 modern sporting rifle, but want more power. That is available in the Rock River Arms LAR-8 series, and this year it will introduce the LAR-8 Predator HP (High Power) in calibers 7.62mm/.308 Win., 7mm-08 Rem. and .243 Win. The rifle is now suitable for everything from big game to varmints.

The Predator features a 20-inch free-floating match-grade bead-blasted lightweight stainless-steel barrel, housed in a free-float aluminum handguard.

**ROCK RIVER ARMS LAR-8 PREDATOR HP**

A forged flat-top A4 upper receiver is ready to take optical sights. The trigger mechanism is the Rock River Arms two-stage model. Rock River Arms claims MOA accuracy from the barrel/free-float combo. The stock is the standard A2 design, and the empty gun weight is 8.6 pounds. The overall length is 40 inches. The gun is shipped with one magazine, a case, a manual and Rock River's limited lifetime warranty. **(866-980-7625; rockriverarms.com)**

## RUGER

Three new rifles join the Ruger lineup this year, highlighted by a 6.8 SPC version of the SR-556 piston-driven modern sporting rifle. The 6.8 SPC (Special Purpose Cartridge) was originally developed for military consideration. The object was to create a cartridge that provided increased striking power over that of the 5.56mm, while maintaining a cartridge case size that allowed it to achieve the same magazine capacity in the M-16/M-4 rifle.

The 6.8 SPC has proven to be a popular choice for those pursuing deer with MSRs, and the new Ruger

SR-556/6.8 offers it in a two-stage piston-driven platform that retains all the features of the original SR-556, including the one-piece bolt carrier, mid-length gas system and four-position gas regulator that allows the user to adjust the piston system to varying ammunition pressures (or even turn it into a single-shot, if desired). Other features include a chrome-lined hammer-forged barrel in a heavy (.850) contour, Troy Industries Folding Battlesights, Quad Rail and rail covers, Hogue Monogrip and six-position adjustable stock. The SR-556/6.8 also has a 16 ½-inch barrel with a 1-in-10 twist rate, with the standard SAAMI 6.8 SPC chambering threaded 5/8-24 and capped with Ruger's Mini- 14/556 flash suppressor. Empty weight is 7.75 pounds. The rifle is shipped with one 5-round magazine, two 25-round mags and a padded carrying case. SRP: $1,995.

The popular Mini-Thirty (chambered for the 7.62x39mm round) gets an upgrade this year with the addition of the Mini-Thirty Tactical. This new model features a 16 1/8-inch blued barrel with a flash suppressor. The stock is black synthetic. Empty weight

**RUGER SR-556**

**RUGER MINI-THIRTY TACTICAL**

is a trim 6.75 pounds; overall length is 37.5 inches. The sighting system included an adjustable ghost ring rear sight with a non-glare protected-post front sight. Ruger's scope bases are machined into the receiver, and a set of matching Ruger rings is included. The side ejection of the cartridge cases allows for clearance of even low-mounted optics.

Rimfire fans will want to check out the new Ruger 10/22 FS rifle. This version features the company's SR-556/ Mini-14-style flash suppressor. The suppressor is removable and allows users to attach an assortment of muzzle accessories. The precision-rifled cold-hammer-forged alloy-steel barrel measures 16 1/8 inches and is finished in black matte. With a black synthetic stock, the rifle weighs 4.3 pounds empty. Overall length is 36 ¼ inches, and the rifle's length of pull is 13.5 inches. It is shipped with a scope-base adapter and a single rotary magazine. Additional magazines are available as accessories. **(928-541-8893; ruger.com)**

## UBERTI

The rolling block is a classic Western design, originally chambered for the .45-70 Govt. This year, Uberti adds a scaled-down rimfire version that is 36 inches in length and weighs 4.5 pounds. Features include an A-Grade walnut stock with a rubber butt pad, and the rifle will be offered in .22LR, .22 WMR and the 17 HMR. **(301-283-6300; uberti.com)**

## WEATHERBY

Rifle-and-scope combo packages have proven popular with many consumers because they simplify the buying decision. This year, Weatherby teams up with Simmons to offer one that should be well-received.

The new Vanguard Synthetic Combo pairs the proven Vanguard bolt-action rifle with a Simmons 3.5-10x40mm scope that features Simmons TrueZero technology. The TrueZero windage and elevation adjustments lock tightly to prevent point-of-impact shifts, while the TruPlex reticule provides quick target acquisition.

All Vanguard rifles are backed with Weatherby's accuracy guarantee of 1.5-inch or better three-shot groups at 100 yards, from a cold barrel, when using premium factory ammunition in non-Weatherby calibers or Weatherby factory ammunition. The Vanguard Synthetic rifle features a fully adjustable trigger, 24-inch hammer-forged barrel and black injection-molded composite Monte Carlo stock with a low-desity recoil pad. The Vanguard offers a one-piece machined bolt with a fully enclosed bolt sleeve that surrounds the cartridge case head with three rings of steel.

The Vanguard Synthetic Combo is available in .243 Win., .270 Win., .308 Win., 30-06 Springfield, .257 Weatherby Mag. and .300 Weatherby Mag. It will be offered in right-hand actions only, with black matte metalwork. The empty rifle weight is 7.25 pounds. SRP for the full Combo package—which includes the rifle, scope and Leupold Rifleman rings and bases—is $629. **(805-227-2600; weatherby.com)**

## WINCHESTER

In 2010, Winchester re-introduced the classic Model 94 lever-action as a limited-edition model to commemorate the 200th anniversary of the birth of Oliver Winchester. This year will see two additional Model 94 rifles added to the product line.

The Model 94 Sporter features a 24-inch half-round, half-octagon blued barrel. The stock (finished with satin oil) is the traditional straight grip with a crescent butt and finely checkered blue-steel buttplate with double-line bordering. The receiver is drilled and tapped for optics. Available calibers are .30-30 Win. and .38-55 Win. SRP: $1,299.99.

The Model 94 Short Rifle has a deeply blued 20-inch round barrel. The stock is straight-grip walnut

**WINCHESTER M94 SPORTER**

with a rifle-style forearm and black grip cap. Other features include a full-length tubular magazine, traditional semi-buckhorn rear sights and a Marble Arms gold-bead front sight. The receiver is drilled and tapped for optics. It will be available in .30-30 Win. SRP: $1,129.99.

Two popular historical Winchester lever-action rifles—the Model 1886 Short Rifle and the Model 1892 Carbine—will also appear in the product line for 2011. The Model 1886 Short Rifle features a deeply blued receiver, 24-inch barrel, matching blued lever, end cap and steel crescent buttplate. The straight-grip Grade 1 walnut stock is satin-finished. A full-length tubular magazine holds six .45-70 Govt. rounds. The receiver is drilled and tapped for optics. SRP: $1,269.

The Model 1892 Carbine features a 20-inch round deeply blued barrel with matching finish on the receiver and lever. The walnut stock features a straight grip and satin finish. It will be offered with a full-length magazine and chambered for .45 Long Colt, .44-40 Win., .44 Mag. and .357 Mag. SRP: $1,069.99.

Although classic lever guns are big news at Winchester this year, they have not ignored bolt-action fans, especially the younger ones. New in the Model 70 bolt-action line-up for 2011 is the Featherweight Compact, designed for the smaller-framed shooters. The Compact Model 70 action uses the pre-'64 controlled-round feed system, three-position safety, jeweled bolt body and knurled bolt handle, and features the M.O.A. Trigger System, which is easily adjusted by the user. The 20-inch barrel is housed in a satin-fished checkered-walnut stock with a Pachmayr Decelerator recoil pad. The action is drilled and tapped for optics. The average weight of the Compact Model 70 is 6.5 pounds, and it will be offered in .22-250 Rem., .243 Win., 7mm-08 Rem. and .308 Win. SRP: $899.99.
**(801-876-3440; winchesterguns.com)**

# SHOTGUNS 2011

The next 365 days promise to be a large and varied year for shotgunners. On the tactical/home-defense front, there are a wealth of new models are specifically directed toward the youth market.

Waterfowlers also will see a number of interesting new models, including more than a few in 20-gauge, a reflection of the advances made in alternative shot in recent years. Those who favor slugs for deer will find new models designed specifically for modern sabot slugs and optical sights. Several new semi-autos make their appearance, and for those upland gunners who yearn for a slick little 28-gauge, the new Weatherby semi-auto is worth a long look.

## BROWNING ARMS

The big news in Browning shotguns this year is the return of the A-bolt-action 12-gauge 3-inch shotgun that looks, and handles, like the Browning A-Bolt rifle and features the same 60-degree bolt lift, top tang safely and crisp trigger. It provides a 22-inch fully rifled barrel designed for use with sabot slugs with a 1-in-28 twist rate. An adjustable rear sight and a Truglo Marble fiber-optic front sight are standard, and the receiver is drilled and tapped for optics. The hinged floorplate accommodates a detachable magazine (2+1 capacity).

It will be available in three models. The A-Bolt Hunter features a satin-finished walnut stock and low-luster blued barrel and receiver. The A-Bolt Stalker features a composite stock with textured gripping surfaces and Dura-Touch armor coating. The Mossy Oak Break-Up Infinity model features the same camo finish on the stock as well as a low-luster blued barrel and receiver. SRP: $1,099.99 to $1,239.

Browning's gas-operated 12-gauge Maxus line will see the addition of a number of new models that include the Maxus Hunter, Maxus All-Purpose Mossy

**BROWNING A-BOLT STALKER**

Oak Break-Up Infinity, Maxus Rifled Deer Mossy Oak Break-Up Infinity, Maxus Rifled Deer Stalker, Maxus Sporting Carbon and Maxus Sporting. The Maxus Hunter and Maxus Sporting each feature a high-gloss walnut stock and a laser-engraved satin-nickel-finished receiver. The Hunter will be offered in 3.5- and 3-inch chambers with 26-, 28- and 30-inch-long barrels. SRP: $1,419.99 to $1,559.99. The Maxus Sporting will be offered in a 3-inch chamber with 28- or 30-inch barrels. SRP: $1,629.99.

The Maxus Carbon Fiber Sporting (SRP: $1,419) features a carbon-fiber finish on the top and bottom of the receiver and barrel. The stock and forearm also have the fiber finish as well as Dura-Touch Armor Coating with textured gripping surfaces. It will have 3-inch chamber and will be offered in 28- or 30-inch barrel lengths.

To accommodate smaller-framed shooters, Browning offers the Micro Midas smoothbore line for 2011. All models will be available in 12- or 20-gauge with 24- or 26-inch barrels. The satin-finished walnut stock features a 13-inch length of pull. SRP: $1,069, Silver Hunter Micro Midas semi-auto; $1,469.99, Citori Satin Hunter Micro Midas over/under. All Micro Midas firearms will, for a limited time, be covered by the Browning Growth Insurance Program. Customers who purchase a new Micro Midas will be eligible to purchase a full-size stock at 50 percent off the retail price. **(801-876-2711; browning.com)**

## CZ-USA

A pair of over/unders and an upgraded semi-auto make up CZ's new smoothbore offering this year. The CZ-USA Wingshooter blends old-world craftsmanship with an extensively engraved look. Each model features heavily engraved scrollwork with a special sideplate design. The stock is an upper-grade Turkish walnut with 18 lpi checkering, Schnabel forend and knurled trigger pad. The action is a boxlock-framed design with selective mechanical triggers and coil-spring operated hammers. The 28-inch chrome-lined barrels are threaded for interchangeable choke tubes, and five tubes are provided with each gun. Available in 12-gauge ($999), 20-gauge ($999), 28-gauge ($1,040) and .410 bore ($1,040); all but the 28-gauge feature 3-inch chambers.

**CZ 912**

The CZ-USA 2011 Limited Edition over/under will be available in a 50-gun run and features 28-inch barrels with a No. 3 grade Circassian walnut stock and buttstock, and Schnabel forend. The silver-engraved gun incorporates selective mechanical triggers, boxlock-frame design, coil-spring-operated hammers, chrome-lined barrels threaded for interchangeable choke tubes (five supplied with each gun) and 3-inch chambers. It will be available in 12-, 20-, 28-gauge and .410 bore. SRP: $2,499.

The new CZ 912 recoil-operated semi-auto shotgun will be available in 12-gauge with 28-inch chrome-lined barrel threaded for interchangeable choke tubes (five tubes supplied). The walnut-stocked smoothbore features a gloss black finish on the metalwork. CZ claims the recoil system will handle a wide variety of 12-gauge loads while allowing for simpler maintenance. The CZ 912 weighs 7.3 pounds, and includes a fiber-optic front bead. SRP: $509. **(913-321-1811; cz-usa.com)**

## LEGACY SPORTS INTERNATIONAL

The new 12-gauge Escort Extreme (SRP: $623) is a gas-operated semi-auto designed for the toughest weather conditions and chambered for 3-inch magnum shells (but will also handle most 2 ¾-inch loads). It features a black synthetic stock with a black nylon recoil pad with raised textured grip panels on the pistol grip and forend.

The 28-inch chrome-lined barrel is rated for steel shot and has a black chrome external finish. The action features a magazine cut-off button that allows a chambered round to be quickly removed without feeding another round from the magazine. It's a handy feature on a hunting gun. A raised rib and brass front bead provide an excellent sighting plane. The capacity of the tubular magazine is 4+1.

Threaded for interchangeable choke tubes, in keeping with the Extreme label, sling swivels for easy transportation are standard.

Slug hunting for deer, especially in the East and Southeast, where most deer are harvested at under 200 yards, continues to grow in popularity. The new Escort Slug Gun is available in either a semi-auto or pump-action gun. Regardless of the model, each barrel features 1-in-26 twist cut rifling designed specifically for sabot slugs (traditional lead slugs are not recommended) and utilizes a machined cantilever scope-mount base on the barrel, which is made from match-grade steel.

The scope rail also includes an integral fiber-optic sight system for those that prefer iron sights.

The semi-auto versions are available in 12- or 20-gauge, with 22-inch barrels, with a blued finished. SRP: $623. The pump versions are offered in 12- and 20-gauge, and also offer 22-inch barrels. SRP: $497. **(775-828-0555; legacysports.com)**

## MOSSBERG

For 2011, Mossberg offers an interesting mix of tactical, turkey and youth-oriented shotguns. Dedicated to younger shooters, the 510 Mini Camo is a miniaturized version of the Mossberg 500 pump shotgun and is available in 20-gauge or .410. It features a length of pull from 10.5 to 11.5 inches. The 18.5-inch barrel is equipped with dual bead sights and includes a set of interchangeable Accu-Chokes. The synthetic stock is finished in Mossy Oak Infinity camo. SRP: $422.

The home-defense shotgun has been a hot topic, and a hot seller, in recent years. Mossberg brings out six new models this year. The SA-20 Tactical is a 20-gauge autoloader with a quick-load shell elevator. The 20-inch barrel features ghost ring sights and includes a Picatinny rail on the top of the receiver, plus a three-sided rail mounted below the barrel to allow for mounting virtually any combination of lights and laser designators. The SA-20 tactical will be available with two stock styles—a standard full-length stock ($510) and a full-length stock with a pistol grip ($516).

For those who prefer the 12-gauge, Mossberg has four new models this year. The Home Security 12-gauge (HS-12) is the over/under Maverick model with a 18.5-inch barrels in a matte finish and a black synthetic stock. It features a rear top Picatinny rail to allow for the mounting lights or lasers, but does have a rear sighting groove cut into it that mates with the front fiber-optic sight.

A front bottom-forend Picatinny rail expands the light- and laser-mounting opportunities. It will be available with both barrels in fixed-cylinder choke ($494) or with fixed-choked barrels (IC on top and modified below). SRP: $507.

Pump-gun enthusiasts have five new models of the venerable Model 500 pump in 12-gauge. The Mossberg 500 Rail Tactical features a six-shot capacity, 18.5-inch Cylinder-choked barrel with a bead front

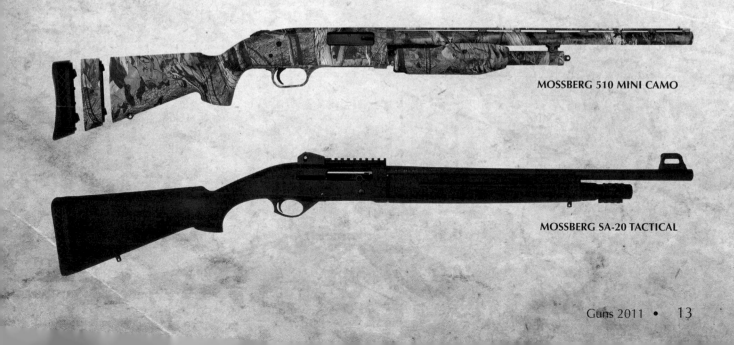

MOSSBERG 510 MINI CAMO

MOSSBERG SA-20 TACTICAL

sight, a six-position adjustable stock and three rails on the forend. It is finished in matte blue. SRP: $553. The Mossberg 500 Rail Persuader offers an eight-shot capacity, 20-inch Cylinder-bored barrel, bead front sight, a black full-length synthetic stock with rails and a matte blue finish. SRP: $435. The Mossberg 500 Rail Tactical features an eight-shot magazine capacity, 20-inch barrel with ghost ring sights and a Cylinder bore. Also on board, a six-position adjustable stock, matte blue finish and tactical rails. SRP: $590.

The Mossberg 590A1 features a six-position adjustable stock with a tri-rail forend. Sights are a ghost ring system. The heavy Cylinder-bore barrel is 18.5 inches long, and the gun incorporates a magazine cut-off and Parkerized finish. SRP: $789. The Mossberg 590 9-Shot offers a 20-inch Cylinder-bore barrel with a heat shield, bead front sight, tri-rail forend and a matte blue finish with a Speedfeed buttstock. SRP: $597.

Turkey hunters weren't ignored this year, and the popular sport sees four new 12-gauge pump guns in the Turkey Thug series. The Mossberg 500 Turkey Thug model features a 24-inch ported barrel with a XX-Full choke, ventilated rib, adjustable fiber-optic sights, a user-adjustable trigger and a black synthetic stock. SRP: $409. The Mossberg 535 features a 20-inch barrel with an X-factor ported choked tube, adjustable fiber-optic sights, user-adjustable trigger, a camouflage Picatinny rail, adjustable stock with the new Mossy Oak Infinity camo finish and a 30mm Tru-Glo red-dot sight (mounted and bore sighted). SRP: $671. The same model is available without the 30mm Tru-Glo sight for $612.

The 3.5-inch chambered Mossberg 835 is available with a 20-inch over-bored barrel, adjustable fiber-optics sights, X-factor ported choke tube, user-adjustable trigger, Picatinny camo rail, 30mm Tru-Glo red-dot sight (mounted and bore sighted) and a synthetic stock finished with Mossy Oak Infinity camo. SRP: $642. **(203-230-5300; mossberg.com)**

**REMINGTON VERSAMAX**

## REMINGTON ARMS

Remington shotguns have been a standard benchmark for shotgunners for more than 100 years, and this year Remington announces a major new operating action addition to its line-up. The initial VersaMax models will be 12-gauge with a 28-inch barrel. They will be available with either a black synthetic stock with gray overmolded grips, or a Mossy Oak Duck Blind full-camo version with black overmolded grips. The next models (available this month) will be 26-inch barreled versions with the black synthetic stock and gray over-molded grips, and the same barrel length in Realtree AP full camo finish. All models feature Remington's soft-touch finish on the stocks and forend. All black synthetic models will ship with five Flush Pro Bore choke tubes (Full, Improved Modeified, Modified, Light Modified and Improved Cylinder). The camo versions ship with four choke tubes (Improved Cylinder, Modified, Full and Extra Full). All VersaMax models are rated for steel/tungsten alternative shot.

The heart of the VersaMax operating action is the new Remington patented gas-piston system. It consists of seven gas ports and two gas pistons. Remington claims they soften recoil (in some cases, with some 12-gauge loads, to below that of many 20-gauge guns) while providing a self-cleaning action for easier maintenance and reliability. The gas-piston system, according to Remington, regulates the gas pressure based upon the length of the shell for flawless functioning with any 12-gauge load.

Designed for heavy field use, the anodized aluminum receiver is combined with a TriNyte coated barrel, nickel-plated bore, nickel-Teflon-plated internal gas-system components, stainless-steel magazine tubes, aluminum action tube and nickel-plated springs. The VersaMax stock is designed to be fully adjustable to fit the individual gun to the individual shooter. The stock features an extra-thick SuperCell recoil pad and an adjustable length-of-pull spacer kit that allows the stock length to be increased by up to 1 inch. Adjustable drop and cast-on/cast-off allows changes in those areas, while an interchangeable padded cheek comb insert allows for height-of-comb adjustments. Sling swivels are standard. Magazine capacity is 3+1 for 2 ¾- and 3-inch loads; and 2+1 for 3 ½-inch shells. SRP: $1,399, black synthetic; $1,599, camo. **(336-548-8820; Remington.com)**

## WEATHERBY

For 2011, Weatherby not only expands its popular line of home-defense shotguns, but it also introduces a slick little 28-gauge semi-auto that should be the darling of those who pursue quail, woodcock, ruffed grouse and doves. Named after the framed dove region of Argentina, the 28-gauge semi-auto Entre Rios features a specially designed scaled-down frame that is perfectly sized to the 28-gauge shell. The CNC-machined aircraft-grade alloy receiver reduces the weight to a very trim 5.25 pounds. It will be available with a 26- or 28-inch barrel. The Entre Rios features a hand-selected walnut stock with cut checkering on the pistol grip and forend. The stock is finished in a high gloss; the metalwork is high-gloss blued. Length of pull is 14 3/8 inches.

The balance is designed to be slightly muzzle-heavy, which experienced wingshooters feel is an advantage on a lightweight gun for a smooth swing and follow-through. A drop-out trigger system simplifies cleaning, and the barrel is chrome-lined. The barrel features lengthened forcing cones for improved patterns and a ventilated top rib. A nice feature is that the barrels are threaded for Weatherby's Multi-Choke system (which is compatible with the Briley

thread pattern), and each Rios is shipped with a Skeet, Improved Cylinder and Modified tube. SRP: $749.

The home-defense smoothbore market will see Weatherby's Threat Response (TR) line increase with three new models: the SA-459 TR semi-auto, the PA-08 TR pump-action and the PA-459 Digital pump.

The semi-auto SA-459 TR is available in 12- and 20-gauge. It has a pistol-grip stock with a rubber-textured grip area. The length of pull is 13.5 inches to facilitate handling in close quarters. The defensive-length barrel is chrome-lined for easy cleaning. If one desires to mount optics (lights or lasers), a Picatinny rail is installed on the receiver and includes a ghost ring-style rear sight that is adjustable for windage and elevation in conjunction with the front bead. The black, synthetic injection-molded stock is matched by black matte metal finishing. SRP: $659. The PA-08 TR (SRP: $368) is designed as a popularly priced 12-gauge home-defense shotgun. It features a dual-action-bar pump action. A lightweight traditional stock of black injection-molded synthetic composite combines with a 19-inch chrome-lined fixed-choke barrel and black matte metal finish. A white blade front sight is easily visible, even in low light

The PA-459 Digital offers the same dual-action pump action as the other PA-459 series shotguns, but is designed to do double duty as a home-defense shotgun and close-range varmint gun. The injection-molded synthetic stock is finished in a universal digital camouflage pattern with metalwork in black-matte finish. The stock provides a piston grip-style buttstock, with a 13.5-inch length of pull, and a low-density recoil pad. It features a 19-inch chrome-lined barrel that is threaded for a removable, ported cylinder-choke tube. An extended forend and bolt release allows for quick operation of the pump action. A mil-spec Picatinny rail

**WEATHERBY SA-459 TR**

is installed on the receiver to allow the mounting of lights or lasers. The rail includes a LPA-style ghost ring sight (adjustable for windage and elevation) that mates with a white blade front sight. Available in 12-gauge only, the PA-08 TR Digital weighs 7 pounds and has an overall length of 39 inches. SRP: $499 **(800-227-2600; weatherby.com)**

## WINCHESTER REPEATING ARMS

For 2011, Winchester introduces a new version of the Super X pump-action shotgun as well as major line increases in the Super X3 semi-auto line. On the pump-action side, the new SPX 12-gauge Waterfowl model will be offered in Mossy Oak Duck Blind camo, in 26- or 28-inch barrel lengths. The SXP Waterfowl features a hard-chrome chamber and bore and Winchester's Speed Plug system; it's also threaded to accept the full line of Invector-Plus choke tubes. SRP: $539.99.

The 12-gauge SX3 Sporting Adjustable is designed for clay-target games, but should perform well in the game fields. It features a lightweight aluminum-alloy receiver, and the barrel is configured to a lightweight profile with a ventilated rib. The walnut stock and forearm have an oil-like satin finish, and the buttstock features an adjustable comb to allow shooters to achieve a perfect zero point for their particular build and shooting style. It will be available in barrel lengths of 28, 30 and 32 inches, and is shipped with five extended Signature choke tubes and a fitted ABS hard case. SRP: $1,629.99. An SX3 Composite 20-gauge, featuring 26- or 28-inch barrels, will be available for $1,139.99

Those who favor slugs for deer may want to look at the new SX3 Cantilever Deer 20-Gauge. It features a 22-inch rifled barrel (designed for modern sabot slugs) with a Weaver-style cantilever rail that allows for easy optics mounting. It also includes an adjustable rear rifle sight with a Tru-Glo fiber-optic front sight for those that prefer iron sights. The stock is a composite material with Dura-Touch coating. The new SX3 20-gauge Waterfowl models will come in Mossy Oak Duck Blind camo with Dura-Touch Armor Coating on the composite stock and forearm. They will be offered in 26- and 28-inch barrel lengths. SRP: $1,339. An All-Purpose Field SX3 (26- or 28-inch barrels) will be offered in Mossy Oak Break-Up Infinity camo.

**WINCHESTER SX3 SPORTING ADJUSTABLE**

Turkey hunters will be interested in the SX3 NWTF Extreme Turkey model. It will be offered in 12-gauge 3.5-inch chamber and 20-gauge 3-inch.

Both will come in Mossy Oak Break-Up Infinity camo with Dura-Touch Armor Coating on the composite stock and forearm, and both will feature an adjustable rear sight. **(801-876-3737; winchesterguns.com)**

# HANDGUNS 2011

It's impossible to ignore the fact that 2011 is the 100th anniversary of the classic 1911 John Browning design. The manufacturers certainly have not. Call this the "Year of the 1911." Numerous models of this venerable pistol—from basic to exotic—make an appearance this year, including a surprising number in .22LR rimfire chambering.

At the same time, revolvers haven't been ignored; DA fans will welcome the return of the Dan Wesson, while SA fans will find a number of new compact models. Some new Action Pistol-oriented 9mms and .40 S&Ws also make their debut, and the trend toward pint-size .380 ACPs continues with a new polymer-frame model from SIG.

## AMERICAN TACTICAL IMPORTS

The Year of the 1911 will be further fueled by a number of new models imported by ATI. The new FX45 series consists of five different 1911 .45 ACP models, manufactured by Shooters Arms Manufacturing in the Philippines.

The ATI FX Military is a traditional full-size standard 1911. It weighs 37 ounces and is 8.5 inches long. It features a standard 5-inch barrel, all steel parts, a black-matte military-style slide stop and thumb safety, solid mahogany grip panels and 8+1 magazine capacity (compatible with aftermarket magazines). SRP: $449.95.

The ATI FX GI is a Commander-sized 1911. Weighing in at 32 ounces, it is 7.9 inches long

**ATI FX THUNDERBOLT**

and uses a 4.25-inch barrel. It offers the same 8+1 magazine capacity as the military model, as well as the same controls, mahogany grips and sights. SRP: $449.95.

The ATI FX Thunderbolt is a full-size 1911 constructed of chrome steel parts. It is a good choice for self-defense or sport. It weighs 39 ounces, and features a 5-inch barrel with a Picatinny rail on the dust cover to allow the use of lights or lasers. Sights are adjustable LPA Bomar-style in a three-white-dot pattern. Textured mahogany grips are standard, as well as the 8+1 magazine capacity. SRP: $699.95.

Two compact 1911s also join the line-up. The Titan Blue ($519.95) features carbon-steel construction; the Titan Stainless ($599.95) is a stainless-steel construction. Both weigh in at 28 ounces, are 6.9 inches long and feature 3.13-inch barrels that operate with a two-stage recoil spring system. Each is equipped with low-profile rear sight with a military-style slide

stop and thumb safety is standard, as are mahogany grip panels. Magazine capacity is 7+1.

If the .45 ACP is a bit more caliber than desired, shooters will want to look at the GSG-1911. A member of the German Sporting Guns family, the GSG-1911 features the same weight and feel as the classic 1911, but the 5-inch threaded barrel is chambered for .22LR high-velocity loads. The detachable magazine has a capacity of 10 rounds. ATI guarantees a 5-pound trigger pull. The gun will be available in a standard model with classic wood grips; it can also be had with black polymer grips, a faux suppressor and a Picatinny rail. SRP: starts at $359.95.
**(800-290-0065; americantactical.us)**

## BROWNING ARMS

In celebration of the 100th anniversary of the classic 1911, Browning will introduce a scaled-down .22LR version in 2011. The new Browning 1911-22 is

**BROWNING 1911-22 A1**

made in the U.S. It will include a special first-year-of-production collector's certificate, and will be shipped with a limited-edition commemorative canvas-and-leather zipped case.

The framed and slide are machined from aluminum alloy and finished in black matte. The barrel has a stainless-steel barrel block and target crown. The blow-back-action design has a single-action trigger, fixed sights, 10-round magazine, manual thumb safety and grip safety. The grip panels are brown composite. An A1 version will be offered in a 4.25-inch barrel length and a weight of 15.5 ounces. A Compact version features a 3 5/8-inch barrel and weighs 15 ounces. SRP: $599.99. **(801-876-2711; browning.com)**

## CHARTER ARMS

Two new personal-defense models, each of which utilizes a frame made of 7075 aircraft-quality aluminum for improved strength and reduce weight, are being added to the 2011 line. The Off Duty HP .38 Special and Undercover Lite .38 Special are available in a high-polish stainless-steel finish with a matte black frame and feature a five-shot 2-inch barrel. Each weighs 14 ounces, has serrated front and rear notched sights, and comes with combat rubber-grip panels that can be changed to accept a Crimson Trace LaserGrip. The Off Duty has an internal DA hammer, which allows the firearms to be shot through the pocket without snagging; the Undercover Lite model has an external standard hammer. Both models are ideal choices for concealed carry. SRP: $404.

Two revolvers specially designed for women shooters are also being added to the line. The Chic Lady and the Chic Lady Off Duty are finished in a high-polish stainless-steel pink anodized aluminum frame and come in a faux alligator pink attaché case with high polished stainless-steel trim. Other features include a rubber grip (which can be changed out to accept a Crimson Trace LaserGrip), 2-inch barrel, 5-shot capacity, a serrated front sight and quick-release cylinder. Each weighs 13 ounces. The Chic Lady has a standard hammer; the Chic Lady Off Duty has an internal DA hammer. Both models have a hammer-blocked safety system that ensures the revolver cannot be fires unless the trigger is held in the full rear position when the hammer falls. SRP: $436, Chic Lady; $446, Chic Lady Off Duty. **(203-922-1652; charterarms.com)**

## CZ-USA

Two new models designed specifically for action sports competition make up CZ's new handgun offerings for 2011. The 9mm Checkmate is an upper-end competition pistol designed for USPSA/IPSC competition in either the Open Class or Limited Class.

The Checkmate comes from the factory configured for Open Class competition with a barrel threaded for an included/mounted four-port compensator, a 6 MOA C-More red-dot sight and an ambidextrous aluminum rear slide racker. A spare barrel is included, along with a front sight adapter, which replaces the compensator to allow use in the Limited Class, and a rear sight, which replaces the slide racker handle when switching from Open to Limited Class configuration. A big-stick 26-round magazine and three 20-round magazines are included, and the gun comes in a hard case to contain all the interchangeable parts. Additional features include four slide stop pins without the slide lock feature, two slide stops with the slide lock feature (which allows a shooter to customize the slide lock feature to his shooting style), a competition hammer, aluminum magwell, ambidextrous manual thumb safeties, under-cut trigger guard and lightweight aluminum alloy grips. The all-steel pistol is finished in black matte. SRP: $3,164.

The 9mm CZ 75 SP-01 has proved popular in USPSA/IPSC competition, and this year the CZ Custom Shop offers the gun in a two-tone finish. Based upon

**CZ 75 SP-01**

the Shadow Target, it wears the same competition fixed sights, slim-line aluminum competition grips and is supplied with 19-round magazines. SRP: $1,199. **(913-321-1811; cz-usa.com)**

## DAN WESSON

This year's new offerings include a compact-carry 1911 .45 ACP, a new series of upper-end 1911 pistols designed for sport and self-defense and the return of the Dan Wesson interchangeable-barrel double-action revolver. Available in .357 Magnum, the new Dan Wesson 715 double-action revolver is a recreation of the Dan Wesson revolvers that earned high marks for accuracy. The new 715 retains the ability to swap barrels and grips with any previous Dan Wesson revolver in the 15-2 and later series models. The tensioned barrel, forward crane lock and rear ball detent contribute to consistent cylinder/barrel alignment, one reason that the Dan Wesson was considered one of the most accurate DA revolvers available. The clockwise rotating cylinder turns into the frame to reduce stress and wear on the crane assembly to maintain that accuracy.

Built on a heavy frame using 416 stainless-steel construction, the 715 features a transfer bar safety, Hogue finger-groove grips and an adjustable rear target sight with interchangeable front-sight blades. A 6-inch barrel with a heavy vent-shroud profile is standard, but accessory barrels from 2.5 to 10 inches are easily interchangeable with any previous Dan Wesson series of 15-2 or later (as are grip styles), and are available

from Dan Wesson. The 715 is shipped with the appropriate wrench kit to change barrels and packed in a Pistol Pack hard case with compartments for three additional barrel assemblies.

On the semi-auto side, Dan Wesson has brought out its compact Guardian model in .45 ACP. The Guardian combines the best features of its Bobtail Commander and CCO, and the bobtail frame helps reduce printing when carrying concealed. An alloy frame, with a Commander-length barrel, helps to reduce weight. It is finished in matte black with tritium sights. SRP: $1,590.

The new Dan Wesson Elite Series is an upper-end 1911 platform designed for serious sport or self-defense. It consists of three models: the Titan, Mayhem and the Havoc.

The Titan is chambered for the 10mm and built on a high-capacity version of the 1911 platform. It features a 5-inch Schuemann match-grade barrel in a flat-top lightened slide, with Snake Scale serrations forward and rear. A tactical accessory rail is incorporated on the dust cover. Bomar-style heavy-duty night sights are standard. Additional features include a hand-fit slide and frame match, Keonig Ultra Low Mass Hammer, CNC-cut 25 lpi checkering, custom competition G-10 low-profile grips, ambidextrous thumb safeties and a black matte finish. A Dawson competition magwell is an option, and 18-round magazines are shipped with the gun.

The .40 S&W Mayhem is purpose-built for USPSA/IPSC Limited Division competition on an all-steel frame. It features a 6-inch slide and barrel that

**DAN WESSON GUARDIAN .45 ACP**

has been lightened to match the weight of a 5-inch barreled gun, but provided the sight radius of a 6-inch barrel. The bull barrel and tactical rail on the dust cover contribute to what Dan Wesson calls "good weight" (muzzle-forward balance). Additional features include a black matte finish, ambidextrous manual safeties, Bomar-style fiber-optic adjustable sights, a Schuemann match-grade barrel, slide serrations forward and rear, custom competition G-10 grips, competition magwell, ultra-low mass hammer, hand-fit slide and frame and cnc-25-lpi cut checkering. The gun is shipped with two 18-round magazines (21-round magazines are an option).

The Havoc model is purpose-designed for USPSA/ISPC Open Class competition. Built on an all-steel high-capacity 1911 frame and finished in black matte, it features fixed iron sights, but also incudes an ultra-low Barry 45-degree C-More mount. Available in .38 Super or 9mm, it offers ambidextrous manual safeties, Schuemann match-grade barrel (threaded for an included Craig six-port "Mach 6" cone compensator), Dawson ICE or EWG competition magwell, ultra-low mass-hammer, CNC-cut 25 lpi checkering, Tri-Topped lightened slide for the 5-inch barrel, a hand-fit slide and frame and G-10 custom grip panels. Two 21-round magazines are supplied, and magazines that hold 24, 27 or 29 rounds are available. **(913-321-1811; cz-usa.com)**

## GLOCK

Continuing to advance the revolutionary Glock design, the new Gen 4 Glock features a smaller grip than previous models, as well as Rough Textured Frame (RTF) surface stippling. An interchangeable

**GEN 4 GLOCK**

backstrap system (easily swapped and secured with a single pin) allows a considerable amount of hand-fitting to the individual user. Magazine-release catches have been enlarged and are now easily reversible for right- or left-handed shooters. The new Gen 4 Glock magazines incorporate two mag-release cut-outs to allow ambidextrous operation of the magazine releases. A dual-recoil spring system replaces the original single model. **(770-432-1202; glock.com)**

## HECKLER & KOCH

First introduced in 2007, the P30 series is becoming the cornerstone of the H&K handgun line. Featuring interchangeable backstraps and side-panel grips in small, medium and large sizes, it can easily be fit to any shooter's hand. Ambidextrous slide and magazine release levers make it well-suited to southpaws, and an integral Picatinny rail allows the installation of light/laser aiming devices. The modular design allows the user to select from a DA trigger system or a traditional DA/SA system, with a decocking button.

For 2011, H&K will add a long-slide model in .40 S&W, featuring a lightweight LEM (Law Enforcement Modification) trigger. **(706-568-1906; hk-usa.com)**

## KAHR ARMS

For 2011, Kahr will introduce two of its most popular models with Crimson Trace LG-437 grips direct from the factory. The .380 ACP KP38331 has a 2.5-inch Lothar Walther match-grade barrel, black polymer frame, matte stainless-steel slide and 6+1 capacity. It is shipped with two stainless-steel six-round magazines.

The .45 ACP PM4543L has a 3.14-inch Lothar Walther match-grade barrel with polygonal rifling, a 5+1 capacity and a black polymer frame with matte stainless-steel slide. It is shipped with two 5-round stainless-steel magazines.

Both will be factory-equipped with the LG-437 laser grips. The grips give the user the choice of either two No. 357 silver oxide batteries or a single 1/3N 3-volt lithium battery. The LG-437 features windage and elevation adjustments. Each laser-equipped gun will be shipped with a sight-adjusting allen wrench, sight cleaner, batteries and Crimson Trace decal. The laser changes the gun's profile, and standard holsters for these guns will not fit the new models, but Kahr has had holsters designed specifically for them. **(845-735-4500; kahr.com)**

## PARA USA

In keeping with the "Year of the 1911" theme, Para introduces a number of new and useful models based on the venerable 1911 design. In their popular Expert series, the new Para GI LCT is a 4.25-inch version of the Expert. It features a full-beaver-tail-grip safety, a fiber-optic front sight and a fixed two-dot rear sight.

For Single Action Shooting Society competitors who want to compete in the new Wild Bunch division, Para is bringing out the 1911 SASS Wild Bunch pistol. It conforms to all division rules with its traditional hammer and grip safety, solid trigger, seven-round magazines and standard sights. The sights are in a three-dot pattern, so the pistol can be used in either the modern or traditional divisions. All traditional shooters need do is black out dots. SRP: $789. USPSA shooters will want to look at the new 1911 Single Stack limit. Designed for USPSA Single Stack competition, it features a 5-inch match-grade barrel with an integral ramp, fiber-optic front sight and a fully adjustable rear sight, skeletonized hammer, competition trigger that is adjustable for over-travel, ambidextrous slide lock, extended beavertail safety and Para's Sterling finish. SRP: $1,298.

Also new is the 18-9 9mm Limited Model with a fiber-optic front sight, fully adjustable rear sight, front strap checkering and Sterling finish. The compact Warthog series sees the addition of the Hawg 7, a flat single-stack with a 3.5-inch barrel and seven-round magazines.

**PARA USA 1911 SASS WILD BUNCH PISTOL**

To celebrate the 100th anniversary of the 1911, Para is bringing out two models—one traditional, one modern. The 1911 100th Anniversary model is a standard 1911 with 5-inch stainless steel barrel, standard extractor, traditional spur hammer, three-dot sights, solid trigger and traditional slide lock and grip safety. It is shipped with two 7-round magazines, and is finished in black PK2 with an engraved slide. SRP: $1,399.

The 14-45 100th Anniversary is a modern version with a 5-inch stainless-steel integral ramped barrel. Features include a Power Extractor, 14-round magazines, fiber-optic front sight and adjustable rear competition sight, skeletonized hammer, competition trigger that is adjustable for over-travel, ambidextrous slide lock, extended beavertail-grip safety and a stainless-steel frame with integral light rail finished in black PK2, with an engraved 100th anniversary slide. The two anniversary guns will also be available in a limited number of boxed two-pistol sets. **(704-930-7600; para-usa.com)**

## REMINGTON ARMS

In 1917, the U.S. Ordnance Department issued an order to Remington-UMC to manufacture 500,000 1911s for the American Expeditionary Forces in WWI. The first Remington-UMC-produced pistols were delivered in August 1918. On November 11, 1918, the Armistice ending WWI was signed and the contract was suspended. In all, Remington-UMC produced 21,677 1911 pistols for the military, and those soldiers/ sailors/ Marines who received them were glad they did.

Now, Remington is bringing that gun back, and with a few improvements. The Remington R1 is an A1 variant of the original 1911, with modern upgrades. Like the original, the 1911 R1 has a flat mainspring housing, short trigger and double diamond grips. The modern enhancements include a lowered and flared ejection port, beveled magazine well, loaded chamber indicator, high-profile fixed sights in a three-white-dot pattern and a match-grade stainless-steel barrel and bushing. The 1911 R1 also sports a Series 80-style firing pin block safety.

The 1911 R1 will be shipped in a custom carry case with two 7-round magazines and a barrel bushing wrench. SRP: $699. **(336-548-8820; remington.com)**

**ROSSI RANCH HAND LEVER ACTION PISTOL**

## ROSSI

Many years ago, there was a popular network TV show featuring actor Steve McQueen playing the role of bounty hunter Josh Randell. Though many may not remember the specifics of the show, they surely remember that his sidearm was a cut-down Winchester lever-action rifle carried in a custom holster on his right side. In an age when every Western TV star had to have some sort of custom sidearm, his stood out, and a lot of shooters thought it was about the coolest gun going. For those that would like to have one, Rossi provides a similar model this year. The Rossi Ranch Hand Lever Action Pistol is about as close as you'll get to Josh Randall's gun. The six-shot lever-action repeating centerfire pistol is a cut-down lever-action rifle fed from the traditional tubular magazine, but manufactured as a handgun in compliance with all federal laws.

It features a matte blue with a Brazilian hardwood stock, with an oversize loop lever. The receiver is investment-cast. The barrel is 12 inches long, and the overall gun length is 24 inches. The empty weight is 4 pounds. Sights consist of a rear adjustable buckhorn, with a milled front post with a brass insert. It will be available in .357 Magnum, .45 Long Colt or .44 Magnum, and all models feature the Taurus Security System. SRP: $536. **(305-474-0401; rossiusa.com)**

## RUGER

The Ruger SR9 was the manufacturer's first foray into the polymer-frame pistol arena, and this year you'll see a .40 S&W chambered version. The new SR40 is built in the same glass-filled nylon frame as the SR9, and the ambidextrous operating controls, trigger system and reversible backstrap are identical to those found on the SR9. The only major difference is that the SR40 adds a bit of weight to the hardened stainless-steel slide by increasing its width by .060 inches. The new SR40 weighs 27.25 ounces and has a 4.1-inch barrel, fully adjustable three-dot sights, integral accessory rail on the dust cover, visual and tactile chamber-loaded indicator and magazine disconnect. It is shipped with two 15-round flush-fit magazines. **(928-541-8892; ruger.com)**

**RUGER SR40**

**SIG P290**

## SIG SAUER

The popular sub-compact semi-auto .380 ACP market expands this year with the introduction of the SIG P290. Designed specifically as a back-up carry gun, it features a hammer-fired DA action that provides repeat-strike capability. The polymer frame is made in the U.S., and the slide is machined from solid stainless-steel billet. The standard single-stack magazine provides a 6+1 capacity, and an optional eight-round extended magazine is available. The gun has interchangeable grip inserts to allow a degree of custom fitting to the user, and features drift-adjustable SIGLITE sights or a high-contrast black sight. SRP: $757 to $787. **(603-772-2302; sigsauer.com)**

## UBERTI

The Cattleman El Patron Cowboy Mounted Shooter (CMS) is a factory custom-tuned full-size SA revolver available in six new configurations with shorter barrels that are ideal for use in mounted Cowboy competition. The El Patron model features a new hammer profile that is easier to cock one-handed.

All new models feature either a stainless-steel or color case-hardened framed, steel backstraps and trigger guards. Other features include checkered walnut grips and wider (easy-to-see) front and rear sights. Stainless-steel models (.357 Magnum and .45

Long Colt) will come with a 3.5-inch barrel. SRP: $739. Color case-hardened models (.357 Magnum and .45 Long Colt) will be available with 3.5- or 4-inch barrels. SRP: $599.

The bird's head grip was originally designed for Colt derringers, but proved popular enough that it was later offered in full-sized SA models. For 2011, Uberti brings back the "Bird's Head Colt" in its new 1873 Cattleman NM Stallion Bird's Head model ($569). This small-framed revolver is chambered for .38 Special. The six-shot SA features a short barrel. **(301-283-6300; uberti.com)**

## UMAREX USA

Umarex USA is also celebrating John Browning's 1911 with one of the more interesting takes on the concept—a .22LR Colt replica. Identical in appearance to the 1911 .45 ACP, this rimfire version will be available as a standard model and a rail model. Both feature fixed sights (drift-adjustable for windage), manual thumb safety, grip safety internal extractor and a pinned ejector. SRP: starts at $399.

Umarex will also expand its presence in the U.S. firearms market with the Turkish-made 1911 Regent series. **(479-646-4210; umarexusa.com)**

**UBERTI CATTLEMAN EL PATRON CMS**

# NEW Products: **Rifles**

ANSCHUTZ 1907A

## ANSCHUTZ 1907A
*Action*: Bolt
*Stock*: Aluminum
*Barrel*: 32.28 in.
*Sights*: None
*Weight*: 13.2 lb.
*Caliber*: .22 LR
*Magazine*: None
*Features*: Match 54 action; heavy, cylindrical barrel; match two stage or single stage trigger; safety signal pin.
**MSRP** . . . . . . . . . . . . . . . . . . **$3511**

## ANSCHUTZ 1907 IN WALNUT
*Action*: Bolt
*Stock*: Walnut
*Barrel*: 32.28 in.
*Sights*: None
*Weight*: 10.78 lb.
*Caliber*: .22 LR
*Magazine*: None
*Features*: Match 54 action; heavy, cylindrical barrel; match two stage or single stage trigger; safety signal pin.
**MSRP** . . . . . . . . . . . . . . . . . . **$3090**

ANSCHUTZ 1907 IN WALNUT

## ARMALITE M-15 22
*Action*: Semi-automatic
*Stock*: Synthetic
*Barrel*: 16 in.
*Sights*: None
*Weight*: N/A
*Caliber*: .22 LR Carbine
*Magazine*: 25 rounds
*Features*: Manganese black nitride steel barrel; forged flattop with picattiny rail; black stock; collapsing buttstock; anodized aluminum upper and lower receiver.
**MSRP** . . . . . . . . . . . . . . . . . . . **$749**

ARMALITE M-15 22

BARRETT MRAD

## BARRETT MRAD

*Action*: Bolt action repeater
*Stock*: Synthetic
*Barrel*: 24.5 in.
*Sights*: None
*Weight*: 14.8 lb.
*Caliber*: .338 Lapua Magnum
*Magazine*: Detachable box, 10-rounds
*Features*: Fluted barrel; multi-role brown finish stock; folding stock; adjustable cheek piece and buttplate; includes two 10-round magazines, two sling loops, and three adjustable accessory rails.
**MSRP** . . . . . . . . . . . . . . . . . . **$6000**

## BARRETT M107A1

*Action*: Semi-automatic
*Stock*: Synthetic
*Barrel*: 57in
*Sights*: Flip-up iron sights
*Weight*: 30.9 lb.
*Caliber*: .50BMG
*Magazine*: Detachable box, 10-rounds
*Features*: Chrome-lined barrel, Flat Dark Earth stock; suppressor-ready muzzle break; M1913 optics rail; detachable, adjustable lightweight bipod legs; lightweight monopod.
**MSRP** . . . . . . . . . . . . . . . . . **$12,000**

## BENELLI R1

*Action*: Semi-automatic
*Stock*: Synthetic
*Barrel*: 24 in.
*Sights*: None
*Weight*: 7.3 lb.
*Caliber*: .338 Win. Mag.
*Magazine*: Detachable box, 3+1
*Features*: GripTight coating; Picatinny rail; raised comb; black synthetic stock.
**MSRP** . . . . . . . . . . . . . . . . . . **$1109**

BARRETT M107A1

BENELLI R1 RIFLE

## BLASER R8 PROFESSSIONAL

*Action*: Straight-pull bolt-action
*Stock*: Black synthetic stock
*Barrel*: 20.5 in., 23 in., 25.75 in.
*Sights*: None
*Weight*: 6.4 lb.
*Caliber*: .222 Rem. to .338 Win. Mag.

*Magazine*: Detachable box, 3-rounds with lock
*Features*: Synthetic stock in black; standard taper barrel; no removable trigger assembly; recoil pad; palm swell; integrated receiver.
**MSRP** . . . . . . . . . . . . . . . . . . . **$3250**

BLASER-R8 PROFESSIONAL

# NEW Products: **Rifles**

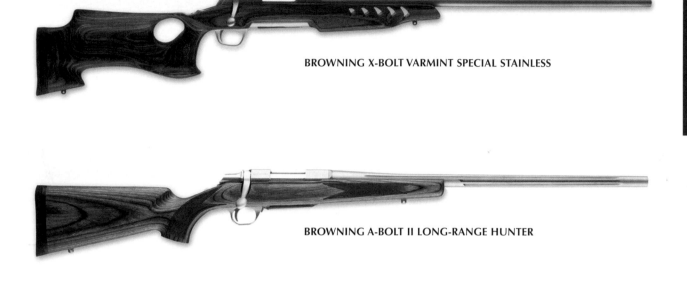

BROWNING X-BOLT VARMINT SPECIAL STAINLESS

BROWNING A-BOLT II LONG-RANGE HUNTER

BROWNING BLR WHITE GOLD MEDALLION

## BROWNING X-BOLT VARMINT SPECIAL STAINLESS

*Action*: Bolt
*Stock*: Altamont Paladin, Black Laminated
*Barrel*: 24 in., 26 in.
*Sights*: None
*Weight*: 8 lb. 8 oz.–8 lb. 11 oz.
*Caliber*: .223 Rem., .22-250 Rem., .243 Win., 7mm-08 Rem., .308 Win., .300 WSM, .270 WSM, 7mm WSM
*Magazine*: Detachable rotary box
*Features*: Stainless steel, free-floating barrel; adjustable feather trigger; top-tang safety; bolt unlock button; inflex technology recoil pads; sling swivel studs installed.
**MSRP** . . . . . . . . . . . . .$1069– $1109

## BROWNING A-BOLT II LONG-RANGE HUNTER

*Action*: Bolt
*Stock*: Grey laminate
*Barrel*: 26 in.
*Sights*: None
*Weight*: 8 lb. 5 oz.
*Caliber*: 7mm Rem. Mag., .300 Win. Mag., .300 RUM
*Magazine*: Detachable box
*Features*: Steel, matte blued finish receiver; drilled and tapped for scope mounts; grip panels; adjustable trigger; hinged floorplate; top-tang safety; recoil pad; sling swivel studs installed.
**MSRP** . . . . . . . . . . . . . . . . . $939

## BROWNING BLR WHITE GOLD MEDALLION

*Action*: Lever-action
*Stock*: Walnut, pistol grip
*Barrel*: 20 in., 22 in.
*Sights*: Open
*Weight*: 6 lb. 8oz.–6 lb. 12oz.
*Caliber*: .243 Win., 7mm-08 Rem., .308 Win., .300 WSM, .270 WSM
*Magazine*: Detachable box
*Features*: Aircraft-grade aluminum receiver with nickel finish; high-relief engraving on receiver; drilled and tapped for scope mounts; crowned muzzle; stainless steel barrel; stock comes in Grade IV/ V walnut with a checkered pistol grip and forearm; rosewood fore-end cap; silver pistol grip cap; adjustable sights; recoil pad; sling swivel studs installed.
**MSRP** . . . . . . . . . . . . . $1339–$1419

BROWNING MICRO MIDAS X-BOLT

## BROWNING MICRO MIDAS X-BOLT

*Action*: Bolt
*Stock*: Walnut
*Barrel*: 20 in.
*Sights*: None
*Weight*: 6 lb. 1 oz.
*Caliber*: .243 Win., 7mm-08 Rem., 308 Win., .22-250 Rem.
*Magazine*: Detachable rotary magazine
*Features*: Drilled and tapped for scope mounts, low-luster blued finish, free floating barrel; adjustable feather trigger; top tang safety.
**MSRP**. . . . . . . . . . . . . . . . . . **$479**

## BROWNING X-BOLT MEDALLION, LEFT HAND

*Action*: Bolt
*Stock*: Walnut
*Barrel*: 22 in., 23 in., 24 in., 26 in.
*Sights*: Open
*Weight*: 6 lb. 6 oz.–7 lb.
*Caliber*: .223 Rem., .22-250 Rem., .243 Win., .308 Win., .25-06 Rem., .270 Win., .280 Rem., .30-06 Spfld., 7mm Rem. Mag., .300 Win. Mag., .338 Win. Mag., .300 WSM, .270 WSM, 7mm WSM, .325 WSM
*Magazine*: Detachable box
*Features*: Gloss finish walnut stock, rosewood forend grip and pistol cap; Inflex Technology recoil pad; adjustable feather trigger; drilled and tapped for scope mounts.
**MSRP**. . . . . . . . . . . . . **$1000–$1040**

## BUSHMASTER .308 ORC

*Action*: Semi-automatic
*Stock*: Synthetic
*Barrel*: 16 in. (carbine), 20 in., (rifle)
*Sights*: None
*Weight*: 7.75 lb.
*Caliber*: .308 Win., 7.62 NATO
*Magazine*: Detachable box, 20-rounds
*Features*: Milled gas block; heavy, chrome lined barrel; A2 Birdcage flash hider; receiver length Picatinny optics rail with two 0.5 in. optic raisers; heavy oval hand guards; six position telescoping stock; shipped in lockable hard case with yellow saftey block; black web sling included.
**MSRP**. . . . . . . . . . . . . . . . . . **$1418**

BUSHMASTER .308 ORC

## BUSHMASTER MOE .308 MID-LENGTH

*Action*: Semi-automatic
*Stock*: Synthetic
*Barrel*: 16 in.
*Sights*: Magpul MSBUS rear flip sight
*Weight*: 6.1 lb.
*Caliber*: .308 Win., 7.62 NATO
*Magazine*: Detachable box, 20-rounds
*Features*: Receiver length Picatinny optics rail; Magpul MOE polymer mid-length handguard; Magpul MOE adjustable buttstock with strong A-frame design; rubber buttplate; Magpul MOE vertical grip; MOE enhanced trigger guards; shipped in lockable hard case with yellow safety block; stock comes in black, flat dark earth or OD green.
**MSRP**. . . . . . . . . . . . . . . . . . **$1448**

BUSHMASTER .308 HUNTER

# NEW Products: **Rifles**

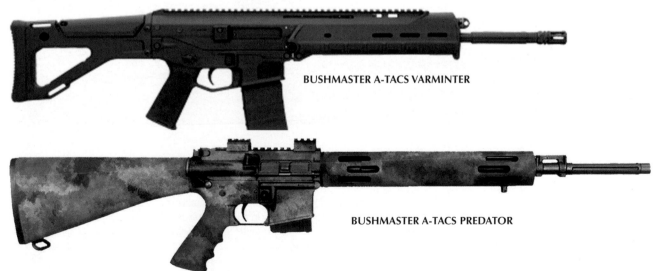

**BUSHMASTER ARC BASIC FOLDER**

## BUSHMASTER .308 HUNTER/ .308 VISTA HUNTER

*Action*: Semi-automatic
*Stock*: Synthetic
*Barrel*: 20 in.
*Sights*: None
*Weight*: 8.2 lb.
*Caliber*: .308 Win., 7.62 NATO
*Magazine*: Detachable box, 5-rounds
*Features*: Two riser blocks, A2 grip on Vista; free-floating, ventend aluminum fore-end; MOE trigger guard for gloved finger.
**Hunter**: . . . . . . . . . . . . . . . . **$1518**
**Vista**:. . . . . . . . . . . . . . . . . **$1618**

## BUSHMASTER ARC BASIC FOLDER

*Action*: Semi-automatic
*Stock*: Composite
*Barrel*: 16.5 in.
*Sights*: None
*Weight*: N/A

*Caliber*: .223/5.56mm NATO to 6.8mm Rem. SPC
*Magazine*: 30 round PMAG
*Features*: Cold hammer forged barrel with melonite coating; A2 birdcage-type hider;  tool-less, quick-change barrel system available in 10.5 in., 14.5 in., and 16.5 in.; quick and easy multi-caliber bolt carrier assembly; free floating MIL-STD 1913 monolithic top rail for optic mounting; high-impact composite hand guard with heat shield; ambidextrous controls; composite stock comes in black or coyote.
**MSRP** . . . . . . . . . . . . . . . . . **$2343**

## BUSHMASTER A-TACS VARMINTER

*Action*: Semi-automatic
*Stock*: Synthetic
*Barrel*: 24 in.
*Sights*: None

*Weight*: 8.4 lb.
*Caliber*: 5.56mm or .223 Rem.
*Magazine*: Detachable box, 5-rounds
*Features*: Coated in A-Tacs digital camoflage; free-floated barrel with a vented aluminum fore-end; two-stage compeition trigger.
**MSRP** . . . . . . . . . . . . . . . . . **$1474**

## BUSHMASTER A-TACS PREDATOR

*Action*: Semi-automatic
*Stock*: Synthetic
*Barrel*: 20 in.
*Sights*: None
*Weight*: 8 lb.
*Caliber*: 5.56mm or .223 Rem.
*Magazine*: Detachable box, 5-rounds
*Features*: Coated in A-Tacs digital camoflage; fluted extra-heavy barrel w/ competition muzzle crown; two-stage compeition trigger.
**MSRP** . . . . . . . . . . . . . . . . . **$1459**

**BUSHMASTER A-TACS VARMINTER**

**BUSHMASTER A-TACS PREDATOR**

COLT SPORTER CARBINE SP6920

COLT SP901

## COLT SPORTER CARBINE RIFLES SP6920, SP6940

*Action*: Semi-automatic
*Stock*: Combat-style, synthetic
*Barrel*: 16.1 in.
*Sights*: None
*Weight*: 5.95 lb.--6.6 lb.
*Caliber*: 5.56 NATO x .223
*Magazine*: Detachable box, 20-rounds
*Features*: Black stock with matte finish; optional removable carry handle; bayonet lug and flash hider; chrome lined barrel.
**MSRP** . . . . . . . . . . . . . **$1155–$1500**

## COLT SP901

*Action*: Semi-automatic
*Stock*: Collapsible
*Barrel*: 16.1 in.
*Sights*: Flip-up front, adjustable post, flip-up rear
*Weight*: 9.4 lb.
*Caliber*: .308 Win.

*Magazine*: Detachable box 20-rounds
*Features*: Matte black, bayonette lug and flash hider; ambidextrous controls; accepts Mil-spec 5.56 Colt uppers.
**MSRP** . . . . . . . . . . . . . . . . . . . **N/A**

COOPER FIREARMS M56 JACKSON GAME

## COOPER FIREARMS M56

*Action*: Bolt
*Stock*: Walnut
*Barrel*: 22 in.
*Sights*: None
*Weight*: 8.25 lb.
*Caliber*: .257 Weatherby Mag., .264 Winchester Mag., .270 Weatherby Mag., 7mm Rem. Mag., 7mm Weatherby Mag., 7mm Shooting Times Westerner, .300 H&H, .300 Win. Mag., .300 Weatherby Mag., .308 Norma Mag., 8mm Rem. Mag., .338 Win. Mag., .340 Weatherby Mag.
*Magazine*: Detachable box, 3-rounds
*Features*: Fully adjustable single stage trigger; AA Carlo walnut stock with 4-panel Cooper southwestern style on classic model; custom Classic model features AAA carlo stock with ebony tip and Len Brownel wrap around western fleur; Pachmayr rubber butt pad

| | |
|---|---|
| **Classic:** | **$2795** |
| **Custom Classic:** | **$3495** |
| **Western Classic:** | **$4395** |
| **Jackson Game:** | **$2995** |
| **Jackson Hunter:** | **$2795** |
| **Excalibur:** | **$2895** |

# NEW Products: **Rifles**

CZ 512 SEMI-
AUTOMATIC RIMFIRE
RIFLE

CZ 557

CZ 455 LUX

## CZ 512 SEMI-AUTOMATIC RIMFIRE RIFLE

*Action*: Semi-automatic
*Stock*: Laquered beech wood
*Barrel*: 20.7 in.
*Sights*: Adjustable
*Weight*: 5.89 lb.
*Caliber*: .22 LR, .22 WMR
*Magazine*: Detachable box, 5-rounds
*Features*: Operates on blow back breech system; equipped with a manual safety; scope rails mounted to receiver.
**MSRP** . . . . . . . . . . . . . $449–$479

## CZ 557 SPORTER

*Action*: Bolt
*Stock*: Walnut
*Barrel*: 20.6 in.
*Sights*: Integral scope dovetails
*Weight*: 7.8 lb.
*Caliber*: .30-06
*Magazine*: Detachable box
*Features*: Sports a checkered American pattern on hardwood stock; matte finished blue steel; fully Adjustable trigger; short extractor; hammer forged barrel; forged receiver.
**MSRP** . . . . . . . . . . . . . . . . . N/A

## CZ 455 LUX

*Action*: Bolt
*Stock*: Walnut
*Barrel*: 20.6 in.
*Sights*: Open
*Weight*: 6.1 lb.
*Caliber*: .22 LR, .22 WMR
*Magazine*: Detachable box, 5-rounds
*Features*: Interchangable barrel system; adjustable trigger; hammer forged barrel and billet machined receiver; adjustable iron sights; Lux pattern walnut stock.
**MSRP** . . . . . . . . . . . . . $420–$448

## DPMS AR-10 REPR

*Action*: Semi-automatic
*Stock*: Synthetic
*Barrel*: 18 in.
*Sights*: None
*Weight*: 9.5 lb.
*Caliber*: 7.62 NATO
*Magazine*: Detachable box
*Features*: Two-stage match grade trigger; dark earth Magpul PRS stock; Houge rubber grip with finger grooves; A3 style flattop; ambi-selector installed; milled from solid billet of aluminum; AAC flash hider/suppressor adapter.
**MSRP** . . . . . . . . . . . . . . . . . . **$2519**

DPMS AR-10 REPR

HARRINGTON & RICHARDSON
STAINLESS ULTRA HUNTER

## HARRINGTON & RICHARDSON STAINLESS ULTRA HUNTER

*Action*: Hinged breech
*Stock*: Laminate
*Barrel*: 24 in.
*Sights*: None

*Weight*: 8 lb.
*Caliber*: .45-70
*Magazine*: None
*Features*: Cinnamon laminate stock with thumbhole pistol grip, swivel studs and rubber rifle butt pad.
**MSRP** . . . . . . . . . . . . . . . . **$516.91**

HARRINGTON & RICHARDSON HANDI-RIFLE

## HARRINGTON & RICHARDSON HANDI-RIFLE

*Action*: Hinged breech
*Stock*: Walnut finish hardwood stock
*Barrel*: 22 in.
*Sights*: 3-9x32 scope included
*Weight*: 7 lb.
*Caliber*: .233 Rem.

*Magazine*: None
*Features*: Blued finish; scope mount rail and hammer extension; bore-sighted bull barrel; Monte Carlo grip; ventilated recoil pad.
**MSRP** . . . . . . . . . . . . . . . . **$313.69**

# NEW Products: **Rifles**

## HECKLER & KOCH MR556 A1

*Action*: Autoloading
*Stock*: Synthetic
*Barrel*: 16.50 in.
*Sights*: Open
*Weight*: 8.91 lb.
*Caliber*: 5.56 x 44mm
*Magazine*: Detachable box, 10- or 20-rounds
*Features*: Free-floating four-quadrant rail system; four MIL-STD 1913 Picatinny rails; two-stage trigger; retractable buttstock.
**MSRP** . . . . . . . . . . . . . . . . . **$3295**

HECKLER & KOCH
MR556 A1

HOWA TALON

## HOWA TALON

*Action*: Bolt
*Stock*: Thumbhole polymer and alloy
*Barrel*: 22 in., 24 in.
*Sights*: Optional scope package
*Weight*: 8.3 lb.
*Caliber*: .270 Win. Fluted, .30-06 Fluted, .300 Win. Mag. Fluted, 7mm Rem. Mag. Fluted
*Magazine*: Internal box, 3- to 5-rounds
*Features*: Two-stage dual Knoxx recoil system; combo includes 4-6 x 44 scope; ambidextrous stock that reduces felt recoil by 70%; blued barrel.
**Standard:** . . . . . . . . . . . . . . . **$980**
**Magnum:** . . . . . . . . . . . . . . **$1019**

## J.P. SAUER S 303 CLASSIC XT

*Action*: Autoloading
*Stock*: Synthetic stock with anti-slip elastomer inlays
*Barrel*: 20 in., 22 in.

*Sights*: Yellow triangle rear sight; red dot front sight
*Weight*: 7.3 lb.
*Caliber*: .30-06, .300 Win. Mag.
*Magazine*: Detachable box, 2- or 5-rounds
*Features*: Light-metal receiver; manual cocking safety; straight comb stock for either left or right-handed shooters; rust protection with Nitrobond-X finish.
**MSRP** . . . . . . . . . . . . . . . . . **N/A**

J.P. SAUER S 303 CLASSIC XT

**LAZZERONI L2010LLT LONG MAGNUM SPORTER**

## LAZZERONI L2012LLT LONG MAGNUM

**Action**: Bolt
**Stock**: Graphite/composite
**Barrel**: 24 in., 25 in., 26 in.
**Sights**: None
**Weight**: 7.3 lb.–10.9 lb.
**Caliber**: Lite: 6.53 (.257) Scramjet, 7.82 (.308) Warbird, 7.21(.284) Firebird, 8.59 (.338) Titan; Sporter: 6.53 (.257) Scramjet, 7.82 (.308) Warbird, 7.21(.284) Firebird, 8.59 (.338) Titan; Thumbhole: 6.53 (.257)

Scramjet, 7.82 (.284) Warbird, 7.21 (.284) Firebird, 8.59 (.338) Titan; Tactical: 7.82(.308) Warbird, 8.59(.338) Titan; Dangerous Game: 9.53 (.375) Saturn, 12.04 (.475) Bibamufu, 10.57 (.416) Meteor
**Magazine**: 4 rounds in one chamber; Tactical: 6 rounds, one in chamber 5 in detachable box.
**Features**: All new precision CNC-machined chrome-moly receiver; one-piece diamond-fluted bolt shaft;

stainless steel match-grade button-barrel; custom molded hand-bedded graphite/ composite stock designs; precision-machined aluminum-alloy floorplate/ trigger guard assembly; Jewel competition trigger; Vais muzzle brake; Limbsaver recoil pad.
**Lite or Sporter:** . . . . . . . . . **$5999.99**
**Thumbhole:** . . . . . . . . . . . . **$6499.99**
**Tactical:** . . . . . . . . . . . . . . . **$7999.99**
**Dangerous Game:** . . . . . . . **$7999.99**

**LES BAER MONOLITH .308 SEMI-AUTO SWAT MODEL**

## LES BAER MONOLITH .308 SEMI-AUTO SWAT MODEL

**Action**: Autoloading
**Stock**: Synthetic
**Barrel**: 20 in. (optional 18 in., 24 in.)
**Sights**: None

**Weight**: 9.04 lb.
**Caliber**: .308
**Magazine**: 20-round Magpaul
**Features**: Gissele two stage trigger group; LBC Steel gas block with

Picatinny rail on top; LBC bench rest, stainless steel barrel; Magpul PRS stock in black; Special Versa Pod and adapater; DuPont S coating in barrel.
**MSRP** . . . . . . . . . . . . . . . . . . **$3690**

# NEW Products: **Rifles**

LES BAER .308 SEMI-AUTO MATCH RIFLE

## LES BAER .308 SEMI-AUTO MATCH RIFLE
*Action*: Autoloading
*Stock*: Synthetic
*Barrel*: 18 in. or 20 in.
*Sights*: None
*Weight*: 11.2 lb.
*Caliber*: .308
*Magazine*: 20-round Magpaul
*Features*: No forward assist; Picatinny style flat top rail; LBC Carrier, chromed; chromed precision bolt; Gissele two stage trigger group; steel gas block; LBC Custom grip; Harris Bipod; Dupont S coating on barrel; Enforcer muzzle brake; Magpul stock.
**MSRP . . . . . . . . . . . . . . . . . $3290**

## MARLIN X7VH
*Action*: Bolt
*Stock*: Walnut
*Barrel*: 26 in.
*Sights*: None
*Weight*: 7.75 lb.
*Caliber*: 22-250 Rem., 308 Win.
*Magazine*: 4+1-rounds
*Features*: Pro-Fire adjustable trigger; fluted bolt; two-position safety; red cocking indicator; pillar-bedded satin-finished walnut with raised cheek piece; Soft-Tech recoil pad.
**MSRP . . . . . . . . . . . . . . . . $396.95**

## MARLIN 336 DELUXE
*Action*: Lever
*Stock*: Walnut
*Barrel*: 20 in.
*Sights*: Open
*Weight*: 7 lb.
*Caliber*: 30-30 Win.
*Magazine*: Tubular magazine, 6-rounds
*Features*: Highly polished blue finish; hammer block safety; #1 Grade full fancy American black walnut stock; adjustable semi-buckhorn folding rear sights and front ramp sights with brass bead and Wide-Scan hood; solid top receiver tapped for scope mount.
**MSRP . . . . . . . . . . . . . . . . $483.52**

MARLIN X7VH

MARLIN 336 DELUXE

NEW PRODUCTS

MARLIN XT-22

MARLIN XT-22TSR

MARLIN 1894 CSBL

## MARLIN XT-22

*Action*: Bolt
*Stock*: Hardwood
*Barrel*: 22 in.
*Sights*: Open
*Weight*: 6 lb.
*Caliber*: 22 LR
*Magazine*: Clip, 7-rounds
*Features*: Pro-Fire adjustable trigger; micro-groove rifling; blued bolt action; thumb safety; red cocking indicator; Monte carlo walnut-finished hardwood with swivel studs; full pistol grip; tough Mar-Shield Finish; adjustable rear sight and front ramp sights; receiver grooved for scope mount, drilled and tapped for scope bases.
**MSRP** . . . . . . . . . . . . . . . **$221–$326**

## MARLIN XT-22TSR

*Action*: Bolt
*Stock*: Synthetic
*Barrel*: 22 in.
*Sights*: Open
*Weight*: 6 lb.
*Caliber*: 22 S, L, LR
*Magazine*: Tubular magazine, 25 S, 19 L, and 17 LR rounds
*Features*: Pro-Fire adjustable trigger; stainless steel bolt action; thumb safety; red cocking indicator; black synthetic stock with palm swell; full pistol grip,molded in swivels and stippled grip areas; stainless steel barrel; adjustable semi-buckhorn folding rear sight; front ramp sight with

high visiblity orange front sight post; cutaway wide-scan hood.
**MSRP** . . . . . . . . . . . . . . . **$221–$326**

## MARLIN 1894 CSBL

*Action*: Lever
*Stock*: Grey/black laminate
*Barrel*: 16.25 in.
*Sights*: Open
*Weight*: 6 lb.
*Caliber*: 44 Special, .44 Mag.
*Magazine*: Tubular magazine, 8-rounds
*Features*: Stainless steel finish; lever action with big loop lever; XS ghost ring with front post sight and scout scope mount.
**MSRP** . . . . . . . . . . . . . . . . . . **$1061**

# NEW Products: **Rifles**

## MOSSBERG 702 PLINKSTER BANTAM
*Action*: Autoloader
*Stock*: Synthetic
*Barrel*: 18 in., 21 in.
*Sights*: Rear sight
*Weight*: 4.1 lb.
*Caliber*: .22LR
*Magazine*: Detachable box, 10-rounds
*Features*: Fold down rear sight; synthetic stock comes in black or pink; blue finish on barrel and metal.
**MSRP . . . . . . . . . . . . . . . $162–$199**

## MOSSBERG TACTICAL .22
*Action*: Autoloader
*Stock*: Synthetic
*Barrel*: 18 in.
*Sights*: None
*Weight*: 5 lb.
*Caliber*: .22 LR
*Magazine*: Detachable box, 10- or 25-rounds
*Features*: Six position adjustable stock or a fixed A2 Style stock; Picatinny rail and carry-handle.
**MSRP . . . . . . . . . . . . . . . . . . . $276**

## MOSSBERG HUNTER
*Action*: Autoloader
*Stock*: Synthetic
*Barrel*: 20 in.
*Sights*: None
*Weight*: N/A
*Caliber*: 5.56/.223 Rem.
*Magazine*: Detachable box, 5-rounds
*Features*: A4 flat top upper with Picatinny rail; single-stage trigger; shell deflector ramp behind ejection port; available in black or mossy oak treestand camo on just the forend and stock or on entire rifle.
**MSRP . . . . . . . . . . . . . . . $922–1010**

**MOSSBERG 702 PLINKSTER BANTAM**

**MOSSBERG TACTICAL .22**

## NOSLER M48 VARMINT
*Action*: Bolt
*Stock*: Composite
*Barrel*: 24 in.
*Sights*: None
*Weight*: 7.25 lb.
*Caliber*: .22-250 Rem.
*Magazine*: Internal box, 4 rounds
*Features*: Onyx black stock with slate metal finish; Rifle Basix trigger; glass pillar-bedded Kevlar and carbon-Fiber stock with teflon overcoat; match-grade stainless Pac-Nor, full free-floated hand lapped barrel.
**MSRP . . . . . . . . . . . . . . . . . . $2995**

**NOSLER M48 VARMINT**

NOSLER M48 TROPHY GRADE

NOSLER M48 SPORTER

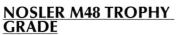

REMINGTION 700 SPS CAMO

## NOSLER M48 TROPHY GRADE

*Action*: Bolt
*Stock*: Composite
*Barrel*: 24 in., 24.75 in.
*Sights*: None
*Weight*: 6.5 lb.–7.5 lb.
*Caliber*: .243 Win., .257 Roberts, 7mm-08 Rem., .280 Ack Imp., .338 Win. Mag., .35 Whelen
*Magazine*: Internal box, 3-or-4 rounds
*Features*: Black w/ grey aluminum-bedded Bell and Carson stock; match-grade Pac-Nor chrome moly barrel; two-position safety; crisp, custom 3-pound Rifle Basix trigger; CeraKote and Micro Slick finishes.
**MSRP . . . . . . . . . . . . . . . . . . $1795**

## NOSLER M48 SPORTER

*Action*: Bolt
*Stock*: Kevlar and carbon fiber
*Barrel*: 24 in.
*Sights*: None
*Weight*: 6.5 lb.–7.5 lb.
*Caliber*: .22-250 Rem., .257 Roberts +P, 6.5-284 Norma, .270 Win., .280 Ack Imp., .30-06, .300 Win. Mag., .228 Win. Mag., .35 Whelen
*Magazine*: Internal box, 3- or 4-rounds
*Features*: Onyx black stock with slate metal finish; Rifle Basix trigger; glass pillar-bedded Kevlar and Carbon-Fiber stock with teflon overcoat; Cerakote and Micro Slick finishes prevent corrosion and weather damage; match-grade stainless Pac-Nor, fully free-floated hand lapped barrel.
**MSRP . . . . . . . . . . . . . . . . . . $2995**
**Left Hand: . . . . . . . . . . . . . . . $3195**

## REMINGTON 700 SPS CAMO

*Action*: Bolt
*Stock*: Synthetic
*Barrel*: 20 in., 22 in., 24 in.
*Sights*: None
*Weight*: 7 lb.–7.37 lb.
*Caliber*: .270 Win. , .30-06 Spgfld., 7mm Rem. Mag., .300 Win. Mag., .243 Win., .243 Win., 7mm-08 Rem.,
*Magazine*: None
*Features*: Hammer-forged barrel; X-Mark Pro externally adjustable trigger system; SuperCell recoil pad; synthetic stock in Mossy Oak Break-Up infinity pattern; Hogue over-molded grips; receivers tapped and drilled for scope mounts.
**MSRP . . . . . . . . . . . . . . . . . . $754**

REMINGTON 700 CDL DM

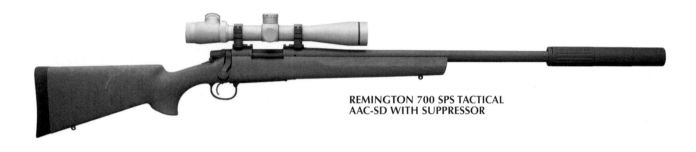

REMINGTON 700 SPS TACTICAL
AAC-SD WITH SUPPRESSOR

REMINGTON 700 CDL

## REMINGTON 700 CDL DM

*Action*: Bolt
*Stock*: Walnut, synthetic
*Barrel*: 24 in., 26 in.
*Sights*: None
*Weight*: 7.3 lb.–7.6 lb.
*Caliber*: .243 Win., 7mm-08 Rem., 270 Win., .30-06 Spgfld., 7mm Rem. Mag., .300 Win. Mag.
*Magazine*: Detachable box
*Features*: Receiver machined from solid-steel bar stock; X-Mark Pro externally adjustable trigger system; walnut stock with satin finish.
**MSRP** . . . . . . . . . . . . . . . . . . **$1020**

## REMINGTON 700 SPS TACTICAL AAC-SD

*Action*: Bolt
*Stock*: Synthetic
*Barrel*: 20 in.
*Sights*: None
*Weight*: 7.3 lb.–7.6 lb.
*Caliber*: .308 Win.
*Magazine*: Internal box
*Features*: Heavy barrel with threaded muzzle; Accepts AAC and other threaded flash hiders, muzzle brakes and supressors; Hogue overmolded ghillie green pillar bedded stock; X-mark pro adjustable trigger; optional Leupold Mark IV Scope.
**MSRP** . . . . . . . . . . . . . . . . . . **$757**

## REMINGTON 700 CDL SF LIMTED EDITION

*Action*: Bolt
*Stock*: Walnut, synthetic
*Barrel*: 24 in., 26 in.
*Sights*: None
*Weight*: 7.4 lb.–7.6 lb.
*Caliber*: 6mm Rem., .270 Win., 7mm Rem. Mag., .30-06 Spfld., .300 WSM
*Magazine*: Internal box
*Features*: Adjustable X-Mark Pro Trigger system; Receiver machined from solid-steel bar stock; stainless steel barrel.
**MSRP** . . . . . . . . . . . . . . . . . . **$1178**

## REMINGTON 700 XCR II CAMO (ROCKY MOUNTAIN ELK FOUNDATION EDITION)

*Action*: Bolt
*Stock*: Synthetic
*Barrel*: 24 in., 26 in.
*Sights*: Iron sights on 375 chamberings
*Weight*: 7.4 lb.–7.6 lb.
*Caliber*: .25-06 Rem., .270 Win., .280 Rem., .30-06 Spfld., 7mm Rem. Mag., .300 WSM, .300 Win. Mag., .338 Win. Mag., 7mm Rem. Ultra Mag., .300 Rem. Ultra Mag., .338 Ultra Mag., .375 H&H, .375 Rem. Ultra Mag.
*Magazine*: Internal box
*Features*: Engraved floorplate; synthetic stock in Realtree AP camo; drilled and tapped for scope mounting; rubber overmolding on grip and forestock; SuperCell recoil pad; TriNyte Corrosion-Control System; X-Mark Pro Trigger system.
**MSRP . . . . . . . . . . . . . . . . . . $1063**

## REMINGTON MODEL SEVEN SYNTHETIC

*Action*: Bolt
*Stock*: Synthetic
*Barrel*: 18 in., 20 in.
*Sights*: None
*Weight*: 6.1 lb.–6.5 lb.
*Caliber*: .223 Rem., .243 Win., .260 Rem., 7mm-08 Rem., .308 Win.
*Magazine*: Internal box
*Features*: Synthetic black stock; compact design for fast handling; cylindrical receiver design.
**MSRP . . . . . . . . . . . . . . . . . . $681**

**REMINGTON 700 XCR II CAMO**

**REMINGTON SEVEN SYNTHETIC**

**REMINGTON R-15 VTR BYRON SOUTH EDITION**

## REMINGTON R-15 VTR BYRON SOUTH EDITION

*Action*: Semi-automatic
*Stock*: Synthetic
*Barrel*: 18 in.
*Sights*: None
*Weight*: 6.75 lb.
*Caliber*: .223 Rem.
*Magazine*: 5-rounds
*Features*: Two-stage compeition trigger, receiver length Picatinny rail; coyote brown stock; ERGO grip; Yankee Hill customizable free floating tube; full advantage MAX HD-1 camo.
**MSRP . . . . . . . . . . . . . . . . . . $1772**

# NEW Products: **Rifles**

NEW PRODUCTS

ROCK RIVER LAR-8 PREDATOR HP

ROCK RIVER RRA LAR COYOTE CARBINE

ROCK RIVER LAR-40 MID-LENGTH A2

## ROCK RIVER LAR-8 PREDATOR HP

*Action*: Semi-automatic
*Stock*: Synthetic
*Barrel*: 20 in.
*Sights*: None
*Weight*: 8.6 lb.
*Caliber*: .308 Win., 7mm-08 Rem., .243 Win.
*Magazine*: Detachable box
*Features*: Forged A4 receiver with forward assist and port door; stainless steel barrel; gas block sight base; two-stage trigger; Hogue rubber Grip; RRA aluminum free float tube; A2 buttstock.
**MSRP** . . . . . . . . . . . . . . . . . . $1535

## ROCK RIVER RRA LAR-40 MID-LENGTH A2 & A4

*Action*: Semi-automatic
*Stock*: Synthetic
*Barrel*: 16 in.
*Sights*: None
*Weight*: 7.5 lb. (A2) & 7.1 lb. (A4)
*Caliber*: .40 S&W
*Magazine*: 1-round
*Features*: A2 flash hider; single-stage trigger; RRA tactical CAR stock with Hogue grip.
**A2:** . . . . . . . . . . . . . . . . . . . . $1140
**A4:** . . . . . . . . . . . . . . . . . . . . $1125

## ROCK RIVER RRA LAR-6.8 COYOTE CARBINE

*Action*: Semi-automatic
*Stock*: Synthetic
*Barrel*: 16 in.
*Sights*: None
*Weight*: 7 lb.
*Caliber*: 6.8mm SPC II
*Magazine*: 1-round
*Features*: Smith Vortex flash hider; chrome moly barrel; RRA two-stage match trigger.
**MSRP** . . . . . . . . . . . . . . . . . . $1200

## ROCK RIVER PDS CARBINE

*Action*: Semi-automatic
*Stock*: Synthetic
*Barrel*: 16 in.
*Sights*: None
*Weight*: 7.4 lb.
*Caliber*: .223 Rem.
*Magazine*: Detachable box
*Features*: Ambidextrous non-reciprocating charging handle; A2 flash hider; RRA two-stage trigger; Hogue rubber grip.
**MSRP . . . . . . . . . . . . . . . . . . $1685**

## ROSSI 92 CARBINE .45 COLT STAINLESS

*Action*: Lever
*Stock*: Wood
*Barrel*: 20 in.
*Sights*: Open
*Weight*: 5 lb.
*Caliber*: .45 Colt
*Magazine*: Tubular magazine, 10+1rounds
*Features*: Stainless steel or blued round barrel; crescent buttplates and extended front sight; used for brush hunting and wilderness packing; recoil absorbing butt pad.
**MSRP . . . . . . . . . . . . . . . . . . . $577**

ROCK RIVER PDS CARBINE

ROSSI 92 CARBINE .45 COLT STAINLESS

ROSSI CIRCUIT JUDGE TACTICAL SYNTHETIC

## ROSSI CIRCUIT JUDGE TACTICAL SYNTHETIC

*Action*: Revolver
*Stock*: Synthetic
*Barrel*: 18.5 in.
*Sights*: Red fiber optic front sight
*Weight*: N/A

*Caliber*: .45 LC, .410 Ga.
*Features*: This gun utilizes the revolver and extends its range for hunting and shooting. One can fire .410 Ga. 3-inch Magnum shotshells, .410 Ga. shotshells 2.5-inch, and . 45 colt ammunition in any order, without switching barrels. It includes modern features like yoke detent, transfer bar, and the Taurus Security System.
**MSRP . . . . . . . . . . . . . . . . . . . . $633**

# NEW Products: **Rifles**

## RUGER GUNSITE SCOUT RIFLE

*Action*: Bolt
*Stock*: Laminate
*Barrel*: 16.50 in.
*Sights*: Post front sight, adjustable rear
*Weight*: 7 lb.
*Caliber*: .308 Win.
*Magazine*: Detachable box, 10-rounds
*Features*: Flash suppressor, Picatinny rail; recoil pad; accurate sighting system; integral scope mounts; Mauser-type Extractor; developed with Gunsite and features their logo.
**MSRP**.................... **$995**

## RUGER M77 COMPACT MAGNUM

*Action*: Bolt
*Stock*: Walnut
*Barrel*: 20 in.
*Sights*: Brass bead front sight, adjustable U rear sight
*Caliber*: .300 RCM
*Magazine*: 3-rounds
*Features*: Ergonomic walnut stock with pistol grip; LC6 Trigger; Mauser-type

Extractor; Hingeds steel floorplate; integral scope mounts; three-positions safety; sling swivel studs.
**MSRP**.................... **$914**

## RUGER SR-556

*Action*: Autoloading
*Stock*: Synthetic
*Barrel*: 16.5 in.
*Sights*: Open
*Weight*: 7.75 lb.
*Caliber*: 6.8 SPC
*Magazine*: Detachable, 5-rounds or 25
*Features*: Two-stage piston-driven platform that retains all the features of the original SR-556; one-piece bolt carrier; mid-length gas system and four-position gas regulator that allows the user to adjust the piston system to various ammunition pressures or turn it to single shot; chrome-lined hammer-forged barrel; Troy Industries folding battlesights; quad rail and rail covers; Hogue Monogrip; six-position adjustable stock.
**MSRP:** .................. **$1995**

## RUGER MINI-THIRTY TACTICAL

*Action*: Autoloading
*Stock*: Synthetic
*Barrel*: 16.1 in.
*Sights*: Adjustable
*Weight*: 6.75 lb.
*Caliber*: 7.62 x 39mm
*Magazine*: 5 rounds
*Features*: Black synthetic stock; blued barrel with a flash supperssor; adjustable ghost ring rear sight, non-glare protected-post front sight.
**MSRP**.................... **$949**

## RUGER 10/22-FS TACTICAL

*Action*: Autoloading
*Stock*: Synthetic
*Barrel*: 16.1 in.
*Sights*: None
*Weight*: 4.3 lb.
*Caliber*: .22 LR
*Magazine*: Rotary box, 10-rounds
*Features*: Removable mini-14-style flash suppressor; precision-rifled cold-hammer-forged alloy-steel barrel in black matte finish; black synthetic stock.
**MSRP**.................... **$316**

RUGER SR-556

RUGER 10/22-FS TACTICAL

RUGER MINI-THIRTY TACTICAL

SAKO 85 SAFARI

## SAKO 85 SAFARI

**Action**: Bolt
**Stock**: Walnut
**Barrel**: 24.2 in.
**Sights**: Front bead, adjustable iron sights rear

**Weight**: 9 lb.
**Caliber**: .375 H&H Mag.
**Magazine**: Detachable box, 6-rounds
**Features**: Free-floating barrel; ergonomic walnut stock with checkering; staggered, two-row

magazine with total control latch; single-set adjustable trigger; steel trigger guard; 2-way Sako safety stocks both trigger and bolt handle; Pachmayr recoil pad.
**MSRP** . . . . . . . . . . . . . . . . . . **$1598**

SIG SAUER SIG 522 COMANDO

## SIG SAUER SIG 522 COMANDO

**Action**: Semi-automatic
**Stock**: Tactical synthetic
**Barrel**: 16 in.
**Sights**: Mini red dot
**Weight**: 6 lb. 2 oz.

**Caliber**: .22 LR
**Magazine**: Detachable box, 10- or 25-rounds

**Features**: Removable inert training suppressor.
**MSRP** . . . . . . . . . . . . . . . . . . **$600**

# **Rifles**

SIG SAUER SIG 516 PRECISION MARKSMAN

## SIG SAUER SIG 516 PRECISION MARKSMAN

**Action**: Semi-automatic
**Stock**: Tactical synthetic
**Barrel**: 18 in.
**Sights**: None

**Weight**: 7.7 lb.
**Caliber**: 5.56 x 45mm NATO
**Magazine**: Detachable box, 10-rounds
**Features**: Gas piston operating system; three-position gas regulator; free-floating military grade chrome lined

barrel; M1913 Picatinny flat top upper; aircraft grade aluminum upper & lower receiver with hard coat anodize finish.
**MSRP**. . . . . . . . . . . . . . . . . . . **$1734**

SIG SAUER SIG 716 PATROL RIFLE

## SIG SAUER SIG 716 PATROL RIFLE

**Action**: Semi-automatic
**Stock**: Tactical synthetic
**Barrel**: 16 in.

**Sights**: None
**Weight**: 9.3 lb.
**Caliber**: 7.62 x 51mm Nato
**Magazine**: Detachable box, 20-rounds
**Features**: Short stroke pushrod

operating system; M1913 Mil-Std rail; free-floating barrel; aluminum quad rail forend; telescoping stock.
**MSRP**. . . . . . . . . . . . . . . . . . . **$1866**

## SIG SAUER SIG M400

**Action**: Semi-automatic
**Stock**: Synthetic
**Barrel**: 16 in.
**Sights**: Adjustable front post, dual aperature
**Weight**: 5.59 lb.
**Caliber**: 5.56 x 45mm NATO
**Magazine**: Detachable box, 30-rounds

**Features**: Military grade, chrome-lined barrel, flat top upper with M1913 accessory rail.
**MSRP** . . . . . . . . . . . . . . . . . . . **$1065**

SIG SAUER SIG M400

SMITH & WESSON M&P 15 PS

## SMITH & WESSON M&P 15 PS

**Action**: Semi-automatic
**Stock**: Synthetic
**Barrel**: 16 in.
**Sights**: None
**Weight**: 6.5 lb.
**Caliber**: 5.56mm NATO

**Magazine**: Fixed box, 10-rounds
**Features**: Short-stroke-piston operating system; one-piece Op rod; adjustable and removable gas plug; one-piece carrier; Picatinny gas block; single-stage trigger.
**MSRP** . . . . . . . . . . . . . . . . . . . **$1359**

# NEW Products: **Rifles**

**SMITH & WESSON M&P 15T**

**UBERTI 1871 ROLLING BLOCK HUNTER CARBINE**

## SMITH & WESSON M&P 15T
*Action*: Semi-automatic
*Stock*: Synthetic
*Barrel*: 16 in.
*Sights*: Folding Magpul
*Weight*: 6.85 lb.
*Caliber*: 5.56mm NATO
*Magazine*: Detachable box, 30-rounds
*Features*: 10 in. patent pending, anti-twist, free-floating quad rail; Melonite barrel; chromed bolt carrier and gas key; gas operated; single-stage trigger.
**MSRP** . . . . . . . . . . . . . . . . . . $1469

## 1860 HENRY RIFLE WITH STANDARD ENGRAVING
*Action*: Lever
*Stock*: Walnut
*Barrel*: 24.25 in.
*Sights*: Open
*Weight*: 9.2 lb.
*Caliber*: .45 LC
*Magazine*: under-barrel tube, 9–13 rounds
*Features*: Standard engraved brass; octagonal barrel with blue finish.
**MSRP** . . . . . . . . . . . . . . . . . . $1525

## UBERTI 1871 ROLLING BLOCK HUNTER
*Action*: Rolling block
*Stock*: Walnut
*Barrel*: 22 in.
*Sights*: Adjustable
*Weight*: 4.5 lb.
*Caliber*: .22 LR, .22 Mag., .17 HMR
*Magazine*: None
*Features*: Round blue barrel; brass trigger guard; case-hardened frame; A-grade walnut stock with rubber butt pad.
**MSRP** . . . . . . . . . . . . . . . . . . $699

WEATHERBY VANGUARD SYNTHETIC COMBO

WINCHESTER 94 SPORTER

WINCHESTER 94 SHORT RIFLE

## WEATHERBY VANGUARD SYNTHETIC COMBO

*Action*: Bolt
*Stock*: Synthetic
*Barrel*: 24 in.
*Sights*: Simmons 3.5-10x40mm scope
*Weight*: 7.25 lb.
*Caliber*: .243 Win., .270 Win., .308 Win., .30-06 Spfld., .257 Weatherby Mag., .300 Weatherby Mag.
*Magazine*: 3+1, 5+1 rounds
*Features*: Fully adjustable trigger; hammer-forged barrel; black injection-molded composite Monte Carlo stock; low density recoil pad.
**MSRP** . . . . . . . . . . . . . . . . . . . **$629**

## WINCHESTER 94 SPORTER

*Action*: Lever
*Stock*: Walnut
*Barrel*: 24 in.
*Sights*: None
*Weight*: 7 lb. 8oz.
*Caliber*: .30-30 Win., .38-55 Win.
*Magazine*: 8-rounds
*Features*: Half-round, half-octagon blued barrel; straight grip with a crescent butt and finely checkered blue-steel buttplate with double-line bordering; drilled and tapped for optics.
**MSRP** . . . . . . . . . . . . . . . . **$1299.99**

## WINCHESTER 94 SHORT RIFLE

*Action*: Lever
*Stock*: Walnut
*Barrel*: 20 in.
*Sights*: None
*Weight*: 6 lb. 12oz.
*Caliber*: .30-30 Win.
*Magazine*: Under barrel tube, 7-rounds
*Features*: Straight grip; rifle-style forearm and black grip cap; semi-buckhorn rear sights, Marble Arms gold-bead front sight; drilled and tapped for optics.
**MSRP** . . . . . . . . . . . . . . . . **$1129.99**

# NEW Products: **Rifles**

**WINCHESTER 1886 SHORT RIFLE**

**WINCHESTER 1892 CARBINE**

**WINCHESTER 70 FEATHERWEIGHT COMPACT**

## WINCHESTER 1886 SHORT RIFLE
*Action*: Lever
*Stock*: Walnut
*Barrel*: 24 in.
*Sights*: None
*Weight*: 8 lb. 6oz.
*Caliber*: .45-70 Govt.
*Magazine*: Tubular mag., 6-rounds
*Features*: Deeply blued receiver and lever; end cap and steel crescent buttplate; straight grip.
**MSRP**. . . . . . . . . . . . . . . . . **$1269**

## WINCHESTER 1892 CARBINE
*Action*: Lever
*Stock*: Walnut
*Barrel*: 20 in.
*Sights*: None
*Weight*: 6 lb.
*Caliber*: .45 Long Colt, .44-40 Win., .44 Mag., .357 Mag.
*Magazine*: 10-rounds
*Features*: Round, deeply blued finish on receiver and lever; straight grip and satin walnut finish.
**MSRP**. . . . . . . . . . . . . . . . . **$1069.99**

## WINCHESTER 70 FEATHERWEIGHT COMPACT
*Action*: Bolt
*Stock*: Walnut
*Barrel*: 20 in.
*Sights*: None
*Weight*: 6.5 lb.
*Caliber*: .22-250 Rem., .243 Win., 7mm-08 Rem., .308 Win.
*Magazine*: 5-rounds
*Features*: Pachmayr declerator recoil pad; action is drilled and tapped for optics.
**MSRP**. . . . . . . . . . . . . . . . . **$899.99**

CROSMAN .357 BENJAMIN ROGUE

STOEGER X-20 SUPPRESSOR

STOEGER X-50 AIR RIFLE COMBO

### CROSMAN BENJAMIN ROUGE .357

*Power*: Electro pre-charged pneumatic
*Stock*: Synthetic
*Overall length*: 48 in.
*Sights*: None
*Weight*: 9.8 lb.
*Caliber*: .357
*Features*: Uses electronic valve technology to provide precise regulation of pressure and provide more shots per fill through the control of pressure; rifled steel barrel; velocity up to 700–1000 fps; has built in LCD screen to control eValve and trigger; sling studs; fill adaptor; degassing tool; magazine holds 6 shots.
**MSRP** . . . . . . . . . . . . . . . . . . **$1500**

### STOEGER X-20 SUPPRESSOR

*Power*: Spring-piston/break action
*Stock*: Black synthetic
*Overall length*: 43 in.
*Sights*: 4 x 32 illuminated red green scope
*Weight*: 7 lb.
*Caliber*: .177
*Features*: Air flow control system; adjustable two-stage trigger; integral dovetail scope rail on receiver; non-slip, deluxe rubber recoil pad; Monte Carlo-style, black synthetic stock with checkering; rifled, blued steel barrel.
**MSRP** . . . . . . . . . . . . . . . . . . **$219.99**

### STOEGER X-50 AIR RIFLE COMBO

*Power*: Spring-piston/ breech-loading
*Stock*: Black synthetic
*Overall length*: 50 in.
*Sights*: 3-9 x 40 parallax adjustable scope with rings
*Weight*: 9.9 lb.
*Caliber*: .177
*Features*: Ergonomic cocking grip; rifled blue-steel barrel; synthetic Monte Carlo-style stock; ambidextrous automatic safety.
**MSRP** . . . . . . . . . . . . . . . . . . **$279.99**

# NEW Products: **Black Powder**

## CVA OPTIMA
*Action*: Break-action muzzleloader
*Stock*: Synthetic
*Barrel*: 26 in.
*Sights*: None
*Weight*: 6.65 lb.
*Caliber*: .50, .45
*Magazine*: None
*Features*: 416 stainless steel, fluted barrel; bullet guiding muzzle; stock

CVA OPTIMA

comes in FiberGrip black or Realtree hardwoods green camo; QRBP; reversible hammer spur; CrushZone

recoil pad; DuraSight dead-on one-piece scope mount.
**MSRP . . . . . . . . . . $269.95–$339.95**

## EMF 1873 PONY EXPRESS
*Lock*: Caplock revolver
*Stock*: Walnut express grips
*Barrel*: 3.5 in.
*Sights*: Fixed
*Weight*: 2 lb.
*Bore/ Caliber*: .45 LC
*Features*: Casehardened steel; checkered walnut express grips; turned down hammer.
**MSRP . . . . . . . . . . . . . . . . . . $625**

## EMF HARTFORD 1863 POCKET REMINGTON
*Lock*: Caplock revolver
*Stock*: Walnut
*Barrel*: 3.5 in.
*Sights*: Fixed
*Weight*: 1 lb. 5oz.
*Bore/ Caliber*: .36
*Features*: Steel frame, blued barrel.
**MSRP . . . . . . . . . . . . . . . . . . . . $295**

## EMF ALCHIMISTA II
*Lock*: Caplock revolver
*Stock*: Walnut
*Barrel*: 4.75 in.
*Sights*: Fixed
*Weight*: 2.1 lb.
*Bore/ Caliber*: .357
*Features*: Standard casehardening; checkered walnut grips.
**MSRP . . . . . . . . . . . . . . . . . . . $605**

**EMF HARTFORD- PONY EXPRESS 45 L LARGE**

**EMF HARTFORD- 1863 POCKET REMINGTON**

**PEDERSOLI SIDE-BY-SIDE SHOTGUN LA BOHEMIENNE**

## PEDERSOLI SIDE-BY-SIDE SHOTGUN LA BOHEMIENNE
*Lock*: Hinged breech muzzleloading
*Stock*: Checkered walnut
*Barrel*: 28 in.

*Choke*: Mod choke tubes
*Weight*: 7 lb.
*Bore/ Caliber*: 12 ga.
*Features*: Rust brown finish barrel; interchangable chokes; color case

hardened framel; hand-Engraved locks.
**MSRP . . . . . . . . . . . . . . . . . . $1914**

## PEDERSOLI DERINGER PHILADELPHIA

*Lock*: Flintlock
*Stock*: Walnut
*Barrel*: 3.06 in.
*Sights*: None
*Weight*: .54 lb.
*Bore/ Caliber*: .45
*Features*: Reproduction of the popular pocket pistols originally manufactured by John Henry Deringer. Brass furniture; case hardned lock..
**MSRP** . . . . . . . . . . . . . . . . . . . **$476**

## TAYLOR'S & CO. LE MAT CAVALRY

*Lock*: Traditional caplock
*Stock*: Walnut
*Barrel*: 8 in.
*Sights*: Fixed
*Weight*: 5 lb.
*Bore/ Caliber*: .44, 20 Ga.
*Features*: Blue steel finish; nine shot .44 caliber revolver with a 20 Ga. Single shot barrel was a favorite among Confederate cavalry troops; Case hardened hammer and trigger; lanyard ring; trigger guard with spur.
**MSRP** . . . . . . . . . . . . . . . . . . . **$1136**

## TRADITIONS PURSUIT ULTRA LIGHT XLT

*Lock*: Hinged breech muzzleloading
*Stock*: Black synthetic or Mossy Oak Treestand camo
*Barrel*: 28 in. fluted
*Sights*: Metal fiber optic
*Weight*: 5.9 lb.
*Bore/ Caliber*: .50
*Features*: Accelerator breech plug; drilled and tapped for scopes; 209 shotgun primer igntion; black synthetic or Soft Touch camoflage stock with CeraKote finish; speed load system.
**MSRP** . . . . . . . . . . . . . . . . . . . **$329**

## TRADITIONS VORTEK MUZZLELOADER

*Action*: Break-action, muzzleloader
*Stock*: Synthetic
*Barrel*: 28 in.
*Sights*: Williams metal fiber optics sights
*Weight*: 12.5 lb.
*Caliber*: .50
*Magazine*: None
*Features*: Black synthetic thumbhole stock; accelerator breech plug; comfort-grip overmolding; sling swivel studs; stainless steel barrels in stainless or blued finish; drilled and tapped for scope.
**MSRP** . . . . . . . . . . . . . . . . . . . **$449**

PEDERSOLI DERINGER PHILADELPHIA

TAYLOR'S & CO. LE MAT CAVALRY

TRADITIONS PURSUIT ULTRA LIGHT XLT

TRADITIONS VORTEK MUZZLELOADER

AYA BOXLOCK ROUND ACTION

BENELLI VINCI CORDOBA

BENELLI SUPER VINCI

BENELLI SUPER BLACK EAGLE II

## AYA BOXLOCK ROUND ACTION
*Action*: Side-by-side hammerless boxlock ejector
*Stock*: Walnut
*Barrel*: 28 in., with other lengths to order
*Chokes*: Screw-in tubes
*Weight*: 6 lb. 10oz.
*Bore/ Gauge*: 12, 16, 20, 28, .410
*Magazine*: None
*Features*: Double locking mechanism with replaceable hinge pin; disc set firing pins; double trigger; chopper lump barrels with concave rib; special floral and scroll engraving available in color hardened, old silver, or white finish; automatic safety; walnut stock.
*MSRP* . . . . . . . . . . . . . . . . . . $7722

## BENELLI VINCI CORDOBA
*Action*: Inerta operated semi-automatic
*Stock*: Synthetic with GripTight coating

*Barrel*: 28 in., 30 in.
*Chokes*: Extended Crio chokes
*Weight*: 7 lb.–7.1 lb.
*Bore/ Gauge*: 12
*Magazine*: 4+1
*Features*: Crio Ported Barrels; ComforTech Gel recoil pad and comb insert; heavy duty magazine cap; black synthetic stock; red bar front sight and metal bead mid sight.
*MSRP* . . . . . . . . . . . . . . . . . . $2009

## BENELLI SUPER VINCI
*Action*: Inerta operated semi-automatic
*Stock*: Synthetic
*Barrel*: 26 in., 28 in.
*Chokes*: Crio chokes (C, IC, M, IM, F)
*Weight*: 6.9 lb.–7 lb.
*Bore/ Gauge*: 12
*Magazine*: 3+1
*Features*: In-line inertia driven system; englarged trigger and trigger guard for use with gloves; ComforTech Plus recoil pad; QuadraFit shim kit; drilled

and tapped for scopes; synthetic stock in black, Realtree APG camo, or Realtree MAX-4 camo.
*MSRP* . . . . . . . . . . . . . . $1649–$1759

## BENELLI SUPER BLACK EAGLE II
*Action*: Inerta operated semi-automatic
*Stock*: Synthetic
*Barrel*: 24 in.
*Chokes*: Custom XTF extended choke
*Weight*: 7.1 lb.
*Bore/ Gauge*: 12
*Magazine*: 3+1
*Features*: Burris FastFire sight; Comfortech Gel recoil pad and comb insert; larger trigger guard for use with gloves; EDM Ported Crio Barrel; Comfortech synthetic stock with Realtree APG finish.
*MSRP* . . . . . . . . . . . . . . . . . . $2879

**BROWNING CYNERGY MOSSY OAK BREAK-UP INFINITY**

## BROWNING CYNERGY SATIN COMPOSITE

*Action*: Over/under
*Stock*: Composite
*Barrel*: 26 in., 28 in.
*Chokes*: Three Invector-Plus choke tubes (F, M, IC)
*Weight*: 7 lb. 6 oz.–7 lb. 8 oz.
*Bore/ Gauge*: 12
*Magazine*: None
*Features*: Steel receiver; MonoLock Hinge; matte blued finish barrel; reverse striker ignition system; impact ejectors; top-tang barrel selector/ safety; black composite with rubber over molding in grip areas; Dura-Touch Armor Coating; adjustable comb; ivory bead front sight; recoil pad
*MSRP* . . . . . . . . . . . . . . . . . . **$1739**

## BROWNING CYNERGY MOSSY OAK BREAK-UP INFINITY

*Action*: Over/under
*Stock*: Composite
*Barrel*: 26 in., 28 in.
*Chokes*: Three Invector-Plus Choke tubes (F, M, IC)
*Weight*: 7 lb. 6 oz., 7 lb. 8 oz.

*Bore/ Gauge*: 12
*Magazine*: None
*Features*: Steel receiver with MonoLock Hinge; Composite stock in Mossy Oak Break-Up Infinity camo finish; ventilated top and side ribs; Reverse Striker igniton system; ivory front and mid bead sights; Medium Inflex recoil pad.
*MSRP* . . . . . . . . . . . . . . . . . . **$1999**

## BROWNING CITORI HERITAGE

*Action*: Over/under
*Stock*: Walnut
*Barrel*: 28 in., 30 in., 32 in.
*Chokes*: Three Invector-Plus choke tubes (F, M, IC)
*Weight*: 6 lb. 9oz.
*Bore/ Gauge*: 28
*Magazine*: None
*Features*: Steel side plate receiver with nitride finish; high-relief gold enhanced engraving; lightning style buttstock and forearm with walnut stock; back buttplate; elite grade ABS case; single-selective trigger.
*MSRP* . . . . . . . . . . . . . . . . . . **$5939**

## BROWNING A-BOLT HUNTER

*Action*: Bolt
*Stock*: Walnut
*Barrel*: 22 in.
*Chokes*: None
*Weight*: 7 lb. 2oz.
*Bore/ Gauge*: 12
*Magazine*: Detachable, 2+1
*Features*: Sling swivel studs; satin finish walnut stock with checkered forearm; low-luster blued finish, steel receiver; drilled and tapped for scope mounts.
*MSRP* . . . . . . . . . . . . . . . . . . **$1200**

## BROWNING A-BOLT STALKER

*Action*: Bolt
*Stock*: Composite
*Barrel*: 22 in.
*Chokes*: None
*Weight*: 7 lb.
*Bore/ Gauge*: 12
*Magazine*: Detachable, 2+1
*Features*: Black composite ( Stalker model); Mossy Oak Break-Up Infinity composite (Infinity Camo Model); textured gripping surfaces; Dura-touch armor coating; sling swivel studs installed; recoil pad; Truglo/ Marble's fiber optic front sight, adjustable rear sight.
**Stalker:** . . . . . . . . . . . . . . . . **$1100**
**Infinity Camo:** . . . . . . . . . . . . **$1240**

**BROWNING CITORI HERITAGE**

**BROWNING A-BOLT STALKER MODEL**

BROWNING MAXUS HUNTER

## BROWNING MAXUS HUNTER

*Action*: Autoloader, gas operated
*Stock*: Composite
*Barrel*: 26 in., 28 in., 30 in.
*Chokes*: Three Invectus-Plus
*Weight*: 6 lb. 15oz.–7 lb. 1oz.
*Bore/ Gauge*: 12
*Magazine*: None
*Features*: Aluminum alloy receiver with durable satin nickel finish; laser engraving of pheasant and mallard on receiver; Inflex Technology recoil pad; ivory front bead sight.
**MSRP . . . . . . . . . . . . . $1420–$1560**

## BROWNING MAXUS SPORTING

*Action*: Autoloader, gas operated
*Stock*: Walnut
*Barrel*: 28 in., 30 in.
*Chokes*: Five Invector-Plus choke tubes
*Weight*: 7 lb.
*Bore/ Gauge*: 12
*Magazine*: None
*Features*: Aluminum alloy receiver with durable satin nickel finish; laser engraving of game birds transforming into clay birds; speed lock forearm; ivory mid-bead sight, HiVix Tri-Comp fiber-optic front sight.
**MSRP . . . . . . . . . . . . . . . . . . $1630**

BROWNING MAXUS SPORTING

BROWNING SILVER HUNTER MICRO MIDAS

## BROWNING SILVER HUNTER MICRO MIDAS

*Action*: Autoloader, gas operated
*Stock*: Walnut
*Barrel*: 24 in., 26 in.
*Chokes*: Three Invector-Plus choke tubes
*Weight*: 6 lb.–7 lb. 5 oz.
*Bore/ Gauge*: 12, 20
*Magazine*: None
*Features*: Semi-humpback receiver design with silver finish; ivory front bead sight.
**MSRP . . . . . . . . . . . . . . . . . . . $1070**

## BROWNING BPS ALL WEATHER HIGH CAPACITY

*Action*: Bottom ejection pump
*Stock*: Composite
*Barrel*: 20 in.
*Chokes*: None
*Weight*: 7 lb. 8 oz.
*Bore/ Gauge*: 12
*Magazine*: 5-round capacity
*Features*: Black composite on All Weather with matte finish; top tang safety; forged and machined steel receiver, satin nickel finish; HiViz Tactical fiber-optic front sight.
**MSRP . . . . . . . . . . . . . . . . . . . . . $689**

BROWNING BPS ALL WEATHER HIGH CAPACITY

# NEW Products: Shotguns

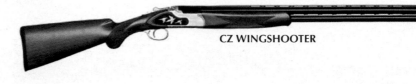

**CZ WINGSHOOTER**

## CZ WINGSHOOTER

**Action**: Over/under
**Stock**: Turkish walnut
**Barrel**: 28 in.
**Chokes**: 5 interchangable choke tubes
**Weight**: 6 lb.–7.4 lb.
**Bore/ Gauge**: 12, 20, 28, .410
**Magazine**: None
**Features**: Single trigger; black chrome barrel finish; box-lock frame; Schnable forend; manual tang safety.

12-Ga: .................... $999
20-Ga: .................... $999
28-Ga: .................. $1040
.410 bore: .............. $1040

**CZ LIMITED EDITION OVER/UNDER**

## CZ LIMITED EDITION OVER/UNDER

**Action**: Over/under
**Stock**: Circassian walnut
**Barrel**: 28 in.
**Chokes**: 5 interchangable choke tubes
**Bore/ Gauge**: 12, 20, 28, .410
**Magazine**: None
**Features**: Schnable forend and buttstock; silver-engraved gun incorporates selective mechanial triggers; box-lock-frame design; coil-spring-operated hammers; chrome-lined barrels threaded for interchangable choke tubes.
MSRP .................... $2499

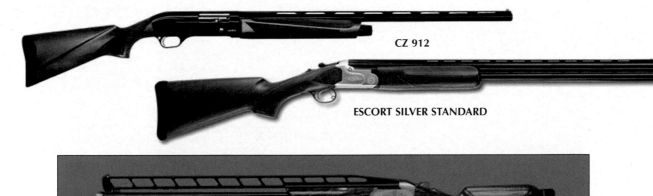

**CZ 912**

**ESCORT SILVER STANDARD**

**Krieghoff K-80 ACS**

## CZ 912

**Action**: Recoil-operated semi-automatic
**Stock**: Walnut
**Barrel**: 28 in.
**Chokes**: 5 interchangable choke tubes
**Weight**: 7.3 lb.
**Bore/ Gauge**: 12
**Magazine**: 4+1
**Features**: Fiber optic front bead; features a gloss black finish on metalwork; cross bolt safety; chrome lined barrel; aluminum frame.
MSRP .................... $509

## ESCORT SILVER SYNTHETIC SHORTY

**Action**: Over/under
**Stock**: Synthetic
**Barrel**: 18 in.
**Chokes**: Multi choke
**Weight**: 7 lb.
**Bore/ Gauge**: 12
**Magazine**: None
**Features**: Nickel plated receiver; adjustable comb; auto safety; blued tang lever, barrel selector switch and trigger guard; soft rubber synthetic stock with cobblestone grip inserts.
MSRP .................... $663

## KRIEGHOFF K-80 ACS

**Action**: Over/under
**Stock**: Walnut
**Barrel**: 30 in., 32 in., 34 in.
**Chokes**: 8 factory steel choke tubes
**Weight**: 8.75 lb.
**Bore/ Gauge**: 12
**Magazine**: None
**Features**: White pearl front bead and metal center bead sight; Case hardened action, nickel plated steel receiver with Nitride Silver finish; Single selective trigger
From: .................... $16490

## LEGACY SPORTS ESCORT AVERY WATERFOWL EXTREME

*Action*: Autoloader
*Stock*: Synthetic
*Barrel*: 28 in.
*Chokes*: Interchangable chokes
*Weight*: 7.4 lb.
*Bore/ Gauge*: 12
*Magazine*: Tubular, 5+1
*Features*: Designed for the toughest weather conditions; black synthetic stock with a black nylon recoil and raised textured grip panels on the pistol grip and forend; black chrome external finish; raised rib; brass front bead.
**MSRP . . . . . . . . . . . . . . . . . . $784**

## LEGACY SPORTS ESCORT SLUG GUN

*Action*: Autoloader or pump
*Stock*: Synthetic
*Barrel*: 22 in.
*Chokes*: Rifled barrel
*Weight*: 5.9 lb.–6.95 lb.
*Bore/ Gauge*: 12 or 20
*Magazine*: None
*Features*: Fiber optic sights; tough, black polymer stock; large button side release.
**Autoloader: . . . . . . . . . . . . . . $623**
**Pump: . . . . . . . . . . . . . . . $497**

MOSSBERG 500 TURKEY

MOSSBERG 935 MAGNUM TURKEY GUN

MOSSBERG 510 MINI CAMO

## MOSSBERG 500 TURKEY

*Action*: Pump
*Stock*: Synthetic
*Barrel*: 24 in.
*Chokes*: Accu-Choke tubes (XX-Full)
*Weight*: 7.25 lb.–8.25 lb.
*Bore/ Gauge*: 12
*Magazine*: 6- or 7-rounds
*Features*: Adjustable front sight; synthetic finish in mossy oak break-up infinity camo; ported barrel; ambidextrous thumb-operated safety; includes gun lock.
**MSPR . . . . . . . . . . . . . . $435–$472**

## MOSSBERG 935 MAGNUM TURKEY GUN

*Action*: Autoloader
*Stock*: Synthetic
*Barrel*: 24 in.
*Chokes*: Mulit-full tube chokes
*Weight*: 7.5 lb.
*Bore/ Gauge*: 12
*Magazine*: 5-rounds
*Features*: Overbored barrel; synthetic stock in New Mossy Oak Break-up Infinity camo; adjustable fiber optic sights; quick-empty magazine button; wide ventilated rib.
**MSRP . . . . . . . . . . . . . . . . . . $769**

## MOSSBERG 510 MINI CAMO

*Action*: Pump
*Stock*: Synthetic
*Barrel*: 18.5 in.
*Chokes*: Interchangable Accu-Choke tubes
*Weight*: 5 lb.
*Bore/ Gauge*: 20 or .410
*Magazine*: 3- or 4-rounds
*Features*: Dual bead sights; synthetic stock comes in Mossy Oak Infinity Camo.
**MSRP . . . . . . . . . . . . . . . . . . $375**

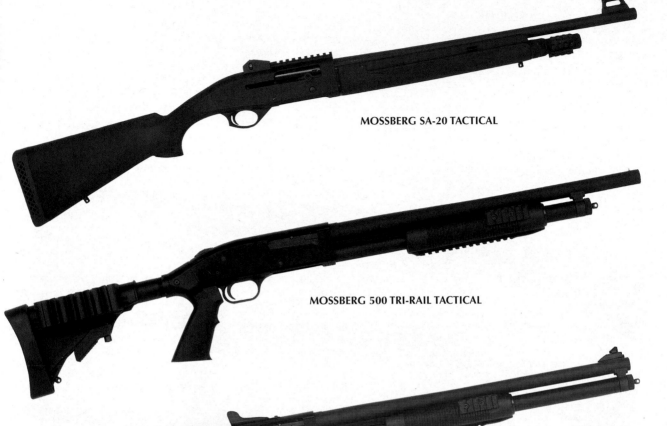

MOSSBERG SA-20 TACTICAL

MOSSBERG 500 TRI-RAIL TACTICAL

MOSSBERG 500 TRI-RAIL PERSUADER

## MOSSBERG SA-20 TACTICAL
*Action*: Autoloader
*Stock*: Synthetic
*Barrel*: 20 in.
*Chokes*: Cylinder bore
*Weight*: 6 lb.
*Bore/ Gauge*: 20
*Magazine*: 5-rounds
*Features*: Quick-load shell elevator; ghost ring sights; Picatinny rail on top of receiver, plus three-sided rail mount below the barrel; standard full-length stock or full-length stock with a pistol grip.
**MSRP**. . . . . . . . . . . . . . . . . . . . **$510**

## MOSSBERG 500 TRI-RAIL TACTICAL
*Action*: Pump
*Stock*: Synthetic
*Barrel*: 18.5 in.
*Chokes*: Cylinder-choked barrel
*Weight*: 6.75 lb.
*Bore/ Gauge*: 12
*Magazine*: 6-rounds
*Features*: Bead front sight; matte black synthetic, adjustable stock; tri-rail forend.
**MSRP**. . . . . . . . . . . . . . . . . . . . **$553**

## MOSSBERG 500 TRI-RAIL PERSUADER
*Action*: Pump
*Stock*: Synthetic
*Barrel*: 20 in.
*Chokes*: Cylinder bore
*Weight*: 7 lb.
*Bore/ Gauge*: 12
*Magazine*: 8-rounds
*Features*: Ghost ring sights; six position adjustable stock; matte blue finish; tri-rail forend.
**MSRP**. . . . . . . . . . . . . . . . . . . . **$590**

MOSSBERG 590A1

MOSSBERG MODEL 535

REMINGTON 1100 COMPETITION
SYNTHETIC

## MOSSBERG 590A1

*Action*: Pump
*Stock*: Synthetic
*Barrel*: 18.5 in.
*Chokes*: Cylinder bore
*Weight*: 7.25 lb.
*Bore/ Gauge*: 12
*Magazine*: 9-rounds
*Features*: Six-position adjustable stock
with a tri-rail forend; ghost ring sights;
Parkarized finish; Speedfeed, black
stock; heavy barrel wall; Blackwater
logo.
**MSRP . . . . . . . . . . . . . . . . . . . $683**

## MOSSBERG 535

*Action*: Pump
*Stock*: Synthetic
*Barrel*: 20 in.
*Chokes*: X-factor ported choke tube
*Weight*: 7 lb.
*Bore/ Gauge*: 12
*Magazine*: 6-rounds
*Features*: Adjustable fiber-optic sights;
user-adjustable trigger; camoflage
Picatinny rail; adjustable stock with
Mossy Oak Infinity camo finish; Tru-
Glo red-dot sight.
**MSRP . . . . . . . . . . . . . . . . . . . $671**

## REMINGTON 1100
## COMPETITION SYNTHETIC

*Action*: Autoloading
*Stock*: Synthetic
*Barrel*: 30 in.
*Chokes*: 5 extended Briley (Target)
choke tubes (Skeet, IC, LM, M, Full)
*Weight*: 8.12 lb.
*Bore/ Gauge*: 12
*Magazine*: None
*Features*: Nickel-Teflon finish on
receiver and all internal parts; barrel
has 10mm target-style rib; adjustable
comb and cast adjustment options;
high-gloss blued barrel; fully
adjustable target-style stock with recoil
reduction; synthetic polymer stock and
forend finished with carbon graphite
apperance; twin target-style bead
sights.
**MSRP . . . . . . . . . . . . . . . . . . . $1180**

# NEW Products: Shotguns

## REMINGTON VERSA MAX SYNTHETIC

**Action**: Autoloading
**Stock**: Synthetic
**Barrel**: 26 in., 28 in.
**Chokes**: 5 Flush Mount Pro Bore chokes (F, M, IM, LB, IC)
**Weight**: 7.5 lb.–7.7 lb.
**Bore/ Gauge**: 12
**Magazine**: 3+1 or 2+1 rounds
**Features**: Remington patented gas-piston system; synthetic stock and forend with grey overmolded grips, comes in black or a Mossy Oak duck blind camo; drilled and tapped receiver; englarged trigger guard opening and larger safety for easier use with gloves; TriNyte Barrel and nickel-Teflon plated internal components.
**Black synthetic:** . . . . . . . . . . . **$1399**
**Camo:** . . . . . . . . . . . . . . . . . **$1599**

## ROSSI "TUFFY" SINGLE-SHOT

**Action**: Single-shot
**Stock**: Synthetic
**Barrel**: 18.5 in.
**Chokes**: None
**Weight**: 3 lb.
**Bore/Gauge**: .410 Ga.
**Magazine**: None
**Features**: Matte nickel finish with steel construction; black synthetic stock with thumbhole grip; buttstock shell holder with window; Taurus Security System.
**MSRP** . . . . . . . . . . . . . . . . . . . . **$172**

REMINGTON VERSA MAX SYNTHETIC

STOEGER 3500

TRISTAR HUNTER EX

ROSSI TUFFY SINGLE SHOT

## STOEGER 3500

**Action**: Semi-automatic
**Stock**: Synthetic
**Barrel**: 24 in., 26 in., 28 in.
**Chokes**: Screw-in choke tubes (C, IC, M, F, XFT) and wrench
**Weight**: 7.45 lb.–7.65 lb.
**Bore/ Gauge**: 12
**Magazine**: 4+1 rounds
**Features**: Synthetic stock comes in black or camo finish in Advantage Max-4, Realtree APG, Intertia Drive system; recoil reducer; red-bar front sight; Weaver scope base; includes shim kit.
**MSRP** . . . . . . . . . . . . . . . . . . . **$679**

## TRISTAR HUNTER EX SYNTHETIC

**Action**: Over/under
**Stock**: Synthetic
**Barrel**: 28 in.
**Chokes**: 3 Beretta style tubes
**Weight**: 7 lb.
**Bore/ Gauge**: 12
**Magazine**: None
**Features**: Synthetic stock comes in half camo finish; 3 in. extractor; fiber optic sight; sling swivel studs; chrome-lined barrels.
**MSRP** . . . . . . . . . . . . . . . . . . . **$559**

### TRISTAR THE SETTER

*Action*: Over/Under
*Stock*: Walnut
*Barrel*: 28 in.
*Chokes*: Beretta style chokes (IC, M, F)
*Weight*: 7.4 lb.
*Bore/Gauge*: 12
*Magazine*: None
*Features*: Double trigger, extractor shotgun; laser-cut checkering; solid steel receiver; brass bead front sight; chrome lined barrels.
**MSRP** . . . . . . . . . . . . . . . . . . . . **$444**

### TRISTAR COBRA FIELD PUMP

*Action*: Pump
*Stock*: Synthetic
*Barrel*: 28 in.
*Chokes*: 1 Berreta style choke (M)
*Weight*: 6.9 lb.
*Bore/ Gauge*: 12
*Magazine*: None
*Features*: Fiber optic front sight; extended forearm to keep out dirt; sling swivel studs.
**MSRP** . . . . . . . . . . . . . . . . . . . . **$319**

### WEATHERBY SA-08 ENTRE RIOS

*Action*: Semi-automatic
*Stock*: Walnut
*Barrel*: 26 in., 28 in.
*Chokes*: 3 application tubes (SK, IC, M)
*Weight*: 5.25 lb.
*Bore/ Gauge*: 28
*Magazine*: 5-rounds
*Features*: Walnut stock with high gloss finish and metalwork.
**MSRP** . . . . . . . . . . . . . . . . . . . . **$749**

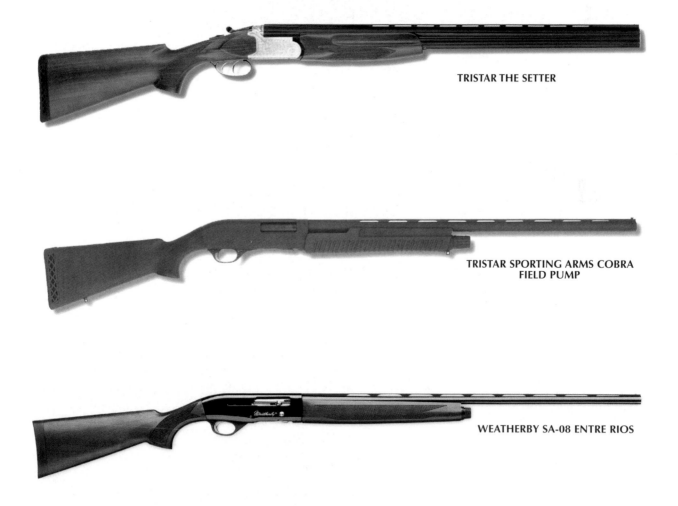

TRISTAR THE SETTER

TRISTAR SPORTING ARMS COBRA FIELD PUMP

WEATHERBY SA-08 ENTRE RIOS

### WEATHERBY PA-459 DIGITAL TR

**Action**: Pump
**Stock**: Synthetic
**Barrel**: 18.5 in.
**Chokes**: Ported cylinder-choke tubes
**Weight**: 7 lb.
**Bore/ Gauge**: 12
**Magazine**: 5+1 or 4+1 rounds
**Features**: Injection-molded synthetic stock with universal digital camoflage finish; metalwork in black-matte finish; pistol-grip style buttstock; chrome-lined barrel; extended forend; Picatinny rail; LPA-style ghost ring rear sights, white blade front sight.
**MSRP** . . . . . . . . . . . . . . . . . . . **$499**

WEATHERBY PA-459 DIGITAL TR

WEATHERBY SA-459 TR

WEATHERBY PA-08 TR

### WEATHERBY SA-459 TR

**Action**: Semi-automatic
**Stock**: Synthetic
**Barrel**: 18.5 in.
**Chokes**: Ported cylinder choke tube
**Weight**: 7 lb.
**Bore/ Gauge**: 12, 20
**Magazine**: 5+1 rounds
**Features**: Pistol grip stock with a rubber textured area; chrome lined barrel; Picatinny rail for mounting scopes and optics; ghost ring Style rear sight, front bead sight; black synthetic injection-molded stock is matched by black matte metal finishing.
**MSRP** . . . . . . . . . . . . . . . . . . . **$659**

### WEATHERBY PA-08 TR

**Action**: Pump
**Stock**: Synthetic
**Barrel**: 19 in.
**Chokes**: Cylinder
**Weight**: 6.75 lb.
**Bore/ Gauge**: 12
**Magazine**: None
**Features**: Dual-action bar pump; black, injection-molded synthetic composite stock; black metal finish; white blade front sight.
**MSRP** . . . . . . . . . . . . . . . . . . . **$368**

## WINCHESTER SUPER X3 CANTILEVER DEER 20 GA.

*Action*: Autoloader
*Stock*: Composite
*Barrel*: 22 in.
*Chokes*: Screw-in tubes
*Weight*: 7 lb. 8oz.
*Bore/ Gauge*: 20
*Magazine*: 4-rounds
*Features*: Active Valve System; Weaver-style rail; adjustable rear sight, Truglo fiber-optic front sight; durable gunnmetal gray Perma-Cote UT surface finish on barrel and receiver; Dura-Touch Armor coating on the black composite stock and forearm; sling swivels.
**MSRP**. . . . . . . . . . . . . . . . . . **$1199**

## WINCHESTER SUPER X3 WATERFOWL 20 GA.

*Action*: Autoloader
*Stock*: Composite
*Barrel*: 26 in., 28 in.
*Chokes*: Invector-Plus three choke tubes (F, M, IC)
*Weight*: 6 lb. 10 oz.–6 lb. 12oz.
*Bore/ Gauge*: 20
*Magazine*: 4-rounds
*Features*: HD Mossy Oak Duck Blind camo finish on composite stock; Dura-Touch Armor coating finish; sling swivel studs.
**MSRP**. . . . . . . . . . . . . . . . . . **$1339**
**(12 Ga. option available at $1479.99)**

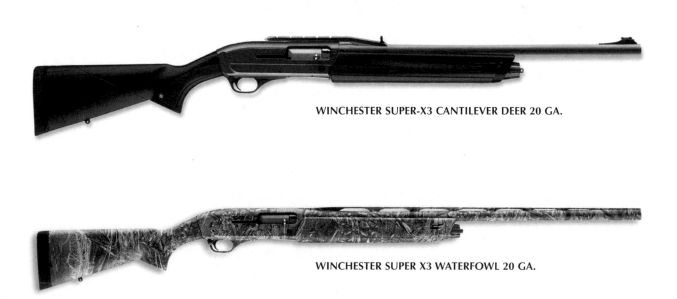

**WINCHESTER SUPER-X3 CANTILEVER DEER 20 GA.**

**WINCHESTER SUPER X3 WATERFOWL 20 GA.**

# NEW Products: **Shotguns**

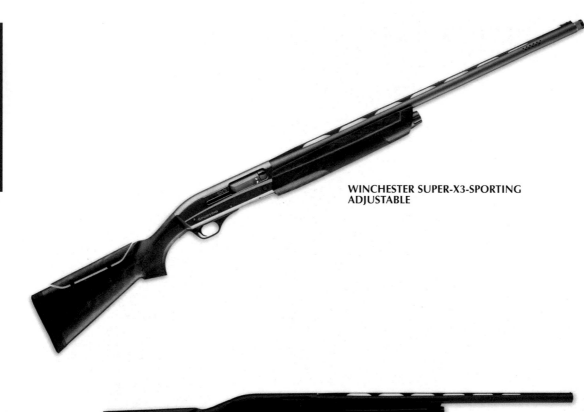

**WINCHESTER SUPER-X3-SPORTING ADJUSTABLE**

**WINCHESTER SX3 BLACK FIELD**

## WINCHESTER SUPER X3 SPORTING ADJUSTABLE

*Action*: Autoloader
*Stock*: Walnut
*Barrel*: 28 in., 30 in., 32 in.
*Chokes*: Five extended signature choke tubes
*Weight*: 7 lb. 6oz.–7 lb. 10oz.
*Bore/ Gauge*: 12
*Magazine*: Holds up to 4-rounds depending on shell size
*Features*: Aluminum-alloy receiver, and barrel; ventilated rib; buttstock features an adjustable comb; chrome plated chamber and bore; Pachmayr decelerator recoil pad; molded red case included.
**MSRP . . . . . . . . . . . . . . . . . $1629.99**

## WINCHESTER SX3 BLACK FIELD

*Action*: Autoloader
*Stock*: Walnut
*Barrel*: 26 in.–28 in.
*Chokes*: Three Invector Plus choke tubes (F, M, IC)
*Weight*: 6 lb. 6 oz.–6 lb. 14 oz.
*Bore/Gauge*: 12, 20
*Magazine*: None
*Features*: White bead front sight; Pachmayr Decelerator recoil pad; satin finish stock; ambidextrous safety; ventilated rib barrel with matte blued finish; aluminum alloy receiver with black anodized finish.
**MSRP . . . . . . . . . . . . . . . . . . . $1069**

## AMERICAN TACTICAL IMPORTS FX 45 MILITARY 1911

*Action*: Semi-automatic
*Grips*: Mahogany
*Barrel*: 5 in.
*Sights*: Fixed
*Weight*: 37 oz.
*Caliber*: .45 ACP
*Capacity*: 8+1 rounds
*Features*: Steel parts; black matte military-style fixed front and rear sights; military-style slide stop and thumb safety, solid mahogany grip panels.
**MSRP**. . . . . . . . . . . . . . . . **$449.95**

AMERICAN TACTICAL IMPORTS FX 45 MILITARY 1911

## AMERICAN TACTICAL IMPORTS FX 45 GI 1911

*Action*: Semi-automatic
*Grips*: Mahogany
*Barrel*: 4.25 in.
*Sights*: Fixed
*Weight*: 32oz.
*Caliber*: .45 ACP
*Capacity*: 8+1 rounds
*Features*: Steel parts; black matte military-style fixed front and rear sights; military-style slide stop and thumb safety, solid mahogany grip panels.
**MSRP**. . . . . . . . . . . . . . . . **$449.95**

AMERICAN TACTICAL IMPORTS FX 45 GI 1911

## AMERICAN TACTICAL IMPORTS FX 45 THUNDERBOLT 1911

*Action*: Semi-automatic
*Grips*: Mahogany
*Barrel*: 5 in.
*Sights*: Fixed
*Weight*: 39 oz.
*Caliber*: .45 ACP
*Capacity*: 8+1 rounds
*Features*: Picatinny rail; steel parts; solid maghogany grips.
**MSRP**. . . . . . . . . . . . . . . . **$699.95**

AMERICAN TACTICAL IMPORTS FX 45 THUNDERBOLT 1911

# NEW Products: **Handguns**

AMERICAN TACTICAL
IMPORTS FX 45 TITAN BLUE

## AMERICAN TACTICAL IMPORTS FX 45 TITAN BLUE & STAINLESS

*Action*: Semi-automatic
*Grips*: Mahogany
*Barrel*: 3.13 in.
*Sights*: Fixed
*Weight*: 28 oz.
*Caliber*: .45 ACP
*Capacity*: 7+1 rounds
*Features*: Carbon-steel construction or stainless-steel construction; two-stage recoil spring system; low-profile rear sights with a dovetailed front sight; military-style slide stop and thumb safety; bull barrel.
**Titan Blue:** . . . . . . . . . . . . . . . **$519.95**
**Titan Stainless:** . . . . . . . . . . **$599.95**

## AMERICAN TACTICAL IMPORTS GSG-1911 PISTOL

*Action*: Semi-automatic
*Grips*: Classic wood (standard), or black polymer grips
*Barrel*: 5 in.
*Sights*: Fixed
*Weight*: 39.5 oz.
*Caliber*: .22 LR
*Capacity*: 10 rounds
*Features*: Picatinny rail; faux suppressor.
**MSRP** . . . . . . . . . . . . . . . . **$359.95**

AMERICAN TACTICAL
IMPORTS GSG-1911 PISTOL

BOND ARMS BOND RANGER

## BOND ARMS BOND RANGER

*Action*: Single-action
*Grips*: Black Ash Star grips
*Barrel*: 4.25 in.
*Sights*: Blade front and fixed rear
*Weight*: 23.5 oz.
*Caliber*: .410/45LC with 3 in. chambers
*Capacity*: 2-rounds
*Features*: Interchangable barrels; automatic extractor; retracting firing pins; crossbolt safety; spring-loaded cammed locking lever; stainless steel with satin polish finish.
**MSRP** . . . . . . . . . . . . . . . . . . . **$499**

## BROWNING 1911-22 A1

*Action*: Autoloader
*Grips*: Brown composite
*Barrel*: 4.25 in.
*Sights*: Fixed sights
*Weight*: 1 lb.
*Caliber*: 22 LR
*Capacity*: 10+1 rounds
*Features*: Alloy frame in matte blued finish; stainless steel barrel block with matte blued finish; blowback action; single-action trigger; detachable magazine; manual thumb safety; grip safety.
**MSRP** . . . . . . . . . . . . . . . . . . . **$600**

BROWNING 1911-22 A1

**BROWNING 1911 COMMEMORATIVE CASED-SET**

## BROWNING 1911 COMMEMORATIVE CASED SET

*Action*: Autoloader
*Grips*: Checkered double-diamond walnut
*Barrel*: 4.25 in.
*Sights*: Fixed sights
*Weight*: 1 lb.
*Caliber*: 22 LR
*Capacity*: 10+1-rounds
*Features*: Display case is velvet-lined walnut. Printed glass top proclaims the 100th anniversary of the famous John M. Browning design of the 1911. Both pistols come packaged in a 1911–2011 Commemorative Limited Edition pistol rug. Features alloy frame with gloss blued finish; gold enhanced engraving on slide; CRMO steel barrel with blued finish; single-action trigger; manual thumb safety; grip safety; circa 1913 Government contract configuration.
**MSRP** . . . . . . . . . . . . . . . . . . **$4669**

**CHARTER ARMS HELLER COMMEMORATIVE**

## CHARTER ARMS HELLER COMMEMORATIVE .44 BULLDOG

*Action*: DA revolver
*Grips*: Walnut
*Barrel*: 2.5 in.
*Sights*: Fixed sight
*Weight*: 12 oz.
*Caliber*: .44 Special
*Capacity*: 5-rounds
*Features*: This fully engraved .44 Bulldog commemorates the historic win of the US Supreme Court case "Heller vs D.C." In this case, the Supreme Court struck down Washington D.C.'s handgun ban and affirmed the Second Amendment as an individual right. Only 250 models will be made. Each firearm will be packaged with an engraved knife, hardcase with etched glass top, and certificate of authenticity.
**MSRP** . . . . . . . . . . . . . . . . . . **$1595**

# NEW Products: **Handguns**

## CHARTER ARMS OFF DUTY HP .38 SPECIAL & UNDERCOVER LITE .38 SPECIAL

*Action*: DA revolver
*Grips*: Crimson Trace LaserGrip
*Barrel*: 2 in.
*Sights*: Serrated front, rear notch sights
*Weight*: 12 oz.
*Caliber*: .38 Special +P
*Capacity*: 5-rounds
*Features*: High-polish stainless-steel finish; matte black frame; Off Duty model has internal DA hammer; Undercover Lite has external standard hammer.
**MSRP:** . . . . . . . . . . . . . . . . . . **$428**

**CHARTER ARMS UNDERCOVER LITE .38 SPECIAL**

**CHARTER ARMS CHIC LADY**

## CHARTER ARMS THE CHIC LADY & CHIC LADY OFF DUTY

*Action*: DA revolver
*Grips*: Rubber
*Barrel*: 2 in.
*Sights*: Fixed
*Weight*: 12 oz.
*Caliber*: .38 Special
*Capacity*: 5-rounds
*Features*: High-polish stainless-steel pink anodized aluminum frame; comes in a faux alligator pink attache case with high-polish stainless-steel trim; serrated front sight; quick-release cylinder.
**Chic Lady:** . . . . . . . . . . . . . . . . **$492**
**Chic Lady Off Duty:** . . . . . . . . . **$446**

## COLT 1911 100TH ANNIVERSARY MODEL

*Action*: Autoloader
*Grips*: Walnut
*Barrel*: 5 in.
*Sights*: Fixed
*Weight*: 39 oz.
*Caliber*: .45 ACP
*Capacity*: 7+1-rounds
*Features*: Quantity limted to 750 units; finished in polished royal blue on all surfaces; smooth Cocobolo grips with 100th anniversary gold plated medallions; comes in glass topped, walnut display case with french fitted red lining and Serpentine Colt etched in glass panel; slide is enhanced with scroll engraving and is decorated with historic Colt symbols highlighted in 24kt. gold.
**MSRP** . . . . . . . . . . . . . . . . . . . **$2295**

**COLT 1911 100 ANNIVERSARY MODEL**

## COLT NEW FRONTIER
*Action*: Single-action revolver
*Grips*: Walnut stock with gold medallions
*Barrel*: 4.75 in., 5.5 in., 7.5 in.
*Sights*: Ramp style front sight; adjustable rear sight
*Weight*: 46 oz.
*Caliber*: .357 Mag., .44 Special, .45 Colt
*Capacity*: 6 rounds
*Features*: Royal blue barrel and cylinder; flat top case colored frame.
**MSRP** . . . . . . . . . . . . . . . . . . **$1455**

**COLT NEW FRONTIER**

**CZ MODEL 75**

## CZ 75 TS CZECHMATE
*Action*: Autoloader
*Grips*: Aluminum
*Barrel*: 5.4 in.
*Sights*: Fixed, C-more red dot sight
*Weight*: 3 lb.
*Caliber*: 9mm
*Capacity*: 20-or 26-rounds
*Features*: Built upon a modified version of the CZ 75 TS frame; interchangable parts allow the user to quickly configure the gun for both roles; features a single-action trigger mechanism; red-dot sight; includes spare barrel; includes three 20-round magazines and one 26-round magazine; all-steel pistol is finished in black matte.
**MSRP** . . . . . . . . . . . . . . . . . . **$3164**

**CZ MODEL 75 SP-01**

## CZ MODEL 75 SP-01
*Action*: Autoloader
*Grips*: Rubber
*Barrel*: 4.7 in.
*Sights*: 3-dot tritium night sights
*Weight*: 2.4 lb.
*Caliber*: 9mm Luger
*Capacity*: 18-rounds
*Features*: Based upon the Shadow Target; decocking lever; safety stop on hammer; firing pin safety; steel frame.
**MSRP** . . . . . . . . . . . . . . . . . . **$648**

# NEW Products: **Handguns**

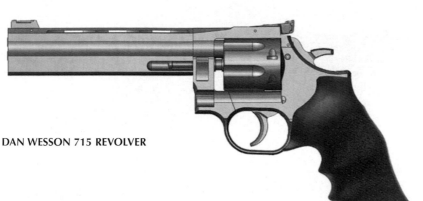

**DAN WESSON 715 REVOLVER**

## DAN WESSON 715 REVOLVER

*Action*: Double-action revolver
*Grips*: Finger grooved Hogue rubber grip
*Barrel*: 6 in.
*Sights*: Interchangable front blade sights
*Weight*: 46oz.
*Caliber*: .357 Mag.
*Capacity*: 6 rounds
*Features*: Features the ability to swap barrels and grips with any previous Dan Wesson revolver in the 15-2 and later series models; tensioned barrel; transfer bar safety; front crane latch and rear ball detent.
**MSRP** . . . . . . . . . . . . . . . . . . **$1169**

**DAN WESSON GUARDIAN .45 ACP**

## DAN WESSON GUARDIAN .45 ACP

*Action*: Autoloader
*Grips*: Stippled shadow
*Sights*: Novak Low Mount style, Night Sights
*Weight*: 1.8 lb.
*Caliber*: .45 ACP
*Capacity*: 8-rounds
*Features*: Bobtail alloy frame; commander length barrel; finished in matte black with tritium sights.
**MSRP** . . . . . . . . . . . . . . . . . . **$1590**

## ED BROWN KOBRA CARRY LIGHTWEIGHT

*Action*: Autoloader
*Grips*: Cocobolo wood
*Barrel*: 5 in.
*Sights*: Fixed dovetail front night sight with high visibility white outlines
*Weight*: 27oz.
*Caliber*: .45 ACP
*Capacity*: 7+1-rounds
*Features*: Lightweight aluminum frame and Bobtail housing; all other components are steel; exclusive snakeskin treatment on forestrap and housing; matte finished Gen III coated slide for low glare.
**MSRP** . . . . . . . . . . . . . . **$2920–$2995**

**ED BROWN KOBRA**

## GEN 4 GLOCK

*Action*: Autoloader
*Grips*: Synthetic
*Barrel*: 4.02 in.
*Sights*: Fixed
*Weight*: 21.16 oz.
*Caliber*: .45 ACP
*Capacity*: 15-rounds
*Features*: Rough textured frame; Interchangable backstrap system; two magazine-release catches for ambidextrous operation; dual-recoil spring system replaces the originial single spring model.
**Fixed Sights:** . . . . . . . . . . . . . **$649**
**Adjustable:** . . . . . . . . . . . . . . **$667**
**Steel Model:** . . . . . . . . . . . . . **$671**

GEN 4 GLOCK

## HECKLER & KOCH P30 LIGHTWEIGHT LEM

*Action*: Autoloader
*Grips*: Polymer
*Barrel*: 3.86 in.
*Sights*: Fixed
*Weight*: 1.60 lb.
*Caliber*: 9mm, .40 S&W
*Capacity*: 10, 13, or 15 rounds
*Features*: Interchangable backstraps and side panel grips in small, medium, and large sizes; ambidextrous slide and magazine releases levers; integral Picatinny rail; modular design allows DA trigger or DA/SA system, with a decocking button.
**MSRP** . . . . . . . . . . . . . . . . . . **$1023**

HECKLER & KOCH P30
LIGHTWEIGHT LEM

## HERITAGE ROUGH RIDER EXOTIC GRIP

*Action*: Single-action revolver
*Grips*: Exotic cocobolo
*Barrel*: 4.75 in.
*Sights*: Fixed
*Weight*: 31oz.
*Caliber*: .22–9mm Shot combo
*Capacity*: 9-rounds
*Features*: Machined barrel is micro-threaded; frame finish comes in smooth silver satin, deep matte black, low gloss black satin, or case hardened finish.
**MSRP** . . . . . . . . . . . . . . . . . . **$279.99**

HERITAGE ROUGH RIDER
EXOTIC GRIP

# NEW Products: **Handguns**

KAHR CM 9

KAHR KP3833

KAHR PM4543

## KAHR CM9

*Action*: Autoloader
*Grips*: Textured polymer
*Barrel*: 3 in.
*Sights*: Adjustable
*Weight*: 14 oz.
*Caliber*: 9mm
*Capacity*: 6+1 rounds
*Features*: Trigger cocking double-action; lock breech; Browning-type recoil lug; passive striker block; no magazine disconnect; drift adjustable, white bar-dot combat sights; black finish; matte stainless steel slide.
**MSRP** . . . . . . . . . . . . . . . . . . . **$565**

## KAHR KP3833

*Action*: Autoloader
*Grips*: Textured polymer
*Barrel*: 2.5 in.
*Sights*: Adjustable
*Weight*: 9.97 oz.
*Caliber*: .380 ACP
*Capacity*: 6+1 rounds
*Features*: Lothar Walther match-grade barrel; black polymer frame; matte stainless-steel slide; passive striker block.
**MSRP** . . . . . . . . . . . . . . . . . . . **$758**

## KAHR PM4543L

*Action*: Autoloader
*Grips*: LG-437 laser grip
*Barrel*: 3.14 in.
*Sights*: Adjustable drift, white bar-dot combat sights
*Weight*: 17.3 oz.
*Caliber*: .45 ACP
*Capacity*: 5+1 rounds
*Features*: Lothar Walther match-grade barrel, with polygonal rifling; black polymer frame; matte stainless-steel slide; browning-type recoil lug.
**MSRP** . . . . . . . . . . . . . . . . . . . **$805**

## PARA ORDNANCE PXT WARTHOG

*Action*: Autoloader
*Grips*: Black plastic
*Barrel*: 3 in.
*Sights*: Fiber-optic front, 2-Dot rear
*Weight*: 24 oz.
*Caliber*: .45 ACP
*Capacity*: 10+1 rounds
*Features*: Spurred hammer; single-action; ramped barrel; alloy receiver.
**MSRP** . . . . . . . . . . . . . . . . . . . . **$999**

PARA ORDNANCE PXT WARTHOG

## PARA ORDNANCE PXT HAWG 7

*Action*: Autoloader
*Grips*: Black plastic
*Barrel*: 3.5 in.
*Sights*: Fiber-optic front, 2-dot rear
*Weight*: 32oz.
*Caliber*: .45 ACP
*Capacity*: 7+1 rounds
*Features*: Integral ramp Match barrel; stainless steel frame; spurred hammer; Griptor grasping grooves for added recoil control.
**MSRP** . . . . . . . . . . . . . . . . . . . . **$919**

PARA ORDNANCE PXT HAWG 7

## PARA ORDNANCE GI LCT

*Action*: Single-action
*Grips*: Checkered composite
*Barrel*: 4.25 in.
*Sights*: Fiber-optic front, 2-Dot rear
*Weight*: 28oz.
*Caliber*: .45 ACP
*Capacity*: 8+1 rounds
*Features*: Full-beaver-tail-grip safety; fiber optic front sight, fixed two-dot rear sight; alloy receiver w/ covert black finish.
**MSRP** . . . . . . . . . . . . . . . . . . . . **$849**

PARA ORDNANCE GI LCT

# NEW Products: Handguns

## PARA ORDNANCE 1911 SASS WILD BUNCH PISTOL

*Action*: Single-action
*Grips*: Checkered composite
*Barrel*: 5 in.
*Sights*: 3-dot
*Weight*: 39 oz.
*Caliber*: .45 ACP
*Capacity*: 7+1 rounds
*Features*: Three-dot sight; conforms to all division rules with its traditional hammer, grip safety, solid trigger, and standard sights.
**MSRP** . . . . . . . . . . . . . . . . . . . **$789**

PARA ORDNANCE 1911 SASS
WILD BUNCH PISTOL

## PARA ORDNANCE 1911 SINGLE STACK LIMITED

*Action*: Single-action
*Grips*: Cocobolo wood
*Barrel*: 5 in.
*Sights*: Adjustable, fiber-optic
*Weight*: 39oz.
*Caliber*: .45 ACP
*Capacity*: 8+1 rounds
*Features*: Match-grade barrel; integral ramp; fiber optic front sight, fully adjustable rear sight; skeleotnized hammer; adjustable, competition trigger; ambidextrous slide lock; extended beavertail safety and Para's Sterling finish.
**MSRP** . . . . . . . . . . . . . . . . . . **$1298**

PARA ORDNANCE 1911 SINGLE
STACK LIMITED

## PARA ORDNANCE 18-9 9MM LIMITED

*Action*: Single-action
*Grips*: Black plastic
*Barrel*: 5 in.
*Sights*: Adjustable, Fiber-optic
*Weight*: 40 oz.
*Caliber*: 9mm
*Capacity*: Full Capacity: 18+1 rounds; Restricted Capacity: 10+1
*Features*: Fiber-optic front sight; fully adjustable rear; front strap checkering and stainless finish.
**MSRP** . . . . . . . . . . . . . . . . . . **$1289**

PARA ORDNANCE 18-9 LIMITED

**REMINGTON M 1911 R1
CENTENNIAL**

**ROCK RIVER LAR-PDS PISTOL**

**ROSSI RANCH HAND**

## REMINGTON M 1911 R1 CENTENNIAL

*Action*: Autoloading
*Grips*: Rosewood laminate
*Barrel*: 5.5 in.
*Sights*: Fixed
*Weight*: 38.5 oz.
*Caliber*: .45 Auto
*Capacity*: 7-rounds
*Features*: Short trigger; double diamond grips; modern enhancements include a lowered and flared ejection port; beveled magazine well; Loaded chamber indicator; high-profile fixed sights in a three white-dot pattern; match grade stainless-steel barrel.
**MSRP . . . . . . . . . . . . . . . . . $1250**

## ROCK RIVER LAR-PDS PISTOL

*Action*: Gas-operated autoloader with PPS (Performance Piston System) AR style
*Grips*: Hogue rubber
*Barrel*: 8 in. chrome moly
*Sights*: MS 1913 rail
*Weight*: 5 lb.
*Caliber*: 5.56mm Nato chamber for 5.56mm & .223
*Capacity*: 30-rounds
*Features*: A2 flash hider; aluminum tri-rail handguard; ambidextrous non-reciprocating charging handle.
**MSRP . . . . . . . . . . . . . $1335–$1485**

## ROSSI RANCH HAND

*Action*: Lever-action repeating pistol
*Grips*: Walnut
*Barrel*: 12 in.
*Sights*: Gold-bead front sight w/ adjustable buckhorn rear sight
*Weight*: 4 lb.
*Caliber*: .357 Mag., .45 Long Colt, .44 Mag.
*Capacity*: 6-rounds
*Features*: Matte blued finish; Brazilian hardwood stock; oversize loop lever; investment-cast receiver.
**MSRP . . . . . . . . . . . . . . . . . . . $536**

# NEW Products: **Handguns**

**RUGER LCP CENTERFIRE PISTOL CRIMSON TRACE LASERGUARD**

## RUGER LCP CENTERFIRE PISTOL CRIMSON TRACE LASERGUARD

*Action*: Double-action autoloader
*Grips*: Black, glass-filled nylon
*Barrel*: 2.75 in.
*Sights*: Fixed, Crimson Trace Laserguard
*Weight*: 10oz.
*Caliber*: .380 Auto
*Capacity*: 6+1 rounds
*Features*: Blued, alloy slide and barrel.
**MSRP**. . . . . . . . . . . . . . . . . . . **$548**

**RUGER SP101 CRIMSON TRACE LASERGRIPS**

## RUGER SP101 CRIMSON TRACE LASERGRIPS

*Action*: Double-action revolver
*Grips*: Crimson Trace Lasergrips
*Barrel*: 2.25 in.
*Sights*: Fixed
*Weight*: 25 oz.
*Caliber*: .357 Mag.
*Capacity*: 5-rounds
*Features*: Stainless steel frame with satin finish.
**MSRP**. . . . . . . . . . . . . . . . . . . **$799**

**RUGER SR40**

## RUGER SR40

*Action*: Autoloader
*Grips*: Black, high performance, glass-filled nylon
*Barrel*: 4.1 in.
*Sights*: Adjustable 3-dot
*Weight*: 27.25 oz.
*Caliber*: .40 S&W
*Capacity*: 10- or 15-rounds
*Features*: Glass-filled nylon frame; ambidextrous operating controls; trigger system and reversible; fully adjustable three-dot sights; integral accessory rail; backstraps are identical to SR9; Nitridox Pro Black or Brushed Stainless finish.
**MSRP**. . . . . . . . . . . . . . . . . . . **$525**

SIG SAUER P290

## SIG SAUER P290
*Action*: Autoloader
*Grips*: Black polymer
*Barrel*: 2.9 in.
*Sights*: Siglite or contrast Sights
*Weight*: 20.5 oz.
*Caliber*: 9mm
*Capacity*: 6+1 rounds
*Features*: Polymer frame; slide is machined from solid stainless-steel billet; interchangable grips; features drift-adjustable Siglite sights or high-contrast black sight.
**MSRP** . . . . . . . . . . . . . . . . . . . . **$758**

## STI INTL. APERIO
*Action*: Autoloader
*Grips*: STI patented modular polymer
*Barrel*: 5 in.
*Sights*: Dawson fiber optic front mounted on barrel, STI adjustable rear
*Weight*: 39 oz.
*Caliber*: 9mm, .40 S&W, .45 ACP
*Capacity*: N/A
*Features*: Full length stainless steel bar stock slide features STI's unique sabertooth rear cocking serrations; Schuemann barrel; STI Recoil Master; STI long curved trigger; blued finish with two toned blue/stainless steel slide.
**MSRP** . . . . . . . . . . . . . . . . . . . **$2690**

STI INTL. APERIO

## STI INTL. 100TH ANNIVERSARY PISTOL SET
*Action*: Autoloader
*Grips*: Wood (1911 model), STI patented modular polymer (2011 model)
*Barrel*: 5 in.
*Sights*: Classic 1911 front and rear sights (1911 model); Dawson fiber optic front, STI adjustable rear (2011 model)
*Weight*: N/A
*Caliber*: .45 ACP
*Capacity*: N/A
*Features*: This limited edition set comes with a traditional GI style 1911 and a pistol built on STI's patented 2011 high capacity. Both slides feature STI 100th Anniversary special engravings; the 1911 model features a fully ramped match grade barrel, a traditional beavertail grip saftey, GI-style one piece guide rod, ambidextrous thumb safeties, and a hot blue finish with gold-colored inlay. The 2011 model features a ramped bull barrel, high rise beavertail grip safety, ambidextrous thumb safties, a STI Recoil Master guide rod and a hard chrome finish with gold-colored inlay.
**MSRP** . . . . . . . . . . . . . . . . . . . **$4154**

STI INTL. 100TH ANNIVERSARY EDITION

# NEW Products: **Handguns**

**STOEGER COUGAR COMPACT**

## STOEGER COUGAR COMPACT

*Action*: DA/SA
*Grips*: Black plastic
*Barrel*: 3.6 in.
*Sights*: Quick read 3-dot sights
*Weight*: 32 oz.
*Caliber*: 9mm
*Capacity*: 13+1 rounds
*Features*: Ambidextrous safety; rotary-locking principal; Bruniton matte black finish.
**MSRP** . . . . . . . . . . . . . . . . . . . . **$449**

**TAURUS 638 PRO COMPACT**

## TAURUS PT638 PRO COMPACT

*Action*: Autoloading
*Grips*: Synthetic
*Barrel*: 3.25 in.
*Sights*: Adjustable rear sight
*Weight*: 28 oz.
*Caliber*: .380 ACP
*Capacity*: 15+1 rounds
*Features*: Matte or blue stainless finish; Taurus security system; loaded chamber indicator; ambidextrous manual safety.
**MSRP** . . . . . . . . . . . . . . . . . . . . **$483**

## TAURUS 740 G2 SLIM

*Action*: DA/SA autoloader
*Grips*: Polymer
*Barrel*: 3.20 in.
*Sights*: Adjustable rear sight, low profile front sights
*Weight*: 19 oz.
*Caliber*: .40
*Capacity*: 6+1 rounds
*Features*: Blue finish; loaded chamber indicator for added safety; extended hi-cap magazine; contoured ambidextrous thumb rests and Finger Indexing Taurus Memory Pads.
**MSRP** . . . . . . . . . . . . . . . . . . . . **$483**

# NEW Products: **Handguns**

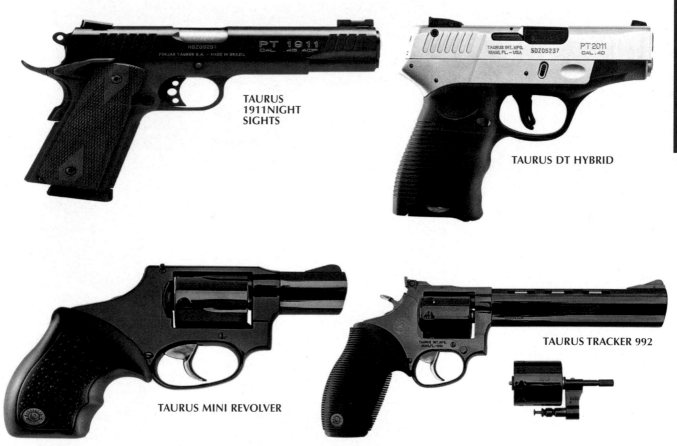

**TAURUS 1911NIGHT SIGHTS**

**TAURUS DT HYBRID**

**TAURUS MINI REVOLVER**

**TAURUS TRACKER 992**

## TAURUS 1911 NIGHT SIGHT

*Action*: Autoloader
*Grips*: Checkered wood
*Barrel*: 5 in.
*Sights*: Novak night sights, fiber optic front sight
*Weight*: 40 oz.
*Caliber*: .45 ACP
*Capacity*: 8+1 rounds
*Features*: Blue finish; Taurus security system; custom fit frame and barrel; skeleton serrated trigger; target hammer; ambidextrous safety; beavertail grip safety with memory pad.
**MSRP . . . . . . . . . . . . . . . . . . . . .N/A**

## TAURUS DT HYBRID

*Action*: SA/DA autoloader

*Grips*: Polymer
*Barrel*: 3.2 in.
*Sights*: Adjustable rear sight
*Weight*: 24 oz.
*Caliber*: .40
*Capacity*: 11+1 rounds
*Features*: Matte stainless steel finish; stainless steel construction; purchase of new Taurus firearm includes free one year membership in the NRA.
**MSRP . . . . . . . . . . . . . . . . . . . . $449**

## TAURUS 380 MINI REVOLVER

*Action*: Revolver
*Grips*: Rubber
*Barrel*: 1.75 in.
*Sights*: Adjustable rear sight
*Weight*: 15.5 oz.
*Caliber*: .380 ACP

*Capacity*: 5 rounds
*Features*: Double action trigger; fully enclosed hammer; blue or matte stainless finish; bobbed hammer.
**MSRP . . . . . . . . . . . . . . . $430–$461**

## TAURUS TRACKER 992

*Action*: SA/DA revolver
*Grips*: Rubber with ribs
*Barrel*: 6.5 in.
*Sights*: Fixed front
*Weight*: 55 oz.
*Caliber*: .22 LR
*Capacity*: 9 rounds
*Features*: Stainless steel construction; blue finish; easily transforms from a .22 LR to .22 Mag. through its removable cylinder.
**MSRP . . . . . . . . . . . . . . . . . . . $545**

## TAURUS 809

*Action*: Autoloader
*Grips*: Checkered polymer
*Barrel*: 4 in.
*Sights*: Fixed
*Weight*: 30.2oz.
*Caliber*: 9mm
*Capacity*: 17+1 rounds
*Features*: Black Tennifer finish; smooth trigger type; strike two capability.
**MSRP** . . . . . . . . . . . . . . . . . . . **$656**

## UBERTI THE OUTFITTER 1873

*Action*: SA revolver
*Grips*: Wood
*Barrel*: 7.5 in.
*Sights*: Fixed
*Weight*: 2.4 lb.
*Caliber*: .45 LC
*Capacity*: 6-rounds
*Features*: Stainless steel finish; steel backstrap and trigger guard.
**MSRP** . . . . . . . . . . . . . . . . . . . **$568**

TAURUS 809

UBERTI 1873 CATTLEMAN BIRDS HEAD, OLD MODEL

## UBERTI 1873 CATTLEMAN BIRDS HEAD, OLD MODEL

*Action*: Single-action revolver
*Grips*: Checkered walnut
*Barrel*: 3.5 in.
*Sights*: Fixed, open
*Weight*: 2 lb.
*Caliber*: .38 Spl.
*Capacity*: 6-rounds
*Features*: Fluted barrel; full matte blue finish; scaled-down stallion frame; steel backstrap and trigger guard.
**MSRP** . . . . . . . . . . . . . . . . . . . **$569**

# NEW Products: **Handguns**

## UBERTI 1873 EL PATRON COWBOY MOUNTED SHOOTER (CMS)

*Action*: Single-action revolver
*Grips*: Checkered walnut
*Barrel*: 3.5 in., 4 in.
*Sights*: EasyView sights
*Weight*: 2.3 lb.
*Caliber*: .45 Colt, .357 Mag.
*Capacity*: 6-rounds
*Features*: Blued or stainless steel finish; optional case-hardened frame; fluted barrel; fitted with U.S.-made Wolff springs; numbered cylinders.
**Blued:** . . . . . . . . . . . . . . . . . . **$599**
**Stainless steel:** . . . . . . . . . . . . . **$749**

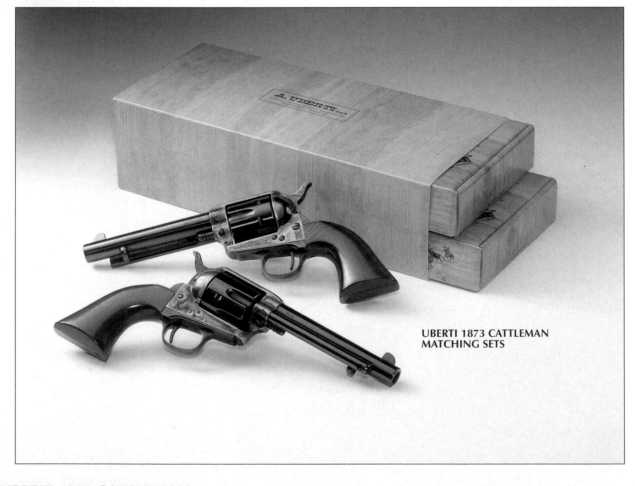

UBERTI 1873 CATTLEMAN
MATCHING SETS

## UBERTI 1873 CATTLEMAN MATCHING SETS

*Action*: Single-action revolver
*Grips*: Walnut
*Barrel*: 5.5 in.

*Sights*: Fixed, open
*Weight*: 2.3 lb.
*Caliber*: .45 Colt and .357 Mag.
*Capacity*: 6-rounds
*Features*: Fluted barrel; blue case-

hardened frame; steel backstrap; trigger guard; the set shares matching serial numbers.
**MSRP** . . . . . . . . . . . . **$1059 per set**

# NEW Products: Handloading Equipment

HORNADY LOCK-N-LOAD BENCH SCALE

## HORNADY LOCK-N-LOAD BENCH SCALE

**Features**: Made from the same high-quality, precision load cell found on the Lock-N-Load Auto Charge, the high performance Lock-N-Load Bench Scale is the perfect addition to your reloading bench. With a capacity of 1500 grains, you can weigh powder, bullets, cases, cartridges, and more. The large LCD display is easy to read and weighs precisely to one tenth (0.1) of a grain. Included are two calibration weights, AC adaptor, 220V adaptor, and metal powder pan.
**MSRP . . . . . . . . . . . . . . . . . $120.88**

HORNADY LOCK-N-LOAD BULLET FEEDER

## HORNADY LOCK-N-LOAD BULLET FEEDER

**Features**: The new Lock-N-Load Bullet Feeder is designed as an accessory for the Hornady Lock-N-Load AP reloading press, but can be used with any other press with 7/8"-14 die threads. Coupled with the Lock-N-Load Case Feeder, you'll realize dramatic increases in efficiency and reloading speed (up to 50% faster)! The bullet feeder die is case-activated, which means the bullet will only feed upon contact with a case. The collets are made of solid steel and durable enough for years of reloading. The setup and caliber changeovers are quick and easy, and there are no special tools required for adjustments. The easy-feed bullet hopper holds up to 200 pistol bullets and features an adjustable center plate and bullet feed-wipers to ensure smooth feeding.
**MSRP . . . . . . . . . . . . . . . . . $350.91**

HORNADY LOCK-N-LOAD CASE PREP ASSISTANT

## HORNADY LOCK-N-LOAD CASE PREP ASSISTANT

**Features**: Make case preparation faster and easier than ever with the new Lock-N-Load Power Case Prep Assistant. Its durable brushed-aluminum housing and high torque, low-speed motor will provide years of dependable use. Included are chamfer and deburr tools, with plenty of onboard storage for optional case prep accessories like our primer pocket cleaners, case neck brushes, and any other 8-32 thread tools. Unit is compatible with 110V or 220V power.
**MSRP . . . . . . . . . . . . . . . . . $120.88**

# NEW Products: **Handloading Equipment**

## LYMAN CASE PREP MULTI-TOOL

*Features*: The unique new case prep accessory provides the reloader with all the essential Case Prep Accessories in one compact, double-ended storage handle. Both ends of the handle are threaded to allow two tool heads to be mounted simultaneously. Plus the hollow, knurled handle unthreads in the center to store all parts and function equally well as two separate handles. The compact aluminum storage handle contains: An outside deburring tool, a VLD inside deburring tool, both large and small primer pocket cleaners and reamers.

**MSRP** . . . . . . . . . . . . . . . . . . **$24.95**

LYMAN CASE PREP MULTI-TOOL

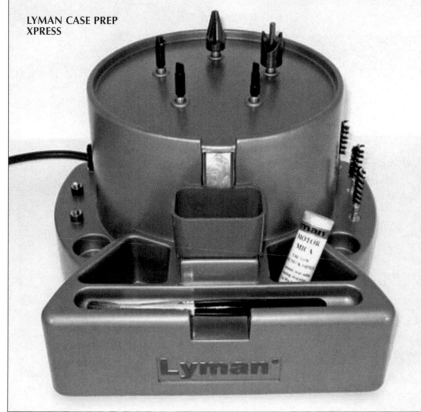

LYMAN CASE PREP XPRESS

## LYMAN CASE PREP XPRESS

*Features*: Lyman introduces one of the most complete electric case prep systems yet developed. It features all the most popular case prep accessories driven by a high-torque gear motor. The Case Prep Xpress allows the reloader to have five different case prep tools mounted vertically and powered, ready to instantly perform the desired operation. Every commonly used case prep tool is included with the substantial five-position power base. In addition, a side-mounted, inside neck lube station is also part of the base with four neck brushes and Mica lube. For easy cleanup of fouling and brass shavings, a convenient removable dump pan is designed inside.

**115 V Model MSRP** . . . . . . . **$149.95**
**230 V Model MSRP** . . . . . . . **$156.00**

# NEW Products: Handloading Equipment

## LYMAN MASTER RELOADING KIT

*Features*: The complete reloading kit compares in price to other starter kits, but is the first one that includes a state-of-the-art digital scale like the Lyman 1000 Grain. The new reloader can choose the turret T-Mag. or single stage Crusher press kit and get all the high-end Lyman tools and accessories needed to start turning out top-quality reloads. The only additional items needed are the dies and shellholder. Lyman's Trimmer Plus Case Conditioning Kit makes a perfect addition once the reloader is ready to further improve the performance of his reloads. The Lyman Master Reloading Kit includes a 7.8 in. x 14 Adapter, 1000 grain electronic scale, #55 powder measure, a universal priming arm, a powder funnel, and an auto primer feed system.

**T-Mag. Master Kit MSRP:. . . $479.95**
**Crusher Master Kit MSRP:. . $425.00**

## RCBS AR SERIES DIES

*Features*: The new RCBS AR Series is a must for the progressive reloader. It features a Small Base sizing die and a new Taper Crimp seating die. This combination makes reloading easier for AR-style or semi-auto shooters. The Small Base sizer guarantees that the cartridge will rechamber. The Taper Crimp Seater is more forgiving when various case lengths are loaded at the same time. Case neck crimp bulges and buckled shoulders are virtually eliminated when Taper crimping is used with cannelured bullets.
**MSRP. . . . . . . . . . . . $36.00–$68.00**

**RCBS AR SERIES DIES**

## RCBS POWDER TRICKLER-2

*Features*: Today's trend is to use electronic scales to measure powder charges. Many of these scales have scale pans that are positioned out of reach of existing powder tricklers. The Powder Trickler—2 solves this problem by adding a height-adjustable, non-skid base and powder tube extension.
**MSRP. . . . . . . . . . . . $17.82–$24.83**

## RCBS CARBIDE REPLACEMENT TOOLS

*Features*: Replacement carbide-tipped cutters for your Case Trimmer, 3-Way Cutter, and Trim Mate Chamfer or Debur tool. These carbide-tipped tools cut clean and stay sharp for a lifetime of use.
**MSRP. . . . . . . . . . . . $36.00–$45.00**

**RCBS POWDER TRICKLER-2**

**LYMAN MASTER RELOADING KIT**

**RCBS CARBIDE REPLACEMENT TOOLS**

# NEW Products: **Handloading Equipment**

## RCBS BULLET FEED DIE-PISTOL

**Features**: Crank out ammo again in no time. RCBS's new Pistol Bullet Feed Die allows the progressive pistol loader to leave the feed die set up on the removable die plate for quick caliber changeovers. The popular RCBS® Bullet Feeder shortens reloading sessions while increasing load rates by approximately 50%. Rather than reinstalling on die plates and adjusting Bullet Fingers and Guides, simply install another Bullet Feed Die to save even more time during caliber changeovers. Includes one set of Bullet Fingers and retaining clip.

**MSRP** . . . . . . . . . . . . . . . . . .**$23.00**

NEW PRODUCTS

**RCBS BULLET FEED DIE-PISTOL**

# NEW Products: **Optics**

By Thomas McIntyre

## ALPEN

Established in 1997, Alpen has tried to combine quality and affordability in its sport optics. And this year it has come out with its new Apex XP ("Xtreme Performance") line of mid-priced fully multi-coated riflescopes. The XP series is said to be able to withstand a recoil shock of 1000 gs, so it ought to be capable of surviving magnum-load rifles. Made fully waterproof and fogproof with a one-piece tube construction, the XP includes zero-reset windage and elevation dials. A fast-focus eyepiece is standard with a "bullet-drop-compensating" (BDC) reticle also standard on most models. Side-focus parallax adjustment comes with the scopes, as well. The XP is available in a variety of 1-inch and 30mm tubes and in such configurations as the 1.5-6x42mm with a 30mm tube suitable for turkey hunting and slug guns; a 3-9x40mm scope with a 1-inch tube and ¼ MOA adjustments, useful for all-around big-game hunting; and a 30mm 6-24x50mm long-range and varmint scope with ⅛ MOA click adjustments. The XP also offers several illuminated red-dot reticles models including a 30mm tube 4-16x56mm. Sunshades are included with all scopes and a matte-black finish is standard, but there is also a 1-inch 2-10x44mm in Mossy Oak Break-Up Infinity finish. All the XPs are backed by a "no fault," "no questions asked" Alpen lifetime warranty.

ALPEN APEX XP 3-9X40

ALPEN APEX XP 4-16X56 IR

ALPEN APEX XP 6-24X50

ALPEN APEX XP 2-10X44 MOSSY
OAK BREAK-UP INFINITY

# NEW Products: Optics

## BSA

It's hard not to be impressed by the history of BSA, the British Small Arms Company, Limited. Although BSA's optics division was started in 1996, only a year before Alpen was founded, the company's roots go back over three hundred years to the English court of William and Mary in the late 17th century. It was then that King William III, dependent on military arms purchased from his native Holland and worried both about invasion and the necessity of shooting Catholics, was told about the skilled gunsmiths located in Birmingham; an order was placed with them for the production of 200 "snaphance" (an older version of the flintlock) muskets a month at seventeen shillings "ready money" apiece. The actual public company was formed in 1861, adopting the symbol of three crossed rifles, or the "Piled Arms" trademark. From the Boer War through World War II, BSA was a major supplier of British military weapons, including service rifles, Sten guns, anti-tank rifles, and a half-million Browning machine guns carried on Spitfire and Hurricane fighter planes. BSA continues to produce sporting firearms and an expanding line of sports optics. For 2011, BSA has a new moderately priced Gold Star line of riflescopes in a variety of configurations. These include the 1-6x24mm for (at 1X) close-range full-view shooting with both eyes open; a 2-12x44mm for general big-game hunting; and a long-range 4-24x50mm. All come in black matte and use 1-inch tubes, have fully multi-coated optics, fast-focus eyepiece, side parallax adjustment on some models, a listed 4-inch eye relief, and come with the "EZ Hunter" reticle that is gauged to various points of hold for the trajectories of a range

of popular factory calibers from 40-grain .204 Ruger to 225-grain .338 Winchester Magnum. The waterproof and fogproof scopes also include a limited lifetime warranty.

## BUSHNELL

Bushnell Performance Optics has been marketing and manufacturing binoculars, riflescopes, and spotting scopes for some sixty years. And for this year they've taken their top-of-the-line Elite 6500 riflescope and offered it to "personnel" (military, police, and to private shooters who want a high-tech, hard-use scope and have $1000 to spend) by giving it a tactical treatment. The fogproof and waterproof Elite

Tactical comes in both 1-inch and 30mm tube diameters and in a variety of configurations from 10x40mm fixed to 6-24x50mm variable. Some of the scopes feature 6.5 magnification range, similar to the Elite 6500. All come with tactical target-adjustment turrets and non-glare black-matte finish as well as "blacked-out" cosmetics for concealment. All the Elite Tacticals have fully multi-coated (with Bushnell "Ultra Wide Band Coating") optics and RainGuard HD moisture-shedding exterior coating, along with illuminated and non-illuminated mil-dot reticles. They come with a 3-inch sunshade and are covered by Bushnell's limited lifetime warranty.

**BUSHNELL ET1040**

**BUSHNELL ET6245**

**BSA GOLD STAR 2-12X**

### CABELA'S

Cabela's has partnered with the Czech optics manufacturer Meopta to make its new Euro line of riflescopes. These 1-inch-tube variable scopes are computer-numerically-controlled machined from a single billet of aircraft aluminum and bead blasted before undergoing ELOX (electrolytic oxidation) anodization for a reduced-glare black matte, abrasion-resistant finish. The scopes are available in configurations ranging from 3-9x42mm to 4-12x50 and 6-18x50mm, with objectives on the 6-18s equipped with parallax adjustment. Lenses are fully multi-coated, using ion-assisted coatings. The scopes are listed as having 3 ¾ inches of eye relief; fields of view that span from 36.3 feet to 6.1 feet at 100 yards, depending on power setting and objective diameter; have fast-focus eyepieces; and are waterproof and fogproof. Elevation and windage turrets are finger adjustable in ¼ MOA clicks. The Euro scopes also offer two reticle options, the "D" for duplex and for $50 more the "EXT" glass-etched hash-marked "extended range" for individual holds out to 500 yards. The Euro scopes come with Cabela's 60-day free-trial-period guarantee. www.cabelas.com

### EOTECH

In 1996, EOTech introduced its holographic sighting technology for use in sport shooting and hunting, and in 2001 extended their "holographic weapons sight" (HWS) in military and law-enforcement applications. In 2005, EOTech was acquired by L-3 Communications, and it hasn't lost sight of its roots in hunting and recreational shooting. This year it came out with what it claims to be the first-ever holographic sight designed specifically for rimfire rifles, the XPS2-RF. It's made for small-game hunting, high-speed target shooting, and plinking. Its integrated base mounts to any ⅜-inch dovetail rails found on most rimfire rifles (but which also means it will not mount on 1-inch Weaver-style or 1913 rails). For a shorter sight length and shortened base, the HWS uses a single transverse CR123 lithium battery, with an average battery life of 600 hours at the 12-rheostat setting, covered by an O-ring tethered cap. The sight "halo" is 30x23mm in dimension, and the reticle is a 65 MOA circle with a 1 MOA aiming dot. The sight's water-resistant and comes with a 2-year warranty. www.eotech-inc.com

### KRUGER

Along with hunting optics, Sisters, Oregon-based Kruger Optical offers optics for tactical applications, including spotting scopes, riflescopes, and the new 1-8x40mm Dual Tactical Sight Gen II. The DTS uses two different sighting systems through a 38x50.8mm window, one a 1X reflex

**EOTECH XPS2-RF**

**KRUGER- 1-8X40 DTS GEN II**

**CABELA'S EURO RIFLESCOPE**

sight with a 1 MOA red dot and a 60 MOA circle. The dot-sight function has six brightness levels with "off" settings between each level. Flipping a lever engages what seems to be a reflex-camera mirror system and turns the sight into a 40mm scope that can be used at 2X or 8X with a mil-dot ranging reticle. The sight features a patent-pending, extended-range elevation system for long-range impact adjustments, with resettable clicks and a Geneva-style revolution counter, and the locking windage and elevation adjustments are ¼ MOA and independent for both sighting systems. The main rectangular-shaped 10½-inch body of the sight around the mechanics is made from a carbon-fiber composite shell for reduced weight. The DTS mounts on a Picatinny rail, is stated to be waterproof and fogproof, and has a limited lifetime warranty. Krugeroptical.com

## LEATHERWOOD/ HI-LUX OPTICS

Leatherwood offers affordable riflescopes that are built to withstand tough weather conditions, terrain, and recoil. Features include a revolutionary larger erector housing that allows greater transmission of light through the scope tube, making the ATR scopes brighter. The added room also allows for additional windage and elevation adjustment. Plus the all-new addition of the "Tri-Center" spring tension suspension insures positive scope adjustment and that your scope holds alignment.

New this year is the Top Angle Series 7-30x50 which has a larger diameter turrent housing that offers additional windage-elevation adjustment in ¼ MOA clicks. All surfaces of the lense are fully multi-coated. The Top Angle objective lens focuses rather than needing adjustment on the objective lens bell. It comes with a mildot reticle for determining range

The Malcom Series Long 6x32 in. scope is a modern copy of the Model 1855 W. Malcom riflescopes. It comes with early-style mounts for scoping original and replica 19th century

**LEATHERWOOD/HI-LUX M1000 ART**

**LEATHERWOOD/ HI-LUX CMR**

**LEATHERWOOD/
HI-LUX MALCOLM
LONG 6 X 32 INCH**

breech loading rifles (Sharps, rolling block, high wall, etc.) or late period long-range percussion muzzleloading bullet rifles. Objective, ocular and internal lenses are fully multi-coated for maximum light transition through a ¾ inch steel scope tube. Interchangable front extension tubes allows this mid 1800s period-correct scope to be mounted on rifles with barrels of 30 to 34 inches.

The CMR (Close Medium Range) Series 1-4x24 scope has all of its surfaces mutli-coated, zero locking turrets, large external target-style windage and elevation adjustment knobs, and Power-ring extended lever handle for power change. It features a fast eye-piece focus, CMR ranging reticle for determining range and also BDC hold over value good for .223, .308, and other calibers. It comes with a green or red illuminated. The Turret is adjustable in ½ MOA clicks.

The M-1000 Auto Ranging trajectory (ART) 2.5-10x44 scope compensates for the bullet drop automatically by using an external cam system. It can be calibrated for most centerfire rifle cartridges—from .223 to .50 BMG. The shooters sets the multi-caliber cam for the different cartridges being used. The M-1000 scope comes with mount and rings. The scope reticle is the "No-Math Mil Dot."

The Toby Bridge High Performance Muzzleloading 3-9x40 scope is designed for in-line ignition muzzleloaders and saboted bullets. It offers multiple reticles for shooting at ranges out to 250 yards. The scope is shipped with a chart providing points of impact at different ranges when using the longer range cross-bar reticles with different bullets at different velocities. All lens surfaces are mutli-coated for maximum light transmission.

**LEATHERWOOD/HI-LUX TOP ANGLE FOCUS**

**LEATHERWOOD/HI-LUX TOBY BRIDGES HIGH-PERFORMANCE MUZZLELOADING 3-9 X 40**

# NEW Products: **Optics**

## LEUPOLD

Leupold began manufacturing optical equipment–surveying instruments–exactly a century ago and were among the first, if not the first, to nitrogen-purge riflescopes to prevent internal fogging. Leupold's latest model, the VX-R, is certainly fogproof and waterproof, but has more to offer than that. The scope uses a fiber-optic LED illumination system employing the FireDot Reticle System, which is available in FireDot Duplex, FireDot Circle, Ballistic FireDot, and FireDot 4, with the dot within the reticle illuminated while the rest of the reticle is non-illuminated. The VX-R uses what Leupold calls its "Motion Sensor Technology" (MST) that employs a single-touch button to activate the illumination, offering eight different intensity settings, including a high-low indicator. The reticle will automatically switch to "stand-by mode" after five minutes of inactivity, then reactivate whenever the rifle is moved. The VX-R is powered by a CR-2032 coin cell battery. Windage and elevation are adjustable in ¼ MOA finger clicks, and the erector assembly uses twin bias springs. The extended-focus-range eyepiece is one-turn adjustable. The lenses are lead-free glass and the exterior surfaces have an ion-assisted coating to help prevent scratches. The VX-Rs have 30mm tubes and are available in configurations ranging from 1.25-4x20mm to 3-9x40mm "custom dial system" (CDS) that can be matched to your rifle's ballistics, and a long-range 4-12x50mm. Comes with a limited lifetime warranty on optics and a two-year warranty on electronics.

**LEUPOLD VX-R 4-12X40**

**MINOX ZA3**

**MINOX ZA5**

## MINOX

Minox does seem able to blend the look and feel of European optics (although at least some of the mechanical parts are made in a large Asian nation that shall remain nameless) with a reasonable price. In 2010, Minox branched out into riflescopes with its ZA3/ZA5 lines, offering 3X and 5X magnification ranges, respectively. This year Minox has added a number of new configurations, including a 30mm tube in the ZA5 6-30x56mm SF (side-focus parallax adjustment). Other configurations include the ZA3 3-9x50mm and ZA5s in 2-10x50mm, 3-15x50mm SF, and 1.5-8x32mm. These are all 1-inch-tube matte-black scopes and are available with Plex, German #4, BDC, and XR-BDC for the extreme-range bullet-drop-compensating reticle, and the "Versa-Plex" reticle in the 1.5-8X ZA5. The Versa-Plex combines a circle reticle, like that on a turkey scope, with the duplex crosshairs used for big game.

Windage and elevation on the 1.5-8X each have 90 minutes of travel (and range between 36 and 72 minutes on the other configurations) in finger-adjustable positive ¼ MOA clicks, and the turrets can be reset to zero. The scopes all have a generous rubber-armored well-marked power ring, and a rubber-ringed eyepiece that feels tight but focuses smoothly without the need for a locking ring. Waterproof and fogproof, the ZA3 and ZA5s have limited lifetime warranties.

# NEW Products: **Optics**

## NIKON

There are a number of new products from Nikon. Waterproof and fogproof, the ProStaff riflescopes are available in 3-9x40mm black matte with Nikoplex reticle (also in 2-7x32– and in Shotgun Hunter with BDC 200 reticle–4-12x40, and 3-9x50 and in silver, RealTree APG and with BDC reticle). Has multi-coated lenses and comes with ¼ MOA hand-turn reticle adjustments with "Zero-Reset" turrets and a quick-focus eyepiece. The 40 and 50mm scopes are adaptable for sunshades. Also waterproof and fogproof is the new laser range-finding scope, the M-223 Laser IRT 2.5-10x40mm. The M-223 provides the equivalent horizontal range to the target, features one-touch laser technology that keeps ranging and displaying distance for 12 seconds with a button push, and has an integral mount for Picatinny rails. There is also a remote control that can be attached to most firearms. With the BDC 600 reticle, circle aiming points and hash marks are available to correspond to the trajectory of the .223 Rem. 5.56 NATO round with 55-grain polymer tip bullet at approximately 3240 fps from ranges from 100 to 600 yards. Finally there's Bolt XR 3x32 BDC crossbow scope. Fogproof and waterproof, the Bolt XR with multi-coated lenses has 3 ²⁄₅ inches of eye relief and a quick-focus eyepiece with ±4 diopter adjustment. The BDC 60 reticle has aiming points out to 60 yards based upon velocity of approximately 305 feet-per-second. Adjustment increments are ¼ inch at 20 yards.

## STEINER

New from Steiner, and an expansion from their binocular line, are their Military Tactical scopes, said to have been developed in cooperation with "Special Forces" and international weapons experts. Available in 3-12x50, 3-12x56, and 4-16x50mm configurations (with a 5-25x56 and a 30mm tube, true 1X 1-4x24 both scheduled for introduction later in 2011), the Steiners are manufactured from a solid one-piece 34mm tube of 6061 T-6 aerospace aluminum which offers high strength, good workability, land high resistance to corrosion. Uses Steiner HD XP optics with hydrophobic protective coating. Windage and elevation adjustments are .1 mil and guaranteed repeatable with "True-Zero" stop for retune to zero. Has a side-mounted parallax adjustment and a side-mounted illumination control with 11 brightness settings and

**NIKON M-223 LASER IRT 2.5-10X40MM**

**NIKON BOLT XR 3X32**

# NEW Products: **Optics**

automatic shutoff. The front-focal-plane scopes use the G2 mildot illuminated reticle, the illuminated stadia subtending 10 mils vertically and horizontally, suitable for both CQB and long-range conditions. The list price is a cool four grand, but "real world" cost is around $2500.

## TRIJICON

Trijicon's noted for its fiber-optic battery-free illuminated-reticle scopes and reflex sights. The new compact, lightweight adjustable LED RMR (Ruggedized Miniature Reflex) red-dot sight, though, is powered by a standard CR2032 lithium battery; battery life is estimated for up to four years and can be left on for 25 days straight. It has eight brightness levels, including a "Super Bright" setting. The housing's an investment-cast aircraft-aluminum alloy with a hard-coat anodized finish. It has windage and elevation adjusters with audible clicks to allow for quick setting. Offered with 3.25 MOA (RM06) and 6.5 MOA (RM07) aiming points. It's waterproof to a pressure of 20 meters; can be mounted on a handgun, rifle, shotgun, or bow; and it has a two-year warranty.

## WEAVER

The newest offerings from Weaver this year include the addition of a 2-7x32mm scope to the 40/44 line. It

**STEINER 4X16-50MM**

has fully multi-coated lenses, one-piece 1-inch tube construction, and is waterproof and fogproof. The Buck Commander scopes, made with whitetail hunters in mind and bearing the "imprimatur" of Duck, now Buck, Commander Willie Robertson, have a new 2-8x36mm scope for shotgun and muzzle loader. Also with fully multi-coated lenses with finger-adjustable turrets that can be reset to zero. It's fogproof and waterproof, as well, and has the options of Dual X and Command X ballistic-drop-compensation reticle. For new tactical scopes there's the Tactical 1-5x24mm for AR platforms. The reticle is an

**TRIJICON RM06**

illuminated glass-etched first-focal-plane "close intermediate range tactical" (CIRT) with the crosshairs referenced to 20-inch shoulder width for ranging. The horizontal crosshairs are segmented in milliradians for

**WEAVER TACTICAL 3-15X50 MM**

**WEAVER 40-44 2-7X32**

**WEAVER TACTICAL 1-5X24**

windage leads, while the ballistic-drop calculations in the vertical crosshairs are matched to the .223 round. The 1-5x24 has a one-piece-construction 30mm tube, as does the Tactical 3-15x50mm Illuminated Long-Range Scope. The reticle of the 3-15x50 is the "enhanced mildot ranging" (EMDR), glass etched with first focal plane and "open-center" subtention for target acquisition. The center crosshairs are 15 percent narrower for reduced target subtention—in other words, to cover less of the—target at long ranges. Uses mil dots and hash marks for fractions of mils. Like all of the scopes above, the 3-15x50 is waterproof and fogproof; and it has a side-focus parallax adjustment, reset-to-zero external turret adjustments, and ten illumination settings, five red and five green.

# NEW Products: **Ammunition**

## BARNES VOR-TX AMMUNITION

*Features*: Provides maximum tissue and bone destruction, pass-through penetration, and devestating energy transfer. Multiple grooves in the bullet's shank reduce pressure and improve accuracy. Bullets open instantly on contact causing the nose to peel back into four sharp-edged copper petals destroying tissue, bone, and vital organs for a quick, humane kill. Handgun, Safari, and rifle line.
*Available in*: Rifle Line: 25-06, .270 WSM, 7mm-08, 30-06 Sprg., .300 WSM, .300 Win. Mag., .300 Rum, .338 Win. Mag., 45/70 Govt.; Safari Line: .375 H&H, .416 Rem. Mag., .416 Rigby, .458 Win. Mag., .458 Win. Mag., .458 Lott, .470 Nitro, .500 Nitro; Handgun Line: .375 Mag., .44 Mag., .45 Colt
MSRP . . . . . . . **Available on request**

## BARNES MATCH BURNERS BULLETS

*Features*: Lead core match-grade bullets with a long boat-tail design and a high ballistic coefficient. Designed with compeititive shooters in mind, the Match Burners are made to aid in consistent marksmenship.
*Available in*: .223, 6mm, 6.5mm, .30
MSRP . . . . . . . . . . . . .**$20.49–$33.99**

## BARNES M/LE BULLET LINE-RRLP

*Features*: Barnes's new RRLP (Reduced Ricochet, Limited Penetration) bullets feature a frangible, powdered-metal copper-tin core inside a guilding metal jacket. The bullets are lead-free, often a requirement in military and LE practice environments. These open-tip bullets won't come apart in mid-air, even at very high velocities and extreme rates of spin. They combine accuracy with explosive fragmentation, and won't destroy steel practice targets. Frangible bullets lacking a protective jacket tend to break apart inside auto-loading rifles. A major selling point for RRLP bullets is that they remain intact under the rigors of autoloader feeding and firing. They eliminate the primary cause of jammed actions and plugged barrels often experienced in firing frangible ammunition. These multi-purpose bullets are designed for shooting steel targets, competition, plinking, hunting, and home defense.
*Available in*: 50 BMG- 750 gr.
MSRP . . . . . . . . . . . . .**$19.88–$26.99**

## BARNES M/LE BULLET LINE-TAC-XP

*Features*: TAC-XP pistol bullets perform exceptionally well in FBI test protocols. All-copper construction prevents contamination of lead-free practice environments. Deep nose cavity ensures maximum expansion after passing through standard barriers.
*Available in*: 10mm/ 40 S&W- 125 gr.
MSRP . . . . . . . . . . . .**$27.99–$32.99**

BARNES VOR-TX AMMUNITION

BARNES MATCH BURNERS BULLETS

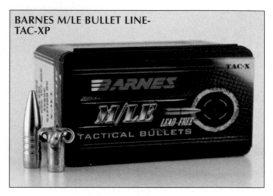

BARNES M/LE BULLET LINE-TAC-XP

### CCI .22 LONG RANGE AR TACTICAL

*Features*: This load is designed specifically for AR-style guns being offered in .22 Long Rifle chambering. These rounds get excellent accuracy including 1.5 inches at 100 yards for 10-shot groups. This target bullet has a copper-plated round nose for smooth feeding. CCI case, priming, and bullet lube combined with clean-burning powder. 375 rounds per box.
*Available in*: .22 Long Rifle; 40-gr.
**4 Box package:. . . . . . . . . . . .$99.99**
**Per box. . . . . . . . . . .$19.99–$25.00**

### GLASER SAFETY SLUG

*Features*: The slug was originally designed for use by Sky Marshals on airplanes. Today the slug is recommended for anyone concerned with over-penetration. The Safety slug uses a copper jacket and it is filled with a compresssed load of either #12 or #6 lead shot. It is then capped with a Blue or Silver ball that enhances feeding and reloading.
*Available in*: .32 Auto-55 gr., .357 Mag.- 80gr, .40 S&W-115gr., .308 Win.- 130 gr.
**Box 6:. . . . . . . . . . . .$20.16–$28.93**

### DPX RIFLE AND HANDGUN

*Features*: DPX is a solid copper hollowpoint bullet that combines the best of the lightweight high speed JHPs and the heavyweight, deep penetrating JHPs. The copper bullet construction makes it conquer hard barriers like auto glass and steel while still maintaining its integrity. This is an optimum load for Law Enforcement. Lead-free projectile. Reduced recoil due to lighter weight projectile. Deep penetration on soft tissue 12–17 inches.
*Available in*: Rifle: 32 Auto-60grain, 44 S&W Special- 200 gr., 480 Ruger-275 gr.;  Handgun: 375 JDJ- 235 gr. & 270-gr.
**Box 20:. . . . . . . . . . .$34.19–$85.67**

### ENVIRON-METAL AMMUNITION HEVI-SHOT MAGNUM BLEND

*Features*: New Hevi-13 Pattern-Density Technology. A breakthrough science that packs more lethal pellets in your pattern. 40 percent more lethal pellets on target, which means more clean kills.
*Available in*: 20 Ga.
**Box 5:. . . . . . . . . . . . . $9.99–$17.49**

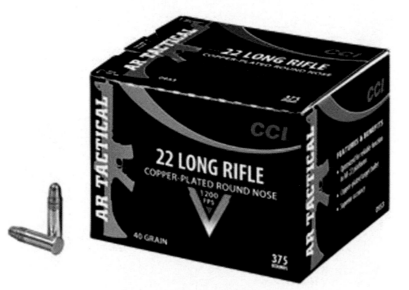

**CCI .22 LONG RANGE AR TACTICAL**

**ENVIRON-METAL AMMUNITION HEVI-SHOT MAGNUM BLEND**

# NEW Products: Ammunition

### FEDERAL MAG-SHOK HEAVYWEIGHT TURKEY

*Features*: Heavyweight shot features a density of 15 grams per cubic centimeter—a third more dense than lead. When combined with the patented Flitecontrol wad, you get tight patterns and lethal shots that allow you to take birds a little bit beyond your typical range. Try the #7 shot for more pellets on target—it matches the density of a #5 lead pellet out to 40 yards.
*Available in*: 20 Ga.; 2.75 in.; 1 1/8 oz.; Shot size 7; Velocity 1,100
**Box 5:. . . . . . . . . . . .$16.99–$28.99**

### FEDERAL BLACK CLOUD HIGH VELOCITY

*Features*: As a natural extension of the Black Cloud waterfowl line, the new Black Cloud High Velocity pumps up the speed and lethal performance for waterfowl hunters everywhere. Boasting higher velocities, increased energy and shorter lead times, the new High Velocity offerings bring a renewed sense of excitement to the duck blind.
*Available in*: 12 Ga.; 3 in.; 1 1/8 oz.; Shot Sizes 3, 4
**Box 25:. . . . . . . . . . .$18.99–$29.04**

### FEDERAL TOP GUN TARGET 12 GA. PINK HULL

*Features*: These special edition pink hull 12-gauge 2-3/4-inch #8 target loads are part of an important mission to find a cure for breast cancer. A portion of the Federal Top Gun sales go directly to search for a cure. These shells are for the volume shooter who needs consistent peformance at a resonable price.
*Available in*: 12 Ga; 2 3/4 in.; 1 1/8 oz.; Shot size 7.5, 8, 9
**Box 25:. . . . . . . . . . . . . . . . . $6.99**

**FEDERAL MAG-SHOK HEAVYWEIGHT TURKEY**

**FEDERAL BLACK CLOUD HIGH VELOCITY**

**FEDERAL TOP GUN TARGET 12-GAUGE PINK HULL**

## FEDERAL GUARD DOG HOME DEFENSE

*Features*: Protect your home and loved ones with a cartridge designed exclusively for home defense. Guard Dog packs the terminal performance that stops threats while reducing over-penetration through walls. Guard Dog is the new benchmark for defending home and family.

*Available in*: 9mm Luger- 105 gr., 40 S&W-135gram, 45 Auto Guard Dog-165 gr.

**Box:** . . . . . . . . . . . . .**$23.20–$32.01**

**FEDERAL GUARD DOG BULLETS BOX**

## FEDERAL FUSION SAFARI

*Features*: From the makers of the world's hottest deer bullet comes Fusion Safari. Fusion's advanced molecular tehnique of electro-chemically applying the jacket to the core means consistent toughness. With enhanced aerodynamics, internal skiving, and suberb accuracy, these bullets provide great performance on a variety of safari animals. Fusion Safari bullets offer high weight retention to ensure deep penetration.

*Available in*: .375 H&H, .416 Rem., .416 Rigby, .458 Win., .458 Lott

**Box 20:** . . . . . . . . . . .**$60.99–$79.00**

**FEDERAL FUSION SAFARI**

## FIOCCHI CANNED HEAT CENTERFIRE RIFLE AMMO

*Features*: One of the most innovative and effective ways to store ammunition long-term. Canned Heat ammo is packed in an oxygen-free nitrogen gas atmosphere to prevent rust and deterioration over time. The cans have an enamel coating inside and out to insulate against electrolysis and prevent corrosion. They stack and store easily, come with resealable plastic lids, and hold up better over time than conventional cardboard packaging.

*Available in*: .223 Rem.- 55 gr.

**Box 30:** . . . . . . . . . . . . . . . . .**$13.99**

**FIOCCHI CANNED HEAT CENTERFIRE AMMUNITION**

# NEW Products: **Ammunition**

## FIOCCHI COWBOY ACTION LINE

*Features*: Our Cowboy Action Line new bullet coating will allow not only a smoother functionality in tubular magazines, but also a saving in production costs.
*Available in*: .38 Special, .357 Mag., .44 Special, .44 S&W, .44-40, .45 Colt, .32 S&W Short, .38 S&W Long, .380 Long. ( 30-30 Win. Rifle caliber toward the end of the year)
**MSRP**. . . . . . . . . . . . . . . . . . . **N/A**

## FIOCCHI LAW ENFORCEMENT LINE

*Features*: This new and greatly enhanced line will be released later this year. Many of the Law Enforcement Line will be offered in two forms of packaging, standard and canned, which will give agencies a safer, longer storage solution with greater accountability.
*Available in*: Shotshells Lethal, Shotshells Less than Lethal, Chemitracer Training Shotshells, Pistol Centerfire Frangible Line, Pistol Centerfire non-toxic packing EMB (expansion mono-block) duty bullets, Pistol Centerfire Training and Frangible line, Rifle non-toxic Tundra core bullets, Rifle Centerfire Training and Sniper Line.
**MSRP**. . . . . . . . . . . . . . . . . . . **N/A**

HOGDON POWDERS
LEVEREVOLUTION

## FIOCCHI CYALUME CHEMI TRACER SHOTSHELL

*Features*: The most advanced training aid for trap, skeet, and sporting clay shooters, the Fiocchi Chemical Tracer, powered by Cyalume, provides a daytime visible trace that travels with the cloud of shot as it hits or misses the clay bird. The Chemical Tracer is non-incendiary, non-toxic, and meets EPA and Consumer Safety compliance. It leaves no residue in the barrel and is non-corrosive.
*Available in*: 12 Ga.; ¾ oz.; Shot size: 8
**Box/ Can 10:**. . . . . . . . . . . . .**$19.99**

## SCORPION FUNNEL POINT

*Features*: Scorpion Funnel Point Mag. Bullets are known for having excellent expansion and take-down. This bullet is offered on a limited time basis.
*Available in*: .40 caliber- 200 gr.
**Box 50:**. . . . . . . . . . . . . . . . .**$18.99**

## HODGDON LEVEREVOLUTION POWDER

*Features*: Hodgdon Powder Company and Hornady Manufacturing have teamed together to answer the frequently asked reloading question; "Can I buy the powder used in Hornady LEVERevolution factory ammunition?" Yes, this is the same spherical propellant used in Hornady's innovative and award-winning high performance factory ammunition. This propellant meters flawlessly and makes lever action cartridges like the .30-30 Winchester yield velocities in excess of 100 fps over any published handloads, with even greater gains over factory ammunition. Other cartridges include the .35 Remington, .308 Marlin Express, .338 Marlin Express, and the .25-35 Winchester.
*Available in*: .25-35 Win., 30-30 Win., 308 Marlin Express, .338 Marlin Express, 338 Federal, 35 Remington
**1 LB:**. . . . . . . . . . . . .**$20.71–$26.00**

## HODGDON SUPERFORMANCE

*Features*: This is another of the spherical powders created by

Hodgdon Powder Company and Hornady Manufacturing. Superformance delivers striking velocities in cartridges like the 22-250 Remington, 243 Winchester, and 300 Winchester Short Magnum. Velocities well in excess of 100 fps over the best published handloads and even larger gains over factory ammunition! Because this propellant is tailored for specific applications, the number of cartridges and bullets is limited.
*Available in*: .22-250 Rem., .243 Win., .243 Win. Super Short Mag., 6mm Rem., .25 Win. Super Short Mag., .300 Win. Short Mag., .300 Ruger Compact mag.
**1 LB:**. . . . . . . . . . . . .**$33.99–$38.99**

## HORNADY .257 WEATHERBY MAG. CUSTOM

*Features*: Millions of successful hunts have proven the accuracy and deadly knockdown power of the famous Hornady InterBond and GMX bullets that are loaded into the 257 Weatherby Custom rifle cartridge. Each cartridge is loaded to ensure optimal pressure, velocity, and consistencey. Much of the brass is made by Hornady. The rest is carefully selected for reliable feeding, corrosion resistance, hardness, and the ability to withstand maximum chamber pressure. Like the powder, each primer is carefully matched to individual loads, and specially selected for their ability to quickly, completely, and reliably ignite the powder charge.
*Available in*: .275 Weatherby Mag.- 110 gr. Interbond; 257 Weatherby Mag.- 90 gr. GR GMX
**Box 20:**. . . . . . . . . . .**$54.73–$61.75**

**HORNADY 257 WEATHERBY MAG. CUSTOM**

## HODGDON SUPERFORMANCE MATCH

*Features*: Superformance Match Ammunition achieves muzzle velocities 100–200 fps faster than ANY conventional ammunition. Amazing ammunition performance starts with outstanding bullets, and Hornady AMAX and Boattail Hollow Point Match bullets, now featuring revolutionary new AMP (Advanced Manufacturing Process) bullet jackets, raise the standard. Topped with the finest bullets, Superformance Match ammunition marries the very best cartridge cases with extremely stable propellants that are custom-blended for each individual load to provide true ammunition performance enhancement.

*Available in*: 223 Rem.- 75gr. GR BTHP; 5.56 Nato-75 gr. BTHP; 308 Win.- 168 gr. A-Max; 308 Win.- 178 gr. BTHP

**Box 20:** . . . . . . . . . . .$26.27–$38.68

## HODGDON .300 WHISPER

*Features*: Originally developed and pioneered by J. D. Jones of SSK Industries, the 300 Whisper is a highly efficient cartridge based on the 221 Remington case necked up to .308. Reknowned as a subsonic cartridge for use with suppressed guns, the 300 Whisper from Hornady is available in both supersonic and subsonic loads. Compatible with guns chambered for the 300 AAC Blackout, the 300 Whisper from Hornady is a reliable performer with or without a suppressor and brings a new level of flexibility to the AR-15 platform.

*Available in*: 300 Whisper- 110 gr. V-Max (Very low recoil—ideal for youth and women); 300 Whisper- 208 grain A-Max (Tactical offering when silence is necessary)

**Box 20:** . . . . . . . . . . . . . . . . . .$33.00

## HORNADY STEEL MATCH

*Features*: Featuring Hornady Match rifle bullets or HAP (Hornady Action Pistol) handgun bullets, Steel Match ammunition is loaded at the Hornady factory with optimized propellant for each load that provides consistency and the highest levels of accuracy. Utilizing polymer-coated steel cartridge cases, and non-corrosive berdan primers, Steel Match ammunition delivers Hornady quality and performance, but with an economical price.

*Available in*: 9mm Luger-125 gr. HAP; 40 S&W- 180 gr. HAP; 45 Auto-230 gr. HAP; 223 Rem.- 55 gr.HP; 30 M1 carbine- 110 gr. FMJ; 308 Win.- 155 gr. BTHP

**Box 50:** . . . . . . . . . . .$27.19–$56.99

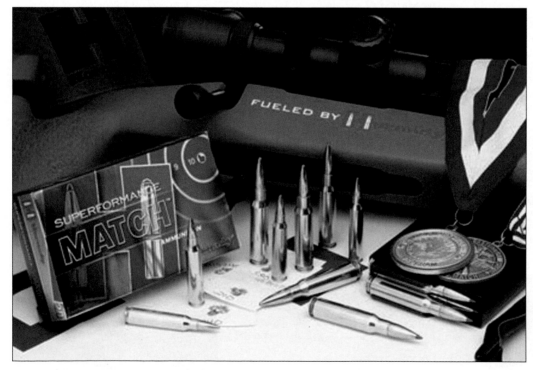

HORNADY SUPERFORMANCE MATCH

HORNADY STEEL MATCH

# NEW Products: Ammunition

## HORNADY CRITICAL DEFENSE

**Features**: The Hornady Critical Defense line of personal defense ammunition has added .22 WMR, 8x18 Makarov, .44 Special, and .45 Colt to the lineup. Loaded with the patented FTX bullet, these bullets provide consistent expansion through heavy clothing, and won't plug up like conventional hollow points. Unaffected by thick and heavy clothing, including denim and leather. Clean-burning and stable propellants reduce recoil in lightweight handguns,

**HORNADY LEVEREVOULTION BULLETS LOADED WITH MONOFLEX**

and perform consistently in all temperatures. Minimal muzzle flash protects night vision. Shiny silver nickel plating prevents corrosion, and is easily visible in low light situations. Bullets are cannelured and crimped to avoid bullet setback.

*Available in*: .22 WMR- 45 gr.; 9x 18mm Makarov- 90 gr.; .44 Special- 165 gr.; .45 colt- 185 gr.

**MSRP . . . . . . . . . . . .$17.53–$27.27**

## HORNADY LEVEREVOULTION BULLETS LOADED WITH MONOFLEX

**Features**: Combining the technologies of the GMX and patented FTX bullet design, the new MonoFlex bullet is a fantastic union of the very latest in bullet design from Hornady. Constructed of gilding metal, MonoFlex bullets won't ever separate, and when recovered, retain 95%+ of their originial weight. Deep

penetration. High weight retention. Unbeatable power. The combined technologies of GMX and FTX have fused to produce the MonoFlex; an accurate, deadly, dependable new choice for lever gun hunters. Up to 250 ft per second faster muzzle velocity than conventional lever gun loads. Up to 40% more energy than traditional flat point loads.

*Available in*: .30-30 Win.- 140 gr.; .308 Marlin Express- 140 gr.; .45-70 Government- 250 gr.

**Box 20: . . . . . . . . . . .$37.61–$52.20**

## HORNADY .22 WMR RIMFIRE

**Features**: Hornady .22 WMR rimfire ammuniton features a 30-grain V-Max bullet that leaves the muzzle at 2.200 feet per second with excellent terminal performance out to 125 yards. Hornady's .22 WMR improves the accuracy of any .22 WMR rifle.

**Box 50: . . . . . . . . . . $15.77–$17.53**

**HORNADY CRITICAL-DEFENSE**

## LAPUA .260 REMINGTON

*Features*: Offering ballistic performance similar to the 6.5x55, this combination could deliver both flat trajectories and pin-point accuracy, giving it a broad appeal to both target shooters and hunters alike. Coupled with the truly superb range of bullets available in this bore size, it was no surprise to see Remington adopt the cartridge as the .260. Despite its incredible list of competitive victories, the .260 isn't just a target round. It has also shown itself to be a fine performer in the field for medium game. Effectively duplicating the ballistic performance of the time-honored 6.5x55, the .260 has already developed a well-earned reputation for dependable stopping power on deer, antelope, and similar game. Given the tremendous selection of bullets for every conceivable application, the .260 is an extraordinarily versatile cartridge. With such a solid history already established in such a short time, Lapua is proud to add the .260 to its line of premier components for the handloader.
*Available in*: .260 Remington, 139 gr.
**MSRP . . . . . . . . . . . .$37.21–$42.99**

HORNADY .22 WMR

## LAPUA SCENAR BULLET

*Features*: This new generation of match bullets has been dubbed the ScenarL, and is a fitting successor to the vaunted Scenar family. Sharing the same aerodynamic profiles as their predecessors, the ScenarL are the perfect choice for any type of competitive shooting. Whether it's ISSF or CISM, Benchrest or F-Class, Silhouette, High Power Across the Course or Long Range, the new ScenarL line will give you the extra edge that takes you to the winners circle. Based on the Scenar's proven track record of competitive successes, Lapua's new ScenarL will deliver the ultimate performance in the most demanding competitive environments every time. Precision craftsmanship, painstaking quality control standards, state of the art manufacturing technology, and advanced ballistic design all combine to make the new ScenarL the very best of the best!
*Available in*: 6mm, 105 gr.
**MSRP . . . . . . . . . . . .$40.95–$50.99**

## NOSLER . 22 CAL. BALLISTIC TIP VARMINT

*Features*: Nosler Ballistic Tip Varmint bullets thrive on ultra-high velocity loads, yet will go the distance with spectacular results all the way down to the lowest practical velocity levels. Fast or slow, near or far, no matter what rifle/cartridge combination you're shooting or what varmint you're shooting at, Nosler Ballistic Tip delivers match-grade accuracy with all

LAPUA SCENAR BULLET

# NEW Products: Ammunition

the performance characteristics serious varminters are looking for.
*Available in*: .22 40 Grain Spitzer, .50 Grain Spitzer, .55 Grain Sptizer
**MSRP:** . . . . . . . . . . .$37.99–$41.99

## NOSLER TROPHY GRADE VARMINT AMMUNITION

*Features*: Trophy Grade VARMINT Ammunition consists of the venerable Ballistic Tip VARMINT bullet or the frangible Ballistic Tip Lead Free along with NoslerCustom Brass. Because of Nosler's unsurpassed quality standards, each piece of brass is checked for correct length, neck-sized, chamfered, trued, and flash holes are checked for proper alignment. Powder charges are meticulously weighed and finished rounds are visually inspected and polished.
*Available in*: .204 Ruger-32 grain; .223 Rem.- 35 grain, 40 grain; 22-250 Rem.- 35 grain, 40 grain
**MSRP** . . . . . . . . . . . .$17.00–$35.99

## PMC FRANGIBLE LINE

*Features*: PMC's frangible ammunition combines their incomparable Sinterfire bullet and reduced-hazard primer. Using a lead-free bullet that shatters into non-toxic dust on impact with anything harder than itself, this product virtually eliminates the danger of ricochet from jacket and bullet fragments. Safe for shooting steel plates from any distance or for close-quarters tactical operations.
*Available in*: 9mm Luger, 40 S&W, 45 Auto, .223 Rem., 5.56 Nato, 7.62 Nato, 50 BMG
**MSRP** . . . . . . . . . . . . . . . . . . **N/A**

## PMC SIDEWINDER

*Features*: PMC lends its strict manufacturing guidelines to the most basic of rifle cartridges, the .22 Long Rifle. The .22 is a fine and enjoyable caliber for shooters of all ages. PMC Sidewinder lets you shoot to your hearts content.
*Available in*: .22 LR
**MSRP** . . . . . . . . . . . .$23.10–$26.99

**NOSLER TROPHY GRADE VARMINT**

## PMC PRECISION LINE

*Features*: PMC's Precision Line incorporates genuine Hornady bullets with precision-drawn cases loaded to stringent manufacturing standards. The result is unparalleled accuracy and consistent performance. It is available in hunting or target versions.
*Available in*: .223 Rem., .243 Rem., .270 Win., 7mm Rem. Mag., .300 Win. Mag., .308 Win., .30-06 Spfld., 30-30 Win.
**MSRP** . . . . . . . . . . . .$22.00–$36.00

## REMINGTON PREMIER NITRO GOLD SPORTING CLAYS TARGET LOADS

*Features*: Remington's Target Loads have taken shot-to-shot consistency to a new performance level, setting the standard at all major skeet, trap, and sporting clays shoots across the country, while providing handloaders with unmatched reloading ease and hull longevity. Available in most gauges, our shells are the most reliable, consistent, and reloadable shells you can shoot. To meet the special demands of avid sporting clays shooters, we developed a new Premier Nitro Gold Sporting Clays target load. At 1300 fps, the extra velocity gives you an added advantage for those long crossers—making target leads closer to normal for ultimate target-crushing satisfaction. Also makes a great high-velocity dove load.
*Available in*: 12, 28, 410 Ga; 2.75 in., 2.5 in.
**MSRP** . . . . . . . . . . . . . $8.49–$9.64

## REMINGTON HYPERSONIC STEEL

**REMINGTON PREMIER NITRO SPORTING CLAYS**

**Features**: Introducing the world's fastest, hardest-hitting steel: the 1,700-fps HyperSonic Steel from Remington. With unprecedented velocity and the highest downrange pattern energies ever achieved, new Remington HyperSonic Steel takes lethality to new heights and lengths, to a level of terminal performance where more birds drop with fewer shots, at the farthest reaches of your abilities.
**Available in**: 10, 12, 20 Ga; 3 in., 3.5 in.
**MSRP**. . . . . . . . . . . .**$17.55–$26.00**

## WINCHESTER BLIND SIDE

**Features**: Winchester Ammunition is introducing one of the most innovative shotshell loads in the brand's 144-year history. The new Blind Side ammunition combines ground-breaking, stacked HEX Shot technology and the new Diamond Cut Wad in the most deadly Winchester waterfowl load available. Loaded with

**REMINGTON HYPERSONIC STEEL**

100 percent HEX Shot, you get more pellets on target, a larger kill zone, and more trauma-inducing pellets than ever before, meaning quick kill shots. Key features include the high packing density and Drylock Super Steel System, that helps to keep your powder dry by sealing out water and moisture.
**Available in**: 12 Ga.; 3, 3.5 in.; Shot size: BB, 2
**Box 25** . . . . . . . . . . .**$22.99–$26.99**

## WINCHESTER SUPER-X POWER CORE 95/5

**Features**: Start with a 95/5 copper alloy, integrate a highly engineered contoured cavity—and you have a new benchmark in lead-free big game cartridges. Introducing the new line of Super-X Power-Core 95/5 centerfire rifle cartridges. Featuring a devastatingly effective bullet with massive initial impact shock plus deep penetration and virtually 100% retained weight, to assure maximum trauma to bone and vitals. Projected hollow point promotes expansion at a variety of ranges.
**Available in**: 223 Rem., 270 Win., 7mm Rem. Mag., 30-30 Win., 30-06 Spgfld., 300 Win. Mag.
**MSRP**. . . . . . . . . . . .**$30.99–$49.99**

**WINCHESTER BLIND SIDE**

# NEW Products: **Ammunition**

## WINCHESTER PDX1 12 DEFENDER

**Features**: The 12-gauge PDX1 Defender ammunition features a distinctive black hull, black oxide high-base head, and 3 pellets of Grex buffered 00 plated buckshot nested on top of a 1 oz. Rifled slug. The result is the ideal, tight-patterning personal defense load. The slug/buckshot combination provides optimum performance at short and long ranges, while compensating for aim error. When it comes to the safety of you and your family, choose the load that delivers innovative, threat-stopping technology.

**Available in**: 12 Ga. 2 ¾ in., ( Also available: .223 Rem.; .410 Ga. 2 ½ in, 3 in.; .380 Auto, .38 Spl. +P, 9mm Luger +P, 9mm Luger, .357 Mag., .357 Sig., .40 S&W, .45 Auto, .45 Colt)
**MSRP** . . . . . . . . . . . .**$22.00–$29.00**

## WINCHESTER POWER MAX BONDED

**Features**: Designed specifically for the whitetail deer hunter, Power Max Bonded delivers maximum performance at an affordable price. The proprietary bonding process welds the lead core to a contoured copper alloy jacket. The aerodynamic profile of the protected hollow point (PHP) bullet design promotes long range accuracy and intiates maximum expansion to provide dramatic knock-down power.

**Available in**: .223 Rem., .270 Win., .270 WSM, 7mm WSM, 7mm Rem. Mag., .30-30 Win., .30-06 Spgfld., .300 WSM, .308 Win., .325 WSM, .338 Win. Mag.
**MSRP** . . . . . . . . . . . . .**$17.00–$29.00**

## WINCHESTER RIMFIRE

**Features**: Rimfire is the most popular ammunition in the world—and it's the ammunition most of us loaded up with when we first started shooting. Rimfire ammunition has come a long way from the simple "lead round nose" rounds we all carried around loose in our pockets. Today, Winchester rimfire ammunition leads the industry in developing and delivering precision technology, highest-quality components, optimum reliability, and superior performance.

**Available in**: .17 HMR, LF .17 HMR, .22 Win. Mag., LF .22 Win. Mag., .22 LR, LF .22 LR
**Box 500:** . . . . . . . . . . . . . . . .**$139.99**

**WINCHESTER PDX1 12 DEFENDER**

**WINCHESTER POWER MAX BONDED**

**WINCHESTER RIMFIRE**

## WINCHESTER E-TIP LEAD FREE

*Features*: Winchester and Nosler have combined technologies to bring hunters a superior hunting load through innovative design. The extremely complex hollow cavity and bullet composition guarantee textbook expansion over a wide range of impact velocities and near 100 percent weight retention. E-Tip ammunition delivers unbeatable terminal performance and accuracy in the field.

*Available in*: .308 Win.- 168 gr.
**MSRP** . . . . . . . . . . . . . . . . . . .**$42.50**

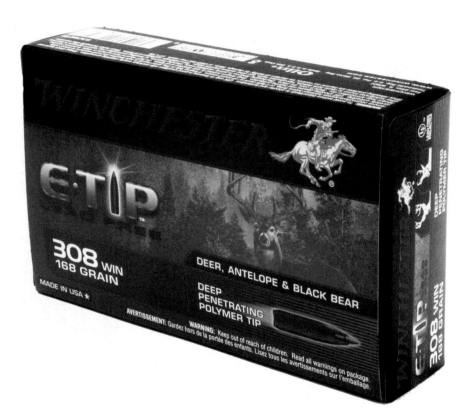

**WINCHESTER E-TIP LEAD FREE**

## ONE SHOT ONLY
—Wayne van Zwoll

For centuries, shooters had to load one shot at a time. Some still prefer single-shot rifles. Here's why!

" . . . Where is the military genius [to] modify the science of war as to best develop the capacities of this terrible engine—the exclusive use of which would enable any government . . . to rule the world?" At one time, this might have been written of the horse, later the atomic bomb. But in an appeal to the U.S. government, Oliver Winchester so described his rimfire Henry. Its advantages as an infantry rifle were to appear during the Civil War, where dismayed Confederates called it "the rifle you loaded on Sunday and fired all week." The .44 Henry could deliver a stream of fifteen bullets (216-grain lead, at 1,025 fps) with just a second's pause between each.

You might think this development would bury all single-shot rifles. It did not. Shortly after war's end, five years before Christian Sharps died of tuberculosis, the Sharps Rifle Manufacturing Company introduced the New Model 1869, its first rifle in metallic chamberings. This single-shot evolved from an 1848 patent Christian Sharps secured for a vertically sliding breech-block operated by an under-lever. The New Model 1869 Sharps was chambered in .40/50, .40/70, .44/77, .45/70, and .50/70. It preceded by only a few

months the New Model 1874 Sharps and soon faded. The 1874 Sharps endured for 12 years after its debut late in 1870—a decade that spanned the height of the market-hunting era. This powerful dropping-block rifle earned a big berth in history as the favorite arm of buffalo hunters.

George Reighard was one. In a 1930 edition of the *Kansas City Star*, he told how he shot bison:

"In 1872 I organized my own outfit . . . to shoot buffaloes for their hides. I furnished the team and wagon and did the killing. [My partners] furnished the supplies and did the skinning, stretching and cooking. They got half the hides and I got the other half. I had two big .50 Sharps rifles with telescopic sights. . . .

"The time I made my biggest kill I lay on a slight ridge, behind a tuft of weeds 100 yards from a bunch of a thousand buffaloes that had come a long distance to a creek, had drunk their fill and then strolled out upon the prairie to rest. . . . After I had killed about twenty-five my gun barrel became hot and began to expand. A bullet from an overheated gun does not go straight, it wobbles, so I put that gun aside and took the other. By the time that became hot the other had cooled, but then the powder smoke in front of me

AMONG THE AUTHOR'S SINGLE-SHOTS, THE RUGER NO. 1 A IS A FAVORITE. THIS 6.5 CREEDEMOOR POINTS FAST!

LONG BARRELS ON SINGLE-SHOTS GIVE YOU HIGH BULLET VELOCITIES IN RIFLES OF AVERAGE OVERALL LENGTH.

was so thick I could not see through it; there was not a breath of wind to carry it away, and I had to crawl backward, dragging my two guns, and work around to another position on the ridge, from which I killed fifty-four more. In one and one-half hours I had fired ninety-one shots, as a count of the empty shells showed afterwards, and had killed seventy-nine buffaloes. . . ."

The Sharps Rifle Company folded in 1880, having failed to market its hammerless 1878 rifle or to design a practical repeater. A prairie emptied by commercial hunters hastened the firm's collapse. By the early 1880s, so many bison had been killed that human scavengers would glean more than three million *tons* of bones from the plains.

The preference of market hunters for single-shots was understandable. Earlier firearms had been muzzle-loaders! People far from services were wary of new and unproven mechanisms. Indeed, after the discovery of fulminates in the early 1800s led to the percussion cap, hunters were slow to accept it. The advantages of generating spark inside the chamber couldn't lure some riflemen from flint ignition. They *knew* flintlocks! Also, the Sharps 1874 (and Remington Rolling Block) seemed a logical follow-up to the iconic plains rifle built by Jacob and Samuel Hawken. In the early 1800s General W. H. Ashley, head of the Rocky Mountain Fur Company, devised the rendezvous to collect furs from trappers on the frontier. Tons of pelts funneled to

JOHN BROWNING DESIGNED A SINGLE-SHOT RIFLE THAT BECAME WINCHESTER'S MODEL 1885. BROWNING PUT ITS VERTICALLY SLIDING LUGS TO USE IN LATER REPEATING RIFLES FOR WINCHESTER, HERE AN 1892.

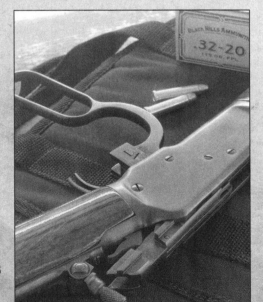

St. Louis, where the Hawken brothers reconfigured the Kentucky rifle for use in the West. Barrels were shorter, for carry on horseback. Bigger bores—50 caliber and up—accepted heavy balls and charge weights to 215 grains, for lethal effect on bison and grizzly bears. Hawken rifles were credited with kills to 300 yards, long shooting then. In 1849, when the California Gold Rush began, you could buy a Hawken rifle for $22.50. That year inventor Walter Hunt devised a curious rifle with a finger-lever that delivered primers like pills behind hollow-base "rocket balls" bearing tiny charges of powder. Hunt's tube-fed Volitional Repeater spawned the Volcanic Rifle, which begat the Henry.

Post-Civil War single-shots could swallow cartridges too big to cycle through repeating actions. The mass around the chamber of a single-shot gave it great strength, and its simple design made it less prone to failure. Reliability and power mattered more in the hunting field than did the quick repeat shots valued by soldiers facing a swarm of men, each much easier to kill than a bison.

John Browning understood this. While still in his twenties, the Utah firearms genius designed and built a dropping-block single-shot rifle. Winchester salesman Andrew McAusland spotted one, used, in 1883. He was so impressed, he sent it to Thomas Bennett, Winchester's president. Bennett had never heard of Browning, but he booked passage on the next train west. He found in Ogden a well-equipped shop run by five brothers barely out of their teens. "I want to buy your rifle," he told John. One rifle? "No, all rights to the rifle." John replied that the price was $10,000—an enormous sum for that time. He quickly accepted Bennett's counter of $8,000. The deal began a 20-year relationship that produced a bonanza of new rifle and shotgun designs for Winchester. The most famous repeating rifles—the 1886, 1892, and 1894—had the vertically sliding lugs of John's single-shot and the storied Sharps.

The Browning rifle became Winchester's Model 1885. It came with either "high-wall" or "low-wall" breech. High, thick steel shoulders provided the strength for big, powerful rounds. Low-wall actions gave the shooter easier breech access with smaller cartridges. Discontinued in 1920, the Model 1885 was later resurrected by Browning as the Japanese-built Model 78, subsequently renamed the Model 1885.

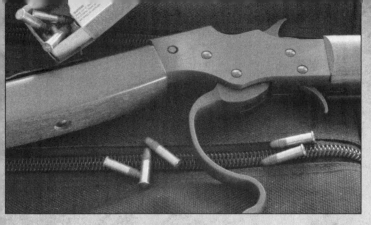

**SAVAGE'S MODEL 30 FAVORITE IS A REINCARNATION OF THE STEVENS FAVORITE, A DROPPING-BLOCK RIMFIRE.**

A mechanism with a sliding breechblock is not an easy thing to manufacture. The hinged-breech or "break-action" design so popular for shotguns was adapted to rifles as steels improved to bottle higher pressures. In my youth, Savage offered its 219 in .22 Hornet and .30-30. Now exposed-hammer rifles like the CVA Apex handle such frisky rounds as the .308 Winchester, with operating pressures above 52,000 psi. My Apex is also accurate. Thompson/Center's Contender and Encore, in pistol and rifle form, thrive partly because each offers many easily interchangeable barrels. Rossi lists its Wizard in twenty-three configurations, including shotgun, muzzle-loader, and rimfire. Harrington & Richardson's Handi-Rifle, an economical hinged-breech rifle, excels as a "first gun" for youngsters. The Savage Model 30 Favorite resurrects the trim dropping-block Stevens .22 of that name.

Low cost hardly applies to all single-shot rifles. The Blaser R95 and Merkel K1 and K2 exhibit figured walnut, beautifully shaped, finished, and fitted. The cocking mechanism of these hammerless rifles operates independently of the hinge. Push ahead to cock; push, then ease the switch back to de-cock. The tilting block that seals the breech provides strong lock-up. Chamberings include magnums. Weight of the K1 Stutzen: just 5 ½ pounds!

In a nod to history, Chiappa (Legacy Sports) markets a line of Sharps 1874 reproductions. Well-made, they have the looks, feel, and features of originals. Short of an Old Reliable on the mantle, a Sharps aficionado can't do better than a rifle from Shiloh Sharps, the Montana company that builds 'em to order, one at a time. The list of accoutrements, finishes, upgrades, chamberings, and barrel contours is very long.

Every Shiloh Sharps rifle I've seen has been beautifully detailed and finished. The actions move silkily. Owners boast of marvelous accuracy.

**MOST SINGLE-SHOT MECHANISMS WILLINGLY ACCEPT RIMMED AND RIMLESS CARTRIDGES. BELTED TOO!**

Dakota Arms offers a "baby" Sharps, each dimension carefully scaled to 80 percent of original. In .22 Hornet, and stocked with fancy walnut, such a rifle is fetching indeed! Dakota also catalogs the Miller single-shot, a lovely dropping-block rifle with a benchrest pedigree. Those I've fired have cut tiny groups. The Miller action accommodates chamberings from .22 rimfire to .404 Jeffery. Dakota's Model 10 single-shot is also of dropping-block design, but trimmer in profile. It is to my mind one of the late Don Allen's most appealing rifles, a truly elegant firearm with exquisite detailing.

But the signature single-shot of the 20th century—and, so far, the 21st—is Ruger's No. 1. Priced at $265 when introduced in 1966, it wore an attractive quarter-rib and a figured walnut stock fashioned by Len Brownell. Five versions featured a wide variety of chamberings. The rifle that inspired the No. 1 was patented by John Farquharson nearly a century before, in 1872. John lived in Daldhu, Scotland. He sold part

**THE RUGER NO. 1 IS A STRONG ACTION AND RELATIVELY SIMPLE. BUT "FITTING IT UP" REQUIRES GREAT SKILL.**

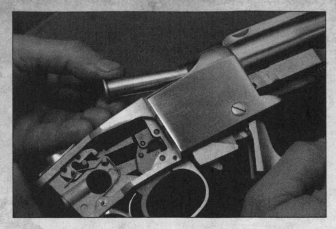

**A CRAFTSMAN AT RUGER'S FACTORY TEST-CHAMBERS A CASE DURING FINAL ADJUSTMENT OF A NO. 1**

**THE AUTHOR STEADIES A RUGER. MAKING THE FIRST SHOT COUNT IS IMPORTANT EVEN IF YOU HAVE MORE BULLETS!**

interest in the rifle to Bristol gunmaker George Gibbs, who manufactured it until the patent expired in 1889. Evidently fewer than 1,000 of these single-shots left Gibbs's shop before the last was delivered in 1910. The Farquharson mechanism found its way into other rifles. Auguste Francotte of Herstal, Belgium copied the action. So did British maker W. J. Jeffery & Co, as early as 1895. In 1904 Jeffery announced an oversize version for the .600 Nitro Express cartridge.

A second mortgage might get you a Gibbs-Farquharson. But Ruger's No. 1 remains within reach of ordinary folks like me. I've hung onto a few—even 7 x 57s, which in the early days had unconscionably long throats. I took a big buck with one in the Wallowa Mountains, then had to follow another deer poorly hit at long range. When on a steep face scree shifted above me, I spun in time to see the buck dash across a chute. The Ruger was up in a wink; my shot boomed as the deer vanished in a dip. I had barely dropped another round into the breech when the buck came tumbling down the chute, end over end. An imperative to make one good shot doesn't always put you at a disadvantage. Truly, it can improve your shooting!

The first opportunity to shoot is almost always the best. Follow-up shots are neither as easy nor as forgiving of poor marksmanship. Guiding hunters, I have noticed that those careful to fill their magazines to capacity are commonly *not* as careful to make the first shot lethal. Hunters who rely on single-shots are declaring from the outset their willingness to bet the trip on one pull of the trigger.

The role of rifle accuracy in killing game is the same, no matter what the mechanism or cartridge. It is a lesser role than we play as marksmen. Number Ones have delivered fine hunting accuracy for me. I've found B and V (Varmint) versions most consistent.

Many have delivered thumb-print groups. Barrel heft gives them an obvious edge over the lighter A version. Still, slender barrels can be accurate. One of the No. 1 A's liabilities (but an endearing feature cosmetically) is its barrel-mounted front swivel stud, shared with the Medium Sporter S and Tropical H rifles. While few hunters rely on a shooting sling, I do. A taut sling affects barrel vibrations during bullet passage. Even on rifles with stock-mounted swivels, sling tension can influence point of impact. Exerted directly on the barrel, it's a force to be reckoned with. When zeroing sporters, I now fire from prone with a tight sling, as that's how I commonly shoot at game.

The forend hanger on Ruger's No. 1 does not ensure a "free-float" condition or consistent contact when you apply sling pressure or press the rifle hard onto a bipod. Forend modifications arrived early. An externally adjustable set screw was one. I installed a rubber hose washer near the rear of the hanger and a brass shim at the forend tip on a No. 1 B in .300 Winchester. The rifle shot well before the treatment, but groups from prone landed much lower than those from a rest. The modified forend cut dispersion in half.

**THE NO. 1 IS AVAILABLE IN A WIDE RANGE OF CHAMBERING, FROM .204 RUGER TO BRITISH EXPRESS ROUNDS.**

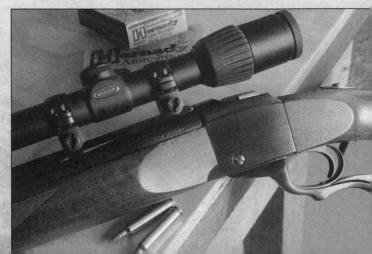

RUGER'S NO. 1 IS CAPABLE OF TIGHT GROUPS. THE V ("VARMINT") VERSION SEEMS ESPECIALLY ACCURATE.

KEN NAGLE LEVELS ONE OF HIS RUGER NO. 1s , THIS WITH A CARBON-FIBER BARREL IN 7MM WSM.

Ruger's No. 1's good looks belie its solid performance. It's the equivalent of a supermodel who likes to cook and change the oil in your pickup. Strong, well balanced, and accurate, the No. 1 has a good trigger. The tang safety is quiet and doesn't spoil the receiver's clean sculpting. The breech-block slides like greased glass in its race. An adjustable extractor lets you choose ejection or a gently raised case. A handloader, I don't mind plucking hulls from the breech. But last fall I was thankful my friend Ken had adjusted his rifle to eject.

Deep in Idaho's central wilderness, we'd seen no elk for most of a week. Then, on a cold, cloudy dawn, we spied a herd with a fine bull. They were nearly a mile below us, on a grassy bench. Ken pressed his No. 1 on me. "Take this. You might need the reach." Swapping my iron-sighted Winchester for that Ruger was my salvation. The only shot I had, after a long scramble, came at 330 yards. The herd was on the move, heading to cover through a cemetery of charred lodgepoles. I flopped prone, snugged the sling, and triggered the No. 1. A 140-grain Nosler AccuBond struck the bull perfectly. I yanked a second round from its loop in the butt sleeve and had it chambered as fast as I'd have cycled a bolt. I fired it and a third; neither was necessary.

The twenty-six-inch barrel of that No. 1 gave the magnum charge of Vihtavuori powder plenty of bore to accelerate the bullet. Compared to bolt-action rifles, short-coupled dropping-blocks deliver about four inches more barrel for a given overall length. That means a higher level of ballistic performance in a rifle that's still nimble in thickets. Truly, not all cartridges need that much tube. Recent No. 1 chamberings include Ruger Compact Magnums and the 6.5 Creedmoor, which perform efficiently in 22-inch bar-

rels. Ruger's Light Sporter version has a 22-inch barrel for standard rounds of modest capacity. This rifle ranks among my all-time favorites. It has a clean, classic but racy look, solid feel with balance that makes it lively and fast to the shoulder. My No. 1A in 6.5 Creedmoor puts Hornady 129-grain SST and 140-grain A-Max bullets over Oehler sky screens at 2,910 and 2,603 fps. For comparison, I fired the same ammo from the 24-inch barrel of a T/C Icon bolt gun. They clocked 2,939 and 2,647—just 30 fps faster.

Another thing I like about the No. 1 is its flat receiver. There's no projecting bolt knob, so the rifle slides easily into cases and scabbards. That trim breech is amazingly adaptable too. It takes rimmed and rimless cases, and belted magnums, from the .22 Hornet to the likes of the .416 Rigby. Its great strength makes it a natural for wildcats and ambitious handloads. Ken barreled one of his No. 1s to a 6.5mm wildcat on the WSM case. "It's throated so I

THE AUTHOR KILLED THIS IDAHO ELK AT 330 YARDS WITH A RUGER NO. 1. HE RELOADED QUICKLY, BUT DIDN'T HAVE TO.

THIS LAST-DAY BULL FELL TO KEN NAGLE AT 380 YARDS
ABOVE THE SALMON RIVER. ONE SHOT ONLY!

FEW BOLT GUNS WERE ENGINEERED FOR THE LIKES OF THE
.404 JEFFERY. RUGER'S NO. 1 ACCEPTS IT EASILY.

can seat bullets out for top speed; 120-grain TSX bullets clock 3,350 fps."

Last fall I visited Ruger's factory to speak with the craftsmen assembling No. 1's. "Each requires a great deal of hand fitting," said a fellow timing the close of the lever. A colleague was fitting buttstocks. As I watched these two deftly adjust and marry the parts on this stout but intricate action, I wondered how Ruger could ever have sold a No. 1 for $265.

You may someday find comfort in a full magazine. But there's no substitute for one well-directed bullet. Carry a single-shot rifle for a season, and you may come to think of additional cartridges as simply extra weight.

LONG CARTRIDGES LIKE THE .300 WEATHERBY CHALLENGE
REPEATERS. THEY'RE NO PROBLEM IN SINGLE-SHOTS.

# FASTEST BOLT RIFLES OF ALL
## —Wayne van Zwoll

F ollow-up shots come as fast as you can aim—with rifles you cycle with your eye to the sight!

Bang! Bang! You'd have thought, just by hearing, that the rifle was an autoloader. In fact, it wore a bolt handle. It leapt back in a blur, snapping forward as fast, readying a second round before the bounce of recoil had left the barrel.

If your rifle doesn't behave this way, you may believe the old bromide that bolt-actions are slow. Hardly. But many shooters run them slowly. And some bolt mechanisms are slower than others.

**A RIFLE THAT STEADIES RIGHT AWAY TRUMPS ONE THAT FLIES TO YOUR SHOULDER BUT DOESN'T SETTLE DOWN.**

The idea behind bolt rifles was the door-latch. At least, such is the legend. In 1867, failing in their bid to supply a French service rifle, Paul and Wilhelm Mauser returned to their native Oberndorf. As the brothers opened a gunshop, the Royal Prussian Military Shooting School tested a Mauser rifle Remington sales agent Samuel Norris had furnished. Impressed, the inspectors asked the Mausers for improvements—and got them. The 11mm Mauser 1871 became the official Prussian shoulder arm. Wilhelm died young in 1882, seven years before Fabrique Nationale d'Armes de Guerre (FN) began building Mauser 1889 rifles for the Belgian government. The 1889 established Paul Mauser as Europe's dominant gun designer. He improved it in 1893 with a staggered-column, fixed-box magazine. By 1895 he had an action that would be perfected as the Model 1898. Within months of its acceptance by the German Army, the 98 became the most popular service arm to that time.

Following World War II, Mauser entered the sporting trade. Its U.S. agent, A. F. Stoeger, Inc. of New York, assigned numbers to the various Mauser actions. By the end of the Depression there were twenty types in four lengths: magnum (9.25"), standard long (8.75"), short (8.50") and "true short" (8.00"). The standard action, designed for the 8 x 57 Mauser and the like, was adapted to other cartridges with the substitution of appropriate magazines—which accounts in part for the many forms of 1898 Mausers listed by Stoeger and purveyors of surplus service rifles. While surplus military Mausers sold cheap, commercial versions did not. In 1939 an M70 Winchester cost $61.25, a Mauser sporter $110 to $250—more for a square-bridge rifle.

**DELIBERATE SHOTS STILL DELIVER THE MOST HITS. LIGHTWEIGHT RIFLES NEED MORE STEADYING THAN SUPPORT.**

**EVEN FAST-FOOTED GAME IS BEST KILLED WITH ONE CAREFUL SHOT. HURRIED SHOOTING IS SELDOM SELECTIVE.**

design his extractor to jump over the rim of a cartridge chambered by hand. But there's roughly .030 extra clearance broached into the right-hand lug race of the receiver ring, should single loading become necessary. Just pinch the extractor spring toward the bolt body as you close the bolt. The extractor makes the jump.

Faster than the Mauser was the Mannlicher-Schoenauer. Actually, M-S rifles were made by Steyr. All of them. Mannlicher and Schoenauer were rifle *designers*, not manufacturing or corporate magnates! Named for a 13th-century town at the confluence of the Steyr and Enns Rivers, Steyr got its start during the 1860s, when young Josef Werndl returned from a stint in the U.S. working for Colt. He applied his fresh knowledge of gun manufacture in his father's shop. In church one day, Josef thought up a new rifle design. Given its genesis, the mechanism was called a "tabernacle breech." Austria's army bought it, and by the end of the 19th century, Steyr had more than 10,000 workers on its payroll! Josef Werndl provided housing for many of them. In 1883 he brought hydro power to the city, making it the first in Europe with electric lights.

Steyr built rifles for other countries too—the Norwegian Krag, even the Mauser. Its Mannlicher-Schoenauer, Model 1903, had a signature split bridge and butterknife bolt handle. Chambered initially in 6.5 x 54, this rifle cycled so effortlessly that with the bolt drawn back, a downward flip of the muzzle could

The Mauser 98 runs loosely, most often with lots of wobble at the end of its throw. But it is easy to manipulate and dead-certain to extract and chamber. You can cycle it as fast as you like without fear of a malfunction. The bottom rim of the 98 Mauser's bolt face is milled flush with the center of the face so case heads can ride smoothly up into the extractor claw. This "controlled-round feed" matters to soldiers. Early snaring of a case precludes double loading and a jam. Mauser did not

**THREE FAST SHOTS WITH A SUPER-SMOOTH STEYR IN 9.3 X 62 NAILED THESE EUROPEAN PIGS FOR THE AUTHOR.**

DETACHABLE BOX MAGAZINES WITH STAGGERED COLUMNS COMBINE SPEED AND CAPACITY. HERE: A STEYR BOX.

it endures test-firing with a full-power load *behind a bullet deliberately lodged halfway up the barrel*! My experience with modern Steyrs bears out the claim of improved accuracy. A Classic version in .270 WSM kept bench groups under .80. One in .338 RCM put three shots into half an inch. A full-stocked Classic in my rack prints sub-minute knots with a lightweight 19-inch barrel in 9.3 x 62. I used that rifle in Austria to nail three driven boars in quick succession. By the way, Steyr began building automobiles in 1918. That year, Josef Wendl died of pneumonia, age 58, after working to protect the city from a flood. In 1934 a merger formed Steyr-Daimler-Puch. The conglomerate dissolved in 1996, leaving firearms production alone under the Steyr name.

My first bolt gun was not built by Steyr or Mauser. At $30, the war-surplus Short Magazine Lee Enfield cost $10 less than a 98, and much less than a Mannlicher-Schoenauer. The SMLE's stamped steel box looked cheap, but fed its ten rounds so smoothly I could cycle *empties*! After re-stocking the rifle and replacing its military blade and notch with Williams open sights, I killed deer with it. My friend Ron had a lever-action 94 Winchester he insisted was faster. Neither of us could waste rounds in speed-shooting contests. So we stuffed our magazines with hulls and shucked furiously on

bring it forward *and rotate it into battery*! A spool magazine fed cartridges fluidly. From the 1903 came a long series of M-S rifles, the last built four decades ago. The Steyrs that replaced them are almost as slick in operation, and they have several advantages. A three-position tang safety serves as bolt release, behind a Mauser-style bridge. The twin-lug lock-up is so stout

STEYR OFFERS ITS SVELTE EUROPEAN-STYLE RIFLES IN MODERN CHAMBERING, LIKE THE FRISKY .270 WSM.

signal until we'd spilled seven. The .303 with its cock-on-closing action proved as fast as the 94 every time!

The 1903 Springfield isn't that fast as issued, though tuned rifles acquit themselves well in rapid-fire stages of the National Match course. I recall '03s and '03A3s for $29.95, back when you could have them delivered by the postman. I still covet Springfields. One in my rack is a military '03 graced with a simple stick of new walnut and a Redfield receiver sight. I took it to Alaska, climbed a mountain, and shot a Dall's ram. On the flats below, it garnered a moose. One bullet each. My other two Springfields wear synthetic stocks and svelte barrels in .30-06 Improved. They wear 3x and 6x scopes, both Leupolds. The first downed a fine six-point Wyoming elk in a thicket. The rifle with the 6x toppled a Utah mule deer.

Winchester's Model 54 borrowed some features of the Springfield. In 1937, the New Haven firm supplanted the 54 with the Model 70, a better rifle and one that gobbled cartridges as long as the .300 and .375 H&H. Don Allen's Dakota 76 endures as a Model 70 sequel, refined but not diluted. A lovely rifle.

During the 1920s, as Winchester puffed its Model 54, Remington was building the Model 30, in profile a well-dressed 1917 Enfield—a sturdy rifle, but neither trim nor fast to operate. The Model 720 replaced it in 1941. Then came war, and it was 1948 before Remington had another bolt-action sporter. The 721 and 722 (long and short versions) featured tubular receivers, stamped bottom metal. Thoughtful re-design in 1962 produced the Remington 700. During the early 1940s, Roy Weatherby used various actions to build rifles for his high-octane cartridges. In 1958, he and Fred Jennie came up with the Mark V. A nine-lug, interrupted-thread bolt head with a full-diameter body gave the Mark V shallow bolt lift and great speed.

Given a lethal first hit, cycling speed hardly matters in a rifle, but not all bullets land where they should, or behave as they ought. "If you can get the strength, reliability, and accuracy of a bolt-action with double the speed, why wouldn't you?" Bernard Knobel knows about speed. A practiced skeet shooter, he thrashed me soundly during an impromptu event at a gun club somewhere in the patchwork of forest and farmland quilting rural Germany. That's where he directs operations for Blaser, a firm that builds truly innovative rifles and shotguns.

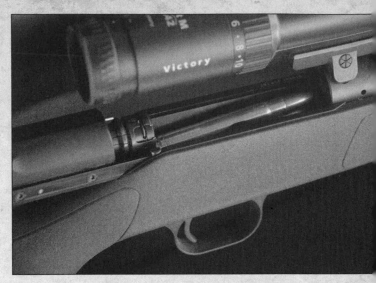

A REAL RACEHORSE, THE STRAIGHT-PULL BLASER R93 (HERE IN .375) IS BEAUTIFULLY FITTED, VERY, VERY SLICK.

Relatively young, by industry standards, Blaser (that's blah'-zer, not blay'-zer) appeared in 1957. Its R93 has since earned plaudits from hunters the world over. This straight-pull bolt rifle offers a broad selection of chamberings on a switch-barrel action noted for trim lines and original engineering. I've used it in Africa, where I quickly learned to like it. The 93's successor, the R8, is named after the year Blaser started making improvements. Bernard insists that neither the R8 nor the R93 fit the German stereotype. "They're *not* over-engineered and under-designed!" he blusters. After using these rifles, I agree.

Norbert Hausman runs Blaser's North American operation from its headquarters in San Antonio. When I saw my first R8, he was quick to assure me the features that distinguished the R93 were all there: hammer-forged barrel; telescoping, radial-head bolt; single-stack magazine tucked into a compact block with a target-quality trigger. That magazine/trigger assembly trims overall length. An R93 with 24-inch barrel is shorter than a Remington 700 with a 22-inch tube!

The 93, and now the R8, don't operate like an ordinary bolt rifle either. You run the bolt with a flick of your hand. From the shoulder. Without losing your sight picture. Back and forth. No rotating required. The thumb-piece that cocks the R8 is its only safety. Shove it up and forward. You're ready to fire. When you want

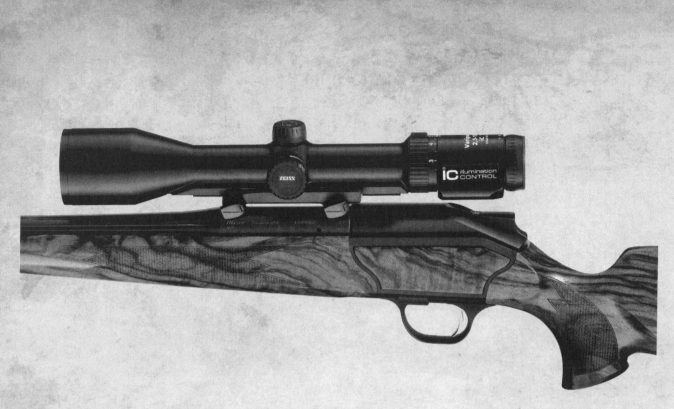

**BLASER'S R8 HAS SLEEK, DISTINCTIVE STYLING, MIRRORED IN ITS QUICK-RELEASE (REPEATABLE!) SCOPE MOUNTS.**

to de-cock, push ahead again, but down slightly, and let it return to the rear. "The R93 and now the R8 are the only bolt rifles you can carry safely at the ready," Norbert points out. "They're not cocked until you're ready to fire."

**THE BLASER R8 HAS A STRAIGHT-PULL BOLT THAT RUNS FASTER THAN YOU CAN RECOVER FROM RECOIL.**

Like its predecessor, the R8 bolt head locks with a collett forced into a circumferential groove in the barrel shank. "But the R8 is stronger," says Norbert, a master gunsmith. "Its locking angle is steeper than the 45 degrees on the R93. Also, a bushing slides into the collett's center for added support. We've tested this mechanism to pressures of 120,000 psi, damaging gauges before the rifles failed."

Blaser barrels come in various lengths, weights, and contours, fluted and not. Most chambers are hammer-forged. Plasma nitriding on barrels increases surface hardness. "Scope rings and base clamps are softer," said Bernhard. "They don't slip from those dimples. Our saddle rings fit so precisely that you can remove the scope and replace it without losing zero."

I went to the range not believing that last claim. Scope removal always means *some* shift in zero.

"Hand it over." A bear of a man with a ready grin, Blaser's Tom Mack snatches the R8 before I had could say no. He frees the Zeiss scope with a couple of tugs on the thumb latches and holds it up like a prize. Hoo boy. I've been flailing at a 5-gallon bucket filled with Texas chalk at 600 yards. This .300 has done my bidding. Now I'll have to re-zero. "Have at," Tom insists, cinching the 6-24 x 56 scope back in place. I sigh and belly into position. Favoring into a 9-o'clock breeze, I press the trigger. A puff of white dust hops into the air.

**WITH PRACTICE, YOU'LL FIRE A BLASER R8 MUCH FASTER THAN YOU CAN A TURN-BOLT RIFLE—AND ACCURATELY!**

"Bingo!" Tom cackles. "Again." I run the Blaser's bolt—a flick of the wrist, even prone. Another Federal load rockets downrange. "Got it again." He's smug now. "One more." I cycle the R-8, fire, hit. "No need to re-adjust, huh?" drawls Tom. "Even at 600 yards."

You can switch Blaser barrels with equal confidence. I'd confirmed that with the R93 in Namibia, replac-ing one barrel with another, previously zeroed. My Norma loads drilled bullseyes at 300 steps. You need but a single tool, a T-handled allen wrench, to change barrels or remove the buttstock. (The wrench supplied with the R8 is 5mm, that with the R93 4mm.)

Like the R93, the R8 has a single-stack polymer magazine. But the R8 magazine/trigger group is hand-detachable as a unit. Just pinch those tabs in front of the guard. You can top-load without removing the box, or re-charge the rifle with pre-loaded magazines from your pocket. Should you wish to lock the magazine in place, there's a sliding tab inside the box. One box accepts all cartridges for which the R8 is chambered (more than two dozen, from .223 to .416 Remington Magnum). But the inner parts, a snap to change by hand, work for *families* of cartridges. For example, a stop abbreviates the bolt throw for rounds shorter than the .30-06. "When you remove the magazine/trigger group," explains Norbert, "the rifle de-cocks automati-cally. It remains non-functional until the assembly is replaced." To protect that assembly while it's out of the R8, Blaser supplies a snug polymer jacket. There's a polymer insert for the receiver.

In Europe, R8s come standard with a trigger pull of 1.6 pounds. U.S. hunters get an equally crisp break at 2.5 pounds. You can special-order a lighter trigger; however, parts must be installed by Blaser, as weight

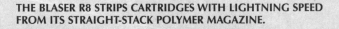

**CLEVERLY ENGINEERED, THE SLICK-FEEDING BLASER R8 HAS A HAND-DETACHABLE MAGAZINE/TRIGGER GROUP.**

**THE BLASER R8 STRIPS CARTRIDGES WITH LIGHTNING SPEED FROM ITS STRAIGHT-STACK POLYMER MAGAZINE.**

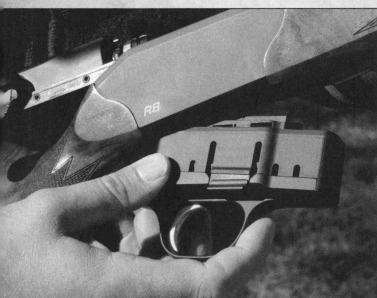

TIGHT GROUPS ON THIS RUNNING BOAR TARGET ILLUSTRATE WHY BLASER'S R8 IS AN IDEAL RIFLE FOR THIS GAME.

adjustment happens in the *receiver*. Like the R93, the R-8 has very fast lock time.

The R8's stock has a straight comb, which, admit Blaser folks, is for most applications better than the hump-back comb traditional in central Europe. It has cast-off at toe and heel, and even 3.5mm in the grip, to make sight alignment quick and easy. As on the R93, the Turkish walnut comes in several grades.

Sub-minute groups at 300 yards have repeatedly shown me that the R8 is accurate! Beyond that, its compact design and excellent balance make it ideal for quick shooting in timber. And that straight-pull bolt is without peer for running boar targets. I've shot those enough to have developed an addiction. The .308 I used most often was beautifully matched with a Zeiss Vari-Point (red dot) scope. The hapless pig got very ragged as it raced back and forth on the rail, brass piling up beside me. No cycling hitches. None.

The only change I'd make in the R8 is at the wrist. The steep European grip works fine offhand, but in prone and sitting my big hand wants room to shift. A more open profile would look better, improve handling.

Handling. As horsepower and gearing can't hurry a sports car through curves without a matching suspension, so a rifle must have the balance and profile to bring the sight back on target as the bolt slams shut. My preference is for a slim stock profile, with an open

WEATHERBY'S MARK V RIFLE HAS LOW BOLT LIFT AND A FULL-DIAMETER BOLT BODY. BOTH IMPROVE CYCLING SPEED.

**DORI RIGGS FIRED FAST IN TIGHT COVER TO TAKE THIS WARTHOG WITH A NEW ULTRA LIGHT ARMS RIFLE.**

grip. The idea isn't to *fill* your hands, but to give them something easy to grasp, and to let them shift slightly if you must swing on a running animal.

Pick up a broomstick. You'll probably find it quick in your hands, and a snap to point. Your rifle's stock should be straight as well as slender, and a tad short. While my arms call for a 14 ½-inch pull, I've come to like, not just accept, standard 13 ⅝ pulls. A stock that's slightly short speeds the rifle to your cheek, because you needn't push the rifle forward to clear your coat. A short stock also better accommodates the odd shooting positions you must sometimes adopt quickly.

Keep the weight low and between your hands. I like a slight tilt to the muzzle to minimize jump during recoil and help settle the rifle against my pulse and the wind. A shallow forend makes sense; so too a slim scope of modest weight, mounted well forward and as low as you can get it. Net rifle weight has a lot to do with the chambering. Rifles violent in recoil not only make you flinch, they're slow on follow-up shots because *you're* slow to get them back on target. Balance matters, no matter the heft.

**THE AUTHOR DOWNED THIS WHITETAIL WITH HOWA IN .243. NOT A LIGHTWEIGHT, THE RIFLE HAS FINE BALANCE.**

Perhaps the thing that gives you the greatest edge in speed is practice. Cycling the mechanism in hunting positions, with dummy rounds, helps a great deal. Cycle often enough *while firing* to trim your recoil-recovery time and ditch the habit of slowly sliding the bolt back to pick out the hull. Do that in the field, and you might as well be toting a single-shot!

**PRACTICE SNATCHING ROUNDS FROM POUCHES AND YOU'LL BECOME A FASTER SHOOTER IN THE FIELD.**

# Anschutz

ANSCHUTZ 1416 D KL

ANSCHUTZ 1416 D HB

ANSCHUTZ 1517

ANSCHUTZ 1710

RIFLES

## 1416 D KL
**Action**: Bolt
**Stock**: Walnut
**Barrel**: 22 in.
**Sights**: Open
**Weight**: 5.94 lb.
**Caliber**: .22 LR
**Magazine**: Detachable box, 5-rounds
**Features**: Folding leaf adjustable sights; laquered walnut wood stock; pistol grip; black butt plate; studs for sling swivel; lateral sliding safety.
**MSRP** . . . . . . . . . . . . . . . . . . **$1099**

## 1416 D HB, 1502 D HB, 1517 D HB
**Action**: Bolt
**Stock**: Walnut
**Barrel**: 23 in.
**Sights**: None
**Weight**: 6.38 lb.

**Caliber**: .22 LR, .17 Mach 2, and .17 HMR respectively
**Magazine**: Detachable box, 5-rounds
**Features**: Folding leaf adjustable sights; beavertailed laquered walnut wood stock; pistol grip; black butt plate; studs for sling swivel; lateral sliding safety.
**1416 D HB, 1507 D HB, 1517 D HB: $1099–$1249**

## 1517
**Action**: Bolt
**Stock**: Walnut
**Barrel**: 22 in.
**Sights**: None
**Weight**: 6.16 lb.
**Caliber**: .17 HMR
**Magazine**: 5-rounds
**Features**: Single or two stage adjustable trigger; optional beavertail stock;

walnut stock comes in classic or Monte Carlo style.
**MSRP** . . . . . . . . . . . . . . . . . . . **$1189**

## 1710
**Action**: Bolt
**Stock**: Walnut
**Barrel**: 22 in.
**Sights**: Open
**Weight**: 7.48 lb.
**Caliber**: .22 LR
**Magazine**: 5-rounds
**Features**: Drilled and tapped for scope mounts; sliding safety catch; two stage or single stage trigger; adjustable folding leaf sights and pear front adjustable ramp; engraved forestock and trigger guard; black plastic butt plate.
**Classic:** . . . . . . . . . . . . . . . **$1959**
**Monte-Carlo:** . . . . . . . . . . **$2089**

# Anschutz

ANSCHUTZ 1827 FORTNER SPRINT

ANSCHUTZ 1903 TARGET SMALL BORE RIFLE

ANSCHUTZ 1907 (IN 1912 STOCK)

## 1827 FORTNER SPRINT

*Action*: Bolt
*Stock*: Biathlon, walnut
*Barrel*: 22 in.
*Sights*: None
*Weight*: 8.14 lb.
*Caliber*: .22 LR
*Magazine*: Detachable box, 5-rounds
*Features*: Combination of an extra light 1827 Fortner barreled action with the stock of the 1827 model; laquered walnut stock with stippled checkering; heavy, cylindrical match barrel; match stage two or single trigger.
**MSRP** . . . . . . . . . . . . . . . . . . **$3568**

## 1903 TARGET SMALL BORE RIFLE

*Action*: Bolt
*Stock*: Hardwood
*Barrel*: 26 in. heavy
*Sights*: None
*Weight*: 9.68 lb.
*Caliber*: .22 LR
*Magazine*: None
*Features*: A match rifle for small bore shooters; anatomically perfect walnut stock with vertically adjustable cheek piece; optional aluminum, hook, or rubber butt plate; aluminum accessories rail.
**MSRP** . . . . . . . . . . . . . . **$885–$1334**

## 1907 (IN 1912 STOCK)

*Action*: Bolt
*Stock*: Standard rifle, walnut
*Barrel*: 32.28 in.
*Sights*: None
*Weight*: 10.78 lb.
*Caliber*: .22 LR
*Magazine*: None
*Features*: Match 54 action; adjustable cheekpiece and hook butt piece; forend rail; match single stage trigger.
**MSRP** . . . . . . . . . . . . . . . . . . **$2809**

## 1770

*Action*: Bolt
*Stock*: Walnut
*Barrel*: 22 in.
*Sights*: Drilled and tapped for scopes
*Weight*: 7.5 lb.
*Caliber*: .223 Rem.
*Magazine*: Detachable, 3-shot, in-line
*Features*: Six locking lug action for strength and reliablility; adjustable, single-stage match trigger; hand-checkered stock with oval cheek piece and rubber butt pad; detachable sling swivel studs.
**MSRP** . . . . . . . . . . . . . . . . . . **$2499**

# Armalite Rifles

## AR-10A2CF CARBINE

*Action*: Semi-automatic
*Stock*: Synthetic
*Barrel*: 16 in.
*Sights*: Open
*Weight*: 9 lb.
*Caliber*: .308
*Magazine*: Detachable box, 10- and 20-rounds
*Features*: Chrome lined barrel; forged A2 receiver; sling; black case; flash suppressor; tactical two stage trigger; black or green stock; stage trigger, flash suppressor.
**MSRP**. . . . . . . . . . . . . . . . . **$1561**

## AR-10A4 CARBINE FORWARD ASSIST

*Action*: Semi-automatic
*Stock*: Synthetic
*Barrel*: 16 in.
*Sights*: None
*Weight*: 9 lb.
*Caliber*: .308
*Magazine*: Detachable box, 10- & 20-rounds
*Features*: Sling; black case; flass suppressor; two stage NM trigger; chrome-lined barrel.
**MSRP**. . . . . . . . . . . . . . . . . **$1657**

## AR-10T

*Action*: Semi-automatic
*Stock*: Synthetic
*Barrel*: 22 in.
*Sights*: None
*Weight*: 9 lb. 10 oz.
*Caliber*: .308
*Magazine*: Detachable box, 10-round mag
*Features*: Triple lapped barrel; NM two stage trigger; black or green stock; Picatinny rail gas block.
**MSRP**. . . . . . . . . . . . . . . . . **$1892**

## AR10 SUPER S.A.S.S.

*Action*: Semi-automatic
*Stock*: Synthetic
*Barrel*: 20 in.
*Sights*: None
*Weight*: 12 lb.
*Caliber*: .308
*Magazine*: Detachable box, 10- & 20-round mag.
*Features*: USMC quick adjustable

**ARMALITE AR-10A2CF CARBINE**

**ARMALITE AR-10A4 CARBINE FORWARD ASSIST**

**ARMALITE AR-10T**

sling; NM two stage trigger; flash suppressor; triple lapped barrel; black stock.
**MSRP**. . . . . . . . . . . . . . . . . **$3078**

## AR-10T CARBINE

*Action*: Semi-automatic
*Stock*: Synthetic
*Barrel*: 16 in.
*Sights*: Open
*Weight*: 8.6 lb.
*Caliber*: .308
*Magazine*: Detachable box, 10- & 20-round mags
*Features*: Free float handguard in black; two stage NM trigger; flash suppressor; black case; black stock.
**MSRP**. . . . . . . . . . . . . . . . . **$1892**

**ARMALITE AR10 SUPER S.A.S.S.**

**ARMALITE AR-10T CARBINE**

RIFLES

# Armalite Rifles

**ARMALITE AR-10 TBNF**

## AR-10 TBNF

*Action*: Semi-automatic
*Stock*: Synthetic
*Barrel*: 20 in.
*Sights*: None
*Weight*: 10 lb. 2 oz.
*Caliber*: .308
*Magazine*: Detachable box, 10-round mags.
*Features*: Free float handguard in black; two stage NM trigger; black case; triple lapped barrel; black or green stock.
**MSRP** . . . . . . . . . . . . . . . . . . **$1892**

## AR-30M

*Action*: Bolt
*Stock*: Synthetic
*Barrel*: 26 in.
*Sights*: Open

*Weight*: 12 lb.
*Caliber*: .300 Win. Magnum
*Magazine*: Detachable box, 5-round mag.
*Features*: Chrome Moly Barrel; hard anodized alumnium, manganese phospated steel finish; forged and machined removable buttstock; Multi-Flute Recoil Check; 10 minute sight base; bi-pod adapter; shilen standard single-stage trigger; black stock.
**MSRP** . . . . . . . . . . . . . . . . . . **$2021**

## AR-50A1 NM

*Action*: Bolt
*Stock*: Synthetic
*Barrel*: 33 in.
*Sights*: None
*Weight*: 33.2 lb.
*Caliber*: .50 BMG

*Magazine*: None
*Features*: Chrome Moly barrel; muzzle brake; 15-minute rail; single-stage trigger.
**MSRP** . . . . . . . . . . . . . . . . . . **$4230**

## M-15 A2

*Action*: Semi-automatic
*Stock*: Synthetic
*Barrel*: 20 in.
*Sights*: Open
*Weight*: 8 lb. 1 oz.
*Caliber*: .223
*Magazine*: Detachable box, 30-rounds
*Features*: Double lapped, chrome-lined barrel; flash suppressor; forged A2 receiver; tactical two-stage trigger; sling; black case; black or green synthetic stock.
**MSRP** . . . . . . . . . . . . . . . . . . **$1150**

**ARMALITE AR-50A1 NM**

**ARMALITE AR-30M**

**ARMALITE M-15 A2**

# Armalite Rifles

### M-15 A2 CARBINE

*Action*: Semi-automatic
*Stock*: Synthetic
*Barrel*: 16 in.
*Sights*: Open
*Weight*: 6 lb. 13 oz.
*Caliber*: .223
*Magazine*: Detachable box, 30-rounds
*Features*: Forged A2 receiver; double lapped, chrome-lined barrel; sling; handguards; black or green synthetic stock; black case; tactical two stage trigger; flash suppressor.
**MSRP . . . . . . . . . . . . . . . . . . $1150**

### M-15 A2 NATIONAL MATCH RIFLE

*Action*: Semi-automatic
*Stock*: Synthetic
*Barrel*: 20 in.
*Sights*: Open
*Weight*: 9 lb. 3 oz.
*Caliber*: .223
*Magazine*: Detachable box, 30-rounds
*Features*: Forged A2 receiver with NM hooded rear sight; triple lapped, stainless steel barrel with NM sleeve; A2 front sight assembly; two stage NM trigger; black or green stock.
**MSRP . . . . . . . . . . . . . . . . . . $1388**

### M-15 SPR II NM

*Action*: Semi-automatic
*Stock*: Synthetic
*Barrel*: 20 in.
*Sights*: None
*Weight*: 9 lb. 7 oz.
*Caliber*: .223
*Magazine*: Detachable box, 30-rounds
*Features*: Forged flattop receiver; triple lapped barrel; A2 flash hider muzzle device; two stage NM trigger; NM carry handle; sling; black case; Picatinny rail; black or green synthetic stock; Picatinny gas block front sight base.
**MSRP . . . . . . . . . . . . . . . . . . $1413**

**ARMALITE M-15 A2 CARBINE**

### M-15 A4 CARBINE

*Action*: Semi-automatic
*Stock*: Synthetic
*Barrel*: 16 in.
*Sights*: None
*Weight*: 6 lb. 7 oz.
*Caliber*: 7.62 x 39mm
*Magazine*: Detachable box, 10-rounds
*Features*: Forged flattop with Picatinny rail; forged aluminum receiver; tactical two stage trigger; A2 flash suppressor; sling; black case; black or green stock.
**MSRP . . . . . . . . . . . . . $1107**

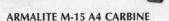

**ARMALITE M-15 A4 CARBINE**

**ARMALITE M-15 A2 NM RIFLE**

# Armalite Rifles

**ARMALITE M-15 A4 CBK WITH OUT CARRY HANDLE**

## SPR MOD 1 LE CARBINE

*Action*: Semi-automatic, short gas system
*Stock*: Synthetic
*Barrel*: 16 in.
*Sights*: 3 detachable rails
*Weight*: 6.5 lb.
*Caliber*: .223
*Magazine*: Detachble box, 30-rounds
*Features*: Muzzle flash suppressor; black synthetic tactical stock; aluminum handguard;  tactical two stage trigger, sling; black case.
**MSRP . . . . . . . . . . . . . . . . . . $1554**

## M-15 A4 CBK W/OUT CARRY HANDLE

*Action*: Semi-automatic
*Stock*: Synthetic
*Barrel*: 16 in.
*Sights*: None
*Weight*: 6 lb. 3 oz.
*Caliber*: .223
*Magazine*: Detachable box, 30-rounds
*Features*: Chrome lined barrel; muzzle flash suppressor; forged flattop; Picatinny rail; tactical two stage trigger; no carry handle; black stock; sling; black case.
**MSRP . . . . . . . . . . . . . . . . . . . $975**

**ARMALITE SPR MOD 1 LE CARBINE**

# Arsenal Rifles

## MTK90 JUBILEE SERIES AK-74

*Action*: Gas-operated autoloader
*Stock*: U.S.-made black polymer
*Barrel*: 16.3 in.
*Sights*: 1000m rear leaf sight and scope rail
*Weight*: 7.3 lb.
*Caliber*: 5.45 x 39.5mm
*Magazine*: 10-shot Russian and 30-shot Bulgarian boxes included
*Features*: Created to celebrate the 35th anniversary of AK-74 and the 90th anniversary of M. T. Kalashnikov; limited edition; Russian-made receiver; includes matching rifle case, gloves, and certificate.
**MSRP . . . . . . . . . . . . . . . . . . . . N/A**

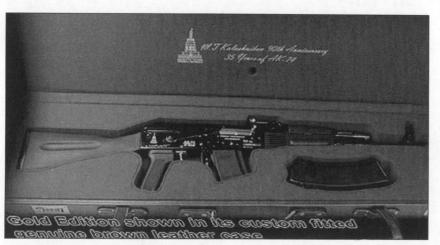

**ARSENAL MTK90 JUBILEE SERIES AK-74**

# Arsenal Rifles

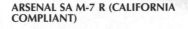

ARSENAL SA RPK-3R

ARSENAL SA M-7 R (CALIFORNIA COMPLIANT)

## SA RPK-3R
**Action**: Gas-operated autoloader
**Stock**: Black polymer or blond wood
**Barrel**: 23.2 in.
**Sights**: Open
**Weight**: 10.5 lb.
**Caliber**: 5.45 x 39.5mm
**Magazine**: 45-round magazine
**Features**: RPK heavy barrel; milled receiver; U.S.-made; paddle style butt-stock and scope rail; includes sling, oil bottle, and cleaning kit,
**MSRP** . . . . . . . . . . . . . **$2500–$2750**

## SA M-7 R (CALIFORNIA COMPLIANT)
**Action**: Gas-operated autoloader
**Stock**: Black polymer
**Barrel**: 16.3 in.
**Sights**: Open
**Weight**: 8.11 lb.
**Caliber**: 7.62 x 39mm
**Magazine**: 10-round U.S.-made magazine
**Features**: Milled receiver; non-detachable magazine; includes muzzle nut, cleaning rod, and bayonet lug.
**MSRP** . . . . . . . . . . . . . **$2000–$2010**

# Auto-Ordnance Rifles

## THOMPSON 1927 A-1
**Action**: Semi-automatic
**Stock**: Walnut, vertical foregrip
**Barrel**: 16.5 in.
**Sights**: Blade front, open rear adjustable
**Weight**: 13 lb.
**Caliber**: .45 ACP
**Magazine**: 30-shot stick
**Features**: Frame and receiver made from solid steel; compensator; optional 50rd drum magazine.
**MSRP:** . . . . . . . . . . . . . . . . . **$1420**
**With 50rd drum, 30 rd stick magazines:** . . . . . . . . . . . . . . . . . . **$1668**
**Lightweight model:** . . . . . . . . **$1286**

AUTO-ORDNANCE THOMPSON 1927 A-1

AUTO-ORDNANCE THOMPSON 1927 A-1 COMMANDO

### THOMPSON 1927 A-1 COMMANDO
*Action*: Semi-automatic
*Stock*: Black finish stock & forend
*Barrel*: 16.5 in.
*Sights*: Blade front, open rear adjustable
*Weight*: 13 lb.
*Caliber*: .45 ACP
*Magazine*: 30-shot stick
*Features*: Frame and receiver made from solid steel; compensator; black nylon sling.
**MSRP . . . . . . . . . . . . . $1393**

AUTO-ORDNANCE THOMPSON 1927 A-1 SBR (SHORT BARREL RIFLE)

### THOMPSON 1927 A-1 SBR (SHORT BARREL RIFLE)
*Action*: Semi-automatic
*Stock*: Walnut, vertical foregrip
*Barrel*: 10.5 in.
*Sights*: Blade front, open rear adjustable
*Weight*: 12 lb.
*Caliber*: .45 ACP
*Magazine*: 30-shot stick
*Features*: Frame and receiver made from solid steel; blue steel finish.
**MSRP . . . . . . . . . . . . . . . $2053**
**W/ detachable butt stock: $2554**

AUTO-ORDNANCE THOMPSON M1

### THOMPSON M1
*Action*: Semi-automatic
*Stock*: Walnut, vertical foregrip
*Barrel*: 16.5 in.
*Sights*: Blade front, fixed battle rear
*Weight*: 8 lb. 11.5 lb.
*Caliber*: .45 ACP
*Magazine*: 30-shot stick

*Features*: Side bolt action; frame and receiver made from solid steel; lightweight model features a frame and receiver made from solid aluminum.
**MSRP . . . . . . . . . . . . . . . . . . . $1334**
**Lightweight Model: . . . . . . . . $1206**

# Auto-Ordnance Rifles

**AUTO-ORDNANCE THOMPSON M1 SBR**

## AOM150

*Action*: Semi-automatic
*Stock*: Walnut; handguard
*Barrel*: 18 in.
*Sights*: Blade front, flip-style rear
*Weight*: 5 lb. 6 oz.
*Caliber*: .30
*Magazine*: 15-shot stick
*Features*: Folding stock; Parkerized finish.
**MSRP** . . . . . . . . . . . . . . . . . . . **$1084**

**AUTO-ORDNANCE AOM160**

## THOMPSON M1 SBR

*Action*: Semi-automatic
*Stock*: Walnut, vertical foregrip
*Barrel*: 10.5 in.
*Sights*: Blade front, fixed battle rear
*Weight*: 10.5 lb.
*Caliber*: .45 ACP
*Magazine*: 30-shot stick
*Features*: Will not accept drum magazines, frame and receiver made from solid steel.
**MSRP** . . . . . . . . . . . . . . . . . . **$1970**

**AUTO-ORDNANCE AOM150**

## AOM160

*Action*: Semi-automatic
*Stock*: Polymer
*Barrel*: 18 in.
*Sights*: Post front sight; flip style rear
*Weight*: 5 lb. 13 oz.
*Caliber*: .30
*Magazine*: 15-shot stick
*Features*: Black polymer folding stock; metal perforated handguard; black oxide finish.
**MSRP** . . . . . . . . . . . . . . . . . . . **$860**

RIFLES

# Barrett

## 82A1

**Action**: Semi-automatic
**Stock**: Synthetic
**Barrel**: 29 in.
**Sights**: Flip-Up Iron Sights or Leupold Scope
**Weight**: 30.9 lb.
**Caliber**: .416 or .50 BMG
**Magazine**: Detachable box, 10-rounds

**Features**: Pelican case; detachable adjustable bipod legs; cleaning kit; carry handle; muzzle brake; M1913 optics rail; chrome-lined barrel.
**MSRP** . . . . . . . . . . . . **$8900–$11700**

## 95

**Action**: Semi-automatic
**Stock**: Synthetic

**Barrel**: 29 in.
**Sights**: Flip-Up Iron Sights
**Weight**: 25 lb.
**Caliber**: .50 BMG
**Magazine**: Detachable box, 5-rounds
**Features**: Pelican case; detachable adjustable bipod legs; cleaning kit; M1913 optics rail.
**MSRP** . . . . . . . . . . . . . . . . . **$6500**

BARRETT 82 A1

BARRETT 95

BARRETT 99

BARRETT 98B

## 99

**Action**: Bolt
**Stock**: Synthetic
**Barrel**: 32 in.
**Sights**: None
**Weight**: 25 lb.
**Caliber**: .416
**Magazine**: None
**Features**: M1913 optics rail; pelican

case; detachable adjustable bipod; cleaning kit.
**MSRP** . . . . . . . . . . . . . . . . . **$3999**

## 98B

**Action**: Bolt
**Stock**: Synthetic
**Barrel**: 27 in.
**Sights**: None

**Weight**: 13.5 lb.
**Caliber**: .338 Lapua Magnum
**Magazine**: Detachable box, 10-rounds
**Features**: Ergonomic pistol grip; muzzle brake; fluted barrel; Harris bi-pod; monopod; cleaning kit; side accessory rail; air/watertight hard case; black stock.
**MSRP** . . . . . . . . . . . . . . . . . **$4799**

# Benelli

**BENELLI R1**

## R1

**Action**: Semi-automatic
**Stock**: AA-Grade satin walnut, synthetic, or Realtree APG
**Barrel**: 22 in. or 24 in.
**Sights**: None
**Weight**: 7.1 lb.–7.3 lb.
**Caliber**: .30-06 Springfield, .300 Win. Mag.
**Magazine**: Detachable box, 3+1(.300 Win. Mag.) 4+1 (.30-.60 Springfield)
**Features**: Picatinny rail; synthetic and APG finish come with griptight coating; raised comb; auto-regulating gas-operated system.
**MSRP** . . . . . . . . . . . . . . **$999–$1219**

## R1 RIFLE COMFORTECH

**Action**: Semi-automatic
**Stock**: Synthetic or Realtree APG
**Barrel**: 24 in.
**Sights**: None
**Weight**: 7.3 lb.
**Caliber**: .03-.06, .300 Win. Mag., .338 Win. Mag.
**Magazine**: Detachable box, 3+1
**Features**: ComforTech recoil absorbing stock system; auto-regulationg gas-operated system; optional interchangable barrels; open sights available; Picatinny rail scope base.
**MSRP** . . . . . . . . . . . . . . **$1109–$1219**

## MR1

**Action**: A.R.G.O (Auto-Regulating-Gas-Operated)
**Stock**: Black Synthetic Tactical pistol grip (ComforTech Optional)
**Barrel**: 16 in.
**Sights**: Military-style aperture sights with Picatinny rail
**Weight**: 7.9 lb.
**Caliber**: .223 Rem.
**Magazine**: Detachable box, 5-shot
**Features**: Self-cleaning stainless piston system with gas port forward of chamber; accepts high-capacity M-16 magazines; hard chrome-lined barrel.
**MSRP** . . . . . . . . . . . . . . **$1299–$1429**

**BENELLI MR1**

# Beretta

**BERETTA RENEGADE SHORT RIFLE**

## 1873 RENEGADE SHORT RIFLE

**Action**: Lever
**Stock**: Walnut
**Barrel**: 20 in.
**Sights**: Gold bead front sight
**Weight**: 7 lb.
**Caliber**: .45 Colt or .357 Mag.
**Magazine**: Under-barrel tube, 10-rounds
**Features**: Straight butt plate; steel-framed ; octagonal barrel; walnut stock with checkered forend.
**MSRP** . . . . . . . . . . . . . . . . . . **$1350**

RIFLES

**BERETTA CX4 STORM**

## CX4 STORM

**Action**: Single-action
**Stock**: Synthetic
**Barrel**: 16.6 in.
**Sights**: Front sight post
**Weight**: 5.75 lb.

**Caliber**: 9mm, .40 S&W, .45 ACP
**Magazine**: Detachable box, 10, 15, 17, 20 (9mm); 10, 11, 12, 14, 17 (40 S&W); 8 (.45ACP)
**Features**: Picatinny rail; allows for reverse ejection and extraction; ideal for lefthanded shooters; adjustable length-of-pull; easy to accessorize.
**MSRP**. . . . . . . . . . . . . . . . . . . . **$915**

# Blaser Rifles

**BLASER TACTICAL 2**

## TACTICAL 2

**Action**: Bolt
**Stock**: Tactical synthetic
**Barrel**: 24.7 in., 25.6 in., 27 in.
**Sights**: None
**Weight**: 11.9 lb.–12.6 lb.

**Caliber**: .338 Lapua, .300 Win. Mag., .308 Win., .223 Rem
**Magazine**: Detachable box, 4- or 5-rounds
**Features**: Fully adjustable ergonomic black stock; interchangable barrel system; adjustable single-stage trigger; M1913 Picatinny receiver rail; bi-pod interface; user-replaceable cold hammer-forged match grade barrel; optional muzzle brake.
**MSRP**. . . . . . . . . . . . . . **$4171–$4612**

# Blaser Rifles

BLASER R8 PROFESSIONAL

BLASER R8 JAEGER

BLASER R93 PRESTIGE

## R8 PROFESSIONAL

**Action**: Straight-pull bolt-action
**Stock**: Matte dark green synthetic stock, pistol grip
**Barrel**: 20.5 in., 23 in., 25.75 in.
**Sights**: None
**Weight**: 6.4 lb.
**Caliber**: .222 Rem. to .338 Win. Mag.
**Magazine**: Detachable box, 3-rounds with lock
**Features**: Shatter-proof, synthetic dark green stock; detachable magazine/ trigger unit; single-stage trigger; quick-release scope mount; ergonomically optimized pistol grip; kickstop optional; precision trigger; black forearm tip; integrated receiver.
**MSRP** . . . . . . . . . . . . . . . . . . . **$3250**

## R8 JAEGER

**Action**: Straight-pull bolt-action
**Stock**: Walnut, pistol grip
**Barrel**: 20.5 in., 23 in., 25.75 in.
**Sights**: None
**Weight**: 6.4 lb.
**Caliber**: .222 Rem. to.338 Win. Mag.
**Magazine**: Detachable box, 3-rounds with lock
**Features**: Cold hammer forged barrels and chambers; black forearm tip; synthetic stock in dark green or walnut, straight comb; manual cocking system; integrated trigger/magazine unit; desmodromic trigger mechanism; original Blaser saddle mount.
**MSRP** . . . . . . . . . . . . . . . . . . . **$3761**

## R93 PRESTIGE

**Action**: Straight-pull bolt-action
**Stock**: Walnut or synthetic
**Barrel**: 20.46 in., 22.71 in., 22.71 in., 25.59 in.
**Sights**: None
**Weight**: 6.61 lb. to 6.83 lb.
**Caliber**: Choice of many popular chamberings
**Magazine**: Detachable box, 3-rounds except 4-rounds in .222 Rem., .223 Rem.; 2-rounds in caliber .300 Rem. Ultra Mag.
**Features**: Straight-pull bolt with expanding collar lockup.
**Prestige:** . . . . . . . . . . . . . . . . **$3737**
**Luxus:** . . . . . . . . . . . . . . . . . **$4594**
**Attache:** . . . . . . . . . . . . . . . . **$6360**
**Left-Hand Versions add $163**

# Blaser Rifles

BLASER R93 PROFESSIONAL

BLASER K95 BARONESSE STUTZEN

## R93 PROFESSIONAL

**Action**: Straight-pull bolt-action
**Stock**: Synthetic
**Barrel**: 25.50 in., (Magnum), 25.59 in. (Ultra Magnum); 27.56 in. (Swiss Kaliber)
**Sights**: None
**Weight**: 6.61 lb. to 6.83 lb.
**Caliber**: .222 Rem., .223 Rem., .22-250, .243 Win., 6 x 62 Freres, .25-06, 6.5 x 5.5, 6.5 x 57, 6.5-284 Norma, 6.5 x 65 RWS, .270 Win., .280 Rem., 7 x 57, 7mm-08, 7 x 64, .308 Win., .30-06, 8 x 57 IS, 8 x 64 S, 8.5 x 63, 9.3 x 62, 6.5 x 68, 7.5 x 55, 8 x 68 S, .257 Weath. Mag., .270 Weath. Mag., 7mm Rem. Mag., .300 Win. Mag., .300 Weath. Mag., .338 Win. Mag., .375 H & H Mag., 7mm STW, .300 Rem. Ultra Mag., 10.3 x 60 R

**Magazine**: In-line box, 3-rounds except: 4-rounds in .22 Rem., .223 Rem; 2-rounds in caliber .300 Rem. Ultra Mag.
**Features**: Anodized barrel; quick-release scope mount; shatter-proof stock comes in natural stone, slate grey, dark green, mossy oak camo; left-handed version optional.
**MSRP** . . . . . . . . . . . . . . . . . . $3039

## K95 BARONESSE STUTZEN

**Action**: Single shot
**Stock**: Walnut
**Barrel**: 19.75 in.
**Sights**: None
**Weight**: 5.7 lb.
**Caliber**: .222 Rem., 5.6 x 50R Mag., 5.6 x 50R, .243 Win., 6.5 x 57R, 7 x 57 R, .308 Win., .30-06, 8 x 57 IRS
**Magazine**: None

**Features**: Octagonal barrel standard, barrels are interchangable; available from grade lexus; split forearm for continuous precision even in extreme weather; black forearm tip.
**MSRP** . . . . . . . . . . . . . . . . . $15335

## S2 DOUBLE RIFLE SAFARI

**Action**: Tilting block, double-barrel
**Stock**: Grained walnut
**Barrel**: 24.4 in.
**Sights**: None
**Weight**: 11 lb. 11 oz.
**Caliber**: .375 H & H Mag., .470 NE, .500/ .416 NE, .500 NE
**Magazine**: None
**Features**: Straight safari stock with Monte Carlo cheek-piece; kickstop; rubber recoil pad; half-beavertail fore-end.
**MSRP** . . . . . . . . . . . . . . . . . $10032

# BPI (CVA)

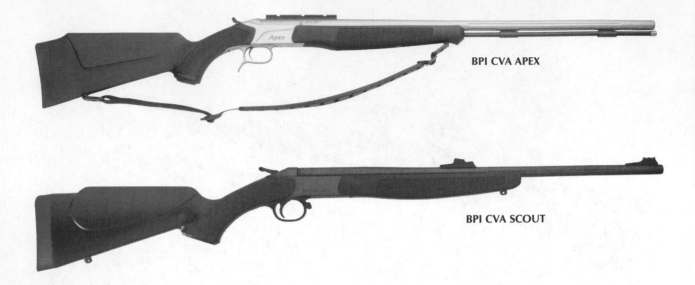

**BPI CVA APEX**

**BPI CVA SCOUT**

## BPI CVA APEX

*Action*: Break-action muzzleloader or center-fire
*Stock*: Ambidextrous synthetic
*Barrel*: 27 in. (muzzleloader), 25 in. (center-fire)
*Sights*: None
*Weight*: 8 lb. (muzzleloader), 7.5 lb. (center-fire)
*Caliber*: 14 different muzzleloading, center-fire, and rimfire calibers: (muzzleloader): .45, .50; (center-fire): .45-70, 7mm-08, .308, .30-06, .300 Win. Mag., .35 Whelen, .270, .243, .223, .222, .22-250; 12 Ga. rifled slug

and 12 Ga. turkey
*Magazine*: None
*Features*: Synthetic stock with rubber grip panels comes in black or Realtree APG camo; stainless steel, fluted Bergara barrel; adjustable trigger; interchangable barrels; CrushZone recoil pad; DuraSight rail mount; QRBP- (quick release breech plug); reversible hammer spur; quake claw sling.
**Muzzleloading Models**
MSRP . . . . . . . . . . . **$619.95–699.95**
**Center-Fire Models**
MSRP . . . . . . . . . . **$659.95–$739.95**

## BPI CVA SCOUT

*Action*: Center-fire, single shot
*Stock*: Ambidextrous synthetic
*Barrel*: 20 in. (compact), 22 in. (standard fluted barrels)
*Sights*: None
*Weight*: 5.8 lb.
*Caliber*: .243, 7mm-08, .270, .30-06, .35 Whelen, .44 Magnum, 12 Ga Slug
*Magazine*: None
*Features*: Stainless steel or blued barrel; black synthetic stock; DuraSight Dead-On Integral scope rail; CrushZone recoil pad; reversible hammer spur; alternate length stocks available.
MSRP . . . . . . . . . . **$329.95–$369.95**

# Brown Precision

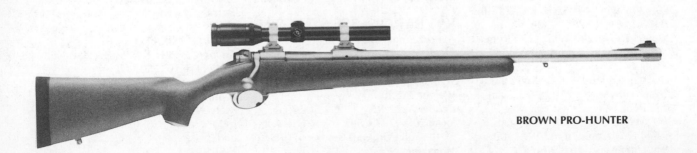

**BROWN PRO-HUNTER**

# Brown Precision

BROWN CUSTOM HIGH COUNTRY

## CUSTOM HIGH COUNTRY

*Action*: Bolt
*Stock*: Composite stock
*Barrel*: Length and contour to order
*Sights*: None
*Weight*: 6.0 lb.
*Caliber*: Any popular standard caliber
*Magazine*: Internal box, 5-rounds
*Features*: Available in custom Remington 700 or Winchester model 70 action; 1.5 in. recoil pad; match grade stainless steel barrel with custom crown; choice of electroless nickel or Teflon finish to all metalwork; choice of stock finish: green, black, grey, brown, or rhino hide finish; choice of scope mounts and scopes.
**Customer Supplied Action: . . $3995**
**MSRP . . . . . . . . . . . . . . . . . $4995**

## LIGHT VARMINTER

*Action*: Bolt
*Stock*: Composite; vertical pistol grip
*Barrel*: Length and contour to order
*Sights*: None
*Weight*: Weight varies on custom options
*Caliber*: Any popular caliber
*Magazine*: Box or single shot
*Features*: Custom Remington 700 or 40x action, available in left or right hand; Shilen match-grade heavy benchrest stainless steel barrel with

custom crown; fiberglass, Kevlar or graphite stock in black, grey, brown or green.
**Customer Supplied Action: . . $3195**
**MSRP . . . . . . . . . . . . . . . . . $4195**

## PRO-HUNTER

*Action*: Bolt
*Stock*: Composite sporter
*Barrel*: Length and contour to order
*Sights*: Front sight banded front ramp with European dovetail and replaceable brass bead; rear sight choice of express sight or custom Dave Talley removeable peep sight
*Weight*: 7 lb.–15 lb.
*Caliber*: Any popular standard caliber, magnum caliber up to .375 H&H
*Magazine*: Internal box, 5-rounds
*Features*: Winchester Model 70 super grade action with controlled feed claw extractor; Shilen select grade stainless steel barrel with custom crown; speed-lock firing pin spring; premium 1 in. recoil-reducing butt pad; custom detached T.N.T scope mount rings and bases.
**Customer Supplied Action: . . $4195**
**MSRP . . . . . . . . . . . . . . . . . $5195**

## PRO-VARMINTER

*Action*: Bolt
*Stock*: Composite; vertical pistol grip

*Barrel*: Length and contour to order
*Sights*: None
*Weight*: Weight varies on custom options
*Caliber*: Any popular caliber
*Magazine*: Box or single shot
*Features*: Custom Remington 700 or 40X action, available in left or right hand; Shilen match grade heavy benchrest stainless steel barrel with custom crown; fiberglass, Kevlar or graphite stock in black, grey, brown or green.
**Customer Supplied Action: . . $3195**
**MSRP . . . . . . . . . . . . . . . . . $4195**

## TACTIAL ELITE

*Action*: Bolt
*Stock*: Composite
*Barrel*: Length and contour to order
*Sights*: None
*Weight*: 9.0 lb.
*Caliber*: .223, .308, .300 Win. Mag., others on special order
*Magazine*: Box, 3- or 5-rounds
*Features*: Fiberglass/Kevlar/Graphite composite target-style stock; custom Remington 700 or 40x action; stainless steel barrel; Teflon metal finish; tuned trigger; optional muzzle brakes, scopes.
**Customer Supplied Action: . . $3995**
**MSRP . . . . . . . . . . . . . . . . . $4995**

# Browning Rifles

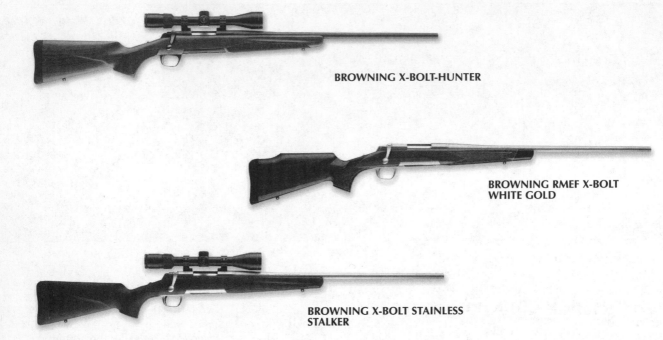

**BROWNING X-BOLT-HUNTER**

**BROWNING RMEF X-BOLT WHITE GOLD**

**BROWNING X-BOLT STAINLESS STALKER**

**BROWNING A-BOLT HUNTER**

## X-BOLT HUNTER

*Action*: Bolt
*Stock*: Satin finish walnut stock
*Barrel*: 22 in., 23 in., 24 in., 26 in.
*Sights*: None
*Weight*: 6.8 lb.–7 lb.
*Caliber*: .243 Win., 7mm-08 Rem., .308 Win., .25-06 Rem., .270 Win., .280 Rem., .30-06 Spfld., 7 Rem. Mag., .388 Win. Mag., .300 WSM, .270 WSM, 7mm WSM, .325 WSM, .223 Rem., .22-250 Rem.
*Magazine*: Detachable rotary box
*Features*: Adjustable feather trigger; top-tang safety with bolt unlock button; sling swivel studs installed; inflex technology recoil pad.
**MSRP**. . . . . . . . . . . . . . .**$840–$880**

## RMEF X-BOLT WHITE GOLD

*Action*: Bolt
*Stock*: Walnut
*Barrel*: 23 in.
*Sights*: None

*Weight*: 7 lb. 3 oz.
*Caliber*: .325 WSM
*Magazine*: Detachable rotary box
*Features*: Monte carlo stock; stainless steel barrel and receiver, receiver etched in gold; raised cheekpiece; inflex technology recoil pad; adjustable feather trigger; top-tang safety with bolt unlock button.
**MSRP**. . . . . . . . . . . . . . . . . **$1440**

## X-BOLT STAINLESS STALKER

*Action*: Bolt
*Stock*: Composite
*Barrel*: 22 in., 23 in., 24 in., 26 in.
*Sights*: None
*Weight*: 6 lb. 3 oz.–6 lb. 13 oz.
*Caliber*: .243 Win., 7mm-08 Rem., .308 Win., .25-06 Rem., .270 Win., .280 Rem., .30-06 Spfld., 7mm Rem. Mag., .300 Win. Mag., .388 Win. Mag., .300 WSM, .270 WSM, 7mm WSM, .325 WSM, .223 Rem., .22-250 Rem.

*Magazine*: Detachable rotary box
*Features*: Composite stock in matte black with textured gripping surfaces; Dura-Touch armor coating; adjustable feather trigger; top-tang safety; bolt unlock button; palm swell.
**MSRP**. . . . . . . . . . . . . . **$1070–$1100**

## A-BOLT HUNTER

*Action*: Bolt
*Stock*: Satin finish walnut
*Barrel*: 26 in.
*Sights*: None
*Weight*: 7 lb. 3 oz.
*Caliber*: 300 Win. Mag.
*Magazine*: Detachable box
*Features*: Steel, low luster blued receiver; adjustable trigger; hinged floorplate; top-tang safety; recoil pad; sling swivel.
**MSRP**. . . . . . . . . . . . . . . . . . . . . **$719**

RIFLES

# Browning Rifles

**BROWNING A-BOLT M-1000 ECLIPSE**

**BROWNING BAR LONGTRAC STALKER**

**BROWNING BAR SAFARI**

## A-BOLT M-1000 ECLIPSE

*Action*: Bolt
*Stock*: Grey laminated
*Barrel*: 26 in.
*Sights*: None
*Weight*: 9 lb. 14 oz.–10 lb.
*Caliber*: .22-250 Rem., 7mm-08
Rem., .308 Win., .300 WSM, .270
WSM, 7mm WSM
*Magazine*: Detachable box
*Features*: Steel, matte blued finish
receiver; drilled and tapped for scope
mounts; hinged floorpate; top-tang
safety; thumbhole grip; Monte Carlo
cheekpiece.
**MSRP . . . . . . . . . . . . . $1270–$1390**

## BAR LONGTRAC STALKER

*Action*: Gas-operated autoloader
*Stock*: Composite
*Barrel*: 22 in., 24 in.
*Sights*: None
*Weight*: 6 lb. 15 oz.–7 lb. 8 oz.
*Caliber*: .270 Win., .30-06 Spfld.,
7mm Rem. Mag., .300 Win. Mag.
*Magazine*: Detachable box
*Features*: Aircraft-grade alloy receiver
with matte blued finish; drilled and
tapped for scope mounts; hammer-
forged; multi-lug rotary bolt; compos-
ite stock in matte black finish; gripping
panels; recoil pad; composite trigger
guard and floorplate.
**MSRP . . . . . . . . . . . . . $1260–$1160**

## BAR SAFARI

*Action*: Gas-operated autoloader
*Stock*: Walnut
*Barrel*: 22 in., 23 in., 24 in.
*Sights*: None
*Weight*: 7 lb. 6 oz.–8 lb. 6 oz.
*Caliber*: .243 Win., .308 Win., .25-06
Rem., .270 Win., .30-06 Spfld., 7mm
Rem. Mag., .300 Win. Mag., .338
Win. Mag., .270 Win. (BOSS), 7mm
Rem. Mag(BOSS), .300 Win. Mag.
(BOSS), .338 Win. Mag. (BOSS), .300
WSM (BOSS), .270 WSM (BOSS),
7mm WSM (BOSS)
*Magazine*: Detachable box
*Features*: Checkered, select gloss finish
walnut stock; steel receiver with blued
finish and scroll engraving; drilled and
tapped for scope mounts; multi-lug
rotary bolt; recoil pad BOSS and
BOSS-CR option; sling swivel studs
installed.
**MSRP . . . . . . . . . . . . . $1150–$1400**

**BROWNING A-BOLT STAINLESS STALKER**

**BROWNING BAR SHORT TRAC**

## A-BOLT STAINLESS STALKER

*Action*: Bolt
*Stock*: Composite
*Barrel*: 22 in., 23 in., 24 in., 26 in.
*Sights*: None
*Weight*: 6 lb. 4 oz.–6 lb. 11 oz.
*Caliber*: .243 Win., 7mm-08 Rem.,
.308 Win., .270 Win., .30-06 Spfld.,
7mm Rem. Mag., .388 Win. Mag.,
.300 WSM, .270 WSM, 7mm WSM,
.325 WSM
*Magazine*: Detachable box
*Features*: Composite stock comes in
matte black, checkered; stainless steel,
matte finish receiver; drilled and
tapped for scope mounts; adjustable
stainless steel trigger; hinged floorplate; top-tang safety; recoil pad;
BOSS and BOSS-CR option.
**MSRP . . . . . . . . . . . . . $799–$1200**

## BAR SHORT TRAC

*Action*: Bolt
*Stock*: Walnut
*Barrel*: 23 in.
*Sights*: None
*Weight*: 7 lb. 4 oz.
*Caliber*: .300 WSM
*Magazine*: Detachable box
*Features*: Satin finish walnut stock with
stylized forearm; aircraft-grade alloy
receiver with blued finish; drilled and
tapped for scope mounts;
interchangable recoil pad.
**MSRP . . . . . . . . . . . . . . . $ 1179**

## BAR LONGTRAC BREAK-UP INFINITY

*Action*: Gas-operated autoloader
*Stock*: Composite
*Barrel*: 22 in., 24 in.
*Sights*: None
*Weight*: 6 lb. 15 oz.–7 lb. 8 oz.
*Caliber*: .270 Win., .30-06 Spfld.,
7mm Rem. Mag., .300 Win. Mag.
*Magazine*: Detachable box
*Features*: Aircraft-grade alloy receiver;
drilled and tapped for scope mounts;
hammer-forged barrel; multi-lug rotary
bolt; composite trigger guard and
floorplate; crossbolt safety; Dura-
Touch Armor coating; composite stock
comes in Mossy Oak camo finishes;
interchangable recoil pad.
**MSRP . . . . . . . . . . . . . $1280–$1390**

**BROWNING BAR LONGTRAC
BREAK-UP INFINITY**

# Browning Rifles

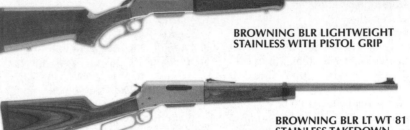

**BROWNING BAR ZENITH BIG GAME**

**BROWNING BAR SHORTTRAC, LEFT HAND**

## BAR ZENITH BIG GAME

*Action*: Gas-operated autoloader
*Stock*: Walnut
*Barrel*: 22 in.
*Sights*: None
*Weight*: 7 lb. 1 oz.
*Caliber*: 7mm WSM
*Magazine*: Detachable box
*Features*: Aircraft-grade alloy receiver with black matte finish; nickel plated sides with European hunting scenes; gloss oil finish, grade 3.0 walnut stock; interchangable recoil pads.
**MSRP . . . . . . . . . . . . . . . . . . $1469**

**BROWNING BLR LIGHTWEIGHT STAINLESS WITH PISTOL GRIP**

**BROWNING BLR LT WT 81 STAINLESS TAKEDOWN**

**BROWNING BAR LIGHTWEIGHT STALKER**

## BAR LIGHTWEIGHT STALKER

*Action*: Gas-operated autoloader
*Stock*: Gas-operated autoloader
*Barrel*: 20 in., 22 in., 23 in., 24 in.
*Sights*: None
*Weight*: 7 lb. 2 oz.–7 lb. 12 oz.
*Caliber*: .243 Win., .308 Win., .270 Win., .30-06 Spfld., .300 WSM, .270 WSM, 7mm WSM., .300 Win. Mag., .338 Win. Mag.
*Magazine*: Detachable box
*Features*: Composite stock in matte black; aircraft-grade alloy receiver in matte blue finish; drilled and tapped for scope mounts; recoil pad; crossbolt safety.
**MSRP . . . . . . . . . . . . . $1140–$1240**

## BAR SHORTTRAC, LEFT HAND

*Action*: Gas-operated autoloader
*Stock*: Walnut
*Barrel*: 22 in., 23 in.
*Sights*: None
*Weight*: 6 lb. 10 oz.–7 lb. 4 oz.
*Caliber*: .243 Win., 7mm-08 Rem., .308 Win., .300 WSM, .270 WSM, 7mm WSM, .325 WSM
*Magazine*: Detachable box
*Features*: Aircaft-grade alloy receiver;

drilled and tapped for scope mounts; hammer-forged barrel; grade II walnut stock with oil finish; stylized, checkered, forearm; sling swivel studs installed; interchangable recoil pad.
**MSRP . . . . . . . . . . . . . . $1190–$1280**

## BLR LIGHTWEIGHT STAINLESS

*Action*: Lever-action
*Stock*: Walnut, pistol grip
*Barrel*: 20 in., 22 in., 24 in.
*Sights*: None
*Weight*: 6 lb. 8 oz.–7 lb. 12 oz.
*Caliber*: .223 Rem., .22-250 Rem., .243 Win., 7mm-08 Rem., .308 Win., .358 Win., .270 Win., .30-06 Spfld., .300 Win. Mag., .300 WSM, .270 WSM, 7mm WSM, .450 Marlin, .325 WSM
*Magazine*: Detachable box
*Features*: Aircraft-grade alloy receiver; drilled and tapped for scope mounts; steel barrel with matte finish; crowned muzzle; adjustable sights; gloss finish walnut stock; sling swivel studs installed; recoil pad.
**MSRP . . . . . . . . . . . . . . $1020–$1100**

**BROWNING BLR LIGHTWEIGHT '81**

## BLR LIGHTWEIGHT '81

*Action*: Lever-action
*Stock*: Walnut, straight grip

*Barrel*: 20 in., 22 in., 24 in.
*Sights*: None
*Weight*: 6 lb. 8 oz.–7 lb. 12 oz.
*Caliber*: .223 Rem., .22-250 Rem., .243 Win., 7mm-08 Rem., .308 Win., .358 Win., .270 Win., .30-06 Spfld., 7mm Rem. Mag., .300 Win. Mag., .300 WSM, .270 WSM, 7mm WSM, .450 Marlin, .325 WSM
*Magazine*: Detachable box
*Features*: Aircaft-grade alloy receiver; drilled and tapped for scope mounts; crowned muzzle; adjustable sights; gloss finish walnut stock; recoil pad.
**MSRP . . . . . . . . . . . . . . . $900–$980**

## BLT LT WT '81 STAINLESS TAKEDOWN

*Action*: Lever-action
*Stock*: Laminate, straight grip
*Barrel*: 20 in., 22 in., 24 in.
*Sights*: Open
*Weight*: 6 lb. 8 oz.–7 lb. 12 oz.
*Caliber*: .223 Rem., .22-250 Rem., .243 Win., 7mm-08 Rem., .308 Win., .358 Win., .270 Win., .30-06 Spfld., 7mm Rem. Mag., .300 Win. Mag., .300 WSM, .270 WSM, 7mm WSM, .450 Marlin, .325 WSM
*Magazine*: Detachable box
*Features*: Aircaft-grade alloy receiver; drilled and tapped for scope mounts; stainless steel barrel with matte finish; gray laminate wood stock in satin finish; recoil pad; separates for storage or transporation; optional Scout-style scope mount; Truglo/Marble's fiber optic front sight.
**MSRP . . . . . . . . . . . . . . $1160–$1240**

# Bushmaster Rifles

**BUSHMASTER PREDATOR**

**BUSHMASTER VARMINTER**

## PREDATOR

*Action*: Semi-automatic
*Stock*: Synthetic, ambidextrious pistol grip
*Barrel*: 20 in.
*Sights*: None
*Weight*: 8.0 lb.
*Caliber*: 5.56mm, .223 Rem.
*Magazine*: Detachable box, 5-rounds (accepts all M16/ AR 15 type)
*Features*: Steel lined fluted barrel; two-stage competition trigger; vented tubular aluminum free-floater forend with bipod stud; shipped with safety block in lockable, foam-padded hard case.
**MSRP . . . . . . . . . . . . . . . . . . $1359**

## VARMINTER

*Action*: Semi-automatic
*Stock*: Synthetic, ambidextrious pistol grip
*Barrel*: 24 in.
*Sights*: None
*Weight*: 8.4 lb.
*Caliber*: 5.56mm, .223 Rem.
*Magazine*: Detachable box, 5-rounds (accepts all M16/ AR 15 type)
*Features*: Competition crowned muzzle; chromemoly vandium steel barrel with full length fluting; two-stage competition trigger; 12 cooling vents in forend; bipod stud installed on forend; black stock with rubberized, non-slip surface; shipped in hard plastic, lockable storage case complete with orange safety bock.
**MSRP . . . . . . . . . . . . . . . . . . $1374**

## STAINLESS VARMINT SPECIAL

*Action*: Semi-automatic
*Stock*: Synthetic, ambidextrious pistol grip
*Barrel*: 24 in.
*Sights*: None
*Weight*: 8.84 lb.
*Caliber*: 5.56mm, .223 Rem.
*Magazine*: Detachable box, 5-rounds (accepts all M16/ AR 15 type)
*Features*: 416 Stainless steel barrel; two-stage competition trigger; vented aluminum, tubular forend that free-floats the barrel; forend bipod stud; mini-risers mounted on the upper receiver to raise scopes; comfortable cheekweld on black stock; ships in Hard plastic, lockable storage case with orange safety block.
**MSRP . . . . . . . . . . . . . . . . . . $1374**

**RIFLES**

**BUSHMASTER STAINLESS VARMINT SPECIAL**

# Bushmaster Rifles

**BUSHMASTER .450 RIFLE**

**BUSHMASTER M4 TYPE CARBINES A3 STYLE**

**BUSHMASTER O.R.C. RIFLE**

### BUSHMASTER .450 RIFLE & CARBINE

*Action*: Semi-automatic
*Stock*: Synthetic, A2 pistol grip
*Barrel*: 16 in. (carbine), 20 in. (rifle)
*Sights*: None
*Weight*: 8.1 lb. (carbine), 8.5 lb. (rifle)
*Caliber*: .450 Bushmaster
*Magazine*: Detachable box, 5-rounds
*Features*: ChroMoly steel barrels; free floating aluminum forends; forged aluminum receivers; solid A2 buttstock with trapdoor storage compartment; Pictatinny rail; black web sling included; shipped in lockable hard plastic case with orange safety block.
Rifle MSRP. . . . . . . . . . . . . . . $1441
Carbine MSRP . . . . . . . . . . . $1426

### M4 TYPE CARBINES

*Action*: Semi-automatic
*Stock*: Synthetic
*Barrel*: 16 in.
*Sights*: Open

*Weight*: 6.22 lb.
*Caliber*: 5.56mm, .223 Rem.
*Magazine*: Detachable box, 30-rounds (accepts all M16/ AR15 type)
*Features*: Six position telestock; "Izzy" flash suppresor; hard chrome lined barrels are designed to acccept M203 grenade launcher; upper receivers available in A2 or A3 configurations; A2 Receiver has 300-800 meter rear sight system; A3 Receiver is mounted with Pictatinny rail, 300-600 Meter rear sight system and removeable carry handle; shipped in lockable hard case with orange safety block.
A2 MSRP . . . . . . . . . . . . . . . $1150
A3 MSRP . . . . . . . . . . . . . . . $1224

### O.R.C (OPTICS READY CARBINE)

*Action*: Semi-automatic
*Stock*: Synthetic
*Barrel*: 16 in.
*Sights*: None
*Weight*: 6 lb.
*Caliber*: 5.56mm, .223 Rem.
*Magazine*: Detachable box, 30-rounds (accepts any AR type mag)
*Features*: Flat-top upper receiver made for easy optic attachment; chrome lined barrel; A2 Bird cage supressor; receiver length Picatinny optics rail with 0.5" optics risers; milled gas block; heavy oval M4 type hand-guards; shipped in a lockable hard case with orange safety block.
MSRP. . . . . . . . . . . . . . . . . . $1068

### CARBON 15 9MM CARBINE

*Action*: Semi-automatic
*Stock*: Composite
*Barrel*: 16 in.
*Sights*: None
*Weight*: 5.7 lb.
*Caliber*: 9mm NATO
*Magazine*: Detachable box, 30-rounds
*Features*: Carbon fiber composite receivers; birdcage flash hider; chrome moly steel barrel; manganese phospate bolt carrier; Picatinny rail mounted on upper receiver; 6 position telescoping buttstock; shipped in lockable bushmaster carrying case.
MSRP. . . . . . . . . . . . . . . . . . $905

# Bushmaster Rifles

**BUSHMASTER BA50 CARBINE**

**BUSHMASTER BA50**

**BUSHMASTER DCM-XR SERIES COMPETITION RIFLE**

## BA50 CARBINES

*Action*: Bolt
*Stock*: Synthetic
*Barrel*: 22 in.
*Sights*: None
*Weight*: 27 lb.
*Caliber*: .50 BMG
*Magazine*: Detachable box, 10-rounds
*Features*: MIL-STD-1913 rail; steel bipod with folding legs; ErgoGrip deluxe tactical pistol grip; LimbSaver ButtPad; Magpaul PRS adjustable butstock; aluminum receiver; recoil reducing brake.
**MSRP . . . . . . . . . . . . . . . . . . $5262**

## BA50 RIFLES

*Action*: Bolt
*Stock*: Synthetic
*Barrel*: 30 in.
*Sights*: None
*Weight*: 30 lb.
*Caliber*: .50 BMG
*Magazine*: Detachable box, 10-rounds
*Features*: MIL-STD-1913 rail; steel bipod with folding legs; ErgoGrip deluxe tactical pistol GRIP; limbsaver ButtPad; Magpaul PRS adjustable butstock; aluminum receiver; recoil reducing brake.
**MSRP . . . . . . . . . . . . . . . . . . $5299**

## DCM-XR SERIES COMPETITION RIFLES

*Action*: Semi-automatic
*Stock*: Synthetic
*Barrel*: 20 in.
*Sights*: Open, adjustable
*Weight*: 13.06 lb.
*Caliber*: 5.56mm, .223 Rem.
*Magazine*: Detachable box, 10-rounds (accepts all M16/ AR15 type)
*Features*: M16A2 dual aperture rear sight with interchanable apertures; competition front sight; extra heavy competition barrel; barrel is lead lapped and hardened to Rockwell C26 to 32; two stage competition trigger; competition "free floater" tube handguard; shipped in lockable hard case.
**A2 MSRP . . . . . . . . . . . . . . . $1306**
**A3 MSRP . . . . . . . . . . . . . . . $1381**

# Bushmaster Rifles

**BUSHMASTER TARGET MODEL RIFLE**

**BUSHMASTER MOE GAS PISTON CARBINE**

## TARGET MODEL RIFLES

**Action**: Semi-automatic
**Stock**: Synthetic
**Barrel**: 20 in.
**Sights**: None
**Weight**: 8.43 lb. (A2), 8.78 lb. (A3)
**Caliber**: 5.56mm, .223 Rem.
**Magazine**: Detachable box, 30-rounds (accepts all M16 / AR15 type)
**Features**: A3 Upper receiver incorporates Pictatinny rail; A2 upper receiver 300-800 meter rear sight system; A3 receiver has 300–600 meter rear sight system; chromemoly steel or polished stainless steel barrels available in 20 in. or 24 in; shipped in a lockable hard case with orange safety block.

A2 MSRP . . . . . . . . . . . . . . . $1105
A3 MSRP . . . . . . . . . . . . . . . $1187
SSA2 MSRP . . . . . . . . . . . . . $1112
SSA3 MSRP . . . . . . . . . . . . . $1187

## V MATCH RIFLE & CARBINE

**Action**: Semi-automatic
**Stock**: Synthetic
**Barrel**: 16 in. (carbine), 20 in. or 24 in. (rifle)
**Sights**: None
**Weight**: 6.8 lb.(carbine), 8.83 lb. or 7.99 lb. (rifle)
**Caliber**: 5.56mm , .223 Rem.
**Magazine**: Detachable box, 30-rounds (accepts all M16 / AR15 type)
**Features**: Heavy profile, match grade, chrome-lined barrels; tubular aluminum V-match knurled handguard; upper and lower receivers forged from aircraft aluminum; Picatinny rail; shipped in hard plastic, lockable storage case.

16" MSRP . . . . . . . . . . . . . . . $1150
20" MSRP . . . . . . . . . . . . . . . $1165
24" MSRP . . . . . . . . . . . . . . . $1180

## MOE GAS PISTON CARBINE

**Action**: Semi-automatic, pistol grip
**Stock**: Synthetic
**Barrel**: 16 in.
**Sights**: Magpul MSBUS rear flip sight
**Weight**: 6.2 lb.
**Caliber**: 5.56mm, .223 Rem.
**Magazine**: Detachable box, 30-rounds
**Features**: M4 profile barrel with gas piston system; receiver-length Picatinny optics rail; Magpul MBUS rear flip sight; Magpul MOE adjustable buttstock with strong A-frame design; rubber buttplate; Magpul MOE vertical grip; stock available in black, flat dark earth, or OD green furniture.

MSRP . . . . . . . . . . . . . . . . . . . $1396

## CARBON 15 R97F

**Action**: Semi-automatic
**Stock**: Synthetic
**Barrel**: 16 in.
**Sights**: None
**Weight**: 4.3 lb.
**Caliber**: 5.56mm, .223 Rem.
**Magazine**: Detachable box, 30-rounds (accepts all M16 / AR15 type)
**Features**: A2 birdcage supressor; chrome plated bolt carrier; Picatinny optics mounting rail; dual aperture rear; blade front sight; forend sling stud installed.

MSRP . . . . . . . . . . . . . . . . . . . $925

RIFLES

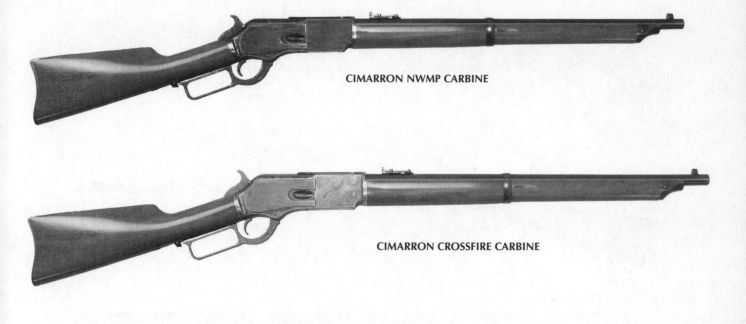

CIMARRON NWMP CARBINE

CIMARRON CROSSFIRE CARBINE

CIMARRON EVIL ROY BRUSH POPPER

## N.W.M.P.(NORTH WEST MOUNTED POLICE) CARBINE

*Action*: Lever
*Stock*: Walnut
*Barrel*: 22 in.
*Sights*: None
*Weight*: 8.95 lb.
*Caliber*: 45-60, 45-75
*Magazine*: Under-barrel tube, 8-rounds
*Features*: Available in walnut stock and all blued metal; reproduction of popular firearm used by mounted police in 1870s.
**MSRP** . . . . . . . . . . . . . . . . . $1780

## CROSSFIRE CARBINE

*Action*: Lever
*Stock*: Walnut
*Barrel*: 22 in.
*Sights*: None
*Weight*: 8.95 lb.
*Caliber*: 45-60, 45-75
*Magazine*: Under-barrel tube, 8-rounds
*Features*: Gun was glorified in the movie "*Crossfire Trail*; case hardened stock with standard blue finish.
**MSRP** . . . . . . . . . . . . . . . . . $1780

## "EVIL ROY" BRUSH POPPER

*Action*: Lever
*Stock*: Walnut
*Barrel*: 18.5 in.
*Sights*: Open
*Weight*: 7.10 lb.–7.30 lb.
*Caliber*: .45 Colt, .44 W.C.F, .357/.38 SP.
*Magazine*: Under-barrel tube, 10-rounds
*Features*: Custom marble sights; Evil Roy signature barrel; leather butt sheath; short stroke kit; walnut straight stock with standard blue finish on metal; case hardened frame.
**MSRP** . . . . . . . . . . . . . . . $1929.35

# Cimarron Rifles

**CIMARRON 1860 CIVILIAN MODEL HENRY**

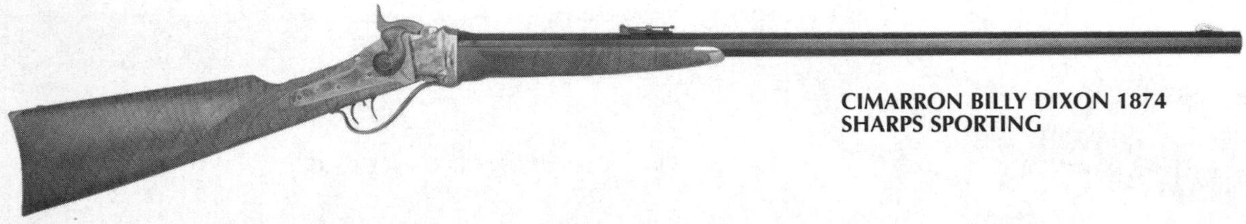

**CIMARRON BILLY DIXON 1874 SHARPS SPORTING**

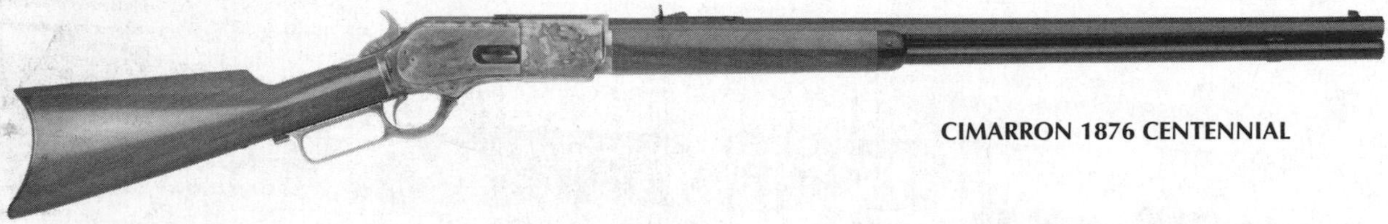

**CIMARRON 1876 CENTENNIAL**

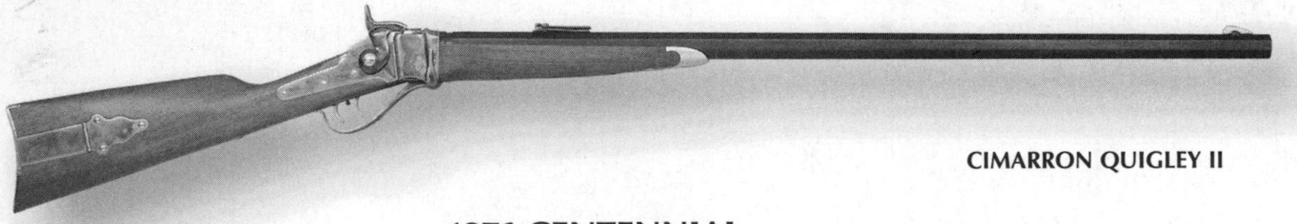

**CIMARRON QUIGLEY II**

## 1860 HENRY CIVILIAN

*Action*: Lever
*Stock*: Walnut
*Barrel*: 24 in.
*Sights*: Open
*Weight*: 9.05 lb., 9.15 lb.
*Caliber*: .45 LC, .44 WCF
*Magazine*: Under-barrel tube, 12-rounds
*Features*: Reproduction of 1860 Civil War Henry rifle; includes military sling swivels; frame comes in charcoal blue or original finish.
**MSRP . . . . . . . . . . . . . . $1483.77
+$78.00 (Charcoal blue finish)
+$84.50 (Original finish)**

## 1876 CENTENNIAL

*Action*: Lever
*Stock*: Walnut
*Barrel*: 28 in.
*Sights*: Open
*Weight*: 9.95 lb.–10.15 lb.
*Caliber*: 45-60, 45-75, 40-60, 50-95
*Magazine*: Under-barrel tube, 10-rounds
*Features*: Reproduction of 1860 Civil War Henry rifle; includes military sling swivels; frame comes in charcoal blue or original finish.
**MSRP . . . . . . .$1681.71–$1745.18**

## BILLY DIXON

*Action*: Dropping block
*Stock*: Walnut, straight grip
*Barrel*: 32 in.
*Sights*: Open
*Weight*: 10.25 lb.–10.65 lb.

38-55
*Magazine*: None
*Features*: Single-shot reproduction; patent markings as on original sharps.
**MSRP . . . . . . . . . . . . . $1370.60**

## QUIGLEY II

*Action*: Dropping block
*Stock*: Walnut, straight grip
*Barrel*: 34 in.
*Sights*: Open
*Weight*: 12.23 lb.–12.55
*Caliber*: .45-70, .45-90, .45-120, .50-90, .45-110
*Magazine*: None
*Features*: Single-shot reproduction; octagonal barrel; pewter nose caps as on original sharps.
**MSRP . . . . . . . . . . . . . $1524.60**

RIFLES

**CIMARRON 1885 HIGH WALL**

## 1885 HIGH WALL
*Action*: Dropping block
*Stock*: Walnut, pistol grip
*Barrel*: 30 in.
*Sights*: Open

*Weight*: 9.27 lb.–10.35 lb.
*Caliber*: .45-70, .40-65, .38-55, .45-90, .30-40 KRAG, .405 Win.
*Magazine*: None
*Features*: Reproduction of the

Winchester single-shot hunting rifle popular in 1880s; standard blue finish on octagonal barrel; single or double set triggers.
**MSRP . . . . . . . . . $112.46–$1320.40**

# Colt Rifles

**COLT MATCH TARGET RIFLE**

**COLT ACCURIZED RIFLE**

## MATCH TARGET RIFLE
*Action*: Semi-automatic
*Stock*: Combat-style, synthetic
*Barrel*: 16.1 in., 20 in.
*Sights*: None
*Weight*: 7.3 lb.–9.25 lb.
*Caliber*: 5.56 NATO x .223
*Magazine*: Detachable box, 9-rounds
*Features*: Flat top with optional carry handle and scope mount; two position-safety; available with free floating monotlithic handguard; available with flip up sights; available with match trigger; black stock with matte finish.
**MSRP . . . . . . . $1173–$1615**

## ACCURIZED RIFLE
*Action*: Semi-automatic
*Stock*: Combat-style, synthetic
*Barrel*: 24 in.
*Sights*: None
*Weight*: 9.0 lb.–9.25 lb.
*Caliber*: 5.56 NATO x .223
*Magazine*: Detachable box, 9-rounds
*Features*: Black stock with matte finish; heavy barrel; target crown muzzle; A2 rifle buttstock; free floating tubular handguard; match trigger.
**MSRP . . . . . . . . . . . . . . . . . . $1374**

# Cooper Firearms

**COOPER LVT**

## LVT (LIGHT VARMINT/ TARGET)

*Action*: Bolt
*Stock*: Walnut
*Barrel*: 24 in.
*Sights*: None
*Weight*: 7.5 lb. on avg.
*Caliber*: .17 HMR, .22 WMR, .17 Mach II, .22 LR
*Magazine*: None
*Features*: Pachmayr rubber butt pad; machined aluminum trigger guard; adjustable single-stage trigger; AA+ Claro walnut stock with checkered 2-panel grip.
**MSRP . . . . . . . . . . . . . . . . . . $1825**

## THE PHOENIX

*Action*: Bolt
*Stock*: Synthetic with Kevlar
*Barrel*: 24 in.
*Sights*: None
*Weight*: 7.5 lb.–8 lb.
*Caliber*: .17 Rem. , .17 Fireball, .204 Ruger, .221 Fireball, .222 Rem., .223 Rem., .223 Rem. Al, 6 x 45, 6 x 47, .20 VarTag, 6.5 Creedmoor, .22 BR, .22-250, .22-250 Al, .220 Swift, 6mm Rem., 6 x 284, 6mm BR, .243 Win.
*Magazine*: None
*Features*: Aircraft-grade aluminum bedding block; Pachmayr rubber butt pad; machined aluminum trigger guard; single-stage trigger; matte stainless steel barrel.
**MSRP . . . . . . . . . . . . . $1525–$1600**

## THE JACKSON SQUIRREL RIFLE

*Action*: Bolt
*Stock*: Walnut
*Barrel*: 22 in.
*Sights*: None
*Weight*: 6.5 lb.
*Caliber*: .17 HMR, .22 WMR, .17 Mach II, .22 LR
*Magazine*: Detachable box, 4-rounds
*Features*: Adjustable single-stage trigger; Pachmayr ruber butt pad; machined aluminum trigger guard; AA + Claro walnut stock with checkered panels on grip.
**MSRP . . . . . . . . . . . . . $1892–$1895**

**COOPER PHOENIX**

**COOPER JACKSON SQUIRREL RIFLE**

# Cooper Firearms

COOPER CLASSIC

COOPER TRP-3

## THE CLASSIC M57, M21, M52

*Action*: Bolt
*Stock*: Walnut
*Barrel*: 22 in.
*Sights*: None
*Weight*: 6 lb.–6.5 lb.
*Caliber*: .17 HMR, .22WMR, .17 Mach II, .22 LR (M 52); .17 Rem., .17 fireball, .204 Ruger, .221 Fireball, .222 Rem., .223 Rem., .223 Rem. AI, 6 x 45, 6 x 47, .20 VarTarg, .17 Squirrel, .17 HeeBee, .17 Ackley Hornet, .22 Hornet, .22 K Hornet, .22 Squirrel, .218 Bee, .218 Mashburn Bee, 6.5 Creedmoor; .30-06, .25-06, .25-06 AI, .30-06, .270, .280, .280 AI, .338-06 (M52)
*Magazine*: None

*Features*: Adjustable single-stage trigger; Pachmayr ruber butt pad; machined aluminum trigger guard; AA Claro walnut stock

**M57 MSRP** . . . . . . . . . . . . . . **$1735**
**M22 MSRP** . . . . . . . . . . . . . . **$1695**
**M52 MSRP** . . . . . . . . . . . . . . **$1755**

## THE TRP-3

*Action*: Bolt
*Stock*: Synthetic
*Barrel*: 24 in.
*Sights*: None
*Weight*: 8 lb.
*Caliber*: 22 LR
*Magazine*: None
*Features*: Adjustable single-stage trigger; Pachmayr ruber butt pad; Cooper Southwestern style checkered 4-panels.
**MSRP** . . . . . . . . . . . . . . . . . **$1595**

## THE VARMINTER, (MODEL 54)

*Action*: Bolt
*Stock*: Walnut
*Barrel*: 22 in.–26 in.
*Sights*: None
*Weight*: 6.5 lb.
*Caliber*: .22-250 Rem., .22-250 AI, .220 Swift, .243 Win., .243 Win. AI, .250 Savage, .250 Sav. AI, .257 Roberts, .257 Rbts AI, .260 Rem., 6.5 Creedmoor, 6.5 x 47 Lupua, 7mm-08, .308 Win.
*Magazine*: Detachable box, 3-rounds
*Features*: AA Carlo walnut stock; Pachmayr rubber pad; adjustable single-stage trigger; stainless steel barrel.
**MSRP** . . . . . . . . . . . . . . . . . **$1855**

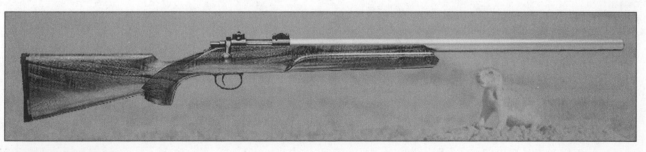

COOPER VARMINTER

# CZ (Ceska Zbrojovka)

**CZ 527**

## 527

**Action**: Bolt
**Stock**: Walnut
**Barrel**: 23.6 in.
**Sights**: Open
**Weight**: 6.2 lb.
**Caliber**: .222 Rem., .223 Rem., .22 Hornet; (American model): .204 Ruger, .221 Fireball; (carbine): 7.62 x 39;
**Magazine**: Detachable box, 5-rounds
**Features**: Hammer forged barrel; controlled round feed; single-set trigger; Turkish walnut stock in Barvarian pattern; Varmint model comes in walnut, Kevlar or laminated; ultralight Predator comes in a synthetic stock with a Blacklands West camo coverage and a black Teflon finish.

| | |
|---|---|
| Lux: | $699 |
| FS: | $748 |
| American: | $699 |
| Left Hand American: | $751 |
| Varmint: | $691–$869 |
| Carbine: | $669 |
| Ultralight Predator: | $832 |

## 550 VARMINT

**Action**: Bolt
**Stock**: Walnut, laminated, Kevlar
**Barrel**: 25.6 in.
**Sights**: Open
**Weight**: 9.7 lb.
**Caliber**: .22-250, .308
**Magazine**: Detachable box, 4-rounds
**Features**: Heavy barreled, two position manual safety; firing pin block and bolt lock.

| | |
|---|---|
| Walnut: | $825 |
| Laminate: | $890 |
| Kevlar: | $961 |

CZ 550 VARMINT

CZ 550

## 550

**Action**: Bolt
**Stock**: Checkered walnut
**Barrel**: 24 in.
**Sights**: Open
**Weight**: 8 lb.
**Caliber**: .22--250, .243 Win., .270 Win., .30-06, .308 Win.; (American) 6.5 x 55, 9.3 x 62; (Medium Lux): 6.5 x 55 Swede
**Magazine**: Detachable box, 4-rounds
**Features**: Adjustable single-set trigger; detachable magazine optional; full stocked model (FS) available; American model includes Pachymar recoil pad.

| | |
|---|---|
| American: | $799–$981 |
| Medium Lux: | $903 |
| FS: | $848–$895 |
| Safari Magnum: | $1179 |

## 550 ULTIMATE HUNTING RIFLE

**Action**: Bolt
**Stock**: Walnut, Kevlar
**Barrel**: 23.6 in.
**Sights**: Open
**Weight**: 7.7 lb.
**Caliber**: .300 Win. Mag
**Magazine**: Fixed, 3-rounds
**Features**: Hammer forged, blued barrel; single stage trigger.

| | |
|---|---|
| MSRP: | $1275 |
| Kevlar: | $1402 |

CZ 550 ULTIMATE HUNTING RIFLE

# CZ (Ceska Zbrojovka)

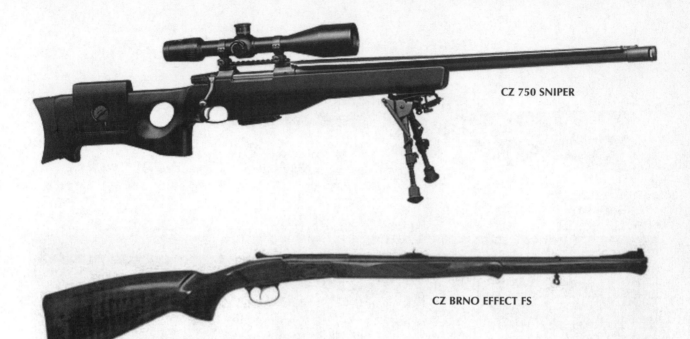

CZ 750 SNIPER

CZ BRNO EFFECT FS

CZ 455 AMERICAN

## 750 SNIPER
*Action*: Bolt
*Stock*: Synthetic thumbhole
*Barrel*: 26 in.
*Sights*: Open
*Weight*: 11.9 lb.
*Caliber*: .308 Win.
*Magazine*: Detachable box, 10-rounds
*Features*: Adjustable comb; underside of forend is fitted with a 220mm long rail for bipod attachament; muzzle brake; thread protector; mirage shield; blued barrel; single stage trigger.
**MSRP** . . . . . . . . . . . . . . . . . . **$1991**

## BRNO EFFECT FS
*Action*: Single-shot
*Stock*: Walnut
*Barrel*: 23.6 in.
*Sights*: Open
*Weight*: 6 lb.
*Caliber*: .30-06 or .308 Win.
*Magazine*: None
*Features*: Select walnut stock (full in FS); big game engravings on receiver; single-set trigger; automatic safety and iron sights.
**MSRP** . . . . . . . . . . . . . . . . . . **$1699**

## 455 AMERICAN
*Action*: Bolt
*Stock*: Walnut
*Barrel*: 20.5 in.
*Sights*: None
*Weight*: 6.1 lb.
*Caliber*: .17 HMR, .22 LR, .22 WMR, Combo .22 LR with .17 HMR replacement bbl
*Magazine*: Detachable box, 5-rounds
*Features*: Cold hammer forged barrel; blued receiver and barrel finish; integrated dovetail scope base; interchangable barrel system; adjustable trigger.
**MSRP** . . . . . . . . . . . . . . . **$396–$531**

# CZ (Ceska Zbrojovka)

CZ 550 URBAN COUNTER-SNIPER

CZ 512 SEMI-AUTO

CZ 550 SAFARI MAGNUM

## 550 URBAN COUNTER-SNIPER
**Action**: Bolt
**Stock**: Synthetic, aluminum bedding block
**Barrel**: 16 in.
**Sights**: None
**Weight**: 8.3 lb.
**Caliber**: .308 Win.
**Magazine**: Detachable box, 10-rounds
**Features**: Floated bull barrel with target crown; surefire muzzle brake; Teflon coating; single-stage trigger.
**MSRP** . . . . . . . . . . . . . . . . . . . **$2404**

## 512 SEMI-AUTO
**Action**: Semi-automatic
**Stock**: Beech
**Barrel**: 20.6 in.
**Sights**: Fixed, adjustable
**Weight**: 5.9 lb.
**Caliber**: .22 LR
**Magazine**: Detachable box, 5-rounds
**Features**: Cold hammer forged barrel; cross bolt safety; dual guide rods for smooth operation; integral dovetail for mounting scopes.
**MSRP** . . . . . . . . . . . . . . . . . . . **$449**

## 550 SAFARI MAGNUM
**Action**: Bolt
**Stock**: Walnut
**Barrel**: 25 in.
**Sights**: Express sights
**Weight**: 9.4 lb.
**Caliber**: .375 H&H Mag., .416 Rigby, .458 Win. Mag.
**Magazine**: Fixed, 3-rounds (.416 Rigby), 5-rounds
**Features**: Hammer forged barrel; single-set trigger; controlled round feed and fixed ejector make the rifle reliable enough for heavy and dangerous game.
**MSRP** . . . . . . . . . . . . . . . . . . . **$1179**

RIFLES

**DAKOTA 10 SINGLE SHOT RIFLE**

## 76 BOLT RIFLE
*Action*: Bolt
*Stock*: Walnut
*Barrel*: 23 in.
*Sights*: None
*Weight*: 6.5 lb.–9.5 lb.
*Caliber*: Classic: .257 Roberts, .260 Rem., .270 Win., .280 Rem., .30-60 Spfld., .300 Dakota, .300 Win. Mag., .300 WSM, .308 Win., .330 Dakota, .416 Rem., 7mm Rem. Mag., 7mm-08 Rem.; Safari: .300 H&H, .375 Dakota, .416 Rem., 7mm Dakota; African: .338 Win. Mag., .375 H&H, .416 Rem., .404 Jeffery, .416 Rigby, .450 Dakota, .458 Lott
*Magazine*: Box, 4-rounds
*Features*: Barrel break-in; custom length pull; optional engraving; point panel checkering; Dakota swivel studs; 1" recoil pad; straddle floorplate; right or left hand configurations; Safari model has front island sight with flip-up night sight; African model has quarter rib sights with banded front sights and flip up night sights.
**Classic: . . . . . . . . . . $5395–$11964**
**Safari: . . . . . . . . . . . . . . . . $6795**
**African: . . . . . . . . . . . $7995–10104**

## 76 LTD. EDITION
*Action*: Bolt
*Stock*: Walnut
*Barrel*: 23 in.
*Sights*: None
*Weight*: 6.5 lb.
*Caliber*: .30-06 Spgfld.
*Magazine*: Box, 4-rounds
*Features*: 100-year banner on floor plate with gold wire border; limited edition checkering patter; stainless steel receiver.
**MSRP . . . . . . . . . . . . . . . . . . $8945**

## 10 SINGLE SHOT
*Action*: Falling block
*Stock*: Walnut
*Barrel*: 23 in.
*Sights*: None
*Weight*: 6 lb.–7 lb.
*Caliber*: .22 LR to .300 Win. (Standard), .338 to .375 H&H (Magnum)
*Magazine*: None
*Features*: Point wrap checkering; scope ring bases installed; custom length of pull; barrel break-in.
**MSRP . . . . . . . . . . . . . . $4695–$7518**

## 97 HUNTER
*Action*: Bolt
*Stock*: Choice of fiberglass, composite, walnut
*Barrel*: 22 in. (short action), 25 in. (long action)
*Sights*: None
*Weight*: 7 lb.
*Caliber*: All weather: .30-06, .338 Win. Mag., .375 H&H, 7mm Rem. Mag., 7mm-08; Long Range: .280 Rem., .338 Win. Mag., 7mm Rem. Mag., 7mm-08
*Magazine*: Blind box
*Features*: Stainless Douglas barrel; black composite stock with two inletted Ken Howell swivel studs; stainless triggerbow.
**All Weather: . . . . . . . . $3595–$4848**
**Long Range: . . . . . . . . $3295–$4310**

**RIFLES**

**DAKOTA 97 HUNTER**

# Dakota Arms Rifles

**DAKOTA LONGBOW TACTICAL**

**DAKOTA SCIMITAR TACTICAL**

## LONGBOW TACTICAL
*Action*: Bolt
*Stock*: A-2 McMillian Fiberglass
*Barrel*: 28 in.
*Sights*: Open
*Weight*: 13.7 lb.
*Caliber*: .338 Lapua Mag., .300 Dakota Mag., .330 Dakota Mag.
*Magazine*: Blind box
*Features*: Machined high strength, steel alloy square bottom action; claw extraction system; Picatinny rail; ergonomic, ambidextrous A-2 McMillian Fiberglass stock in black or olive drab green; full length action bedding; bipod spike in forend; muzzle brake.
**MSRP** . . . . . . . . . . . . . . . . . . . **$4795**

## SCIMITAR TACTICAL
*Action*: Bolt
*Stock*: Dakota KISS polymer stock
*Barrel*: 24 in. (short action), 28 in. (long action)
*Sights*: None
*Weight*: 16 lb.
*Caliber*: .308 Win. (7.62 NATO)
*Magazine*: Detachable box
*Features*: Ergonomic, amidextrous Dakota KISS stock in black polymer finish; full-length action bedding; recessed match-grade crown; secure over-sized bolt knob positioned for tactical use; machine Mil-Std-1912 one-piece optical rail.
**MSRP** . . . . . . . . . . . . . . . . . . **$6295**

## PREDATOR
*Action*: Bolt
*Stock*: Walnut
*Barrel*: 22 in.
*Sights*: None
*Weight*: 8.25 lb.
*Caliber*: .17 VarTarg, .17 Remington, .17 tactical, .20 PPC, .204 Ruger, .221 Rem. Fireball, .22 PPC, .223; Rem., 6mm PPC, 6.5 Grendel: Miller:
*Magazine*: None
*Features*: Available in walnut sporter-style stock or XXX walnut varmint style stock with semi-beavertail forend; checkered grip; recessed target crown; Vaper hone matte bead blast finish on stainless; stainless steel barrel.
**Classic:** . . . . . . . . . . . . . . . . **$4295**
**Serious:** . . . . . . . . . . . . . . . . **$3295**

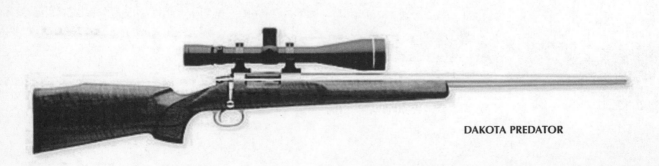

**DAKOTA PREDATOR**

# Dakota Arms Rifles

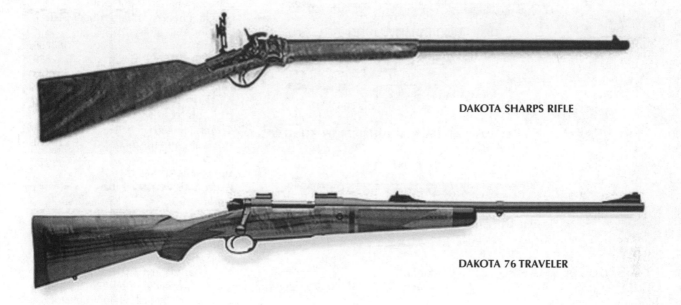

DAKOTA SHARPS RIFLE

DAKOTA 76 TRAVELER

## SHARPS RIFLE
*Action*: Falling block
*Stock*: Walnut
*Barrel*: 26 in.
*Sights*: Open
*Weight*: 8 lb.
*Caliber*: .17 HMR, .22 Hornet, .30-30, .30-40 Krag, .375 H&H
*Features*: Octagon barrel; steel buttplate; single blade rear sight with front bead; matte blue metal finish.

Sharps MSRP . . . . . . . . $5525–$6535
Miller MSRP . . . . . . . . . . . . . $6805

## 76 TRAVELER
*Action*: Bolt
*Stock*: Walnut
*Barrel*: 23 in.
*Sights*: Flip-up
*Weight*: 7.5 lb., Safari: 8.5 lb.
*Caliber*: .22-250 Rem. to .416 Rem; multiple barrel/caliber combinations
*Magazine*: Drop box, 4-rounds
*Features*: Safari has front island sight with flip-up night sight; XXX American black walnut stock; 1 in. black recoil pad; point panel checkering; Dakota swivel studs; takes down into two sections for easy transport for the traveling hunter.

Classic: . . . . . . . . . . . . . . . . $7285
Safari: . . . . . . . . . . . . . . . . . $8450

# Dixie Gun Works

DIXIE 1873 TRAPDOOR OFFICER'S MODEL

## 1873 TRAPDOOR OFFICER'S MODEL BY PEDERSOLI
*Action*: Breechloading
*Stock*: Walnut
*Barrel*: 26 in.
*Sights*: Adjustable
*Weight*: 8 lb.
*Caliber*: .45-70
*Magazine*: None
*Features*: Single-shot rifle; front sight is blued steel with brass bead; rear sight is adjustable tang sight; color case-hardened steel furniture, pewter nose-cap; single set trigger.

MSRP . . . . . . . . . . . . . . . . . . $1600

RIFLES

# Dixie Gun Works

DIXIE SHILOH SHARPS MODEL 1874 LONGE RANGE

DIXIE SHILOH SHARPS MODEL 1874 SPORTING RIFLE

DIXIE SHILOH SHARPS MODEL 1874 SPORTING RIFLE NO. 1

## 1874 SHILOH SHARPS MODEL

*Action*: Breechloading
*Stock*: Walnut, pistol grip
*Barrel*: 34 in. Long Range; 30 in. Sporting Rifle No.1; 26 in. Sporting Rifle
*Sights*: Adjustable
*Weight*: 10 lb.
*Caliber*: .45-70,.30-40 Krag. sporting rifle
*Magazine*: None
*Features*: Long range has Parsons tube scope; sporting model has a spirit level dovetail; part round, part octagonal barrel; frame, lockplate, hammer, and lever have all the original color casehardening; buttstock is mounted with checkered hard rubber plate; double-set triggers.

Long Range: . . . . . . . . . . . . . $3250
No. 1 Sporting Rifle: . . . . . . . $2850
Sporting Rifle: . . . . . . . . . . . $2395

## KODIAK DOUBLE RIFLE BY PEDERSOLI

*Action*: Hinged breech
*Stock*: Walnut, pistol grip
*Barrel*: 24 in.
*Sights*: Flip up sights
*Weight*: 10 lb.–10.75 lb.
*Caliber*: .50, .54, .58 Kodiak, .45-70 Mark IV, .72 Express
*Magazine*: None
*Features*: Express has dovetail, steel ramp with brass bead as front sight; blued barrels; external hammers are rebounding style; double triggers; sling is included; English walnut buttstock and forearm are checkered; rubber recoil pad.

Mark IV:. . . . . . . . . . . . . . . . $4500
Express: . . . . . . . . . . . . . . . . $1200
Kodiak: . . . . . . . . . . . . . . . . $1200

DIXIE KODIAK DOUBLE RIFLE

# DPMS Panther Arms

DPMS LR-204

## LR-204

*Action*: Semi-automatic
*Stock*: Synthetic
*Barrel*: 24 in.
*Sights*: None
*Weight*: 10.25 lb.
*Caliber*: .204 Rueger
*Magazine*: Detachable box, 30-rounds

*Features*: Fluted barrel; standard A2 black stock; aluminum ribbed free float tube; aircraft aluminum alloy, Teflon coated, forged A3 style receiver; nylon web sling included.
MSRP. . . . . . . . . . . $1029

RIFLES

# DPMS Panther Arms

**DPMS ARCTIC PANTHER**

**DPMS BULL 24 SPECIAL**

**DPMS BULL SWEET 16, 20, 24**

## ARCTIC PANTHER

*Action*: Semi-automatic
*Stock*: Synthetic
*Barrel*: 20 in.
*Sights*: None
*Weight*: 9 lb.
*Caliber*: .223 Rem.
*Magazine*: Detachable box, 30-rounds
*Features*: Fluted and black teflon coated barrel; aircraft aluminum alloy, A3 style flattop receiver coated in white; standard A2 black Zytle mil-spec stock; aluminum ribbed free float handguard tube (coated white).
**MSRP** . . . . . . . . . . . . . . . . . **$1099**

## BULL SWEET 16, 20, 24

*Action*: Semi-automatic
*Stock*: Synthetic
*Barrel*: 16 in., 20 in., 24 in.
*Sights*: None
*Weight*: 7.85 lb. (Sweet 16), 9.15 lb. (Bull 20), 9.8 lb. (Bull 24)
*Caliber*: .223 Rem.
*Magazine*: Detachable box, 30-rounds
*Features*: Aircraft aluminum alloy, A3 style flattop receiver coated in black Teflon; aluminum trigger guard; black standard A2 Zytel mil-spec stock; aluminum ribbed free float tube; nylon web sling included.
**Bull Sweet 16:** . . . . . . . . . . . . **$909**
**Bull 20:** . . . . . . . . . . . . . . . . . **$939**
**Bull 24:** . . . . . . . . . . . . . . . . . **$969**

## BULL 24 SPECIAL

*Action*: Semi-automatic
*Stock*: Synthetic; pistol grip
*Barrel*: 24 in.
*Sights*: None
*Weight*: 10.25 lb.
*Caliber*: .233 Rem.
*Magazine*: Detachable box, 30-rounds
*Features*: Aircraft aluminum alloy, A3 style flattop receiver coated in black Teflon; aluminum trigger guard; black standard A2 Zytel mil spec stock with Panther tactical grip; aluminum ribbed free float tube; nylon web sling included; adjustable butt plate.
**MSRP** . . . . . . . . . . . . . . . . . **$1189**

# DPMS Panther Arms

## DCM

**Action**: Semi-automatic
**Stock**: Synthetic
**Barrel**: 20 in.
**Sights**: Adjustable NM sight
**Weight**: 9.35 lb.
**Caliber**: .233 Rem.
**Magazine**: Detachable box, 30-rounds
**Features**: National Match dual aperture rear sight, A2 fixed carry handle; forged aircraft aluminum alloy receiver; receiver coated in Teflon; aluminum trigger guard; standard black A2 Zytel mil stock with trap door assembly; DCM free float hadnguard system
**MSRP** . . . . . . . . . . . . . . . . . . .$ 1099

## PRAIRIE PANTHER KING'S DESERT SHADOW, MOSSY OAK BUSH

**Action**: Semi-automatic
**Stock**: Synthetic
**Barrel**: 20 in.

**Sights**: None
**Weight**: 7.10 lb.
**Caliber**: .223 Rem.
**Magazine**: Detachable box, 20-rounds
**Features**: Target crowned, stainless steel heavy barrel; A3 flattop aircraft aluminum alloy receiver; Magpul winter trigger guard; King's Desert Shadow camo or Mossy Oak Brush camo stock; receiver features durable ceramic over coat in either type of camo; nylon web sling included.
**MSRP** . . . . . . . . . . . . . . . . . . . $1249

## A2 TACTICAL 16-INCH

**Action**: Semi-automatic
**Stock**: Synthetic
**Barrel**: 16 in.
**Sights**: Open
**Weight**: 8.2 lb.
**Caliber**: 5.56 x 45mm
**Magazine**: Detachable box, 30-rounds
**Features**: Chrome-moly steel barrel with A3 flash hider; A2 front and rear sight assembly; forged aircraft aluminum alloy receiver coated in Teflon; black standard A2 Zytel mil stock; nylon web sling included.
**MSRP** . . . . . . . . . . . . . . . . . . . $829

DPMS A2 TACTICAL 16-INCH

DPMS DCM

DPMS PRAIRIE PANTHER KING'S DESERT SHADOW, MOSSY OAK BUSH

RIFLES

# DPMS Panther Arms

## AP4 CAR. MICULEK COMP.

*Action*: Semi-automatic
*Stock*: Synthetic
*Barrel*: 16 in.
*Sights*: Open
*Weight*: 6.9 lb.
*Caliber*: 5.56 x 45mm
*Magazine*: Detachable box, 30-rounds
*Features*: Chrome-moly steel barrel with Miculek compensator; forged aircraft aluminum alloy receiver with Teflon coating; black stock with AP4 6-position, telescoping fiber reinforced polymer; oval, carbine length GlacierGuards.
**MSRP** . . . . . . . . . . . . . . . . . . . . **$989**

## AP4 CARBINE

*Action*: Semi-automatic
*Stock*: Synthetic
*Barrel*: 16 in.
*Sights*: Open
*Weight*: 7.15 lb.
*Caliber*: 5.56 x 45mm
*Magazine*: Detachable box, 30-rounds
*Features*: Chrome-moly steel barrel with A2 flash hider; A3 aircraft aluminum alloy receiver with detachable carrying handle; adjustable rear sight and A2 front sight assembly; black AP4-6 position, telescoping fiber reinforced polymer stock; oval, carbine length GlacierGuards.
**MSRP** . . . . . . . . . . . . . . . . . . . . **$949**

## PANTHER CARBINE A2

*Action*: Semi-automatic
*Stock*: Synthetic
*Barrel*: 11.5, 16 in.
*Sights*: Open
*Weight*: 7.05 lb., 6.9 lb.(A2)
*Caliber*: 5.56 x 45mm
*Magazine*: Detachable box, 30-rounds
*Features*: Chrome-moly steel barrel with flash hider; A3 aircraft aluminum alloy receiver with detachable carrying handle; adjustable rear sight and A2 front sight assembly; DPMS Pardus black stock; oval, carbine length GlacierGuards.
**MSRP** . . . . . . . . . . . . . . . . . . . . **$829**

## LITE 16

*Action*: Semi-automatic
*Stock*: Synthetic
*Barrel*: 16 in.
*Sights*: Open

*Weight*: 6.5 lb.
*Caliber*: 5.56 x 45mm
*Magazine*: Detachable box, 30-rounds
*Features*: Chrome-moly steel barrel with A2 flash hider; A3 aircraft aluminum alloy receiver with detachable carrying handle; A1 front and rear sights; DPMS Pardus carbine black stock; oval, carbine length GlacierGuards.
**MSRP** . . . . . . . . . . . . . . . . . . . . **$759**

DPMS AP4 CARBINE

DPMS CARBINE A2

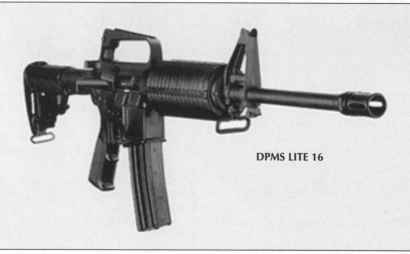

DPMS LITE 16

# DPMS Panther Arms

**DPMS LO-PRO CLASSIC**

**DPMS AP4 6.8MM SPC II PANTHER CARBINE**

**DPMS LR-260**

## CLASSIC

**Action**: Semi-automatic
**Stock**: Synthetic
**Barrel**: 20 in.
**Sights**: Open
**Weight**: 9 lb.
**Caliber**: 5.56 x 45mm
**Magazine**: Detachable box, 30-rounds
**Features**: Chrome-moly steel barrel with A2 flash hider; forged aircraft aluminum alloy receiver with A2 fixed carry handle; black standardized A2 black Zytel mil-spec stock; standard A2 round handguards; dual aperature adjustable rear sights, mil-spec front sight post.
**MSRP** . . . . . . . . . . . . . . . . . . . . $849

## LO-PRO CLASSIC

**Action**: Semi-automatic
**Stock**: Synthetic
**Barrel**: 16 in.
**Sights**: None
**Weight**: 7.9 lb.
**Caliber**: 5.56 x 45mm
**Magazine**: Detachable box, 30-rounds
**Features**: Chrome-moly steel barrel; flattop Lo-Pro, extruded receiver made of aircraft aluminum alloy; semi-auto trigger group; standard A2 black Zytel mil stock with trap door assembly; GlacierGuards.
**MSRP** . . . . . . . . . . . . . . . . . . . . $759

## AP4 6.8MM SPC II PANTHER CARBINE

**Action**: Semi-automatic
**Stock**: Synthetic
**Barrel**: 16 in., 20 in.
**Sights**: Open
**Weight**: 7 lb. (16in) , 9 lb. (20in)
**Caliber**: 6.8 x 43mm Rem. SPC II

**Magazine**: Detachable box, 25-rounds
**Features**: Chrome-moly steel barrel with A2 flash hider; A3 aircraft aluminum alloy receiver with detachable carrying handle; GlacierGuards(16in), A2 length standard handguards (20in); standard A2 front sight assembly; AP4 -6 position, telescoping fiber reinforced polymer stock in black (16in.); Standard A2 black Zytel mil spec stock (20in).
**16-inch:** . . . . . . . . . . . . . . . . $1019
**20-inch:** . . . . . . . . . . . . . . . . $1029

## LR-243L, LR-243

**Action**: Semi-automatic
**Stock**: Synthetic
**Barrel**: 18 in. (LR-243L), 20 in. (LR-243)
**Sights**: None
**Weight**: 7.99 lb.(LR-243L), 10.65 lb. (LR-243)
**Caliber**: .243 Win.
**Magazine**: Detachable box, 19-rounds
**Features**: Custom Miculek compensator, lightweight gasblock (LR-243L); black Tefloned stainless steel barrel

with .308 Panther flash hider (LR-243); A3 flattop lightweight receiver, extruded from T-5 aluminum (LR-243L); A3 flattop thick-walled aluminum receiver (LR-243); two-stage trigger (LR-243L); standard AR-15 trigger group (LR-243); carbon fiber free float tube with bipod stud (LR-243L); standard length ribbed free float handguard tube (LR-243).
**LR-243L:** . . . . . . . . . . . . . . . . . $1499
**LR-243:** . . . . . . . . . . . . . . . . . . $1199

## LR-260

**Action**: Semi-automatic
**Stock**: Synthetic
**Barrel**: 24 in.
**Sights**: None
**Weight**: 11.3 lb.
**Caliber**: .260 Rem.
**Magazine**: Detachable box, 19-rounds
**Features**: 416 stainless steel bull barrel; A3 style flattop receiver made of thick-walled aluminum; standard AR-15 trigger group; standard A2 black Zytel mil-spec stock with trap door assembly; standard length ribbed free float handguard tube.
**MSRP** . . . . . . . . . . . . . . . . . . . . $1199

**RIFLES**

# DPMS Panther Arms

**DPMS RECON CARBINE**

## LR-308
**Action**: Semi-automatic
**Stock**: Synthetic
**Barrel**: 24 in.
**Sights**: None
**Weight**: 11.20 lb.
**Caliber**: .308 Win.
**Magazine**: Detachable box, 19-rounds
**Features**: 416 stainless steel bull barrel; thick-walled aluminum receiver coated with Teflon; internal trigger guard; raised Picatinny rail for easy scope mounting; standard A2 black Zytel mil stock.
**MSRP** . . . . . . . . . . . . . . . . . . $1169

## DPMS RECON CARBINE
**Action**: Semi-automatic
**Stock**: Synthetic
**Barrel**: 16 in.
**Sights**: Magpul BUIS
**Weight**: 9 lb.
**Caliber**: 5.56mm
**Magazine**: Detachable box, 30-rounds
**Features**: Bead-blasted stainless, mid length gas system; semi-auto trigger group; Magpul MOE stock in Teflon black.
**MSRP** . . . . . . . . . . . . . . . . . . $1099

# EMF Replica Rifles

EMF MISSOURI RIVER HAWKEN

EMF DEER HUNTER CARBINE

## MISSOURI RIVER HAWKEN BY PEDERSOLI
**Action**: Single shot
**Stock**: Maple or walnut
**Barrel**: 30 in.
**Sights**: Open
**Weight**: 9.24 lb.
**Caliber**: .45 (optional .50)
**Magazine**: Under-barrel tube, 8-rounds
**Features**: Replica percussion rifle; available in maple or walnut stock in rust brown color finish; barrel features an octagonal cross-section; case hardened color lock; equipped with a double-set trigger.
**Maple:** . . . . . . . . . . . . . . . . . . $1050
**Walnut** . . . . . . . . . . . . . . . . . . $910

## THE DEER HUNTER
**Action**: Lever
**Stock**: Walnut
**Barrel**: 20 in.
**Sights**: Open
**Weight**: 5.5 lb.
**Caliber**: 44 Mag.
**Magazine**: Under-barrel tube
**Features**: Case hardened frame, blued barrel.
**Carbine:** . . . . . . . . . . . . . . . . . $550
**Rifle:** . . . . . . . . . . . . . . . . . . . $580

RIFLES

# E. R. Shaw Rifles

## MARK VII CUSTOM
**Action**: Bolt
**Stock**: Walnut, laminate wood, or synthetic
**Barrel**: 16.25 in. to 26 in.
**Sights**: None
**Weight**: Depends on specifications
**Caliber**: 75 calibers choices from .17 Rem. to .458 Lott
**Magazine**: Internal magazine
**Features**: Right- or left-hand actions; stainless receivers; contour barrels; polished or matte blue finish; recoil pads and swivel studs; choice of 2 barrel contours, stainless steel or blued chromemoly steel.
**MSRP** . . . . . . . . . . . . . . . **$707–$1220**

# Excel Arms

EXCEL ACCELERATOR RIFLE

EXCEL X22R WITH SCOPE

## ACCELERATOR RIFLE
**Action**: Semi-automatic
**Stock**: Polymer composite, pistol grip
**Barrel**: 18 in.
**Sights**: Standard includes red/green dot optic
**Weight**: 8 lb.
**Caliber**: .22 WMR, .17 HMR
**Magazine**: Detachable box, 9-rounds
**Features**: Weaver rail for scope, sights and optics; pin block safety; stainless steel barrel; polymer composite stock available in black or silver shroud.
**Basic MSRP:** . . . . . . . . . . . . . . . **$512**
**Standard MSRP** . . . . . . . . . . . **$549**

## X-22R RIFLE
**Action**: Semi-automatic
**Stock**: Synthetic
**Barrel**: 18 in.
**Sights**: None
**Weight**: 4.75 lb.
**Caliber**: .22 LR high velocity
**Magazine**: Detachable box, 25-rounds, (10-rounds version also available)
**Features**: CNC machined aluminum frame; optional 3-9x40 scope; tapped holes in hand guard for mounting accessory rails; inegral weaver base to mount scopes, sights, and optics.
**X-22R Basic MSRP:** . . . . . . . . . **$461**
**X-22R Scoped MSRP:** . . . . . . . . **$548**
**X-22R 10 RD MSRP:** . . . . . . . . **$461**

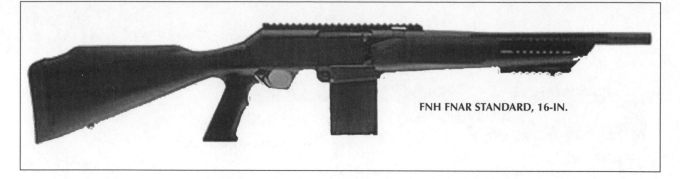

FNH FNAR STANDARD, 16-IN.

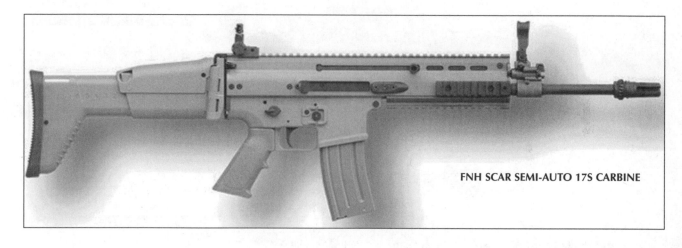

FNH SCAR SEMI-AUTO 17S CARBINE

## STANDARD AND HEAVY

**Action**: Gas-operated autoloader
**Stock**: Matte black synthetic with pistol grip and adjustable comb
**Barrel**: 16 in. or 20 in standard fluted or 20 in. heavy fluted
**Sights**: Receiver mounted rail
**Weight**: 8.8 lb. to 10 lb.
**Caliber**: .308 Win. (7.62 x 51mm Nato)
**Magazine**: 10- or 20-round
**Features**: Extended bolt handle, hammer forged barrel with crown; comes with one magazine, three interchangable recoil pads, three comb inserts and shims for adjusting for cast-on, cast-off and drop at comb.
**MSRP** . . . . . . . . . . . . . . . . . . **$1699**

## SCAR 17S CARBINE

**Action**: Gas-operated autoloader
**Stock**: Tactical, telescoping, side-folding polymer
**Barrel**: 16.25 in.
**Sights**: Adjustable, folding, removable
**Weight**: 8 lb.
**Caliber**: .308 Win. (7.62 x 51mm Nato)
**Magazine**: 10- or 20-round
**Features**: Fully adjustable stock; MIL-STD 1913 optical rail plus three accessory rails for attaching a variety of sights and lasers; free-floating, cold hammer-forged barrel; available in black or flat dark earth.
**MSRP** . . . . . . . . . . . . . . . . . . **$3349**

# Harrington & Richardson Rifles

H&R BUFFALO CLASSIC RIFLE

## CLASSIC BUFFALO RIFLE

**Action**: Hinged breech
**Stock**: Walnut
**Barrel**: 32 in.
**Sights**: Open
**Weight**: 8 lb.
**Caliber**: .45-70
**Magazine**: None
**Features**: Antique color case hardened frame; cut-checkered American black walnut with case colored crescent steel buttplate.
**MSRP** . . . . . . . . . . . . . . . . . . **$479.17**

# Harrington & Richardson Rifles

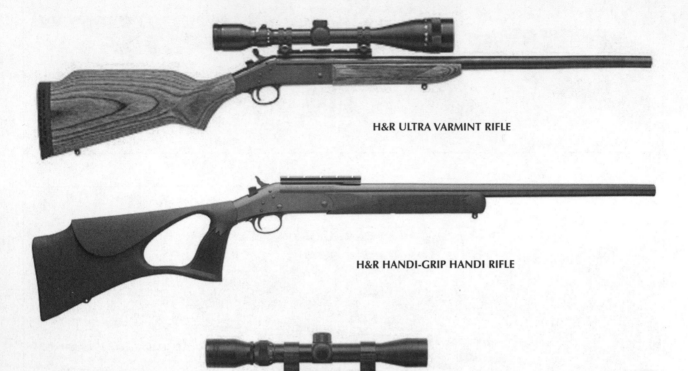

H&R ULTRA VARMINT RIFLE

H&R HANDI-GRIP HANDI RIFLE

H&R SUPERLIGHT HANDI-RIFLE COMPACT WITH SCOPE

## ULTRA VARMINT RIFLE

**Action**: Hinged breech
**Stock**: Cinnamon laminated American hardwood
**Barrel**: 24 in. bull barrel
**Sights**: None
**Weight**: 7 lb.–8 lb.
**Caliber**: .223 Rem., .243 Win.
**Magazine**: None
**Features**: Monte Carlo pistol grip with checkering; sling swivel studs; ventilated recoil pad; scope mount and hammer extension, no iron sights.
**MSRP** . . . . . . . . . . . . . . . . . .$381.36

## HANDI-GRIP HANDI RIFLE

**Action**: Hinged breech
**Stock**: Ambidextrous thumbhole black polymer
**Barrel**: 22, 24, 26 in.
**Sights**: Scope mount rail and hammer extension
**Weight**: 7 lb.
**Caliber**: .204 Ruger, .223 Rem., .22-250 Rem., .308 Win., .45-70 Govt., .243 Win., .35-06 Rem.
**Magazine**: None
**Features**: Molded checkering at grip and forend for sure handling; transfer bar system.
**MSRP:** . . . . . . . . . . . . . . . . . .$341.12

## SUPERLIGHT HANDI-RIFLE COMPACT WITH SCOPE

**Action**: Hinged breech
**Stock**: High-density polymer, matte black
**Barrel**: 20 in.
**Sights**: Open
**Weight**: 5.3 lb.
**Caliber**: .243 Win.
**Magazine**: None
**Features**: Sling swivel studs; recoil pad; ramp front sight, adjustable rear; drilled and tapped for scope rail; includes 3-9x32 scope, factory-mounted and bore sighted.
**MSRP** . . . . . . . . . . . . . . . . . .$35901

# Heckler & Koch Rifles

H&K USC

H&K SL8-6

## USC

**Action**: Autoloading
**Stock**: Synthetic
**Barrel**: 16.13 in.
**Sights**: None
**Weight**: 6.00 lb.
**Caliber**: .45 ACP
**Magazine**: Detachable box, 10-rounds
**Features**: Black reinforced polymer stock; steel barrel; skeletonized butt-stock is topped with rubber cheek rest and recoil pad; Picatinny rails; ambidextrous safety.
**MSRP**. . . . . . . . . . . . . . . . . . $1883

## SL8-6

**Action**: Autoloading
**Stock**: Synthetic
**Barrel**: 20.08 in.
**Sights**: None
**Weight**: 9.26 lb.
**Caliber**: .223 Rem.
**Magazine**: Detachable box, 10-rounds
**Features**: Short Picatinny rail mount; piston-actuated gas operating system; black ergonomic, synthetic stock.
**MSRP**. . . . . . . . . . . . . . . . . . $2449

# Henry Repeating Arms

HENRY BIG BOY

## BIG BOY

**Action**: Lever
**Stock**: Walnut
**Barrel**: 20 in.
**Sights**: Open
**Weight**: 8.68 lb.
**Caliber**: .44 Mag., .45 Colt, .357 Mag.
**Magazine**: Under-barrel tube, 10-rounds
**Features**: Adjustable marble semi-buckhorn rear with white diamond insert and brass beaded front sight; solid top brass receiver, brass buttplate and brass barrel band; straight-grip American walnut stock; octagonal barrel.
**MSRP**. . . . . . . . . . . . . . . . . .$899.95

# Henry Repeating Arms

HENRY GOLDEN BOY

HENRY LEVER ACTION .22

HENRY VARMINT EXPRESS

RIFLES

## GOLDEN BOY

*Action*: Lever
*Stock*: Walnut
*Barrel*: 16.25 (youth), 20 in. (.22, .17 HMR), 20.5 in.(.22 Mag)
*Sights*: Open
*Weight*: 6 lb. (youth), 6.75 lb.
*Caliber*: .22, .22 Mag., .17 HMR
*Magazine*: Under-barrel tube, 16-rounds (LR), 21-rounds (S); 12-rounds (.22 Mag); 11 round (.17 HMR); youth: 12-rounds (.22 LR), 17-rounds (.22 L), 18-rounds .22 (S)
*Features*: American walnut stock; adjustable buckhorn rear sight, beaded front sight; brasslite receiver, brass butt plate and blued barrel.

.22: . . . . . . . . . . . . . . . . . . . . $515
.22 Mag:. . . . . . . . . . . . . . . . . $595
.17 HMR: . . . . . . . . . . . . . . . . $615
.22 Youth: . . . . . . . . . . . . . . . $515

## LEVER ACTION .22

*Action*: Lever
*Stock*: Walnut
*Barrel*: 16.13 in. (carbine, youth), 18.25 in.
*Sights*: Open
*Weight*: 4.5 lb. (carbine, youth), 5.25 lb., 5.5 lb. (Mag.)
*Caliber*: .22, .22 L, .22 LR
*Magazine*: Under-barrel tube, 11-rounds (.22 Mag.), 15-rounds (.22 LR), 17-rounds (.22 L), 18-rounds (.22 S), 21-rounds (.22)
*Features*: Straight-grip American walnut stock; deluxe checkered American walnut stock (.22 Magnum); adjustable rear, hooded front sight; blued round barrel and lever.

Rifle, Youth, Carbine: . . . $325–$340
Magnum:. . . . . . . . . . . . . . . . . $475

## VARMINT EXPRESS

*Action*: Lever
*Stock*: Walnut
*Barrel*: 20 in.
*Sights*: Open
*Weight*: 5.75 lb.
*Caliber*: .17 HMR
*Magazine*: Under-barrel tube, 11-rounds
*Features*: Checkered American walnut stock; Williams Fire Sights; blued round barrel and lever.
MSRP . . . . . . . . . . . . . . . . . . $549.95

# Henry Repeating Arms

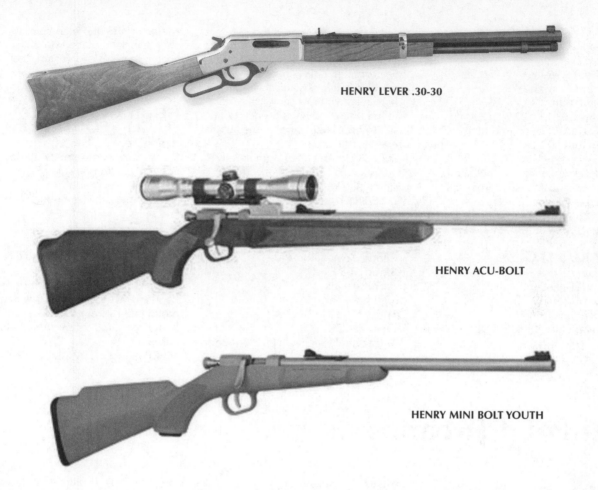

HENRY LEVER .30-30

HENRY ACU-BOLT

HENRY MINI BOLT YOUTH

## FRONTIER T MODEL
*Action*: Lever
*Stock*: Walnut
*Barrel*: 20 in.
*Sights*: Open
*Weight*: 6.25 lb.
*Caliber*: .22 LR, .22 S
*Magazine*: Under-barrel tube, 21-rounds (.22 S), 16-rounds (.22 LR); 12-rounds (.22 Mag.); 11-rounds (.17 HMR)
*Features*: American walnut; marbles fully adjustable semi-buckhorn rear, with reversible white diamond insert and brass beaded front sight; blued barrel and lever.
.22LR, .22S: . . . . . . . . . . . . . . $425
.22Mag.: . . . . . . . . . . . . . . . $539.95
.17HMR: . . . . . . . . . . . . . . . $549.95

## LEVER .30-30
*Action*: Lever
*Stock*: Walnut
*Barrel*: 20 in.
*Sights*: Open
*Weight*: 7 lb.
*Caliber*: .30-30
*Magazine*: 5-rounds
*Features*: Steel round barrel: deluxe checkered American walnut with rubber buttpad; XS Ghost Rings sights; blued steel receiver, drilled and tapped for easy scope mounting. brass octagon barrel: straight-grip American walnut with butt plate; marble fully adjustable semi-buckhorn rear sight, with diamond insert, beaded front-sight; brass receiver, drilled and tapped for easy scope mounting.
**Steel: $749.95; Brass: $969.95**

## ACU-BOLT
*Action*: Bolt
*Stock*: Synthetic
*Barrel*: 20 in.
*Sights*: Open
*Weight*: 4.25 lb.
*Caliber*: .22 LR, .22 Mag., .17 HMR
*Magazine*: None
*Features*: Single-shot; one piece fiberglass synthetic stock; Williams Fire Sights; stainless steel receiver and barrel.
**MSRP**. . . . . . . . . . . . . . . . . $399.95

## MINI BOLT YOUTH
*Action*: Bolt
*Stock*: Synthetic
*Barrel*: 16.25 in.
*Sights*: Open
*Weight*: 3.25 lb.
*Caliber*: .22 LR, .22 S
*Magazine*: None
*Features*: Single-shot; one piece fiberglass synthetic stock in orange or black; Williams Fire Sights; stainless steel receiver and barrel.
**MSRP**. . . . . . . . . . . . . . . . . $249.95

# Henry Repeating Arms

## PUMP-ACTION
*Action*: Pump
*Stock*: Walnut
*Barrel*: 19.75 in.
*Sights*: Open
*Weight*: 6 lb.
*Caliber*: .22 LR, .22 S, .22 Mag.
*Magazine*: Under-barrel tube, 15-rounds (.22 LR, .22 S), 12-rounds (.22 Mag.)
*Features*: American walnut stock; adjustable rear, beaded front sight; blued octagonal barrel.
*MSRP:* . . . . . . . . . . . . . . . . . . . $515
*Mag:* . . . . . . . . . . . . . . . . . . . $595

## MARE'S LEG
*Action*: Lever
*Stock*: Walnut
*Barrel*: 12.9 in.
*Sights*: Open
*Weight*: .4.45 lb. (.22 S/L/LR), 5.79 lb. (.45 Colt)
*Caliber*: .22 S/L/LR, .45 Colt

*Magazine*: Under-barrel tube, 10-rounds (.22 S/L/LR); 5-rounds (.45 Colt)
*Features*: .45 colt: American walnut; marbles fully adjustable semi-buck-horn rear, with reversible white diamond insert and brass beaded front sights; brasslite receiver, brass buttplate and blued barrel.
.22 S/L/ LR: American walnut; fully adjustable rear, with hooded front sight; blue metal barrel and lever.
*.22 S/L/LR:* . . . . . . . . . . . . . . . $360
*.45 Colt:* . . . . . . . . . . . . . . . . $950

## U. S. SURVIVAL
*Action*: Semi-automatic
*Stock*: ABS Plastic
*Barrel*: 16 in.
*Sights*: Open
*Weight*: 2.25 lb.
*Caliber*: .22 LR
*Magazine*: Detachable box, 8-rounds

*Features*: ABS plastic in black; adjustable rear sight, blade front sight; Teflon coated receiver and coated steel barrel.
*MSRP* . . . . . . . . . . . . . . . . . . . $275

## HENRY GOLDEN BOY "EAGLE SCOUT" TRIBUTE
*Action*: Lever
*Stock*: American walnut with Boy Scout medallion on side
*Barrel*: 20 in.
*Sights*: Adjustable semi-buckhorn rear and brass bead front
*Weight*: 6.75 lb.
*Caliber*: .22 LR and .22 short
*Magazine*: 16 round (LR) and 21 round (short)
*Features*: Nickel-plated receiver with hand engraved eagle and Boy Scout motto in 24-karat gold; brass buttplate, barrel band and receiver; blued barrel and lever.
*MSRP* . . . . . . . . . . . . . . . . . $1049.95

# Hi-Point Firearms

## 995 TS
*Action*: Blow-back autoloader
*Stock*: Black, skeleton-style, all weather molded polymer
*Barrel*: 16.5 in.

*Sights*: Ajdustable
*Weight*: 7 lb.
*Caliber*: 9mm
*Magazine*: Detachable box, 10-rounds
*Features*: Sling, swivels, and base mount included; last round lock-open

latch; multiple Picatinny rails; internal recoil buffer.
*MSRP* . . . . . . . . . . . . . . . . . . . $274

# High Standard Rifles

## HAS-15 MIL-SPEC SERIES
*Action*: Gas-operated autoloader
*Stock*: 6-position
*Barrel*: 20 in. (16 in. carbine)
*Sights*: Adjustable
*Weight*: 8 lb. (7.3 lb. carbine)
*Caliber*: 5.56 NATO or 9mm NATO

*Magazine*: Detachable box, 30-rounds
*Features*: Matte black collapsible stock, G.I. style; hard chrome bore; A2 flash holder.
*MSRP* . . . . . . . . . . . . .$862–$1237.50

HIGH STANDARD HAS-15 MIL SPEC SERIES

HOWA/ HOGUE .375 RUGER

HOWA RANCHLAND COMPACT

## HOWA/ HOGUE .375 RUGER RIFLES

*Action*: Bolt
*Stock*: Synthetic
*Barrel*: 20 in., 24 in.
*Sights*: None
*Weight*: 7.75 lb.
*Caliber*: .375 Ruger
*Magazine*: Internal box, 3-rounds
*Features*: Black or green synthetic stock; hinged floor plate; sling swivel studs; black rubber recoil pad; blued receiver, drilled and tapped for scopes.
**$658–$799**

## RANCHLAND COMPACT

*Action*: Bolt
*Stock*: Synthetic
*Barrel*: 20 in.
*Sights*: None
*Weight*: 7.15 lb.–8.75 lb.
*Caliber*: .223, .204 Ruger, .22-250 Rem., .243 Win., .308 Win., 7mm-08
*Magazine*: Internal box
*Features*: Black, green, or sand overmolded stock; includes one-piece scope rail; color match combo option includes Nikko Stirling 3-10x42 Nighteater scope, rings and one-piece base; full camo packages include Desert camo stock, nikko Stirling 3-10x42 Nighteater scope, rings and one-piece base.
**MSRP . . . . . . . . . . . . . . . $643–$768**

## HOWA/ HOGUE RIFLES

*Action*: Bolt
*Stock*: Synthetic
*Barrel*: 20 in., 22 in., 24 in.
*Sights*: None
*Weight*: 7.75 lb.
*Caliber*: Standard Blue, Stainless: .223, .204 Ruger, .22-250 Rem., .243 Win., .308 Win., 7mm-08, 6.5 x 55 SW, .25-06, .270 Win., .30-06 Magnum; Blue, Stainless: .300 Win. Mag., .375 Ruger, .338 Win. Mag., 7mm Rem. Mag.
*Magazine*: Internal box
*Features*: Stainless or blued barrel; synthetic stock comes in black, sand or green with matching Houge soft grip; recoil pad; hinged floor plate; sling; swivel studs.
**Standard Blue: . . . . . . . . . . $625–745**
**Stainless Blue: . . . . . . . . . . . . . $784**
**Magnum Blue: . . . . . . . . . $658–$784**
**Magnum Stainless: . . . . . . . . . $799**

## AMBIVARMINTER & THUMBHOLE VARMINTER

*Action*: Bolt
*Stock*: Laminate
*Barrel*: 24 in.
*Sights*: None
*Weight*: 9.9 lb.
*Caliber*: .223, .204 Ruger, .22-250 Rem., .243 Win., .308 Win.
*Magazine*: Internal box, 5-rounds
*Features*: Nutmeg or woodland stock color; optional thumbhole stock; heavy blued or stainless barrel; black recoil pad; sling swivel studs.
**Blue Barrel: . . . . . . . . . . . . . . $901**
**Stainless Barrel: . . . . . . . . . . $1019**

HOWA THUMBHOLE VARMINTER

RIFLES

# HOWA Rifles

## HOWA TALON

**Action**: Bolt
**Stock**: Thumbhole polymer and alloy
**Barrel**: 20 in., 22 in., 24 in. standard or heavy
**Sights**: Optional scope package
**Weight**: 8.3 lb. to 9.7 lb.
**Caliber**: .223 Rem. To .375 Ruger
**Magazine**: Internal box, 3- to 5-rounds
**Features**: Two-stage dual Knoxx recoil system; combo includes 4-6x44 scope; ambidextrous stock that reduces felt recoil by 70%.

HOWA TALON

Standard:................. $901    Varmint:................. $988
Magnum:................. $939    Scope packages: ..... $1050–$1152

# H-S Precision Rifles

## PRO-SERIES 2000 PHR (PROFESSINAL HUNTER RIFLE)

**Action**: Bolt
**Stock**: Synthetic
**Barrel**: 20 in., 22 in., 24 in., 26 in.
**Sights**: None
**Weight**: 7.75 lb.–8.25 lb.
**Caliber**: All popular magnum calibers up to .375 H&H and .338 Lapua
**Magazine**: Detachable box, 3- or 4-rounds
**Features**: Cheek piece and built-in recoil reduction system; steel barrel; optional muzzle brake; synthetic stock comes in a wide range of color combinations including sand, black, olive, gray, and spruce green.
**MSRP**....... $3045

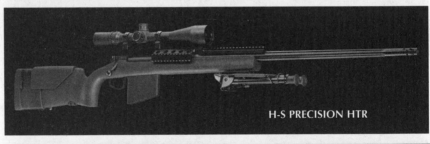

H-S PRECISION PRO-SERIES 2000 PHR

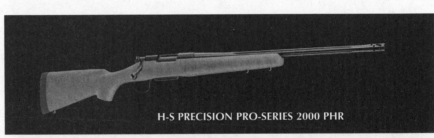

H-S PRECISION HTR

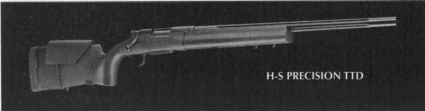

H-S PRECISION TTD

## HTR (HEAVY TACTICAL RIFLE)

**Action**: Bolt
**Stock**: Synthetic
**Barrel**: 20 in., 22 in., 24 in., 26 in.
**Sights**: None
**Weight**: 10.75 lb.–11.25 lb.
**Caliber**: Any standard SAAMI, LR calibers
**Magazine**: Detachable box, 3- or 10-rounds
**Features**: Fully adjustable synthetic stock comes in a wide range of colors combinations including sand, black, olive, gray, and spruce green; heavy fluted barrel.
**MSRP**.................. $3070

## TTD (TAKE-DOWN RIFLE)

**Action**: Bolt
**Stock**: Composite
**Barrel**: 22 in., 24 in.
**Sights**: None
**Weight**: 11.25 lb. –11.75 lb.
**Caliber**: Available in all standard SA SAAMI and LR calibers
**Magazine**: Detachable box, 3- or 4-rounds
**Features**: Stainless steel barrel and floorplate; synthetic stock with full length bedding block chassis system; metal parts are finished in matte black Teflon; wide variety of stock colors including sand, black, olive, gray, and spruce green.
**MSRP**.................. $5000

# Jarrett Custom Rifles

**JARRET ORIGINAL BEANFIELD**

**JARRET PROFESSIONAL HUNTER**

**JARRET WIND WALKER**

## ORIGINAL BEANFIELD
*Action*: Bolt
*Stock*: Synthetic
*Barrel*: Various lengths available
*Sights*: None
*Weight*: Varies depending on options
*Caliber*: Any popular standard or magnum chambering
*Magazine*: Comes with 20-rounds
*Features*: Can build rifle on any receiver provided; optional caliber, stock style, color, muzzle brake, barrel size and taper; includes load data and 20-rounds of custom ammo.
**MSRP . . . . . . . . . . starting at $5380**

## PROFESSIONAL HUNTER
*Action*: Bolt
*Stock*: Synthetic or walnut
*Barrel*: Various lengths available
*Weight*: Varies depending on options
*Caliber*: .375 H&H, .416 Rem., .416 Rigby, .450 Rigby
*Magazine*: Comes with 80-rounds
*Features*: Includes 40-rounds of soft pointed bullets and solids created custom for each gun; ballistics printout

and last three targets the gun shot also provided; optional scopes; .416 Rem. comes with Jarrett tri-lock receiver.
**MSRP . . . . . . . . . starting at $10400**

## WIND WALKER
*Action*: Bolt
*Stock*: Synthetic
*Barrel*: Up to 24 in.
*Sights*: None
*Weight*: 7.5 lb.
*Caliber*: Any popular short-action
*Magazine*: Comes with 20-rounds
*Features*: Jarrett Tri-Lock action; muzzle brake; tally scope mounting system; phenolic resin metal finish with choice of stock colors; ballistic printout included.
**MSRP . . . . . . . . . . starting at $7380**

# J.P. Sauer Rifles

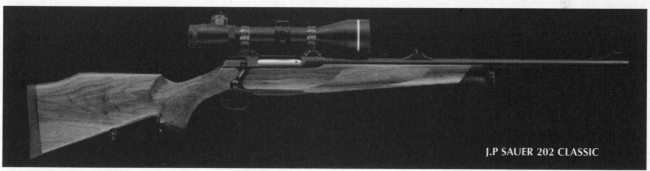

**J.P SAUER 202 CLASSIC**

## S 202 CLASSIC BOLT ACTION RIFLE
*Action*: Bolt
*Stock*: Walnut
*Barrel*: 24 in.
*Sights*: None
*Weight*: 7.7 lb.
*Caliber*: .22, .22 Mag.
*Magazine*: Detachable box, 5-round
*Features*: Features stable, dark tan walnut heart wood; Monte Carlo stock

with cheek piece; luxury wood tip on the forend and pistol grip; polymer-coated steel surface; round bolt handle.
**MSRP . . . . . . . . . . . . . . . . . . $3295**

## S 303 ELEGANCE
*Action*: Autoloading
*Stock*: Walnut
*Barrel*: 20 in., 22 in.
*Sights*: High contrast

*Weight*: 7.16 lb.–7.38 lb.
*Caliber*: .30-06, .300 Win. Mag.
*Magazine*: Detachable box, 2- or 5-rounds
*Features*: Manual cocking at the upper wrist; crisp single-stage trigger; four bolt lugs engage directly into the barrel; free floating barrel.
**MSRP . . . . . . . . . . . . . . . . . . $4498**

**RIFLES**

# Kimber Rifles

## 84M

**Action**: Bolt
**Stock**: Walnut, laminate
**Barrel**: 18 in., 22 in., 24 in.
**Sights**: None
**Weight**: 5 lb. 13 oz.–9 lb.
**Caliber**: Classic: .243 Win., .7mm-08 Rem., .308 Win.; Classic Stainless: .25-06 Rem., .270 Win., .30-06 Sprg.; Classic Select Grade: .223 Rem., .22-250 Rem., .243 Win., .257 Roberts, 7mm-08 Rem., .308 Win.; Varmint: 204 Ruger, .22-250 Rem., LongMaster Classic: .223 Rem., .308Win.; ProVarmint: .204 Ruger, .223 Rem., 22-250 Rem.; SVT: .223 Rem.

**Magazine**: Internal box; Classic, Classic Stainless: 5-rounds; Classic Select Grade, Varmint, ProVarmint, LongMaster Classic, SVT : 6-rounds
**Features**: A-grade walnut stock with checkering panel, or gray laminated stock; recoil pad; sling swivel studs; steel matte blue or satin stainless steel finish; front locking repeater; SVT model has font swivel for bipod.

| | |
|---|---|
| **Classic:** | **$1172** |
| **Classic Stainless:** | **$1223** |
| **Classic Select Grade:** | **$1359** |
| **Varmint:** | **$1255** |
| **LongMaster Classic:** | **$1255** |
| **ProVarmint:** | **$1391** |
| **SVT:** | **$1391** |

## 84M SUPER AMERICA

**Action**: Bolt
**Stock**: Walnut
**Barrel**: 22 in.
**Sights**: None
**Weight**: 5 lb. 10 oz.
**Caliber**: 7mm-08 Rem., .308 Win
**Magazine**: Internal box, 5-rounds
**Features**: AAA-grade walnut stock with checkering panel; recoil pad; sling swivel studs; highly polished blue steel; front locking repeater; adjustable trigger.
**MSRP** . . . . . . . . . . . . . . . . . . . **$2224**

KIMBER 84M CLASSIC

KIMBER 84 MONTANA

KIMBER 84 LONGMASTER VT

KIMBER 8400 WSM

## 84 MONTANA

**Action**: Bolt
**Stock**: Synthetic
**Barrel**: 22 in.
**Sights**: None
**Weight**: 5 lb. 6 oz.
**Caliber**: .204 Ruger, .223 Rem., .243 Win., .257 Roberts, 7mm-08 Rem., .308 Win., .338 Federal
**Magazine**: Internal box, 5-rounds
**Features**: Kevlar-carbon fiber stock in grey; sling swivel studs; 1-inch thick recoil pad; stainless steel barrel with satin finish; stainless steel action with front locking repeater.
**MSRP** . . . . . . . . . . . . . . . . . . . **$1312**

## LONGMASTER VT

**Action**: Bolt
**Stock**: Laminate
**Barrel**: 26 in.
**Sights**: None
**Weight**: 10 lb.
**Caliber**: .22-250 Rem.
**Magazine**: Internal box, 5-rounds
**Features**: Grey laminated stock; front swivel stud for bipod; recoil pad; stainless steel barrel with satin finish; steel action with matte blue finish.
**MSRP** . . . . . . . . . . . . . . . . . . . **$1391**

## 8400 WSM

**Action**: Bolt
**Stock**: Walnut, synthetic

**Barrel**: 24 in.Sights: None
**Weight**: 6 lb. 3 oz.–6 lb. 10 oz.
**Caliber**: .270 WSM, .300 WSM, .325 WSM; SuperAmerica: .270 WSM, .300 WSM
**Magazine**: Internal box, 3-rounds
**Features**: Stock options: A-grade walnut with checkered panels, A-grade French walnut with checkered panels, grey synthetic Kevlar-carbon fiber stock; sling swivel studs; recoil pad; steel barrel with matte blue finish or stainless steel satin finish; front locking repeater; mauser claw extractor.

| | |
|---|---|
| **Classic:** | **$1172** |
| **Classic Stainless:** | **$1223** |
| **Classic Select Grade:** | **$1359** |
| **SuperAmerica:** | **$2240** |
| **Montana:** | **$1312** |

# Kimber Rifles

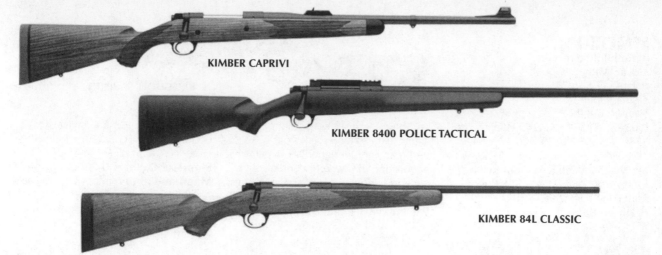

KIMBER CAPRIVI

KIMBER 8400 POLICE TACTICAL

KIMBER 84L CLASSIC

## CAPRIVI

*Action*: Bolt
*Stock*: Walnut
*Barrel*: 24 in.
*Sights*: None
*Weight*: 8 lb. 10 oz.
*Caliber*: .375 H&H Mag., .416 Rem. Mag., .458 Lott
*Magazine*: Internal box, 4-rounds
*Features*: AA-gradle walnut stock with wrap checkering; ebony forend tip; cheekpiece; double cross-bolts; sling swivel studs; front barrel band swivel stud; recoil pad; steel barrel with matte blue finish; front locking repeater; mauser claw extractor; adjustable trigger.
**MSRP** . . . . . . . . . . . . . . . . . . **$3196**

## 8400 POLICE TACTICAL

*Action*: Bolt
*Stock*: Laminate
*Barrel*: 24 in.
*Sights*: None
*Weight*: 8 lb. 12 oz.
*Caliber*: .308 Win., .300 Win. Mag.
*Magazine*: Internal box, 5-rounds
*Features*: Laminated wood stock with black epoxy finish; sling swivel studs; front swivel stud for bipod; recoil pad; steel barrel with matte blue finish; fluted bolt front locking repeater; adjustable trigger.
**MSRP** . . . . . . . . . . . . . . . . . . **$1476**

## 84L CLASSIC

*Action*: Bolt
*Stock*: Walnut (Select Grade features French walnut with ebony forend tip and hand-cut checkering)
*Barrel*: 24 in. match grade
*Sights*: None
*Weight*: 6 lb. 2 oz.
*Caliber*: .270, .30-06 (.25-06 Rem., also in 84L Classic Select Grade)
*Magazine*: Internal box, 5-rounds
*Features*: Full-length Mauser claw exactor; 1 in. Pachmayr recoil pad; full-length match-grade barrel with pillar and glass bedding; match-grade trigger and 3-position wing safety.
**MSRP** . . . . . . . . . . . . . . . . . . **$11720**

# Krieghoff Rifles

## CLASSIC STANDARD

*Action*: Hinged breech
*Stock*: Walnut
*Barrel*: 23.5 in.
*Sights*: Open
*Weight*: 7.25 lb.–8.25 lb.
*Caliber*: 7 x 57 R, 7 x 65 R, .308 Win., .30-06, 8 x 57 JRS, 8 x 75 RS, 8.5 x 75 RS, 9.3 x 74 R
*Magazine*: None
*Features*: European walnut stock with conventional rounded cheekpiece and kaiser grip; adjustable, removable muzzle wedge integrated in the front sight ramp; universal-trigger-system; combi-cocking device; ergonomically shaped "Kickspanner" manual cocking device.
**MSRP** . . . . . . . . . . . . . . . . . . **$9795**

KRIEGHOFF CLASSIC STANDARD

KRIEGHOFF CLASSIC BIG FIVE

## CLASSIC BIG FIVE

*Action*: Hinged breech
*Stock*: Walnut
*Barrel*: 23.5 in.
*Sights*: Open
*Weight*: 9.5 lb.–10.5 lb.
*Caliber*: .375 H&H Mag., .375 Flanged Magnum N.E., .450/.400 NE, .500/.416 N.E., .470 N.E., .500 N.E.
*Magazine*: None
*Features*: Double triggers; V-shaped rear sight with a white, vertical middle line and a pearl front sight; optional Super-Express sight; Monte-Carlo Style cheekpiece; European walnut stock with small game scene engraving; steel trigger and floorplate; straight comb and large recoil pad.
**MSRP** . . . . . . . . . . . . . . . . . . **$12795**

RIFLES

# Krieghoff Rifles

### SEMPRIO

**Action**: Inline repeater
**Stock**: Walnut
**Barrel**: 21.5 in., 25 in.
**Sights**: Open
**Weight**: 6.8 lb.
**Caliber**: .223 Rem., .243 Win., 6.5 x 55SE, 6.5 x 57, .270 Win., 7 x 64, .308 Win., .30-06 Spr., 8 x 57 JS, 9.3 x 62; Magnum calibers: 7mm Rem. Mag., .300 Win. Mag., .375 Ruger
**Magazine**: Detachable box
**Features**: Barrels are plasmanitrated

**KRIEGHOFF SEMPRIO**

and blued to resist corrosion; open sights feature fluorescent front bead and rear sight, designed for target acquisition in low light conditions; accepts various types of scope-mounts; Turkish walnut stock available with or without the Semprio cheek piece;

rubber recoil pad; sling swivels; optional recoil reducer; includes fitted case.

**Standard Caliber:** ......... **$4690**
**Magnum Caliber:** ......... **$4990**

# L.A.R. Rifles

### GRIZZLY BIG BOAR

**Action**: Bolt
**Stock**: Steel
**Barrel**: 36 in.
**Sights**: None
**Weight**: 30.4 lb.
**Caliber**: .50 BMG
**Magazine**: None
**Features**: Bull Pup single-shot; match grade steel barrel; steel receiver; very low recoil; thumb safety and bolt top safety; harris bipod; Weaver scope mount; leather cheeck pad; hard carry case.
**Standard Blue:** ........... **$2350**
**Parkerized:** ............. **$2450**
**Blue with Nickel Trigger Housing Finish:** .................. **$2600**

**L.A.R. GRIZZLY BIG BOAR**

**Full Nickel Finish:** ......... **$2700**
**Stainless Steel Barrel:** ...... **$2600**

### GRIZZLY T-50

**Action**: Bolt
**Stock**: Steel
**Barrel**: 32 in.–36 in.
**Sights**: None
**Weight**: 30.4 lb.

**Caliber**: .50 BMG
**Magazine**: None
**Features**: Bull Pup single-shot; steel stock; aircraft grade aluminum scope mount, bipod and monopod rails; Steel receiver; very low recoil; thumb safety and bolt stop safety; 20 MOA scope mount Picatinny rail; integrated cheek pad; hard carry case.
**MSRP**................... **$3200**

# Lazzeroni Rifles

### L2005-SLT GLOBAL HUNTER

**Action**: Bolt
**Stock**: Graphite/composite
**Barrel**: 22 in.
**Sights**: None
**Weight**: 6.1 lb.

**Caliber**: 6.17 (.243) Spitfire, 6.71 (.264) Phantom, 7.21 (284) Tomahawk, 7.82 (.308) Patriot, 8.59 Galaxy, 9.53(.375) Hellcat, 10.57 (.416) Maverick, 12.04 (.475) Lilmufu
**Magazine**: Internal box, 3-rounds
**Features**: CNC-machined 17R Stainless

steel receiver; match grade button-barrel; Jewel competition trigger; diamond-fluted bolt shaft; titanium firing pin; slim line graphite/composite stock.
**MSRP**................. **$5499.99**

# Legacy Sports International Rifles

### PUMA M-92

**Action**: Lever
**Stock**: Walnut
**Barrel**: 16 in., 20 in., 24 in.
**Sights**: Open
**Weight**: 6.6 lb.
**Caliber**: .45 Colt, .357 Mag., .44/40,

.44Mag.
**Magazine**: Tubular magazine, 16 in. round holds 9-rounds, 20 in. round holds 10-rounds, octagonal barrels hold 10-rounds
**Features**: Octagonal or round steel barrel available; walnut stock with

straight grip; crescent butt plate; Blue barrel; color case receiver; factory magazine tube plug is included limiting it to 5-rounds until removed; high grade Italian walnut stock.
**MSRP**.................$899–990

# Legacy Sports International Rifles

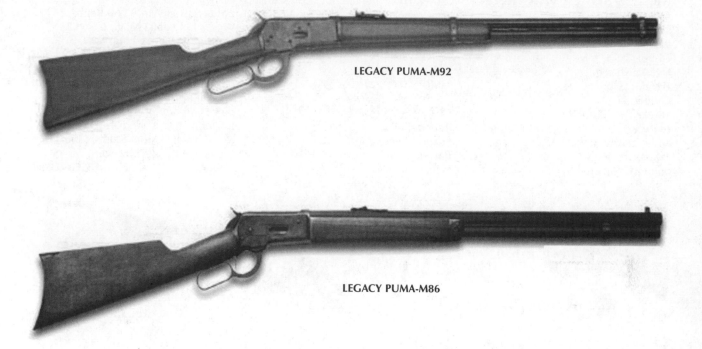

LEGACY PUMA-M92

LEGACY PUMA-M86

LEGACY .22LR SEMI-AUTO

## PUMA M-86

**Action**: Lever
**Stock**: Walnut
**Barrel**: 22 in., 26 in.
**Sights**: Open
**Weight**: 9 lb.
**Caliber**: .45-70
**Magazine**: Tubular magazine, 7- to 8-rounds
**Features**: Octagonal steel barrel; graduated rear and blade front sights; double locking lugs; high-grade Italian walnut stock; standard loop lever.
**MSRP** . . . . . . . . . . . . . . . . . . $1399

## PUMA WILDCAT .22LR SEMI-AUTO RIFLE

**Action**: Semi-automatic
**Stock**: Synthetic, wood
**Barrel**: 16 in., 20 in., 24 in.
**Sights**: Open
**Weight**: 5.5 lb.
**Caliber**: .22 LR
**Magazine**: Detachable box, 10- or 50-rounds
**Features**: Wood, black synthetic stock or new Wildcat stock; Wildcat stock has vertical forend grip and Picatinny rail; optional charging handle and detachable rail; synthetic models are bi-pod compatible with a front swivel stud.
**MSRP** . . . . . . . . . . . . . . . $519–$609

# Les Baer Rifles

### AR .223 SUPER VARMINT
**Action**: Bolt
**Stock**: Synthetic
**Barrel**: 20 in. (optional 18 in., 22 in., 24 in.)
**Sights**: None
**Weight**: 9 lb.
**Caliber**: .223
**Magazine**: 20-rounds
**Features**: Includes targets; LBC forged and precision machined upper and lower receivers; Picatinny style flat top rail; LBC National Match chromed carrier; LBC chromed bolt; LBC extractor; Geissele two-stage trigger group; adjustable free float handguard with locking ring; aluminum gas block; stainless steel barrel; Versa Pod installed.
**MSRP** . . . . . . . . . . . . . . . . . . . **$2290**

### LBC TACTICAL RECON
**Action**: Bolt
**Stock**: Synthetic
**Barrel**: 24 in.
**Sights**: None
**Weight**: 11 lb. 8 oz.
**Caliber**: .308 Win., .260 Rem., .243 Win., .338 Lapua Mag., 6.5 x .284 Norma, .300 Win. Mag.
**Magazine**: Detachable box, 5-rounds
**Features**: Optional enforcer muzzle brake; tactical-style stock in black with vertical pistol grip; adjustable cheek-piece and butt plate; Timney match trigger; match grade barrel coated in matte-black Dupont S finish; Picatinny 1-piece rail; Harris bipod.
**MSRP** . . . . . . . . . . . . . **$3560–$3890**

**LES BAER AR .223 SUPER VARMINT**

**LES BAER LBC TACTICAL RECON**

# Lone Star Rifle Co.

### SPORTING RIFLE
**Action**: Single-shot
**Stock**: Wood
**Barrel**: 28 in. to 34 in.
**Sights**: None
**Weight**: Varies on options
**Caliber**: .22 Hornet, 44-60 Sharps BN, .219 Zipper, .44-77 Sharps BN, .25-20 WCF, .44-90 Sharps St., .25-35, .44-90 Remington, Special 2.4, .30-30, .44-90 remington Special 2.6, .30-40 Krag, .45 Sporting ( .45-50 Peabody ), .32-20, .45-70, .33 Winchester, .45-90, .38-50 Hepburn, .45-100, .38-55, .45-110, .40-50 Straight, .45-120, .40-50 BN, .475 Turnbull, .40-65 Win., .50-70, .40-82 Win., .50-90, .40-90 Sharps St., .50-140, .40-90 Sharps BN, 20 Bore 1 7/8 (rifled), 20 Ga. (rifled)
**Magazine**: None
**Features**: Single-trigger, optional double-set triggers; various barrel configurations ranging from straight round, tapered round, straight octagon, tapered octagon, to 1/2 octagon 1/2 round; optional engraving; standard wood stock, upgrades optional.
**MSRP** . . . . . . . . . . . . . . . . . . . **$2495**

### BUFFALO RIFLE
**Action**: Single-shot
**Stock**: Wood
**Barrel**: 32 in.
**Sights**: Open
**Weight**: 16 lb.
**Caliber**: .50-70, .50-90
**Magazine**: None
**Features**: Period scope can be attached, includes beach combination front sight and combination rear sight; wood stock available in a variety of antique finishes; double-set triggers.
**MSRP** . . . . . . . . . . . . . . . . . . . **$3200**

**RIFLES**

**LONE STAR SPORTING RIFLE**

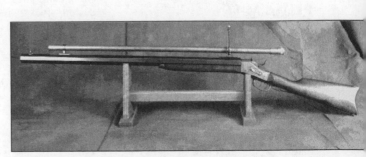
**LONE STAR BUFFALO RIFLE**

# Magnum Research Rifles

## MOUNTAIN EAGLE MAGNUM LITE GRAPHITE

*Action*: Bolt
*Stock*: Composite
*Barrel*: 24 in. Sport Tapper, 26 in. Bull
*Sights*: None
*Weight*: 7.25 lb.–9.1 lb.
*Caliber*: .30-06, .223, .308, .280, 7mm Rem. Mag., .300 Win. Mag., .22/250, .300 WSM, 7mm WSM
*Magazine*: Box, 4- or 5-rounds
*Features*: Adjustable trigger; Kevlar-graphite stock in H-S precision or Hogue OverMolded; open grip; free-floating match-grade barrel; hinged floorplate of solid steel; recoil pad; sling swivel studs; left hand available for most calibers; action has been drilled and tapped for scope.
*MSRP* . . . . . . . . . . . . . . . . . . **$2173**

## MAGNUM LITE

*Action*: Semi-automatic
*Stock*: Composite or laminate
*Barrel*: 17 in., 18 in., 19 in.
*Sights*: None
*Weight*: 4.45 lb.–7.3 lb.
*Caliber*: .22 LR, .22 Win. Mag.
*Magazine*: Box, 9- or 10-rounds
*Features*: 17 in., 19 in. models have graphite barrels; 18 in. barrels come in stainless steel; .22 Win. Mag. version has patented gas-assisted blowback operation; CNC receivers machined from aircraft aluminum; include integral Weaver-type rail for optics; heat treated steel with tight bolt face depth tolerances.
*MSRP* . . . . . . . . . . . . . . . **$665–$819**

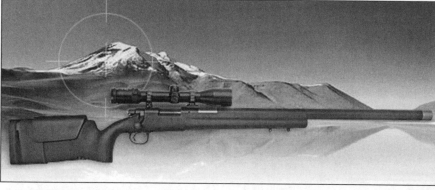

**MAGNUM RESEARCH MOUNTAIN EAGLE**

**MAGNUM RESEARCH MAGNUM LITE**

# Marlin

**MARLIN X7S**

## X7S

*Action*: Bolt
*Stock*: Synthetic
*Barrel*: 22 in.
*Sights*: None
*Weight*: 6.5 lb.
*Caliber*: Long action: .25-06 Rem., .270 Win., .30-06 Spfld.; Short-action: .243 Win., 7mm-08 Rem. and .308 Win. Compact: .243 Win., 7mm-08 Rem., .308 Win.
*Magazine*: 4+1 rounds
*Features*: Pro-fire adjustable trigger; button-fired barrel with a target-style muzzle crown; soft-tech recoil pad; stainless steel barrel and receiver; pillar-bedded black synthetic stock with raised cheek piece; Realtree APG hd stock for X7C long action version; two-position safety; red cocking indicator; fluted bolt design.
*MSRP* . . . . . . . . . . . . . . . . . . **$579.90**

# Marlin

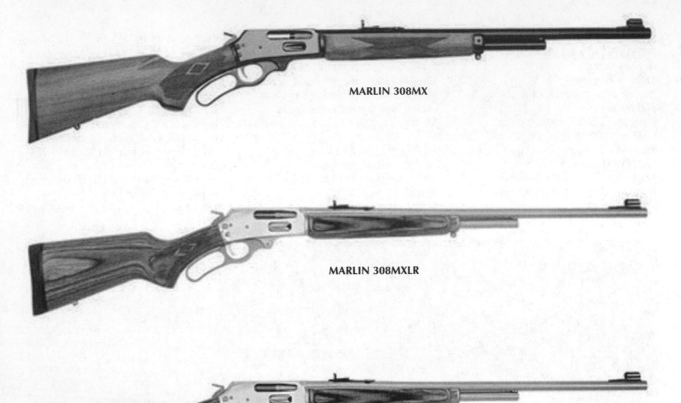

MARLIN 308MX

MARLIN 308MXLR

MARLIN 336XLR

## 308 MARLIN EXPRESS
*Action*: Lever
*Stock*: Walnut or wood laminate with pistol grip
*Barrel*: 22 in., 24 in.
*Sights*: None
*Weight*: 7 lb.
*Caliber*: .308 Marlin Express, .338 Marlin Express
*Magazine*: Tubular magazine, 5-rounds
*Features*: Hammer block safety; American black walnut stock or black/grey laminate with cut checkering; stainless steel receiver; rubber rifle butt pad; Mar-Shield finish; 338 MXLR model: adjustable semi-buckhorn folding rear and ramp front sight with brass bead and Wide-Scan hood; solid top receiver tapped for scope mount; offset hammer spur for scope use.
MSRP . . . . . . . . . . . . . . . . . . . $662.63

## 308MXLR
*Action*: Lever
*Stock*: Laminated hardwood
*Barrel*: 24 in.
*Sights*: Open
*Weight*: 7 lb.
*Caliber*: .308 Marlin Express
*Magazine*: Tubular magazine, 5-rounds
*Features*: Stainless steel receiver, barrel, lever, and trigger guard plate; black/grey laminated hardwood stock with pistol grip and checkering; deluxe recoil pad; nickel plates swivel studs; adjustable semi-buckhorn folding rear sight and brass bead front sight with Wide-Scan hood; receiver tapped for scope mount.
MSRP . . . . . . . . . . . . . . . . . . . $873.98

## 336XLR
*Action*: Lever
*Stock*: Laminated hardwood
*Barrel*: 24 in.
*Sights*: Open
*Weight*: 7 lb.
*Caliber*: .30-30
*Magazine*: Tubular magazine, 5-rounds
*Features*: Stainless steel receiver, barrel, lever, and trigger guard plate; black/grey laminated hardwood stock with pistol grip and checkering; deluxe recoil pad; nickel plates swivel studs; adjustable semi-buckhorn folding rear sight and brass bead front sight with Wide-Scan hood; receiver tapped for scope mount.
MSRP . . . . . . . . . . . . . . . . . . . $873.98

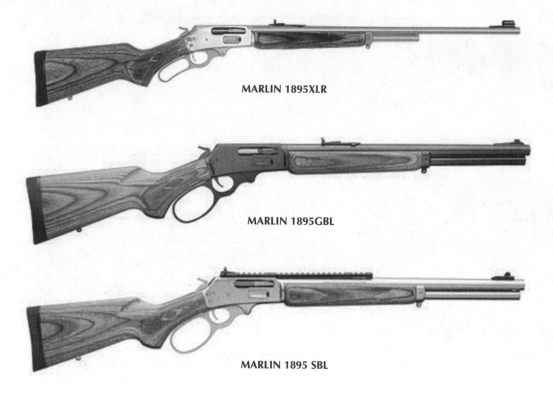

MARLIN 1895XLR

MARLIN 1895GBL

MARLIN 1895 SBL

## 1895XLR

***Action***: Lever
***Stock***: Laminated hardwood
***Barrel***: 24 in.
***Sights***: Open
***Weight***: 7.5 lb.
***Caliber***: .45-70 Govt.
***Magazine***: Tubular magazine, 4-rounds
***Features***: Stainless steel receiver, barrel, lever, and trigger guard plate; black/grey laminated hardwood stock with pistol grip and checkering; deluxe recoil pad; nickel plates swivel studs; adjustable semi-buckhorn folding rear sight and brass bead front sight with Wide-Scan hood; receiver tapped for scope mount.
***MSRP***. . . . . . . . . . . . . . . .**$874.76**

## 1895GBL

***Action***: Lever
***Stock***: Laminate
***Barrel***: 18.5 in.
***Sights***: Open
***Weight***: 7 lb.
***Caliber***: .45-70 Govt.
***Magazine***: Full length tubular

magazine, 6-rounds
***Features***: Lever action with big loop finger lever; deeply blued metal surfaces; hammer block safety; American pistol grip two tone brown laminate stock with cut checkering; ventilated recoil pad; Mar-Shield finish; swivel studs; adjustable semi-buckhorn folding rear sight and ramp front sight with brass bead; receiver tapped for scope mount; offset hammer spur for scope use.
***MSRP***. . . . . . . . . . . . . . . .**$685.21**

## CLASSIC 1895

***Action***: Lever
***Stock***: Walnut
***Barrel***: 22 in.
***Sights***: Open
***Weight***: 7.5 lb.
***Caliber***: .45-70 Govt.
***Magazine***: Tubular magazine, 4-rounds
***Features***: Deeply blued metal surfaces; hammer block safety; American black walnut pistol grip with fluted comb and cut checkering; rubber rifle butt pad; Mar-Shield finish; swivel studs; adjust-

able semi-buckhorn folding rear sight and front ramp sight with brass bead and Wide-scan hood; Model 1985 G has 18.5 in. barrel and straight grip; Model 1985 Cowboy has a 26 in. octagonal barrel and straight grip.
**Classic 1895:** . . . . . . . . . . . .**$649.43**
**1895G:** . . . . . . . . . . . . . . .**$654.01**
**1895G in Stainless Steel:** . . .**$781.34**
**1895 Cowboy:** . . . . . . . . . .**$815.28**

## 1895 SBL

***Action***: Lever
***Stock***: Laminated hardwood
***Barrel***: 18.5 in.
***Sights***: Open
***Weight***: 8 lb.
***Caliber***: .45-70 Govt.
***Magazine***: Full length tubular magazine, 6-rounds
***Features***: Lever action with big loop finger lever; deeply blued metal surfaces; stainless steel barrel and receiver; black/grey laminated hardwood with pistol-grip stock and cut checkering; fluted comb; deluxe recoil pad.
***MSRP***. . . . . . . . . . . . . . . .**$998.81**

# Marlin

MARLIN 444

MARLIN 336SS

MARLIN 1894 DELUXE

RIFLES

## 444
**Action**: Lever
**Stock**: Walnut
**Barrel**: 22 in.
**Sights**: Open
**Weight**: 7.5 lb.
**Caliber**: .444 Marlin
**Magazine**: Tubular magazine, 5-rounds
**Features**: Deeply blued metal surfaces; hammer block safety; American black walnut pistol grip with fluted comb and cut checkering; rubber rifle butt pad; tough Mar-Shield finish; swivel studs; adjustable semi-buckhorn folding rear sight and front ramp sight with brass bead.
**MSRP** . . . . . . . . . . . . . . . . . **$649.43**

## 336C
**Action**: Lever
**Stock**: Walnut
**Barrel**: 20 in.
**Sights**: Open
**Weight**: 7 lb.
**Caliber**: .30-30 Win., .35 Rem.

**Magazine**: Tubular magazine, 6-rounds
**Features**: Deeply blued surfaces; hammer block safety; American black walnut stock with pistol grip and checkering.
**MSRP** . . . . . . . . . . . . . . . . . **$572.39**

## 336SS
**Action**: Lever
**Stock**: Walnut
**Barrel**: 20 in.
**Sights**: Open
**Weight**: 7 lb.
**Caliber**: .30-30 Win., .35 Rem.
**Magazine**: Tubular magazine, 6-rounds
**Features**: Stainless steel receiver, barrel, lever and trigger guard; hammer block safety; American black walnut pistol grip stock with fluted comb and cut checkering; rubber rifle butt pad; adjustable semi-buckhorn folding rear, ramp front sight with brass bead and Wide-Scan hood; solid top receiver tapped for scope mount; offset hammer spur for scope use.
**MSRP** . . . . . . . . . . . . . . . . . **$702.44**

## M 1894 DELUXE
**Action**: Lever
**Stock**: Walnut
**Barrel**: 20 in.
**Sights**: Open
**Weight**: 6.5 lb.
**Caliber**: .44 Rem. Mag., .44 S&W Special
**Magazine**: Tubular magazine, 10-rounds
**Features**: Richly polished deep blued metal surfaces; hammer block safety; #1 grade-fancy American black walnut straight-grip stock with cut checkering; rubber rifle butt pad; tough Mar-Shield finish; blued steel forend cap; swivel studs; adjustable semi-buckhorn folding rear sight and front ramp sight with brass bead and Wide-Scan hood; solid top receiver tapped for scope mount.
**MSRP** . . . . . . . . . . . . . . . . . **$1068**

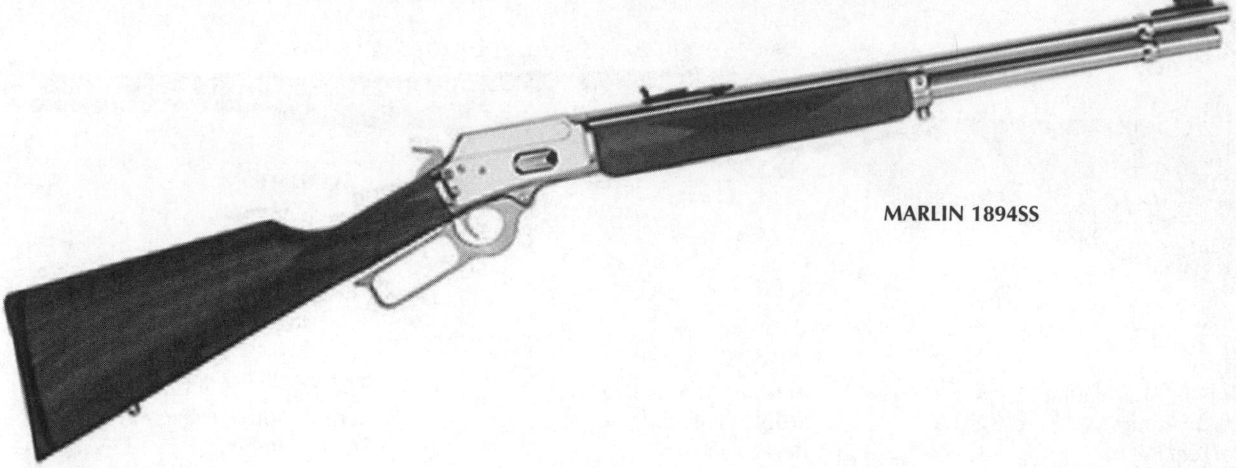

MARLIN 1894SS

## 1894SS

**Action**: Lever
**Stock**: Walnut
**Barrel**: 20 in.
**Sights**: Open
**Weight**: 6 lb.
**Caliber**: .44 Rem. Mag., .44 S&W Special
**Magazine**: Tubular magazine, 10-rounds
**Features**: Lever action with squared finger lever; stainless steel receiver, barrel and lever; straight-grip American black walnut stock with cut checkering; rubber rifle butt pad; tough Mar-Shield finish; nickel-plated steel forend cap; adjustable semi-buckhorn folding rear sight and front ramp sight with brass bead and Wide-Scan hood; solid top receiver tapped for scope mount.
**MSRP** . . . . . . . . . . . . . . . . . . .$828.94

## 1894 COWBOY

**Action**: Lever
**Stock**: Walnut
**Barrel**: 24 in.
**Sights**: Open
**Weight**: 6.5 lb.
**Caliber**: .45 Colt, .357 Mag./.38 Spl., .44 Mag./.44Spl.
**Magazine**: Tubular magazine, 10-rounds
**Features**: Lever action with squared finger lever; deeply blued metal surfaces; straight-grip American black walnut stock; hard rubber butt plate; tough Mar-Shield finish; blued steel forend cap; tapered octagon barrel; adjustable marble semi-buckhorn rear sight and marble carbine front sight; solid top receiver tapped for scope mount.
**MSRP** . . . . . . . . . . . . . . . . . .$966.69

## GOLDEN 39A

**Action**: Lever
**Stock**: Walnut
**Barrel**: 24 in.
**Sights**: Open
**Weight**: 6.5 lb.
**Caliber**: .22 S, L, LR
**Magazine**: Tubular magazine, holds 26 short, 21 long or 19 Long rifle-rounds
**Features**: Rebounding hammer; hammer safety block; one-step takedown; deeply blued metal surfaces; gold plated steel trigger; genuine American black walnut with full pistol grip and forend; blued steel forend cap; swivel studs; rubber rifle butt pad; tough Mar-Shield finish; adjustable semi-buckhorn folding rear sight and front ramp sight with brass bead and Wide-Scan hood.
**MSRP** . . . . . . . . . . . . . . . . . .$668.78

**RIFLES**

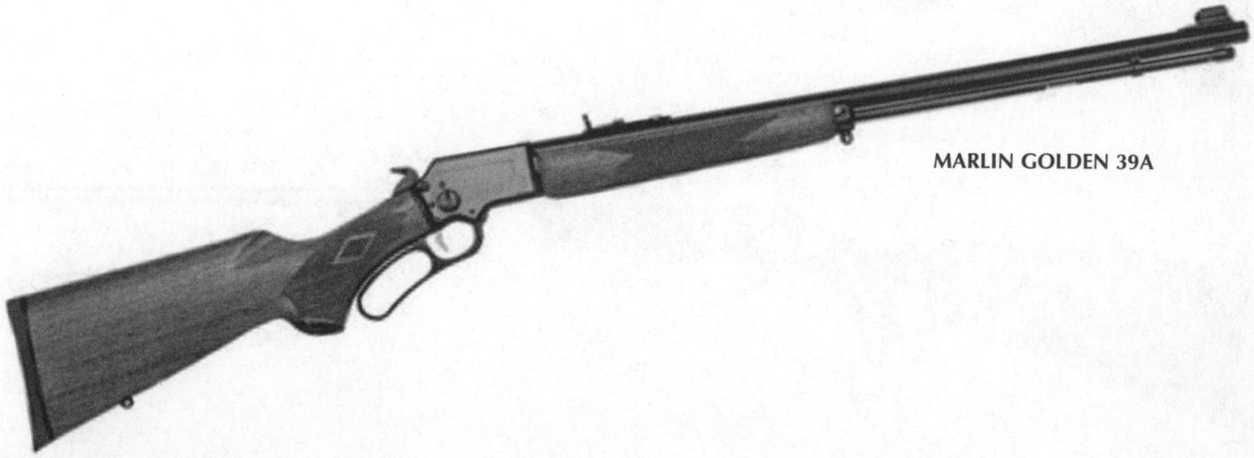

MARLIN GOLDEN 39A

# Marlin

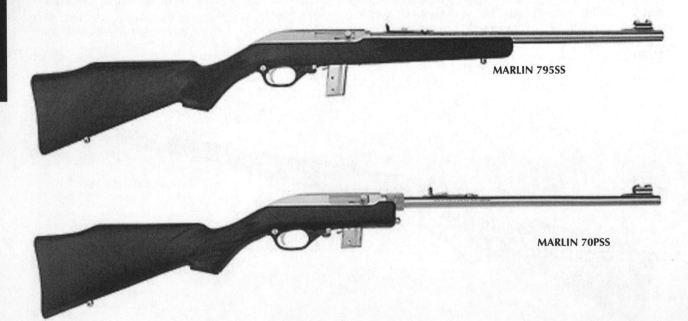

MARLIN 60

## 60

**Action**: Autoloading
**Stock**: Laminated hardwood
**Barrel**: 19 in.
**Sights**: Open
**Weight**: 5.5 lb.
**Caliber**: .22 LR
**Magazine**: Tubular magazine, 14-rounds with patented closure system
**Features**: Manual and automatic "last-shot" bolt hold-opens; receiver top has serrated, non-glare finish; cross-bolt safety; steel charging handle; Monte Carlo walnut-finished laminated hardwood; M60C comes with camoflage patterned Monte Carlo hardwood stock; full pistol grip; tough Mar-Shield finish; adjustable open rear sight, front ramp sight.
**M60**: .................. **$187.46**
**M60C**: .................. **$221.01**
**M60SB**: .................. **$237.70**

## 795SS

**Action**: Autoloading
**Stock**: Synthetic
**Barrel**: 18 in.
**Sights**: Open
**Weight**: 4.5 lb.
**Caliber**: 22 LR
**Magazine**: Clip, 10-rounds
**Features**: Automatic "last-shot" bolt hold-open, manual bolt hold-open; cross-bolt safety; Monte Carlo black fiberglass-filled synthetic with swivel studs and molded in checkering; adjustable open rear sight and front ramp sight; receiver grooved for scope mount.
**MSRP**.................. **$166.25**
**795SS**: .................. **$237.73**

## 70PSS

**Action**: Autoloading
**Stock**: Synthetic
**Barrel**: 16.25 in.
**Sights**: Open
**Weight**: 3.25 lb.
**Caliber**: .22 LR
**Magazine**: Clip, 7-rounds
**Features**: Automatic "last-shot" bolt hold-open; manual bolt hold-open; Monte Carlo black fiberglass-filled synthetic stock with abbreviated fore-end; nickel plated swivel studs; molded-in checkering; adjustable open rear sight; Front ramp sight with high visiblity orange post and cutaway Widescan hood.
**MSRP**.................. **$298.25**

MARLIN 795SS

MARLIN 70PSS

# McMillian Rifles

**MCMILLIAN CUSTOM LEGACY WITH SCOPE**

**MCMILLIAN TAC-338**

## CUSTOM HUNTING RIFLES: LEGACY
*Action*: Bolt
*Stock*: Synthetic
*Barrel*: 22 in., 24 in.
*Sights*: None
*Weight*: 6 lb. 10 oz.–7 lb.
*Caliber*: .270 Win., .308 Win., .30-06, .300 Win. Mag.
*Magazine*: Internal box
*Features*: McMillian classic sporter fiberglass stock with shadowline cheekpice; McMillian G30 custom action in long or short; match-grade stainless steel barrel, with a matte finish and target crown; custom machined one-piece aluminum hinged floorplate; custom Jewell trigger; includes scope base and travel case with rollers.
**MSRP................... $4770**

## TAC-50
*Action*: Bolt
*Stock*: Composite
*Barrel*: 29 in.
*Sights*: None
*Weight*: 26 lb.
*Caliber*: .50 BMG
*Magazine*: Detachable box
*Features*: Bipod; match-grade, stainless steel barrel; muzzle brake; anti-glare Dura Coating; square-surfaced recoil lug; extra long bolt handle; tight benchrest tolerances; saddle cheekpiece; metal finish comes in black, olive, gray, tan, or dark earth to match composite stock.
**MSRP................... $7999**

## TAC-338
*Action*: Bolt
*Stock*: Composite
*Barrel*: 26.5 in.
*Sights*: None
*Weight*: 11 lb.
*Caliber*: .338 Lapua Mag., .338 Norma Mag.
*Magazine*: Detachable box, 1- to 5-rounds
*Features*: G30 McMillan long action; hinged floorplate system; metal finish (to match stock)- black, olive, gray, tan, or dark earth; vanguard case; adjustable cheekpiece; tight benchrest tolerances; square-surfaced recoil lugs; threaded cap provided; match grade, stainless steel barrel with matte finish.
**MSRP................... $5599**

**RIFLES**

**MCMILLIAN TAC-50**

# McMillian Rifles

MCMILLIAN TUBB 2000

## LONG HUNTING RIFLE
*Action*: Bolt
*Stock*: Synthetic
*Barrel*: 24 in., 26 in., 27 in.
*Sights*: None
*Weight*: 9.5 lb.–10 lb.
*Caliber*: .243 Win., 7mm Rem. Mag., 7mm Rem. Ultra Mag., .308 Win., .300 Win. Mag., .338 Lapua Mag.
*Magazine*: Internal box
*Features*: McMillian A-3 fiberglass stock with fixed cheekpiece and recoil pad; McMillian G30 custom long or short action; match grade, stainless steel barrels with matte finish and target crown; hinged steel floorplate; Remington-style trigger; optional box magazine; comes with travel case with rollers.
**LRH .243, .308:** . . . . . . . . . . . **$4899**
**LRH 7mm, .300:** . . . . . . . . . . **$5099**
**LRH .338:** . . . . . . . . . . . . . . . **$5299**

## TUBB 2000
*Action*: Bolt
*Stock*: Synthetic
*Barrel*: Up to 30 in.
*Sights*: None
*Weight*: 12 lb.
*Caliber*: 6XC, .22-250 Rem., 7mm-08 Rem., .308, 6mm BR Rem.
*Magazine*: Box, 10- or 20-rounds
*Features*: Interchangable barrels; stainless steel receiver; full-length Picatinny sight rail; Schneider stainless steel match barrel; aluminum, anodized matte black, adjustable buttstock; disassembles into two pieces; optional bipod.
**MSRP** . . . . . . . . . . . . . . . . . . **$5000**

## 50 LBR
*Action*: Bolt
*Stock*: Synthetic
*Barrel*: 32in
*Sights*: None
*Weight*: 28 lb.
*Caliber*: .50
*Magazine*: Internal box
*Features*: McMillian 50 LBR stock in orange and grey marbling; fluted match barrel with McMillian BR muzzle brake and precision target crown; pillar-bedded action; adjustable Jewell trigger.
**MSRP** . . . . . . . . . . . . . . . . . **$7499**

MCMILLIAN 50 LBR

# McMillian Rifles

MCMILLIAN 40A1

## 40A1
**Action**: Bolt
**Stock**: Composite
**Barrel**: 24 in.
**Sights**: Open
**Weight**: 14.48 lb.
**Caliber**: .308 Win. (7.62 NATO)
**Magazine**: Internal box

**Features**: Steel tubed MST-100 10x scope; Remington trigger; Remington 700 action; McMillan plain HTG stock with molded-in Forest camo; Schneider steel barrels with recessed target crown.
**MSRP** . . . . . . . . . . . . . . . . . . **$8541**

# Merkel

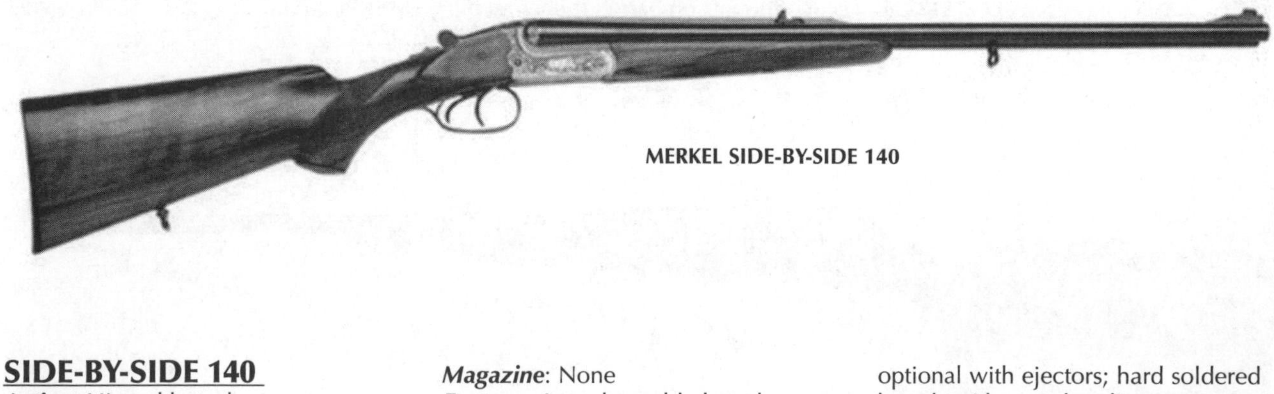

MERKEL SIDE-BY-SIDE 140

## SIDE-BY-SIDE 140
**Action**: Hinged breech
**Stock**: Wood
**Barrel**: 23.6 in.
**Sights**: None
**Weight**: 7.5 lb.
**Caliber**: 7 x 65 R, .30-06, .30 R Blaser, 8 x 57 IRS, 9mm, 3 x 74 R

**Magazine**: None
**Features**: Interchangable barrel options; Anson & Deeley locks; steel action; Greener-style cross bolt and double bottom bite; double-trigger with front set trigger, optional single trigger; automatic trigger safety; optional with ejectors; hard soldered barrels with muzzle adjustment; engraving English arabesque or game scene "JAGD"; rubber butt plate; pistol grip; cheekpiece and hogback comb.
**MSRP** . . . . . . . . . . . . . . . . . . **$11995**

# Merkel

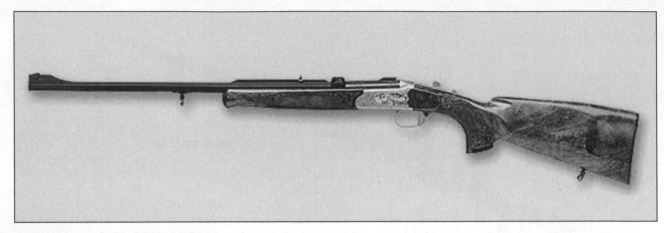

MERKEL AFRICAN SAFARI SERIES M401-2.1

## AFRICAN SAFARI SERIES DOUBLE RIFLE 140-2.1

*Action*: Boxlock
*Stock*: Walnut
*Barrel*: 23.6 in.
*Sights*: Bead front, four-leaf express rear
*Weight*: 10.5 lb.
*Caliber*: .470 NE, .375 H&H, .450/400, .500 NE
*Magazine*: None
*Features*: Classic styling with cheekiece, half-luxus Turkish walnut; hand-engraved, English-style arabesque, gold relief Cape buffalo, tapered, octagonal barrel with rust blue finish.
**MSRP** . . . . . . . . . . . . . . . . . **$12595**

## KR1 SINGLE SHOT RIFLE

*Action*: Bolt
*Stock*: Walnut with hogback comb and Bavarian cheekpiece
*Barrel*: 22.2 in.
*Sights*: None
*Weight*: 6.4 lb.
*Caliber*: .223 Rem., .243 Rem., .270, 30/60, .308, 6.5 x 55, 7mm Rem., 7mm Rem. Mag., .300 Mag., 9.3 x 62
*Magazine*: 3-rounds (short mag. 2-rounds)
*Features*: Short-stroke bolt action; modular design allows for quick disassembly for transport or change of caliber; disassembly has no effect on point of impact; left hand versions available; scope mounts on barrel; rubber recoil pad.
**MSRP** . . . . . . . . . . . . . . . . . **$2595**

## B3 OVER-AND-UNDER RIFLE

*Action*: Over/under
*Stock*: Checkered walnut
*Barrel*: 21.6 in.
*Sights*: Driven-hunt sight with integrated light elements
*Weight*: 6.4 lb.
*Caliber*: .30-06, .30R Blaser, 8 x 57IRS, 9.3 x 74 R
*Magazine*: None
*Features*: Short, light, and responsive; manual cocking mechanism; tilting breech block can be removed without tools; adjustable single-trigger; pistol grip; cheekpiece and hogback comb; rubber butt pad.
**MSRP** . . . . . . . . . . . . . **$5495–$6495**

MERKEL KR1

# Mossberg

## 464 LEVER-ACTION RIFLE

*Action*: Lever
*Stock*: Walnut
*Barrel*: 18 in., 20 in.
*Sights*: Adjustable rifle sights
*Weight*: 5.5 lb.–6.75 lb.
*Caliber*: .33
*Magazine*: 18 in. 14-rounds, 20 in. 7-rounds
*Features*: Adjustable rifle sights; 18 in. model has dovetail receiver; drilled and tapped for scope; walnut stock with optional pistol grip.
**18in:. . . . . . . . . . . . . . . . . . . . $468**
**20in:. . . . . . . . . . . . . . . . $479–$535**

## 4X4 BOLT-ACTION CENTERFIRE RIFLE

*Action*: Bolt
*Stock*: Synthetic
*Barrel*: 24 in.
*Sights*: None
*Weight*: 6.75 lb.
*Caliber*: .25-06 Rem.
*Magazine*: Detachable box, Standard: 5-rounds; Magnum: 4-rounds
*Features*: Classic style, grey laminate stock in Marinecote finish; free-floating, fluted, button rifled barrel with muzzle brake; scoped combos available.
**MSRP . . . . . . . . . . . . . . . . . . . $652**

## 100ATR BOLT-ACTION

*Action*: Bolt
*Stock*: Synthetic
*Barrel*: 22 in.
*Sights*: None
*Weight*: 6.75 lb.–7 lb.
*Caliber*: .270 Win., .30-06, .243 Win., .308 Win.
*Magazine*: Top loading magazine, 4+1 rounds
*Features*: Integral synthetic trigger guard; Weaver-style scope bases; integral swivel studs; free-floating, button-rifled barrels; recessed muzzle crown; barrel finishes include matte blued or Marincote; rugged synthetic stocks include black, camo, and synthetic walnut finshes; rubber recoil pad; free gunlock.
**MSRP . . . . . . . . . . . . . . . $424–$471**

**MOSSBERG 464 LEVER-ACTION RIFLE**

**MOSSBERG 4X4**

RIFLES

Rifles • 189

# Mossberg

### TACTICAL .22 AUTOLOADER

*Action*: Autoloader
*Stock*: Synthetic
*Barrel*: 18 in.
*Sights*: Open
*Weight*: 5 lb.
*Caliber*: .22 LR
*Magazine*: Detachable box, 10- or 25-rounds
*Features*: Integrated A2-style carry handle; rear sight and front post; optional handle mount Picatinny rail; bulled finish barrel; quad-rail forend; adjustable black synthetic stock.
**MSRP**.....................**$276**

### 802 PLINKSTER BOLT-ACTION

*Action*: Bolt
*Stock*: Synthetic or wood
*Barrel*: 18 in., 21 in.
*Sights*: Adjustable rifle sights
*Weight*: 4.1 lb. to 4.6 lb.
*Caliber*: .22 LR
*Magazine*: Detachable magazine, 11-rounds
*Features*: Stock comes in black, pink, or marble pink finish synthetic and wood; receiver grooved to accept ³/₈ in. scope mounts; cross bolt safety and magazine release buttons; free float barrel with blued or brushed chrome finish; includes free gun lock.
**MSRP**.................**$171–$199**

### 817 BOLT-ACTION

*Action*: Bolt
*Stock*: Synthetic or wood
*Barrel*: 21 in.
*Sights*: None
*Weight*: 4.5 lb.–7.5 lb.
*Caliber*: .17 HMR
*Magazine*: Detachable box, 5-rounds
*Features*: Factory mounted Weaver-style scope bases; cross bolt safety and magazine release buttons; free gun lock included; stock available in black, synthetic, or wood; metal finishes include blue or brushed chrome; optional scope; optional muzzle brake.
**MSRP**.................**$190–$364**

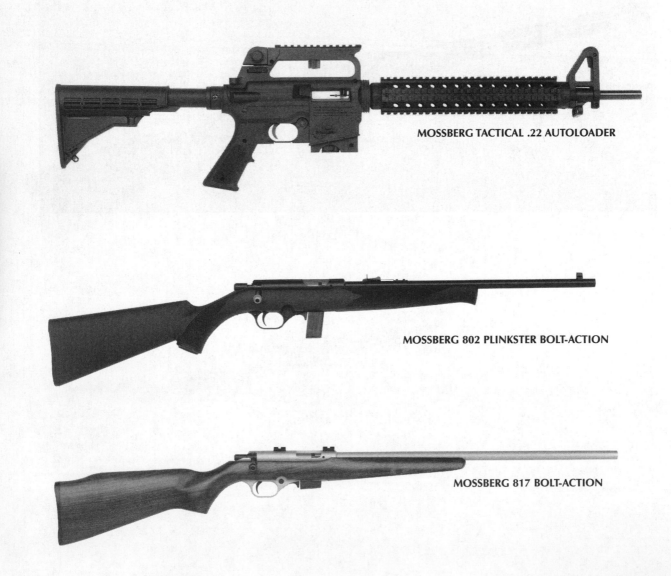

MOSSBERG TACTICAL .22 AUTOLOADER

MOSSBERG 802 PLINKSTER BOLT-ACTION

MOSSBERG 817 BOLT-ACTION

RIFLES

# Navy Arms

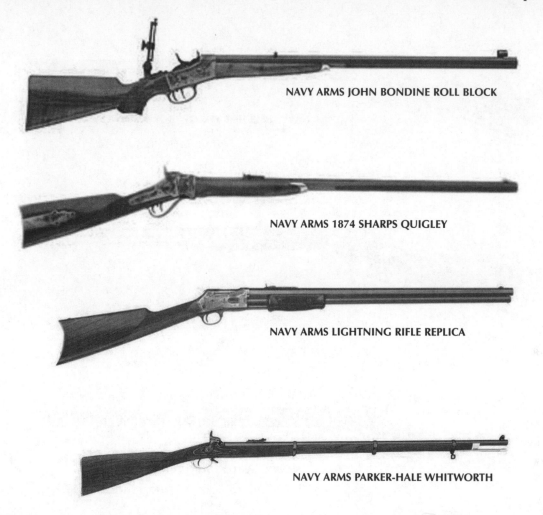

NAVY ARMS JOHN BONDINE ROLL BLOCK

NAVY ARMS 1874 SHARPS QUIGLEY

NAVY ARMS LIGHTNING RIFLE REPLICA

NAVY ARMS PARKER-HALE WHITWORTH

## LIGHTING RIFLE REPLICA

**Action**: Pump
**Stock**: Walnut
**Barrel**: 24 in.
**Sights**: None
**Weight**: 6 lb. 13 oz.
**Caliber**: .357 Mag., .45 Colt, .44-44
**Magazine**: 10-rounds
**Features**: Wood stock features checkered wrists and forends; color case hardened finish; tangs drilled for peep sights; gold bead front sight and smeibuckhorn rear sight; octagonal barrel.
**MSRP** . . . . . . . . . . . . . . . . . . . **$1399**

## JOHN BODINE ROLLING BLOCK

**Action**: Rolling block
**Stock**: Walnut
**Barrel**: 30 in.
**Sights**: Open

**Weight**: 9 lb.
**Caliber**: .45-70 Govt.
**Magazine**: None
**Features**: Double-set trigger; Named for famed shooter from 1800's; Heavy matte finished octagon barrel; "Soule" target rear tang sight; barrel mounted spirit level; globe front sight with interchangable inserts.
**MSRP** . . . . . . . . . . . . . . . . . . . **$1940**

## 1874 SHARPS QUIGLEY

**Action**: Dropping block
**Stock**: Walnut
**Barrel**: 34 in.
**Sights**: None
**Weight**: 13 lb.
**Caliber**: .45-70 Govt.
**Magazine**: None
**Features**: Chrome Vanadium steel forgings; reproduction from movie

"*Quigley Down Under*". Military patchbox; heavy octagonal barrel.
**MSRP** . . . . . . . . . . . . . . . . . . . **$1981**

## PARKER-HALE WHITWORTH

**Action**: Muzzleloading
**Stock**: Walnut
**Barrel**: 36 in.
**Sights**: Open
**Weight**: 10.5 lb.
**Caliber**: .45
**Magazine**: None
**Features**: Hexagonal rifling; walnut stock with checkered wrist and forearm; blued tapered, round barrel; front sight is a blued steel globe with bead post; steel rear sight.
**MSRP** . . . . . . . . . . . . . . . . . . . **$1550**

# Navy Arms

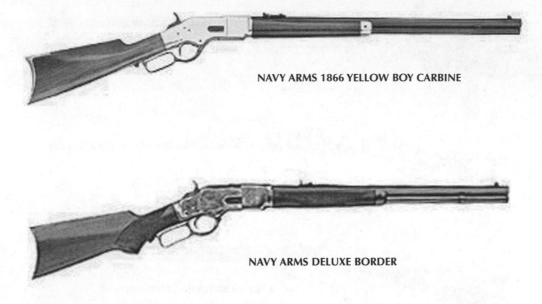

NAVY ARMS 1866 YELLOW BOY CARBINE

NAVY ARMS DELUXE BORDER

NAVY ARMS 1873 WINCHESTER-STYLE

## 1866 YELLOW BOY CARBINE
*Action*: Lever
*Stock*: Walnut
*Barrel*: 19 in.
*Sights*: Open
*Weight*: 7 lb. 4 oz.
*Caliber*: .38 Spl., .44-40, .45 Colt
*Magazine*: Under barrel tube
*Features*: Saddle ring carbine; round barrel; polished brass receiver.
**MSRP** . . . . . . . . . . . . . . . . . . . . **$972**

## 1873 DELUXE BORDER RIFLE
*Action*: Lever
*Stock*: Walnut
*Barrel*: 20 in.
*Sights*: Open
*Weight*: 7 lb. 6 oz.
*Caliber*: .357 Mag., .44-40, .45 Colt
*Magazine*: None
*Features*: Octagonal barrel; walnut stock with a checkered wrist, pistol grip buttstock and forend; blued barrel; color case-hardened receiver.
**MSRP** . . . . . . . . . . . . . . . . . . **$1241**

## 1873 WINCHESTER-STYLE RIFLE
*Action*: Lever
*Stock*: Walnut
*Barrel*: 24.25 in.
*Sights*: Open
*Weight*: 8 lb. 4 oz.
*Caliber*: .357 Mag., .44-40, .45 Colt
*Magazine*: None
*Features*: Lush case-hardened receiver; full octagon barrel; walnut stocks.
**MSRP** . . . . . . . . . . . . . . . . . . **$1132**

NEW ENGLAND SURVIVOR

## SYNTHETIC HANDI-RIFLE

**Action**: Hinged breech
**Stock**: Synthetic
**Barrel**: 22 in.
**Sights**: Open
**Weight**: 7 lb.
**Caliber**: .22 Hornet, .45-70, 44 Mag., .357 Mag., .444 Marlin, .233 Rem., .243 Win., .270 Win., .30-60 Spfld.
**Magazine**: None
**Features**: High-density polymer, black matte finish stock; optional Monte Carlo stock; sling swivel studs; recoil pad; ramp front sight, fully adjustable rear sight; receiver is tapped for scope mount.
**MSRP** . . . . . . . . . . **$274.88–$341.12**

## SPORTSTER

**Action**: Hinged breech
**Stock**: Polymer
**Barrel**: 20 in.
**Sights**: Open
**Weight**: 5.5 lb.
**Caliber**: .22 S, L, LR; .22 WMR
**Magazine**: None
**Features**: Single shot, break-open action with side lever release; high-density polymer, pistol grip, black matte finish, sling swivel studs, recoil pad.
**MSRP** . . . . . . . . . . . . . . . . . **$171.51**
**.22 in. Bull Barrel model:** . . . **$205.77**

## SURVIVOR

**Action**: Hinged breech
**Stock**: Polymer
**Barrel**: 22 in., 24 in.
**Sights**: None
**Weight**: 6.5 lb.
**Caliber**: .223 Rem., .308 Win.
**Magazine**: None
**Features**: Bull Barrel with blued finish; high-density polymer stock with black matte finish, thumbhole design; butt stock storage compartment; sling swivel studs and sling.
**MSRP** . . . . . . . . . . . . . . . . . **$326.55**

NEW ENGLAND SYNTHETIC HANDI-RIFLE

NEW ENGLAND SPORTSTER

RIFLES

# New Ultra Light Arms Rifles

**NEW ULTRA LIGHT 209 MUZZLELOADER**

**NEW ULTRA LIGHT 20 MOUNTAIN RIFLE**

## 209 MUZZLELOADER

**Action**: Bolt
**Stock**: Kevlar/graphite composite
**Barrel**: 24 in.
**Sights**: None
**Weight**: 4.9 lb.
**Caliber**: .45, .50
**Magazine**: None
**Features**: Adjustable Timney trigger; postive primer extraction; button-rifled barrel; Kevlar/ graphite stock comes in various colors; recoil pad; sling swivels; ULA scope mounts; hard case.
**MSRP** . . . . . . . . . . . . . . . . . $1300

## 20 MOUNTAIN RIFLE

**Action**: Bolt
**Stock**: Kevlar/graphite composite
**Barrel**: 22 in.
**Sights**: None
**Weight**: 5 lb.
**Caliber**: .308, .243 Win., 6mm Rem., .257 Roberts, 7mm-08, .284
**Magazine**: Detachable box
**Features**: Available in left hand; choice of stock colors; 20 oz. action; two-position safety.
**MSRP** . . . . . . . . . . . . . . . . . . $3000
**Left handed model:** . . . . . . . . $3100

## 20 RIMFIRE

**Action**: Bolt
**Stock**: Kevlar/graphite composite
**Barrel**: 22 in.
**Sights**: None
**Weight**: 5.25 lb.
**Caliber**: .22 LR
**Magazine**: None or detachable box, 5-rounds
**Features**: Single-shot or repeater; drilled and tapped for scope; recoil pad; sling swivels; color stock options.
**Single shot:** . . . . . . . . . . . . . . $1300
**Repeater:** . . . . . . . . . . . . . . . . $1350

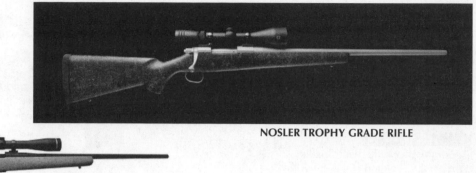

**NOSLER TROPHY GRADE RIFLE**

**NOSLER M48 VARMINT**

**NOSLER M48 LEGACY**

**NOSLER CUSTOM RIFLE**

## M48 TROPHY GRADE RIFLE

*Action*: Bolt
*Stock*: Composite
*Barrel*: 24 in.
*Sights*: None
*Weight*: 6.5 lb.–7.5 lb.
*Caliber*: Short: .243 Win., .257 Roberts +P, .270 WSM, 7mm-08 Rem., .308 Win., .300 WSM, .325 WSM. Long: .270 Win., .280 Ack Imp, .7mm Rem. Mag., .308 Win., .30-06 Spglfd., .300 Win. Mag., .338 Win. Mag., .35 Whelen
*Magazine*: Internal box, 3- or 4-rounds
*Features*: Custom aluminum-bedded Bell and Carson composite stock in black with grey; Pachmayr decelerator; recoil pad; sling swivel studs; Nosler Custom Action with standard scope mount; match-grade Pac-Nor chrome moly barrel; two-position safety; Basix trigger.
**MSRP** . . . . . . . . . . . . . . . . . . . **$1795**

## M48 LEGACY

*Action*: Bolt
*Stock*: Walnut
*Barrel*: 24 in.
*Sights*: None
*Weight*: 7.5 lb.–8 lb.
*Caliber*: Short: .257 Roberts +P, .308 Win., .300 Win. Mag.; Long: .270 Win., .280 Ack Imp, .30-06 Spgfld, .388 Win. Mag., .35 Whelen
*Magazine*: Internal box, 3- or 4-rounds
*Features*: Model 48 action; hand lapped Pac-Nor match-grade chrome moly, fully free-floated barrel; hinged floorplate; custom rifle Basix trigger; Hand oiled black-walnut with 20 LPI checkering; classic American-styled stock with shadow-line cheekpiece; glass-pillar bedded; sling swivel studs; pachmayr decelerator recoil pad.
**MSRP** . . . . . . . . . . . . . . . . . . . **$2195**

## M48 CUSTOM VARMINT

*Action*: Bolt
*Stock*: Composite
*Barrel*: 24 in.
*Sights*: None
*Weight*: 7.25 lb.
*Caliber*: .204 Ruger, .223 Rem., .22-250 Rem.
*Magazine*: Interal box, 4-rounds
*Features*: Coyote Tan stock with slate metal finish; rifle Basix trigger; glass pillar-bedded Kevlar and carbon-fiber stock with Teflon overcoat; match-grade stainless Pac-Nor, full free-floated hand lapped barrel.
**MSRP** . . . . . . . . . . . . . . . . . . . **$2995**

## NOSLER CUSTOM RIFLE

*Action*: Bolt
*Stock*: Walnut
*Barrel*: 24 in., 24.75 in.
*Sights*: Open
*Weight*: 8.25 lb.–8.75 lb.
*Caliber*: .300 WSM, .280 Ack Imp, .338 Win. Mag.
*Magazine*: Internal box, 3- or 4-rounds
*Features*: Leupold Custom Shop; match-grade stainless, fully free-floated hand lapped barrel; 3-stage safety; glass pillar-bedded fancy walnut stock; custom case cruzer by Pelican; custom leather sling.
**MSRP** . . . . . . . . . . . . . . . . . . . **$4195**

RIFLES

# Olympic Arms

**OLYMPIC GAMESTALKER**

## GAMESTALKER

**Action**: Gas-operated autoloader
**Stock**: ACE Skeleton stock in camo
**Barrel**: 22 in. stainless fluted
**Sights**: None
**Weight**: 7.5 lb.
**Caliber**: .243 WSSM, .25 WSSM, .300

OSSM
**Magazine**: Detachable box, 5-rounds
**Features**: Flat-top upper receiver; free-

floating aluminum handguard; ERGO grip; Picatinny rail.
**MSRP** . . . . . . . . . . . . . . . . . . . **$1359**

# Pedersoli Replica

**PEDERSOLI 1763 LEGER CHARLESVILLE**

**PEDERSOLI KODIAK MARK IV**

## 1763 LEGER (1766) CHARLEVILLE

**Action**: Dropping block
**Stock**: Walnut
**Barrel**: 44.7 in.
**Sights**: Open
**Weight**: 10.13 lb.
**Caliber**: .69
**Magazine**: None

**Features**: Creedmoor sight; tunnel front sight; Replica of French infantry musket.
**MSRP** . . . . . . . . . . . . . . . . . . **$1429**

## KODIAK MARK IV

**Action**: Breech loading
**Stock**: Walnut
**Barrel**: 22 in., 24 in.

**Sights**: Open
**Weight**: 9.69 lb.–10.3 lb.
**Caliber**: .45-70; 8 x 57 JRS; 3 x 74 R
**Magazine**: None
**Features**: Double-leaf rear sight in a dovetail; tapered round barrels made of blued steel; select walnut stock with checkering and oil finish.
**MSRP** . . . . . . . . . . . . . . **$5320–$7615**

RIFLES

# Pedersoli Replica

PEDERSOLI 1874 OLD WEST MAPLE

## 1874 SHARPS OLD WEST MAPLE

**Action**: Dropping block
**Stock**: Maple
**Barrel**: 30 in.
**Sights**: None
**Weight**: 11.43 lb.
**Caliber**: .45-70
**Magazine**: None

**Features**: Optional Creedmoor and tunnel sights; brass plate on right side of butt stock can be personalized; forend has wedge plates; pistol grip cap is made of hardened steel.
**MSRP**. . . . . . . . . . . . . . . . . . $2122

PEDERSOLI ROLLING BLOCK TARGET

## ROLLING BLOCK TARGET

**Action**: Dropping block
**Stock**: Walnut
**Barrel**: 30 in.
**Sights**: Open
**Weight**: 10.57 lb.
**Caliber**: .357 Mag., .45-70
**Magazine**: None
**Features**: Octagonal, conical blued barrel; case hardened color frame is equipped with ramp rear sight adjust-

able in elevation; steel butt plate and trigger guard; straight stock and forend made of walnut with oil finish.
**MSRP**. . . . . . . . . . . . . . . . . . $1088

# PGW Defence Technology Rifles

**PGW TIMBERWOLF 338 WITH SUPPRESSOR**

## TIMBERWOLF
*Action*: Bolt
*Stock*: Fiberglass
*Barrel*: 26 in.
*Sights*: None
*Weight*: 15 lb.
*Caliber*: .338 SWS
*Magazine*: 5-rounds
*Features*: Stainless steel Receiver and

bolt; muzzle brake;  3 position safety; 1913 Picatinny rail; A5 fiberglass stock in molded camo; suppressor.
**MSRP** . . . . . . . . . . . . . . . . **$7079.43**

## COYOTE
*Action*: Bolt
*Stock*: Fiberglass
*Barrel*: 24 in.

*Sights*: None
*Weight*: 13.5 lb.
*Caliber*: 7.62 SWS
*Magazine*: 8-rounds
*Features*: Stainless steel receiver and bolt; muzzle brake;  3position safety; 1913 Picatinny rail; A5 fiberglass stock in molded camo; suppressor.
**MSRP** . . . . . . . . . . . . . . . . **$5562.41**

# Puma Rifles

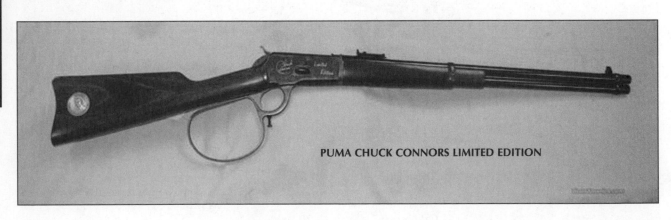

**PUMA CHUCK CONNORS LIMITED EDITION**

## M1892-CHUCK CONNORS LIMITED EDITION
*Action*: Lever
*Stock*: Walnut
*Barrel*: 20 in.
*Sights*: Open

*Weight*: 6.5 lb.
*Caliber*: .45-40
*Magazine*: Full-length tube
*Features*: Limited edition made in Italy by Chiappa Firearms, imported by Legacy Sports. The rifle commemorates the popular 1950s TV show *The*

*Rifleman*. Large loop with set screw in trigger guard; Chuck Connor's signature etched on receiver and laser engraved on stock.
**MSRP** . . . . . . . . . . . . . . . . . . **$1299**

# Purdey Rifles

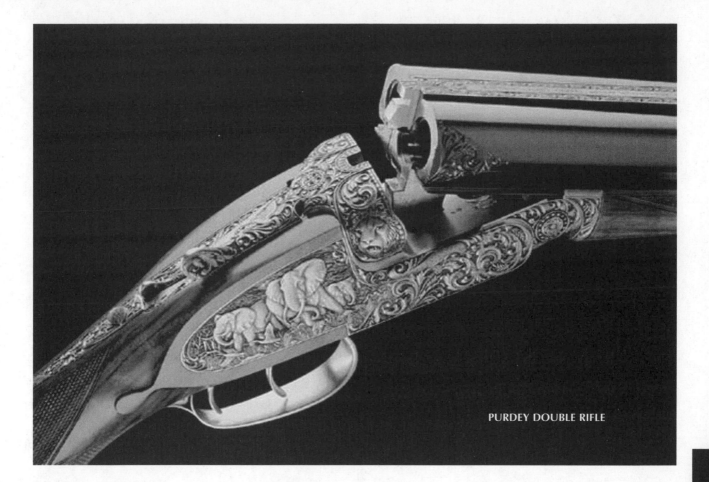

PURDEY DOUBLE RIFLE

## DOUBLE RIFLES

*Action*: Self-opening
*Stock*: Walnut
*Barrel*: 23 in. to 26 in.
*Sights*: Open
*Weight*: 12 lb. 4 oz.
*Caliber*: .375,.416 .470, .475, .500 .577, .600
*Magazine*: None
*Features*: Hinged front trigger; bolted non-qutomatic safety catch; sling Swivels optional; full pistol grip; cheek piece and leather-covered recoil pad; chopper lump barrel construction; express rear sights with bead foresight with flip-up moonsight; optional beavertail forend and telescopic sights.

.375 or smaller: . . . . . . . . .$146033
.416, .470, .475, .500: . . . . .$159941
.557, .600: . . . . . . . . . . . . .$174657

## BOLT ACTION RIFLES

*Action*: Bolt
*Stock*: Walnut
*Barrel*: 25 in.
*Sights*: Open
*Weight*: 10 lb. 8 oz.
*Caliber*: .375 H&H, 7mm Mag.
*Magazine*: None
*Features*: Original Mauser '98 or modern Mauser-type magnum square bridge; model 70 type safety catch for use with telescopic sights; quick detachable claw or Purdey rail mounts depending on type of action and telescopic sight chosen; Purdey's rail mount system with integral recoil bar; Turkish walnut stock with pistol grip; cheek piece and rubber recoil pad; single-trigger.

**Original Mauser Action: . . . $38827**
**Magnum Square Bridge Action (.375 caliber & above): . . . . . . . . . $41253**

RIFLES

# Remington Arms

### R-15 450 BUSHMASTER

*Action*: Semi-automatic, gas action
*Stock*: Synthetic
*Barrel*: 18 in., 22 in.
*Sights*: None
*Weight*: 7.5 lb.–7.75 lb.
*Caliber*: .450 Bushmaster, .30 Rem. AR
*Magazine*: Detachable box, 4-rounds
*Features*: Free-floated, fluted barrel; clean-breaking single-stage trigger; receiver length Picatinny rail; aluminum receiver; synthetic Full Mossy Oak camo stock with ergonomic pistol grip; lockable hard case included.
*MSRP* . . . . . . . . . . . . . . . . . $1276

### R-25

*Action*: Semi-automatic, gas action
*Stock*: Synthetic
*Barrel*: 20 in.
*Sights*: None
*Weight*: 8.75 lb.
*Caliber*: .308 Win., .243 Win., 7mm-08 Remington
*Magazine*: Detachable box, 4 rounds
*Features*: Free-floated, fluted barrel; clean-breaking single-stage trigger; receiver length Picatinny rail; aluminum receiver; synthetic Full Mossy Oak camo stock with ergonomic pistol grip; lockable hard case included.
*MSRP* . . . . . . . . . . . . . . . . . $1631

### 750 WOODSMASTER

*Action*: Semi-automatic, gas action
*Stock*: Walnut, synthetic
*Barrel*: 22 in.
*Sights*: Open
*Weight*: 7.5 lb.
*Caliber*: .270 Win., .30-06 Spfd., .308 Win., .243 Win.
*Magazine*: None
*Features*: American walnut or black synthetic stock and forend; iron sights; receiver drilled and tapped for model 7400 scope mounts; rotary-bolt lock-up; sling swivel studs.
*MSRP* . . . . . . . . . . . . . . . . . $1004

REMINGTON R15 450 BUSHMASTER WITH SCOPE

REMINGTON R-25 RIFLE

REMINGTON 750 WOODSMASTER

RIFLES

# Remington Arms

**REMINGTON 700 VTR A-TACS**

**REMINGTON 700 SPS TACTICAL**

**REMINGTON 700 XCR II**

## 700 VTR A-TACS

*Action*: Bolt
*Stock*: Synthetic or laminate
*Barrel*: 22 in.
*Sights*: None
*Weight*: 7 lb. 1 oz.
*Caliber*: .223 Rem., .308 Win.
*Magazine*: 4-rounds
*Features*: Triangular barrel design; A-TACS camo pattern on synthetic or laminate stock; integral muzzle brake; vents in forend for quick cooling; X-Mark Pro adjustable trigger; dual front swivel studs; concave target-style barrel crown; SuperCell recoil pad.
**MSRP** . . . . . . . . . . . . . . . . . . . . $930

## 700 SPS TACTICAL

*Action*: Bolt
*Stock*: Synthetic
*Barrel*: 20 in.
*Sights*: None
*Weight*: 7.25 lb.–7.7 lb.
*Caliber*: .223 Rem., .308 Win.
*Magazine*: Detachable box
*Features*: Ergonomic tactical stock in black; sling swivel studs; carbon steel barrel is drilled and tapped for sights; metal features blued finish; X-Mark Pro adjustable trigger; supercell recoil pad; semi-beavertail forend; hinged floorplate.
**MSRP** . . . . . . . . . . . . . . . . . . . . $757

## 700 XCR II

*Action*: Bolt
*Stock*: Synthetic
*Barrel*: 24 in., 26 in.
*Sights*: Iron sights on 375 chamberings
*Weight*: 7.4 lb.–7.6 lb.
*Caliber*: .25-06 Rem., .270 Win., .280 Rem., .30-06 Spfld., 7mm Rem. Mag., .300 WSM, .300 Win. Mag., .338 Win. Mag., 7mm Rem. Ultra Mag., .300 Rem. Ultra Mag., .338 Ultra Mag., .375 H&H, .375 Rem. Ultra Mag.
*Magazine*: Internal box
*Features*: Engraved floorplate; synthetic stock in; drilled and tapped for scope mounting; rubber overmolding on grip and forestock; SuperCell recoil pad; TriNyte Corrosion-Control System; X-Mark Pro trigger system.
**MSRP** . . . . . . . . . . . . . . . . . . . . $1005

# Remington Arms

REMINGTON 700 BDL

REMINGTON 700 CDL

REMINGTON 700 MTN LSS

RIFLES

## 700 BDL

**Action**: Bolt
**Stock**: Walnut
**Barrel**: 22 in., 24 in., 26 in.
**Sights**: Open
**Weight**: 7.25 lb.–7.62 lb.
**Caliber**: .243 Win., .270 Win., .30-06 Spgfd., 7mm Rem. Mag., .300 Rem. Ultra Mag.
**Magazine**: Internal box
**Features**: Adjustable X-mark Pro trigger system; walnut stock with black forend cap; Monte Carlo comb with raised cheekpiece and skipline cut checkering; hinged magazine floorplate; sling swivel studs; hooded ramp front sight and adjustable rear sight; cylindical receiver machined from solid-steel bar.
**MSRP** . . . . . . . . . . . . . . . . . . . **$985**

## 700 CDL

**Action**: Bolt
**Stock**: Walnut
**Barrel**: 24 in., 26 in.
**Sights**: None
**Weight**: 7.3 lb.–7.6 lb.
**Caliber**: .243 Win., .270 Win., 7mm-08 Rem., .300 Win. Mag., 7mm Rem. Ultra Mag., .300 Rem. Ultra Mag.
**Magazine**: Internal box
**Features**: Adjustable X-Mark Pro Trigger system; cylindrical receiver machined from solid-steel bar stock; walnut stock with oil finish.
**MSRP** . . . . . . . . . . . . . . . . . . . **$1019**

## 700 MOUNTAIN LSS

**Action**: Bolt
**Stock**: Laminate
**Barrel**: 22 in.
**Sights**: None
**Weight**: 6.5 lb.–6.6 lb.
**Caliber**: .270 Win., 7mm-08 Rem., .30-06 Spfld., .280 Rem.
**Magazine**: Internal box
**Features**: Brown two-tone laminated stock with element resistant, satin finish and checkering; black forend tip and grip cap; hinged floorplate magazine; cylindrical receiver machined from solid-steel bar stock.
**MSRP** . . . . . . . . . . . . . . . . . . . **$1123**

## 700 SENDERO SF II

*Action*: Bolt
*Stock*: Composite
*Barrel*: 26 in.
*Sights*: None
*Weight*: 8.5 lb.
*Caliber*: .264 Win. Mag., 7mm Rem. Mag., .300 Win. Mag., 7mm Rem. Ultra Mag., .300 Rem. Ultra Mag.
*Magazine*: Internal box
*Features*: Composite stock in black with gray webbing, reinforced with aramid fibers; features contoured beavertail forend with ambidextrous finger grooves and palm swells; heavy contour barrels are fluted for rapid cooling; full-length aluminum bedding stocks; twin front swivel studs for sling and bipod; concave target-style barrel crown.
**MSRP** . . . . . . . . . . . . . . . . . . **$1451**

## 700 SPS

*Action*: Bolt
*Stock*: Synthetic
*Barrel*: 24 in., 26 in.
*Sights*: None
*Weight*: 7 lb.–7.6 lb.
*Caliber*: .270 WSM, .300 WSM, .223 Rem., .243 Win., 7mm-08 Rem., .308 Win., .270 Win., .20-06 Spfld., .300 Win. Mag., .300 Rem. Ultra Mag., 7mm Rem. Ultra Mag., 7mm Rem. Mag., .17 Rem. Fireball
*Magazine*: Internal box
*Features*: Black ergonomic synthetic stock; carbon steel sight drilled and tapped for scope mounts; exterior metalwork features matte blued finish; hinged floorplate; swivel studs.
**MSRP** . . . . . . . . . . . . . . . . . . **$702**

## 700 SPS VARMINT

*Action*: Bolt
*Stock*: Synthetic
*Barrel*: 26 in.
*Sights*: None
*Weight*: 8.5 lb.
*Caliber*: .17 Rem. Fireball, .204 Ruger, .223 Rem., .22-250 Rem., .243 Win., .308 Win.
*Magazine*: Internal box, 5-rounds
*Features*: Ergnomic black synthetic stock has a vented beavertail forend; Non-reflective matte blued finish on barrel and receiver; hinged floorplate; sling swivel studs; drilled and tapped for scope mounts.
**MSRP** . . . . . . . . . . . . . . . . . . . **$732**

REMINGTON SENDERO SF II

REMINGTON 700 SPS

REMINGTON 700 SPS VARMINT

RIFLES

# Remington Arms

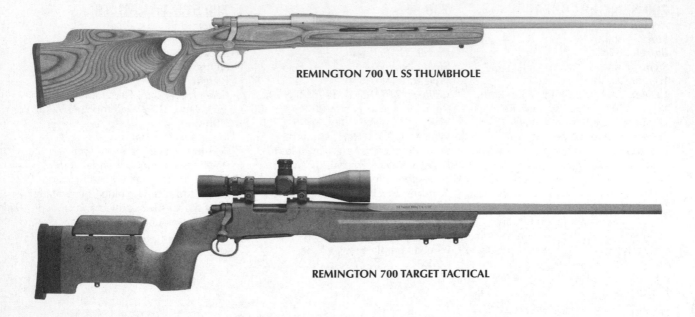

**REMINGTON 700 VL SS THUMBHOLE**

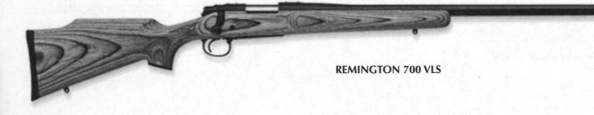

**REMINGTON 700 TARGET TACTICAL**

**REMINGTON 700 VLS**

## 700 VL SS THUMBHOLE
*Action*: Bolt
*Stock*: Laminate
*Barrel*: 26 in.
*Sights*: None
*Weight*: 9.12 lb.
*Caliber*: .204 Ruger, .223 Rem., .22-250 Rem.
*Magazine*: Internal box
*Features*: Laminated thumbhole stock; semi-beaver tail fore-end; heavy contour stainless steel barrel; concave target-style barrel crown; drilled and tapped for scope mount; X-Mark Pro trigger.
**MSRP . . . . . . . . . . . . . . . . . . . $1159**

## 700 TARGET TACTICAL
*Action*: Bolt
*Stock*: Synthetic
*Barrel*: 26 in.
*Sights*: Target
*Weight*: 11.75 lb.
*Caliber*: .308 Win.
*Magazine*: Internal box
*Features*: Triangular VTR barrel configuration; Bell & Carson Medalist Varmint/Tactical stock in black; 5-R hammer-forged tactical target rifling; adjustable length of comb and pull; tactical style bolt knob; X-Mark Pro Adjustable trigger.
**MSRP . . . . . . . . . . . . . . . . . . . $2117**

## 700 VLS
*Action*: Bolt
*Stock*: Laminate
*Barrel*: 26 in.
*Sights*: Target
*Weight*: 9.37 lb.
*Caliber*: .204 Ruger, .22-250 Rem., .223 Rem., .243 Win., .308 Win.
*Magazine*: Internal box
*Features*: Varmint laminated stock; Monte Carlo cheekpiece; beavertail shape fore-end; blued, satin finish metal; concave target-style barrel crown.
**MSRP . . . . . . . . . . . . . . . . . . $1045**

## 700 VTR
*Action*: Bolt
*Stock*: Synthetic
*Barrel*: 22 in.
*Sights*: None
*Weight*: 7.5 lb.
*Caliber*: .223 Rem., .308 Win., .243 Win., .204 Ruger, .223 Rem., .22-250 Rem.
*Magazine*: Internal box
*Features*: Triangular barrel contour; integral muzzle brake; green stock with black overmold grips.
**MSRP** . . . . . . . . . . . . . . . . . . . **$825**

## 770
*Action*: Bolt
*Stock*: Synthetic
*Barrel*: 22 in.
*Sights*: Boresighted 3-9 x 40mm scope
*Weight*: 8.5 lb.–8.6 lb.
*Caliber*: .243 Win., .270 Win., .30-06 Spgfd., 7mm Rem. Mag., .300 Win. Mag., .308 Win.
*Magazine*: Detachable box, standard 4-rounds, magnum 3-rounds
*Features*: Button rifling; ergonomically contoured stock with a raised cheekpiece; textured grips; black synthetic stock; blued or stainless barrel with nickel-plated action & bolt; easy-camming 60 degree bolt; stainless steel barrel.
**MSRP** . . . . . . . . . . . . . . . . . . . **$373**

## 770 STAINLESS CAMO
*Action*: Bolt
*Stock*: Synthetic
*Barrel*: 22 in., 24 in.
*Sights*: Boresighted 3-9x40mm scope
*Weight*: 8.5 lb.
*Caliber*: .270 Win., .30-06 Spfld., 7mm Rem. Mag., .300 Win. Mag.
*Magazine*: Detachable box, standard 4-rounds, magnum 3-rounds
*Features*: Realtree AP HD camo synthetic stock design; molded swing swivel studs; stainless barrel with nickel-plated action & bolt; easy-camming 60 degree bolt.
**MSRP** . . . . . . . . . . . . . . . . . . . **$455**

REMINGTON 700 VTR

REMINGTON 770 WITH SCOPE

RIFLES

REMINGTON 770 STAINLESS CAMO WITH SCOPE

# Remington Arms

REMINGTON SEVEN CDL

## SEVEN CDL
*Action*: Bolt
*Stock*: Walnut
*Barrel*: 20 in., 22 in.
*Sights*: Open
*Weight*: 6.5 lb.–7.3 lb.
*Caliber*: .270 WSM, .350 Rem., .243 Win., .260 Rem., 7mm-08 Rem., .308 Win.
*Magazine*: Internal box
*Features*: SuperCell recoil pad; American walnut CDL stock with sat-in-finished barrel; compact design for fast handling; cylindrical receiver; available in Rem. short-action magnum and Winchester short magnum.
**MSRP . . . . . . . . . . . . . . . . . . . . $998**

## SEVEN PREDATOR
*Action*: Bolt
*Stock*: Synthetic
*Barrel*: 22 in.
*Sights*: None
*Weight*: 7 lb.
*Caliber*: .223 Rem., .22-250 Rem., .243 Win.
*Magazine*: Internal box
*Features*: Mossy Oak Brush camo stock; fluted magnum-contour barrel; X-Mark Pro trigger system.
**MSRP . . . . . . . . . . . . . . . . . . . . $886**

## 7600
*Action*: Pump
*Stock*: Wood
*Barrel*: 22 in.
*Sights*: Open
*Weight*: 7.5 lb.
*Caliber*: .243 Win., 270 Win., .30-06 Spfd., .308 Win.
*Magazine*: Detachable box, 4-rounds
*Features*: Free-floated barrel; Monte Carlo walnut stock with satin finish as standard; metal work has black non-reflective finish; iron sights and drilled and tapped receiver for scope mounts; rotary-bolt lock-up.
**MSRP . . . . . . . . . . . . . . . . . . . . $900**

REMINGTON SEVEN PREDATOR

REMINGTON 7600

RIFLES

## 7600 SYNTHETIC
*Action*: Pump
*Stock*: Synthetic
*Barrel*: 22 in.
*Sights*: Open
*Weight*: 7.5 lb.
*Caliber*: .243 Win., .270 Win., .30-06 Spfd., .308 Win.
*Magazine*: Detachable box, 4-rounds
*Features*: Fiberglass-reinforced synthetic stock and forend; free-floated barrel; metal work has black non-reflective finish; iron sights and drilled and tapped receiver for scope mounts; rotary-bolt lock-up.
**MSRP**. . . . . . . . . . . . . . . . . . . . **$756**

## 597
*Action*: Semi-automatic
*Stock*: Synthetic
*Barrel*: 22 in.
*Sights*: Open
*Weight*: 5.5 lb.
*Caliber*: .22 LR, .22 WMR
*Magazine*: Detachable box, 10-rounds
*Features*: Bolt-guidance system features twin, tool-steel guide rails; sear and hammer are Teflon/nickel-plated; non-glare matte finish; adjustable big game iron sights; last-shot "hold open" bolt for added safety.
**MSRP**. . . . . . . . . . . . . . . . . . . . **$204**

## 597 VTR A-TACTS CS
*Action*: Semi-automatic
*Stock*: Synthetic
*Barrel*: 16 in.
*Sights*: None
*Weight*: 5.5 lb.
*Caliber*: .22 LR, .22 WMR
*Magazine*: Detachable box, 10-rounds
*Features*: Pardus A2 style stock with A-TACS digital camouflage and pistol grip; collapsible design; receiver mounted Picatinny style rail.
**MSRP**. . . . . . . . . . . . . . . . . . . **$618**

**REMINGTON 7600 SYNTHETIC**

**REMINGTON 597 WITH SCOPE**

**REMINGTON 597 VTR A-TACS CAMO**

RIFLES

# Remington Arms

**REMINGTON 552 BDL SPEEDMASTER**

## 552 BDL SPEEDMASTER

*Action*: Semi-automatic
*Stock*: Walnut
*Barrel*: 22 in.
*Sights*: Open
*Weight*: 5.75 lb.
*Caliber*: .22 S, L, LR
*Magazine*: Tubular magazine
*Features*: Adjustable iron sights for open sight plinking; grooved receiver for scope mounts; high-gloss American walnut stock and forend checkering; richly blued carbon-steel barrel; positive cross-bolt safety.
**MSRP. . . . . . . . . .$650**

## 572 BDL FIELDMASTER

*Action*: Pump
*Stock*: Walnut
*Barrel*: 21 in.
*Sights*: Open
*Weight*: 5.75 lb.
*Caliber*: 22 S, L, LR
*Magazine*: Smooth classic side action; high-gloss American walnut stock and forend with cut checkering; richly blued carbon-steel barrel; adjustable iron sights for open sight plinking; receiver grooved for scope mounts; positive cross-bolt safety.
**MSRP. . . . . . . . . .$665**

**REMINGTON 572 BDL FIELDMASTER**

RIFLES

# Rifles Inc.

RIFLES INC. LIGHTWEIGHT STRATA

RIFLES INC. CLASSIC

RIFLES INC. SAFARI

## LIGHTWEIGHT STRATA

**Action**: Bolt
**Stock**: Laminate
**Barrel**: 22 in.–26 in.
**Sights**: None
**Weight**: 4.5 lb.–5.75 lb.
**Caliber**: All popular chamberings up to .375 H&H
**Magazine**: Internal box
**Features**: Customer-supplied Rem. 700 action; match grade stainless steel Lilja barrel; fluted bolt and hollowed-handle; blind or hinged floorplate; matte stainless metal finish, optional black Teflon finish; hand-laminated blend of Kevlar/graphite and boron, pillar glass bedded stock; titanium strata has hand-laminated graphite stock with pillar glass-bedded; custom butt pad; Quiet Slimbrake II muzzle brake.
**Lightweight Strata:**. . . . . . . . . **$2900**
**Lightweight 70:** . . . . . . . . . . **$2800**
**Titanium Strata:** . . . . . . . . . . **$3500**

## CLASSIC

**Action**: Bolt
**Stock**: Laminated fiberglass
**Barrel**: 24 in.–26 in.
**Sights**: None
**Weight**: 6.5 lb.
**Caliber**: All popular chamberings up to .375 H&H
**Magazine**: Internal box
**Features**: Customer-supplied Rem. 700 action; match grade stainless steel Lilja barrel; blind or hinged floorplate; matte stainless metal finish, optional black Teflon finish; black laminated fiberglass, pillar glass-bedded stock.
**MSRP**. . . . . . . . . . . . . . . . . . **$2600**

## SAFARI

**Action**: Bolt
**Stock**: Laminated fiberglass
**Barrel**: 23 in.–25 in.
**Sights**: Optional Express sights
**Weight**: 8.5 lb.
**Caliber**: .375 H&H, 416 Rem. Mag. and other large game cartridges
**Magazine**: Drop box, 4-rounds
**Features**: Customer-supplied Winchester Model 70 Classic action; lapped and face-trued bolt; match grade stainless steel Lilja barrel; Quiet Slimbrake II muzzle brake; hinged floorplate or optional drop box; matte stainless finish, optional black Teflon; double laminated fiberglass, pillar glass-bedded stock; Pachmayr decelerator; optional barrel band.
**MSRP**. . . . . . . . . . . . . . . . . . **$3200**

# Rifles Inc.

RIFLES INC. MASTER'S SERIES

## MASTER'S SERIES

**Action**: Bolt
**Stock**: Laminated fiberglass
**Barrel**: 24 in.–27 in.
**Sights**: None
**Weight**: 7.25 lb.
**Caliber**: All popular chamberings up to .300 Rem. Ultra Mag
**Magazine**: Internal box
**Features**: Customer supplied Rem. .700 action; match grade stainless steel Lilja #5 barrel; hinged floorplate; matte stainless metal finish, optional black Teflon finish; black laminated fiberglass, pillar glass-bedded stock; optional muzzle brake.
**MSRP**. . . . . . . . . . . . . . . . . . **$2900**

## CANYON

**Action**: Bolt
**Stock**: McMillan HTG
**Barrel**: 24 in.
**Sights**: None
**Weight**: 10 lb.
**Caliber**: Most popular calibers
**Magazine**: Internal box
**Features**: Blind or hinged floorplate; customer-supplied Rem. 700 action; match grade stainless steel Lilja #6 barrel; optional muzzle-brake; matte stainless metal finish, optional black Teflon; adjustable cheek piece; custom butt pad.
**MSRP**. . . . . . . . . . . . . . . . . . **$3500**

## PEAR FLAT

**Action**: Bolt
**Stock**: Checkered composite with Pear Flat paint scheme
**Barrel**: 24 in.
**Sights**: None
**Weight**: 6.25 lb.
**Caliber**: 6.5 x 284
**Magazine**: Internal box, 3-rounds
**Features**: Engraved pear on floorplate with individual number (only 100 made); 1-8 twist, 3-groove Lilja barrel; ¾ M.O.A. accuracy.
**MSRP**. . . . . . . . . . . . . . . . . . **$3250 (customer-supplied Remington action)**

# Rock River Rifles

## RRA LAR-8 MID LENGTH A2 RIFLE

**Action**: Semi-automatic
**Stock**: Synthetic
**Barrel**: 16 in.
**Sights**: Open
**Weight**: 8.4 lb.
**Caliber**: .308 / 7.62x51mm NATO
**Magazine**: Detachable box
**Features**: A2 rear sight and front sight with housing rail; A2 flash hider; mid-length handguard; RRA two stage trigger; RRA 6-position tactical CAR stock with Hogue grip in black.
**MSRP**. . . . . . . . . . . . . . . . . . **$1375**

## RRA LAR-458 CAR A4

**Action**: Semi-automatic
**Stock**: Synthetic
**Barrel**: 16 in.
**Sights**: None
**Weight**: 7.6 lb.
**Caliber**: .458 SOCOM
**Magazine**: Detachable box
**Features**: Forged A4 receiver; A2 flash hider; chrome moly bull barrel; varmint gas block with sight rail; RRA two-stage trigger; RRA aluminum free-float tube; A2 pistol grip; A2 buttstock.
**MSRP**. . . . . . . . . . . . . . . . . . **$1150**

RIFLES

# Rogue River Rifle Works

**ROGUE RIVER RIFLE CHIPMUNK**

## CHIPMUNK
*Action*: Bolt
*Stock*: Walnut, laminated
*Barrel*: 16 in., 18 in.
*Sights*: Target
*Weight*: 2.5 lb.

*Caliber*: .22, .22 LR, .22 WMR
*Magazine*: None
*Features*: Designed with younger shooters in mind; single-shot; manual-cocking action; receiver-mounted rear sights; metal with blued finish; post sight on ramp front, fully adjustable peep rear; adjustable trigger; extendable butt plate and front rail.
MSRP . . . . . . . . . . . . . . . . .$164–$349

# Rossi Rifles

**ROSSI R92 .44-40**

**ROSSI YOUTH MATCHED PAIR-CENTERFIRE RIFLE AND SHOTGUN**

## R92 .44-40
*Action*: Lever
*Stock*: Wood
*Barrel*: 20 in., 24 in.
*Sights*: None
*Weight*: 7 lb.
*Caliber*: Most popular calibers: .38/.357 Mag., .44 Mag., .45 Colt, .44-40 Win.
*Magazine*: 12+1 rounds
*Features*: Octagonal barrel with a variety of metal finishes: blue, blue/case-hardened, blue/brass, and stainless; curved butt plate.
MSRP . . . . . . . . . . . . . . . . . . . $577

## YOUTH SIZE CENTERFIRE MATCHED PAIR
*Action*: Break open, single shot
*Stock*: Synthetic
*Barrel*: 22 in., 22 in.
*Sights*: Adjustable fiber optic front (rifle barrels), brass bead front (shotgun)
*Weight*: 5 lb., 6.25 lb.
*Caliber*: 20 Ga./ .44 Mag.
*Magazine*: None
*Features*: Quick-interchangable rifle and shotgun barrels in youth size; matte blue finish.
MSRP . . . . . . . . . . . . . . . . . . . $299

**RIFLES**

# Rossi Rifles

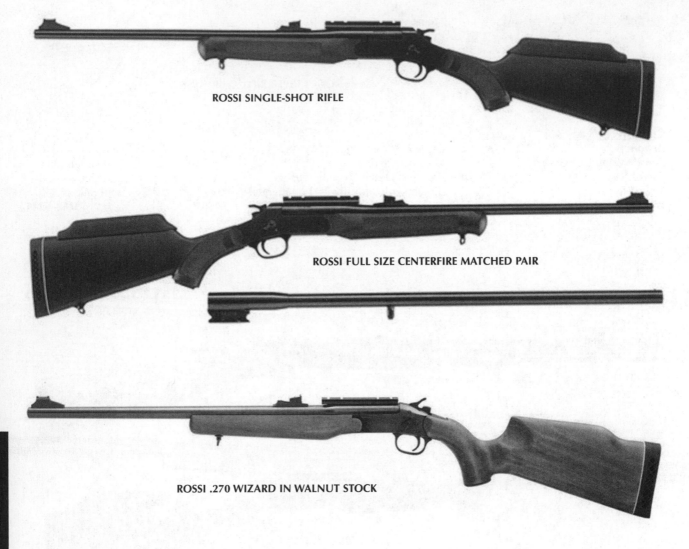

ROSSI SINGLE-SHOT RIFLE

ROSSI FULL SIZE CENTERFIRE MATCHED PAIR

ROSSI .270 WIZARD IN WALNUT STOCK

RIFLES

## SINGLE-SHOT RIFLE

*Action*: Break-open, single-shot
*Stock*: Synthetic
*Barrel*: 23 in.
*Sights*: Adjustable fiber optic front
*Weight*: 7 lb.
*Caliber*: .243 Win.
*Magazine*: None
*Features*: Steel barrel in matte blued finish; equipped with scope rail and hammer extension that accomodates all popular optics; black synthetic stock with removeable cheek piece; soft recoil pad; white line spacer; button rifled barrels; sling swivels.
**MSRP** . . . . . . . . . . . . . . . . . . . . $272

## FULL SIZE CENTERFIRE MATCHED PAIR

*Action*: Break-open, single-shot
*Stock*: Synthetic
*Barrel*: 23 in., 28 in.
*Sights*: Adjustable sights
*Weight*: 5.25 lb.–6.22 lb.
*Caliber*: 12 Ga., .243 Win.
*Magazine*: None
*Features*: Quick-interchangable rifle and shotgun barrels; recoil pad; sling swivels; black synthetic stock; steel barrel with matte blue finish; button rifled barrel.
**MSRP** . . . . . . . . . . . . . . . . . . . . $299

## WIZARD

*Action*: Single-shot
*Stock*: Wood or Hi-Def Green camo
*Barrel*: 23 in.
*Sights*: Fiber optic front sight
*Weight*: 7 lb.
*Caliber*: .270 Win. and other popular calibers, including all shotgun calibers, and .22 Rimfire, .22 Rimfire Mag.
*Magazine*: None
*Features*: Interchangable rifle and barrel system allows barrels to be changed quickly without tools; blued finish, cushioned recoil pad; Monte Carlo stock.
**MSRP** . . . . . . . . . . . . . . . . . . . . $391

ROSSI CIRCUIT JUDGE

ROSSI RIO GRANDE

## CIRCUIT JUDGE
*Action*: DA Revolver
*Stock*: Hardwood
*Barrel*: 18.5 in.
*Sights*: Fiber optic front sight
*Weight*: 4.45 lb.
*Caliber*: 410 GA./ .45 LC
*Magazine*: 5-rounds
*Features*: Shotgun/rifle crossover allows you to fire .410 3-inch Magnum shotshells, .410 2.5-inch shotshells and .45 Colt ammunition in any order without switching barrels; available in smooth-bore shotgun or rifled barrel shotgun; Yoke Detent; transfer bar; Taurus Security System.
**MSRP** . . . . . . . . . . . . . . . . . . . . **$618**

## RIO GRANDE
*Action*: Lever
*Stock*: Hardwood
*Barrel*: 20 in.
*Sights*: Open
*Weight*: 7 lb.
*Caliber*: .30-30 Win.
*Magazine*: 6-rounds
*Features*: Blue or stainless steel barrel; authentic buckhorn sights; Taurus Safety System.
**MSRP** . . . . . . . . . . . . . . . . . . . . **$549**

# Ruger Rifles

RUGER M77 HAWKEYE

## M77 HAWKEYE
*Action*: Bolt
*Stock*: Walnut
*Barrel*: 22 in., 24 in.
*Sights*: None
*Weight*: 7 lb.–8.25 lb.
*Caliber*: .204 Ruger, .22-250 Rem., .223 Rem., .243 Win., 6.5 Creedmoor, .257 Roberts, .270 Win., 7mm Rem. Mag., 7mm-08 Rem., .300 RCM, .30-06 Sprg., .300 Win. Mag., .308 Win., .338 RCM, .338 Win. Mag.
*Magazine*: 5-rounds
*Features*: American walnut stock; alloy steel, satin blued barrel; LCG trigger; positive floor plate latch; integral scope mounts; three-position safety.
**MSRP** . . . . . . . . . . . . . . . . . . . . **$843**

RIFLES

# Ruger Rifles

RUGER M77 HAWKEYE ALASKAN MATTE BLACK

RUGER M77 HAWKEYE ALASKAN STAINLESS STEEL

RUGER M77 HAWKEYE AFRICAN

## M77 HAWKEYE ALASKAN MATTE BLACK
*Action*: Bolt
*Stock*: Synthetic
*Barrel*: 20 in.
*Sights*: Bead front sight, adjustable rear
*Weight*: 8 lb.
*Caliber*: .375 Ruger
*Magazine*: 3-rounds
*Features*: New Hawkeye matte black finish on steel barrel; LC6 trigger; non-rotating, Mauser-type controlled round feed extractor; steel floorplate; three-position safety; integral scope mounts; ergonmic black stock with pistol grip.
MSRP. . . . . . . . . . . . . . . . . . $1095

## M77 HAWKEYE ALASKAN
*Action*: Bolt
*Stock*: Synthetic
*Barrel*: 20 in.
*Sights*: Bead front sight, adjustable rear
*Weight*: 7.75 lb.–8 lb.
*Caliber*: .375 Ruger, .416 Ruger
*Magazine*: 3-rounds
*Features*: Matte stainless steel barrel; LC6 trigger; non-rotating, Mauser-type controlled round feed extractor; steel floorplate; three-position safety; integral scope mounts; ergonmic black stock with pistol grip.
MSRP. . . . . . . . . . . . . . . . . . $1095

## M77 HAWKEYE AFRICAN
*Action*: Bolt
*Stock*: Walnut
*Barrel*: 23 in.
*Sights*: Bead front sight, adjustable rear V notch sight
*Weight*: 7.75 lb.
*Caliber*: .223 Rem., .300 Win. Mag., .338 Win. Mag., 9.3 x 62, .375 Ruger
*Magazine*: 3-, 4- or 5-rounds
*Features*: Walnut stock with pistol grip; LC6 trigger; non-rotating, Mauser-type controlled round feed extractor; steel floorplate; three-position safety; integral scope mounts.
MSRP. . . . . . . . . . . . . . . . . . $1095

# Ruger Rifles

**RUGER M77 PREDATOR**

## M77 PREDATOR
**Action**: Bolt
**Stock**: Green Mountain laminate
**Barrel**: 22 in., 24 in.
**Sights**: None
**Weight**: 7.75 lb.–8.00 lb.

**Caliber**: .204 Ruger, .22-250 Rem., .223 Rem.
**Magazine**: 4- or 5-rounds
**Features**: Hawkeye matte stainless steel finish on barrel; two-stage adjustable target trigger; non-rotating,

Mauser-type controlled round feed extractor; hinged solid-steel floorplate; three-position safety; integral scope mounts; sling swivel studs.
**MSRP**................... **$979**

**RUGER SR-556**

**RUGER SR22**

## SR-556
**Action**: Autoloading
**Stock**: Synthetic
**Barrel**: 16.12 in.
**Sights**: Folding BattleSights
**Weight**: 7.40 lb.–7.94 lb.
**Caliber**: 5.56mm NATO/.223 Rem., 6.8 SPC
**Magazine**: Detachable box, 10-, 25-, or 30-rounds
**Features**: Stock options include black synthetic standard or collapsible; two-

stage piston with adjustable regulator; chrome-lined gas block; quad rail handgaurd; Troy Industries sights; telescoping buttstock; hammer-forged barrel; pistol grip stock; rail covers and soft case.
**MSRP**................... **$1995**

## SR22
**Action**: Autoloading
**Stock**: Synthetic
**Barrel**: 16.12 in.

**Sights**: None
**Weight**: 6.50 lb.
**Caliber**: .22 LR
**Magazine**: Detachable rotary, 10-rounds
**Features**: Black laminate stock in standard or collapsible; AR-style ergonomic Houge monogrip and six-position telescoping buttstock; hammer-forged barrel; round handguard; barrel support block.
**MSRP**................... **$625**

RIFLES

# Ruger Rifles

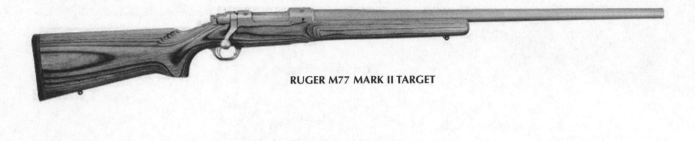

**RUGER M77 MARK II TARGET**

**RUGER 77/17 BLACK LAMINATE**

**RUGER 77/22 WALNUT MODEL**

## M77 MARK II TARGET

*Action*: Bolt
*Stock*: Laminate
*Barrel*: 26 in., 28 in.
*Sights*: None
*Weight*: 9.25 lb.–9.75 lb.
*Caliber*: .204 Ruger, .22-250 Rem., .223 Rem., .243 Win., .25-06 Rem., 6.5 Creedmoor, .308 Win.
*Magazine*: 4- or 5-rounds
*Features*: Black laminate stock; stainless steel barrel; two-stage target trigger; non-rotating, Mauser-type controlled round feed extractor, hinged solid-steel floorplate, three-position safety; intergral scope mounts; sling swivel studs.
**MSRP** . . . . . . . . . . . . . . . . . . . . **$979**

## 77/17

*Action*: Bolt
*Stock*: Walnut or laminate
*Barrel*: 22 in., 24 in.
*Sights*: None
*Weight*: 6.50 lb.–7.50 lb.
*Caliber*: .17 HMR
*Magazine*: Detachable rotary, 9-rounds
*Features*: Stock options include American walnut with blued finish or black laminate with target grey finish; alloy steel or stainless steel barrel; integral scope mounts; three-position safety; sling swivel stud mounts.
**Walnut:** . . . . . . . . . . . . . . . . . . **$793**
**Laminate:** . . . . . . . . . . . . . . . . . **$877**

## 77/22

*Action*: Bolt
*Stock*: Laminate, walnut, synthetic
*Barrel*: 20 in., 24 in.
*Sights*: None
*Weight*: 6 lb.–7.5 lb.
*Caliber*: .22 LR, .22 Mag., .22 LR, .22 Hornet
*Magazine*: Detachable rotary, 6-, 9- or 10-rounds
*Features*: Stock options include black synthetic, American walnut, or brown laminate; alloy steel or stainless steel barrel in target grey, blued, or brushed stainless finish; integral scope mounts; three-position safety; sling swivel studs.
**Walnut, Synthetic:** . . . . . . . . . . **$793**
**Laminate:** . . . . . . . . . . . . . . . . . **$877**

# Ruger Rifles

RUGER 77/ 44 CAMO

RUGER NO.1 LIGHT SPORTER

RUGER NO.1 VARMINTER

RUGER 10/22 CARBINE

## 77/ 44

*Action*: Bolt
*Stock*: Vista Camo, synthentic
*Barrel*: 18.5 in.
*Sights*: Front bead sight, adjustable rear
*Weight*: 5.25 lb.
*Caliber*: .44 Mag.
*Magazine*: Detachable rotary, 4-rounds
*Features*: Stock options include next G1 Vista Camo or black synthetic; stainless steel barrel with brushed steel finish; integral scope mounts; three-position safety; sling swivel studs.
**Vista Camo:** . . . . . . . . . . . . . . **$819**
**Synthetic:** . . . . . . . . . . . . . . . **$793**

## NO.1 LIGHT SPORTER

*Action*: Falling block, single-shot
*Stock*: Walnut
*Barrel*: 22 in.
*Sights*: Front bead sight, adjustable rear

*Weight*: 7 lb.-7.24 lb.
*Caliber*: 6.5 Creedmoor, .30-06 Sprg., .308 Win., .243 Win., .270 Win., .300 RCM, .303 British
*Magazine*: None
*Features*: Falling block breech mechanism, sliding tang safety; sculptured receiver; Ruger scope mounting system; Alexander Henry-style forend; sporting style butt pad; grip cap and sling swivel studs; American walnut stock.
**MSRP** . . . . . . . . . . . . . . . . . . **$1242**

## NO.1 VARMINTER

*Action*: Falling block, single-shot
*Stock*: Walnut
*Barrel*: 24 in.
*Sights*: None
*Weight*: 8.50 lb.–8.75 lb.
*Caliber*: 6.5 Creedmoor, .22-250 Rem., .223 Rem., .25-06 Rem.
*Magazine*: None
*Features*: Falling block breech

mechanism, sliding tang safety; sculptured receiver; Ruger scope mounting system; Alexander Henry-style forend; sporting style buttpad; grip cap and sling swivel studs; American walnut stock.
**MSRP** . . . . . . . . . . . . . . . . . . **$1242**

## 10/22 CARBINE

*Action*: Autoloading
*Stock*: Synthetic or hardwood
*Barrel*: 18.5 in.
*Sights*: Gold bead front sight, adjustable rear
*Weight*: 5 lb.
*Caliber*: .22 LR
*Magazine*: Rotary, 10-rounds
*Features*: Stock comes in black synthetic and hardwood; extended magazine release; push-button manual safety; combination scope base adapter; hammer-forged barrel; polymer trigger housing; aluminum receiver; contoured buttpad; barrel band.
**MSRP** . . . . . . . . . . . . . . . . **$277–$299**

# Ruger Rifles

RUGER 10/22 TARGET

RUGER MINI-14 RANCH RIFLE

RUGER MINI THIRTY RIFLE

RUGER MINI-14 TARGET RIFLE

## 10/22 TARGET
**Action**: Autoloading
**Stock**: Laminate
**Barrel**: 20 in.
**Sights**: None
**Weight**: 7.50 lb.
**Caliber**: .22 LR
**Magazine**: Rotary, 10-rounds
**Features**: Stock comes in black or brown laminate; extended magazine release; push-button manual safety; combination scope base adapter; hammer-forged barrel; polymer trigger housing; aluminum receiver; target trigger; flat butt plate.
**MSRP** . . . . . . . . . . . . . . . . $499–$549

## MINI-14 RANCH RIFLE
**Action**: Autoloading
**Stock**: Hardwood, synthetic
**Barrel**: 18.5 in.
**Sights**: Blade front sight, adjustable rear
**Weight**: 6.75 lb.–7.00 lb.
**Caliber**: 5.6mm NATO/.223 Rem., 6.8 SPC

**Magazine**: 5-rounds, or detachable box, 20-rounds
**Features**: Stock comes in hardwood or black synthetic; garand style action; hammer-forged barrel; sighting system; integral scope mounts; flat butt pad; integral sling swivels on hardwood or black synthetic stocks.
**MSRP** . . . . . . . . . . . . . . . . $881–$966

## MINI THIRTY RIFLE
**Action**: Autoloading
**Stock**: Synthetic
**Barrel**: 16.12 in., 18.5 in.
**Sights**: Blade front sight, adjustable rear
**Weight**: 6.75 lb.
**Caliber**: 7.62 x 39mm
**Magazine**: 5-rounds, or detachable box, 20-rounds
**Features**: Garand style action, hammer-forged barrel; sighting system; integral scope mounts; black synthetic stock; sling swivels; stainless steel or

alloy steel barrel in matte or blued finish.
**MSRP** . . . . . . . . . . . . . . . . $921–$966

## MINI-14 TARGET RIFLE
**Action**: Autoloading
**Stock**: Laminate or Hogue OverMolded
**Barrel**: 22 in.
**Sights**: None
**Weight**: 8.5 lb.–9.5 lb.
**Caliber**: .223 Rem.
**Magazine**: 5-rounds
**Features**: Black laminate with thumb hole stock or black Hogue Over Molded stock; matte stainless finish on stainless steel barrel; garand style action; hammer-forged barrel; integral scope mounts; harmonic dampener; sling swivel studs.
**MSRP** . . . . . . . . . . . . . . . . . $1098

# Sako Rifles

SAKO A7-ST

SAKO M85 KODIAK

SAKO M85 CLASSIC

## A7-ST
**Action**: Bolt
**Stock**: Synthetic
**Barrel**: 22 in., 24 in.
**Sights**: None
**Weight**: 6.5 lb.–7 lb.
**Caliber**: .22-250 Rem., .243 Win., .308 Win., .25-06 Rem., .270 Win., .30-06 SPRG, .300 Win. Mag., .270 WSM, .300 WSM, 7mm-08 Rem., 7mm Rem. Mag.
**Magazine**: 4-rounds
**Features**: Stainless or blued finish
**MSRP**. . . . . . . . . . . . . . . **$935–$980**
**Stainless:** . . . . . . . . . . . . . . . **$1065**

## M85 KODIAK
**Action**: Bolt
**Stock**: Laminated hardwood
**Barrel**: 12.25 in.

**Sights**: Open
**Weight**: 7. 9 lb.
**Caliber**: .338 Win. Mag., .375 H&H Mag.
**Magazine**: Detachable box, 5-rounds
**Features**: Adjustable single-stage trigger; barrel band for front swivel; integral dovetail rails for secure scope mounting; straight stock made of gray matte-lacquered laminated hardwood and reinforced with two cross-bolts; free floating "bull" barrel.
**MSRP**. . . . . . . . . . . . . . . . . . **$1975**

## M85 CLASSIC
**Action**: Bolt
**Stock**: Walnut
**Barrel**: 22.4 in., 24.4 in.
**Sights**: Open
**Weight**: 7 lb.–7.75 lb.

**Caliber**: (S): .243 Win., .260 Rem., 7mm-08 Rem., .308 Win., .338 Federal; (SM) .270 Win. S Mag., .300 Win. S Mag.; (M) .25-06 Rem., 6.5x55 SE, .270 Win., .30-06 Sprg., 9.3x 66 Sako; (L): 7mm Rem. Mag., .300 Win. Mag., .338 Win. Mag., .375 H&H Mag.
**Magazine**: Detachable box, S/M 6-rounds, SM/L 5-rounds
**Features**: Comes in short actions extra short (XS), short (S) and short magnum (SM), medium action (M) and long action (L); straight, classic walnut stock with rosewood forend tip and pistol grip cap; integral rails for scope mounts; free-floating barrel is cold hammer-forged; adjustable single-stage trigger.
**MSRP**. . . . . . . . . . . . . . **$2250–$2360**

# Sako Rifles

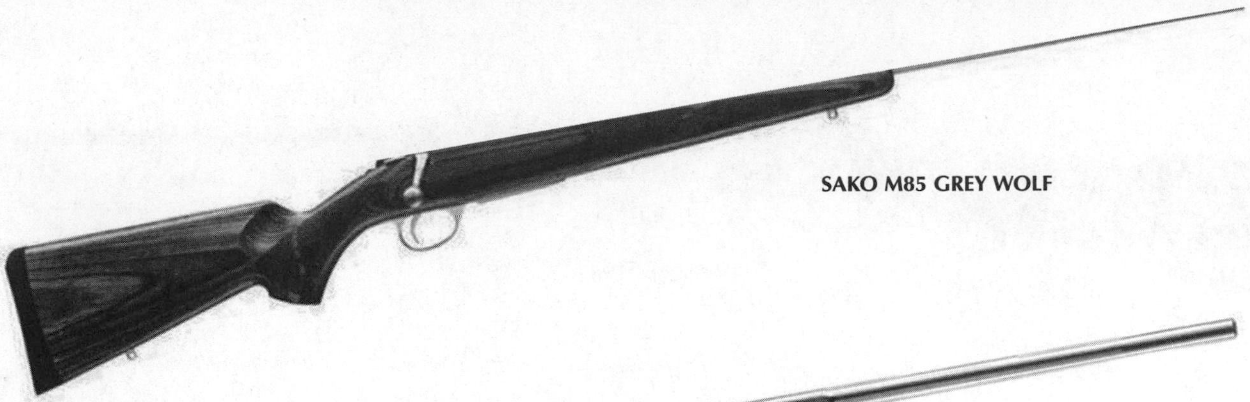

SAKO M85 GREY WOLF

SAKO M85 FINNLIGHT

SAKO TRG 22

## M85 GREY WOLF

**Action**: Bolt
**Stock**: Grey lamintate
**Barrel**: 22 in., 24 in.
**Sights**: None
**Weight**: 7.25 lb.
**Caliber**: .270 Win., .30-06 Sprg, .300 Win. Mag., .270 WSM, .300 WSM, 7mm Rem. Mag.
**Magazine**: 4- or 5-rounds
**Features**: Stainless steel barrel and action; warp-free stock makes the rifle suitable for hunting in extreme conditions.
**MSRP** . . . . . . . . . . . . . . . . . . . $1750

## M85 FINNLIGHT

**Action**: Bolt
**Stock**: Synthetic
**Barrel**: 20.25 in., 22.4 in.
**Sights**: None
**Weight**: 6.2 lb.–6.8 lb.
**Caliber**: (S): .22-250 Rem., .243 Win., .260 Rem., 7mm-08 Rem., .308 Win.; (SM) .270 Win. Short Mag., .300 Win. Short Mag.; (M): .25-06 Rem., 6.5x55 SE, .270 Win., .30-06 Sprg.; (L) 7mm Rem. Mag., .300 Win. Mag.
**Magazine**: Detachable box, S/M 6-rounds, SM/L 5-rounds
**Features**: Comes in short actions short (S) and short magnum (SM), medium action (M) and long action (L); single-stage trigger; 2-way Sako safety locks both trigger and bolt handle; black synthetic stock with soft grey grip areas; pistol grip stock; integral rails for scope mounts; free-floating barrel is cold hammer-forged of stainless steel.
**MSRP** . . . . . . . . . . . . . . $1775–$1865

## TRG 22

**Action**: Bolt
**Stock**: Synthetic
**Barrel**: 20 in., 26 in., 27.1 in.
**Sights**: None
**Weight**: 10.25 lb.–10.75 lb.
**Caliber**: .308 Win., .300 Win. Mag., .338 Lapua Mag.
**Magazine**: Detachable box, 5-, 7- or 10-rounds
**Features**: Double-stage trigger; 2-way Sako safety locks both trigger and bolt handle; base of stock is made of polyurethane with aluminum skeleton; adjustable cheekpiece and buttplate; ambidextrous stock in green or desert tan color; includes integral dovetail on receiver and is drilled and tapped for picatinny rail mounting.
**MSRP** . . . . . . . . . . . . . . . . . . . $4560

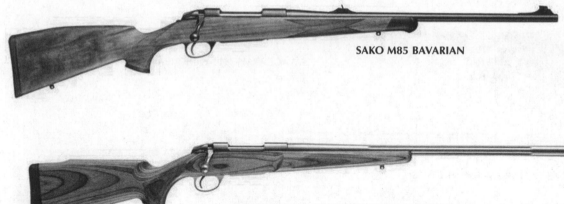

SAKO M85 BAVARIAN

SAKO M85 VARMINT LAMINATED STAINLESS

## M85 BAVARIAN
**Action**: Bolt
**Stock**: Walnut
**Barrel**: 22 in., 24 in.
**Sights**: None
**Weight**: 7 lb.–7.5 lb.
**Caliber**: .308 Win., .270 Win., .30-06 Sprg., .300 Win. Mag., .270 WSM, .300 WSM, 6.5x55 Swede, 7mm-08 Rem., 7mm Rem. Mag.
**Magazine**: 4- or 5-rounds
**Features**: Single-set trigger
**MSRP** . . . . . . . . . . . . . . **$2250–$2360**

## M85 VARMINT LAMINATED STAINLESS
**Action**: Bolt
**Stock**: Laminated hardwood
**Barrel**: 20 in., 23.6 in.
**Sights**: None
**Weight**: 8.6 lb.–9 lb.
**Caliber**: (XS) .204 Ruger, .222 Rem., .223 Rem.; (S) .22-250 Rem., .243 Win., .260 Rem., 7mm-08 Rem., .308 Win., .338 Federal

**Magazine**: Detachable box, XS 7-rounds, S 6-rounds
**Features**: Comes in short actions extra short (XS) and short (S); single-set trigger; 2-way Sako safety locks both trigger and bolt handle; straight stock with wide forend is made of brown mattle aquered laminated hardwoood; integral rail for scope mounts.
**MSRP** . . . . . . . . . . . . . . . . . **$2050**

# Savage Arms Rifles

SAVAGE ARMS M14 CLASSIC

## M14 CLASSIC
**Action**: Bolt
**Stock**: Wood
**Barrel**: 22 in., 24 in.
**Sights**: None
**Weight**: 7.5 lb.–7.75 lb.
**Caliber**: .308 Win., .243 Win., .270 WSM, .300 WSM

**Magazine**: Hinged floorplate, 2- or 4-rounds
**Features**: Drilled and tapped for scope mounts; hinged floorplate; carbon steel barrel with matte blued finish; short action; AccuTrigger; satin finish wood stock.
**MSRP** . . . . . . . . . . . . . . . **$886–$920**

# Savage Arms Rifles

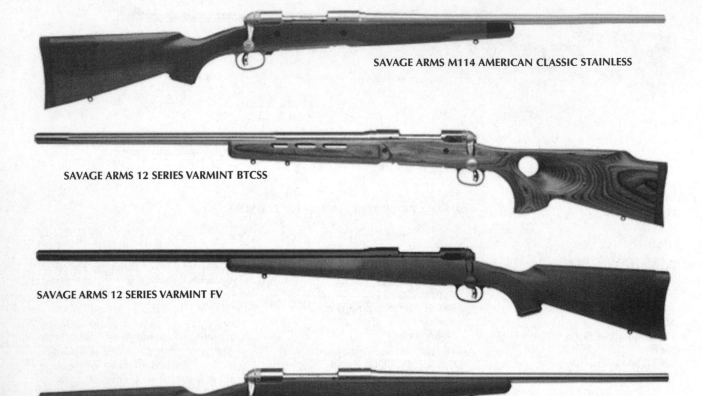

SAVAGE ARMS M114 AMERICAN CLASSIC STAINLESS

SAVAGE ARMS 12 SERIES VARMINT BTCSS

SAVAGE ARMS 12 SERIES VARMINT FV

SAVAGE ARMS  WEATHER WARRIOR 16FCSS

## M114 AMERICAN CLASSIC STAINLESS
**Action**: Bolt
**Stock**: Wood
**Barrel**: 22 in.
**Sights**: None
**Weight**: 7.5 lb.
**Caliber**: .30-06 Spfld., .270 Win., 7mm Rem. Mag.
**Magazine**: Detachable box, 3- or 4-rounds
**Features**: Drilled and tapped for scope mounts; stainless steel barrel with high luster finish; AccuTrigger; wood stock with satin finish; long action.
**MSRP**. . . . . . . . . . . . . . . . . . . **$967**

## 12 SERIES VARMINT BTCSS
**Action**: Bolt
**Stock**: Laminate
**Barrel**: 26 in.
**Sights**: None
**Weight**: 10 lb.
**Caliber**: .204 Ruger, .223 Rem., .22-250 Rem.
**Magazine**: Detachable box, 4-rounds
**Features**: Drilled and tapped for scope mounts; stainless steel barrel with high luster finish; AccuTrigger; wood laminate with thumbhole and satin finish.
**MSRP**. . . . . . . . . . . . . . . . . . **$1105**

## 12 SERIES VARMINT FV
**Action**: Bolt
**Stock**: Synthetic
**Barrel**: 26 in.
**Sights**: None
**Weight**: 8.75 lb.
**Caliber**: .22-250 Ruger, .223 Rem., .204 Ruger
**Magazine**: Internal box, 4-rounds
**Features**: Drilled and tapped for scope mounts; carbon steel barrel with blued satin finish; AccuTrigger; synthetic stock with matte black finish.
**MSRP**. . . . . . . . . . . . . . . . . . . **$698**

## WEATHER WARRIOR SERIES 16FCSS
**Action**: Bolt
**Stock**: Synthetic
**Barrel**: 22 in., 24 in.
**Sights**: None
**Weight**: 6.9 lb.–7.15 lb.
**Caliber**: .204 Ruger, .223 Rem., .308 Win., .7mm-08 Rem., .243 Win., .22-.250 Rem., 6.5 Creedmoor, .260 Rem., .300 WSM, .270 WSM
**Magazine**: Detachable box, 2- or 4-rounds
**Features**: Drilled and tapped for scope mounts; stainless steel barrel with high luster finish; synthetic stock with black matte finish; AccuTrigger.
**MSRP**. . . . . . . . . . . . . . . . . **$801–$834**

SAVAGE ARMS HUNTER SERIES 11BTH

SAVAGE ARMS HUNTER SERIES 11 GCNS

SAVAGE ARMS HUNTER SERIES 111BTH

## WEATHER WARRIOR SERIES 116FSS

**Action**: Bolt
**Stock**: Synthetic
**Barrel**: 22 in.
**Sights**: None
**Weight**: 6.5 lb.
**Caliber**: .270 Win., .30-06 Spfld.
**Magazine**: Internal box, 4-rounds
**Features**: Drilled and tapped for scope mounts; stainless steel barrel with high luster finish; synthetic stock with black matte finish; AccuTrigger.
**MSRP** . . . . . . . . . . . . . . . . . . . $720

## HUNTER SERIES 11BTH

**Action**: Bolt
**Stock**: Wood laminate
**Barrel**: 22 in.
**Sights**: None
**Weight**: 6.75 lb.

**Caliber**: .308 Win., 22-250 Rem., .243 Win., .223 Rem.
**Magazine**: Hinged floorplate, 4-rounds
**Features**: Drilled and tapped for scope mounts; carbon steel barrel with blued satin finish; AccuTrigger; wood laminate stock with thumbhole in satin finish.
**MSRP** . . . . . . . . . . . . . . . . . . . $836

## HUNTER SERIES 11GCNS

**Action**: Bolt
**Stock**: Wood
**Barrel**: 22 in.
**Sights**: None
**Weight**: 6.75 lb.
**Caliber**: .223 Rem., .308 Win., .22-250 Rem., .243 Win.
**Magazine**: Detachable box, 4-rounds
**Features**: Drilled and tapped for scope mounts; stainless steel barrel with high

luster finish; AccuTrigger; wood stock with satin finish; short action.
**MSRP** . . . . . . . . . . . . . . . . . . . $699

## HUNTER SERIES 111BTH

**Action**: Bolt
**Stock**: Wood laminate
**Barrel**: 22 in.
**Sights**: None
**Weight**: 7 lb.
**Caliber**: .270 Win., .25-06 Rem., .30-06 Spfld.
**Magazine**: Hinged floorplate, 4-rounds
**Features**: Drilled and tapped for scope mounts; carbon steel barrel with blued satin finish; AccuTrigger; wood laminate stock with thumbhole in satin finish.
**MSRP** . . . . . . . . . . . . . . . . . . . $836

# Savage Arms Rifles

**SAVAGE ARMS PACKAGE SERIES 10 GLXP3**

**SAVAGE ARMS SPECIALTY SERIES M11 LONGE RANGE HUNTER**

**SAVAGE ARMS 10XP PREDATOR HUNTER PACKAGE BRUSH**

## PACKAGE SERIES 10 GLXP3

*Action*: Bolt
*Stock*: Wood
*Barrel*: 22 in.
*Sights*: 3-9x40mm scope, mounted and bore-sighted
*Weight*: 7.25 lb.
*Caliber*: .243 Win., .222-250 Rem., .223 Rem., .308 Win.
*Magazine*: Internal box, 4-rounds
*Features*: Carbon steel barrel in blued satin finish; left handed model; AccuTrigger; wood stock in satin finish.
**MSRP** . . . . . . . . . . . . . . . . . . . **$691**

## SPECIALTY SERIES M11 LONGE RANGE HUNTER

*Action*: Bolt
*Stock*: Synthetic
*Barrel*: 26 in.
*Sights*: None
*Weight*: 8.4 lb.
*Caliber*: .260 Rem., .308 Win., 6.5 Creedmoor, .300 WSM
*Magazine*: Hinged floorplate, 2- or 4-rounds
*Features*: Drilled and tapped for scope mounts; carbon steel barrel with black matte finish; synthetic stock with black matte finish; AccuTrigger.
**MSRP** . . . . . . . . . . . . . . . **$962–$1001**

## 10XP PREDATOR HUNTER PACKAGE BRUSH

*Action*: Bolt
*Stock*: Synthetic
*Barrel*: 22 in.
*Sights*: 4-12x40mm scope
*Weight*: 8.5 lb.
*Caliber*: .223 Rem., .204 Ruger, .22-250 Rem., .243 Win.
*Magazine*: 4-rounds
*Features*: Mounted and bore-sighted scope; AccuTrigger; carbon steel barrel; synthetic camo stock.
**MSRP** . . . . . . . . . . . . . . . . . . . **$889**

RIFLES

# Savage Arms Rifles

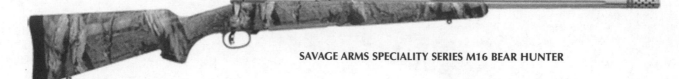

SAVAGE ARMS SPECIALITY SERIES M16 BEAR HUNTER

SAVAGE ARMS SPECAILTY SERIES M220

SAVAGE ARMS LIGHTWEIGHT VARMINTER SERIES M25LV

## SPECIALITY SERIES M16 BEAR HUNTER
*Action*: Bolt
*Stock*: Synthetic
*Barrel*: 23 in.
*Sights*: None
*Weight*: 7.5 lb.
*Caliber*: .325 WSM, .300 WSM
*Magazine*: Hinged floorplate, 2-rounds
*Features*: Drilled and tapped for scope mounts; adjustable muzzle brake; stainless steel barrel; synthetic stock with matte camo finish; AccuTrigger; AccuStock.
**MSRP** . . . . . . . . . . . . . . . . . . . . **$973**

## SPECIALTY SERIES M220, YOUTH, CAMO
*Action*: Bolt
*Stock*: Synthetic
*Barrel*: 22 in.
*Sights*: None
*Weight*: 7.5 lb.
*Caliber*: 20 Ga.
*Magazine*: 2-rounds
*Features*: Drilled and tapped for scope mounts; carbon steel barrel with matte blued finish; AccuTrigger; synthetic stock in matte black finish or camo.
**Standard:** . . . . . . . . . . . . . . . . **$534**
**Camo:** . . . . . . . . . . . . . . . . . . . **$588**
**Youth:** . . . . . . . . . . . . . . . . . . **$534**

## LIGHTWEIGHT VARMINTER SERIES M25LV
*Action*: Bolt
*Stock*: Wood laminate
*Barrel*: 24 in.
*Sights*: None
*Weight*: 8.25 lb.
*Caliber*: .204 Ruger, .22 Hornet, .223 Rem.
*Magazine*: Detachable box, 4-rounds
*Features*: Drilled and tapped for scope mounts; carbon steel barrel with blued satin finish; wood laminate stock with satin finish.
**MSRP** . . . . . . . . . . . . . . . . . . . . **$687**

# Savage Arms Rifles

SAVAGE ARMS TARGET RIFLE SERIES M12 BENCH R

SAVAGE ARMS LAW ENFORCEMENT SERIES M1

SAVAGE ARMS AXIS

## TARGET RIFLE SERIES M12 BENCH REST

**Action**: Bolt, single-shot
**Stock**: Wood laminate
**Barrel**: 29 in.
**Sights**: None
**Weight**: 12.75 lb.
**Caliber**: .308 Win., 6.5 x 284 Norma, 6mm Norma BR
**Magazine**: None
**Features**: Drilled and tapped for scope mounts; stainless steel barrel with high luster finish; wood laminate stock with satin finish; AccuTrigger.
**MSRP** . . . . . . . . . . . . . . . . **$1460**

## LAW ENFORCEMENT SERIES M10BA

**Action**: Bolt
**Stock**: Aluminum
**Barrel**: 24 in.
**Sights**: None
**Weight**: 13.4 lb.
**Caliber**: .308 Win.
**Magazine**: Detachable box, 10-rounds
**Features**: Rail system, #5-48 screws; carbon steel barrel with matte black finish; aluminum stock with matte black finish; AccuTrigger; AccuStock.
**MSRP** . . . . . . . . . . . . . . . . . . **$2132**

## AXIS SERIES

**Action**: Bolt
**Stock**: Synthetic
**Barrel**: 22 in.
**Sights**: None
**Weight**: 6.5 lb.
**Caliber**: .30-06 Spfld., .270 Win., .25-06 Rem., .308 Win., .22-250 Rem., 7mm-08 Rem., .243 Win., .223 Rem.
**Magazine**: Detachable box, 4-rounds
**Features**: New modern design, smooth bolt operation; drilled and tapped for scope mounts; carbon steel barrel with black matte finish; synthetic stock with matte black finish.
**MSRP** . . . . . . . . . . . . . . . . . . **$349**

# Savage Arms Rifles

**SAVAGE ARMS STEVENS 200 LONG**

**SAVAGE ARMS SEMI-AUTOMATIC SERIES 64F**

**SAVAGE ARMS MAGNUM SERIES M93 BRJ**

## STEVENS 200 LONG
*Action*: Bolt
*Stock*: Synthetic
*Barrel*: 22 in., 24 in.
*Sights*: None
*Weight*: 6.75 lb.
*Caliber*: .30-06 Spfld., .270 Win., .300 Win. Mag., 7mm Rem. Mag.
*Magazine*: Internal box, 3- or 4-rounds
*Features*: Drilled and tapped for scope mounts; carbon steel barrel with satin blued barrel; synthetic stock with matte grey finish stock.
**MSRP**. . . . . . . . . . . . . . . . . . . **$415**

## SEMI-AUTOMATIC SERIES 64F
*Action*: Semi-automatic
*Stock*: Synthetic
*Barrel*: 20.5 in.
*Sights*: Open
*Weight*: 5 lb.
*Caliber*: .22 LR
*Magazine*: Detachable box, 10-rounds
*Features*: Drilled and tapped for scope mounts; carbon steel barrel with satin blued finish; synthetic matte black stock.
**MSRP**. . . . . . . . . . . . . . . . . . . **$160**

## MAGNUM SERIES M93 BRJ
*Action*: Bolt
*Stock*: Wood laminate
*Barrel*: 21 in.
*Sights*: None
*Weight*: 7 lb.
*Caliber*: .22 WMR
*Magazine*: 5-rounds
*Features*: Carbon steel barrel in blued satin finish; wood laminate stock; AccuTrigger.
**MSRP**. . . . . . . . . . . . . . . . . . . **$478**

# Savage Arms Rifles

**SAVAGE ARMS SINGLE-SHOT SERIES M CUB T PINK**

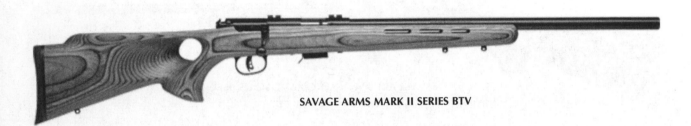

**SAVAGE ARMS MARK II SERIES BTV**

**SAVAGE ARMS 17 SERIES M93R17 CLASSIC T**

## SINGLE SHOT SERIES M CUB T PINK

**Action**: Bolt
**Stock**: Wood laminate
**Barrel**: 16 in.
**Sights**: Rear peep sight
**Weight**: 3.5 lb.
**Caliber**: .22 LR
**Magazine**: None
**Features**: Carbon steel barrel with blued satin finish; pink wood laminate stock with thumbhole; AccuTrigger.
**MSRP** . . . . . . . . . . . . . . . . . . . . $296

## MARK II SERIES BTV

**Action**: Bolt
**Stock**: Wood laminate
**Barrel**: 21 in.
**Sights**: None
**Weight**: 6.5 lb.
**Caliber**: .22 LR
**Magazine**: Detachable box, 5-rounds
**Features**: Carbon steel barrel with blued satin finish; wood laminate stock with thumbhole; AccuTrigger.
**MSRP** . . . . . . . . . . . . . . . . . . . . $418

## 17 SERIES M93R17 CLASSIC T

**Action**: Bolt
**Stock**: Wood
**Barrel**: 24 in.
**Sights**: None
**Weight**: 6.5 lb.
**Caliber**: .17 HMR
**Magazine**: Detachable box, 5-rounds
**Features**: Carbon steel barrel with blued high luster finish; wood stock with high luster finish; AccuTrigger.
**MSRP** . . . . . . . . . . . . . . . . . . . . $640

RIFLES

# Sig Sauer Rifles

**SIG556-SWAT WITH OPTIONAL RAIL COVERS**

SIG556 PATROL

SIG516 PATROL

## SIG556 CLASSIC SWAT

**Action**: Semi-automatic
**Stock**: Tactical synthetic
**Barrel**: 16 in.
**Sights**: Rear rotary diopter sight
**Weight**: 8.2 lb.
**Caliber**: 5.56 x 45mm NATO
**Magazine**: Detachable box, 30-rounds
**Features**: Features full length gas piston operating system; quad rail and rotary diopter sight; black Swiss-type folding stock that adjusts to length; cold hammer-forged barrel; alloy trigger housing; AR style magazine and flash suppressor.
**MSRP** . . . . . . . . . . . . . . . . . . . **$1324**

## SIG556 PATROL

**Action**: Semi-automatic
**Stock**: Tactical synthetic
**Barrel**: 14.4 in.
**Sights**: Rear rotary diopter sight
**Weight**: 7.5 lb.
**Caliber**: 5.56 x 45mm NATO, .223
**Magazine**: Detachable box, 30-rounds
**Features**: A2 type flash suppressor; reduced length gas piston with 2-position gas valve; improved design trigger casing; Swiss type folding stock, adjustable for length; Swiss type reduced lengthy polymer handguards; alloy quad rail reduced length tactical forend; Rdss rotary diopter sight system.
**MSRP** . . . . . . . . . . . . . . . . . . . **$1191**

## SIG516 PATROL

**Action**: Semi-automatic
**Stock**: Tactical synthetic
**Barrel**: 16 in.
**Sights**: None
**Weight**: 7.3 lb.
**Caliber**: 5.56mm NATO
**Magazine**: Detachable box, 30 rounds
**Features**: Gas piston operating system; three-position gas regulator; free-floating military grade chrome lined barrel; M1913 Picatinny flat top upper; aircraft grade aluminum upper & lower receiver with hard coat anodize finish.
**MSRP** . . . . . . . . . . . . . . . . . . . **$1599**

# Smith & Wesson Rifles

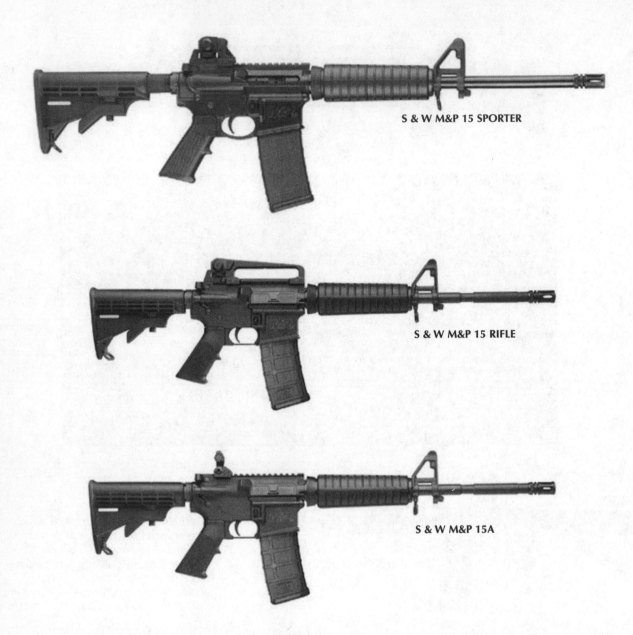

S & W M&P 15 SPORTER

S & W M&P 15 RIFLE

S & W M&P 15A

### M&P 15 SPORTER
**Action**: Semi-automatic
**Stock**: Synthetic
**Barrel**: 16 in.
**Sights**: Adjustable A2 front post, adjustable dual aperature
**Weight**: 6.5 lb.
**Caliber**: 5.56mm NATO
**Magazine**: Detachable box, 10- or 30-rounds
**Features**: 6-position telescopic black stock or fixed stock; chrome-lined gas key and bolt carrier; Flash supressor compensator; two-position safety lever.
**MSRP** . . . . . . . . . . . . . . . . . . . . **$709**

### M&P 15 AND M&P 15A
**Action**: Semi-automatic
**Stock**: Synthetic
**Barrel**: 16 in.
**Sights**: Troy adjustable front post, folding rear battle sight
**Weight**: 6.5 lb.–6.74 lb.
**Caliber**: 5.56 mm NATO, .223
**Magazine**: Detachable box, 30-rounds
**Features**: 6-position telescopic black stock; chrome-lined gas key and bolt carrier; flash supressor compensator; two-position safety lever.
**M&P 15:** . . . . . . . . . . . . . . . . . **$1249**
**M&P 15A:** . . . . . . . . . . . . . . . . **$1289**

# Smith & Wesson Rifles

S & W M&P 15-22

S & W M&P 15 PC

## M&P 15-22

**Action**: Semi-automatic
**Stock**: Synthetic
**Barrel**: 18 in.
**Sights**: Adjustable A2 front post, adjustable dual aperature
**Weight**: 5.4 lb.
**Caliber**: .22 LR
**Magazine**: Detachable box, 10-rounds
**Features**: 6-position collapsible stock; functioning charging handle; two-position receiver mounted safety selector; cartridge case deflector; bolt catch; recessed magazine release button; match grade precision, threaded barrel.
**MSRP** . . . . . . . . . . . . . . . . . . . . $769

## M&P 15 PC

**Action**: Semi-automatic
**Stock**: Synthetic
**Barrel**: 20 in.
**Sights**: None
**Weight**: 8 lb. 2 oz.
**Caliber**: 5.56mm NATO, .233
**Magazine**: Detachable box, 10-rounds
**Features**: Hogue Green pistol grip; A2 buttstock; two-stage trigger; Realtree Advantage Max-1 camo finish stock; chromed gas key and bolt carrier.
**MSRP** . . . . . . . . . . . . . . . . . . . $1539

# Springfield Armory Rifles

## M1A STANDARD

**Action**: Autoloading
**Stock**: Composite or walnut
**Barrel**: 22.6 in.
**Sights**: National Match military front post, adjustable rear aperture sight
**Weight**: 9.3 lb.
**Caliber**: 7.62 x 51mm NATO, .308 Win.
**Magazine**: Detachable box; 10-rounds

SPRINGFIELD ARMORY M1A STANDARD

**Features**: Black fiberglass with rubber buttplate, Mossy Oak stock with metal buttplate or American walnut with original miliatry buttplate; two-stage military trigger.
**MSRP** . . . . . . . . . . . . . . $1640–$1739

# Springfield Armory Rifles

SPRINGFIELD ARMORY M1A NATIONAL MATCH

SPRINGFIELD ARMORY SCOUT RIFLE

SPRINGFIELD ARMORY SOCOM 16

### NATIONAL MATCH M1A
*Action*: Autoloading
*Stock*: Walnut
*Barrel*: 22 in.
*Sights*: Natonal match front military post sight; rear National match hooded aperture
*Weight*: 9.8 lb.
*Caliber*: 7.62 x 51mm NATO, .308 Win.
*Magazine*: Detachable box; 10-rounds
*Features*: Glass bedded; NM gas cylinder; NM recoil spring guide; NM flash suppressor; walnut stock; stainless steel or carbon barrel; two-stage military trigger.
**MSRP . . . . . . . . . . . . . . $2318–$2373**

### SOCOM 16
*Action*: Autoloading
*Stock*: Composite
*Barrel*: 16 in.
*Sights*: Tritium front sight
*Weight*: 8.8 lb.
*Caliber*: 7.62 x 51mm NATO, .308 Win.
*Magazine*: Detachable box, 10-rounds
*Features*: Muzzle brake; forward mounted scope base; two-stage military trigger; composite black or green stock.
**MSRP . . . . . . . . . . . . . $1893–$1905**

### SCOUT SQUAD
*Action*: Autoloading
*Stock*: Walnut, composite
*Barrel*: 18 in.
*Sights*: Natonal match front military post sight; rear military aperature
*Weight*: 9.3 lb.
*Caliber*: 7.62 x 51mm NATO, .308 Win.
*Magazine*: Detachable box, 10-rounds
*Features*: Mounted optical sight base; muzzle stablizers; black or green fiberglass composite, American walnut stock or Mossy Oak camo stock; two-stage military trigger.
**MSRP . . . . . . . . . . . . . $1775–$1893**

RIFLES

# Stag Arms

**STAG ARMS MODEL 8**

## MODEL 8
*Action*: Gas-operated piston autoloader
*Stock*: Synthetic
*Barrel*: Chrome-lined 20 in.
*Sights*: Midwest Industries front and rear flip-up
*Weight*: 6.8 lb.
*Caliber*: 5.56 Nato
*Magazine*: Detachable box, 30-Rounds
*Features*: Right and left-hand available; 6-position collapsible stock.
**MSRP** . . . . . . . . . . . . . . . . . . **$1145**

# Steyr Arms

## MANNLICHER CLASSIC
*Action*: Bolt
*Stock*: European walnut
*Barrel*: 20 in., 23.6 in., 25.6 in.
*Sights*: Open
*Weight*: 7.3 lb.
*Caliber*: .222 Rem., .223 Rem., .243 Win., 6.5 x 55 SE, .270 Win., 7 x 64, 25-06 Rem., .308 Win., .30-06 Spr., 8 x 57 JS, 9.3 x 62, 6.5 x 57
*Magazine*: Detachable box, 3- or 4-rounds

**STEYR MANNLICHER CLASSIC**

*Features*: Set or direct trigger; sights included for full stock only; Bavarian-styled cheekpiece; safe bolt system; case hardening surface finish on European walnut stock.
**Full stock:** . . . . . . . . . . . . . . **$2999**

## MANNLICHER PRO HUNTER
*Action*: Bolt
*Stock*: Synthetic
*Barrel*: 20 in., 23.6 in., 25.6 in.
*Sights*: None
*Weight*: 7.3 lb.–8.2 lb.
*Caliber*: .222 Rem., .223 Rem., .243 Win., 6.5 x 55SE, .25-06Rem., .270 Win., 7 x 64, 7mm-08 Rem., .308 Win., .30-06 Spr., 9.3 x 62, .338 Fed. Mag. Magnum Caliber: .300 Win. Mag., 9.3 x 62, 7mm WSM, .270 WSM, .300 WSM

**STEYR MANNLICHER PROHUNTER**

*Magazine*: Detachable box
*Features*: Direct trigger, optionally set trigger; durable synthetic stock adjusted by spacers; MANNOTM metal surface finish protects agianst corrosion; three-position safety.
**MSRP** . . . . . . . . . . . . . . . . . . **$1150**
**Stainless:** . . . . . . . . . . . . . . . . **$1250**

# Steyr Arms

**STEYR MANNLICHER SCOUT**

## MANNLICHER SCOUT

**Action**: Bolt
**Stock**: Synthetic
**Barrel**: 19 in.
**Sights**: None
**Weight**: 6.6 lb.

**Caliber**: .243 Rem., 7mm-08 Rem., .308 Win.
**Magazine**: Box, 2- or 5-rounds (optional 10-round magazine)
**Features**: Weaver scope mounting rail; set trigger or direct trigger; synthetic

stock in black or grey wood imitation; optional bipod integrated into forearm; matte black or stainless steel finish on barrel.
**MSRP** . . . . . . . . . . . . . . . . . . . **$2099**

**STEYR SSG 08**

## SSG 08

**Action**: Bolt
**Stock**: Synthetic
**Barrel**: 20 in., 23.6 in.
**Sights**: None
**Weight**: 5.5 lb.–5.7 lb.

**Caliber**: .308 Win.
**Magazine**: Box, 10-rounds
**Features**: Direct trigger; Mannox system; high grade aluminum folding stock; adjustable cheek piece and butt plate with height marking; ergonomic

exchangeable pistol grip; UIT rail and Picatinny rail; muzzle brake; versa-pod.
**MSRP** . . . . . . . . . . . . . . . . . . . **$5899**

**STEYR AUG/A3 SA USA**

## AUG/A3 SA USA

**Action**: Semi-automatic
**Stock**: Synthetic
**Barrel**: 16 in.
**Sights**: None
**Weight**: 8.15 lb.
**Caliber**: .223 Rem.
**Magazine**: Detachable transparent box, 30-rounds
**Features**: Synthetic black stock; lateral push-through type, locks trigger; 1913

Picatinny rail; changeable barrel; includes factory Aug sling and cleaning kit that fits inside buttstock.
**MSRP** . . . . . . . . . . . . . . . . . . . **$2295**

RIFLES

SZECSEI & FUCHS DOUBLE-BARREL REPEATER

## DOUBLE BOLT REPEATER

**Action**: Bolt
**Stock**: Turkish walnut
**Weight**: 11.4 lb. round barrel, 13 lb.–15.2 lb. octagonal barrel
**Caliber**: Available in many popular calibers. The larger caliber rifles are available in .17 Cal to .700 Cal. Their most affordable options are the .17 and 22 Cal rifles.
**Magazine**: Detachable box, 4+2-rounds

**Features**: Hungarian inventor Joseph Szecsei developed his innovative design after being charged simultaneously by three elephants in 1989. Built with great care and much handiwork from the finest materials, it follows a design remarkable for its cleverness. While the rifle is not light-weight, it can be aimed quickly and offers more large-caliber firepower than any competitor. The six-shot magazine feeds two rounds simultaneously, both of which can then be fired by two quick pulls of the trigger. Optical sight is secured with titanium mounting; triggers have integrated, noiseless double-firing safety catch; titanium and steel barrels in octagon or round; one piece bolt reloads two rounds.

**Larger caliber rifles
can be purchased at:** . . . . . . $72,000
**Smaller caliber
rifles start at:** . . . . . . . . . . . $38,000

# Tactical Rifles

TACTICAL L.R.

## TACTICAL L.R.
**Action**: Bolt, 700 Rem.
**Stock**: Synthetic
**Barrel**: 18 in. to 26 in.
**Sights**: None
**Weight**: 12 lb.–13.4 lb.

**Caliber**: 7.62 NATO, (.308 Win.)
**Magazine**: Detachable box, 5- or 10-rounds
**Features**: Ergonomic thumbhole stock comes in black or green; raised cheek piece; free floating chrome moly

match grade barrel; ambidextrous sling swivel studs; soft rubber recoil pad; 1913 MIL-STD Picatinny rail; aluminum block chassis stock system; optional bipod.
**MSRP** . . . . . . . . . . . . . . . . . $2950

# Taylor's Firearms

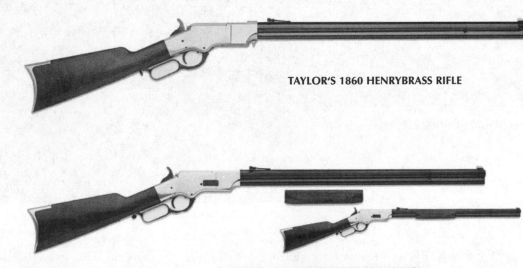

TAYLOR'S 1860 HENRYBRASS RIFLE

TAYLOR'S 1866 WINCHESTER TRANSITION

## 1860 HENRY RIFLE
**Action**: Lever
**Stock**: Walnut
**Barrel**: 24.25 in.
**Sights**: Open
**Weight**: 9.2 lb.
**Caliber**: .44-40
**Magazine**: Under-barrel tube, 9- to 13-rounds

**Features**: Brass frame; octagonal barrel with blue finish; includes sling swivels.
**MSRP** . . . . . . . . . . . . . . . . . $1304

## 1866 WINCHESTER TRANSITION
**Action**: Lever
**Stock**: Walnut

**Barrel**: 24.25 in.
**Sights**: Open
**Weight**: 9 lb. 1 oz
**Caliber**: .45LC, .44-40
**Magazine**: Under-barrel tube
**Features**: Checkered walnut stock with optional checkered forend; crescent buttplate with trapdoor.
**MSRP** . . . . . . . . . . . . . . . . . $1170

RIFLES

# Taylor's Firearms

**TAYLOR'S LIGHTNING RIFLE**

## LIGHTNING SLIDE ACTION RIFLE

**Action**: Slide
**Stock**: Walnut
**Barrel**: 24.25 in., 26 in.
**Sights**: Open
**Weight**: 6.2 lb.–6.5 lb.
**Caliber**: .45 LC, .44-40, .357 Mag.
**Magazine**: Under-barrel tube
**Features**: Case-hardened frame; walnut stock with checkered forend; octagonal barrel.
**MSRP** . . . . . . . . . . . . . . **$1099–$1120**

# Thompson/Center

**THOMPSON/CENTER ENCORE RIFLE**

**THOMPSON/CENTER ENCORE PRO HUNTER**

## ENCORE CENTERFIRE

**Action**: Single-shot, break-open
**Stock**: Walnut, composite
**Barrel**: 24 in., 26 in.
**Sights**: 24 in. model has adjustable sights
**Weight**: 6 lb. 12oz.
**Caliber**: .17 HMR, .22 LR, .204 Ruger, .22 Hornet, .22-250 Rem., .223 Rem., .243 Win., .25-06 Rem., .270 Win., 6.8 Rem., .280 Rem., 7mm-08 Rem., 7mm Rem. Mag., .30-06 Sprg., .308 Win., .300 Win. Mag., .375 H&H Mag., .45/70 Govt.
**Magazine**: None

**Features**: Blued or stainless barrel; black composite stock or American walnut stock; fixed spur hammer; single cheveron receiver; readily interchangable barrels.
**MSRP** . . . . . . . . . . . . . . . **$734–$787**

## ENCORE PRO HUNTER CENTERFIRE

**Action**: Single-shot, break-open
**Stock**: Composite
**Barrel**: 20 in., 28 in.
**Sights**: Optional fiber optic sights and peep sights
**Weight**: 6.25 lb.–7.75 lb.
**Caliber**: .204 Ruger, .223 Ruger, .22-250 Rem., .243 Win., .25-06 Rem., .270 Win., .280 Rem., 7mm Rem. Mag., 7mm-08 Rem., .300 Win. Mag., .308 Win., .30-06 Sprg., .45/70 Govt., .460 S&W, .500 S&W
**Magazine**: None
**Features**: Swing hammer; flextech stock in black or Realtree hardwoods camo; fluted barrel; thumbhole stock optional; Sims recoil pad; engraved stainless steel frame; readily interchangable barrels.
**MSRP** . . . . . . . . . . . . . . . . . . **$970**

# Thompson/Center

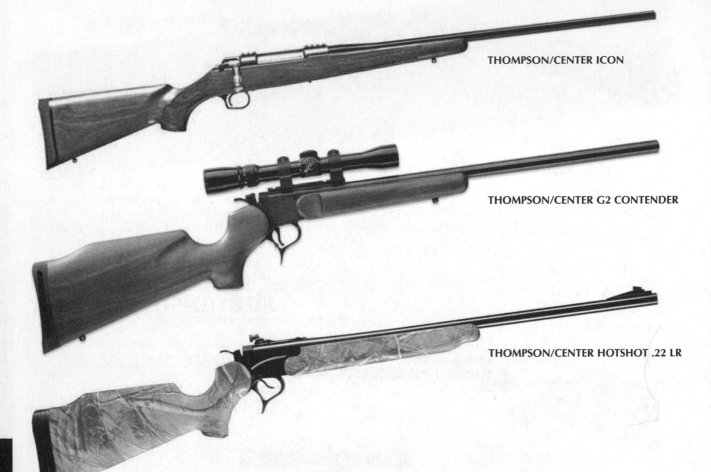

THOMPSON/CENTER ICON

THOMPSON/CENTER G2 CONTENDER

THOMPSON/CENTER HOTSHOT .22 LR

## ICON
*Action*: Bolt
*Stock*: Wood laminated walnut stock or solid walnut
*Barrel*: 24 in.
*Sights*: None
*Weight*: 7.5–7.75 lb.
*Caliber*: .22-250 Rem., .243, .308 Win., .30 TC, 6.5 Creedmore
*Magazine*: Detachable box, 3+1
*Features*: Blued steel barrel; icon weather shield finish; Interlok bedding block system; receiver machined from solid steel.
**MSRP** . . . . . . . . . . . . . . . **$869–$958**

## G2 CONTENDER
*Action*: Single-shot, break-open
*Stock*: Walnut, composite
*Barrel*: 18 in., 23 in.
*Sights*: None

*Weight*: 5.4 lb.
*Caliber*: .17 HMR, .22 LR Match, 5mm Rem. Mag., .204 Ruger, .223 Rem., 6.8 Rem., 7-30 Waters, .30/30 Win., .45/70 Govt.
*Magazine*: None
*Features*: Blued or stainless steel barrel; automatic hammer block with bolt interlock; drilled and tapped for scope mounts; button rifled.
**MSRP** . . . . . . . . . . . . . . . **$805–$835**

## VENTURE PREDATOR
*Action*: Bolt
*Stock*: Composite
*Barrel*: 22 in.
*Sights*: None
*Weight*: 6.75 lb.
*Caliber*: .204 Rug, .223 Rem., .22-250 Rem., .308 Win.
*Magazine*: Detachable box, 3+1

*Features*: Realtree MAX-1 Composite with Hogue panels; adjustable trigger; weather shield bolt handle; Weaver-style scope bases factory installed; adjustable trigger; sling swivel studs.
**MSRP** . . . . . . . . . . . . . . . . . **$670**

## HOTSHOT .22 LR
*Action*: Bolt
*Stock*: Composite
*Barrel*: 19 in.
*Sights*: Peep
*Weight*: 3 lb.
*Caliber*: .22 LR
*Magazine*: None
*Features*: Blued barrel finish; composite stock in black, Realtree AP camo HD, or Realtreee AP camo HD pink; automatic safety.
**MSRP** . . . . . . . . . . . . . . . **$232–$260**

**THOMPSON/CENTER PROHUNTER PREDATOR**

## PROHUNTER PREDATOR
*Action*: Single-shot, break-open
*Stock*: Composite
*Barrel*: 28 in.
*Sights*: None
*Weight*: 7.75 lb.

*Caliber*: .204 Rug, .223 Rem., .22-250 Rem., .308 Win.
*Magazine*: None
*Features*: Realtree MAX-1 camo composite stock and barrel; flextech; mounted and drilled for scopes.
MSRP . . . . . . . . . . . . . . . . . . . . $925

# Tikka Rifles

**TIKKA T3 HUNTER**

**TIKKA T3 SCOUT CTR**

## T3 HUNTER
*Action*: Bolt
*Stock*: Walnut
*Barrel*: 20 in., 22.4 in., 24.4 in.
*Sights*: None
*Weight*: 6.6 lb.–7 lb.
*Caliber*: .204 Ruger, .222 Rem., .223 Rem., .22-250 Rem., .243 Win., .260 Rem., 7mm-08 Rem., .308 Win., .338 Federal, .25-06 Rem., 6.5 x 55 SE, .270 Win., 7 x 64, 30-06 Sprg., 8 x 57 IS, 9.3 x 62, 7mm Rem. Mag., .300 Win. Mag., .338 Win. Mag., .270 Win. Short Mag., .300 Win. Short Mag.
*Magazine*: Detachable box, 4- or 5-rounds

*Features*: Sling swivels; free-floating cold-hammer forged barrel; two locking Lug T3 action; two-stage safety; single-set trigger; walnut stock in oil finish and optional matte laquered stock; integral scope mounts.
MSRP . . . . . . . . . . . . . . . $695–$735

## T3 SCOUT CTR (COMPACT TACTICAL RIFLE)
*Action*: Bolt
*Stock*: Synthetic
*Barrel*: 20 in.
*Sights*: None
*Weight*: 7.9 lb.
*Caliber*: .308 Win., .223 Rem.

*Magazine*: Detachable box, 5-rounds
*Features*: Free-floating cold hammer-forged barrel; two piece bolt with locking lugs; single-stage adjustable trigger; two position safety; black synthetic stock; Picatinny rail; high cheekpiece.
MSRP . . . . . . . . . . . . . . . . . . . . $930

**RIFLES**

# Tikka Rifles

TIKKA T3 LITE

TIKKA T3 BATTUE

TIKKA T3 VARMINT

## T3 LITE
*Action*: Bolt
*Stock*: Synthetic
*Barrel*: 20 in., 22.4 in., 24.4 in.
*Sights*: None
*Weight*: 6 lb.-6.4 lb.
*Caliber*: .204 Ruger, .222 Rem., .223 Rem., .22-250 Rem., .243 Win., .260 Rem., 7mm-08 Rem., .308 Win., .338 Federal, .25-06 Rem., 6.5 x 55 SE, .270 Win., 7 x 64, .30-06 Spfld., 8 x 57 IS, 9.3 x 62, 7mm Rem. Mag., .300 Win. Mag., .338 Win. Mag., .270 Win. Short Mag., .300 Win. Short Mag.
*Magazine*: Detachable box, 4- or 5-rounds
*Features*: Stainless steel bolt; two-stage safety; single-set trigger; fiber glass synthetic stock in black; Weaver scope mount bases; free-floating, cold hammer-forged barrel.
**MSRP**. . . . . . . . . . . . . . .$595–$625

## T3 BATTUE
*Action*: Bolt
*Stock*: Walnut
*Barrel*: 20 in., 22.4 in., 24.4 in.
*Sights*: Battue sight with TruGlo optic fibers
*Weight*: 6.8 lb.
*Caliber*: .308 Win., .338 Federal, 7 x 64, .30-06 Spfld., 8 x 57 IS, 9.3 x 62, .300 Win. Mag., .300 Win. Short Mag.
*Magazine*: Detachable box, 4-rounds
*Features*: Walnut stock oil finished, optional matte-lacaquered stocks; straight stock features ambidextrous palm swell; integral rails for scope mounts; short, free-floating barrel is cold hammer-forged.
**MSRP**. . . . . . . . . . . . . . . . . $1440

## T3 VARMINT
*Action*: Bolt
*Stock*: Syntehtic
*Barrel*: 20 in., 23.75 in.
*Sights*: None
*Weight*: 7.5 lb.–8 lb.
*Caliber*: .204 Ruger, .222 Rem., .223 Rem., .22-250 Rem., .243 Win., .260 Rem., 7mm-08 Rem., .308 Win., .25-06 Rem., 6.5 x 55 SE, .270 Win., 7 x 64, 3.0-06 Spfld.., 8 x 57 IS, 9.3 x 62, 7mm Rem. Mag., .300 Win. Mag., .338 Win. Mag., .270 Win. Short Mag., .300 Win. Short Mag.
*Magazine*: Detachable box, 4-, 5-, 6- or 7-rounds
*Features*: Two locking lug T3 action; stainless steel, free-floating barrel; single-stage trigger; integral rails for scope mounts.
**MSRP**. . . . . . . . . . . . . . . . . . $895

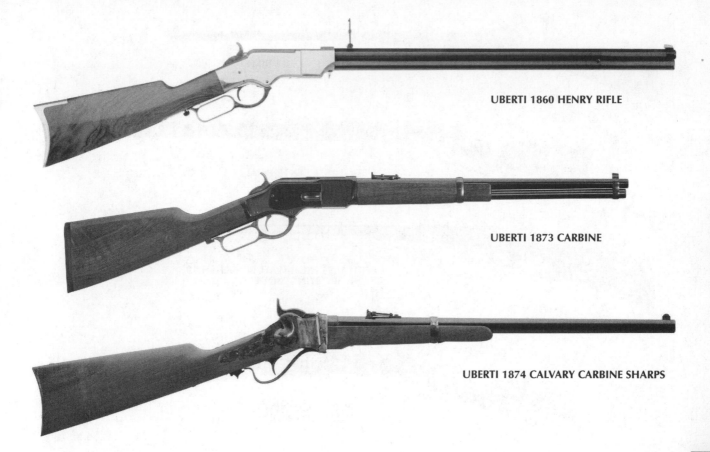

UBERTI 1860 HENRY RIFLE

UBERTI 1873 CARBINE

UBERTI 1874 CALVARY CARBINE SHARPS

## 1860 HENRY RIFLE

**Action**: Lever
**Stock**: Walnut
**Barrel**: 18.5 in., 24.5 in.
**Sights**: Adjustable
**Weight**: 9 lb.
**Caliber**: .45 Colt, .44/40
**Magazine**: Under-barrel tube, 8+1 or 13+1
**Features**: Blue or standard buttplate; case hardened lever and frame; A-grade walnut stock; octagonal barrel.
**MSRP** . . . . . . . . . . . . . **$1399–$1429**

## 1866 YELLOWBOY

**Action**: Lever
**Stock**: Walnut
**Barrel**: 19 in., 20 in., 24.25 in.
**Sights**: Adjustable
**Weight**: 8.2 lb.

**Caliber**: .45 Colt, .44/40, .38 Spl.
**Magazine**: Under-barrel tube, 10+1 or 13+1
**Features**: Brass forend nose cap; solid brass crescent buttplate; case hardened lever; brass frame and buttplate.
**MSRP** . . . . . . . . . . . . . **$1089–$1139**

## 1873 RIFLE & CARBINE

**Action**: Lever
**Stock**: Walnut
**Barrel**: 16.1 in., 18 in., 19 in., 20 in., 24.5 in.
**Sights**: Adjustable
**Weight**: 7.2 lb.–8.2 lb.
**Caliber**: .45 Colt, .357 Mag., .44/44
**Magazine**: Under-barrel tube, 9+1, 10+1, 13+1
**Features**: Octagonal barrel on rifle; round barrel on carbine and trapper;

A-grade walnut with checkered pistol grip and forend.
**Trapper**: . . . . . . . . . . . . . . . . **$1259**
**Rifle**: . . . . . . . . . . . . . **$1259–$1299**
**Carbine**: . . . . . . . . . . . **$1199–$1309**

## 1874 CALVARY CARBINE SHARPS

**Action**: Falling block
**Stock**: Walnut
**Barrel**: 22 in.
**Sights**: Creedmoor Sight
**Weight**: 8 lb.
**Caliber**: .45-70
**Magazine**: None (1-round)
**Features**: Round blue barrel; case-hardened levers and blue buttplate.
**MSRP** . . . . . . . . . . . . . . . . . **$1709**

UBERTI 1874 SHARPS RIFLE

UBERTI 1876 CENTENNIAL

UBERTI 1885 HIGH-WALL SINGLE-SHOT
SPECIAL SPORTING MODEL

UBERTI LIGHTNING-
SHORT RIFLE MODEL

## 1874 SHARPS RIFLE

*Action*: Falling block
*Stock*: Walnut
*Barrel*: 32 in., 34 in.
*Sights*: Creedmoor Sight
*Weight*: 10.25–11 lb.
*Caliber*: .45-70
*Magazine*: None (1-round)
*Features*: Blue octagonal barrel; checkered walnut stock; case-hardened, except extra deluxe model; double set trigger; pewter forend cap.
**Special:** . . . . . . . . . . . . . . . . . **$1859**
**Deluxe:** . . . . . . . . . . . . . . . . . **$2929**
**Down Under:** . . . . . . . . . . . . **$2359**
**Buffalo Hunter:** . . . . . . . . . . **$2359**
**Extra Deluxe:** . . . . . . . . . . . . . **$4289**

## 1876 CENTENNIAL

*Action*: Lever
*Stock*: Walnut

*Barrel*: 28 in.
*Sights*: Adjustable
*Weight*: 10 lb.
*Caliber*: .45-60, .45-75, .50-95
*Magazine*: 11+1 rounds
*Features*: Case-hardened frame and lever; blue buttplate; octagonal barrel; straight stock.
**MSRP** . . . . . . . . . . . . . . . . . . **$1599**

## 1885 HIGH-WALL SINGLE-SHOT

*Action*: Falling block
*Stock*: Walnut
*Barrel*: 28 in., 30 in., 32 in.
*Sights*: Adjustable
*Weight*: 9.3 lb. (carbine), 10 lb.
*Caliber*: .45-70, .45-90, .45-120
*Magazine*: None (1-round)
*Features*: Case-hardened frame and lever; blue buttplate; octagonal barrel;

carbine model has round barrel; carbine and sporting rifle have straight stock.
**Carbine:** . . . . . . . . . . . . . . . . **$969**
**Sporting Rifle:** . . . . . . . **$1049–$1089**
**Special Sporting Rifle:** **$1189–$1219**

## LIGHTNING

*Action*: Pump
*Stock*: Walnut
*Barrel*: 20 in., 24.25 in.
*Sights*: Adjustable
*Weight*: 6.2 lb.–6.5 lb.
*Caliber*: .45 Colt, .357 Mag.
*Magazine*: Under-barrel tube, 10+1 rounds (short rifle), 13+1 rounds (standard)
*Features*: Case-hardened frame and trigger guard; octagonal barrel.
**MSRP** . . . . . . . . . . . . . . . . . . **$1259**

RIFLES

# Uberti

UBERTI SPRINGFIELD TRAPDOOR CARBINE

UBERTI SPRINGFIELD TRAPDOOR RIFLE

UBERTI 1883 BURGESS RIFLE

UBERTI 1871 ROLLING BLOCK
HUNTER CARBINE

RIFLES

## SPRINGFIELD TRAPDOOR CARBINE

**Action**: Hinged breech
**Stock**: Walnut
**Barrel**: 22 in.
**Sights**: Adjustable ladder
**Weight**: 7.3 lb.
**Caliber**: .45-70
**Magazine**: None (1-round)
**Features**: Blue steel, case-hardened breechblock and butt plate; fitted with sliding ring and bar for calvalryman to carry it clipped to carbine sling.
**MSRP**. . . . . . . . . . . . . . . . . . **$1569**

## SPRINGFIELD TRAPDOOR RIFLE

**Action**: Hinged breech
**Stock**: Walnut
**Barrel**: 32.5 in.
**Sights**: Adjustable ladder

**Weight**: 8.8 lb.
**Caliber**: .45-70
**Magazine**: None (1-round)
**Features**: Blue steel, case-hardened breechblock and butt plate.
**MSRP**. . . . . . . . . . . . . . . . . . **$1789**

## 1883 BURGESS RIFLE & CARBINE

**Action**: Lever
**Stock**: Walnut
**Barrel**: 20 in.(carbine), 25.5 in. (rifle)
**Sights**: Fixed
**Weight**: 7.6 lb.–8.1 lb.
**Caliber**: .45 Colt
**Magazine**: Under-barrel tube, 10- or 13-rounds
**Features**: Case-hardened, round barrel; straight grip.
**MSRP**. . . . . . . . . . . . . . . . . . **$1499**

## 1871 ROLLING BLOCK HUNTER CARBINE

**Action**: Rolling block
**Stock**: Walnut
**Barrel**: 22 in.
**Sights**: Fixed
**Weight**: 4.5 lb.
**Caliber**: .38-55, .30-30, .45-70
**Magazine**: None (1-round)
**Features**: Rubber butt pad; case-colored receiver
**MSRP**. . . . . . . . . . . . . . . . . . **$799**

# Volquartsen

**VOLQUARTSEN TF-17**

## TF-17 & TF-22
*Action*: Autoloader
*Stock*: Ambidextrous birch
*Barrel*: 18.5 in.
*Sights*: Picatinny mil-spec rail
*Weight*: 8.5 lb.

*Caliber*: .17 HMR, .22 WMR
*Magazine*: Rotary mag., 9-rounds
*Features*: Blowback design, TG2000 trigger unit with 2.25-lb. pull; black stainless barrel.
**MSRP. . . . . . . . . . . . . . . . . . . . $1041**

# Walther Rifles

**WALTHER G22 CARBINE**

## G22 CARBINE
*Action*: Autoloading
*Stock*: Synthetic
*Barrel*: 20 in.
*Sights*: Adjustable on handle and front strut
*Weight*: 6 lb.
*Caliber*: .22 LR
*Magazine*: Detachable box, 10-rounds
*Features*: Single-action trigger; employs an innovative " Bullpup" design; Weaver-style universal rails for sight mounts, bipods and other acces-

sories; includes Walther safety package with cocking indicator, slide safety and integral lock; available in left hand

models; synthetic stock comes in black or green.
**MSRP. . . . . . . . . . . . . . . . $509–$615**

# Weatherby Rifles

**WEATHERBY MARK V ACCUMARK**

## MARK V ACCUMARK
*Action*: Bolt
*Stock*: Composite
*Barrel*: 24 in., 26 in., 28 in.
*Sights*: None
*Weight*: 7.25 lb.–9 lb.
*Caliber*: .270 Win., .208 Win., .257 Wby. Mag., .270 Wby. Mag., 7mm Rem. Mag., 7mm Wby. Mag., .300 Win. Mag., .300 Wby. Mag., .30-378 Wby. Mag., .340 Wby. Mag., .247 Wby. Mag., .300 Wby. Mag., .30-378 Wby. Mag.

*Magazine*: Box, 2+1, 3+1, 5+1 rounds
*Features*: Adjustable trigger; hand-laminated raised comb, Monte Carlo composite stock with matte gel coat finish and spiderweb accents;

Pachmayr decelerator pad; button rifled; CNC-machined 6061 T-6 aluminum bedding plate; cocking indicator; fluted bolt body.
**MSRP. . . . . . . . . . . . . . . . . . . $1779**

# Weatherby Rifles

**WEATHERBY MARK V DELUXE**

## MARK V DELUXE
**Action**: Bolt
**Stock**: Walnut
**Barrel**: 24 in., 26 in., 28 in.
**Sights**: None
**Weight**: 6.75 lb.–10 lb.
**Caliber**: .270 Win., .308 Win.,
.30-06 Sprg., .257 Wby. Mag.,
.270 Wby. Mag., 7mm Wby. Mag.,
.300 Wby. Mag., .340 Wby. Mag.,
.378 Wby. Mag., .416 Wby. Mag.,
.460 Wby. Mag.
**Magazine**: Box, 2+1, 3+1, 5+1 rounds
**Features**: Adjustable trigger; walnut
Monte Carlo stock with rosewood
forend and pistol grip cap and maple-
wood spacers; blued metalwork in
high luster finish; Pachmayr decelerator pad.
**MSRP**. . . . . . . . . . . . . . . . . . . . **$2260**

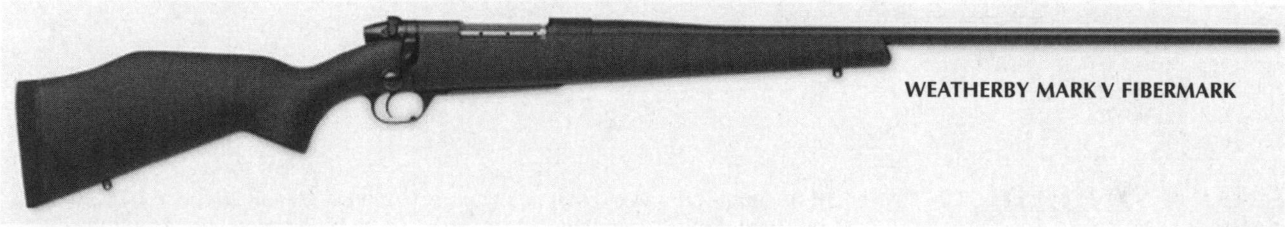

**WEATHERBY MARK V FIBERMARK**

## MARK V FIBERMARK
**Action**: Bolt
**Stock**: Composite
**Barrel**: 24 in., 26 in., 28 in.
**Sights**: None
**Weight**: 8 lb., 8.5 lb.
**Caliber**: .257 Wby. Mag.,
.270 Wby. Mag., 7mm Rem. Mag.,
7mm Wby. Mag., .300 Win. Mag.,
.300 Wby. Mag., .30-378 Wby. Mag.,
.340 Wby. Mag., .375 H&H Mag.
**Magazine**: Box, 2+1, 3+1 rounds
**Features**: Adjustable trigger; pillar-bed-
ded, hand-laminated raised comb
Monte Carlo composite stock with stra-
tegically placed bedding points assures
consistent, repeatable accuracy.
**MSRP**. . . . . . . . . . . . . . . . . . . . **$1476**

**WEATHERBY MARK V
LAZERMARK**

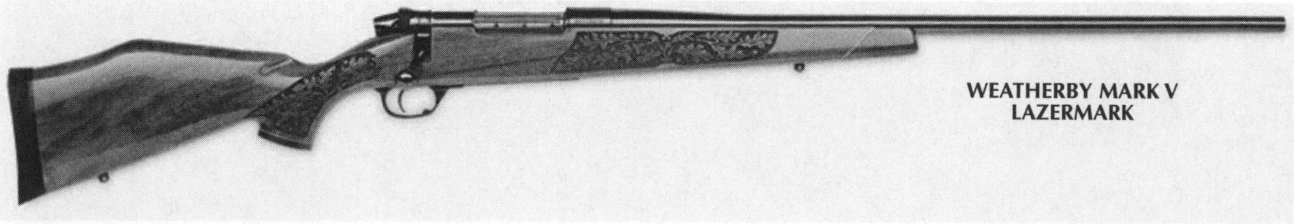

## MARK V LAZERMARK
**Action**: Bolt
**Stock**: Walnut
**Barrel**: 26 in.
**Sights**: None
**Weight**: 8.5 lb.
**Caliber**: .257 Wby. Mag.,
.270 Wby. Mag., 7mm Rem. Mag.,
7mm Wby. Mag., .300 Win. Mag.,
.300 Wby. Mag.
**Magazine**: Box, 3+1 rounds
**Features**: Adjustable trigger; hand-
selected, raised comb Monte Carlo
stock with laser-carved oak leaf pat-
tern; blued metalwork in high luster
finish; Pachmayr decelerator pad.
**MSRP**. . . . . . . . . . . . . . . . . . . . **$2532**

**RIFLES**

WEATHERBY MARK V SPORTER

## MARK V SPORTER

**Action**: Bolt
**Stock**: Walnut
**Barrel**: 24 in., 26 in.
**Sights**: None
**Weight**: 8 lb.
**Caliber**: .257 Wby. Mag.,
.270 Wby. Mag., 7mm Rem. Mag.,
7mm Wby. Mag., .300 Win. Mag.,
.300 Wby. Mag., .340 Wby. Mag.
**Magazine**: Box, 3+1 rounds
**Features**: Adjustable trigger; raised
comb Monte Carlo walnut stock with
satin finish; features fineline diamond
point checkering and rosewood forend
and grip cap; bead blasted, blued met-
alwork with low luster finish;
Pachmayr decelerator pad.
**MSRP** . . . . . . . . . . . . . . . . . . . **$1537**

WEATHERBY MARK V SYNTHETIC

## MARK V SYNTHETIC

**Action**: Bolt
**Stock**: Synthetic
**Barrel**: 24 in., 26 in.
**Sights**: None
**Weight**: 6.75 lb.–8.5 lb.
**Caliber**: .243 Wby. Mag.,
.270 Wby. Mag., .308 Win.,
.30-06 Sprg., .257 Wby. Mag.,
7mm Rem. Mag., 7mm Wby. Mag.,
.300 Win. Mag., .300 Wby. Mag.,
.30-378 Wby. Mag., .340 Wby. Mag.,
.375 H&H Mag.
**Magazine**: Box, 2+1, 3+1, 5+1 rounds
**Features**: Adjustable trigger; lightweight, injection-molded, raised comb
Monte Carlo stock; bead blasted,
matte blued metalwork; button-rifled
barrel; low-density recoil pad.
**MSRP** . . . . . . . . . . . . . . . . . . . **$1235**

WEATHERBY MARK V ULTRAMARK
LIGHTWEIGHT

## MARK V ULTRA LIGHWEIGHT

**Action**: Bolt
**Stock**: Composite
**Barrel**: 24 in., 26 in.
**Sights**: None
**Weight**: 5.75 in.–6.75 in.
**Caliber**: .243 Win., .240 Wby. Mag.,
.25-06 Rem., .270 Win.,
7mm-08 Rem., .308 Win.,
.30-06 Sprg., .257 Wby. Mag.,
7mm Rem. Mag., 7mm Wby. Mag.,
.300 Win. Mag., .257 Wby. Mag.,
.300 Wby. Mag.
**Magazine**: Box, 3+1, 5+1 rounds
**Features**: Adjustable trigger; contoured
fluted stainless steel barrel, blackened
to reduce glare; Bell & Carlson composite stock with spiderweb accents;
CNC-machined 6061 T-6 aluminum
bedding plate; one-piece forged bolt;
Pachmayr decelerator pad.
**MSRP** . . . . . . . . . . . . . . . . . . . **$1919**

RIFLES

# Weatherby Rifles

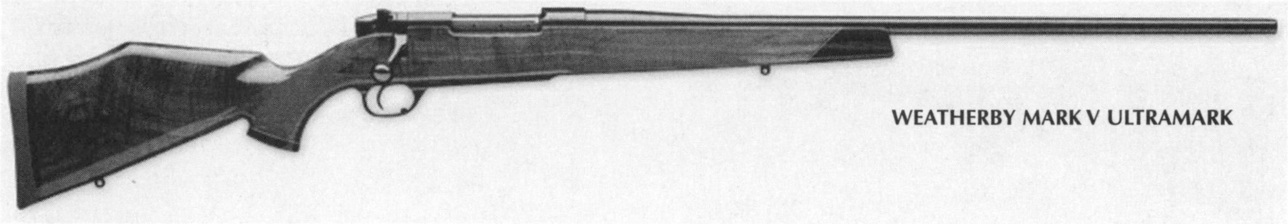

WEATHERBY MARK V ULTRAMARK

## MARK V ULTRAMARK
**Action**: Bolt
**Stock**: Walnut
**Barrel**: 26 in.
**Sights**: None
**Weight**: 8.5 lb.

**Caliber**: .257 Wby. Mag., .300 Wby. Mag.
**Magazine**: Box, 3+1 rounds
**Features**: Adjustable trigger; hand-selected, AAA fancy exhibition grade walnut stock; features 20 LPI checker-ing, maplewood/ebony spacers and rosewood forend and grip caps; blued metalwork in high luster finish; Pachmayr decelerator pad.
**MSRP**...................**$3044**

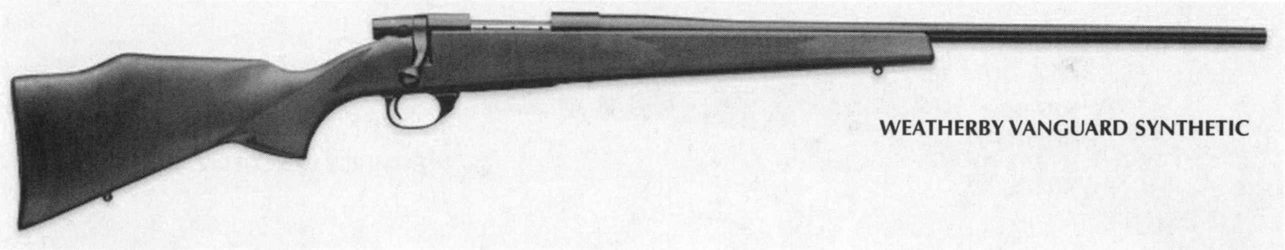

WEATHERBY VANGUARD SYNTHETIC

## VANGUARD SYNTHETIC
**Action**: Bolt
**Stock**: Synthetic
**Barrel**: 24 in.
**Sights**: None
**Weight**: 7.25 lb.
**Caliber**: .223 Rem., .22-250 Rem.,

.243 Win., .25-06 Rem., .270 Win., 7mm-08 Rem., .308 Win., .30-06 Sprg., .257 Wby. Mag., .270 WSM, 7mm Rem. Mag., .300 Win. Mag., .300 WSM, .300 Wby. Mag., .338 Win. Mag.
**Magazine**: Box 3+1, 5+1 rounds

**Features**: Adjustable trigger; injection-molded, Monte Carlo composite stock; matte black metalwork; hammer-forged barrel.
**MSRP**...................**$469**

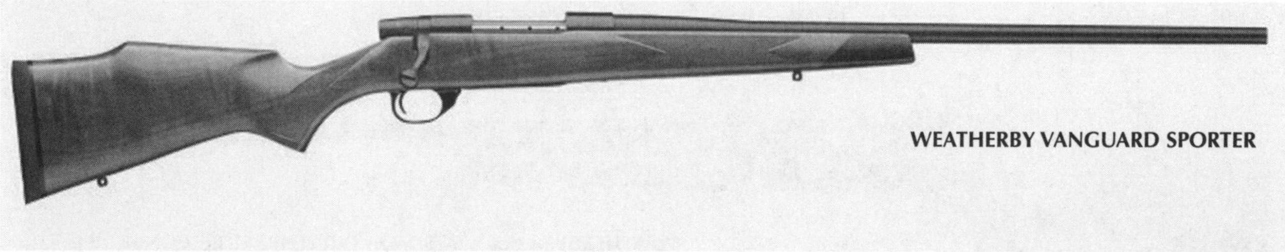

WEATHERBY VANGUARD SPORTER

## VANGUARD SPORTER
**Action**: Bolt
**Stock**: Walnut
**Barrel**: 24 in.
**Sights**: None
**Weight**: 7.5 lb.
**Caliber**: .223 Rem., .22-250 Rem., .243 Win., .25-06 Rem., .270 Win.,

7mm-08 Rem., .308 Win., .30-06 Sprg., .257 Wby. Mag., .270 WSM, 7mm Rem. Mag., .300 Win. Mag., .300 WSM, .300 Wby. Mag., .338 Win. Mag.
**Magazine**: Box 3+1, 5+1 rounds
**Features**: Adjustable trigger; factory-tuned, fully adjustable trigger; raised

comb, Monte Carlo stock with satin urethane finish; hand-selected a fancy grade Turkish walnut; rosewood forend; low luster, matte black metal-work; fineline diamond point checker-ing; low density recoil pad.
**MSRP**...................**$754**

**WEATHERBY VANGUARD VARMINT SPECIAL**

## VANGUARD VARMINT SPECIAL
**Action**: Bolt
**Stock**: Composite
**Barrel**: 22 in.
**Sights**: None

**Weight**: 8 lb.
**Caliber**: .223 Rem., .22-250 Rem., .308 Win.
**Magazine**: Box, 5+1 rounds
**Features**: Adjustable trigger; Monte Carlo composite stock with tan pebble

grain finish and black spiderwebbing; matte black metalwork; features recessed target crown to enhance accuracy and protect rifling.
**MSRP** . . . . . . . . . . . . . . . . . . . . **$713**

**WEATHERBY VANGUARD PREDATOR**

## VANGUARD PREDATOR
**Action**: Bolt
**Stock**: Composite
**Barrel**: 22 in.
**Sights**: None
**Weight**: 8 lb.

**Caliber**: .223 Rem., .22-250 Rem., .308 Win.
**Magazine**: Box, 5+1 rounds
**Features**: Adjustable trigger; injection-molded composite stock and metalwork feature natural gear camo

pattern; #3 contour barrel; low density recoil pad; features recessed target crown to enhance accuracy and protect rifling.
**MSRP** . . . . . . . . . . . . . . . . . . . . **$866**

**WEATHERBY MARK V SUB-MOA TRR (THREAT RESPONSE RIFLE)**

## MARK V SUB-MOA TRR (THREAT RESPONSE RIFLE)
**Action**: Bolt
**Stock**: Hand-laminated with 3-position buttstock
**Barrel**: 26 in.

**Sights**: None
**Weight**: 9 lb.
**Caliber**: .300 Win. Mag., .300 Wby. Mag., .30-378 Wby. Mag., .338-378 Wby. Mag.
**Magazine**: Drop box, +1 capacity

**Features**: Guaranteed to shoot a 3-shot group of .99 in. or less; hand-tuned, fully-adjustable trigger; stock has bi-pod attachment.
**MSRP** . . . . . . . . . . . . . . . . . . . . **$4019**

RIFLES

# Weatherby Rifles

**WEATHERBY VANGUARD
SYNTHETIC DBM**

## VANGUARD SYNTHETIC DBM
*Action*: Bolt
*Stock*: Injection-molded Monte Carlo
*Barrel*: 24 in.

*Sights*: None
*Weight*: 7 lb.
*Caliber*: .25-06 Rem., .270 Win., .30-06 Spfld.
*Magazine*: Detachable box, 3-rounds

*Features*: Matte black metalwork; low density recoil pad; adjustable trigger.
**MSRP . . . . . . . . . . . . . . . . . . . . $599**

**WEATHERBY VANGUARD SPORTER DBM**

## VANGUARD SPORTER DBM
*Action*: Bolt
*Stock*: Walnut Monte Carlo
*Barrel*: 24 in.

*Sights*: None
*Weight*: 7 lb.
*Caliber*: .25-06 Rem., .270 Win., .30-06 Spfld.
*Magazine*: Detachable box, 3-rounds

*Features*: Rosewood forend; raised comb; satin urethane finish; matte black metalwork; adjustable trigger.
**MSRP . . . . . . . . . . . . . . . . . . . . $809**

**WEATHERBY VANGUARD YOUTH**

## VANGUARD YOUTH
*Action*: Bolt
*Stock*: Injection-molded Monte Carlo
*Barrel*: 20 in.
*Sights*: None

*Weight*: 6.5 lb.
*Caliber*: .223 Rem., .22-250 Rem., .243 Win., 7mm-08 Rem., .308 Win.
*Magazine*: Internal box, 5-rounds

*Features*: Removable spacer to allow stock to be lengthened as shooter grows; low-density recoil pad.
**MSRP . . . . . . . . . . . . . . . . . . . . $523**

**RIFLES**

## ALASKAN CO-PILOT

**Action**: Lever
**Stock**: Walnut
**Barrel**: 16,18.5, or 20 in.
**Sights**: Fiber optic front bead, ghost ring sight
**Weight**: 6.5 lb.

*Caliber*: .457 Mag., .45-70, .50 Alaskan, .30-30, .35 Rem., .44 Mag., .357, .45 Colt
*Magazine*: Under-barrel tube
*Features*: 1859 Marlin action; features the Trigger Happy kit; Pachmayr decelerator pad; includes soft carry case;

WWG recoil control porting system; WWG bear proof ejector installed; mil-spec Parkerized finish.
**.457 Mag./ 45–70:** .......... **$1980**
**.50 Alaskan:** .............. **$2230**
**30–30, 35 Rem., 44 Mag.,**
**357 and 45 Colt:** .......... **$1999**

# Wilson Combat

**WILSON COMBAT M-4T TACTICAL CARBINE**

## M-4T TACTICAL CARBINE

**Action**: Autoloader
**Stock**: Collapsible, 6-position tactical
**Barrel**: 16.25 in. target-grade
**Sights**: Optional quad rail

*Weight*: 6.9 lb.
*Caliber*: .223 Rem.
*Magazine*: Detachable box, 30-rounds
*Features*: 2 MOA at 100 yards guaranteed; single stage trigger; pistol grip

stock comes in tan, green, gray or black; CNC-machined receiver, muzzle brake.
**MSRP** .................. **$2000**

RIFLES

# Winchester Rifles

## M70

*Action*: Bolt
*Stock*: Walnut
*Barrel*: 22, 24, 26 in.
*Sights*: None
*Weight*: 6 lb. 12oz.–8.25 lb.
*Caliber*: .243 Win., 7mm-08 Rem., .308 Win., .325 WSM, .270 Win., .30-06 Spfld., .300 Win. Mag., .338 Win. Mag., .300 WSM, .270 WSM, .416 Rem. Mag., .458 Win. Mag., .375 H&H Mag.
*Magazine*: 3+1, 5+1 rounds
*Features*: M.O.A Trigger System; pre-64 controlled round feeding, 3-position safety; blade-ejector type; black Pachmayr decelerator.
**Super Grade**: . . . . . . . . **$1329–$1379**
**Featherweight**: . . . . **$899.99–$949.99**
**Sporter**: . . . . . . . . . **$899.99–$949.99**
**Safari Express**: . . . . . . . . . . . . **$1349**

## SUPER X RIFLE-SXR

*Action*: Autoloader
*Stock*: Walnut
*Barrel*: 22, 24 in.
*Sights*: None
*Weight*: 7 lb. 4oz.–7 lb. 8oz.
*Caliber*: .30-06 Spfld., .300 Win. Mag., .300 WSM, .270 WSM
*Magazine*: 3+1, 4+1 rounds
*Features*: Hammer-forged barrel; enlarged trigger guard; crossbolt safety.
**MSRP** . . . . . . . . . . . . . . . . . . . **$979**

WINCHESTER SUPER X RIFLE-SXR

## WILDCAT BOLT-ACTION .22

*Action*: Bolt
*Stock*: Checkered hardwood
*Barrel*: 21 in.
*Sights*: None
*Weight*: 4 lb. 8oz.
*Caliber*: .22
*Magazine*: 5- or 10-rounds
*Features*: Checkered black synthetic Winchester buttplate and matching grip cap; Schnabel forend and steel sling swivel studs.
**MSRP** . . . . . . . . . . . . . . . . . . . **$259**

WINCHESTER WILDCAT BOLT-ACTION .22

## WILDCAT TARGET/ VARMINT .22

*Action*: Bolt
*Stock*: Checkered hardwood
*Barrel*: 21 in.
*Sights*: None
*Weight*: 5 lb. 8oz.
*Caliber*: .22
*Magazine*: 5- or 10-rounds
*Features*: Drilled and tapped receiver; grooved for scope mounting; adjustable trigger; dual front steel swivel studs.
**MSRP** . . . . . . . . . . . . . . . . . . . **$309**

WINCHESTER WILDCAT TARGET VARMINT .22

## M70 COYOTE LIGHT

*Action*: Bolt
*Stock*: Composite
*Barrel*: 24 in.
*Sights*: None
*Weight*: 7 lb. 8oz.
*Caliber*: 7mm WSM
*Magazine*: 3-rounds
*Features*: Bipod mounting studs; matte-blued receiver and medium-heavy fluted stainless barrel mount; Pachmayr decelerator.
**MSRP** . . . . . . . . . . . . . . . . . . . **$1099**

WINCHESTER 70 COYOTE LIGHT

## M70 ULTIMATE SHADOW

*Action*: Bolt
*Stock*: Composite
*Barrel*: 22 in., 24 in.
*Sights*: None
*Weight*: 6 lb. 8oz.–6 lb. 12oz.
*Caliber*: .300 WSM, .270 WSM, 7mm WSM, .223 WSSM, .243 WSSM, .25 WSSM, .325 WSM
*Magazine*: 3–rounds
*Features*: Features integrated, rubberized oval-dot gripping surfaces; pistol grip; controlled round feed action.
**MSRP** . . . . . . . . . . . . . . . . **$817–$838**

WINCHESTER M70 ULTIMATE SHADOW

## SUPER X RIFLE
**Action**: Autoloader
**Stock**: Walnut
**Barrel**: 22 in., 24 in.
**Sights**: None
**Weight**: 7 lb. 4oz.
**Caliber**: .30-06 Spfld., .300 Win. Mag., .300 WSM, .270 WSM
**Magazine**: 3- or 4-rounds
**Features**: Receiver is drilled and tapped for scope mounting bases; enlarged trigger guard; crossbolt safety; single-stage trigger.
**MSRP** . . . . . . . . . . . . . . . $939–$969

**WINCHESTER SUPER X RIFLE**

## 94 HIGH GRADE
**Action**: Lever
**Stock**: Walnut
**Barrel**: 24 in.
**Sights**: Marble's gold bead front sight
**Weight**: 8 lb.
**Caliber**: .30-30 Win.
**Magazine**: 8-rounds
**Features**: Deeply blued half-round, half octagonal barrel; commemorates the 200th anniversary of Oliver Winchester's birth; high grade walnut and deep scroll engraving on receiver; custom grade has gold inlays.
**MSRP** . . . . . . . . . . . . . . . . . $1469

## 70 SAFARI EXPRESS
**Action**: Bolt
**Stock**: Satin-finished checkered walnut with deluxe cheekpiece
**Barrel**: 24 in.
**Sights**: Hooded-blade front and express-style rear
**Weight**: 9 lb.
**Caliber**: 375 H&H Mag., 416 Rem. Mag., 458 Win. Mag., 375 H&H Mag.
**Magazine**: 3-rounds
**Features**: Pre-'64 type claw extractor; Pachmayr decelerator recoil pad; barrel band front swivel base; dual recoil lugs and three-position safety; M.O.A. trigger system; matte blued finish; two steel crossbolts and one-piece steel trigger guard and hinged floorplate.
**MSRP** . . . . . . . . . . . . . $1149–$1189

**WINCHESTER 1886 EXTRA LIGHT GRADE I**

## 1886 EXTRA LIGHT GRADE I
**Action**: Lever
**Stock**: Walnut
**Barrel**: 22 in.
**Sights**: None
**Weight**: 7 lb. 4oz.
**Caliber**: .45-70
**Magazine**: 4-shot tube
**Features**: Deeply blued receiver, lever, and barrel; top-tang safety.
**MSRP** . . . . . . . . . . . . . . . . . $1269

**WINCHESTER 1859 GRADE I**

## 1895 GRADE I
**Action**: Lever
**Stock**: Walnut with checkering and Schnabel forend
**Barrel**: 24 in.
**Sights**: Adjustable buckhorn rear and blade front
**Weight**: 8 lb.
**Caliber**: .30-06 Spfld., .405 Win.
**Magazine**: 4-shot internal box
**Features**: Limited production rifle designed by John Browning; Teddy Roosevelt favored the original 1895 for big game hunting.
**MSRP** . . . . . . . . . . . . . . . . . $1179

**RIFLES**

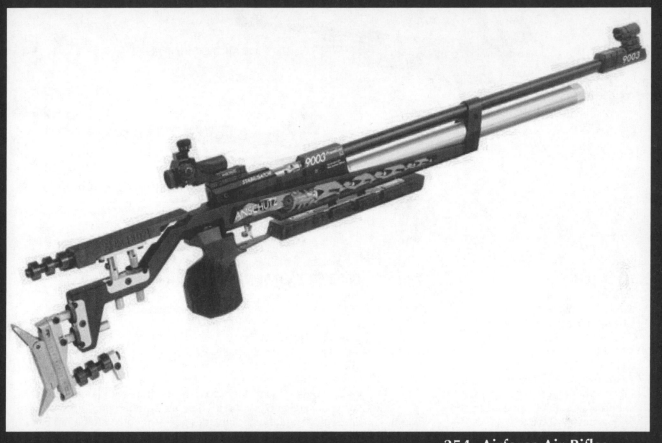

AIRFORCE AIR 8001 JUNIOR

AIRFORCE AIR 8002 COMPRESSED AIR ALU

## 8001 JUNIOR

*Power*: Compressed air
*Stock*: Laminate
*Overall Length*: 26.38 in.
*Sights*: Open, includes sight set 6834
*Weight*: 8.14 lb.
*Caliber*: .177
*Features*: Laminated wood in blue and orange with aluminum buttplate stock; cylindrical match grade barrel; comes with accessory box.
**MSRP . . . . . . . . . . . . . . . . . . . .N/A**

## 8002 S2 COMPRESSED AIR ALU

*Power*: Compressed air
*Stock*: Aluminum and synthetic pistol grip or laminted wood pistol grip
*Overall Length*: 30.7 in.
*Sights*: Open, includes sight set 6834
*Weight*: 10.12 lb.
*Caliber*: .177
*Features*: Aluminum stock in silver and blue with laminated wood or synthetic pistol grip; blue air cylinder; ProGrip cheekpiece and forend; includes accessory box; aluminum accessory rail.
**MSRP . . . . . . . . . . . . . . . . . . . .N/A**

AIRFORCE AIR THE EDGE

## THE EDGE

*Power*: Pre-charged pneumatic
*Stock*: Composite
*Overall Length*: 35 in.-40 in.
*Sights*: TS1 peep sight system

*Weight*: 6.1 lb.
*Caliber*: .177
*Features*: Ambidextrious cocking Knob; regulated air system; adjustable length of pull; adjustable forend;

hooded front sight only or front and rear sight available; two-stage adjustable trigger; composite stock in red or blue finish.
**MSRP . . . . . . . . . . . $545.95–$679.95**

AIR RIFLES

# Airforce Air Rifles

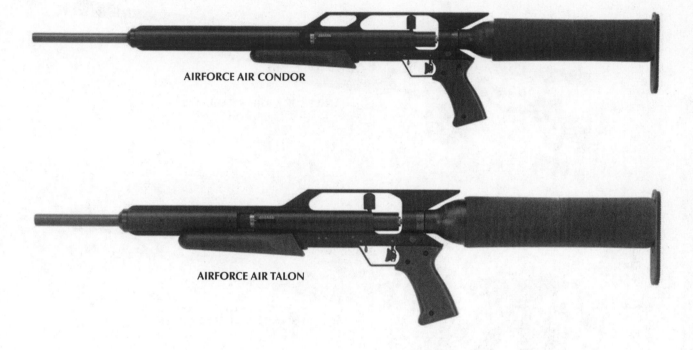

AIRFORCE AIR CONDOR

AIRFORCE AIR TALON

AIRFORCE AIR TALON SS

## CONDOR
*Power*: Pre-charged pneumatic, user adjustable
*Stock*: Composite
*Overall Length*: 38.7 in.
*Sights*: None
*Weight*: 6.5 lb.
*Caliber*: .25, .22, .20, .177
*Features*: Black, red, or, blue composite stock; integral extended scope rail; detachable air tank; Lothar Walther barrel; pressure relief device; adjustable power.
**MSRP** . . . . . . . . . . . . . . . . . .$649.95

## TALON
*Power*: Compressed air
*Stock*: Composite
*Overall Length*: 32.6 in.
*Sights*: None
*Weight*: 5.5 lb.
*Caliber*: .25, .22, .20, .177
*Features*: Lothar Walther barrel; pressure relief device; adjustable power; detachable air tank; black composite stock.
**MSRP** . . . . . . . . . . . . . . . . . .$529.75

## TALON SS
*Power*: Compressed air
*Stock*: Composite
*Overall Length*: 32.7 in.
*Sights*: None
*Weight*: 5.25 lb.
*Caliber*: .25, .22, .20, .177
*Features*: Lothar Walther barrel; pressure relief device; adjustable power; detachable air tank; black, red, or blue composite stock; multiple mounting rails; two-stage trigger; has innovative muzzle cap that strips away air turbulance and reduces discharge sound levels.
**MSRP** . . . . . . . . . . . . . . . . . .$551.50

# Anschutz Air Rifles

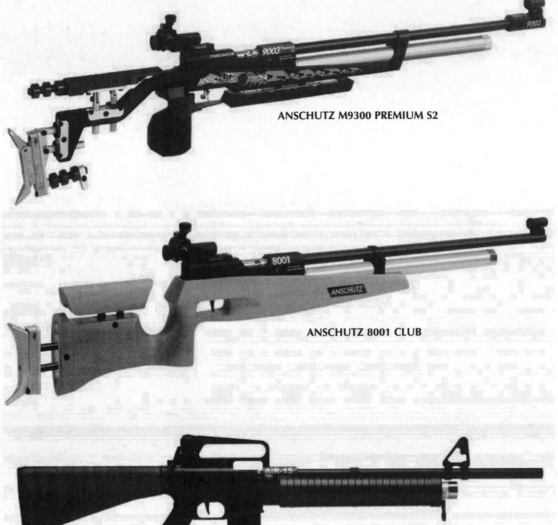

**ANSCHUTZ M9300 PREMIUM S2**

**ANSCHUTZ 8001 CLUB**

**ANSCHUTZ AIR-15**

## M9003 PREMIUM S2
*Power*: Compressed air
*Stock*: Aluminum or walnut
*Overall Length*: 30.7 in.
*Sights*: Open, includes sight set 6834
*Weight*: 9.68 lb.
*Caliber*: .177
*Features*: Black aluminum stock or walnut; pistol grip; Soft Link shock absorber pads; adjustable fore-end stock, cheekpiece and buttplate; includes plastic rifle case; valve and valve body coated with gold; steel match barrel; aluminum accessory rail on stock.
**MSRP** . . . . . . . . . . . . . . . . . . . . . .N/A

## 8001 CLUB
*Power*: Compressed air
*Stock*: Walnut
*Overall Length*: 30.7 in.
*Sights*: Open, includes sight set 6834
*Weight*: 8.36 lb.
*Caliber*: .177
*Features*: Walnut stock with stippled checkering and non-stained aluminum or rubber butt plate; adjustable trigger; match grade barrel.
**MSRP** . . . . . . . . . . . . . . . . . . . . . .N/A

## AIR-15
*Power*: Compressed air
*Stock*: Synthetic
*Overall Length*: 26.3 in.
*Sights*: Front sight post and rear sight
*Weight*: 9.37 lb.
*Caliber*: .177
*Features*: Receiver sleeve, front sight housing, carry handle and hand guard are machined from solid aluminum; butt stock, pistol grip and sling swivels are Bushmaster parts; removable compressed air cylinder may be filled with either an air compressor or standard scuba tank.
**MSRP** . . . . . . . . . . . . . . . . . . . .N/A

# Beeman Air Rifles

**BEEMAN R1**

**BEEMAN R9**

**BEEMAN HW97 MKII**

## R1, R1 CARBINE
*Power*: Spring piston
*Stock*: Hardwood
*Overall Length*: 45.2 in., 42 in.
*Sights*: Adjustable
*Weight*: 8.3 lb.–8.8 lb.
*Caliber*: .22, .20, .177; Carbine: .177, .20
*Features*: Beech stained hardwood stock; adjustable two-stage trigger; automatic safety.
Carbine: . . . . . . . . . . . . . . **$649.95**
Elite: . . . . . . . . . . . . . . . . **$799.95**

## R9, R9 DELUXE
*Power*: Spring piston
*Stock*: Hardwood
*Overall Length*: 43 in.
*Sights*: Adjustable
*Weight*: 7.3 lb.–7.5 lb.
*Caliber*: .20, .177
*Features*: Beech stained hardwood stock with Monte Carlo cheekpiece; ambidextrous rifle; soft rubber butt plate; adjustable two-stage trigger; automatic safety; R9 deluxe has hand checkered panels, pistol cap, carved Monte Carlo cheekpiece and interchangable globe front sight.
MSRP. . . . . . . . . . . . . . . . . **$449.95**
Elite: . . . . . . . . . . . . . . . . **$549.95**

## HW 97 MKII
*Power*: Spring piston
*Stock*: Hardwood
*Overall Length*: 44.1 in.
*Sights*: Adjustable
*Weight*: 9.2 lb.
*Caliber*: .177, .20
*Features*: Underlever cocking method; blued steel action, barrel and cocking lever; Beech Sporter stock which features tapered forend, high comb, cut checkering on the pistol grip and a soft rubber recoil pad; grooved receiver for optical sights; adjustable two-stage trigger; automatic safety.
Elite: . . . . . . . . . . . . . . . . **$699.95**
Thumbstock: . . . . . . . . . . . **$829.95**

## BENJAMIN DISCOVERY
*Power*: Dual fuel compressed air
*Stock*: Walnut
*Overall Length*: 39 in.
*Sights*: Fiber optic front sight, adjustable rear
*Weight*: 5 lb. 2 oz.
*Caliber*: .22 or .177
*Features*: Rifled steel barrel; velocity up to 900 fps; cross bolt safety; built-in pressure gauge.
MSRP. . . . . . . . . . . . . . . . . . **$269**

## 760 PUMPMASTER
*Power*: Pneumatic pump
*Stock*: Synthetic
*Overall Length*: 33.5 in.
*Sights*: Fiber optic front sight, adjustable rear
*Weight*: 2.75 lb.
*Caliber*: .177
*Features*: Cross bolt safety; BB up to 625 fps; pellet up to 600 fps.
MSRP. . . . . . . . . . . . . . . . . . **$34.99**

# Crosman Air Rifles

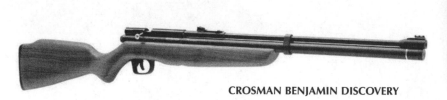

**CROSMAN BENJAMIN DISCOVERY**

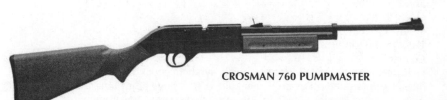

**CROSMAN 760 PUMPMASTER**

**AIR RIFLES**

# Crosman Air Rifles

CROSMAN RECRUIT

CROSMAN PHANTOM 1000

## RECRUIT
*Power*: Pneumatic pump
*Stock*: Synthetic
*Overall Length*: 38.25 in.
*Sights*: Fiber optic front sight, adjustable rear
*Weight*: 2.95 lb.
*Caliber*: .177
*Features*: Adjustable butt stock; adjustable synthetic stock; 11mm dovetail scope rail; cross bolt safety.
**MSRP**.................**$69.99**

## PHANTOM 1000
*Power*: Spring piston
*Stock*: Synthetic
*Overall Length*: 44.5 in.
*Sights*: Fiber optic front sight, adjustable rear
*Weight*: 6.02 lb.
*Caliber*: .177
*Features*: All-weather, synthetic black stock and forearm; features a checkered grip and forearm; velocity up to 1,000 fps; rifled steel barrel; two-stage adjustable trigger.
**MSRP**.................**$99.99**

CROSMAN QUEST 1000

## TAC 1 EXTREME
*Power*: Spring piston
*Stock*: Synthetic
*Overall Length*: 44.5 in.
*Sights*: Optical or red dot
*Weight*: 6.02 lb.
*Caliber*: .22
*Features*: Features an all-weather black, synthetic stock with pistol grip design and padded adjustable cheekpiece; two-stage adjustable trigger; ambidextrous; CenterPoint 3-9x32mm scope features dual-illuminated reticle, flashlight, bipod, and laser sight.
**MSRP**.................**$279.99**

## QUEST 1000
*Power*: Spring piston
*Stock*: Synthetic
*Overall Length*: 45 in.
*Sights*: Open
*Weight*: 6 lb. 32 oz.
*Caliber*: .177
*Features*: Two-stage adjustable trigger; velocity up to 100 fps.
**MSRP**.................**$99.99**

# Crosman Air Rifles

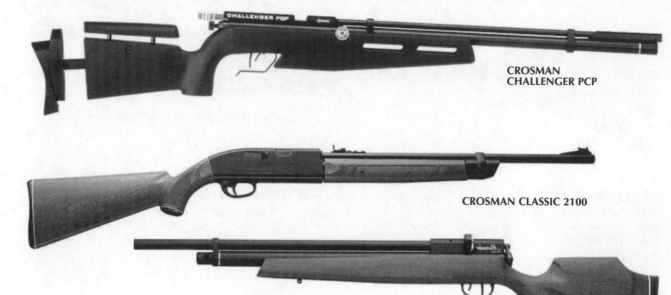

CROSMAN
CHALLENGER PCP

CROSMAN CLASSIC 2100

CROSMAN MARAUDER

## CHALLENGER PCP
*Power*: Dual fuel: pre-charged pneumatic pump and CO2
*Stock*: Synthetic
*Overall Length*: 40 in.
*Sights*: Open
*Weight*: 7.3 lb.
*Caliber*: .177
*Features*: Two-stage match grade adjustable trigger; Lothar Walther barrel; adjustable cheekpiece and buttpiece; black synthetic stock; 11mm scope mount rails; ambidextrous.
**MSRP**. . . . . . . . . . . . . . . .**$529.99**

## CLASSIC 2100
*Power*: Pneumatic pump
*Stock*: Synthetic
*Overall Length*: 39.75 in.
*Sights*: Visible impact front sight, adjustable rear
*Weight*: 4 lb. 13 oz.
*Caliber*: .177
*Features*: Cross bolt safety; BB up to 755 fps, Pellet up to 725 fps.
**MSRP**. . . . . . . . . . . . . . . . . .**$62.99**

## MARAUDER
*Power*: Pre-charged pneumatic
*Stock*: Hardwood
*Overall Length*: 43 in.
*Sights*: None
*Weight*: 7 lb. 8 oz.
*Caliber*: .177
*Features*: Crosman custom-choked barrel and internal shroud for unsurpassed accuracy and ultra-quiet operation; two-stage adjustable match grade trigger; rifle can be filled with Benjamin hand pump or a high pressure tank; velocity up to 1100 fps; ambidextrious hardwood stock.
**MSRP**. . . . . . . . . . . . . . . .**$509.99**

CROSMAN M 2260

## M 2260
*Power*: $CO_2$
*Stock*: Hardwood
*Overall Length*: 39.75 in.
*Sights*: Fixed front sight, peep rear sight
*Weight*: 4 lb. 12 oz.
*Caliber*: .22
*Features*: Velocity up to 600 fps; rifled steel barrel.
**MSRP**. . . . . . . . . . . . . . . . . .**$83.84**

AIR RIFLES

# Crosman Air Rifles

CROSMAN AIRSOURCE 1077

## AIRSOURCE 1077
*Power*: Airsource $CO_2$ cylinder
*Stock*: Synthetic
*Overall Length*: 36.88 in.

*Sights*: Fiber optic front sight, adjustable rear
*Weight*: 3 lb. 11 oz.
*Caliber*: .177

*Features*: Rifled steel barrel; cross bolt safety; all-weather black synthetic stock; velocity up to 625 fps.
MSRP . . . . . . . . . . . . . . . . . . $102.99

# CZ (Ceska Zbrojovka) Air Rifles

## CZ 200 T
*Power*: Pre-charged pneumatic
*Stock*: Walnut
*Overall Length*: 36.5 in.

*Sights*: None
*Weight*: 6.6 lb.
*Caliber*: .177
*Features*: Compact receiver with a

fixed or removable compressed air reservoir; hammer-forged barrel.
MSRP . . . . . . . . . . . . . . . . . . . $429

# Daisy Air Rifles

DAISY POWERLINE M500 BREAK BARREL

## POWERLINE M1000 BREAK BARREL
*Power*: Break barrel/spring piston
*Stock*: Wood
*Overall Length*: 45.75 in.
*Sights*: TruGlo fiber-optic front, micro adjustable rear
*Weight*: 6.6 lb.
*Caliber*: .177
*Features*: Rifle comes with 4x32 air rifle scope; rear button safety; solid stained wood stock; velocity up to 1000 fps; rifled steel barrel.
MSRP . . . . . . . . . . . . . . . . . . $149.99

## POWERLINE M500 BREAK BARREL
*Power*: Break barrel/spring piston
*Stock*: Wood
*Overall Length*: 45.7 in.
*Sights*: Hooded front sight with blade and ramp, micro-adjustable rear
*Weight*: 6.6 lb.
*Caliber*: .177
*Features*: Rifle comes with 4 x 32 air rifle scope; auto rear button safety; solid stained wood stock; velocity up to 490 fps; rifled steel barrel.
MSRP . . . . . . . . . . . . . . . . . . $149.99

AIR RIFLES

DAISY POWERLINE M901

DAISY POWERLINE M880

DAISY POWERLINE TARGETPRO 953

## POWERLINE M901

**Power**: Multi-pump pneumatic
**Stock**: Composite
**Overall Length**: 37.5 in.
**Sights**: Fiber-optic front, adjustable rear
**Weight**: 3.70 lb.
**Caliber**: .177
**Features**: Rifled steel barrel; black advanced composite stock; dovetail mounts for optics.
**MSRP**...................$99.99

## POWERLINE M880

**Power**: Multi-pump pneumatic
**Stock**: Molded woodgrain
**Overall Length**: 37.6 in.
**Sights**: Truglo fiber-optic front, adjustable rear
**Weight**: 3.70 lb.
**Caliber**: .177
**Features**: Woodgrain, Monte Carlo stock and forearm; rifled steel barrel; crossbolt trigger block; velocity up to 750 fps; engineering resin with dovetail mount for scope.
**MSRP**...................$74.99

## POWERLINE TARGETPRO 953

**Power**: Pneumatic single-pump cocking lever
**Stock**: Composite
**Overall Length**: 37.75 in.
**Sights**: Front and rear optics
**Weight**: 6.40 lb.
**Caliber**: .177
**Features**: Full-length, match-style black composite stock; rifled high-grad steel barrel; die-cast metal reeiver; manual crossbolt trigger block with red indicator.
**MSRP**................$129.99

DAISY AVANTI M887 GOLD MEDALIST

## AVANTI M887 GOLD MEDALIST

**Power**: CO2 single shot bolt
**Stock**: Laminated hard wood
**Overall Length**: 39.5 in.
**Sights**: Front globe sight with changeable aperture inserts; rear diopter sight with micrometer
**Weight**: 7.30 lb.
**Caliber**: .177
**Features**: Laminated hardwood stock; Lothar Walther rifled high-grade steel barrel; manual, crossbolt trigger block; includes scope rail adapter.
**MSRP**.................$754.99

## M853 LEGEND

**Power**: Single-pump pneumatic
**Stock**: Hardwood
**Overall Length**: 38.5 in.
**Sights**: Hooded front with interchangable aperture inserts; micrometer adjustable rear
**Weight**: 5.50 lb.
**Caliber**: .177
**Features**: Diecast receiver with dovetail scope mount; Lothar Walther rifled high-grade steel barrel; full-length, sporter-style hardwood with adjustable length.
**MSRP**................$529.99

AIR RIFLES

# Gamo Air Rifles

## BIG CAT 1200
*Power*: Break-barrel, spring-piston
*Stock*: Synthetic
*Overall Length*: 43.3 in.
*Sights*: 4 x 32 scope
*Weight*: 6.1 lb.
*Caliber*: .177
*Features*: Tough all weather molded synthetic stock; ventilated rubber pad for recoil; twin cheek pads; non-slip texture design on grip and forearm; manual trigger system; fluted barrel; two-stage adjustable trigger.
**MSRP . . . . . . . . . . . . . . . . . $169.95**

## WHISPER
*Power*: Break-barrel, spring-piston
*Stock*: Synthetic
*Overall Length*: 46 in.
*Sights*: Fiber optic front sight with sight guard; Liber optic adjustable rear sight
*Weight*: 5.28 lb.
*Caliber*: .177
*Features*: Raised rail scope mount with 39 x 40 scope; second stage adjustable trigger; manual safety; non-removable noise dampener; black synthetic all-weather stock; ventilated rubber butt plate; non-slip checkering on grip and forearm
**MSRP . . . . . . . . . . . . . . . . . $299.99**

## DYNAMAX
*Power*: Pre-charge pneumatic
*Stock*: Tactical synthetic
*Overall Length*: 38.2 in.
*Sights*: Red-dot
*Weight*: 8.75 lb. with scope
*Caliber*: .177
*Features*: Removeable rotary magazine; match-quality, full-floated barrel; black synthetic tactical stock; two-stage adjustable trigger; fingertip cocking system.
**MSRP . . . . . . . . . . . . . . . . . $699.95**

## RECON
*Power*: Break-barrel, spring-piston
*Stock*: Synthetic
*Overall Length*: 37.2 in.
*Sights*: 4 x 20 scope
*Weight*: 4.63 lb.
*Caliber*: .177
*Features*: All-weather black molded synthetic stock; ventliated rubber butt pad; twin cheek pads; automatic cocking safety system.
**MSRP . . . . . . . . . . . . . . . . . $139.95**

# RWS Air Rifles

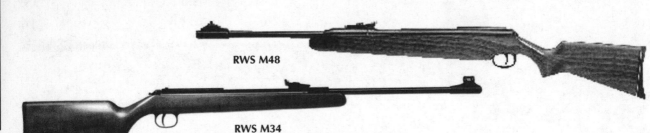

RWS M48

RWS M34

## M48
*Power*: Side lever/spring-piston
*Stock*: Hardwood
*Overall Length*: 42.5 in.
*Sights*: Adjustable rear sight
*Weight*: 8.5 lb.
*Caliber*: .177
*Features*: Extended breech stock to reduce recoil; fixed barrel system; adjustable trigger; automatic safety; includes RWS 4 x 32 scope and mounts.
**MSRP . . . . . . . . . . . . . . . . . $545.99**

## M34, M34 PRO COMPACT
*Power*: Break-barrel, spring-piston
*Stock*: Hardwood, synthetic
*Overall Length*: 45 in.
*Sights*: 4 x 32 scope
*Weight*: 7.5 lb.–8 lb.
*Caliber*: .22 or .177
*Features*: Polished with blued metalwork; full sized hardwood stock; two-stage adjustable trigger; automatic safety; finely rifled barrel; 34 Pro: large muzzle brake.
**MSRP . . . . . . . . . . . . . . . . . $390**
**M34 Pro Compact: . . . . . . . . $326.25**

RWS M54

RWS M350 MAG

RWS SCHUTZE

## M54

**Power**: Side lever/spring-piston
**Stock**: Hardwood
**Overall Length**: 43.7 in.
**Sights**: Adjustable rear sight
**Weight**: 9 lb.
**Caliber**: .22
**Features**: Adjustable trigger; scope rail; Monte Carlo hardwood stock with cheek piece and checkering; automatic safety.
**MSRP** . . . . . . . . . . . . . . . . . **$754.99**

## M350 MAG

**Power**: Break-barrel, spring-piston
**Stock**: Hardwood
**Overall Length**: 48.3 in.
**Sights**: 4 x 32 scope
**Weight**: 8.2 lb.
**Caliber**: .22
**Features**: Two-stage trigger; mounted scope rail.
**MSRP** . . . . . . . . . . . . . . . . . . . **$519**

## SCHUTZE

**Power**: Break-barrel, spring-piston
**Stock**: Hardwood
**Overall Length**: 41 in.
**Sights**: TruGlo fiber optic sights
**Weight**: 5.7 lb.
**Caliber**: .177
**Features**: Classic straight hardwood stock; ambidextrous safety.
**MSRP** . . . . . . . . . . . . . . . . . **$215.50**

## X-5

**Power**: Break-barrel, spring-piston
**Stock**: Hardwood, black synthetic
**Overall Length**: 41 in.
**Sights**: Hooded front sight with red, fiber optic insert; rear fiber-optic
**Weight**: 5.7 lb.
**Caliber**: .177
**Features**: Automatic, ambidextrous safety mounted on back of receiver; Monte Carlo-style stock; integral dovetail scope rail on receiver.
**MSRP**. . . . . . . . . . . . . . . . . .$125.00

**STOEGER X-5**

# AYA Shotguns

AYA NO. 37

AYA NO. 4/53

AYA IMPERIAL

## NO. 37
**Action**: Over/under sidelock
**Stock**: Walnut
**Barrel**: 28 in.
**Chokes**: Screw-in tubes
**Weight**: 7.5 lb.
**Bore/Gauge**: 12
**Magazine**: None
**Features**: Double underlocking lugs and double crossbolt; chopper lump chrome nickel steel barrels; gold-lined cocking indicators; gold-washed internal lock parts; double-trigger with hinged-front trigger; fine rose and scroll game scene, or bold relief engraving on action plates; full pistol grip walnut stock.
**MSRP** . . . . . . . . . . . $19658–$29380

## NO. 4/53
**Action**: Side-by-side hammerless box-lock ejector
**Stock**: Walnut
**Barrel**: 28 in., with other lengths to order
**Chokes**: Screw-in tubes
**Weight**: 6 lb. 10 oz.
**Bore/Gauge**: 12, 16, 20, 28, .410
**Magazine**: None
**Features**: Double locking mechanism with replaceable hinge pin; disc set firing pins; double-trigger; chopper lump barrels with concave rib; light scroll engraving; metal finish available in hardened, old silver, or white finish; automatic safety.
**MSRP** . . . . . . . . . . . . . . . . . . $5292

## IMPERIAL
**Action**: Side-by-side hammerless side-lock
**Stock**: Walnut
**Barrel**: 28 in., with other lengths to order
**Chokes**: Screw-in tubes
**Weight**: 6.75 lb.
**Bore/Gauge**: 12, 16, 20, 28, .410
**Magazine**: None
**Features**: Forged steel action with double locking mechanism and gas vents; gold washed internal lock parts; gold lined cocking indicators; optional selective or non-selective single-trigger; concave rib; straight hand, finely checkered walnut stock; gold initial oval.
**MSRP** . . . . . . . . . . . . . . . . . $25012

BENELLI CORDOBA COMFORTECH 12 GA.

BENELLI CORDOBA COMFORTECH 20 GA.

BENELLI LEGACY

SHOTGUNS

## CORDOBA COMFORTECH 12 GA.
**Action**: Inerta operated semi-automatic
**Stock**: Synthetic
**Barrel**: 28 in., 30 in.
**Chokes**: Extended Crio chokes
**Weight**: 7 lb.
**Bore/Gauge**: 12
**Magazine**: 4+1rounds
**Features**: Black or Realtree MAX-4 camo synthetic stock; Crio ported barrels; ComforTech gel recoil pad and comb insert; heavy duty magazine cap.
**MSRP** . . . . . . . . . . . . . **$1949–$2119**

## CORDOBA COMFORTECH- 20 GA
**Action**: Inerta operated semi-automatic
**Stock**: Synthetic
**Barrel**: 28 in., 30 in.
**Chokes**: Extended Crio chokes

**Weight**: 7 lb.
**Bore/Gauge**: 20
**Magazine**: 4+1 rounds
**Features**: Black synthetic stock; Crio ported barrels; ComforTech gel recoil pad and comb insert; heavy duty magazine cap.
**MSRP** . . . . . . . . . . . . . . . . . **$1939**

## VINCI PLUS
**Action**: Inerta operated semi-automatic
**Stock**: Synthetic
**Barrel**: 24 in., 26 in., 28 in.
**Chokes**: Crio chokes (C, IC, M, IM, F)
**Weight**: 6.8 lb.–6.9 lb.
**Bore/Gauge**: 12
**Magazine**: 3+1 rounds
**Features**: Stock in black, Realtree APG, Realtree APG HD steadygrip, or Realtree MAX-4 camo; red bar front sight and metal mid-bead sight; drilled and tapped for scope mounting;

ComforTech plus recoil pads.
**MSRP** . . . . . . . . . . . . . . **$1379–$1479**

## LEGACY
**Action**: Inerta operated semi-automatic
**Stock**: Walnut
**Barrel**: 24 in., 26 in., 28 in.
**Chokes**: Crio choke (C, IC, M, IM, F); 28 guage: (C & M)
**Weight**: 4.9 lb.–7.4 lb.
**Bore/Gauge**: 12, 20, 28
**Magazine**: 4+1, 28 Ga.: 2+1
**Features**: Satin walnut with Weathercoat or AA-grade stock; classic game scene etchings on receiver; red front sight and metal mid-bead sight.
**MSRP** . . . . . . . . . . . . . . **$1795–$1989**

# Benelli Shotguns

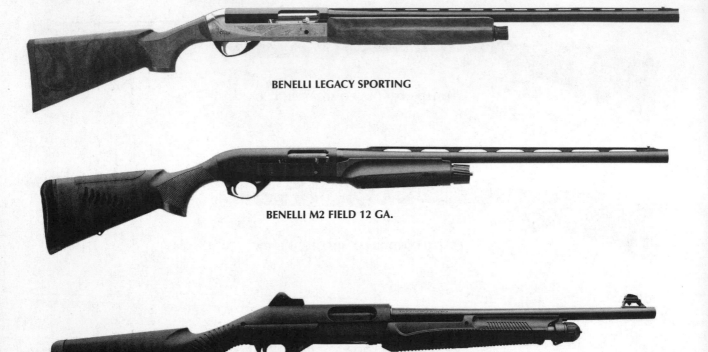

BENELLI LEGACY SPORTING

BENELLI M2 FIELD 12 GA.

BENELLI NOVA PUMP TACTICAL

## LEGACY SPORTING
**Action**: Inerta operated semi-automatic
**Stock**: Walnut
**Barrel**: 28 in., 30 in.
**Chokes**: Extended Crio chokes (C, CI, M, IM, F)
**Weight**: 7.4 lb.–7.5 lb.
**Bore/Gauge**: 12
**Magazine**: 4+1 rounds
**Features**: Acid-etched game scenes on receiver plates; AA-grade walnut stock; red front sight and metal mid-bead sight.
**MSRP** . . . . . . . . . . . . . . . . . . . . $2369

## M2 FIELD 12 GA.
**Action**: Inerta operated semi-automatic
**Stock**: Synthetic, walnut
**Barrel**: 21 in., 24 in., 26 in., 28 in.
**Chokes**: Crio chokes (IC, M, F)
**Weight**: 6.9 lb.–7.2 lb.

**Bore/Gauge**: 12
**Magazine**: 3+1 rounds
**Features**: ComforTech gel recoil pad and comb insert; ComforTech shim kit; red bar front sight; stock comes in satin walnut, black synthetic, Realtree APG, and Realtree MAX-4 Camo.
**Synthetic**: . . . . . . . . . . . . . . . $1319
**Camo**: . . . . . . . . . . . . . . . . . $1429
**Walnut**: . . . . . . . . . . . . . . . . $1269

## M2 FIELD 20 GA.
**Action**: Inerta operated semi-automatic
**Stock**: Synthetic
**Barrel**: 24 in., 26 in.
**Chokes**: Crio chokes (IC, M, F)
**Weight**: 7.1 lb.–7.2 lb.
**Bore/Gauge**: 20
**Magazine**: 3+1 rounds
**Features**: ComforTech gel recoil pad and comb insert; ComforTech shim kit;

red bar front sight; synthetic stock in Realtree Max-4 Camo or matte black finish.
**Synthetic**: . . . . . . . . . . . . . . . $1379
**Realtree APG**: . . . . . . . . . . . . $1489

## NOVA PUMP TACTICAL
**Action**: Pump
**Stock**: Synthetic
**Barrel**: 18.5 in.
**Chokes**: Fixed cylinder choke
**Weight**: 7.2 lb.
**Bore/Gauge**: 12
**Magazine**: 4+1 rounds
**Features**: Available with ghost-ring or open rifle sights; push-button shell stop grooved grip surface stocks in black synthetic stock.
**MSRP** . . . . . . . . . . . . . . . $409–$449

# Benelli Shotguns

BENELLI NOVA H20 PUMP

BENELLI SPORT II

BENELLI SUPER
BLACK EAGLE II

BENELLI SUPERNOVA FIELD

## NOVA H2O PUMP

*Action*: Pump
*Stock*: Synthetic
*Barrel*: 18.5 in.
*Chokes*: Fixed cylinder choke
*Weight*: 7.2 lb.
*Bore/Gauge*: 12
*Magazine*: 4+1 rounds
*Features*: Available with ghost-ring or open rifle sights; push-button shell stop; grooved grip surface black syntethic stock.
MSRP . . . . . . . . . . . . . . . . . . . . $629

## SPORT II

*Action*: Inerta operated semi-automatic
*Stock*: Walnut
*Barrel*: 28 in., 30 in.
*Chokes*: Extended Crio chokes (C, CI, M, IM, F)
*Weight*: 6.3 lb.–7.3 lb.

*Bore/Gauge*: 12, 20
*Magazine*: 4+1 rounds
*Features*: Red bar front sight and metal bead mid sight; Crio ported barrels; ComforTech gel recoil pad and comb insert; heavy duty magazine cap.
MSRP . . . . . . . . . . . . . . . . . . . . $1759

## SUPER BLACK EAGLE II

*Action*: Inerta operated semi-automatic
*Stock*: Walnut, synthetic
*Barrel*: 24 in., 26 in., 28 in.
*Chokes*: Crio choke (C, IC, M, IM, F)
*Weight*: 7.1 lb.–7.3 lb.
*Bore/Gauge*: 12
*Magazine*: 3+1 rounds
*Features*: Red bar front sight and metal mid-bead sight; ComforTech gel recoil pad and comb insert; larger trigger guard for use with gloves; stock in black synthetic, Realtree Max-4 camo,

Realtree APG camo, or walnut.
MSRP . . . . . . . . . . . . . . . . . . . $1609
With SteadyGrip: . . . . . . . . . . $1839

## SUPERNOVA FIELD

*Action*: Pump
*Stock*: Synthetic
*Barrel*: 24 in., 26 in., 28 in.
*Chokes*: Standard choke (IC, M, F)
*Weight*: 7.8 lb.–8.0 lb.
*Bore/Gauge*: 12
*Magazine*: 4+1 rounds
*Features*: Stock comes in black synthetic, Realtree APG camo, or Realtree Max-4 camo; receiver drilled and tapped for scope mounting; standard chokes; vented recoil pad.
**Comfortech Stock:** . . . . . $529–$639
**SteadyGrip stock:** . . . . . . . . . . $659

# Benelli Shotguns

BENELLI SUPERSPORT

BENELLI ULTRA LIGHT

## SUPERSPORT
**Action**: Inerta operated semi-automatic
**Stock**: Synthetic
**Barrel**: 28 in., 30 in.
**Chokes**: Extended Crio chokes (C, IC, M, IM, F)
**Weight**: 6.3 lb.–7.3 lb.
**Bore/Gauge**: 12, 20
**Magazine**: 4+1 rounds
**Features**: Stock comes in black SuperSport Carbon Fiber Finish; red bar front sight and metal mid-bead sight; Crio ported barrels; ComforTech gel recoil pad and comb insert.
**MSRP** . . . . . . . . . . . . . . . . . . **$2069**

## ULTRA LIGHT
**Action**: Inerta operated semi-automatic
**Stock**: Walnut
**Barrel**: 24 in., 26 in.
**Chokes**: Crio chokes (IC, M, F)
**Weight**: 5.2 lb.–6.1 lb.
**Bore/Gauge**: 12, 20
**Magazine**: 2+1 rounds
**Features**: Weather-coated walnut stock; red bar front sight and metal mid-bead sight; gel recoil pad; option of checkered Montefeltro forend or ultra light forend.
**MSRP** . . . . . . . . . . . . . . . . . . **$1599**

# Beretta Shotguns

BERETTA 471 SILVER
HAWK ENGLISH STOCK

## 471 SILVER HAWK & 471 ENGL. SILVER HAWK
**Action**: Side-by-side
**Stock**: Walnut
**Barrel**: 26 in., 28 in.
**Chokes**: Fixed mod and full
**Weight**: 6.5 lb.
**Bore/Gauge**: 12, 20
**Magazine**: 3+1 rounds
**Features**: Monoblock by a laser system; boxlock; satin chromed or cas-colored receiver; single-selective trigger or double-triggers; automatic ejectors; straight or pistol grip; extensive scroll and leaf engraving and a gold-filled hawk's head on top lever; beavertail forend on standard stock; splinter forend on English stock.
**MSRP** . . . . . . . . . . . . . . . . . . **$3850**

SHOTGUNS

# Beretta Shotguns

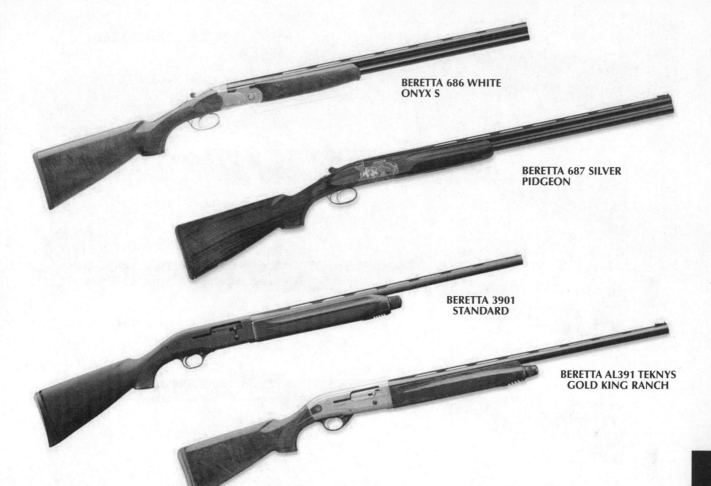

BERETTA 686 WHITE ONYX S

BERETTA 687 SILVER PIDGEON

BERETTA 3901 STANDARD

BERETTA AL391 TEKNYS GOLD KING RANCH

## 686 WHITE ONYX

**Action**: Over/under
**Stock**: Walnut
**Barrel**: 26 in., 28 in.
**Chokes**: Screw-in tubes
**Weight**: 6.8 lb.–7.7 lb.
**Bore/Gauge**: 12, 20, 28
**Magazine**: 3+1 rounds
**Features**: Includes case and accessories; boxlock; 3 in. chambers; single-selective triggers; top mounted bolt-lug design; satin nickel frame in dura-jewel finish.
**MSRP** . . . . . . . . . . . . . . . . . $2075

## 687 SILVER PIGEON V

**Action**: Over/under
**Stock**: Walnut
**Barrel**: 28 in.

**Chokes**: Screw-in tubes
**Weight**: 6.8 lb.
**Bore/Gauge**: 12, 20, 28, .410
**Magazine**: 3+1 rounds
**Features**: Oil-finished walnut stock detailed with gold game bird inlays and a gold Beretta medallion underneath; color-case finish; single-selective trigger; 3-inch chambers.
**MSRP** . . . . . . . . . . . . . . . . . $3775

## 3901 STANDARD

**Action**: Semi-automatic
**Stock**: Synthetic
**Barrel**: 28 in.
**Chokes**: Screw-in tubes
**Weight**: 7.6 lb.
**Bore/Gauge**: 12
**Magazine**: 3-rounds
**Features**: Soft-shooting gas system;

high-strength steel alloy hammer-forged barrel; Mobilechoke versatility.
**MSRP** . . . . . . . . . . . . . . . . . .$645.

## AL391 TEKNYS GOLD KING RANCH

**Action**: Semi-automatic
**Stock**: Walnut
**Barrel**: 26 in., 28 in.
**Chokes**: Screw-in tubes
**Weight**: 5.9 lb.–7.3 lb.
**Bore/Gauge**: 12, 20
**Magazine**: 3-rounds
**Features**: Self-compressing gas system; Optima Bore overbored barrels (12 Ga.); OptimaChoke flush tubes; checkered stocks and forends with "Running W" pattern.
**MSRP** . . . . . . . . . . . . . . . . . $2075

# Beretta Shotguns

BERETTA AL391 URIKA 2 MAX-4

BERETTA A391 XTREMA 2

BERETTA 686 SILVER PIGEON S KING RANCH

BERETTA SV10 PERENNIA III 12 GA.

## AL391 URIKA 2 MAX-4

*Action*: Semi-automatic
*Stock*: Synthetic
*Barrel*: 28 in.
*Chokes*: OptimaChoke Plus Flush choke tube
*Weight*: 6.6 lb.
*Bore/Gauge*: 12
*Magazine*: 3-rounds
*Features*: 3 in. chamber; gas operating system with self-cleaning and self-compensating valve; synthetic stock in Max-4 HD camo; OptimaBore overbored barrel.
**MSRP . . . . . . . . . . . . . $1125–$1500**

## A391 XTREMA 2

*Action*: Semi-automatic
*Stock*: Synthetic
*Barrel*: 26 in., 28 in.
*Chokes*: Screw-in tubes
*Weight*: 7.8 lb.
*Bore/Gauge*: 12

*Magazine*: 4+1 rounds
*Features*: Gas operation system with exhaust valve; self-cleaning gas cylinder and piston; self-cleaning exhaust valve; stainless steel barrel and receiver; optional kick-off hydraulic dampening reduction system; synthetic stock comes in black, AP camo, and Max-4 camo.
**MSRP . . . . . . . . . . . . . $1350–$1700**

## 686 SILVER PIGEON S KING RANCH

*Action*: Over/under
*Stock*: Walnut
*Barrel*: 26 in., 28 in.
*Chokes*: Mobilchoke flush screw-in tube
*Weight*: 6.2 lb.–6.7 lb.
*Bore/Gauge*: 20, 28
*Magazine*: 2-rounds
*Features*: Scroll work on the receiver in nickel finish; walnut stock with checkered comb and Schanbel forend;

3.5 in. chamber; front bead sight; automatic safety; rubber butt plate.
**MSRP . . . . . . . . . . . . . . . . . . $2800**

## SV10 PERENNIA III 12 GA.

*Action*: Over/under
*Stock*: Walnut
*Barrel*: 26 in., 28 in.
*Chokes*: OptimaChoke HP Extended choke tubes
*Weight*: 7.3 lb.
*Bore/Gauge*: 12
*Magazine*: None
*Features*: Optional kick-off hydraulic dampening reduction system; sling swivels; plastic pad; Optimabore high-performance cold, hammer-forged barrels; automatic safety; chrome-lined bore and chamber.
**MSRP . . . . . . . . . . . . . . . . . . $2600**

# Beretta Shotguns

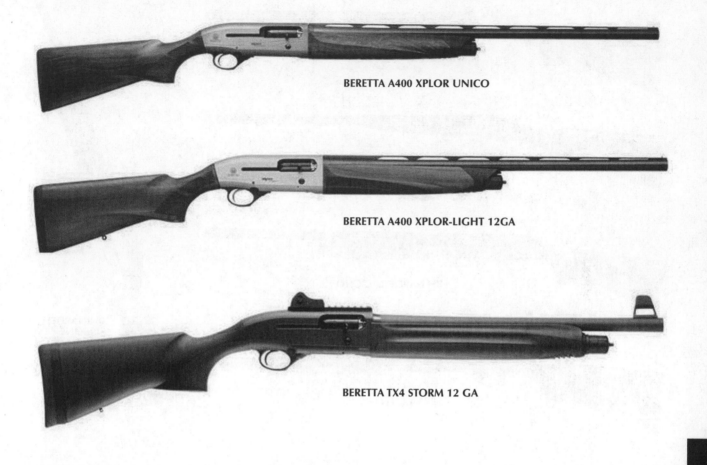

**BERETTA A400 XPLOR UNICO**

**BERETTA A400 XPLOR-LIGHT 12GA**

**BERETTA TX4 STORM 12 GA**

## A400 XPLOR UNICO
*Action*: Semi-automatic
*Stock*: Walnut and polymer
*Barrel*: 26 in., 28 in.
*Chokes*: OptimaChoke screw-in tube
*Weight*: 6.6 lb.–7 lb.
*Bore/Gauge*: 12
*Magazine*: None
*Features*: Single-selective trigger; green receiver; walnut stock with polymer forend insert, trigger guard and kick-off interface; 3.5-in. chamber; metal bead front sight.
**MSRP** . . . . . . . . . . . . . . . . . . $1625

## A400 XPLOR LIGHT 12 GA.
*Action*: Over/under
*Stock*: Walnut and polymer
*Barrel*: 26 in., 28 in.
*Chokes*: OptimaChoke screw-in tube

*Weight*: 6.2 lb.–6.6 lb.
*Bore/Gauge*: 12
*Magazine*: None
*Features*: Steelium barrel design, walnut stock with polymer forend insert, trigger guard and kick-off interface; 3-in. chamber; blink operating system; Micro-Core recoil pad.
**MSRP** . . . . . . . . . . . . . . . . . . $1400

## TX4 STORM 12 GA.
*Action*: Semi-automatic
*Stock*: Synthetic
*Barrel*: 18 in.
*Chokes*: OptimaBore HP-Cylinder
*Weight*: 6.4 lb.
*Bore/Gauge*: 12
*Magazine*: 5+1 rounds
*Features*: Adjustable length of pull with ½-in. spacers; Picatinny rail; soft

rubber grip inlays on the stock and forend.
**MSRP** . . . . . . . . . . . . . . . . . . $1450

## DT 10 TRIDENT L SPORTING
*Action*: Over/under
*Stock*: Walnut
*Barrel*: 30 in., 32 in.
*Chokes*: OptimaChoke choke tube
*Weight*: 8 lb.
*Bore/Gauge*: 12
*Magazine*: 2-rounds
*Features*: Ergonomic top lever; detachable trigger; cross-bolt locking system; receiver is embelleished by fine floral scroll engraving; rubber buttplate; checkered walnut stock.
**MSRP** . . . . . . . . . . . . . . . . . . $9650

**SHOTGUNS**

# Bernardelli Shotguns

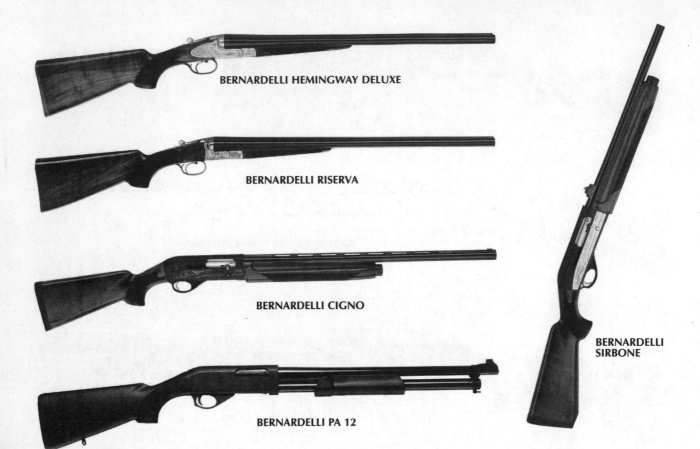

BERNARDELLI HEMINGWAY DELUXE

BERNARDELLI RISERVA

BERNARDELLI CIGNO

BERNARDELLI SIRBONE

BERNARDELLI PA 12

## HEMINGWAY DELUXE
*Action*: Side-by-side
*Stock*: Walnut
*Barrel*: 24 in., 26 in., 27 in., 28 in., 29 in.
*Chokes*: Fixed cylinder chokes
*Weight*: 6.1 lb.–6.2 lb.
*Bore/Gauge*: 12, 20
*Magazine*: None
*Features*: Simple or automatic extractors; double trigger or single trigger with selector; beavertail butt stock; forged steel frame; English walnut stock with pistol grip.
**MSRP: . . . . . . . . Price on Request**

## RISERVA
*Action*: Side-by-side
*Stock*: Walnut
*Barrel*: 24 in., 26 in., 27 in., 28 in., 29 in.
*Chokes*: Fixed cylinder chokes
*Weight*: 6.83 lb.
*Bore/Gauge*: 12
*Magazine*: None

*Features*: Forged steel frame; double trigger or single trigger with selector; simple or automatic extractor; English walnut stock with pistol grip; beavertail butt stock.
**MSRP: . . . . . . . . Price on Request**

## CIGNO
*Action*: Semi-automatic
*Stock*: Walnut
*Barrel*: 24 in., 26 in., 28 in., 30 in.
*Chokes*: Steel chokes (M, F, IM, IC, CYL, F)
*Weight*: 6.83 lb.
*Bore/Gauge*: 12
*Magazine*: 2+1, 4+1 rounds
*Features*: Select walnut stock with pistol grip; rubber recoil pad; includes carrying case; receiver is black anodized and finely sand blasted.
**MSRP: . . . . . . . . Price on Request**

## PA 12
*Action*: Pump
*Stock*: Synthetic

*Barrel*: 20 in.
*Chokes*: Steel cylinder chokes
*Weight*: 6 lb.
*Bore/Gauge*: 12
*Magazine*: 6+1 rounds
*Features*: Synthetic black matte stock; shipped in carton box; steel barrel
**MSRP: . . . . . . . . Price on Request**

## SIRBONE
*Action*: Semi-automatic
*Stock*: Walnut
*Barrel*: 24 in., 26 in., 28 in., 30 in.
*Chokes*: Steel chokes (M, F, IM, IC, CYL, F)
*Weight*: 6.83 lb.
*Bore/Gauge*: 12
*Magazine*: 2+1, 4+1 rounds
*Features*: Optical fiber front sight with rear sight dovetail optical fiber; select walnut stock with pistol grip; rubber recoil pad.
**MSRP: . . . . . . . . Price on Request**

# Blaser Shotguns

BLASER F3 20 GA.

BLASER F3 GAME

## F3 20 GA.
**Action**: Over/under
**Stock**: Walnut
**Barrel**: 30 in., 32 in.
**Chokes**: Briley Spectrum screw-in chokes
**Weight**: 7.25 lb.
**Bore/Gauge**: 20
**Magazine**: None
**Features**: Internal block system; ergonomically optimized, adjustable trigger blade; Triplex Bore design; ejection-ball-system; balancer.
**MSRP**. . . . . . . . . . . . . . . . . . . $6895

## F3 GAME
**Action**: Over/under
**Stock**: Walnut
**Barrel**: 27 in., 28 in., 29 in.
**Chokes**: Briley Spectrum choke (SK, IC, Mod., I.Mod., Full)
**Weight**: 7.3 lb.
**Bore/Gauge**: 12, 20, 28
**Magazine**: None
**Features**: Sporting stock, forearm with Schnabel; internal block system; ergonomically optimized, adjustable trigger blade; Triplex Bore design; ejection-ball-system; balancer.

| | |
|---|---|
| **Standard:**. . . . . . . . . . . . . . | **$6895** |
| **Luxus:** . . . . . . . . . . . . . . . . | **$8495** |
| **Super Luxus:** . . . . . . . . . . . | **$12475** |
| **Baronesse:**. . . . . . . . . . . . . | **$13475** |
| **Exclusive:**. . . . . . . . . . . . . . | **$15575** |
| **Super Exclusive:**. . . . . . . . . | **$23750** |
| **Imperial:** . . . . . . . . . . . . . . | **$29950** |

# Browning Shotguns

BROWNING MAXUS STALKER

## MAXUS STALKER
**Action**: Autoloader, gas operated
**Stock**: Composite
**Barrel**: 26 in., 28 in.
**Chokes**: Three Invector-Plus choke tubes
**Weight**: 6 lb. 14 oz.
**Bore/Gauge**: 12
**Magazine**: None

**Features**: Magazine cut-off, matte black composite stock with pistol grip; speed lock forearm; textured gripping surfaces; Dura Touch armor coating; Inflex technology recoil pads; lightning trigger system; ventilated rib; duck blind has Mossy Oak camo finish.
**Maxus Stalker:**. . . . . . . $1200–$1390
**Duck Blind:** . . . . . . . . . $1340–$1540

SHOTGUNS

# Browning Shotguns

**BROWNING CYNERGY CLASSIC TRAP UNSINGLE COMBO WITH ADJUSTABLE COMB**

**BROWNING CYNERGY SPORTING**

**BROWNING CYNERGY CLASSIC FIELD**

**BROWNING CYNERGY CLASSIC TRAP**

## CYNERGY CLASSIC TRAP UNSINGLE COMBO
**Action**: Single-shot and over/under
**Stock**: Walnut
**Barrel**: 30 in., 32 in.
**Chokes**: Four Invector-Plus Midas Grade choke tubes
**Weight**: 8 lb. 13 oz.–8 lb. 15 oz.
**Bore/Gauge**: 12
**Magazine**: None
**Features**: Steel receiver with MonoLock Hinge; double and single barrel sets included; reverse striker ignition system; impact ejectors; top-tang barrel selector/safety; gloss finish Monte Carlo grade III/IV walnut stock with right-hand palm swell.
**MSRP** . . . . . . . . . . . . . . . . . . . **$5720**

## CYNERGY SPORTING
**Action**: Over/under
**Stock**: Walnut
**Barrel**: 28 in., 30 in., 32 in.
**Chokes**: Three Invecto-Plus choke tubes
**Weight**: 6 lb. 4 oz.–8 lb. 1 oz.
**Bore/Gauge**: 12, 20
**Magazine**: None
**Features**: Reverse striker ignition system; impact ejectors; top-tang barrel selector/safety; gloss oil finish on grade III/IV walnut; steel receiver; inflex technology recoil pad system; HiViz pro-comp fiber-optic sight.
**MSRP** . . . . . . . . . . . . . **$3960–$3990**

## CYNERGY CLASSIC FIELD
**Action**: Over/under
**Stock**: Walnut
**Barrel**: 26 in., 28 in.
**Chokes**: Three Invector-Plus choke tubes on 12 and 20; Three standard Invector chokes on 28 and .410

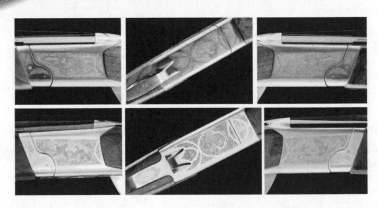

**BROWNING CYNERGY CLASSIC FIELD GRADE III**

**Weight**: 6 lb. 4oz.–7 lb. 13oz.
**Bore/Gauge**: 12, 20, 28, .410
**Magazine**: None
**Features**: Reverse striker ignition system; impact ejectors; top-tang barrel selector/safety; gloss oil finish on grade III/IV walnut; steel receiver; ivory front and mid-bead sights.
**MSRP** . . . . . . . . . . . . . **$2430–$2460**

## CYNERGY CLASSIC TRAP
**Action**: Over/ under
**Stock**: Walnut
**Barrel**: 30 in., 32 in.
**Chokes**: Three Invector-Plus Midas Grade choke tubes
**Weight**: 8 lb.10 oz.–8 lb. 12 oz.
**Bore/Gauge**: 12
**Magazine**: None
**Features**: Reverse striker ignition system; impact ejectors; top-tang barrel selector/ safety; Monte Carlo walnut stock with right-hand palm swell; HiViz pro-comp fiber-optic sight.
**MSRP** . . . . . . . . . . . . . . . . . . . **$3780**

## CYNERGY CLASSIC FIELD GRADE III
**Action**: Over/under
**Stock**: Walnut
**Barrel**: 26 in., 28 in.
**Chokes**: Three Invector-Plus choke tubes
**Weight**: 6 lb. 8 oz.–8 lb. 1 oz.
**Bore/Gauge**: 12, 20
**Magazine**: None
**Features**: Steel receiver with MonoLock Hinge; full coverage high-relief engraving; ventilated top and side ribs; reverse striker ignition system; gloss finish Grade III/IV walnut; recoil pad on 12 gauge model.
**MSRP** . . . . . . . . . . . . . **$3820–$3860**

BROWNING CYNERGY FEATHER

BROWNING CYNERGY FIELD

BROWNING GOLD LIGHT 10 GA

## CYNERGY CLASSIC FIELD GRADE IV

*Action*: Over/under
*Stock*: Walnut
*Barrel*: 26 in., 28 in.
*Chokes*: Three Invector-Plus
*Weight*: 6 lb. 8 oz.–8 lb. 1 oz.
*Bore/Gauge*: 12, 20
*Magazine*: None
*Features*: Steel receiver with MonoLock Hinge; full coverage high-relief engraving; ventilated top and side ribs; reverse striker ignition system; gloss finish grade V/VI walnut; recoil pad on 12 gauge model.
*MSRP* . . . . . . . . . . . . . . **$5800–$5830**

## CYNERGY FEATHER

*Action*: Over/under
*Stock*: Walnut
*Barrel*: 26 in., 28 in.
*Chokes*: Three Invector-Plus choke tubes on 12 and 20, Standard Invector on 28 and .410
*Weight*: 5 lb. 8 oz.–6 lb. 13 oz.
*Bore/Gauge*: 12, 20, 28, .410
*Magazine*: None
*Features*: Lightweight alloy receiver; gold enhanced grayed finish; MonoLock Hinge; reverse striker

ignition system; top-tang barrel selector/safety; inflex technology recoil pad system; ivory front and mid-bead sights.
*MSRP* . . . . . . . . . . . . . . **$2750–2780**

## CYNERGY CLASSIC SPORTING

*Action*: Over/under
*Stock*: Walnut
*Barrel*: 28 in., 30 in., 32 in.
*Chokes*: Three Invector-Plus Midas Grade choke tubes on 12 and 20; Three Standard Invector chokes on 28 and .410
*Weight*: 6 lb. 4 oz.–7 lb. 15 oz.
*Bore/Gauge*: 12, 20, 28, .410
*Magazine*: None
*Features*: Steel receiver; ventilated top and side ribs; reverse striker ignition system; impact ejectors; top-tang barrel selector/safety; gloss oil finish grade III/IV walnut; HiViz pro-comp fiber-optic sight.
*MSRP* . . . . . . . . . . . . . . **$3510–$3550**

## CYNERGY FIELD

*Action*: Over/under
*Stock*: Walnut
*Barrel*: 26 in., 28 in.

*Chokes*: Three Invector-Plus choke tubes on 12 and 20; Standard Invector on 28 and .410
*Weight*: 6 lb. 1 oz.-7 lb. 11 oz.
*Bore/Gauge*: 12, 20, 28, .410
*Magazine*: None
*Features*: Steel receiver with MonoLock Hinge; reverse striker ignition system; impact ejectors; oil finish walnut stock; ivory front and mid-bead sights
*MSRP* . . . . . . . . . . . . . . **$2680–$2710**

## GOLD LIGHT 10 GA.

*Action*: Autoloader, gas operated
*Stock*: Composite
*Barrel*: 26 in., 28 in.
*Chokes*: Three Standard Invector choke tubes
*Weight*: 9 lb. 9 oz.–9 lb. 10 oz.
*Bore/Gauge*: 10
*Magazine*: 4+1 rounds
*Features*: Aluminum alloy receiver; ventilated rib barrel; composite stock and forearm in Mossy Oak camo or Mossy Oak duck blind camo; DuraTouch armor coating.
*MSRP* . . . . . . . . . . . . . . . . . **$1640**

# Browning Shotguns

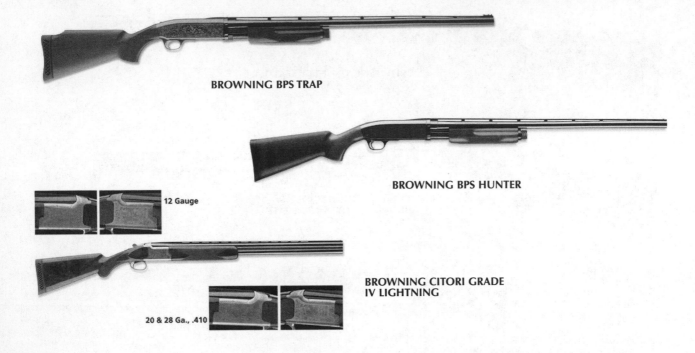

BROWNING BPS TRAP

BROWNING BPS HUNTER

12 Gauge

BROWNING CITORI GRADE IV LIGHTNING

20 & 28 Ga., .410

## BPS TRAP
**Action**: Bottom ejection pump
**Stock**: Walnut
**Barrel**: 30 in.
**Chokes**: Three Invector-Plus choke tubes
**Weight**: 8 lb. 2 oz.
**Bore/Gauge**: 12
**Magazine**: None
**Features**: Satin finish walnut stock with raised comb; forged and machined steel receiver with engraving; dual steel action bars; top-tang safety; magazine cut-off; HiViz procomp fiber-optic sight with mid-bead.
**MSRP** . . . . . . . . . . . . . . . . . . . . $780

## BPS HUNTER
**Action**: Bottom ejection pump
**Stock**: Walnut
**Barrel**: 26 in., 28 in.
**Chokes**: Three Invector-Plus choke tubes with 12 and 20 gauges; Standard Invectors with 16, 28 and .410
**Weight**: 6 lb. 15 oz.–7 lb. 11 oz.
**Bore/Gauge**: 12, 16, 20, 28, .410
**Magazine**: None
**Features**: Satin Finish walnut stock; forged and machined steel receiver; ventilated rib barrel; top-tang safety.
**MSRP** . . . . . . . . . . . . . . . $620–$660

## BPS RIFLED DEER HUNTER
**Action**: Bottom ejection pump
**Stock**: Walnut
**Barrel**: 22 in.
**Chokes**: Screw-in tubes
**Weight**: 7 lb. 4 oz.–7 lb. 10 oz.
**Bore/Gauge**: 12, 20
**Magazine**: None
**Features**: Satin-finish walnut stock; Forged and machined steel receiver; thick-walled barrel for slug ammunition only; dual steel action bars.
**MSRP** . . . . . . . . . . . . . . . . $750–$760

## BT-99 CONVENTIONAL
**Action**: Bottom ejection pump
**Stock**: Walnut
**Barrel**: 32 in., 34 in.
**Chokes**: Screw-in tubes
**Weight**: 8 lb. 3 oz.–8 lb. 5 oz.
**Bore/Gauge**: 12
**Magazine**: None
**Features**: Satin finish walnut stock with beavertail forearm; steel receiver with blued finish; high-post ventilated rib.
**MSRP** . . . . . . . . . . . . . . . . . . . $1340

## CITORI LIGHTNING
**Action**: Over/under
**Stock**: Walnut
**Barrel**: 26 in., 28 in.
**Chokes**: Three Invector-Plus choke

tubes on 12 and 20, Three Standard Invector tubes on 28 and .410
**Weight**: 6 lb. 7 oz.–8 lb. 2 oz.
**Bore/Gauge**: 12, 20, 28, .410
**Magazine**: None
**Features**: Walnut stock with pistol grip; ventilated rib; single-selective trigger; hammer ejectors; top-tang barrel selector/ safety; ivory front bead sight.
**MSRP** . . . . . . . . . . . . . . $1900–$1960

## CITORI GRADE IV LIGHTNING AND VII LIGHTNING
**Action**: Over/under
**Stock**: Walnut
**Barrel**: 26 in., 28 in.
**Chokes**: Three Invector-Plus choke tubes
**Weight**: 6 lb. 8 oz.–8 lb. 3 oz.
**Bore/Gauge**: 12, 20, 28, .410
**Magazine**: None
**Features**: Steel grayed finish receiver with full coverage engraving; blued finish on lightning VII; ventilated rib barrel; single selective trigger; hammer ejectors; lightning-style walnut stock and forearm.
**MSRP** . . . . . . . . . . . . . . $3340–$3420

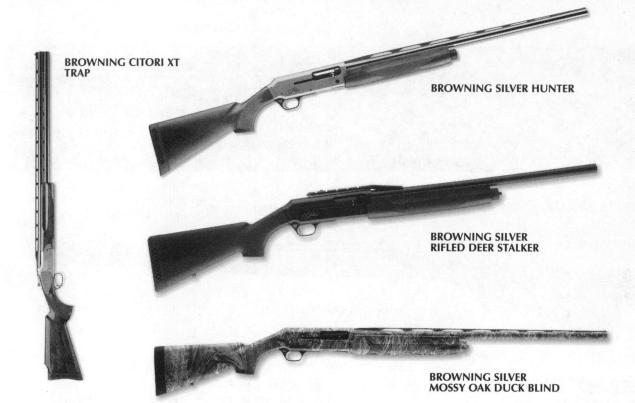

BROWNING CITORI XT TRAP

BROWNING SILVER HUNTER

BROWNING SILVER RIFLED DEER STALKER

BROWNING SILVER MOSSY OAK DUCK BLIND

## CITORI 625 SPORTING

**Action**: Over/under
**Stock**: Walnut
**Barrel**: 28 in., 30 in., 32 in.
**Chokes**: Five Diamond Grade Extended Invector-Plus choke tubes on 12 and 20. Standard Invector on 28 and .410
**Weight**: 6 lb. 15 oz.–8 lb. 2 oz.
**Bore/Gauge**: 12, 20, 28, .410
**Magazine**: None
**Features**: Steel receiver with high-relief engraving with gold embellishment; single-selective trigger; hammer ejectors; top-tang barrel selector/safety; sporting recoil pad; triple trigger system; HiViz pro-comp fiber optic sight.
**MSRP**. . . . . . . . . . . . . **$3560–$3580**

## CITORI XT TRAP

**Action**: Over/under
**Stock**: Walnut
**Barrel**: 30 in., 32 in.
**Chokes**: Three Invector-Plus choke tubes
**Weight**: 8 lb. 6 oz.–8 lb. 8 oz.
**Bore/Gauge**: 12
**Magazine**: None

**Features**: Triple trigger system; HiViz pro-comp sight; steel receiver with gold accented engravings; ventilated barrel; walnut stock with close radius pistol grip and right-hand palm swell; semi-beavertail forearm with finger grooves.
**MSRP**. . . . . . . . . . . . . . . . . **$2820**

## SILVER HUNTER

**Action**: Autoloader, gas operated
**Stock**: Walnut
**Barrel**: 26 in., 28 in., 30 in.
**Chokes**: Three Invector-Plus choke tubes
**Weight**: 6 lb. 5 oz.–7 lb. 9 oz.
**Bore/Gauge**: 12, 20
**Magazine**: None
**Features**: Aluminum alloy receiver; ventilated rib barrel; satin finish walnut stock.
**MSRP**. . . . . . . . . . . . . **$1070–$1270**

## SILVER RIFLED DEER STALKER

**Action**: Autoloader, gas operated
**Stock**: Composite
**Barrel**: 22 in.

**Chokes**: None
**Weight**: 7 lb. 12 oz.
**Bore/Gauge**: 12
**Magazine**: None
**Features**: Aluminum alloy receiver; semi-humpback design; thick-walled barrel for slug ammunition only; matte black composite stock and forearm; Dura-Touch armor coating; cantilever scope mount.
**MSRP**. . . . . . . . . . . . . . . . . **$1220**

## SILVER MOSSY OAK DUCK BLIND

**Action**: Autoloader, gas operated
**Stock**: Composite
**Barrel**: 26 in., 28 in.
**Chokes**: Three Invector-Plus choke tubes
**Weight**: 7 lb. 8 oz.–7 lb. 9 oz.
**Bore/Gauge**: 12
**Magazine**: None
**Features**: Aluminum alloy receiver; Mossy Oak duck blind camo finish composite stock and foream; Dura-Touch armor coating; ventilated rib barrel.
**MSRP**. . . . . . . . . . . . . . . . . **$1360**

SHOTGUNS

# Caesar Guerini Shotguns

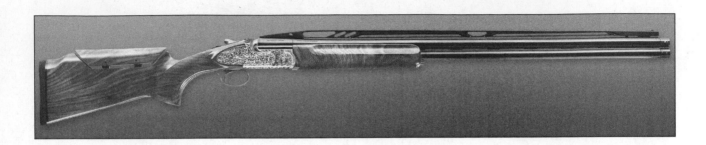

**CAESAR GUERINI MAXUM IMPACT**

**CAESAR GUERINI ELLIPSE EVO**

SHOTGUNS

## MAXUM IMPACT
*Action*: Over/under
*Stock*: Checkered walnut with adjustable cheekpiece
*Barrel*: 30 in. to 34 in.
*Chokes*: Maxis choke system
*Weight*: 7 lb. 11 oz.–8 lb. 7 oz.
*Bore/Gauge*: 12 or 20
*Magazine*: None
*Features*: Engraved receiver; 17mm-tall D.T.S. rib for more upright shooting; 5 in. dual conicial forcing cones; selective and non-selective triggers available; left hand available.
**MSRP . . . . . . . . . . . . . . $7695–$9895**

## ELLIPSE EVO
*Action*: Over/Under
*Stock*: Walnut
*Barrel*: 28 in.
*Chokes*: 5 choke tube options
*Weight*: 6 lb.–7 lb. 4 oz.
*Bore/Gauge*: 12, 20, 28
*Magazine*: None
*Features*: Single trigger; rounded forend; chrome lined barrel; non-ventilated center rib; hand polished coin finish receiver with Invisalloy protective finish.
**MSRP . . . . . . . . . . . . . $5605–$7365**

# Charles Daly Shotguns

## FIELD HUNTER
*Action*: Autoloader
*Stock*: Synthetic
*Barrel*: 24 in., 26 in., 28 in.
*Chokes*: Screw-in tubes
*Weight*: 7.5 lb.
*Bore/Gauge*: 12, 20, 28
*Magazine*: 2 rounds
*Features*: Black or camo Synthetic stock with Integrated grips; 2.75-in. and 3-in. chamber.
**MSRP . . . . . . . . . . . . . . . . . . $429**

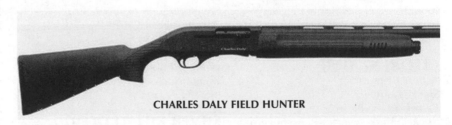

**CHARLES DALY FIELD HUNTER**

# Charles Daly Shotguns

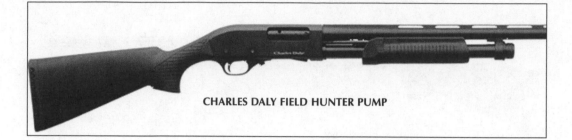

CHARLES DALY FIELD HUNTER PUMP

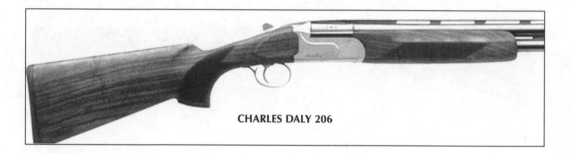

CHARLES DALY 206

## FIELD HUNTER PUMP

*Action*: Pump
*Stock*: Synthetic
*Barrel*: 18 in. through 30 in.
*Chokes*: Screw-in tubes
*Weight*: 7.0 lb.
*Bore/Gauge*: 12, 20
*Magazine*: 4-rounds
*Features*: Black or camo synthetic stock with optional nickel finish; integrated grips; ventilated rib.
**MSRP**................$219

## 206

*Action*: Over/under
*Stock*: Walnut
*Barrel*: 26 in., 28 in., 30 in
*Chokes*: Screw-in tubes
*Weight*: 6.8 lb.
*Bore/Gauge*: 12
*Magazine*: 2 rounds
*Features*: Select Turkish walnut stock; single selective trigger.
**MSRP**................$700

# Connecticut Shotgun Mfg. Co.

## A-10 AMERICAN

*Action*: Sidelock over/under
*Stock*: Checkered Amerian black walnut
*Barrel*: 26 in.–32 in.
*Chokes*: 5 TruLock tubes
*Weight*: 6.5 lb.–7.5 lb.
*Bore/Gauge*: 12, 20, or, 28
*Magazine*: None
*Features*: Finely engraved, cut checkering; ventilated rib; pistol grip or straight grip; auto ejectors, single-selective trigger; Galazan pad.
**Standard Grade:** .........$7995
**Deluxe Grade add** ........$1000
**Plantinum Edition add** ......$8505

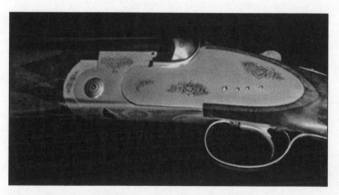

CONNECTICUT SHOTGUN MFG CO. A-10 AMERICAN

# CZ Shotguns

**CZ 712 UTILITY**

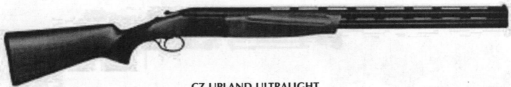

**CZ UPLAND ULTRALIGHT**

**CZ REDHEAD CUSTOM ENHANCED**

## 712 SEMI AUTO
*Action*: Semi-automatic
*Stock*: Walnut
*Barrel*: 26 in., 28 in.
*Chokes*: Screw-in chokes (IC, M, F, C, IM)
*Weight*: 7.3 lb.
*Bore/Gauge*: 12
*Magazine*: 4+1 rounds
*Features*: 3 in. chamber; cross bolt safety; matte black chrome barrel finish; matte anodized receiver finish; gas operated system; chrome-lined barrel.
MSRP . . . . . . . . . . . . . . . . . . . . . $471

## 712 UTILITY
*Action*: Semi-automatic
*Stock*: Synthetic
*Barrel*: 20 in.
*Chokes*: Screw-in chokes (F, IM, M, IC, C)
*Weight*: 6.6 lb.
*Bore/Gauge*: 12
*Magazine*: 4+1 rounds
*Features*: 3 in. chamber cross bolt safety; black synthetic stock; matte chrome black barrel.
MSRP . . . . . . . . . . . . . . . . . . . . . $471

## UPLAND ULTRALIGHT
*Action*: Over/under
*Stock*: Turkish walnut
*Barrel*: 26 in., 28 in.
*Chokes*: Multi
*Weight*: 6 lb.
*Bore/Gauge*: 12
*Magazine*: None
*Features*: Lightweight, black alloy receiver; vent rib.
MSRP . . . . . . . . . . . . . . . . . . . $713

## REDHEAD CUSTOM ENHANCED
*Action*: Over/under
*Stock*: Circassian walnut, hand rubbed finish with Schnabel forend
*Barrel*: 28 in.
*Chokes*: Multi
*Weight*: 7.9 lb.
*Bore/Gauge*: 12
*Magazine*: None
*Features*: Hand-cut checkering, silver receiver, 3.5 to 4 lb. trigger pull.
MSRP . . . . . . . . . . . . . . . . . . . $818

# Escort Shotguns

ESCORT SILVER STANDARD

ESCORT XTREME

## SILVER STANDARD
*Action*: Over/under
*Stock*: Walnut
*Barrel*: 28 in.
*Chokes*: Choke tubes (M, IC, F)
*Weight*: 7.65 lb.
*Bore/Gauge*: 12
*Magazine*: None
*Features*: 3-in. chamber; Turkish walnut stock; Trio recoil pad; blued tang lever; barrel selector switch and trigger guard; auto safety; nickel plated receiver; blued barrel.
**MSRP . . . . . . . . . . . . . . . . . . . . . $773**

## XTREME
*Action*: Semi-automatic
*Stock*: Synthetic
*Barrel*: 22 in., 24 in., 26 in., 28 in., 30 in.
*Chokes*: Steel chokes (F, IM, M, IC, CYL)
*Weight*: 7 lb.
*Bore/Gauge*: 12
*Magazine*: 4+1 rounds
*Features*: Hiviz Spark sights; rubber recoil pad; manual cross safety button; black synthetic stock with rubber inlays.
**MSRP . . . . . . . . . . . . . . . . . . . . $499**

# Fausti Stefano

## DEA ROUND BODY
*Action*: Side-by-side
*Stock*: Oil-finished select walnut
*Barrel*: 28 in.
*Chokes*: Fixed or interchangable choke tubes

*Weight*: 6 lb. 3 oz.
*Bore/Gauge*: 12,16, 20, 24, 28, 36, .410
*Magazine*: None
*Features*: English-style round-body action and stock; low-profile case-

colored receiver; selective ejectors and extractors.
**From: . . . . . . . . . . . . . . . . . . . . $3895**

# Flodman Shotguns

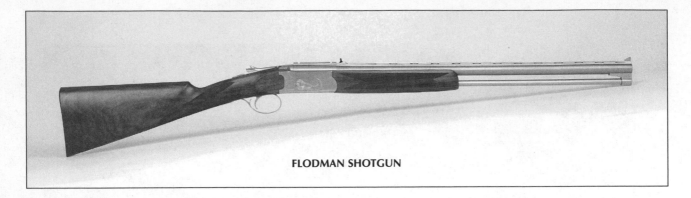

**FLODMAN SHOTGUN**

## FLODMAN SHOTGUN
**Action**: Over/under
**Stock**: Walnut
**Barrel**: 28 in.-34 in.
**Chokes**: Multichoke

**Weight**: 6.2–8.4 lb.
**Bore/Gauge**: 12, 20
**Magazine**: None
**Features**: Boxlock offered in any standard gauge or rifle/shotgun combination; walnut stock with pistol grip; auto or manual safety; stainless steel barrel
**MSRP** . . . . . . . . . . . . . . . . . . $24727

# Franchi Shotguns

**FRANCHI 48AL FIELD 20 GA.**

**FRANCHI 720 COMPETITION 20 GA.**

## 48AL FIELD AND DELUXE
**Action**: Autoloader
**Stock**: Walnut
**Barrel**: 24 in., 26 in., 28 in.
**Chokes**: Screw-in tubes Standard (IC, M, F, wrench), Optional (C, IC, M, IM, F)
**Weight**: 5.4 lb.–6.7 lb.
**Bore/Gauge**: 20, 28
**Magazine**: 4+1 rounds
**Features**: Matte blue steel barrel; polished steel barrel on deluxe model; satin walnut stock on Field model; A-grade satin walnut on Deluxe model; optional custom-fitted hard case.
**Field**: . . . . . . . . . . . . . . . . . . . $839
**Deluxe**: . . . . . . . . . . . . . $939–$1109

## 720 COMPETITION
**Action**: Autoloader
**Stock**: Walnut
**Barrel**: 28 in.
**Chokes**: Screw-in tubes (C, IC, M)
**Weight**: 6.2 lb.
**Bore/Gauge**: 20
**Magazine**: 4+1 rounds
**Features**: Twin shock absorber gel-insert recoil pad; walnut with weathercoat finish; front mid-bead sights.
**MSRP** . . . . . . . . . . . . . . . . . . $1109

SHOTGUNS

# Franchi Shotguns

**FRANCHI I-12 WATERFOWL**

**FRANCHI I-12 UPLAND FIELD**

**FRANCHI I-12 SPORTING**

## I-12 WATERFOWL

**Action**: Autoloader
**Stock**: Walnut, synthetic
**Barrel**: 24 in., 26 in., 28 in.
**Chokes**: Screw-in tubes (C, IC, M, IM, F)
**Weight**: 7.5 lb.–7.7 lb.
**Bore/Gauge**: 12
**Magazine**: 4+1 rounds
**Features**: Walnut stock or synthetic stock in black, Max-4 or APG HD camo finishes; twin shock absorber gel-insert recoil pad; red bar front sight.
**MSRP**. . . . . . . . . . . . . . .$839–$939

## I-12 UPLAND FIELD

**Action**: Autoloader
**Stock**: Walnut
**Barrel**: 28 in.
**Chokes**: Screw in tubes (C, IC, M, IM, F)
**Weight**: 7.7 lb.
**Bore/Gauge**: 12
**Magazine**: 4+1 rounds
**Features**: Walnut stock with pistol grip; red bar front sight; twin shock absorber system.
**Limited**: . . . . . . . . . . . . . . . . $1699
**Standard:**. . . . . . . . . . . . . . . . $939

## I-12 SPORTING

**Action**: Autoloader
**Stock**: Walnut
**Barrel**: 30 in.
**Chokes**: Screw-in tubes (C, IC, M, IM, F)
**Weight**: 6.5 lb.
**Bore/Gauge**: 12
**Magazine**: None
**Features**: Walnut stock with weather-coat finish; twin shock absorber gel-insert recoil pad; optional custom-fitted hard case; red bar sight.
**MSRP**. . . . . . . . . . . . . . . . . . $1329

# Harrington & Richardson Shotguns

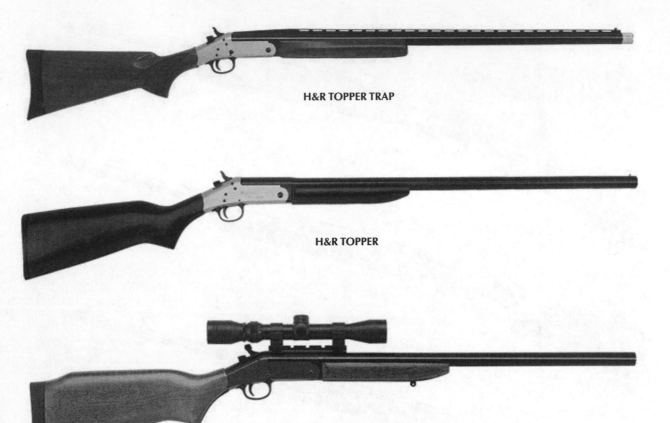

**H&R TOPPER TRAP**

**H&R TOPPER**

**H&R ULTRA LIGHT SLUG HUNTER**

SHOTGUNS

## TOPPER TRAP

*Action*: Break-open, single-shot
*Stock*: Walnut
*Barrel*: 30 in.
*Chokes*: Screw-in Imp. Mod. Extended choke
*Weight*: 7 lb.
*Bore/Gauge*: 12
*Magazine*: None
*Features*: Select trap stock from American Walnut Company with fluted comb, pistol grip, cut checkering and deluxe Pachmayr trap recoil pad; two white trap-bead sights.
**MSRP . . . . . . . . . . . . . . . . . . $424.25**

## TOPPER

*Action*: Hinged single-shot
*Stock*: Hardwood
*Barrel*: 26 in., 28 in.
*Chokes*: Modified (12 Ga., 20 Ga.) and full chokes ( .410 Bore)
*Weight*: 5 lb.–6 lb.
*Bore/Gauge*: 12, 20, .410
*Magazine*: None
*Features*: American hardwood with black finish and pistol grip; Deluxe model has black walnut stock with checkering; brass-bead front sight; nickel-finished receiver; automatic ejectors.
**Topper: . . . . . . . . . . . . . . . $164.47**
**Deluxe Classic: . . . . . . . . . $242.53**

## ULTRA LIGHT SLUG HUNTER

*Action*: Break-open, single-shot
*Stock*: Hardwood
*Barrel*: 24 in.
*Chokes*: None
*Weight*: 5.25 lb.
*Bore/Gauge*: 12, 20
*Magazine*: None
*Features*: American hardwood with walnut finish, full pistol grip, recoil pad and sling swivel studs; Ultragon rifling; scope base included.
**MSRP . . . . . . . . . . . . . . . . . . $227.30**

# Harrington & Richardson Shotguns

**H&R TAMER 20 GA.**

## ULTRA SLUG HUNTER
*Action*: Hinged single-shot
*Stock*: Hardwood
*Barrel*: 24 in.
*Chokes*: None
*Weight*: 8 lb.–9 lb.
*Bore/Gauge*: 12, 20
*Magazine*: None
*Features*: Walnut stained American hardwood Monte Carlo pistol grip stock; sling swivels; nylon sling; ventilated recoil pad; drilled and tapped for scope mount rail; optional 3-9 x 32 scope.
**MSRP. . . . . . . . . . . . . . . . . .$290.87**

## TAMER 20 GA.
*Action*: Hinged single-shot
*Stock*: High density polymer
*Barrel*: 20 in.
*Chokes*: Modified choke
*Weight*: 6 lb.
*Bore/Gauge*: 20
*Magazine*: None
*Features*: High density polymer stock with matte black finish, pistol grip and thumbhole design with storage compartment.
**MSRP. . . . . . . . . . . . . . . . .$185.85**

# Ithaca Shotguns

**ITHACA DEERSLAYER II**

## DEERSLAYER II
*Action*: Pump
*Stock*: Walnut
*Barrel*: 24 in.
*Chokes*: None
*Weight*: 6.8 lb.–8.4 lb.

*Bore/Gauge*: 12, 20
*Magazine*: 4+1 rounds
*Features*: Thumbhole or standard black walnut Monte Carlo stock; fat deluxe checkered forend; sling swivel studs; Pachmayr 750 decelerator recoil pad;

matte blued finish on barrel; gold-plated trigger; Marble Arms rifle sights; drilled and tapped for Weaver #62 scope rail.
**MSRP. . . . . . . . . . . . . . . . . . . $899**

# Ithaca Shotguns

**ITHACA 37 TRAP**

## 37 TRAP
**Action**: Pump
**Stock**: Walnut
**Barrel**: 30 in.
**Chokes**: Briley choke tubes

**Weight**: 7.8 lb.
**Bore/Gauge**: 12
**Magazine**: 4+1 rounds
**Features**: Bottom ejection; 3-in.

chamber; gold plated tubes; walnut Monte Carlo stock; vent rib barrel; classic game scene engraving.
**MSRP** . . . . . . . . . . . . . . . . . . . . **$549**

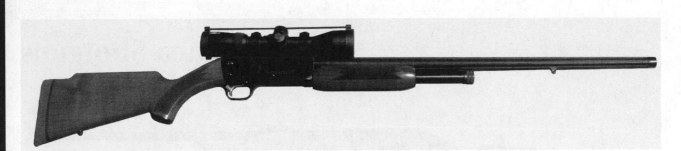

**ITHACA DEERSLAYER III**

## DEERSLAYER III
**Action**: Pump
**Stock**: Walnut
**Barrel**: 20 in., 26 in., 28 in.
**Chokes**: None
**Weight**: 8.1 lb.–9.5 lb.

**Bore/Gauge**: 12, 20
**Magazine**: 4+1 rounds
**Features**: Heavy-walled, fluted, fixed barrel in blue matted finish; walnut Monte Carlo stock with optional thumbhole; Pachmayr 750 decelerator

recoil pad; sling swivel studs; gold-plated trigger; Weaver #62 rail pre-installed on receiver.
**MSRP** . . . . . . . . . . . . . . . . . . **$1189**

# Ithaca Shotguns

**ITHACA 37 DEFENSE SYNTHETIC**

## 37 DEFENSE

*Action*: Pump
*Stock*: Synthetic, walnut
*Barrel*: 18.5 in., 20 in.

*Chokes*: None
*Weight*: 6.5 lb.–7.1 lb.
*Bore/Gauge*: 12, 20
*Magazine*: 4+1, 7+1 rounds
*Features*: Choice of walnut or black

synthetic stock; 3 in. chamber; matte blued finish barrel; Pachmayr decelerator recoil pad.
**Walnut:** . . . . . . . . . . . . . .**$529–$549**
**Synthetic:** . . . . . . . . . . . .**$499–$519**

**ITHACA M37 FEATHERLIGHT**

## M37 FEATHERLIGHT

*Action*: Pump
*Stock*: Walnut
*Barrel*: 26 in., 28 in., 20 in.
*Chokes*: 3 Briley choke tubes

(F, M, IC, and wrench)
*Weight*: 6.1 lb.–7.6 lb.
*Bore/Gauge*: 12, 16, 20, 28
*Magazine*: 4+1 rounds
*Features*: Solderless Barrel System; classic game scene engraving; fancy

black walnut stock and forend; black walnut stock with semi-pistol butt stock; Truglo red front sight; Pachmayr 752 decelerator recoil pad.
**MSRP:** . . . . . . . . . . . . . . . . . . . **$859**

SHOTGUNS

# Krieghoff Shotguns

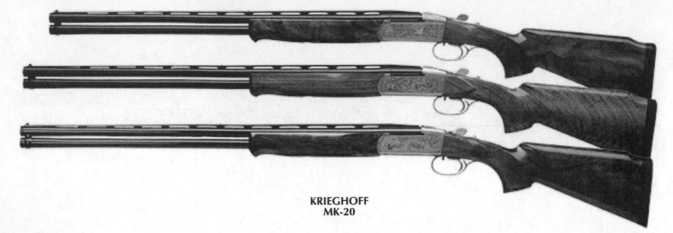

**KRIEGHOFF
MK-20**

## MK-20

**Action**: Over/under
**Stock**: Walnut
**Barrel**: 30 in., 32 in.
**Chokes**: 5 choke tubes (C, S, IC, LM, M, LIM, IM, F)
**Weight**: 7.5 lb.

*Bore/Gauge*: 20, 28, .410
*Magazine*: None
*Features*: Top-tang push safety button; classic scroll engraving; white pearl front bead and metal center bead; single selective mechanical trigger; hand-checkered select European walnut stock with satin epoxy finish.

| | |
|---|---|
| 20 Ga.: . . . . . . . . . . . . . . . . | **$10695** |
| 28 Ga: . . . . . . . . . . . . . . . | **$10850** |
| 410 Ga: . . . . . . . . . . . . . . . | **$10850** |
| 20/28 Ga set w/ 10 choke tubes & 2 Bbl hard case: . . | **$14845** |
| 3 Ga. set w/ 15 choke tubes & 3 Bbl hard case: . . | **$19015** |

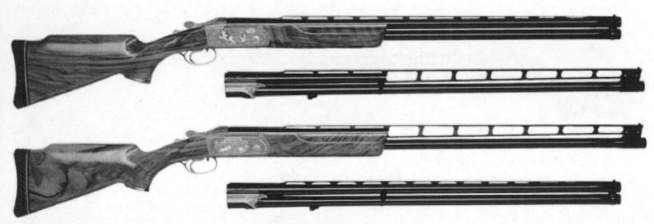

**KRIEGHOFF MK80**

## MK-80

**Action**: Over/under
**Stock**: Walnut
**Barrel**: 30 in., 32 in., 34 in.
**Chokes**: Steel or titanium choke tubes (C, S, IC, LM, M, LIM, IM, F, SF)
**Weight**: 8.25 lb.

*Bore/Gauge*: 12
*Magazine*: None
*Features*: White pearl front sight and metal center bead; nickel-plated steel receiver with satin-grey finish; single-select trigger; top tang push button

safety; fine-checkered Turkish walnut.
**Skeet & Sporting Standard
Models:** . . . . . . . . . **$9470–$10995**

SHOTGUNS

# Legacy Sports Shotguns

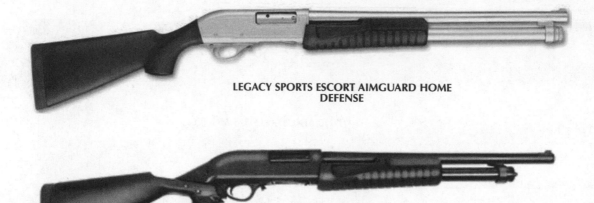

LEGACY SPORTS ESCORT AIMGUARD HOME DEFENSE

LEGACY SPORTS CITADEL TACTICAL SHOTGUNS WITH TALON STOCK

## ESCORT AIMGUARD HOME DEFENSE

**Action**: Autoloader or pump
**Stock**: Pistol grip butt stock with rubber grip and 2-round built-in shell holder
**Barrel**: 18 in.
**Chokes**: Cylinder bore
**Weight**: 5.5 lb.
**Bore/Gauge**: 12
**Magazine**: Tubular, 5-rounds
**Features**: Drilled and tapped and installed upper Picatinny rail; ghost ring rear sight with windage and elevation adjustments, fiber optic front sight; large, easily accessible slide release, black matte finish.

**Pump**: . . . . . . . . . . . . . . . $349–$449
**Autoloader**: . . . . . . . . . . . . . . $590

## CITADEL TACTICAL SHOTGUNS

**Action**: LE pump
**Stock**: Spec-ops or Talon stock
**Barrel**: 18.75 in.
**Chokes**: None
**Weight**: 6 lb.
**Bore/Gauge**: 12
**Magazine**: Detachable, 5- or 10-rounds
**Features**: Short combat; available with traditional tube magazine, 7-rounds with a 20 in. barrel.

**MSRP**. . . . . . . . . . . . . . . $466–$632

# Ljutic Shotguns

LJUTIC MONO GUN

## MONO GUN

**Action**: Single barrel
**Stock**: Walnut
**Barrel**: 32 in.–34 in.
**Chokes**: Optional screw-in chokes (Fixed, Ljutic SIC, Briley SIC)
**Weight**: 10 lb.
**Bore/Gauge**: 740, 12
**Magazine**: None
**Features**: Comes with American walnut wood; optional roll over combs and cheekpieces; various upgrades available.

**Mono**. . . . . . . . . . . . . . . . . . . $7495
**Stainless**. . . . . . . . . . . . . . . . $8495

# Ljutic Shotguns

LJUTIC ADJUSTABLE RIB MONO GUN

LJUTIC PRO 3

## ADJUSTABLE RIB MONO GUN

*Action*: Single barrel
*Stock*: Walnut
*Barrel*: 34 in.
*Chokes*: Fixed or Ljutic SIC
*Weight*: 10 lb.
*Bore/Gauge*: 740, 12
*Magazine*: None
*Features*: "One Touch" adjustable rib allows you to change your point-of-impact; adjustable comb stock.

**Adjustable Rib . . . . . . . . . . . $7995**
**Stainless Adjustable . . . . . . . . $8995**

## PRO 3

*Action*: Single barrel
*Stock*: Walnut
*Barrel*: 34 in.
*Chokes*: 4 Briley Series 12 chokes
*Weight*: 9 lb.
*Bore/Gauge*: 740, 12
*Magazine*: None
*Features*: Aluminum baseplate; interchangable 2 pad system; adjustable comb; English or American walnut stock; screw-in hinge pin; stainless or blued barrel.

**Blued barrel: . . . . . . . . . . . . $8995**
**Stainless. . . . . . . . . . . . . . . $9995**

## ADJUSTABLE PRO 3

*Action*: Single barrel
*Stock*: Walnut
*Barrel*: 34 in.
*Chokes*: Fixed or Ljutic SIC
*Weight*: 9 lb.
*Bore/Gauge*: 740, 12
*Magazine*: None
*Features*: "One Touch" adjustable rib; adjustable comb stock; adjustable chokes.

**Adjustable: . . . . . . . . . . . . . $9520**
**Stainless: . . . . . . . . . . . . . . $10520**

# Marocchi Shotguns

## MODEL 100

*Action*: Over/ under
*Stock*: Walnut
*Barrel*: 28 in.- 32 in.
*Chokes*: Trap (Imp. Mod/ Full); Sporter (Multichoke), Skeet( SK/SK); Electrocibles (Mulitchokes); Double Trap (Multichoke/ Full)
*Weight*: 7.2 lb.- 8.1 lb.

*Bore/Gauge*: 12
*Magazine*: None
*Features*: Steel action; single adjustable trigger; mechanically assisted ejector system; steel barrels; boss type locking system; walnut stock available in various grades

**MSRP. . . . . . . . . . . . . . . . . . $3250**

SHOTGUNS

# Merkel Shotguns

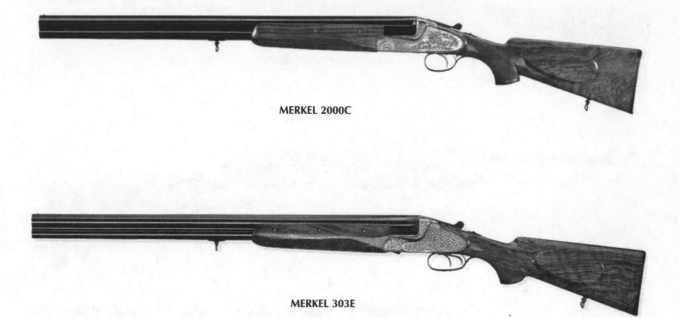

**MERKEL 2000C**

**MERKEL 303E**

## 45E
**Action**: Side-by-side
**Stock**: Wood
**Barrel**: 27 in., 28 in.
**Chokes**: Steel-shot proofed chokes
**Weight**: 6.17 lb.
**Bore/Gauge**: 12, 20
**Magazine**: None
**Features**: English stock finished with fine hand-cut checkering at buttplate; silver monogram plate; steel action is grey nitrated; Anson & Deely locks; Greener-style cross bolt and double bottom bite; double trigger; automatic safety.
**MSRP** . . . . . . . . . . . . . . . . . . $4595

## 2000C
**Action**: Over/under
**Stock**: Wood
**Barrel**: 27 in., 28 in.
**Chokes**: 2 interchangable chokes steel-shot proofed
**Weight**: 6.8 lb.

**Bore/Gauge**: 12/76, 20/76
**Magazine**: None
**Features**: Disconnectable ejectors; arabesque engraving; Anson & Deely locks in steel receiver; Kersten cross bolt; selective single trigger, adjustable in length; manual safety; wood stock with pistol grip and cheekpiece.
**MSRP** . . . . . . . . . . . . . . . . . . $8495

## 303E
**Action**: Over/under
**Stock**: Wood
**Barrel**: 27 in., 28 in.
**Chokes**: Steel-shot proofed chokes
**Weight**: 6.8 lb.
**Bore/Gauge**: 12/76, 20/76
**Magazine**: None
**Features**: Sidelocks with V-springs; Kersten cross bolt with double conventional bottom bite; double trigger; front trigger articulated; optional

selective single trigger; engraving English arabesque; luxury grade walnut stock with pistol grip; optional English styled stock
**MSRP** . . . . . . . . . . . . . . . . . . $4995

## 60E
**Action**: Side-by-side
**Stock**: Wood
**Barrel**: 27 in., 28 in.
**Chokes**: Steel-shot proofed chokes
**Weight**: 6.2 lb.–6.8 lb.
**Bore/Gauge**: 12/76, 20/76
**Magazine**: None
**Features**: Detachable sidelocks; steel action; Greener-style cross bolt and double bottom bite; double trigger; automatic safety; pistol grip wood stock and cheekpiece.
**MSRP** . . . . . . . . . . . . . . . . . . $5500

# Mossberg Shotguns

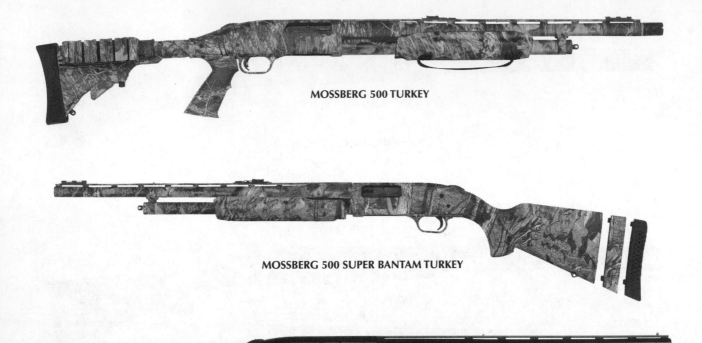

**MOSSBERG 500 TURKEY**

**MOSSBERG 500 SUPER BANTAM TURKEY**

**MOSSBERG 510 MINI SUPER BANTAM**

## 500 MARINER J.I.C (JUST IN CASE)

*Action*: Pump
*Stock*: Synthetic
*Barrel*: 18.5 in.
*Chokes*: Cyclinder bore chokes
*Weight*: 5.5 lb.
*Bore/Gauge*: 12
*Magazine*: 6-rounds
*Features*: Bead sight; Marinecote metal finish; comes with multi-tool, survival knife and Cordura carrying case; gun lock; swivel studs; black synthetic stock.
*MSRP*.....................$580

## 500 TURKEY

*Action*: Pump
*Stock*: Synthetic
*Barrel*: 24 in.
*Chokes*: Accu-Choke tubes (XX-Full)

*Weight*: 7.25 lb.
*Bore/Gauge*: 12, 20
*Magazine*: 6-rounds
*Features*: Adjustable front sight; synthetic finish in Mossy Oak camo; ported barrel; ambidextrous thumb-operated safety; includes gun lock.
*MSRP*.....................$435

## 500 SUPER BANTAM TURKEY

*Action*: Pump
*Stock*: Synthetic
*Barrel*: 20 in.
*Chokes*: Interchangable Accu-Choke (X-full and wrench)
*Weight*: 5.25 lb.
*Bore/Gauge*: 20
*Magazine*: 6-rounds
*Features*: Adjustable synthetic stock in Mossy Oak Break-up Infinity camo or

Hardwoods HD green camo; adjustable fiber optic sights; drilled and tapped for scopes; gun lock.
*MSRP*.....................$435

## 510 MINI SUPER BANTAM

*Action*: Pump
*Stock*: Synthetic
*Barrel*: 18.5 in.
*Chokes*: Accu-set in 20 Ga., Fixed-Mod. in .410 Bore
*Weight*: 5 lb.
*Bore/Gauge*: 410, 20
*Magazine*: 3 (.410) and 4 (20 Ga.)
*Features*: Good choice for petite or younger shooter; adjustable synthetic stock in black; blue barrel finish; dual bead sights.
*MSRP*.....................$375

# Mossberg Shotguns

**MOSSBERG 500 SLUGSTER WITH LPA TRIGGER**

**MOSSBERG 835 ULTI-MAG**

**MOSSBERG SUPER BANTAM SLUGSTER**

SHOTGUNS

## 500 SLUGSTER WITH LPA TRIGGER

*Action*: Pump
*Stock*: Synthetic
*Barrel*: 24 in.
*Chokes*: None
*Weight*: 7 lb.
*Bore/Gauge*: 12
*Magazine*: 6 rounds
*Features*: Fully rifled bore; integral scope base; LPA (Lightning Pump Action) trigger system providing creep-free rifle-like trigger; ported barrel; ambidextrous thumb-operated safety.
**MSRP** . . . . . . . . . . . . . . . . . . . . . **$499**

## 500 SUPER BANTAM SLUGSTER

*Action*: Pump
*Stock*: Synthetic
*Barrel*: 24 in.
*Chokes*: None
*Weight*: 5.25 lb.
*Bore/Gauge*: 20
*Magazine*: 6-rounds
*Features*: Fully rifled bore; adjustable synthetic stock; blue or Realtree AP finish; drilled and tapped for scopes; ported barrels; adjustable rifle sights.
**MSRP** . . . . . . . . . . . . . . . **$375–$435**

## 835 ULTI-MAG

*Action*: Pump
*Stock*: Synthetic
*Barrel*: 24 in.
*Chokes*: Ulti-full tube chokes
*Weight*: 7.5 lb.
*Bore/Gauge*: 12
*Magazine*: 6-rounds
*Features*: Overbored, ported barrel; synthetic stock comes in Woodlands, Mossy Oak Break-up Infinity or Hardwoods HD green camo; ambidextrous, thumb-operated safety; drilled and tapped for scope mounts.
**MSRP** . . . . . . . . . . . . . . . **$516–$541**

# Mossberg Shotguns

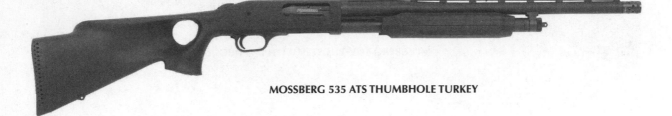

**MOSSBERG 535 ATS THUMBHOLE TURKEY**

**MOSSBERG 935 MAGNUM TURKEY GUN**

**MOSSBERG SILVER RESERVE FIELD**

SHOTGUNS

### 535 ATS THUMBHOLE TURKEY
*Action*: Pump
*Stock*: Synthetic
*Barrel*: 20 in.
*Chokes*: Interchangable, X-Factor Ptd choke tube
*Weight*: 7 lb.
*Bore/Gauge*: 12
*Magazine*: 6-rounds
*Features*: Adjustable front sights; synthetic thumbhole stock comes in black with matte blue metal finish, Mossy Oak Break-up Infinity or Hardwoods HD green camo; Ventilated rib barrel; includes gun lock.
**MSRP**. . . . . . . . . . . . . . . .$456–$522

### 935 MAGNUM TURKEY GUN
*Action*: Autoloader
*Stock*: Synthetic
*Barrel*: 24 in.
*Chokes*: Ulti-full tube chokes
*Weight*: 7.5 lb.
*Bore/Gauge*: 12
*Magazine*: 5-rounds
*Features*: Overbored barrel; synthetic stock in Mossy Oak Break-Up or ; Quick-empty magazine button; hardwoods HD Green camo; adjustable fiber optic sights; wide ventilated rib.
**MSRP**. . . . . . . . . . . . . . . . . . . . $769

### SILVER RESERVE FIELD
*Action*: Over/under
*Stock*: Walnut
*Barrel*: 26 in.
*Chokes*: 5 sports tubes, fixed modified choke on 410 bore
*Weight*: 6 lb.–7.7 lb.
*Bore/Gauge*: 12, 20, 28, 410
*Magazine*: None
*Features*: Blued barrels, silver receiver with gold game scene; satin finish on select black walnut stock; precision machined receiver; chrome plated bores; dual locking lugs; front bead sight.
**MSRP**. . . . . . . . . . . . . . . . . . . . $672

# New England Arms / FAIR Shotguns

**NEW ENGLAND/FAIR PARDNER PUMP SHOTGUN**

**NEW ENGLAND/FAIR TRACKER II**

**NEW ENGLAND/FAIR PARDNER SINGLE-SHOT**

SHOTGUNS

## PARDNER PUMP SHOTGUN

**Action**: Pump
**Stock**: Walnut
**Barrel**: 26 in., 28 in.
**Chokes**: Screw-in modified choke
**Weight**: 7.5 lb.
**Bore/Gauge**: 12, 20
**Magazine**: 5-rounds
**Features**: American walnut stock with grooved and ventilated recoil pad; bead front sight; drilled and tapped for scope base; chrome-plated bolt; vent-rib barrel.
**MSRP** . . . . . . . . . . . . . . . . . **$253.70**

## TRACKER II

**Action**: Single-shot
**Stock**: Hardwood
**Barrel**: 24 in.
**Chokes**: Rifled bore choke
**Weight**: 5.25 lb
**Bore/Gauge**: 12, 20
**Magazine**: None
**Features**: Adjustable rifle sights; American hardwood with walnut finish; full pistol grip; recoil pad; sling swivel studs.
**MSRP** . . . . . . . . . . . . . . . . . **$227.30**

## PARDNER SINGLE-SHOT

**Action**: Break-open single-shot
**Stock**: Hardwood
**Barrel**: 22 in., 26 in., 28 in., 32 in.
**Chokes**: Modified or full (12 Ga., 20 Ga.), Modified (28 Ga.), Full (12 Ga., 410 Bore)
**Weight**: 5 lb.–6 lb.
**Bore/Gauge**: 12, 20, 28, 410
**Magazine**: None
**Features**: American hardwood, walnut finish with pistol grip; bead front sight; side lever release; automatic ejection; transfer bar safety system.
**Compact:** . . . . . . . . . . . . . . **$161.99**
**Standard:** . . . . . . . . **$150.42–$168.48**

# New England Arms / FAIR Shotguns

**NEW ENGLAND/FAIR PARDNER TURKEY**

## PARDNER TURKEY
*Action*: Break-open single-shot
*Stock*: Synthetic, hardwood
*Barrel*: 24 in.
*Chokes*: Extra-full screw-in chokes, full in camo 12 Ga.
*Weight*: 6 lb.–9 lb.
*Bore/Gauge*: 10, 12

*Magazine*: None
*Features*: American hardwood stock in black matte finish or with camo pattern; pistol grip; ventilated rubber recoil pad; sling swivel studs; sling; bead sights; drilled and tapped for scope mount.
*MSRP* . . . . . . . . . . . $217.91–$309.56

# Perazzi Shotguns

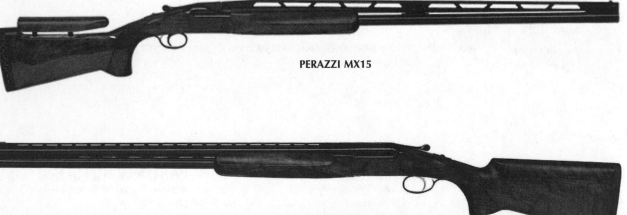

**PERAZZI MX15**

**PERAZZI MX8**

## MX8
*Action*: Over/under
*Stock*: Walnut
*Barrel*: 29 in., 30 in., 31 in.
*Chokes*: Interchangable chokes
*Weight*: 7.3 lb.
*Bore/Gauge*: 12, 20
*Magazine*: None
*Features*: Custom walnut stock with beavertail forend; half ventilated side ribs on barrel; removable trigger with flat or coil springs; blue or nickel plating; sporting, skeet and trap models; 28 Ga. and 410 models also available
*MSRP* . . . . . . . . . . . . . . . . . $5213

## MX15
*Action*: Hinged single shot
*Stock*: Walnut
*Barrel*: 32 in., 34 in., 35 in.

*Chokes*: Fixed chokes
*Weight*: 8.4 lb.
*Bore/Gauge*: 12
*Magazine*: None
*Features*: Removable trigger group; adjustable rib with 6 notches; tapered barrel; stock with adjustable comb in wood or rubber; beavertail forend; adjustable point of impact.
*MSRP* . . . . . . . . . . . . . . . . . . $9594

SHOTGUNS

# Purdey Shotguns

## OVER/UNDER GUN

*Action*: Over/under
*Stock*: Walnut
*Barrel*: 26 in. to 30 in.
*Chokes*: Interchangable choke tubes
*Weight*: 4 lb. 14 oz.–7 lb. 8 oz.
*Bore/Gauge*: 12, 16, 20, 28, 410
*Magazine*: None
*Features*: Available in round, square, or ultra-round action shapes; available with double or non-selective single triggers and automatic safety catch; demi-bloc construction; solid game rib with hand matted finish; Turkish walnut with straight, semi, or full pistol grip; gold oval or inlaid gold letters.

12, 16, 20 Ga.: . . . . . . . . . . .$116646
28 Ga.: . . . . . . . . . . . . . . . .$123218
.410: . . . . . . . . . . . . . . . . . .$125682

## SIDE-BY-SIDE GAME GUN

*Action*: Side-by-side
*Stock*: Walnut
*Barrel*: 26 in. to 30 in.
*Chokes*: Interchangable choke tubes
*Weight*: 4 lb. 10oz.–6 lb. 12oz.
*Bore/Gauge*: 10, 12, 16, 20, 28, .410
*Magazine*: None
*Features*: Built on self-opening system; available with double or non-selective single triggers and automatic safety catch; Turkish walnut in straight, semi, or full pistol grip; gold oval or inlaid gold letters; traditional splinter or beavertail forends available.

12, 16, 20 Ga.: . . . . . . . . . . . $99395
28 Ga.: . . . . . . . . . . . . . . . . .$101449
.410: . . . . . . . . . . . . . . . . . .$105967
10 Ga.: . . . . . . . . . . . . . . . . .$105967

# Remington Shotguns

REMINGTON 870 EXPRESS SUPER MAG TURKEY WATERFOWL

REMINGTON MODEL 870 EXPRESS

## 870 EXPRESS SUPER MAG. TURKEY/ WATERFOWL

*Action*: Pump
*Stock*: Synthetic
*Barrel*: 26 in.
*Chokes*: Wingmaster HD Waterfowl and Turkey Extra Full Rem. chokes
*Weight*: 7.25 lb.
*Bore/Gauge*: 12
*Magazine*: None
*Features*: Synthetic stock in full Mossy Oak Bottomland camo; HiVix fiber-optics; supercell recoil pad; drilled and tapped receiver.

MSRP . . . . . . . . . . . . . . . . . . . $620

## 870 EXPRESS

*Action*: Pump
*Stock*: Synthetic, hardwood laminate, or camo
*Barrel*: 18 in.–28 in.
*Chokes*: Modified Remington choke, Extra full Rem.
*Weight*: 6 lb.–7.25 lb.
*Bore/Gauge*: 12, 20
*Magazine*: 2- to 7-rounds depending on model
*Features*: Single-bead sight; standard express finish on barrel and receiver; rubber recoil pad; twin action bars ensure smooth, reliable non-binding action; solid steel receiver; optional thumbhole stock in some models.

Express. . . . . . . . . . . . . . . . . . . $411
Express Syn. Deer . . . . . . . . . . $ 457
Express Tactical . . . . . . . . . . . . $572
Turkey Camo . . . . . . . . . . . . . . $485
Express Super Mag. . . . . . . . . . $462
Express SPS Shurshot
Express Synthetic Super Slug . . $829
Express Super Mag.
Waterfowl Camo . . . . . . . . . . . $620

# Remington Shotguns

**REMINGTON 870 SPS SHURSHOT SYNTHETIC TURKEY**

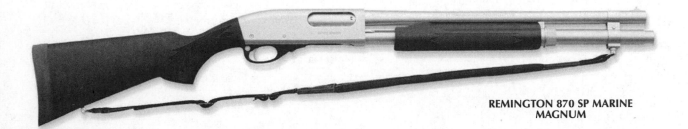

**REMINGTON 870 SP MARINE MAGNUM**

**REMINGTON 870 SHURSHOT SYNTHETIC SUPER SLUG**

## 870 SPS SHURSHOT SYNTHETIC TURKEY

*Action*: Pump
*Stock*: Synthetic
*Barrel*: 23 in.
*Chokes*: Wingmaster HD extended Rem. choke
*Weight*: 7.5 lb.
*Bore/Gauge*: 12
*Magazine*: None
*Features*: Synthetic stock covered in Realtree APG HD camo; features ShurShot synthetic pistol-grip stock; adjustable Truglo fiber-optic sights; receiver drilled and tapped for scope mounts.
**MSRP** . . . . . . . . . . . . . . . . . . . . **$671**

## 870 SP MARINE MAGNUM

*Action*: Pump
*Stock*: Synthetic
*Barrel*: 18 in.
*Chokes*: Cylinder chokes
*Weight*: 7.5 lb.
*Bore/Gauge*: 12
*Magazine*: 6-rounds
*Features*: Single-bead front sight; padded Cordura; sling swivels; electroless nickel plating covers all metal; twin action bars ensure smooth, reliable non-binding action.
**MSRP** . . . . . . . . . . . . . . . . . . . . **$829**

## 870 SHURSHOT SYNTHETIC SUPER SLUG

*Action*: Pump
*Stock*: Synthetic
*Barrel*: 25 in.
*Chokes*: Screw-in tubes
*Weight*: 7.8 lb.
*Bore/Gauge*: 12
*Magazine*: None
*Features*: Ambidextrous ShurShot pistol-grip synthetic stock; rubberized overmolding; SuperCell recoil pad; receiver is drilled and tapped; Weaver rail; sling swivels.
**MSRP** . . . . . . . . . . . . . . . . . . . . **$829**

# Remington Shotguns

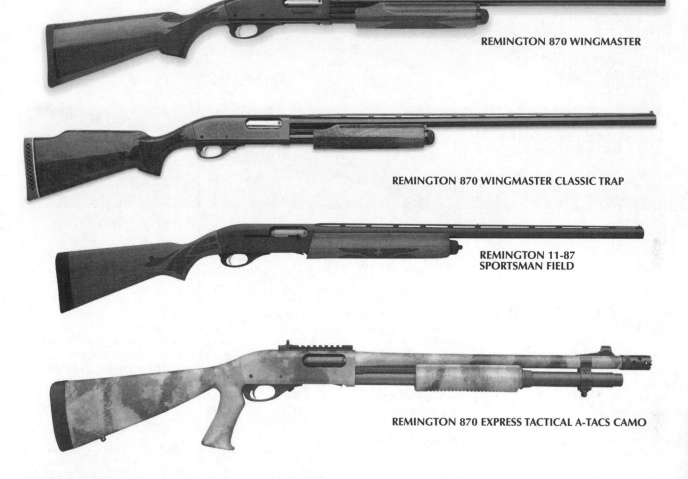

REMINGTON 870 WINGMASTER

REMINGTON 870 WINGMASTER CLASSIC TRAP

REMINGTON 11-87 SPORTSMAN FIELD

REMINGTON 870 EXPRESS TACTICAL A-TACS CAMO

## 870 WINGMASTER
**Action**: Pump
**Stock**: Walnut
**Barrel**: 25 in.
**Chokes**: Screw-in tubes
**Weight**: 6 lb.–6.25 lb.
**Bore/Gauge**: 12, 20, 28, 410
**Magazine**: None
**Features**: Twin action bars for non-binding action; receiver machined from solid billet of steel; highly polished and richly blued receiver; wide array of barrel and choke options.
**MSRP** . . . . . . . . . . . . . . . . . . . . . $818

## 870 WINGMASTER CLASSIC TRAP
**Action**: Pump
**Stock**: Walnut
**Barrel**: 30 in.
**Chokes**: Screw-in tube, Rem. choke

**Weight**: 8.25 lb.
**Bore/Gauge**: 12
**Magazine**: None
**Features**: American walnut, Monte Carlo stock; forend with deep cut checkering and a high-gloss finish; twin bead sights; three specialized trap Rem. choke tubes; twin action bars ensure smooth, reliable non-binding action; choke vent rib barrel.
**MSRP** . . . . . . . . . . . . . . . . . . $1081

## 11-87 SPORTSMAN FIELD
**Action**: Autoloading
**Stock**: Walnut
**Barrel**: 26 in., 28 in.
**Chokes**: Rem. Modified choke
**Weight**: 7.25 lb.–8.25 lb.
**Bore/Gauge**: 12, 20
**Magazine**: None
**Features**: Solid walnut stock and

forend with satin finish and fleur-de-lis checkering; nickel-plated bolt and gold-plated trigger; vent rib with dual bead sights.
**MSRP** . . . . . . . . . . . . . . . . . . . . . $845

## 870 EXPRESS TACTICAL A-TACS CAMO
**Action**: Pump
**Stock**: Synthetic
**Barrel**: 18.5 in.
**Chokes**: Screw-in tube
**Weight**: 7.5 lb.
**Bore/Gauge**: 12
**Magazine**: None
**Features**: Synthetic stock covered in A-TACS digitized camo; tactical Rem. choke SpeedFeed IV; pistol grip stock; SuperCell recoil pad; adjustable XS ghost ring sight rail with removable with bead front sight; Picatinny-style rail.
**MSRP** . . . . . . . . . . . . . . . . . . . . . $685

# Remington Shotguns

REMINGTON 887 NITRO MAG. CAMO COMBO

REMINGTON 1100 CLASSIC TRAP

## 887 NITRO MAG. CAMO COMBO
*Action*: Autoloading
*Stock*: Synthetic
*Barrel*: 22 in., 28 in.
*Chokes*: Screw-in tubes
*Weight*: 7 lb.–7.25 lb.
*Bore/Gauge*: 12
*Magazine*: None
*Features*: Synthetic camo stock with ArmorLokt coating; SuperCell recoil pad; HiViz front sight; contoured grip panels; sling swivel
**MSRP** . . . . . . . . . . . . . . . . . . . . **$728**

## 1100 CLASSIC TRAP
*Action*: Autoloading
*Stock*: Walnut
*Barrel*: 30 in.
*Chokes*: Screw-in tubes
*Weight*: 8.25 lb.
*Bore/Gauge*: 12
*Magazine*: None
*Features*: American walnut stock with cut-checkering; bead blasted top and bottom radius; blued finish on receiver and barrel; gold triggers and gold embellishments on receiver.
**MSRP** . . . . . . . . . . . . . . . . . . **$1270**

# Renato Gamba Shotguns

## DAYTONA 12GA
*Action*: Autoloading
*Stock*: Walnut
*Barrel*: 30 in.
*Chokes*: Screw-in chokes
*Weight*: 9 lb.
*Bore/Gauge*: 12
*Magazine*: None
*Features*: Single-selective trigger; checkered pistol grip with adjustable comb; walnut stock; checkered Scnabel; hard rubber pad; single brass-bead sight; includes hard case and two trigger systems.
**MSRP** . . . . . . . . . . . . . . . . . . **$5800**

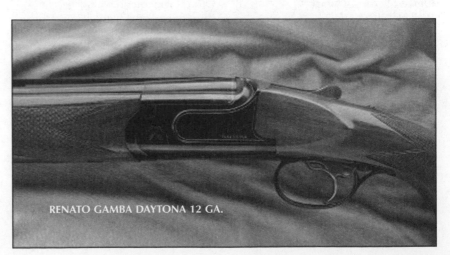

RENATO GAMBA DAYTONA 12 GA.

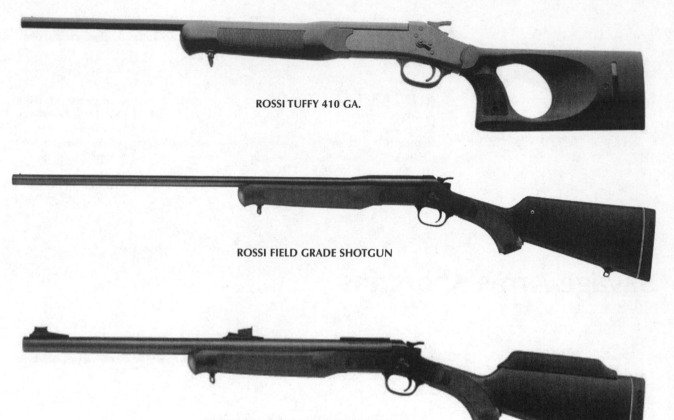

ROSSI TUFFY 410 GA.

ROSSI FIELD GRADE SHOTGUN

ROSSI YOUTH RIFLED BARREL SLUG GUN

## TUFFY 410 GA.
*Action*: Single-shot, hinged breech
*Stock*: Synthetic
*Barrel*: 18.5 in.
*Chokes*: Screw-in chokes
*Weight*: 3 lb.
*Bore/Gauge*: 410
*Magazine*: None
*Features*: Black synthetic stock with thumbhole grip; Taurus security system; matte blue metal finish or matte nickel; steel receiver.
**MSRP**. . . . . . . . . . . . . . .$164–$172

## FIELD GRADE SHOTGUN
*Action*: Single-shot, break-open
*Stock*: Synthetic

*Barrel*: 28 in.
*Chokes*: Modified screw-in chokes
*Weight*: 3.75 lb.–5.25 lb.
*Bore/Gauge*: 12, 20, 410
*Magazine*: None
*Features*: Steel receiver; black synthetic stock with grips; blue finish metal; transfer bar safety action.
**Full size:** . . . . . . . . . . . . . . . . . **$131**
**Youth 22 in. Barrel:** . . . . . . . . **$138**

## YOUTH RIFLED BARREL SLUG GUN
*Action*: Single-shot, break-open
*Stock*: Synthetic
*Barrel*: 23 in.
*Chokes*: Screw-in tubes

*Weight*: 6.25 lb.
*Bore/Gauge*: 12
*Magazine*: None
*Features*: Steel receiver; black synthetic stock with grips; blue matte finish on metal; removable cheekpiece; trifecta three-barrel youth gun includes either .243 Win. or .44 Mag. barrel with fiber optic sights or .22 long rifle barrel with adjustable fiber optics and 20 Ga. shot gun barrel with brass bead front sight.
**MSRP**. . . . . . . . . . . . . . . . . . . . **$225**

# Ruger Shotguns

**RUGER RED LABEL SHOTGUN**

## RED LABEL SHOTGUNS
*Action*: Over/under
*Stock*: Walnut
*Barrel*: 26 in., 28 in., 30 in.
*Chokes*: 5 screw-in tubes (F, M, IC)
*Weight*: 7.25 lb.–7.75 lb.
*Bore/Gauge*: 12, 20, 28
*Magazine*: None

*Features*: Stainless steel receiver; tang safety; barrel selector; brass bead front sight; hammer-forged barrels; compact locking system; blued barrel finish; walnut stock with pistol or straight grip.
**Standard or All-Weather: . . . . $2015**
**Engraving: . . . . . . . . . . . . . . $2245**

# Savage Arms Shotguns

**SAVAGE ARMS STEVENS 512 GOLD WING**

**SAVAGE ARMS STEVENS 350 PUMP FIELD**

## STEVENS 512 GOLD WING
*Action*: Over/under
*Stock*: Walnut
*Barrel*: 26 in.
*Chokes*: None
*Weight*: 6 lb.–8 lb.
*Bore/Gauge*: 12, 20, 28, 410
*Magazine*: None
*Features*: Vent rib with front sight bead; carbon steel barrel; blued metal finish.
**Standard:. . . . . . . . . . . . . . . . $665**
**Youth: . . . . . . . . . . . . . . . . . $665**

## STEVENS 350 PUMP FIELD
*Action*: Pump
*Stock*: Synthetic
*Barrel*: 28 in.
*Chokes*: None
*Weight*: 8.2 lb.
*Bore/Gauge*: 12
*Magazine*: Internal box, 5-rounds
*Features*: Vent rib, bead sights; carbon steel barrel; blued metal finish; matte black synthetic stock.
**MSRP. . . . . . . . . . . . . . . . . . . $294**

SHOTGUNS

# Savage Arms Shotguns

SAVAGE ARMS STEVENS 350 PUMP SECURITY

SAVAGE ARMS 220

## STEVENS 350 PUMP SECURITY
**Action**: Pump
**Stock**: Synthetic
**Barrel**: 18.25 in.
**Chokes**: None
**Weight**: 7.6 lb.
**Bore/Gauge**: 12
**Magazine**: Internal box, 5-rounds
**Features**: Bead sights; carbon steel barrel with matte blued finish; synthetic stock in matte black finish.
**MSRP** . . . . . . . . . . . . . . . . . . . . **$264**

## 220
**Action**: Bolt
**Stock**: Synthetic
**Barrel**: 22 in.
**Chokes**: None
**Weight**: 7.5 lb.
**Bore/Gauge**: 20
**Magazine**: None
**Features**: Drilled and tapped for scope mounts; carbon steel barrel with matte blued finish; AccuTrigger; black synthetic stock with matte finish.
**MSRP** . . . . . . . . . . . . . . . . . . . . **$534**

# SKB Shotguns

SKB 505

## 505
**Action**: Over/under
**Stock**: Walnut
**Barrel**: 26 in., 28 in., 30 in.
**Chokes**: Standard series choke tube system A (IC, M, F) or B (SK, IC, M)
**Weight**: 6 lb. 11oz.–8 lb. 9oz.
**Bore/Gauge**: 12, 20, 28
**Magazine**: None
**Features**: Select American walnut stock with cut checkering; fitted butt pad on 12 Ga. model; single-selective trigger; rolled engraving patter; inertia triggers; Greener-style cross bolt lock; full side ribs on barrel; metal front bead sights.
**MSRP** . . . . . . . . . . . . . . . . . . . . **$1429**

# Smith & Wesson Shotguns

**S&W ELITE GOLD GRADE I**

**S&W ELITE SILVER GRADE I**

## ELITE GOLD GRADE I

**Action**: Side-by-side
**Stock**: Walnut
**Barrel**: 28 in.
**Chokes**: Improved Cylinder/Mod. bore
**Weight**: 6.7 lb.
**Bore/Gauge**: 20
**Magazine**: None
**Features**: Ivory sight with mid-bead; Prince of Wales walnut stock; features the S&W trigger plate; true bone-charcoal case hardening; hand-engraved receiver, English scroll.
**MSRP** . . . . . . . . . . . . . . . . . . **$2380**

## ELITE SILVER GRADE I

**Action**: Over/under
**Stock**: Walnut
**Barrel**: 30 in.
**Chokes**: 5 thin-wall, English Teague-style choke tubes (Cylinder, Improved Cylinder, Modified, Improved Modified, Full)
**Weight**: 7.8 lb.

**Bore/Gauge**: 12
**Magazine**: None
**Features**: Ivory sight with mid-bead; Prince of Wales walnut stock; features the S&W trigger plate; true Bone-charcoal case hardening; hand-engraved receiver, English scroll.
**MSRP** . . . . . . . . . . . . . . . . . . **$2380**

# Stoeger Shotguns

**STOEGER DOUBLE DEFENSE**

## DOUBLE DEFENSE

**Action**: Side-by-side
**Stock**: Hardwood
**Barrel**: 20 in.
**Chokes**: Screw-in chokes (IC/IC fixed)

**Weight**: 6.5 lb.
**Bore/Gauge**: 12, 20
**Magazine**: None
**Features**: Black hardwood stock; fiber optic front sight; ported barrels; two

Picatinny rails; single trigger design; tang-mounted automatic safety.
**MSRP** . . . . . . . . . . . . . . . . . . **$479**

SHOTGUNS

# Stoeger Shotguns

STOEGER 2000 REALTREE APG HD

STOEGER COACH GUN

STOEGER CONDOR

## 2000

**Action**: Semi-automatic
**Stock**: Synthetic, walnut
**Barrel**: 18.5 in., 24 in., 26 in., 28 in.,
**Chokes**: Screw-in chokes (C, IC, M, F, XFT)
**Weight**: 6.5 lb.–7.2 lb.
**Bore/Gauge**: 12
**Magazine**: 4+1 rounds
**Features**: Stock comes in walnut and synthetic with black, Realtree Max-4, and Realtree APG finishes; red bar front sight; intertia drive system; recoil reducer; red-bar front sight; Weaver scope base; includes shim kit; pistol grip.
**MSRP** . . . . . . . . . . . . . . . . $499–$579

## COACH GUN

**Action**: Side-by-side
**Stock**: Walnut, hardwood
**Barrel**: 20 in.
**Chokes**: Fixed chokes (IC, M)
**Weight**: 6.3 lb.–6.5 lb.
**Bore/Gauge**: 12, 20, 410
**Magazine**: None
**Features**: A-grade satin or black finished hardwood stock; brass bead sights; nickel or blue metal finish.
**MSRP** . . . . . . . . . . . . . . . $399–$479

## CONDOR

**Action**: Over/under
**Stock**: Walnut
**Barrel**: 22 in.,26 in., 28 in.

**Chokes**: Screw-in and fixed chokes on 12 Ga., 20 Ga. (IC, M), on 16 Ga. (M, F), and on 410 (F&F )
**Weight**: 5.5 lb.–7.4 lb.
**Bore/Gauge**: 12, 16, 20, 410
**Magazine**: None
**Features**: Walnut stock; brass bead sight; single-trigger; auto-ejectors.
**Condor:** . . . . . . . . . . . . . . . . . **$399**
**Condor Supreme:** . . . . . . . . . . **$599**
**Condor Youth:** . . . . . . . . . . . . **$399**

# Stoeger Shotguns

STOEGER CONDOR SUPREME COMBO

STOEGER CONDOR COMPETITION

STOEGER CONDOR COMPETITION COMBO

## CONDOR SUPREME COMBO

**Action**: Over/under
**Stock**: Walnut
**Barrel**: 26 in./28 in.
**Chokes**: Screw-in (IC, M)
**Weight**: 6.8 lb.–7.4 lb.
**Bore/Gauge**: 12, 20
**Magazine**: None
**Features**: Walnut stock; brass bead sight; comes with extractors and has a non–selectable trigger.
**MSRP** . . . . . . . . . . . . . . . . . . . $599

## CONDOR COMPETITION

**Action**: Over/under
**Stock**: Walnut
**Barrel**: 30 in.
**Chokes**: Screw-in (IC, M, F)
**Weight**: 7.3 lb.–7.8 lb.
**Bore/Gauge**: 12, 20
**Magazine**: None
**Features**: Walnut stock; brass bead with silver mid-bead sight; single-selective trigger; automatic ejector; ported barrel.
**MSRP** . . . . . . . . . . . . . . . . . . . $649

## CONDOR COMPETITION COMBO

**Action**: Over/under
**Stock**: Walnut
**Barrel**: 30 in.
**Chokes**: Screw-in (IC, M, F)
**Weight**: 7.8 lb.–7.3 lb.
**Bore/Gauge**: 12, 20
**Magazine**: None
**Features**: Walnut stock; brass bead with silver mid-bead sight; single-selective trigger; automatic ejector; ported barrel; fully adjustable comb.
**MSRP** . . . . . . . . . . . . . . . . . . . $849

# Stoeger Shotguns

**STOEGER CONDOR OUTBACK**

**STOEGER P350 APG**

**STOEGER P350 MAX-4, CAMO**

**STOEGER P350 BLACK SYNTHETIC**

## CONDOR OUTBACK
*Action*: Over/under
*Stock*: Walnut, hardwood
*Barrel*: 20 in.
*Chokes*: Screw-in (IC, M)
*Weight*: 6.5 lb.–7 lb.
*Bore/Gauge*: 12, 20
*Magazine*: None
*Features*: Notched rear sight and fixed blade front sight; shell extractor; single trigger; A-grade satin walnut or black finished hardwood.
**MSRP . . . . . . . . . . . . . . . $399–$449**

## P350 PUMP
*Action*: Pump
*Stock*: Walnut
*Barrel*: 18.5 in., 24 in., 26 in., 28 in.
*Chokes*: Screw-in (C, IC, M, F, XFT)
*Weight*: 6.4 lb.–6.9 lb.
*Bore/Gauge*: 12
*Magazine*: 4+1 rounds
*Features*: Red-bar front sight and metal bead mid-sight; shipped with limiter plug installed; synthetic stock comes in black, Realtree APG, or Realtree Max-4 HD; ergonomic forend.

**Synthetic:** . . . . . . . . . . . . . . . **$349**
**Realtree Max-4 Camo:** . . . . . . . **$449**
**Realtree APG:** . . . . . . . . . . . . . **$449**
**Trealtree APG Steady Grip:** . . . **$449**
**Synthetic Pistol Grip:** . . . . . . . . **$349**

# Stoeger Shotguns

**STOEGER UPLANDER**

## UPLANDER
*Action*: Side by side
*Stock*: Walnut
*Barrel*: 22 in. (youth), 26 in., 28 in., 28.in.
*Chokes*: Screw-in and fixed tubes
*Weight*: 6.5 lb.–7.5 lb.
*Bore/Gauge*: 12, 16, 20, 28, 410

*Magazine*: None
*Features*: Brass-bead sights; A-grade satin walnut stock; tang-mounted safety; single or double triggers; extractors included.
**Uplander:** . . . . . . . . . . . . . . . . **$399**
**Uplander Supreme:** . . . . . . . . . **$499**
**Uplander Youth:** . . . . . . . . . . . **$399**
**Uplander Supreme Combo:** . . **$679**

# Thompson/Center

## PROHUNTER TURKEY
*Action*: Hinged-breech single-shot
*Stock*: AP camo with Flextech
*Barrel*: 24 in. or 26 in.
*Chokes*: T/C extra full
*Weight*: 6.25 lb.–6.75 lb.

*Bore/Gauge*: 12 or 20
*Magazine*: None
*Features*: Fiber optic sights; 14 in. length pull
**MSRP** . . . . . . . . . . . . . . . . . . . **$937**

# Tristar Sporting Arms Shotguns

**TRISTAR SPORTING ARMS COBRA TACTICAL PUMP**

## COBRA TACTIAL PUMP
*Action*: Pump
*Stock*: Synthetic
*Barrel*: 20 in.
*Chokes*: Screw-in tubes
*Weight*: 6.3 lb.

*Bore/Gauge*: 12
*Magazine*: 5+1 rounds
*Features*: Faux extended magazine tube; spring-loaded forearm; synthetic stock in matte black; 3-in. chamber.
**MSRP** . . . . . . . . . . . . . . . . . . . **$304**

# Verona Shotguns

**VERONA 501 SERIES TWO BARREL SET**

## 501 SERIES TWO BARREL SET

*Action*: Over/under
*Stock*: Walnut
*Barrel*: 28 in.
*Chokes*: 5 interchangable chokes per barrel (F, M, IM, IC, SK)
*Weight*: 6.35 lb.
*Bore/Gauge*: 20, 28

*Magazine*: None
*Features*: Oil-finished, walnut stock with round pistol grip and rounded forend; chrome receiver with gold inlay; monobloc barrel construction; bottom locking bolt system on a double trough; automatic safety.
*MSRP*. . . . . . . . . . . . . . . . . $3242

**VERONA 662 SERIES SIDE-BY-SIDE**

## 662 SERIES SIDE-BY-SIDE

*Action*: Side-by-side
*Stock*: Walnut
*Barrel*: 26 in., 28 in.
*Chokes*: 5 interchangable chokes per barrel (F, M, IM, IC, SK)
*Weight*: 5 lb.–7.1 lb.
*Bore/Gauge*: 12, 20, 28
*Magazine*: None
*Features*: Oil–finished, walnut stock

with round pistol grip and rounded forend; standard case hardened; chrome receiver with gold inlay; monobloc barrel construction; bottom locking bolt system on a double trough; automatic safety.
*MSRP*. . . . . . . . . . . . . . $2826–$3574

SHOTGUNS

# Weatherby Shotguns

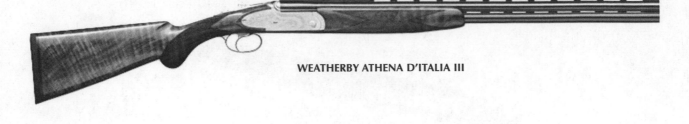

WEATHERBY ATHENA D'ITALIA III

WEATHERBY ORION D'ITALIA I

WEATHERBY PA-08 UPLAND

## ATHENA D'ITALIA III
**Action**: Over/under
**Stock**: Walnut
**Barrel**: 26 in., 28 in.
**Chokes**: Screw-in tubes (IC, M, F)
**Weight**: 6.5 lb.–8 lb.
**Bore/Gauge**: 12, 20
**Magazine**: None
**Features**: Oil-finished walnut stock with 20 LPI checkering; chrome-plated false sideplates feature gamebird scene in gold plate overlay on side and bottom of receiver; pierced and engraved top lever; trigger guard features Weatherby "Flying W" engraved with gold fill; monobloc barrel.
**MSRP** . . . . . . . . . . . . . . . . . . **$2599**

## ORION D'ITALIA I
**Action**: Over/under
**Stock**: Walnut
**Barrel**: 26in, 28in
**Chokes**: Screw-in tubes (IC, M, F)
**Weight**: 6.5 lb.-8 lb.
**Bore/Gauge**: 12, 20
**Magazine**: None
**Features**: Walnut stock with high luster finish; all metalwork is blued; gold-plated trigger; ventilated mid-and top-rib dissipates heat; trigger guard features Weatherby "flying W" engraved with gold fill.
**MSRP** . . . . . . . . . . . . . . . . . . **$1699**

## PA-08 UPLAND
**Action**: Pump
**Stock**: Walnut
**Barrel**: 26 in., 28 in.
**Chokes**: Screw-in tubes (IC, M, F)
**Weight**: 6.5 lb.
**Bore/Gauge**: 12
**Magazine**: None
**Features**: Walnut stock with gloss finish; gloss black finish on metalwork; vented top dissapates heat and aids in target acquisition; chrome-lined barrels.
**MSRP** . . . . . . . . . . . . . . . . . . . **$409**

# Weatherby Shotguns

**WEATHERBY SA-08 UPLAND**

**WEATHERBY SA-08 DELUXE**

## SA-08 UPLAND
*Action*: Semi-automatic
*Stock*: Walnut
*Barrel*: 26 in., 28 in.
*Chokes*: Screw-in tubes (IC, M, F)
*Weight*: 6 lb.–6.75 lb.
*Bore/Gauge*: 12, 20
*Magazine*: None
*Features*: Walnut stock with satin finish; matte black finish on metalwork; vented top rib dissapates heat and aids in target acquisition; dual valve system.
**MSRP** . . . . . . . . . . . . . . . . . . . **$733**

## SA-08 DELUXE
*Action*: Semi-automatic
*Stock*: Walnut
*Barrel*: 26 in., 28 in.
*Chokes*: Screw-in tubes (IC, M, F)
*Weight*: 6 lb.–6.75 lb.
*Bore/Gauge*: 12, 20
*Magazine*: None
*Features*: Walnut stock with high gloss finish and metalwork; vented top rib dissipates heat and aids in target acquisition; dual valve system.
**MSRP** . . . . . . . . . . . . . . . . . . . **$754**

# Winchester

**WINCHESTER 101**

**WINCHESTER SUPER X3 COMPOSITE**

## 101
*Action*: Over/under
*Stock*: Walnut
*Barrel*: 26 in., 28 in., 30 in., 32 in.
*Chokes*: Invector-Plus choke system, 3 tubes
*Weight*: 6 lb. 12 oz.–7 lb.
*Bore/Gauge*: 12
*Magazine*: None
*Features*: Solid brass-bead front sight; deep relief receiver engraving; high-gloss grade II/ III walnut stock; vented Pachmayr decelerator pad with classic white line spacer.
**Field**: . . . . . . . . . . . . . . . . . . **$1789**
**Sporting**: . . . . . . . . . . . . . . . **$2199**

## SUPER X3 COMPOSITE
*Action*: Autoloader
*Stock*: Composite
*Barrel*: 26 in., 28 in.
*Chokes*: Invector-Plus choke tube system (F, M, IC)
*Weight*: 6 lb. 10 oz.–7 lb. 2oz.
*Bore/Gauge*: 12, 20
*Magazine*: Tubular magazine
*Features*: Dura-Touch Armor Coating; gunmetal gray perma-cote UT finish to metal surfaces; recoil pad; sling swivel studs.
**MSRP** . . . . . . . . . . . . . . **$1139–$1276**

SHOTGUNS

# Winchester

WINCHESTER SUPER X3
CANTILEVER DEER

WINCHESTER SUPER X3
WALNUT FIELD

WINCHESTER SUPER X PUMP BLACK SHADOW FIELD

WINCHESTER SUPER X3-RIFLED
DEER CANTILEVER

WINCHESTER SX3 NWTF
EXTREME TURKEY

SHOTGUNS

## SUPER X3 CANTILEVER DEER

**Action**: Autoloader
**Stock**: Composite
**Barrel**: 22 in.
**Chokes**: Screw-in tubes
**Weight**: 7 lb. 12 oz.
**Bore/Gauge**: 12
**Magazine**: 4-rounds
**Features**: Active Valve System; Weaver-style rail; adjustable rear sight, Truglo fiber-optic front sight; durable gunmetal gray perma-cote UT surface finish on barrel and receiver; Dura-Touch armor coating on the black composite stock and forearm; sling swivels.
**MSRP** . . . . . . . . . . . . . . . . . . $1219

## SUPER X3 WALNUT FIELD

**Action**: Autoloader
**Stock**: Walnut
**Barrel**: 26 in., 28 in.
**Chokes**: Invector-Plus choke tube system
**Weight**: 6 lb. 6 oz.–6 lb. 14 oz.
**Bore/Gauge**: 12, 20
**Magazine**: 4-rounds
**Features**: Active Valve System; Pachmayr decelerator recoil pad; gunmetal gray perma-cote UT metal surface finish; nickel finish bolts; walnut stock.
**MSRP** . . . . . . . . . . . . . . . . . . $1219

## SUPER X PUMP DEFENDER

**Action**: Autoloader
**Stock**: Composite
**Barrel**: 18 in.
**Chokes**: Fixed cylinder choked barrel
**Weight**: 6 lb. 4oz.
**Bore/Gauge**: 12
**Magazine**: 5+1 rounds
**Features**: Uses Foster-type slugs; non-glare metal surfaces with a tough black composite stock; deeply grooved forearm for control and stability.
**MSRP** . . . . . . . . . . . . . . . . . . $379.99

## SUPER X3 WATER FOWL

**Action**: Autoloader
**Stock**: Composite
**Barrel**: 26 in., 28 in.
**Chokes**: Three choke tubes (F, M, IC)
**Weight**: 7 lb. –7 lb. 2 oz.
**Bore/Gauge**: 12
**Magazine**: 4-rounds
**Features**: HD Mossy Oak duck blind camo finish on composite stock; Dura-Touch armor coating finish; sling swivel studs.
**MSRP** . . . . . . . . . . . . . . . . . . $1479

## SUPER X PUMP BLACK SHADOW FIELD

**Action**: Pump
**Stock**: Composite
**Barrel**: 26 in., 28 in.
**Chokes**: Invector-Plus chokes
**Weight**: 6 lb. 12 oz.–6 lb. 14 oz.
**Bore/Gauge**: 12
**Magazine**: None
**Features**: Non-glare matte finish on barrel; durable black composite stock and forearm.
**MSRP** . . . . . . . . . . . . . . . . . . $429.99

## SX3 NWTF EXTREME TURKEY

**Action**: Autoloader
**Stock**: Composite
**Barrel**: 24 in.
**Chokes**: Invector-Plus Extra-Full Extended Turkey choke tube
**Weight**: 7 lb. 2oz.–7 lb. 8oz.
**Bore/ Gauge**: 12, 20
**Magazine**: Holds up to 4 rounds depending on shell size
**Features**: Mossy Oak Break-Up Infinity Camo with Dura-Touch Armor coating; adjustable rear sight.
**MSRP** . . . . . . . . . . $1399.99–$1419.99

## SUPER X3 RIFLED DEER CANTILEVER

**Action**: Autoloader
**Stock**: Composite
**Barrel**: 22 in.
**Chokes**: Screw-in tubes
**Weight**: 7 lb.
**Bore/ Gauge**: 12
**Magazine**: None
**Features**: Gas operated with Active Valve System; aluminum alloy receiver; composite stock with Mossy Oak Break-up Infinity camo finish; Inflex technology recoil pad; Dura-Touch Armor Coating; Truglo fiber optic front sight.
**MSRP** . . . . . . . . . . . . . . . . . . $1269

# Accu-Tek Handguns

ACCU-TEK
AT-380 II

## AT-380 II
**Action**: Semi-automatic
**Grips**: Composite
**Barrel**: 2.8 in.
**Weight**: 23.5 oz.
**Caliber**: .380 ACP
**Capacity**: 6+1 rounds
**Features**: Stainless steel construction; adjustable rear sight; one hand manual safety blocks; stainless steel magazine.
**MSRP** . . . . . . . . . . . . . . . . . . . . . **$275**

## HC-380
**Action**: Semi-automatic
**Grips**: Composite
**Barrel**: 2.8 in.
**Weight**: 26 oz.
**Caliber**: .380 ACP
**Capacity**: 13-rounds
**Features**: Adjustable rear sight; black checkered grip; one hand manual safety block; includes two magazines and cable lock
**MSRP** . . . . . . . . . . . . . . . . . . . . **$314**

ACCU-TEK HC-380

# American Derringer Handguns

AMERICAN DERRINGER
MODEL 1

## MODEL 1
**Action**: Hinged breech
**Grips**: Rosewood or stag
**Barrel**: 3 in.
**Weight**: 15 oz.
**Caliber**: .45, .410
**Capacity**: 2-rounds
**Features**: Single-action; automatic barrel selection; manually operated hammer-blcok safety
**MSRP** . . . . . . . . . . . . . . . . . . . . . **$705**

HANDGUNS

# American Derringer Handguns

AMERICAN DERRINGER
MODEL 4

AMERICAN DERRINGER
MODEL 6

## MODEL 4
*Action*: Hinged breech
*Grips*: Rosewood
*Barrel*: 4.1 in
*Weight*: 16.5 oz.
*Caliber*: .375 Mag., 357 Max., 45-70, .45 Colt/.410, .44 Mag.
*Capacity*: 2-rounds
*Features*: Satin or high polish stainless steel finish; single-action; automatic barrel selection; manually operated hammer-block type safety.
**MSRP** . . . . . . . . . . . . . . . . . . . **$760**

## MODEL 6
*Action*: Hinged breech
*Grips*: Rosewood, walnut, black
*Barrel*: 6 in.
*Weight*: 21 oz.
*Caliber*: .357 Mag., .45 Auto, .45 Colt/.410
*Capacity*: 2-rounds
*Features*: Satin or high polish stainless steel finish; single-action; automatic barrel selection; manually operated hammer-block type safety.
**MSRP** . . . . . . . . . . . . . . . . . . . **$860**

AMERICAN DERRINGER
MODEL 8

AMERICAN DERRINGER
MODEL 7

## MODEL 8
*Action*: Hinged breech
*Grips*: Rosewood, walnut, black
*Barrel*: 6 in.
*Weight*: 24 oz.
*Caliber*: .357 Mag., .45 Auto, .45 Colt/.410
*Capacity*: 2-rounds
*Features*: Satin or high polish stainless steel finish; single-action; automatic barrel selection; manually operated hammer-block type safety
**MSRP** . . . . . . . . . . . . . . . . . . . **$910**

## MODEL 7 LIGHTWEIGHT & ULTRA LIGHTWEIGHT
*Action*: Hinged breech
*Grips*: Blackwood
*Barrel*: 3 in.
*Weight*: 7.5 oz.
*Caliber*: .44 Special, .380 Auto, .38 Special, .32 Magnum/.32 S&W Long, .22 LR, .22 Mag.
*Features*: Grey matte finish; single-action; automatic barrel selection; manually operated hammer-block type safety.
**MSRP** . . . . . . . . . . . . . . . . . . . **$705**

HANDGUNS

# Auto-Ordnance

### M 1911A1
*Action*: Autoloader
*Grips*: Brown checkered plastic, checkered wood grips
*Barrel*: 5 in.
*Weight*: 39 oz.
*Caliber*: .45 ACP
*Capacity*: 7+1-rounds
*Features*: Single-action 1911 Colt design; WWII Parkerized; stainless steel or blued finish metal.
**MSRP** . . . . . . . . . . . . . . . **$627–$658**

AUTO-ORDNANCE
M 1911A1

# Beretta Handguns

BERETTA 21
BOBCAT

BERETTA 3032
TOMCAT

BERETTA 84FS
CHEETAH

BERETTA 85 FS
CHEETAH

### 21 BOBCAT
*Action*: Autoloader
*Grips*: Plastic
*Barrel*: 2.4 oz.
*Weight*: 11.5 oz.
*Caliber*: .22 LR, .25 ACP
*Capacity*: 7- or 8-rounds
*Features*: Double-action; tip-up barrel; stainless steel slide and barrel; alloy gray frame; other metal parts come in black or inox finish.
**Black Finish:** . . . . . . . . . . . . . **$335**
**Inox Finish:** . . . . . . . . . . . . . **$420**

### 3032 TOMCAT
*Action*: Autoloader
*Grips*: Plastic
*Barrel*: 2.5 in.
*Weight*: 14.5 oz.
*Caliber*: .32 ACP, .380
*Capacity*: 7+1-round
*Features*: Double-action; tip-up barrel latch; Inox has stainless steel slide and barrel; titanium alloy frame in black or gray; double or single trigger.
**MSRP** . . . . . . . . . . . . . . . **$435–$555**

### 84FS CHEETAH
*Action*: Autoloader
*Grips*: Plastic
*Barrel*: 3.8 in.
*Weight*: 23.3 oz.
*Caliber*: .380 Auto
*Capacity*: 10- or 13-rounds
*Features*: Optional wood grips; ambidextrous safety; steel barrel with hard chromed bore; open slide design; firing pin block; reversible magazine release; anodized alloy frame with matte black finish or nickel; combat-style trigger guard; double action trigger.
**MSRP** . . . . . . . . . . . . . . . **$770–$830**

### 85FS CHEETAH
*Action*: Autoloader
*Grips*: Plastic
*Barrel*: 3.8 in.
*Weight*: 23.3 oz.
*Caliber*: .380 Auto
*Capacity*: 8+1 rounds
*Features*: Optional wood grips; ambidextrous safety; steel barrel with hard chromed bore; open slide design; firing pin block; reversible magazine release; anodized alloy frame with matte black finish or nickel; combat-style trigger guard; double action trigger.
**MSRP** . . . . . . . . . . . . . . . **$770–$830**

HANDGUNS

**BERETTA PX4 STORM COMPACT**

**BERETTA PX4 STORM FULL SIZE**

**BERETTA 87 CHEETAH**

**BERETTA 87 TARGET**

**BERETTA STAMPEDE BLUE**

**BERETTA 90-TWO TYPE F**

## PX4 STORM COMPACT

*Action*: Autoloader
*Grips*: Plastic
*Barrel*: 3.2 in.
*Weight*: 27.3 oz.
*Caliber*: 9mm, .40 S&W
*Capacity*: 12- or 15-rounds; full size magazines 9mm: 17- or 20-rounds, .40: 14- or 17-rounds; restricted capacity: 10-rounds
*Features*: Ambidextrous side stop lever; integral Picatinny MIL-STD-1913 rail; Bruiton non-reflective black coating; visible automatic firing pin block.
**MSRP. . . . . . . . . . . . . . . . . . . $550**

## PX4 STORM FULL SIZE

*Action*: Autoloader
*Grips*: Plastic
*Barrel*: 4 in.
*Weight*: 27.7 oz.
*Caliber*: 9mm, .40 S&W
*Capacity*: 14- or 17-rounds, restricted capacity: 10-rounds
*Features*: Picatinny MIL STD-1913 rail; innovative locked-breech with a rotating barrel system; visible automatic firing pin block; ambidextrous safety; reversible magazine release.
**MSRP. . . . . . . . . . . . . . . . . . . $550**

## 87 CHEETAH

*Action*: Autoloader
*Grips*: Wood
*Barrel*: 3.8 in.
*Weight*: 23.3 oz.
*Caliber*: .22 LR
*Capacity*: 7+1 rounds
*Features*: Steel barrel with hard chromed bore; open slide design; firing pin block; ambidextrous safety; reversible magazine release; matte black finish; combat-style trigger guard; double-action trigger.
**MSRP. . . . . . . . . . . . . . . . . . . $845**

## 87 TARGET

*Action*: Autoloader
*Grips*: Plastic
*Barrel*: 5.9 in.
*Weight*: 20.1 oz.
*Caliber*: .22 LR
*Capacity*: 10+1 rounds
*Features*: Optional wood grips; ambidextrous safety; steel barrel with hard chromed bore; open slide design; firing pin block; reversible magazine release; anodized alloy frame with matte black finish or nickel; combat-style trigger guard; double action trigger.
**MSRP. . . . . . . . . . . . . . . . . . . $880**

## STAMPEDE

*Action*: Single-action revolver
*Grips*: Polymer, plastic, or walnut
*Barrel*: 4.75 in. –7.5 in.
*Weight*: 36.8 oz.–38.4 oz.
*Caliber*: .45 Colt, .357 Mag.
*Capacity*: 6-rounds
*Features*: Color-case hardened frame; blue, charcol blue, Inox, or Old West finish; transfer-bar safety system.
**Blued: . . . . . . . . . . . . . . . . . . $575**
**Deluxe: . . . . . . . . . . . . . . . . . $695**
**Nickel: . . . . . . . . . . . . . . . . . . $625**
**Marshal Old West: . . . . . . . . . . $650**
**Stampede Old West: . . . . . . . . $650**

## 90-TWO TYPE F

*Action*: Autoloader
*Grips*: Technopolymer single-piece wraparound, standard or slim size
*Barrel*: 4.9 in.
*Weight*: 32.5 oz.
*Caliber*: 9mm, .40 S&W
*Capacity*: 12- or 17-rounds, restricted capacity 10-rounds
*Features*: Slide serrations; Guigiaro design grips; removable front sight; internal recoil buffer; Picatinny mil-STD-1913 rail.
**MSRP. . . . . . . . . . . . . . . . . . . $795**

**HANDGUNS**

# Beretta Handguns

**BERETTA 92FS TYPE M9A1**

**BERETTA 92 A1**

**BERETTA 9 COMMERCIAL**

**BERETTA U22 NEOS**

HANDGUNS

## 92FS TYPE M9A1
*Action*: Autoloader
*Grips*: Plastic
*Barrel*: 4.9 in.
*Weight*: 33.9 oz.
*Caliber*: 9mm
*Capacity*: 15+1 rounds, restricted capacity 10+1 rounds
*Features*: Picatinny MIL-STD-1913 rail; magazine well beveled; sand-resistant magazine.
**MSRP**.....................$750

## 9 COMMERCIAL
*Action*: Autoloader
*Grips*: Plastic
*Barrel*: 4.9 in.
*Weight*: 33.3 oz.
*Caliber*: 9mm
*Capacity*: 15-rounds, Restricted capacity 10+1 rounds
*Features*: Has distinctive military-style markings; chrome-lined bore; double-action; automatic firing pin block; ambidextrous manual safety; lightweight forged alluminum alloy frame w/combat-style trigger guard.
**MSRP**.....................$650

## 92 A1
*Action*: Autoloader
*Grips*: Plastic
*Barrel*: 4.9 in.
*Weight*: 34.4 oz.
*Caliber*: 9mm, .40 S&W
*Capacity*: 12- or 17-rounds; restricted capacity 10-rounds
*Features*: Removable front sight; MIL-STD-1913, internal recoil buffer; captive recoil spring assembly.
**MSRP**.....................$690

## U22 NEOS
*Action*: Autoloader
*Grips*: Plastic
*Barrel*: 4.5 in. or 6 in.
*Weight*: 31.7 oz.–36.2 oz.
*Caliber*: .22 LR
*Capacity*: 10+1 rounds
*Features*: Single-action; removable colored grip inserts; deluxe model features adjustable trigger, replacable sights; optional 7.5 in. barrel.
**U22 Neos:**.................$275
**Inox:**.....................$375

# Bersa Handguns

**BERSA THUNDER 9 COMPACT**

**BERSA THUNDER 380**

**BERSA 45 THUNDER ULTRA COMPACT**

**BERSA THUNDER 380 CONCEALED CARRY**

## THUNDER 9 ULTRA COMPACT

*Action*: Autoloader
*Grips*: Black polymer
*Barrel*: 3.25 in.
*Weight*: 23 oz.
*Caliber*: 9mm
*Capacity*: 10+1, or 13+1 rounds
*Features*: Picatinny rail; precision machined lightweight alloy; ambidextrous safety; lifetime service contract; intergral locking system; anatomically designed polymer grips; double-action; available in matte or duotone finish.
Matte: . . . . . . . . . . . . . . . . . . . $517
Duotone:. . . . . . . . . . . . . . . . . $525

## THUNDER 40 ULTRA COMPACT

*Action*: Autoloader
*Grips*: Black polymer
*Barrel*: 3.25 in.
*Weight*: 23 oz.
*Caliber*: .40 S&W
*Capacity*: 10+1 rounds
*Features*: Picatinny rail; precision machined lightweight alloy; ambidextrous safety; lifetime service contract; intergral locking system; anatomically designed polymer grips; double-action; available in matte or duotone finish.
Matte: . . . . . . . . . . . . . . . . . . . $517
Duotone:. . . . . . . . . . . . . . . . . $525

## THUNDER 45 ULTRA COMPACT

*Action*: Autoloader
*Grips*: Black polymer
*Barrel*: 3.6 in.
*Weight*: 27 oz.
*Caliber*: .45 ACP
*Capacity*: 7+1 rounds
*Features*: Double-action; Picatinny rail; precision machined lightweight alloy; ambidextrous safety; lifetime service contract; intergral locking system; anatomically designed polymer grips; double-action; available in matte or duotone finish.
Matte: . . . . . . . . . . . . . . . . . . . $517
Duotone:. . . . . . . . . . . . . . . . . $525

## THUNDER 380

*Action*: Autoloader
*Grips*: Black polymer
*Barrel*: 3 in.
*Weight*: 20 oz.
*Caliber*: .380 ACP
*Capacity*: 7+1 rounds
*Features*: Combat-style trigger guard; extended slide release; micro-polished bore with sharp, deep rifling; intergral locking system; available in matte, satin nickel, or duotone finish.
Matte: . . . . . . . . . . . . . . . . . . . $335
Duotone:. . . . . . . . . . . . . . . . . $325

## THUNDER 380 CONCEALED CARRY

*Action*: Autoloader
*Grips*: Black polymer
*Barrel*: 3.2 in.
*Weight*: 16.4 oz.
*Caliber*: .380 ACP
*Capacity*: 8+1 rounds
*Features*: Extra low profile sights; combat-style trigger guard; slim slide release; intergral locking system.
Matte: . . . . . . . . . . . . . . . . . . . $349
Duotone:. . . . . . . . . . . . . . . . . $365

# Bond Arms Handguns

**BOND ARMS SNAKE SLAYER IV**

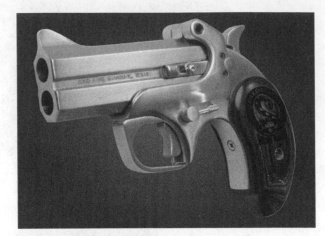

**BOND ARMS SNAKE SLAYER**

**BOND ARMS CENTURY 2000**

## SNAKE SLAYER IV

*Action*: Single-action
*Grips*: Extended custom rosewood
*Barrel*: 4.25 in.
*Weight*: 23.5 oz.
*Caliber*: .410/45 LC with 3 in. chambers
*Capacity*: 2-rounds
*Features*: Automatic extractor; interchangable barrels; rebounding hammer; retracting firing pins; crossbolt safety; spring-loaded cammed locking lever; trigger guard; stainless steel with satin polish finish.
**MSRP**. . . . . . . . . . . . . . . . . . . **$499**

## SNAKE SLAYER

*Action*: Single-action
*Grips*: Extended custom rosewood
*Barrel*: 3.5 in.
*Weight*: 22 oz.
*Caliber*: .410/45 LC with 3 in. chambers
*Capacity*: 2-rounds

*Features*: Interchangable barrels; automatic extractor; rebounding hammer; retracting firing pins; crossbolt safety; spring-loaded cammed locking lever; trigger guard; stainless steel with satin polish finish.
**MSRP**. . . . . . . . . . . . . . . . . . . **$469**

## TEXAS DEFENDER

*Action*: Single-action
*Grips*: Custom laminated black ash or rosewood
*Barrel*: 3 in.
*Weight*: 20 oz.
*Caliber*: 45 Colt/.410 Shot Shell (rifled), .357 Mag./.38 Spl, .357 Max, .45 ACP, .45 Colt, .45 Glock Auto, 44-40 Win., .40 S&W, 10mm, 32 H&R Mag., .22 LR
*Capacity*: 2-rounds
*Features*: Interchangable barrels; auto-

matic extractor; rebounding hammer; retracting firing pins; crossbolt safety; spring-loaded cammed locking lever; trigger guard; stainless steel with satin polish finish.
**MSRP**. . . . . . . . . . . . . . . . . . . **$399**

## CENTURY 2000

*Action*: Single-action
*Grips*: Custom laminated black ash or rosewood
*Barrel*: 3.5 in.
*Weight*: 21 oz.
*Caliber*: .410/45LC
*Capacity*: 2-rounds
*Features*: Interchangable barrels; automatic extractor; rebounding hammer; retracting firing pins; crossbolt safety; spring-loaded cammed locking lever; trigger guard; stainless steel with satin-polish finish.
**MSRP**. . . . . . . . . . . . . . . . . . . **$420**

# Browning Handguns

BROWNING BUCK MARK PLUS

BROWNING BUCK MARK
LITE GREEN

BROWNING HI-POWER
STANDARD

BROWNING BUCK MARK
PRACTICAL URX

## BUCK MARK SERIES
*Action*: Autoloader
*Grips*: Composite, black
*Barrel*: 5.5 in.–7.25 in.
*Weight*: 2 lb. 2 oz.–2 lb. 7 oz.
*Caliber*: 22 LR
*Capacity*: 10+1 rounds
*Features*: Alloy, matte blued finish receiver; tapered barrel; blowback action; single-action trigger; URX ambidextrous grip in contour models; cocobolo, ambidex grip on Hunter model; lite gray model has matte gray barrel finish and Truglo/marble fiber-optic front sight.
**Camper:** . . . . . . . . . . . . . . . . **$359**
**Stainless:** . . . . . . . . . . . . . . . . **$400**
**Contour 5.5 URX:** . . . . . . . . . . **$519**
**Contour 7.25 URX:** . . . . . . . . . **$540**
**Hunter:** . . . . . . . . . . . . . . . **$469.99**
**Lite Gray 5.5:** . . . . . . . . . . . **$549.99**

## BUCK MARK PLUS
*Action*: Autoloader
*Grips*: Rosewood, black laminated, or walnut ultragrip DX ambidextrous
*Barrel*: 5.5 in.–7.25 in.
*Weight*: 2 lb. 2 oz.
*Caliber*: .22 LR

*Capacity*: 10+1 rounds
*Features*: Matte blue, polished barrel flats; blowback action; single-action trigger.
**Walnut** . . . . . . . . . . . . . . . . . . . **$510**
**Rosewood** . . . . . . . . . . . . . . . . **$510**
**Black laminated:** . . . . . . . . . . . **$550**

## HI-POWER STANDARD
*Action*: Autoloader
*Grips*: Select walnut, cut checkering
*Barrel*: 4.6 in.
*Weight*: 2 lb.
*Caliber*: 9mm
*Capacity*: 10+1 rounds
*Features*: Locked breech action; single-action trigger; ambidextrous thumb safety; extra magazine; steel, polished blue finish barrel.
**MSRP** . . . . . . . . . . . . . . **$1100–$1030**

## BUCK MARK LITE GREEN
*Action*: Autoloader

*Grips*: Ultragrip RX ambidextrous
*Barrel*: 5.5 in.
*Weight*: 1 lb. 12 oz.
*Caliber*: .22 LR
*Capacity*: 10+1 rounds
*Features*: Matte green finish; fluted barrel; alloy sleeved barrel; matte black grips and receiver; single action trigger.
**MSRP** . . . . . . . . . . . . . . . . . . . **$550**

## BUCK MARK PRACTICAL URX
*Action*: Autoloader
*Grips*: Ultragrip RX ambidextrous
*Barrel*: 5.5 in.
*Weight*: 2 lb. 2oz.
*Caliber*: 22 LR
*Capacity*: 10+1 rounds
*Features*: Tapered bull barrel with matte blued finish; matte gray finish receiver.
**MSRP** . . . . . . . . . . . . . . . . . . . **$420**

# Charles Daly Handguns

**CHARLES DALY
1911 A-1**

**CHARLES DALY M-5
GOVERNMENT**

## 1911 A-1
*Action*: Autoloader
*Grips*: Hand checkered double dia-
mond hardwood grips
*Barrel*: 5 in.
*Weight*: 38.5 oz.
*Caliber*: .45 ACP
*Capacity*: 6+1 rounds
*Features*: Stainless steel frame avail-
able in various finishes.
**MSRP** . . . . . . . . . . . . . . . . . . . . **$619**

## M-5
*Action*: Autoloader
*Grips*: Checkered black
*Barrel*: 5 in.
*Weight*: 33.5 oz.
*Caliber*: .40 SW, .45 ACP
*Capacity*: 10+1 rounds
*Features*: Stainless steel frame available in various finishes; single-action; poly-
mer frame; tapered bull barrel and full-length guide rod; thumb safety; dove-
tailed sights on Ultra model.
**Government:** . . . . . . . . . . . . . . **$699**
**Commander:** . . . . . . . . . . . . . **$699**
**IPSC:** . . . . . . . . . . . . . . . . . . **$1500**
**Ultra X:** . . . . . . . . . . . . . . . . . **$725**

# Charter Arms Handguns

## .38 UNDERCOVER
*Action*: DA revolver
*Grips*: Checkered compact rubber or
Crimson Trace lasergrips
*Barrel*: 2 in.
*Weight*: 16 oz.
*Caliber*: .38 Special +P
*Capacity*: 5-rounds
*Features*: Stainless steel frame; blue or
stainless finish; compact and light-
weight, this revolver is ideal for con-
cealed carry situations; 3-point cylin-
der lock-up.
**Blue Standard:** . . . . . . . . . . . . . **$352**
**Stainless Standard:** . . . . . . . . . **$365**
**Blue DAO:** . . . . . . . . . . . . . . . . **$360**
**Stainless DAO:** . . . . . . . . . . . . . **$372**
**Crimson Trace:** . . . . . . . . . . . . **$636**

**CHARTER ARMS
.38 UNDERCOVER**

**CHARTER ARMS .38
UNDERCOVER LITE**

## .38 UNDERCOVER LITE
*Action*: DA revolver
*Grips*: Rubber, compact
*Barrel*: 2 in.
*Weight*: 12 oz.
*Caliber*: .38 Special +P
*Capacity*: 5-rounds
*Features*: Frame is constructed from
aircraft-grade aluminum and steel; tra-

ditional spurred hammer; optional
DAO (double action trigger); black,
red, green, or stainless finishes.
**Black DAO:** . . . . . . . . . . . . . . . **$428**
**Alum. Standard:** . . . . . . . . . . . **$404**
**Red & Stainless:** . . . . . . . . . . . . **$422**
**Cougar Pink & Stainless:** . . . . . **$443**
**Shamrock:** . . . . . . . . . . . . . . . . **$470**

**324** • Shooter's Bible 103rd Edition

www.skyhorsepublishing.com

# Charter Arms Handguns

**CHARTER ARMS
UNDERCOVER ON DUTY**

**CHARTER ARMS.357 MAG.
PUG**

## UNDERCOVER ON DUTY
*Action*: DA revolver
*Grips*: Rubber; Crimson Trace lasergrips
*Barrel*: 2 in.
*Weight*: 12 oz.
*Caliber*: .38 Special +P
*Capacity*: 5-rounds
*Features*: Unique hammer block design; constructed of heat-treated aluminum; allows single-action and double-action operations while minimizing the risk of snagging the hammer on clothing; standard or Crimson Trace grip.
**Standard:** . . . . . . . . . . . . . . . . **$410**
**Crimson Trace Grip:** . . . . . . . **$664**

## .357 MAG. PUG
*Action*: DA revolver
*Grips*: Rubber; Crimson Trace lasergrips
*Barrel*: 2.2 in. or 4 in.
*Weight*: 23 oz.
*Caliber*: .357 Mag.
*Capacity*: 5-rounds
*Features*: Traditional spurred hammer and full-size grips; optional crimson trace grip; stainless steel frame; blue finish.
**Standard:** . . . . . . . . . . . . . . . . **$396**
**Crimson:** . . . . . . . . . . . . . . . . . **$665**
**Stainless:** . . . . . . . . . . . . . . . . . **$400**
**Stainless DAO:** . . . . . . . . . . . . **$404**
**Target:** . . . . . . . . . . . . . . . . . . . **$479**

## .32 H&R UNDERCOVERETTE
*Action*: DA revolver
*Grips*: Rubber; Crimson Trace lasergrips
*Barrel*: 2 in.
*Weight*: 12 oz.
*Caliber*: .32 H&R
*Capacity*: 5-rounds
*Features*: Gun with less kick for women; standard or Crimson Trace grip; two-tone pink, stainless, or lavender finish; high-grade cast aluminum revolver features.
**Standard Grip Pink Lady:** . . . . . **$428**
**Crimson Trace Grip:** . . . . . . . . **$570**
**Lavender Lady:** . . . . . . . . . . . . **$428**
**Stainless Standard:** . . . . . . . . . **$378**

## BULLDOG
*Action*: DA revolver
*Grips*: Rubber; Crimson Trace laser-grips
*Barrel*: 2.5 in. or 4 in. in Target model
*Weight*: 21 oz.
*Caliber*: .44 Special
*Capacity*: 5-rounds
*Features*: Stainless steel frame; optional DAO trigger; standard hammer; stainless or blue finish.
**Stainless Standard:** . . . . . . . . . **$426**
**Blue DAO:** . . . . . . . . . . . . . . . . **$465**
**Target Bulldog:** . . . . . . . . . . . . **$479**
**Crimson Bulldog:** . . . . . . . . . . **$696**

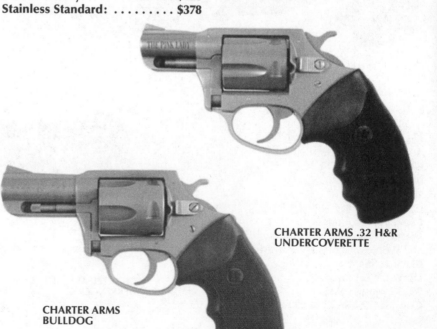

**CHARTER ARMS .32 H&R
UNDERCOVERETTE**

**CHARTER ARMS
BULLDOG**

# Charter Arms Handguns

## .22 PATHFINDER

*Action*: DA revolver
*Grips*: Rubber; Crimson Trace laser-grips
*Barrel*: 2 in.
*Weight*: 19 oz.
*Caliber*: .22 LR, .22 Mag.
*Capacity*: 6-rounds
*Features*: Stainless steel frame

**Stainless Steel:** . . . . . . . . . . . . . **$369**
**.22 Mag.:** . . . . . . . . . . . . . . . . . **$410**
**Target .22 Mag.:** . . . . . . . . . . . . **$459**
**Target Combo:** . . . . . . . . . . . . **$548**
**Target .22 LR:** . . . . . . . . . . . . . **$412**

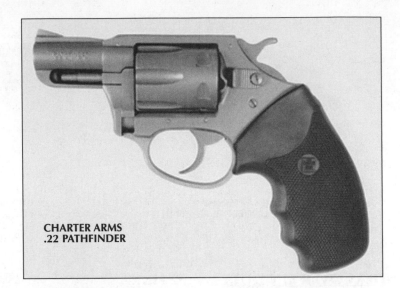

**CHARTER ARMS
.22 PATHFINDER**

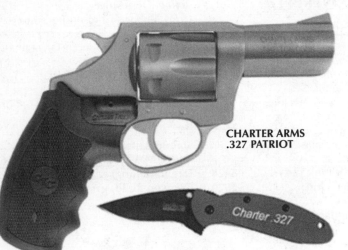

**CHARTER ARMS
.327 PATRIOT**

## .327 PATRIOT

*Action*: DA revolver
*Grips*: Rubber; Crimson Trace laser-grips
*Barrel*: 2.2 in. or 4 in.
*Weight*: 21 oz.–23 oz.
*Caliber*: .327 Federal Mag.
*Capacity*: 6-rounds
*Features*: Stainless steel frame; satin stainless finish; standard hammer; packaged with free Kershaw Scallion folding knife.

**Crimson Patriot:** . . . . . . . . . . . **$570**
**Patriot:** . . . . . . . . . . . . . . . . . **$432**
**Target Patriot:** . . . . . . . . . . . . . **$484**

## DIXIE DERRINGER

*Action*: DA revolver
*Grips*: Rubber
*Barrel*: 1.1 in.
*Weight*: 6 oz.
*Caliber*: .22 Mag., .22 LR
*Capacity*: 5-rounds
*Features*: Stainless steel frame; black and stainless, stainless, or finish.

**Black & SS:** . . . . . . . . . . . . . . . **$221**
**LR:** . . . . . . . . . . . . . . . . . . . . . . **$211**
**SS .22 Mag.:** . . . . . . . . . . . . . . . **$221**
**Combo .22 LR/.22 Mag.:** . . . . . **$264**

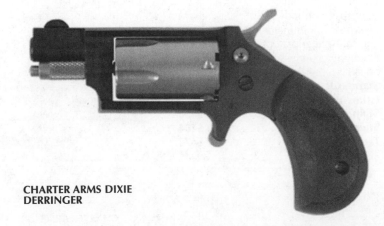

**CHARTER ARMS DIXIE
DERRINGER**

HANDGUNS

# Cimarron Handguns

**CIMARRON 1872 OPEN TOP**

**CIMARRON BISLEY**

**CIMARRON LIGHTNING SA**

## 1872 OPEN TOP
**Action**: Single-action revolver
**Grips**: Walnut
**Barrel**: 5.5 in., 7.5 in.
**Weight**: 40 oz.
**Caliber**: .44 Special; .44 Colt & Russian, .45 Schofield, .45 Colt, .38 Colt & Special
**Capacity**: 6-rounds
**Features**: Forged, color case-hardened frame; charcoal blue, standard blue, or original barrel finish.
**Army Grip:**.............**$562.91**
**Navy Grip:**.............**$518.36**

## BISELY
**Action**: Single-action revolver
**Grips**: Walnut
**Barrel**: 4.75 in., 5.5 in., 7.5 in.
**Weight**: 40.3 oz., 40.6 oz., 44 oz.
**Caliber**: .45 LC, .44 Special, .44 WCF, .357 Magnum
**Capacity**: 6-rounds
**Features**: Reproduction of the original Colt Bisley; forged, color case-hardened frame; blue, charcol blue, or nickel finish.
**MSRP**.................**$637.18**

## GEORGE ARMSTRONG CUSTER 7TH U.S. CALVARY MODEL
**Action**: Single-action revolver
**Grips**: Walnut
**Barrel**: 7.5 in.
**Weight**: 40.4 oz.
**Caliber**: .45 LC
**Capacity**: 6-rounds
**Features**: Old model case-hardened with 7th Cavalry markings; made with 1 piece of walnut with OWA (Ainsworth) cartouche; blue, charcoal blue or nickel barrel finish.
**MSRP**...........**$607.47–$757.93**

## LIGHTNING SA
**Action**: Single-action revolver
**Grips**: Walnut
**Barrel**: 3.5 in., 4.75 in., or 5.5 in.
**Weight**: 28.5 oz., 29.5 oz., 30.75 oz.
**Caliber**: .38 Special, .22 LR, .41 Colt, 32-20/.32 H&R Dual Cylinder
**Capacity**: 6-rounds
**Features**: Forged, pre-war color case-hardened frame; charcoal blue, standard blue, or original barrel finish; walnut stock smooth or checkered.
**MSRP**...........**$533.21–$666.88**

HANDGUNS

# Cimarron Handguns

CIMARRON MODEL P JR.

CIMARRON THUNDERER

## P 1873
**Action**: Single-action revolver
**Grips**: Walnut
**Barrel**: 4.75 in., 5.5 in., 7.5 in.
**Weight**: 44 oz.
**Caliber**: 32 WCF, 38 WCF, .357 Mag., 44 WCF, .44 Special, .45 LC, .45LC/.45 ACP Dual Cylinder
**Capacity**: 6-rounds
**Features**: Fashioned after the 1873 Colt SAA; standard blue, charcoal blue, or original finish.
**MSRP** . . . . . . . . . **$548.06–$666.88**

## P JR.
**Action**: Single-action revolver
**Grips**: Walnut
**Barrel**: 3.5 in., 4.75 in., 5.5 in.
**Weight**: 35.2 oz.
**Caliber**: .41 Colt .38 Special, .22 LR, .41 Colt, 32-20/.32 H&R Dual Cylinder
**Capacity**: 6-rounds
**Features**: Fashioned after the 1873 Colt SAA, but on a smaller scale; color case-hardened frame; blue, charcoal

blue, or nickel finish.
**MSRP** . . . . . . . . . **$507.48–$637.18**

## NEW SHERIFF MODEL
**Action**: Single-action revolver
**Grips**: Walnut, black hard rubber
**Barrel**: 3.5 in.
**Weight**: 33.5 oz.
**Caliber**: . 45 LC, 44 WCF, .357 Mag.
**Capacity**: 6-rounds
**Features**: Forged, color case-hardened frame; standard blue barrel finish.
**MSRP** . . . . . . . . . . . . . . . . **$546.08**

## THUNDERER
**Action**: Single-action revolver
**Grips**: Walnut, ivory, mother of pearl, or black hard rubber
**Barrel**: 3.5 in. w/ ejector, 4.75 in., 5.5 in., 7.5 in.
**Weight**: 38 oz., 40 oz., 40.75 oz., 43.60 oz.,
**Caliber**: .45 LC, .44 Special, 44 WCF,

.357 Mag., .45LC/45 ACP Dual Cylinder
**Capacity**: 6-rounds
**Features**: Designed in 1990 by Cimarron founder & president "Texas Jack" Harvey; forged, color case-hardened frame; blue, charcoal blue, or nickel finish.
**MSRP** . . . . . . . . . . **$592.62–$696.59**

## U.S. ARTILLERY MODEL
**Action**: Single-action revolver
**Grips**: Walnut
**Barrel**: 5.5 in.
**Weight**: 40 oz.
**Caliber**: .45 LC
**Capacity**: 6-rounds
**Features**: Old model case-hardened with U.S. Artillery markings; stock is a solid piece of walnut with RAC cartouche; blue, charcoal blue, or original finish.
**MSRP** . . . . . . . . . . **$607.47–$681.73**

# Citadel Handguns

## 1911 PISTOLS

*Action*: Autoloader
*Grips*: Full size or compact, wood, or Houge synthetic grips
*Barrel*: 3.5 in., 5 in.
*Weight*: 2.1 lb.–2.35 lb.
*Caliber*: .45 ACP, .38 Super
*Capacity*: 6- or 8-rounds
*Features*: Wounded Warrior Project Model includes laser cut wood grips with WWP insignia and inscription "Never Forget" and engraved commemorative slide; matte black, brush nickel, or polished nickel finish; optional Hogue wrap-around grip in black, green, or sand; available in compact and full sized models; comes with lockable, hard plastic case.

**.45 ACP: Compact: . . . . . $723–$815**
**CS with Hogue Black,**
**Sand, or Green: . . . . . . . . . . . $773**
**Full Size: . . . . . . . . . . . . . $723–$815**
**Wounded Warior Project: . . . $1047**
**.38 Super: Black: . . . . . . . . . . . $665**
**Brush Nickel: . . . . . . . . . . . . . $848**
**Polished Nickel: . . . . . . . . . . . $914**

**CITADEL 1911 PISTOLS**

# Colt Handguns

## SERIES 70

*Action*: Autoloader
*Grips*: Double diamond rosewood grips
*Barrel*: 5 in.
*Weight*: 39 oz.
*Caliber*: .45 ACP
*Capacity*: 7+1 rounds
*Features*: Spur hammer; single-action; blue or brushed steel finish; carbon steel or stainless steel frame; short steel trigger; original series 70 firing system with titanium firing pin.

**Blued: . . . . . . . . . . . . . . . . . $974**
**Brushed Steel: . . . . . . . . . . . $1007**

## 1991 SERIES

*Action*: Autoloader
*Grips*: Rosewood or composite
*Barrel*: 5 in.
*Weight*: 39 oz.
*Caliber*: .45 ACP
*Capacity*: 7+1 rounds
*Features*: Beveled magazine well; single and double action; carbon steel, aluminum alloy, or stainless steel frame; standard or beavertail grip

**COLT SERIES 70**

safety; blue, black anodized, brushed stainless steel, bright stainless steel frame finish.

**MSRP . . . . . . . . . . . . . . . $942–$1224**

## XSE SERIES

*Action*: Autoloader
*Grips*: Checkered, double diamond rosewood
*Barrel*: 5 in.
*Weight*: 39 oz.
*Caliber*: .45 ACP
*Capacity*: 8+1 rounds
*Features*: Front and rear slide serrations; extended ambidextrous thumb safeties; enhanced hammer; new roll marking and enhanced tolerances; single-action; white dot carry sights; bea-

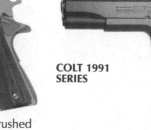

**COLT 1991 SERIES**

**COLT XSE**

vertail safety grip; blue, brushed stainless steel, Teflon coated, or black anodized finish; carbon steel, stainless steel or aluminum alloy frame.

**MSRP . . . . . . . . . . . . . . $1012–$1188**

HANDGUNS

# Colt Handguns

**COLT GOLD CUP SERIES**

**COLT DEFENDER**

**COLT RAIL GUN**

**COLT SINGLE ACTION ARMY**

**COLT 175TH ANNIVERSARY SINGLE ACTION ARMY**

**COLT NEW AGENT DAO**

## GOLD CUP SERIES

*Action*: Autoloader
*Grips*: Black composite
*Barrel*: 5 in.
*Weight*: 39 oz.
*Caliber*: .45 ACP
*Capacity*: 8+1 rounds
*Features*: Beveled magazine well; beavertail grip safety; black wrap-around grips; wide aluminum 3-hole trigger adjustable for over travel; stainless steel frame finish and material; enhanced hammer.
MSRP. . . . . . . . . . . . . . . . . . **$1103**

## DEFENDER

*Action*: Autoloader
*Grips*: Rubber finger-grooved
*Barrel*: 5 in.
*Weight*: 30 oz.
*Caliber*: .45 ACP
*Capacity*: 7+1 rounds
*Features*: Beveled magazine well; black skeletonized aluminum trigger; series 80 firing system; beavertail grip and standard thumb safety; stainless steel slide, Teflon coated receiver; aluminum alloy frame.
MSRP. . . . . . . . . . . . . . . . . . **$995**

## SINGLE ACTION ARMY

*Action*: Single-action revolver
*Grips*: Black composite Eagle grips
*Barrel*: 4.75 in., 5.5 in., 7.5 in.
*Weight*: 46 oz.
*Caliber*: .32/20, .38 Special, .38/40,

.357 Mag., .44/40, .45 Colt
*Capacity*: 6-rounds
*Features*: Case-colored frame; transfer bar; 2nd generation-style cylinder bushing; features 175th anniversary rollmark; blue or nickel finishes.
MSRP. . . . . . . . . . . . . **$1290–$1490**

## RAIL GUN

*Action*: Autoloader
*Grips*: Double diamond rosewood or blackened rosewood grips
*Barrel*: 5 in.
*Weight*: 39 oz.
*Caliber*: .45 ACP
*Capacity*: 8+1 rounds
*Features*: Stainless steel, blackened receiver/brushed slide, blackened receiver and slide frame finish options; stainless steel frame material; Colt upswept beavertail with palm swell; enhanced hammer; M1913 Picatinny rail; National Match barrel; single slide tactical thumb safety.
MSRP. . . . . . . . . . . . . . . . . . **$1075**

## NEW AGENT DAO

*Action*: DAO autoloader
*Grips*: Double diamond slim fit grips
*Barrel*: 3 in.
*Weight*: 39 oz.
*Caliber*: .45 ACP

*Capacity*: 7+1 rounds
*Features*: Double action only; black anodized frame with beveled magazine well; front strap serrations.
MSRP. . . . . . . . . . . . . . . . . . **$992**

## FRONTIER SIX SHOOTER

*Action*: Single-action revolver
*Grips*: Black composite Eagle grips
*Barrel*: 4.75 in., 5.5 in., 7.5 in.
*Weight*: 46 oz.
*Caliber*: .44/40
*Capacity*: 6-rounds
*Features*: The revival of the Colt Peacemaker classic.
MSRP. . . . . . . . . . . . . . . . . . **$1455**

## COLT 175TH ANNIVERSARY SINGLE ACTION ARMY

*Action*: Single-action revolver
*Grips*: Black composite
*Barrel*: 4.75 in., 5.5 in., 7.5 in.
*Weight*: 46 oz.
*Caliber*: .45 ACP
*Capacity*: 6-rounds
*Features*: Black powder-style frame with all metal surfaces polished and finished in Colt royal blue; guns are embellished with selective gold plating; limited to production of 175 units.
MSRP. . . . . . . . . . . . . . . . . . **$1580**

HANDGUNS

# CZ Handguns

## 75 COMPACT

**Action**: Autoloader
**Grips**: Plastic
**Barrel**: 3.8 in.
**Weight**: 2 lb.
**Caliber**: 9mm Luger
**Capacity**: 14-rounds
**Features**: Black polycoat, dual tone, satin nickel frame finishes; manual safety; steel frame; high capacity double column magazines; hammer forged barrels.
**Black Polycoat**: . . . . . . . . . . . . $518
**Dual Tone, Satin Nickel**: . . . . . $559

CZ 75 COMPACT

## 75

**Action**: Autoloader
**Grips**: Plastic
**Barrel**: 4.7 in.
**Weight**: 2.2 lb.
**Caliber**: .40 S&W, 9mm
**Capacity**: .40 S&W: 10-rounds, 9mm: 16-rounds
**Features**: Steel frame; high capacity double column magazines; hammer forged barrels; ergonomic grip and controls; double action or single action; firing pin block safety; black polycoat, dual tone, satin nickel finshes.
**.40 S&W**: . . . . . . . . . . . . . $546–$615
**9mm**: . . . . . . . . . . . . . . . $499–$559

CZ 75

## 75 KADET

**Action**: Autoloader
**Grips**: Plastic
**Barrel**: 4.7 in.
**Weight**: 2.4 lb.
**Caliber**: .22 LR
**Capacity**: 10-rounds
**Features**: Cold hammer-forged steel barrel; manual safety; 3-dot sighting system; double- or single-action; high-capacity double-column magazines; firing-pin block safety; black polycoat frame finish.
**MSRP** . . . . . . . . . . . . . . . . . . $678

CZ 75 KADET

# CZ Handguns

## 83

*Action*: Autoloader
*Grips*: Plastic
*Barrel*: 3.8 in.
*Weight*: 1.8 lb.
*Caliber*: .32 Auto, .380 Auto
*Capacity*: .380 Auto: 12-rounds, .32 Auto: 15-rounds
*Features*: Ambidextrous manual sear block safety; rebounding hammer safety; single action or double action; glossy blue or satin nickel finish available.
**.32 Auto:** . . . . . . . . . . . . . . . . **$444**
**.380 Auto:** . . . . . . . . . . . **$444–$479**

CZ 83

CZ 85 COMPACT

## 85 COMPACT

*Action*: Autoloader
*Grips*: Plastic
*Barrel*: 4.7 in.
*Weight*: 2.2 lb.
*Caliber*: 9mm Luger
*Capacity*: 16-rounds
*Features*: Manual safety; safety stop on hammer; steel frame; extended magazine release; ambidextrous slide stop; black polycoat, dual tone, satin nickel finish; single or double action.
**Black Polycoat:** . . . . . . . . . . . **$604**
**Dual Tone & Satin Nickel:** . . . . **$630**

## 97

*Action*: Autoloader
*Grips*: Plastic
*Barrel*: 4.8 in.
*Weight*: 2.5 lb.
*Caliber*: .45 ACP
*Capacity*: 10-rounds
*Features*: Manual safety; cold hammer forged barrel; single or double action.
**Black Polycoat:** . . . . . . . . . . . **$644**
**Glossy Blue:** . . . . . . . . . . . . . . **$700**

CZ 97

**CZ 2075 RAMI**

**CZ P-07 DUTY**

**CZ P-01**

**CZ 75 SP-01 SHADOW TARGET**

**CZ 75 SA TARGET**

## 2075 RAMI

*Action*: Autoloader
*Grips*: Rubber
*Barrel*: 4.7 in.
*Weight*: 1.6 lb.
*Caliber*: .40 S&W, 9mm Luger
*Capacity*: .40 S&W: 7- or 9-rounds, 9mm: 14-rounds
*Features*: Operates in selective DA and SA mode depending on shooter's preferences; firing pin block; manual safety; double-stack magazine; black polycoat alloy frame; cold hammer forged.
**.40 S&W:** . . . . . . . . . . . . . . . . . **$604**
**9mm Luger:** . . . . . . . . . . . . . **$585**

## P-01

*Action*: Autoloader
*Grips*: Rubber
*Barrel*: 3.8 in.
*Weight*: 1.8 lb.
*Caliber*: 9mm Lueger
*Capacity*: 14-rounds

*Features*: Decocking lever; safety stop on hammer; firing pin safety; black polycoat frame finish; black or pink grips; single or double action.
**MSRP** . . . . . . . . . . . . . . . . . . . **$598**

## P-07 DUTY

*Action*: DAO autoloader
*Grips*: Polymer
*Barrel*: 3.8 in.
*Weight*: 1.7 lb.
*Caliber*: .40 S&W, 9mm Luger
*Capacity*: .40 S&W: 12-rounds, 9mm: 16-rounds
*Features*: Omega double- or single-action trigger; cold hammer forged barrel; accessory rail and two magazines included.
**.40 S&W:** . . . . . . . . . . . . . . . . . **$487**
**9mm:** . . . . . . . . . . . . . . . . . . . **$467**

## 75 SP-01 SHADOW TARGET

*Action*: Autoloader
*Grips*: Cocobolo

*Barrel*: 4.7 in.
*Weight*: 2.4 lb.
*Caliber*: 9mm
*Capacity*: 18-rounds
*Features*: Single- or double-action; manual safety; steel frame; TRT rear sight; competition springs; CZ custom stianless guide rod.
**MSRP** . . . . . . . . . . . . . . . . . . . **$1199**

## 75 SA TARGET

*Action*: Single-action autoloader
*Grips*: CZ custom shop aluminum
*Barrel*: 4.7 in.
*Weight*: 2.2 lb.
*Caliber*: 9mm
*Capacity*: 16-rounds
*Features*: Single-action; extended manual safety; black polycoat receiver finish; cold-hammer forged barrel.
**MSRP** . . . . . . . . . . . . . . . . . . . **$1182**

**HANDGUNS**

# Dan Wesson Firearms

**DAN WESSON GUARDIAN**

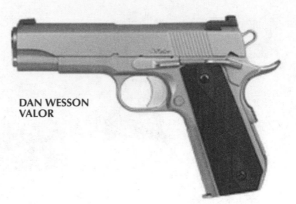

**DAN WESSON VALOR**

## GUARDIAN
*Action*: Single-action autoloader
*Grips*: Stippled shadow, wood
*Barrel*: 4.3 in.
*Weight*: 1.8 lb.
*Caliber*: 9mm Luger
*Capacity*: 9-rounds
*Features*: Thumb safety, grip safety; match grade barrel; forged aluminum frame.
**MSRP**. . . . . . . . . . . . . . . . . . **$1530**

## VALOR
*Action*: Single-action autoloader
*Grips*: Slim Line G10
*Barrel*: 4.3 in.
*Weight*: 2.2 lb.
*Caliber*: .45 ACP
*Capacity*: 8-rounds
*Features*: Matte black duty receiver finish; manual thumb safety; forged stainless steel frame.
**MSRP**. . . . . . . . . . . . . . . . . . **$2040**

# Downsizer Handguns

## WSP (WORLD'S SMALLEST PISTOL)
*Action*: Tip-up hinged breech
*Grips*: Composite
*Barrel*: 2.10 in.
*Weight*: 11 oz.
*Caliber*: .357 Mag., .38 SP, .45 ACP
*Capacity*: 1-round
*Features*: Double-action; stainless steel frame & barrel; internal firing pin block.
**MSRP**. . . . . . . . . . . . . . . . . . **$499**

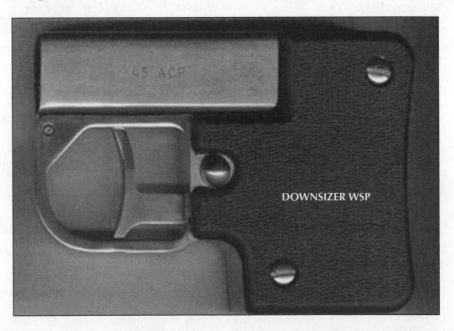

**DOWNSIZER WSP**

# Ed Brown Handguns

## CLASSIC CUSTOM

**Action**: Autoloader
**Grips**: Cocobolo wood
**Barrel**: 5 in.
**Weight**: 40 oz.
**Caliber**: .45 ACP
**Capacity**: 7+1 rounds
**Features**: Single-action; single-stack government model frame; special mirror finished side; two-piece guide rod for smoother cycling and easier disassembly; stainless or blue finish.
MSRP . . . . . . . . . . . . . . . . . . $3155

## EXECUTIVE CARRY

**Action**: Autoloader
**Grips**: Checkered cocobolo wood
**Barrel**: 4.25 in.
**Weight**: 35 oz.
**Caliber**: .45 ACP
**Capacity**: 7+1 rounds
**Features**: Frame modified with an innovative Ed Brown Bobtail; stainless or blue frame finish with stainless, black, or blue slide finish; fixed dovetail 3-dot night sights with high visibility white outlines.
MSRP . . . . . . . . . . . . . . $2645–$2720

## EXECUTIVE ELITE

**Action**: Autoloader
**Grips**: Checkered cocobolo wood
**Barrel**: 5 in.
**Weight**: 38 oz.
**Caliber**: .45 ACP
**Capacity**: 7+1 rounds
**Features**: Single stack government model frame; matte finished slide for low glare, with traditional square cut serrations on rear of slide only; blue or stainless finish.
MSRP . . . . . . . . . . . . . . $2395–$2470

## KOBRA

**Action**: Autoloader
**Grips**: Cocobolo wood
**Barrel**: 5 in.
**Weight**: 38 oz.
**Caliber**: .45 ACP
**Capacity**: 7+1 rounds
**Features**: Single stack government model frame; John Browning traditional design; exclusive snakeskin treatment on forestrap and mainspring housing; matte finished slide for low glare; 3-dot night sights with high visibility white outlines; blue or stainless finish.
MSRP . . . . . . . . . . . . . . $2195–$2270

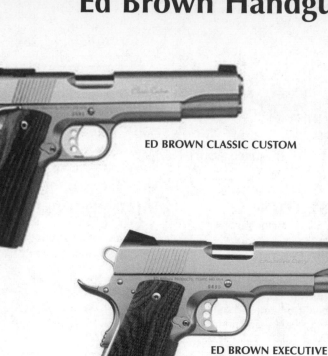

ED BROWN CLASSIC CUSTOM

ED BROWN EXECUTIVE CARRY

ED BROWN EXECUTIVE ELITE STAINLESS BLUE

ED BROWN KOBRA

HANDGUNS

# EMF Handguns

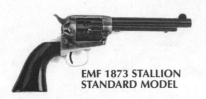

**EMF 1873 STALLION STANDARD MODEL**

**EMF 1875 REMINGTON OUTLAW**

**EMF CALIFORNIAN**

### 1873 STALLION
*Action*: Single-action revolver
*Grips*: Walnut
*Barrel*: 5.5 in.
*Weight*: 48 oz.
*Caliber*: .22 LR
*Capacity*: 10-rounds
*Features*: Case-hardened steel frame with a brass backstrap and trigger guard.
**MSRP** . . . . . . . . . . . . . . . . . $480

### 1875 REMINGTON OUTLAW
*Action*: Single-action revolver
*Grips*: Walnut
*Barrel*: 7.5 in.
*Weight*: 48 oz.
*Caliber*: .45 LC
*Capacity*: 6-rounds
*Features*: Case-hardened colored steel frame.
**MSRP** . . . . . . . . . . . . . . . . . $450

### CALIFORNIAN
*Action*: Single-action revolver
*Grips*: Walnut
*Barrel*: 4.75 in., 5.5 in., 7.5 in.
*Weight*: 48 oz.
*Caliber*: .45 LC, .375, .44/40
*Capacity*: 6-rounds
*Features*: Standard case-hardening; steel frame.
**MSRP** . . . . . . . . . . . . . . $450–$495

# Entréprise Arms Handguns

**ENTRÉPRISE ELITE**

**ENTRÉPRISE MEDALIST**

### ELITE
*Action*: Autoloader
*Grips*: Composite
*Barrel*: 3.25 in., 4.25 in., or 5 in.
*Weight*: 36 oz.–40 oz.
*Caliber*: .45 ACP
*Capacity*: 10- or 14-rounds
*Features*: 3 hi-visible dot sights; black oxide finish; extended thumb lock; match grade disconnector with polished contact points; hardened steel magazine release; adjustable anti-lash match trigger.
**MSRP** . . . . . . . . . . . . . . . .$699.90

### MEDALIST
*Action*: Autoloader
*Grips*: Composite
*Barrel*: 5 in.
*Weight*: 40 oz.
*Caliber*: .40 Cal, .45 ACP
*Capacity*: 10- or 14-rounds
*Features*: Widebody frame; adjustable anti-lash match trigger; high ride beavertail grip safety; 410 chrome moly steel firing-pin; match extractor.
**MSRP** . . . . . . . . . . . . . . $979–$1099

# European American Armory Handguns

## WITNESS

*Action*: Autoloader
*Grips*: Rubber
*Barrel*: 4.5 in.
*Weight*: 33 oz.
*Caliber*: 9mm, .38 Super, .40 S&W, 10mm, .45 ACP, .45/22, 9mm/22
*Capacity*: 10+1, 15+1, or 17+1 rounds
*Features*: Wonder finish, windage adjustable sight; double or single action; steel frame; integral accessory rail.
**Standard:** .................. **$571**
**Combo:** ................... **$669**

## WITNESS COMPACT

*Action*: Autoloader
*Grips*: Rubber
*Barrel*: 3.6 in.
*Weight*: 30 oz.
*Caliber*: 9mm, .38 Super, .40 S&W, 10mm, .45 ACP
*Capacity*: 8+1, 12+1, or 14+1 rounds
*Features*: Wonder finish, windage adjustable sight; double or single action; steel frame; integral accessory rail; blue finish.
**MSRP** ..................... **$571**

## WITNESS HUNTER

*Action*: Autoloader
*Grips*: Rubber
*Barrel*: 6 in.
*Weight*: 41 oz.
*Caliber*: 10mm, .45 ACP
*Capacity*: 10+1 or 15+1 rounds
*Features*: Single-action with over-travel stop; extended manual safety; super sight; cone barrel, slide lockup; checkered non-slip frame; drilled and tapped for scope mount; auto firing pin block.
**MSRP** ..................... **$1205**

## BOUNTY HUNTER

*Action*: Single-action revolver
*Grips*: Walnut
*Barrel*: 4.5, 6.75 in., 7.5 in.
*Weight*: 39 oz.–41 oz.
*Caliber*: .44 Mag., .22 LR/22 WMR, .45 LC
*Capacity*: 6- or 8-rounds
*Features*: Transfer bar safety; steel or alloy frame; blue, silver, case color, or ivory/blue finish.
**Nickel:** ............... **$456–$489**
**Blue:** ................ **$324–$359**
**Case Color:** ........... **$456–$489**
**Ivory/Blue:** ........... **$456–$489**

**EUROPEAN AMERICAN WITNESS STEEL FULL SIZE**

**EUROPEAN AMERICAN WITNESS STEEL COMPACT**

**EUROPEAN AMERICAN WITNESS HUNTER**

**EUROPEAN AMERICAN BOUNTY HUNTER IN NICKEL**

HANDGUNS

# Firestorm Handguns

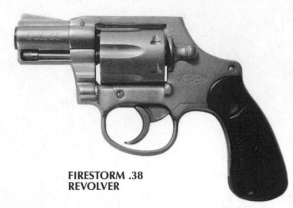

**FIRESTORM .38
REVOLVER**

**FIRESTORM .380/22
DUO-TONE**

## .38 REVOLVER

*Action*: Double-action revolver
*Grips*: Black wood boot
*Barrel*: 2 in.
*Weight*: 24 oz.
*Caliber*: .38 Special
*Capacity*: 6-rounds
*Features*: Steel frame/cylinder; double action; satin-nickel, polished-nickel, or Parkerized finish; bobbed hammer.
**MSRP** . . . . . . . . . . . . . . . . . . . **$364**

## .380/22

*Action*: Autoloader
*Grips*: Rubber wrap-around
*Barrel*: 3.5 in.
*Weight*: 18.9 oz.–20 oz.
*Caliber*: .22 LR, .380 ACP
*Capacity*: .380 ACP: 7+1-rounds, .22 LR: 10+1-rounds
*Features*: Alloy frame/steel slide; duotone or matte black finish; combat-style trigger guard; extended slide release.
**MSRP** . . . . . . . . . . . . . . . . . . . **$334**

# FNH USA Handguns

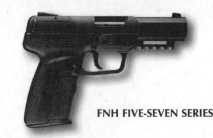

**FNH FIVE-SEVEN SERIES**

**FNH FNP-9 SERIES**

## FIVE-SEVEN SERIES

*Action*: Autoloader
*Grips*: Plastic
*Barrel*: 4.75 in.
*Weight*: 20.8 oz.
*Caliber*: 5.7 x 28mm
*Capacity*: 10- or 20-round
*Features*: Integrated accessory rail for mounting tactical lights or lasers; reversible magazine button; ambidextrous manual safety levers; hammer-forged, chrome lined barrel; choice of adjustable three dot target sights or fixed C-More systems; available with matte black, olive drab green, or flat dark earth.
**MSRP** . . . . . . . . . . . . . . . . . . . **$1299**

## FNP-9 SERIES

*Action*: Autoloader
*Grips*: Plastic
*Barrel*: 4 in.
*Weight*: 24.7 oz.
*Caliber*: 9mm
*Capacity*: 10- or 16-rounds
*Features*: Interchangable arched and flat backstrap inserts; double or single action with decocker; integrated accessory rail for mounting tactical lights or lasers; full-length guide rod and flat-coil recoil spring; reversible magazine button; loaded chamber indicator on external extractor.
**MSRP** . . . . . . . . . . . . . . . . . . . **$649**

# FNH USA Handguns

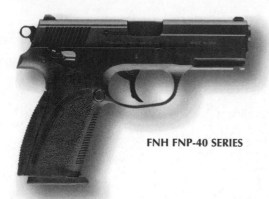

**FNH FNP-40 SERIES**

**FNH FNP-45 TACTICAL**

## FNP-40
*Action*: Autoloader
*Grips*: Plastic
*Barrel*: 4 in.
*Weight*: 26.7 oz.
*Caliber*: .40 S&W
*Capacity*: 10- or 14-rounds
*Features*: Interchangable arched and flat backstrap inserts; integrated accessory rail; full-length guide rod and flat-coil recoil spring; reversible magazine button; cold hammer-forged stainless steel barrel; available in matte black industrial tool finish.
**MSRP . . . . . . . . . . . . . . . . . . . $649**

## FNX-9/FNX-40
*Action*: Autoloader
*Grips*: Interchangable backstraps with lanyard eyelets
*Barrel*: 4 in.
*Weight*: 22 oz. (9mm) and 24 oz. (.40)
*Caliber*: 9mm and .40 S&W
*Capacity*: 17-rounds (9mm), 14-rounds (.40)
*Features*: Ergonomic polymer black frame with low bore axis; checkered and ribbed grip panels; stainless steel slide and hammer-forged stainless barrel; DA/SA ambidextrous operating controls.
**MSRP . . . . . . . . . . . . . . . . . . . $699**

## FNP-45 TACTICAL
*Action*: Autoloader
*Grips*: Checkered polymer with interchangable backstraps
*Barrel*: 5.3 in.
*Weight*: 33.6 oz.
*Caliber*: .45 ACP
*Capacity*: 15-rounds
*Features*: DA/SA operation with decocker/manual safety; polymer frame in flat dark earth with low bore axis for reduced felt recoil; comes with three magazines and nylon soft case.
**MSRP . . . . . . . . . . . . . . . $795–$1395**

# Freedom Arms Handguns

**FREEDOM ARMS 83 PREMIER GRADE**

## 83 PREMIER GRADE
*Action*: Single-action revolver
*Grips*: Hardwood
*Barrel*: 4.75 in., 6 in., 7.5 in., 10 in.
*Weight*: 52.5 oz.
*Caliber*: .500 Wyoming Express, .475 Linebaugh, .454 Casull, .44 Remington Mag., .41 Remington Mag., .357 Mag.
*Capacity*: 5-rounds
*Features*: Adjustable sight models are drilled and tapped for scope mounts; stainless steel, brush finish, and impregnated hardwood grips.
**MSRP . . . . . . . . . . . . . $2229–$2320**

## 83 RIMFIRE
*Action*: Single-action revolver
*Grips*: Hardwood
*Barrel*: 10 in.
*Weight*: 55.5 oz.
*Caliber*: .22 LR match grade chambers
*Capacity*: 5-rounds
*Features*: Drilled and tapped for scope mounts; stainless steel frame; matte finish.
**MSRP . . . . . . . . . . . . . . . . . . . $2137**

# Freedom Arms Handguns

## 97 PREMIER GRADE

*Action*: Single-action revolver
*Grips*: Laminated hardwood
*Barrel*: 4.5 in., 5.5 in., 7.5 in., or 10 in.
*Weight*: 39 oz.
*Caliber*: .45 Colt, .44 Special, .41 Rem. Mag., .357 Mag., .327 Fed., .224-32 FA, .22 LR, .17 HMR,
*Capacity*: 5- or 6-rounds
*Features*: Impregnated hardwood grips; stainless steel frame; brush stainless finish.
**MSRP . . . . . . . . . . . . . $1750–$1907**

## M2008 SINGLE SHOT

*Action*: Hinged breech with top slide latch
*Grips*: Impregnated hardwood
*Barrel*: 10 in. to 16 in.
*Weight*: 63 oz.
*Caliber*: .223 Rem. To .375 Win.
*Capacity*: 1-round
*Features*: Hammer block safety; stainless matte finish.
**MSRP . . . . . . . . . . . . . . . . . . $1495**

**FREEDOM ARMS 97 PREMIER GRADE**

# Glock Handguns

GLOCK G17

GLOCK G19

GLOCK G26

## STANDARD PISTOL G17, G20, G21, G22, G31, G37

*Action*: Autoloader
*Grips*: Composite
*Barrel*: 4.49 in.
*Weight*: 22.04 oz.–27.68 oz.
*Caliber*: 9mm, .40, 10mm Auto, .45 G.A.P., .45 Auto, .380 Auto, .357
*Capacity*: 10-, 13-, 15-, 17-rounds
*Features*: Double action; safe action trigger system; G20 model has recoil-damping Glock hi-tech polymer.
**G17, G22, G31: . . . . . . . . . . . . $599**
**G20, G21: . . . . . . . . . . . . . . . $637**
**G37: . . . . . . . . . . . . . . . . . . . $614**

## COMPACT PISTOLS G19, G23, G38, G25, G32

*Action*: Autoloader
*Grips*: Composite
*Barrel*: 4.02 in.
*Weight*: 20.99 oz.–24.16 oz.
*Caliber*: 9mm, .40, .45 G.A.P., .380 Auto, .357
*Capacity*: 8-, 10-, 13-, 15-rounds
*Features*: Trigger safety; double-action.
**MSRP: . . . . . . . . . . . . . . . $614–$621**

## SUBCOMPACT PISTOLS G26, G27, G29, G39, G30, G28, G33

*Action*: Autoloader
*Grips*: Composite
*Barrel*: 3.46 in.–3.78 in.
*Weight*: 18.66–24.69 oz.
*Caliber*: 9mm, .40, 10mm Auto, .45 G.A.P., .45 Auto, .380 Auto, .357
*Capacity*: 6-, 9-, 10-rounds
*Features*: Trigger safety; double-action.
**MSRP . . . . . . . . . . . . . . . . $599–$637**

HANDGUNS

# Glock Handguns

**GLOCK G36**

**GLOCK G34**

## SUBCOMPACT SLIMLINE G36

*Action*: Autoloader
*Grips*: Synthetic
*Barrel*: 3.78 in.
*Weight*: 20.11 oz.
*Caliber*: .45 Auto
*Capacity*: 6-rounds
*Features*: Safe action system; single stack magazine for slim grip.
**MSRP . . . . . . . . . . . . . . . . . . . . $637**

## COMPETITION G34, G35

*Action*: Autoloader
*Grips*: Synthetic
*Barrel*: 5.32 in.
*Weight*: 22.92 oz.–24.5 oz.
*Caliber*: 9mm, .40
*Capacity*: 15-, 17-rounds
*Features*: Safe action system; hexagonal barrel; right hand; extended barrel.
**MSRP . . . . . . . . . . . . . . . . . . . $679**

# Hammerli Handguns

**HAMMERLI SP20**

**HAMMERLI X-ESSE**

## SP20 TARGET PISTOL

*Action*: Autoloader
*Grips*: Synthetic
*Barrel*: 4.6 in.
*Weight*: 40 oz.
*Caliber*: .22 LR, .32 S&W
*Capacity*: 5-rounds
*Features*: Front end magazine.
**.32 S&W: . . . . . . . . . . . . . . . $2099**
**.22 LR: . . . . . . . . . . . . . . . . . $1899**

## X-ESSE STANDARD

*Action*: Autoloader
*Grips*: Composite
*Barrel*: 4.5 in., 6 in.
*Weight*: 36 oz.
*Caliber*: .22 LR
*Capacity*: 10-rounds
*Features*: Single-action, two-stage trigger; rail for scope mount.
**MSRP . . . . . . . . . . . . . . . . . . . . $799**

# Heckler & Koch Handguns

**H&K P30**

**H&K P2000**

**H&K 23**

**H&K USP COMPACT**

**H&K UPS**

## P30
**Action**: Autoloader
**Grips**: Polymer
**Barrel**: 6.95 in.
**Weight**: 1.63 lb.
**Caliber**: 9mm, .40 S&W
**Capacity**: 12-rounds
**Features**: Corrosion proof fiber-reinforced polymer frame; multiple trigger firing modes; HK recoil reduction system; blued finish; Picatinny rail; ambidextrous magazine release levers and side release.
**MSRP** . . . . . . . . . . . . . . . . . . . **$1005**

## P2000 & P2000 SK
**Action**: Autoloader
**Grips**: Polymer
**Barrel**: 3.26 in.–3.66 in.
**Weight**: 1.49 lb.–1.62 lb.
**Caliber**: 9mm, .40 S&W, .357 SIG
**Capacity**: 9- to 13-rounds
**Features**: LEM trigger system; double-action; pre-cock hammer; ambidextrous magazine release and inter-

changable grip straps; mounting rail.
**P2000**: . . . . . . . . . . . . . . . . . . **$941**
**P2000 SK**: . . . . . . . . . . . . . . . . **$983**

## MARK 23
**Action**: Autoloader
**Grips**: Polymer
**Barrel**: 5.9 in.
**Weight**: 42 oz.
**Caliber**: .45 ACP
**Capacity**: 10+1 rounds
**Features**: Threaded O-ring barrel with polygonal bore profile; match grade trigger; one piece machined steel slide; frame mounted decocking lever and separate ambidextrous safety lever; HK recoil reduction system; ambidextrous magazine release lever.
**MSRP** . . . . . . . . . . . . . . . . . . **$2310**

## USP COMPACT
**Action**: Autoloader
**Grips**: Polymer
**Barrel**: 3.58 in.–3.80 in.
**Weight**: 1.60 lb.–1.74 lb.

**Caliber**: 9mm, .40 S&W, .45 Auto
**Capacity**: 12–rounds
**Features**: Corrosion proof fiber-reinforced polymer frame; ambidextrous magazine release lever; grooved target triggers; can be converted to any of nine trigger firing modes.
**MSRP** . . . . . . . . . . . . . . . **$941–$1086**

## USP
**Action**: Autoloader
**Grips**: Polymer
**Barrel**: 4.25 in.–4.41 in.
**Weight**: 1.70–1.96 lb.
**Caliber**: 9mm, .40 S&W, .45 Auto
**Capacity**: 12-rounds
**Features**: Browning-type action with a patented recoil reduction system; double and single action modes; available in nine trigger/firing mode configurations; fiber-reinforced polymer frame; blued finish; ambidextrous magazine release trigger.
**MSRP** . . . . . . . . . . . . . . . **$902–$983**

# Heritage Handguns

## ROUGH RIDER BIG BORE

*Action*: Single-action revolver
*Grips*: Cocobolo
*Barrel*: 4.5 in., 5.5 in., 7.5 in.
*Weight*: 38 oz.
*Caliber*: .357, .45
*Capacity*: 6-rounds
*Features*: Patterned after 1873 Colt; blue, nickel, stainless, and blue/color-case hardened finishes are available; frame mounted intertia firing pin and transfer bar.
**MSRP** . . . . . . . . . . . . . . . **$479–$549**

## ROUGH RIDER SMALL BORE

*Action*: Single-action revolver
*Grips*: Cocobolo
*Barrel*: 3.5 in., 4.75 in., 6.5 in., 9 in.
*Weight*: 31 oz.
*Caliber*: .22 LR & .22 Mag.
*Capacity*: 6-rounds
*Features*: Machined barrel is micro-

**HERITAGE ROUGH RIDER SMALL BORE**

threaded; optional cocobolo grips include white mother of pearl, black mother of pearl, or green camo laminate grips; frame finish comes in

smooth silver satin, deep matte black, low gloss black satin, or case-hardened finish.
**MSRP** . . . . . . . . . . . **$229.99–$279.99**

# High Standard Handguns

## G-MAN MODEL

*Action*: Autoloader
*Grips*: Cocobolo wood
*Barrel*: 5 in.
*Weight*: 39 oz.
*Caliber*: .45 ACP
*Capacity*: 8+1 rounds
*Features*: Custom fit match grade stainless barrel and National Match bushing; polished feed ramp; throated barrel; slotted hammer; STI lightweight trigger with overtravel stop; colt-style safety grip; black Teflon finish.
**MSRP** . . . . . . . . . . . . . . . . . . . **$1395**

## OLYMPIC

*Action*: Autoloader
*Grips*: Cocobolo wood
*Barrel*: 5.5 in.
*Weight*: 44 oz.
*Caliber*: .22 Short
*Capacity*: 10+1 rounds
*Features*: Lightweight aluminum alloy slide; precision carbon steel frame; drilled and tapped for scopes; single-action.
**MSRP** . . . . . . . . . . . . . . . . . . . **$875**

**HIGH STANDARD VICTOR**

**HIGH STANDARD SUPERMATIC TROPHY**

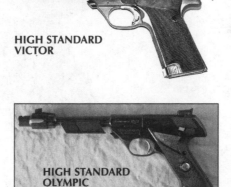

**HIGH STANDARD OLYMPIC**

*Features*: Features gold plated components—trigger, safety, slide stop, and magazine catch; adjustable trigger; checkered deluxe grips; blue finish.
**MSRP** . . . . . . . . . . . . . . . **$845–$895**

## VICTOR

*Action*: Autoloader
*Grips*: Walnut
*Barrel*: 4.5 in., 5.5 in.
*Weight*: 45 oz.
*Caliber*: .22 LR
*Capacity*: 10+1 rounds
*Features*: Removable aluminum rib; drilled and tapped for scopes; optional slide conversion kit for .22 short.
**MSRP** . . . . . . . . . . . . . . . . . . . **$845**

## SUPERMATIC TROPHY

*Action*: Autoloader
*Grips*: Walnut
*Barrel*: 5.5 in., 7.25 in.
*Weight*: 44 oz.
*Caliber*: .22 LR
*Capacity*: 10+1 rounds

# High Standard Handguns

## SUPERMATIC CITATION

**Action**: Autoloader
**Grips**: Walnut
**Barrel**: 5.5 in.
**Weight**: 54 oz.
**Caliber**: .22 LR
**Capacity**: 10+1 rounds
**Features**: Durable Parkerized finish and black epoxy-finished wood; ambidextrous grips; drilled and tapped for scopes; includes letter authenticating it as a 10X.
**MSRP** . . . . . . . . . . . . . . . . . . $1095

## US MODEL 1911 CUSTOM

**Action**: Autoloader
**Grips**: Walnut
**Barrel**: 5 in.

**HIGH STANDARD
SUPERMATIC CITATION .22LR**

**Weight**: 40 oz.
**Caliber**: .45 ACP
**Capacity**: 7+1 rounds
**Features**: Beveled magazine well; match trigger with overtravel stop; available in stainless steel, blued, or Parkerized finish.
**MSRP** . . . . . . . . . . . . . . . . . . $995

# Hi-Point Handguns

**HI-POINT MODEL CF-380**

**HI-POINT MODEL C-9**

## MODEL .45 ACP & .40 S&W

**Action**: Autoloader
**Grips**: Polymer
**Barrel**: 4.5 in.
**Weight**: 35 oz.
**Caliber**: .40 S&W, .45 ACP
**Capacity**: 10-rounds
**Features**: Polymer frame; quick on-off thumb safety; operations safety sheet; +P rated; free extra rear peep sight; free trigger lock; black finish.
**MSRP** . . . . . . . . . . . . . . . . . . $199.95

## MODEL C-9

**Action**: Autoloader
**Grips**: Polymer
**Barrel**: 3.5 in.
**Weight**: 29 oz.
**Caliber**: 9mm
**Capacity**: 8- or 10-rounds
**Features**: Polymer frame; last round lock open; quick on-off thumb safety; free trigger lock; free extra peep sight; black finish.
**MSRP** . . . . . . . . . . . . . . . . . . $165

## MODEL CF-380

**Action**: Autoloader
**Grips**: Polymer
**Barrel**: 3.5 in.
**Weight**: 29 oz.
**Caliber**: .380 ACP
**Capacity**: 8- or 10-rounds
**Features**: High-impact polymer frame; black powder coat with chrome rail; durable, easy-grip finish; quick on-off thumb safety; free extra rear peep sight.
**MSRP** . . . . . . . . . . . . . . . . . . $140

HANDGUNS

# Kahr Handguns

KAHR CW .45 ACP

KAHR P-9 SERIES

KAHR PM9

KAHR P40

## CW45

*Action*: Autoloader
*Grips*: Textured polymer
*Barrel*: 3.64 in.
*Weight*: 19.7 oz.
*Caliber*: .45 ACP
*Capacity*: 6+1 rounds
*Features*: Trigger cocking double-action; lock breech; Browning-type recoil lug; passive striker block; no magazine disconnect; drift adjustable , white bar-dot combat rear sight, pinned in polymer front sight; black finish; matte stainless steel slide.
**MSRP** . . . . . . . . . . . . . . . . . . . **$606**

## PM45

*Action*: Autoloader
*Grips*: Textured polymer
*Barrel*: 3.64 in.
*Weight*: 18.5 oz.
*Caliber*: .45 ACP
*Capacity*: 6+1 rounds
*Features*: Trigger cocking double action; lock breech; Browning-type recoil lug; passive striker block; no magazine disconnect; drift adjustable, white bar-dot combat sights; black

polymer frame, matte blackened stainless steel slide.
**MSRP** . . . . . . . . . . . . . . . . . . . **$855**

## P9 SERIES

*Action*: Autoloader
*Grips*: Textured polymer
*Barrel*: 3.6 in.
*Weight*: 15 oz.
*Caliber*: 9mm
*Capacity*: 7+1 rounds
*Features*: Trigger cocking DAO; lock breech; Browning-type recoil lug; passive striker block; no magazine disconnect; black polymer frame.
**P9 Polymer, Matte Stainless:** . . **$739**
**P9 Black:** . . . . . . . . . . . . . . . . **$786**
**P9 Black with Night Sights:** . . . **$903**

## PM9 SERIES

*Action*: Autoloader
*Grips*: Textured polymer
*Barrel*: 3 in.
*Weight*: 14 oz.
*Caliber*: 9mm
*Capacity*: 6+1 or 7+1 rounds
*Features*: Trigger cocking DAO; lock breech; Browning-type recoil lug; pas-

sive striker block; no magazine disconnect; black polymer frame.
**PM9:** . . . . . . . . . . . . . . . . . . . . **$786**
**PM9 Night Sights:** . . . . . . . . . . **$908**
**PM9 Black:** . . . . . . . . . . . . . . . . **$837**
**PM9 Black with Night Sights:** . . **$958**
**PM9 w/CT Laser Sight:** . . . . . . . **$991**
**PM9 Black Rose:** . . . . . . . . . . **$1049**
**PM9 w/External Safety & LCI:** . . **$924**
**PM9 w/Night Sights,**
**External Safety & LC:** . . . . . . . **$1049**

## P40 SERIES

*Action*: Autoloader
*Grips*: Textured polymer
*Barrel*: 3.6 in.
*Weight*: 16.8 oz.
*Caliber*: .40 S&W
*Capacity*: 6+1 rounds
*Features*: Trigger cocking DAO; lock breech; Browning-type recoil lug; passive striker block; no magazine disconnect; black polymer frame.
**P40:** . . . . . . . . . . . . . . . . . . . . **$739**
**P40 w/Night Sights:** . . . . . . . . . **$857**
**P40 Black:** . . . . . . . . . . . . . . . . **$786**
**P40 Black w/Night Sights:** . . . . **$903**

# Kahr Handguns

## P45 SERIES
**Action**: Autoloader
**Grips**: Textured polymer
**Barrel**: 3.64 in.
**Weight**: 18.5 oz.
**Caliber**: .45 ACP
**Capacity**: 5+1, 6+1 rounds
**Features**: Trigger cocking DAO; lock breech; Browning-type recoil lug; passive striker block; no magazine disconnect; black polymer frame.
**P45:** . . . . . . . . . . . . . . . . . . . . . . $805
**P45 Black:** . . . . . . . . . . . . . . . $855
**P45 w/Night Sights:** . . . . . . . . . $921
**P45 Black w/Night Sights:** . . . . $973

## P380
**Action**: Autoloader
**Grips**: Textured polymer
**Barrel**: 2.5 in.
**Weight**: 9.97 oz.
**Caliber**: .380 ACP
**Capacity**: 6+1 rounds
**Features**: Trigger cocking DAO; lock breech; Browning-type recoil lug; passive striker block; no magazine disconnect; black polymer frame, matte stainless steel slide; premium Lothar Walther match grade barrel.
**MSRP** . . . . . . . . . . . . . . . . . . . . $649

**KAHR P380**

# Kel-Tec Handguns

KEL-TEC P-3AT

KEL-TEC P-11

KEL-TEC P-32

## P-3AT
**Action**: Autoloader
**Grips**: Polymer
**Barrel**: 2.7 in.
**Weight**: 8.3 oz.
**Caliber**: .380 Auto
**Capacity**: 6+1 rounds
**Features**: Double action only; steel barrel and slide; aluminum frame; transfer bar.
**Blued Finish:** . . . . . . . . . . . . . . $318
**Parkerized Finish:** . . . . . . . . . . $361
**Hard Chrome Finish:** . . . . . . . . $377

## P-11
**Action**: Autoloader
**Grips**: Polymer
**Barrel**: 3.1 in.
**Weight**: 14 oz.
**Caliber**: 9mm
**Capacity**: 10+1 rounds, Optional 12-rounds

KEL-TEC PF-9

**Features**: Double-action only; steel barrel and slide; aluminum frame; locked breech; high impact polymer Dupont grips.
**Blued Finish:** . . . . . . . . . . . . . . $333
**Parkerized Finish:** . . . . . . . . . . $377
**Hard Chrome Finish:** . . . . . . . . $390

## P-32
**Action**: Autoloader
**Grips**: Polymer
**Barrel**: 3.1 in.
**Weight**: 6.6 oz.

**Caliber**: 32 Auto
**Capacity**: 7+1 rounds
**Features**: Steel barrel and slide; locked breech mechanism.
**Blued Finish:** . . . . . . . . . . . . . . $318
**Parkerized Finish:** . . . . . . . . . . $361
**Hard Chrome Finish:** . . . . . . . . $377

## PF-9
**Action**: Autoloader
**Grips**: Polymer
**Barrel**: 3.1 in.
**Weight**: 12.7 oz.
**Caliber**: 9mm
**Capacity**: 7+1 rounds
**Features**: Firing mechanism is double-action only with an automatic hammer block safety; grips available in black, grey, and olive drab; rear sight is a new design and is adjustable for windage.
**Blued Finish:** . . . . . . . . . . . . . . $333
**Parkerized Finish:** . . . . . . . . . . $377
**Hard Chrome Finish:** . . . . . . . . $390

# Kel-Tec Handguns

## SUB RIFLE 2000
*Action*: Autoloader
*Grips*: Polymer
*Barrel*: 16.1 in.
*Weight*: 64 oz.
*Caliber*: 9mm and .40 S&W
*Capacity*: 10+1 rounds
*Features*: Self-loading carbine for pistol cartridges; by rotating the barrel upwards and back, it can be reduced to a size of "16x7" to facilitate secure storage.
**MSRP** . . . . . . . . . . . . . . . . . . . **$409**

## PMR-30
*Action*: SA autoloader
*Grips*: Nylon
*Barrel*: 4.3 in.
*Weight*: 13.6 oz.
*Caliber*: .22 WMR
*Capacity*: 30-rounds
*Features*: Blowback/locked breech system; lightweight but Full size; urethane recoil buffer; disassembles for cleaning with removal of one pin.
**MSRP** . . . . . . . . . . . . . . . . . . . **$415**

**KEL-TEC SUB RIFLE 2000 FOLDED**

**KEL-TEC SUB RIFLE 2000**

**KEL-TEC PMR-30**

# Kimber Handguns

**KIMBER STAINLESS PRO RAPTOR II**

**KIMBER TACTICAL ENTRY II**

## STAINLESS PRO RAPTOR II
*Action*: Autoloading, recoil operated
*Grips*: Zebra wood, scale pattern
*Barrel*: 4 in.
*Weight*: 35 oz.
*Caliber*: .45 ACP
*Capacity*: 8-rounds
*Features*: Stainless steel slide and frame with satin-silver finish; match grade barrel; ambidextrous thumb safety; full-length guide rod.
**MSRP** . . . . . . . . . . . . . . . . . . . **$1359**

## TACTICAL ENTRY II
*Action*: Autoloading, recoil operated
*Grips*: Laminated double diamond, Kimber logo
*Barrel*: 5 in.
*Weight*: 40 oz.
*Caliber*: .45 ACP
*Capacity*: 7-rounds
*Features*: Ambidextrous thumb safety; full-length guide rod; stainless steel frame and slide; matte gray Kim Pro II frame finish.
**MSRP** . . . . . . . . . . . . . . . . . . . **$1428**

HANDGUNS

# Kimber Handguns

**KIMBER ULTRA CARRY II**

**KIMBER ULTRA CDP II**

**KIMBER COMPACT STAINLESS II**

### ULTRA CARRY II
*Action*: Autoloading, recoil operated
*Grips*: Black synthetic double Diamond
*Barrel*: 3 in.
*Weight*: 25 oz.
*Caliber*: .45 ACP
*Capacity*: 7-rounds
*Features*: Black matte finish; aluminum frame; steel slide; full-length guide rod.
**MSRP . . . . . . . . . . . . . . . . . . . . $888**

### ULTRA CDP II
*Action*: Autoloader
*Grips*: Rosewood double diamond
*Barrel*: 3 in.
*Weight*: 25 oz.
*Caliber*: .45 ACP
*Capacity*: 7-rounds
*Features*: Ambidextrous thumb safety; full-length guide rod; matte black Kim Pro frame finish; aluminum frame; stainless steel slide and barrel; match grade trigger.
**MSRP . . . . . . . . . . . . . . . . . . . $1318**

### COMPACT STAINLESS II
*Action*: Autoloader
*Grips*: Black synthetic double diamond
*Barrel*: 4 in.
*Weight*: 27 oz.
*Caliber*: .45 ACP
*Capacity*: 7-rounds
*Features*: Full-length guide rod; aluminum frame in satin silver finish; steel match grade barrel; aluminum match grade trigger.
**MSRP . . . . . . . . . . . . . . . . . . $1009**

**KIMBER CUSTOM II**

**KIMBER ECLIPSE ULTRA II**

**KIMBER GOLD MATCH II**

### CUSTOM II
*Action*: Autoloader
*Grips*: Black synthetic double diamond
*Barrel*: 5 in.
*Weight*: 38 oz.
*Caliber*: .45 ACP
*Capacity*: 7-rounds
*Features*: Full-length guide rod; aluminum frame in matte black finish; steel match grade barrel; aluminum match grade trigger.
**MSRP . . . . . . . . . . . . . . . . . . . . $828**

### ECLIPSE ULTRA II
*Action*: Autoloader
*Grips*: Laminated double diamond
*Barrel*: 3 in.
*Weight*: 38 oz.
*Caliber*: .45 ACP
*Capacity*: 7-rounds
*Features*: Full-length guide rod; stainless steel frame with brush polished finish; stainless steel slide; match grade steel barrel; aluminum match grade trigger.
**MSRP . . . . . . . . . . . . . . . . . . . $1236**

### GOLD MATCH II
*Action*: Autoloader
*Grips*: Rosewood double diamond
*Barrel*: 5 in.
*Weight*: 38 oz.
*Caliber*: .45 ACP
*Capacity*: 8-rounds
*Features*: Premium aluminum, match grade trigger; full length guide rod; steel frame with highly polished blue finish; stainless steel, match grade barrel.
**MSRP . . . . . . . . . . . . . . . . . . . $1345**

HANDGUNS

# Kimber Handguns

### STAINLESS PRO TLE (LG)
*Action*: Autoloader
*Grips*: Tactical gray double diamond, Crimson Trace lasergrips
*Barrel*: 4 in.
*Weight*: 36 oz.
*Caliber*: .45 ACP
*Capacity*: 7-rounds
*Features*: Full-length guide rod; stainless steel frame with satin silver; match grade steel barrel; aluminum match grade trigger.
MSRP . . . . . . . . . . . . . . . . . $1462

### ULTRA CRIMSON CARRY II
*Action*: Autoloading, recoil operated
*Grips*: Rosewood double diamond, Crimson Trace lasergrips
*Barrel*: 3 in.
*Weight*: 25 oz.
*Caliber*: .45 ACP
*Capacity*: 7-rounds
*Features*: Full-length guide rod; aluminum frame in satin silver finish; steel match grade barrel; aluminum match grade trigger.
MSRP . . . . . . . . . . . . . . . . . $1156

### SUPER CARRY PRO
*Action*: Autoloader
*Grips*: Micarta/laminated rosewood
*Barrel*: 4 in.
*Weight*: 28 oz.
*Caliber*: .45 ACP
*Capacity*: 8-rounds
*Features*: Ambidextrous thumb safety; carry melt; full-length guide rod; aluminum frame in satin silver; super carry serations; high cut under trigger guard; steel match grade barrel; aluminum match grade trigger.
MSRP . . . . . . . . . . . . . . . . . $1530

### STAINLESS ULTRA TLE II
*Action*: Autoloader
*Grips*: Tactical gray double diamond
*Barrel*: 3 in.
*Weight*: 25 oz.
*Caliber*: .45 ACP
*Capacity*: 7-rounds
*Features*: Full-length guide rod; front strap checkering; aluminum frame with satin silver finish; steel match grade barrel; aluminum match grade trigger.
MSRP . . . . . . . . . . . . . . . . . $1210

KIMBER STAINLESS PRO TLE (LG)

KIMBER ULTRA CRIMSON CARRY II

KIMBER SUPER CARRY PRO

KIMBER STAINLESS ULTRA TLE II

### SOLO CARRY
*Action*: Autoloader
*Grips*: Black synthetic checkered/smooth
*Barrel*: 2.7 in.
*Weight*: 17 oz.
*Caliber*: 9mm
*Capacity*: 6-rounds
*Features*: Aluminum finish frame; stainless steel barrel; single action striker trigger.
MSRP . . . . . . . . . . . . . . . . . $747

KIMBER SOLO CARRY

# Magnum Research Handguns

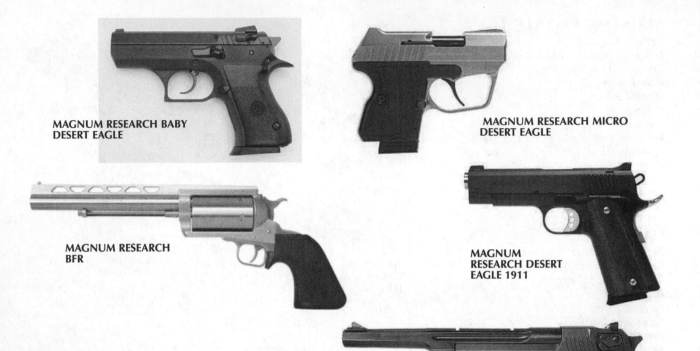

MAGNUM RESEARCH BABY
DESERT EAGLE

MAGNUM RESEARCH MICRO
DESERT EAGLE

MAGNUM RESEARCH
BFR

MAGNUM
RESEARCH DESERT
EAGLE 1911

MAGNUM RESEARCH
MARK XIX DESERT EAGLE

## BABY DESERT EAGLE

*Action*: Autoloader
*Grips*: Plastic composite
*Barrel*: 3.64 in., 3.93 in., 4.52 in.
*Weight*: 1 lb. 10.8 oz.–2 lb. 6.6 oz.
*Caliber*: 9mm, .40 S&W, .45 ACP
*Capacity*: 10-, 12-, 13-, 15-rounds
*Features*: Black steel or polymer frame; slide safety; decocker; double and single action; polygonal rifling; Picatinny rail.
**MSRP**. . . . . . . . . . . . . . . . . . . **$630**

## BFR (BIG FRAME REVOLVER)

*Action*: Single-action revolver
*Grips*: Rubber, optional wood
*Barrel*: 7.5 in.
*Weight*: 3.6 lb.–5.3 lb.
*Caliber*: Long Cylinder: .30/30 Win., .444 Marlin, .45 Long Colt/.410, .45/70 Gov't., .450 Marlin, .460 S&W Mag., .500 S&W Mag.; Short Cylinder: .22 Hornet, .454 Casull, .480 Ruger/.475 Linebaugh, .50 AE
*Capacity*: 5-rounds
*Features*: Both long and short-cylinder models are made of stainless steel; barrels are stress-relieved and cut rifled; current production revolvers are shipped with rubber grips and Weaver-style scope mount
**MSRP**. . . . . . . . . . . . . . . . . . . **$1050**

## MARK XIX DESERT EAGLE

*Action*: Autoloader
*Grips*: Plastic composite
*Barrel*: 6 in. or 10 in.
*Weight*: 62.4 oz.–71.4 oz.
*Caliber*: .357 Mag., .44 Mag., .50 A.E.
*Capacity*: 7-, 8-, 9-rounds
*Features*: Gas operated; polygonal rifling; integral scope bases.
**Black 6 in.:**. . . . . . . . . . . . . . **$1563;**
**Black 10 in.:**. . . . . . . . . . . . . . **$1650**

## MICRO DESERT EAGLE

*Action*: Autoloader
*Grips*: Black polymer
*Barrel*: 2.22 in.
*Weight*: 14 oz.
*Caliber*: .380 Auto (9mm Browning)
*Capacity*: 6-rounds
*Features*: Gas-assisted blowback system; alloy frame; steel slide; oversized trigger guard; nickel finish.
**MSRP**. . . . . . . . . . . . . . . . . . . **$479**

## MR. EAGLE "FAST ACTION"

*Action*: Autoloader

*Grips*: Black polymer
*Barrel*: 4 in. (9mm), 4.15 in. (.40)
*Weight*: 24.8 oz. (9mm), 26.4 oz. (.40 S&W)
*Caliber*: 9mm or .40 S&W
*Capacity*: 10 or 15 (9mm), 10 or 12 (.40 SUW)
*Features*: 6-groove filing; hammer forged barrel; full Picatinny rail; ergonomic polymer grip frame; four separate safety devices.
**MSRP**. . . . . . . . . . . . . . . . . . . **$699**

## DESERT EAGLE 1911

*Action*: Autoloader
*Grips*: Checkered wood
*Barrel*: 5 in. or 4.3 in.
*Weight*: 36 oz. (5 in. barrel), 32 oz. (4.3 in. barrel)
*Caliber*: .45 ACP
*Capacity*: 8-rounds
*Features*: Grip safety; extended thumb safety; blued finish.
**MSRP**. . . . . . . . . . . . . . . . . . . **$799**

# MOA Handguns

## MAXIMUM
*Action*: Hinged breech
*Grips*: Walnut
*Barrel*: 8.5 in., 10.5 in., 14 in.
*Weight*: 3 lb. 8 oz.–4 lb. 3 oz.
*Caliber*: Most rifle chamberings from .22 Hornet to .375 H&H
*Capacity*: Single shot
*Features*: Falling block action; free floating barrel; multiple length barrels; receiver tapped for scope mounts.
**Blued barrel:** . . . . . . . . . . . . . . **$865**
**Stainless barrel:** . . . . . . . . . . . **$966**

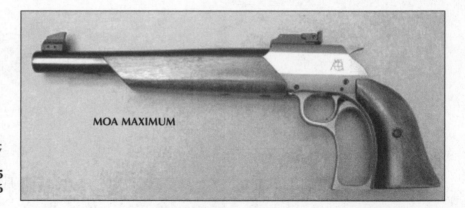

MOA MAXIMUM

# Navy Arms Handguns

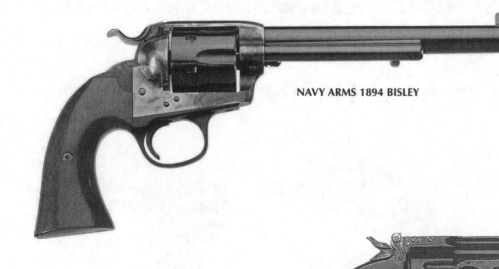

NAVY ARMS 1894 BISLEY

NAVY ARMS 1875
SCHOFIELD CAVALRY

## 1875 SCHOFIELD CAVALRY
*Action*: Single-action revolver
*Grips*: Walnut
*Barrel*: 5 in.
*Weight*: 2 lb. 3oz.
*Caliber*: .45 Colt
*Capacity*: 6-rounds
*Features*: Top-break action, automatic ejectors; rear notch and high blade front sight.
**MSRP** . . . . . . . . . . . . . . . . . . . **$899**

## 1894 BISLEY
*Action*: Single-action revolver
*Grips*: Walnut
*Barrel*: 4.8 in., 5.5 in., 7.5 in.
*Weight*: 45 oz.– 48 oz.

*Caliber*: .44-40, .45 Colt
*Capacity*: 6-rounds
*Features*: Bisley grip case-colored frame.
**MSRP** . . . . . . . . . . . . . . . . . . . **$572**

# Nighthawk Custom Handguns

## 10-8 GUN

*Action*: Autoloader
*Grips*: VZ Diamondback grips, in green or black linen Micarta
*Barrel*: 5 in.
*Weight*: 38 oz.
*Caliber*: .45 ACP
*Capacity*: 8+1 rounds
*Features*: Front and rear grasping grooves on slide.
**MSRP** . . . . . . . . . . . . . . . . . . **$2595**

NIGHTHAWK CUSTOM 10-8 GUN

# North American Arms Handguns

## PUG MINI-REVOLVER

*Action*: Revolver
*Grips*: Rubber
*Barrel*: 1 in.
*Weight*: 6.4 oz.
*Caliber*: .22 Mag.
*Capacity*: 5-rounds
*Features*: Oversized pebble-textured rubber grips enable the handler to keep a firm grip.
**White Dot Sight:** . . . . . . . . . . . **$299**
**Tritium Sight:** . . . . . . . . . . . . . **$319**

## GUARDIAN .32

*Action*: Autoloader
*Grips*: Polymer
*Barrel*: 2.5 in.
*Weight*: 13.5 oz.
*Caliber*: .32 ACP
*Capacity*: 6+1 rounds
*Features*: Stainless steel; double action; integral locking system safety.
**MSRP** . . . . . . . . . . . . . . . . . . . **$402**

## GUARDIAN .380

*Action*: Autoloader
*Grips*: Composite

NORTH AMERICAN
PUG MINI-REVOLVER

NORTH AMERICAN GUARDIAN .32

NORTH AMERICAN
GUARDIAN .380

*Barrel*: 2.49 in.
*Weight*: 18.72 oz.
*Caliber*: .380 ACP
*Capacity*: 6+1 rounds
*Features*: Stainless steel; double action; integral locking system safety.
**MSRP** . . . . . . . . . . . . . . . . . . . **$449**

HANDGUNS

# North American Arms Handguns

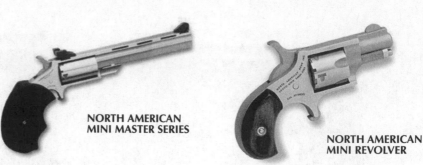

NORTH AMERICAN
MINI MASTER SERIES

NORTH AMERICAN
MINI REVOLVER

## MINI MASTER SERIES REVOLVER

*Action*: Single-action revolver
*Grips*: Rubber
*Barrel*: 2 in. or 4 in.
*Weight*: 8.8 oz. (2 in.), or 10.7 oz. (4 in.)
*Caliber*: .22 LR, .22 Mag., .17 MACH 2, .17 HMR
*Capacity*: 5-rounds
*Features*: Conversion cylinder or adjustable sights available.

**.22 LR, .22 Mag. w/
Fixed Sights:** . . . . . . . . . . . . . $284
**Conversion w/Fixed Sights:** . . . $319
**.22 LR, .22 Mag. w/
Adjustable Sights:** . . . . . . . . . $314
**Conversion w/
Adjustable Sights:** . . . . . . . . . $349

## MINI REVOLVER

*Action*: Single-action revolver
*Grips*: Laminated rosewood
*Barrel*: 1.2 in.
*Weight*: 5 oz.
*Caliber*: .22 Short, .22 LR, .22 Mag.
*Capacity*: 5-rounds
*Features*: Features NAA's safety cylinder so Mini-Revolver can be carried fully loaded.
**.22:** . . . . . . . . . . . . . . . . . . . . . $199
**.22 LR:** . . . . . . . . . . . . . . . . . . . $199
**.22 Mag:** . . . . . . . . . . . . . . . . . $214

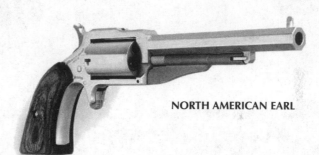

NORTH AMERICAN EARL

## THE EARL 1860-4

*Action*: SA revolver
*Grips*: Rosewood
*Barrel*: 4 in. heavy octagonal
*Weight*: 8.6 oz.
*Caliber*: .22 Mag.
*Capacity*: 5-rounds
*Features*: 1860's style mini-revolver resembles 150-yr-old percussion revolver.
**MSRP** . . . . . . . . . . . . . . . . . . . . $289

# Olympic Arms Handguns

## COHORT

*Action*: Autoloader
*Grips*: Walnut, fully checkered
*Barrel*: 4 in. bull
*Weight*: 36 oz.
*Caliber*: .45 ACP
*Capacity*: 7+1 rounds
*Features*: Single-action on 1911 Colt design; short slide on a full size frame; grooved frame front strap; satin bead blast finish.
**MSRP** . . . . . . . . . . . . . . . . . . . $1033

OLYMPIC ARMS COHORT

# Olympic Arms Handguns

**OLYMPIC ARMS
ENFORCER**

**OLYMPIC ARMS
MATCHMASTER**

**OLYMPIC ARMS
WESTERNER**

## ENFORCER
*Action*: Autoloader
*Grips*: Smooth, laser etched widow icon, walnut
*Barrel*: 4 in. bull
*Weight*: 35 oz.
*Caliber*: .45 ACP
*Capacity*: 6+1 rounds
*Features*: Single-action on 1911 Colt design; satin bead blast finish; hooked frame trigger guard; Triplex counter-wound self-contained spring recoil system.
**MSRP . . . . . . . . . . . . . . . . . $1033.50**

## MATCHMASTER
*Action*: Autoloader
*Grips*: Smooth, laser etched scorpion icon, walnut
*Barrel*: 5 in.
*Weight*: 40 oz.–44 oz.
*Caliber*: .45 ACP
*Capacity*: 7+1 rounds
*Features*: Single-action on 1911 Colt design; satin bead blast or Parkerized finish; grooved frame front strap.
**5 in.: . . . . . . . . . . . . . . . . . . $903.50**
**6 in.: . . . . . . . . . . . . . . . . . . $975**

## WESTERNER
*Action*: Autoloader
*Grips*: Smooth, laser etched Westerner icon, ivory color
*Barrel*: 5 in.
*Weight*: 39 oz.
*Caliber*: .45 ACP
*Capacity*: 7+1 rounds
*Features*: Single-action; color case-hardened frame and slide; stainless steel barrel; round frame trigger guard; straight front frame strap.
**MSRP . . . . . . . . . . . . . . . . . . . $1039**

# Para Ordnance/Para USA Handguns

**PARA ORDNANCE PXT 1911**

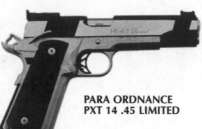

**PARA ORDNANCE PXT 14 .45 LIMITED**

**PARA ORDNANCE PXT SSP**

## PXT 1911 LTC

*Action*: Single-action autoloading
*Grips*: Cocobolo wood with gold medallion
*Barrel*: 4.25 in.
*Weight*: 35 oz.
*Caliber*: .45 ACP
*Capacity*: 8+1 rounds
*Features*: Match-grade integral ramped stainless barrel; single-action trigger; regal finish; steel receiver.
**MSRP . . . . . . . . . . . . . . . . . . . $999**

## PXT 14 .45 LIMITED

*Action*: Single-action autoloader
*Grips*: Polymer
*Barrel*: 5 in.
*Weight*: 40 oz.
*Caliber*: .45 ACP
*Capacity*: 10+1 (restricted), 14+1 (full) rounds
*Features*: Spurred hammer; comes in either full or restricted capacity models; stainless steel receiver; sterling frame finish.
**MSRP . . . . . . . . . . . . . . . . . $1289**

## PXT SSP

*Action*: Autoloader
*Grips*: Cocobolo wood
*Barrel*: 5 in.
*Weight*: 39 oz.
*Caliber*: .45 ACP
*Capacity*: 8+1 rounds
*Features*: Luminous fiber optic front sight with fixed 3-dot system; single-action single stack.
**MSRP . . . . . . . . . . . . . . . . . . . $999**

**PARA ORDNANCE GI EXPERT**

**PARA ORDNANCE PDA**

**PARA ORDNANCE PXT LDA COMPANION**

## GI EXPERT

*Action*: Single-action autoloader, recoil operated
*Grips*: Checkered composite
*Barrel*: 5 in.
*Weight*: 39 oz.
*Caliber*: .45 ACP
*Capacity*: 8+1 rounds
*Features*: Stainless steel barrel; grip safety; skeletonized spur hammer to prevent hammer bite; covert black finish.
**MSRP . . . . . . . . . . . . . . . . . . . $659**

## PDA

*Action*: Double-action autoloader
*Grips*: Cocobolo wood
*Barrel*: 3 in.
*Weight*: 24 oz.
*Caliber*: 9mm, .45 ACP
*Capacity*: 9mm: 8+1 rounds, .45 ACP: 6+1 rounds
*Features*: Spurless hammer; alloy receiver, duo-tone finish; match grade barrels; .45 ACP model has a lda trigger.
**9mm: . . . . . . . . . . . . . . . . . . $1249**
**.45 ACP: . . . . . . . . . . . . . . . . $1299**

## PXT LDA COMPANION

*Action*: Autoloader
*Grips*: Black plastic
*Barrel*: 3.5 in.
*Weight*: 32 oz.
*Caliber*: .45 ACP
*Capacity*: 7+1 rounds
*Features*: Spurless hammer; stainless receiver; covert black finish; lda trigger system.
**MSRP . . . . . . . . . . . . . . . . . . . $999**

# Puma Handguns

PUMA M-1873

PUMA M-1911-22

## M-1873

*Action*: Single-action revolver
*Grips*: Walnut, synthetic
*Barrel*: 4.75 in., 5.5 in., 7.5 in.
*Weight*: 2.2 lb.–2.4 lb.
*Caliber*: .22 LR, Extra cylinder .22 Mag.
*Capacity*: 6-rounds
*Features*: Antique or matte black finish; TGT extra cylinder on all models but 4.75 in. barrel; checkered grips; key operated, hammer block safety; side loading gate.
**MSRP** . . . . . . . . . . . . . . . . **$224–$333**

## M-1911-22

*Action*: SA autoloader
*Grips*: Walnut
*Barrel*: 4.75 in.
*Weight*: 2.1 lb.
*Caliber*: .22 LR
*Capacity*: 10-rounds
*Features*: Key operated safety; blued finish; rimfire version of M-1911.
**MSRP** . . . . . . . . . . . . . . . . . . . **$323**

# Rossi Handguns

## R351 AND R352

*Action*: Double-action revolver
*Grips*: Rubber
*Barrel*: 2 in.
*Weight*: 24 oz.
*Caliber*: .38 Spl.
*Capacity*: 5-rounds
*Features*: Blue or stainless steel finish; checkered grips; forged steel frame.
**R351:** . . . . . . . . . . . . . . . . . . . **$389**
**R352:** . . . . . . . . . . . . . . . . . . . **$452**

ROSSI R351

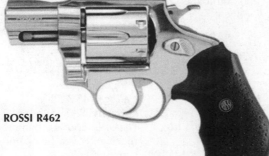

ROSSI R462

## R462 AND R461

*Action*: Double-action revolver
*Grips*: Rubber
*Barrel*: 2 in.
*Weight*: 26 oz.
*Caliber*: .357 Mag.
*Capacity*: 6-rounds
*Features*: Blue or stainless steel finish; checkered grips; forged steel frame.
**R461:** . . . . . . . . . . . . . . . . . . . **$389**
**R462:** . . . . . . . . . . . . . . . . . . . **$452**

# Rossi Handguns

ROSSI R851

ROSSI R972

## R851
**Action**: Double-action revolver
**Grips**: Rubber
**Barrel**: 4 in.
**Weight**: 32 oz.
**Caliber**: .38 Spl.
**Capacity**: 6-rounds
**Features**: Adjustable rear sight; blue finish; forged steel frame.
**MSRP** . . . . . . . . . . . . . . . . . . . . $389

## 972
**Action**: Double-action revolver
**Grips**: Rubber
**Barrel**: 6 in.
**Weight**: 35 oz.
**Caliber**: .357 Mag.
**Capacity**: 6-rounds
**Features**: Stainless steel finish; deep contoured finger grooves in the grip for solid grasp and comfort; frame forged from steel.
**MSRP** . . . . . . . . . . . . . . . . . . . . $508

# Ruger Handguns

RUGER MARK III HUNTER

RUGER LCP CENTERFIRE PISTOL

## RUGER MARK III HUNTER
**Action**: SA autoloading, recoil operated
**Grips**: Cocobolo wood
**Barrel**: 4.5 in., 6.88 in.
**Weight**: 38 oz.–41 oz.
**Caliber**: .22 LR
**Capacity**: 10-rounds
**Features**: Stainless steel frame with stain finish; fluted bull barrel; visible loaded chamber indicator.
**MSRP** . . . . . . . . . . . . . . . . . . . . $638

## LCP CENTERFIRE PISTOL
**Action**: Double-action autoloader
**Grips**: Black, glass-filled nylon
**Barrel**: 2.75 in.
**Weight**: 9.4 oz.
**Caliber**: .380 Auto
**Capacity**: 6+1 rounds
**Features**: Blued, alloy slide and barrel.
**MSRP** . . . . . . . . . . . . . . . . . . . . $373

# Ruger Handguns

**RUGER LCR**

**RUGER .22 CHARGER**

**RUGER BISLEY**

**RUGER BISLEY VAQUERO**

**RUGER GP100 STANDARD**

**RUGER MARK III STANDARD**

## LCR (LIGHTWEIGHT COMPACT REVOLVER)

*Action*: DA revolver
*Grips*: Houge Tamer and Crimson Trace lasergrips
*Barrel*: 1.8 in.
*Weight*: 13 oz.–17.1 oz.
*Caliber*: .38 Spl., .357 Mag.
*Capacity*: 5-rounds
*Features*: Advanced Target grey cylinder finish; option of replaceable, pinned ramp or XS standard dot tritium front sight.
MSRP . . . . . . . . . . . . . . . $575–$792

## .22 CHARGER STANDARD

*Action*: Autoloader
*Grips*: Black laminate
*Barrel*: 10 in.
*Weight*: 3.50 lb.
*Caliber*: .22 LR
*Capacity*: 10-rounds
*Features*: Cross bolt safety; extended magazine release; combination Weaver-style and tip-off sight mount; bipod; alloy steel frame with matte

black finish.
MSRP . . . . . . . . . . . . . . . . . . . $380

## BISLEY

*Action*: Single-action revolver
*Grips*: Hardwood
*Barrel*: 7.5 in.
*Weight*: 48 oz.–50 oz.
*Caliber*: .44 Mag., .45 Colt
*Capacity*: 6-rounds
*Features*: Blued alloy steel frame
MSRP . . . . . . . . . . . . . . . . . . . $724

## BISLEY VAQUERO

*Action*: Single-action revolver
*Grips*: Simulated ivory
*Barrel*: 5.5 in.
*Weight*: 41 oz.–45 oz.
*Caliber*: .45 Colt, .357 Mag.
*Capacity*: 6-rounds
*Features*: Stainless steel frame with high-gloss stainless finish.
MSRP . . . . . . . . . . . . . . . . . . . $779

## GP100

*Action*: Double-action revolver

*Grips*: Black Hogue Monogrip
*Barrel*: 3 in., 4.2 in., 6 in.
*Weight*: 36 oz.–45 oz.
*Caliber*: .327 Fed. Mag., .357 Mag.
*Capacity*: 6-rounds
*Features*: Satin stainless or blued finish; stainless steel or alloy steel frame; cushioned rubber grip; transfer bar; triple-locking cylinder.
MSRP . . . . . . . . . . . . . . . $659–$729

## MARK III STANDARD

*Action*: Autoloader
*Grips*: Checkered plastic
*Barrel*: 4.75 in., 6 in.
*Weight*: 35 oz., 37 oz.
*Caliber*: .22 LR
*Capacity*: 10-rounds
*Features*: Steel frame with blued finish; loaded chamber indicator; manual safety; internal cylindrical bolt.
MSRP . . . . . . . . . . . . . . . . . . . $362

# Ruger Handguns

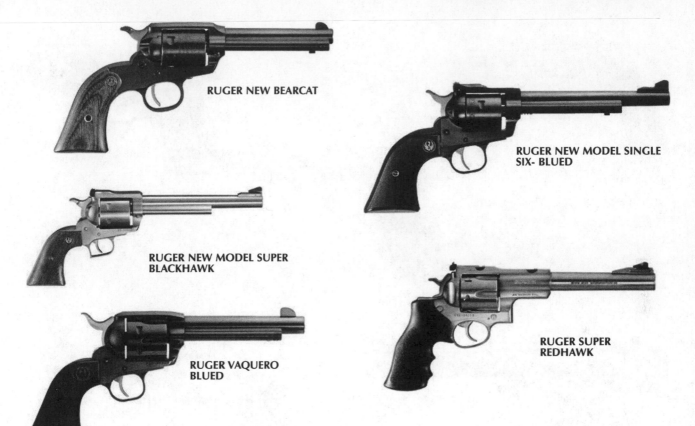

RUGER NEW BEARCAT

RUGER NEW MODEL SINGLE SIX- BLUED

RUGER NEW MODEL SUPER BLACKHAWK

RUGER SUPER REDHAWK

RUGER VAQUERO BLUED

## NEW BEARCAT
*Action*: Single-action revolver
*Grips*: Hardwood
*Barrel*: 4.2 in.
*Weight*: 24 oz.
*Caliber*: .22 LR
*Capacity*: 6-rounds
*Features*: Alloy steel with blued finish or stainless steel frame with satin stainless finish; decorative cylinder; transfer bar mechanism; features one-piece frame reminiscent of old Remington Civil War-era revolvers
**Alloy Steel:** . . . . . . . . . . . . . . **$542**
**Stainless Steel:** . . . . . . . . . . . . **$584**

## NEW MODEL SINGLE SIX BLUED
*Action*: Single-action revolver
*Grips*: Black checkered hard rubber
*Barrel*: 6.5 in.
*Weight*: 35 oz.
*Caliber*: .17 HMR
*Capacity*: 6-rounds
*Features*: Alloy Steel frame with blued finish; transfer bar mechanism.
**MSRP** . . . . . . . . . . . . . . . . . . . **$550**

## NEW MODEL SUPER BLACKHAWK
*Action*: Single-action revolver
*Grips*: Hardwood
*Barrel*: 4.62 in., 5.5 in., 7.5 in., 10.5 in.
*Weight*: 45 oz.–48 oz.
*Caliber*: .44 Mag.
*Capacity*: 6-rounds
*Features*: Alloy steel or stainless steel frame; blued or satin stainless finish; transfer bar mechanism; Western-style grip.
**MSRP** . . . . . . . . . . . . . . . **$695–$739**

## VAQUERO BLUED
*Action*: Single-action revolver
*Grips*: Black checkered
*Barrel*: 4.62 in., 5.5 in.
*Weight*: 40 oz.–43 oz.
*Caliber*: .45 Colt, .357 Mag.
*Capacity*: 6-rounds
*Features*: Blued finish alloy steel; reverse indexing pawl; ejector rod head; transfer bar mechanism; internal lock; sights.
**MSRP** . . . . . . . . . . . . . . . . . . . **$699**

## REDHAWK
*Action*: Double-action revovler
*Grips*: Hardwood or black Hogue Monogrip
*Barrel*: 4.2 in., 5.5 in., 7.5 in.
*Weight*: 46 oz.–54 oz.
*Caliber*: .44 Mag., .45 Colt
*Capacity*: 6-rounds
*Features*: Satin stainless finish; triple-locking cylinder; single spring mechanism; easy sighting; stainless steel construction; dual chambering; transfer bar.
**MSRP** . . . . . . . . . . . . . . . **$949–$999**

## SUPER REDHAWK
*Action*: Double-action revolver
*Grips*: Black Hogue Tamer Monogrip
*Barrel*: 7.5 in., 9.5 in.
*Weight*: 53 oz.–58 oz.
*Caliber*: .44 Mag., .454 Casull
*Capacity*: 6-rounds
*Features*: Satin stainless finish; tripple-locking cylinder; integral scope system; corrosion-resistant; extended frame; dual chambering; transfer bar.
**MSRP** . . . . . . . . . . . . . . . . . . . **$999**

HANDGUNS

# Ruger Handguns

**RUGER SP101**

**RUGER P-SERIES**

**RUGER SR9C**

**RUGER 22 45 RP**

**RUGER GP100LE IN .327 FED. MAG.**

## SP101
*Action*: Double-action revolver
*Grips*: Black rubber
*Barrel*: 2.25 in., 3.06 in.
*Weight*: 25 oz.- 28 oz.
*Caliber*: .357 Mag., .327 Fed. Mag., .38 Spl.
*Capacity*: 5- or 6-rounds
*Features*: Stainless steel frame with satin finish; cushioned rubber grip; grip frame; transfer bar; triple-locking cylinder.
**MSRP**. . . . . . . . . . . . . . . . . . . . $629

## P-SERIES
*Action*: Autoloader
*Grips*: Black polymer
*Barrel*: 3.9 in., 4.20 in.,
*Weight*: 27 oz.–29 oz.
*Caliber*: .45 Auto, 9mm Luger
*Capacity*: 8+1 rounds

*Features*: Stainless or blued barrel; ambidextrous manual safety; slide; grip frame; contoured grip.
**P345**: . . . . . . . . . . . . . . . .$595–$636
**P95**: . . . . . . . . . . . . . . . .$393–$424

## SR9C
*Action*: DA autoloader
*Grips*: Black, glass-filled, nylon
*Barrel*: 3.5 in.
*Weight*: 23.4 oz.
*Caliber*: 9mm Luger
*Capacity*: 10- or 17-rounds
*Features*: Compact version of SR9; black alloy or brushed stainless 6-groove rifling; high visibility sights; accessory mounting rail.
**MSRP**. . . . . . . . . . . . . . . . . . . . $525

## RUGER 22/45 RP
*Action*: SA autoloder

*Grips*: Checkered cocobolo
*Barrel*: 5.5 in. bull
*Weight*: 33 oz.
*Caliber*: .22 LR
*Capacity*: 10-rounds
*Features*: Replacable panels; Zytel polymer frame; blued finish; classic 1911-style pistol.
**MSRP**. . . . . . . . . . . . . . . . . . . . $380

## GP100 LE IN .327 FED. MAG.
*Action*: DA revolver
*Grips*: Black with Hogue Monogrip
*Barrel*: 4.2 in.
*Weight*: 40 oz.
*Caliber*: .327 Fed. Mag.
*Capacity*: 7-rounds
*Features*: Stainless medium frame; cushioned grips.
**MSRP**. . . . . . . . . . . . . . . . . . . . $729

# Sig Sauer Handguns

## P238 NITRON

**Action**: Single-action autoloading
**Grips**: Fluted polymer
**Barrel**: 2.7 in.
**Weight**: 15.2 oz.
**Caliber**: .380 ACP (9mm Short)
**Capacity**: 6-rounds
**Features**: Nitron slide finish; beavertail style frame.
**MSRP** . . . . . . . . . . . . . . . . . . . . **$679**

**SIG SAUER P238 N**

## P250

**Action**: Locked breech DAO semi-auto
**Grips**: Interchangable polymer
**Barrel**: 4.7 in.
**Weight**: 29.4 oz.
**Caliber**: 9mm, .357 Sig, .40 S&W, .45 ACP
**Capacity**: 10-, 14-, 17-rounds
**Features**: Interchangable polymer grip shell with stainless insert; nitron slide finish; interchangable grip sizes and calibers.
**Contrast**: . . . . . . . . . . . . . . . . . **$450**
**Night Sights**: . . . . . . . . . . . . . **$521**

## P220

**Action**: Autoloader
**Grips**: Polymer, laminated, or custom shop wood
**Barrel**: 4.4 in.
**Weight**: 30.4 oz.–31.2 oz.
**Caliber**: .45 ACP
**Capacity**: 8-rounds
**Features**: Nitron finish, light-weight alloy frame; accessory rail.
**Standard**: . . . . . . . . . . . . . . . . . **$976**
**Night Sights**: . . . . . . . . . . . . . **$1050**
**Two-tone DAK**: . . . . . . . . . . **$1079**
**Equinox**: . . . . . . . . . . . . . . . . **$1200**

**SIG SAUER P250**

## P226

**Action**: Autoloader
**Grips**: One-piece ergo grip, Extreme model features Hogue custom G10 grips
**Barrel**: 4.4 in.
**Weight**: 34 oz.
**Caliber**: 9mm, .357 Sig, .40 S&W
**Capacity**: 9mm: 10- or 15-rounds; .357 Sig: 10- or 12-rounds, .40 S&W: 10- or 12-rounds
**Features**: Double and single action; black hard anodized frame finish; nitron slide finish; accessory rail; Navy model features an anchor engraved on slide; Extreme model features SRT trigger and front cocking serrations.
**Standard**: . . . . . . . . . . . . . . . . . **$976**
**Night Sights**: . . . . . . . . . . . . . **$1050**
**Navy**: . . . . . . . . . . . . . . . . . . . . **$1020**
**Extreme**: . . . . . . . . . . . . . . . . **$1129**

**SIG SAUER P220**

HANDGUNS

# Sig Sauer Handguns

SIG SAUER P229

SIG SAUER SP2022

## P229
**Action**: Autoloader
**Grips**: Black polymer factor grips
**Barrel**: 3.9 in.
**Weight**: 32 oz.
**Caliber**: 9mm, .40 S&W, .357 Sig
**Capacity**: 9mm: 10- or 15-rounds; .357 Sig: 10- or 12-rounds, .40 S&W: 10- or 12-rounds
**Features**: Black hard anodized frame finish; nitron slide finish; accessory rail.
**MSRP** . . . . . . . . . . . . . . . . . . . . **$976**
**Night Sights:** . . . . . . . . . . . . **$1050**

## SP2022
**Action**: Autoloader
**Grips**: Polymer
**Barrel**: 3.9 in.
**Weight**: 29 oz.
**Caliber**: 9mm, .40 S&W
**Capacity**: 10- or 15-rounds (9mm), 10- or 12-rounds (.40 S&W)
**Features**: Accessory rail; wear-resistant polymer frame; black polymer frame finish; nitron slide finish.
**MSRP** . . . . . . . . . . . . . . . . . . . . **$494**
**Night Sights:** . . . . . . . . . . . . . **$566**

SIG SAUER P239

SIG SAUER MOSQUITO

## P239
**Action**: Autoloader
**Grips**: Polymer, Tactical model features black polymer factory grips
**Barrel**: 3.6 in., 4 in.
**Weight**: 29.5 oz.
**Caliber**: 9mm, .40 S&W, .357 Sig
**Capacity**: 8-rounds (9mm), 7-rounds (.40 S&W, .357 Sig)
**Features**: Black polymer factor grips; black hard anodized frame finish; nitron frame finish; double and single-action trigger.
**Contrast Sights:** . . . . . . . . . . . **$840**

**Night Sights:** . . . . . . . . . . . . . . **$912**
**Tactical:** . . . . . . . . . . . . . . . . . **$963**

## SP232
**Action**: Autoloader
**Grips**: Polymer
**Barrel**: 3.6 in.
**Weight**: 17.6 oz.
**Caliber**: .380 ACP
**Capacity**: 7-rounds
**Features**: Black polymer factor grips; blued finish.
**MSRP** . . . . . . . . . . . . . . . . . . . . **$649**
**Night Sights:** . . . . . . . . . . . . . . **$720**

## MOSQUITO
**Action**: Autoloader
**Grips**: Black polymer
**Barrel**: 5.5 in.
**Weight**: 24.6 oz.
**Caliber**: .22 LR
**Capacity**: 10-rounds
**Features**: Integrated accessory rail; rugged blowback system; fixed barrel; superior ergonomic grip; internal locking device; slide mounted ambidextrous safety; blued slide finish; black polymer frame finish.
**MSRP** . . . . . . . . . . . . . . . . . . . . **$390**

HANDGUNS

# Sig Sauer Handguns

SIG SAUER P238
SPECIAL EDITION
NITRON

SIG SAUER
P250 2SUM

## 1911
*Action*: Autoloader
*Grips*: Custom shop wood grips, aluminum grips on Platnium Elite model
*Barrel*: 5 in.
*Weight*: 41.6 oz.
*Caliber*: .45 ACP
*Capacity*: 8-rounds
*Features*: Accessory rail; beavertail frame; single-action; checkered grip; match grade barrel, hammer/sear set and trigger; stainless finish on stainless model; duo-tone finish on Platinum Elite model.
**Nitron:** . . . . . . . . . . . . . . . . . . $1070
**Stainless:** . . . . . . . . . . . . . . . . $1099
**Platinum Elite:** . . . . . . . . . . . $1170

## P250 2SUM
*Action*: DA autoloader
*Grips*: black polymer
*Barrel*: 4.7 in.
*Weight*: 29.4 oz.
*Caliber*: 9mm, .40 S&W
*Capacity*: 17 (full-size 9mm), 14 (full-size .40 S&W)
*Features*: Full size P250 with all the components to rapidly convert it to the P250 subcompact with 3.6 in. barrel (24.9 oz.)
**MSRP** . . . . . . . . . . . . . . . . . . . . $713
**Night Sights:** . . . . . . . . . . . . . $814

## P238 SPECIAL EDITION NITRON
*Action*: SA autoloader
*Grips*: Rosewood
*Barrel*: 2.7 in.
*Weight*: 15 oz. alloy frame, 20 oz. stainless frame
*Caliber*: .380 ACP
*Capacity*: 6 round
*Features*: Expanded P238 concealed carry pistol line; options include rainbow titanium finish; natural stainless or nitron finish; two-tone with flat black anodized top, as well as new grip styles.
**MSRP** . . . . . . . . . . . . . . . . . . . . $679

# Smith & Wesson Handguns

## CLASSIC M57 AND M58
*Action*: DA N-frame revolver
*Grips*: Checkered square-butt walnut
*Barrel*: 4 in., 6 in.
*Weight*: 40.8 oz.
*Caliber*: .41 Magnum
*Capacity*: 6-rounds
*Features*: Bright blue or nickel finish; carbon steel frame; classic style thumbpiece; color case wide spur hammer; color case wide serrated target trigger
**M57:** . . . . . . . . . . . . . . . $979-$1153
**M58:** . . . . . . . . . . . . . . . $969-$1146

S&W M57

# Smith & Wesson Handguns

**S&W M14**

**S&W M18 COMBAT MASTERPIECE**

**M27 CLASSIC**

**S&W M10**

**S&W M29**

**S&W M22 CLASSIC**

**S&W M22 CLASSIC OF 1917**

## M14
**Action**: DA K-frame revolver
**Grips**: Wood
**Barrel**: 6 in.
**Weight**: 35 oz.
**Caliber**: .38 S&W Special +P
**Capacity**: 6-rounds
**Features**: Carbon steel frame and cylinder; nickel or bright blue finish; medium sized frame; exposed hammer; single or double action.
Nickel:. . . . . . . . . . . . . . . . . $1106
Blue: . . . . . . . . . . . . . . . . . . $909

## M18 COMBAT MASTERPIECE
**Action**: DA K-frame revolver
**Grips**: Wood
**Barrel**: 4 in.
**Weight**: 37.6 oz.
**Caliber**: .22 LR
**Capacity**: 6-rounds
**Features**: Carbon steel frame and cylinder; blue finish.
MSRP. . . . . . . . . . . . . . . . . . $919

## M27 CLASSIC
**Action**: Single/double action revolver
**Grips**: Checkered square butt walnut
**Barrel**: 4 in.
**Weight**: 48.5 oz.
**Caliber**: .357 Mag., .38 S&W Special +P
**Capacity**: 6-rounds
**Features**: Carbon steel frame; bright nickel or blue finish.
Nickel:. . . . . . . . . . . . . . . . . $1193
Blue: . . . . . . . . . . . . . . . . . . $1029

## M10
**Action**: Single or double-action revolver
**Grips**: Wood
**Barrel**: 4 in.
**Weight**: 36 oz.
**Caliber**: .38 S&W Special +P
**Capacity**: 6-rounds
**Features**: Carbon steel frame; carbon steel cylinder; blue finish; medium size frame; exposed hammer.
MSRP. . . . . . . . . . . . . . . . . . $719

## M29
**Action**: Revolver
**Grips**: Checkered square butt walnut;

6 in. model features Altamont Service walnut grips
**Barrel**: 4 in., 6 in.
**Weight**: 48.5 oz.
**Caliber**: .44 Mag., .44 S&W Special
**Capacity**: 6-rounds
**Features**: Carbon steel frame with nickel finish.
4 in.: . . . . . . . . . . . . . . . . . . $1019
6in.:. . . . . . . . . . . . . . . . . . . $1219

## M22 CLASSIC
**Action**: Revolver
**Grips**: Altamont wood
**Barrel**: 4 in.
**Weight**: 36.8 oz.
**Caliber**: .45 ACP
**Capacity**: 6-rounds
**Features**: Carbon steel frame and cylinder; blue finish.
MSRP. . . . . . . . . . . . . . . . . . $1090

## M22 CLASSIC OF 1917
**Action**: Revolver
**Grips**: Altamont wood
**Barrel**: 5.5 in.
**Weight**: 37.2 oz.
**Caliber**: .45 ACP
**Capacity**: 6-rounds
**Features**: Carbon steel frame and cylinder; blue finish.
MSRP. . . . . . . . . . . . . . . . . . $999

# Smith & Wesson Handguns

S&W M36

S&W M40

S&W M42

S&W M60

S&W M317

S&W M325
NIGHT GUARD

## M36
**Action**: Revolver
**Grips**: Wood
**Barrel**: 1.8 in.
**Weight**: 19.5 oz.
**Caliber**: .38 S&W Special +P
**Capacity**: 5-rounds
**Features**: Small-sized frame; exposed hammer; carbon steel frame and cylinder; blue or nickel finish; single or double action.
**Blue:** .................... **$729**
**Nickel:** ................... **$749**

## M40
**Action**: Hammerless revolver
**Grips**: Wood
**Barrel**: 1.8 in.
**Weight**: 21 oz.
**Caliber**: .38 S&W Special +P
**Capacity**: 5-rounds
**Features**: Small-sized frame; internal hammer; double action only; blue finish; carbon steel frame and cylinder.
**MSRP** .................... **$877**

## M42
**Action**: Hammerless revolver
**Grips**: Wood
**Barrel**: 1.8 in.
**Weight**: 14.4 oz.
**Caliber**: .38 S&W Special +P
**Capacity**: 5-rounds
**Features**: Matte black finish; aluminum alloy frame, carbon steel cylinder; double action only.
**MSRP** .................... **$861**

## M60
**Action**: Revolver
**Grips**: Synthetic
**Barrel**: 3 in.
**Weight**: 24.5 oz.
**Caliber**: .357 Mag., .38 S&W Special +P
**Capacity**: 5-rounds
**Features**: Stainless steel finish; single or double-action; stainless steel frame and cylinder.
**MSRP** .................... **$759**

## M317
**Action**: Revolver
**Grips**: Synthetic
**Barrel**: 1.8 in.
**Weight**: 10.8 oz.
**Caliber**: .22 LR
**Capacity**: 8-rounds
**Features**: Aluminum alloy frame and cylinder; clear coat finish; small frame with exposed hammer; double or single-action.
**MSRP** .................... **$699**

## M325 NIGHT GUARD
**Action**: Single/double action revolver
**Grips**: Synthetic
**Barrel**: 2.75 in.
**Weight**: 28 oz.
**Caliber**: .45 ACP
**Capacity**: 6-rounds
**Features**: Scandium alloy frame; stainless steel cylinder; large-size frame; exposed hammer; matte black finish.
**MSRP** .................... **$1049**

# Smith & Wesson Handguns

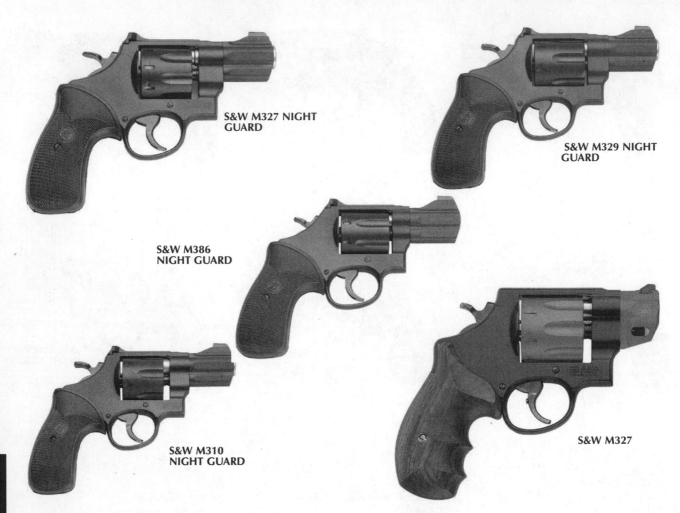

S&W M327 NIGHT GUARD

S&W M329 NIGHT GUARD

S&W M386 NIGHT GUARD

S&W M310 NIGHT GUARD

S&W M327

### M327 NIGHT GUARD
*Action*: Single/double action revolver
*Grips*: Synthetic
*Barrel*: 2.5 in.
*Weight*: 27.6 oz.
*Caliber*: .357 Mag., .38 S&W Special +P
*Capacity*: 8-rounds
*Features*: Scandium alloy frame; stainless steel cylinder; large-size frame; exposed hammer; matte black finish.
**MSRP** . . . . . . . . . . . . . . . . . **$1049**

### M329 NIGHT GUARD
*Action*: Single/double action revolver
*Grips*: Synthetic
*Barrel*: 2.5 in.
*Weight*: 29.3 oz.
*Caliber*: .44 Mag., .44 S&W Special
*Capacity*: 6-rounds
*Features*: Scandium alloy frame; stainless steel cylinder; large-size frame;

exposed hammer; matte black finish.
**MSRP** . . . . . . . . . . . . . . . . . **$1049**

### M386 NIGHT GUARD
*Action*: Single/double action revolver
*Grips*: Synthetic
*Barrel*: 2.5 in.
*Weight*: 24.5 oz.
*Caliber*: .357 Mag., .38 S&W Special +P
*Capacity*: 7-rounds
*Features*: Scandium alloy frame; stainless steel cylinder; medium-size frame; exposed hammer; matte black finish.
**MSRP** . . . . . . . . . . . . . . . . . **$979**

### M310 NIGHT GUARD
*Action*: Single/double action revolver
*Grips*: Synthetic
*Barrel*: 2.75 in.
*Weight*: 28 oz.
*Caliber*: 10mm, .40 S&W
*Capacity*: 6-rounds

*Features*: Scandium alloy frame; stainless steel cylinder; large-size frame; exposed hammer; matte black finish.
**MSRP** . . . . . . . . . . . . . . . . . **$1185**

### M327
*Action*: Revolver
*Grips*: Wood
*Barrel*: 2 in.
*Weight*: 24.3 oz.
*Caliber*: .357 Mag., .38 S&W Special +P
*Capacity*: 8-rounds
*Features*: Color case with overtravel stop; color case tear drop with pinned sear; large frame size; exposed hammer; matte black finish; scandium alloy frame and titanium alloy cylinder; polish button rifling; smooth double action with Wolff mainspring.
**MSRP** . . . . . . . . . . . . . . . . . **$1269**

# Smith & Wesson Handguns

S&W M627

S&W M325
THUNDER RANCH

S&W M327
TRR8

## M627
**Action**: Single/double action revolver
**Grips**: Synthetic
**Barrel**: 4 in.
**Weight**: 41.2 oz.
**Caliber**: .357 Mag., .38 S&W Special +P
**Capacity**: 8-rounds
**Features**: Stainless steel frame and cylinder; matte stainless; large-size frame; exposed hammer.
**MSRP** . . . . . . . . . . . . . . . . . . . $969

## M325 THUNDER RANCH
**Action**: Single/double action revolver
**Grips**: Synthetic
**Barrel**: 4 in.
**Weight**: 31 oz.
**Caliber**: .45 ACP
**Capacity**: 6-rounds
**Features**: Scandium alloy frame; stainless steel cylinder; matte black.
**MSRP** . . . . . . . . . . . . . . . . . . . $1289

## M327 TRR8
**Action**: Single/double action revolver
**Grips**: Synthetic
**Barrel**: 5 in.
**Weight**: 35.3 oz.
**Caliber**: .357 Mag., .38 S&W Special +P
**Capacity**: 8-rounds
**Features**: Scandium alloy frame; stainless steel cylinder; matte black; large-size frame; exposed hammer; equipment rails.
**MSRP** . . . . . . . . . . . . . . . . . . . $1289

S&W M329 XL
HUNTER

S&W M386 XL
HUNTER

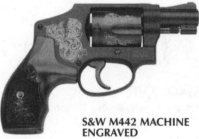

S&W M442 MACHINE
ENGRAVED

## M329 XL HUNTER
**Action**: Single/double action revolver
**Grips**: Synthetic
**Barrel**: 6.5 in.
**Weight**: 33 oz.
**Caliber**: .44 Mag., .44 S&W Special
**Capacity**: 6-rounds
**Features**: Scandium alloy frame; stainless steel cylinder; matte black; large-size frame; exposed hammer.
**MSRP** . . . . . . . . . . . . . . . . . . . $1138

## M386 XL HUNTER
**Action**: Single/double action revolver
**Grips**: Synthetic
**Barrel**: 6 in.
**Weight**: 30 oz.
**Caliber**: .357 Mag., .38 S&W Special +P
**Capacity**: 7-rounds
**Features**: Scandium alloy frame; stainless steel cylinder; matte black; medium-size frame; exposed hammer.
**MSRP** . . . . . . . . . . . . . . . . . . . $899

## M442
**Action**: Double action revolver
**Grips**: Synthetic
**Barrel**: 1.87 in.
**Weight**: 15 oz.
**Caliber**: .38 S&W Special +P
**Capacity**: 5-rounds
**Features**: Aluminum alloy frame; stainless steel cylinder; matte black finish; small-size frame; internal hammer; cylinder cut for moon clips.
**MSRP** . . . . . . . . . . . . . . . . . . . $469

## M442 MACHINE ENGRAVED
**Action**: Double action revolver
**Grips**: Engraved wood
**Barrel**: 1.8 in.
**Weight**: 15 oz.
**Caliber**: .38 S&W Special +P
**Capacity**: 5-rounds
**Features**: Aluminum alloy frame; stainless steel barrel/cylinder; matte black.
**MSRP** . . . . . . . . . . . . . . . . . . . $709

HANDGUNS

# Smith & Wesson Handguns

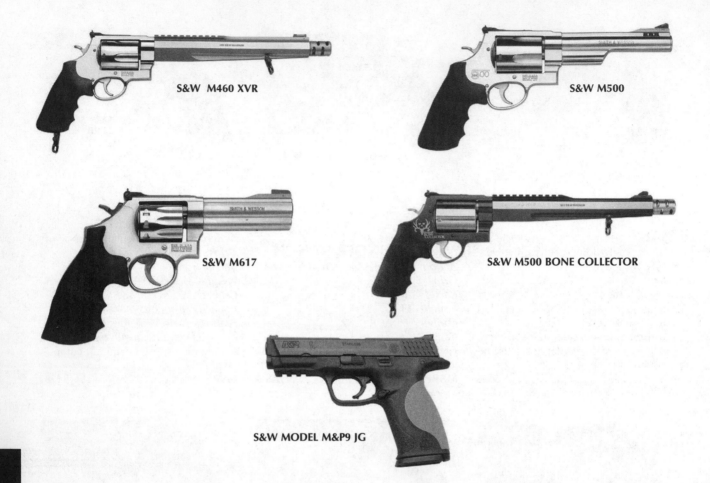

S&W M460 XVR

S&W M500

S&W M617

S&W M500 BONE COLLECTOR

S&W MODEL M&P9 JG

## M460 XVR
**Action**: Single/double action revolver
**Grips**: Synthetic
**Barrel**: 10.5 in.
**Weight**: 82.5 oz.
**Caliber**: .460 S&W Mag.
**Capacity**: 5-rounds
**Features**: Satin stainless finish; stainless steel frame and cylinder; X-large-size frame; exposed tear drop chrome hammer; .312 chrome trigger; multi-caliber capability: .454 Casull, .45 Colt; integral Weaver base for optic mounting.
**MSRP** . . . . . . . . . . . . . . . . . . . $1519

## M500
**Action**: SA/DA action revolver
**Grips**: Synthetic
**Barrel**: 6.5 in.
**Weight**: 60.7 oz.
**Caliber**: .500 S&W Mag.
**Capacity**: 5-rounds
**Features**: Stainless steel frame and cyl-

inder; stain stainless finish; integral compensator; internal lock; recoil tamed with effective muzzle compensator.
**MSRP** . . . . . . . . . . . . . . . . . . $1249

## M 500 BONE COLLECTOR
**Action**: Single/double action revolver
**Grips**: Synthetic
**Barrel**: 10.5 in.
**Weight**: 82 oz.
**Caliber**: .500 S&W Mag.
**Capacity**: 5-rounds
**Features**: Stainless steel frame and cylinder; X-large frame with exposed hammer; limited run of 1,000 pieces; two-tone finish.
**MSRP** . . . . . . . . . . . . . . . . . . $1389

## M617
**Action**: Single/double-action K-frame revolver

**Grips**: Synthetic
**Barrel**: 4 in.
**Weight**: 38.9 oz.
**Caliber**: .22 LR
**Capacity**: 10-rounds
**Features**: Stainless steel frame and cylinder with satin stainless finish; medium-size frame with exposed hammer.
**MSRP** . . . . . . . . . . . . . . . . . . . $829

## MODEL M&P9 JG
**Action**: Autoloader, striker fire action
**Grips**: Interchangable palm swell grip sizes, black and pink
**Barrel**: 4.25 in.
**Weight**: 24 oz.
**Caliber**: 9mm
**Capacity**: 17+1 rounds
**Features**: Polymer frame; stainless steel barrel and slide; black melonite finish; breast cancer awareness ribbon engraved on slide; designed in collaboration with Julie Goloski-Golob.
**MSRP** . . . . . . . . . . . . . . . . . . . $619

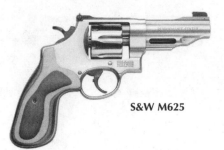

**S&W M625**

**S&W M629**

**S&W M629 V-COMP**

**S&W M640**

**S&W M686**

**S&W M686 SSR**

## M625
*Action*: SA/DA revolver
*Grips*: Hogue combat laminate, red, white & blue
*Barrel*: 4 in.
*Weight*: 42 oz.
*Caliber*: .45 ACP
*Capacity*: 6-rounds
*Features*: Stainless steel frame and cylinder with satin stainless finish; deep cut broached rifling; chambered charge holes; PC trigger with stop.
*MSRP* . . . . . . . . . . . . . . . . . $1049

## M625 JM
*Action*: SA/DA revolver
*Grips*: Jerry Miculek wood
*Barrel*: 4 in.
*Weight*: 40.3 oz.
*Caliber*: .45 ACP
*Capacity*: 6-rounds
*Features*: Stainless steel frame and cylinder; matte stainless; large-size frame; exposed hammer; Miculek style .265 wide grooved speed trigger; low reflection bead blast finish.
*MSRP* . . . . . . . . . . . . . . . . . $979

## M629
*Action*: SA/DA revolver
*Grips*: Synthetic

*Barrel*: 5 in.
*Weight*: 44.3 oz.
*Caliber*: .44 Mag., .44 S&W Special
*Capacity*: 6-rounds
*Features*: Stainless steel frame and cylinder with satin stainless finish; exposed hammer.
*MSRP* . . . . . . . . . . . . . . . . . $989

## M629 V-COMP
*Action*: SA/DA revolver
*Grips*: Synthetic
*Barrel*: 4 in.
*Weight*: 40.3 oz.
*Caliber*: .44 Mag., .44 S&W Special
*Capacity*: 6-rounds
*Features*: Stainless steel frame and cylinder with matte finish; removable compensator and cap muzzle protector; chambered charge holes; ball detent lock-up; chromed hammer and trigger with overtravel stop.
*MSRP* . . . . . . . . . . . . . . . . . $1509

## M640
*Action*: Double-action revolver
*Grips*: Synthetic
*Barrel*: 2.1 in.
*Weight*: 23 oz.
*Caliber*: .357 Mag., .38 S&W Special +P
*Capacity*: 5-rounds

*Features*: Stainless steel frame and cylinder; satin stainless finish.
*MSRP* . . . . . . . . . . . . . . . . . $729

## M686
*Action*: Revolver
*Grips*: Synthetic
*Barrel*: 2.5 in.
*Weight*: 34.7 oz.
*Caliber*: .357 Mag., .38 S&W Special +P
*Capacity*: 6-rounds
*Features*: Stainless steel frame and cylinder; satin stainless finish; exposed hammer; single and double-action; built on L frame.
*MSRP* . . . . . . . . . . . . . . . . . $829

## M686 SSR
*Action*: Revolver
*Grips*: Wood
*Barrel*: 4 in.
*Weight*: 38.3 oz.
*Caliber*: .357 Mag., .38 S&W Special +P
*Capacity*: 6-rounds
*Features*: Stainless steel frame and barrel with satin finish; exposed hammer; chambered charge holes; bossed mainspring; ergonomic grip to force high-hand hold; custom barrel with recessed precision crown.
*MSRP* . . . . . . . . . . . . . . . . . $969

**HANDGUNS**

# Smith & Wesson Handguns

**S&W M945**

**S&W M&P 9MM**

**S&W M&P 45**

**S&W M&P 40 COMPACT**

**S&W M&P 357**

## M945
**Action**: Autoloader
**Grips**: Wood
**Barrel**: 5 in.
**Weight**: 40.9 oz.
**Caliber**: .45 ACP
**Capacity**: 8+1 rounds
**Features**: Stainless steel frame and slide; serrated match hammer; single-action; competition match with travel overstop; two-tone finish; beveled magazine well.
MSRP . . . . . . . . . . . . . . . . . . $2410

## M&P 9MM
**Action**: Autoloader
**Grips**: Polymer
**Barrel**: 4.25 in.
**Weight**: 24 oz.
**Caliber**: 9mm
**Capacity**: 17+1 rounds
**Features**: Zytel polymer frame, stainless steel barrel/slide and structural components; optional Tritium sights; black Melonite finish.
MSRP . . . . . . . . . . . . . . . . . . $569

## M&P 45
**Action**: Autoloader
**Grips**: Polymer
**Barrel**: 4.5 in.
**Weight**: 29.6 oz.
**Caliber**: .45 ACP
**Capacity**: 10+1 rounds
**Features**: Zytel polymer frame, stainless steel barrel/slide and structural components; black Melonite finish; CA compliant; 3 interchangable palm-swell grip sizes.
MSRP . . . . . . . . . . . . . . . . . . $619

## M&P 40 COMPACT
**Action**: Autoloader
**Grips**: Polymer
**Barrel**: 3.5 in.
**Weight**: 21.9 oz.
**Caliber**: .40 S&W
**Capacity**: 10-rounds
**Features**: 3 interchangable palm swell grip sizes; black Melonite; thumb safety.
MSRP . . . . . . . . . . . . . . . . . . $569

## M&P 357
**Action**: Autoloader
**Grips**: Polymer
**Barrel**: 4.25 in.
**Weight**: 25.5 oz.
**Caliber**: .357 Auto
**Capacity**: 15-rounds
**Features**: 3 interchangable palm swell grip sizes; black Melonite; thumb safety; polymer frame/stainless steel barrel and slide.
MSRP . . . . . . . . . . . . . . . . . . $727

## M&P R8
**Action**: Autoloader
**Grips**: Polymer
**Barrel**: 5 in.
**Weight**: 36.3 oz.
**Caliber**: .357 Mag., .38 S&W Special +P
**Capacity**: 8-rounds
**Features**: Single or double action; scandium alloy frame; stainless steel cylinder; integral accessory Picatinny style rail; precision barrel forcing cone.
MSRP . . . . . . . . . . . . . . . . . . $1289

# Smith & Wesson Handguns

**S&W M SW1911 PD**

**S&W BODYGUARD 38**

**S&W BODYGUARD 380**

**HANDGUNS**

## M SW1911

*Action*: Autoloader
*Grips*: Wood
*Barrel*: 4.25 in.
*Weight*: 29.6 oz.
*Caliber*: .45 ACP
*Capacity*: 7+1 rounds
*Features*: Single-action; scandium alloy frame; stainless steel slide; two-tone finish; compact extended slide.
**MSRP**. . . . . . . . . . . . . . . . . . **$1139**

## M SW1911 PD

*Action*: Autoloader
*Grips*: Herrett's tactical oval walnut stocks with gunsite and S&W logos
*Barrel*: 4.25 in.

*Caliber*: .45 ACP
*Capacity*: 8+1 rounds
*Features*: Black Melonite finish; scandium alloy frame; stainless steel slide; beveled edges for carry use; solid match aluminum trigger; GI spec recoil guide; non-reflective, black matte finish.
**MSRP**. . . . . . . . . . . . . . . . . . **$1229**

## BODYGUARD 38

*Action*: DA revolver
*Grips*: Matte black synthetic
*Barrel*: 1.9 in.
*Weight*: 4.3 oz.
*Caliber*: .38 S&W Special +P
*Capacity*: 5-rounds

*Features*: Stainless steel cylinder with PVD coating.
**MSRP**. . . . . . . . . . . . . . . . . . **$509**

## BODYGUARD 380

*Action*: DA autoloader
*Grips*: Polymer
*Barrel*: 2.75 in.
*Weight*: 11.85 oz.
*Caliber*: .380 Auto
*Capacity*: 6+1 rounds
*Features*: Manual thumb safety external takedown lever; external slide stop; barrel and slide stainless with Melonite finish; integrated Insight laser sighting system.
**MSRP**. . . . . . . . . . . . . . . . . . **$399**

# Springfield Armory Handguns

## EMP ENHANCED MICRO PISTOL

*Action*: Autoloader
*Grips*: Thinline cocobolo hardwood
*Barrel*: 3 in.
*Weight*: 26 oz.
*Caliber*: 9mm
*Capacity*: 3–9 rounds
*Features*: Forged stainless steel, satin finish; dual spring recoil system with full length guide rod.
MSRP . . . . . . . . . . . . . . $1345–$1424

## RANGE OFFICER

*Action*: Autoloader
*Grips*: Cocobolo
*Barrel*: 5 in.
*Weight*: 40 oz.
*Caliber*: .45 ACP
*Capacity*: 2–7 rounds
*Features*: Standard guide rod; forged steel frame with blued finish; stainless match grade barrel.
MSRP . . . . . . . . . . . . . . . . . . $939

## GI FULL SIZED

*Action*: Autoloader
*Grips*: US engraved, hardwood
*Barrel*: 5 in.
*Weight*: 39 oz.
*Caliber*: .45 ACP
*Capacity*: 5–7 rounds
*Features*: Forged steel, Parkerized frame and slide; GI style recoil system; standard ejection port; arched mainspring housing with lanyard loop.
MSRP . . . . . . . . . . . . . . . . . . $656

## LOADED MICRO-COMPACT

*Action*: Autoloader
*Grips*: Thinline cocobolo hardwood
*Barrel*: 3 in.
*Weight*: 26 oz.
*Caliber*: .45 ACP
*Capacity*: 2–6 rounds
*Features*: Stainless steel match grade, fully supported ramped bull barrel; forged aluminum alloy with integral accessory rail frame; black hardcoat anodized; dual spring with full length guide rod.
MSRP . . . . . . . . . . . . . . . . . . $1349

## LIGHTWEIGHT CHAMPION OPERATOR

*Action*: Autoloader
*Grips*: Cocobolo hardwood
*Barrel*: 4 in.
*Weight*: 31 oz.
*Caliber*: .45 ACP
*Capacity*: 2–7 rounds
*Features*: Stainless steel match grade, fully supported ramped bull barrel; long aluminum match grade trigger; forged aluminum alloy with integral accessory rail; black hardcoat anodized; dual spring with full length guide rod.
MSRP . . . . . . . . . . . . . . . . . . $1011

SPRINGFIELD ARMORY EMP ENHANCED MICRO PISTOL

SPRINGFIELD ARMORY RANGE OFFICER

SPRINGFIELD ARMORY GI FULL SIZED

SPRINGFIELD ARMORY LIGHTWEIGHT CHAMPION OPERATOR

HANDGUNS

# Springfield Armory Handguns

## MIL-SPEC FULL SIZE STAINLESS

*Action*: Autoloader
*Grips*: Cocobolo hardwood and black plastic
*Barrel*: 5 in.
*Weight*: 39 oz.
*Caliber*: .45 ACP
*Capacity*: 2–7 rounds
*Features*: Forged stainless steel, matte-rounds with polished flats; GI style recoil system.
MSRP.....................$843

## LOADED FULL SIZE TROPHY MATCH STAINLESS STEEL

*Action*: Autoloader
*Grips*: Cocobolo hardwood
*Barrel*: 5 in.
*Weight*: 40 oz.
*Caliber*: .45 ACP
*Capacity*: 2–7 rounds
*Features*: Wide-mouth magazine well; tuned trigger; checkered front strap; forged stainless steel frame; 2 piece full length guide rod.
MSRP...................$1605

## TRP (TACTICAL RESPONSE PISTOL)

*Action*: Autoloader
*Grips*: G10 Composite
*Barrel*: 5 in.
*Weight*: 42 oz.
*Caliber*: .45 ACP
*Capacity*: 2–7 rounds
*Features*: Forged steel frame with black Armory Kote; 2 piece full length guide rod; wide-mouth magazine well; tuned trigger.
MSRP...................$1777

## USA XD (M)

*Action*: DA autoloader
*Grips*: Polymer
*Barrel*: 3.8 in. or 4.5 in. match-grade
*Weight*: 28 oz. (29–30 oz. in 4.5 in.)
*Caliber*: 9mm, .40 S&W
*Capacity*: 19 (9mm), 16 (.40 S&W)
*Features*: "M" features include carrying case, two magazines, paddle holster, mag. loader, double mag. pouch and 3 interchangable backstraps and two magazines. "All-Terrain" texture and deep slide serrations are standard.
9mm:.................$697–$815
40 S&W:..............$697–$876

**SPRINGFIELD ARMORY MIL-SPEC FULL SIZE STAINLESS**

**SPRINGFIELD ARMORY LOADED FULL SIZE TROPHY MATCH STAINLESS STEEL**

**SPRINGFIELD ARMORY TRP ARMORY KOTE**

HANDGUNS

# STI International Handguns

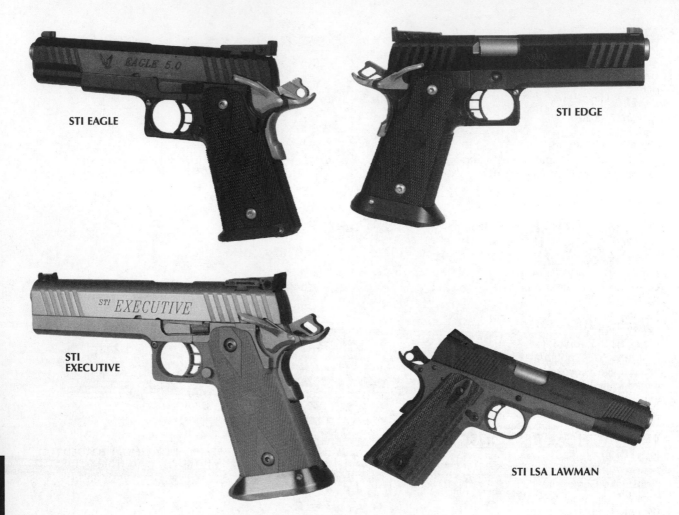

STI EAGLE

STI EDGE

STI EXECUTIVE

STI LSA LAWMAN

## EAGLE 5.0

*Action*: Autoloader
*Grips*: STI patented modular polymer
*Barrel*: 5 in.
*Weight*: 33.5 oz.
*Caliber*: 9mm, .357 Sig, .38 Super, .40 S&W, .45 ACP
*Capacity*: 10+1 rounds
*Features*: Stainless STI grip, ambi thumb, ramped bull barrel; STI patented modular steel frame; STI rear serrations; blue finish.
**MSRP** . . . . . . . . . . . . . . . . **$1944.25**

## EDGE

*Action*: Autoloader
*Grips*: STI patented modular polymer with aluminum magwell
*Barrel*: 5 in.
*Weight*: 38.5 oz.
*Caliber*: 9mm, .38 Super, .40 S&W, .45ACP
*Capacity*: 6+1 rounds
*Features*: STI fully supported, ramped bull barrel; stainless STI grip and ambi slided thumb; STI recoil master guide rod; blue finish.
**MSRP** . . . . . . . . . . . . . . . . **$1994**

## EXECUTIVE

*Action*: Autoloader
*Grips*: STI Patented modular polymer with stainless magwell
*Barrel*: 5 in.
*Weight*: 39.5 oz.
*Caliber*: .40 S&W
*Capacity*: 10+1 rounds
*Features*: Stainless STI grip, ambi thumb, ramped bull barrel; STI patent-ed modular steel, long wide frame; STI rear serrations; blue finish.
**MSRP** . . . . . . . . . . . . . . . . . **$2464**

## LAWMAN

*Action*: Autoloader
*Grips*: Color matched polymer panels
*Barrel*: 5 in.
*Weight*: 37 oz.
*Caliber*: .45 ACP
*Capacity*: 6+1 rounds
*Features*: STI blue grip and single sided thumb safety, STI high rise bea-vertail; STI one piece full length guide rod; black finish is traditional blued, two tone finish is polymer coated.
**MSRP** . . . . . . . . . . . . . . . . . **$1419**

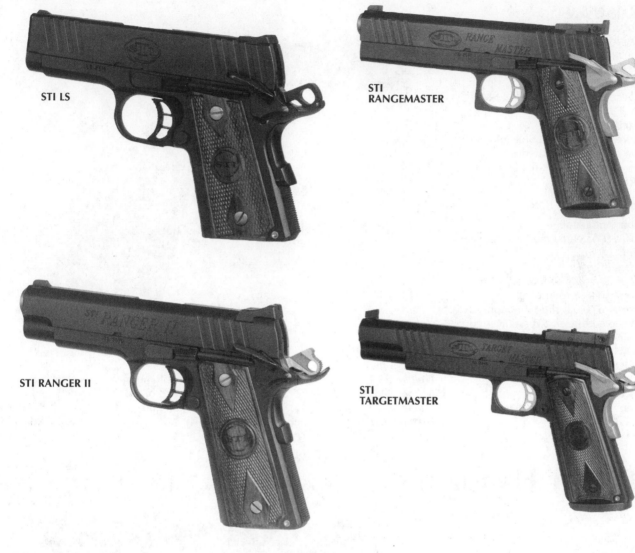

**STI LS**

**STI RANGEMASTER**

**STI RANGER II**

**STI TARGETMASTER**

## LS
*Action*: Autoloader
*Grips*: Rosewood Thin Panels
*Barrel*: 3.4 in.
*Weight*: 28 oz.
*Caliber*: 9mm
*Capacity*: 6+1 rounds
*Features*: STI compact, steel, stippled front strap; STI bullet style front and rear serrations; STI Recoil Master guide rod; flat blue finish.
**MSRP**................**$991.61**

## RANGEMASTER
*Action*: Autoloader
*Grips*: STI logo, checkered, cocobolo, standard thickness
*Barrel*: 5 in.
*Weight*: 41.2 oz.

*Caliber*: 9mm, .45 ACP
*Capacity*: N/A
*Features*: STI long curved trigger; ramped bull barrel; STI polished stainless grip and ambi thumb; STI recoil-master guide rod; matte blue finish.
**MSRP**................. **$1521**

## RANGER II
*Action*: Autoloader
*Grips*: STI logo, checkered, cocobolo, thin
*Barrel*: 4.15 in.
*Weight*: 33oz.
*Caliber*: 9mm, .40 S&W, .45 ACP
*Capacity*: 7+1 rounds
*Features*: STI long curved trigger with stainless bow; STI Hi-Rise blue grip and

single sided thumb safeties; blue finish.
**MSRP**................. **$1110**

## TARGETMASTER
*Action*: Autoloader
*Grips*: STI logo, checkered, cocobolo, standard thickness
*Barrel*: 6 in.
*Weight*: 44 oz.
*Caliber*: 9mm, .45 ACP
*Capacity*: N/A
*Features*: STI long curved trigger; STI stainless grip and ambi sided thumb; STI two piece rail guide rod; matte blue finish.
**MSRP**................. **$1695**

HANDGUNS

# STI International Handguns

### TROJAN 5.0

**Action**: Autoloader
**Grips**: STI logo, checkered, cocobolo, thin
**Barrel**: 5 in.
**Weight**: 36 oz.
**Caliber**: 9mm, .38 Super, .40 S&W, .45ACP
**Capacity**: N/A
**Features**: STI standard blue grip and single slided thumb safeties; STI one piece steel guide rod; flat blue finish.
**MSRP**.................... **$1110**

### VIP

**Action**: Autoloader
**Grips**: STI patented modular polymer
**Barrel**: 3.9 in.
**Weight**: 30 oz.
**Caliber**: 9mm, .40 S&W, .45 ACP
**Capacity**: 10+1 rounds
**Features**: STI rear slide serrations; STI long curved trigger; STI stainless grip and single sided thumb; matte blue slide with blue steel frame.
**MSRP**.................. **$1645.85**

### ECLIPSE

**Action**: SA autoloader
**Grips**: Black polymer

**STI VIP**

**Barrel**: 3 in. ramped, bull contour
**Weight**: 23.1 oz.
**Caliber**: .45 ACP, .40 S&W
**Capacity**: 10-rounds
**Features**: 2011 double stack pistol; double-column magazine; steel frame; singlesided blued thumb safety and beavertail grip safety.
**MSRP**.................... **$1825**

# Stoeger Handguns

### COUGAR

**Action**: SA/DA action
**Grips**: Black plastic
**Barrel**: 3.6 in.
**Weight**: 32 oz.–32.5 oz.
**Caliber**: .45 ACP, .40 S&W, 9mm
**Capacity**: 8+1, 11+1, 15+1 rounds
**Features**: Ambidextrous safety; rotary-locking principal: available in a non-glare Bruniton silver steel slide with an anodized alloy matte-silver frame or two-tone style, featuring a matte Bruniton black steel slide combined with an anodized alloy matte-silver frame.
**MSRP**................ **$449–$499**

**STOEGER COUGAR**

# Swiss Arms Handguns

## P210

**Action**: Single-action autoloader
**Grips**: Custom wood
**Barrel**: 4.7 in.
**Weight**: 37.4 oz.
**Caliber**: 9mm
**Capacity**: 8-rounds
**Features**: Durable nitron frame and slide finish; chrome-moly barrel; carbon steel slide; frame machined from solid billet steel; slide magazine release.
**MSRP** . . . . . . . . . . . . . . . . . . **$2199**

SWISS ARMS P210

# Taurus Handguns

## M22 PLY/M25 PLY

**Action**: Double-action autoloading, recoil operated
**Grips**: Polymer
**Barrel**: 2.3 in.
**Weight**: 10.8 oz.
**Caliber**: .22 LR
**Capacity**: 8+1-, 9+1 rounds
**Features**: Polymer/blue steel construction; blue steel finish; tip-up barrel.
**MSRP** . . . . . . . . . . **Price on Request**

TAURUS M22 PLY

## M709 SLIM

**Action**: SA/DA autoloading, recoil operated
**Grips**: Checkered polymer
**Barrel**: 3 in.
**Weight**: 19 oz.
**Caliber**: 9mm
**Capacity**: 7+1 rounds
**Features**: Blue and matte stainless steel finish.
**MSRP** . . . . . . . . . . . . . . . . . . . . **$498**

## M738 TCP

**Action**: Double-action autoloader
**Grips**: Checkered polymer
**Barrel**: 2.84 in.
**Weight**: 9 oz.
**Caliber**: .380 ACP
**Capacity**: 6+1 rounds
**Features**: Titanium construction; compact frame; smooth trigger.
**MSRP** . . . . . . . . . . . . . . . . . . . . **$453**

TAURUS M738 TCP

# Taurus Handguns

**TAURUS JUDGE PUBLIC DEFENDER**

**TAURUS 24-7 OSS STAINLESS STEEL**

**TAURUS M709 B**

**TAURUS M856**

**TAURUS M24-7**

**TAURUS M44SS6**

HANDGUNS

## JUDGE PUBLIC DEFENDER

**Action**: Double-action revolver
**Grips**: Rubber
**Barrel**: 2.5 in.
**Weight**: 28.2 oz.
**Caliber**: .45/.410
**Capacity**: 5-rounds
**Features**: Blue finish; firing pin block, transfer bar; available in carbon steel or stainless steel frame with the option of a titanium cylinder; features a reduced profile hammer.
**MSRP** . . . . . . . . . . . . . . . . . . . . **$570**

## 24/7 OSS STAINLESS STEEL

**Action**: SA/DA action autoloader
**Grips**: Rubber grip overlay
**Barrel**: 4 in.
**Weight**: 28.2 oz.
**Caliber**: .40
**Capacity**: 15+1 rounds
**Features**: Firing pin block; manual safety; trigger block; polymer steel construction with stainless steel finish.
**MSRP** . . . . . . . . . . . . . . . . . . . . **$514**

## M709 B

**Action**: Autoloader
**Grips**: Checkered polymer
**Barrel**: 3 in.
**Weight**: 19 oz.
**Caliber**: 9mm
**Capacity**: 7+1 rounds
**Features**: Steel construction; blue finish; single and double action.
**MSRP** . . . . . . . . . . . . . . . . . . . . **$483**

## M856

**Action**: Revolver
**Grips**: Rubber
**Barrel**: 2 in.
**Weight**: 13.2 oz.–22 oz.
**Caliber**: .38 Special, .38 Special +P
**Capacity**: 6-rounds
**Features**: Offered in several configurations including a Hy-Lite magnesium model in .38 special and standard version (.38 special +P) in blue or matte stainless; Taurus security system allows users to securely lock the gun.
**MSRP** . . . . . . . . . . . . . . . . **$441–$492**

## M24/7

**Action**: Autoloader
**Grips**: Rubber grip overlay
**Barrel**: 4 in.
**Weight**: 27.2 oz.
**Caliber**: .40
**Capacity**: 10+1-rounds
**Features**: Double-action; firing pin block; manual safety; trigger block; polymer/steel construction with blue finish.
**MSRP** . . . . . . . . . . . . . . . . . . . . **$475**

## M44

**Action**: Autoloader
**Grips**: Soft rubber
**Barrel**: 4 in., 6.5 in., 8.4 in.
**Weight**: 45 oz.–57oz.
**Caliber**: .44 Mag.
**Capacity**: 6-rounds
**Features**: Transfer bar; ported barrel; matte stainless steel finish; double and single-action.
**4 in.**: . . . . . . . . . . . . . . . . . . . **$650**
**6.5 in.**: . . . . . . . . . . . . . . . . . . **$666**
**8.4 in.**: . . . . . . . . . . . . . . . . . . **$666**

## M82

**Action**: Autoloader
**Grips**: Rubber
**Barrel**: 4 in.
**Weight**: 36.5 oz.
**Caliber**: .38 SPL +P
**Capacity**: 6-rounds
**Features**: Transfer bar; steel construction with blue finish; single/double-action trigger.
**MSRP** . . . . . . . . . . . . . . . . . . . . **$424**

# Taurus Handguns

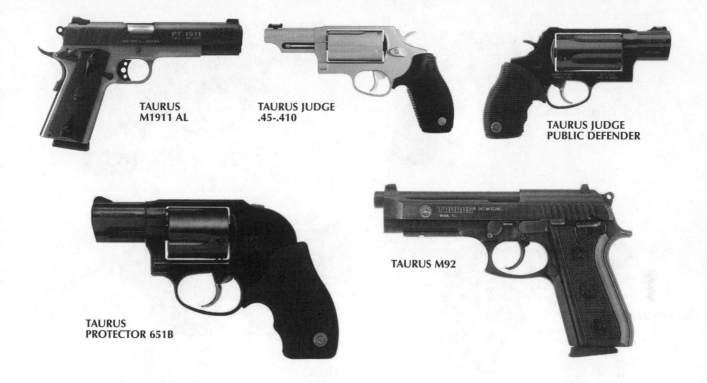

**TAURUS M1911 AL**

**TAURUS JUDGE .45-.410**

**TAURUS JUDGE PUBLIC DEFENDER**

**TAURUS M92**

**TAURUS PROTECTOR 651B**

## M1911 AL
*Action*: Autoloader
*Grips*: Checkered black
*Barrel*: 5 in.
*Weight*: 33 oz.
*Caliber*: .45 ACP
*Capacity*: 8+1 rounds
*Features*: Steel/alloy construction with blue/gray finish; single-action; forged slide and frame; ventilated trigger type.
**MSRP . . . . . . . . . . . . . . . . . . . . $837**

## JUDGE .45/.410
*Action*: Double/Single-action revolver
*Grips*: Taurus Ribber Grips
*Barrel*: 3 in.
*Weight*: 29 oz.
*Caliber*: .45/.410
*Capacity*: 5-rounds
*Features*: Firing pin block, transfer bar safety; compact frame; matte stainless steel finish; steel construction.
**MSRP . . . . . . . . . . . . . . . . . . . . $592**

## JUDGE PUBLIC DEFENDER
*Action*: Revolver
*Grips*: Rubber
*Barrel*: 2 in.
*Sights*: Fixed

*Weight*: 26oz.
*Caliber*: .410 GA/ .45 LC
*Capacity*: 5-rounds
*Features*: Titanium construction; blue steel finish; carbon steel and stainless steel frame; double and single-action; optional titanium cylinder; features a reduced profile hammer.
**MSRP . . . . . . . . . . . . . . . . . . . $570**

## PROTECTOR 651B
*Action*: Double/single action revolver
*Grips*: Rubber, polymer
*Barrel*: 2 in.
*Weight*: 19.7 oz.–25 oz.
*Caliber*: .357 Mag.
*Capacity*: 5-rounds
*Features*: Stainless steel construction; blue finish or matte stainless steel finish; single and double action.
**Blue, Steel: . . . . . . . . . . . . . . $433**
**Stainless, Polymer: . . . . . . . . $461**
**Stainless, Steel: . . . . . . . . . . . $480**

## M92
*Action*: Autoloader
*Grips*: Checkered rubber or rosewood
*Barrel*: 5 in.
*Weight*: 34 oz.

*Caliber*: 9mm
*Capacity*: 10+1 rounds
*Features*: Blue, stainless steel with gold or stainless finish; steel/alloy construction; firing pin block, hammer decocker, manual safety.
**Rubber grips, Blue steel: . . . . . $571**
**Rubber grips, Stainless: . . . . . . $589**
**Rosewood, Stainless: . . . . . . . . $670**

## MODEL 94/941
*Action*: Revolver
*Grips*: Rubber
*Barrel*: 2 in.
*Weight*: 24 oz.
*Caliber*: .22 Mag. .22 LR
*Capacity*: 8-, 9-rounds
*Features*: Steel construction; blue or matte stainless steel finish; single and double action; transfer bar.
**Blue: . . . . . . . . . . . . . . . . . . . . $405**
**Magnum, Blue: . . . . . . . . . . . . $430**
**Stainless: . . . . . . . . . . . . . . . . $477**
**Magnum, Stainless Steel: . . . . $477**

**HANDGUNS**

# Taurus Handguns

**TAURUS M608**

**TAURUS M905**

**TAURUS 22B**

Tip-up Barrel

**TAURUS MILLENNIUM PRO BP**

## M605 B2

**Action**: Revolver
**Grips**: Rubber
**Barrel**: 2 in.
**Weight**: 24 oz.
**Caliber**: .357 Mag.
**Capacity**: 5-rounds
**Features**: Transfer bar safety; steel construction with blue finish; single-double action trigger.
**MSRP** . . . . . . . . . . . . . . . . . . . . . **$424**

## M608

**Action**: Revolver
**Grips**: Rubber
**Barrel**: 4 in., 6.5 in., 8.4 in.
**Weight**: 44 oz.–51 oz.
**Caliber**: .357 Mag.
**Capacity**: 8-rounds
**Features**: Matte stainless steel finish; transfer bar; large frame; steel frame; Taurus security system; porting.
**Stainless, 4 in.:** . . . . . . . . . . . **$615**
**Stainless, 6.5 in. or 8.4 in.:** . . . **$641**

## M905

**Action**: Revolver

**Grips**: Rubber
**Barrel**: 2 in.
**Weight**: 22.2 oz.
**Caliber**: 9mm
**Capacity**: 5-rounds
**Features**: Blue finish; transfer bar; steel frame; porting; Taurus security system.
**Blue:** . . . . . . . . . . . . . . . . . . . **$443**
**Stainless Steel:** . . . . . . . . . . . **$480**

## M22B

**Action**: Autoloader
**Grips**: Checkered-wood
**Barrel**: 2.75 in.
**Weight**: 12.3 oz.
**Caliber**: .22 LR
**Capacity**: 8+1 rounds
**Features**: Steel/alloy frame with blue finish; manual safety; tip-up barrel; Taurus security system.
**MSRP** . . . . . . . . . . . . . . . . . . . . **$262**

## M945

**Action**: Autoloader
**Grips**: Checkered rubber, rosewood, mother of pearl

**Barrel**: 4.25 in.
**Weight**: 29.5 oz.
**Caliber**: .45 ACP
**Capacity**: 8+1 rounds
**Features**: Steel/alloy frame; blue, or stainless steel finish with or without gold; firing pin block; hammer decocker; manual safety; loaded chamber indicator.
**Blue:** . . . . . . . . . . . . . . . . . . . **$658**
**Stainless Steel:** . . . . . . . . . . . . **$674**
**Rosewood, Stainless
Steel/Gold:** . . . . . . . . . . . . . . **$727**
**Mother of Pearl:** . . . . . . . . . . **$743**

## MILLENNIUM PRO BP

**Action**: Autoloader
**Grips**: Checkered polymer
**Barrel**: 3.25 in.
**Weight**: 18.7 oz.
**Caliber**: 9mm
**Capacity**: 10+1 rounds
**Features**: Firing pin block; manual safety; polymer/steel frame with blue finish; loaded chamber indicator; Taurus security system.
**MSRP** . . . . . . . . . . . . . . . . . . . . **$441**

## RAGING BULL 416 SS6

*Action*: Revolver
*Grips*: Rubber w/cushioned Insert
*Barrel*: 6.5 in.
*Weight*: 53 oz.
*Caliber*: .41 Mag.
*Capacity*: 6-rounds
*Features*: Steel construction with stainless steel finish; transfer bar; dual lock-up cylinder; porting; Taurus security system.
**MSRP** . . . . . . . . . . . . . . . . . . . **$780**

## TRACKER

*Action*: Revolver
*Grips*: Rubber with ribs
*Barrel*: 4 in.
*Weight*: 34oz.–34.8oz.
*Caliber*: .41 Mag., .44 Mag.
*Capacity*: 5-rounds
*Features*: Matte stainless steel finish; transfer bar; steel frame; porting.
**.41 Mag.:** . . . . . . . . . . . . . . . . . **$597**
**.44 Mag., Blue:** . . . . . . . . . . . . **$581**
**.44 Mag., Stainless:** . . . . . . . . . **$632**

## M24/7 G2

*Action*: DA/SA autoloader
*Grips*: Checkered polymer with metallic inserts, and 3 interchangable backstraps
*Barrel*: 4.2 in.
*Weight*: 28 oz.
*Caliber*: 9mm, .40, .45 ACP
*Capacity*: 15 (9mm), 13 (.40), 10 (.45 ACP)
*Features*: Blued or stainless steel; DA/SA trigger system; SA or DA only; contoured thumb rests; Picatinny accessory rail.
**MSRP** . . . . . . . . . . . . . . . . . . . **$498**

## 740 SLIM /SLIM 708

*Action*: DA/SA autoloader
*Grips*: Polymer metallic inserts
*Barrel*: 3.2 in.
*Weight*: 19 oz.
*Caliber*: .380 ACP or .40
*Capacity*: 7 (.380), 6 (.40)
*Features*: Sub-compact pistol in blued or stainless steel; loaded chamber indicator; low-profile sights; short, crisp DA/SA trigger pull.
**MSRP** . . . . . . . . . . . . . . . . . . . **$483**

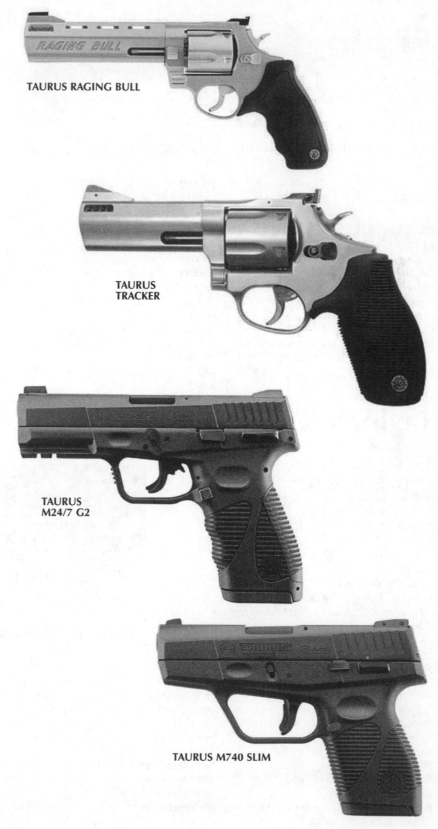

TAURUS RAGING BULL

TAURUS TRACKER

TAURUS M24/7 G2

TAURUS M740 SLIM

HANDGUNS

# Taurus Handguns

**TAURUS PUBLIC DEFENDER ULTRA-LITE**

**TAURUS PUBLIC DEFENDER POLYMER**

**TAURUS RAGING JUDGE MAGNUM**

### PUBLIC DEFENDER ULTRA-LITE

*Action*: DA revolver
*Grips*: Rubber
*Barrel*: 2.5 in.
*Weight*: 20.7 oz.
*Caliber*: .410 ga./.45LC
*Capacity*: 5-rounds
*Features*: Blue or stainless; generous profile hammer; fiber optic front sight.
**MSRP . . . . . . . . . . . . . . . . . . . . . $680**

### PUBLIC DEFENDER POLYMER

*Action*: DA revolver
*Grips*: Rubber
*Barrel*: 2.5 in.
*Weight*: 27 oz.
*Caliber*: .45/.410
*Capacity*: 5-rounds
*Features*: Newest version of the Judge; polymer frame, blued or stainless finish; target hammer and trigger; fires both .410 shotshells and .45 Colt ammunition.
**MSRP . . . . . . . . . . . . . . . . . . . . . $570**

### RAGING JUDGE MAGNUM

*Action*: DA revolver
*Grips*: Soft cushion insert
*Barrel*: 3 in. (or 6 in.)
*Weight*: 60.6oz. (72.7 oz. with 6 in. barrel)
*Caliber*: .410 ga./.45 LC/.454 Casull
*Capacity*: 6-rounds
*Features*: Stainless steel finish; "Raging Bull" backstrap for added cushioning.
**MSRP . . . . . . . . . . . . . . . . . . . . . $936**

# Taylor's & Company Handguns

### SMOKE WAGON

*Action*: Single-action revolver
*Grips*: Checkered wood
*Barrel*: 4.75 in., 5.5 in.
*Weight*: 2.5 lb.
*Caliber*: .38 Sp., .357 Mag., .45 LC, .44-40
*Capacity*: 6-rounds
*Features*: Low profile hammer; deluxe edition model includes custom tuning, cutom hammer and base pin springs; jig-cut positive angles on trigger and sears; wire bolt and trigger springs.
**Standard: . . . . . . . . . . . . . . . . . $485**
**Deluxe: . . . . . . . . . . . . . . . . . $620**

**TAYLOR'S & COMPANY SMOKE WAGON**

### RUNNIN' IRON

*Action*: SA revolver
*Grips*: Checkered walnut
*Barrel*: 3.5 in. to 5.5 in.
*Weight*: 39 oz.
*Caliber*: .45 LC or .357 Mag.
*Capacity*: 6-rounds
*Features*: Designed for the sport of mounted shooting; offered in stainless or blue finish with low, wide hammer spur; checkered, one-piece gunfighter style grips in walnut or black polymer; wide trigger and extra clearance at front and rear of cylinder.
**Stainless w/wood grips: . . . . . . $780**
**Blue w/wood grips: . . . . . . . . . $650**
**Stainless w/black polymer grips: . . . . . . . . . . . . $810**

**TAYLOR'S & COMPANY RUNNIN' IRON BLUE FINISH**

HANDGUNS

# Thompson/Center Handguns

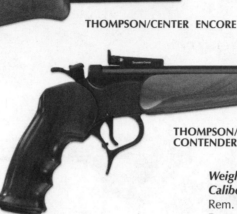

THOMPSON/CENTER ENCORE

THOMPSON/CENTER G2
CONTENDER 12IN.

## ENCORE

**Action**: Single shot, break open design
**Grips**: Walnut or rubber
**Barrel**: 12 or 15 in.
**Weight**: 4.25 lb.–4.5 lb.
**Caliber**: 204 Ruger, 223 Rem., 22-250 Rem., 243 Win., 25-06 Rem., 270 Win., 7mm-08 Rem., 308 Win., 30-06 Sprg., 45-70 Govt., 44 Rem. Mag., 45 Colt/410, 17 HMR, 22 LR, 460 S&W, 500 S&W
**Capacity**: 1-round
**Features**: Interchangable barrels; button rifled; drilled and tapped for T/C scope mounts; adjustable trigger for overtravel; ambidextrous pistol grip

with finger grooves and butt cap; matching forend; blued or stainless steel finish; patented automatic hammer block with bolt interlock.
**MSRP:** . . . . . . . . . . . . . . . **$720–$768**

## G2 CONTENDER

**Action**: Single shot, break open design
**Grips**: Walnut or rubber
**Barrel**: 12 in. or 14 in.

**Weight**: 3.5 lb.–3.75 lb.
**Caliber**: .22 LR Match, .357 Mag., .44 Rem. Mag., .45/410 Vent Rib, .223 Rem., .17 HMR, .204 Ruger, .22 Hornet, 6.8 Rem., 7-30 Waters, 30/30 Win., 45/70 Gov't, 30-30 Win.
**Capacity**: 1-round
**Features**: 45/410 models include removable choke tube and wrench; stainless steel or walnut frame; manual firing pin selector; button rifled; drilled and tapped for T/C scope mounts.
**MSRP:** . . . . . . . . . . . . . . . . . . **$776**

## 1851 NAVY CONVERSION

**Action**: Single-action revolver
**Grips**: Walnut
**Barrel**: 4.75 in., 5.5 in., 7.5 in.
**Weight**: 2.6 lb.
**Caliber**: .38 Spl.
**Capacity**: 6-rounds
**Features**: Case-hardened frame octagonal barrel; brass backstrap and trigger guard; conversion revolver frames are retro-fitted with loading gates to accommodate metallic cartridges like the originals.
**MSRP**. . . . . . . . . . . . . . . . . . . **$539**

## 1860 ARMY CONVERSION

**Action**: Single-action revolver
**Grips**: Walnut
**Barrel**: 4.75 in., 5.5 in., 8 in.
**Weight**: 2.6 lb.
**Caliber**: .38 Spl., .45 Colt
**Capacity**: 6-rounds
**Features**: Case-hardened frame; round barrel; steel backstrap and trigger guard; conversion revolver frames are retro-fitted with loading gates to accommodate metallic cartridges like the originals.
**MSRP**. . . . . . . . . . . . . . . . . . . **$559**

# Uberti Handguns

UBERTI 1851 NAVY CONVERSION LG

UBERTI 1860 ARMY CONVERSION LG

# Uberti Handguns

UBERTI 1871-1872 OPEN-TOP

UBERTI 1873 CATTLEMAN
CHISHOLM

UBERTI 1873 STALLION STEEL
TARGET

### 1871-1872 OPEN-TOP
*Action*: Single-action revolver
*Grips*: Walnut
*Barrel*: 4.75 in., 5.5 in., 7.5 in.
*Weight*: 2.6 lb.
*Caliber*: .38 Spl., .45 Colt
*Capacity*: 6-rounds
*Features*: 1872 model has steel back-strap and trigger guard; 1871 model has brass backstrap and trigger guard; case-hardened frame; round barrel; blue finish conversion revolver frames are retro-fitted with loading gates to accommodate metallic cartridges like the originals.
1872: . . . . . . . . . . . . . . . . . . . . $539
1871: . . . . . . . . . . . . . . . . . . . . $509

### 1873 CATTLEMAN BIRD'S HEAD
*Action*: Single-action revolver
*Grips*: Walnut
*Barrel*: 3.5 in., 4.75 in., 5.5 in.
*Weight*: 2.2 lb.
*Caliber*: .45 Colt, .357 Mag.
*Capacity*: 6-rounds
*Features*: Case-hardened frame, steel backstrap and trigger guard; blue finish; bird head shape grip.
MSRP. . . . . . . . . . . . . . . . . . . . $559

### 1873 CATTLEMAN CHISHOLM
*Action*: Single-action revolver

*Grips*: Checkered walnut
*Barrel*: 4.75 in., 5.5 in.
*Weight*: 2.3 lb.
*Caliber*: .45 Colt
*Capacity*: 6-rounds
*Features*: Complete matte finished steel; fluted barrel.
MSRP. . . . . . . . . . . . . . . . . . . $539

### 1873 CATTLEMAN DESPERADO
*Action*: Single-action revolver
*Grips*: Bison horn-style
*Barrel*: 4.75 in., 5.5 in.
*Weight*: 2.3 lb.
*Caliber*: .45 Colt
*Capacity*: 6-rounds
*Features*: Full nickel plated steel; fluted barrel.
MSRP. . . . . . . . . . . . . . . . . . . $799

### 1873 SINGLE-ACTION CATTLEMAN
*Action*: Single-action revolver
*Grips*: Walnut
*Barrel*: 4.75 in., 5.5 in., 7.5 in.
*Weight*: 2.3 lb.
*Caliber*: .45 Colt, .44/40, .357 Mag.
*Capacity*: 6-rounds
*Features*: Case-hardened frame; brass or steel backstrap and trigger guard; blue, nickel or stainless steel finish; fluted barrel.

Blue, Brass: . . . . . . . . . . . . . . $489
Blue, Steel: . . . . . . . . . . . . . . $519
Nickel: . . . . . . . . . . . . . . . . . . $629
Stainless Steel: . . . . . . . . . . . . $679
Charcoal Blue: . . . . . . . . . . . . . $599
Calvalry & Artillery Cattleman: $649
Blue New Model: . . . . . . . $599–$639

### 1873 STALLION/STALLION TARGET
*Action*: Single-action revolver
*Grips*: Walnut
*Barrel*: 4.75 in., 5.5 in.
*Weight*: 2 lb.
*Caliber*: .22 LR, .22 LR/Mag.
*Capacity*: 6-rounds
*Features*: Case-hardened frame; brass or steel backstrap and trigger guard; blue finish; fluted barrel.
MSRP. . . . . . . . . . . . . . . . $429–$569

### 1875 OUTLAW & FRONTIER
*Action*: Single-action revolver
*Grips*: Walnut
*Barrel*: 5.5 in.(Frontier), 7.5 in.
*Weight*: 2.5 lb., 2.8 lb.
*Caliber*: .45 Colt
*Capacity*: 6-rounds
*Features*: Case-hardened or full nickel plated steel frame; steel backstrap and trigger guard; fluted barrel.
Outlaw: . . . . . . . . . . . . . . . . . . $549
Outlaw Nickel: . . . . . . . . . . . . $639
Frontier: . . . . . . . . . . . . . . . . . $549

# Uberti Handguns

## 1873 CATTLEMAN BISLEY

**Action**: Single-action revolver
**Grips**: Bisley target style walnut
**Barrel**: 4.75 in., 5.5 in.
**Weight**: 2.5 lb.
**Caliber**: .45 Colt, .357 Mag.
**Capacity**: 6-rounds
**Features**: Case-hardened frame; steel backstrap and trigger guard; blue finish; fluted barrel.
**MSRP** . . . . . . . . . . . . . . . . . . . **$589**

UBERTI 1873 CATTLEMAN BISLEY

## 1890 SINGLE ACTION POLICE REVOLVER

**Action**: Single-action revolver
**Grips**: Walnut with lanyard ring
**Barrel**: 5.5 in.
**Weight**: 2.6 lb.
**Caliber**: .45, .357 Mag.
**Capacity**: 6-rounds
**Features**: Blue steel frame, backstrap and trigger guard; fluted barrel.
**MSRP** . . . . . . . . . . . . . . . . . . . **$569**

UBERTI 1890 POLICE

## TOP BREAK REVOLVERS

**Action**: Single-action revolver
**Grips**: Walnut or pearl-style
**Barrel**: 3.5 in., 5 in., 7 in.
**Weight**: 2.5 lb.
**Caliber**: .45 Colt, .38 Spl., .44/40
**Capacity**: 6-rounds
**Features**: Full nickel plated steel or blue steel frame and blackstrap; case-hardened trigger guard; fluted barrel.
**Pearl-style Grip:** . . . . . . . . . . . **$1399**
**Walnut Grip:** . . . . . . . . . . . . . **$1049**

UBERTI TOP BREAK REVOLVER

## NEW MODEL RUSSIAN REVOLVER

**Action**: Single-action revolver
**Grips**: Walnut or ivory style with lanyard ring
**Barrel**: 6.5 in.
**Weight**: 2.5 lb.
**Caliber**: .45 Colt, .44 Russ
**Capacity**: 6-rounds
**Features**: Full nickel plated steel or blue steel frame and blackstrap; case-hardened trigger guard; fluted barrel.
**Blue Steel:** . . . . . . . . . . . . . . . **$1059**
**Nickel:** . . . . . . . . . . . . . . . . . . **$1399**

UBERTI NEW MODEL RUSSIAN REVOLVER

## 1873 CATTLEMAN CALLAHAN NM

**Action**: Single-action revolver
**Grips**: Walnut, black or mother-of-pearl synthetic
**Barrel**: 4.75 in., 6 in.
**Weight**: 42 oz.
**Caliber**: .44 Mag.
**Capacity**: 6-rounds
**Features**: Blue, stainless, case-hardened or Old West finish; target model has angled front target sight and adjustable notched rear blade sight.
**MSRP** . . . . . . . . . . . . . . . **$599**

UBERTI 1873 CATTLEMAN CALLAHAN NM

# U.S. Firearms

U.S. FIREARMS THE ORIGINAL RODEO

U.S. FIREARMS SHOOTING MASTER MAGNUM

U.S. FIREARMS OLD ARMORY ORIGINAL SERIES 1ST GENERATION

U.S. FIREARMS SPARROWHAWK

## THE ORIGINAL RODEO
*Action*: Single-action revolver
*Grips*: US hard rubber
*Barrel*: 4.75 in., 5.5 in.
*Caliber*: .45 Colt, .38 Special
*Capacity*: 6-rounds
*Features*: Handcrafted with cowboy action in matte blue, glare-reducing finish; standard white sided hammer; cross-pin frame style.
MSRP . . . . . . . . . . . . . . . . . . . $760

## SHOOTING MASTER MAGNUM
*Action*: Single-action revolver
*Grips*: US hard rubber
*Barrel*: 7.5 in.
*Caliber*: .357 S&W Mag.
*Capacity*: 6-rounds
*Features*: Heavy magnum frame; full dome blue finish.
MSRP . . . . . . . . . . . . . . . . . . $1495

## OLD ARMORY ORIGINAL SERIES 1ST GENERATION
*Action*: Single-action revolver
*Grips*: US hard rubber or walnut
*Barrel*: 4.75 in., 5.5 in., 7.5 in.
*Caliber*: .45 Colt
*Capacity*: 6-rounds
*Features*: Historically correct OEM 1st generation; frame window is smaller; smally cylinder profile correct for early Colt production; early flutes and beveled cylinder; choice of B.P. frame, V notch or cross pin frame V notch.
MSRP from . . . . . . . . . . . . . . $2095

## SPARROWHAWK
*Action*: Single-action revolver
*Grips*: US hard rubber
*Barrel*: 7.5 in.
*Caliber*: .327 Fed. Mag.
*Capacity*: 8-rounds
*Features*: Full dome blue; new scaled .32 caliber frame; includes removable firing pin.
MSRP . . . . . . . . . . . . . . . . . . $1495

# Walther Handguns

**WALTHER PPS**

**WALTHER P22**

**WALTHER P99AS**

## PPS (POLICE PISTOL SLIM)

**Action**: Striker fire action autoloader
**Grips**: Black polymer
**Barrel**: 3.2 in.
**Weight**: 19.4 oz. (9mm), 20.8 oz. (.40S&W)
**Caliber**: 9mm, 40 S&W
**Capacity**: 6- and 8-rounds (9mm), 5- and 7-rounds (.40 S&W)
**Features**: Ambidextrous magazine release; loaded chamber and cocking indicators; small and large backstrap; trigger safety; Walther quicksafe safety
**First Edition 9mm**: . . . . . . . . . $665
**.40 S&W**: . . . . . . . . . . . . . . $735
**9mm**: . . . . . . . . . . . . . . . . . $735

## P22

**Action**: Double action autoloader
**Grips**: Polymer
**Barrel**: 3.4 in. or 5 in.
**Weight**: 19.6 oz.
**Caliber**: .22 LR
**Capacity**: 10+1 rounds
**Features**: Interchangable frame back straps; ambidextrous controls; integrated trigger lock, loaded chamber indicator; fixed barrel; blue, nickel, or brushed chrome finishes.
**MSRP** . . . . . . . . . . . . . . . $375–$446

## P99 COMPACT QA

**Action**: Striker fire action autoloader
**Grips**: Polymer
**Barrel**: 4.4 in.
**Weight**: 18.7 oz.
**Caliber**: 9mm, 40 S&W
**Capacity**: 10-rounds (9mm), 8-rounds (.40 S&W)
**Features**: Flat-bottom magazine butt plate, finger rest magazine buttplate; molded with a Weaver-style rail; interchangable backstraps; hammerless striker system and integral safety devices come standard.
**MSRP** . . . . . . . . . . . . . . . . . $825

## PKK AND PKK/S

**Action**: Autoloader
**Grips**: Polymer; optional Crimson Trace Grip
**Barrel**: 3.5 in.
**Weight**: 20.8 oz.
**Caliber**: .380 and .32 ACP
**Capacity**: 7-rounds
**Features**: Firing pin safety; manual safety with decocking function; double and single action trigger; extended beavertail.
**MSRP** . . . . . . . . . . . . . . . . . . $626
**Stainless, Crimson Trace Grip**:  $862

## P99AS

**Action**: DA autoloader
**Grips**: Black polymer frame and grips
**Barrel**: 4 in. stainless steel with Tenifer finish
**Weight**: 21 to 23 oz.
**Caliber**: 9mm or .40 S&W
**Capacity**: 15 (9mm), 12 (.40 S&W)
**Features**: The first pistol with a firing pin block combines advantages of a traditional DA pull with SA trigger and a decocking button safety integrated into slide, allowing users the ability to decock the striker, preventing inadvertent firing in both DA and SA mode.
**MSRP** . . . . . . . . . . . . . . . . . . $825

# Wildey Handguns

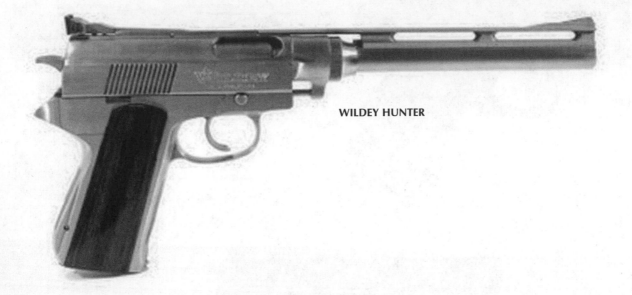

**WILDEY HUNTER**

## HUNTER

**Action**: Autoloader
**Grips**: Hardwood
**Barrel**: 5 in., 6 in., 7 in., 8 in., 10 in., 12 in., 14 in. and 18 in.
**Weight**: Starts at 64 oz.

**Caliber**: .45 Win. Mag., .44 Auto Mag., .45 Wildey Mag. and .475 Wildey Mag.
**Capacity**: 7+1 rounds
**Features**: Selective single or autoloading capability; patented gas operation system; fixed barrel; stainless construction; ventilated rib with interchangable front sights, red, orange, and black; single action trigger mechanism; patented hammer block and trigger block.
**MSRP**.......... **$1828.95–2410.95**
**18 in., Sillhouette:**....... **$3038.95**

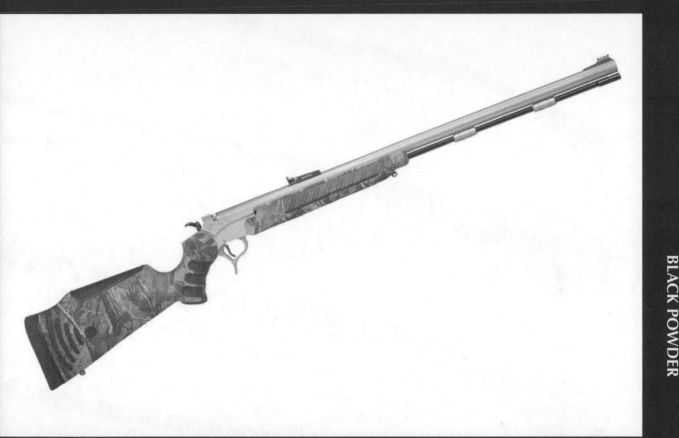

# Cabela's Black Powder

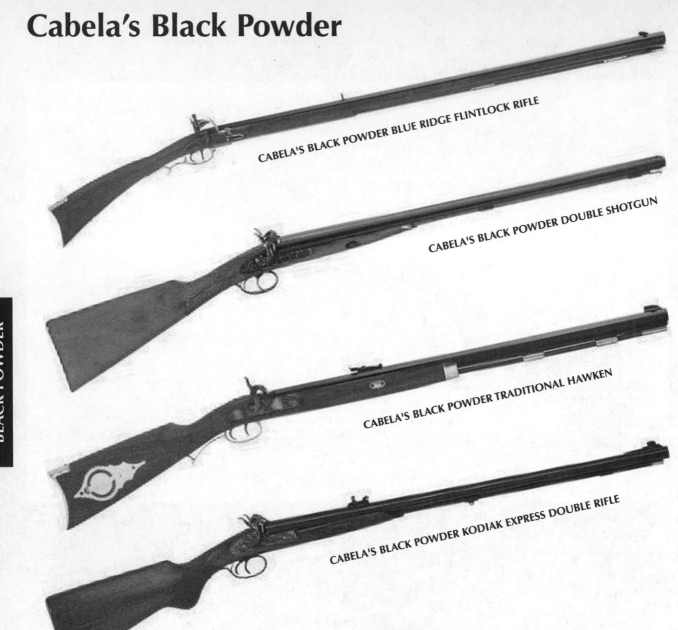

CABELA'S BLACK POWDER BLUE RIDGE FLINTLOCK RIFLE

CABELA'S BLACK POWDER DOUBLE SHOTGUN

CABELA'S BLACK POWDER TRADITIONAL HAWKEN

CABELA'S BLACK POWDER KODIAK EXPRESS DOUBLE RIFLE

## BLUE RIDGE FLINTLOCK RIFLE
*Lock*: Side-hammer caplock
*Stock*: Walnut
*Barrel*: 39 in., 48 in.
*Sights*: None
*Weight*: 7.25 lb.–7.75 lb.
*Bore/ Caliber*: .32, .36, .45, .50, and .54
*Features*: Double-set triggers; buttplate and trigger guard are polished brass; browned octagonal barrels.
**MSRP** . . . . . . . . . **$749.99**

## DOUBLE SHOTGUN
*Lock*: Traditional caplock
*Stock*: Checkered walnut
*Barrel*: 28.5 in.
*Sights*: None
*Weight*: 7 lb.
*Bore/ Caliber*: 12 Ga., 10 Ga.
*Features*: Chrome-lined double-barrels; screw-in chokes (x-full, modified, and improved cylinder); engraved locks; blued.
**MSRP** . . . . . . . . . **$899.99**

## TRADITIONAL HAWKEN PERCUSSION RIFLE
*Lock*: Traditional cap or flint
*Stock*: Walnut
*Barrel*: 29 in.
*Sights*: Adjustable, open
*Weight*: 9 lb.
*Bore/ Caliber*: .40, .54
*Features*: Brass trigger guards, curved buttplates, forend caps, ferrules and ramrods fittings; case-hardened locks contain hefty coil springs; solid hoooked breech and latch pin; adjustable double-set triggers.
**MSRP** . . . . . . . . . **$429.99**

## KODIAK EXPRESS DOUBLE RIFLE
*Lock*: Traditional caplock
*Stock*: Walnut, pistol grip
*Sights*: Adjustable, open
*Weight*: 9.3 lb.
*Bore/ Caliber*: .72, .50
*Features*: Fully adjustable double folding rear leaf sights and ramp front; lock, top tang and trigger guard are polished and engraved.
**MSRP** . . . . . . . . . **$1199.99**

# CVA Black Powder

CVA BLACK POWDER WOLF WITH SCOPE AND STARTER KIT

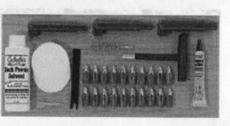

CVA BLACK POWDER ACCURA V2

CVA BLACK POWDER APEX

## OPTIMA 209 AND OPTIMA PRO 209
*Lock*: In-line
*Stock*: Synthetic or camo
*Barrel*: 26 in., 29 in.
*Sights*: Adjustable fiber optic
*Weight*: 6.65 lb.
*Bore/ Caliber*: .45, .50
*Features*: 416 stainless steel; fluted barrel; bullet guiding muzzle; ambidextrous thumbhole or standard stock; quick release breech plug; reversible hammer spur; CrushZone recoil pad; durasight DEAD-ON one-piece scope mount.
**Optima, Synthetic/ Black:....$259.95–$269.95**
**Stainless Steel/ Realtree Hdwds Green**
**HD camo: ...... $339.95**

## ACCURA V2
*Lock*: Hinged breech muzzleloading
*Stock*: Composite stock in standard or thumbhole w/ SoftTouch coating and rubber grip panels
*Barrel*: 27 in. 416 stainless Bergara
*Sights*: DuraSight fiber optic sight
*Weight*: 7.3 lb.
*Bore/ Caliber*: .45, .50
*Features*: Quick-release breech plug, CrushZone recoil pad, drilled and tapped for scope mount.
**MSRP......... $479.99**

## WOLF W/ SCOPE AND STARTER KIT
*Lock*: Hinged breech muzzleloading
*Stock*: Black or hardwoods camo
*Barrel*: 24 in. blued
Sights: DuraSight fiber optic sight; includes a 3-9 x 40mm duplex scope
*Weight*: 6.25 lb.
*Bore/ Caliber*: .50
*Features*: Starter kit has key components to get you started; new tool-free QR breech plug system; compact or standard stock, CrushZone recoil pad, reversible hammer spur.
**MSRP........... $319**

## APEX
*Lock*: Hinged breech muzzleloading
*Stock*: Synthetic or camo
*Barrel*: 27 in.
*Sights*: DuraSight rail mount
*Weight*: 8 lb.
*Bore/ Caliber*: .50
*Features*: Multibarrel interchangable rifle system; ambidextrous butt stock; 416 stainless steel Bergara barrels; quick-release breech plug; quake claw sling; CrushZone recoil pad.
**MSRP....$599.99–$649.99**

# Dixie Black Powder

DIXIE BLACK POWDER MODEL U.S. 1816 FLINTLOCK MUSKET

DIXIE BLACK POWDER 1853 THREE-BAND ENFIELD

DIXIE BLACK POWDER NEW MODEL 1859 MILITARY SHARPS CARBINE

## MODEL U.S. 1816 SPRINGFIELD MUSKET
*Lock*: Traditional flintlock
*Stock*: Walnut
*Barrel*: 42 in.
*Sights*: Fixed
*Weight*: 9.8 lb.
*Bore/ Caliber*: .69
*Features*: Most common military flint-lock from U.S. armories, complete with bayonet lug and swivels.
**MSRP**................... $1595

## 1853 THREE-BAND ENFIELD
*Lock*: Traditional caplock
*Stock*: Walnut
*Barrel*: 39 in.
*Sights*: Fixed
*Weight*: 10.25 lb.
*Bore/ Caliber*: .58
*Features*: Color case-hardened lock; single trigger; single swivels; steel ram-rod.
**MSRP**................... $875

## SHARPS NEW MODEL 1859 MILITARY CARBINE
*Lock*: Dropping block
*Stock*: Walnut
*Barrel*: 22 in.
*Sights*: Adjustable open
*Weight*: 8 lb.
*Bore/ Caliber*: .54
*Features*: Steel furniture; color case-hardened; single trigger; single barrel band; saddle bar with ring
**MSRP**................... $1200

DIXIE BLACK POWDER
SCREW BARREL PISTOL

## SCREW BARREL PISTOL
*Lock*: Traditional caplock
*Stock*: European walnut
*Barrel*: 3 in.
*Sights*: None
*Weight*: .75 lb.
*Bore/ Caliber*: .44
*Features*: Color case-hardened lock; single folding trigger; combination nipple/barrel wrench included.
**MSRP**................... $185

## FR4055 SPANISH MUSKET

**Lock**: Flintlock muzzleloading
**Stock**: Full, European walnut 56 in.
**Barrel**: Smoothbore
**Sights**: Steel stud front
**Weight**: 10 lb.
**Bore/ Caliber**: .68 round ball
**Features**: Brass butt plate, triggerguard, and barrel bands; bright steel side-plates; steel ramrod.
**MSRP** . . . . . . . . . . . . . . . . . . $1400

## 1851 NAVY

**Lock**: Caplock revolver
**Stock**: Walnut
**Barrel**: 7.5 in.
**Sights**: Fixed
**Weight**: 2.5 lb.
**Bore/ Caliber**: .36, .44
**Features**: Octagonal barrel; brass or steel frame.
**Steel**: . . . . . . . . . . . . . . . . . . . . $215
**Brass**: . . . . . . . . . . . . . . . . . . . . $220

## 1851 NAVY SHERIFF'S

**Lock**: Caplock revolver
**Stock**: Walnut
**Barrel**: 5.5 in.
**Sights**: None
**Weight**: 2 lb.
**Bore/ Caliber**: .44
**Features**: Brass guard; case-hardened frame and blued barrel.
**MSRP** . . . . . . . . . . . . . . . . . . . . $215

## 1858 REMINGTON ARMY REVOLVER

**Lock**: Caplock revolver
**Stock**: Walnut
**Barrel**: 8 in.
**Sights**: Fixed
**Weight**: 2.5 lb.
**Bore/ Caliber**: .44
**Features**: Brass or stainless steel frame; blued barrel optional.
**Brass Frame**: . . . . . . . . . . . . . . $210
**Blued Steel Frame:** . . . . . . . . . $260
**Stainless Frame:** . . . . . . . . . . . $390

## 1860 ARMY REVOVLER

**Lock**: Caplock revolver
**Stock**: Walnut
**Barrel**: 8 in.
**Sights**: Fixed
**Weight**: 2.6 lb.
**Bore/ Caliber**: .44
**Features**: Case-hardened frame; blued barrel.
**Brass Frame:** . . . . . . . . . . . . . . $215
**Steel**: . . . . . . . . . . . . . . . . . . . . $245

DIXIE BLACK POWDER FR4055 SPANISH MUSKET

# EMF Hartford Black Powder

EMF HARTFORD BLACK POWDER 1851 NAVY

EMF HARTFORD BLACK POWDER 1851 NAVY SHERIFF'S

EMF HARTFORD BLACK POWDER 1858 REMINGTON ARMY REVOLVER

EMF HARTFORD BLACK POWDER 1860 ARMY REVOLVER

BLACK POWDER

# Lyman Black Powder

LYMAN MUSTANG BREAKAWAY 209 MAGNUM

LYMAN DEERSTALKER

LYMAN GREAT PLAINS RIFLE

## MUSTANG BREAKAWAY 209 MAGNUM
*Lock*: In-line
*Stock*: Hardwood
*Barrel*: 26 in.
*Sights*: Fiber optic front and rear
*Weight*: 11 lb.
*Bore/ Caliber*: .50
*Features*: Pachmayr "Decelerator" recoil pad; comes drilled and tapped for Weaver-style bases; hammerless; removable, stainless breech plug & easy take-down; "magnetized" primer retention system.
**MSRP** . . . . . . . . . . . . . . . . . . . **$525**

## DEERSTALKER RIFLE
*Lock*: Traditional cap or flint
*Stock*: Walnut
*Barrel*: 24 in.
*Sights*: Fiber optic front and rear
*Weight*: 10.4 lb.
*Bore/ Caliber*: .50 or .54
*Features*: Quiet single trigger; metal blackened to avoid glare; black rubber recoil pad.
**MSRP** . . . . . . . . . . **$449.95–$584.95**

## GREAT PLAINS RIFLE
*Lock*: Traditional cap or flint
*Stock*: Walnut
*Barrel*: 32 in.
*Sights*: Adjustable open
*Weight*: 11.6 lb.
*Bore/ Caliber*: .50 or .54
*Features*: Double-set triggers; Hawken style percussion "snail" with clean out screw; separate ramrod entry thimble and nose cap; reliable coil spring lock with correct lock plate.
**MSRP** . . . . . . . . . . **$689.95–$744.95**

# Lyman Black Powder

LYMAN BLACK POWDER PLAINS PISTOL

## TRADE RIFLE
*Lock*: Traditional cap or flint
*Stock*: Walnut
*Barrel*: 28 in.
*Sights*: Adjustable open
*Weight*: 10.8 lb.
*Bore/ Caliber*: .50 or .54
*Features*: Brass furniture; were originally developed for the early Indian fur trade
**MSRP . . . . . . . . . . $499.95–$539.95**

## PLAINS PISTOL
*Lock*: Traditional caplock
*Stock*: Walnut
*Barrel*: 6 in.
*Sights*: Fixed
*Weight*: 3.1 lb.
*Bore/ Caliber*: .50 or .54
*Features*: Blackened iron furniture; polished brass trigger guard and ramrod tips; hooked patent breech takes down quickly for easy cleaning; thimble is recessed into the rib; detachable belt hook; spring-loaded trigger. **Plains Pistol: $359.95**
**Kit: . . . . . . . . . . . . . . . . . . . $299.95**

# Markesbery Black Powder

MARKESBERY BLACK POWDER POLAR BEAR

## BLACK BEAR
*Lock*: In-line
*Stock*: Two-piece walnut, synthetic or laminated
*Barrel*: 24 in.
*Sights*: Bead front, open fully adjustable rear
*Weight*: 6.5 lb.
*Bore/ Caliber*: .36, .45, .50, .54
*Features*: Grizzly Bear model comes with thumbhole stock; Brown Bear comes with one-piece thumbhole stock, both checkered; aluminum ramrod; Monte Carlo comb.
**Black Bear: . . . . . . . $536.63–$556.27**
**Brown Bear: . . . . . . $658.83–$680.07**
**Grizzly Bear: . . . . . $642.96–$664.20**

## POLAR BEAR
*Lock*: In-line
*Stock*: Laminated, hardwood, or laminate
*Barrel*: 24 in.
*Sights*: Adjustable open
*Weight*: 7.8 lb.
*Bore/ Caliber*: .36, .45, .50, .54
*Features*: One-piece stock with Monte Carlo comb; interchangable barrel system; outer-line ignition system; cross-bolt double safety.
**MSRP . . . . . . . . . . $539.01–$570.56**

BLACK POWDER

# Navy Arms Black Powder

## 1805 HARPER'S FERRY PISTOL

*Lock*: Traditional flintlock
*Stock*: Walnut
*Barrel*: 10 in.
*Sights*: Fixed
*Weight*: 2.75 lb.
*Bore/ Caliber*: .58
*Features*: The first U.S. Marshall pistol; browned, rifled barrel.
**MSRP** . . . . . . . . . . . . . . . . . . . . **$495**

NAVY ARMS BLACK POWDER 1805 HARPER'S FERRY PISTOL

# Pedersoli Black Powder

PEDERSOLI BLACK POWDER SWISS MATCH STANDARD FLINTLOCK

PEDERSOLI BLACK POWDER GIBBS SHOTGUN

PEDERSOLI BLACK POWDER HOWDAH HUNTER PISTOL

## GIBBS SHOTGUN

*Lock*: Standard percussion
*Stock*: Walnut
*Barrel*: 32.3 in.
*Sights*: None
*Weight*: 8.59 lb.
*Bore/ Caliber*: 12 Ga.
*Features*: Octagonal to round barrel; case-hardened color-finished lock; grip and forend caps with ebony inserts; pistol grip stock.
**MSRP** . . . . . . . . . . . . . . . . . . . . **$1409**

## SWISS MATCH STANDARD FLINTLOCK

*Lock*: Traditional flintlock
*Stock*: Walnut
*Barrel*: 30.8 in.
*Sights*: Adjustable
*Weight*: 16.3 lb.
*Bore/ Caliber*: .40
*Features*: Octagonal conical profile barrel with rust brown finish; lock is case hardened; steel ramrod; double-set trigger; steel hook butt plate.
**MSRP** . . . . . . . . . . . . . . . . . . . . **$3104**

## HOWDAH HUNTER PISTOL

*Lock*: Standard percussion
*Stock*: Walnut
*Barrel*: 11.25 in.
*Sights*: None
*Weight*: 5.07 lb.
*Bore/ Caliber*: 20 Ga., or .50 cal.
*Features*: Engraved locks with wild animal scenes; case-hardened color finish; checkered walnut pistol grip with steel butt cap.
**20 Ga.:** . . . . . . . . . . . . . . . . . . . **$745**
**.50 cal.:** . . . . . . . . . . . . . . . . . . . **$823**
**.58 cal:** . . . . . . . . . . . . . . . . . . . **$835**
**20x50:** . . . . . . . . . . . . . . . . . . . **$809**

# Pedersoli Black Powder

## LE PAGE TARGET FLINTLOCK PISTOL

*Lock*: Traditional flintlock
*Stock*: Walnut
*Barrel*: 10.5 in.
*Sights*: Adjustable
*Weight*: 2.64 lb.
*Bore/ Caliber*: .44 or .45
*Features*: Smoothbore .45 available; adjustable single set trigger; brightly polished lock with a roller Frizzen spring.
**MSRP** . . . . . . . . . . . . . . . . . . . **$1110**

**PEDERSOLI BLACK POWDER LE PAGE TARGET FLINTLOCK PISTOL**

## MANG IN GRAZ

*Lock*: Traditional caplock
*Stock*: Walnut
*Barrel*: 11.4 in.
*Sights*: Fixed
*Weight*: 2.65 lb.
*Bore/ Caliber*: .38 or .44
*Features*: Fluted grip; octagonal, rifled barrel in brown rust finish; adjustable single set trigger; breech plug shows a typical mask of the period; barrel and tang enriched with gold inlays.
**MSRP** . . . . . . . . . . . . . . . . . . . **$1581**

**PEDERSOLI BLACK POWDER MANG IN GRAZ**

## MORTIMER TARGET RIFLE

*Lock*: Flintlock
*Stock*: English-style European walnut
*Barrel*: 36. 4 in.
*Sights*: Target
*Weight*: 10.13 lb.
*Bore/ Caliber*: .54
*Features*: Case-colored lock; stock has cheek piece and hand checkering; 7-groove barrel.
**MSRP** . . . . . . . . . . . . . . . . . . . **$1630**

**PEDERSOLI BLACK POWDER MORTIMER TARGET RIFLE**

**PEDERSOLI BLACK POWDER TYRON TARGET STANDARD RIFLE**

## TYRON TARGET STANDARD RIFLE

*Lock*: Traditional caplock

*Stock*: Walnut
*Barrel*: 36.4 in.
*Sights*: Adjustable open
*Weight*: 9.7 lb.

*Bore/ Caliber*: .45, .50, .54
*Features*: Creedmoor version with aperature sight available.
**MSRP** . . . . . . . . . . . . . . . . . . . **$1028**

# Savage Arms Black Powder

SAVAGE ARMS BLACK POWDER MODEL 10ML

## MODEL 10ML-11 MUZZLELOADER

**Lock**: In-line
**Stock**: Synthetic, camo, or laminated
**Barrel**: 24 in.
**Sights**: Adjustable fiber optics
**Weight**: 7.75 lb.

**Bore/ Caliber**: .50
**Features**: Bolt-action mechanism; drilled and tapped for scope mounts; AccuTrigger; free floating barreled action; sling swivel studs; stock comes in black synthetic, Realtree Hardwoods HD camoflauge synthetic or brown laminate; blued or stainless steel barrel.

**Black Synthetic, Blued:** . . . . . . $660
**Black Synthetic, Stainless Steel:** . . . . . . . . . . . . $738
**Camo, Stainless:** . . . . . . . . . . $787
**Laminate, Stainless:** . . . . . . . . $839

# Shiloh Sharps Black Powder

SHILOH SHARPS BLACK POWDER MODEL 1863 SHARPS

SHILOH SHARPS BLACK POWDER MODEL 1874 TARGET CREEDMOOR

## MODEL 1863 RIFLE

**Lock**: Traditional caplock
**Stock**: Walnut
**Barrel**: 30 in.
**Sights**: Adjustable open
**Weight**: 9.5 lb.
**Bore/ Caliber**: .50 or .54
**Features**: Sporting model has half-stock; double set trigger on military model with 3-band full stock; military steel buttstock on all models.

**Sporting rifle:** . . . . . . . . . . . $1800
**Carbine rifle:** . . . . . . . . . . . . $1800
**Military rifle:** . . . . . . . . . . . . $2092

## MODEL 1874 TARGET CREEDMOOR RIFLE

**Lock**: Black powder cartridge
**Stock**: Walnut
**Barrel**: 32 in.
**Sights**: V aiming rear sight; blade front sight
**Weight**: 9 lb.
**Bore/ Caliber**: All popular black powder cartridges from .38-55 to .50-90
**Features**: Pistol grip; single trigger; AA finish; polished barrel; octagon barrel; pewter tip.
**MSRP** . . . . . . . . . . . . . . . . . . . $2743

BLACK POWDER

# Taylor's & Co. Black Powder

TAYLOR'S & CO. 1847 WALKER

TAYLOR'S & CO. 1848 DRAGOONS

## 1848 DRAGOONS
*Lock*: Traditional caplock
*Stock*: Walnut
*Barrel*: 7.5 in. round
*Sights*: Fixed
*Weight*: 4 lb.–4 lb. 14 oz.
*Bore/ Caliber*: .44
*Features*: These dragoon revolvers were first used by the U.S. Army's Mounted Rifles 1st Cavalry in 1833. soon they went on to see considrable use during the 1850s and during the Civil War.; blue finish; 6-round capacity.
**1st Model, 2nd Model:** ...... **$350**
**3rd Model:**............... **$358**

## 1847 WALKER
*Lock*: Traditional caplock
*Stock*: Walnut
*Barrel*: 9 in.
*Sights*: Fixed
*Weight*: 4 lb. 12 oz.
*Bore/ Caliber*: .44
*Features*: Blue finish; round barrel.
**MSRP** .................... **$380**

# Thompson/Center Black Powder

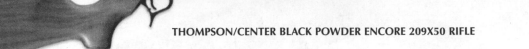

THOMPSON/CENTER BLACK POWDER ENCORE 209X50 RIFLE

THOMPSON/CENTER BLACK POWDER TRIUMPH BONE COLLECTOR

THOMPSON/CENTER BLACK POWDER FIRE STORM

THOMPSON/CENTER BLACK POWDER ENCORE ENDEAVOR PROHUNTER XT

BLACK POWDER

## ENCORE PRO HUNTER 209
*Lock*: In-line
*Stock*: FlexTech in camo or synthetic
*Barrel*: 28 in.
*Sights*: Fiber optic
*Weight*: 7.2 lb.
*Bore/ Caliber*: .50
*Features*: Stainless steel finish; interchangable fluted barrels; thumbhole or standard stock in black or Realtree Hardwoods camo
MSRP . . . . . . . . . . . . . . . . . . . . $925

## TRIUMPH BONE COLLECTOR
*Lock*: In-line
*Stock*: Composite, black or Realtree

AP HD camo
*Barrel*: 28 in.
*Sights*: Adjustable fiber optic
*Weight*: 6.5 lb.
*Bore/ Caliber*: .50
*Features*: Blued, stainless, and weather shield finish; speed brech XT.
MSRP . . . . . . . . . . . . . . . . $672–$716

## FIRE STORM
*Lock*: Traditional cap or flint
*Stock*: Composite
*Barrel*: 26 in.
*Sights*: Steel fiber optic sights
*Weight*: 7.0 lb.
*Bore/ Caliber*: .50
*Features*: Aluminum ramrod; single

trigger with large trigger guard bow; Fire Storm positive ignition; magnum capabilities.
MSRP . . . . . . . . . . . . . . . $567–$634

## ENCORE ENDEAVOR PROHUNTER XT
*Lock*: Hinged breech muzzleloading
*Stock*: Camo or black FlexTech with SIMS recoil pad
*Barrel*: Stainless, fluted 28 in.
*Sights*: Fiber optic
*Weight*: 8.25 lb.
*Bore/ Caliber*: .50
*Features*: 209 ignition primer, swing hammer, power rod, QLA muzzle system; speed breech XT.
MSRP . . . . . . . . . . . . . . . $612–$655

# Thompson/Center Black Powder

## IMPACT
**Lock**: Hinged breech muzzleloading
**Stock**: Black or LongLeaf camo
**Barrel**: Blued 28 in.
**Sights**: Fiber optic
**Weight**: 6.5 lb.
**Bore/ Caliber**: .50
**Features**: Triple lead thread breech plug;
1in adjustable buttstock.
**MSRP** . . . . . . . . . . . . . . .**$276–$382**

## NORTHWEST EXPLORER
**Lock**: Dropping-breech
**Stock**: Black composite or Realtree Hardwoods camo
**Barrel**: 28 in. blued
**Sights**: Adjustable
**Weight**: 7 lb.
**Bore/ Caliber**: .50
**Features**: Design meets legal regulations of Western States; exposed breech system; #11 cap ignition and metal sights; QLA (Quick Load Accurizor); weather shield coating available.
**MSRP** . . . . . . . . . . . . . . .**$381–$470**

# Traditions Black Powder

## YANKEE REVOLVER 1851 NAVY
**Lock**: Caplock
**Stock**: Walnut
**Barrel**: 7.5 in.
**Sights**: Fixed
**Weight**: 2.5 lb.
**Bore/ Caliber**: .44
**Features**: Octagonal barrel and lever style loader; brass, antiqued or old silver frame and guard
**Brass** . . . . . . . . . . . . . . . . . . . **$221**
**Antiqued:** . . . . . . . . . . . . . . . **$389**
**Old Silver:** . . . . . . . . . . . . . . . **$325**

TRADITIONS BLACK POWDER
YANKEE 1851 NAVY REVOLVER

## 1858 ARMY REVOLVER
**Lock**: Caplock
**Stock**: Walnut
**Barrel**: 8 in.
**Sights**: Fixed
**Weight**: 2.75 lb.
**Bore/ Caliber**: .44
**Features**: Octagonal barrel and lever style loader; steel frame and guard; top strap/ post sights
**MSRP** . . . . . . . . . . . . . . . . . . . **$325**

TRADITIONS BLACK POWDER
1858 ARMY REVOLVER

## 1860 ARMY REVOVLER
**Lock**: Caplock
**Stock**: Walnut
**Barrel**: 8 in.
**Sights**: Fixed
**Weight**: 2.75 lb.
**Bore/ Caliber**: .44
**Features**: Blued barrel; steel frame; brass guard; has hammer/ blade sights
**Walnut, steel:** . . . . . . . . . . . . . **$295**
**Ivory, Nickel:** . . . . . . . . . . . . . . **$339**
**Antiqued:** . . . . . . . . . . . . . . . **$439**

TRADITIONS BLACK POWDER
1860 ARMY REVOLVER

# Traditions Black Powder

## CROCKETT PISTOL

**Lock**: Traditional caplock
**Stock**: Hardwood
**Barrel**: 15 in.
**Sights**: Fixed
**Weight**: 2.0 lb.
**Bore/ Caliber**: .32
**Features**: Blued, octagonal barrel.
**MSRP** . . . . . . . . . . . . . . . . . . . . **$229**

TRADITIONS BLACK POWDER
CROCKETT PISTOL

## KENTUCKY PISTOL

**Lock**: Traditional caplock
**Stock**: Hardwood
**Barrel**: 10 in.
**Sights**: Fixed
**Weight**: 2.5 lb.
**Bore/ Caliber**: .50
**Features**: Brass furniture; case colored sidelock and brass ramrod thimble.
**MSRP** . . . . . . . . . . . . . . . . . . . . **$219**

TRADITIONS BLACK POWDER
KENTUCKY PISTOL

TRADITIONS BLACK POWDER
DEERHUNTER RIFLE SYNTHETIC

TRADITIONS BLACK POWDER
FRONTIER MUZZLELOADER

## DEERHUNTER RIFLE

**Lock**: Traditional caplock or flint
**Stock**: Synthetic or hardwood
**Barrel**: 24 in.
**Sights**: Lite Optic adjustable sights
**Weight**: 6.0 lb.
**Bore/ Caliber**: .32, .50, .54
**Features**: Octagonal performance barrels; blued or nickel barrel finish; percussion models are drilled and tapped to accept scope mounts; non-slip recoil pad; stock comes in black synthetic, Mossy Oak Treestand camo, or hardwood.
**Flint, Synthetic, Blued**: . . . . . . **$279**
**Flint, Camo:** . . . . . . . . . . . . . . **$359**

**Flint, Hardwood, Blued:** . . . . . **$339**
**Cap, Hardwood, Blued:** . . . . . . **$299**
**Cap, Synthetic, Blued:** . . . . . . . **$249**

## FRONTIER MUZZLELOADER

**Lock**: Traditional flintlock and cap
**Stock**: Hardwood
**Barrel**: 28 in.
**Sights**: V rear sight and blade
**Weight**: 7.8 lb.
**Bore/ Caliber**: .50
**Features**: Octagonal blued barrel; colored hardware and solid brass furniture.
**MSRP** . . . . . . . . . . . . . . . . . . . . **$419**

BLACK POWDER

# Traditions Rifles

BLACK POWDER

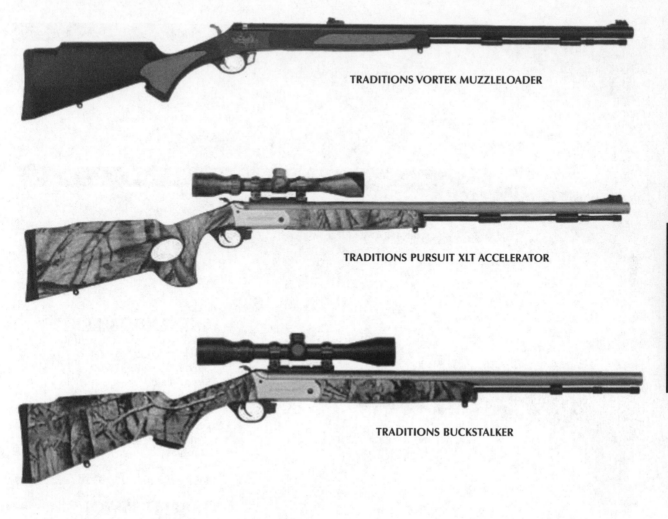

**TRADITIONS VORTEK MUZZLELOADER**

**TRADITIONS PURSUIT XLT ACCELERATOR**

**TRADITIONS BUCKSTALKER**

## VORTEK MUZZLELOADER

*Action*: Break-action, muzzleloader
*Stock*: Synthetic
*Barrel*: 28 in.
*Sights*: Williams metal fiber optics sights
*Weight*: 12.5 lb.
*Caliber*: .50
*Magazine*: None
*Features*: Black synthetic or soft touch Mossy Oak treestand camo stock with optional thumbhole; accelerator breech plug; comfort-grip overmolding; sling swivel studs; stainless steel barrels in stainless or blued finish; drilled and tapped for scope.
**MSRP . . . . . . . . . . . . . . . . $339–$589**
**Thumbhole: . . . . . . . . . . . . . . $419**

## PURSUIT XLT ACCELERATOR

*Action*: Break-action, muzzleloader
*Stock*: Synthetic
*Barrel*: 28 in.
*Sights*: Tru-Glo fiber optics sights
*Weight*: 7.5 lb.
*Caliber*: .50
*Magazine*: None
*Features*: Drilled and tapped for sights; solid aluminum ramrod; sling swivel studs; Monte Carlo-style stock in Mossy Oak treestand camo pattern; dual safety system; PAS-projectile alignment system; quick relief recoil pad.
**MSRP . . . . . . . . . . . . . . . . . . . $429**

## BUCKSTALKER

*Action*: Break-action, muzzleloader
*Stock*: Synthetic
*Barrel*: 24 in.
*Sights*: Tru-Glo fiber optics sights
*Weight*: 7.5 lb.
*Caliber*: .50
*Magazine*: None
*Features*: Dual safety system; nickel guard coating; synthetic black or G1 vista camo stock; nickel or blue finish barrel; Monte Carlo stock; drilled and tapped for a scope; sling swivel studs.
**MSRP . . . . . . . . . . . . . . . . $189–$229**

**BLACK POWDER**

TRADITIONS BLACK POWDER
PENNSYLVANIA RIFLE

TRADITIONS BLACK POWDER
SHENANDOAH RIFLE

TRADITIONS BLACK POWDER
WILLIAM PARKER PISTOL

## SHENANDOAH RIFLE
*Lock*: Traditional cap or flint
*Stock*: Walnut
*Barrel*: 33.5 in.
*Sights*: Fixed
*Weight*: 7.2 lb.
*Bore/ Caliber*: .50
*Features*: Brass stock inlay ornamentation, inletted patch box, nosecap, thimbles and trigger guard; double-set triggers; octagonal barrel.
**MSRP** . . . . . . . . . . . . . . . . . . . **$599**

## TRAPPER PISTOL
*Lock*: Traditional cap or flint
*Stock*: Hardwood
*Barrel*: 9.75 in.
*Sights*: Primitive-style adjustable rear sight
*Weight*: 2.9 lb.
*Bore/ Caliber*: .50
*Features*: Octagonal blued barrel; doubleset triggers.
**MSRP** . . . . . . . . . . . . . . . . . . . **$299**

## WILLIAM PARKER PISTOL
*Lock*: Traditional caplock
*Stock*: Walnut
*Barrel*: 10.4 in.
*Sights*: Fixed
*Weight*: 2.5 lb.
*Bore/ Caliber*: .50
*Features*: Polished steel barrel; checkered grip with brass furniture.
**MSRP** . . . . . . . . . . . . . . . . . . . **$399**

## HAWKEN WOODSMAN RIFLE
*Lock*: Traditional cap or flint
*Stock*: Hardwood
*Barrel*: 28 in.
*Sights*: Adjustable rear hunting sight
*Weight*: 7.8 lb.
*Bore/ Caliber*: .50
*Features*: Hooked breech for easy barrel removal; double-set triggers in an oversized glove-fitting trigger guard; inletted solid brass patch box; left hand model available; octagonal blued barrel.
**MSRP** . . . . . . . . . . . . . . . . . . . **$469**

## PENNSYLVANIA RIFLE
*Lock*: Traditional cap or flint
*Stock*: Walnut
*Barrel*: 20 in.
*Sights*: Adjustable primitive style rear sight
*Weight*: 8.5 lb.
*Bore/ Caliber*: .50
*Features*: Brass stock inlay ornamentation and toe plate; cheekpiece; solid brass patch box.
**MSRP** . . . . . . . . . . . . . . . . . . . **$719**

# Traditions Black Powder

**TRADITIONS BLACK POWDER TRACKER 209**

**TRADITIONS BLACK POWDER PURSUIT LT BREAK-OPEN**

**TRADITIONS BLACK POWDER VORTEK ULTRA LIGHT**

## TRACKER 209
*Lock*: In-line
*Stock*: Synthetic
*Barrel*: 22 in.
*Sights*: Light optic adjustable sights
*Weight*: 6.5 lb.
*Bore/ Caliber*: .50
*Features*: Removable 209 primer ignition; projectile alignment system; in-line bolt with a quiet thumb safety; removable breech plug system; rugged synthetic ramrod.
**Nickel. . . . . . . . . . . . . . . . . . $189;**
**Blued: . . . . . . . . . . . . . . . . . . $169**

## PURSUIT LT BREAK-OPEN
*Lock*: Break-open
*Stock*: Synthetic
*Barrel*: 28 in.
*Sights*: Tru-Glo Fiber Optic Sights
*Weight*: 6.75 lb.
*Bore/ Caliber*: .50
*Features*: 209 Shotgun ignition primer; Monte Carlo style stock; drilled and tapped for scopes; sling swivels studs; thumbhole stocks available; solid aluminum ramrod; dual safety system; nickel guard coating; Quick Relief recoil pads.
**MSRP. . . . . . . . . . . . . . . . . . . $289**

## VORTEK ULTRA LIGHT
*Lock*: Hinged breech muzzleloading
*Stock*: Synthetic black Hogue Overmold or Realtree AP camo
*Barrel*: 28 in.
*Sights*: Fixed, green
*Weight*: 6.25 lb.
*Bore/ Caliber*: .50
*Features*: Drop-out trigger assembly; recoil pad; 3-pound factory trigger; frame and barrel have CeraKote finish.
**MSRP. . . . . . . . . . . . . . . . . . . $499**

# Traditions Black Powder

## VORTEK PISTOL
**Lock**: Hinged breech muzzleloading
**Stock**: Select hardwood
**Barrel**: 13 in.
**Sights**: Fixed open
**Weight**: 3.25 lb.
**Bore/ Caliber**: .50
**Features**: 209 primer ignition, accelerator breech plug; CeraKote finish on frame and barrel.
**MSRP** . . . . . . . . . . . . . . . . . . . . $369

## PURSUIT XLT
**Lock**: Hinge breech muzzleloading
**Stock**: Realtree Tree Stand camo, Monte Carlo style
**Barrel**: 28 in. fluted, nickel plated or camo
**Sights**: Metal fiber optic
**Weight**: 7.5 lb.
**Bore/ Caliber**: .50
**Features**: Alloy, lightweight frame, aluminum ramrod; QuickRelief recoil pad; SoftTouch rubberized coating on stock; 209 ignition primer; drilled and tapped for scope mounts; sling swivel.
**MSRP** . . . . . . . . . . . . . . . . . . . . $377
**Camo:** . . . . . . . . . . . . . . . . . . . $399

TRADITIONS BLACK POWDER
VORTEK PISTOL

TRADITIONS BLACK POWDER
PURSUIT ULTRA LIGHT XLT

# Uberti Black Powder

## 1847 WALKER
**Lock**: Caplock revolver
**Stock**: Walnut
**Barrel**: 9 in.
**Sights**: Fixed, open
**Weight**: 4.5 lb.
**Bore/ Caliber**: .44
**Features**: Case-hardened frame, steel backstrap, brass trigger guard; blue finish.
**MSRP** . . . . . . . . . . . . . . . . . . . . $429

UBERTI BLACK POWDER 1847 WALKER

## 1848 DRAGOON
**Lock**: Caplock revolver
**Stock**: Walnut
**Barrel**: 7.5 in.
**Sights**: Fixed, open
**Weight**: 4.1 lb.
**Bore/ Caliber**: .44
**Features**: Case-hardened frame; steel or brass backstrap and trigger guard; engraved.
**MSRP** . . . . . . . . . . . . . . . . . $409–429

UBERTI BLACK POWDER 1848 DRAGOON

## 1851 NAVY REVOLVER
**Lock**: Caplock revolver
**Stock**: Walnut
**Barrel**: 7.5 in.
**Sights**: Fixed, open
**Weight**: 2.6 lb.
**Bore/ Caliber**: .36
**Features**: Color case-hardened frame; oval or squareback trigger guard; brass or steel backstrap and trigger guard; octagonal barrel (Leech- Rigdon model has round barrel).
**MSRP** . . . . . . . . . . . . . . . . . $329–$349

UBERTI BLACK POWDER 1851
NAVY REVOLVER

# Uberti Black Powder

**UBERTI BLACK POWDER 1860 ARMY REVOLVER**

## 1860 ARMY REVOLVER
**Lock**: Caplock revolver
**Stock**: Walnut
**Barrel**: 7.5 in.
**Sights**: Fixed, open
**Weight**: 2.6 lb.
**Bore/ Caliber**: .44
**Features**: Case-hardened frame, steel backstrap, brass trigger guard; blue finish; round barrel.
**Steel & Brass Model:** . . . . . . . . $339
**Fluted Steel:** . . . . . . . . . . . . . . $349

**UBERTI BLACK POWDER-1861 NAVY REVOLVER**

## 1861 NAVY REVOLVER
**Lock**: Caplock revolver
**Stock**: Walnut
**Barrel**: 7.5 in.
**Sights**: Fixed, open
**Weight**: 2.6 lb.
**Bore/ Caliber**: .36
**Features**: Case-hardened frame, steel or brass backstrap and trigger guard.
**Steel:** . . . . . . . . . . . . . . . . . . . $349
**Civil Brass:** . . . . . . . . . . . . . . . $329

**UBERTI BLACK POWDER 1862 POCKET NAVY**

## 1862 POCKET NAVY
**Lock**: Caplock revolver
**Stock**: Walnut
**Barrel**: 5.5 in. or 6.5 in.
**Sights**: Fixed, open
**Weight**: 1.7 lb.
**Bore/ Caliber**: .36
**Features**: Case-hardened frame; brass backstrap and trigger guard; octagonal, blued barrel.
**MSRP** . . . . . . . . . . . . . . . . . . . $349

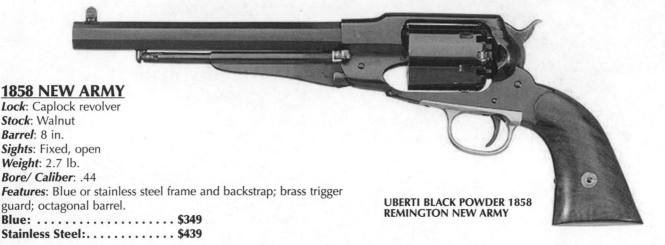

## 1858 NEW ARMY

*Lock*: Caplock revolver
*Stock*: Walnut
*Barrel*: 8 in.
*Sights*: Fixed, open
*Weight*: 2.7 lb.
*Bore/ Caliber*: .44
*Features*: Blue or stainless steel frame and backstrap; brass trigger guard; octagonal barrel.
**Blue:** . . . . . . . . . . . . . . . . . . . **$349**
**Stainless Steel:** . . . . . . . . . . . . **$439**

**UBERTI BLACK POWDER 1858 REMINGTON NEW ARMY**

**UBERTI BLACK POWDER 1862 POLICE REVOLVER**

## 1862 POLICE REVOLVER

*Lock*: Caplock revolver
*Stock*: Walnut
*Barrel*: 5.5 in. or 6.5 in.
*Sights*: Fixed, open
*Weight*: 1.6 lb.
*Bore/ Caliber*: .36
*Features*: Case-hardened frame; brass backstrap and trigger guard; fluted round barrel.
**MSRP** . . . . . . . . . . . . . . . . . . . . **$349**

BLACK POWDER

# Uberti Black Powder

## 1848-1849 POCKET REVOLVERS
*Lock*: Caplock revolver
*Stock*: Walnut
*Barrel*: 4 in.
*Sights*: Fixed, open
*Weight*: 1.5 lb.
*Bore/ Caliber*: .31
*Features*: Case-hardened frame; brass backstrap and trigger guard; blue octagonal barrel; engraved.
**MSRP . . . . . . . . . . . . . . . . . . . . $339**

**UBERTI BLACK POWDER
1849 POCKET REVOLVER**

# Alpen Optics Scopes

## By Thomas McIntyre

**ALPEN APEX XP
2-10X44MM**

## APEX XP
## 2-10X44MM

Alpen Apex XP Extreme Performance
Radical Hunter Series Riflescope
2-10x44mm with Mossy Oak Camo,
Model #4054 (also in matte black in
3-9x40, 2-10x44, and 4-16x44)
**Weight**: 17 oz.
**Length**: 14 in.
**Power**: 2x-10X
**Objective Diameter**: 44mm
**Main Tube Diameter**: 1 in
**Exit Pupil**: 15mm-4.4mm
**Field of View**: 40 ft-9 ft @ 100 yds
**Twilight Factor**: 9.4-21
**Eye Relief**: 3 ⁴/₅ inches
**Waterproof**: Yes
**Fogproof**: Yes
***Lifetime No-Fault Warranty***
***Product Description***: The Alpen Apex
XP riflescope series features fully
multi-coated optical design, one-
piece-tube construction, and zero reset
windage and elevation dials with ¼
MOA click adjustments (⅛ MOA in the
4-16x44). A fast-focus eye piece is
standard, and all come with side-focus
parallax adjustments. Reticles include
the BDC, WBDC-A, and WBDC-B.
Also comes with a 4 inch detachable
sun shade.
**MSRP:** . . . . . . . . . . . . . . . . . . . **$500**

## APEX XP
## 6-24X50MM

Alpen Apex XP Extreme Performance
6-24x50mm, matte black (also in 1.5-
6x42, and in red-dot illuminated-reti-
cle 1.5-6x42, 2.5-10x50, and 4-16x56)
**Weight**: 24 oz.
**Length**: 15 ½ in.
**Width**: 2 ½ in.
**Power**: 6X-24X
**Objective Diameter**: 50mm
**Main Tube Diameter**: 30mm
**Exit Pupil**: 8mm-2mm
**Field of View**: 16 ft-4 ft @ 100 yds
**Twilight Factor**: 17.3-34.6
**Eye Relief**: 3 ½ inches
**Waterproof**: Yes
**Fogproof**: Yes
***Lifetime No-Fault Warranty***

***Product Description***: Similar features
to those on the 1-inch tube model XP.
The 6-24x50 and the 4-16x56 have ⅛
MOA adjustment increments, while
the others have ¼ MOA.
**MSRP:** . . . . . . . . . . . . . . . . . . **$530**

## KODIAK

Alpen Kodiak 3.5-10x50, matte black,
Model #2060 (also in 1.5-4x32,
3-9x32, 4x32, 3-9x40, 4-12x40, and
6-24x50
**Weight**: 21 oz.
**Length**: 13 ⅕ in.
**Width**: 2 in.
**Power**: 3.5X-10X
**Objective Diameter**: 50mm
**Main Tube Diameter**: 1 in.
**Exit Pupil**: 13.5mm-4.9mm
**Field of View**: 35 ft-12 ft @ 100 yds
**Twilight Factor**: 13.2-22.4
**Eye Relief**: 3 in.
**Waterproof**: Yes
**Fogproof**: Yes
***Limited Lifetime Warranty***
***Product Description***: The Alpen
Kodiak riflescope series features multi-
coated optical design. It has oversized
zero-reset windage and elevation dials
adjustable in ¼ MOA (⅛ MOA in the
6-24x50) clicks and comes with the
AccuPlex Tapered duplex-style reticle.
A fast-focus eye piece is standard.
**MSRP:** . . . . . . . . . . . . . . . . . . **$195**

**ALPEN APEX XP
6-24X50MM**

**ALPEN KOPIAK**

SCOPES

# Bushnell Outdoor Products

## BONE COLLECTOR

Bushnell Bone Collector 3-9x40mm DOA 600 Reticle (also in 3-9x40mm DOA 250 Reticle)
**Weight**: 13 oz.
**Length**: 12 $^3/_5$ in.
**Power**: 3-9X
**Objective Diameter**: 40mm
**Main Tube Diameter**: 1 in.
**Eye Relief**: 3 $^1/_3$ in.
**Exit Pupil**: 13.3-4.4mm
**Field of View**: 33.8-11.5 ft @ 100 yds
**Twilight Factor**: 10.95-18.97
**Waterproof**: Yes
**Fogproof**: Yes
**Product Description**: The Bushnell Bone Collector Edition advertises 90-percent light transmission with the "Ultra Wide Band Coating" and RainGuard HD technologies. Made from a one-piece aluminum tube with a fast-focus eyepiece. The Bushnell DOA reticle technology featuring the Rack Bracket for ranging distance and judging a buck's trophy quality is available in two configurations–the DOA 600 for centerfire rifles and the DOA 250 for muzzleloaders. The scope has ¼ MOA adjustment increments and a 50 MOA range of adjustment for windage and elevation.
**MSRP**: . . . . . . . . . . . . . . . . .$569.95

## ELITE 3-9X40MM

Bushnell Elite 3-9x40mm Multi-X Reticle (matte finish) (also in 1.25-4x24mm, 2.5-10x40mm, 2.5-10x50mm, 4-16x40mm Multi-X Reticle, 4-16x40mm DOA 600 Reticle, 4-16x50mm, 6-24x40mm Mil-Dot Reticle, 6-24x40mm Multi-X Reticle, 8-32x40mm, Multi-X Reticle, 2-7x32mm, 3-10x40mm, 3-9x40mm Gloss Finish, 3-9x40mm Silver Finish, 3-9x40mm FireFly Reticle, 3-9x40mm DOA 600 Reticle, 3-9x50mm Multi-X Reticle, 3-9x50mm DOA 600 Reticle, 3-9x50mm FireFly Reticle)
**Weight**: 13 oz.
**Length**: 12.6 in.
**Power**: 3-9X
**Objective Diameter**: 40mm
**Main Tube Diameter**: 1 in.
**Eye Relief**: 3 $^2/_5$ in.
**Exit Pupil**: 13.33-4.44mm
**Field of View**: 33.8-11.5 ft @ 100 yds
**Twilight Factor**: 10.95-18.97
**Waterproof**: Yes
**Fogproof**: Yes
**"No Questions Asked" One-Year Elite Warranty and Limited Lifetime Warranty**
**Product Description**: The Elite family of one-piece-tube riflescopes includes fully multi-coated optics, with Bushnell's "Ultra Wide Band Coating"; and the lenses are treated with moisture shedding RainGuard HD. The fingertip windage and elevation adjustments are audible and resettable and in ¼ MOA increments. And the Elites are available in an extensive selection of variable-power, objective, and reticle configurations.
**MSRP**: . . . . . . . . . . . . . . . . .$398.95

## ELITE TACTICAL

Bushnell Elite Tactical 3-12x44mm (also in 10x44mm, 2.5-16x42mm, 4.5-30x50mm, 5-15x40mm, 6-24x50mm Mil-Dot Reticle, 6-24x50mm Illuminated Mil-Dot)
**Weight**: 24.4 oz.
**Length**: 13 in.
**Power**: 3-12X
**Objective Diameter**: 44mm
**Main Tube Diameter**: 30mm
**Eye Relief**: 3 ¾ in.
**Exit Pupil**: 14.66-3.66mm
**Field of View**: 36- 10 ft @ 100 yds
**Twilight Factor**: 11.48-22.97

**BUSHNELL BONE COLLECTOR**

**Waterproof**: Yes
**Fogproof**: Yes
**"No Questions Asked" One-Year Elite Warranty and Limited Lifetime Warranty**
**Product Description**: This year Bushnell's taken their top-of-the-line Elite 6500 riflescope and offered it to "personnel" (military, police, and to private shooters who want a high-tech, hard-use scope and have $1000 to spend) by giving it a tactical treatment. Along with the 1-inch fogproof and waterproof 3-12x44 Elite Tactical comes in a variety of configurations from 10x40mm fixed to 6-24x50mm variable. Some of the scopes feature 6.5X magnification range, similar to the Elite 6500. All come with tactical target-adjustment turrets and non-glare black-matte finish as well as "blacked-out" cosmetics for concealment. All the Elite Tacticals have fully multi-coated (with Bushnell "Ultra Wide Band Coating") optics and RainGuard HD moisture-shedding exterior coating, along with illuminated and non-illuminated mildot reticles.
**MSRP**: . . . . . . . . . . . . . . . .$1435.95

**BUSHNELL ELITE 3-9X40MM**

**BUSHNELL ELITE TACTICAL**

# Bushnell Outdoor Products

**BUSHNELL ELITE 6500**

**BUSHNELL TROPHY XLT**

**BUSHNELL TROPHY XLT 2-7x36MM CROSSBOW SCOPE WITH DOA RETICLE**

## ELITE 6500

Bushnell Elite 6500 2.5-16x50mm Mil-Dot Reticle (also in 1.25x-8x32mm, 2.5-16x42mm Fine Multi-X Reticle, 2.5-16x42mm Mil-Dot Reticle, 2.5-16x50mm FMX Reticle, 4.5-30x50mm DOA 600 Reticle, 4.5-30x50mm Fine Multi-X Reticle, 4.5-30x50mm Mil-Dot Reticle)
**Weight**: 21 oz.
**Length**: 13 ½ in.
**Power**: 2.5-16X
**Objective Diameter**: 50mm
**Mai Tube Diameter**: 30mm
**Eye Relief**: 3 $^9/_{10}$ in
**Exit Pupil**: 20-3.12mm
**Field of View**: 42-7 ft @ 100 yds
**Twilight Factor**: 11.18-28.28
**Waterproof**: Yes
**Fogproof**: Yes
**"No Questions Asked" One-Year Elite Warranty and Limited Lifetime Warranty**
**Product Description**: The Elite 6500 series features a 6.5-times range of magnification. Lenses have a 60-layer "Ultra Wide Band Coating" with an advertised 91 percent total light transmission through the scope, and are treated with permanent, water-repellent RainGuard HD coating. Windage and elevation adjustments are in ¼ MOA increments and do not require a tool and are audible. The variable Elite 6500s come in a variety of power, objective, and reticle configurations.
**MSRP:** . . . . . . . . . . . . . . . . $1242.95

## TROPHY XLT
Bushnell Trophy XLT 3-9x40mm Mil-Dot Reticle (also in 3-9x40mm DOA 250 Reticle Matte Finish, 3-9x40mm DOA 250 Reticle Camo Finish, 3-9x40mm DOA 600 Reticle, 3-9x40mm Multi-X Reticle Gloss Finish, 3-9x40mm Multi-X Reticle Silver Finish, 3-9x40mm Multi-X Reticle Matte Finish, 3-9x40mm Circle-X Reticle, 3-9x50mm, 4-12x40mm DOA 600 Reticle, 4-12x40mm Multi-X Reticle, 1-4x24mm, 1.5-6x42mm, 1.5-6x44mm, 3-12x56mm, 1.75-4x32mm Camo Finish, 1.75-4x32mm Matte Finish, 2-6x32mm Matte Finish, 2-6x32mm Silver Finish, 2-7x36mm DOA Crossbow Reticle, 2-7x36mm DOA 200 Reticle, 3-9x40mm DOA 200 Reticle, 6-18x50mm)
**Weight**: 14.1 oz.
**Length**: 11 $^9/_{10}$ in.
**Power**: 3-9X
**Objective Diameter**: 40mm
**Main Tube Diameter**: 1 in.
**Eye Relief**: 4 in.
**Exit Pupil**: 13.3-4.4mm
**Field of View**: 40-13 ft @ 100 yds
**Twilight Factor**: 10.95-18.97
**Waterproof**: Yes
**Fogproof**: Yes
**Product Description**: The Trophy XLT features fully multi-coated optics that are advertised to produce 91 percent total-light transmission. It has a one-piece tube with an integrated saddle. Has ¼ MOA fingertip windage and elevation adjustments with a range of adjustment of 80 MOA. Comes with Butler Creek flip-up scope covers.
**MSRP:** . . . . . . . . . . . . . . . . $204.95

## TROPHY XLT CROSSBOW SCOPE
Bushnell Trophy XLT 2-7x 36mm Crossbow Scope with DOA Reticle
**Weight**: 14.3 oz.

**Length**: 13 in.
**Power**: 2-7X
**Objective Diameter**: 36mm
**Main Tube Diameter**: 1 in.
**Exit Pupil**: 13.3-4.4mm
**Eye Relief**: 5 in.
**Twilight Factor**: 8.5-15.9
**Field of View**: 33-11 ft @ 100 yds
**Waterproof**: Yes
**Fogproof**: Yes
**Limited Lifetime Warranty**
**Product Description**: The Bushnell crossbow scope is a new addition to the Trophy XLT line of riflescopes. The Trophy XLT features fully multi-coated optics housed in a one-piece tube with an integrated mounting saddle. The included Butler Creek flip-up caps shield the lenses. Bushnell advertises 91 percent light transmission, and the specialized DOA Crossbow reticle and ¼ MOA fingertip windage and elevation adjustments allow for extended-range shooting out to 60 yards.
**MSRP:** . . . . . . . . . . . . . . . . $227.95

# Cabela's

## 5X ALPHA

Cabela's 5X Alpha Riflescope
3-15x40mm
**Weight**: 12 oz.
**Length**: 12 $^2/_5$ in.
**Power**: 3-15X
**Objective Diameter**: 40mm
**Main Tube Diameter**: 1 in.
**Exit Pupil**: 13.33-2.66mm
**Field of View**: 31.5-6.3 ft @ 100 yards
**Twilight Factor**: 10.95-24.49
**Eye Relief**: 4 in.
**Waterproof**: Yes
**Fogproof**: Yes
**Product Description**: The Alpha riflescopes in 5X optical zoom and the EXT bullet drop reticle for long-range accuracy out to 500 yards. The other reticles are matched to bullet drop at 300, 400, and 500 yards. Pine Ridge lenses are multicoated for enhanced light transmission and image clarity. Scopes are waterproof, shockproof and fogproof for all-weather performance. Windage and elevation adjustments are ¼ MOA clicks.
**MSRP**: . . . . . . . . . . . . . . . .$244.99

## 30MM TACTICAL CLASSIC

Cabela's 30mm Tactical Classic 6-18 SF x50mm EXT (also with Duplex reticle and in 2.5-10X50 and 8-32 SF x50 with both EXT and Duplex reticles)
**Weight**: 17.5 oz.
**Length**: 13 ¼ in.
**Power**: 6-18X
**Objective Diameter**: 50mm
**Main Tube Diameter**: 30mm
**Exit Pupil**: 8.33-2.77mm
**Field of View**: 15.88-5.24 ft @ 100 yards
**Twilight Factor**: 17.32-30
**Eye Relief**: 4 in.
**Waterproof**: Yes
**Fogproof**: Yes
**Product Description**: Made with the larger, tactical-grade three-dimensionally forged 30mm tube and with Guidetech broadband lens technology. All components are machined to military-grade tolerances. Low-profile turrets with ¼ MOA click windage and elevation adjustments for the 2.5-10 power models and a $^1/_8$ MOA click windage and elevation adjustments for the 6-18 and 8-32 power models.

Hard-blasted anodized finish and moisture- and dust-repelling lenses.
**MSRP**: . . . . . . . . . . . . . . . .$369.99

## ALASKAN GUIDE

Cabela's Alaskan Guide 1-inch 3-10x40mm EXT– "extended range" (also in 4-12x44SF–side-focus parallax adjustment–and 6-18x50SF EXT, and 3-10x40, 4-12x44SF, and 6-18x50SF Duplexes)
**Weight**: 13.5 oz.
**Length**: 12 $^2/_5$ in.
**Power**: 3-10X
**Objective Diameter**: 40mm
**Main Tube Diameter**: 1 in.
**Exit Pupil**: 13.33-4mm
**Field of View**: 33.65-10.48 ft @ 100 yards
**Twilight Factor**: 10.95-20
**Eye Relief**: 3 ¾ in.
**Waterproof**: Yes
**Fogproof**: Yes
**Product Description**: This scope use "Guidetech" broadband lens coating

**CABELA'S 5X ALPHA**

technology. The body is a three-dimensionally forged one-piece tube. All components are machined to military-grade tolerances. Low-profile turrets with ¼ MOA click windage and elevation adjustments. Hard-blasted anodized finish for durability and corrosion resistance. Moisture- and dust-repelling lenses.
**MSRP**: . . . . . . . . . . . . . . . .$269.99

**CABELA'S 30MM TACTICAL CLASSIC RIFLESCOPE**

**CABELA'S ALASKAN GUIDE**

SCOPES

# Cabela's

## ALASKAN GUIDE PREMIUM

Cabela's Alaskan Guide Premium 3-9x40mm (also in 4-12x40 and 6-20x40 with adjustable objective– AO)

**Weight**: 13 oz.
**Length**: 12 $^2/_5$ in.
**Power**: 3-9X
**Objective Diameter**: 40mm
**Main Tube Diameter**: 1 in.
**Exit Pupil**: 13.33-4.44mm
**Field of View**: 33.2-11.1 ft @ 100 yards
**Twilight Factor**: 10.95-18.97
**Eye Relief**: 3 ½ in.
**Waterproof**: Yes
**Fogproof**: Yes
**Limited Lifetime Warranty**
**Product Description**: The lens surface is fully multi-coated. A one-piece aluminum tube; power adjustment is rubber coated; positive-click increments on the fast-focus eyepiece; metal-to-metal contact between the windage and elevation adjustments and the erector tube; and ½ MOA adjustments. The AO ring on the higher magnification scopes is knurled.
**MSRP:** . . . . . . . . . . . . . . . . .**$299.99**

## EURO SCOPE

**Product Name and Model**: Cabela's Euro Riflescope 3-9x42mm EXT (also with Duplex reticle, and in 4-12x50 and 6-18x50 with EXT and Duplex reticles)
**Weight**: 16 oz.
**Length**: 12 $^2/_5$ in.
**Power**: 3-9X
**Objective Diameter**: 42mm
**Main Tube Diameter**: 1 in.
**Exit Pupil**: 14-4.66mm
**Field of View**: 36.3-12.1 ft @ 100 yards
**Twilight Factor**: 11.22-19.44
**Eye Relief**: 3 ¾ in.
**Waterproof**: Yes
**Fogproof**: Yes
**Product Description**: Cabela's has partnered with the Czech optics manufacturer Meopta to make its new Euro line of rifle scopes. These 1 inch tube variable scopes are CNC machined from a single billet of aircraft-aluminum and bead blasted before undergoing ELOX (electrolytic oxidation) anodization for a reduced-glare black

**CABELA'S ALASKAN GUIDE PREMIUM**

**CABELA'S LEVER-ACTION RIFLESCOPE**

matte, abrasion-resistant finish. The scopes are available in configurations ranging from 3-9x42mm to 4-12x50 and 6-18x50mm, with objectives on the 6-18s equipped with parallax adjustment. Lenses are fully multi-coated using ion-assisted coatings. The scopes is listed as having 3 ¾ inches of eye relief; fields of view that span from 36.3 feet to 6.1 feet at 100 yards, depending on power setting and objective diameter; have fast-focus eyepieces; and are waterproof and fogproof. Elevation and windage turrets are finger adjustable in ¼ MOA clicks. The Euro scopes also offer two reticle options, the "D" for duplex and for $50 more the "EXT" glass-etched hash-marked "extended range" for individual holds out to 500 yards. And the Euro scopes come with Cabela's 60 day free-trial-period guarantee.
**MSRP:** . . . . . . . . . . . . . . . . .**$449.99**

## LEVER ACTION
Cabela's Lever Action 3-9x40mm .30-30 Winchester Reticle (also in .308 Marlin, .338 Marlin Express, .444 Marlin, .35 Remington, and .45-70 Govt. reticles)
**Weight**: 14.64 oz.
**Length**: 13 in.
**Power**: 3-9X
**Objective Diameter**: 40mm
**Main Tube Diameter**: 1 in.
**Exit Pupil**: 13.33-4.44mm
**Field of View**: 30.55-9.6 ft @ 100 yards
**Twilight Factor**: 10.95-18.97
**Eye Relief**: 5 ½ in.
**Waterproof**: Yes
**Fogproof**: Yes
**Product Description**: These scopes are tailored for use with Hornady LEVERevolution, Flex Tip bullet-technology ammunition. The scopes are outfitted with Ballistic Glass Reticles specifically engineered for use with a particular Hornady LEVERevolution round. An extra-long, 5½ inch eye relief facilitates mounting on traditional lever-action rifles. Comes with 200 and 300 yard horizontal lines to hold dead-on at those ranges with 100 yard zero. Besides the .30-30 Winchester regulated for the 160 grain LEVERevolution round, other models are available for use with LEVERevolution ammunition in .45-70 (modern rifles only) using a 325-grain bullet, .444 Marlin using a 265-grain bullet, .308 Marlin using a 160-grain bullet, .35 Rem. using a 200-grain bullet, .338 Marlin using a 200-grain bullet and .44 Mag. using a 225-grain bullet. The tube is machined aluminum and lenses are multi-coated. Windage and elevation are adjustable in ¼ MOA clicks.
**MSRP:** . . . . . . . . . . . . . . . . .**$99.99**

**CABELA'S EURO SCOPE**

## RIMFIRE RIFLESCOPE

Cabela's Rimfire Riflescope 3-9x40mm with Duplex reticle (also in 4x32)
**Weight**: 13.4 oz.
**Length**: 12 in.
**Power**: 3-9X
**Objective Diameter**: 40mm
**Main Tube Diameter**: 1 in.
**Exit Pupil**: 13.33-4.44mm
**Field of View**: 37.7-12.4 ft @ 100 yards
**Twilight Factor**: 10.95-18.97
**Eye Relief**: 4 in.
**Waterproof**: Yes
**Fogproof**: Yes
**Product Description**: For hunting, target shooting, or plinking with a rimfire rifle. Parallax-free at 50 yards. Multi-coated glass optics. Extended eye relief and an expanded exit pupil. Low-profile windage and elevation turrets.
**MSRP**: . . . . . . . . . . . . . . . . . .**$79.99**

**CABELA'S RIMFIRE RIFLESCOPE**

## SHOTGUN/BLACK-POWDER

Cabela's Shotgun/Black-Powder 2.5-7x32mm with Diamond reticle (also with Duplex reticle and in camo, and in 2.5x32 fixed power with Diamond reticle)
**Weight**: 12.2 oz.
**Length**: 11 ⁴/₅ in.
**Power**: 2.5-7X
**Objective Diameter**: 32mm
**Main Tube Diameter**: 1 in.
**Exit Pupil**: 12.8-4.57mm
**Field of View**: 40.03-14.15 ft @ 100 yards
**Twilight Factor**: 8.94-14.96
**Eye Relief**: 4 in.
**Waterproof**: Yes
**Fogproof**: Yes
**Product Description**: For use with slug guns and muzzleloading rifles. Has extended eye relief and an expanded exit pupil to promote faster target acquisition. Uses rigid machined-aluminum tube and has low-profile turrets for windage and elevation adjustments. Also available in Seclusion 3D camouflage.
**MSRP**: . . . . . . . . . . . . . . . . . .**$69.99**

**CABELA'S SHOTGUN/BLACK POWDER**

**SCOPES**

# Cabela's

## ALASKAN GUIDE

Cabela's Alaskan Guide 30mm 3-12 SF x52mm with Rangefinding reticle (also in 4-16 SF x52, and both with side-focus parallax adjustment and with Duplex and EXT reticles)
**Weight**: 21.9 oz.
**Length**: 14 in.
**Power**: 3-12X
**Objective Diameter**: 52mm
**Main Tube Diameter**: 30mm
**Exit Pupil**: 17.33-4.33mm
**Field of View**: 31.5-7.8 ft @ 100 yards
**Twilight Factor**: 12.48-24.97
**Eye Relief**: 4 in.
**Waterproof**: Yes
**Fogproof**: Yes
**Product Description**: The features on these scopes are similar to those on the other Alaskan Guide rifles with the addition of the 30mm tube and 52mm objective for added light gathering and enhanced field of view with less aberration.
**MSRP**: . . . . . . . . . . . . . . . . .$269.99

## PINE RIDGE

Cabela's Pine Ridge .17 Tactical 3-12 SF x40mm with Target Dot reticle (also with Duplex reticle and in 3-9x40 with Duplex reticle)
**Weight**: 16.2 oz.
**Length**: 13 $2/5$ in.
**Power**: 3-12X
**Objective Diameter**: 40mm
**Main Tube Diameter**: 1 in.
**Exit Pupil**: 13.3 3-3.33mm
**Field of View**: 29.42-7.33 ft @ 100 yards
**Twilight Factor**: 10.95-21.9
**Eye Relief**: 4 in.
**Waterproof**: Yes
**Fogproof**: Yes
**Product Description**: Redesigned in 2010 with new low-profile knurled turrets for windage and elevation adjustments. Incrementally calibrated to adjust for bullet drop out to 300 yards. Fully coated optics. The 3-12x40 features side-focus parallax adjustment and is available with the Target Dot reticle, with Duplex also available. Uses lighter, smaller "egg-shell" eyepiece.
**MSRP**: . . . . . . . . . . . . . . . . .$119.99

## POWDERHORN MUZZLELOADER

Cabela's Powderhorn Muzzleloader 3-10x40mm (also in silver and camo)
**Weight**: 11.6 oz.
**Length**: 12 $1/5$ in.
**Power**: 3-10X
**Objective Diameter**: 40mm
**Main Tube Diameter**: 1 in.
**Exit Pupil**: 13.33-4mm
**Field of View**: 31.5-10.5 ft @ 100 yards
**Twilight Factor**: 10.95-20
**Eye Relief**: 3 ¾ in.
**Waterproof**: Yes
**Fogproof**: Yes
**Product Description**: The ballistic reticle of the Powderhorn scope is regulated to match bullet drop. When the scope is sighted in at 100 yards at 10X, the next bar down is calibrated for a drop at 150 yards and the lowest bar down for 250 yards. Loading data is based on the 250-grain saboted bullet and 150 grains of Triple Se7en FFg powder. Scope multi-coated lenses and hand-turn ¼ MOA click adjustments.
**MSRP**: . . . . . . . . . . . . . . . . .$119.99

**CABELA'S ALASKAN GUIDE 30MM RIFLESCOPE**

**CABELA'S POWDERHORN MUZZLELOADER SCOPE**

SCOPES

# Carl Zeiss Sports Optics

ZEISS CONQUEST 3-9X40

ZEISS CONQUEST 6.5-20X50 TARGET

ZEISS VICTORY DIAVARI 1.5-6X42

## CONQUEST 3-9X40

**Weight**: 15.17 oz.
**Length**: 12 9/10 in.
**Main Body Tube Diameter**: 1 in.
**Power**: 3-9X
**Objective Diameter**: 40mm
**Exit Pupil**: 13.3-4.4mm
**Field of View**: 34-11 ft @ 100 yards
**Twilight Factor**: 8.5-19.0
**Eye Relief**: 4 in.
**Waterproof**: Yes
**Fogproof**: Yes
**Product Description**: The Conquest 3-9x40 is a classic, all-purpose scope with excellent light gathering ability. It offers wide fields of view, brilliant contrast and high resolution images, and is perfect for shotguns, muzzle loaders, and centerfire rifles. Conquest riflescopes are available with a variety of reticles including the Rapid-Z® Ballistic Reticle.
**MSRP:** . . . . . . . . . . . . . . . . .**$399.99**
**(with #20 reticle, also in 3-9x40; 3.5-10x44, 4.5-14x44, 3-9x50, 3.5-10x50, 4.5-14x50, 6.5-20x50, 3-12x56)**

## CONQUEST 6.5-20X50

**Weight**: 21.83 oz.
**Length**: 15 3/5 in.
**Main Body Tube Diameter**: 1 in.
**Power**: 6.5-20X
**Objective Diameter**: 50mm
**Exit Pupil**: 7.7-2.5mm
**Field of View**: 18-6 ft @ 100 yards
**Twilight Factor**: 18-31.6
**Eye Relief**: 3 ½ in.
**Waterproof**: Yes
**Fogproof**: Yes
**Product Description**: The high-magnification Zeiss Conquest 6.5-20x50 includes parallax adjustment for varmints or long-range shooting. Available with either target or hunting turret and with a variety of reticles including the Rapid-Z® 800 and

Rapid-Z 1000® Ballistic Reticles.
**MSRP:** . . . . . . . . **Starting at $999.99**
**(with #4 or #20 reticle)**

## VICTORY DIAVARI 1.5

Victory Diavari 1.5-6x42 T (also in 2.5-10x50 T, 3-12x56 T, 4-16x50 T FL, 6-24x56 T FL and 6-24x72 T FL)
**Weight**: 15.52 oz.
**Length**: 12 ¼ in.
**Main Body Tube Diameter**: 30mm
**Power**: 1.5-6X
**Objective Diameter**: 42mm
**Exit Pupil**: 15.0mm-7.0mm
**Field of View**: 72-23 ft @ 100 yards
**Twilight Factor**: 4.2-15.9
**Eye Relief**: 3 ½ in.
**Waterproof**: Yes

**Fogproof**: Yes
**Product Description**: Zeiss Victory Diavari riflescopes come with LotuTec® lens coating and ZEISS T multi-coating. The 1.5-6x42 is an compact, lightweight, low profile scope designed for fast target acquisition. Available with railmount and with illumination on select models. And with FL glass where shown
**MSRP:** . . . . . . . . . . . . . . . . .**$1649.99**

SCOPES

# Carl Zeiss Sports Optics

**ZEISS VICTORY DIARANCE 2.5-10X50**

**ZEISS VICTORY VARIPOINT 1.1-4X24**

**ZEISS VICTORY DIARANGE M 2.5-10X50**

**ZEISS VICTORY VARIPOINT 3-12X56**

## VICTORY DIARANGE M 2.5-10X50

Victory Diarange M 2.5-10x50 T* (also in 3-12x56 T*)
**Weight**: 31.75 oz.
**Length**: 13 ⅕ in.
**Width**: 56.5mm (rail mount)
**Power**: 2.5-10X
**Objective Diameter**: 50mm
**Exit Pupil**: 15-5mm
**Field of View**: 43 ½-12 ft @ 100 yards
**Twilight Factor**: 7.1-22.4
**Eye Relief**: 3 ½ in.
**Waterproof**: Yes to 400 mbar
**Fogproof**: Yes
***Transferable Limited Lifetime Warranty on optics and mechanics.***
**Electronics**: 5 Years
**Product Description**: The Victory Diarange M series riflescope laser-ranges from 10 yds to 999 yds (depending on the size of the object, reflectivity, angle of impact and weather conditions) with a measuring accuracy of ± 1 yd at ranges up to 600 yards and ± 0.5% at ranges beyond 600 yards in a measuring time of 0.5 seconds. The Diarange can be used in temperatures between -13° to 122° F. Available with illuminated #43 Mil Dot and illuminated Rapid-Z® 600 & 800 reticles.
**MSRP:** . . . . . . . . . . . . . . . . $3949.99

## VICTORY DIAVARI 6-24

**Product Name and Model**: Victory Diavari 6-24x72 T* FL
**Weight**: 37.39 oz.
**Length**: 14 9/10 in.
**Main Body Tube Diameter**: 34mm
**Power**: 6-24X
**Objective Diameter**: 72mm
**Exit Pupil**: 12.-3.mm
**Field of View**: 18 ³/₁₀- 5 ¹/₁₀ ft @ 100 yards
**Twilight Factor**: 16.9-41.6
**Eye Relief**: 3 ½ in.
**Waterproof**: Yes
**Fogproof**: Yes
**Product Description**: The 6-24x72 T* Diavari FL riflescope uses a FL glass objective and LotuTec® coating. Available with two ballistic-compensation options—BDC Ballistic Turret and Rapid Z® Ballistic reticle. The Victory 6-24x72 T* FL is designed for tactical marksmen, varmint or predator hunters, and long-range hunters and shooters. This scope also features parallax compensation and ¼ MOA lockable windage and elevation turrets. Available with illumination on select models.
**MSRP:** . . . . . . . . . . . . . . . . $3399.99

## VICTORY VARIPOINT 1.1-4X24

Victory Varipoint 1.1-4x24 T* (also in 1.5-6x42 T*, 2.5-10x50 T* and 3-12x56 T*)
**Weight**: 15.87 oz.
**Length**: 11 ⁴/₅ in.
**Main Body Tube Diameter**: 30mm
**Power**: 1.1-4X
**Objective Diameter**: 24mm
**Exit Pupil**: 14.8-6.0mm
**Field of View**: 108-31 ft @ 100 yards
**Twilight Factor**: 3.1-9.8
**Eye Relief**: 3 ½ in.
**Waterproof**: Yes
**Fogproof**: Yes
**Product Description**: The ZEISS Victory Varipoint has an illuminated red-dot reticle for fast target acquisition. It also uses LotuTec® "hydrophobic" lens coating.
**MSRP:** . . . . . . . . . . . . . . . $2199.99

## VICTORY VARIPOINT 3-12X56

Victory Varipoint 3-12x56 T*
**Weight**: 21.34 oz.
**Length**: 14 in.
**Main Body Tube Diameter**: 30mm
**Power**: 3-12X
**Objective Diameter**: 56mm
**Exit Pupil**: 14.7mm-4.7mm
**Field of View**: 37 ½-10 ½ ft @ 100 yards
**Twilight Factor**: 8.5-25.9
**Eye Relief**: 3 ½ in.
**Waterproof**: Yes
**Fogproof**: Yes
**Product Description**: The large objective lens of the Victory Varipoint 3-12x56 T* is traditional for European scopes that are often used from shooting towers in low light. With illuminated red-dot reticle.
**MSRP:** . . . . . . . . . . . . . . . $2399.99

**SCOPES**

# Leatherwood/Hi-Lux Optics

LEATHERWOOD/HI-LUX
CMR SERIES 1-4X24

## CLOSE MEDIUM RANGE—CMR SERIES 1-4X24MM

**Weight**: 16.5 oz
**Length**: 10 $\frac{1}{5}$ in.
**Main Body Tube Diameter**: 30mm
**Power**: 1-4X
**Objective Diameter**: 24mm
**Exit Pupil**: 11.1-6mm
**Field of View**: 94.8-26.2 ft @ 100 yards
**Twilight Factor**: 4.89-9.79
**Eye Relief**: 3 in.
**Waterproof**: Yes
**Fogproof**: Yes
**Product Description**: All surfaces of all lenses are fully multi-coated; zero-locking turrets; large external target-style windage and elevation adjustment knobs; power-ring extended lever handle for power change; fast eye-piece focus; CMR ranging reticle for determining range and also BDC hold over value good for .223, .308, and other calibers; green or red illuminated reticle; turrets adjustable in ½ MOA clicks.
**MSRP** . . . . . . . . . . . . . . . . . . . $399

## TOP ANGLE SERIES 7-30X50MM (ALSO IN 3-12X50 AND 4-16X50)

**Weight**: 29.8 oz
**Length**: 17 $\frac{1}{5}$ in.
**Main Body Tube Diameter**: 30mm
**Power**: 7-30X

LEATHERWOOD/HI-LUX TOP
ANGLE SERIES 7-30X50MM

**Objective Diameter**: 50mm
**Exit Pupil**: 6.9-2.3mm
**Field of View**: 10.6-3.5 ft @ 100 yards
**Twilight Factor**: 18.70-38.72
**Eye Relief**: 3$\frac{1}{3}$ in.
**Waterproof**: Yes
**Fogproof**: Yes
**Limited Lifetime Warranty**
**Product Description**: All surfaces of all lenses are fully multi-coated; larger diameter turret housing offers additional windage-elevation adjustment in ¼ MOA clicks; top-angle objective lens focus rather than adjustment on the objective lens bell; and mildot reticle for determining range.
**MSRP** . . . . . . . . . . . . . . . . . . . $449

SCOPES

# Leatherwood/Hi-Lux Optics

LEATHERWOOD/HI-LUX TOBY BRIDGES SERIES HIGH PERFORMANCE MUZZLELOADING 3-9X40MM

LEATHERWOOD/HI-LUX M-1000 AUTO RANGING TRAJECTORY 2.5-10X44MM

LEATHERWOOD/HI-LUX WM. MALCOLM SERIES LONG 6X 32 INCH

## TOBY BRIDGES SERIES HIGH PERFORMANCE MUZZLELOADING 3-9X40MM, MATTE BLACK (ALSO AVAILABLE IN SILVER FINISH)

*Weight*: 15.8 oz
*Length*: 12 ½ in.
*Main Body Tube Diameter*: 1 in.
*Power*: 3-9X
*Objective Diameter*: 40mm
*Exit Pupil*: 13.3-4.4mm
*Field of View*: 39-13 ft @ 100 yards
*Twilight Factor*:
*Eye Relief*: 3 ¼ in.
*Waterproof*: Yes
*Fogproof*: Yes
*Limited Lifetime Warranty*
*Product Description*: The TB/ML scope is designed in-line ignition muzzleloaders and saboted bullets. It offers multiple reticles for shooting at ranges out to 250 yards. The scope is shipped with a chart providing points of impact at different ranges when using the longer range cross-bar reticles with different bullets at different velocities. All lens surfaces are multi-coated for maximum light transmission.
**MSRP** . . . . . . . . . . . . . . . . . .**$179.00**
**(Blue-black), $189.00 (Silver)**

## WM. MALCOLM SERIES LONG 6X 32 INCH (ALSO IN 3X 17 INCH AND 6X 18-IN. SHORT MALCOLMS)

*Weight*: 32.5 oz
*Length*: 30 ½ in. (without front mount extension tube)
*Main Body Tube Diameter*: ¾ in.
*Power*: 6X
*Objective Diameter*: 16mm
*Exit Pupil*: 5.8mm
*Field of View*: 10 ft @ 100 yards
*Twilight Factor*:
*Eye Relief*: 4 in.
*Waterproof*: Yes
*Fogproof*: Yes
*Product Description*: A modern copy of the Model 1855 W. Malcolm riflescopes, comes with early-style mounts for scoping original and replica 19th century breechloading rifles (Sharps, rolling block, high wall, etc.) or late period long-range percussion muzzleloading bullet rifles. Objective, ocular, and internal lenses are fully multi-coated for maximum light transition through a ¾ inch (steel) scope tube. Interchangeable front extension tubes allows this mid 1800s period-correct scope to be mounted on rifles with barrels of 30 to 34 inches.
**MSRP** . . . . . . . . . . . . . . . . . .**$439.00**

## M-1000 AUTO RANGING TRAJECTORY 2.5-10X44MM.

*Weight*: 25.2 oz
*Length*: 13 ¹/₅ in
*Main Body Tube Diameter*: 1 in.
*Power*: 2.5-10X
*Objective Diameter*: 44mm
*Exit Pupil*: 10.2-4mm
*Field of View*: 47.2-11.9 ft @ 100 yards
*Twilight Factor*: 10.5-21
*Eye Relief*: 3 ¹/₁₀ in.
*Waterproof*: Yes
*Fogproof*: Yes
*Limited Lifetime Warranty*
*Product Description*: Leatherwood/Hi-Lux M-1000 Auto Ranging Trajectory 2.5-10x44 scope compensate for the bullet drop automatically by using an external cam system. It can be calibrated for most centerfire rifle cartridges–from .223 to .50 BMG. The shooter sets the multi-caliber cam for the different cartridges being used. The M-1000 scope comes with mount and rings. The scope reticle used is the "No-Math Mil-Dot."
**MSRP** . . . . . . . . . . . . . . . . . .**$459.00**

# Leupold & Stevens

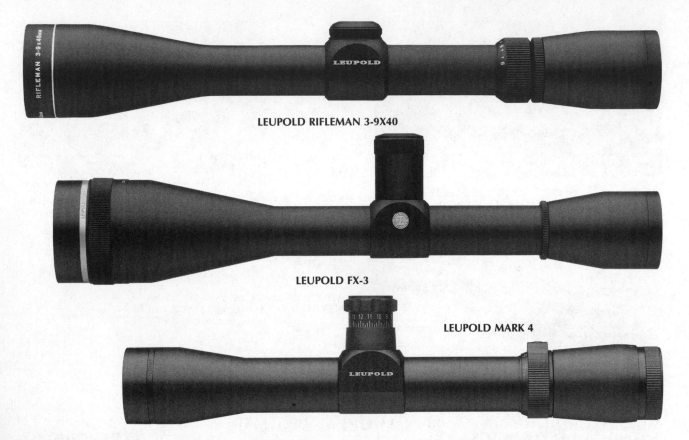

**LEUPOLD RIFLEMAN 3-9X40**

**LEUPOLD FX-3**

**LEUPOLD MARK 4**

## RIFLEMAN

Rifleman 3-9x40mm (also in 2-7x33, 4-12x40, and 3-9x50)
**Weight**: 12.6 oz.
**Length**: 12 $\frac{1}{3}$ in.
**Power**: 3.3-8.5X
**Objective Diameter**: 40mm
**Main Tube Diameter**: 1 in.
**Exit Pupil**: 12-4.7mm
**Field of View**: 329-131 ft @ 1000 yards
**Twilight Factor**: 10.95-18.97
**Eye Relief**: 4.2-3.7 in.
**Waterproof**: Yes
**Fogproof**: Yes
**Product Description**: The Leupold Rifleman series features fully coated lenses for excellent low light brightness, durable waterproof construction.

## FX-3

FX-3 6X42mm Adjustable Objective Competition Hunter (also available in 12x40mm Adjustable Objective Target, 25x40mm Adjustable Objective Silhouette, 30x40mm Adjustable Objective Silhouette and 6x42mm)
**Weight**: 15 oz.

**Length**: 12 $\frac{1}{5}$ inches
**Main Body Tube Diameter**: 1 in.
**Power**: 6X
**Objective Diameter**: 42mm
**Exit Pupil**: 7mm
**Field of View**: 17.3 ft @ 100 yards
**Twilight Factor**: 15.87
**Eye Relief**: 4 $\frac{2}{5}$ in.
**Waterproof**: Yes
**Fogproof**: Yes
**Product Description**: The FX-3 fixed-power riflescope features Leupold's Xtended Twilight Lens System. DiamondCoat 2 helps increase light transmission and provides maximum scratch resistance. Blackened lens edges helps reduce glare and improve resolution and contrast. Windage and elevation adjustments are ¼ MOA.
**MSRP**: . . . . . . . . . . . . . . . . . .$469.99

## MARK 4

Mark 4 2.5-8x36mm MR/T M1 riflescope (also available in 1.5-5x20mm, 1.5-5x20mm M2 and 2.5-8x36mm M2 models)
**Weight**: 16 oz.
**Length**: 11 $\frac{1}{3}$ in.

**Main Body Tube Diameter**: 30mm
**Power**: 2.5-8X
**Objective Diameter**: 36mm
**Exit Pupil**: 14.4-4.5
**Field of View**: 35.5-13.6 ft @ 100 yds
**Twilight Factor**: 9.48-16.97
**Eye Relief**: 3 $\frac{7}{10}$ - 3.0 in.
**Waterproof**: Yes
**Fogproof**: Yes
**Product Description**: The Leupold Mark 4 2.5-8x36mm Mid Range/Tactical M1 riflescope features the Xtended Twilight Lens System and DiamondCoat 2 for maximum scratch resistance. The M1 dials are ¼ MOA for windage and elevation. They are finger-adjustable with audible, tactile clicks. Illuminated Mil Dot and Tactical Milling Reticle (TMR) options are offered, along with a non-illuminated TMR version. Flip-open lens covers are standard.
**MSRP**: . . . . . . . . . . . . . . . . . .$949.99
**($1099.99 with illuminated reticle)**

# Leupold & Stevens

## PRISMATIC HUNTING

Prismatic Hunting 1x14mm, matte black (also in "Dark Earth" anodized finish and with Circle Plex or DCD reticles)
**Weight**: 12 oz.
**Length**: 4 ½ in.
**Main Body Tube Diameter**: 30mm
**Power**: 1X
**Field of View**: 83 ft @ 100 yards
**Eye Relief**: 3 in.
**Waterproof**: Yes
**Fogproof**: Yes
**Product Description**: Leupold's Prismatic 1x14mm riflescope provides the fast target acquisition of a non-magnifying red dot sight with a wide field of view. Key features include an etched-glass reticle that is visible with or without illumination, ½ MOA finger-adjustable windage and elevation dials, and a focusing eyepiece. In addition to the hunting model, including a National Wild Turkey Federation model, the Prismatic is available in a tactical version.
**MSRP**: . . . . . . . . . . . . . . . . .$479.99

## DELTAPOINT REFLEX SIGHT

**Weight**: 0.6 oz.
**Length**: 1 ⅔ in.
**Width**: 1 in.

**Height**: 1 ⅖ in.
**Sight Size**: 3.5 MOA Dot, 7.5 MOA Delta
**Waterproof**: Yes
**Fogproof**: Yes
**Product Description**: Leupold's DeltaPoint Reflex Sight can be used on handguns, shotguns, and AR-style rifles. It comes in a kit that includes numerous mounting options. Includes an aspheric lens, motion activation, auto-brightness sensor, locking elevation and windage adjustment system, and a magnesium housing. Two reticle options are available: 7.5 MOA Delta and 3.5 MOA Dot.
**MSRP**: . . . . . . . . . . . . . . . .$399.99 **(cross-slot mount), $449.99 (all mounts)**

## MARK AR

Mark AR 3-9x40mm T2 riflescope (also available in 1.5-4x20mm, 4-12x40mm Adjustable Objective T2 and 6-18x40mm Adjustable Objective T1 models)
**Weight**: 12.5 oz.
**Length**: 12 ⅖ inches
**Main Body Tube Diameter**: 1 in.

**Power**: 3-9X
**Objective Diameter**: 40mm
**Exit Pupil**: 13.33-4.44mm
**Field of View**: 32.3-14 ft @ 100 yds
**Twilight Factor**: 10.95-18.97
**Eye Relief**: 4 ⁷⁄₁₀ - 3 ⁷⁄₁₀ in.
**Waterproof**: Yes
**Fogproof**: Yes
**Product Description**: The Leupold Mark AR riflescope features a Multicoat 4 lens system for a bright sight picture. The ½ MOA T2 elevation adjustment includes a pre-engraved Bullet Drop Compensation (BDC) dial to match the ballistics of most 55-grain loads, including the .223 Remington and 5.56 NATO. Other features include a lockable fast-focus eyepiece and a large power selector dial with aggressive knurling to provide a sure grip in all conditions.

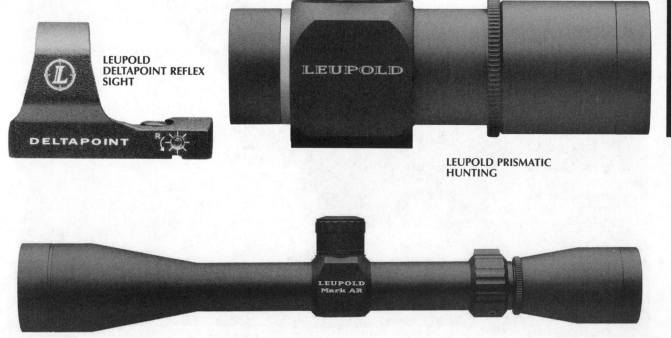

LEUPOLD DELTAPOINT REFLEX SIGHT

DELTAPOINT

LEUPOLD PRISMATIC HUNTING

LEUPOLD MARK AR

SCOPES

## MARK 4 CQ/T

Mark 4 CQ/T 1-3x14mm
**Weight**: 17.5 oz.
**Length**: 8 4/5 in.
**Main Body Tube Diameter**: 2 9/10 in.
**Power**: 1-3X
**Objective Diameter**: 30mm
**Exit Pupil**: 30-10mm
**Field of View**: 112-41 ft @ 100 yds
**Twilight Factor**: 3.74-6.48
**Eye Relief**: 2 4/5 - 2 in.
**Waterproof**: Yes
**Fogproof**: Yes
**Product Description**: The Leupold Mark 4 Close Quarters/Tactical (CQ/T) riflescope combines a red dot at close range with a variable-power optic. Its Circle Dot reticle is visible with or without illumination or batteries. Eleven reticle-illumination settings. The CQ/T has slotted ½ MOA click adjustments for windage and elevation.
MSRP:. . . . . . . . . . . . . . $899.99

## VX-3

VX-3 3.5-10x40mm and CDS (custom dial system) Model (also in 1.5-5x20, 1.5-5x20 IR, 1.75-6x32, 2.5-8x36, 4.5-14x40, 4.5-14x40 CDS, 4.5-14x40 SF, 4.5-14x40 AO, 6.5-20x40 AO, 6.5-20x40 EFR, 6.5-20x40 SF, 3.5-10x50, 3.5-10x50 CDS, 3.5-10x50 IR, 3.5-10x50 IR Metric, 4.5-14x50, 4.5-14x50 SF, 4.5-14x50 SF IR, 6.5-20x50 SF Target, and 8.5-23x50 SF Target)
**Weight**: 12.6 oz.
**Length**: 12 2/3 in.
**Power**: 3.3-9.7X (actual)
**Objective Diameter**: 40mm
**Main Tube Diameter**: 1 in.
**Exit Pupil**: 12.1-4.1mm
**Field of View**: 298-110 ft @ 1000 yards
**Twilight Factor**: 11.83-20
**Eye Relief**: 4 2/5-3 3/5 in.
**Waterproof**: Yes
**Fogproof**: Yes
**Product Description**: The Leupold VX-3 series features Leupold's X-Tended Twilight Lens System for high light transmission, finger adjustable ¼ MOA windage and elevation dials, abrasion-resistant Diamond Coat 2 external lens coatings, a dual spring erector assembly, and available CDS dial options and illuminated reticles.

## VX-II

VX-II 3-9x40mm (also in 1-4x20, 4-12x40 AO, 6-18x40 AO and Target, 3-9x50, 4-12x50)
**Weight**: 12 oz.
**Length**: 12 2/5 in.
**Power**: 3.3-8.6X (actual)
**Objective Diameter**: 40mm
**Main Tube Diameter**: 1 in.
**Exit Pupil**: 12-4.6mm
**Field of View**: 323-140 ft @ 1000 yards
**Twilight Factor**: 10.95-18.97
**Eye Relief**: 4 7/10 - 3 7/10 in.
**Waterproof**: Yes
**Fogproof**: Yes
**Product Description**: The Leupold VX-II series features Leupold's Multicoat 4 Lens System for 92% light transmission and coin click ¼ MOA windage and elevation dials.

LEUPOLD VX-3

LEUPOLD MARK 4 CQ/T

LEUPOLD VX-II

SCOPES

# Millett Optics Scopes

## DMS-1

Millett DMS-1 1-4x24mm A-TACS
Finish (also in 1-4x24mm Matte Finish)
*Power*: 1-4X
*Objective Diameter*: 24mm
*Main Tube Diameter*: 30mm
*Eye Relief*: 3 ½ in.
*Exit Pupil*: 24-6mm
*Field of View*: 90-23 ft @ 100 yds
*Twilight Factor*: 4.89-9.79
*Waterproof*: Yes
*Fogproof*: Yes
*Limited Lifetime Warranty*
*Product Description*: The low-light
Designated Marksman Riflescope
(DMS) features a Donut Dot illuminat-
ed reticle with the "donut" subtending
18 MOA for ranges as close as three
meters, and the illuminated dot 1
MOA for medium to extended ranges
out to 500 yards. The featured A-TACS
model offers the best in concealment
technology.
**MSRP:** . . . . . . . . . . . . . . . . .**$450.95**

MILLET DMS-1

MILLETT TRS

## LRS

Millett LRS 6-25x56mm Illuminated
Mil-DotBar Reticle Matte Finish .1 Mil
(also in 6-25x 56mm Mil-DotBar
Reticle .25 Click Value, 6-25x 56mm
Mil-DotBar Reticle .1 Mil Click Value,
6-25x 56mm Illuminated Mil-DotBar
Reticle A-TACS Finish, Millet LRS
6-25x 56mm Illuminated Mil-DotBar
Reticle Matte Finish .25 Click Value)
*Power*: 6-25X
*Objective Diameter*: 56mm
*Main Tube Diameter*: 35mm
*Eye Relief*: 3 in.
*Exit Pupil*: 9.33-2.24mm
*Twilight Factor*: 18.33-37.41
*Waterproof*: Yes
*Fogproof*: Yes
*Limited Lifetime Warranty*
*Product Description*: The Millet LRS is
built for extreme-duty and extended-
range for calibers such as the .50 BMG
and .338 Lapua. Massively built with a
one-piece 35mm tube and 56mm
objective, it has precision controls
with 140 MOA range of adjustment.
The Millett LRS riflescope line features
several glass-etched Mil-DotBar reticle
and click value configurations. The
scope is available in a matte or
A-TACS (Advanced Tactical
Concealment System) finish.
**MSRP:** . . . . . . . . . . . . . . . . .**$854.95**

## TRS

Millett TRS-1 4-16x50mm .1 mil Click
Value (also in 4-16x50mm .25 Click
Value Matte Finish, 4-16x50mm .25
Click Value A-TACS Finish, 10x50mm
.25 Click Value, 10x50mm .1 mil Click
Value)
*Power*: 4-16X
*Objective Diameter*: 50mm
*Main Tube Diameter*: 30mm
*Eye Relief*: 3 ½ in.
*Exit Pupil*: 12.5-3.12mm
*Twilight Factor*: 14.14-28.28
*Waterproof*: Yes

*Fogproof*: Yes
*Limited Lifetime Warranty*
*Product Description*: The Mil-DotBar
reticle system functions as a standard
Mil-Dot with the addition of a thin line
for easier alignment for rangefinding
and holdover. The illuminated reticle is
green and adjustable for brightness.
The optics are multi-coated and the
scope has a side-focus parallax adjustment knob. Five models are available,
including a fixed 10x50mm model and
several 4-16x50mm models finished in
either matte or A-TACS (Advanced
Tactical Concealment System).
**MSRP:** . . . . . . . . . . . . . . . . .**$567.95**

MILLET LRS

# MINOX USA Inc.

## MNX ZA 3

ZA 3 3-9x40 (also in 3-9x50)
**Weight**: 12.3 oz.
**Length**: 12 ³/₁₀ in.
**Main Tube Diameter**: 1 in.
**Power**: 3-9X
**Objective Diameter**: 40mm
**Exit Pupil**: 13.33-4.44mm
**Field of View**: 31.5 ft @ 100 yards
**Twilight Factor**: 10.95-18.97
**Eye Relief**: 4.0 in.
**Waterproof**: Yes
**Fogproof**: Yes
**"Full Coverage" Lifetime Warranty**
**Product Description**: Fully multi-coated Schott-glass lenses with 3-times magnification zoom range.

MINOX MNX ZA3

## MNX ZA 5

ZA 5 4-20x50 SF (also in 1.5-8x32, 2-10x40, 2-10x50, 3-15x42, 4-20x56, 6-30x56)
**Weight**: 19.2 oz.
**Length**: 13 ½ in.
**Main Tube Diameter**: 1 in (30mm in 6-30x56)
**Power**: 4-20X
**Objective Diameter**: 50mm
**Exit Pupil**: 0.49mm
**Field of View**: 23.6 ft @ 100 yards
**Twilight Factor**: 14.14-31.62

MINOX MNX ZA5

**Eye Relief**: 4 in.
**Waterproof**: Yes
**Fogproof**: Yes
**"Full Coverage" Lifetime Warranty**

**Product Description**: Fully multi-coated Schott-glass lenses with 5-times magnification zoom range.
**MSRP:**.................$839

# Nightforce Optics, Inc.

## 3.5-15X50 NXS

**Weight**: 30 oz.
**Length**: 14 ⁴/₅ in.
**Main Tube Diameter**: 30mm
**Power**: 3.5-15
**Objective Diameter**: 50mm

**Exit Pupil**: 14.3-3.6mm
**Field of View**: 27.6 ft @ 100 yds-7.3 ft @ 100 yds
**Twilight Factor**: 13.22-27.38
**Eye Relief**: 3 ⁹/₁₀ in.

**Waterproof**: Yes
**Fogproof**: Yes
**Product Description**: Developed for use on military small arms, proven in the harshest combat conditions around the globe. An excellent choice for all-around hunting and by professional shooters. Low mounting profile, a full 110 MOA of internal adjustment, applicable to a wide range of applications. Available with .250 MOA and .1 Mil-Radian adjustments, and one of several scopes offered with Nightforce's patented ZeroStop, which provides an instant return to the shooter's chosen zero point under any conditions, just by feel.
**MSRP:** ................. $1591

NIGHTFORCE 3.5-15X50

SCOPES

# Nightforce Optics, Inc.

## 1-4X24 NXZ COMPACT

**Weight**: 17 oz.
**Length**: 8 ⅘ in.
**Main Tube Diameter**: 30mm
**Power**: 1-4
**Objective Diameter**: 24mm
**Exit Pupil**: 1-6mm
**Field of View**: 100 ft @ 100 yds-25 ft @ 100 yds
**Twilight Factor**: 4.89-9.79
**Eye Relief**: 3 ½ in.
**Waterproof**: Yes
**Fogproof**: Yes
**Product Description**: Originally designed for military and CQB (close-quarters battle) applications, it is ideal for the hunter pursuing dangerous or running game at close quarters. A low profile complements big bore bolt action and double rifles. One of the few true one-power variable scopes in the world, making it as quick as open sights yet vastly more precise. The shooter can keep both eyes open for instant target acquisition in high-stress situations.
**MSRP**: . . . . . . . . . . . . . . . . . . $1252

## 2.5-10X32 NXS COMPACT

**Weight**: 19 oz.
**Length**: 12 in.
**Main Tube Diameter**: 30mm
**Power**: 2.5-10
**Objective Diameter**: 32mm
**Exit Pupil**: 13.3-3.3mm
**Field of View**: 44 ft @ 100 yds-11 ft @ 100 yds
**Twilight Factor**: 8.94-17.88
**Eye Relief**: 3 ⅖ in.
**Waterproof**: Yes
**Fogproof**: Yes
**Product Description**: The optimum in size-to-weight performance. Light in weight, low in profile, it will not over-whelm even a delicate rifle yet provides low-light performance that exceeds most optics with much larger objective lenses. Large exit pupil for fast target acquisition and no parallax or focusing issues. Available with the Nightforce Velocity 600 yard reticle, which provides precise shot placement to 600 yards with no guessing at holdover.
**MSRP**: . . . . . . . . . . . . . . . . . . $1345

NIGHTFORCE 1-4x24

NIGHTFORCE 1-4x24

NIGHTFORCE 2.5-10x32

# Nightforce Optics, Inc.

## NXS 3.5-15 X 56

3.5-15 x 56mm NXS
**Weight**: 31 oz.
**Length**: 14 $\frac{2}{5}$ in.
**Main Tube Diameter**: 30mm
**Power**: 3.5-15
**Objective Diameter**: 56mm
**Exit Pupil**: 14.5-4mm
**Field of View**: 27.6 ft @ 100 yds-7.3 ft @ 100 yds
**Twilight Factor**: 14-28.98
**Eye Relief**: 3 $\frac{4}{5}$ in.
**Waterproof**: Yes
**Fogproof**: Yes
**Product Description**: The top choice for law enforcement snipers. The large objective lens increases resolution and exit pupil size for quick target acquisition and optimal performance at twilight. Especially appropriate for tactical teams that may not have a dedicated night vision scope. This configuration also makes it ideal for hunters and sport shooters wanting a scope that will perform in the shadows. Large field of view allows quick recovery from recoil for an accurate second shot.
**MSRP**: . . . . . . . . . . . . . . . . . $1591

## NIGHTFORCE 5.5-22X50

Nightforce 5.5-22x50mm NXS
**Weight**: 31 oz.
**Length**: 15 $\frac{1}{10}$ in.
**Main Tube Diameter**: 30mm
**Power**: 5.5-22
**Objective Diameter**: 50mm
**Exit Pupil**: 9.1-2.3mm
**Field of View**: 17.5 ft @ 100 yds-4.7 ft @ 100 yds
**Twilight Factor**: 16.58-33.16
**Eye Relief**: 3 $\frac{4}{5}$ in.
**Waterproof**: Yes
**Fogproof**: Yes
**Product Description**: Originally developed for the U.S. military's extreme long range shooting and hard target interdiction. Plenty of eye relief and 100 MOA of elevation travel make it ideal for use on the .50 BMG, allowing accurate shots to 2000 yards and beyond. Slim profile, easily adaptable to a wide range of mounting systems. Superb resolution at high magnification has made the 5.5-22x50 extremely popular for long-range hunting.
**MSRP**: . . . . . . . . . . . . . . . . . $1751

NIGHTFORCE
NXS 3.5-15x56

NIGHTFORCE 5.5-22X50

SCOPES

# Nightforce Optics, Inc.

NIGHTFORCE 5.5-22X56

NIGHTFORCE 8-32X56

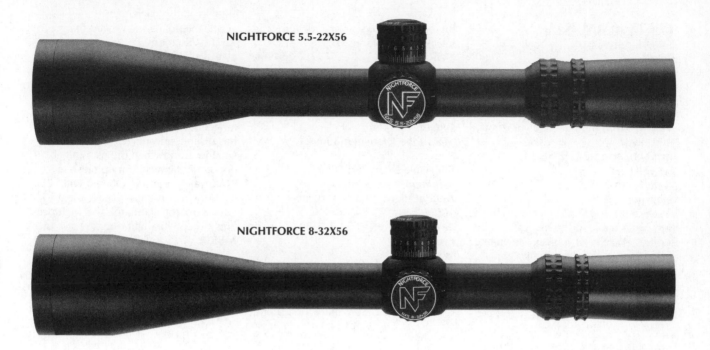

## 5.5-22X56
5.5-22x56mm NXS
**Weight**: 32 oz.
**Length**: 15 $^1/_5$ in.
**Main Tube Diameter**: 30mm
**Power**: 5.5-22
**Objective Diameter**: 56mm
**Exit Pupil**: 10.2-2.5mm
**Field of View**: 17.5 ft. @ 100 yds-4.7 ft. @ 100 yds
**Twilight Factor**: 17.54-35.09
**Eye Relief**: 3 $^9/_{10}$ in
**Waterproof**: Yes
**Fogproof**: Yes
**Product Description**: Advanced field tactical riflescope for long-range applications. Maximum clarity and resolution across the entire magnification range, exceptional low-light performance. Available with ZeroStop technology and .125 and .250 MOA or .1 Mil-Radian adjustments.
**MSRP**: . . . . . . . . . . . . . . . . . $1751

## 8-32X56
8-32x56mm NXS
**Weight**: 34 oz.
**Length**: 15 $^9/_{10}$ in.
**Main Tube Diameter**: 30mm

**Power**: 8-32
**Objective Diameter**: 56mm
**Exit Pupil**: 7-1.8mm
**Field of View**: 12.1 ft @ 100 yds-3.1 ft @ 100 yds
**Twilight Factor**: 21.16-42.33
**Eye Relief**: 3 $^4/_5$ in.
**Waterproof**: Yes
**Fogproof**: Yes
**Product Description**: For long-range hunting, competition, and target shooting. A choice of five different reticles for the shooter's chosen application. For pushing the "long-range" envelope to two miles and beyond, maximizing the potential of the newest high-performance cartridges. Offered with .125 MOA, .250 MOA or .1 Mil-Radian Hi-Speed adjustments. ZeroStop also available.
**MSRP**: . . . . . . . . . . . . . . . . . $1883

## 8-32X56 BR
Nightforce 8-32x56mm Precision Benchrest (also in 12-42x56mm)
**Weight**: 36 oz.
**Length**: 16 $^3/_5$ in.
**Main Tube Diameter**: 30mm
**Power**: 8-32
**Objective Diameter**: 56mm

**Exit Pupil**: 5.6-1.7mm
**Field of View**: 9.4 ft @ 100 yds-3.1 ft @ 100 yds
**Twilight Factor**: 21.16-42.33
**Eye Relief**: 2 $^9/_{10}$ in.
**Waterproof**: Yes
**Fogproof**: Yes
**Product Description**: A new Heavy Gun World Record was set with this scope in September, 2010, by Matt Kline—10 shots, 2.815 inches. This breaks the previous world record of 3.044 inches, also set with a Nightforce scope. Nightforce Precision Benchrest models are known for superior resolution, allowing fine detail to be distinguished at extreme ranges. An adjustable objective allows extra-fine focus for parallax adjustment from 25 yards to infinity. Target adjustments are calibrated in true .125 MOA ($^1/_8$ click) values, and can be re-indexed to zero after sighting in. Includes an eyepiece that allows for fast reticle focusing and a glass-etched illuminated reticle, with eight different reticles for specific applications and maximum precision at extreme ranges.
**MSRP**: . . . . . . . . . . . . . . . . . $1275

# Nightforce Optics, Inc.

## 12-42X56MM NXS

**Weight**: 34 oz.
**Length**: 16 ¹/₁₀ in.
**Main Tube Diameter**: 30mm
**Power**: 12-42
**Objective Diameter**: 56mm
**Exit Pupil**: 4.7-1.3mm
**Field of View**: 8.2 ft @ 100 yds-2.4 ft @ 100 yds
**Twilight Factor**: 25.92-48.49
**Eye Relief**: 3 ⁴/₅ in.
**Waterproof**: Yes
**Fogproof**: Yes
**Product Description**: Optical resolution comparable to the highest quality spotting scopes, with unsurpassed clarity across the entire magnification range. Specifically designed for optimum resolution under all conditions, even at maximum magnification, where other scopes often lose resolving power. A scope for rapidly growing F-Class competitions.
**MSRP**: . . . . . . . . . . . . . . . . . . **$1964**

## 3.5-15X50 F1 NXS

Nightforce 3.5-15x50mm F1 NXS
**Weight**: 30 oz.
**Length**: 14 ⁴/₅ in.
**Main Tube Diameter**: 30mm
**Power**: 3.5-15
**Objective Diameter**: 50mm
**Exit Pupil**: 11.5-3.2mm
**Field of View**: 28 ft @ 100 yds-8.7 ft @ 100 yds
**Twilight Factor**: 13.22-27.38
**Eye Relief**: 3 ¹/₅ in.
**Waterproof**: Yes
**Fogproof**: Yes
**Product Description**: First focal plane reticle design, developed at the request of the U.S. military for a scope applicable to a wide range of targets at various distances. Five specialized reticles available to maximize first focal plane design. Since the reticle remains in the same visual proportion to the target across the entire magnification range, it is especially appropriate with rangefinding reticle designs. The F1 has distinct advantages in high-stress situations and when the user might encounter targets from up close to 1000 yards or more. Offered with .250 MOA or .1 Mil-Radian adjustments, with ZeroStop standard. Also includes Nightforce Ultralight rings.
**MSRP**: . . . . . . . . . . . . . . . . . . **$2410**

NIGHTFORCE 12-42X56

NIGHTFORCE 3.5-15X50 F1 NXS

# Nikon Sport Optics

## SLUGHUNTER

SlugHunter 1.65-5x36mm matte with BDC 200 reticle (also in 3-9x40 and in RealTree APG)

**Weight**: 13.58 oz.
**Length**: 11 $^1/_7$ in.
**Main Body Tube Diameter**: 1 in.
**Power**: 1.65-5X
**Objective Diameter**: 36mm
**Exit Pupil**: 7.2 (at 5x)mm
**Field of View**: 45.3-15.1 ft @ 100 yards
**Twilight Factor**: 7.7-13.41
**Eye Relief**: 5 in.
**Waterproof**: Yes
**Fogproof**: Yes
**Product Description**: The compact SlugHunter 1.65-5x36 features an increased exit pupil for low-light performance and a 75-yard parallax setting. Available with the BDC 200 trajectory-compensating reticle, with "ballistic circle" aiming points, calibrated for the lower power range and smaller objective and for aerodynamic polymer-tipped slugs. Has lead- and arsenic-free "Eco-Glass" multi-coated optics, hand-turn ¼ MOA click adjustments, and quick-focus eyepiece.
**MSRP**: . . . . . . . . . . . . . . . . . **$320.95**

## MONARCH

Monarch 2.5-10x42mm Nikoplex (also available in 2-8x30, 3-12x42, 4-16x42, 5-20x44, 2.5-10x50, 4-16x50, 6-24x50, and 8-32x50, in matte and silver with ED glass, SF–side focus–mildot, and fine crosshair with dot)

**Weight**: 16.6 oz.
**Length**: 12 $^3/_5$ in.
**Main Body Tube Diameter**: 1 in.
**Power**: 2.5-10X
**Objective Diameter**: 42mm
**Exit Pupil**: 16.8-4.2mm
**Field of View**: 40.3-10.1 ft @ 100 yards
**Twilight Factor**: 10.24-20.49
**Eye Relief**: 4.0 - 3.8 in.
**Waterproof**: Yes
**Fogproof**: Yes
**Product Description**: This Monarch offers a wide magnification range and enhanced ring spacing for mounting on rifles including magnum-length actions. The Monarch is available with the see-through "ballistic circle" BDC reticle. With Ultra ClearCoat optical system, the Monarch is adaptable for a sunshade and can be customized with accessory target-style windage and elevation adjustment knobs and caps.
**MSRP**: . . . . . . . . . . . . . . . . . **$550.95**

## MONARCH DOT SIGHT VSD 1X30MM

**Weight**: 7.8 oz. (without batteries)
**Length**: 3 $^4/_5$ in.
**Power**: 1X
**Objective Diameter**: 30mm
**Exit Pupil**: 30mm
**Twilight Factor**: 5.5
**Eye Relief**: Unlimited
**Waterproof**: Yes
**Fogproof**: Yes
**Limited Lifetime Warranty**
**Product Description**: The Monarch Dot Sight VSD's (Variable Sized Dot) offers selections of 1, 4, 6, 8, or 10 MOA dot size. Includes 11-position rheostat and integral mounting system attachable to any Weaver-style base. Waterproof, fogproof, and shockproof (except battery chamber). Objective and ocular lenses are 30mm and are multi-coated.
**MSRP**: . . . . . . . . . . . . . . . . . **$274.95**

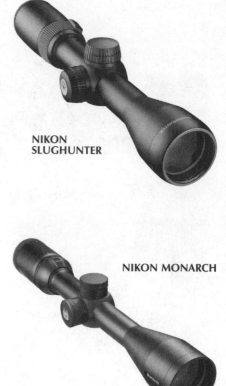

NIKON
SLUGHUNTER

NIKON MONARCH

NIKON MONARCH
DOT SIGHT VSD

**NIKON M-223 LASER IRT**

**NIKON ENCORE**

## M-223 LASER IRT

**Product Name and Model**: M-223 Laser IRT 2.5-10x40mm
**Length**: 12 $\frac{1}{5}$ in.
**Power**: 2.5-10X
**Objective Diameter**: 40mm
**Exit Pupil**: 16-4mm
**Field of View**: 23.6-7.3 ft @ 100 yards
**Twilight Factor**: 10-20
**Eye Relief**: 3 ½ in.
**Waterproof**: Yes
**Fogproof**: Yes
**Product Description**: The M-223 Immediate Ranging Technology riflescope combines a Nikon laser rangefinder with the M-223 BDC 600 reticle. The M-223 IRT provides the equivalent horizontal range to the target and features one-touch laser technology that keeps ranging and displaying distance for 12 seconds with a single push of the button. Low-profile mounts attach to Picatinny Rails. Remote control laser activator can be affixed to most firearms. Has a zoom control with the reference numbers viewable from the shooter's position.
**MSRP:** . . . . . . . . . . . . . . . . **$1150.95**

## ENCORE

Encore 2.5-8x28 EER in silver with BDC reticle (and in 2x20 and in matte)
**Weight**: 11.46 oz.
**Length**: 9 $\frac{4}{5}$ in.
**Main Body Tube Diameter**: 1 in.
**Power**: 2.5-8X
**Objective Diameter**: 28mm
**Exit Pupil**: 3.5mm
**Field of View**: 13.1-4.1 ft @ 100 yards
**Twilight Factor**: 8.36
**Eye Relief**: 12 - 30 (at 2.5x), 9 - 13 (at 8x) in
**Waterproof**: Yes
**Fogproof**: Yes
**Product Description**: The 2.5-8x28 EER (Extended Eye Relief) scope, engineered for arm's length shooting, features Nikon's BDC reticle and is built for the severe recoil of hunting, varmint, and competition handgun shooting, advertised to withstand the recoil of calibers up to S&W .500 Magnum. With the Nikon Ultra ClearCoat optical system and quick-focus eyepiece.
**MSRP:** . . . . . . . . . . . . . . . . . **$454.95**

# Nikon Sport Optics

**NIKON MONARCH X**

**NIKON M-223**

## MONARCH X

Monarch X 2.5-10x44mm SF Nikoplex
(also in 4-16x50 with mildot and dual-
illuminated mildot)
**Weight**: 23.5 oz.
**Length**: 13 $^9/_{10}$ in.
**Power**: 2.5-10X
**Objective Diameter**: 44mm
**Main Body Tube Diameter**: 30mm
**Exit Pupil**: 17.6-4.4mm
**Field of View**: 42-10 ½ ft @ 100 yards
**Twilight Factor**: 10.24-20.49
**Eye Relief**: 3 ½-3 $^4/_5$ in.
**Waterproof**: Yes
**Fogproof**: Yes
**Product Description**: The Monarch X
series offers Nikoplex, Mildot, or Dual
Illuminated Mildot reticle options.
Lenses use the Ultra ClearCoat system.
Four-time magnification range with
easy-to-grip adjustment knobs and a
one-piece 30mm body tube milled
from aircraft grade aluminum. Hand-
turn ¼ MOA windage and elevation
adjustments and side-focus parallax
adjustment.
**MSRP**: . . . . . . . . . . . . . . . $1760.95

## M-223

M-223 3-12x42SF Nikoplex with
Rapid Action Turret (also in 1-4x20
and 2-8x32 and with BDC 600 reticle)
**Weight**: 19.93 oz.
**Length**: 13 $^1/_{10}$ in.
**Main Body Tube Diameter**: 1 in.
**Power**: 3-12X
**Objective Diameter**: 42mm
**Exit Pupil**: 14-3.5mm
**Field of View**: 33.6-8.4 ft @
100 yards

**Twilight Factor**: 11.22-22.44
**Eye Relief**: 4-3 $^4/_5$ in.
**Waterproof**: Yes
**Fogproof**: Yes
**Product Description**: The M-223
3-12x42 has side-focus parallax adjustment from zero out to 600 yards. With
Nikon's Rapid Action Turret technology
based on a .223/5.56mm 55-grain
polymer tipped bullet. Has a 4-time
zoom range, one-piece main body
tube and "Ultra ClearCoat" optics.
Variable-magnification reference numbers are viewable from the shooter's
position.
**MSRP**: . . . . . . . . . . . . . . . . $620.95

## TURKEYPRO BTR

TurkeyPro BTR 1.65-5x36mm Mossy
Oak Break-Up (also in RealTree APG
and matte)
**Weight**: 13.58 oz.
**Length**: 11 $^1/_7$ in.
**Main Body Tube Diameter**: 1 in.
**Power**: 1.65-5X
**Objective Diameter**: 36mm
**Exit Pupil**: 21.8-7.2mm
**Field of View**: 45.3-15.1 ft @ 100
yards
**Twilight Factor**: 7.7-13.41
**Eye Relief**: 5 in.
**Waterproof**: Yes
**Fogproof**: Yes
**Product Description**: This is Nikon's
dedicated turkey-hunting scope with
the Ballistic Turkey Reticle, or BTR,
which subtends a turkey's head from
crown to wattles at 5x (larger circle)
and at 1.65x (smaller circle) at 40 yards.
Also includes the ARD (Anti-Reflective
Device) lens cap technology to elimi-
nate glare.
**MSRP**: . . . . . . . . . . . . . . . . $420.95

**NIKON TURKEYPRO BTR**

# Nikon Sport Optics

**NIKON BUCKMASTERS 1X20**

## BUCKMASTERS 1X20 BLACK POWDER WITH NIKOPLEX

**Weight**: 10.6 oz.
**Length**: 9 $\frac{1}{10}$ in.
**Main Body Tube Diameter**: 1 in.
**Power**: 1x
**Objective Diameter**: 20mm
**Exit Pupil**: 20mm
**Field of View**: 52 ½ ft @ 75 yards
**Twilight Factor**: 4.47
**Eye Relief**: 4 $\frac{3}{10}$-13 in.
**Waterproof**: Yes
**Fogproof**: Yes
**Warranty**: Lifetime
**Product Description**: For muzzleloading hunting where only 1 power scopes are allowed. Uses Nikon's Brightvue multi-coating with a stated 92-percent light transmission. Has hand-turn ½ MOA positive-click adjustments, plus quick-focus eyepiece.
**MSRP**: . . . . . . . . . . . . . . . . $252.95

## PROSTAFF

ProStaff 3-9x40mm matte with Nikoplex (also in 2-7x32–and in Shotgun Hunter with BDC 200 reticle–3-9x40, 4-12x40, and 3-9x50 and in silver, RealTree APG and with BDC reticle)
**Weight**: N/A
**Length**: 12 $\frac{2}{5}$ in.
**Main Body Tube Diameter**: 1 in.
**Power**: 3x-9x
**Objective Diameter**: 40mm
**Exit Pupil**: 13.3-4.4mm
**Field of View**: 33.8-11.3 ft @ 100 yards
**Twilight Factor**: 10.95-18.97
**Eye Relief**: 3 $\frac{3}{5}$-3 $\frac{3}{5}$ in
**Waterproof**: Yes
**Fogproof**: Yes

**NIKON PROSTAFF**

**Product Description**: The ProStaff riflescopes are available in 3-9x40mm black matte with Nikoplex reticle (also in 2-7x32–and in Shotgun Hunter with BDC 200 reticle–4-12x40, and 3-9x50 and in silver, RealTree APG and with BDC reticle). Has multi-coated lenses and comes with ¼ MOA hand-turn reticle adjustments with "Zero-Reset" turrets and a quick-focus eyepiece.
**MSRP**: . . . . . . . . . . . . . . . . $232.95

## COYOTE SPECIAL

Coyote Special 3-9x40 in Mossy Oak Brush with BDC Predator reticle (also in 4.5-14x40 and in matte and RealTree Max-1)
**Weight**: 16 oz.
**Length**: 13 $\frac{1}{10}$ in.
**Main Body Tube Diameter**: 1 in.
**Power**: 3-9x
**Objective Diameter**: 40mm
**Exit Pupil**: 13.3-4.4mm
**Field of View**: 35.7-11.9 ft @ 100 yards
**Twilight Factor**: 10.95-18.97
**Eye Relief**: 3 $\frac{2}{5}$-3 $\frac{2}{5}$ in.
**Waterproof**: Yes
**Fogproof**: Yes
**Product Description**: Nikon's 3-9x40 Coyote Special utilizes the BDC Predator Reticle for ranges out to 450 yards and beyond. The open BDC's ballistic circles don't obscure the target. Has multi-coated lenses; hand-turn ¼ MOA click adjustments; quick-focus eyepiece and lead- and arsenic-free "Eco-Glass." Uses the ARD (Anti Reflective Device) scope cover to eliminate glare but permit shooting.
**MSRP**: . . . . . . . . . . . . . . . . $416.95

## BUCKMASTERS 3-9X40

Buckmasters 3-9x40mm RealTree APG Nikoplex (also in 4.5-14x40, 6-18x40, 3-9x50, and 4-12x50, and in matte

**NIKON COYOTE SPECIAL**

# Nikon Sport Optics

and silver with BDC, mildot, and fine crosshair with dot)
**Weight**: 16.1 oz.
**Length**: 13 $\frac{1}{10}$ in.
**Main Body Tube Diameter**: 1 in.
**Power**: 3x-9x
**Objective Diameter**: 40mm
**Exit Pupil**: 13.3-4.4mm
**Field of View**: 35.7-11.9 ft @ 100 yards
**Twilight Factor**: 10.95-18.97
**Eye Relief**: 3 $\frac{3}{5}$ - 3 $\frac{3}{5}$ in.
**Waterproof**: Yes
**Fogproof**: Yes
**Product Description**: Built for centerfire rifle, muzzleloader, or rimfire, the Buckmasters 3-9x40 has Brightvue multi-coating, quick-focus eyepiece, hand-turn ¼ MOA click adjustments,

and is adaptable for a sunshade.
**MSRP**: . . . . . . . . . . . . . . . . . **$342.95**

## OMEGA

Omega 1.65-5x36mm Muzzleloading Riflescope in matte with BDC 250 reticle (also in 3-9x40 and in silver and RealTree APG and with Nikoplex and BDC 300 reticles)
**Weight**: 13.58 oz.
**Length**: 11 $\frac{1}{2}$ in.
**Main Body Tube Diameter**: 1 in.
**Power**: 1.65x-5x
**Objective Diameter**: 36mm
**Exit Pupil**: 7.2 (at 5x)mm
**Field of View**: 45.3-15.1 ft @ 100 yards
**Twilight Factor**: 7.7-13.41
**Eye Relief**: 5 in.
**Waterproof**: Yes

**Fogproof**: Yes
**Warranty**: Lifetime
**Product Description**: At 5X the Omega gives the maximum useful exit pupil of 7.2mm. Available with a BDC 250 trajectory-compensating reticle, designed specifically for the lower power range and smaller objective, uses "ballistic circles" for aiming points; 100-yard parallax; compact size; with hand-turn ¼ MOA click adjustments and quick-focus eyepiece.
**MSRP**: . . . . . . . . . . . . . . . . . **$320.95**

**NIKON OMEGA**

**NIKON BUCKMASTERS 3-9X40**

## BOLT XR 3X32 BDC

**Weight**: 11.2 oz.
**Length**: 8 $\frac{1}{10}$ in.
**Main Body Tube Diameter**: 1 in.
**Power**: 3x
**Objective Diameter**: 32mm
**Exit Pupil**: 10.7mm
**Field of View**: 35.6 ft @ 100 yards
**Twilight Factor**: 9.79
**Eye Relief**: 3 $\frac{4}{5}$ in.
**Waterproof**: Yes
**Fogproof**: Yes
**Product Description**: The Bolt XR features fully multi-coated 3x Nikon optics, a large ocular, 3.4-inches of eye relief and quick focus eye-piece with ±4 diopter adjustment. The BDC 60 reticle offers aiming points out to 60 yards based upon velocity of approximately 305 fps. Has ¼ inch at 20 yards adjustments with a 150 MOA adjustment range (at 100 yards). Quick focus eyepiece with ±4 Diopter Zero-Reset Turrets that allow sight-in at 20 yards, then lift the spring-loaded adjustment knob, rotate to pre-set "zero", and re-engage. Parallax-free at 20 yards.
**MSRP:** . . . . . . . . . . . . . . . .**$218.95**

## MONARCH GOLD

Monarch Gold 2.5-10x50mm SF BDC (also in 1.5-6x42 and 2.5x10x56 and with Nikoplex and German #4 reticles)
**Weight**: 21.2 oz.
**Length**: 13 in.
**Main Body Tube Diameter**: 30mm
**Power**: 2.5-10x
**Objective Diameter**: 50mm
**Exit Pupil**: 19.2-5.2mm

**Field of View**: 38.8-10 ½ ft @ 100 yards
**Twilight Factor**: 11.18-22.36
**Eye Relief**: 4 $\frac{1}{10}$-4 in.
**Waterproof**: Yes
**Fogproof**: Yes
**Product Description**: The Monarch Gold riflescope advertises an Ultra ClearCoat optical system that offers a bright, sharp, flat sight picture and light transmission up to its theoretical maximum—95 percent. With larger internal lenses for less spherical abber-ation. The locking side focus adjustment dials out parallax. Milled from aircraft grade aluminum, with a quick-focus eyepiece and hand-turn ¼ MOA windage and elevation adjustments.

**NIKON MONARCH GOLD**

**NIKON BOLT XR**

# Pentax Imaging Co.

## GAMESEEKER

Gameseeker 30 3-10x40mm (89750) (also in 4-16x50, 6-24x50, and 8.5-32x50)
**Weight**: 15.2 oz.
**Length**: 13 $\frac{1}{10}$ in.
**Main Tube Diameter**: 30mm
**Power**: 3x-10x
**Objective Diameter**: 40mm
**Exit Pupil**: 13.3-4mm
**Field of View**: 35.6-10.5 ft @ 100 yards
**Twilight Factor**: 10.95-20
**Eye Relief**: 4 $\frac{2}{5}$-3 $\frac{1}{5}$ in.
**Waterproof**: Yes
**Fogproof**: Yes
**Product Description**: A 30mm variable scope with fully multi-coated optics and a bullet-drop-compensating "Precision Plex" reticle.
**MSRP**: . . . . . . . . . . . . . . . . . . . **$179**

## GAMESEEKER II

PENTAX Gameseeker II 4-16x 50mm (PP) (89744) (also in 2-7x32, 3-9x40, 4-12x40, 3-9x50, and 5-10x56, and P and LPP reticles)
**Weight**: 16.1 oz.
**Length**: 13 $\frac{9}{10}$ in.
**Main Tube Diameter**: 1 in.
**Power**: 4x-16x
**Objective Diameter**: 50mm
**Exit Pupil**: 12.5-3.125mm
**Field of View**: 26 $\frac{1}{5}$-6 $\frac{4}{5}$ ft @ 100 yards
**Twilight Factor**: 14.14-28.28
**Eye Relief**: 3 in.
**Waterproof**: Yes
**Fogproof**: Yes
**Product Description**: This scope features a one-piece, 1-inch tube with finger-adjustable windage and elevation turrets and fully multi-coated optics.
**MSRP**: . . . . . . . . . . . . . . . . . . . **$149**

**PENTAX GAMESEEKER**

**PENTAX GAMESEEKER II**

# Pentax Imaging Co.

## LIGHTSEEKER

Lightseeker 30 3-10x40 (BP) (89606) *(also in 4-16x50 and 6-24x50, and with Mil Dot reticle)*
**Weight**: 20 oz.
**Length**: 13 $\frac{1}{10}$ in.
**Main Tube Diameter**: 30mm
**Power**: 3-10x
**Objective Diameter**: 40mm
**Exit Pupil**: 13.3-4.0mm
**Field of View**: 34-14 ft @ 100 yards
**Twilight Factor**: 10.95-20
**Eye Relief**: 3 ½ - 4 in.
**Waterproof**: Yes
**Fogproof**: Yes
**Product Description**: A 30mm tube scope with finger-adjustable windage and elevation turrets, and side parallax adjustment. Fully multi-coated optics.
**MSRP**: . . . . . . . . . . . . . . . . . . . **$519**

## LIGHTSEEKER XL

Lightseeker XL 4-16x44 (BP) (89619) *(also in 3-9x40 and 2.5-10x50, and with P and Twilight Plex reticles)*
**Weight**: 23 oz.
**Length**: 14 in.
**Main Tube Diameter**: 1 in.
**Power**: 4x-16x
**Objective Diameter**: 44mm
**Exit Pupil**: 11-2.8mm

**Field of View**: 24-8 ft @ 100 yards
**Twilight Factor**: 9.4-26.5
**Eye Relief**: 3 ½-4 in.
**Waterproof**: Yes
**Fogproof**: Yes
**Product Description**: A 1-inch-tube riflescope with finger-adjustable windage and elevation turrets, fully multi-coated optics, and "European-style" eyepieces.
**MSRP**: . . . . . . . . . . . . . . . . . . **$459**

**PENTAX LIGHTSEEKER XL**

**PENTAX LIGHTSEEKER**

# Redfield

## REVOLUTION

Revolution 3-9x40mm (also available in 2-7x33, 3-9x50, and 4-12x40)
**Weight**: 12.6 oz.
**Length**: 12 ⅓ in.
**Main Body Tube Diameter**: 1 in.
**Power**: 3-9X
**Objective Diameter**: 40mm
**Exit Pupil**: 12.1-4.7mm
**Field of View**: 32.9-13.1 ft @ 100 yards
**Twilight Factor**:
**Eye Relief**: 3 $\frac{7}{10}$-4 $\frac{1}{5}$ in.

**Waterproof**: Yes
**Fogproof**: Yes
***"Redfield Riflescope Full Lifetime Warranty" (does not cover unauthorized repair, alteration, or misuse)***
**Product Description**: The Redfield Revolution riflescope comes with a black matte finish and either a 4-Plex or Accu-Range reticle. Key features include the Illuminator Lens System with premium lenses and vapor-depo-

sition multi-coatings for a bright, crisp sight picture. The Accu-Trac windage and elevation adjustment system has resettable stainless steel ¼ MOA finger click adjustments. Uses a "Rapid Target Acquisition" (RTA) lockable eyepiece.
**MSRP**: . . . . . . . . . . . . . . . . .**$159.99 with 4-Plex reticle ($169.99 with Accu-Range reticle)**

**REDFIELD REVOLUTION**

SCOPES

# Schmidt & Bender

SCHMIDT & BENDER 3-12X50MM KLASSIK

SCHMIDT & BENDER 2.5-10X40MM
SUMMIT

SCHMIDT & BENDER 3-12X42MM
PRECISION HUNTER

## 3-12X50MM KLASSIK

Schmidt & Bender 3-12x50mm Klassik
Illuminated (also in illuminated-reticle
2.5-10x56 and 3-12x42, and in non-
illuminated 2.5-10x40, 3-12x42, and
4-16x 50 which is also available with
the Varmint No. 8 Dot reticle)
**Weight**: 21.66 oz.
**Length**: 13 ¾ in.
**Power**: 3-12X
**Objective Diameter**: 50mm
**Main Tube Diameter**: 30mm
**Exit Pupil**: 4.2-14.4mm
**Field of View**: 33.3-11.4 ft @ 100
yards
**Twilight Factor**: 8.5-24.5
**Eye Relief**: 3 ¹/₇ in
**Waterproof**: Yes
**Fogproof**: Yes
*30 Year Parts and Service Warranty*
*Product Description*: All of the
Klassik variables have generous
objectives for greater light transmis-
sion. Schmidt & Bender offers an
exceptional variety of reticles in illu-
minated, non-illuminated, and var-
mint. Adjustments on the 3-12x50 are
⅓ MOA; the 4-16x50 has ¼
MOA increments.
**MSRP:** . . . . . . . . . . . . . . . . . . $2279

## 2.5-10X40MM SUMMIT

**Weight**: 16.8 oz.
**Length**: 13 ¹/₅ in.
**Power**: 2.5-10X
**Objective Diameter**: 40mm
**Main Tube Diameter**: 1 in.
**Exit Pupil**: 16-4mm
**Field of View**: 12.3 – 40.4 ft @ 100
yards
**Twilight Factor**: 14-20
**Eye Relief**: 3.93 in.
**Waterproof**: Yes
**Fogproof**: Yes
*30 Year Parts and Service Warranty*
*Product Description*: The Summit is
built for the American market with its
1-inch tube. Adjustments are ¼ MOA,
and the field of view is a wide 40 feet
at 100 yards at the 2.5X setting.
**MSRP:** . . . . . . . . . . . . . . . . . . $1499

## 3-12X42MM PRECISION HUNTER

Schmidt & Bender 3-12x42mm
Precision Hunter (also in 3-12x50 and
4-16x50)
**Weight**: 19.90 oz.
**Length**: 13 ⅔ in.
**Power**: 3-12X
**Objective Diameter**: 42mm
**Main Tube Diameter**: 30mm
**Exit Pupil**: 3.5-14mm
**Field of View**: 31.5-11.4 ft @ 100
yards
**Twilight Factor**: 8.5-22.4
**Eye Relief**: 3 ½ inches
**Waterproof**: Yes
**Fogproof**: Yes
*30 Year Parts and Service Warranty*
*Product Description*: An enhanced
model 3-12x42 Klassik designed for
longer ranges. Features the P3 reticle
with bullet-drop compensated elevation knob. Originally designed for military and tactical use, the mil-dots can
be used for estimating holdover at longer distances, as well as for windage
allowance and for leading moving targets. Adjustments are in ⅓ MOA; the
4-16x50's clicks are ¼ MOA and the
scope has a third-turret parallax adjustment.
**MSRP:** . . . . . . . . . . . . . . . . . . $2099

SCOPES

**SCHMIDT & BENDER 1.5-6X42MM
ZENITH FLASH DOT**

## 1.5-6X 42MM ZENITH FLASH DOT

Schmidt & Bender 1.5-6x 42mm Zenith Flash Dot (also in 1.1-4x24, 1-8x24, 3-12x50, and 2.5-10x56 with Flash Dot and in 1.1-4x24, 1.5-6x42, 1-8x24, 3-12x50, and 2.5-10x56 with non-illuminated reticle)
*Weight*: 21.52 oz.
*Length*: 12 ⅓ in.
*Power*: 1.5-6X
*Objective Diameter*: 42mm
*Main Tube Diameter*: 30mm
*Exit Pupil*: 28-7mm
*Field of View*: 60-19.5 ft @ 100 yards
*Twilight Factor*: 4.2-15.9
*Eye Relief*: 3 ½ inches
*Waterproof*: Yes
*Fogproof*: Yes
*30 Year Parts and Service Warranty*
*Product Description*: The Zenith line runs from dangerous-game scopes up through long-range, low-light configurations. The Flash Dot reticle in the center of the crosshairs performs like the front bead sight on a shotgun when illuminated—it comes with adjustable brightness levels—that can pick up running or charging game. The Flash Dot can also be shut off to use the scope in the non-illuminated mode. The click values on the windage and elevation adjustments are ½ MOA on the 1.1-4x24 and ⅓ MOA on the rest.
**MSRP:** . . . . . . . . . . . . . . . . . $2349

## 12.5-50X56MM FIELD TARGET

Schmidt & Bender 12.5-50x56mm Field Target
*Weight*: 40.56 oz.
*Length*: 16 ⅖ in.
*Power*: 12.5-50X
*Objective Diameter*: 56mm
*Main Tube Diameter*: 30mm
*Exit Pupil*: 4.55-1.18mm

*Field of View*: 10.5-2.7 ft @ 100 yards
*Twilight Factor*: 26.5-53
*Eye Relief*: 2 ¾ in.
*Waterproof*: Yes
*Fogproof*: Yes
*30 Year Parts and Service Warranty*
*Product Description*: Built for field-target shooting. "Field target" is a form of competitive outdoor air-gun shooting that originated in the United Kingdom. It employs metallic silhouettes at ranges of 8 to 55 yards. Most shots can be taken freestyle from any position, but a certain number must be taken either standing or kneeling. The "kill zone"

**SCHMIDT & BENDER 12.5-50X56 FIELD TARGET**

on target may be as small as 25mm, making high-powered telescopic sights necessary. Ranging is also essential; and a high-magnification scope has a shallow depth of field, so the parallax side-focus wheel can be used as a reference for gauging the distance to the target and adjusting the trajectory. The Schmidt & Bender 12.5-50x56 comes with an extra-large focus wheel to range distances from 7 to 70 meters. The scope also has an illuminated reticle with brightness settings adjustable from 1 to 11.
**MSRP:** . . . . . . . . . . . . . . . . . $3199

**SCOPES**

# Schmidt & Bender

### 4-16X42 PM II/LP
Schmidt & Bender 4-16x42 PM II/LP
(also in 30mm 10x42 and 34mm
3-12x50 with non-illuminated reticle,
and in 34mm tube 4-16x42, 3-12x50,
4-16x50, and 5-25x56 with illuminat-
ed reticle an LP turret system, and the
5-25x56 PMII /LP MTC LT for extreme
long ranges, along with illuminated
reticle 4-16x50 and 12-50x56 without
LP system)
**Weight**: 30.86 oz.
**Length**: 15 ½ in.
**Power**: 4-16X
**Objective Diameter**: 42mm
**Main Tube Diameter**: 34mm
**Exit Pupil**: 10.5-2.6mm
**Field of View**: 22.5-7 ft @ 100 yards
**Twilight Factor**: 11.3-25.9
**Eye Relief**: 3 ½ in.
**Waterproof**: Yes
**Fogproof**: Yes
*30 Year Parts and Service Warranty*
*Product Description*: Designed at the
request of the US Military. Includes
color coded elevation turret. All mod-
els include an illuminated reticle and
parallax adjustment, except the 10x42.
The LP turret system features a color-
coded elevation knob for instant refer-
ence to the elevation setting.
**MSRP**: . . . . . . . . . . . . . . . . . . **$2999**

### 6X42MM KLASSIK FIXED
Schmidt & Bender 6x42mm Klassik
Fixed (also in 10x42 and 8x56)
**Weight**: 16.67 oz.
**Length**: 13 $^7/_{10}$ in.
**Width**: 2 $^1/_{10}$ in.
**Power**: 6X
**Objective Diameter**: 42mm
**Main Tube Diameter**: 1 in.
**Exit Pupil**: 7mm
**Field of View**: 21 ft @ 100 yds
**Twilight Factor**: 15.8
**Eye Relief**: 3 $^1/_7$ in.
**Waterproof**: Yes
**Fogproof**: Yes
*30 Year Parts and Service Warranty*
*Product Description*: Simple and eco-
nomical, fixed 6-power magnification
applicable to a wide range of hunting
situations. Windage and elevation
adjustments are in $^1/_3$ MOA incre-
ments. The classic European 8x56 con-
figuration offers maximum light trans-
mission.
**MSRP**: . . . . . . . . . . . . . . . . . . **$1189**

### POLICE MARKSMAN
Schmidt & Bender Police Marksman
1.1-4x20 PM Locking Short Dot (also
in 1.1-4x20 and 1-8x24 Short Dots
and 1.1-4x24 PM Zenith Short Dot LE)
**Weight**: 20.11 oz.
**Length**: 10 $^3/_5$ in.
**Power**: 1.1-4X
**Objective Diameter**: 20mm
**Main Tube Diameter**: 30mm
**Exit Pupil**: 14-5mm
**Field of View**: 96-30 ft @ 100 yds
**Twilight Factor**: 4.69-8.94
**Eye Relief**: 3 ½ in.
**Waterproof**: Yes
**Fogproof**: Yes
*30 Year Parts and Service Warranty*
*Product Description*: Includes locking
turrets and CQB reticle. M855, 75 gr.
TAP, and M118LR calibration rings
standard.
**MSRP**: . . . . . . . . . . . . . . . . . . **$2549**

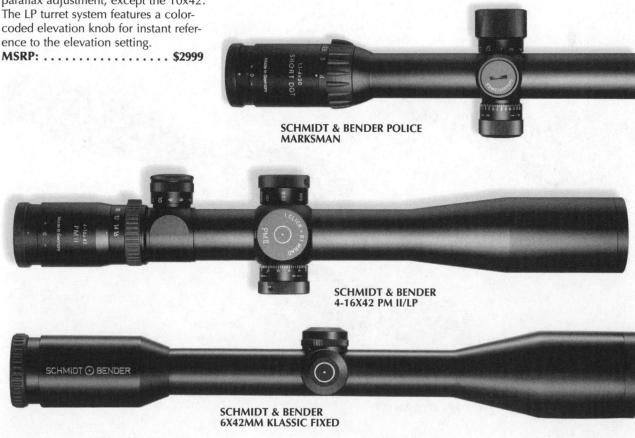

**SCHMIDT & BENDER POLICE
MARKSMAN**

**SCHMIDT & BENDER
4-16X42 PM II/LP**

**SCHMIDT & BENDER
6X42MM KLASSIC FIXED**

## .44 MAG

Simmons .44 Mag. 3-10x44mm (also in 4-12x44mm, 6-21x44mm .25 Click Value, 6-21x44mm .125 Click Value TruPlex Reticle, 6-21x44mm .125 Click Value Mil-Dot Reticle, 6-24x44mm)
*Weight*: 11.3 oz.
*Power*: 3-10x
*Objective Diameter*: 44mm
*Main Tube Diameter*: 1 in.
*Eye Relief*: 3 ¾ in.
*Exit Pupil*: 14.66-4.4mm
*Field of View*: 33-9.4 ft @ 100 yds
*Twilight Factor*: 11.48-20.97
*Waterproof*: Yes
*Fogproof*: Yes
*Product Description*: With its 44mm objective, Simmons Signature .44 Mag. riflescope has a wide field of view with brightness delivered via multi-coated optics. The QTA (Quick Target Acquisition) eyepiece makes target acquisition easy and fast. Comes with TrueZero windage and elevation adjustment system.
*MSRP*: . . . . . . . . . . . . . . . . .$165.95

## PREDATOR QUEST

Simmons Predator Quest 6-25x50mm (also in 4.5-18x44mm)
*Weight*: 17 oz.
*Power*: 6-25x
*Objective Diameter*: 50mm
*Main Tube Diameter*: 30mm
*Exit Pupil*: 8.33-2mm
*Twilight Factor*: 17.32-35.35
*Field of View*: 14-4 ft @ 100 yds
*Eye Relief*: 3 ⁹⁄₁₀ in
*Waterproof*: Yes
*Fogproof*: Yes
*Product Description*: Inspired by Les Johnson and his popular TV show, the Simmons Predator Quest series. Multi-coated lenses produce bright, high-contrast images and fingertip-adjustable turrets promote quick aim modifications. The Predator Quest has a side focus adjustment for rapid target acquisition and a versatile TruPlex reticle.
*MSRP*: . . . . . . . . . . . . . . . . .$364.95

## PROHUNTER

Simmons ProHunter 3-9x40mm Illuminated TruPlex Reticle (also in 4x32mm, 1.5-5x32mm, 3-9x40mm TruPlex Reticle, 4x32mm, 2-6x32mm Matte Finish, 2-6x32mm Silver Finish)
*Weight*: 10.8 oz.
*Power*: 3-9x
*Objective Diameter*: 40mm
*Main Tube Diameter*: 1 in.
*Eye Relief*: 3 ¾ in.
*Exit Pupil*: 13.33-4.44mm
*Field of View*: 31.4-11 ft @ 100 yds
*Twilight Factor*: 10.95-18.97
*Waterproof*: Yes
*Fogproof*: Yes
*Product Description*: Simmons ProHunter has multi-coated optics and is available in seven configurations. The ProHunter series features TrueZero windage and elevation adjustment system for a locked-in zero and raised tab on the power change ring for easy grip and surer adjustments.
*MSRP*: . . . . . . . . . . . . . . . . .$186.95

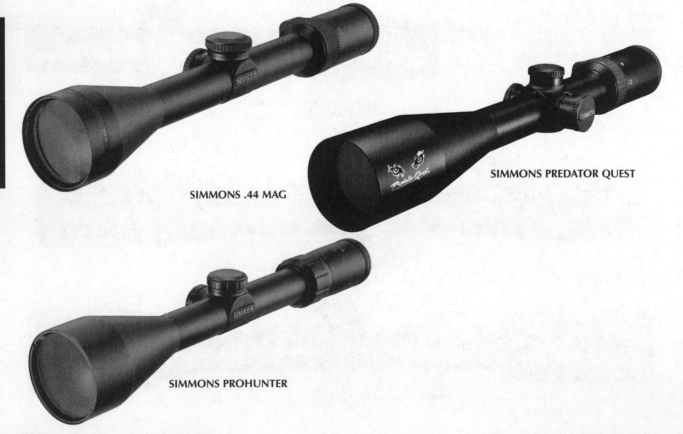

SIMMONS .44 MAG

SIMMONS PREDATOR QUEST

SIMMONS PROHUNTER

# Simmons

## PROTARGET

Simmons ProTarget 3-9x40mm (also in 3-12x40mm, 6-18x40mm)
*Weight*: 20.4 oz.
*Power*: 3-9x
*Objective Diameter*: 40mm
*Main Tube Diameter*: 1 in.
*Eye Relief*: 3 $^9/_{10}$ in.
*Exit Pupil*: 13.33-4.44mm
*Field of View*: 31-10.5 ft @ 100 yds
*Twilight Factor*: 10.95-18.97
*Waterproof*: Yes
*Fogproof*: Yes
*Product Description*: Calibrated for either .22 LR or .17 HMR, the Simmons ProTarget series offers precision optics for mid- to long-range shooting. Multi-coated optics provide bright, sharp images, and the TruPlex Reticle makes it easier to pinpoint the smallest targets with a rimfire rifle. Comes with fingertip-adjustable turrets with a side focus available on the higher magnification models.
*MSRP*: . . . . . . . . . . . . . . . . .$191.95

**SIMMONS PROTARGET**

# Swarovski Optik

## Z3 RIFLESCOPE

Z3 Riflescope 3-10x42 (also in 3-9x36 and 4-12X50)
*Weight*: 12.7 oz
*Length*: 12 $^3/_5$
*Main Tube Diameter*: 1 in.
*Power*: 3-10X
*Objective Diameter*: 42mm
*Exit Pupil*: 12.6-4.2mm
*Field of View*: 33-11.7 ft @ 1000 yds.
*Twilight Factor*: 11.22-20.49
*Eye Relief*: 3 ½ in.
*Waterproof*: Yes
*Fogproof*: Yes
*Product Description*: Z3 riflescopes have a 3X zoom factor and are the lightest riflescopes in the Swarovski Optik line., a perfect fit for many of today's lightweight rifles. Available reticles for the Z3 include the 4A, Plex, BRX/BRH (3-10X and 4-12X), and ML in the 3-10X. Ballistic turrets are available in the 4-12X.
*MSRP*: . . . . . . . . . . . . . . . . .$1276.67

## Z5 RIFLESCOPE

Z5 Riflescope 5-25x52 (also in 3.5-18x44)
*Weight*: 17.5 oz.
*Length*: 14 $^3/_5$ in.
*Main Tube Diameter*: 1 in.
*Power*: 5-25X
*Objective Diameter*: 52mm
*Exit Pupil*: 9.6-2.1mm
*Field of View*: 21.9-4.5 ft @ 100 yards
*Twilight Factor*: 16.12-36.05
*Eye Relief*: 3 ¾ in
*Waterproof*: Yes
*Fogproof*: Yes
*Product Description*: The Z5 Riflescope line features a 5X zoom factor, a third parallax-adjustment turret, and long eye relief, with reticles available in #4, Plex, Fine in the 5-25X, and BRX/BRH. Also available with the ballistic turrets.
*MSRP*: . . . . . . . . . . . . . . . .$1765.56

**SWAROVSKI
Z5 RIFLESCOPE**

**SWAROVSKI
Z3 RIFLESCOPE**

# Swarovski Optik

## Z6 RIFLESCOPE

Z6 Riflescope 2-12X50 (also in 1-6x24, 1.7-10x42, 2,5-15X44, 2.5-15X56, 3-18X50, and 5-30X50, and in illuminated)
**Weight**: 18.3 oz.
**Length**: 13 $\frac{2}{5}$ in.
**Width**: in.
**Main Tube Diameter**: 30mm

**Power**: 2-12X
**Objective Diameter**: 50mm
**Exit Pupil**: 25-4.17mm
**Field of View**: 63.0-10.5 ft @100 yds
**Twilight Factor**: 10-24.49
**Eye Relief**: 3.74 in.
**Waterproof**: Yes
**Fogproof**: Yes
**Product Description**: The Z6 line of

riflescopes feature a 6X zoom factor, long eye relief, adjustable parallax, on and HD glass on select high magnification models. Also available with illuminated reticles which have a spare battery stored in the turret cap. Available, as well, with a wide selection of reticles.
**MSRP**: . . . . . . . . . . . . . . . . $2265.56

SWAROVSKI Z6 RIFLESCOPE

# Trijicon Inc.

## ACCUPOINT

Trijicon AccuPoint 3-9x40 (also in 1.25-4x24, and in 30mm in 1-4 x 24, 1.25-4 x 24, 5-20 x 50, and 2.5-10 x 56)
**Weight**: 13.4 oz.
**Length**: 12 $\frac{2}{5}$ in.
**Main Tube Diameter**: 1-in tube
**Power**: 3-9X
**Objective Diameter**: 40mm
**Exit Pupil**: 13.3 to 4.4mm

**Field of View**: 6.45 to 2.15
**Twilight Factor**: 10.95-18.97
**Eye Relief**: 3 $\frac{3}{5}$ in.
**Waterproof**: Yes
**Fogproof**: Yes
**Product Description**: The Trijicon AccuPoint riflescope combines the illumination characteristics of Tritium with the light-gathering capabilities of fiber for a battery-free dual-illuminated. Has Trijicon's Manual Brightness

Adjustment Override, multi-layer-coated, quick-focus eyepiece, long-eye relief, and windage and elevation adjustments. Built from aircraft hard-anodized aluminum with black-matte finish. Available reticles include BAC Triangle, Standard Cross-Hair with Dot, Mil-Dot Cross-Hair with Dot, and German #4 in red, green, and amber illumination.
**MSRP**: . . . . . . . . . . . . . . . . . . $900

TRIJICON ACCUPOINT

# Weaver Optics

## SUPER SLAM
**Weight**: 14.0 oz.-24 oz.
**Length**: 10.31 in.-13.31 in.
**Power**: 1-5x, 2-10x, 3-15x, 4-20x
**Objective Diameter**: 42-50mm
**Main Tube Diameter**: 1 in.
**Exit Pupil**: 11.4-4.9mm to 10.5-2.44mm
**Field of View**: 100-19.9 ft @ 100 yds-24.5-4.9 ft @ 100 yds
**Twilight Factor**: 16
**Eye Relief**: 4.25 in.-3.98 in.
**Waterproof**: Yes
**Fogproof**: Yes
**Product Description**: Engineered to meet the strict standards of the legendary Weaver name, the new Super Slam scopes are loaded with all the latest technological advances of modern high-end optics. If you know and trust the Weaver name, you'll be impressed with this new line of premier riflescopes designed for the serious big game hunter and shooter.
**MSRP:** . . . . . . . . . **$786.95–$999.49**

WEAVER SUPER SLAM

## CLASSIC K SERIES
**Weight**: 9.8 oz.-15.3 oz.
**Length**: 19.17 in.-13.5 in.
**Width**: 3 in.
**Power**: 4x, 6x, 8x
**Objective Diameter**: 38mm
**Main Tube Diameter**: 1 in.
**Exit Pupil**: 6.3mm to 9.5mm
**Field of View**: 8.5 ft @ 100 yds-26.8 ft @ 100 yds
**Twilight Factor**: 15.1
**Eye Relief**: 3.15 in.-9.45 in.
**Waterproof**: Yes
**Fogproof**: Yes
**Product Description**: Crafted from a one-piece aircraft-grade aluminum tube, the Classic K-Series fixed power scopes are built to take heavy recoil punishment and hold zero to 10,000 rounds from a .375 H&H magnum rifle. Classic K-Series fixed scopes present a consistent field of view that's perfect for open field hunting and are among the easiest scopes any instinctive shooter will ever use—regardless of the range.
**MSRP:** . . . . . . . . . **$265.49–$395.49**

WEAVER CLASSIC K SERIES

## CLASSIC RIMFIRE
**Weight**: 8.75 oz.-12 oz.
**Length**: 10.22 in.-11.50 in.
**Width**: 3 in.
**Power**: 2.5-7x, 3-9x, 4x
**Objective Diameter**: 28mm
**Main Tube Diameter**: 1 in.
**Exit Pupil**: 9.9-4mm, 10.6mm, 7mm
**Field of View**: 40.3-14.6 ft @ 100 yds, 33.2-11 ft @ 100 yds, 25.2 ft @ 100 yds
**Twilight Factor**: 14
**Eye Relief**: 3.58 in., 3.62 in.
**Waterproof**: Yes
**Fogproof**: Yes
**Product Description**: Every Classic Rimfire scope incorporates many of the exact same features found on Weaver's top-of-the-line models. Designed to bring out the best in rimfire and adult air rifles, the Classic Rimfire comes in variable and fixed power models—with fully multi-coated, non-glare lenses that produce edge-sharp, low-light brightness, even in the duskiest of conditions. All scopes feature rugged, aircraft-grade, one-piece aluminum construction. Waterproof, fogproof, and shockproof, the Classic Rimfire is designed to withstand the multi-directional recoil from the heaviest spring-loaded adult airguns. Parallax is set at 50 yards for ideal rimfire target acquisition and accuracy.
**MSRP:** . . . . . . . . . **$188.49–$357.95**

WEAVER CLASSIC RIMFIRE

SCOPES

# Weaver Optics

**WEAVER 40/44 SHOTGUN & MUZZLELOADER**

## 40/44 SHOTGUN & MUZZLELOADER

**Weight**: 14.0 oz.-24 oz.
**Length**: 10.31 in.-13.31 in.
**Width**: Power: 2-7x
**Objective Diameter**: 32mm
**Main Tube Diameter**: 1 in.
**Exit Pupil**: 15-5.4mm
**Field of View**: 44.7-12.7 ft @ 100 yds
**Eye Relief**: 3.5 in.

**Waterproof**: Yes
**Fogproof**: Yes
**Product Description**: For those hunters venturing afield with a shotgun or muzzleloader, Weaver has you covered. Weaver's dedicated shotgun and muzzleloader scopes are engineered specifically for the unique performance of these firearms and give hunters maximum performance out of these short-to medium-range guns.
**MSRP**: . . . . . . . . . . $181.49, $191.49

**SCOPES**

# Weaver Optics

## CLASSIC HANDGUN
**Weight**: 6.4 oz.-9.1 oz.
**Length**: 8.19 in.-9.29 in.
**Power**: 1.5-4x, 2x, 2.5-8x, 4x
**Objective Diameter**: 20mm, 28mm
**Main Tube Diameter**: 1 in.
**Exit Pupil**: 11.4-4.9 to 10.5-2.44
**Field of View**: 100-19.9/33.3-6.6 to 24.5-4.9/8.2-1.6
**Eye Relief**: 23.31 in., 24.13 in., 24.53 in., 26.86 in.
**Waterproof**: No
**Fogproof**: No
**Product Description**: Handguns demand a scope that is built to withstand the brutal, shot-after-shot pounding from today's most powerful revolvers and single-shot pistols. Designed for the tremendous recoil of 1,000 rounds from a .454 Casull revolver,

Weaver's Classic Handgun scopes deliver the goods on rugged, reliable, repeatable accuracy.
**MSRP**: . . . . . . . . . . $259.49–$339.49

**WEAVER CLASSIC HANDGUN**

# Browning
By Thomas McIntyre

## BUCK MARK REFLEX SIGHT
**Power**: 1X
**Field of View**: 47 ft @ 100 yards
**Eye Relief**: Unlimited
**Product Description**: The Buck Mark has an aluminum housing, four red reticle patterns, a seven-position brightness rheostat powered by a lithium battery, and mounts on a standard Weaver-style base.
**MSRP** . . . . . . . . . . . . . . . . . .**$49.99**

**BROWNING BUCK MARK REFLEX SIGHT**

# Carl Zeiss Sports Optics

## COMPACT POINT
**Weight**: 2.64 oz.
**Length**: 2¼ in.
**Width**: 1 in.
**Power**: 1.05X
**Halo Size**: 23x16 mm
**Waterproof**: Yes
**Fogproof**: Yes
**Transferable Limited Lifetime Warranty on Mechanics, 5 Year Warranty on Electronics**
**Product Description**: Approximately 25-percent larger than the average reflex sight, the Compact Point uses an illuminated red dot for target acquisition and LotuTec moisture-resistant coating on the lens. Available for Picatinny or Weaver-style mounts and suitable for hunting rifles, AR-style weapons, shotguns, and handguns.
**MSRP** . . . . . . . . . . . . . . . . . .**$499.99**

**ZEISS COMPACT POINT**

## Z-POINT (RED DOT REFLEX SIGHT)

**Weight**: 5.65 oz
**Length**: 2 ½ in.
**Width**: 1 ²/₅ in.
**Power**: 1X
**Waterproof**: Yes
**Fogproof**: Yes
**Transferable Limited Lifetime Warranty on Mechanics, 5 Year Warranty on Electronics**
**Product Description**: This acquisition sight for shotguns, rifles, and handguns uses a dual-source illumination: a solar cell for daylight hours and battery power for dark, extending the overall the life of the battery. The red dot automatically adapts to the brightness of the surroundings and can also be regulated manually. Available for Weaver or Picatinny mounts.
**MSRP** . . . . . . . . . . . . . . . . . $574.99

ZEISS Z-POINT

# Davide Pedersoli & C.

DAVIDE PEDERSOLI USA 473

## U.S. MODEL 1879 SPRINGFIELD TRAPDOOR REAR SIGHT, MODEL USA 473

**Product Description**: Sometimes referred to as "Buckhorn" style. Used on Trapdoor rifles from 1874 until superseded by Buffington style in 1884. Side ramps are graduated to 500 yards and the ladder to 1500 yards. Slide has windage adjustment.
**MSRP** . . . . . . . . . . . . . . . . . . . $147

## "SOULE TYPE" MIDDLE RANGE SET, MODEL USA 170

**Elevation Adjustment**: 3 in.
**Product Description**: Wooden-box set including Soule XL Middle Range Sight; Tunnel Front Sight with a micro- metric screw for windage adjustment, spirit level, and fifteen interchangeable inserts; professional "Hadley Style" Eyepiece with eight varying diameter viewing holes, depending on available light, on a rotating disk which can be selected without disassembling or loosening the eyepiece, and a rubber ring on the eyepiece; six interchangeable glass bubbles (spirit level) with different colors for varying light conditions.
**MSRP** . . . . . . . . . . . . . . . . . . . $848

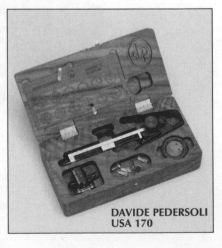

DAVIDE PEDERSOLI USA 170

SIGHTS

# Davide Pedersoli & C.

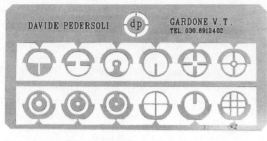

**DAVIDE PEDERSOLI USA 425**

**DAVIDE PEDERSOLI-USA 430**

**DAVIDE PEDERSOLI USA 409**

**DAVIDE PEDERSOLI USA 428**

SIGHTS

## SPIRIT LEVEL TUNNEL SIGHT ADJUSTABLE WITH 12 INSERTS SET, MODEL USA 425

*Product Description*: Spirit level tunnel sight with micrometer adjustment for windage, equipped with twelve interchangeable inserts.

**MSRP** . . . . . . . . . . . . . . . . . . . . . **$229**

## FIBER OPTIC FRONT AND REAR SIGHT, MODEL USA 409

*Product Description*: Front sight and rear sight set for muzzleloading rifles (Model 410 for breechloaders). Front sight with dovetail base; rear sight with base for octagonal barrel.

**MSRP** . . . . . . . . . . . . . . . . . . . . . **$127**

## ENGLISH REAR SIGHT, MODEL USA 428

*Product Description*: Rear sight with convex base, with two adjustable and folding leaves.

**MSRP** . . . . . . . . . . . . . . . . . . . . . **$142**

## UNIVERSAL CREEDMOOR SIGHT, MIDDLE AND LONG RANGE, MODELS USA 465 AND 430

*Distance between the two mounting holes*: $2^3/_{16}$ up to $2^5/_{16}$ in.
*Elevation Adjustments*: 2 and 3 in.
*Product Description*: Tang sight with elevation and windage adjustment in the eye piece. For long-distance target shooting both with muzzle-loading and breech-loading rifles.

**MSRP** . . . . . . . . . . . . . . . . . **$244–$248**

## HD7 RED DOT SIGHT

**Weight**: 13 oz.
**Length**: 5½ in.
**Width**: 2¾ in.
**Power**: 1X
**Objective Diameter**: 34mm
**Field of View**: 44 ft @ 100 yards with 4 inches of eye relief
**Eye Relief**: Unlimited
**Waterproof**: Yes
**Fogproof**: Yes

**Limited Lifetime Warranty**
**Product Description**: The HD7 comes with an integral Picatinny rail and reversible mounting pins for bullpup-style firearms. It is shockproof and has two modes of operation (manual & "Auto-Brightness") with 12 brightness settings in the reticle control, four operator-selectable reticles based on a 2 MOA dot (2 MOA dot, 25 MOA circle-crosshair, 25 MOA crosshair, and 25 MOA circle with 2 MOA dot) with ½ MOA click adjustments. Parallax free, it is powered by one AAA battery, providing over 1000 hours of life in high and nearly 5000 hours when the Auto-Brightness mode is employed and has a two-hour auto shutoff. The frame is cast aluminum armored in chemical rubber and is available with a 2X screw-in eyepiece.
**MSRP** . . . . . . . . . . . . . . . . . . . **$249**

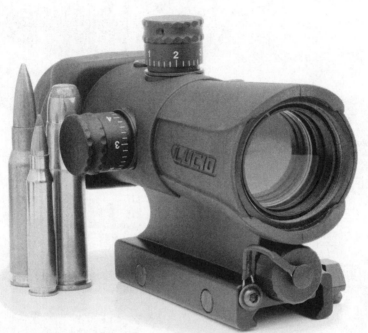

LUCID HD7 RED DOT SIGHT

# Pentax Imaging Co.

## GAMESEEKER DOT SIGHT HS-20 (89702)

**Weight**: 3.4 oz.
**Length**: 3⁹⁄₁₀ in.
**Width**: 2 in.
**Power**: 1X
**Halo Size**: 33x22 mm
**Dot Size**: 5 MOA
**Field of View**: 55-50 ft @ 100 yards
**Waterproof**: Yes
**Fogproof**: Yes
**Limited Lifetime Warranty**
**Product Description**: Has 5 MOA dot with 11 brightness settings and 72 hours of continuous battery use. Uses continuous, non-click adjustments. With Weaver-style mounting system.
**MSRP** . . . . . . . . . . . . . . . . . . . **$59**

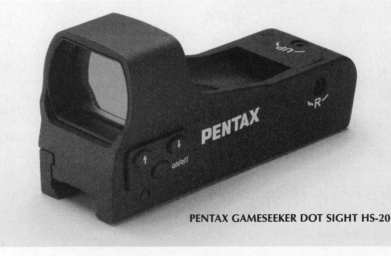

PENTAX GAMESEEKER DOT SIGHT HS-20

SIGHTS

# Pentax Imaging Co.

## GAMESEEKER DOT SIGHT RD-10 (89701)

*Weight*: 7.07 oz.
*Length*: 3⁴/₅ in.
*Tube Diameter*: 39 mm
*Power*: 1X
*Objective Diameter*: 30 mm
*Dot Size*: 4 MOA
*Field of View*: 54 ft @ 100 yards
*Waterproof*: Yes
*Fogproof*: Yes
*Limited Lifetime Warranty*
*Product Description*: A reflex sight with a 4 MOA dot, 11 brightness settings, 72 hours continuous battery life, and continuous windage and elevation adjustments. With Weaver-style mounting system.
MSRP . . . . . . . . . . . . . . . . . . . . . $69

PENTAX GAMESEEKER
DOT SIGHT RD-10

# Trijicon Inc.

## TRIJICON RMR™ ADJUSTABLE LED RM06 (ALSO IN DUAL-ILLUMINATED RMR WITH 13.0 MOA DOT, 7.0 MOA DOT, 9.0 MOA DOT, AND TRIANGLE-RETICLE RMR LED WITH 3.25 MOA DOT AND 8.0 MOA DOT)

*Weight*: 1.2 oz.
*Length*: 45 mm
*Power*: 1X
*Dot Size*: 3.25 MOA
*Waterproof*: Yes
*Fogproof*: Yes
*Limited Lifetime Warranty*
*Product Description*: Electronic reflex sight with a military-grade investment-cast aircraft-aluminum-alloy and hard-coat anodized-finish housing. With eight brightness levels powered by a long-life lithium battery.
MSRP . . . . . . . . . . . . . . . . . . . . . $675

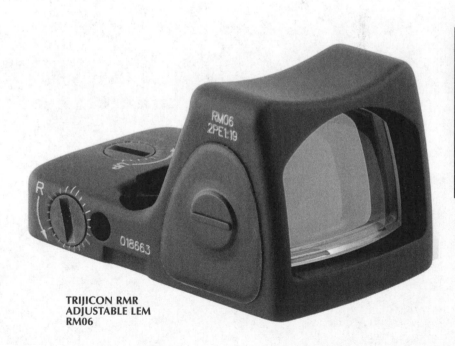

TRIJICON RMR
ADJUSTABLE LEM
RM06

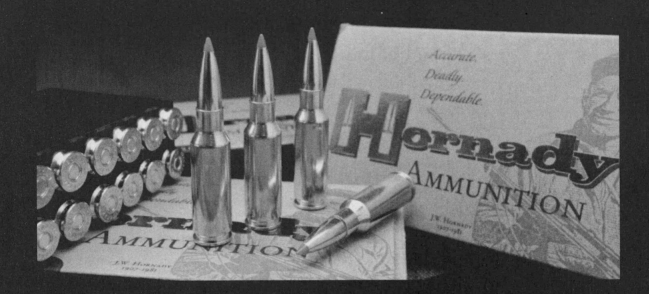

# Barnes Ammunition

**BARNES BUSTER BULLET**

**BARNES LRX BULLETS**

**BARNES SPIT-FIRE T-EZ**

## BUSTER BULLETS

**Features**: Deep penetrating hunting bullets for handguns and lever rifles. Features a thick copper jacket and a heavy lead core resulting in minimal expansion and maximum weight retention.
**Available in**: .44 Mag., 454 Casull, 45/70, 500 S&W
**MSRP** . . . . . . . . . . . . **$48.99–$59.49**

## TRIPPLE-SHOCK X (TSX) BULLETS

**Features**: Delievers a triple impact. One when it first strikes game, another as the bullet begins opening, and a third devastating impact when the specifically engineered cavity fully expands to deliver extra shock and maximum transferred energy.
**Available in**: .22, .224, .6mm, .25, 6.5mm, 6.8mm, .270, 7mm .224 (223/5.56)
**MSRP** . . . . . . . . . . . . **$26.64–$35.66**

## LRX BULLETS

**Features**: Long-Range X bullets increase B.C. values by increasing ogive and boat tail lengths to improve the bullet's long-range ballistic performance. Manufacturered with 100-per-cent copper, lead-free bodies. The polymer tip initiates expansion and causes the nose cavity to open instantly on contact, doubling the bullet's original diameter, while creating four sharp petals that cause internal damage.
**Available in**: .30, .338 Lapua, .7mm
**MSRP** . . . . . . . . . . . . **$38.99–$46.99**

## BANDED SOLIDS

**Features**: These bullets feature rings cut into the shank to reduce presures and allow higher velocities. They are designed to penetrate large, dangerous game with their wider meplat because they won't deflect on heavy bone. No lead core or jacket to separate on impact. Round nose or flat nose solids available.
**Available in**: .223, .6mm, .25, 6.5mm, .270, 7mm, .30, .338, 9.3mm, .375, .410
**MSRP** . . . . . . . . . . . . **$17.91–$58.17**

## XPB BULLETS

**Features**: All-copper bullets for increased penetration over conventional jacketed lead-core bullets; these lead-free bullets provide superior expansion and weight retention. Ideal for hunting or self-defense. Retain virtually 100-percent of their originial weight.
**Available in**: .357 Mag., .41 Mag., .45 Colt, .454 Casull, .460 S&W, .480 Ruger, .500 S&W
**MSRP** . . . . . . . . . . . . **$15.49–$24.99**

## SPITZ-FIRE T-EZ

**Features**: Resdesigned sabot reduces the ramrod pressure needed to load and seat these .50-caliber, flat based bullets. Polymer tip enhances expansion and boosts BC for superior long-range ballistics. Six sharp cutting petals emerge on impact to maximize shock and penetration.
**Available in**: .50
**MSRP** . . . . . . . . . . . . **$31.99–$91.00**

## VARMINT GRENADE

**Features**: Created by technology developed exclusively for military applications, the new Varmint Grenade bullet features a highly frangible, copper-tin composite core. Remains intact at ultra-high velocities, yet fragments explosively on impact.
**Available in**: .204, .22 Hornet, .22
**MSRP** . . . . . . . . . . . . **$17.77–$52.99**

## BLACK HILLS COWBOY PISTOL AMMUNITION

*Features*: Designed to meet the needs of cowboy-action shooters with its new virgin brass and premium-qality hard-cast bullets. Velocities are moderate to provide low recoil and excellent accuracy.

*Available in*: .32-20, .38 Long Colt, .39 Spl., .357 Mag., .38-40, .44-40, .44 Russian, .44 Spl., .44 Colt, .45 Schofield, .38-55, .45-70,
**MSRP** . . . . . . . . . . . . **$27.99–$37.99**

BLACK HILLS COWBOY PISTOL AMMUNITION

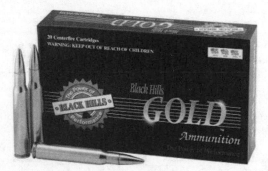

BLACK HILLS GOLD

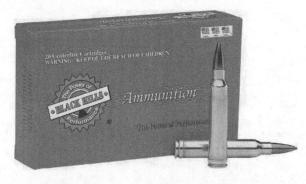

BLACK HILLS NEW FACTORY RIFLE AMMUNITION

## REMANUFACTURED .223 REMINGTON VARMINT GRENADE

*Features*: Ammunition designed for the practice shooter in mind, with incredible accuracy for a great price point. It's the same ammunition used by the U.S. Army Marksmanship Unit in 600-yd. matches. It has the capability to produce 2 in. groups at 300 meters. 50 rounds per box.

*Available in*: .223 Rem. (Also available in molycoat)
**MSRP** . . . . . . . . . . . . **$31.99–$41.99**

## BLACK HILLS GOLD LEAD-FREE RIFLE AMMUNITION

*Features*: Coupling the finest components in the industry with bullets by Barnes, these lead-free non-toxic rounds set a new standard for high-performance hunting ammunition. 20 rounds per box.

*Available in*: .22-250, .243 Win., .25-06 Rem., .260 Rem., .270 Win., 6.5-.284 Norma, 7mm Rem. Mag., .300 Win. Mag., .308 Win., .30-06, .300 Win. Short Mag.
**MSRP** . . . . . . . . . . . . **$39.99–$52.99**

## FACTORY NEW HANDGUN AMMUNITION

*Features*: Relied upon by the United States Military in all four branches for its reliablity.

*Available in*: .32 H&R Mag., .380 Automatic, 9mm Luger, .38 Spl., .357 Mag., .40 S&W, .44 Mag., .45 Auto Rim, .45 ACP
**MSRP** . . . . . . . . . . . . **$34.99–$49.99**

## FACTOR NEW RIFLE AMMUNITION

*Features*: Coupling the finest components in the industry with bullets by manufacturers such as Hornady, Barnes and Nosler, these rounds set a new standard for high-performance hunting ammunition. 20 rounds per box.

*Available in*: .223 Rem., .308 Win. Match, . 300 Win. Mag., .338 Lapua, .338 Norma Magnum
**MSRP** . . . . . . . . . . . . **$29.99–$124.99**

# Brennake USA Ammuntion

## CLASSIC MAGNUM SLUGS

**Features**: Invented by Wilhelm Brenneke in 1898, the classic is the ancestor of all modern shotgun slugs. Today this state of the art slug provides long-range stopping power, consistently flat trajectories, and a patented B.E.T. was column.
**Available in**: 12 Ga., 16 Ga.
MSRP . . . . . . . . . . . . . .$8.99–$11.99

## BLACK MAGIC MAGNUM AND SHORT MAGNUM

**Features**: The Black Magic Magnum and Black Magic Short Magnum are two of the most powerful cartridges available on the market, offering tremendous knockdown power up to 100/60 yards. The clean speed coating reduces lead fouling inside the barrel by almost 100-percent.
**Available in**: 12 Ga. (2 ¾ in.), 12 Ga. (3 in.)
MSRP . . . . . . . . . . . . . .$9.99–$10.99

## K.O. SLUG

**Features**: The K.O. is an improved Foster type slug with excellent penetration. Range up to 60 yds, for all barrel types.
**Available in**: 12 Ga. (2 ¾ in.)
MSRP . . . . . . . . . . . . . . . . . .$5.99

## HEAVY FIELD SHORT MAGNUM SLUGS- GREEN LIGHTNING

**Features**: The original "Emerald" slug with patented B.E.T wad and famous stopping power. For all barrel types; range up to 100 yards.
**Available in**: 12 Ga., 20 Ga. (2 ¾ in.)
MSRP . . . . . . . . . . . . . .$7.99–$9.29

## GOLD MAGNUM SLUGS

**Features**: Designed for long distance and accuracy; Gold Magnum is designed for rifled barrels only, it is one of the heaviest and most accurate slugs on the market. It has broad ribs for optimum guidance in the rifled barrel and a special coating to reduce lead fouling. Range 100+ yards.

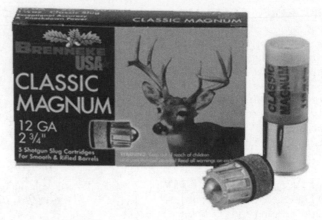

**BRENNAKE CLASSIC MAGNUM SLUGS 12 GA**

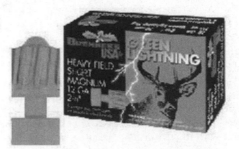

**BRENNAKE HEAVY FIELD SHORT MAGNUM GREEN LIGHTNING SLUGS**

**Available in**: 12 Ga. (3 in.)
MSRP . . . . . . . . . . . . . . . . . .$11.99

## SUPERSABOT

**Features**: The SuperSabot has a movable core, lead free construction and an effective range up to more than 100 yards. It mushrooms up to 1 in.
**Available in**: 12 Ga. (2 ¾ in.), 12 Ga. (3 in.)
MSRP . . . . . . . . . . .$15.98–$17.79

## K.O. SABOT

**Features**: One of the most affordable sabots on the market, it offers 58-percent more frontal area than standard .50 cal slugs, resulting in massive energy transfer. Deep penetration, expansion up to .9 inches. Range up to 100 yards.
**Available in**: 12 Ga. (2 ¾ in.), 12 Ga. (3 in.)
MSRP . . . . . . . . . . . . . . . . . .$13.29

## .22 WIN. MAG. MAXI MAG

*Features*: A favorite of varmint shooters. 40 grain TMJ flat nose at 1875 ft/sec, or 40 grain jacketed HP at 1875 ft/sec. Both loads give over 1400 ft/sec from a 6-inch revolver. Clean-burning propellants keep actions cleaner. Sure-fire CCI priming. Reusable plastic box with dispenser lid.
*Available in*: .22 Win. Mag.
**Box 50** . . . . . . . . . . . **$13.99–$14.99**

## LONG HV AND SHORT HV

*Features*: Designed for rimfire guns that require .22 Long and .22 Short ammunition. Clean-burning propellants keep actions cleaner. Sure-fire CCI priming. Resusable plastic box with dispenser lid.
*Available in*: .22 short 29 gr solid lead bullet; .22 short 27 gr hollow point bullet; .22 Long 29 gr solid lead bullet
**Long HV:** . . . . . . . . . . . . . . . .**$8.99**
**Short HV100:** . . . . . . . . .**$7.95–$9.95**

## MINI-MAG. HV

*Features*: CCI's first rimfire product and still most popular. Mini-Mag. hallow points are high-velocity products and offer excellent all-around performance for small game and varmints. Clean-burning propellants keep actions cleaner. Sure-fire CCI priming. Reusable plastic box with dispenser lid
*Available in*: .22 Long Rifle; 40-grain gileded round nose; 36 grain gilded lead hollow point
**Box 100:** . . . . . . . . . . . .**$5.88–$6.89**

## HMR TNT

*Features*: CCI extends the usefulness of the exciting 17 Hornady Magnum Rimfire by offering the first hollow point loading. A 17 grain Speer TNT hollow point answers requests from varmint hunters and gives explosive performance over the 17's effective

**CCI .22 MINI-MAG. HV**

range. Clean-burning propellants keep actions cleaner. Sure-fire CCI priming. Reusable plastic box with dispenser lid.
*Available in*: .17 HMR- 17 grain TNT hollow point
**MSRP** . . . . . . . . . . . . . . . . .**$13.99**

## PISTOL MATCH

*Features*: Designed expressly for high-ended semi-auto match pistols. Single-die tooling and great care in assembly lets you wring the last bit of accuracy from your precision pistol. Clean-burning propellants keep actions cleaner. Sure-fire CCI priming. Reusable plastic box with dispenser

lid.
*Available in*: .22 LR - 40 grain lead round nose bullet
**Box 50:** . . . . . . . . . . . . . .**$6.90–$7.90**

## V-MAX 17 MACH 2

*Features*: The 17 Mach 2 is a .22 LR CCI Stinger case necked down to hold a 17 caliber bullet. CCI loads a super accurate 17-grain polymer-tipped bullet, and drives it 60-percent faster than a .22 Long Rifle 40-grain hollow-point. The loaded cartridge is no longer than a 22 Long rifle, greatly expanding the gun actions that can accomodate .17 caliber rimfire cartridges. Reusable 50-count plastic box that protects and dispenses five cartridges at a time.
*Available in*: .17 Mach 2 (V-Max also aviale in 17 HMR and .22 Mag. RF)
**Box 50:** . . . . . . . . . . . . . . . . .**$8.99**

## GREEN TAG

*Features*: Our first and still most popular match rimfire product. Tight manufacturing and accuracy specs mean you get the consistency and accuracy that the unforgiving field of compeition demands. And we load our rimfire match ammo to leave the muzzle sub-sonic. That means no buffeting in the transonic zone. Clean-burning propellants keep actions cleaner. Sure-fire CCI priming. Reusable plastic box with dispenser lid.
*Available in*: .22 LR - 40 grain lead round nose
**Box 100:** . . . . . . . . . . . . . . . .**$13.44**

## SELECT .22LR

*Features*: The 22 Long Rifle Select is build for semi-automatic compeition. Reliable operation, accuracy and consistency make Select an ideal choice for compeition shooters.
*Available in*: .22 LR
**Box 100:** . . . . . . . . . . . . . . . .**$11.69**

# Cor-Bon Ammunition

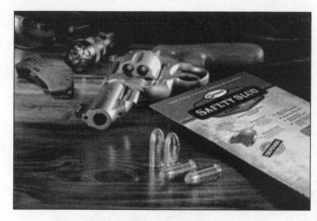

COR-BON GLASER SAFETY SLUG

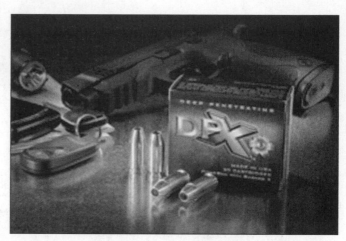

COR-BON DXP

### GLASER SAFETY SLUG

*Features*: The slug was originally designed for use by Sky Marshals on airplanes. Today the slug is reccommended for anyone concerned with over penetration. The Safety slug uses a copper jacket and it is filled with a compresssed load of either #12 or #6 lead shot. It is then capped with a round polymer ball that enhances feeding and reloading.
*Available in*: .25Auto, .32 NAA, .380 Auto, 9mm Makarov, 9mm Luger +P, .38 Super Auto, .38 Special Std., .38 Special +P, .357 Sig, 10mm Auto, .400 Corbon, .44 S&W Special, .44 Mag., 45 Auto +P, .45 Colt +P, .223, 7.62x39, .30-06 Sprg.
**Box 6:. . . . . . . . . . . $17.59–$28.93**

### DPX

*Features*: DPX is a solid copper hollowpoint bullet that combines the best of the lightweight high speed JHPs and the heavyweight, deep penetrating JHPs. The copper bullet construction makes it conquer hard barriers like auto glass and steel while still main-

taining its integrity. This is an optimum load for Law Enforcement. Lead free projectile. Reduced recoil due to lighter weight projectile. Deep penetration on soft tissue 12-17 inches.
*Available in*: 9mm Luger +P, 9x23, 10mm Auto, .357 Mag., .357 Sig, 3.8 Auto +P, .38 Special +P, .380 Auto, .400 Corbon, .40 S&W, .45 GAP, .45 Auto Rim, .45 Auto, 45 Auto +P, .44 Rem. Mag., .44 S&W Special, .45 Colt +P, .454 Casull, .480 Ruger, 7.62x39, .41 Rem. Mag., .460 S&W Mag., .500 S&W Special, .500 S&W Mag.
**Box 20:. . . . . . . . . . . $39.57–$59.16**

### POW'RBALL

*Features*: Designed for finicky feeding pistols, Pow'Rball is a great choice for your semi auto pistols or revolvers. Reliable feeding and consistent reliable expansion. Deeper soft tissue penetration. Custom scored jacket. Proprietary polymer ball and patented lead core
*Available in*: .32 Auto, .380 Auto, 9mm Makarov, 9mm Luger +P, 9x23, 10mm Auto, .357 Mag., .357 Sig, .38

Special +P, 38 Super +P, .400 Corbon, .40 S&W, .45 GAP, .45 Auto +P
**Box 20:. . . . . . . . . . . $27.37–$33.15**

### CORBON HUNTER

*Features*: Hunting ammunition for serious handgun hunters. Corbon maufactures Bonded Core Soft Point ammunition that retains optimum weight and integrity. These provide reliable expansion, coupled with deep penetration. The Penetrator features a heavy full copper jacket enclosed in a hard linotype lead core. Our Hard Cast bullets are precision cast from hard linotype lead and have the prove flat, LBT nose design. Both loads cause a through and through hole, penetrating the thickest hides and breaking the heaviest bone.
*Available in*: .460 S&W Mag., .460 Rowland, 10mm Auto, .300 Whisper, .357 Mag., .41 Rem. Mag., .44 Auto Mag., .440 Corbon, .44 Rem. Mag., .444 Marlin, .45 Colt +P, .454 Casull, .45-70 Govt., .460 Rowland, .460 S&W Mag., .475 Turnbull, .500 S&W Mag., 7.62x39
**Box 12:. . . . . . . . . . . $35.10–$98.07**

**ENVIRON-METAL HEVI-SHOT**

**ENVIRON-METAL HEVI-SHOT
MAGNUM BLEND**

### HEVI-SHOT DEAD COYOTE

*Features*: With these Hevi-Shot T-shot loads, you can be deadly at ranges you never thought possible with a 12 gauge. The 3 in. load pounds out 50 pellets at 1,350 feet-per-second. Each pellet is molded perfectly round to minimize the effects of air resistance and keep your pattern together. 10-percent heavier than lead, 54-percent denser than steel. Each 50 rounds includes a dry-storage box.
*Available in*: 12 Ga. (3 in., 3.5 in.)
**Box 50:** . . . . . . . . . . $169.99–$179.99

### HEVI-SHOT CLASSIC DOUBLES

*Features*: Optimized for your fixed chokes and fine classic doubles. Denser than steel but soft like lead which means you get deeper penetration. USFWS approved non-toxic shot. 45-percent more on target pellets than steel. Belted sphere for maximum pellet mass. Buffered and nano-treated pellets for tight patterns. Weather-resistant crimp.
*Available in*: 12 Ga., 16 Ga., 20 Ga., 28 Ga., 410 Ga.
**Box 10:** . . . . . . . . . . . . $22.99–$31.99

### HEVI-SHOT MAGNUM BLEND

*Features*: Take advantage of Pattern-density technology with Hevi Shot Magnum Blend. Put more lethal pellets in your pattern with a combination of No. 5, 6, and 7 Hevi-13 shot, and boost your lethal range by 14 to 17%. Buffered and moly-coated pellets produce a denser pattern than conventional shot. Hevi-13 delivers 40-percent more knockdown energy and up to 40-percent longer range than lead shells.
*Available in*: 12 Ga.
**Box 5: $7.99–$26.99**

# Federal Ammunition

## Handgun Ammunition

### CASTCORE
*Features*: Heavyweight, flat-nosed, hard cast-lead bullet that smashes through bone.
*Available in*: .375 Mag., .41 Rem., Mag., .44 Rem. Mag. (Vital-Shok)
**.375: $24.00**
**.44: $35.99**
**.41: $35.99**

### FULL METAL JACKET
*Features*: Good choice for range practice and reducing lead fouling in the barrel. Jacket extends from the nose to the base, preventing bullet expansion and barrel leading. Primarily as military ammunition for recreational shooting.
*Available in*: .25 Auto, .32 Auto, .380 Auto, 9mm Makarov, 9mm Luger, 9x21mm, .38 Super +P, .357 Sig, .38 Special, .40 S&W, 10mm Auto, .45 G.A.P., .45 Auto (American Eagle)
**MSRP . . . . . . . . . . . . . .$9.99–$21.99**

### HYDRA-SHOK
*Features*: Unique center-post design delivers controlled expansion, and the notched jacket provides efficient energy transfer to penetrate barriers while retaining stopping power. Deep penetration satisfies even the FBI's stringent testing requirements.
*Available in*: .32 Auto, .327 Federal Magnum, .380 Auto, 9mm Luger, .38 Spl., 38 Spl. +P, .357 Mag., .40 S&W, 10mm Auto, .44 Rem. Mag., .45 G.A.P., .45 Auto (Premium Personal Defense)
**MSRP . . . . . . . . . . . . $19.99–$32.99**

### JACKETED HOLLOW POINT
*Features*: Ideal personal defense round in revolvers and semi-autos. Quick, positive expansion. Jacket ensures smooth feeding into autoloading firearms.
*Available in*: .32 H&R Mag., 9mm Luger, .38 Super +P (American Eagle), .357 Sig, .357 Mag. (Premium Personal Defense, Power- Shok), .40 S&W (Personal Defense), .41 Rem. Mag., 44 Rem. Mag. (Power-Shok, American Eagle), .45 Auto (Personal Defense)
**MSRP . . . . . . . . . . . . . $16.99–$22.99**

**FEDERAL PREMIUM CASTCORE .357 MAG**

### LEAD ROUND NOSE
*Features*: Great training round for practicing at the range. 100 lead with no jacket. Excellent accuracy and is very economical.
*Available in*: .32 S&W Long (Champion), .38 Special (American Eagle)
**MSRP . . . . . . . . . . . . $21.99–$38.99**

### LEAD SEMI-WADCUTTER
*Features*: Most popular all-around choice for target and personal defense, a versatile design which cuts clean holes in targets and efficiently transfers energy.
*Available in*: .32 H&R Magnum (Champion)
**MSRP . . . . . . . . . . . . . . . .$15.29**

### SEMI-WADCUTTER HOLLOW POINT
*Features*: For both small game and personal defense. Hollow point design promotes uniform expansion.
*Available in*: .44 Special, .45 Colt (Champion)
**MSRP . . . . . . . . . . . . $18.99–$22.00**

## Rifle Ammunition

### BARNES TRIPLE-SHOCK X-BULLET (TSX)
*Features*: Superior expansion and deep penetration. The all-copper design provides high weight retention.
*Available in*: 9.3x62 Mauser, 9.3x74 R, .370 Sako Mag., .375 H&H Mag., .416 Rigby, .416 Rem. Mag., .458 Win. Mag., 458 Win. Mag., .458 Lott, .470 Nitro Express, .500 Nitro Express 3 (Cape-Shok)
**MSRP . . . . . . . . . . . . . $36.99–$65.99**

### FULL METAL JACKET BOAT-TAIL
*Features*: Accurate, non-expanding bullets. Flat shooting trajectory, leave a small exit hole in game, and put clean holes in paper. Smooth, reliable feeding into semi-automatics too.
*Available in*: .223 Rem. (Power-Shok, American Eagle), .308 Win., 30-06 Spring (American Eagle)
**MSRP . . . . . . . . . . . . . .$8.49–11.39**

**fusion lite**

### NOSLER ACCUBOND
*Features*: Combines the terminal performance of a bonded bullet with the accuracy and retained energy of a Ballistic Tip.
*Available in*: .270 Win., .270 Win. Short Mag., 7mm Rem. Mag., .300 Win. Mag., .300 Win. Short Mag., .338 Federal, .338 Rem. Ultra Mag., .338 Win. Mag., .375 H&H Mag. (Vital-Shok)
**MSRP . . . . . . . . . . . . . . . .$44–$60**

### NOSLER BALLISTIC TIP
*Features*: Fast, flat-shooting wind-defying performance. Long-range shots at varmints, predators and small to medium game. Color-coded polycarbonate tip provides easy identification, prevents deformation in the magazine and drives back on impact for expansion.
*Available in*: .204 Ruger, .223 Rem., .220 Swift, .243 Win., 25-06 Rem., .260 Rem., .270 Win., 270 Win. Short Mag., 7mm-08 Rem., 280 Rem., 7mm Rem. Mag., 7mm Win. Short Mag., .308 Win., 30-06 Spring., .300 Win. Short Mag.
**Box 20: . . . . . . . . . . . . .24.00–$34.36**

## NOSLER PARTITION

*Features*: Proven choice for medium to large game animals. Partioned copper jacket allows the front half of the bullet to mushroom, while the rear core remains intact, driving forward for deep penetration and stopping power.
*Available in*: .223 Rem., .22-250 Rem., .243 Win., 6mm Rem., 257 Roberts +P, .25-06 Rem., .270 Win., .270 Win. Short Mag., 7mm Mauser (Vital-Shok)
**Box20**: . . . . . . . . . . . **$25.65–$52.70**

## SIERRA GAMEKING BOAT-TAIL

*Features*: Long ranges are its speciality. Excellent choice for everything from varmints to big game animals. Tapered, boat-tail design provides extremely flat trajectories. Higher downrange velocity for more energy at the point of impact. Reduced wind drift.
*Available in*: .223 Rem., .22-250 Rem., .243 Win. (Vital-Shok)
**Box 20**: . . . . . . . . . . . **$28.49–$38.00**

## SOFT POINT

*Features*: Proven performer on small game and thin-skinned medium game. Aerodynamic tip for a flat trajectory. Exposed soft point expands rapidly for hard hits, even as velocity slows at longer ranges.
*Available in*: .22 Hornet (V-Shok), .222 Rem., .22-250 Rem., .243 Win., 6mm Rem., 6.5x55 Swedish, .270 Win., .270 Win. Short Mag., 7mm Rem. Mag., 7mm Win. Short Mag., 7.62x39 Soviet, .300 Savage, .308 Win., .30-06 Spring., .300 Win. Short Mag., .303 British, 8mm Mauser, .375 H&H Mag. (Power-Shok), .338 Federal(American Eagle)
**Box 50**: . . . . . . . . . . . **$23.30–$27.00**

## SOFT POINT FLAT NOSE

*Features*: Great for thick cover, it expands reliably and penetrates deep on light to medium game. The flat nose prevents accidental discharge.
*Available in*: .30-30 Win., .32 Win. Spl.
**Box 20**: . . . . . . . . . . . **$14.99–$16.95**

## SOFT POINT ROUND NOSE

*Features*: The choice in heavy cover.

Large exposed tip, good weight retention and specially tapered jacket provide controlled expansion.
*Available in*: .270 Win., 7mm Mauser, .30 Carbine, .30-30 Win., .35 Rem
**Box 20**: . . . . . . . . . . . **$12.00–$25.99**

## TROPHY BONDED BEAR CLAW

*Features*: Ideal for medium to large dangerous game. The jacket and core are 100% fusion-bonded for reliable bullet expansion from 25 yards to extreme ranges. Bullet retains 95% of its weight for deep penetration. Hard solid copper base tapering to a soft, copper nose section for controlled expansion.
*Available in*: 7mm Rem. Mag., 300 Win. Mag., .388 Win. Mag., .35 Whelen (Vital-Shok), .375 H&H Mag., .416 Rigby, .416 Rem. Mag., .458 Mag., .458 Win. Mag., .458 Lott, .470 Nitro Express (Cape-Shok)
**Box 20**: . . . . . . . . . . . **$41.99–$64.99**

## TROPHY BONDED SLEDGEHAMMER

*Features*: Use it on the largest, most dangerous game in the world. Jack Carter design maximizes stopping power. Bonded bronze solid with a flat nose that minimizes deflection off bone and muscle for a deep straight wound channel.
*Available in*: .375 H&H Mag., .416 Rigby, .416 Rem. Mag., .458 Win. Mag., .458 Lott, .470 Nitro Express (Cape-Shok)
**Box 20**: . . . . . . . . . . . **$105–$243.00**

**Shotgun Ammunition**

## PERSONAL DEFENSE SHOT SHELLS

*Features*: The Judge from Taurus has emerged as a very popular handgun for Personal Defense. This specialized gun has been without a specialized load—until now.
*Available in*: 410 Ga. $7/16$ oz.; 2.5 in; Shot size 4
**MSRP** . . . . . . . . . . . **$11.00–$14.99**

## PRAIRE STORM SHOTSHELLS (FS)

*Features*: Since its debut last year,

upland hunters have praised Prairie Storm lead loads. For 2011, Federal Premium extends the capabilities for this successful ammunition and brings hunters steel options designed specifically for upland birds. These new high velocity loads give upland hunters ideal patterns using patented and rear-braking Flitecontrol wad and lethal flit-estopper (FS) steel
*Available in*: 12 , 20 Ga.; 1⅛ or ⅞ oz.; Shot sizes 3, 4
**MSRP** . . . . . . . . . . . **$15.99–$19.00**

## GAME-SHOK UPLAND GAME LOAD

*Available in*: 12, 16, 20 Ga.; 2.75 in.; Shot sizes 6, 8, 7.5
**Box 25**: . . . . . . . . . . . **$7.46–$10.23**

## GAME-SHOK UPLAND HEAVY FIELD

*Available in*: 12, 16, 20 Ga.; 2.75 in.; Shot sizes 6, 8, 7.5
**Box 25**: . . . . . . . . . . . **$9.36–$11.49**

## GAME-SHOK UPLAND HI-BRASS

*Available in*: 12, 16, 20, .410 Ga.; 2.5 in., 2.75 in., 3 in.; Shot sizes 4, 5, 6, 7.5, 8
**Box 25**: . . . . . . . . . . . **$10.67–$15.55**

## PREMIUM BLACK CLOUD STEEL

*Available in*: 12 Ga.; 3, 3.5 in.; shot sizes 2, BB, BBB
**Box 25**: . . . . . . . . . . . **$14.00–$25.00**

## PREMIUM GOLD MEDAL TARGET- EXTRA-LITE PAPER (LR)

*Available in*: 12 Ga.; 2.75 in.; Shot sizes 7.5, 8
**Box 25**: . . . . . . . . . . . **$36.50–$38.99**

## PREMIUM GOLD MEDAL TARGET- EXTRA-LITE PLASTIC (LR)

*Available in*: 12 Ga.; 2.75 in.; Shot sizes 7.5, 8
**Box 25**: . . . . . . . . . . . **$11.45–$12.99**

## PREMIUM GOLD MEDAL TARGET- HANDICAP PAPER HV

# Federal Ammunition

*Available in*: 12 Ga.; 2.75 in.; Shot sizes 7.5, 8

**Box 25:** . . . . . . . . . . . **$11.30–$12.99**

## PREMIUM GOLD MEDAL TARGET- HANDICAP PLASTIC HV

*Available in*: 12 Ga.; 2.75 in.; Shot sizes 7.5, 8

**Box 25:** . . . . . . . . . . . . . . . . **$18.50**

## PREMIUM GOLD MEDAL TARGET- INTERNATIONAL PAPER

*Available in*: 12 Ga.; 2.75 in.; Shot sizes 7.5

**Box 25:** . . . . . . . . . . . **$10.50–$13.00**

## PREMIUM GOLD MEDAL TARGET- INTERNATIONAL PLASTIC

*Available in*: 12 Ga.; 2.75 in.; Shot sizes 7.5, 8

**Box 25:** . . . . . . . . . . . **$11.00–$12.99**

## PREMIUM GOLD MEDAL TARGET- PAPER

*Available in*: 12 Ga.; 2.75 in.; Shot sizes 7.5, 8, 9

**Box 25:** . . . . . . . . . . . . **$9.00–$13.00**

## PREMIUM GOLD MEDAL TARGET- PLASTIC

*Available in*: 12, 20, 28, 410 Ga.; 2.5 in., 2.75 in.; Shot sizes 7.5, 8, 8.5, 9

**Box 25:** . . . . . . . . . . . . **$8.00–$10.50**

## PREMIUM GOLD MEDAL TARGET- SPORTING CLAYS

*Available in*: 12 Ga.; 2.75 in.; Shot sizes 7.5, 8, 8.5

**Box 25:** . . . . . . . . . . . . **$8.00–$10.50**

## PREMIUM MAG-SHOK- HEAVYWEIGHT TURKEY

*Available in*: 12 Ga.; 3, 3.5 in.; Shot sizes 5, 6, 7

**Box 5:** . . . . . . . . . . . . **$16.99–$39.00**

## PREMIUM MAG-SHOK- HIGH VELOCITY LEAD

*Available in*: 10, 20 Ga.; 3, 3.5 in.; Shot sizes 4, 5, 6

**Box 10:** . . . . . . . . . . . **$16.00–$24.86**

## PREMIUM MAG-SHOK LEAD WITH FLITECONTROL

*Available in*: 12 Ga.; 3, 3.5 in.; Shot sizes 4, 5, 6

**Box 10:** . . . . . . . . . . **$ 12.00–$18.99**

## PREMIUM MAG-SHOK HEAVY HIGH VELOCITY STEEL

*Available in*: 12 Ga.; 2.75, 3, 3.5 in.; Shot sizes 4, 5, 6

**Box 10:** . . . . . . . . . . . **$16.00–$25.17**

## PREMIUM ULTRA-SHOK HEAVY HIGH VELOCITY STEEL

*Available in*: 10, 12 Ga.; 2.75, 3, 3.5 in.; Shot sizes 1, 2, 3, 4, BB, BBB, T

**Box 25:** . . . . . . . . . . . **$18.71–$25.99**

## PREMIUM ULTRA-SHOK HEAVYWEIGHT

*Available in*: 12 Ga.; 3, 3.5 in.; Shot sizes 2, 4, BB

**Box 10:** . . . . . . . . . . . **$22.99–$38.99**

## PREMIUM ULTRA-SHOK HIGH DENSITY WATERFOWL

*Available in*: 10, 12, 20 ga.; 3, 3.5 in.; Shot sizes 2, 4, BB

**Box 10:** . . . . . . . . . . . **$21.00–$33.00**

## PREMIUM ULTRA-SHOK HIGH VELOCITY STEEL

*Available in*: 12, 16, 20 Ga.; 2.75, 3, 3.5 in.; Shot sizes 1, 2, 3, 4, 6, BB, BBB, T

**Box 25:** . . . . . . . . . . . **$12.00–$25.17**

## PREMIUM ULTRA-SHOK SUBSONIC HIGH DENSITY

*Available in*: 12 Ga.; 2.75 in.; Shot sizes BB

**Box 25:** . . . . . . . . . . . **$16.99–$21.00**

## PREMIUM WING-SHOK FLYER LOADS

*Available in*: 12 Ga.; 2.75 in.; Shot sizes 7.5

**Box 25:** . . . . . . . . . . . **$17.00–$23.95**

## PREMIUM WING-SHOK HIGH BRASS

*Available in*: 28 Ga.; 2.75 in.; Shot sizes 6, 7.5, 8

**Box 25:** . . . . . . . . . . . **$18.00–$21.00**

## PREMIUM WING-SHOK HIGH VELOCITY

*Available in*: 12 Ga.; 2.75 in.; 2.75, 3 in.; Shot sizes: 4, 5, 6, 7.5

**Box 25:** . . . . . . . . . . . **$14.00–$19.00**

## PREMIUM WING-SHOK HIGH VELOCITY- PHEASANT

*Available in*: 12, 20 Ga.; 2.75 in.; Shot sizes 4, 5, 6, 7.5

**Box 25:** . . . . . . . . . . . **$13.00–$19.46**

## PREMIUM WING-SHOK HIGH VELOCITY- QUAIL FOREVER

*Available in*: 12, 20 Ga.; 2.75 in.; Shot sizes 7.5, 8

**Box 25:** . . . . . . . . . . . **$15.00–$19.46**

## PREMIUM WING-SHOK MAGNUM

*Available in*: 10, 12, 16, 20 Ga.: 2.75, 3, 3.5 in.; Shot sizes 2, 4, 5, 6, BB

**Box 25:** . . . . . . . . . . . **$17.99–$32.00**

## SPEED-SHOK STEEL

*Available in*: 12, 20 Ga.; 2.75, 3, 3.5 in.; Shot sizes 2, 3, 4, 6, 7, BB

**Box 25:** . . . . . . . . . . . **$6.00–$12.00**

## STRUT-SHOK

*Available in*: 12 Ga.; 3, 3.5 in.; Shot sizes 2, 3, 4, 6, 7, BB

**Box 10:** . . . . . . . . . . . **$8.00–$14.00**

## TOP GUN SUBSONIC

*Available in*: 12 Ga.; 2.75 in.; Shot sizes 7.5

**Box 25:** . . . . . . . . . . . **$6.00–$7.99**

## TOP GUN TARGET

*Available in*: 12, 20 Ga.; 2.75 in.; Shot sizes 7, 7.5, 8, 9

**Box 25:** . . . . . . . . . . . **$5.00–$7.00**

## TOP GUN TARGET STEEL

*Available in*: 20 Ga.; 2.75 in.; Shot sizes 7

**Box 25:** . . . . . . . . . . . . . . . **$7.00**

**Shotgun Ammunition Slugs**

## FUSION SABOT SLUGS

*Features*: Electro-chemical process applies a copper jacket to the lead core one molecule at a time. Yields a pefectly uniform jacket.
*Available in*: 20 Ga.; 3 in., ⅝oz. Loads; 2.75 in. And 3 in., 12 Ga. Loads

**Box 12:** . . . . . . . . . . . . **$7.00–$11.99**

## POWER-SHOK RIFLED SLUG

*Features*: Hollow point slug type
*Available in*: 10,12,16,20,410 Ga.;

2.5, 2.75, 3, 3.5 in.
**Box 5:** . . . . . . . . . . . . . .**$4.00–$7.00**

## POWER-SHOK SABOT SLUG

*Features*: Sabot hollow point slug type
*Available in*: 12 Ga.; 2.75 in.; 1 oz. Slug wt.
**Box 5:** . . . . . . . . . . . . . .**$4.28–$8.99**

## PREMIUM VITAL-SHOK BARNES EXPANDER

*Features*: Barnes Sabot slug type
*Available in*: 12, 20 Ga.; 2.75, 3 in.; ⅝, ¾, 1oz. Slug wt.
**Box 20:** . . . . . . . . . . .**$37.99–$68.99**

## PREMIUM VITAL-SHOK TRUBALL RIFLED SLUG

*Features*: Truball rifled slug type
*Available in*: 12, 20 Ga.; 2.75 in.; .75, 1 oz. slug wt.
**Box 5:** . . . . . . . . . . . . . .**$3.91–$5.52**

## VITAL-SHOK TROPHY BONDED TIP

*Features*: Built on the Trophy Bonded Bear Claw platform to provide deep

penetration and high weight retention. Sleek profile, with tapered heel and translucent polymer tip. Nickel-plated. Available as component and in Federal loaded ammunition.
*Available in*: .270 Win., .270 Win. Short Mag., .270 Weatherby Mag., 7mm-08 Rem., .280 Rem., 7mm Rem. Mag., 7mm Win. Short Mag., 7mm Weatherby Mag., 7mm STW, .308 Win., .30-06 Spfld., .300 H&H Mag., .300 Win. Short Mag., .300 Weatherby Mag., .300 Rem. Ultra Mag., .338 Federal
**Box 20:** . . . . . . . . . . . .**$32.00–$46.00**

## NYCLAD BULLETS

*Features*: These 3-inch Premium Personal Defense handgun .410 loads offer a unique wad system for the rifled barrel and pattern great. Hollow point tip.

*Available in*: .38 Special- 125 Grains
**Box 20:** . . . . . . . . . . . .**$14.49–$20.00**

## V-SHOK HEAVYWEIGHT COYOTE

*Features*: Hardcore varmint hunters will be amazed at the patterns they get with this 3 inch 1.5 oz. load. Federal's exclusive Flitecontrol wad is at work again with this new offering. The engineers have taken the same delivery system in Vital-Shok buckshot, Black Cloud and Mag-Shok turkey loads and created a devastating predator load.
*Available in*: 12 Ga.; Shot size BB; 1.5 oz.
**Box 5:** . . . . . . . . . . . . .**$19.91–$27.59**

## BLACK CLOUD FS WATERFOWL

*Features*: Flightcontrol wad provides controlled release of Flitestopper (FS)

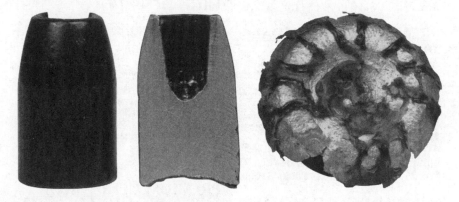

**FEDERAL NYCLAD BULLETS**

**FEDERAL V-SHOK HEAVYWEIGHT COYOTE**

# Federal Ammunition

steel pellets. Increases downrange pellet energy. FS Steel Shot design cuts on impact. Payload of Premium Steel (60%) and FS Steel (40%) gives excellent patterns. Adds 10-15 yards distance to typical waterfowl shots.
*Available in*: 10, 12, 20 Ga.
**Box 25:** . . . . . . . . . . . . **$16.99–$29.99**

## .327 MAGNUM

*Features*: Federal Premium has partnered with Ruger to introduce a new personal defense revolver cartridge designed to deliver .357 Magnum ballistics from .32-caliber diameter platform. The .327 Federal Magnum is designed for use in lightweight, small-frame revolvers like the Ruger SP101. The ammunition is available in Federal Premium 85-gr Hydra-Shok JHP, American Eagle 100-gr SP and Speer 115-gr Gold Dot HP.
*Available in*: .327 Fed. Mag.
**Box 20:** . . . . . . . . . . . . **$16.00–$21.00**

## TNT GREEN

*Features*: TNT Green brings non-tox technology to the Federal Premium

**FEDERAL BLACK CLOUD FS WATERFOWL**

**.327 FEDERAL MAGNUM**

# Federal Ammunition

V-Shok varmint hunting line. This is a totally lead-free bullet that couples explosive expansion with match-grade accuracy.
*Available in*: .22 Hornet, .204 Ruger, .222 Rem., .22-250 Rem.
**Box 20:. . . . . . . . . . . $19.00–$27.00**

## VITAL-SHOK TROPHY BONDED TIP

*Features*: You spend all year dreaming of the moment of truth—why trust it to anything less than the best. Vital-Shok is available with the world's finest big game bullets, from the unrivaled Trophy Bonded family to Nosler, Sierra, and Barnes. Match that with world-class brass, select powders and legendary primers and you get ammunition you can truly believe in.
*Available in*: .270 Win., .270 Win. Short Mag., .270 Weatherby Mag., 7mm-08 Rem., .280 Rem., 7mm Rem. Mag., 7mm Win. Short Mag.
**Box 20:. . . . . . . . . . . $46.89–$57.62**

**FEDERAL TNT GREEN**

# Federal Fusion Ammunition

## 200-GRAIN .338 FEDERAL

*Features*: Fusion has added a 200-grain, .338 Federal Offering to its deer-focused rifle ammo lineup. This round (currently chambered by six major rifle manufacturers) will have a 200-grain (2660 fps.) load. The round is built on the .308 case and features a .338 diameter projectile.
*Available in*: .338 Fed. - 200 Grain
**Box 20:. . . . . . . . . . . $22.72–$27.26**

## FUSION RIFLE AMMO

*Features*: This specialized deer bullet electrochemically joins pure copper to an extreme pressure-formed core to ensure optimum performance. The result is high terminal energy on impact that radiates lethal shock throughout the target. This energy is optimized through mass weight retention, a top secretive tip-skiving process and superior bullet integrity. Try Fusion Lite for less recoil with full lethality to 200-yards.
*Available in*: .223 Rem., .22-250 Rem., .243 Win., .25-06 Rem., .243 Win., 6.5x55 Swedish, .260 Rem., .270

**200-GRAIN .338 FEDERAL**

Win., .270 Win. Short Mag., 7mm-08 Rem., .280 Rem., 7mm Rem. Mag., 7mm Win. Short Mag., 7.62x39mm Soviet, .30-30 Win., .308 Win., .30-06 Spring., 300 Win. Mag., .300 Win. Short Mag., .338 Federal, .338 Win. Mag., .35 Federal, .338 Win. Mag. .35 Whelen, .375 H&H Mag., 416 Rigby, .416 Rem. Mag., .45-70 Govt. .458 Win. Mag., .458 Lott
**Box 20:. . . . . . . . . $19.99–$46.99**

**FEDERAL FUSION RIFLE AMMO**

# Fiocchi Ammunition

## Handgun Ammunition

### 7.63 MAUSER PISTOL CARTRIDGE

*Features*: The 7.63 Mauser cartridge was first introduced by Waffenfabrik Mauser, Orbendorf, Germany in 1869 in the famous C-96 "Broomhandle" Mauser Pistol. The C-96 was the first semi-automatic pistol to see wide spread military use. Fiocchi Ammunition now offers classic pistol ammunition to owners of historic handguns. The 88-grain Full Metal Jacket has a muzzle velocity of 1, 425 fps and 400 ft-lbs energy at the muzzle, impressive for a 110-year-old cartridge.The ammunition is available for classic American and European cartridges
*Available in*: 7.63 Mauser
**Box 50:** . . . . . . . . . . . **$32.49–$36.99**

### CENTERFIRE HANDGUN LINE

*Features*: New Expanding Mono-block bullet load in 9x19 pistol ammo. XTP loads in 9mm, .38 Special, .357 SIG, .44 Special (Cowboy Action), .44 Magnum and .45 ACP.
**MSRP:** . . . . . . . . **Prices on request**

## Rifle Ammunition

### EXTREMA .223 REM. HVA

*Features*: Fiocchi now offers the extremely popular .223 Remington cartridge loaded with super accurate and deadly Hornady V-Max 50-grain bullets in Fiocchi's Extrema rifle ammunition line. Extrema 223 Remington HVA has unmatched terminal ballistics that will make the cartridge a favorite of both the Western prairie dog and Eastern ground hog hunter.
*Available in*: .223 Rem- 50 grain
**Box 20:** . . . . . . . . . . . . . . . .**$11.00**

### CENTERFIRE RIFLE LINE

*Features*: This ammunition is constructed by using top quality components that are manufactured by RWS, including non-corrosive, boxer-primed, reloadable brass cases.
*Available in*: 4.6x30 H&K, .222 Rem., .204 Ruger, Canned .223 Rem., .223 Rem., .22-250 Rem., .243 Win., 6.5

FIOCCHI TUNDRA COMPOSITION SHOT

Swedish, .270 Win., .30-30 Win., .300 Win. Mag., .308 Win., Canned .308 Win., .30-06 Spring., 7.62x39 Soviet
**Box 50:** . . . . . . . . . . . . .**$9.00–$12.25**

## Shotgun Ammunition

### LIGHT WHITE RHINO

*Features*: Competition shells made especially for target shooters.
*Available in*: 12 Ga.; 1- 1⅛ oz.;  shot size 2.75 in.
**Box 25:** . . . . . . . . . . . .**$8.25–$13.99**

### TUNDRA COMPOSITION SHOT

*Features*: It's heavier than bismuth for dead-on-delivery performance. Spherical nonbrittle Tundra compound deforms on impact, just like lead. Use with any choke, even full.
*Available in*: 12, 20 Ga.; 2.75 in., 3 in.; Shot size 2, 4, BB
**Box 10:** . . . . . . . . . . .**$22.99–$28.99**

### PREMIUM NICKEL PLATED HUNTING LOADS

*Features*: Fiocchi offers the hunter a wide selection of hunting loads that incorporate nickel plated shot to help make hunting more successful. Nickel plated shot gives the hunter such benefits as denser, more consistent patterns with fewer spray pellets and increased range and penetration than non-plated shot.
*Available in*: 1.25 oz. Helice loads (12 Ga., 2.75 in., shot sizes 7, 7.5, 8); 1.5, 1.75, 2.4 oz. Turkey Loads (12 Ga., 2.75, 3 and 3.5 in., shot sizes 4, 5, 6); 7/8 to 1.75 oz. Golden Pheasant Loads (12, 20, 16, 28 Ga., 2.75 and 3 in., shot sizes 4, 5, 6, 7.5, 8); and Buckshot Loads (12 Ga., 2.75 in., shot sizes 00 Buck, 4 Buck)
**Box 25:** . . . . . . . . . . . . . .**$6–$14.11**

# Fiocchi Ammunition

## PREMIUM TARGET LOADS

**Features**: Specifically for compeititive shooters. Our Target Load Line is the offspring of a 50 year tradition of supporting the world of trap, skeet and now sporting clays, FITASC and Compaq.
**Available in**: 1 and 1⅛ oz. Paper Target Loads (12 Ga., 2.75 in., shot sizes 7.5, 8, 8.5); 1⅛ oz. and 1 oz. Premium Target Loads (12, 20, 28, 410 Ga., 2.5 and 2.75 in., shot sizes 7.5, 8, 8.5, 9); 1 and 1⅛ oz. Multi-sport Loads (12 Ga., 2.75 in., shot sizes 7.5, 8, 9); 1 ¼ oz. Helice Loads (12 Ga., 2.75 in., shot sizes 7, 7.5, 8); 1⅛ oz. Power Spreaders (12 Ga., 2.75 in., shot sizes 8, 8.5); 1oz. Interceptor Spreaders (12 Ga., 2.75 in., Shot sizes 8, 8.5); ⅞ and 1 oz. Steel Target Loads (12, 20 ga., 2.75 in., shot sizes 7); and ¾ and ⅛ oz. Ultra Low Recoil Training Loads (12, 20 Ga., 2.75 in., Shot sizes 7.5, 8)
**MSRP**: . . . . . . . . . . . . . . . . . .$8.43

## STEEL HUNTING LOADS

**Features**: Fiocchi steel shot hunting loads are manufactured with a combination of treated steel shot, protective wads and the appropriate powders to deliver a consistent dense pattern that is easy on your gun barrel but hard on your target.

**Available in**: 1⅛ to 1⅝ oz., 2 ¾ to 3 ½ in. 12 Ga. loads in shot sizes 1, 2, 3, 4, BB, BBB, T; ⅞ oz. , 3 in. 20 Ga. Loads in shot sizes 2, 3, 4
**MSRP** . . . . . . . . . . . . $13.10–$17.99

## UPLAND GAME AND FIELD LOADS

**Features**: Fiocchi offers a full line of hunting loads from Dove Loads to powerful Hi Brass Loads.
**Available in**: ¾ to 1²/₄ oz. High Velocity Loads (12, 20, 16, 28, 410 Ga., 2 ¾ and 3 in., Shot sizes 4, 5, 6, 7.5, 8, 9); 1 to 1.25 oz. Field Loads (12, 20, 16 Ga., 2.75 in., shot sizes 4, 5, 6, 7.5, 8, 9); ½ to 1⅛ oz. Dove Loads (12, 20, 16, 28, 410 Ga., 2 to 3.25 in., shot sizes 6, 7.5, 8, 9); and ¼ to 1¹/₁₆ oz. Specialty Shotshell Loads (Flobert 9 Rimfire, 24, 32 Ga., 1.75 and 2.5 in., shot sizes 6, 7.5, 8, 9)
**Box 25**: . . . . . . . . . . . $13.99–$16.95

## WHITE RHINO SHOTSHELLS

**Features**: Fiocchi's White Rhino uses B&P (Baschieri & Pellagri) wads and 5-percent antimony lead shot. Its additional 50 feet per second velocity over standard trap loads make it a favorite for "Handicap trap" for those long distance shots on the sporting clays

course. The B&P shot cup, with its softer plastic and better sealing ability, means there's less gas escaping around the wad ensuring higher velocity.
**Available in**: 12 Ga., 2.75 in., 1 ⅛ oz.
**Box 25**: . . . . . . . . . . . . . . . . . .$8.67

## GOLDEN PHEASANT SHOT SHELLS

**Features**: Golden Pheasants shot shells utilize a special hard, nickel-plated lead shot, based on Fiocchi's strict ballistic tolerances that ensure proven shot consistency—resulting in deeper penetration, longer ranges and much tighter patterns.
**Available in**: 12, 16, 20, 28 Ga.
**MSRP** . . . . . . . . . . . . . $15.46–$19.48

## GOLDEN WATERFOWL SHOT SHELLS

**Features**: Fiocchi Steel shot hunting loads are manufactured with a combination of treated steel shot, protective wads and the appropriate powders to deliver a consistent dense pattern that is easy on your gun barrel but hard on your target.
**Available in**: 12 Ga., 3 in., 1 ¼ oz.; Shot sizes BBB, BB, 1, 2, 3, 4
**MSRP** . . . . . . . . . . . . . $16.87–$19.93

# Hodgdon (and IMR and Winchester) Powders

## EXTREME RIFLE POWDER-H4895

**Features**: This is a most versatile rifle powder. This member of the Extreme Extruded line powder is great for 17 Remington, 250-3000 Savage, 308 Winchester and 458 Winchester, to name just a few. It is amazingly accurate in every cartridge where it is listed in our data. It had its origin in the 30-06 as a military powder and was the first powder Bruce Hodgdon sold

to the loading public. Available in 1 lb. & 8 lb. containers.
**1 LB**: . . . . . . . . . . . . . $21.71–$29.97

## IMR SMOKELESS RIFLE POWEDERS- 8208 XBR

**Features**: The latest in the versatile IMR line of fine propellants, this accurate metering, super short grained extruded rifle powder was designed expressly for match, varmint, and AR sniper cartridges. Ideally suited for

cartridges like the 223 Remington/5.56mm, 308 Winchester/7.62mm NATO and the 6mm PPC, shooters will find IMR 8208 XBR totally insensitive to changes in temperature, while yielding max velocities and "tack driving" accuracy. Clearly, the competitor's "choice" and the Varmint Hunter's "dream powder".
**1 LB**: . . . . . . . . . . . . . $29.97–$40.99

# Hornady Ammunition

**HORNADY .357 MAG**

### .300 RCM AND .338 RCM

**Features**: Most magnum cartridges require 24- to 26-inch-long barrels to achive advertised performance. Hornady Ruger Compact Magnum cartridges achieve true magnum levels of velocity, accuracy and terminal peformance in short action guns featuring a compact 20-inch barrel. Based on the beltless .375 Ruger case, the .300 and .338 RCMs feature cartridge geometry that provides for an extremely efficient cartridge case.

**Box 20:**. . . . . . . . . . . . . . . . .**$43.91**

### .32 WIN. SPECIAL

**Features**: Hornady's .32 Winchester Special LEVERevolution cartridge features a 165 grain Flex Tip eXpandtin (FXT) bullet that delivers a muzzle velocity of 2,410 fps. This velocity combined with an impressive ballistic coefficient allows the .32 Winchester Special LEVERevolution to be effective out to 300 yards.

**Box 20:**. . . . . . . . . . . . . . . . .**$30.39**

### .357 MAG/ .44 MAG

**Features**: The .357 and .44 Magnum LEVERevolution catridges feature 140 and 225 grain FTX bullets, launching at 850 to 1,900 fps respectively. Now hunters who use both handguns and lever guns no longer have to use two different cartridges to get results.

**Box 20:**. . . . . . . . . . . . . . . . .**$27.79**

### 450 NITRO EXPRESS 3.25 INCH

**Features**: Hornady's .450 Nitro Express 3.25 in. amunniton features a 480 grain bullet with a muzzle velocity of 2,150 fps. Hornady's .450 NE offers two bullet styles—the Dangerous Game Solid (DGS), a non-expanding solid for deep penetration and the 480 grain Dangerous Game eXpanding (DGX) that expands to allow more energy to be transferred upon impact.

**Box 20:**. . . . . . . . . . . . . . . . .**$129.81**

### 6.5 CREEDMOOR

**Features**: Originally developed from the ground up to give competitive shooters a factory-loaded cartridge that would allow them to compete and win. in the highest levels of competitive shooting. With pedigree firmly rooted in precision shooting, the 6.5 Creedmoor is making its way into the world of hunting. Chambered by both Ruger and DPMS in hunting rifles, the 6.5 Creedmoor is making its debut as a hunting round in our new Superformance™ line of ammunition. Loaded with both the new 120 grain GMX® and the venerable 129 grain SST®, the 6.5 Creedmoor brings a world of precision-based performance to the hunting arena, and its light recoil make it a dream to shoot for extended periods. It's perfect for any North American game up to and including Elk.

**Box 20:**. . . . . . . . . . . .**$34.77–$38.28**

### 50 CAL SABOT LOW DRAG WITH 45 CAL 250 SST BULLET

**Features**: Hornady's Low Drag Sabot with 150 grain reduces loading effort while preserving terminal performance. The SST-ML High Speed Low Drag Sabot fully engages the rifling to deliver pinpoint accuracy at 200 yards and beyond.

**Box 20:**. . . . . . . . . . . . . . . . .**$16.99**

### 500 SMITH & WESSON XTP MAG

**Features**: The XTP Mag., with 350 grain, delievers dead-on accuracy and reliable expansion for deep, terminal penetration at a wide range of velocities. Heavier jacket stands up to the high pressure and velocities of the highest performance handgun cartridges.

**Box 20:** . . . . . . . . . . . . . . . . .**$48.91**

## 6.8MM SPC BTHP & V-MAX

**Features**: Developed at the request of the U.S. Special Forces. Perfect sporting cartridge for game up to the size of whitetail and mule deer. Same power class as the .300 Savage, but delivers a flatter trajectory and less recoil. Features either a 110 gr. BTHP bullet, specifically designed for the cartridge, or a proven 110 gr. V-Max bullet. 110 gr. BTHP delivers excellent expansion and maximum energy transfer at all velocities, while the 110 gr. VMAX has all the characteristics of our Varmint Express ammo—flat trajectories and rapid, violent expansion.

**MSRP** . . . . . . . . . . . . . . . . . .**$28.75**

## 9.3 X 74R

**Features**: Hornady InterLock and FMJ (Full Metal Jacket) bullets have reached legendary status among safari hunters, and we've raised the bar again with the introduction of the best large game bullets we've ever seen—the DGS (Dangerous Game Solid) and the DGX (Dangerous Game eXpanding). Both bullets are made with a hard lead/antimony alloy cone, surrounded by a copper clad steel jacket. These bullets feature a flat meplat for straighter penetration and create more energy transfer than a simple round profile bullet. Hornady Dangerous Game Series ammunition is designed specifically for large game and safari hunting. These cartridges feature both classic bullets, like the 270 gr InterLock Spire Point-Recoil Proof, as well as our new flagship DGS and DGX bullets. All ammunition is designed to work well in all rifles, and meticulous attention was devoted to ensure that ammunition like the 450/400 Nitro Express 3", and 450 Nitro Express 3-¼" regulate properly in both classic doubles and their younger counterparts.

**MSRP** . . . . . . . . . . . . . . . . . .**$91.33**

## 17 HMR HP XTP

**Features**: This new XTP bullet was purposed and designed as a hunting load for less pelt damage. The polymer tip of the V-Maz bullet delievers more than tack-driving accuracy at long range—it also creates dramatic expasion on impact. Has a 20 grain XTP bullet.

**MSRP** . . . . . . . . . . . . . . . . . .**$17.24**

## 17 HORNADY MACH 2

**Features**: Provides target-erasing accuracy and a frozen clothesline trajectory—nearly seven inches flatter at 150 yards than a standard High Velocity 22 Long Rifle cartridge. Delivers 2,100 fps, far outperforming a standard High Velocity 22 Long Rifle's 1,255 fps velocity at the muzzle.

**Box 50:** . . . . . . . . . . . .**$9.91–$11.65**

## .30 TC

**Features**: Designed for Thompson Center's Icon bolt-action rifle. Hornady perfected the balance between case volume, bore volume and burn rates for both the 150- and 165-grain offerings. Slightly smaller in capacity than the 308 Winchester, but delivers ballistic performance exceeding the 30-06. With a muzzle velocity of 3000 fps, the 150-grain load out performs the 308 Win. by 180 fps and outperforms the 30-06 by nearly 100 fps. Provides a 15% reduction in perceived recoil, ultra-smooth feeding, full magazine capacity, a short bolt throw, longer barrel life and delivers full ballisitic potential in a short action case.

**Box 20:** . . . . . . . . . . . . . . . . .**$34.77**

## 204 RUGER, 45-GR. SP

**Features**: Designed to provide controlled expansion for deeper penetration on larger varmints. Built around Hornady's proven Spire Point design, the 204 45 grain SP cartridge provides flat trajectories, enhanced penetration and a new dimension to the 204 Ruger's personality.

**Box 20:** . . . . . . . . . . . . . . . . .**$25.01**

## .375 RUGER

**Features**: Delivers performance that exceeds the .375 H&H. Designed to provide greater knockdown power with a shorter catridge from a standard action and a 20 in. Barrel. Improves on the velocity of the .375 H&H by 150 fps. Three different loads, including a 270-grain Spire Point Recoil-Proof, 300-grain Round Nose and a 300-grain FMJ-RN. Longer ogive and less exposed lead which helps protect the bullet from deformation under recoil in rifle magazines.

**MSRP** . . . . . . . . . . . . . . . . . .**$73.52**

## 405 WINCHESTER 300-GR. INTERLOCK SP

**Features**: Millions of successful hunts have proven the accuracy and deadly knockdown power of the famous Hornady InterLock, SST and InterBond bullets we load into every Hornady Custom rifle cartridge. Each cartridge is loaded to ensure optimal pressure, velocity and consistency, from lot to lot. Much of the brass is made by Hornady, the rest carefully selected for

**HORNADY 500 SMITH & WESSON BULLET CUTAWAY**

# Hornady Ammunition

reliable feeding, corrosion resistance, hardness and the ability to withstand maximum chamber pressure.
**Box 50:** . . . . . . . . . . . . . . . . .**$56.27**

## 40 BUSHMASTER 250 GR FTX LEVEREVOLUTION

**Features**: Nicknamed "The Thumper," the 450 Bushmaster is the most radical cartridge ever chambered in production AR-15 type firearms. Hornady brings big bore performance to the most popular semi-automatic rifle in America — opening a whole new world of hunting to the battle-proven platform. The 450 Bushmaster fires Hornady's 0.452" 250 gr. SST-ML featuring Hornady's Flex Tip™ technology. The overall cartridge matches the 223 Remington at 2.250", but uses a specially designed magazine. The SST's sleek profile makes for surprisingly flat trajectories and tremendous downrange energy.
**Box 50:** . . . . . . . . . . . . . . . . .**$39.35**

## 450/400 NITRO EXPRESS 3IN. 400 GR. DGS

**Features**: Hornady InterLock and FMJ (Full Metal Jacket) bullets have reached legendary status among safari hunters, and we've raised the bar again with the introduction of the best large game bullets we've ever seen - the DGS (Dangerous Game Solid) and the DGX (Dangerous Game eXpanding). Both bullets are made with a hard lead/antimony alloy cone, surrounded by a copper clad steel jacket. These bullets feature a flat meplat for straighter penetration and create more energy transfer than a simple round profile bullet. Hornady Dangerous Game Series ammunition is designed specifically for large game and safari hunting. These cartridges feature both classic bullets, like the 270 gr InterLock Spire Point-Recoil Proof, as well as our new

flagship DGS and DGX bullets. All ammunition is designed to work well in all rifles, and meticulous attention was devoted to ensure that ammunition like the 450/400 Nitro Express 3", and 450 Nitro Express 3-¼" regulate properly in both classic doubles and their younger counterparts.
**Box 20:** . . . . . . . . . . . . . . . . .**$117.93**

## LEVEREVOULTION AMMUNITION

**Features**: Hornady brings you an innovation in ammunition performance featuring state of the industry patented, FTX (Flex Tip eXpanding) and MonoFlex bullets that are safe in your tubular magazine. Its higher ballistic coefficient delivers dramatically flatter trajectories for fantastic downrange energy increases and amazing bullet expansion at all ranges. Up to 250 feet per second faster muzzle velocity than conventional lever gun loads. Up to 40% more energy than traditional flat point loads. The innovative LEVERevolution bullet design may require a newer magazine follower to provide best possible functioning of the last round out of the magazine. These magazine followers may be purchased from the manufacturer of your firearm. For optimum performance we do not recommend storing LEVERevolution ammunition in tubular magazines for extended periods, as this can result in tip deformation.

**Available in**: 30-30 Win., 308 Marlin Express, 32 Win. Special, 338 Marlin Express, 35 Rem., 357 Mag., 357 Mag., 44 Mag., 444 Marlin, 45-70 Gov't., 450 Marlin
**Box 20:** . . . . . . . . . . . .**$25.41–$45.97**

## SST SHOTGUN SLUG

**Features**: The sharp point increases the ballistic coefficient of the FTX, allowing it to fly faster, farther and on a flatter trajectory. On impact, the Flex Tip initiates expansion at all velocities. The SST Shotgun Slug delivers true 200 yard accuracy and you'll achieve sub-2" groups at 100 yards. No other slug gun ammo can come close to the performance of the SST. The 12 GA 300 gr FTX delivers a crushing 1793 ft/lbs of energy at 100 yards and the smaller, 20 GA 250 gr FTX delivers an impressive 1200 ft/lbs of energy at the same distance.
**Available in**: 12, 20 Ga.
**Box 5:** . . . . . . . . . . . . . . . . . .**$15.87**

**HORNADY LEVEREVOULTION BULLETS LOADED WITH MONOFLEX**

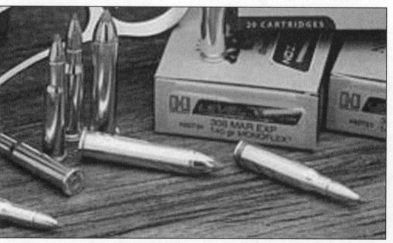

# Jarrett Rifles Ammunition

### TROPHY AMMUNITION
**Features**: Jarrett's high-performance cartridges are in 10-round boxes. The cases are from Norma with Jarrett's headstamp
**Available in**: 243 Win. 85gr. Sierra HPBT, 243 Win. 85gr. Nosler Partition, 270 Win. 140gr. Nosler Accubond,

270 Win. 150gr. Swift A Frame, 7mm Rem. Mag. 140gr. Nosler Ballistic Tip, 7mm Rem. Mag. 160gr. Nosler Accubond, 7mm Rem. Mag. 175gr. Swift A Frame, 30-06 Sprg. 165gr. Nosler Ballistic Tip, 30-06 Sprg. 180gr. Swift Scirocco, 300 WM 165gr. HPBT, 300 WM 180gr. Nosler Accubond,

300 WM 200gr. Nosler Partition, 300 Jarrett 165gr. Nosler Ballistic Tip, 300 Jarrett 180gr. Nosler Accubond, 300 Jarrett 200gr. Nosler Partition, 375 H&H 300gr. Swift A Frame, 375 H&H 300gr. TCCI Solid, 416 Rem. Mag. 400gr. Swift A Frame, 416 Rem. Mag. 400gr. TCCI Solid
**Box 10:** . . . . . . . . . . . **$26.68–$76.05**

# Kynoch Ammunition

### RIFLE AMMUNITION
**Features**: Today, in addition to manufacturing most of the well-known British proprietary big game cartridges using modern components that duplicate the performance of the original ammunition, Kynamco also provides a varied range of services and products for non-hunting purposes including commercial, industrial, veterinary, and other sporting applications. Extensive hunting ammunition development has covered both the established ranges dating back to the turn of the century and manufacture of new developments such as the new Holland & Holland .700" NE and Rigby .450" Rimless NE cartridges. Much work, in close conjunction with the Proof Houses, has been devoted to duplicating original loads to ensure that, when fired from older guns, and particularly double rifles, new 'KYNOCH' ammunition does not necessitate the re-regulation for both grouping and point of aim. The choice of bullet has also been the subject of exhaustive testing, both for external and terminal ballistic perfor-

mance, and 'KYNOCH' hunting ammunition is now standardised on Woodleigh soft nosed and solid bullets, recognised world-wide as the most reliable big game bullets currently manufactured. Kynamco offers virtually the whole range of classic British Nitro Express from its purpose-built factory which incorporates loading laboratories, workshops, temperature and humidity controlled storage and its own 100 metre, three lane range for proofing and testing the ammunition. This facility also enables customers to test the ammunition in their own guns and to store them when not on safari. Kynamco also manufactures a wide range of special cartridges for commercial/industrial applications together with the manufacture of the famous S. W. Silver range of traditional recoil pads and the sales of a wide variety of shooting memorabilia.
**Available in**: .240 H&H Flanged, .425 Westley Richards, 6.5 Mannlicher Schoenauer, .450 Nitro Express, 9.5 Mannlincher Schoenauer, .450 Nitro for Black, .300 H&H Flanged, .450 No. 2 Nitro Express, .300 H&H Belted

Magnum, .450 Rigby, .303 British, .500/ 450 Nitro Express, .310 Cadet, .577/ 450 Martini Henry, .318 Rimless, .500/ 465 Nitro Express, .333 Jeffery Flanged, .458 Win. Mag., .333 Rimless Nitro Express, .458 Lott, .35 Win., .470 Capstick, .350 Rigby, .470 Nitro Express, .400/ 350 Nitro Express & .350 Rigby No. 2, .475 Nitro Express, .400/ 360 Purdey, .475 No. 2 Nitro Express, .400/ 360 Westley Richards, .476 Westley Richards Nitro Express, .360 No. 2 Nitro Express, .500 Jeffery Nitro Express, .375 2.5 in. Nitro Express, .500 Nitro Express 3 in., .375 H&H Flanged, .500 3 in. Nitro for Black, .375 H&H Belted Mag., .500 3.25 in. Nitro for Black, .400/ 375 Belted Nitro Express, .505 Gibbs, .400 Purdey, .577 3 in. Nitro Express, .450/ 400 Mag. Nitro Express, .577 2.75 in. Soft Nose, .450/400 3.25 in. Nitro for Black, .577 3 in. Nitro for Black, .450/400 Nitro Express, .577 Snider, .404 Jeffery Rimless Nitro Express, .600/ 577 REWA, .405 Win., .600 Nitro Express, .416 Rigby, .700 Nitro Express
**MSRP** . . . . . . . . . . . . . **$32.00–$83.98**

# Lapua Ammunition

### LAPUA NATURALIS
**Features**: Lapua Naturalis and Mega Bullets: the mushrooming of bullet starts immediately on impact. The opening process is started by the valve at the tip of bullet, leading the bullet to expand symmetrically and without shattering. This gives a maximal shock effect to the hunted game. The top premium copper bullet will make its work and retains up to 100% of its weight

after the impact. The factory loaded ammunition is available in most popular calibers used by the Scandinavian type of hunters. The Naturalis bullets are sold for the handloaders worldwide in 7 different diameters.
**Available in**: .243 Win., 6.5x55 SE, .308 Win., .30-06 Spring., .338 Lapua Mag., 9.3x62
**MSRP** . . . . . . . . . . . **$87.99–$118.99**

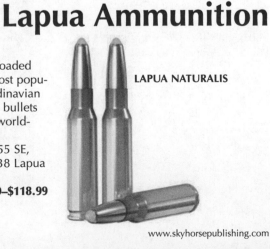
LAPUA NATURALIS

# Lapua Ammunition

## MEGA BULLETS

**Features**: The Lapua Mega is a soft point bullet designed for big game hunting. The bullet features a lead core and copper jacket which are mechanically bonded together. The Mega bullet has also a long jacket that protects core and prevents premature bullet expansion or breakage when bullet goes through light brush or grass cover. Mechanical bonding means that core is firmly locked inside the jacket and will not separate even on hardest impact. The Mega bullet has very high, up to 97% retaining weight after impact on game. It typically more than doubles on impact, causing an immediate shock effect. The Mega bullet family includes 5 bullets which are available in 6.5mm, .30 and 9.3mm calibers. Ammunition is loaded in the most popular big game calibers used in Scandinavia.
**Available in**: 6.5x55 SE, .308 Win., .30-06 Spring., 7.62x53R/ 54R, 9.3x62
**MSRP** . . . . . . . . . . . . . $40.99–$69.99

## .308 PALMA CASE

**Features**: Lapua is proud to introduce the new .308 Win. Palma case. Developed in conjunction with the US Palma team, the small rifle primer case is designed to deliver enhanced long-range accuracy for the most demanding competitive applications.
**Box 100:** . . . . . . . . . . . . . . . . .$82.99

## VIHTAVUORI POWDERS

**Features**: Lapua recommends Finnish-made Vihtavuori powders for reloading. These powders ensure clean burning and repeatable shooting properties in all weathers and conditions. They have uniform and superb quality based on full control of the whole production chain beginning from the production of nitrocellulose to the bottling of the end product. The selection covers more that 20 different types—a right choice for all disciplines, guns and shooting styles.
**Available in**: 26 different powder types ranging from rifles to handguns.
**MSRP** . . . . . . . . . . . . . . . . . . .$34.95

# Magtech Ammunition

## CLEANRANGE

**Features**: CleanRange loads are specifically designed to eliminate airborne lead and the need for lead retrieval at indoor ranges. That means an overall cleaner shooting environment and lower maintenance cost for trap owners, as well as cleaner guns and brass casing for shooters. CleanRange ammunition was developed using a state-of-the-art combination of high-tech, lead-free primers and specially designed Fully Encapsulated Bullets. This unique mix of components eliminates lead and heavy metal exposure at the firing point. No more lead in the air.
**Available in**: .38 SPL, .380 Auto, 9mm Luger, .40 S&W, .45 Auto
**Box 50:** . . . . . . . . . . . . $17.95–$28.48

MAGTECH CLEAN RANGE

## COWBOY ACTION

**Features**: "Old West" Cowboy Action loads were developed specifically for cowboy action shooting enthusiasts. These flat-nose bullets deliver reliable knockdown power that puts steel targets dwon on the first shot. Superior components and construction assure trouble-free performance in both single-action revolvers and lever-action rifles.
**Available in**: .38 SPL, .357 Mag., .44 SPL, .45 Colt, .44- 40 Win.
**Box 50:** . . . . . . . . . . . . $19.00–$35.99

## FIRST DEFENSE

**Features**: Magtech First Defense rounds are designed with a 100% solid copper bullet, unlike traditional hollow points that contain a lead core covered by a copper jacket. Copper jackets could tear away when fired, causing a loss of weight and a corresponding loss of power. However, Magtech First Defense solid copper bullets have no jacket to split or tear away, ensuring every round you fire meets its target with maximum impact and effectiveness. Trust the bullet that delivers deep penetration and devastating expansion. . . the kind that stops a threat in its tracks.

MAGTECH FIRST DEFENSE

**Available in**: 9mm Luger, .38 SPL +P, .380 Auto, .357 Mag., .40 S&W, .45 Auto+P

**Box 20:** . . . . . . . . . . . $16.00–$22.00

## GUARDIAN GOLD

**Features**: Thanks to its tremendous stopping power, deep penetration, awesome mushrooming and dead-on accuracy, Guardian Gold is fast-becoming a favorite among those seeking reliable, affordable personal protection. Simply put, Guardian Gold gives you the advantage against those who may seek to do harm to you or your family. Every round of Guardian Gold undergoes an extensive quality control process before it ever leaves the factory. After passing initial inspection, each case is primed with reliable ignition primers, loaded with the finest clean burning propellants, and assembled with the specified bullet. Only after passing each and every stage is the loaded round approved for final packaging.

**Available in**: 9mm Luger, 9mm Luger+P, 38 SPL+P, .380 Auto+P, .357 Mag., .40 S&W, .45 Auto+P

**Box 20:** . . . . . . . . . . . $14.99–$17.58

## SPORT SHOOTING

**Features**: Magtech pistol and revolver ammunition is ideal for all of your recreational shooting needs. Each cartridge is assembled using only the highest quality components and rigorous quality control is exercised in every stage of the manufacturing process. Originally designed to be the ultimate high performance law enforcement and self-defense handgun bullet, the 100% solid copper hollow-point projectile also meets the crtical requirement of stopping power for handgun hunting applications . The bullet features a six-petal hollow-point

specifically designed to deliver tight groups, superior expansion, and increased penetration over jacketed lead-core bullets. The one piece design of the solid copper bullet delivers virtually 100% weight retention, even though some of the toughest bone and tissue structure of your favorite thin skinned, big game animal.

**Available in**: .223 FMJ 55gr BT, 25 Auto 50 Grain Full Metal Jacket, .308 FMJ 150gr BT, 30 Carbine 110 Grain Full Metal Jacket, 30 Carbine 110 Grain Soft Point, 32 Auto 71 Grain Full Metal Jacket, 32 Auto 71 Grain Jacketed Hollow Point, 32 Auto 71 Grain Lead Round Nose, 32 S&W 85 Grain Lead Round Nose, 32 S&W 98 Grain Lead Round Nose, 32 S&W 98 Grain Lead Wad Cutter, 32 S&W 98 Grain Semi Jacketed Hollow Point, .357 Mag. 158 SJSP Flat, 357 Magnum 125 Grain Full Metal Jacket Flat, 357 Magnum 158 Grain Full Metal Jacket Flat, 357 Magnum 158 Grain Lead Semi Wad Cutter, 357 Magnum 158 Grain Semi Jacketed Hollow Point, 357 Magnum 158 Grain Semi Jacketed Soft Point Flat, 357 Magnum 158 Grain Semi Jacketed Soft Point Flat, .380 Auto 95 FMJ, 380 Auto 95 Grain Full Metal Jacket, 380 Auto 95 Grain Jacketed Hollow Point, 380 Auto 95 Grain Lead Round Nose,38 SPL 125 Grain Full Metal Jacket Flat, 38 SPL 125 Grain Lead Round Nose,38 SPL 125 Grain Semi Jacketed Hollow Point, 38 SPL 125 Grain Semi Jacketed Soft Point Flat, 38 SPL 130 Grain Full Metal Jacket, 38 SPL 148 Grain Lead Wad Cutter, 38 SPL 158 Grain Full Metal Jacket Flat, 38 SPL 158 Grain Lead Round Nose, 38 SPL 158 Grain Lead Semi Wad Cutter, 38 SPL 158 Grain Semi Jacketed Hollow Point, 38 SPL 158 Grain Semi Jacketed Hollow Point, 38 SPL 158 Grain Semi Jacketed Soft Point Flat, 38 SPL 158 Grain Semi Jacketed Soft Point Flat, .38 SPL 158 LRN, 38 Super Auto 130 Grain Full Metal Jacket, 38 S&W 146 Grain Lead Round Nose, 40 S&W 155 Grain Jacketed Hollow Point, 40 S&W 160 Grain Lead Semi Wad Cutter, 40 S&W 165 Grain Full Metal Jacket Flat, .40 S&W 180 FMJ, .40 S&W 180 FMJ, 40 S&W 180 Grain Jacketed Hollow Point, 44 Rem. Mag. 240 Grain Full Metal Jacket Flat, 44 Rem. Mag. 240 Grain Semi Jacketed Soft Point Flat, 454 Casull 240 Grain Semi Jacketed Soft Point Flat, 454 Casull 260 Grain Full Metal Jacket Flat, 454 Casull 260 Grain Semi Jacketed Soft Point Flat, 45 Auto 200 Grain Lead Semi Wad Cutter, .45 Auto 230 FMJ, 45 Auto 230 Grain Full Metal Jacket Semi Wad Cutter, .45GAP FMJ 230gr, 500 S&W 325 Grain Semi Jacketed Soft Point Flat,500 S&W 400 Grain Semi Jacketed Soft Point Flat, .500 S&W Light Loading SJSP 325gr, 50 BMG M33 624 Full Metal Jacket, 9mm Luger 115 FMJ, 9MM Luger 115 Grain Jacketed Hollow Point, 9MM Luger 115 Grain Jacketed Hollow Point,9MM Luger 124 Grain Full Metal Jacket, 9MM Luger 124 Grain Jacketed Soft Point, 9MM Luger 124 Grain Lead Round Nose, 9MM Luger 147 Grain Full Metal Jacket Flat, 9MM Luger 147 Grain Jacketed Hollow Point Sub, 9MM Luger 95 Grain Jacketed Soft Point Flat, 9MM Luger 95 Grain Jacketed Soft Point Flat w/o Grooves, 9x21mm 124 Grain Full Metal Jacket, 9x21mm 124 Grain Lead Round Nose, 45 Auto 230 Grain Full Metal Jacket, 40 S&W 180 Grain Full Metal Jacket Flat, 9MM Luger 115 Grain Full Metal Jacket

**Box 50:** . . . . . . . . . . . $15.00–$26.00

## TROPHY GRADE HUNTING AMMUNITION

**Features**: Manufactured to Nosler's strictest quality standards, Trophy Grade Ammunition uses NoslerCustom Brass and Nosler Bullets to attain optimum performance, no matter where your hunting trip takes you. Whether you want your ammunition loaded with AccuBond, Partition Ballistic Tip

or , E-Tip, NoslerCustom Trophy Grade Ammunition will have the right load for the right game.

**Available in**: 243 Win., 25-06 Rem, 257 Roberts +P, 257 Wby, 6.5x55 Mauser, 260 Rem, 6.5x55 Mauser, 260 Rem, 6.5-284 Norma, 264 Win. Mag., 270 Win., 270 WSM, 7mm-08 Rem,

280 Ack Imp, 7mm SAUM, 7mm Rem. Mag., 7mm STW, 7mm Rum, 308 Win., 30-06 Spfld, 300 H&H Mag., 300 Win. Mag., 300 Win. Mag., 300 WSM, 300 SAUM, 300 Rum, 300 Wby, 325 WSM, 338 Rum, 35 Whelen, 375 H&H Mag

**Box 20:** . . . . . . . . . . . $29.00–$57.00

# Nosler Ammunition

**NOSLER TROPHY GRADE HUNTING AMMUNITION**

## MATCH GRADE AMMUNITION

**Features**: NoslerCustom Match Grade Ammunition consists of Nosler's precisely-designed Custom Competition bullet along with NoslerCustom Brass. Because of Nosler's unsurpassed quality standards, each piece of brass is checked for correct length, neck-sized, chamfered, trued and flash holes are checked for proper alignment. To further ensure our reputation for quality and consistency, powder charges are meticulously weighed and finished rounds are visually inspected and polished.

**Available in**: 300 Win
**Box 20**: . . . . . . . . . . . . **$18.00–$30.00**

## BALLISTIC TIP VARMINT

**Features**: Nosler Ballistic Tip Varmint bullets thrive on ultra-high velocity loads, yet will go the distance with spectacular results all the way down to the lowest practical velocity levels.

Fast or slow, near or far, no matter what rifle/cartridge combination you're shooting or what varmint you're shooting at, Nosler Ballistic Tip delivers match-grade accuracy with all the performance characteristics serious varminters are looking for.

**Available in**: .204, .6mm, .25
**MSRP** . . . . . . . . . . . . . **$19.00–$37.99**

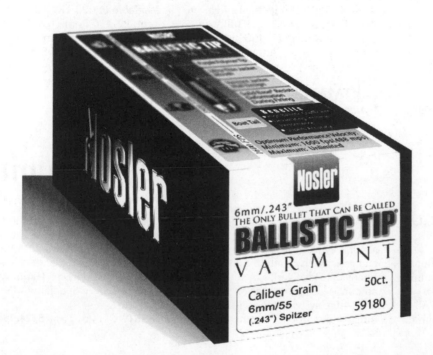

**NOSLER BALLISTIC TIP VARMINT**

## AFRICAN PH AMMO

**Features**: The concept behind Norma's AFRICAN PH range is different. Based on many generations of experience of reputable African Professional Hunters, this range of cartridges has been developed with the aim to optimize ballistic criteria such as Bullet Momentum, Sectional Density and Deep, Straight-line, Bone-breaking Penetration. These factors in turn, are responsible for KO or Knock Out Value, probably the most important ballistic criterion of all, for stopping a determined charge from one of Africa's Big Five. Loaded cartridges with Woodleigh softnose and solid bullets, in chamberings popular for dangerous game, including .375 H&H, .404 Jeffery, .416 Rem. Mag., .416 Rigby, .450 Rigby, .458 Lott, .470 NE, .500 NE, .505 Gibbs.
MSRP . . . . . . . . . . $129.99–$229.99

NORMA AFRICAN PH AMMO

## KALAHARI PLAINS GAME

**Features**: Two of the most challenging environments to hunt in are deserts and mountains where long shots are common and the game often runs out of sight after the shot. Ideally, the bullet should exit the animal, giving an immediate blood spoor for the PH or tracker to follow. The unique bullet design of Kalahari sets the new standard. It is loaded with selected lots of powder to ensure the highest possible velocity within safe pressures to give the flattest trajectory attainable. It also gives the best possible ballistic coefficient and lowest wind drift achievable at normal hunting ranges. Bullet expansion is controlled and restricted–only the front third of the bullet will expand. Six razor-edged petals will separate from the shank for maximum wounding effect, leaving the rear part of the bullet unimpeded, guaranteeing deep penetration. Lastly, the proprietary coating almost eliminates metal fouling in the bore – the usual curse of other copperbased monolithic hollowpoints.
**Available in**: 270 Winchester - 120 gr; 270 Win. Short Magnum- 120 gr.; 7x64- 125 gr., 280 Rem.- 125 gr.; 7mm Rem. Mag.- 125 gr; 308 Win.- 150 gr., 30-06 Spfld.- 150 gr.; 300 Win. Mag.- 155gr; 300 Win. Short Mag.- 155 gr
MSRP . . . . . . . . . . . . . . . . . . . . .N/A

## JAKTMATCH

**Features**: Target ammunition should have the same quality as your hunting cartridges. Many hunters also use Jaktmatch to hunt birds and small game so we have no reason to distinguish between hunting and target cartridges. All components in the Jaktmatch cartridges are the highest quality. The fired cases provide the reloader with a top quality product to reload.
**Available in**: .22 LR, .222 Rem, .223 Rem, 22-250 Rem., 6.5x55, .270 Win., .270 WSM, 7mm Rem. Mag., .308 Win., .30-06, .300 WSM, .300 Win. Mag., 8x57 JS, .338 Win. Mag., 9.3x 57, 9.3x62
MSRP . . . . . . . . . . . . . . . . . . . . .N/A

# PMC Ammunition

## BRONZE LINE- HANDGUN

**Features**: The same quality and dependability built into our Starfire ammunition is incorporated throughout our extensive line of PMC training ammunition and standard hollow point or soft point ammunition. All PMC cartridges must pass through the rigorous inspection of our electronic powder check station. This station accurately measures the propellant charge in each round. If the propellant in any cartridge varies by a tiny amount—just two tenths of one grain—the system stops and that cartridge is discarded. No other ammunition manufacturer can truthfully assure you greater uniformity and reliability.
**Available in**: 25 Auto, 32 Auto, 380 Auto, 38 Special, 38 Special +P, 9mm Luger, 357 Magnum, 10mm Auto, 40 S&W, 44 S&W Special, 44 Rem. Mag., 45 Auto
MSRP . . . . . . . . . . $124.99–$459.99

# PMC Ammunition

## BRONZE LINE-RIFLE

**Features**: For shooters and hunters who appreciate affordable quality ammunition, the PMC Bronze Line offers reliable performance for every shooting application, from target shooting to hunting. This long-popular ammunition line makes it possible for hunters and riflemen to enjoy high volume shooting without emptying their wallets. Bronze ammunition is available in Full Metal Jacket (FMJ) bullet types .223A Remington, .308B Winchester and .50A in commercial and military packaging.
*Available in*: .223 Rem, .30 Carbine, .308 Win., 7.62x 39, 50 Caliber
**MSRP . . . . . . . . . . . . . $11.00–$19.73**

PMC BRONZE LINE HANDGUN AMMUNITION

## GOLD LINE, STARFIRE

**Features**: The secret of Starfire's impressive performance lies in a unique, patented rib-and-flute hollow point cavity design that is like no other. Upon impact, the pre-notched jacket mouth begins to peel back, separating into five uniform copper petals and allowing expansion to begin. Pressure from incoming material creates lateral pressure on the ribs in the cavity wall, forcing them apart and allowing nearly instantaneous expansion of the lead core to the depth of the deep hollow point cavity. The sharp ribs are then exposed and form the leading edge of the expanded bullet, helping it cut its way through. The result is broad temporary and permanent wound cavities and impressive stopping power.
*Available in*: .380 Auto, .38 Special +P, .357 Mag., 9mm Luger, 40 S&W, 44 Rem. Mag., 45 Auto
**MSRP . . . . . . . . . . . . . $14.47–$21.81**

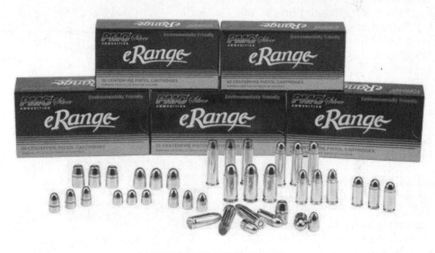

PMC SILVER LINE, ERANGE

## SILVER LINE, ERANGE

**Features**: PMC's eRange environmentally friendly ammunition utilizes a reduced hazard primer that is the first of this type in the industry, an encapsulated metal jacket (EMJ) bullet which completely encloses the surface of the bullet core with precision made copper alloy, and powder with clean burning characteristics and smooth fire for increased barrel life. PMC frangible bullets disintegrate on contact with harder material. They're ideal for training exercises and environments where ricochets and over-penetration are unacceptable.
*Available in*: .380 Auto, .38 Special, .357 Mag., 9mm Luger, 40 S&W, 44 Rem. Mag., 45 Auto
**MSRP . . . . . . . . . . . . . $15.00–$30.99**

## "ONE SHOT" HIGH VELOCITY PHEASANT LOADS

**Features**: In both 3" and 2 ¾", 12- and 20-gauge, these maximum velocity loads deliver a knockout punch of copper plating around extra-hard lead shot. Their specially designed plastic wads incorporate an innovative shot cup that ensures dense, uniform patterns needed to buckle late-season game birds and animals made fat by winter and wary by hunting pressure.
*Available in*: 12 and 20 ga., shot sizes 4, 5, 6, 7.5
**MSRP . . . . . . . . . . . . . $16.00–$18.29**

## X-TAC RIFLE AMMUNITION

**Features**: PMC's exacting adherence to precise specifications of military and law-enforcement organizations assures that X-TAC ammunition will perform perfectly in that fraction of a second when a serious threat arises and your life is on the line. Self-defense depends on reliable, consistent ammunition.
*Available in*: 5.56mm FMJ- 55 grain; 5.56mm LAP- 62 grains
**MSRP . . . . . . . . . . . . . $6.00–$9.12**

## PREMIER .30 REM. AR

*Features*: A short, 30-caliber round whose 125-grain bullets match the speed of .308 150s, for hunting deer-size game with the AR-15 modular repeating rifle. Ammo comes with Core-Lokt and AccuTip bullets (125 grains) and, in UMC loads, with full metal case (123 grains) bullets.
**MSRP**. . . . . . . . . . . . . .**$21.99–38.00**

## PREMIER COPPER SOLID

*Features*: This polymer-tipped, lead-free, copper bullet is of boat-tail design and delivers extremely deep penetration with nearly 100% weight retention and has a sleek ogive profile.
*Available in*: 243 Win., 270 Win., 7mm Rem. Mag., 30-30 Win., 30-06 Spfld., 300 Win. Mag., 300 Rem. Ultra Mag., 300 Win. Mag., 308 Win.
**MSRP**. . . . . . . . . . . . .**$13.00–$46.00**

## .308 MARLIN EXPRESS

*Features*: Core-Lokt: Progressively tapered copper jacket is locked to a solid lead core promoting controlled expansion and high weight retention.
**MSRP**. . . . . . . . . . . . .**$20.00–$27.00**

## ACCUTIP BONDED SABOT SLUG

*Features*: Guided by our new Power Port Tip, the AccuTip Bonded Sabot Slug delivers a degree of accuracy and terminal performance unmatched by any other we tested. In field testing, this huge .58-caliber slug produced gaping wound channels and crumpled every deer it touched with a single shot. From 5 to 200 yards, it yields perfect mushrooms and over 95% weight retention thanks to its spiral nose cuts, bonded construction and high-strength cartridge brass jacket. With performance as revolutionary as its appearance, this is one tip sure to get stunning results. Designed for fully rifled barrels only.
*Available in*: 12 or 20 ga; 2.75 in. or 3 in.
**MSRP**. . . . . . . . . . . . .**$11.65–$21.99**

## PREMIER DISINTEGRATOR VARMINT

*Features*: Frangible bullet design with iron/tin bullet core (no lead), designed

REMINGTON PREMIER .30 REM. AR

REMINGTON PREMIER COPPER SOLID

REMINGTON ACCUTIP BONDED SABOT SLUG

REMINGTON PREMIER DISINTEGRATOR VARMINT

# Remington Ammunition

to disintegrate up on impact on varmints.
*Available in*: .223 Rem, .22-250 Rem.
**MSRP . . . . . . . . . . . . $20.00–$26.99**

## PREMIER ACCUTIP

*Features*: Featuring precision-engineered polymer tip bullets designed for match-grade accuracy (sub minute-of-angle), Premier AccuTip offers an unprecedented combination of super-flat trajectory an deadly down-range performance.
*Available in*: 300 WSM, 30 Rem. AR, 300 Rem. Ultra Mag., 270 WSM, 300 WSM, 223 Rem., 243 Win., 260 Rem., 270 Win., 280 Rem., 7mm Rem. Mag., 30-06 Spgfld., 300 Win. Mag., 308 Win., 7mm-08 Rem., 30-06 Spfld.,
**MSRP . . . . . . . . . . . . $20.00–$37.00**

## POWER LEVEL AMMUNITION

*Features*: The hardest-hitting flattest-shooting magnum cartridges in history are now the world's most versatile. New Power Level Ammunition allows you to incrementally tailor the performance of your 7mm or 300 Ultra Mag™ rifle to the species and terrain you're hunting, similar to the way shotgunners use 2 ¾", 3" and 3 ½" shells. Plus, point of impact between Power Levels is within 2" at 200 yards, meaning little or no scope adjustment when you change levels. Now when you choose the 7mm or 300 Ultra Mag.,™ you're getting three guns in one.
**Box 20: . . . . . . . . . . . $32.00–$78.94**

## PREMIER CORE-LOKT ULTRA BONDED

*Features*: The bonded bullet retains up to 95% of its original weight with maximum penetration and energy transfer. Featuring a progressively tapered jacket design, the Core-Lokt Ultra Bonded bullet initiates and controls expansion nearly 2x.
*Available in*: 260 Rem, 7mm-08 Rem., 30-30 Win., 30-06 Spfld., 300 Savage, 303 British, 308 Win., 32 Win. Special, 35 Rem., 35 Wheelen, 25-06 Rem., 338 Win. Mag., 243 Win., 270 Win., 7mm Rem. Mag., 30-30 Win., 30-06 Spfld., 308 Win., 308 Marlin Express, 35 Rem., 7mm Rem. SA Ultra

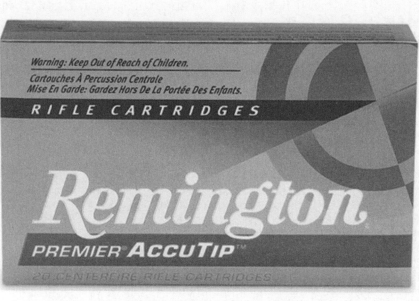

**REMINGTON PREMIER ACCUTIP**

**REMINGTON PREMIER CORE-LOKT ULTRA BONDED**

Mag., 450 Bushmaster, 338 Rem. Ultra Mag., 300 Rem. Short Action Ultra Mag., 9.3x62mm, 280 Rem., 257 Roberts, 30-40 Krag, 280 Rem., 44-40 Win., 7mm STW, 270 WSM, 300 Rem. Ultra Mag., 7mm Mauser, 6mm Rem., 280 Rem., 6.5 Rem. Mag., 8mm Mauser, 7x 64 Brenneke, 6.5x55 Swedish, 300 Wby Mag., 375 Rem. Ultra Mag., 350 Rem. Mag., 7mm Rem. Ultra Mag., 300 WSM, 30 Rem. AR, 364 Win. Mag., 300 Win. Mag.
**Box 50: . . . . . . . . . . . $17.00–$39.00**

### Centerfire Rifle Ammunition

## MANAGED RECOIL

**Features**: Managed-Recoil Ammunition delivers Remington Field proven hunting performance out to 200 yards with half the recoil. Bullets provide 2x expansion with over 75% weight retention on shots inside 50 yards and out to 200 yards.
**Available in**: 260 Rem., 270 Win., 30-06 Spfld., 300 Rem. Ultra Mag., 30-30 Win., 300 Win. Mag., 7mm Rem. Mag., 7mm-08 Rem., 308 Win.
**MSRP** . . . . . . . . . . . **$14.00–$27.00**

## PREMIER A-FRAME

**Features**: Whether it's whitetails with a 270 Win., or Cape Buffalo with a 416 Remington Magnum, you want your first shot to do the job. That's why we load the dual-core A-Frame bullets, so that you can expect reliable expansion at long-range decreased velocities, but without over-expansion at short-range high velocities. The combination of A-Frame construction and proprietary bonding process produces extremely uniform, controlled expansion to 2x caliber with nearly 100% weight retention. All Premier A-Frame components receive multiple inspections: primers are pre-inspected five times for ignition reliability; each round is receiver-gauged, and cases are nickel-plated for precision feeding and extraction. You simply can't buy a better factory-loaded medium- to big-game ammunition.
**Available in**: 300 Rem. Ultra Mag. (Power Level III), 7mm STW, 8mm Rem. Mag., 270 Win., 7mm Rem. Ultra Mag. ( Power Level III), 375 H&H Mag., 300 Win. Mag., 30-06 Spfld., 416 Rem. Mag., 338 Rem. Ultra mag., 375 Rem. Ultra Mag.
**MSRP** . . . . . . . . . . . **$40.00–$85.00**

## PREMIER MATCH

**Features**: Loaded with match-grade bullets, this ammunition employs special loading practices to ensure world-class performanc and accuracy with every shot.
**Available in**: 308 Win., 223 Rem., 6.8 Rem. SPC, 223 Rem, 300 Win. Mag., 223 Rem., 300 Rem. Short Action

Ultra Mag., 6.8mm Rem. SPC
**MSRP** . . . . . . . . . . . **$24.00–$27.49**

## PREMIER SCIROCCO BONDED

**Features**: The Swift Scirocco Bonded bullet combines polymer tip ballistics with weight retention. The expansion generating polymer tip and the boat tail base defy air resistance at the front end, and reduce drag at the back.
**Available in**: 300 Ultra Mag., 300 Rem. Ultra mag., 7mm Rem. Mag., 30-06 Spfld., 243 Win., 270 Win., 300 Win. Mag., 7mm Rem. Mag. (Power Level III), 300 WSM
**MSRP** . . . . . . . . . . . **$37.00–$47.00**

### Handgun Ammunition

## DISINTEGRATOR CTF

**Features**: Truly the ultimate choice for all lead-free training scenarios. Utilizing jacketless, copper tin frangible bullets, the Disintegrator CTF delivers complete breakup at distances as close as 5 feet with no splashback, no jacket fragments and absolutely no lead residue. Disintegrator CTF bullets are formed from powder using a compaction and sintering process that eliminates the need for a jacket to house the bullet core. When these completely frangible bullets strike a barrier, they're instantly reduced to dust-sized particles, dramatically reducing hazard to bystanders. Highly frangible design prolongs the life of target traps and backstops, and our Heavy Metal Free (HMF) primer offers the best shelf life available with a non-toxic primer.
**Available in**: 38 Special (+P), 9mm (+P), 40 S&W, 45 Auto
**MSRP** . . . . . . . . . . . **$36.00–$57.50**

## EXPRESS PISTOL AND REVOLVER AMMUNTION

**Features**: Remington's exceptionally broad line of handgun ammunition covers a comprehensive range of calibers, bullet weights and bullet styles. Available styles include: Full Metal Case, Lead Round Nose, Jacketed Hollow Point, Lead Hollow Point, Semi-Jacketed Hollow Point, Semi-Wadcutter Lead, Soft Point and

Wadcutter Match.
**Available in**: 45 Auto, 25 Auto, 32 S&W, 32 S&W Long, 32 Auto, 357 Mag., 9mm Luger, 380 Auto, 357 Sig., 38 S&W, 38 Special, 41 Rem. Mag., 9mm Luger, 40 S&W, 38 Short Colt, 44 S&W Special, 45 Colt, 44 Rem. Mag., 45 Colt, 44 Rem. Mag., 357 Mag
**MSRP** . . . . . . . . . . . **$13.00–$41.00**

## GOLDEN SABER HPJ

**Features**: Dead-serious bullet innovation. A superior bullet for when the stakes are at their highest. Designed for law enforcement and personal defense, the Golden Saber High Performance Jacket successfully combines: match-type accuracy, deep penetration, maximum expansion and near 100% weight retention. Cases nickel-plated for reliable feed, function and extraction.
**Available in**: 357 Mag., 380 Auto, 9mm Luger, 9mm Luger (+P), 40 S&W, 45 Auto, 45 Auto (+P)
**MSRP** . . . . . . . . . . . **$14.00–$31.99**

### Rimfire Ammunition

## .22 RIMFIRE TARGET

**Features**: Whether it's getting young shooter started, practice plinking, small-game hunting or keeping match shooters scoring high, Remington's rimfire quality stands tall. As in their centerfire ammo they put the maxiumum level of quality into their .22s so you can get the maximum performance out of them.
**Available in**: .22 LR
**MSRP** . . . . . . . . . . . **$7.00–$12.73**

## MAGNUM RIMFIRE

**Features**: Whether it's shooting metallic silhouette targets or hunting small game, these Magnum rimfire cartridges deliver exceptional performance and unmatched reliability. Our Premier Gold Box Rimfire ammunition features sleek AccuTip-V bullets available in either 17 HMR or 22 Win. Mag. Our standard line of Magnum rimfire ammunition gives shooters the choice of either a Jacketed Hollow Point for quick expansion or a Pointed Soft Point for optimum penetration. Both of

# Remington Ammunition

these 40-grain bullets generate 1,910 feet-per-second muzzle velocities and retain excellent downrange energies.
*Available in*: .22 Mag.
MSRP . . . . . . . . . . . . $10.00–$21.00

## PREMIER GOLD BOX RIMFIRE

*Features*: This ammunition uses the AccuTip- V bullet with precision- engineered polymer tip for match-type accuracy, high on-game energy, and rapid expansion.
*Available in*: 17 HMR, .22 Win. Mag., 17 Mach 2 Rimfire
MSRP . . . . . . . . . . . . $15.09–$18.99

## REMINGTON-ELEY COMPETITION RIMFIRE MATCH EPS

*Features*: When it comes to competition-grade rimfire ammunition, there's only one name good enough to share the Remington® brand – Eley. Building on the rimfire expertise of Eley, Ltd., and its reputation among dedicated rimfire shooters as the world's most accurate and reliable ammunition, Remington and Eley offer three grades of their premier 22 Long Rifle ammunition. For the finest performance available Remington/Eley Match EPS offers the ultimate in rimfire accuracy. This match grade load features Eley's innovative Tenex EPS-profile bullet—ideal for aspiring top class shooters and training at the highest level.
*Available in*: .22 Long Rifle
MSRP . . . . . . . . . . . . $9.99–$15.99

**Shotgun Ammunition**

## EXPRESS EXTRA LONG RANGE UPLAND LOADS

*Features*: For the broadest selection in game-specific Upland shotshells, Remington Upland Loads are the perfect choice. The hunter's choice for a wide variety of game-bird applications, available from 12-gauge to .410 bore, with shot size options ranging from BB's all the way down to 9s—suitable for everything from quail to farm predators. Long considered to be some of the best-balanced, best-patterning upland field loads available, our family of shotshells offer great selections for upland bird hunting. Available in: 12

Ga., 16 Ga., 20 Ga., 410 Ga
MSRP . . . . . . . . . . . . $12.75–$14.27

## GUN CLUB TARGET LOADS

*Features*: Excellent choice for economical shooting. Loaded with Gun Club Grade Shot, Premier STS Primers, and Power Piston One-Piece Wads, these high-quality shells receive the same care in loading as top-of-the-line Premier STS and Nitro 27 shells. Many shooters are discovering that they can get acceptable reloading life while stretching their shooting dollar.
*Available in*: 12 Ga., 20 Ga; 2.75 in; Shot sizes 7.5, 8, 9
MSRP . . . . . . . . . . . . $5.00–$6.00

## LEAD GAME LOADS

*Features*: For a wide variety of field gaming, these budget-stretching loads include the same quality components as other Remington shotshells, and are available in four different gauges to match up with your favorite upland shotguns.
*Available in*: 12, 16, 20, 410 Ga.; 2.75 in., 2.5 in.; Shot sizes 6, 7.5, 8
MSRP . . . . . . . . . . . . $7.00–$17.00

## MANAGED RECOIL STS TARGET LOADS

*Features*: Managed- Recoil STS target loads offer dramaticaly reduced recoil- 40% less in the 12-gauage load- with target-grinding STS consistency and pattern density. Ideal for new shooters and high-volume practice.
*Available in*: 12, 20 ga.; 2.75 in.; Shot sizes 8.5
MSRP . . . . . . . . . . . . $8.41

## NITRO TURKEY BUFFERED LOADS

*Features*: These loads contain Nitro Mag. extra-hard lead shot that is as hard and round as copper-plated shot. Nitro Turkey Magnums will pattern as well as other copper-plated, buffered loads without the higher cost. Utilizing a specially blended powder recippe and Remington's advanced Power Piston one-piece wad, the loads delivers a full 1⅞ oz. payload at 1210 fps while delivering 80% pattern densities with outstanding knockdown power.
*Available in*: 12, 20 Ga.; 2.75 in.,

3 in., 3.5 in.
MSRP . . . . . . . . . . . . $8.00–$12.00

## NITRO-MAG. BUFFERED MAGNUM TURKEY LOADS

*Features*: The original buffered magnum shotshells from Remington. The shot charge is packed with a generous amount of shock-absorbing polymer buffering and surrounded by our patented Power Piston wad to protect the specially hardened shot all the way down the barrel for dense, even patterns and uniform shot strings.
*Available in*: 12, 20 Ga.; 2 ¾ in., 3 in.
MSRP . . . . . . . . . . . . $22.99–$31.99

## NITRO PHEASANT LOADS

*Features*: Uses Remington's own Copper-Lokt copper-plated lead shot with high antimony content. Hard shot stays rounder for truer flight, tighter patterns, and greater penetration. Available in both high-velocity and magnum loadings.
*Available in*: 12, 20 Ga.; 2.75 in., 3 in.; shot sizes 4, 5, 6
MSRP . . . . . . . . . . . . $15.00–$20.99

## NITRO-STEEL HIGH VELOCITY MAGNUM WATERFOWL LOADS

*Features*: Greater hull capacity means heavier charges and larger pellets, which makes these loads ideal for large waterfowl. Nitro-Steel delivers denser patterns for greater lethality and is zinc-plated to prevent corrosion.
*Available in*: 10, 12, 16, 20 Ga.; 2.75 in., 3 in., 3.5 in.; Shot sizes T, BBB, BB, 1234
MSRP . . . . . . . . . . . . $16.95–$24.06

## PHEASANT LOADS

*Features*: For the broadest selection in game-specific Upland shotshells, Remington Upland Loads are the perfect choice. Their high-velocity and long-range performance are just right for any pheasant hunting situation. Standard high-base payloads feature Power Piston one-piece wads.
*Available in*: 12, 16, 20 ga.; 2.75 in.; Shot sizes 4, 5, 6, 7.5
MSRP . . . . . . . . . . . . $11.22–$19.99

## PREMIER DUPLEX

## MAGNUM COPPER-PLATED BUFFERED TURKEY LOADS

**Features**: Remington is proud to offer shotshell ammunition for the turkey hunter who appreciates dense patterns, deep penetration, and range flexibility. Premier Duplex has No. 4 size shot carefully layered on top of No. 6 shot. When ranges vary, they combine retained energy and penetration from the larger pellets with pattern density from the smaller ones. Duplex patterns are extremely well balanced. If gobblers are your game, you'd better stock up on the copper-plated, buffered magnum shells early.
**Available in**: 12 ga.; 2.75 in., 3 in.; Shot sizes 4x6
**MSRP**. . . . . . . . . . . . **$11.00–$19.00**

## PREMIER HIGH-VELOCITY MAGNUM COPPER-PLATED BUFFERED TURKEY LOADS

**Features**: Utilizing a specially blended powder recipe, Remington's advanced Power Piston one piece wad and hardened copper plated shot, these new high velocity loads result in extremely dense patterns and outstanding knockdown power at effective ranges.
**Available in**: 12 ga.; 3, 3.5 in.; Shot sizes 4, 5, 6
**MSRP**. . . . . . . . . . . . **$13.45–$18.99**

## PREMIER MAGNUM COPPER-PLATED BUFFERED TURKEY LOADS

**Features**: Premier Magnum Turkey Loads provide that extra edge to reach out with penetrating power and dense, concentrated patterns. Its magnum-grade, Copper-Lokt shot is protected by our Power Piston wad and cushioned with special polymer buffering. Available with some of the heaviest payloads of 4s, 5s, and 6s on the market.
**Available in**: 10, 12, 20 ga.; 2.75 in., 3 in., 3.5 in.; Shot sizes 4, 5, 6
**MSRP**. . . . . . . . . . . . **$11.79–$18.90**

## PREMIER NITRO 27 TARGET LOADS

**Features**: Remington's Target Loads have taken shot-to-shot consistency to a new performance level, setting the standard at all major skeet, trap, and sporting clays shoots across the country, while providing handloaders with unmatched reloading ease and hull longevity. Available in most gauges, our shells are the most reliable, consistent and most reloadable shells you can shoot. Designed specifically for back-fence trap and long-range sporting clays. Delivers consistent handicap velocity and pattern uniformity. New, improved powder loading significantly reduces felt recoil while retaining high velocity—both factors allow avid trap shooters to stay fresh for the shootoff. They score just as high on fast-moving doves.
**Available in**: 12 Ga; 2.75 in.; Shot Size 7.5, 8
**MSRP**. . . . . . . . . . . . . . **$5.87–$9.87**

## PREMIER STS TARGET LOADS

**Features**: STS Target Loads have taken shot-to-shot consistency to a new performance level, setting the standard at all major skeet, trap, and sporting clays shooting across the country, while providing handloaders with unmatched reloading ease and hull longevity. Available in most gauges our Premier STS shells are the most relaible, consistent and most reloadable shells you can shoot.
**Available in**: 12, 20, 28, .410 Ga.; 2.5 in., 2.75 in., 3 in., 3.75 in.; Shot sizes 7.5, 8, 8.5, 9
**MSRP**. . . . . . . . . . . . . . . . . . **$8.00**

## SHURSHOT HEAVY FIELD AND HEAVY DOVE LOADS

**Features**: A sure bet for all kinds of upland game, ShurShot loads have earned the reputation as one of the best-balanced, best-pattering upland field loads available. And for good reason. These shells combine an ideal balance of powder charge and shot payload to deliver effective velocities and near-perfect patterns with mild recoil for high-volume upland hunting situations.
**Available in**: 12, 20 Ga.; 2.75 in.; shot sizes 6, 7.5, 8
**MSRP**. . . . . . . . . . . . . . **$7.94–$12.00**

## SHURSHOT HIGH BASE PHEASANT LOADS

**Features**: The ShurShot High Base Pheasant loads deliver an ideal combination of velocity and payload. Loaded with our reliable Power Piston Wad and hard lead shot.
**Available in**: 12 Ga.; 2.75 in.; Shot sizes 4, 5
**MSRP**. . . . . . . . . . . . **$12.00–$16.85**

## SPORT LOADS

**Features**: Remington Sport Loads are an economical, multi-purpose utility load for a variety of shotgunning needs. Loaded with Power Piston wads, and plastic Unibody hulls, these shells perform effectively for skeet trap and sporting clays, as well as quail, doves, and woodcock.
**Available in**: 12, 20 Ga.; 2.75 in.; Shot sizes 8
**MSRP**. . . . . . . . . . . . . . **$7.22–$14.00**

## SPORTSMAN HI-SPEED STEEL WATERFOWL LOADS

**Features**: Sportsman Hi-Speed Steel's sealed primer, high quality steel shot, and consistent muzzle veocities combine to provide reliability in adverse weather, while delivering exceptional pattern density and retained energy. A high-speed steel load that is ideal for short-range high-volume shooting during early duck seasons, or over decoys.
**Available in**: 10, 12, 20 Ga.; 2.75 in., 3, 3.5 in.; shot sizes BB, 1, 2, 3, 4, 6, 7
**MSRP**. . . . . . . . . . . . **$12.92–$24.00**

## WINGMASTER HD TURKEY LOADS

**Features**: Comprised of tungsten, bronze and iron, Wingmaster HD pellets are specifically engineered with a density of 12 grams/cc, 10 percent denser than lead. Wingmaster HD loads also feature a precise balance of payload and velocity that provide turkey hunters with a shotshell that generates nearly 200 ft.-lbs more energy at 40 yds. than competitive tungsten based shot. This results in deeper penetrating pellets.
**Available in**: 10, 12, 20 Ga.; 2.75 in., 3 in., 3.5 in.; shot sizes 2, 4, 6, BB, T
**MSRP**. . . . . . . . . . . . **$14.00–$34.93**

# Remington Ammunition

## WINGMASTER HD WATERFOWL LOADS

**Features**: Wingmaster HD nontoxic shot stretches the kill zone with an ultra-tuned combination of density, shape and energy. At 12 grams/cc, it's 10% denser than lead and the scientfically proven optimum density for pellet count and pattern density. Plus, its smooth round shape delivers awesome aerodynamics and sustained payload energy. Wingmaster HD is also 16% softer than Premier Heavi-Shot, which makes it easier on your barrel. And it's more responsive to chokes, allowing you to open up the pattern for close-range hunting or stretch the shotgun range to its farthest reaches. Also available in Turkey and Predator Loads.
**Available in**: 10,12, 20 Ga.; 2.75 in., 3 in., 3.5 in.; Shot sizes T, BB 2, 3, 6
**MSRP** . . . . . . . . . . . . $17.00–$26.81

**Shotgun Ammunition (Buckshot)**

## EXPRESS BUCKSHOT AND EXPRESS MAGNUM BUCKSHOT

**Features**: A combination of heavy cushioning behind the shot column and a granulated polymer buffering helps maintain pellet roundness for tight, even patterns.
**Available in**: 12, 20 Ga.; 2.75 in., 3, 3.5 in.; Shot sizes 0,00,000, 1, 3, 4
**MSRP** . . . . . . . . . . . . . . $4.00–$9.00

## MANAGED-RECOIL EXPRESS BUCKSHOT

**Features**: With less felt recoil than full velocity loads, Express Managed-Recoil Buckshot is an ideal close-range performer. Less recoil means second shot recovery is quicker, allowing the user to get back on target more easily. These loads are buffered for dense patterns, allowing for highly effective performance at up to 40 yards.
**Available in**: 12 Ga.; 2.75 in.; Shot sizes 00
**MSRP** . . . . . . . . . . . . . . . . . . . $4.99

**Shotgun Ammunition (slugs)**

## BUCKHAMMER LEAD SLUGS

**Features**: Specifically designed for rifled barrels and rifled choke tubes, these high-performance slugs are capable of producing 3-inch or better groups at 100-yards with nearly 100% weight retention and controlled expansion to nearly one-inch in diameter. Unlike traditional sabot slugs, the BuckHammer's unique attached stabilizer allows for a full bore diameter lead slug that delivers devastating terminal performance with unsurpassed accuracy.
**Available in**: 12, 20 Ga.; 2.75 in., 3 in.
**MSRP** . . . . . . . . . . . . . $4.22–$13.99

## MANAGED-RECOIL BUCKHAMMER LEAD SLUGS

**Features**: Buckhammer lead slugs generate 40% less felt-recoil without sacrificing its devastating on-game performance. Specially designed for fully rifled barrels and rifled choke tubes, these lower-recoil slugs still deliver the same outstanding accuracy as our standard Buckhammer loads with near 100% weight retention and controlled expansion to nearly 1-inch in diameter. For use at the range or in the field the Managed Recoil Buckhammer slug maintains an impressive 1032 ft-lbs of deer-stopping energy at 100-yds.
**Available in**: 12, 20 Ga.; 2.75 in.
**MSRP** . . . . . . . . . . . . . $6.00–$10.99

## MANAGED-RECOIL COPPER SOLID SABOT SLUGS

**Features**: With 40% less recoil, these slugs are perfect for anyone who wants outstanding on-game results without the rearward punch. Or, use them to sight-in, then step up to full loads. There's no finer slug load for young or recoil-sensitive hunters.
**Available in**: 12, 20 ga.; 2.75 in., 3 in.
**MSRP** . . . . . . . . . . . . $14.00–$19.97

## PREMIER CORE-LOKT ULTRA BONDED SABOT SLUGS

**Features**: Ultra-high velocities deliver devastating on-game performance and the tightest groups—1.8 in.—of any shotgun slug with ultra-flat trajectories. Remington patented spiral nose cuts ensure consistent 2x expansion over a wide range of terminal velocities, while the sleek, ogive nose delivers high down-range energy retention. The 385-grain bonded bullet yields near 100% weight retention. Flattest shooting slug in existence—10% better than the nearest competition. Designed for use in fully rifled barrels only.
**Available in**: 12, 20 ga.; 2.75 in., 3 in.
**MSRP** . . . . . . . . . . . . $17.79–$19.99

## SLUGGER HIGH VELOCITY SLUGS

**Features**: This is the first high-velocity Foster-style lead slug. This higher velocity slug exits the barrel at 1800 fps, 13% faster than standard 1 oz. slugs. The ⅞ oz. Slugger High Velocity delivers 200ft-lbs more energy at 50 yards with flatter trajectory on deer than standard 1 oz. slugs. Designed for the avid deer hunter using smooth bore guns.
**Available in**: 12, 20 Ga.; 2.75 in., 3 in.
**MSRP** . . . . . . . . . . . . . $4.00–$5.89

## SLUGGER MANAGED-RECOIL RIFLED SLUGS

**Features**: Slugger Managed-Recoil Rifled Slugs offer remarkably effective performance but with 45% less felt recoil than full velocity Sluggers. With effective energy out of 80 yards, these 1 oz. Slugs easily handle the majority of shotgun deer hunting ranges.
**Available in**: 12 Ga.; 2.75 in.
**MSRP** . . . . . . . . . . . . . $4.00–$6.38

## SLUGGER RIFLED SLUGS

**Features**: Remington redesigned their 12-gauge Slugger Rifled Slug for a 25% improvement in accuracy. Also, at 1760 fps muzzle velocity, the 3 in. 12-GA. Magnum slugs shoot 25% flatter than regular 12-Ga. Slugs. Packed in convenient, easy-carrying 5-round boxes. Also available in a reduced recoil loading.
**Available in**: 12, 16, 20, .410 Ga.; 2.75 in., 3 in.
**MSRP** . . . . . . . . . . . . . $4.00–$5.00

**AMMUNITION**

## Centerfire Cartridges

### .375 H&H MAG. UNI

*Features*: This cartridge is loaded with a 301-grain RWS UNI bullet. It leaves the muzzle at 2,590 fps and produces 4,468ft./lbs of muzzle energy. It has a softer lead tip core united to a harder heavier tail core section. The harder rear core is blended to join with the softer front to retard its mushrooming ability and to increase its penetration force. Deep penetration, followed by delayed shock, is a very effective and reliable technique for taking large, dangerous game. The RWS UNI bullet contains a hard nickel-plated jacket with a deep groove cut into its mid-section to initiate the delayed fragmentation effect. The torpedo-shaped tail, with its large base area, improves the external-ballistic performance by giving the projectile precise flight stability. After deeply penetrating and fragmenting, the residual body of the projectile is designed to continue through the animal's body making a clean exit after transferring its high amount of energy.
**Box 20:** . . . . . . . . . . . **$75.00–$78.99**

### 6.5X55 DK 140-GRAIN

*Features*: In 1894, both Sweden and Norway adopted this cartridge as their standard military cartridge. Nowadays, this cartridge is highly popular around the world, as a hunting and target shooting cartridge at distances up to 300 meters. It is a highly dynamic cartridge with a flat trajectory. The intrinsic accuracy is excellent. As a hunting cartridge it is very suitable for all medium to light red deer or wild boar. When used wth the 8.2 gram KS or 9.1 gram DK bullets it becomes an all-round hunting cartridge.
**Box 20:** . . . . . . . . . . . **$21.97–$33.00**

### 7MM REM. MAG. ID CLASSIC

*Features*: The 7mm Rem. Mag. is a very good and highly accurate cartridge up to 300 meters. Its field of application primarily covers medium-sized game up to 150 kg live weight. It is a very good cartridge for use in the mountains, thanks to the flat trajectory, and is ideal for hunting chamois, ibex and moufflon. The 10.3 gram EVO bullet can be used as an all-round bullet, and the damage to the meat when used on roe deer is within acceptable limits.
**MSRP** . . . . . . . . . . . . . **$31.19–$41.29**

## Rimfire Cartridges

### .22 LR HV HOLLOW POINT

*Features*: This higher velocity hollow point offers the shooter greater shocking power in game. Suitable for both small game and vermin.
**Box 50:** . . . . . . . . . . . . **$8.58–$10.00**

### .22 LR RIFLE MATCH

*Features*: Perfect for the club level target competitor. Accurate and affordable.
**Box 50:** . . . . . . . . . . . **$10.00–$14.00**

### .22 LR SUBSONIC HOLLOW POINT

*Features*: Subsonic ammunition is a favorite ammunition of shooters whose shooting range is limited to where the noise of a conventional cartridge would be a problem.
**Box 500** . . . . . . . . . . . **$67.48–$81.99**

### .22 LR TARGET RIFLE

*Features*: An ideal training and field cartridge, the .22 Long Rifle Target also excels in informal competitions. The target .22 provides the casual shooter with accuracy at an economical price.
**Box 50:** . . . . . . . . . . . . **$8.69–$11.00**

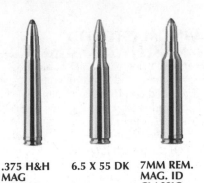

.375 H&H MAG    6.5 X 55 DK    7MM REM. MAG. ID CLASSIC

### .22 MAGNUM FULL JACKET

*Features*: Outstanding penetration characteristics of this cartridge allow the shooter to easily tackle game where penetration is necessary.
**Box 50:** . . . . . . . . . . . . . . . **$31.99**

### .22 MAGNUM HOLLOW POINT

*Features*: The soft point allows good expansion on impact, while perserving the penetration characterisitcs necessary for larger vermin and game.
**Box 50:** . . . . . . . . . . . . . . . **$30.99**

### .22 R50

*Features*: For competitive shooters demanding the ultimate in precision. This cartridge has been used to establish several world records and is used by Olympic Gold Medalists.
**Box 50:** . . . . . . . . . . . **$14.45–$19.03**

### .22 SHORT R25

*Features*: Designed for world class Rapid Fire Pistol events, this cartridge provides the shooter with outstanding accuracy and minimal recoil. Manufactured to exacting standards, so the shooter can be assured of consistent performance.
**Box 50:** . . . . . . . . . . . . . . . **$14.49**

# Sierra Ammunition

### MATCHKING BULLETS

*Features*: For serious rifle competition, you'll be in championship company with MatchKing bullets. The hollow point boat tail design provides that extra margin of ballistic performance match shooters need to fire long ranges under adverse conditions. Our exacting tolerances assure record-breaking accuracy you can depend on.

*Available in*: .224, 6mm, .257, 6.5mm, .277, .284, .308, .311, .323, .338
**MSRP** . . . . . . . . . . . . . **$19.49–$33.99**

# Sierra Ammunition

### PRO-HUNTER

**Features**: The traditional, flat base design of the Pro-Hunter has been skillfully blended with Sierra's world-famous accuracy. Our custom-tapered Pro-Hunter jacket design helps assure maximum expansion, optimum weight retention and deep penetration for game-stopping, one-shot performance.

**Available in**: .243, .257, 6.5mm, .277, 7mm, .30-30, .308, .311, 8mm, .338, .375, .458
**MSRP** . . . . . . . . . . . . **$17.00–$25.99**

# Swift Ammunition

### SCIROCCO II

**Features**: Scirocco II bonded is the perfect bullet design for today's fast, flat-shooting, long-range cartridges. Its secant ogive, 15-degree boat tail base and Signature Black Tip create a sleek, aerodynamic profile that helps maintain down-range velocities and flat trajectories. The extra heavy tapering jacket wall with an internally bonded lead core provides structural integrity, reliable expansion, and penetration with 80%+ weight retention.
**Available in**: .224, 6mm, .25, 6.5mm, .270, 7mm, .30, .338
**Box 100:** . . . . . . . . . . **$56.75–$69.00**

### A-FRAME

**Features**: With its unique cross-member jacket design and the bonded front core, the Swift A-Frame™ Bullet has become famous for its ability to combine three critical performance features – controlled expansion to 2X original diameter, deep penetration and 95% weight retention at all velocities. This has made it the bullet that hunters shoot with confidence, at any game, of any size, close up or far off.
**Available in**: .510, .505 Gibbs, .357, .41, .44, .45, .50, 9.3mm
**MSRP** . . . . . . . . . . . **$55.00–$114.50**

# Weatherby Ammunition

### BARNES TSX

**Features**: Upon its introduction, the Barnes X Bullet was generally regarded as a quantum leap in bullet design, retaining virtually all of its weight upon impact and delivering superior terminal performance with lighter weight bullets. TSX takes the X bullet to the next level. Get greater penetration and more one-shot kills with the world's deadliest hunting bullet. Specially designed nose cavity opens instantly into four petals on impact. Offers faster expansion than traditional lead-core bullets. Retains virtually 100% of its original weight. 100% copper construction. Precisely positioned rings relieve firing pressure, allowing the TSX to be loaded at higher velocities. Reduces fouling for easier cleaning of the bore.
**Available in**: .240, .257, .270, 7mm, .300, .30, .338, .340, .378, .416, .460
**MSRP** . . . . . . . . . . . **$66.00–$141.00**

### NORMA SPITZER

**Features**: This value-priced bullet is ideal for most medium to big game from antelope to elk. The half-jacked, lead alloy core features a classic Spitzer design with exposed lead tip. A field-proven, economical alternative to other premium-priced bullets. Specially designed for high velocity cartridges, maintaining superior accuracy. Retains 60%-70% of mass for deep penetration and larger wound channels.
**Available in**: .257, .270, .300
**MSRP** . . . . . . . . . . . . **$31.66–$72.99**

# Winchester Ammunition

### BONDED PDX1 HANDGUN AMMUNITION

**Features**: The new Winchester Supreme Elite Bonded PDX1, which was chosen by the FBI as their primary service round, is now available in a full line of popular handgun calibers. The Bonded PDX1 is engineered to maximize terminal ballistics, as defined by the demanding FBI test protocol, which simulates real-world threats. The new Winchester Bonded PDX is offered in 9mm, 40 Smith & Wesson, 45 automatic and .38 special.
**Available in**: 380 Auto, 38 Special +P, 40 S&W, 45 Colt, 45 Auto, 9mm Luger +P, 9mm Luger
**MSRP** . . . . . . . . . . . . **$16.99–$28.99**

**WINCHESTER BONDED
PDX1 HANDGUN AMMO**

## SUPER-X POWER MAX BONDED BULLETS

**Features**: Super-X Power Max Bonded is specifically designed for the white-tail deer hunter and takes the time-proven jacketed bullet design to a new level of performance at an affordable price. Key features of the Super-X bullet include: protected hollow point PHP design, lead core bonded to jacket with proprietary process, massive frontal area of mushroom is more than double original diameter, lead remains bonded to jacket after impact.
**Available in**: 243 Win., 270 Win., 270 WSM, 30-06 Spfld., 300 WSM, 300 Win. Mag., 300 WSM, 30-30 Win., 308 Win., 300 Win. Mag., 7mm Rem. Mag., 7mm WSM
**MSRP** . . . . . . . . . . . . . $18.99–$23.99

**WINCHESTER SUPER-X POWER MAX BONDED BULLETS**

## .22 XPEDITER

**Features**: The Xpediter, part of the Supreme line, is Winchester's fastest 22 long rifle varmint and small game round. The lighting-fast copper plated 32-grain lead hollow point bullet achieves an ultra-high muzzle velocity of 1,640 feet per second. The Xpediter is flat shooting with explosive upset. The deep hollow point allows for maximum terminal effect. 50 round plastic pack.
**MSRP** . . . . . . . . . . . . . . $5.00–$9.99

**WINCHESTER 22 XPEDITER**

## SUPREME ELITE DUAL BOND HANDGUN AMMO

**Features**: The Supreme Elite Dual Bond offers a large hollow point cavity, which provides consistent upsets at a variety of ranges and impact velocities. The heavy outer jacket is mechanically bonded to the inner bullet. The inner bullet utilizes a proprietary bonding process which welds the lead core to a second jacket which results in a design that provides for a combination of knockdown power, solid penetration and significant tissue damage while retaining nearly 100% of the original weight.
**Available in**: 454 Cassull, 460 S&W Mag., 500 S&W Mag.
**MSRP** . . . . . . . . . . . . $18.00–$50.99

**WINCHESTER DUAL BOND HANDGUN AMMO**

# Winchester Ammunition

## E- TIP

*Features*: The E-Tip lead-free bullet from Winchester Ammunition is a product developed for big-game hunters and complies with current state non-toxic regulations. Co-developed with Nosler, this bullet features an E2 energy expansion cavity, which promotes consistent upset at a variety of impact ranges. The bullet is made of gilding metal instead of pure copper, which helps prevent barrel fouling and provides for a high performance sporting bullet that is lead-free. The polycarbonate tip prevents deformation in the magazine, boosts aerodynamic efficiency and intiates expansion.
*Available in*: 270 WSM, 270 Win., 30-06 Spfld., 300 WSM, 300 Win. Mag., 308 Win., 7mm Rem. Mag.
MSRP . . . . . . . . . . . . $37.00–$56.00

WINCHESTER E-TIP LEAD FREE

## RACKMASTER SLUG

*Features*: The RackMaster system design consists of a new hard-hitting lead nose and the innovative WinGlide rear projectile stabilizer, engineered specifically to improve in-bore alignment and enhance down-range accuracy. RackMaster delivers high accuracy, hard-hitting knockdown performance to hunters shooting shotguns with either smooth bore, rifled choke tube or fully-rifled barrels.
*Available in*: 12, 20 Ga.; 2.75 in., 3 in.
MSRP . . . . . . . . . . . . . $6.00–$15.99

WINCHESTER RACKMASTER SLUG

## XP3 SABOT SHOTGUN SLUG

*Features*: The Supreme Elite XP3 Sabot Slug is the most accurate, hard-hitting long-range slug ever developed by Winchester specifically for rifled-barreled shotguns.
*Available in*: 12 Ga.; 2.75 in., 3 in.; 300 Grain
MSRP . . . . . . . . . . . $11.00–$15.99

**handgun ammunition**

## COWBOY LOADS LEAD

*Features*: Designed for cowboy action shooters who need high accuracy and consistent performance.
*Available in*: 38 Special, 44-40 Winchester, 44 S&W Special, 45 Colt
MSRP . . . . . . . . . . . $32.00–$38.99

## SUPER-CLEAN NT

*Features*: Specially designed jacketed soft point tin core bullet shoots and performs like lead. Meets the totally non-toxic needs of indoor ranges.
*Available in*: 9mm, 40 S&W
MSRP . . . . . . . . . . . $38.91–$52.96

## SUPER-X FULL METAL JACKET

*Available in*: 30 Luger
Box 50: . . . . . . . . . . . . . . . . $57.99

## SUPER-X JHP

*Available in*: 357 Mag., 38 Special +P,

454 Casull, 45 Winchester Mag., 460 S&W Mag.
MSRP . . . . . . . . . . . . $38.00–$50.92

## SUPER-X BLANK- BLACK POWDER

*Available in*: 32 S&W
MSRP . . . . . . . . . . . . . . . . . $36.49

## SUPER-X BLANK- SMOKELESS

*Available in*: 38 Special
MSRP . . . . . . . . . . . $31.00–$41.33

## SUPER- X EXPANDING POINT
*Available in*: 25 Auto
**MSRP . . . . . . . . . . . . $25.00–$37.99**

## SUPER-X HOLLOW SOFT POINT
*Available in*: 30 Carbine, 44 Rem. Mag.
**MSRP . . . . . . . . . . . . $17.00–$26.00**

## SUPER-X JACKETED SOFT POINT
*Available in*: .357 Mag.
**Box 50: . . . . . . . . . . . $18.00–$37.40**

## SUPER- X LEAD ROUND NOSE
*Available in*: 32 Short Colt, 32 S&W Long, 32 S&W, 38 Special, 38 S&W, 44 S&W Special, 45 Colt
**MSRP . . . . . . . . . . . . $18.00–$34.00**

## SUPER-X LEAD SEMI-WAD CUTTER
*Available in*: .38 Special
**MSRP . . . . . . . . . . . . $17.65–$37.87**

## SUPER-X LEAD SEMI-WAD CUTTER HP
*Available in*: .38 Special +P
**MSRP . . . . . . . . . . . . . . . $19.00**

## SUPER-X MATCH
*Available in*: .38 Special Super Match
**MSRP . . . . . . . . . . . . $36.49–$46.59**

## SUPER-SILVERTIP HOLLOW POINT
*Available in*: 10mm Auto, 32 Auto, 357 Mag., 380 Auto, 38 Super Auto +P, 38 Special +P, 38 Special, 40 S&W, 41 Rem. Mag., 44 S&W, 45 Auto, 45 Colt, 45 G.A.P., 9x23 Winchester, 9mm Luger
**MSRP . . . . . . . . . . . . $21.00–$39.17**

## SUPER-X JACKETED HOLLOW POINT
*Available in*: 500 S&W
**MSRP . . . . . . . . . . . . $39.99–$56.44**

## SUPER-X LEAD FLATNOSE
*Available in*: .45 Colt
**MSRP . . . . . . . . . . . . . . . $6.99**

## SUPREME PARTITION GOLD
*Features*: Proven partition technology, consistent, dramatic bullet expansion, deep penetration regardless of barrel length, maximum weight retention.
*Available in*: 357 Mag., 44 Rem. Mag., 454 Casull, 460 S&W Mag.
**MSRP . . . . . . . . . . . . . $14.00–$34.00**

## SUPREME PLATINUM TIP HOLLOW POINT
*Features*: Patented notched reserve taper bullet jacket, plated heavy wall jacket and two-part hollow point cavity for uniform bullet expansion, massive energy depot.
*Available in*: 41 Rem. Mag., 44 Rem. Mag., 454 Casull, 500 S&W
**MSRP . . . . . . . . . . . . . $21.00–$31.49**

## SUPREME T-SERIES
*Features*: Reverse Taper Jacket design; consistent, reliable bullet expansion through common barrier test events; excellent accuracy; positive functioning.
*Available in*: 380 Auto, 38 Special +P, 38 Special, 40 S&W, 45 Auto, 9mm Luger
**MSRP . . . . . . . . . . . . . . . . . $34.35**

## WINCLEAN
*Features*: The patented lead and heavy-metal free primers, Brass Enclosed Base bullets and clean-burning propellants not only eliminate airborne lead at the firing point, they also generate less barrel, action and shell case residue.
*Available in*: Brass Enclosed Base (357 Sig WinClean, 380 Auto, 40 S&W, 45 Auto, 45 GAP, 9mm Luger, 9mm Luger WinClean), Jacketed Soft Point (357 Mag., 38 Special)
**MSRP . . . . . . . . . . . . . $17.00–$27.25**

## SUPREME ELITE BONDED PDX1
*Features*: The new Winchester Supreme Elite Bonded PDX1, which was chosen by the FBI as their primary service round, is now available in a full line of popular handgun calibers. The Bonded PDX1 is engineered to maximize terminal ballistics, as defined by the demanding FBI test protocol, which simulates real-world threats. The new Winchester Bonded PDX is offered in 9mm, 40 Smith & Wesson, 45 automatic and .38 special.
*Available in*: .380 Auto, 38 Special +P, 40 S&W, 45 Colt, 45 Auto, 9mm Luger +P, 9mm Luger
**MSRP . . . . . . . . . . . . . $15.99–$22.99**

**rifle ammunition**

## SUPER-X FLAT POINT
*Available in*: 405 Winchester
**Box 20: . . . . . . . . . . . . . . . . . $45.99**

## SUPER-X HOLLOW POINT
*Available in*: 204 Ruger, 218 Bee, 22 Hornet, 30-30 Win.
**MSRP . . . . . . . . . . . . . $20.61–$35.00**

## SUPER-X HOLLOW SOFT POINT
*Available in*: 30 Carbine, 44 Rem. Mag.
**MSRP . . . . . . . . . . . . . $17.00–$21.00**

## SUPER-X JACKETED SOFT POINT
*Available in*: 357 Mag.
**MSRP . . . . . . . . . . . . . . . . . $37.40**

## SUPER-X JHP
*Available in*: 45-70 Gov't
**MSRP . . . . . . . . . . . . . $9.00–$17.00**

## SUPER-X LEAD
*Available in*: 32-20 Win.
**MSRP . . . . . . . . . . . . . $7.00–$18.00**

## SUPER-X POSITIVE EXPANDING POINT
*Available in*: 25-06 Rem., 25 WSSM
**MSRP . . . . . . . . . . . . . $24.00–$49.99**

## SUPER-X POWER POINT
*Available in*: 22-250 Remington, 223 Remington, 223 WSSM, 243 Winchester, 243 WSSM, 257 Roberts + P, 264 Winchester Magnum, 270 Winchester, 270 Winchester, 270 WSM, 284 Winchester, 300 Savage, 30-06 Springfield, 30-06 Springfield, 300 WSM, 300 WSM Winchester Short Mag., 30-30 Winchester, 30-30 Winchester, 30-30 Win., 303 British, 30-40 Krag, 307 Winchester, 308 Winchester, 308 Winchester, 300 Winchester Magnum, 300 Winchester Magnum, 325 Winchester Short Magnum, 32 Winchester Special, 338 Winchester Magnum, 356 Winchester, 35 Remington, 375 Winchester, 6mm Remington, 7mm-08 Remington, 7mm

# Winchester Ammunition

Mauser (7 x 57), 7mm Remington Magnum, 7mm Remington Magnum, 7mm WSM, 8mm Mauser (8 x 57
**MSRP** . . . . . . . . . . . **$22.00–$43.33**

## SUPER-X SILVERTIP
*Available in*: .250 Savage, .270 Winchester, .30-06 Springfield, .30-30 Winchester, .308 Winchester, .348 Winchester, .358 Winchester
**MSRP** . . . . . . . . . . . **$15.00–$35.00**

## SUPER- X SILVERTIP HOLLOW POINT
*Available in*: .44 Rem. Mag.
**Box 20** . . . . . . . . . . . **$17.00–$39.00**

## SUPER-X SOFT POINT
*Available in*: .22 Hornet, .25-20 Winchester, .25-35 Winchester, .38-40 Winchester, .38-55 Winchester, .44-40 Winchester, .458 Winchester, 6.5x55 Swedish, 7.62x39mm Russian
**Box 20:** . . . . . . . . . . . **$27.00–$59.00**

## SUPER-X SUPER CLEAN NT (TIN)
*Available in*: 5.56mm
**Box 50:** . . . . . . . . . . . **$5.00–$10.00**

## SUPREME ACCUBOND CT
*Features*: Fully bonded lead alloy core, high weight retention, pinpoint accuracy, boattail design, Lubalox coating/ red polymer tip
*Available in*: .25-06 Remington, .25 WSSM, .270 Winchester, .270 WSM, .30-06 Springfield, .300 Winchester Magnum, .300 WSM, .325 Winchester Short Magnum, .338 Winchester Magnum, 7mm Remington Magnum, 7mm WSM
**Box 50:** . . . . . . . . . . . **$26.00–$45.00**

## SUPREME BALLISTIC SILVERTIP
*Features*: Solid based boat tail design delivers excellent long range accuracy. In .22 calibers, the Ballistic plastic polycarbonate Silvertip bullet initiates rapid fragmentation. In medium to larger calibers special jacket contours extend range and reduce cross-wind drift. Harder lead core ensures proper bullet expansion.
*Available in*: .22-250 Rem., .223 Rem., .204 Ruger, .223 WSSM, .243 Win.,

.25-06 Rem., 25 WSSM, .270 WSM, .280 Rem., .300 Win. Mag., .30-06 Spfld., .300 WSM, .30-30 Win., .308 Win., .325 Win. Short Mag., .338 Win. Mag., 7mm Rem. Mag., 7mm-08 Rem., 7mm Rem. Mag., 7mm WSM
**MSRP** . . . . . . . . . . . **$25.00–$35.00**

## SUPREME E-TIP
*Available in*: .270 WSM, .270 Win., .30-06 Spfld., .300 WSM, .300 Win. Mag., .308 Win., 7mm Rem. Mag.
**MSRP** . . . . . . . . . . . **$37.00–$46.99**

## SUPREME NOSLER PARTITION AND NOSLER SOLID
*Available in*: .375 H&H, .416 Rigby, .416 Rem.-Mag., .458 Win. Mag.
**MSRP** . . . . . . . . . . . **$66.99–$133.00**

## SUPREME HOLLOWPOINT BOATTAIL MATCH
*Available in*: 308 Win. Match
**Box 20:** . . . . . . . . . . . **$32.25–$46.86**

## SUPREME PARTITION GOLD
*Features*: Proven partition technology, consistent, dramatic bullet expansion, deep penetration regardless of barrel length, maximum weight retention.
*Available in*: .45-70 Govt
**Box 20:** . . . . . . . . . . . **$31.99–$46.00**

## SUPREME ELITE XP3
*Features*: The new XP3 bullet starts with a 2-stage expansion design, then combines all the best-known bullet technology into one bullet. It delivers precision accuracy, awesome knock-down power, and deep penetration all in one package—and it's as effective on thin-skinned game, like deer and antelope, as it is on tough game, like elk, moose, bear, and African animals, at short and long ranges.
*Available in*: 243 Win., 270 WSM, 270 Win., 30-06 Spfld., 300 WSM, 300 Win. Mag., 308 Win., 325 WSM, 7mm Rem. Mag., 7mm WSM
**Box 20:** . . . . . . . . . . . **$39.99–$52.99**

**rimfire ammunition**

## DYNAPOINT
*Available in*: .22 LR
**MSRP** . . . . . . . . . . . **$9.99–$14.24**

## SUPREME JHP AND SUPREME V-MAX
*Available in*: .22 Win. Mag. ( JHP), 17 HMR (V-Max)
**Box 50:** . . . . . . . . . . . **$11.00–$18.00**

## SUPER-X #12 SHOT
*Available in*: .22 LR
**Box 50:** . . . . . . . . . . . **$8.40–$12.95**

## SUPER-X BLANK
*Available in*: .22 Short
**Box 50:** . . . . . . . . . . . **$6.95**

## SUPER-X FULL METAL JACKET
*Available in*: .22 Win. Mag.
**Box 50:** . . . . . . . . . . . **$8.98–$11.99**

## SUPER-X JHP
*Available in*: .17 HMR, .22 Win. Mag.
**Box 50:** . . . . . . . . . . . **$9.58–$14.99**

## SUPER-X LEAD HOLLOW POINT
*Available in*: .22 LR
**Box 50:** . . . . . . . . . . . **$8.99–$13.99**

## SUPER-X LEAD ROUND NOSE
*Available in*: .22 LR, .22 Long, .22 Short
**Box 100:** . . . . . . . . . . . **$7.49**

## SUPER-X LEAD ROUND NOSE, STANDARD VELOCITY
*Available in*: .22 LR
**Box 50:** . . . . . . . . . . . **$3.48**

## SUPER-X POWER-POINT
*Available in*: .22 LR
**Box 20:** . . . . . . . . . . . **$22.75–$33.06**

## SUPER-X POWER-POINT, LEAD HOLLOW POINT
*Available in*: .22LR
**Box 100:** . . . . . . . . . . . **$7.19**

## XPERT LEAD HOLLOW POINT
*Available in*: .22LR
**Box 500:** . . . . . . . . . . . **$17.75–$35.99**

## WILDCAT DYNAPOINT PLATED
*Available in*: .22 Win. Mag.
**Box 50:** . . . . . . . . . . . **$9.00**

# Winchester Ammunition

## WILDCAT LEAD FLAT NOSE
*Available in*: .22 WRF
**Box 50:** . . . . . . . . . . . .**$6.22–$10.13**

## WILDCAT LEAD ROUND NOSE
*Available in*: .22 LR
**Box 500:** . . . . . . . . . . . . . . .**$26.99**

**shotgun ammunition**

## AA TARGET LOADS
*Features*: The hunter's choice for a wide variety of game-bird applications, available in an exceptionally broad selection of loadings, from 12-gauge to .410 bore, with shot size options ranging from BB's all the way down to 9s—suitable for everything from quail to farm predators.
*Available in*: 12, 20, 28, .410 ga.; 2½, 2¾; shot sizes 7½, 8, 8½, 9
**Box 25:** . . . . . . . . . . . .**$8.00–$10.99**

## SUPER-TARGET LOADS
*Available in*: 12, 20 ga.; 2¾in.; Shot sizes 7, 7.5, 8
**Box 25:** . . . . . . . . . . . . . .**$5.85–$7.83**

## SUPER-X GAME AND FIELD LOADS
*Available in*: 12, 16, 20, 28, .410 ga.; 2½, 2¾, 3 in.; shot sizes 4, 5, 6, 7½, 8, 8½
**Box 25:** . . . . . . . . . . .**$13.11–$16.99**

## SUPER-X SUPER PHEASANT LOADS
*Available in*: 12, 20 Ga.; 2 ¾, 3 in.; Shot size 4, 5, 6
**Box 25:** . . . . . . . . . . .**$10.40–$15.11**

## SUPER-X SUPER PHEASANT STEEL LOADS
*Available in*: 12 Ga.; 3 in.; Shot size 4
**Box 25:** . . . . . . . . . . .**$16.72–$24.29**

## SUPER-X TRIALS AND BLANKS
*Available in*: 10, 12 Ga.; 2 ¾, 2 7/8 in.; Shot sizes (blank)
**Box 25:** . . . . . . . . . . .**$16.68–$21.42**

## SUPER-X TURKEY LOADS
*Available in*: 12 Gag.; 2 ¾, 3 in.; Shot sizes 4, 5, 6
**Box 25:** . . . . . . . . . . .**$8.00–$13.66**

## SUPER-X WATERFOWL LOADS
*Available in*: 10, 12, 20 ga.; 2¾, 3, 3½ in.; shot sizes T, BBB, BB, 1, 2, 3, 4
**Box 25:** . . . . . . . . . . .**$17.00–$23.00**

## SUPREME GAME AND FIELD LOADS
*Available in*: 12, 20 Ga.; 2 ¾, 3 in.; Shot size 4, 5, 6
**Box 25:** . . . . . . . . . . .**$28.00–$36.75**

## SUPREME TURKEY LOADS
*Available in*: 10, 12 20 ga.; 2¾, 3, 3 ½ in.; shot sizes 4, 5, 6
**Box 10:** . . . . . . . . . . . .**$9.90–$17.00**

## SUPREME ELITE XTENDED RANGE HD COYOTE
*Available in*: 12 ga.; 3 in.; shot sizes B
**Box 5:** . . . . . . . . . . . .**$12.22–$19.99**

## SUPREME ELITE XTENDED RANGE HD TURKEY
*Available in*: 12 Ga.; 2 ¾, 3, 3 ½ in.; Shot size 4, 5, 6
**Box 10:** . . . . . . . . . . .**$33.70–$41.41**

## SUPREME ELITE XTENDED RANGE HD WATERFOWL
*Available in*: 12, 20 Ga.; 2 ¾, 3, 3 ½ in.; Shot size 2, 4, B
**Box 10:** . . . . . . . . . . .**$16.00–$27.00**

## WINLITE LOW RECOIL, LOW NOISE TARGET LOADS
*Available in*: 12, 20 Ga.; 2 ¾ in.; Shot size 8
**Box 25:** . . . . . . . . . . . . . . . . . .**$9.66**

## XPERT HI-VELOCITY STEEL LOADS
*Available in*: 12, 16, 20, 28, .410 ga.; 2¾, 3, 3 ½ in.; shot sizes BB, 1, 2, 3, 4
**Box 25:** . . . . . . . . . . .**$11.58–$16.63**

## XPERT STEEL LOADS
*Available in*: 12, 20, 28, 410 Ga.; 2 ¾ in.; Shot size 6, 7
**Box 25:** . . . . . . . . . . .**$10.00–$15.00**

**shotgun ammunition (buckshot)**

## SUPER-X BUCKSHOT
*Available in*: 12, 16, 20, .410 ga.; 2½, 2¾, 3, 3 ½ in.; shot sizes 4, 3, 1, 00, 000
**Box 5:** . . . . . . . . . . . . . .**$3.00–$8.00**

## SUPREME BUCKSHOT
*Available in*: 12 Ga.; 2 ¾, 3, 3 ½ in.; Shot size 4, 00
**Box 5:** . . . . . . . . . . . .**$11.31–$15.86**

## WINLITE LOW RECOIL BUCKSHOT
*Available in*: 12 Ga.; 2 ¾
**Box 5:** . . . . . . . . . . . . . .**$4.71–$13.29**

**shotgun ammunition (slugs)**

## SUPER-X SLUGS
*Available in*: 12, 16, 20, .410 ga.; 2½, 2¾, 3 in.; 1/5, ¼, 5/8, ¾, 1 oz.
**Box 15:** . . . . . . . . . . .**$10.90–$16.02**

## SUPREME ELITE XP3 SABOT SHOTGUN SLUGS
*Available in*: 12 ga.; 2¾, 3 in.; 300 gr.
**Box 5:** . . . . . . . . . . . . .**$11.00–$15.99**

## SUPREME PLATINUM TIP HOLLOW POINT SLUGS
*Available in*: 12, 20 Ga.; 2 ¾ in.; 260Gr or 400 Gr
**Box 5:** . . . . . . . . . . . . .**$10.99–$16.99**

## SUPREME RACKMASTER RIFLED SLUGS
*Available in*: 12, 20 Ga.; 2 ¾, 3 in.; 1 1/8, 7/8 oz.
**Box 5:** . . . . . . . . . . . . . . .**$6.99–$8.99**

## SUPREME WINCHESTER SLUGS
*Available in*: 12, 20 Ga.; 2 ¾, 3 in.; 385 Gr. or 260g
**Box 5:** . . . . . . . . . . . . .**$6.00–$12.00**

## WINLITE LOW RECOIL SLUGS
*Available in*: 12 Ga.; 2 ¾ in.; 400 Gr. or 1 oz.
**Box 5:** . . . . . . . . . . . . .**$4.00–$16.99**

# muzzleloading ammunition
## Barnes Bullets

### EXPANDER MZ MUZZLELOADER BULLETS AND ALIGNERS

*Features*: Semi-spitzer ogive, boat-tail base. Six copper petals w/ double-diameter expansion. Full weight retention.
*Available in*: .45- 195gr, .50-250, 300gr., .54-275, 325gr.
**Box 24:. . . . . . . . . . . $28.86–$34.64**

### SPIT-FIRE MZ

*Features*: A streamlined semi-spitzer ogive, boattail base and tack-driving accuracy make the Barnes Spit-Fire MZ a great choice for difficult long shots. Deadly at high and low velocities. Six razor-sharp copper petals create massive shock, deep penetration, and double-diameter expansion. Retains virtually 100 percent of its original weight. Available in .50 caliber, 245- and 285-grain bullets in 15-

BARNES EXPANDER MZ

and 24-bullet packs.
*Available in*: .50 - 245 or 285gr.
**Box 24:. . . . . . . . . . . $30.44–$31.49**

### SPIT-FIRE TMZ

*Features*: Boattail, all copper with polymer tip. Expands at 1050 fps.; remains intact at extreme velocities.
*Available in*: .50- 250 or 290 gr.
**Box 24:. . . . . . . . . . . $33.59–$35.69**

# CVA

### POWERBELT COPPER

*Features*: Thin copper plating reduces bore friction while allowing for optimal bullet expansion. Available in four tip designs: Hollow Point, AeroTip, Flat Point and Steel Tip.
*Available in*: .45 caliber (175,195, 195, 225, 225, 275, 275 gr.); 50 caliber (223, 245, 295, 348, 405 gr.); .54 caliber (295, 348, 405, 444 gr.)
**MSRP. . . . . . . . . . . . . $15.00–$22.00**

### POWERBELT PLATINUM AEROTIP

*Features*: Proprietary hard plating and aggressive bullet taper design for improved ballistic coefficient. A large size fluted gas check produces higher and more consistent pressures.
*Available in*: .45 caliber (223, 300 gr.); .50 caliber (270, 300, 338 gr.)
**MSRP. . . . . . . . . . . . . $21.00–$26.99**

### POWERBELT PURE LEAD

*Features*: Pure lead, available in four different grain weights in Hollow Point and 444 in. Flat Point.
*Available in*: .50 caliber (295, 348, 405 gr.); .54 caliber (295, 348, 405 gr.)
**MSRP. . . . . . . . . . . . . $15.00–$24.99**

# Federal Fusion Ammunition

### FUSION MUZZLELOADER SLUGS

*Features*: The Fusion bullet process now is available for hunters using .50-caliber muzzleloaders. A .45-caliber slug is offered in three grain weights paired with a .50-cal crush rib

sabot. The Fusion bullet is deep penetrating, with high weight retention at 95 percent and high accuracy. In addition, the crush rib sabot reduces loading friction up to 50 percent.
*Available in*: 50 caliber in 240, 260 and 300 gr.
**MSRP. . . . . . . . . . . . . . . . . .$15.45**

FEDERAL FUSION MUZZLELOADER SLUGS

# Harvester

## SABER TOOTH BELTED BULLETS
**Features**: Copper-Clad belted bullets in Harvester Crush Rib Sabot.
**Available in**: .50 Cal in 250, 270, 300 gr.
**Box 15**:. . . . . . . . . . . . . . . . .$11.99

HARVESTER SABER TOOTH BELTED BULLETS

## SCORPION
**Features**: Electroplated copper plating does not separate from lead core. Loaded in Harvester Crush Rib Sabots.
**Available in**: Funnel Point Mag. and Polymer Ballistic Tip- .50 Caliber (240, 260, 300 Gr.); .54 caliber (240, 260, 300 gr.)
**Box 12**:. . . . . . . . . . . .$8.99–$11.49

## SCORPION PT GOLD
**Features**: Scorpion PT Gold Ballistic Tip Bullets are electroplated with copper plating that does not separate from lead core. The PT Gold offers greater accuracy at longer ranges than a hollow point. The 3% antimony makes the bullet harder than pure lead.
**Available in**: .50 Caliber- 260 and 300 grain sizes
**MSRP**. . . . . . . . . . .$11.00–$20.00
**Per box of 12 or 50**

HARVESTER SCORPION PT GOLD

# Hornady Mfg. Co.

HARVESTER GREAT PLAINS MAXI HOLLOW BASE HOLLOW POINTS

## GREAT PLAINS MAXI HOLLOW BASE, HOLLOW POINTS (HB-HP)
**Features**: Pre-scored hollow points, a short ogive and three diameter bearing surface.
**Available in**: .50 Cal in 385 gr.; 54 Cal in 425 gr.
**Box 20**:. . . . . . . . . . . . . . . . .$12.28

## HP/XTP BULLET/ SABOT
**Features**: Hornady XTP bullet/sabot combination with controlled expansion XTP bullet.
**Available in**: .45 Cal. In 200 gr.; .50 Cal in 180, 240, 300 gr.
**Box 20**:. . . . . . . . . . . .$13.37–$16.47

# Knight Rifles

## JACKETED BULLETS WITH SABOTS
**Features**: Copper jacketed, hollow point bullet with sabot.
**Available in**: .50 cal. - 260 gr.
**Box 20**:. . . . . . . . . . . . . . . . .$16.50

KNIGHT JACKETED BULLETS WITH SABOTS

## LEAD BULLETS WITH SABOTS
**Features**: Pure lead bullet with sabot.
**Available in**: .50 cal. - 310 gr.
**Box 20**:. . . . . . . . . . . . . . . . .$12.00

## RED HOT BULLETS
**Features**: Saboted Barnes solid copper bullet with superior expansion.
**Available in**: .45cal- 175, 195gr., .50cal.- 200, 250gr., .52 cal.- 275,

KNIGHT FTX BULLETS

375gr.; .54 cal.-275, 375gr.
**MSRP:** . . . . . . . . . . .$15.00–$26.00

## FTX BULLETS
**Features**: Copper bullet with patented Flex Tip Design and Sabot
**Available in**: .52 Cal- 325 gr.
**Box 18**:. . . . . . . . . . . . . . . . .$23.00

## POLYMER-TIP BOAT-TAIL BULLETS
**Features**: Sabot with all copper polymer tip bullet; expands into six razor-sharp copper petals while retaining 100% of original weight.
**Available in**: .50 Cal- 250, 290 gr.
**Box 18**:. . . . . . . . . . . . . . . . .$26.00

## SPITZER BOAT-TAIL BULLETS
**Features**: Sabot loaded with Barnes Spitzer Boat-tail bullet.
**Available in**: .50 Cal- 245, 285gr.
**Box 18**:. . . . . . . . . . . . . . . . .$23.99

# MDM

### DYNO-CORE MAGNUM MUZZLELOADING BULLETS

**Features**: The Dyno-Core Magnum uses a polymer tip and base that is surrounded by a grooved lead cylinder. Upon impact, the tip is driven back into the bullet causing tremendous expansion. This full-bore conical bullet is pre-lubricated with Dyno-Kote, a dry lube finish with no greasy, wax-based lubricants, for easy loading and quick follow-up shots.
**MSRP** . . . . . . . . . . . . **$12.00–$14.59**

### DYNO-CORE PREMIUM MUZZLELOADING BULLETS

**Features**: The Dyno-Core Premium, a non-lead muzzleloading bullet that uses dual core tungsten technology to enhance performance. Terminal ballistics resemble those found in centerfire rifle bullets. This is a saboted non-lead bullet with a copper jacket, offered in an easy-to-load Tri-Petal sabot.
**Available in**: 50 caliber, 222 grains and 285 grains
**MSRP** . . . . . . . . . . . . **$13.00–$15.00**

MDM DYNO-CORE PREMIUM

# Nosler

### BLACK POWDER PARTITION- HG SABOT

**Features**: HG Sabot with Nosler Partition jacketed hollow point bullet.
**Available in**: .50 Cal.- 250, 260, 300gr.
**MSRP** . . . . . . . . . . . . . . . . . **$13.95**

# Thompson/Center Arms

### MAGNUM EXPRESS SABOTS

**Features**: Mag. Express Sabots separate from the projectile quickly. Sabots are available preassembled with XTP bullets.
**Available in**: .50 cal- 240, 300 gr., .54 cal.- 250 gr.
**MSRP** . . . . . . . . . . . . **$15.64–$18.12**

### MAXIBALL SUPERIOR PENETRATION

**Features**: Maximum expansion on deer-size game. Lubricating grooves (maxi wide grooves).
**Available in**: .50 cal- 320, 370 gr.
**MSRP** . . . . . . . . . . . . **$16.50–$17.20**

### MAXI-HUNTER

**Features**: Maximum expansion on deer sized game. Lubricating grooves (maxi hunter multiple grooves).
**Available in**: .50 cal- 275 gr.
**MSRP** . . . . . . . . . . . . . . . . . **$16.40**

### SHOCKWAVE SABOTS

**Features**: Polymer tip spire point bullet with sabot. Incorporates harder lead core with walls interlocked with the jacket for maximum weight retention and expansion. Available with spire point or bonded bullets.
**Available in**: .50 cal- 200, 250, 300 gr., .45cal- 200 gr.
**MSRP** . . . . . . . . . . . . **$14.62–$22.64**

THOMPSON/CENTER MAXI-HUNTER

THOMPSON/CENTER SHOCKWAVE SABOTS

# Winchester

### MUZZLELOADING SUPREME PLATINUM TIP BULLETS & SABOTS

**Features**: The new Platinum Tip Hollow Point bullet includes Winchester's patented reverse taper jacket and notching technology that delivers expansion and on-target energy delivery.
**Available in**: .50 cal- 260gr., .54cal- 400gr.
**Box 30:** . . . . . . . . . . . . . . . . . **$37.49**

WINCHESTER MUZZLELOADING SUPREME PLATINUM TIP SABOT

THOMPSON/CENTER MAXIBALL SUPERIOR PENETRATION

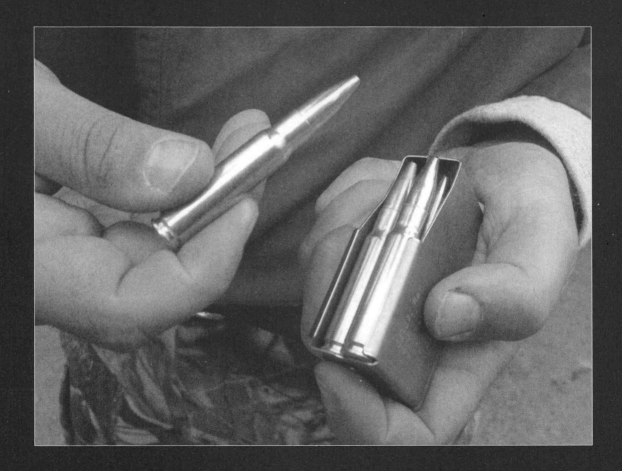

# BULLETS

## Barnes Bullets

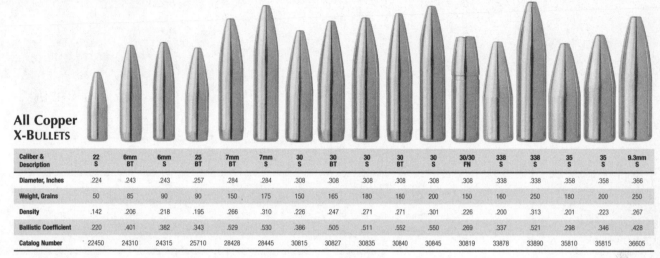

### All Copper X-Bullets

| Caliber & Description | 22 S | 6mm BT | 6mm S | 25 BT | 7mm BT | 7mm S | 30 S | 30 BT | 30 S | 30 BT | 30 S | 30/30 FN | 338 S | 338 S | 35 S | 35 S | 9.3mm S |
|---|---|---|---|---|---|---|---|---|---|---|---|---|---|---|---|---|---|
| Diameter, Inches | .224 | .243 | .243 | .257 | .284 | .284 | .308 | .308 | .308 | .308 | .308 | .308 | .338 | .338 | .358 | .358 | .366 |
| Weight, Grains | 50 | 85 | 90 | 90 | 150 | 175 | 150 | 165 | 180 | 180 | 200 | 150 | 160 | 250 | 180 | 200 | 250 |
| Density | .142 | .206 | .218 | .195 | .266 | .310 | .226 | .247 | .271 | .271 | .301 | .226 | .200 | .313 | .201 | .223 | .267 |
| Ballistic Coefficient | .220 | .401 | .382 | .343 | .529 | .530 | .386 | .505 | .511 | .552 | .550 | .269 | .337 | .521 | .298 | .346 | .428 |
| Catalog Number | 22450 | 24310 | 24315 | 25710 | 28428 | 28445 | 30815 | 30827 | 30835 | 30840 | 30845 | 30819 | 33878 | 33890 | 35810 | 35815 | 36605 |

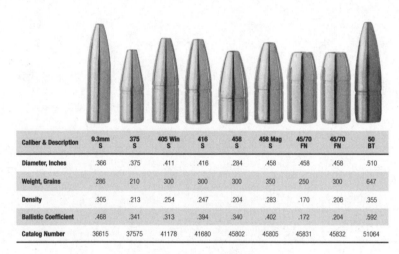

| Caliber & Description | 9.3mm S | 375 S | 405 Win S | 416 S | 458 S | 458 Mag S | 45/70 FN | 45/70 FN | 50 BT |
|---|---|---|---|---|---|---|---|---|---|
| Diameter, Inches | .366 | .375 | .411 | .416 | .284 | .458 | .458 | .458 | .510 |
| Weight, Grains | 286 | 210 | 300 | 300 | 300 | 350 | 250 | 300 | 647 |
| Density | .305 | .213 | .254 | .247 | .204 | .283 | .170 | .206 | .355 |
| Ballistic Coefficient | .468 | .341 | .313 | .394 | .340 | .402 | .172 | .204 | .592 |
| Catalog Number | 36615 | 37575 | 41178 | 41680 | 45802 | 45805 | 45831 | 45832 | 51064 |

> **LEGEND**
> **BMG** – Browning Machinegun
> **BT** – Boattail
> **FB** – Flat Base
> **FMJ** – Full Metal Jacket
> **FN** – Flat Nose
> **RN** – Round Nose
> **S** – Spitzer
> **SP** – Soft Point

**From: $27.52–$39.99**

### Triple-Shock X-Bullet

| Caliber & Description | 22 FB | 6mm BT | 25 BT | 25 FB | 6.5mm FB | 270 BT | 270 BT | 7mm BT | 7mm FB | 30 BT | 30 BT | 30 BT | 30 FB | 338 BT | 338 FB |
|---|---|---|---|---|---|---|---|---|---|---|---|---|---|---|---|
| Diameter, Inches | .224 | .243 | .257 | .257 | .264 | .277 | .277 | .284 | .308 | .308 | .308 | .308 | .308 | .338 | .338 |
| Weight, Grains | 53 | 85 | 100 | 115 | 130 | 130 | 140 | 140 | 160 | 180 | 168 | 180 | 200 | 185 | 225 |
| Density | .151 | .206 | .216 | .249 | .266 | .242 | .261 | .248 | .283 | .226 | .253 | .271 | .301 | .231 | .281 |
| Ballistic Coefficient | .231 | .333 | .420 | .429 | .479 | .466 | .497 | .5477 | .508 | .428 | .476 | .552 | .550 | .437 | .482 |
| Catalog Number | 22443 | 24341 | 25742 | 25743 | 26442 | 27742 | 27744 | 28444 | 28446 | 30841 | 30844 | 30846 | 30848 | 33843 | 33846 |

**From: $28.00–$55.00**

# Barnes Bullets

**LEGEND**
- **BMG** – Browning Machinegun
- **BT** – Boattail
- **FB** – Flat Base
- **FMJ** – Full Metal Jacket
- **FN** – Flat Nose
- **RN** – Round Nose
- **S** – Spitzer
- **SP** – Soft Point

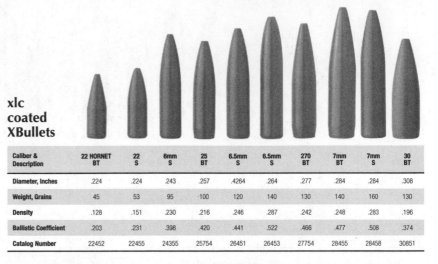

## xlc coated XBullets

| Caliber & Description | 22 HORNET BT | 22 S | 6mm S | 25 BT | 6.5mm S | 6.5mm S | 270 BT | 7mm BT | 7mm S | 30 BT |
|---|---|---|---|---|---|---|---|---|---|---|
| Diameter, Inches | .224 | .224 | .243 | .257 | .4264 | .264 | .277 | .284 | .284 | .308 |
| Weight, Grains | 45 | 53 | 95 | 100 | 120 | 140 | 130 | 140 | 160 | 130 |
| Density | .128 | .151 | .230 | .216 | .246 | .287 | .242 | .248 | .283 | .196 |
| Ballistic Coefficient | .203 | .231 | .398 | .420 | .441 | .522 | .466 | .477 | .508 | .374 |
| Catalog Number | 22452 | 22455 | 24355 | 25754 | 26451 | 26453 | 27754 | 28455 | 28458 | 30851 |

**From: $23.54–$51.45**

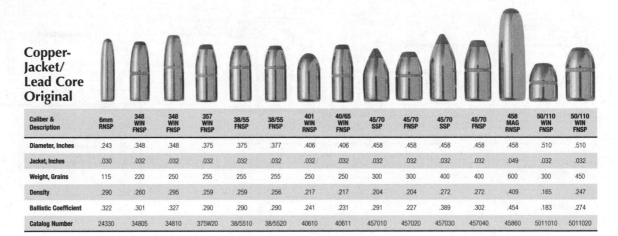

## Copper-Jacket/ Lead Core Original

| Caliber & Description | 6mm RNSP | 348 WIN FNSP | 348 WIN FNSP | 357 WIN FNSP | 38/55 FNSP | 38/55 FNSP | 401 WIN RNSP | 40/65 WIN FNSP | 45/70 SSP | 45/70 FNSP | 45/70 SSP | 45/70 FNSP | 458 MAG RNSP | 50/110 WIN FNSP | 50/110 WIN FNSP |
|---|---|---|---|---|---|---|---|---|---|---|---|---|---|---|---|
| Diameter, Inches | .243 | .348 | .348 | .375 | .375 | .377 | .406 | .406 | .458 | .458 | .458 | .458 | .458 | .510 | .510 |
| Jacket, Inches | .030 | .032 | .032 | .032 | .032 | .032 | .032 | .032 | .032 | .032 | .032 | .032 | .049 | .032 | .032 |
| Weight, Grains | 115 | 220 | 250 | 255 | 255 | 255 | 250 | 250 | 300 | 300 | 400 | 400 | 600 | 300 | 450 |
| Density | .290 | .260 | .295 | .259 | .259 | .256 | .217 | .217 | .204 | .204 | .272 | .272 | .409 | .165 | .247 |
| Ballistic Coefficient | .322 | .301 | .327 | .290 | .290 | .290 | .241 | .231 | .291 | .227 | .389 | .302 | .454 | .183 | .274 |
| Catalog Number | 24330 | 34805 | 34810 | 375W20 | 38/5510 | 38/5520 | 40610 | 40611 | 457010 | 457020 | 457030 | 457040 | 45860 | 5011010 | 5011020 |

**From: $15.07–$25.99**

## Solids

| Caliber & Description | 22 FB | 22 FB | 6mm BT | 25 BT | 7mm BT | 7mm FB | 30 FB | 30 BT | 30 FB | 338 BT | 9.3mm S | 577 NITRO FN | 50 BMG BT | 50 BMG BT | 50 BMG BT | 50 BMG BT | 600 NITRO FB |
|---|---|---|---|---|---|---|---|---|---|---|---|---|---|---|---|---|---|
| Diameter, Inches | .224 | .224 | .243 | .257 | .284 | .284 | .308 | .308 | .308 | .338 | .366 | .585 | .510 | .510 | .510 | .510 | .620 |
| Weight, Grains | 45 | 50 | 75 | 90 | 150 | 100 | 125 | 165 | 220 | 250 | 286 | 750 | 750 | 750 | 750 | 800 | 900 |
| Density | .128 | .142 | .181 | .195 | .266 | .177 | .188 | .248 | .331 | .313 | .305 | .313 | .412 | .412 | .412 | .439 | .334 |
| Ballistic Coefficient | .212 | .235 | .330 | .324 | .529 | .343 | .372 | .481 | .305 | .326 | .342 | .351 | 1.070 | — | — | 1.095 | .380 |
| Catalog Number | 22401 | 22402 | 24301 | 25720 | 28428 | 28401 | 30812 | 30822 | 30842 | 33825 | 36612 | 58520 | 510750A | 510750 | 510750T | 510800A | 62020 |

**From: $19.00–$55.99**

# Barnes Bullets

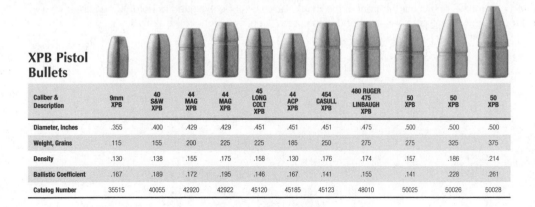

## XPB Pistol Bullets

| Caliber & Description | 9mm XPB | 40 S&W XPB | 44 MAG XPB | 44 MAG XPB | 45 LONG COLT XPB | 44 ACP XPB | 454 CASULL XPB | 480 RUGER 475 LINBAUGH XPB | 50 XPB | 50 XPB | 50 XPB |
|---|---|---|---|---|---|---|---|---|---|---|---|
| Diameter, Inches | .355 | .400 | .429 | .429 | .451 | .451 | .451 | .475 | .500 | .500 | .500 |
| Weight, Grains | 115 | 155 | 200 | 225 | 225 | 185 | 250 | 275 | 275 | 325 | 375 |
| Density | .130 | .138 | .155 | .175 | .158 | .130 | .176 | .174 | .157 | .186 | .214 |
| Ballistic Coefficient | .167 | .189 | .172 | .195 | .146 | .167 | .141 | .155 | .141 | .228 | .261 |
| Catalog Number | 35515 | 40055 | 42920 | 42922 | 45120 | 45185 | 45123 | 48010 | 50025 | 50026 | 50028 |

**LEGEND**

| | |
|---|---|
| BMG | – Browning Machinegun |
| BT | – Boattail |
| FB | – Flat Base |
| FMJ | – Full Metal Jacket |
| FN | – Flat Nose |
| RN | – Round Nose |
| S | – Spitzer |
| SP | – Soft Point |

**From: $14.00–$26.99**

# Berger Bullets

Famous for their superior performance in benchrest matches, Berger bullets also include hunting designs. From .17 to .30, all Bergers feature 14 jackets with wall concentricity tolerance of .0003. Lead cores are 99.9% pure and swaged in dies to within .0001 of round. Berger's line includes several profiles: Match, Low Drag, Very Low Drag, Length Tolerant and Maximum-Expansion, besides standard flat-base and standard boat-tail.

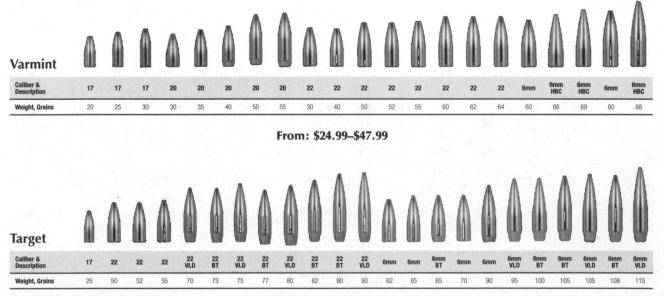

## Varmint

| Caliber & Description | 17 | 17 | 17 | 20 | 20 | 20 | 20 | 20 | 22 | 22 | 22 | 22 | 22 | 22 | 22 | 22 | 6mm | 6mm HBC | 6mm HBC | 6mm | 6mm HBC |
|---|---|---|---|---|---|---|---|---|---|---|---|---|---|---|---|---|---|---|---|---|---|
| Weight, Grains | 20 | 25 | 30 | 30 | 35 | 40 | 50 | 55 | 30 | 40 | 50 | 52 | 55 | 60 | 62 | 64 | 60 | 66 | 69 | 80 | 88 |

**From: $24.99–$47.99**

## Target

| Caliber & Description | 17 | 22 | 22 | 22 | 22 VLD | 22 BT | 22 VLD | 22 BT | 22 VLD | 22 BT | 22 BT | 22 VLD | 6mm | 6mm | 6mm BT | 6mm | 6mm | 6mm VLD | 6mm BT | 6mm BT | 6mm VLD | 6mm BT | 6mm VLD |
|---|---|---|---|---|---|---|---|---|---|---|---|---|---|---|---|---|---|---|---|---|---|---|---|
| Weight, Grains | 25 | 50 | 52 | 55 | 70 | 73 | 75 | 77 | 80 | 82 | 90 | 90 | 62 | 65 | 65 | 70 | 90 | 95 | 100 | 105 | 105 | 108 | 115 |

**From: $32.22–$50.99**

# Hornady Bullets

The 200-grain .40 and 250- and 300-grain .45 bullets are meant for use in sabot sleeves. They feature a jacketed lead core with the signature red polymer tip. The SST has led also to Hornady's newest big game bullet, the Interbond. Essentially, it's an SST with a thicker jacket that has an inner "expansion control ring" near the front of the shank. Jacket and core are also bonded to ensure deep penetration and high weight retention. Though it typically opens to double its initial diameter, the Interbond bullet can be expected to hold 90 percent of its weight in the animal.

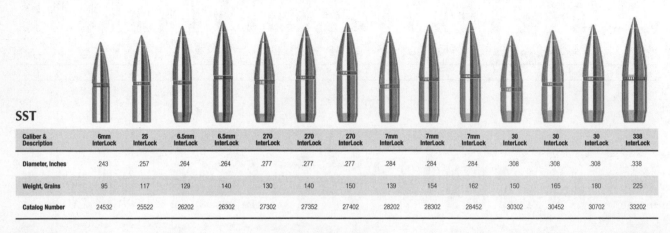

## InterBond

| Caliber & Description | 270 | 7mm | 7mm | 30 | 3 0 | 30 | 338 | 375 RN | 416 RN | 45 RN |
|---|---|---|---|---|---|---|---|---|---|---|
| Diameter, Inches | .277 | .284 | .284 | .308 | .308 | .308 | .338 | .375 | .416 | .458 |
| Weight, Grains | 130 | 139 | 154 | 150 | 165 | 180 | 225 | 300 | 400 | 500 |
| Catalog Number | 27309 | 28209 | 28309 | 30309 | 30459 | 30709 | 33209 | 37209 | 41659 | 45049 |

**From: $46.93–$63.48**

**LEGEND**
BT – Boattail
HBC – High Ballistic Coefficient
VLD – Very Low Drag

## SST

| Caliber & Description | 6mm InterLock | 25 InterLock | 6.5mm InterLock | 6.5mm InterLock | 270 InterLock | 270 InterLock | 270 InterLock | 7mm InterLock | 7mm InterLock | 7mm InterLock | 30 InterLock | 30 InterLock | 30 InterLock | 338 InterLock |
|---|---|---|---|---|---|---|---|---|---|---|---|---|---|---|
| Diameter, Inches | .243 | .257 | .264 | .264 | .277 | .277 | .277 | .284 | .284 | .284 | .308 | .308 | .308 | .338 |
| Weight, Grains | 95 | 117 | 129 | 140 | 130 | 140 | 150 | 139 | 154 | 162 | 150 | 165 | 180 | 225 |
| Catalog Number | 24532 | 25522 | 26202 | 26302 | 27302 | 27352 | 27402 | 28202 | 28302 | 28452 | 30302 | 30452 | 30702 | 33202 |

**From: $33.33–$52.13**

HANDLOADING

# Hornady Bullets

## V-Max

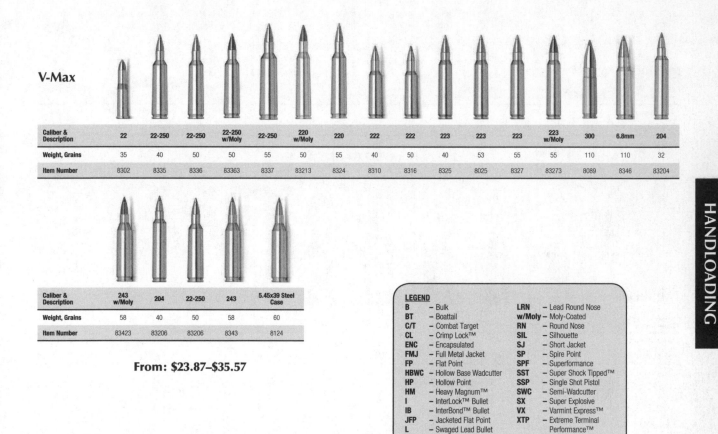

| Caliber & Description | 22 | 22-250 | 22-250 | 22-250 w/Moly | 22-250 | 220 w/Moly | 220 | 222 | 222 | 223 | 223 | 223 | 223 w/Moly | 300 | 6.8mm | 204 |
|---|---|---|---|---|---|---|---|---|---|---|---|---|---|---|---|---|
| Weight, Grains | 35 | 40 | 50 | 50 | 55 | 50 | 55 | 40 | 50 | 40 | 53 | 55 | 55 | 110 | 110 | 32 |
| Item Number | 8302 | 8335 | 8336 | 83363 | 8337 | 83213 | 8324 | 8310 | 8316 | 8325 | 8025 | 8327 | 83273 | 8089 | 8346 | 83204 |

| Caliber & Description | 243 w/Moly | 204 | 22-250 | 243 | 5.45x39 Steel Case |
|---|---|---|---|---|---|
| Weight, Grains | 58 | 40 | 50 | 58 | 60 |
| Item Number | 83423 | 83206 | 83206 | 8343 | 8124 |

**From: $23.87–$35.57**

## Traditional Varmint

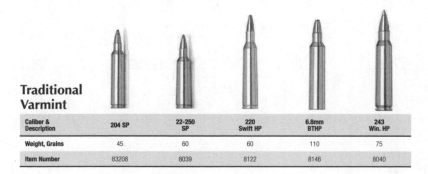

| Caliber & Description | 204 SP | 22-250 SP | 220 Swift HP | 6.8mm BTHP | 243 Win. HP |
|---|---|---|---|---|---|
| Weight, Grains | 45 | 60 | 60 | 110 | 75 |
| Item Number | 83208 | 8039 | 8122 | 8146 | 8040 |

**From: $25.01–$33.00**

# Hornady Bullets

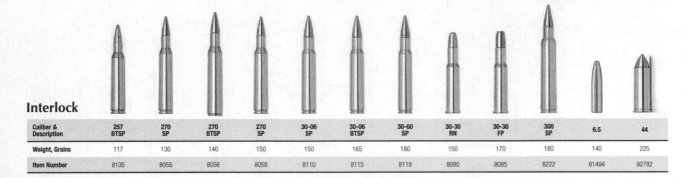

## Interlock

| Caliber & Description | 257 BTSP | 270 SP | 270 BTSP | 270 SP | 30-06 SP | 30-06 BTSP | 30-60 SP | 30-30 RN | 30-30 FP | 300 SP | 6.5 | 44 |
|---|---|---|---|---|---|---|---|---|---|---|---|---|
| Weight, Grains | 117 | 130 | 140 | 150 | 150 | 165 | 180 | 150 | 170 | 180 | 140 | 225 |
| Item Number | 8135 | 8055 | 8056 | 8058 | 8110 | 8115 | 8118 | 8080 | 8085 | 8222 | 81494 | 92782 |

**From: $27.37–$57.24**

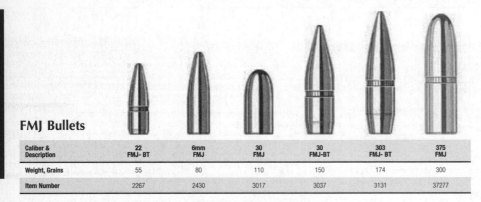

## FMJ Bullets

| Caliber & Description | 22 FMJ-BT | 6mm FMJ | 30 FMJ | 30 FMJ-BT | 303 FMJ-BT | 375 FMJ |
|---|---|---|---|---|---|---|
| Weight, Grains | 55 | 80 | 110 | 150 | 174 | 300 |
| Item Number | 2267 | 2430 | 3017 | 3037 | 3131 | 37277 |

**From: $18.71–$36.37**

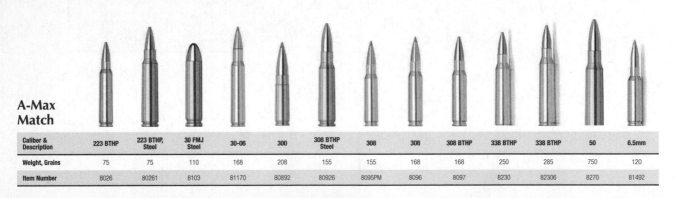

## A-Max Match

| Caliber & Description | 223 BTHP | 223 BTHP, Steel | 30 FMJ Steel | 30-06 | 300 | 308 BTHP Steel | 308 | 308 | 308 BTHP | 338 BTHP | 338 BTHP | 50 | 6.5mm |
|---|---|---|---|---|---|---|---|---|---|---|---|---|---|
| Weight, Grains | 75 | 75 | 110 | 168 | 208 | 155 | 155 | 168 | 168 | 250 | 285 | 750 | 120 |
| Item Number | 8026 | 80261 | 8103 | 81170 | 80892 | 80926 | 8095PM | 8096 | 8097 | 8230 | 82306 | 8270 | 81492 |

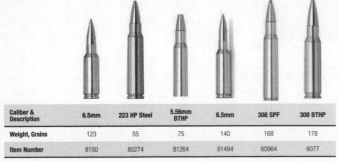
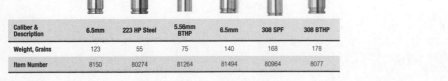

| Caliber & Description | 6.5mm | 223 HP Steel | 5.56mm BTHP | 6.5 | 308 SPF | 308 BTHP |
|---|---|---|---|---|---|---|
| Weight, Grains | 123 | 55 | 75 | 140 | 168 | 178 |
| Item Number | 8150 | 80274 | 81264 | 81494 | 80964 | 8077 |

**From: $24.52–$111.67**

# Hornady Bullets

## Handgun Bullets

### XTP Bullets

| Caliber & Description | 30 RN | 30 HP | 32 HP | 32 HP | 32 HP | 9mm HP | 9mm HP | 38 HP | 9mm HP | 38 FP | 9mm HP | 38 HP | 38 HP | 38 FP | 38 HP | 38 HP |
|---|---|---|---|---|---|---|---|---|---|---|---|---|---|---|---|---|
| Diameter, Inches | 0.308 | 0.309 | 0.312 | 0.312 | 0.312 | 0.355 | 0.355 | 0.357 | 0.355 | 0.357 | 0.355 | 0.357 | 0.357 | 0.357 | 0.357 | 0.357 |
| Weight, Grains | 86 | 90 | 60 | 85 | 100 | 90 | 115 | 110 | 124 | 125 | 147 | 125 | 140 | 158 | 158 | 180 |
| Item Number | 3100 | 31000 | 32010 | 32050 | 32070 | 35500 | 35540 | 35700 | 35571 | 35730 | 35580 | 35710 | 35740 | 35780 | 35750 | 35771 |

| Caliber & Description | 9x18mm HP | 10mm HP | 10mm HP | 10mm HP | 41 HP | 44 HP | 44 HP | 44 CL-SIL | 44 HP | 44 HP | 45 HP | 45 HP | 45 HP | 45 | 45 HP | 45 HP |
|---|---|---|---|---|---|---|---|---|---|---|---|---|---|---|---|---|
| Diameter, Inches | 0.365 | 0.400 | 0.400 | 0.400 | 0.410 | 0.430 | 0.430 | 0.430 | 0.430 | 0.300 | 0.451 | 0.451 | 0.451 | 0.452 | 0.452 | 0.452 |
| Weight, Grains | 95 | 155 | 180 | 200 | 210 | 180 | 200 | 240 | 240 | 300 | 185 | 200 | 230 | 240 | 250 | 300 |
| Item Number | 36500 | 40000 | 40040 | 40060 | 41000 | 44050 | 44100 | 4425 | 44200 | 44280 | 45100 | 45140 | 45160 | 45220 | 45200 | 45230 |

| Caliber & Description | 45 | 475 MAG | 475 | 50 | 500 MAG | 500 FP |
|---|---|---|---|---|---|---|
| Diameter, Inches | 0.452 | 0.475 | 0.475 | 0.500 | 0.500 | 0.500 |
| Weight, Grains | 300 | 325 | 400 | 300 | 350 | 500 |
| Item Number | 45235 | 47500 | 47550 | 50101 | 50100 | 50105 |

**From: $20.11–$55.95**

### FMJ Bullets

| Caliber & Description | 9mm FMJ-RN | 9mm FMJ-RN | 10mm FMJ-FP | 45 C SWC | 45 FMJ-RN | 45 FMJ-FP | 45 FMJ-RN |
|---|---|---|---|---|---|---|---|
| Diameter Inches | 0.355 | 0.355 | 0.400 | 0.451 | 0.451 | 0.451 | 0.451 |
| Weight, Grains | 115 | 124 | 180 | 185 | 230 | 230 | 230 |
| Item Number | 35557 | 355771 | 400471 | 45137 | 45177 | 451871 | 451771 |

**From: $21.73–$128.80**

# Hornady Bullets

## HAP Bullets

| Caliber & Description | 9mm HAP | 9mm HAP | 9mm HAP | 10mm HAP | 10mm HAP | 45 HAP | 45 HAP | 44 Mag JSP |
|---|---|---|---|---|---|---|---|---|
| Diameter, Inches | 0.356 | 0.356 | 0.356 | 0.400 | 0.400 | 0.451 | 0.451 | 0.429 |
| Weight, Grains | 125 | 121 | 125 | 180 | 180 | 230 | 230 | 186 |
| Item Number | 355721 | 35530B | 35572B | 400421 | 40042B | 451611 | 45161B | |

**From: $96.08–$540.00**

## Frontier/Lead Bullets

| Caliber & Description | 32 HBWC | 32 SWC | 38 | 38 HBWC | 38 LRN | 38 SWC | 38 SWC HP | 44 Cowboy | 44 Cowboy |
|---|---|---|---|---|---|---|---|---|---|
| Diameter, Inches | 0.314 | 0.314 | 0.358 | 0.358 | 0.358 | 0.358 | 0.358 | 0.427 | 0.430 |
| Weight, Grains | 90 | 90 | 140 | 148 | 158 | 158 | 158 | 205 | 180 |
| Item Number | 10028 | 10008 | 10078 | 10208 | 10508 | 10408 | 10428 | 11208 | 11058 |

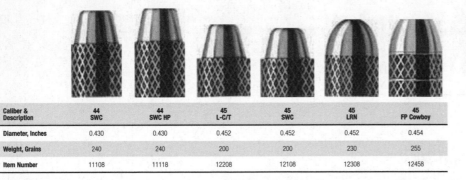

| Caliber & Description | 44 SWC | 44 SWC HP | 45 L-C/T | 45 SWC | 45 LRN | 45 FP Cowboy |
|---|---|---|---|---|---|---|
| Diameter, Inches | 0.430 | 0.430 | 0.452 | 0.452 | 0.452 | 0.454 |
| Weight, Grains | 240 | 240 | 200 | 200 | 230 | 255 |
| Item Number | 11108 | 11118 | 12208 | 12108 | 12308 | 12458 |

**From: $31.31–$49.48**

---

**LEGEND**

| | | | |
|---|---|---|---|
| B | – Bulk | LRN | – Lead Round Nose |
| BT | – Boattail | w/Moly | – Moly-Coated |
| C/T | – Combat Target | RN | – Round Nose |
| CL | – Crimp Lock™ | SIL | – Silhouette |
| ENC | – Encapsulated | SJ | – Short Jacket |
| FMJ | – Full Metal Jacket | SP | – Spire Point |
| FP | – Flat Point | SST | – Super Shock Tipped™ |
| HBWC | – Hollow Base Wadcutter | SSP | – Single Shot Pistol |
| HP | – Hollow Point | SWC | – Semi-Wadcutter |
| HM | – Heavy Magnum™ | SX | – Super Explosive |
| I | – InterLock™ Bullet | VX | – Varmint Express™ |
| IB | – InterBond™ Bullet | XTP | – Extreme Terminal Performance™ |
| JFP | – Jacketed Flat Point | | |
| L | – Swaged Lead Bullet | +P | – Plus Pressure |
| LM | – Light Magnum™ | | |

# Lapua Bullets

Lapua precision bullets are made from the best raw materials and meet the toughest precision specifications. Each bullet is subject to visual inspection and tested with advanced measurement devices.

### D46
The D46 bullet is manufactured to the strictest tolerances for concentricity, uniformity of shape and weight. It has shot its way to the record books since the 1930's all the way to the 21st century.
**From: $41.00–$45.49**

### D166
The Lapua's unique D166 construction has remained the same since the late 1930s: Superb accurate FMJBT bullet for 7.62mm (.311) cartridges.
**From: $45.49**

### FMJ SPITZER
Whether you require bullets for training, competitions or serious hunting situations you can really trust the performance of Lapua's FMJ bullet family. Ten rounds loaded with Lapua's .30 S374 8.0/123gr FMJ bullet from 100m can easily achieve groupings less than 30mm. Reliability means that every shot you fire will hit the target.
**From: $39.99–$90.99**

### HOLLOW POINT
This HPCE bullet cuts a clean and easily distinguishable hole in your target. With ten rounds (G477 in .308 Win.) fired at 100 meters, this bullet typically achieves groupings of under 25mm- sometimes even less than 15mm.
**From: $32.49–$118.00**

### LOCK BASE
A distinctive Full Metal Jacket Boat Tail bullet that has many applications, from sport shooting to battlefield. Streamlined ballistic shape combined with patented base design.
**From: $37.00–$64.99**

### MEGA
The Lapua Mega is for hunting big game. This bullet is at its best in the field and typically more than duplicates on impact, causing an immediate shock effect in your quarry. The Mega is a soft point bullet with a protective copper jacket – traditional hunting performance. This ensures that the bullet's lead alloy core remains intact when shooting through brush or branch. The mechanical bonding locks the lead alloy in place, allowing the bullet to achieve up to 97% weight retention. The Mega product family covers the most popular calibers in Scandinavia including 9 products.
**From: $40.99–$48.49**

### SCENAR
The first choice for serious target competition. Lapua Scenar hollow point boat tail bullets have given superb results at long ranges and bench rest shooting. The Scenar bullets have the IBS World Record in 600 yard Heavy Gun 5-shot group (0.404") and also hold the official world ISSF record of 600 out of 600 possible, an unbeatable score. All Scenar bullets are also available in Coated Silver Jacket version.
**From: $39.00–$118.00**

LAPUA D46

LAPUA D166

LAPUA FMJ S

LAPUA HOLLOW POINT

LAPUA LOCK BASE

LAPUA MEGA

LAPUA SCENAR

## 7MM-CALIBER 120 GR. SPITZER BALLISTIC TIP

Nosler has added the 7mm-caliber, 120-grain Ballistic Tip to its lineup for deer, sheep, and antelope hunters. The more you hunt, the more you start to realize how unpredictable and unforgiving nature can be. This is why Nosler engineered the Ballistic Tip Hunting bullet to be very predictable and extremely forgiving. It all starts with the Nosler Ballistic Tip. The tip is made from polymer and is color coded by caliber. It is designed to resist deformation in the magazine and initiate expansion upon impact. The fully tapered jacket allows for a controlled expansion. The special lead alloy core that has made Nosler Ballistic Tip famous adds to the terminal performance as it is dispersed into the target. The net result is 50–60% weight retention and full terminal performance. The final features of the Nosler Ballistic Tip are the heavy jacketed base that acts as a platform for a large diameter mushroom coupled with the Nosler Solid Base. The Solid Base allows the bullet to withstand ultra velocities while the boat tail design combined with the polymer tip allows for extreme long range accuracy and easier loading for the hand loader.
**MSRP:** . . . . . . . . . . . **Box 50: $21.00**

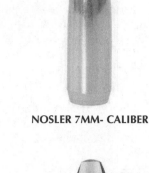

**NOSLER 7MM- CALIBER**

## .458 PARITION

Nosler now offers the largest Parition bullet to date. Designed for .458 Winchester Magnum and .460 Weatherby Magnum, the .458 partition is ideal for dangerous game like Cape buffalo. It provides excellent accuracy, controlled expansion and weight retention. When the front lead is released it causes tissue damage by fragmentation, while the mushroomed bullet penetrates enough to exit the animal or stop under the skin on the off-side hide.
**MSRP:** . . . . . . . . . . . **Box 25: $80.60**

**NOSLER .458**

## E-TIP 6.8MM- 85GR. SPITZER

New to the line up is the 6.8mm, 85 grain Spitzer. The Nosler E-Tip is a lead-free bullet built on a highly concentric gliding metal frame. The polycarbonate tip prevents deformation in the magazine, boosts aerodynamic efficiency, and initiates expansion. Nosler's exclusive Energy Expansion Cavity allows for immediate and uniform expansion yet retains 95%+ weight for improved penetration. E-Tip also features a precisely formed boat tail that serves to reduce drag and provides a more efficient flight profile for higher retained energy at long range. The E-Tip's alloy provides less fouling.
**MSRP:** . . . . . . . . . . . **Box 50: $31.00**

**NOSLER E-TIP**

## SOLIDS

Nosler Solid Bullets feature a unique design and homogenous lead-free alloy construction to provide an impressively straight wound channel. Engineered with multiple seating grooves, Solids provide optimal load versatility with minimal fouling. Nosler Solids are designed to match the ballistic performance of the Nosler Partition bullets in the same caliber and weight, resulting in near identical points of impact for both bullets at typical hunting ranges. For dangerous game, hunters can use a Partition load on the first shot, followed by Solids and have confidence in shot placement and bullet performance. Available in the following calibers: 9.3mm, .375, .30.416, .458, 470 NE.
**MSRP:** . . . . . .**Box 25: $39.95–$84.00**

**NOSLER SOLIDS**

# Nosler Bullets

## Custom Competition

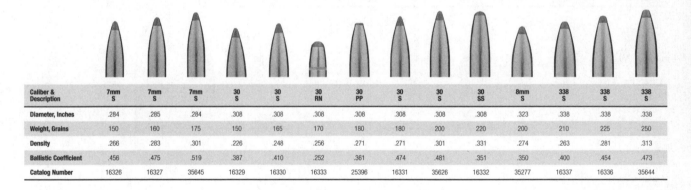

| Caliber & Description | 22 HPBT | 22 HPBT | 22 HPBT | 22 HPBT | 6mm HPBT | 6mm HPBT | 6.5mm HPBT | 6.8mm HPBT | 30 HPBT | 30 HPBT | 30 HPBT | 30 HPBT | 8mm HPBT | 45 JHP |
|---|---|---|---|---|---|---|---|---|---|---|---|---|---|---|
| Diameter, Inches | .220 | .224 | .224 | .224 | 0.243 | 0.243 | .264 | .277 | .308 | .308 | 0.308 | 0.308 | 0.323 | .451 |
| Weight, Grains | 52 | 69 | 77 | 80 | 105 | 107 | 140 | 115 | 155 | 168 | 175 | 190 | 200 | 185 |
| Density | .148 | .196 | .219 | .228 | 0.254 | 0.259 | .287 | .214 | 233 | .253 | 0.264 | 0.286 | 0.274 | .130 |
| Ballistic Coefficient | .220 | .305 | .340 | .415 | 0.517 | 0.525 | .529 | .375 | .450 | .462 | 0.505 | 0.53 | 0.52 | .142 |
| Catalog Number | 53294 | 17101 53065 | 22421 53064 | 25116 53080 | 53614 | 49742 | 26725 | 45357 | 53155 53169 | 53164 53168 | 53952 | 53412 | 49524 | 44847 |

**Box 100: $24.00–$39.00**

## Partition

| Caliber & Description | 22 S | 6mm S | 6mm S | 6mm S | 25 S | 25 S | 25 S | 6.5mm S | 6.5mm S | 6.5mm S | 270 S | 270 S | 270 S | 270 SS |
|---|---|---|---|---|---|---|---|---|---|---|---|---|---|---|
| Diameter, Inches | .220 | .243 | .243 | .243 | .257 | .257 | .257 | .264 | .264 | .264 | .277 | .277 | .277 | .277 |
| Weight, Grains | 60 | 85 | 95 | 100 | 100 | 115 | 20 | 100 | 125 | 140 | 130 | 140 | 150 | 160 |
| Density | .171 | .206 | .230 | .242 | .216 | .249 | .260 | .205 | .256 | .287 | .242 | .261 | .279 | .298 |
| Ballistic Coefficient | .228 | .315 | .365 | .384 | .377 | .389 | .391 | .326 | .449 | .490 | .416 | .432 | .465 | .434 |
| Catalog Number | 16316 | 16314 | 16315 | 35642 | 16317 | 16318 | 35643 | 16319 | 16320 | 16321 | 16322 | 35200 | 16323 | 16324 |

| Caliber & Description | 7mm S | 7mm S | 7mm S | 30 S | 30 S | 30 RN | 30 PP | 30 S | 30 S | 30 SS | 8mm S | 338 S | 338 S | 338 S |
|---|---|---|---|---|---|---|---|---|---|---|---|---|---|---|
| Diameter, Inches | .284 | .285 | .284 | .308 | .308 | .308 | .308 | .308 | .308 | .308 | .323 | .338 | .338 | .338 |
| Weight, Grains | 150 | 160 | 175 | 150 | 165 | 170 | 180 | 180 | 200 | 220 | 200 | 210 | 225 | 250 |
| Density | .266 | .283 | .301 | .226 | .248 | .256 | .271 | .271 | .301 | .331 | .274 | .263 | .281 | .313 |
| Ballistic Coefficient | .456 | .475 | .519 | .387 | .410 | .252 | .361 | .474 | .481 | .351 | .350 | .400 | .454 | .473 |
| Catalog Number | 16326 | 16327 | 35645 | 16329 | 16330 | 16333 | 25396 | 16331 | 35626 | 16332 | 35277 | 16337 | 16336 | 35644 |

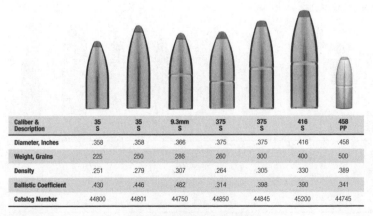

| Caliber & Description | 35 S | 35 S | 9.3mm S | 375 S | 375 S | 416 S | 458 PP |
|---|---|---|---|---|---|---|---|
| Diameter, Inches | .358 | .358 | .366 | .375 | .375 | .416 | .458 |
| Weight, Grains | 225 | 250 | 286 | 260 | 300 | 400 | 500 |
| Density | .251 | .279 | .307 | .264 | .305 | .330 | .389 |
| Ballistic Coefficient | .430 | .446 | .482 | .314 | .398 | .390 | .341 |
| Catalog Number | 44800 | 44801 | 44750 | 44850 | 44845 | 45200 | 44745 |

**Box 50: $29.00–$80.60**

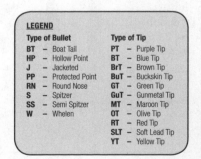

**LEGEND**

| Type of Bullet | | Type of Tip | |
|---|---|---|---|
| BT | – Boat Tail | PT | – Purple Tip |
| HP | – Hollow Point | BT | – Blue Tip |
| J | – Jacketed | BrT | – Brown Tip |
| PP | – Protected Point | BuT | – Buckskin Tip |
| RN | – Round Nose | GT | – Green Tip |
| S | – Spitzer | GuT | – Gunmetal Tip |
| SS | – Semi Spitzer | MT | – Maroon Tip |
| W | – Whelen | OT | – Olive Tip |
| | | RT | – Red Tip |
| | | SLT | – Soft Lead Tip |
| | | YT | – Yellow Tip |

## Ballistic Tip Hunting

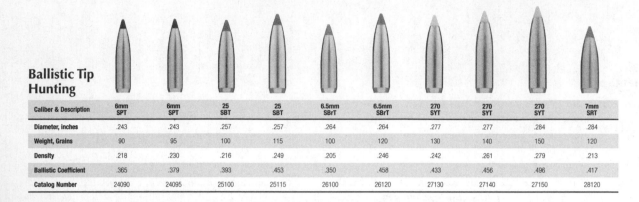

| Caliber & Description | 6mm SPT | 6mm SPT | 25 SBT | 25 SBT | 6.5mm SBrT | 6.5mm SBrT | 270 SYT | 270 SYT | 270 SYT | 7mm SRT |
|---|---|---|---|---|---|---|---|---|---|---|
| Diameter, inches | .243 | .243 | .257 | .257 | .264 | .264 | .277 | .277 | .284 | .284 |
| Weight, Grains | 90 | 95 | 100 | 115 | 100 | 120 | 130 | 140 | 150 | 120 |
| Density | .218 | .230 | .216 | .249 | .205 | .246 | .242 | .261 | .279 | .213 |
| Ballistic Coefficient | .365 | .379 | .393 | .453 | .350 | .458 | .433 | .456 | .496 | .417 |
| Catalog Number | 24090 | 24095 | 25100 | 25115 | 26100 | 26120 | 27130 | 27140 | 27150 | 28120 |

| Caliber & Description | 7mm SRT | 7mm SRT | 30 SRT | 30 SRT | 30 SRT | 30 SRT | 8mm SGuT |
|---|---|---|---|---|---|---|---|
| Diameter, inches | .284 | .284 | .308 | .308 | .308 | .308 | .323 |
| Weight, Grains | 140 | 150 | 125 | 150 | 165 | 180 | 180 |
| .248 | .248 | .266 | .188 | .226 | .248 | .271 | .247 |
| Ballistic Coefficient | .485 | .493 | .366 | .435 | .475 | .507 | .357 |
| Catalog Number | 28140 | 28150 | 30125 | 30150 | 30165 | 30180 | 32180 |

**Box 50: $19.00–$25.00**

## Ballistic Tip Varmint

| Caliber & Description | 204 | 204 | 22 SOT | 22 SOT | 22 SOT | 22 SOT | 22 SOT | 6mm SPT | 6mm SPT | 6mm SPT | 25 SBT |
|---|---|---|---|---|---|---|---|---|---|---|---|
| Diameter, inches | .204 | .204 | .224 | .224 | .227 | .224 | .224 | .243 | .243 | .243 | .257 |
| Weight, Grains | 32 | 40 | 40 | 40 | 45 | 50 | 55 | 55 | 70 | 80 | 85 |
| Density | .110 | .137 | .137 | .114 | .128 | .142 | .157 | .133 | .169 | .194 | .183 |
| Ballistic Coefficient | .206 | .239 | .239 | .221 | .144 | .238 | .267 | .276 | .31o | .329 | .329 |
| Catalog Number | 35216 | 52111 | 52111 | 39510 39555 | 35487 | 39522 39557 | 39526 39560 | 24055 39565 | 39532 39570 | 24080 | 43004 |

**Box 100: $24.00–$58.00**

## CT Ballistic Silvertip Hunting

| Caliber & Description | 6mm S | 25 S | 25 S | 270 S | 270 S | 7mm S | 7mm S | 30 S | 30 RN | 30 S | 30 S | 8mm S | 338 S |
|---|---|---|---|---|---|---|---|---|---|---|---|---|---|
| Diameter, inches | .243 | .257 | .257 | .277 | .277 | .284 | .284 | .308 | 0.308 | .308 | .308 | 0.323 | .338 |
| Weight, Grains | 95 | 85 | 115 | 130 | 150 | 140 | 150 | 150 | 150 | 168 | 180 | 180 | 200 |
| Density | .230 | .183 | .249 | .242 | .279 | .248 | .266 | .226 | 0.226 | .253 | .271 | 0.247 | .250 |
| Ballistic Coefficient | .379 | .329 | .453 | .433 | .496 | .485 | .493 | .435 | 0.232 | .490 | .507 | 0.394 | .414 |
| Catalog Number | 51040 | 51045 | 51050 | 51075 | 51100 | 51105 | 51110 | 51150 | 51165 | 51160 | 51170 | 51693 | 51200 |

**Box 50: $25.00–$30.00**

# Nosler Bullets

## Accubond

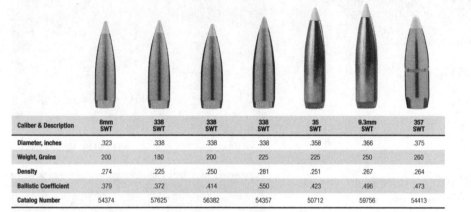

| Caliber & Description | 6mm S | 25 SWT | 6.5mm SWT | 6.5mm | 270 SWT | 270 SWT | 7mm SWT | 7mm SWT | 30 SWT | 30 SWT | 30 SWT | 30 SWT |
|---|---|---|---|---|---|---|---|---|---|---|---|---|
| Diameter, inches | 0.243 | .257 | .264 | | .277 | .277 | .284 | .284 | .308 | .308 | .308 | .308 |
| Weight, Grains | 90 | 110 | 130 | 140 | 130 | 140 | 140 | 160 | 150 | 165 | 180 | 200 |
| Density | 0.218 | .238 | .266 | | .242 | .261 | .248 | .283 | .226 | .248 | .271 | .301 |
| Ballistic Coefficient | 0.376 | .418 | .488 | | .435 | .496 | .485 | .531 | .435 | .475 | .507 | .588 |
| Catalog Number | 56357 | 53742 | 56902 | | 54987 | 54765 | 59992 | 54932 | 56719 | 55602 | 54825 | 54618 |

| Caliber & Description | 8mm SWT | 338 SWT | 338 SWT | 338 SWT | 35 SWT | 9.3mm SWT | 357 SWT |
|---|---|---|---|---|---|---|---|
| Diameter, inches | .323 | .338 | .338 | .338 | .358 | .366 | .375 |
| Weight, Grains | 200 | 180 | 200 | 225 | 225 | 250 | 260 |
| Density | .274 | .225 | .250 | .281 | .251 | .267 | .264 |
| Ballistic Coefficient | .379 | .372 | .414 | .550 | .423 | .496 | .473 |
| Catalog Number | 54374 | 57625 | 56382 | 54357 | 50712 | 59756 | 54413 |

**Box 50: $29.00–$56.00**

## Sporting handgun

| Caliber & Description | 38 JHP | 41 JHP | 44 JHP | 44 JHP | 44 JHP | 44 JHP | 45 Colt JHP |
|---|---|---|---|---|---|---|---|
| Diameter, Inches | .357 | .410 | .429 | .429 | .429 | .429 | .451 |
| Weight, Grains | 158 | 210 | 200 | 240 | 240 | 300 | 250 |
| Density | .177 | .178 | .155 | .186 | .186 | .233 | .176 |
| Ballistic Coefficient | .182 | .170 | .151 | .173 | .177 | .206 | .177 |
| Catalog Number | 44841 | 43012 | 44846 | 44842 | 44868 | 42069 | 43013 |

**Box 250: $47.00–$60.00**

# Sierra Bullets

## 7MM- 180 GR. HPBT MATCHKING

Sierra now offers a 7mm 180 grain HPBT MatchKing bullet. In response to requests from top level F-Class shooters, Sierra has designed an all new MatchKing to provide a higher weight/higher B.C. alternative in our 7mm line. This bullet's 12 caliber secant ogive and lengthened boat tail make it the perfect choice for the discerning 7mm long range shooter. Sierra recommends at least a 1 in 8 inch twist barrel to stabilize this bullet.
**Box 100: $40.01; Box 500: $197.87**

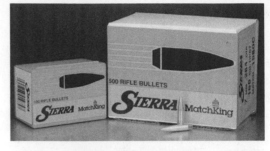

**SIERRA 7MM MATCHKING**

## .25 CAL.- 70GR. AND 90GR. BLITZKING

Sierra presents its 2 newest members of their BlitzKing line; the 25 caliber 70 (flat base) & 90 (boat tail) grain BlitzKing bullets. Created to fill the demand for the longer range varmint crowd taking over where our current .20-6mm BlitzKings leave off. These bullets will be available in boxes of 100 bullets and 500 bullets.
**Box 100: $28.46–$29.36; Box 500: $140.93–$173.43**

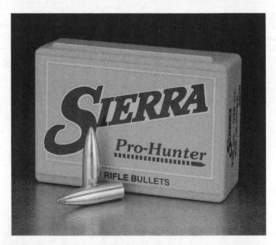

**SIERRA .25 CAL.- 70GR. AND 90GR. BLITZKING**

## .338 CALIBER- 225GR. SPT PRO-HUNTER

Sierra is pleased to introduce the newest member of their Pro-Hunter line; the .338 caliber 225 grain SPT Pro-Hunter. The flat based design and lighter weight of this projectile make it a great choice for medium & large game. Combine that with Sierra's world-renowned accuracy, and you have a perfect choice for those hunters seeking a reduced recoil alternative where a heavier bullet is not required.
**Box 50: $24.62**

**SIERRA .338 CALIBER- 225GR. SPT PRO-HUNTER**

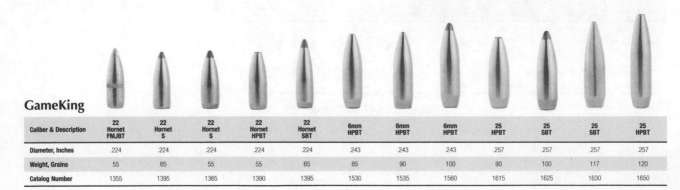

### GameKing

| Caliber & Description | 22 Hornet FMJBT | 22 Hornet S | 22 Hornet S | 22 Hornet HPBT | 22 Hornet SBT | 6mm HPBT | 6mm HPBT | 6mm HPBT | 25 HPBT | 25 SBT | 25 SBT | 25 HPBT |
|---|---|---|---|---|---|---|---|---|---|---|---|---|
| Diameter, Inches | .224 | .224 | .224 | .224 | .224 | .243 | .243 | .243 | .257 | .257 | .257 | .257 |
| Weight, Grains | 55 | 65 | 55 | 55 | 65 | 85 | 90 | 100 | 90 | 100 | 117 | 120 |
| Catalog Number | 1355 | 1395 | 1365 | 1390 | 1395 | 1530 | 1535 | 1560 | 1615 | 1625 | 1630 | 1650 |

# Sierra Bullets

## GameKing (cont.)

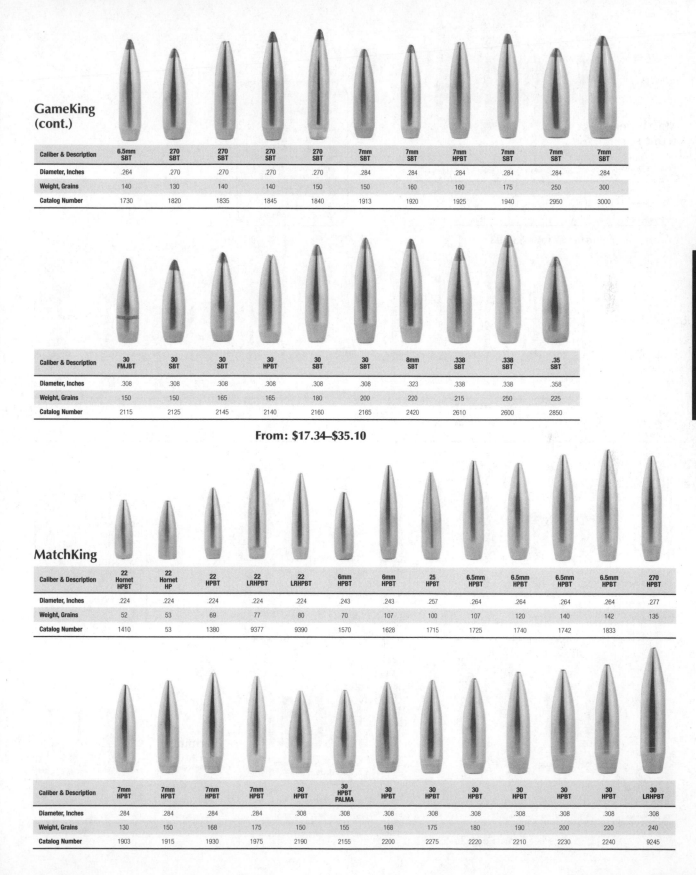

| Caliber & Description | 6.5mm SBT | 270 SBT | 270 SBT | 270 SBT | 270 SBT | 7mm SBT | 7mm SBT | 7mm HPBT | 7mm SBT | 7mm SBT | 7mm SBT |
|---|---|---|---|---|---|---|---|---|---|---|---|
| Diameter, Inches | .264 | .270 | .270 | .270 | .270 | .284 | .284 | .284 | .284 | .284 | .284 |
| Weight, Grains | 140 | 130 | 140 | 140 | 150 | 150 | 160 | 160 | 175 | 250 | 300 |
| Catalog Number | 1730 | 1820 | 1835 | 1845 | 1840 | 1913 | 1920 | 1925 | 1940 | 2950 | 3000 |

| Caliber & Description | 30 FMJBT | 30 SBT | 30 SBT | 30 HPBT | 30 SBT | 30 SBT | 8mm SBT | .338 SBT | .338 SBT | .35 SBT |
|---|---|---|---|---|---|---|---|---|---|---|
| Diameter, Inches | .308 | .308 | .308 | .308 | .308 | .308 | .323 | .338 | .338 | .358 |
| Weight, Grains | 150 | 150 | 165 | 165 | 180 | 200 | 220 | 215 | 250 | 225 |
| Catalog Number | 2115 | 2125 | 2145 | 2140 | 2160 | 2165 | 2420 | 2610 | 2600 | 2850 |

**From: $17.34–$35.10**

## MatchKing

| Caliber & Description | 22 Hornet HPBT | 22 Hornet HP | 22 HPBT | 22 LRHPBT | 22 LRHPBT | 6mm HPBT | 6mm HPBT | 25 HPBT | 6.5mm HPBT | 6.5mm HPBT | 6.5mm HPBT | 6.5mm HPBT | 270 HPBT |
|---|---|---|---|---|---|---|---|---|---|---|---|---|---|
| Diameter, Inches | .224 | .224 | .224 | .224 | .224 | .243 | .243 | .257 | .264 | .264 | .264 | .264 | .277 |
| Weight, Grains | 52 | 53 | 69 | 77 | 80 | 70 | 107 | 100 | 107 | 120 | 140 | 142 | 135 |
| Catalog Number | 1410 | 53 | 1380 | 9377 | 9390 | 1570 | 1628 | 1715 | 1725 | 1740 | 1742 | 1833 | |

| Caliber & Description | 7mm HPBT | 7mm HPBT | 7mm HPBT | 7mm HPBT | 30 HPBT | 30 HPBT PALMA | 30 HPBT | 30 HPBT | 30 HPBT | 30 HPBT | 30 HPBT | 30 HPBT | 30 LRHPBT |
|---|---|---|---|---|---|---|---|---|---|---|---|---|---|
| Diameter, Inches | .284 | .284 | .284 | .284 | .308 | .308 | .308 | .308 | .308 | .308 | .308 | .308 | .308 |
| Weight, Grains | 130 | 150 | 168 | 175 | 150 | 155 | 168 | 175 | 180 | 190 | 200 | 220 | 240 |
| Catalog Number | 1903 | 1915 | 1930 | 1975 | 2190 | 2155 | 2200 | 2275 | 2220 | 2210 | 2230 | 2240 | 9245 |

# Sierra Bullets

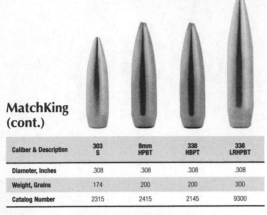

## MatchKing (cont.)

| Caliber & Description | 303 S | 8mm HPBT | 338 HBPT | 338 LRHPBT |
|---|---|---|---|---|
| Diameter, Inches | .308 | .308 | .308 | .308 |
| Weight, Grains | 174 | 200 | 200 | 300 |
| Catalog Number | 2315 | 2415 | 2145 | 9300 |

**From: $21.40–$38.02**

**LEGEND**
BT – Boattail
FMJ – Full Metal Jacket
FN – Flat Nose
FPJ – Full Profile Jacket
HP – Hollow Point
JFP – Jacketed Flat Point
JHC – Jacketed Hollow Cavity
JHP – Jacketed Hollow Point
JSP – Jacketed Soft Point
RN – Round Nose
S – Spitzer
SMP – Semi-Pointed
SSP – Single Shot Pistol

## Pro-Hunter

| Caliber & Description | 6mm S | 25 S | 25 S | 6.5mm HP | 270 S | 270 S | 7mm S | 7mm S | 7mm HPFN | 30 (03-03) HPFN | 30 (03-03) FNPJ | 30 (03-03) FNPJ |
|---|---|---|---|---|---|---|---|---|---|---|---|---|
| Diameter, Inches | .243 | .257 | .257 | .264 | .277 | .277 | .284 | .284 | .284 | .308 | .308 | .308 |
| Weight, Grains | 150 | 100 | 117 | 120 | 110 | 130 | 120 | 140 | 300 | 125 | 150 | 170 |
| Catalog Number | 1540 | 1620 | 1640 | 1720 | 1810 | 1830 | 1900 | 1910 | 8900 | 2020 | 2000 | 2010 |

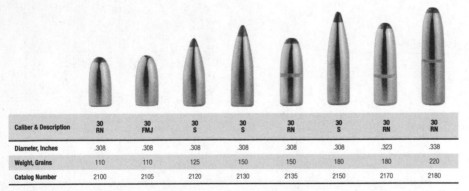

| Caliber & Description | 30 RN | 30 FMJ | 30 S | 30 S | 30 RN | 30 S | 30 RN | 30 RN |
|---|---|---|---|---|---|---|---|---|
| Diameter, Inches | .308 | .308 | .308 | .308 | .308 | .308 | .323 | .338 |
| Weight, Grains | 110 | 110 | 125 | 150 | 150 | 180 | 180 | 220 |
| Catalog Number | 2100 | 2105 | 2120 | 2130 | 2135 | 2150 | 2170 | 2180 |

**LEGEND**
BT – Boattail
FMJ – Full Metal Jacket
FN – Flat Nose
FPJ – Full Profile Jacket
HP – Hollow Point
JFP – Jacketed Flat Point
JHC – Jacketed Hollow Cavity
JHP – Jacketed Hollow Point
JSP – Jacketed Soft Point
RN – Round Nose
S – Spitzer
SMP – Semi-Pointed
SSP – Single Shot Pistol

| Caliber & Description | 303 S | 303 S | 303 S | 8mm S | 8mm S | 30 S | 35 RN | 375 FN | 45-70 HP- FN |
|---|---|---|---|---|---|---|---|---|---|
| Diameter, Inches | .311 | .311 | .311 | .323 | .323 | 0.338 | .358 | .375 | 0.458 |
| Weight, Grains | 125 | 150 | 180 | 150 | 175 | 225 | 200 | 200 | 300 |
| Catalog Number | 2305 | 2300 | 2310 | 2400 | 2410 | 2620 | 2800 | 2900l | 8900 |

**From: $21.36–$31.81**

## Varminter

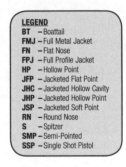

| Caliber & Description | 22 Hornet | 22 Hornet | 22 Hornet | 22 Hornet |
|---|---|---|---|---|
| Diameter, Inches | .223 | .223 | .223 | .223 |
| Weight, Grains | 40 | 45 | 40 | 45 |
| Catalog Number | 1100 | 1110 | 1200 | 1210 |

**HANDLOADING**

# Sierra Bullets

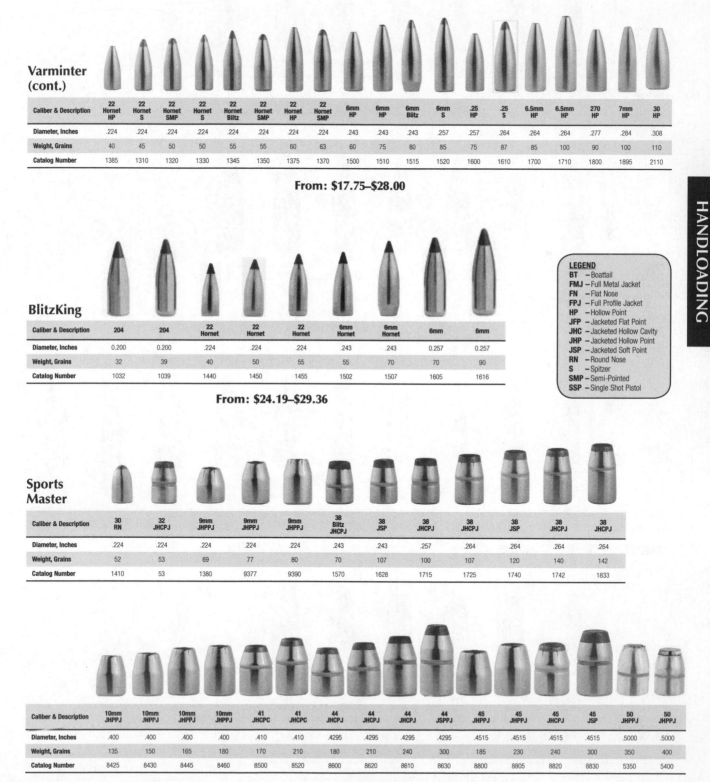

## Varminter (cont.)

| Caliber & Description | 22 Hornet HP | 22 Hornet S | 22 Hornet SMP | 22 Hornet S | 22 Hornet Blitz | 22 Hornet SMP | 22 Hornet HP | 22 Hornet SMP | 6mm HP | 6mm HP | 6mm Blitz | 6mm S | .25 HP | .25 S | 6.5mm HP | 6.5mm HP | 270 HP | 7mm HP | 30 HP |
|---|---|---|---|---|---|---|---|---|---|---|---|---|---|---|---|---|---|---|---|
| Diameter, Inches | .224 | .224 | .224 | .224 | .224 | .224 | .224 | .224 | .243 | .243 | .243 | .257 | .257 | .264 | .264 | .264 | .277 | .284 | .308 |
| Weight, Grains | 40 | 45 | 50 | 50 | 55 | 55 | 60 | 63 | 60 | 75 | 80 | 85 | 75 | 87 | 85 | 100 | 90 | 100 | 110 |
| Catalog Number | 1385 | 1310 | 1320 | 1330 | 1345 | 1350 | 1375 | 1370 | 1500 | 1510 | 1515 | 1520 | 1600 | 1610 | 1700 | 1710 | 1800 | 1895 | 2110 |

**From: $17.75–$28.00**

## BlitzKing

| Caliber & Description | 204 | 204 | 22 Hornet | 22 Hornet | 22 Hornet | 6mm Hornet | 6mm Hornet | 6mm | 6mm |
|---|---|---|---|---|---|---|---|---|---|
| Diameter, Inches | 0.200 | 0.200 | .224 | .224 | .224 | .243 | .243 | 0.257 | 0.257 |
| Weight, Grains | 32 | 39 | 40 | 50 | 55 | 55 | 70 | 70 | 90 |
| Catalog Number | 1032 | 1039 | 1440 | 1450 | 1455 | 1502 | 1507 | 1605 | 1616 |

**From: $24.19–$29.36**

**LEGEND**
- **BT** – Boattail
- **FMJ** – Full Metal Jacket
- **FN** – Flat Nose
- **FPJ** – Full Profile Jacket
- **HP** – Hollow Point
- **JFP** – Jacketed Flat Point
- **JHC** – Jacketed Hollow Cavity
- **JHP** – Jacketed Hollow Point
- **JSP** – Jacketed Soft Point
- **RN** – Round Nose
- **S** – Spitzer
- **SMP** – Semi-Pointed
- **SSP** – Single Shot Pistol

## Sports Master

| Caliber & Description | 30 RN | 32 JHCPJ | 9mm JHPPJ | 9mm JHPPJ | 9mm JHPPJ | 38 Blitz JHCPJ | 38 JSP | 38 JHCPJ | 38 JHCPJ | 38 JSP | 38 JHCPJ | 38 JHCPJ |
|---|---|---|---|---|---|---|---|---|---|---|---|---|
| Diameter, Inches | .224 | .224 | .224 | .224 | .224 | .243 | .243 | .257 | .264 | .264 | .264 | .264 |
| Weight, Grains | 52 | 53 | 69 | 77 | 80 | 70 | 107 | 100 | 107 | 120 | 140 | 142 |
| Catalog Number | 1410 | 53 | 1380 | 9377 | 9390 | 1570 | 1628 | 1715 | 1725 | 1740 | 1742 | 1833 |

| Caliber & Description | 10mm JHPPJ | 10mm JHPPJ | 10mm JHPPJ | 10mm JHPPJ | 41 JHCPC | 41 JHCPC | 44 JHCPJ | 44 JHCPJ | 44 JHCPJ | 44 JSPPJ | 45 JHPPJ | 45 JHPPJ | 45 JHCPJ | 45 JSP | 50 JHPPJ | 50 JHPPJ |
|---|---|---|---|---|---|---|---|---|---|---|---|---|---|---|---|---|
| Diameter, Inches | .400 | .400 | .400 | .400 | .410 | .410 | .4295 | .4295 | .4295 | .4295 | .4515 | .4515 | .4515 | .4515 | .5000 | .5000 |
| Weight, Grains | 135 | 150 | 165 | 180 | 170 | 210 | 180 | 210 | 240 | 300 | 185 | 230 | 240 | 300 | 350 | 400 |
| Catalog Number | 8425 | 8430 | 8445 | 8460 | 8500 | 8520 | 8600 | 8620 | 8610 | 8630 | 8800 | 8805 | 8820 | 8830 | 5350 | 5400 |

**From: $18.68–$30.33**

## Boat Tail Bullets

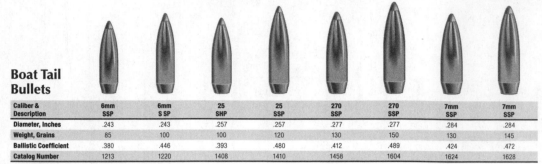

| Caliber & Description | 6mm SSP | 6mm S SP | 25 SHP | 25 SSP | 270 SSP | 270 SSP | 7mm SSP | 7mm SSP |
|---|---|---|---|---|---|---|---|---|
| Diameter, Inches | .243 | .243 | .257 | .257 | .277 | .277 | .284 | .284 |
| Weight, Grains | 85 | 100 | 100 | 120 | 130 | 150 | 130 | 145 |
| Ballistic Coefficient | .380 | .446 | .393 | .480 | .412 | .489 | .424 | .472 |
| Catalog Number | 1213 | 1220 | 1408 | 1410 | 1458 | 1604 | 1624 | 1628 |

*Match bullets are not recommended for use on game animals.*

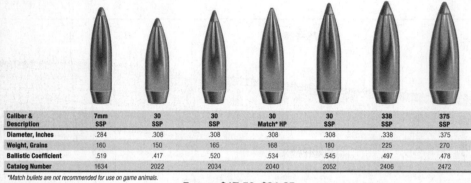

| Caliber & Description | 7mm SSP | 30 SSP | 30 SSP | 30 Match* HP | 30 SSP | 338 SSP | 375 SSP |
|---|---|---|---|---|---|---|---|
| Diameter, Inches | .284 | .308 | .308 | .308 | .308 | .338 | .375 |
| Weight, Grains | 160 | 150 | 165 | 168 | 180 | 225 | 270 |
| Ballistic Coefficient | .519 | .417 | .520 | .534 | .545 | .497 | .478 |
| Catalog Number | 1634 | 2022 | 2034 | 2040 | 2052 | 2406 | 2472 |

*Match bullets are not recommended for use on game animals.*

**From: $17.59–$31.85**

## Grand Slam

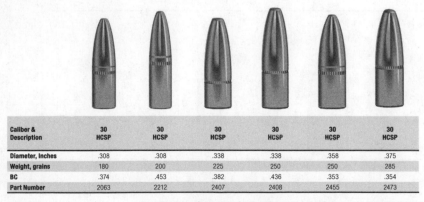

| Caliber & Description | 6mm SP | 25 HCSP | 6.5mm HCSP | 270 HCSP | 270 HCSP | 7mm HCSP | 7mm HCSP | 7mm HCSP | 30 HCSP | 30 HCSP |
|---|---|---|---|---|---|---|---|---|---|---|
| Diameter, Inches | .243 | .257 | .264 | .277 | .277 | .284 | .284 | .284 | .308 | .308 |
| Weight, grains | 100 | 120 | 140 | 130 | 150 | 145 | 160 | 175 | 150 | 165 |
| BC | .327 | .356 | .385 | .332 | .378 | .353 | .389 | .436 | .295 | .354 |
| Part Number | 1222 | 1415 | 1444 | 1465 | 1608 | 1632 | 1638 | 1643 | 2026 | 2038 |

| Caliber & Description | 30 HCSP | 30 HCSP | 30 HCSP | 30 HCSP | 30 HCSP | 30 HCSP |
|---|---|---|---|---|---|---|
| Diameter, Inches | .308 | .308 | .338 | .338 | .358 | .375 |
| Weight, grains | 180 | 200 | 225 | 250 | 250 | 285 |
| BC | .374 | .453 | .382 | .436 | .353 | .354 |
| Part Number | 2063 | 2212 | 2407 | 2408 | 2455 | 2473 |

**From: $19.00–$47.03**

# Speer Bullets

## Hot-Cor Bullets*

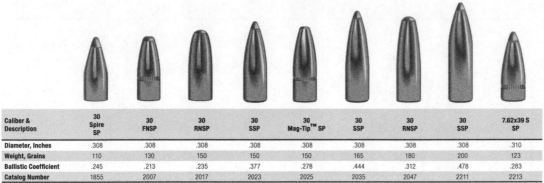

| Caliber & Description | 25 SPFN | 25 SSP | 25 SSP | 25 SSP | 6.5mm SSP | 6.5mm SSP | 270 SSP | 270 SSP | 7mm SSP | 7mm SPFN | 7mm SSP |
|---|---|---|---|---|---|---|---|---|---|---|---|
| Diameter, Inches | 0.257 | .257 | .257 | .257 | .264 | .264 | .277 | .277 | .284 | 0.284 | .284 |
| Weight, grains | 75 | 87 | 100 | 120 | 120 | 140 | 130 | 150 | 130 | 130 | 145 |
| BC | 0.133 | .300 | .334 | .405 | .392 | .498 | .383 | .455 | .368 | 0.257 | .416 |
| Part Number | 1237 | 1241 | 1405 | 1411 | 1435 | 1441 | 1459 | 1605 | 1623 | 1625 | 1629 |
| Bullets/box | 100 | 100 | 100 | 100 | 100 | 100 | 100 | 100 | 100 | 100 | 100 |
| Bullet Construction | HC | HC | HC | HC | HC | HC | HC | HC | HC | HC | HC |

* Not recommended for lever-action rifles.

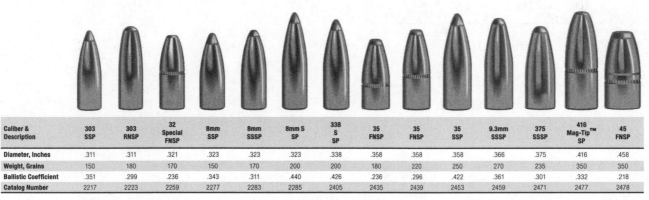

| Caliber & Description | 30 Spire SP | 30 FNSP | 30 RNSP | 30 SSP | 30 Mag-Tip™ SP | 30 SSP | 30 RNSP | 30 SSP | 7.62x39 S SP |
|---|---|---|---|---|---|---|---|---|---|
| Diameter, Inches | .308 | .308 | .308 | .308 | .308 | .308 | .308 | .308 | .310 |
| Weight, Grains | 110 | 130 | 150 | 150 | 150 | 165 | 180 | 200 | 123 |
| Ballistic Coefficient | .245 | .213 | .235 | .377 | .278 | .444 | .312 | .478 | .283 |
| Catalog Number | 1855 | 2007 | 2017 | 2023 | 2025 | 2035 | 2047 | 2211 | 2213 |

* Not recommended for lever-action rifles.

| Caliber & Description | 303 SSP | 303 RNSP | 32 Special FNSP | 8mm SSP | 8mm SSSP | 8mm S SP | 338 S SP | 35 FNSP | 35 FNSP | 35 SSP | 9.3mm SSSP | 375 SSSP | 416 Mag-Tip™ SP | 45 FNSP |
|---|---|---|---|---|---|---|---|---|---|---|---|---|---|---|
| Diameter, Inches | .311 | .311 | .321 | .323 | .323 | .323 | .338 | .358 | .358 | .358 | .366 | .375 | .416 | .458 |
| Weight, Grains | 150 | 180 | 170 | 150 | 170 | 200 | 200 | 180 | 220 | 250 | 270 | 235 | 350 | 350 |
| Ballistic Coefficient | .351 | .299 | .236 | .343 | .311 | .440 | .426 | .236 | .296 | .422 | .361 | .301 | .332 | .218 |
| Catalog Number | 2217 | 2223 | 2259 | 2277 | 2283 | 2285 | 2405 | 2435 | 2439 | 2453 | 2459 | 2471 | 2477 | 2478 |

**From: $20.00–$32.55**

## Jacketed HP Bullets

| Caliber & Description | 22 Hornet-HP | 45 HP |
|---|---|---|
| Diameter, Inches | 0.224 | 0.458 |
| Weight, Grain | 33 | 300 |
| Ballistic Coefficient | 0.079 | 0.206 |
| Catalog Number | 1014 | 2482 |

**From: $15.99–$64.78**

# Speer Bullets

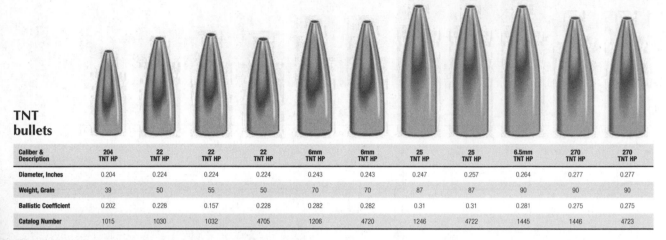

## TNT bullets

| Caliber & Description | 204 TNT HP | 22 TNT HP | 22 TNT HP | 22 TNT HP | 6mm TNT HP | 6mm TNT HP | 25 TNT HP | 25 TNT HP | 6.5mm TNT HP | 270 TNT HP | 270 TNT HP |
|---|---|---|---|---|---|---|---|---|---|---|---|
| Diameter, Inches | 0.204 | 0.224 | 0.224 | 0.224 | 0.243 | 0.243 | 0.247 | 0.257 | 0.264 | 0.277 | 0.277 |
| Weight, Grain | 39 | 50 | 55 | 50 | 70 | 70 | 87 | 87 | 90 | 90 | 90 |
| Ballistic Coefficient | 0.202 | 0.228 | 0.157 | 0.228 | 0.282 | 0.282 | 0.31 | 0.31 | 0.281 | 0.275 | 0.275 |
| Catalog Number | 1015 | 1030 | 1032 | 4705 | 1206 | 4720 | 1246 | 4722 | 1445 | 1446 | 4723 |

| Caliber & Description | 7mm TNT HP | 7mm TNT HP | 30 TNT HP | 30 TNT HP |
|---|---|---|---|---|
| Diameter, Inches | 0.284 | 0.284 | 0.308 | 0.308 |
| Weight, Grain | 110 | 110 | 125 | 125 |
| Ballistic Coefficient | 0.338 | 0.338 | 0.326 | 0.326 |
| Catalog Number | 1616 | 4724 | 1986 | 4725 |

**From: $20.00–$169.99**

## Special Purpose Bullets*

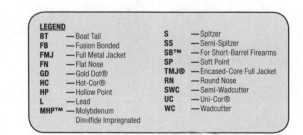

| Caliber & Description | 30 SPRN | 30 HP | 45 SPFN |
|---|---|---|---|
| Diameter, Inches | 0.308 | 0.308 | 0.458 |
| Weight, Grain | 100 | 110 | 400 |
| Ballistic Coefficient | 0.124 | 0.136 | 0.214 |
| Catalog Number | 1805 | 1835 | 2479 |

**From: $15.00–$30.89**

### LEGEND

| | | | |
|---|---|---|---|
| BT | — Boat Tail | S | — Spitzer |
| FB | — Fusion Bonded | SS | — Semi-Spitzer |
| FMJ | — Full Metal Jacket | SB™ | — For Short-Barrel Firearms |
| FN | — Flat Nose | SP | — Soft Point |
| GD | — Gold Dot® | TMJ® | — Encased-Core Full Jacket |
| HC | — Hot-Cor® | RN | — Round Nose |
| HP | — Hollow Point | SWC | — Semi-Wadcutter |
| L | — Lead | UC | — Uni-Cor® |
| MHP™ | — Molybdenum Disulfide Impregnated | WC | — Wadcutter |

**HANDLOADING**

# Speer Bullets

## GOLD DOT BULLETS

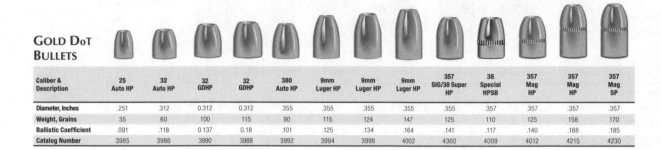

| Caliber & Description | 25 Auto HP | 32 Auto HP | 32 GDHP | 32 GDHP | 380 Auto HP | 9mm Luger HP | 9mm Luger HP | 9mm Luger HP | 357 SIG/38 Super HP | 38 Special HPSB | 357 Mag HP | 357 Mag HP | 357 Mag SP |
|---|---|---|---|---|---|---|---|---|---|---|---|---|---|
| Diameter, Inches | .251 | .312 | 0.312 | 0.312 | .355 | .355 | .355 | .355 | .355 | .357 | .357 | .357 | .357 |
| Weight, Grains | 35 | 60 | 100 | 115 | 90 | 115 | 124 | 147 | 125 | 110 | 125 | 158 | 170 |
| Ballistic Coefficient | .091 | .118 | 0.137 | 0.18 | .101 | .125 | .134 | .164 | .141 | .117 | .140 | .168 | .185 |
| Catalog Number | 3985 | 3986 | 3990 | 3988 | 3992 | 3994 | 3998 | 4002 | 4360 | 4009 | 4012 | 4215 | 4230 |

| Caliber & Description | 40/10mm HP | 40/10mm HP | 40/10mm HP | 41 Mag HP | 44 Special HP | 44 Mag HP | 44 Mag SP | 45 Auto Gold Dot HP | 45 Auto Gold Dot HP | 45 Auto Gold Dot HP |
|---|---|---|---|---|---|---|---|---|---|---|
| Diameter, Inches | .400 | .400 | .400 | .410 | .429 | .429 | .429 | .451 | .451 | .451 |
| Weight, Grains | 155 | 165 | 180 | 210 | 200 | 210 | 240 | 185 | 200 | 230 |
| Ballistic Coefficient | .123 | .138 | .143 | .183 | .145 | .154 | .175 | .109 | .138 | .143 |
| Catalog Number | 4400 | 4397 | 4406 | 4430 | 4427 | 4428 | 4456 | 4470 | 4478 | 4483 |

†=475 Linebaugh is a registered trademark of Timothy B. Sundles

**From: $18.00–$36.00**

## Jacketed Bullets

| Caliber & Description | 32 327 Magnum JHP | 9mm 38 Auto 380 FN JSP | 38 Spl. 357 Magnum JHP | 38 Spl. 357 Magnum JSP | 38 Spl. 357 Magnum JHP | 38 Spl. 357 Magnum JHP | 38 Spl. 357 Magnum JHP | 38 Spl. 357 Magnum JSP | 38 Spl. 357 Magnum JSP | 41 Mag JHP | 44 JHP |
|---|---|---|---|---|---|---|---|---|---|---|---|
| Diameter, Inches | 0.312 | 0.355 | 0.357 | 0.357 | 0.357 | 0.357 | 0.357 | 0.357 | 0.357 | 0.41 | 0.429 |
| Weight, Grain | 100 | 124 | 110 | 125 | 125 | 140 | 158 | 158 | 158 | 200 | 200 |
| Ballistic Coefficient | 0.138 | 0.115 | 0.113 | 0.129 | 0.129 | 0.152 | 0.163 | 0.164 | 0.163 | 0.163 | 0.158 |
| Catalog Number | 3980 | 3997 | 4007 | 4011 | 4013 | 4203 | 4211 | 4217 | 4732 | 4421 | 4423 |

# Speer Bullets

## Jacketed Bullets (cont.)

| Caliber & Description | 44 Mag JHP | 44 Mag JSP | 44 Mag JSP | 45 Colt JHP | 45 Colt 460 JHP | 45 Colt 460 JHP | 50 JHP |
|---|---|---|---|---|---|---|---|
| Diameter, Inches | 0.429 | 0.429 | 0.429 | 0.451 | 0.451 | 0.451 | 0.186 |
| Weight, Grain | 240 | 240 | 300 | 225 | 260 | 300 | 325 |
| Ballistic Coefficient | 0.163 | 0.169 | 0.213 | 0.169 | 0.183 | 0.199 | 0.169 |
| Catalog Number | 4424 | 4454 | 4463 | 4469 | 4481 | 4485 | 4495 |

**From: $12.00–$67.53**

## Lead Handgun Bullets

| Caliber & Description | 32 S&W HBWC | 9mm Luger RN | 38 Bevel-Base WC | 38 Hollow-Base WC | 38 SWC | 38 SWC HP | 38 RN | 44 SWC | 45 Auto SWC | 45 Auto RN | 45 Colt SWC |
|---|---|---|---|---|---|---|---|---|---|---|---|
| Diameter, Inches | .314 | .356 | .358 | .358 | .358 | .358 | .358 | .430 | .452 | .452 | .452 |
| Weight, grains | 98 | 125 | 148 | 148 | 158 | 158 | 158 | 240 | 200 | 230 | 250 |
| Part No | – | 4601 | 4605 | 4617 | 4623 | 4627 | 4647 | 4660 | 4677 | 4690 | 4683 |
| Box Count | – | 100 | 100 | 100 | 100 | 100 | 100 | 100 | 100 | 100 | 100 |
| Bulk Part No. | 4600 | 4602 | 4606 | 4618 | 4624 | 4628 | 4648 | 4661 | 4678 | 4691 | 4684 |
| Bulk Count | 1000 | 500 | 500 | 500 | 500 | 500 | 500 | 500 | 500 | 500 | 500 |

**From: $17.00–$69.84**

**LEGEND**

| | | | |
|---|---|---|---|
| BT | —Boat Tail | S | —Spitzer |
| FB | —Fusion Bonded | SS | —Semi-Spitzer |
| FMJ | —Full Metal Jacket | SB™ | —For Short-Barrel Firearms |
| FN | —Flat Nose | SP | —Soft Point |
| GD | —Gold Dot® | TMJ® | —Encased-Core Full Jacket |
| HC | —Hot-Cor® | RN | —Round Nose |
| HP | —Hollow Point | SWC | —Semi-Wadcutter |
| L | —Lead | UC | —Uni-Cor® |
| MHP™ | —Molybdenum Disulfide Impregnated | WC | —Wadcutter |

HANDLOADING

**516** • Shooter's Bible 103rd Edition

www.skyhorsepublishing.com

# Swift Bullets

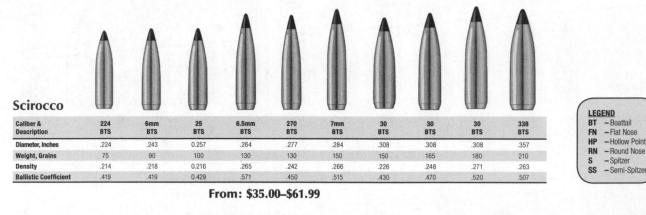

### Scirocco

| Caliber & Description | 224 BTS | 6mm BTS | 25 BTS | 6.5mm BTS | 270 BTS | 7mm BTS | 30 BTS | 30 BTS | 30 BTS | 338 BTS |
|---|---|---|---|---|---|---|---|---|---|---|
| Diameter, Inches | .224 | .243 | 0.257 | .264 | .277 | .284 | .308 | .308 | .308 | .357 |
| Weight, Grains | 75 | 90 | 100 | 130 | 130 | 150 | 150 | 165 | 180 | 210 |
| Density | .214 | .218 | 0.216 | .265 | .242 | .266 | .226 | .248 | .271 | .263 |
| Ballistic Coefficient | .419 | .419 | 0.429 | .571 | .450 | .515 | .430 | .470 | .520 | .507 |

**From: $35.00–$61.99**

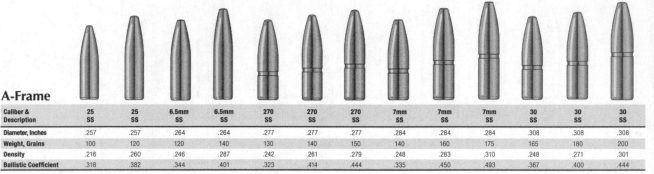

### A-Frame

| Caliber & Description | 25 SS | 25 SS | 6.5mm SS | 6.5mm SS | 270 SS | 270 SS | 270 SS | 7mm SS | 7mm SS | 7mm SS | 30 SS | 30 SS | 30 SS |
|---|---|---|---|---|---|---|---|---|---|---|---|---|---|
| Diameter, Inches | .257 | .257 | .264 | .264 | .277 | .277 | .277 | .284 | .284 | .284 | .308 | .308 | .308 |
| Weight, Grains | 100 | 120 | 120 | 140 | 130 | 140 | 150 | 140 | 160 | 175 | 165 | 180 | 200 |
| Density | .216 | .260 | .246 | .287 | .242 | .261 | .279 | .248 | .283 | .310 | .248 | .271 | .301 |
| Ballistic Coefficient | .318 | .382 | .344 | .401 | .323 | .414 | .444 | .335 | .450 | .493 | .367 | .400 | .444 |

## The Swift Bullet Company

The Scirocco rifle bullet starts with a tough, pointed polymer tip that reduces air resistance, prevents tip deformation, and blends into the radius of its secant ogive nose section. A moderate 15-degree boat-tail base reduces drag and eases seating. The thick base prevents bullet deformation during launch. Scirocco's shape creates two other significant advantages. One is an extremely high ballistic coefficient. The other, derived from the secant ogive nose, is a comparatively long bearing surface for a sharply pointed bullet, a feature that improves rotational stability.

Inside, the Scirocco has a bonded-core construction with a pure lead core encased in a tapered, progressively thickening jacket of pure copper. Pure copper was selected because it is more malleable and less brittle than less expensive gilding metal. Both jacket and core are bonded by Swift's proprietary process so that the bullet expands without break-up as if the two parts were the same metal. In tests, the bullet mushroomed effectively at velocities as low as 1440 fps, yet stayed together at velocities in excess of 3,000 fps, with over 70 percent weight retention.

The Swift A-Frame bullet, with its midsection wall of copper, is still earning praise for its deep-driving dependability in tough game. Less aerodynamic than the Scirocco, it produces a broad mushroom while carrying almost all its weight through muscle and bone. Available in a wide range of weights and diameters, it is also a bonded-core bullet.

## .25 SIROCCO-100GR.

Swift now offers the 100-grain .25 caliber Scirocco bullet as part of the Scirocco II bonded line. The new addition is the perfect bullet design for today's fast, flat-shooting, long-range cartridges. Its secant ogive, 15-degree boat tail base and Signature Black Tip create a sleek, aerodynamic profile that helps maintain down-range velocities and flat trajectories. The extra heavy tapering jacket wall with an internally bonded lead core provides structural integrity, reliable expansion and penetration with 80%+ weight retention.
**Box 100: . . . . . . . . . . . . . . . . $57.75**

HANDLOADING

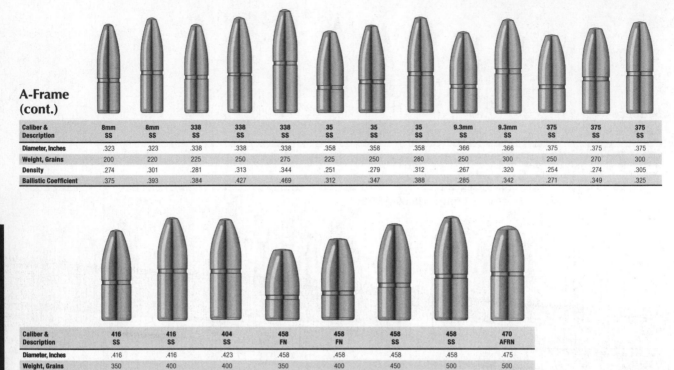

## A-Frame (cont.)

| Caliber & Description | 8mm SS | 8mm SS | 338 SS | 338 SS | 338 SS | 35 SS | 35 SS | 35 SS | 9.3mm SS | 9.3mm SS | 375 SS | 375 SS | 375 SS |
|---|---|---|---|---|---|---|---|---|---|---|---|---|---|
| Diameter, Inches | .323 | .323 | .338 | .338 | .338 | .358 | .358 | .358 | .366 | .366 | .375 | .375 | .375 |
| Weight, Grains | 200 | 220 | 225 | 250 | 275 | 225 | 250 | 280 | 250 | 300 | 250 | 270 | 300 |
| Density | .274 | .301 | .281 | .313 | .344 | .251 | .279 | .312 | .267 | .320 | .254 | .274 | .305 |
| Ballistic Coefficient | .375 | .393 | .384 | .427 | .469 | .312 | .347 | .388 | .285 | .342 | .271 | .349 | .325 |

| Caliber & Description | 416 SS | 416 SS | 404 SS | 458 FN | 458 FN | 458 SS | 458 SS | 470 AFRN |
|---|---|---|---|---|---|---|---|---|
| Diameter, Inches | .416 | .416 | .423 | .458 | .458 | .458 | .458 | .475 |
| Weight, Grains | 350 | 400 | 400 | 350 | 400 | 450 | 500 | 500 |
| Density | .289 | .330 | .319 | .238 | .72 | .307 | .341 | .329 |
| Ballistic Coefficient | .321 | .367 | .375 | .170 | .258 | .325 | .361 | .364 |

**From: $41.81–$122.58**

### LEGEND
**BT** — Boattail
**FN** — Flat Nose
**HP** — Hollow Point
**RN** — Round Nose
**S** — Spitzer
**SS** — Semi-Spitzer

## A-Frame Hunting Revolver Bullets

| Caliber & Description | 44 HP | 44 HP | 44 HP | 45 HP | 45 HP | 45 HP |
|---|---|---|---|---|---|---|
| Diameter, Inches | .430 | .430 | .430 | .452 | .452 | .452 |
| Weight, Grains | 240 | 280 | 300 | 265 | 300 | 325 |
| Density | .185 | .216 | .232 | .185 | .210 | .227 |
| Ballistic Coefficient | .119 | .139 | .147 | .129 | .153 | .171 |

**From: $27.87–$54.11**

# Woodleigh Premium Bullets

## FULL METAL JACKET

Fashioned from gilding metal-clad steel 2mm thick, jackets on FMJ bullets are heavy at the nose for extra impact resistance. The jacket then tapers toward the base to assist rifling engraving. **From: $41.49–$190.00**

## WELDCORE SOFT NOSE

A product of Australia, Woodleigh Weldcore Soft Nose bullets are made from 90/100 gilding metal (90% copper; 10% zinc) 1.6 mm thick. Maximum retained weight is obtained by fusing the pure lead to the gilding metal jacket. **From: $36.49–$194.92**

**98% & 95% RETAINED WEIGHT 300 WIN MAG 180GR PP**

**458 X 500GN SN RECOVERED FROM BUFFALO**

**270 WIN 150GN PP 86% RETAINED WEIGHT**

**94% RETAINED WEIGHT 300 WIN MAG 180GR PP**

**500/465 RECOVERED FROM BUFFALO**

| Caliber Diameter | Type | Weight Grain | SD | BC |
|---|---|---|---|---|
| 6.5mm | PP SN | 140 | .287 | .444 |
| .264 | PP SN | 160 | .328 | .509 |
| 270 Win | PP SN | 130 | .242 | .409 |
| .277 | PP SN | 150 | .279 | .463 |
| | PP SN | 180 | .334 | .513 |
| 7mm | PP SN | 140 | .248 | .436 |
| .284 | PP SN | 160 | .283 | .486 |
| | PP SN | 175 | .310 | .510 |
| 275 H&H | PP SN | 160 | .277 | .474 |
| .287 | PP SN | 175 | .304 | .509 |
| 308 | PP SN | 150 | .226 | .310 |
| .308 | PP SN | 165 | .248 | .320 |
| | PP SN | 180 | .271 | .376 |
| | RN SN | 220 | .331 | .367 |
| | FMJ | 220 | .331 | .359 |
| 30-30 | FN SN | 150 | 0.226 | 0.246 |
| .308 | | | | |
| 30/06 | PP SN | 240 | 0.361 | 0.401 |
| 300 Mag. | PP SN | 180 | .271 | .435 |
| .308 | PP SN | 200 | .301 | .362 |
| 303 British | PP SN | 174 | .255 | .362 |
| .312 | RN SN | 215 | .316 | .359 |
| 325 (8mm) | PP SN | 200 | 0.274 | 0.406 |
| .323 | PP SN | 220 | .301 | .448 |
| 8x57 | RN SN | 200 | 0.283 | 0.331 |
| .318 | | | | |
| 318 | RN SN | 250 | .328 | .420 |
| .330 | FMJ | 250 | .328 | .364 |
| 333 Jeffery | RN SN | 250 | .322 | .335 |
| .333 | RN SN | 300 | .386 | .418 |
| | FMJ | 300 | .386 | .418 |
| 338 Fed | PP SN | 180 | .226 | .361 |
| .338 | PP SN | 200 | .251 | .401 |
| 33 Win. | FN SN | 200 | 0.246 | 0.234 |
| .338 | | | | |
| 338 Mag | PP SN | 225 | .281 | .425 |
| .338 | RN SN | 250 | .313 | .332 |
| | PP SN | 250 | .313 | .431 |
| | FMJ | 250 | .313 | .326 |
| | RN SN | 300 | .375 | .416 |
| | FMJ | 300 | .375 | .414 |
| 348 Win. | FN SN | 250 | 0.295 | 0.281 |
| .348 | | | | |
| 358 | RN SN | 225 | 0.251 | 0.263 |
| .358 | PP SN | 225 | .251 | .372 |
| | FMJ | 250 | .251 | .263 |
| | RN SN | 250 | .279 | .300 |
| | PP SN | 275 | .279 | .400 |
| | PP SN | 310 | .307 | .450 |
| | RN SN | 310 | .346 | .458 |
| | FMJ | | .346 | .458 |

| Caliber Diameter | Type | Weight Grain | SD | BC |
|---|---|---|---|---|
| 9.3 | RN SN | 250 | .267 | .281 |
| .366 | PP SN | 250 | .267 | .381 |
| | RN SN | 286 | .305 | .321 |
| | PP SN | 286 | .305 | .396 |
| | FMJ | 286 | .305 | .305 |
| | RN SN | 320 | .341 | .359 |
| | PP SN | 320 | .341 | .457 |
| | FMJ | 320 | .341 | .341 |
| 375 Mag. | PP SN | 235 | .239 | .310 |
| .375 | RN SN | 270 | .274 | .250 |
| | PP SN | 270 | .274 | .370 |
| | RN SN | 300 | .305 | .277 |
| | PP SN | 300 | .305 | .380 |
| | FMJ | 300 | .305 | .275 |
| | RN SN | 350 | .356 | .321 |
| | PP SN | 350 | .356 | .400 |
| | FMJ | 350 | .356 | .307 |
| 338 Fed | PP SN | 180 | .226 | .361 |
| .338 | PP SN | 200 | .251 | .401 |
| 33 Win. | FN SN | 200 | 0.246 | 0.234 |
| .338 | | | | |
| 338 Mag | PP SN | 225 | .281 | .425 |
| .338 | RN SN | 250 | .313 | .332 |
| | PP SN | 250 | .313 | .431 |
| | FMJ | 250 | .313 | .326 |
| | RN SN | 300 | .375 | .416 |
| | FMJ | 300 | .375 | .414 |
| 348 Win. | FN SN | 250 | 0.295 | 0.281 |
| .348 | | | | |
| 358 | RN SN | 225 | .251 | .263 |
| .358 | PP SN | 225 | .251 | .327 |
| | FMJ | 225 | .251 | .263 |
| | RN SN | 250 | .279 | .300 |
| | PP SN | 250 | .279 | .400 |
| | PP SN | 275 | .307 | .450 |
| | RN SN | 310 | .346 | .458 |
| | FMJ | 310 | .346 | .458 |
| 9.3 | RN SN | 250 | .267 | .281 |
| .366 | PP SN | 250 | .267 | .381 |
| | RN SN | 286 | .305 | .321 |
| | PP SN | 286 | .305 | .396 |
| | FMJ | 286 | .305 | .305 |
| | RN SN | 320 | .341 | .359 |
| | PP SN | 320 | .341 | .457 |
| | FMJ | 320 | .341 | .341 |
| 375 Mag. | PP SN | 235 | .239 | .310 |
| .375 | RN SN | 270 | .274 | .250 |
| | PP SN | 270 | .274 | .370 |
| | RN SN | 300 | .305 | .277 |
| | PP SN | 300 | .305 | .380 |
| | FMJ | 300 | .305 | .275 |
| | RN SN | 350 | .356 | .321 |
| | PP SN | 350 | .356 | .400 |
| | FMJ | 350 | .356 | .307 |
| 400 Purdey | RN SN | 230 | .200 | .181 |
| .405 | | | | |
| 450/400 Nitro | RN SN | 400 | 0.344 | 0.307 |
| .408 | | | | |

# Woodleigh Premium Bullets

| Caliber Diameter | Type | Weight Grain | SD | BC |
|---|---|---|---|---|
| 0.411 | RN SN | 400 | 0.338 | 0.307 |
| 450/400 Ruger .410 | RN SN | 400 | 0.338 | 0.307 |
| 0.408 | FMJ | 400 | 0.344 | 0.300 |
| .410 Ruger | FMJ | 400 | 0.338 | 0.300 |
| 405 Win. .412 | RN SN | 300 | 0.252 | 0.194 |
| 416 Rigby .416 | PP SN | 340 | 0.281 | 0.330 |
| | RN SN | 410 | .338 | .307 |
| | FMJ | 410 | .338 | .300 |
| | RN SN | 450 | .371 | .338 |
| | FMJ | 450 | .371 | .330 |
| 416 Rem. .416 | RN SN | 400 | .330 | .305 |
| | FMJ | 400 | .330 | .300 |
| | RN SN | 450 | .371 | .338 |
| | FMJ | 450 | .371 | .330 |
| 404 Jeffery .422 | RN SN | 350 | .281 | .293 |
| | RN SN | 400 | .321 | .335 |
| | FMJ | 400 | .321 | .330 |
| | RN SN | 450 | .361 | .360 |
| | FMJ | 450 | .361 | .355 |
| 10.75x68mm .423 | RN SN | 347 | .277 | .290 |
| | FMJ | 347 | .277 | .288 |
| 444 Marlin .430 | FN SN | 280 | 0.216 | 0.186 |
| 425 Westly Richards .435 | RN SN | 410 | 0.31 | |
| | FMJ | 410 | 0.31 | 0.222 |
| | | | | 0.221 |
| 11.2 Schuler .440 | RN SN | 401 | 0.296 | 0.325 |
| 458 Mag .458 | PP SN | 400 | 0.272 | 0.34 |
| | RN SN | 480 | .327 | .328 |
| | FMJ | 480 | .327 | .325 |
| | RN SN | 500 | .341 | .310 |
| | PP SN | 500 | .341 | .378 |
| | FMJ | 500 | .341 | .310 |
| | RN SN | 550 | .375 | .340 |
| | FMJ | 550 | .375 | .326 |
| 450 BPE .458 | RN SN | 350 | 0.238 | 0.25 |
| 45/70 .458 | FN SN | 405 | 0.276 | 0.204 |
| | FN SN | 300 | .205 | .196 |
| 450 Nitro .458 | RN SN | 480 | 0.327 | 0.328 |
| | FMJ | 480 | .327 | .325 |
| 465 Nitro .468 | RN SN | 480 | 0.313 | 0.334 |
| | FMJ | 480 | .313 | .330 |
| 470 Nitro .474 | RN SN | 500 | .318 | .374 |
| | FMJ | 500 | .318 | .370 |
| 476 Westly Richards .476 | RN SN | 520 | .328 | .385 |
| | FMJ | 520 | .328 | .380 |
| 475 No. 2 .483 | RN SN | 480 | .294 | .309 |
| | FMJ | 480 | .294 | .300 |
| 500 S&W MAG .500 | FN SN | 400 | 0.229 | 0.182 |
| 505 Gibbs .505 | RN SN | 525 | .294 | .345 |
| | FMJ | 525 | .294 | .340 |
| | PP SN | 600 | .336 | .360 |
| | FMJ | 600 | .336 | .360 |
| 500 Jeffery .510 | RN SN | 535 | .294 | .350 |
| | PP SN | 535 | .294 | .310 |
| | FMJ | 535 | .294 | .340 |
| | PP SN | 600 | .330 | .350 |
| | FMJ | 600 | .330 | .355 |
| 500 BP .510 | RN SN | 440 | 0.242 | 0.255 |
| 50 Alaskan & 50/110 WIN .510 | FN SN | 500 | 0.275 | 0.219 |
| 500 Nitro .510 | RN SN | 450 | .247 | .257 |
| | RN SN | 570 | .313 | .368 |
| | FMJ | 570 | .313 | .350 |
| 577 BP Express .585 | RN SN | 650 | 0.271 | 0.292 |
| 577 Nitro .585 | RN SN | 650 | 0.271 | 0.292 |
| 0.584 | FMJ | 650 | 0.272 | 0.292 |
| 0.585 | RN SN | 750 | 0.313 | 0.346 |
| 0.584 | FMJ | 750 | 0.314 | 0.351 |
| 600 Nitro .620 | RN SN | 900 | .334 | .371 |
| | FMJ | 900 | .334 | .334 |
| 700 Nitro .700 | RN SN | 1000 | .292 | .340 |
| | FMJ | 1000 | .292 | .340 |

# POWDERS

## Accurate Powder

| Price | | NG* | Avgerage Length/Thickness in./mm. | Avgerage Diameter inches | Avgerage Diameter millimeters | Bulk Density gram/cc | VMD cc/grain | Comparative Powders*** Ball | Comparative Powders*** Extruded |
|---|---|---|---|---|---|---|---|---|---|
| **BALL PROPELLANTS - Handguns/Shotshell** | | | | | | | | | |
| $15.99 | No. 2 Imp. | 14.0 | — | 0.018 | 0.457 | 0.650 | 0.100 | WIN 231 | |
| $17.99 | No. 5 | 18.0 | — | 0.027 | 0.686 | 0.950 | 0.068 | WIN 540 | |
| $17.99 | No. 7 | 12.0 | — | 0.012 | 0.305 | 0.985 | 0.066 | WIN 630 | |
| $17.99 | No. 9 | 10.0 | — | 1.015 | 0.381 | 0.935 | 0.069 | WIN 296 | |
| $18.99 | 1680 | 10.0 | — | 0.014 | 0.356 | 0.950 | 0.068 | WIN 680 | |
| $18.99 | Solo 4100 | 10.0 | — | 0.011 | 0.279 | 0.960 | 0.068 | WIN 296 | |
| **BALL PROPELLANTS - Rifle** | | | | | | | | | |
| $18.99 | 2230 | 10.0 | — | 0.022 | 0.559 | 0.980 | 0.066 | BL C2, WIN 748 | |
| $18.99 | 2460 | 10.0 | — | 0.022 | 0.559 | 0.990 | 0.065 | BL C2, WIN 748 | |
| $18.99 | 2520 | 10.0 | — | 0.022 | 0.559 | 0.970 | 0.067 | — | |
| $18.99 | 2700 | 10.0 | — | 0.022 | 0.559 | 0.960 | 0.068 | WIN 760 | |
| $18.99 | MAGPRO | 9.0 | — | 0.030 | 0.762 | 0.970 | 0.067 | — | |
| **EXTRUDED PROPELLANTS - Shotshell/Handguns** | | | | | | | | | |
| $14.99 | Nirto 100 | 21.0 | 0.010/ 0.254 | 0.058 | 1.473 | 0.505 | 0.128 | — | |
| $14.99 | Solo 1000 | — | 0.010/ 0.254 | 0.052 | 1.321 | 0.510 | 0.127 | — | |
| **EXTRUDED PROPELLANTS - Rifle/handgun** | | | | | | | | | |
| $22.99 | 5744 | 20.00 | 0.048/ 1.219 | 0.033 | 0.838 | 0.880 | 0.074 | — | |
| **EXTRUDED PROPELLANTS - Rifle** | | | | | | | | | |
| $20.99 | 2015 | — | 0.039/ 0.991 | 0.031 | 0.787 | 0.880 | 0.074 | — | |
| $20.99 | 2495 | — | 0.068/ 1.727 | 0.029 | 0.737 | 0.880 | 0.074 | — | |
| $20.99 | 4064 | — | 0.050/ 1.270 | 0.035 | 0.889 | 0.890 | 0.072 | — | |
| $20.99 | 4350 | — | 0.083/ 0.038 | 0.038 | 0.965 | 0.890 | 0.072 | — | |
| $20.99 | 3100 | — | 0.083/ 0.038 | 0.038 | 0.965 | 0.920 | 0.070 | — | |

*NG-NItroglycerin  ***For comparison only, not a loading recommendation

# Alliant Smokeless Powders

### 20/28 SMOKLESS SHOTSHELL POWDER

Attention sub-gauge shooters. Alliant Powder now offers a new propellant to satisfy your shooting passion. Introducing 20/28, a powder designed to deliver competition-grade performance to 20 and 28 gauge clay target shooters. Extremely clean burning with proven lot-to-lot consistency, 20/28 is sure to elevate any sub-gauge shooter's confidence.

**MSRP:**
  (1lb.) **$18.29**
  (4lb.) **$64.99**
  (8lb.) **119.29**

### 410

Cleanest .410 bore powder on the market.
**1lb: $18.29**
**4lbs: $64.57**
**8lbs: $119.29**

### 2400

Legendary for its performance in .44 magnum and other magnum pistol loads. Originally developed for the .22 Hornet, it's also the shooter's choice for .410 bore. *Available in 8 lb., 4 lb. and 1 lb. canisters.*
**1lb: $18.99**
**4lbs: $60.93**
**8lbs: $122.04**

### AMERICAN SELECT

This ultra-clean burning premium powder makes a versatile target load and superior 1 oz. load for improved clay target scores. Great for Cowboy Action handgun loading, too. *Available in 8 lb., 4 lb. and 1 lb. canisters.*
**1lb: $17.59**
**4lbs: $58.95**
**8lbs: $118.29**

### BLUE DOT

The powder of choice for magnum lead shotshell loads. 10, 12, 16 and 20 ga. Consistent and accurate. Doubles as magnum handgun powder. *Available in 5 lb. and 1 lb. canisters.*
**1lb: $17.59**
**5lbs: $77.99**

### BULLSEYE

America's best known pistol powder. Unsurpassed for .45 ACP target loads. *Available in 8 lb., 4 lb. and 1 lb. canisters.*
**1lb: $ 17.59**
**4lbs: $60.05**
**8lbs: $113.29**

### E3

The first of a new generation of high performance powders.
**1lb: $17.59**
**4lb: $64.58**
**8lbs: $115.29**

### GREEN DOT

It delivers precise burn rates for uniformly tight patterns, and you'll appreciate the lower felt recoil. Versatile for target and field. *Available in 8 lb., 4 lb. and 1 lb. canisters.*
**1lb: $17.59**
**4lbs: $63.12**
**8lbs: $113.29**

### HERCO

Since 1920, a proven powder for heavy shotshell loads, including 10, 12, 16, 20 and 28 ga. target loads. The ultimate in 12 ga., 1¼ oz. upland game loads. *Available in 8 lb., 4 lb. and 1 lb. canisters.*
**1lb: $15.59**
**4lbs: $58.94**
**8lbs: $113.29**

### PISTOL POWDER

Designed for high performance in semi-automatic pistols (9mm, .40 S&W and .357 SIG). *Available in 4 lb. and 1 lb. canisters.*
**1lb: $15.76**
**4lbs: $ 60.05**

HANDLOADING

# Alliant Shotshell Powders

### RED DOT
America's #1 choice for clay target loads, now 50% cleaner. Since 1932, more 100 straights than any other powder. *Available in 8 lb., 4 lb. and 1 lb. canisters.*
1lb: $17.00
4lbs: $69.99
8lbs: $108.99

### RELODER 7
Designed for small caliber varmint loads, it meters consistently and meets the needs of the most demanding bench rest shooter. Great in .45-70 and .450 Marlin. *Available in 5 lb. and 1 lb. canisters.*
1lb: $25.99
5lbs: $111.44

### RELODER 10X
Best choice for light bullet applications in .222 Rem, .223 Rem, .22-250 Rem and key bench rest calibers. Also great in light bullet .308 Win. loads. *Available in 5 lb. and 1 lb. canisters*
1lb: $21.44
5lbs: $83.55

### RELODER 15
An all-around medium speed rifle powder. It provides excellent .223 and .308 cal. performance. Selected as the powder for U.S. Military's M118 Special Ball Long Range Sniper Round. *Available in 5 lb. and 1 lb. canisters.*
1lb: $21.99
5lbs: $99.80

### RELODER 19
Provides superb accuracy in most medium and heavy rifle loads and is the powder of choice for 30-06 and .338 calibers. *Available in 5 lb. and 1 lb. canisters.*
1lb: $25.99
5lbs: $98.77

### RELODER 22
This top performing powder for big-game loads provides excellent metering and is the powder of choice for .270, 7mm magnum and .300 Win. magnum. *Available in 5 lb. and 1 lb. canisters.*
1lb: $ 24.99
5lbs: $97.00

### RELODER 25
This powder for big-game hunting features improved slower burning and delivers the high-energy heavy magnum loads needed. *Available in 5 lb. and 1 lb. canisters.*
1lb: $21.13
5lbs: $99.00

### STEEL
Designed for waterfowl shotshells. Gives steel shot high velocity within safe pressure limits for 10 and 12 ga. loads. *Available in 4 lb. and 1 lb. canisters.*
1lb: $17.95
4lbs: $59.95

### UNIQUE
Shotgun/handgun powder for 12, 16, 20 and 28 ga. loads. Use with most hulls, primers and wads. *Available in 8 lb., 4 lb. and 1 lb. canisters.*
1lb: $16.95
4lbs: $68.99
8lbs: $120.99

### CLAYS
Tailored for use in 12 ga., $^7/_8$ oz., 1 oz. and $1^1/_8$ oz. loads. Performs well in many handgun applications, including .38 Special, .40 S&W and 45 ACP. Perfect for $1^1/_8$ oz. and 1 oz. loads.

| | |
|---|---|
| **14oz.:** | **$15.95** |
| **4lbs:** | **$66.00** |
| **8lbs:** | **$112.95** |

### CLAYS, INTERNATIONAL
Ideal for 12 and 20 ga. autoloaders who want reduced recoil.

| | |
|---|---|
| **14oz.:** | **$15.95** |
| **4lbs:** | **$62.95** |
| **8lbs:** | **$113.95** |

### CLAYS, UNIVERSAL
Loads nearly all of the straight-wall pistol cartridges as well as 12 ga. $1^1/_4$ oz. thru 28 ga. $^3/_4$ oz. target loads.

| | |
|---|---|
| **1lb:** | **$18.95** |
| **4lb:** | **$65.95** |
| **8lb:** | **$119.95** |

### EXTREME BENCHMARK
A fine choice for small rifle cases like the .223 Rem and PPC competition rounds. Appropriate also for the 300-30 and 7x57.

| | |
|---|---|
| **1lb:** | **$21.95** |
| **8lbs:** | **$143.95** |

### EXTREME H50 BMG
Designed for the 50 Browning Machine Gun cartridge. Highly insensitive to extreme temperature changes.

| | |
|---|---|
| **1lb:** | **$26.99** |
| **8lbs:** | **$162.99** |

### EXTREME H322
This powder fills the gap between H4198 and BL-C9(2). Performs best in small to medium capacity cases.

| | |
|---|---|
| **1lb:** | **$29.97** |
| **8lbs:** | **$156.95** |

### EXTREME H1000 EXTRUDED POWDER
Fills the gap between H4831 and H870. Works especially well in over-bore capacity cartridges (1,000-yard shooters take note).

| | |
|---|---|
| **1lb:** | **$23.95** |
| **8lbs:** | **$165.50** |

# Hodgdon Smokeless Powder

### EXTREME H4198
H4198 was developed especially for small and medium capacity cartridges.
1lb:. . . . . . . . . . . . . . . . . . . $23.95
8lbs:. . . . . . . . . . . . . . . . . . $156.95

### EXTREME H4350
Gives superb accuracy at optimum velocity for many large capacity metallic rifle cartridges.
1lb:. . . . . . . . . . . . . . . . . . . $22.59
8lbs:. . . . . . . . . . . . . . . . . . $165.95

### EXTREME H4831
Outstanding performance with medium and heavy bullets in the 6mm's, 25/06, 270 and Magnum calibers. Also available with shortened grains (H4831SC) for easy metering.
1lb:. . . . . . . . . . . . . . . . . . . $23.80
8lbs:. . . . . . . . . . . . . . . . . . $155.00

### EXTREME H4895
4895 gives desirable performance in almost all cases from 222 Rem. to 458 Win. Reduced loads, to as low as 3/5 maximum, still give target accuracy.
1lb:. . . . . . . . . . . . . . . . . . . $26.99
8lbs:. . . . . . . . . . . . . . . . . . $165.50

### EXTREME VARGET
Features small extruded grain powder for uniform metering, plus higher velocities/ normal pressures in such calibers as .223, 22-250, 306, 30-06, 375 H&H.
1lb:. . . . . . . . . . . . . . . . . . . $21.95
8lbs:. . . . . . . . . . . . . . . . . . $156.95

### H110
A spherical powder made especially for the 30 M1 carbine. H110 also does very well in 357, 44 spec., 44 Mag. or 410 ga. shotshell. Recommended for consistent ignition.
From:. . . . . . . . . . . . . . . . . . $21.00

### HP38
A fast pistol powder for most pistol loading. Especially recommended for mid-range 38 specials.
1lb:. . . . . . . . . . . . . . . . . . . $17.95
8lbs:. . . . . . . . . . . . . . . . . . $131.50

### HS-6 AND HS-7
HS-6 and HS-7 for Magnum field loads are unsurpassed. Deliver uniform charges and are dense to allow sufficient wad column for best patterns.
1lb:. . . . . . . . . . . . . . . . . . . $19.49
8lbs:. . . . . . . . . . . . . . . . . . $125.99

### LONGSHOT
Spherical powder for heavy shotgun loads.
1lb:. . . . . . . . . . . . . . . . . . . $19.95
4lbs:. . . . . . . . . . . . . . . . . . . $81.25
8lbs:. . . . . . . . . . . . . . . . . . $129.95

### PYRODEX PELLETS
Both rifle and pistol pellets eliminate powder measures, speeds shooting for black powder enthusiasts.
From:. . . . . . . . . . . . . . $9.00–$28.99

### RETUMBO
Designed for such cartridges as the 300 Rem. Ultra Mag., 30-378 Weatherby, the 7mm STW and other cases with large capacities and small bores. Expect up to 40-100 feet per second more velocity than other magnum powders.
1lb:. . . . . . . . . . . . . . . . . . . $23.00
8lbs:. . . . . . . . . . . . . . . . . . $143.95

### SPHERICAL BL-C2
Best performance is in the 222, .308 other cases smaller than 30/06.
1lb:. . . . . . . . . . . . . . . . . . . $21.95
8lbs:. . . . . . . . . . . . . . . . . . $145.99

### SPHERICAL H335
Similar to BL-C(2), H335 is popular for its performance in medium capacity cases, especially in 222 and 308 Winchester.
1lb:. . . . . . . . . . . . . . . . . . . $22.95
8lbs:. . . . . . . . . . . . . . . . . . $143.99

### SPHERICAL H380
Fills a gap between 4320 and 4350. It is excellent in 22/250, 220 Swift, the 6mm's, 257 and 30/06.
1lb:. . . . . . . . . . . . . . . . . . . $24.99
8lbs:. . . . . . . . . . . . . . . . . . $143.80

### SPHERICAL H414
In many popular medium to medium-large calibers, pressure velocity relationship is better.
1lb:. . . . . . . . . . . . . . . . . . . $21.90
8lbs:. . . . . . . . . . . . . . . . . . $145.95

### TITEGROUP
Excellent for most straight-walled pistol cartridges, incl. 38 Spec., 44 Spec., 45 ACP. Low charge weights, clean burning; position insensitive and flawless ignition.
1lb:. . . . . . . . . . . . . . . . . . . $17.95
4lbs:. . . . . . . . . . . . . . . . . . . $63.95
8lbs:. . . . . . . . . . . . . . . . . . $119.95

### TITEWAD
This 12 ga. flattened spherical shotgun powder is ideal for $7/8$ oz., 1 oz. and $1 1/8$ oz. loads, with minimum recoil and mild muzzle report. The fastest fuel in Hodgdon's line.
1lb:. . . . . . . . . . . . . . . . . . . $24.97
4lbs:. . . . . . . . . . . . . . . . . . . $59.95
8lbs:. . . . . . . . . . . . . . . . . . $114.83

### TRIPLE SEVEN
Hodgdon Powder Company offers its sulfur-free Triple Seven powder in 50-grain pellets. Formulated for use with 209 shotshell primers, Triple Seven leaves no rotten egg smell, and the residue is easy to clean from the bore with water only. The pellets are sized for 50- caliber muzzleloaders and can be used singly (for target shooting or small game) as well as two at a time.
From:. . . . . . . . . . . . . . $15.00–$26.99

HANDLOADING

## RIFLE POWDERS

**IMR 3031**—A propellant with many uses, IMR 3031 is a favorite of 308 match shooters using 168 grain match bullets. It is equally effective in small-capacity varmint cartridges from .223 Remington to .22-250 Remington and a great .30-30 Winchester powder.

1lb:.....................$21.95
8lbs:...................$154.95

**IMR 4198**—This fast-burning rifle powder gives outstanding performance in cartridges like the .222 Remington, 221 Fireball, .45-70 and .450 Marlin.

1lb:.....................$23.95
8lbs:...................$154.95

**IMR 4227**—The choice for true magnum velocities and performance. In rifles, this powder delivers excellent velocity and accuracy in such cartridges as the .22 Hornet and .221 Fireball.

1lb:.....................$21.95
8lbs:...................$139.95

**IMR 4320**—Short granulation, easy metering and perfect for the .223 Remington, .22-250 Remington, .250 Savage and other medium burn rate cartridges. It has long been a top choice for the vintage .300 Savage cartridge.

1lb:.....................$23.58
8lbs:...................$154.95

**IMR 4350**—The number one choice for the new short magnums, both Remington and Winchester versions. For magnums with light to medium bullet weights, IMR 4350 is the best choice.

1lb:.....................$23.95
8lbs:...................$154.95

**IMR 4895**—Originally a military powder featured in the .30-06, IMR 4895 is extremely versatile. From .17 Remington to the .243 Winchester to the .375 H&H Magnum, accuracy and performance are excellent. In addition, it is a long-time favorite of match shooters.

1lb:.....................$23.95
8lbs:...................$154.95

**IMR 7828**—The big magnum powder. This slow burner gives real magnum performance to the large overbored magnums, such as the .300 Remington

Ultra Mag, the .30-378 Weatherby Magnum and 7mm Remington Ultra Magnum.

1lb:.....................$23.95
8lbs:...................$154.95

## HANDGUNS & SHOTGUN POWDERS

**"Hi Skor" 700-X**—This extruded flaketype powder is ideally suited for shotshells in 12 and 16 ga. where clay target and light field loads are the norm. It doubles as an excellent pistol target powder for such cartridges as the .38 Special, .45 ACP and many more.

1lb:.....................$17.99
4lbs:...................$69.37
8lbs:...................$121.99

**"Hi Skor" 800-X**—This large-grained flake powder is at its best when used in heavy field loads from 10 ga. to 28 ga. In handgun cartridges, 800-X performs superbly in cartridges such as the 10mm Auto, .357 Magnum and .44 Remington Magnum.

1lb:.....................$18.79
4lbs:...................$65.99
8lbs:...................$122.99

**PB**—Named for the porous base structure of its grains by which the burning rate is controlled, PB is an extremely

clean-burning, single-base powder. It gives very low pressure in 12 and 20 ga. shotshell target loads and performs well in a wide variety of handgun loads.

1lb:.....................$20.69
4lbs:...................$84.99
8lbs:...................$162.29

**SR 4756**—This fine-grained, easy-metering propellant has long been a favorite of upland and waterfowl handloaders. SR4756 performs extremely well in the big handgun cartridges.

1lb:.....................$20.38
8lbs:...................$134.36

**SR 4759**—This bulky handgun powder works great in the magnums, but really shines as a reduced load propellant for rifle cartridges. Its large grain size gives good loading density for reduced loads, enhancing velocity uniformity.

1lb:.....................$22.49
8lbs:...................$134.36

**SR 7625**—SR7625 covers the wide range of shotshells from 10 ga. to 28 ga. in both target and field loadings. This versatile powder is equally useful in a large array of handgun cartridges for target, self-defense and hunting loads.

1lb:.....................$23.78
8lbs:...................$176.70

# Ramshot Powders

Ramshot (Western Powders, Inc.) powders are all double-base propellants, meaning they contain nitrocellulose and nitroglycerine. While some spherical or ball powders are known for leaving plenty of residue in barrels, these fuels burn very clean. They meter easily, as do all ball powders. Plastic canisters are designed for spill-proof use and include basic loading data on the labels.

**RAMSHOT BIG GAME** is a versatile propellant for cartridges as diverse as the .30-06 and the .338 Winchester, and for light-bullet loads in small-bore magnums.

**1lb:** . . . . . . . . . . . . . . . . . . . . **$19.99**
**8lb:** . . . . . . . . . . . . . . . . . . . **$139.99**

**RAMSHOT COMPETITION** is for the clay target shooter. A fast-burning powder comparable to 700-X or Red Dot, it performs well in a variety of 12 ga. target loads, offering low recoil, consistent pressures and clean combustion

**1lb:** . . . . . . . . . . . . . . . . . . . . **$16.99**
**4lbs:** . . . . . . . . . . . . . . . . . . . **$49.99**
**8lbs:** . . . . . . . . . . . . . . . . . . **$119.95**

**RAMSHOT ENFORCER** is a match for high-performance handgun hulls like the .40 Smith & Wesson. It is designed for full-power loading and high velocities. Ramshot X-Terminator, a fast-burning rifle powder, excels in small-caliber, medium-capacity cartridges. It has the versatility to serve in both target and high-performance varmint loads.

**1lb:** . . . . . . . . . . . . . . . . . . . . **$19.99**
**4lbs:** . . . . . . . . . . . . . . . . . . . **$69.99**
**8lbs:** . . . . . . . . . . . . . . . . . . **$115.90**

**RAMSHOT MAGNUM** is the slowest powder of the Western line, and does its best work in cartridges with lots of case volume and small to medium bullet diameter. It is the powder of choice in 7mm and .30 Magnums.

**1lb:** . . . . . . . . . . . . . . . . . . . . **$21.49**
**8lb:** . . . . . . . . . . . . . . . . . . . **$142.95**

**RAMSHOT SILHOUETTE** is ideal for the 9mm handgun cartridge, from light to heavy loads. It also works well in the .40 Smith & Wesson and combat loads for the .45 Auto.

**1lb:** . . . . . . . . . . . . . . . . . . . . **$19.99**
**4lbs:** . . . . . . . . . . . . . . . . . . . **$73.50**

**RAMSHOT TAC** was formulated for tactical rifle cartridges, specifically the .223 and .308. It has produced exceptional accuracy with a variety of bullets and charge weights.

**1lb:** . . . . . . . . . . . . . . . . . . . . **$17.99**
**8lb:** . . . . . . . . . . . . . . . . . . . **$142.99**

**RAMSHOT TRUE Blue** was designed for small- to medium-size handgun cartridges. Similar to Winchester 231 and Hodgdon HP-38, it has enough bulk to nearly fill most cases, thereby better positioning the powder for ignition.

**1lb:** . . . . . . . . . . . . . . . . . . . . **$20.00**
**8lb:** . . . . . . . . . . . . . . . . . . . **$94.99**

**RAMSHOT X-TERMINATOR** is a clean burning powder designed for the .222 Rem., 223 Rem. and .22 Benchrest calibers.

**1lb:** . . . . . . . . . . . . . . . . . . . . **$19.99**
**8lb:** . . . . . . . . . . . . . . . . . . . **$139.99**

**RAMSHOT ZIP** a fast-burning target powder for cartridges like the .38 Special and .45 ACP, gives competitors uniform velocities.

**1lb:** . . . . . . . . . . . . . . . . . . . . **$17.49**
**8lb:** . . . . . . . . . . . . . . . . . . . **$67.99**

# VihtaVuori Powders

**N110**—A very fast-burning propellant that can be used in applications that previously used Hercules 2400, Hodgdon H110 or Winchester 296. Typical applications include: .22 Hornet, .25-20 Winchester, .357 S&W Magnum, .357 Maximum, .44 Magnum and .45 Winchester Magnum.
**1lb:** . . . . . . . . . . . . . . . . . . . . . **$32.65**

**N120**—A limited application propellant. This speed develops higher pressure than N110 in order to optimize burning. Burning rate falls near the various 4227s. It works well with light bullets in .22 caliber cartridges.
**1lb:** . . . . . . . . . . . . . . . . . . . . . **$32.65**

**N130**—Burning rate is between IMR 4227 and the discontinued Winchester 680. This is the powder used in factory-loaded .22 and 6mm PPC.
**1lb:** . . . . . . . . . . . . . . . . . . . . . **$32.56**
**2lbs:** . . . . . . . . . . . . . . . . . . . . . **$58.76**

**N133**—This powder's speed is very close to IMR 4198 in quickness. Thus, it is ideal for the .222 Remington, .223 Remington, .45-70 Government and other applications where a relatively fast-burning rifle propellant is needed.
**1lb:** . . . . . . . . . . . . . . . . . . . . . **$32.65**
**8lbs:** . . . . . . . . . . . . . . . . . . . . . **$209.92**

**N135**—This is a moderate-burning propellant. It will fit applications similar to Hercules Reloader 12, IMR-4895 or IMR 4064. Applications range from the .17 Remington to the .458 Winchester.
**1lb:** . . . . . . . . . . . . . . . . . . . . . **$32.65**
**2lb:** . . . . . . . . . . . . . . . . . . . . . **$64.00**

**N140**—This powder can usually be used in place of Hercules Reloader 15, IMR 4320 and Hodgdon H380. Applications include: .222 Remington Magnum, .22-250 Remington (factory powder), .30-.30 Winchester, .308 Winchester, .30-06 Springfield, .375 H&H Magnum and so on.
**1lb:** . . . . . . . . . . . . . . . . . . . . . **$32.65**
**8lb:** . . . . . . . . . . . . . . . . . . . . . **$209.92**

**N150**—This is a moderately slow powder that can help refine rifle cartridge ballistics when N140 is too fast and N160 is too slow. Works well in many applications previously filled by 760, H414 and IMR 4350.
**1lb:** . . . . . . . . . . . . . . . . . . . . . **$32.65**
**8lb:** . . . . . . . . . . . . . . . . . . . . . **$209.92**

**N160**—A relatively slow powder ideally suited to many magnum and standard rounds requiring a slow propellant. It has characteristics that make it work well for applications previously using various 4350s, Hercules Reloader 19 and the various 4831s. For example, some ideal applications are: .243 Winchester, .25-06 Remington, .264 Winchester Magnum, .270 Winchester (factory load), 7mm Remington Magnum, .30-06 Springfield, .300 Winchester Magnum, .338 Winchester Magnum, .375 H&H Magnum, etc.
**1lb:** . . . . . . . . . . . . . . . . . . . . . **$32.65**
**2lbs:** . . . . . . . . . . . . . . . . . . . . . **$64.00**
**8lbs:** . . . . . . . . . . . . . . . . . . . . . **$209.92**

**N165**—A very slow-burning magnum propellant for use with heavy bullets. Applications begin with heavy bullets in the .30-06, and include the .338 Winchester Magnum.

**1lb:** . . . . . . . . . . . . . . . . . . . . . **$32.65**

**N170**—VihtaVuori's slowest speed propellant and the slowest canister reloading powder generally available from any manufacturer.
**1lb:** . . . . . . . . . . . . . . . . . . . . . **$32.65**

**N500 Series**—VihtaVuori calls powders that have nitroglycerol added (maximum 25%) producing the high energy NC-powders that form the N500 series. Geometrically the powders in the N500 series are equal to the N100 series. Although these powders have a higher energy content, they do not cause greater wear to the gun. This is because the surface of the powder has been treated with an agent designed to reduce barrel wear. N500 series powders work well at different temperatures.

**N530**—Burning rate close to N135. Especially for .223 Remington. Excellent also for .45-70 Government
**1lb:** . . . . . . . . . . . . . . . . . . . . . **$34.99**
**2lbs:** . . . . . . . . . . . . . . . . . . . . . **$68.00**

**N540**—Burning rate like N140. Especially for the .308 Winchester.
**1lb:** . . . . . . . . . . . . . . . . . . . . . **$34.99**
**2lbs:** . . . . . . . . . . . . . . . . . . . . . **$68.00**

**N550**—Burning rate like N150. Especially for the .308 Winchester and .30-06 Springfield.
**1lb:** . . . . . . . . . . . . . . . . . . . . . **$34.99**

**N560**—Burning rate like N160. Especially for .270 Winchester and 6.5 x 55 Swedish Mauser.
**1lb:** . . . . . . . . . . . . . . . . . . . . . **$34.99**

# ACCESSORIES

# Battenfeld Technologies

### FRANKFORD MICRO RELOADING SCALE
The Micro Reloading Scale is the perfect accessory for reloaders who want a light, accurate, portable scale. The unit is suitable for use on the reloading bench, yet is at home on the shooting range or in the field. The Micro Reloading Scale weighs objects up to 750 grains. It is accurate within ± .1 grains. The digital scale can be set to read in grains, grams, ounces, ct, dwt or ozt. It comes with a protective sleeve and is small enough to fit in your shirt pocket. A calibration weight and batteries are also included.
**MSRP:** . . . . . . . . . . . . . . . . . . .**$49.99**

HANDLOADING

# Dillon Precision Reloaders

DILLON
RL550B

DILLON SL900

## RL 550B

The RL550B is able to load rifle as well as pistol cartridges The RL550B uses standard 7/8 by 14 thread per inch dies, as long as they deprime in the size die. Manually indexed shell-plate. Manually fed cases and bullets Capable of loading 400 to 600 rounds per hour. It has 4 stations and includes a caliber conversion kit, powder measure with large and small powder bars, one toolhead, one prime system and small priming parts and one loaded cartridge catch bin.
**MSRP:** .................$429.95

## SL 900 SHOT SHELL RELOADER

This shot shell reloader reloads 12, 20 and 28 guage loaders. It has automatic indexing, auto powder and priming systems. Features easily adjustable, case-activated powder and shot systems that eliminate troublesome bushing changes along with spilled powder and shot. The powder measure is the same proven design used on our metallic cartridge reloaders, renowned for its accuracy (within one-tenth of a grain) and consistency. New adjustable shot dispenser uses the same design principle, with an extra large hopper that holds 25 pounds of shot. The frame is a heavy duty O-frame design, precision CNC machined to exacting tolerances. Switching from one gauge to another is easy, because the SL 900 features Dillon's famous interchangeable toolhead design. The toolhead assembly simply slides out of the frame, keeping all your critical die and measurement adjustments intact and comes with factory adjusted dies.
**MSRP:** .................$844.95

# Dillon Precision Reloaders

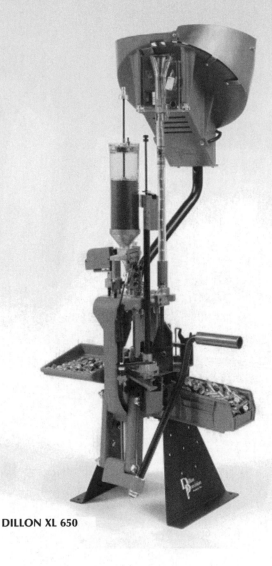

**DILLON THE SQUARE DEAL B**

**DILLON XL 650**

## SQUARE DEAL B

Designed to produce up to 400 or 500 handgun rounds per hour. The Square Deal B comes with a factory adjusted carbide die set. Square Deal B is available in all popular handgun calibers and you can change from one caliber to another in minutes with a Square Deal B caliber conversion kit. Features: Automatic indexing; auto powder/priming systems; available in 14 handgun calibers; loading dies standard.
**MSRP:** . . . . . . . . . . . . . . . . .$370.95

## XL 650

The XL 650 loads virtually every popular pistol and rifle cartridge utilizing standard dies. The optional powder charge check die on the third station sounds an alarm if the powder charge in a round is out of limits, either high or low. An exclusive primer system uses a rotary indexing plate that positively controls each primer and keeps a steel shield between the primers and the operator. Features: Automatic indexing; five-station interchangeable tool-head; auto powder / priming systems; uses standard 7/8" x 14" dies rotary indexing plate for primers.
**MSRP:** . . . . . . . . . . . . . . . . .$556.95

# Forster Reloading (FR)

## CO-AX RELOADING PRESS M B3

Designed to make reloading easier and more accurate, this press offers the following features: Snap-in and snap-out die change; positive spent primer catcher; automatic self-acting shell holder; floating guide rods; top priming device seats primers to factory specifications; uses any standard 7/8" x 14" dies. It now offers a short-throw handle for when you don't need lots of leverage.

**MSRP:** . . . . . . . . . . . . . . . . . **$408.00**

## BENCHREST SEATER DIES

Bench Rest Rifle Dies are glass-hard and polished mirror-smooth with special attention given to headspace, tapers and diameters. Sizing die has an elevated expander button to ensure better alignment of case and neck.

**Original Bench Rest Seater Die: $87.00+**
**Ultra Micrometer Seater Die: $120.00+**
**Custom: $87.00+**

## ULTRA MICROMETER SEATER DIE

Ultra Micrometer Seater Die for 204 Ruger. Forster's Ultra Micrometer Seater Die includes all the popular straight line seating features of our original Bench Rest Seater Die plus an ultra-accurate micrometer adjustment feature for adjusting bullet seating depth. The Forster Ultra allows you to adjust seating depth to .001" or even .0005" increments. Much of the trial and error that was once associated with seating accurate rounds is eliminated with the Ultra Seater Die. After you have seated your bullet close to the desired depth and measured it, simply adjust the micrometer stem down to the desired depth and the cartridge will be exactly the length you need. Fine tuning of your rounds to bring them out close to the lands of your rifling is simple with the Ultra Micrometer Die. If you use different brands and styles of bullets in the same rifle, make note of your "optimal bullet depth setting" for each bullet and save that information for future loading.

**MSRP:** . . . . . . . . . . . . . . . . . **$95.00**

## .50 BMG TRIMMER

50 BMG Case Trimmer Instructions. Case Trimmer, for .50 BMG only - includes one pilot # 510 & case rim holder (no collet required). Enthusiasts of the .50 Cal BMG cartridge now have access to a reloading tool to help them economize on the high cost of ammunition. The .50 BMG Case Trimmer is designed specifically for the reloading needs of .50 Cal BMG shooters. It does not require a collet, but it comes complete with a #510 pilot and rim holder.

**MSRP:** . . . . . . . . . . . . . . . . . **$124.00**

## CLASSIC CASE TRIMMER

Case Trimmer Classic (collet and pilot not included). Larger than our Original Case Trimmer, our Classic was the first production model trimmer on the market to accommodate a large range of classic cartridges. It's suitable for more than three-hundred different big bore calibers from popular big game rifles to classic black powder calibers (the Classic

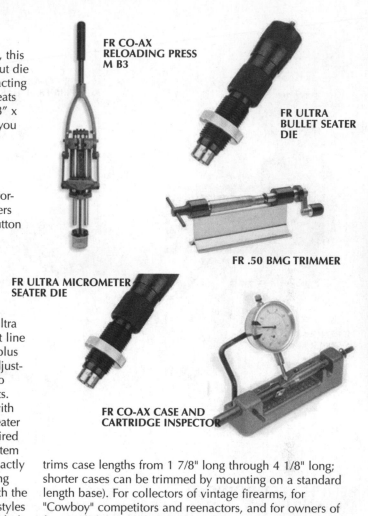

FR CO-AX RELOADING PRESS M B3

FR ULTRA BULLET SEATER DIE

FR .50 BMG TRIMMER

FR ULTRA MICROMETER SEATER DIE

FR CO-AX CASE AND CARTRIDGE INSPECTOR

trims case lengths from 1 7/8" long through 4 1/8" long; shorter cases can be trimmed by mounting on a standard length base). For collectors of vintage firearms, for "Cowboy" competitors and reenactors, and for owners of fine English single and double rifles chambered in hard hitting calibers like 500 Nitro Express, .416 Rigby, 50 Sharps, .475 Nitro Exp, etc., this is the hand case trimmer that will allow accurate reloading. Collets #5 through #8 fit the Classic Case Trimmer. Collets and pilots for the Classic Case Trimmer are available separately. See collet and pilot search.

**MSRP:** . . . . . . . . . . . . . . . . . **$116.00**

## CO-AX CASE AND CARTRIDGE INSPECTOR

Accurate performance from your ammunition is absolutely dependent on uniformity of both the bullet and the case. Achieving that uniformity is not possible without an accurate, reliable measuring device. Forster's exclusive Co-Ax Case & Cartridge Inspector provides you with the ability to ensure uniformity by measuring three critical dimensions: neck wall thickness, case neck concentricity, and bullet runout. Measurements are in increments of one-thousandth of an inch so accuracy is superb. The Inspector is unique because it checks both the bullet and case alignment in relation to the centerline (axis) of the entire cartridge or case. The .17 caliber pilot is not compatible with this tool.

**MSRP:** . . . . . . . . . . . . . . . . . **$110.00**

# Forster Reloading

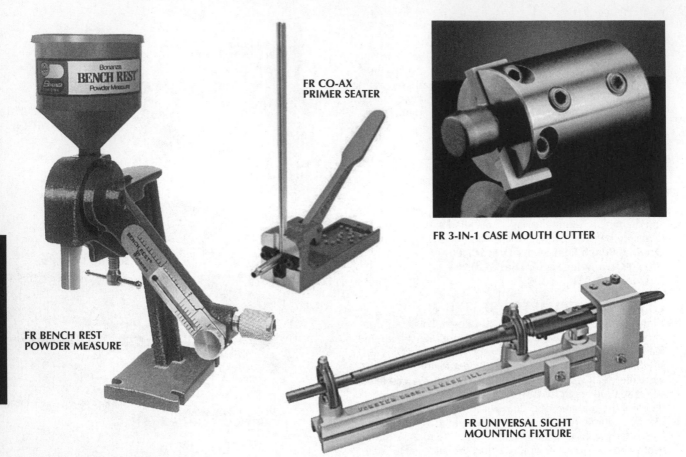

FR CO-AX PRIMER SEATER

FR 3-IN-1 CASE MOUTH CUTTER

FR BENCH REST POWDER MEASURE

FR UNIVERSAL SIGHT MOUNTING FIXTURE

## BENCH REST POWDER MEASURE

The superior design of our Bench Rest Powder Measure throws uniform charges. The charge arm/operating handle meters the powder and dispenses a flow of powder that is free from extremes in variation while minimizing powder shearing. The powder hopper's built-in baffle feeds powder into the charge arm very uniformly. Our Bench Rest measure can throw consistent charges from 2 1/2 grains of Bulls-Eye to 95 grains of 4320. Convenient and simple to use.
MSRP: . . . . . . . . . . . . . . . . $149.00

## CO-AX PRIMER SEATER

There are other primer seaters on the market, but none quite like our exclusive Forster Co-Ax Primer Seater. Unlike other seaters, ours is designed so the operator can eliminate all slop when working with a specific cartridge. That translates into perfect seat-ing, reliable ignition and reduced misfires. No additional shell holders are required. The E-Z-Just jaws close to securely grip most modern rifle and pistol cases with a rim thickness of .045" to .072". Other features include a built-in primer flipper tray. Large and small primer tubes have an open slot and primers stack sideways for added safety.
MSRP: . . . . . . . . . . . . . . . . .$97.00

## UNIVERSAL SIGHT MOUNTING FIXTURE

The Forster Universal Sight Mounting Fixture was designed to meet the exacting requirements of gunsmiths who drill and tap holes for the mounting of scope mounts, receiver sights and shotgun beads. The fixture will accommodate any single barrel long gun including bolt actions, lever actions and pump actions as long as the barrel can be laid into the "V" blocks of the fixture. Tubular magazine guns can be drilled. The body is quality manufactured from an aluminum casting, then precision machined. The two "V" blocks are made from hardened steel accurately ground on the "V" as well as the shaft. The blocks are adjustable for height. Universal Site Mounting Fixture includes 6-48 bushings.
MSRP: . . . . . . . . . . . . . . . . .$465.00

## 3-IN-1 CASE MOUTH CUTTER

This carbide case trimmer accessory performs three functions simultaneously: It trims the case to length, chamfers the inside of the case to an angle of 14 degrees and the outside of the mouth at 30 degrees. Blades never need sharpening if used on brass only. The 3-in-1 Cutter is curently available for three bullet diameters .224, .243, .308.
MSRP: . . . . . . . . . . . . . . . . .$81.00

# Hornady

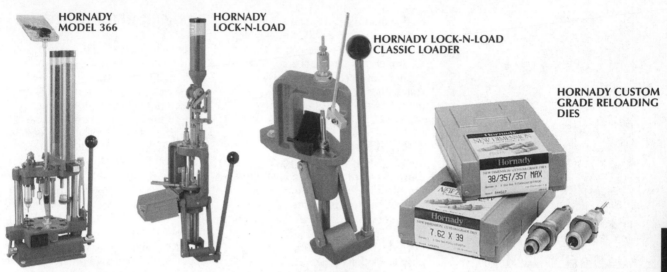

HORNADY
MODEL 366

HORNADY
LOCK-N-LOAD

HORNADY LOCK-N-LOAD
CLASSIC LOADER

HORNADY CUSTOM
GRADE RELOADING
DIES

## 366 AUTO PROGRESSIVE RELOADER

The 366 Auto features full-length resizing with each stroke, automatic primer feed, swing-out wad guide, three-state crimping featuring Taper-Loc for factory tapered crimp, automatic advance to the next station and automatic ejection. The turntable holds 8 shells for 8 operations with each stroke. Automatic charge bar loads shot and powder, dies and crimp starters for 6 point, 8 point and paper crimps.

**12, 20, 28 Ga.:** . . . . . . . . . . . **$670.16**
**.410:** . . . . . . . . . . . . . . . . . . . **$789.91**

## LOCK-N-LOAD AP RELOADING PRESS

The Lock-N-Load Automatic Progressive reloading press features the Lock-N-Load bushing system. Dies and powder measure are inserted into Lock-N-Load die bushings. The bushings remain with the die and powder measure and can be removed in seconds. Other features include: deluxe powder measure, automatic indexing, off-set handle, power-pac linkage, case ejector, five die bushings, shell-plate, primer catcher, Positive Priming System, powder drop, Deluxe Powder Measure, automatic primer feed.

**MSRP:** . . . . . . . . . . . . . . . **$503.58**

## LOCK-N-LOAD CLASSIC LOADER

Lock-N-Load is available on Hornady's single stage and progressive reloader models. This bushing system locks the die into the press like a rifle bolt. Instead of threading dies in and out of the press, you simply lock and unlock them with a slight twist. Dies are held firmly in a die bushing that stays with the die and retains the die setting. Features: easygrip handle; O-style high-strength.

**MSRP:** . . . . . . . . . . . . . . . . **$146.38**
**Lock-N-Load Classic**
    **Press Kit:** . . . . . . . . . . . . **$382.71**

## CUSTOM GRADE RELOADING DIES

For ultra-precise alignment and match-winning performance from your press, you'll want Hornady's Match Grade New Dimension Dies. The neck size die features interchangeable, self-centering neck size bushings (available in .002" increments) that eliminate the chance of oversizing your case necks and overworking the brass. Some calibers are available in two styles: full-length sizing and shoulder bump neck size. Both styles feature interchangeable neck sizing bushings.

**MSRP:** . . . . . . . . . . **$53.20–$100.00**

## HANDHELD PRIMING TOOL

This portable tool primes new or cleaned cases — no need to use your press. Very useful for priming large quantities of cases before processing through a loader. The pliers-style design gives you more leverage, less fatigue and a better feel than thumb-operated styles. Holds both small and large primers right side up for proper feeding. Uses standard Hornady shell holders, and a converter is available for RCBS shells.

**MSRP:** . . . . . . . . . . . . . . . . . **$47.15**

## UNIVERSAL SHELL HOLDERS

Shell Holders for the single stage press have been improved. The mouth of the shell holder has been widened with a radius to allow easier case insertion while maintaining maximum contact area once the case is in the shell holder. Made for use in any tool designed to use a shell holder.

**MSRP:** . . . . . . . . . . . . . . . . . . **$8.97**

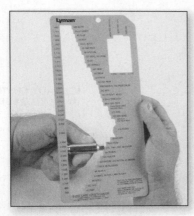

**LYMAN E-ZEE CASE GAUGE II**

## E-ZEE CASE GUAGE II

This improved version measures the case length of over 70 popular rifle and pistol cases. Many new cartridges are included, like the Winchester Short Mags, 204 Ruger, 500 S&W and others. Precisely made, this rugged metal gauge makes sorting cases quick, easy and accurate.
**MSRP:** . . . . . . . . . . . . . . . . . .$19.95

## MODEL 1200 DPS II (DIGITAL POWDER SYSTEM)

Imagine precisely weighing every charge you load nearly as fast as using a measure. With Lyman's new DPS 3, it can be a reality. This is the fastest powder system ever. In addition, the new Auto-Repeat Setting throws a precise charge automatically each time the pan is put in place. The DPS 3 is weighing your next charge while you're seating the bullet on your last charge. Now change powders faster and easier. Automatically throws the next charge each time the pan is put in place.
**MSRP:** . . . . . . . . . $399.95–$410.00

## CRUSHER II RELOADING PRESS

Our new Crusher II is the ideal press for reloading both rifle and pistol cartridges. The Crusher starts with a 1" diameter ram, compound linkage and a 4 1/2" press opening, which makes even the largest magnum cartridges easy to load. Its classic "O" frame design takes all standard 7/8" x 14 dies. The Crusher II is equipped with hardened and ground linkage pins and retaining rings for a smooth and tight operation. The new base design has 14 square inches of "machined flat" surface area with 3 mounting bolt holes (vs. 2 slots for Rock ChuckerT) for perfect rigid mounting. The Crusher's ball handle mounts for either right or left-handed operation.
**MSRP:** . . . . . . . . . . . . . . . . . $166.50

## CRUSHER II PRO KIT

Includes press, loading block, case lube kit, primer tray, Model 500 Pro scale, powder funnel and Lyman Reloading Handbook.
**MSRP:** . . . . . . . . . . . . . . . . .$449.95

## T-MAG II RELOADING PRESS

America's favorite high-speed turret press has been reengineered and upgraded to offer unmatched versatility, power, and precision. The T-Mag II has a new Hi-Tech iron frame with state of the art silver hammertone powder coat finish for guaranteed durability. Lyman's improved Turret Retention System allows smooth indexing while maintaining rock solid turret support. The new turret handle makes indexing easier than ever. The T-Mag II's six station turret head lets the reloader mount up to six different reloading dies at one time. Like more expensive progressive presses, the turret head detaches to easily change calibers while retaining precise set-up. The turret handle doubles as a turret-removing wrench. No tools required. Obtain extra turret heads and have all your favorite calibers set up to reload. The T-Mag II features a "flat machined" base that mounts easily to a wood or metal bench. Compound leverage assures a powerful and smooth operation. The handle mounts for either right or left hand use. The T-Mag II uses standard 7/8" x 14 dies and can be used for reloading rifle or pistol cases. It comes with universal priming arm, primer catcher, and turret handle.
**MSRP:** . . . . . . . . . . . . . . . . .$237.50

**HANDLOADING**

**LYMAN MODEL 1200 DPS II**

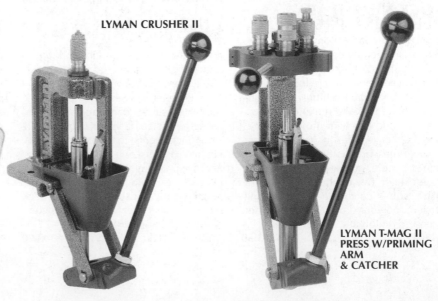

**LYMAN CRUSHER II**

**LYMAN T-MAG II PRESS W/PRIMING ARM & CATCHER**

# Lyman Reloading Tools

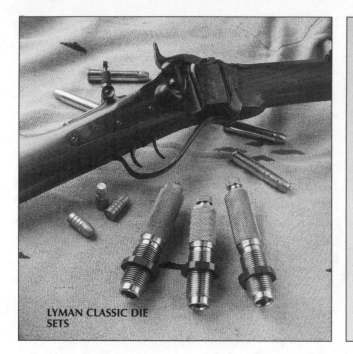

LYMAN CLASSIC DIE SETS

LYMAN STEEL 3 DIE SET FOR 5.7X28MM FN

### 3-DIE CARBIDE PISTOL DIE SETS

Lyman originated the Tungsten Carbide (T-C) sizing die and the addition of extra seating screws for pistol die sets and the two step neck expanding die. Multi-Deluxe Die sets offer these features; a one-piece hardened steel decapping rod and extra seating screws for all popular bullet nose shapes; all-steel construction.
**MSRP:** . . . . . . . . . . . . . . . . . .**$62.50**

### CLASSIC DIE SETS

Lyman Products offers new reloading dies sets for .40-60 Win, .45-65 Win and .45-75 Win cartridges. These cartridges have become popular with the introduction of the new '76 Winchester lever action reproductions. Most importantly, these new dies have been carefully engineered to modern standards to provide precise reloads with either black or smokeless powder.
**MSRP:** . . . . . . . . . . . . . . . . . .**$64.95**

### STEEL 3 DIE SET FOR 5.7X28MM FN PISTOL CARTRIDGE

Lyman has added a new die set for the 5.7x28mm FN pistol cartridge. Offered for those shooters who want to enjoy

the economy and accuracy advantages of reloading this unique new pistol round, these new dies are precisely dimensioned to load ammo that will provide accurate and reliable function in autoloaders.
**MSRP:** . . . . . . . . . . . . . . . . . .**$44.95**

### RIFLE DIE SETS

Lyman precision rifle dies feature fine adjustment threads on the bullet seating stem to allow for precision adjustments of bullet seating depth. Lyman dies fit all popular presses using industry standard 7/8" x 14" threads, including RCBS, Lee, Hornady, Dillon, Redding, and others. Each sizing die for bottle-necked rifle cartridges is carefully vented. This vent hole is precisely placed to prevent air traps that can damage cartridge cases. Each sizing die is polished and heat-treated for toughness.

### RIFLE 2-DIE SETS

Set consists of a full-length resizing die with de-capping stem and neck expanding button and a bullet-seating die for loading jacketed bullets in bottlenecked rifle cases. For those who load cast bullets, use a neck-expanding die, available separately.
**MSRP:** . . . . . . . . . . . . . . . . . .**$41.50**

### RIFLE 3-DIE SETS

Straight wall rifle cases require these three die sets consisting of a full length resizing die with decapping stem, a two step neck expanding (M) die and a bullet seating die. These sets are ideal for loading cast bullets due to the inclusion of the neck-expanding die.
**MSRP:** . . . . . . . . . . . . . . . . . .**$64.95**

### PREMIUM CARBIDE 4-DIE SETS FOR PISTOLS

Lyman 4-Die Sets feature a separate taper crimp die and powder charge/expanding die. The powder charge/expand die has a special hollow 2-step neck expanding plug which allows powder to flow through the die from a powder measure directly into the case. The powder charge/expanding die has a standard 7/8" x 14" thread and will accept Lyman's 55 Powder Measure, or most other powder measures.
**MSRP:** . . . . . . . . . . . . . . . . . .**$79.95**

# Lyman Reloading Tools

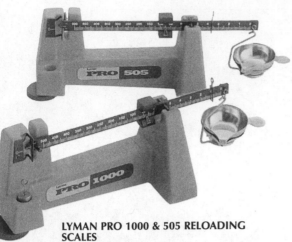

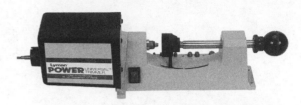

LYMAN PRO 1000 & 505 RELOADING
SCALES

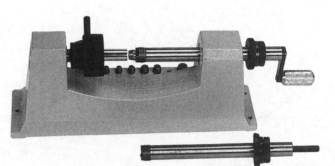

LYMAN ACCU-TRIMMER

LYMAN UNIVERSAL TRIMMER WITH
NINE PILOT MULTI-PACK
WITH POWER ADAPTER

HANDLOADING

## PRO 1000 & 505 RELOADING SCALES

Features include improved platform system; hi-tech base design of high impact styrene; extra-large, smooth leveling wheel; dual agate bearings; larger damper for fast zeroing; built-in counter weight compartment; easy-to-read beam.

**Pro 1000 Scale:** . . . . . . . . . . . **$84.95**
**Pro 500 Scale:** . . . . . . . . . . . **$69.95**

## ACCU-TRIMMER

Lyman's Accu-Trimmer can be used for all rifle and pistol cases from .22 to .458 Winchester Magnum. Standard shellholders are used to position the case, and the trimmer incorporates standard Lyman cutter heads and pilots. Mounting options include bolting to a bench, C-clamp or vise.

**MSRP:** . . . . . . . . . . . . . . . . **$62.95**

## UNIVERSAL POWER TRIMMER

The Lyman Power Trimmer is powered by a fan-cooled electric motor designed to withstand the severe demands of case trimming. The unit, which features the Universal Chuckhead, allows cases to be positioned for trimming or easy removal. The Power Trimmer package includes Nine-Pilot Multi-Pack, two cutter heads and a pair of wire end brushes for cleaning primer pockets. Other features include safety guards, on-off rocker switch, heavy cast base with receptacles for nine pilots and bolt holes for mounting on a work bench. Power Trimmer is available for 110 or 220 volt systems.

**MSRP:** . . . . . . . . . . . . . . . . . **$325.00**
**230 Volt Model:** . . . . . . . . . **$333.50**

## UNIVERSAL TRIMMER

This trimmer with patented chuckhead accepts all metallic rifle or pistol cases, regardless of rim thickness. To change calibers, simply change the case head pilot. Other features include coarse and fine cutter adjustments, an oil-impregnated bronze bearing, and a rugged cast base to assure precision alignment. Optional carbide cutter available.

**MSRP** . . . . . . . . . . . . . . . . . . **$99.95**
**Universal Trimmer**
    **Power Pack Combo:** . . . . **$116.50**
**Universal Trimmer**
    **Power Adapter:** . . . . . . . . **$24.95**

# Lyman Reloading Tools

**LYMAN TURBO TWIN TUMBLER**

**LYMAN MODEL 2500 PRO MAGNUM TUMBLER**

**LYMAN .40-60 WINCHESTER BULLET MOLD**

**LYMAN 55 CLASSIC BLACK POWDER MEASURE**

## MODEL 1200 CLASSIC TURBO TUMBLER

This case tumbler features an improved base and drive system, plus a stronger suspension system and built-in exciters for better tumbling action and faster cleaning.

**Model 1200 Classic:** . . . . . . . . $67.95
**Model 1200 Auto-Flo:** . . . . . . $110.00

## MODEL 2500 PRO MAGNUM TUMBLER

The Lyman 2500 Pro Magnum tumbler handles up to 900 .38 Special cartridges at once.

**MSRP:** . . . . . . . . . . . . . . . . . $99.95
**W/ Auto Flow Feature:** . . . . . $139.95

## TURBO TWIN TUMBLER

The Twin features Lyman 1200 Pro Tumbler with an extra 600 bowl system. Reloaders may use each bowl interchangeably for small or large capacity loads. 1200 Pro Bowl System has a built-in sifter lid for easy sifting of cases and media at the end of the polishing cycle. The Twin Tumbler features the Lyman Hi-Profile base design with built-in exciters and anti-rotation pads for faster, more consistent tumbling action.

**MSRP:** . . . . . . . . . . . . . . . . . $88.00

## .40-60 WINCHESTER BULLET MOLD

The .40-60 Winchester cartridge has become popular with the introduction of the '76 Winchester lever action reproductions. The mold is a proven ideal design that was popular back when these big-bore, lever-action rifles were originally introduced. It has been carefully updated and dimensioned to modern standards for precise reloads with either black or smokeless powder.

**MSRP:** . . . . . . . . . . . . . . . . . $81.25

## 55 CLASSIC BLACK POWDER MEASURE

Lyman's 55 Classic Powder Measure is ideal for the Cowboy Action Competition or black powder cartridge shooters. The one-pound-capacity aluminum reservoir and brass powder meter eliminate static. The internal powder baffle assures highly accurate and consistent charges. The 24" powder compacting drop tube allows the maximum charge in each cartridge. Drop tube works on calibers 38 through 50 and mounts easily to the bottom of the measure.

**Model with Tubes:** . . . . . . . . $164.95
**Powder Drop Tubes only:** . . . $35.95

# Lyman Reloading Tools

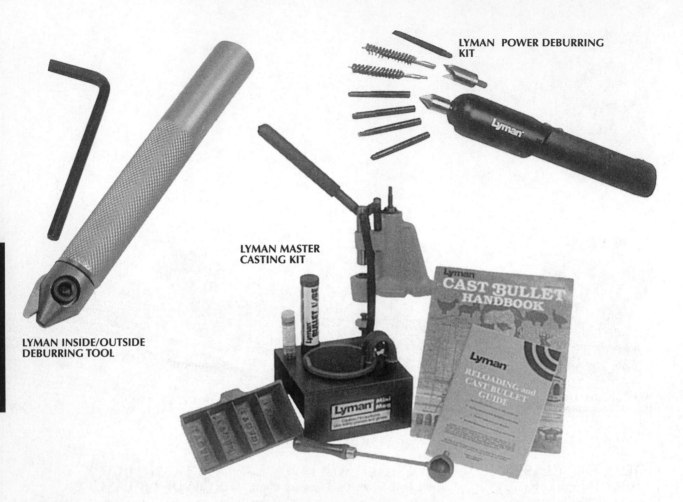

**LYMAN POWER DEBURRING KIT**

**LYMAN MASTER CASTING KIT**

**LYMAN INSIDE/OUTSIDE DEBURRING TOOL**

## OUTSIDE NECK TURNING TOOL

For both Lyman's Universal Trimmer and AccuTrimmer. Provides the user with a simple-to-operate tool that guarantees neck wall thickness and outside neck diameter. Essential for case reforming. Improves accuracy. Adjustable cutter (for length of cut and rate of feed) removes minimum brass to attain uniformity. Cutter blade can be adjusted to any diameter from .195" to .405". Comes with two extra cutting blades. Mandrels from .22 to .375. Includes six mandrel Multi-Pack (for .22, .243, .25, .270, 7mm, and .30 calibers). (Not adaptable to Power Trimmer.) Replacement parts and additional mandrels also available.
**MSRP . . . . . . . . . . . . . . . . . . $38.25**

## INSIDE/OUTSIDE DEBURRING TOOL

This tool features an adjustable cutting blade that adapts easily to the mouth of any rifle or pistol case from .22 to .45 caliber with a simple hex wrench adjustment. Inside deburring is completed by a conical internal section with slotted cutting edges, thus providing uniform inside and outside deburring in one simple operation. The deburring tool is mounted on an anodized aluminum handle that is machine-knurled for a sure grip.
**MSRP . . . . . . . . . . . . . . . . . . $16.50**

## MASTER CASTING KIT

Designed especially to meet the needs of blackpowder shooters, this kit features Lyman's combination round ball

and maxi ball mould blocks. It also contains a combination double cavity mould, mould handle, mini-mag furnace, lead dipper, bullet lube, a user's manual and a cast bullet guide. Kits are available in .45, .50 and .54 caliber.
**MSRP . . . . . . . . . . $244.95–$255.00**

## POWER DEBURRING KIT

Features a high torque, rechargeable power driver plus a complete set of accessories, including inside and outside deburr tools, large and small reamers and cleaners and case neck brushes. No threading or chucking required. Set also includes battery recharger and standard flat and Phillips driver bits.
**MSRP . . . . . . . . . . . . . . . . . . $62.50**

# Lyman Reloading Tools

LYMAN REVOLUTION ROTATING GUN VISE

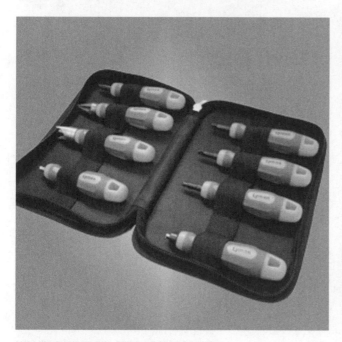

LYMAN UNIVERSAL PREP ACCESSORY SET

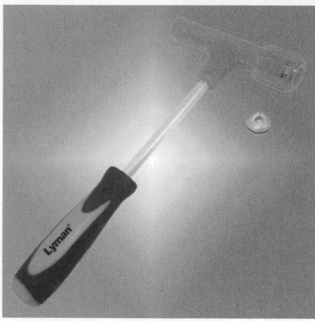

LYMAN MAGNUM INERTIA BULLET PULLER

## REVOLUTION ROTATING GUN VISE

This versatile gun vise is engineered with a full range of adjustments; it tilts, clamps and has inserts to securely hold any firearm. The padded contact points protect the firearm during cleaning, maintenance or gunsmithing, even bore sighting.

MSRP . . . . . . . . . . . . . . . . . .$92.00

## UNIVERSAL PREP ACCESSORY SET

This new accessory features all the items necessary for quality case preparation in one deluxe set. Includes both large and small primer pocket reamers, primer pocket cleaners, outside deburring tool, inside (VLD) chamfer tool and large and small primer pocket uniformer tools. All individual items have their own molded handle with rubber insert for sure grip. Includes custom zippered case for storage or easy transport to the range.

MSRP . . . . . . . . . . . . . . . . . .$69.95

## MAGNUM INERTIA BULLET PULLER

Safely strips loaded rounds in seconds without damage to bullet or case. Features newly engineered head design that allows use on full range of calibers from tiny 5.7 X 28FN to the largest Magnums. New "full-size" ergonomic molded handle with rubber insert for comfort and sure grip. Traps components with just a few raps on the bench.

MSRP . . . . . . . . . . . . . . . . . .$21.50

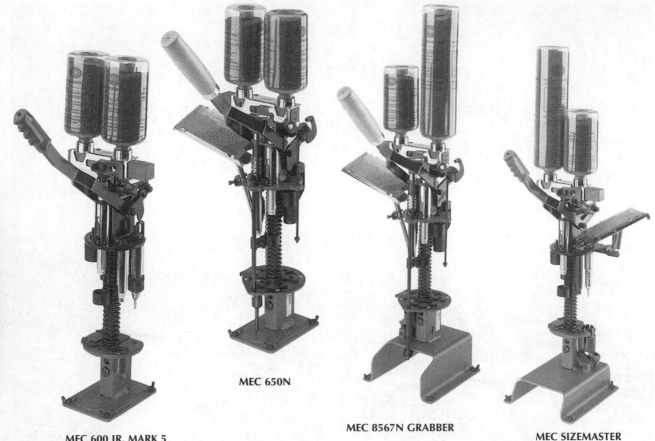

MEC 650N

MEC 600 JR. MARK 5

MEC 8567N GRABBER

MEC SIZEMASTER

## 600 JR. MARK 5

This single-stage reloader features a cam-action crimp die to ensure that each shell returns to its original condition. MEC's 600 Jr. Mark 5 can load 6 to 8 boxes per hour and can be updated with the 285 CA primer feed. Press is adjustable for 3 in. shells.

**MSRP:** . . . . . . . . . **$165.32–$181.06**

## 650N

This reloader works on 6 shells at once. A reloaded shell is completed with every stroke. The MEC 650 does not resize except as a separate operation. Automatic primer feed is standard. Simply fill it with a full box of primers and it will do the rest. Reloader has 3 crimping stations: the first one starts the crimp, the second closes the crimp, and the third places a taper on the shell. Available in 12, 16, 20 and 28 ga. and .410 bore. No die sets available.

**MSRP:** . . . . . . . . . **$311.02–$340.64**

## 8567N GRABBER

This reloader features 12 different operations at all 6 stations, producing finished shells with each stroke of the handle. It includes a fully automatic primer feed and Auto-Cycle charging, plus MEC's exclusive 3-stage crimp. The "Power Ring" resizer ensures consistent, accurately sized shells without interrupting the reloading sequence. Simply put in the wads and shell casings, then remove the loaded shells with each pull of the handle. Optional kits to load 3 in. shells and steel shot make this reloader tops in its field. Resizes high and low base shells. Available in 12, 16, 20, 28 ga. and .410 bore.

**MSRP:** . . . . . . . . . **$438.02–$479.74**

## SIZEMASTER

Sizemaster's "Power Ring" collet resizer returns each base to factory specifications. This resizing station handles brass or steel heads, both high and low base. An 8-fingered collet squeezes the base back to original dimensions, then opens up to release the shell easily. The E-Z Prime auto primer feed is standard equipment (not offered in .410 bore). Press is adjustable for 3 in. shells and is available in 10, 12, 16, 20, 28 ga. and .410 bore. Die sets are available at: $88.67 ($104.06 in 10 ga.).

**MSRP:** . . . . . . . . . **$238.38–$261.08**

# MEC Reloading

**MEC STEELMASTER**

**MEC 9000H**

**MEC 9000G**

## STEELMASTER

Equipped to load steel shotshells as well as lead ones. Every base is resized to factory specs by a precision "power ring" collet. Handles brass or steel heads in high or low base. The E-Z prime auto primer feed dispenses primers automatically and is standard equipment. Separate presses are available for 12 ga. 2¾", 3", 3½" and 10 ga.

**Steelmaster**
    **10 or 12 Ga:** .... **$269.77–$282.03**
**Steelmaster 12 Ga:** ........ **$282.03**

## 9000 SERIES

MEC's 9000 Series features automatic indexing and finished shell ejection for quicker and easier reloading. The factory set speed provides uniform movement through every reloading stage. Dropping the primer into the reprime station no longer requires operator "feel." The reloader requires only a

minimal adjustment from low to high brass domestic shells, any one of which can be removed for inspection from any station. Can be set up for automatic or manual indexing. Available in 12, 16, 20 and 28 ga. and .410 bore. No die sets are available.

**9000GN:** ......... **$527.43–$577.67**
**9001HN without**
    **P&H:** ......... **$590.39–$646.62**
**9000HN:** ........ **$1077.32–$1128.63**

# MTM Case-Gard Handloading

## MINI DIGITAL RELOADING SCALE

From first time reloaders to competitive gun and archery shooters, MTM Case-Gard introduces a pocket-sized scale that is sure to satisfy all levels of sportsmen. It features a powder pan, custom designed to facilitate bullet, powder, and arrow weighing. It has up

to a 750 grain capacity. It measures in grains, grams, carats, and ounces. The high-impact, plastic sensory cover doubles as a large powder pan. Great for the reloading bench or a well-equipped shooting box, the DS-750 is packed with features that shooting sportsmen need.

**From:** ............. **$28.74–$39.99**

**MTM MINI DIGITAL RELOADING SCALE**

# Nosler Reloading

### CUSTOM BRASS

Nosler now offers cartridge brass in 257 Weatherby, 7mm Rem. Ultra Mag., 8x57 JS Mauser, and 350 Rem. Mag. The cartridge brass is made to exact dimensional standards and tolerances for maximum accuracy/consistency and long case life. Flash holes are deburred, and necks are deburred and chambered. Packaged in custom boxes of 50.

**257 Weatherby:** . . . . . . . . . . .**$77.00**
**7mm Rem. Ultra Mag.:** . . . . .**$60.00**
**8x57 JS Mauser:** . . . . . . . . . . .**$75.00**
**350 Rem. Mag.:** . . . . . . . . . . .**$75.00**

# RCBS Reloading Tools

**RCBS ROCK CHUCKER SUPREME PRESS**

**RCBS UNIVERSAL PRIMER ARM 2**

**RCBS AMMOMASTER-2 SINGLE STAGE PRESS**

## ROCK CHUCKER SUPREME PRESS

With its easy operation, outstanding strength and versatility, a Rock Chucker Supreme press serves beginner and pro alike. It can also be upgraded to a progressive press with an optional Piggyback conversion unit.

- Heavy-duty cast iron for easy case-resizing
- Larger window opening to accommodate longer cartridges
- 1" ram held in place by 12½ sq. in. of rambearing surface

- Ambidextrous handle
- Compound leverage system
- ⅞" x 14" thread for all standard reloading dies and accessories

**MSRP** . . . . . . . . . . . . . . . . .**$196.95**

## UNIVERSAL PRIMER ARM 2

Designed for fast and accurate primer seating. Primer plugs and sleeves included for large and small rifle and pistol primers. Universal primer for Rock Chucker Press.

**MSRP:** . . . . . . . . . . . . . . . . . .**$16.95**

## AMMOMASTER-2 SINGLE STAGE PRESS

The AmmoMaster offers handloaders the freedom to configure a press to particular needs and preferences. It covers the complete spectrum of reloading, from single stage through fully automatic progressive reloading, from .25 Auto to .50 caliber. The AmmoMaster Auto has all the features of a five-station press.

**MSRP:** . . . . . . . . . . . . . . . . .**$351.95**

# RCBS Reloading Tools

RCBS
GRAND
SHOTSHELL
PRESS

RCBS MINI-
GRAND
SHOTSHELL
PRESS

RCBS
PRO-2000
PROGRESSIVE
PRESS

## AMMOMASTER
## .50BMG PACK

The Pack includes the press, dies and accessory items needed, all in one box. The press is the Ammo Master Single Stage rigged for 1½" dies. It has a 1½" solid steel ram and plenty of height for the big .50. The kit also has a set of RCBS .50 BMG , 1½" reloading dies, including both full-length sizer and seater. Other items are a shell holder, ram priming unit and a trim die.
**MSRP:** . . . . . . . . . . . . . . . . .**$765.95**

## GRAND SHOTSHELL
## PRESS

Tthe combination of the Powder system and shot system and Case Holders allows the user to reload shells without fear of spillage. The powder system is case-actuated: no hull, no powder. Cases are easily removed with universal 12 and 20 ga. case holders allowing cases to be sized down to the rim. Priming system: Only one primer feeds at a time. Steel size ring: Provides complete resizing of high and low base hulls. Holds 25 lbs. of shot and 1½ lbs. of powder. Lifetime warranty.
**MSRP:** . . . . . . . . . . . . . . . . . **$1025.95**
**Grand Conversion Kit:** . . . . . **$489.95**

## MINI-GRAND
## SHOTSHELL PRESS

The Mini-Grand shotgun press, a seven-station single-stage press, loads 12 and 20 ga. hulls, from 2¾ to 3½ in. in length. It utilizes RCBS, Hornady and Ponsness Warren powder and shot bushings, with a half-pound capacity powder hopper and 12½ lb. capacity shot hopper. The machine will load both lead and steel shot.
**MSRP:** . . . . . . . . . . . . . . . . .**$169.95**

## ROCK CHUCKER
## SUPREME MASTER KIT

The Rock Chucker Master Reloading Kit includes all the tools and accessories needed to start handloading: Rock Chucker Press; RCBS 505 Reloading Scale; Speer Manual #13; Uniflow Powder Measure; deburring tool; case loading block; Primer Tray-2; hand priming tool; powder funnel; case lube pad; case neck brushes; fold-up hex key set; Trim Pro Manual Case Trimmer Kit.
**MSRP:** . . . . . . . . . . . . . . . . .**$458.95**

## PARTNER PRESS

Easy-to-use, durable press in a compact package. Features compound linkage, durable steel links, priming arm. Reloads most standard calibers.
**Partner Press:** . . . . . . . . . . . .**$93.95**
**Partner Press Reloading Kit:** **$236.95**

## PRO-2000
## PROGRESSIVE PRESS

Constructed of cast iron, the Pro-2000 features five reloading stations. The case-actuated powder measure assures repeatability of dispensing powder. A Micrometer Adjustment Screw allows precise return to previously recorded charges. All dies are standard 7/8" x 14", including the Expander Die. The press incorporates the APS Priming System. Allows full-length sizing in calibers from .32 Auto to.460 Weatherby Mag.
**MSRP:** . . . . . . . . . . . . . . . . .**$673.95**
**Deluxe Reloading Kit:** . . . .**$1212.95**

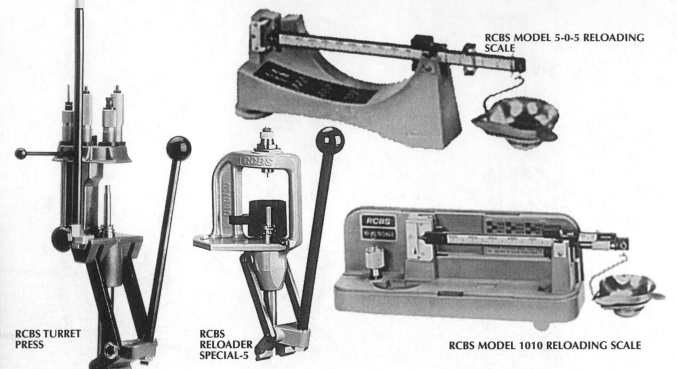

RCBS MODEL 5-0-5 RELOADING SCALE

RCBS TURRET PRESS

RCBS RELOADER SPECIAL-5

RCBS MODEL 1010 RELOADING SCALE

HANDLOADING

## TURRET PRESS

With pre-set dies in the six-station turret head, the Turret Press can increase production from 50 to 200 rounds per hour. The frame, links, and toggle block are constructed of cast iron and the handle offers compound leverage for full-length sizing of any caliber from .25 ACP to .460 Weatherby Magnum. Six stations allow for custom set-up. The quick-change turret head makes caliber changes fast and easy. This press accepts all standard 7/8" x 14" dies and shell holders.

**MSRP:** . . . . . . . . . . . . . . . . **$284.95**
**Turret Deluxe Reloading Kit: $559.95**

## RELOADER SPECIAL-5 PRESS

The Reloader Special press features a ball handle and primer arm so that cases can be primed and resized at the same time. Other features include a compound leverage system; solid aluminum "O" frame offset; corrosion-resistant baked-powder finish; 7/8" x 14" thread for all standard reloading dies and accessories; optional Piggyback II conversion unit.

**MSRP:** . . . . . . . . . . . . . . . . **$160.95**

## PIGGYBACK III CONVERSION KIT

The Piggyback III conversion unit moves from single-stage reloading to 5-station, manual-indexing, progressive reloading in one step. The Piggyback III will work with the RCBS Rock Chucker, Reloader Special-3 and Reloader Special-5.

**MSRP:** . . . . . . . . . . . . . . . . **$508.95**

## MODEL 5-0-5 RELOADING SCALE

This 511-grain capacity scale has a three-poise system with widely spaced, deep beam notches. Two smaller poises on right side adjust from 0.1 to 10 grains, larger one on left side adjusts in full 10-grain steps. The scale uses magnetic dampening to eliminate beam oscillation. The 5-0-5 also has a sturdy die-cast base with large leveling legs. Self-aligning agate bearings support the hardened steel beam pivots for a guaranteed sensitivity to 0.1 grains.

**MSRP:** . . . . . . . . . . . . . . . . **$115.95**

## MODEL 1010 RELOADING SCALE

Normal capacity is 510 grains, which can be increased without loss of sensitivity by attaching the included extra weight up to 1010 grains. Features include micrometer poise for quick, precise weighing, special approach-toweight indicator, easy-to-read graduation, magnetic dampener, agate bearings, anti-tip pan and a dustproof lid snaps on to cover scale for storage. Sensitivity is guaranteed to 0.1 grains.

**MSRP:** . . . . . . . . . . . . . . . . **$195.95**

# RCBS Reloading Tools

**RCBS CHARGEMASTER 1500**

**RCBS RANGEMASTER 750**

**RCBS APS PRIMER STRIP LOADER**

**RCBS CHARGEMASTER COMBO**

**RCBS RC-130 MECHANICAL SCALE**

## CHARGEMASTER 1500 SCALE

High performance reloading scale with 1500-grain capacity. Scale reads in grains or grams; calibration weights included. Available in 110 or 220 volt—AC adaptor included. Can be upgraded to an automatic dispensing system with the RCBS ChargeMaster.
**MSRP:** ................$246.95

## CHARGEMASTER COMBO

Performs as a scale or as a complete powder dispensing system. Scale can be removed and used separately. Dispenses from 2.0 to 300 grains. Reads and dispenses in grains or grams. Stores up to 30 charges in memory for quick recall of favorite loads. 110 volt or 220 volt adaptor included.
**MSRP:** .................$470.95

## RANGEMASTER 750 SCALE

Compact, lightweight and portable with 750-grain capacity. Scale reads in grams or grains; calibration weights included. Accurate to ± 0.1 of a grain; fast calibration; Powered by AC or 9 volt battery—AC adaptor included. 110 or 220 volt model available.
**MSRP:** .................$156.95

## RC-130 MECHANCIAL SCALE

The RC130 features a 130-grain capacity and maintenance-free movement, plus a magnetic dampening system for fast readings. A 3-poise design incorporates easy adjustments with a beam that is graduated in increments of 10 grains and 1 grain. A micrometer poise measures in 0.1-grain increments with accuracy to ±0.1 grain.
**MSRP:** .................$56.95

## APS PRIMER STRIP LOADER

For those who keep a supply of CCI primers in conventional packaging, the APS primer strip loader allows quick filling of empty strips. Each push of the handle seats 25 primers.
**MSRP:** .................$38.95

# RCBS Reloading Tools

**RCBS ELECTRONIC DIGITAL MICROMETER**

**RCBS SHELL HOLDER RACK**

**RCBS HAND PRIMING TOOL**

**RCBS TRIM PRO CASE TRIMMER**

## ELECTRONIC DIGITAL MICROMETER
Instant reading; large, easy to read numbers for error reduction with instant inch/millimeter conversion; zero adjust at any position; thimble lock for measuring like objects; replaceable silver oxide cell—1.55 Volt; auto off after 5 minutes for longer battery life; adjustment wrench included; fitted wooden storage cases.
**MSRP:** . . . . . . . . . . . . . . . . .**$156.95**

## HAND PRIMING TOOL
A patented safety mechanism separates the seating operation from the primer supply, virtually eliminating the possibility of tray detonation. Fits in your hand for portable primer seating. Primer tray installation requires no contact with the primers. Uses the same RCBS shell holders as RCBS presses. Made of cast metal.
**MSRP:** . . . . . . . . . . . . . . . . .**$49.95**

## SHELL HOLDER RACK
RCBS has developed the Shell Holder Rack to give reloaders another unique way to stay organized. This item allows shooters quick and easy access to all shell holders, and eliminates digging through several loose holders to find the right one. The Shell Holder Rack has twelve positions that hold two shell holders on each post. There is also

room to store six Trim Pro Shell Holders as well. Its clear cover keeps out the dust and dirt while allowing you to see what is stored in the rack. This rack can also be mounted on the wall or used on the bench. The wall mount spacing allows it to be hung off of standard 1-in. pegboard hooks as well. The support legs angle the bottom out for wall mounting or the top up for bench use. Several Shell Holder Racks can be snapped together if more shell holder storage is needed, and stickers are included to label shell holder posts.
**MSRP:** . . . . . . . . . . . . . . . . .**$15.95**

## POW'R PULL BULLET PULLER
The RCBS Pow'r Pull bullet puller features a three-jaw chuck that grips the case rim—just rap it on any solid surface like a hammer, and powder and bullet drop into the main chamber for re-use. A soft cushion protects bullets from damage. Works with most centerfire cartridges from .22 to .45 (not for use with rimfire cartridges)
**MSRP:** . . . . . . . . . . . . . . . . .**$19.95**

## TRIM PRO CASE TRIMMER
Cases are trimmed quickly and easily. The lever-type handle is more accurate to use than draw collet systems. A flat plate shell holder keeps cases locked in place and aligned. A micrometer fine

adjustment bushing offers trimming accuracy to within .001 in. Made of die-cast metal with hardened cutting blades.
**Power 120 Vac Kit:** . . . . . . . .**$358.95**
**Manual Kit:** . . . . . . . . . . . . .**$129.95**
**Trim Pro Case Trimmer Stand:** . . . . . . . . .**$25.95**

## PRECISION BI-POD
Quick-adjust telescoping legs of 6061 T6 alloy secure your rifle for accurate shooting on uneven ground. Range of movement: 7 to 10 inches, with 25 degrees of cant. Skid-resistant polyurethane feet grip slick surfaces. Tool-free mounting adapts this bipod to any Picatinny rail. Paddle locks make for quick, easy deployment. Hard-coating anodizing ensures tough use.
**MSRP:** . . . . . . . . . . . . . . . . .**$219.95**

## BULLET FEEDER- RIFLE KIT (PROGRESSIVE PRESS)
Designed to fit most progressive presses with 7/8". platform holes, this automatic unit features a rotating collator that orients the bullets to drop itno the feed mechanism/seat die. Choose .22 or .30. The hopper holds 250 .22 caliber bullets over .30s. Powdered by 110-240 VAC, the unit comes with plug adapters for foreign outlets.
**MSRP:** . . . . . . . . . . . . . . . . .**$613.95**
**Also available Bullet Feeder- Pistol Kit:** . . . . . .**$526.95**

# Redding Reloading Tools

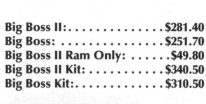

REDDING BIG
BOSS RELOADING
PRESS

REDDING
T-7 TURRET
PRESS

REDDING
ULTRAMAG
RELOADING
PRESS

## HANDLOADING PRESSES

## BOSS RELOADING PRESS

This "O" type reloading press features a rigid cast iron frame whose 36 degree offset provides the best visibility and access of comparable presses. Its "Smart" primer arm moves in and out of position automatically with ram travel. The priming arm is positioned at the bottom of ram travel for lowest leverage and best feel. Model 721 accepts all standard 7/8" x 14" threaded dies and universal shell holders.

**MSRP:** . . . . . . . . . . . . . . . . . **$198.90**
**Boss Reloading Kit:** . . . . . . **$257.70**

## BIG BOSS RELOADING PRESS

A larger version of the Boss reloading press built on a heavier frame with a longer ram stroke for reloading magnum cartridges. It features a 1-in. diameter ram with over 3.8 inches of stroke; Smart primer arm; offset ball handle; heavy duty cast iron frame; heavy duty compound linkage; steel adapter bushing accepts all standard 7/8" x 14" threaded dies.

**Big Boss II:** . . . . . . . . . . . . . **$281.40**
**Big Boss:** . . . . . . . . . . . . . . . **$251.70**
**Big Boss II Ram Only:** . . . . . . **$49.80**
**Big Boss II Kit:** . . . . . . . . . . **$340.50**
**Big Boss Kit:** . . . . . . . . . . . . **$310.50**

## T-7 TURRET PRESS

The Redding T-7 Turret Press has a 7-station turret head that is easily turned to set the next die in place. With the addition of additional turret heads (sold separately), a reloader can switch between calibers without readjusting depth. The cast iron construction and stout compound linkage allow for reloading magnum cartridges with ease.

**MSRP:** . . . . . . . . . . . . . . . . . **$436.80**
**Turret Kit:** . . . . . . . . . . . . . **$495.30**

## ULTRAMAG RELOADING PRESS

The UltraMag is the heavy duty workhorse of the Redding line, and is a nononsense high quality press. It is our favorite for large jobs and we highly recommend it for the reloader needing a large frame press. The leverage system on this press (unlike most others)

is connected to the top of the press frame which gives it literally tons of pressure without the usual concerns of press frame deflection or misalignment. This is an expensive press, but one we feel is worth the money, especially for long magnum cartridges.

**MSRP $454.80**
**Kit, includes shell holder and one set of 10A dies:** . . . . . **$513.90**

## DIES & BUSHINGS

## BODY DIES

Designed to full-length resize the case body and bump the shoulder position for proper chambering without disturbing the case neck. They are intended for use only to resize cases that have become increasingly difficult to chamber after repeated firing and neck sizing. Small Base Body Dies are available in .223 Rem, 6mm P.P.C, 6mm B. R. Rem, 6mm/284 Win, .260 Rem, 6.5mm/284 Win, .284 Win, .308 Win, .30-06.

**Category I:** . . . . . . . . . . . . . . **$40.68**
**Category II:** . . . . . . . . . . . . . **$50.40**
**Category III:** . . . . . . . . . . . . **$61.80**

# Redding Reloading Tools

**REDDING COMPETITION BULLET SEATING DIE**

**REDDING NECK SIZING DIES**

**REDDING COMPETITION BUSHING - STYLE NECK SIZING DIE**

**REDDING PISTOL TRIM DIES**

## COMPETITION BULLET SEATER DIE FOR HANDGUN & STRAIGHT-WALL RIFLE CARTRIDGES

The precision seating stem moves well down into the die chamber to accomplish early bullet contact. The seating stem's spring loading provides positive alignment bias between the tapered nose and the bullet ogive. Thus spring loading and bullet alignment are maintained as the bullet and cartridge case move upward until the actual seating of the bullet begins. The Competition Bullet Seating Die features dial-in micrometer adjustment calibrated in .001-in. increments, is infinitely adjustable and has a "zero" set feature that allows setting desired load to zero. The die is compatible with all progressive reloading presses and has industry standard 7/8" x 14" threaded extended die bodies. An oversize bell-mouth chamfer with smooth radius has been added to the bottom of the die.

**MSRP:** . . . . . . . . . . . . . . . . .**$116.40**

## COMPETITION BUSHING-STYLE NECK SIZING DIE

This die allows you to fit the neck of your case perfectly in the chamber. As in the Competition Seating Die, the cartridge case is completely supported and aligned with the sizing bushing and remains supported in the sliding sleeve as it moves upward while the resizing bushing self-centers on the case neck. The micrometer adjustment of the bushing position delivers precise control to the desired neck length. All dies are supplied without bushings.

**Category I:** . . . . . . . . . . . . . .**$153.72**
**Category II:** . . . . . . . . . . . . .**$183.24**
**Category III:** . . . . . . . . . . . .**$226.68**

## FORM & TRIM DIES

Redding trim dies file trim cases without unnecessary resizing because they are made to chamber dimensions. For case forming and necking brass down from another caliber, Redding trim dies can be the perfect intermediate step before full length resizing.

**Series A:** . . . . . . . . . . . . . . . .**$40.68**
**Series B:** . . . . . . . . . . . . . . . .**$56.40**
**Series C:** . . . . . . . . . . . . . . . .**$69.00**
**Series D:** . . . . . . . . . . . . . . . .**$76.20**

## NECK SIZING BUSHINGS

Redding Neck Sizing Bushings are available in two styles. Both share the same external dimensions (½" O.D. x 3/8" long) and freely interchange in all

Redding Bushing style Neck Sizing Dies. They are available in .001" size increments throughout the range of .185" thru .365", covering all calibers from .17 to .338.

**Heat Treated Steel:** . . . . . . . .**$19.56**
**Titanium Nitride Treatment:** .**$34.80**
**Storage Box:** . . . . . . . . . . . . . .**$3.72**

## NECK SIZING DIES

These dies size only the necks of bottleneck cases to prolong brass life and improve accuracy. These dies size only the neck and not the shoulder or body, fired cases should not be interchanged between rifles of the same caliber. Available individually or in Deluxe Die Sets.

**Series A:** . . . . . . . . . . . . . . . .**$45.30**
**Series B:** . . . . . . . . . . . . . . . .**$61.50**
**Series C:** . . . . . . . . . . . . . . . .**$78.30**
**Series D:** . . . . . . . . . . . . . . . .**$88.20**

## PISTOL TRIM DIES

Redding trim dies for pistol calibers allow trimming cases without excessive resizing. Pistol trim dies require extended shellholders.

**Series A:** . . . . . . . . . . . . . . . .**$40.68**
**Series B:** . . . . . . . . . . . . . . . .**$56.40**
**Series C:** . . . . . . . . . . . . . . . .**$69.00**
**Series D:** . . . . . . . . . . . . . . . .**$76.20**

HANDLOADING

# Redding Reloading Tools

REDDING
PROFILE
CRIMP DIES

REDDING
TAPER &
CRIMP DIES

REDDING MODEL 1400-XT CASE TRIMMING LATHE

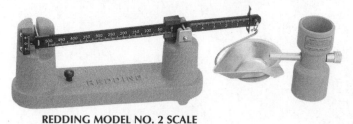

REDDING MODEL NO. 2 SCALE

## PROFILE CRIMP DIES

For handgun cartridges which do not head-space on the case mouth. These dies were designed for those who want the best possible crimp. Profile crimp dies provide a tighter, more uniform roll type crimp, and require the bullet to be seated to the correct depth in a previous operation.

Series A: . . . . . . . . . . . . . . . .$36.30
Series B: . . . . . . . . . . . . . . . .$36.30
Series C: . . . . . . . . . . . . . . . .$54.60
Series D: . . . . . . . . . . . . . . . .$61.50

## TAPER & CRIMP DIES

Designed for handgun cartridges which head-space on the case mouth where conventional roll crimping is undesirable. Also available for some revolver cartridges, for those who prefer the uniformity of a taper crimp. Available in the following rifle calibers: .223 Rem., 7.62MM x 39, .30-30, .308 Win, .30-06, .300, Win Mag.

Series A: . . . . . . . . . . . . . . . .$36.30
Series B: . . . . . . . . . . . . . . . .$36.30
Series C: . . . . . . . . . . . . . . . .$54.60
Series D: . . . . . . . . . . . . . . . .$61.50

## TYPE S- BUSHING STYLE DIES

The new Type S - Bushing Style Neck Sizing Die provides reloaders with a simple means to precisely control case neck size and tension. The Type-S features: interchangeable sizing bushings available in .001 in. increments; adjustable decapping rod with standard size button; self-centering resizing bushing; decapping pin retainer. All dies are supplied without bushings.

Category I: . . . . . . . . . . . . . . .$79.50
Category II: . . . . . . . . . . . . . . .$97.50
Category III: . . . . . . . . . . . .$119.88

## NATIONAL MATCH DIE SET

Redding now offers a specialized die set for the military match shooter. Available in 223 Rem, 308 Win and 30-06 Springfield, the set includes a Full-Length Sizing Die a Competition Bullet Seating Die and a Taper Crimp Die.

MSRP: . . . . . . . . . . . . . . . . .$216.30

## G-RX PUSH THRU BASE SIZING DIE

The new G-Rx Carbide push thru base sizing die is designed to restore fired cases from 40 S&W autoloading pistols that exhibit a bulge near the base without the need for case lube. By passing the case completely through the new G-Rx Carbide Die, the bulge is removed and the case may be returned to service.

MSRP: . . . . . . . . . . . . . . . . . $102.30

### CASE TRIMMERS

## MODEL 1400-XT CASE TRIMMING LATHE

This unit features a universal collet that accepts all rifle and pistol cases. The frame is cast iron with storage holes in the base for extra pilots. Coarse and fine adjustments are provided for case length. The Master Case Trimmer also features: six pilots (.22, 6mm, .25, .270, 7mm and .30 cal.); universal collet; two neck cleaning brushes (.22 through .30 cal.); two primer pocket cleaners (large and small); tin coated replaceable cutter; accessory power screwdriver adaptor.

Case Trimming Lathe: . . . . .$141.30
Pilots: . . . . . . . . . . . . . . . . . .$6.30

### POWDER SCALES

## MODEL NO. 2 POWDER AND BULLET SCALE

Model No. 2 features 505-grain capacity and .1-grain accuracy, a dampened beam and hardened knife edges and milled stainless bearing seats for smooth, consistent operation and a high level of durability.

MSRP: . . . . . . . . . . . . . . . . .$125.70

**REDDING
CARBIDE SIZE
BUTTON KIT**

**REDDING MODEL
10X-PISTOL AND SMALL
RIFLE MEASURE**

**HANDLOADING**

## HANDLOADING ACCESSORIES

### VERSA PAK RELOADING KIT

As the name implies, the Versa Pak was created for versatility, offering all of the products a serious handloader needs (without the press and dies) at a substantial savings over the cost of the individual items. This allows the first time or seasoned handloader to improve his or her experience with, not just the best equipment, but equipment best suited to his or her individual needs. The Versa Pak includes all the items listed in the Pro Pak (less press and dies) plus a Model 3 Master Powder Measure, a 1400 XT Case Trimmer, Imperial Dry Neck Lube in Application Media, a starter size of Imperial Sizing Die Wax and our DVD, "Advanced Handloading, Beyond the Basics". When mated with any Redding press and dies (many available in discounted packages), you can build the right package for a lifetime of service whether you intend to load for handgun or the big Sharps rifle cases.

**MSRP:** . . . . . . . . . . . . . . . $5568.50

### CARBIDE SIZE BUTTON KITS

Make inside neck sizing smoother and easier without lubrication. Now die sets can be upgraded with a carbide size button kit. Available for bottleneck cartridges .22 thru .338 cal. The carbide size button is free-floating on the decap rod, allowing it to self-center in the case neck. Kits contain: carbide size button, retainer and spare decapping pin. These kits also fit all Type-S dies.
**MSRP: $39.00**

### MODEL 3 POWDER MEASURE

The Model 3 has a micrometer metering chamber in front for easy setting and reading. The frame is precision machined cast iron with hand-honed fit between the frame and hard surfaced drum to easily cut and meter powders. The Model 3 features a large capacity clear powder reservoir; seethrough drop tube; body w/ standard 7/8" x 14" thread to fit mounting bracket and optional bench stand; cast mounting bracket included.
**MSRP:** . . . . . . . . . . . . . . . . $190.90

# Redding Reloading Tools

**REDDING MODEL
BR-30 MEASURE**

**REDDING EZ FEED
SHELLHOLDERS**

## COMPETITION MODEL 10X-PISTOL AND SMALL RIFLE POWDER MEASURE

MSRP: . . . . . . . . . . . . . . . .$285.60

## COMPETITION MODEL BR-30 POWDER MEASURE

Combines all of the features of Competition Model BR-30, with a drum and metering unit designed to provide uniform metering of small charge weights. To achieve the best metering possible at the targeted charge weight of approximately 10 grains, the diameter of the metering cavity is reduced and the metering

plunger is given a hemispherical shape. Charge range: 1 to 25 grains. Drum assembly easily changed from right to left-handed operation.
MSRP: . . . . . . . . . . . . . . . .$285.60

## MATCH-GRADE POWDER MEASURE MODEL 3BR

Interchange Universal- or pistol-metering chambers. Measures charges up to 100 grains. Unit is fitted with lock ring for fast dump with large clear plastic reservoir. See-through drop tube accepts all calibers from .22 to .600. Precision-fitted rotating drum is critically honed to prevent powder escape. Knife-edged powder chamber shears

coarse-grained powders with ease, ensuring accurate charges.
**Model 3BR Pistol Metering
      Chamber:** . . . . . . . . . . . .$73.50
**Model 3BR Universal Metering
      Chamber:** . . . . . . . . . . . .$73.50
**Powder Measure Mounting
      Bracket:** . . . . . . . . . . . . . .$21.75

# Redding Reloading Tools

**REDDING EXTENDED SHELLHOLDERS**

**REDDING HEADSPACE & BULLET COMPARATOR**

## SHELLHOLDERS

### EZ FEED SHELLHOLDERS

Redding shellholders are of a Universal "snap-in" design recommended for use with all Redding dies and presses, as well as all other popular brands. They are precision machined to very close tolerances and heat-treated to fit cases and eliminate potential resizing problems. The outside knurling makes them easier to handle and change.
**MSRP:** . . . . . . . . . . . . . . . . . .**$12.00**

### EXTENDED SHELLHOLDERS

Extended shellholders are required when trimming short cases under 1½ in. O.A.L. They are machined to the same tolerances as standard shellholders, except they're longer.
**MSRP:** . . . . . . . . . . . . . . . . . .**$19.80**

## HANDLOADING TOOLS

### INSTANT INDICATOR HEADSPACE & BULLET COMPARATOR

The Instant Indicator checks the headspace from the case shoulder to the base. Bullet seating depths can be compared and bullets can be sorted by checking the base of bullets to give dimension. Case length can be measured. Available for 33 cartridges from .222 Rem to .338 Win. Mag., including new WSSM cartridges.
**W/ Dial Indicator:** . . . . . . . .**$174.30**
**W/o Dial Indicator:** . . . . . . .**$134.70**
**1 in. Dial Indicator:** . . . . . . . .**$44.10**

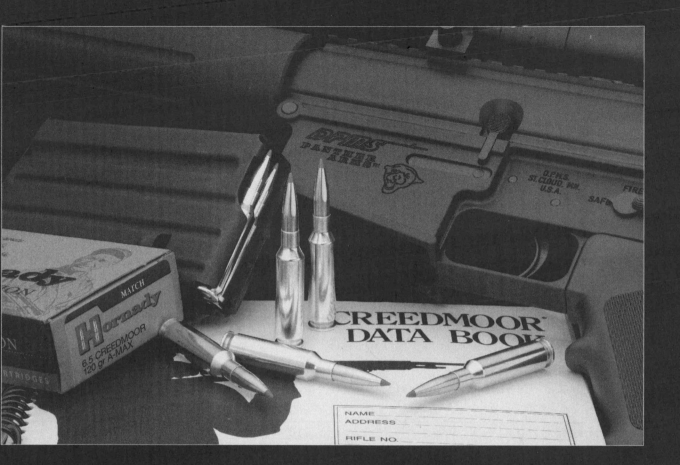

## 554 CENTERFIRE RIFLE BALLISTICS

## 586 CENTERFIRE HANDGUN BALLISTICS

# Centerfire Rifle Ballistics

## Comprehensive Ballistics Tables for Currently Manufactured Sporting Rifle Cartridges

No more collecting catalogs and peering at microscopic print to find out what ammunition is offered for a cartridge, and how it performs relative to other factory loads! *Shooter's Bible* has assembled the data for you, in easy-to-read tables, by cartridge. Of course, this section will be updated on a regular basis to bring you the latest information.

Data is taken from manufacturers' charts; your chronograph readings may vary. Listings are current as of February the year *Shooter's Bible* appears (not the cover year). Listings are not intended as recommendations. For example, the data for the .44 Magnum at 400 yards shows its effective range is much shorter. The lack of data for a 285-grain .375 H&H bullet beyond 300 yards does not mean the bullet has no authority farther out. Besides ammunition, the rifle, sights, conditions and shooter ability all must be considered when contemplating a long shot. Accuracy and bullet energy both matter when big game is in the offing.

Barrel length affects velocity, and at various rates depending on the load. As a rule, figure 50 fps per inch of barrel, plus or minus, if your barrel is longer or shorter than 22 inches.

Bullets are given by make, weight (in grains) and type. Most type abbreviations are self-explanatory: BT=Boat-Tail, FMJ=Full Metal Jacket, HP=Hollow Point, SP=Soft Point—except in Hornady listings, where SP is the firm's Spire Point. TNT and TXP are trademarked designations of Speer and Norma. XLC identifies a coated Barnes X bullet. HE indicates a Federal High Energy load, similar to the Hornady LM (Light Magnum) and HM (Heavy Magnum) cartridges.

Arc (trajectory) is based on a zero range published by the manufacturer, from 100 to 300 yards. If a zero does not fall in a yardage column, it lies halfway between—at 150 yards, for example, if the bullet's strike is "+" at 100 yards and "-" at 200.

## .17 REMINGTON TO .221 REMINGTON FIREBALL

| cartridge bullet | range, yards: | 0 | 100 | 200 | 300 | 400 |
|---|---|---|---|---|---|---|
| **.17 Remington** | | | | | | |
| Rem. 20 AccuTip BT | velocity, fps: | 4250 | 3594 | 3028 | 2529 | 2081 |
| | energy, ft-lb: | 802 | 574 | 407 | 284 | 192 |
| | arc, inches: | | +1.3 | +1.3 | -2.5 | -11.8 |
| Rem. 20 Fireball | velocity, fps | 4000 | 3380 | 2840 | 2360 | 1930 |
| | energy, ft-lb | 710 | 507 | 358 | 247 | 165 |
| | arc, inches: | | +1.6 | +1.5 | -2.8 | -13.5 |
| Rem. 25 HP Power-Lokt | velocity, fps: | 4040 | 3284 | 2644 | 2086 | 1606 |
| | energy, ft-lb: | 906 | 599 | 388 | 242 | 143 |
| | arc, inches: | | +1.8 | 0 | -3.3 | -16.6 |
| **.204 Ruger** | | | | | | |
| Federal 32 Nosler Ballistic Tip | velocity, fps | 4030 | 3465 | 2968 | 2523 | 2119 |
| | arc, inches | | +0.7 | 0 | -4.7 | -14.9 |
| Hornady 32 V-Max | velocity, fps: | 4225 | 3632 | 3114 | 2652 | 2234 |
| | energy, ft-lb: | 1268 | 937 | 689 | 500 | 355 |
| | arc, inches: | | +0.6 | 0 | -4.2 | -13.4 |
| Hornady 40 V-Max | velocity, fps: | 3900 | 3451 | 3046 | 2677 | 2335 |
| | energy, ft-lb: | 1351 | 1058 | 824 | 636 | 485 |
| | arc, inches: | | +0.7 | 0 | -4.5 | -13.9 |
| Rem. 32 AccuTip | velocity, fps: | 4225 | 3632 | 3114 | 2652 | 2234 |
| | Energy, ft-lb: | 1268 | 937 | 689 | 500 | 355 |
| | Arc, inches: | | +0.6 | 0 | -4.1 | -13.1 |
| Rem. 40 AccuTip | velocity, fps: | 3900 | 3451 | 3046 | 2677 | 2336 |
| | energy, ft-lb: | 1351 | 1058 | 824 | 636 | 485 |
| | arc, inches: | | +0.7 | 0 | -4.3 | -13.2 |
| Win. 32 Ballistic Silver Tip | velocity, fps: | 4050 | 3482 | 2984 | 2537 | 2132 |
| | energy, ft-lb | 1165 | 862 | 632 | 457 | 323 |
| | arc, inches | | +0.7 | 0 | -4.6 | -14.7 |
| Win. 34 HP | velocity, fps: | 4025 | 3339 | 2751 | 2232 | 1775 |
| | energy, ft-lb: | 1223 | 842 | 571 | 376 | 238 |
| | arc, inches: | | +0.8 | 0 | -5.5 | -18.1 |

| cartridge bullet | range, yards: | 0 | 100 | 200 | 300 | 400 |
|---|---|---|---|---|---|---|
| **.218 Bee** | | | | | | |
| Win. 46 Hollow Point | velocity, fps: | 2760 | 2102 | 1550 | 1155 | 961 |
| | energy, ft-lb: | 778 | 451 | 245 | 136 | 94 |
| | arc, inches: | | 0 | -7.2 | -29.4 | |
| **.22 Hornet** | | | | | | |
| Hornady 35 V-Max | velocity, fps: | 3100 | 2278 | 1601 | 1135 | 929 |
| | energy, ft-lb: | 747 | 403 | 199 | 100 | 67 |
| | arc, inches: | | +2.8 | 0 | -16.9 | -60.4 |
| Rem. 35 AccuTip | velocity, fps: | 3100 | 2271 | 1591 | 1127 | 924 |
| | energy, ft-lb: | 747 | 401 | 197 | 99 | 66 |
| | arc, inches: | | +1.5 | -3.5 | -22.3 | -68.4 |
| Rem. 45 Pointed Soft Point | velocity, fps: | 2690 | 2042 | 1502 | 1128 | 948 |
| | energy, ft-lb: | 723 | 417 | 225 | 127 | 90 |
| | arc, inches: | | 0 | -7.1 | -30.0 | |
| Rem. 45 Hollow Point | velocity, fps: | 2690 | 2042 | 1502 | 1128 | 948 |
| | energy, ft-lb: | 723 | 417 | 225 | 127 | 90 |
| | arc, inches: | | 0 | -7.1 | -30.0 | |
| Win. 34 Jacketed HP | velocity, fps: | 3050 | 2132 | 1415 | 1017 | 852 |
| | energy, ft-lb: | 700 | 343 | 151 | 78 | 55. |
| | arc, inches: | | 0 | -6.6 | -29.9 | |
| Win. 45 Soft Point | velocity, fps: | 2690 | 2042 | 1502 | 1128 | 948. |
| | energy, ft-lb: | 723 | 417 | 225 | 127 | 90 |
| | arc, inches: | | 0 | -7.7 | -31.3 | |
| Win. 46 Hollow Point | velocity, fps: | 2690 | 2042 | 1502 | 1128 | 948. |
| | energy, ft-lb: | 739 | 426 | 230 | 130 | 92 |
| | arc, inches: | | 0 | -7.7 | -31.3 | |
| **.221 Remington Fireball** | | | | | | |
| Rem. 50 AccuTip BT | velocity, fps: | 2995 | 2605 | 2247 | 1918 | 1622 |
| | energy, ft-lb: | 996 | 753 | 560 | 408 | 292 |
| | arc, inches: | | +1.8 | 0 | -8.8 | -27.1 |

| cartridge bullet | range, yards: | 0 | 100 | 200 | 300 | 400 |
|---|---|---|---|---|---|---|

## .222 Remington

| cartridge bullet | range, yards: | 0 | 100 | 200 | 300 | 400 |
|---|---|---|---|---|---|---|
| Federal 50 Hi-Shok | velocity, fps: | 3140 | 2600 | 2120 | 1700 | 1350 |
| | energy, ft-lb: | 1095 | 750 | 500 | 320 | 200 |
| | arc, inches: | | +1.9 | 0 | -9.7 | -31.6 |
| Federal 55 FMJ boat-tail | velocity, fps: | 3020 | 2740 | 2480 | 2230 | 1990 |
| | energy, ft-lb: | 1115 | 915 | 750 | 610 | 484. |
| | arc, inches: | | +1.6 | 0 | -7.3 | -21.5 |
| Hornady 40 V-Max | velocity, fps: | 3600 | 3117 | 2673 | 2269 | 1911 |
| | energy, ft-lb: | 1151 | 863 | 634 | 457 | 324 |
| | arc, inches: | | +1.1 | 0 | -6.1 | -18.9 |
| Hornady 50 V-Max | velocity, fps: | 3140 | 2729 | 2352 | 2008 | 1710. |
| | energy, ft-lb: | 1094 | 827 | 614 | 448 | 325 |
| | arc, inches: | | +1.7 | 0 | -7.9 | -24.4 |
| Norma 50 Soft Point | velocity, fps: | 3199 | 2667 | 2193 | 1771 | |
| | energy, ft-lb: | 1136 | 790 | 534 | 348 | |
| | arc, inches: | | +1.7 | 0 | -9.1 | |
| Norma 50 FMJ | velocity, fps: | 2789 | 2326 | 1910 | 1547 | |
| | energy, ft-lb: | 864 | 601 | 405 | 266 | |
| | arc, inches: | | +2.5 | 0 | -12.2 | |
| Norma 62 Soft Point | velocity, fps: | 2887 | 2457 | 2067 | 1716 | |
| | energy, ft-lb: | 1148 | 831 | 588 | 405 | |
| | arc, inches: | | +2.1 | 0 | -10.4 | |
| PMC 50 Pointed Soft Point | velocity, fps: | 3044 | 2727 | 2354 | 2012 | 1651 |
| | energy, ft-lb: | 1131 | 908 | 677 | 494 | 333 |
| | arc, inches: | | +1.6 | 0 | -7.9 | -24.5 |
| PMC 55 Pointed Soft Point | velocity, fps: | 2950 | 2594 | 2266 | 1966 | 1693 |
| | energy, ft-lb: | 1063 | 822 | 627 | 472 | 350 |
| | arc, inches: | | +1.9 | 0 | -8.7 | -26.3 |
| Rem. 50 Pointed Soft Point | velocity, fps: | 3140 | 2602 | 2123 | 1700 | 1350. |
| | energy, ft-lb: | 1094 | 752 | 500 | 321 | 202 |
| | arc, inches: | | +1.9 | 0 | -9.7 | -31.7 |
| Rem. 50 HP Power-Lokt | velocity, fps: | 3140 | 2635 | 2182 | 1777 | 1432. |
| | energy, ft-lb: | 1094 | 771 | 529 | 351 | 228 |
| | arc, inches: | | +1.8 | 0 | -9.2 | -29.6 |
| Rem. 50 AccuTip BT | velocity, fps: | 3140 | 2744 | 2380 | 2045 | 1740 |
| | energy, ft-lb: | 1094 | 836 | 629 | 464 | 336. |
| | arc, inches: | | +1.6 | 0 | -7.8 | -23.9 |
| Win. 40 Ballistic Silvertip | velocity, fps: | 3370 | 2915 | 2503 | 2127 | 1786 |
| | energy, ft-lb: | 1009 | 755 | 556 | 402 | 283 |
| | arc, inches: | | +1.3 | 0 | -6.9 | -21.5 |
| Win. 50 Pointed Soft Point | velocity, fps: | 3140 | 2602 | 2123 | 1700 | 1350 |
| | energy, ft-lb: | 1094 | 752 | 500 | 321 | 202 |
| | arc, inches: | | +2.2 | 0 | -10.0 | -32.3 |

## .223 Remington

| cartridge bullet | range, yards: | 0 | 100 | 200 | 300 | 400 |
|---|---|---|---|---|---|---|
| Black Hills 40 Nosler B. Tip | velocity, fps: | 3600 | | | | |
| | energy, ft-lb: | 1150 | | | | |
| | arc, inches: | | | | | |
| Black Hills 50 V-Max | velocity, fps: | 3300 | | | | |
| | energy, ft-lb: | 1209 | | | | |
| | arc, inches: | | | | | |
| Black Hills 52 Match HP | velocity, fps: | 3300 | | | | |
| | energy, ft-lb: | 1237 | | | | |
| | arc, inches: | | | | | |
| Black Hills 55 Softpoint | velocity, fps: | 3250 | | | | |
| | energy, ft-lb: | 1270 | | | | |
| | arc, inches: | | | | | |
| Black Hills 60 SP or V-Max | velocity, fps: | 3150 | | | | |
| | energy, ft-lb: | 1322 | | | | |
| | arc, inches: | | | | | |
| Black Hills 60 Partition | velocity, fps: | 3150 | | | | |
| | energy, ft-lb: | 1322 | | | | |

| cartridge bullet | range, yards: | 0 | 100 | 200 | 300 | 400 |
|---|---|---|---|---|---|---|
| | arc, inches: | | | | | |
| Black Hills 68 Heavy Match | velocity, fps: | 2850 | | | | |
| | energy, ft-lb: | 1227 | | | | |
| | arc, inches: | | | | | |
| Black Hills 69 Sierra MK | velocity, fps: | 2850 | | | | |
| | energy, ft-lb: | 1245 | | | | |
| | arc, inches: | | | | | |
| Black Hills 73 Berger BTHP | velocity, fps: | 2750 | | | | |
| | energy, ft-lb: | 1226 | | | | |
| | arc, inches: | | | | | |
| Black Hills 75 Heavy Match | velocity, fps: | 2750 | | | | |
| | energy, ft-lb: | 1259 | | | | |
| | arc, inches: | | | | | |
| Black Hills 77 Sierra MKing | velocity, fps: | 2750 | | | | |
| | energy, ft-lb: | 1293 | | | | |
| | arc, inches: | | | | | |
| Federal 50 Jacketed HP | velocity, fps: | 3400 | 2910 | 2460 | 2060 | 1700 |
| | energy, ft-lb: | 1285 | 940 | 675 | 470 | 320 |
| | arc, inches: | | +1.3 | 0 | -7.1 | -22.7 |
| Federal 50 Speer TNT HP | velocity, fps: | 3300 | 2860 | 2450 | 2080 | 1750 |
| | energy, ft-lb: | 1210 | 905 | 670 | 480 | 340 |
| | arc, inches: | | +1.4 | 0 | -7.3 | -22.6 |
| Federal 52 Sierra MatchKing BTHP | velocity, fps: | 3300 | 2860 | 2460 | 2090 | 1760 |
| | energy, ft-lb: | 1255 | 945 | 700 | 505 | 360 |
| | arc, inches: | | +1.4 | 0 | -7.2 | -22.4 |
| Federal 55 Hi-Shok | velocity, fps: | 3240 | 2750 | 2300 | 1910 | 1550 |
| | energy, ft-lb: | 1280 | 920 | 650 | 445 | 295 |
| | arc, inches: | | +1.6 | 0 | -8.2 | -26.1 |
| Federal 55 FMJ boat-tail | velocity, fps: | 3240 | 2950 | 2670 | 2410 | 2170 |
| | energy, ft-lb: | 1280 | 1060 | 875 | 710 | 575 |
| | arc, inches: | | +1.3 | 0 | -6.1 | -18.3 |
| Federal 55 Sierra GameKing BTHP | velocity, fps: | 3240 | 2770 | 2340 | 1950 | 1610 |
| | energy, ft-lb: | 1280 | 935 | 670 | 465 | 315 |
| | arc, inches: | | +1.5 | 0 | -8.0 | -25.3 |
| Federal 55 Trophy Bonded | velocity, fps: | 3100 | 2630 | 2210 | 1830 | 1500. |
| | energy, ft-lb: | 1175 | 845 | 595 | 410 | 275 |
| | arc, inches: | | +1.8 | 0 | -8.9 | -28.7 |
| Federal 55 Nosler Bal. Tip | velocity, fps: | 3240 | 2870 | 2530 | 2220 | 1920 |
| | energy, ft-lb: | 1280 | 1005 | 780 | 600 | 450 |
| | arc, inches: | | +1.4 | 0 | -6.8 | -20.8 |
| Federal 55 Sierra BlitzKing | velocity, fps: | 3240 | 2870 | 2520 | 2200 | 1910 |
| | energy, ft-lb: | 1280 | 1005 | 775 | 590 | 445 |
| | arc, inches: | | +-1.4 | 0 | -6.9 | -20.9 |
| Federal 62 FMJ | velocity, fps: | 3020 | 2650 | 2310 | 2000 | 1710 |
| | energy, ft-lb: | 1225 | 970 | 735 | 550 | 405 |
| | arc, inches: | | +1.7 | 0 | -8.4 | -25.5 |
| Federal 64 Hi-Shok SP | velocity, fps: | 3090 | 2690 | 2325 | 1990 | 1680 |
| | energy, ft-lb: | 1360 | 1030 | 770 | 560 | 400 |
| | arc, inches: | | +1.7 | 0 | -8.2 | -25.2 |
| Federal 69 Sierra MatchKing BTHP | velocity, fps: | 3000 | 2720 | 2460 | 2210 | 1980 |
| | energy, ft-lb: | 1380 | 1135 | 925 | 750 | 600 |
| | arc, inches: | | +1.6 | 0 | -7.4 | -21.9 |
| Hornady 40 V-Max | velocity, fps: | 3800 | 3305 | 2845 | 2424 | 2044 |
| | energy, ft-lb: | 1282 | 970 | 719 | 522 | 371 |
| | arc, inches: | | +0.8 | 0 | -5.3 | -16.6 |
| Hornady 53 Hollow Point | velocity, fps: | 3330 | 2882 | 2477 | 2106 | 1710 |
| | energy, ft-lb: | 1305 | 978 | 722 | 522 | 369 |
| | arc, inches: | | +1.7 | 0 | -7.4 | -22.7 |
| Hornady 55 V-Max | velocity, fps: | 3240 | 2859 | 2507 | 2181 | 1891. |
| | energy, ft-lb: | 1282 | 998 | 767 | 581 | 437 |
| | arc, inches: | | +1.4 | 0 | -7.1 | -21.4 |
| Hornady 55 TAP-FPD | velocity, fps: | 3240 | 2854 | 2500 | 2172 | 1871 |
| | energy, ft-lb: | 1282 | 995 | 763 | 576 | 427 |

# Centerfire Rifle Ballistics

## .223 REMINGTON TO .22-250 REMINGTON

| cartridge bullet | range, yards: | 0 | 100 | 200 | 300 | 400 |
|---|---|---|---|---|---|---|
| | arc, inches: | | +1.4 | 0 | -7.0 | -21.4 |
| Hornady 55 Urban Tactical | velocity, fps: | 2970 | 2626 | 2307 | 2011 | 1739 |
| | energy, ft-lb: | 1077 | 842 | 650 | 494 | 369 |
| | arc, inches: | | +1.5 | 0 | -8.1 | -24.9 |
| Hornady 60 Soft Point | velocity, fps: | 3150 | 2782 | 2442 | 2127 | 1837. |
| | energy, ft-lb: | 1322 | 1031 | 795 | 603 | 450 |
| | arc, inches: | | +1.6 | 0 | -7.5 | -22.5 |
| Hornady 60 TAP-FPD | velocity, fps: | 3115 | 2754 | 2420 | 2110 | 1824 |
| | energy, ft-lb: | 1293 | 1010 | 780 | 593 | 443 |
| | arc, inches: | | +1.6 | 0 | -7.5 | -22.9 |
| Hornady 60 Urban Tactical | velocity, fps: | 2950 | 2619 | 2312 | 2025 | 1762 |
| | energy, ft-lb: | 1160 | 914 | 712 | 546 | 413 |
| | arc, inches: | | +1.6 | 0 | -8.1 | -24.7 |
| Hornady 75 BTHP Match | velocity, fps: | 2790 | 2554 | 2330 | 2119 | 1926 |
| | energy, ft-lb: | 1296 | 1086 | 904 | 747 | 617 |
| | arc, inches: | | +2.4 | 0 | -8.8 | -25.1 |
| Hornacy 75 TAP-FPD | velocity, fps: | 2790 | 2582 | 2383 | 2193 | 2012 |
| | energy, ft-lb: | 1296 | 1110 | 946 | 801 | 674 |
| | arc, inches: | | +1.9 | 0 | -8.0 | -23.2 |
| Hornady 75 BTHP Tactical | velocity, fps: | 2630 | 2409 | 2199 | 2000 | 1814 |
| | energy, ft-lb: | 1152 | 966 | 805 | 666 | 548 |
| | arc, inches: | | +2.0 | 0 | -9.2 | -25.9 |
| PMC 40 non-toxic | velocity, fps: | 3500 | 2606 | 1871 | 1315 | |
| | energy, ft-lb: | 1088 | 603 | 311 | 154 | |
| | arc, inches: | | +2.6 | 0 | -12.8 | |
| PMC 50 Sierra BlitzKing | velocity, fps: | 3300 | 2874 | 2484 | 2130 | 1809 |
| | energy, ft-lb: | 1209 | 917 | 685 | 504 | 363 |
| | arc, inches: | | +1.4 | 0 | -7.1 | -21.8 |
| PMC 52 Sierra HPBT Match | velocity, fps: | 3200 | 2808 | 2447 | 2117 | 1817 |
| | energy, ft-lb: | 1182 | 910 | 691 | 517 | 381 |
| | arc, inches: | | +1.5 | 0 | -7.3 | -22.5. |
| PMC 53 Barnes XLC | velocity, fps: | 3200 | 2815 | 2461 | 2136 | 1840 |
| | energy, ft-lb: | 1205 | 933 | 713 | 537 | 398. |
| | arc, inches: | | +1.5 | 0 | -7.2 | -22.2 |
| PMC 55 HP boat-tail | velocity, fps: | 3240 | 2717 | 2250 | 1832 | 1473 |
| | energy, ft-lb: | 1282 | 901 | 618 | 410 | 265 |
| | arc, inches: | | +1.6 | 0 | -8.6 | -27.7 |
| PMC 55 FMJ boat-tail | velocity, fps: | 3195 | 2882 | 2525 | 2169 | 1843 |
| | energy, ft-lb: | 1246 | 1014 | 779 | 574 | 415 |
| | arc, inches: | | +1.4 | 0 | -6.8 | -21.1 |
| PMC 55 Pointed Soft Point | velocity, fps: | 3112 | 2767 | 2421 | 2100 | 1806 |
| | energy, ft-lb: | 1182 | 935 | 715 | 539 | 398 |
| | arc, inches: | | +1.5 | 0 | -7.5 | -22.9 |
| PMC 64 Pointed Soft Point | velocity, fps: | 2775 | 2511 | 2261 | 2026 | 1806. |
| | energy, ft-lb: | 1094 | 896 | 726 | 583 | 464 |
| | arc, inches: | | +2.0 | 0 | -8.8 | -26.1 |
| PMC 69 Sierra BTHP Match | velocity, fps: | 2900 | 2591 | 2304 | 2038 | 1791 |
| | energy, ft-lb: | 1288 | 1029 | 813 | 636 | 492 |
| | arc, inches: | | +1.9 | 0 | -8.4 | -25.3 |
| Rem. 50 AccuTip BT | velocity, fps: | 3300 | 2889 | 2514 | 2168 | 1851 |
| | energy, ft-lb: | 1209 | 927 | 701 | 522 | 380 |
| | arc, inches: | | +1.4 | 0 | -6.9 | -21.2 |
| Rem. 55 Pointed Soft Point | velocity, fps: | 3240 | 2747 | 2304 | 1905 | 1554 |
| | energy, ft-lb: | 1282 | 921 | 648 | 443 | 295 |
| | arc, inches: | | +1.6 | 0 | -8.2 | -26.2 |
| Rem. 55 HP Power-Lokt | velocity, fps: | 3240 | 2773 | 2352 | 1969 | 1627 |
| | energy, ft-lb: | 1282 | 939 | 675 | 473 | 323 |
| | arc, inches: | | +1.5 | 0 | -7.9 | -24.8 |
| Rem. 55 AccuTip BT | velocity, fps: | 3240 | 2854 | 2500 | 2172 | 1871 |
| | energy, ft-lb: | 1282 | 995 | 763 | 576 | 427 |
| | arc, inches: | | +1.5 | 0 | -7.1 | -21.7 |
| Rem. 55 Metal Case | velocity, fps: | 3240 | 2759 | 2326 | 1933 | 1587 |
| | energy, ft-lb: | 1282 | 929 | 660 | 456 | 307 |

| cartridge bullet | range, yards: | 0 | 100 | 200 | 300 | 400 |
|---|---|---|---|---|---|---|
| | arc, inches: | | +1.6 | 0 | -8.1 | -25.5 |
| Rem. 62 HP Match | velocity, fps: | 3025 | 2572 | 2162 | 1792 | 1471 |
| | energy, ft-lb: | 1260 | 911 | 643 | 442 | 298 |
| | arc, inches: | | +1.9 | 0 | -9.4 | -29.9 |
| Rem. 69 BTHP Match | velocity, fps: | 3000 | 2720 | 2457 | 2209 | 1975 |
| | energy, ft-lb: | 1379 | 1133 | 925 | 747 | 598 |
| | arc, inches: | | +1.6 | 0 | -7.4 | -21.9 |
| Win. 40 Ballistic Silvertip | velocity, fps: | 3700 | 3166 | 2693 | 2265 | 1879. |
| | energy, ft-lb: | 1216 | 891 | 644 | 456 | 314 |
| | arc, inches: | | +1.0 | 0 | -5.8 | -18.4 |
| Win. 45 JHP | velocity, fps: | 3600 | | | | |
| | energy, ft-lb: | 1295 | | | | |
| | arc, inches: | | | | | |
| Win. 50 Ballistic Silvertip | velocity, fps: | 3410 | 2982 | 2593 | 2235 | 1907. |
| | energy, ft-lb: | 1291 | 987 | 746 | 555 | 404 |
| | arc, inches: | | +1.2 | 0 | -6.4 | -19.8 |
| Win. 53 Hollow Point | velocity, fps: | 3330 | 2882 | 2477 | 2106 | 1770 |
| | energy, ft-lb: | 1305 | 978 | 722 | 522 | 369 |
| | arc, inches: | | +1.7 | 0 | -7.4 | -22.7 |
| Win. 55 Pointed Soft Point | velocity, fps: | 3240 | 2747 | 2304 | 1905 | 1554 |
| | energy, ft-lb: | 1282 | 921 | 648 | 443 | 295 |
| | arc, inches: | | +1.9 | 0 | -8.5 | -26.7 |
| Win. 55 Super Clean NT | velocity, fps: | 3150 | 2520 | 1970 | 1505 | 1165 |
| | energy, ft-lb: | 1212 | 776 | 474 | 277 | 166 |
| | arc, inches: | | +2.8 | 0 | -11.9 | -38.9 |
| Win. 55 FMJ | velocity, fps: | 3240 | 2854 | | | |
| | energy, ft-lb: | 1282 | 995 | | | |
| | arc, inches: | | | | | |
| Win. 55 Ballistic Silvertip | velocity, fps: | 3240 | 2871 | 2531 | 2215 | 1923 |
| | energy, ft-lb: | 1282 | 1006 | 782 | 599 | 451 |
| | arc, inches: | | +1.4 | 0 | -6.8 | -20.8 |
| Win. 64 Power-Point | velocity, fps: | 3020 | 2656 | 2320 | 2009 | 1724 |
| | energy, ft-lb: | 1296 | 1003 | 765 | 574 | 423 |
| | arc, inches: | | +1.7 | 0 | -8.2 | -25.1 |
| Win. 64 Power-Point Plus | velocity, fps: | 3090 | 2684 | 2312 | 1971 | 1664 |
| | energy, ft-lb: | 1357 | 1024 | 760 | 552 | 393 |
| | arc, inches: | | +1.7 | 0 | -8.2 | -25.4 |

## .5.6 x 52 R

| cartridge bullet | | 0 | 100 | 200 | 300 | 400 |
|---|---|---|---|---|---|---|
| Norma 71 Soft Point | velocity, fps: | 2789 | 2446 | 2128 | 1835 | |
| | energy, ft-lb: | 1227 | 944 | 714 | 531 | |
| | arc, inches: | | +2.1 | 0 | -9.9 | |

## .22 PPC

| cartridge bullet | | 0 | 100 | 200 | 300 | 400 |
|---|---|---|---|---|---|---|
| A-Square 52 Berger | velocity, fps: | 3300 | 2952 | 2629 | 2329 | 2049 |
| | energy, ft-lb: | 1257 | 1006 | 798 | 626 | 485 |
| | arc, inches: | | +1.3 | 0 | -6.3 | -19.1 |

## .225 Winchester

| cartridge bullet | | 0 | 100 | 200 | 300 | 400 |
|---|---|---|---|---|---|---|
| Win. 55 Pointed Soft Point | velocity, fps: | 3570 | 3066 | 2616 | 2208 | 1838. |
| | energy, ft-lb: | 1556 | 1148 | 836 | 595 | 412 |
| | arc, inches: | | +2.4 | +2.0 | -3.5 | -16.3 |

## .224 Weatherby Magnum

| cartridge bullet | | 0 | 100 | 200 | 300 | 400 |
|---|---|---|---|---|---|---|
| Wby. 55 Pointed Expanding | velocity, fps: | 3650 | 3192 | 2780 | 2403 | 2056 |
| | energy, ft-lb: | 1627 | 1244 | 944 | 705 | 516 |
| | arc, inches: | | +2.8 | +3.7 | 0 | -9.8 |

## .22-250 Remington

| cartridge bullet | | 0 | 100 | 200 | 300 | 400 |
|---|---|---|---|---|---|---|
| Black Hills 50 Nos. Bal. Tip | velocity, fps: | 3700 | | | | |
| | energy, ft-lb: | 1520 | | | | |
| | arc, inches: | | | | | |
| Black Hills 60 Nos. Partition | velocity, fps: | 3550 | | | | |
| | energy, ft-lb: | 1679 | | | | |
| | arc, inches: | | | | | |

BALLISTICS

| cartridge bullet | range, yards: | 0 | 100 | 200 | 300 | 400 |
|---|---|---|---|---|---|---|
| Federal 40 Nos. Bal. Tip | velocity, fps: | 4150 | 3610 | 3130 | 2700 | 2300 |
| | energy, ft-lb: | 1530 | 1155 | 870 | 645 | 470 |
| | arc, inches: | | +0.6 | 0 | -4.2 | -13.2 |
| Federal 40 Sierra Varminter | velocity, fps: | 4000 | 3320 | 2720 | 2200 | 1740 |
| | energy, ft-lb: | 1420 | 980 | 660 | 430 | 265 |
| | arc, inches: | | +0.8 | 0 | -5.6 | -18.4 |
| Federal 55 Hi-Shok | velocity, fps: | 3680 | 3140 | 2660 | 2220 | 1830 |
| | energy, ft-lb: | 1655 | 1200 | 860 | 605 | 410 |
| | arc, inches: | | +1.0 | 0 | -6.0 | -19.1 |
| Federal 55 Sierra BlitzKing | velocity, fps: | 3680 | 3270 | 2890 | 2540 | 2220 |
| | energy, ft-lb: | 1655 | 1300 | 1020 | 790 | 605 |
| | arc, inches: | | +0.9 | 0 | -5.1 | -15.6 |
| Federal 55 Sierra GameKing BTHP | velocity, fps: | 3680 | 3280 | 2920 | 2590 | 2280 |
| | energy, ft-lb: | 1655 | 1315 | 1040 | 815 | 630 |
| | arc, inches: | | +0.9 | 0 | -5.0 | -15.1 |
| Federal 55 Trophy Bonded | velocity, fps: | 3600 | 3080 | 2610 | 2190 | 1810. |
| | energy, ft-lb: | 1585 | 1155 | 835 | 590 | 400. |
| | arc, inches: | | +1.1 | 0 | -6.2 | -19.8 |
| Hornady 40 V-Max | velocity, fps: | 4150 | 3631 | 3147 | 2699 | 2293 |
| | energy, ft-lb: | 1529 | 1171 | 879 | 647 | 467 |
| | arc, inches: | | +0.5 | 0 | -4.2 | -13.3 |
| Hornady 50 V-Max | velocity, fps: | 3800 | 3349 | 2925 | 2535 | 2178 |
| | energy, ft-lb: | 1603 | 1245 | 950 | 713 | 527 |
| | arc, inches: | | +0.8 | 0 | -5.0 | -15.6 |
| Hornady 53 Hollow Point | velocity, fps: | 3680 | 3185 | 2743 | 2341 | 1974. |
| | energy, ft-lb: | 1594 | 1194 | 886 | 645 | 459 |
| | arc, inches: | | +1.0 | 0 | -5.7 | -17.8 |
| Hornady 55 V-Max | velocity, fps: | 3680 | 3265 | 2876 | 2517 | 2183 |
| | energy, ft-lb: | 1654 | 1302 | 1010 | 772 | 582 |
| | arc, inches: | | +0.9 | 0 | -5.3 | -16.1 |
| Hornady 60 Soft Point | velocity, fps: | 3600 | 3195 | 2826 | 2485 | 2169 |
| | energy, ft-lb: | 1727 | 1360 | 1064 | 823 | 627 |
| | arc, inches: | | +1.0 | 0 | -5.4 | -16.3 |
| Norma 53 Soft Point | velocity, fps: | 3707 | 3234 | 2809 | 1716 | |
| | energy, ft-lb: | 1618 | 1231 | 928 | 690 | |
| | arc, inches: | | +0.9 | 0 | -5.3 | |
| PMC 50 Sierra BlitzKing | velocity, fps: | 3725 | 3264 | 2641 | 2455 | 2103 |
| | energy, ft-lb: | 1540 | 1183 | 896 | 669 | 491 |
| | arc, inches: | | +0.9 | 0 | -5.2 | -16.2 |
| PMC 50 Barnes XLC | velocity, fps: | 3725 | 3280 | 2871 | 2495 | 2152 |
| | energy, ft-lb: | 1540 | 1195 | 915 | 691 | 514. |
| | arc, inches: | | +0.9 | 0 | -5.1 | -15.9. |
| PMC 55 HP boat-tail | velocity, fps: | 3680 | 3104 | 2596 | 2141 | 1737 |
| | energy, ft-lb: | 1654 | 1176 | 823 | 560 | 368 |
| | arc, inches: | | +1.1 | 0 | -6.3 | -20.2 |
| PMC 55 Pointed Soft Point | velocity, fps: | 3586 | 3203 | 2852 | 2505 | 2178 |
| | energy, ft-lb: | 1570 | 1253 | 993 | 766 | 579 |
| | arc, inches: | | +1.0 | 0 | -5.2 | -16.0 |
| Rem. 50 AccuTip BT (also in EtronX) | velocity, fps: | 3725 | 3272 | 2864 | 2491 | 2147 |
| | energy, ft-lb: | 1540 | 1188 | 910 | 689 | 512 |
| | arc, inches: | | +1.7 | +1.6 | -2.8 | -12.8 |
| Rem. 55 Pointed Soft Point | velocity, fps: | 3680 | 3137 | 2656 | 2222 | 1832 |
| | energy, ft-lb: | 1654 | 1201 | 861 | 603 | 410 |
| | arc, inches: | | +1.9 | +1.8 | -3.3 | -15.5 |
| Rem. 55 HP Power-Lokt | velocity, fps: | 3680 | 3209 | 2785 | 2400 | 2046. |
| | energy, ft-lb: | 1654 | 1257 | 947 | 703 | 511 |
| | arc, inches: | | +1.8 | +1.7 | -3.0 | -13.7 |
| Rem. 60 Nosler Partition (also in EtronX) | velocity, fps: | 3500 | 3045 | 2634 | 2258 | 1914 |
| | energy, ft-lb: | 1632 | 1235 | 924 | 679 | 488 |
| | arc, inches: | | +2.1 | +1.9 | -3.4 | -15.5 |
| Win. 40 Ballistic Silvertip | velocity, fps: | 4150 | 3591 | 3099 | 2658 | 2257 |
| | energy, ft-lb: | 1530 | 1146 | 853 | 628 | 453 |
| | arc, inches: | | +0.6 | 0 | -4.2 | -13.4 |

| cartridge bullet | range, yards: | 0 | 100 | 200 | 300 | 400 |
|---|---|---|---|---|---|---|
| Win. 50 Ballistic Silvertip | velocity, fps: | 3810 | 3341 | 2919 | 2536 | 2182 |
| | energy, ft-lb: | 1611 | 1239 | 946 | 714 | 529. |
| | arc, inches: | | +0.8 | 0 | -4.9 | -15.2 |
| Win. 55 Pointed Soft Point | velocity, fps: | 3680 | 3137 | 2656 | 2222 | 1832 |
| | energy, ft-lb: | 1654 | 1201 | 861 | 603 | 410 |
| | arc, inches: | | +2.3 | +1.9 | -3.4 | -15.9 |
| Win. 55 Ballistic Silvertip | velocity, fps: | 3680 | 3272 | 2900 | 2558 | 2240 |
| | energy, ft-lb: | 1654 | 1307 | 1027 | 799 | 613 |
| | arc, inches: | | +0.9 | 0 | -5.0 | -15.4 |
| Win. 64 Power-Point | velocity, fps: | 3500 | 3086 | 2708 | 2360 | 2038 |
| | energy, ft-lb: | 1741 | 1353 | 1042 | 791 | 590 |
| | arc, inches: | | +1.1 | 0 | -5.9 | -18.0 |

## .220 Swift

| cartridge bullet | range, yards: | 0 | 100 | 200 | 300 | 400 |
|---|---|---|---|---|---|---|
| Federal 52 Sierra MatchKing BTHP | velocity, fps: | 3830 | 3370 | 2960 | 2600 | 2230 |
| | energy, ft-lb: | 1690 | 1310 | 1010 | 770 | 575 |
| | arc, inches: | | +0.8 | 0 | -4.8 | -14.9 |
| Federal 55 Sierra BlitzKing | velocity, fps: | 3800 | 3370 | 2990 | 2630 | 2310. |
| | energy, ft-lb: | 1765 | 1390 | 1090 | 850 | 650 |
| | arc, inches: | | +0.8 | 0 | -4.7 | -14.4 |
| Federal 55 Trophy Bonded | velocity, fps: | 3700 | 3170 | 2690 | 2270 | 1880 |
| | energy, ft-lb: | 1670 | 1225 | 885 | 625 | 430 |
| | arc, inches: | | +1.0 | 0 | -5.8 | -18.5 |
| Hornady 40 V-Max | velocity, fps: | 4200 | 3678 | 3190 | 2739 | 2329 |
| | energy, ft-lb: | 1566 | 1201 | 904 | 666 | 482 |
| | arc, inches: | | +0.5 | 0 | -4.0 | -12.9 |
| Hornady 50 V-Max | velocity, fps: | 3850 | 3396 | 2970 | 2576 | 2215. |
| | energy, ft-lb: | 1645 | 1280 | 979 | 736 | 545 |
| | arc, inches: | | +0.7 | 0 | -4.8 | -15.1 |
| Hornady 50 SP | velocity, fps: | 3850 | 3327 | 2862 | 2442 | 2060. |
| | energy, ft-lb: | 1645 | 1228 | 909 | 662 | 471 |
| | arc, inches: | | +0.8 | 0 | -5.1 | -16.1 |
| Hornady 55 V-Max | velocity, fps: | 3680 | 3265 | 2876 | 2517 | 2183 |
| | energy, ft-lb: | 1654 | 1302 | 1010 | 772 | 582 |
| | arc, inches: | | +0.9 | 0 | -5.3 | -16.1 |
| Hornady 60 Hollow Point | velocity, fps: | 3600 | 3199 | 2824 | 2475 | 2156 |
| | energy, ft-lb: | 1727 | 1364 | 1063 | 816 | 619 |
| | arc, inches: | | +1.0 | 0 | -5.4 | -16.3 |
| Norma 50 Soft Point | velocity, fps: | 4019 | 3380 | 2826 | 2335 | |
| | energy, ft-lb: | 1794 | 1268 | 887 | 605 | |
| | arc, inches: | | +0.7 | 0 | -5.1 | |
| Rem. 50 Pointed Soft Point | velocity, fps: | 3780 | 3158 | 2617 | 2135 | 1710 |
| | energy, ft-lb: | 1586 | 1107 | 760 | 506 | 325 |
| | arc, inches: | | +0.3 | -1.4 | -8.2 | |
| Rem. 50 V-Max boat-tail (also in EtronX) | velocity, fps: | 3780 | 3321 | 2908 | 2532 | 2185 |
| | energy, ft-lb: | 1586 | 1224 | 939 | 711 | 530 |
| | arc, inches: | | +0.8 | 0 | -5.0 | -15.4 |
| Win. 40 Ballistic Silvertip | velocity, fps: | 4050 | 3518 | 3048 | 2624 | 2238. |
| | energy, ft-lb: | 1457 | 1099 | 825 | 611 | 445 |
| | arc, inches: | | +0.7 | 0 | -4.4 | -13.9 |
| Win. 50 Pointed Soft Point | velocity, fps: | 3870 | 3310 | 2816 | 2373 | 1972 |
| | energy, ft-lb: | 1663 | 1226 | 881 | 625 | 432 |
| | arc, inches: | | +0.8 | 0 | -5.2 | -16.7 |

## .223 WSSM

| cartridge bullet | range, yards: | 0 | 100 | 200 | 300 | 400 |
|---|---|---|---|---|---|---|
| Win. 55 Ballistic Silvertip | velocity, fps: | 3850 | 3438 | 3064 | 2721 | 2402 |
| | energy, ft-lb: | 1810 | 1444 | 1147 | 904 | 704 |
| | arc, inches: | | +0.7 | 0 | -4.4 | -13.6 |
| Win. 55 Pointed Softpoint | velocity, fps: | 3850 | 3367 | 2934 | 2541 | 2181 |
| | energy, ft-lb: | 1810 | 1384 | 1051 | 789 | 581 |
| | arc, inches: | | +0.8 | 0 | -4.9 | -15.1 |
| Win. 64 Power-Point | velocity, fps: | 3600 | 3144 | 2732 | 2356 | 2011 |
| | energy, ft-lb: | 1841 | 1404 | 1061 | 789 | 574 |
| | arc, inches: | | +1.0 | 0 | -5.7 | -17.7 |

**BALLISTICS**

# Centerfire Rifle Ballistics

## 6MM PPC TO .243 WINCHESTER

| cartridge bullet | range, yards: | 0 | 100 | 200 | 300 | 400 |
|---|---|---|---|---|---|---|
| **6mm PPC** | | | | | | |
| A-Square 68 Berger | velocity, fps: | 3100 | 2751 | 2428 | 2128 | 1850 |
| | energy, ft-lb: | 1451 | 1143 | 890 | 684 | 516 |
| | arc, inches: | | +1.5 | 0 | -7.5 | -22.6 |
| **6x70 R** | | | | | | |
| Norma 95 Nosler Bal. Tip | velocity, fps: | 2461 | 2231 | 2013 | 1809 | |
| | energy, ft-lb: | 1211 | 995 | 810 | 654 | |
| | arc, inches: | | +2.7 | 0 | -11.3 | |
| **6.8mm SPC** | | | | | | |
| Hornady 110 V-Max | velocity, fps: | 2550 | 2319 | 2100 | 1893 | 1700 |
| | energy, ft-lb: | 1588 | 1313 | 1077 | 875 | 706 |
| | arc, inches: | | +2.5 | 0 | -10.4 | -30.6 |
| **.243 Winchester** | | | | | | |
| Black Hills 55 Nosler B. Tip | velocity, fps: | 3800 | | | | |
| | energy, ft-lb: | 1763 | | | | |
| | arc, inches: | | | | | |
| Black Hills 95 Nosler B. Tip | velocity, fps: | 2950 | | | | |
| | energy, ft-lb: | 1836 | | | | |
| | arc, inches: | | | | | |
| Federal 70 Nosler Bal. Tip | velocity, fps: | 3400 | 3070 | 2760 | 2470 | 2200 |
| | energy, ft-lb: | 1795 | 1465 | 1185 | 950 | 755. |
| | arc, inches: | | +1.1 | 0 | -5.7 | -17.1 |
| Federal 70 Speer TNT HP | velocity, fps: | 3400 | 3040 | 2700 | 2390 | 2100 |
| | energy, ft-lb: | 1795 | 1435 | 1135 | 890 | 685 |
| | arc, inches: | | +1.1 | 0 | -5.9 | -18.0 |
| Federal 80 Sierra Pro-Hunter | velocity, fps: | 3350 | 2960 | 2590 | 2260 | 1950 |
| | energy, ft-lb: | 1995 | 1550 | 1195 | 905 | 675 |
| | arc, inches: | | +1.3 | 0 | -6.4 | -19.7 |
| Federal 85 Sierra GameKing BTHP | velocity, fps: | 3320 | 3070 | 2830 | 2600 | 2380 |
| | energy, ft-lb: | 2080 | 1770 | 1510 | 1280 | 1070 |
| | arc, inches: | | +1.1 | 0 | -5.5 | -16.1 |
| Federal 90 Trophy Bonded | velocity, fps: | 3100 | 2850 | 2610 | 2380 | 2160. |
| | energy, ft-lb: | 1920 | 1620 | 1360 | 1130 | 935 |
| | arc, inches: | | +1.4 | 0 | -6.1 | -19.2 |
| Federal 100 Hi-Shok | velocity, fps: | 2960 | 2700 | 2450 | 2220 | 1990 |
| | energy, ft-lb: | 1945 | 1615 | 1330 | 1090 | 880 |
| | arc, inches: | | +1.6 | 0 | -7.5 | -22.0 |
| Federal 100 Sierra GameKing BTSP | velocity, fps: | 2960 | 2760 | 2570 | 2380 | 2210 |
| | energy, ft-lb: | 1950 | 1690 | 1460 | 1260 | 1080 |
| | arc, inches: | | +1.5 | 0 | -6.8 | -19.8 |
| Federal 100 Nosler Partition | velocity, fps: | 2960 | 2730 | 2510 | 2300 | 2100 |
| | energy, ft-lb: | 1945 | 1650 | 1395 | 1170 | 975. |
| | arc, inches: | | +1.6 | 0 | -7.1 | -20.9 |
| Hornady 58 V-Max | velocity, fps: | 3750 | 3319 | 2913 | 2539 | 2195 |
| | energy, ft-lb: | 1811 | 1418 | 1093 | 830 | 620 |
| | arc, inches: | | +1.2 | 0 | -5.5 | -16.4 |
| Hornady 75 Hollow Point | velocity, fps: | 3400 | 2970 | 2578 | 2219 | 1890 |
| | energy, ft-lb: | 1926 | 1469 | 1107 | 820 | 595 |
| | arc, inches: | | +1.2 | 0 | -6.5 | -20.3 |
| Hornady 100 BTSP | velocity, fps: | 2960 | 2728 | 2508 | 2299 | 2099 |
| | energy, ft-lb: | 1945 | 1653 | 1397 | 1174 | 979 |
| | arc, inches: | | +1.6 | 0 | -7.2 | -21.0 |
| Hornady 100 BTSP LM | velocity, fps: | 3100 | 2839 | 2592 | 2358 | 2138 |
| | energy, ft-lb: | 2133 | 1790 | 1491 | 1235 | 1014 |
| | arc, inches: | | +1.5 | 0 | -6.8 | -19.8 |
| Norma 80 FMJ | velocity, fps: | 3117 | 2750 | 2412 | 2098 | |
| | energy, ft-lb: | 1726 | 1344 | 1034 | 782 | |
| | arc, inches: | | +1.5 | 0 | -7.5 | |
| Norma 100 FMJ | velocity, fps: | 3018 | 2747 | 2493 | 2252 | |
| | energy, ft-lb: | 2023 | 1677 | 1380 | 1126 | |
| | arc, inches: | | +1.5 | 0 | -7.1 | |

| cartridge bullet | range, yards: | 0 | 100 | 200 | 300 | 400 |
|---|---|---|---|---|---|---|
| Norma 100 Soft Point | velocity, fps: | 3018 | 2748 | 2493 | 2252 | |
| | energy, ft-lb: | 2023 | 1677 | 1380 | 1126 | |
| | arc, inches: | | +1.5 | 0 | -7.1 | |
| Norma 100 Oryx | velocity, fps: | 3018 | 2653 | 2316 | 2004 | |
| | energy, ft-lb: | 2023 | 1563 | 1191 | 892 | |
| | arc, inches: | | +1.7 | 0 | -8.3 | |
| PMC 80 Pointed Soft Point | velocity, fps: | 2940 | 2684 | 2444 | 2215 | 1999 |
| | energy, ft-lb: | 1535 | 1280 | 1060 | 871 | 709 |
| | arc, inches: | | +1.7 | 0 | -7.5 | -22.1 |
| PMC 85 Barnes XLC | velocity, fps: | 3250 | 3022 | 2805 | 2598 | 2401 |
| | energy, ft-lb: | 1993 | 1724 | 1485 | 1274 | 1088 |
| | arc, inches: | | +1.6 | 0 | -5.6 | 16.3 |
| PMC 85 HP boat-tail | velocity, fps: | 3275 | 2922 | 2596 | 2292 | 2009 |
| | energy, ft-lb: | 2024 | 1611 | 1272 | 991 | 761 |
| | arc, inches: | | +1.3 | 0 | -6.5 | -19.7 |
| PMC 100 Pointed Soft Point | velocity, fps: | 2743 | 2507 | 2283 | 2070 | 1869 |
| | energy, ft-lb: | 1670 | 1395 | 1157 | 951 | 776 |
| | arc, inches: | | +2.0 | 0 | -8.7 | -25.5 |
| PMC 100 SP boat-tail | velocity, fps: | 2960 | 2742 | 2534 | 2335 | 2144 |
| | energy, ft-lb: | 1945 | 1669 | 1425 | 1210 | 1021 |
| | arc, inches: | | +1.6 | 0 | -7.0 | -20.5 |
| Rem. 75 AccuTip BT | velocity, fps: | 3375 | 3065 | 2775 | 2504 | 2248 |
| | energy, ft-lb: | 1897 | 1564 | 1282 | 1044 | 842 |
| | arc, inches: | | +2.0 | +1.8 | -3.0 | -13.3 |
| Rem. 80 Pointed Soft Point | velocity, fps: | 3350 | 2955 | 2593 | 2259 | 1951 |
| | energy, ft-lb: | 1993 | 1551 | 1194 | 906 | 676 |
| | arc, inches: | | +2.2 | +2.0 | -3.5 | -15.8 |
| Rem. 80 HP Power-Lokt | velocity, fps: | 3350 | 2955 | 2593 | 2259 | 1951 |
| | energy, ft-lb: | 1993 | 1551 | 1194 | 906 | 676 |
| | arc, inches: | | +2.2 | +2.0 | -3.5 | -15.8 |
| Rem. 90 Nosler Bal. Tip (also in EtronX) or Scirocco | velocity, fps: | 3120 | 2871 | 2635 | 2411 | 2199 |
| | energy, ft-lb: | 1946 | 1647 | 1388 | 1162 | 966 |
| | arc, inches: | | +1.4 | 0 | -6.4 | -18.8 |
| Rem. 95 AccuTip | velocity, fps: | 3120 | 2847 | 2590 | 2347 | 2118 |
| | energy, ft-lb: | 2053 | 1710 | 1415 | 1162 | 946 |
| | arc, inches: | | +1.5 | 0 | -6.6 | -19.5 |
| Rem. 100 PSP Core-Lokt (also in EtronX) | velocity, fps: | 2960 | 2697 | 2449 | 2215 | 1993 |
| | energy, ft-lb: | 1945 | 1615 | 1332 | 1089 | 882 |
| | arc, inches: | | +1.6 | 0 | -7.5 | -22.1 |
| Rem. 100 PSP boat-tail | velocity, fps: | 2960 | 2720 | 2492 | 2275 | 2069 |
| | energy, ft-lb: | 1945 | 1642 | 1378 | 1149 | 950 |
| | arc, inches: | | +2.8 | +2.3 | -3.8 | -16.6 |
| Speer 100 Grand Slam | velocity, fps: | 2950 | 2684 | 2434 | 2197 | |
| | energy, ft-lb: | 1932 | 1600 | 1315 | 1072 | |
| | arc, inches: | | +1.7 | 0 | -7.6 | -22.4 |
| Win. 55 Ballistic Silvertip | velocity, fps: | 4025 | 3597 | 3209 | 2853 | 2525 |
| | energy, ft-lb: | 1978 | 1579 | 1257 | 994 | 779 |
| | arc, inches: | | +0.6 | 0 | -4.0 | -12.2 |
| Win. 80 Pointed Soft Point | velocity, fps: | 3350 | 2955 | 2593 | 2259 | 1951. |
| | energy, ft-lb: | 1993 | 1551 | 1194 | 906 | 676 |
| | arc, inches: | | +2.6 | +2.1 | -3.6 | -16.2 |
| Win. 95 Ballistic Silvertip | velocity, fps: | 3100 | 2854 | 2626 | 2410 | 2203 |
| | energy, ft-lb: | 2021 | 1719 | 1455 | 1225 | 1024 |
| | arc, inches: | | +1.4 | 0 | -6.4 | -18.9 |
| Win. 95 Supreme Elite XP3 | velocity, fps | 3100 | 2864 | 2641 | 2428 | 2225 |
| | energy, ft-lb | 2027 | 1730 | 1471 | 1243 | 1044 |
| | a rc, inches | | +1.4 | 0 | -6.4 | -18.7 |
| Win. 100 Power-Point | velocity, fps: | 2960 | 2697 | 2449 | 2215 | 1993 |
| | energy, ft-lb: | 1945 | 1615 | 1332 | 1089 | 882 |
| | arc, inches: | | +1.9 | 0 | -7.8 | -22.6. |
| Win. 100 Power-Point Plus | velocity, fps: | 3090 | 2818 | 2562 | 2321 | 2092 |
| | energy, ft-lb: | 2121 | 1764 | 1458 | 1196 | 972 |
| | arc, inches: | | +1.4 | 0 | -6.7 | -20.0 |

BALLISTICS

| cartridge bullet | range, yards: | 0 | 100 | 200 | 300 | 400 |
|---|---|---|---|---|---|---|

## 6mm Remington

| cartridge bullet | | 0 | 100 | 200 | 300 | 400 |
|---|---|---|---|---|---|---|
| Federal 80 Sierra Pro-Hunter | velocity, fps: | 3470 | 3060 | 2690 | 2350 | 2040 |
| | energy, ft-lb: | 2140 | 1665 | 1290 | 980 | 735 |
| | arc, inches: | | +1.1 | 0 | -5.9 | -18.2 |
| Federal 100 Hi-Shok | velocity, fps: | 3100 | 2830 | 2570 | 2330 | 2100 |
| | energy, ft-lb: | 2135 | 1775 | 1470 | 1205 | 985 |
| | arc, inches: | | +1.4 | 0 | -6.7 | -19.8 |
| Federal 100 Nos. Partition | velocity, fps: | 3100 | 2860 | 2640 | 2420 | 2220 |
| | energy, ft-lb: | 2135 | 1820 | 1545 | 1300 | 1090 |
| | arc, inches: | | +1.4 | 0 | -6.3 | -18.7 |
| Hornady 100 SP boat-tail | velocity, fps: | 3100 | 2861 | 2634 | 2419 | 2231 |
| | energy, ft-lb: | 2134 | 1818 | 1541 | 1300 | 1088 |
| | arc, inches: | | +1.3 | 0 | -6.5 | -18.9 |
| Hornady 100 SPBT LM | velocity, fps: | 3250 | 2997 | 2756 | 2528 | 2311 |
| | energy, ft-lb: | 2345 | 1995 | 1687 | 1418 | 1186 |
| | arc, inches: | | +1.6 | 0 | -6.3 | -18.2 |
| Rem. 75 V-Max boat-tail | velocity, fps: | 3400 | 3088 | 2797 | 2524 | 2267 |
| | energy, ft-lb: | 1925 | 1587 | 1303 | 1061 | 856 |
| | arc, inches: | | +1.9 | +1.7 | -3.0 | -13.1 |
| Rem. 100 PSP Core-Lokt | velocity, fps: | 3100 | 2829 | 2573 | 2332 | 2104. |
| | energy, ft-lb: | 2133 | 1777 | 1470 | 1207 | 983 |
| | arc, inches: | | +1.4 | 0 | -6.7 | -19.8 |
| Rem. 100 PSP boat-tail | velocity, fps: | 3100 | 2852 | 2617 | 2394 | 2183. |
| | energy, ft-lb: | 2134 | 1806 | 1521 | 1273 | 1058 |
| | arc, inches: | | +1.4 | 0 | -6.5 | -19.1 |
| Win. 100 Power-Point | velocity, fps: | 3100 | 2829 | 2573 | 2332 | 2104 |
| | energy, ft-lb: | 2133 | 1777 | 1470 | 1207 | 983 |
| | arc, inches: | | +1.7 | 0 | -7.0 | -20.4 |

## .243 WSSM

| cartridge bullet | | 0 | 100 | 200 | 300 | 400 |
|---|---|---|---|---|---|---|
| Win. 55 Ballistic Silvertip | velocity, fps: | 4060 | 3628 | 3237 | 2880 | 2550 |
| | energy, ft-lb: | 2013 | 1607 | 1280 | 1013 | 794 |
| | arc, inches: | | +0.6 | 0 | -3.9 | -12.0 |
| Win. 95 Ballistic Silvertip | velocity, fps: | 3250 | 3000 | 2763 | 2538 | 2325 |
| | energy, ft-lb: | 2258 | 1898 | 1610 | 1359 | 1140 |
| | arc, inches: | | +1.2 | 0 | 5.7 | 16.9 |
| Win. 95 Supreme Elite XP3 | velocity, fps | 3150 | 2912 | 2686 | 2471 | 2266 |
| | energy, ft-lb | 2093 | 1788 | 1521 | 1287 | 1083 |
| | arc, inches | | +1.3 | 0 | -6.1 | -18.0 |
| Win. 100 Power Point | velocity, fps: | 3110 | 2838 | 2583 | 2341 | 2112 |
| | energy, ft-lb: | 2147 | 1789 | 1481 | 1217 | 991 |
| | arc, inches: | | +1.4 | 0 | -6.6 | -19.7 |

## .240 Weatherby Magnum

| cartridge bullet | | 0 | 100 | 200 | 300 | 400 |
|---|---|---|---|---|---|---|
| Wby. 87 Pointed Expanding | velocity, fps: | 3523 | 3199 | 2898 | 2617 | 2352 |
| | energy, ft-lb: | 2397 | 1977 | 1622 | 1323 | 1069 |
| | arc, inches: | | +2.7 | +3.4 | 0 | -8.4 |
| Wby. 90 Barnes-X | velocity, fps: | 3500 | 3222 | 2962 | 2717 | 2484 |
| | energy, ft-lb: | 2448 | 2075 | 1753 | 1475 | 1233 |
| | arc, inches: | | +2.6 | +3.3 | 0 | -8.0 |
| Wby. 95 Nosler Bal. Tip | velocity, fps: | 3420 | 3146 | 2888 | 2645 | 2414 |
| | energy, ft-lb: | 2467 | 2087 | 1759 | 1475 | 1229 |
| | arc, inches: | | +2.7 | +3.5 | 0 | -8.4 |
| Wby. 100 Pointed Expanding | velocity, fps: | 3406 | 3134 | 2878 | 2637 | 2408 |
| | energy, ft-lb: | 2576 | 2180 | 1839 | 1544 | 1287 |
| | arc, inches: | | +2.8 | +3.5 | 0 | -8.4 |
| Wby. 100 Partition | velocity, fps: | 3406 | 3136 | 2882 | 2642 | 2415 |
| | energy, ft-lb: | 2576 | 2183 | 1844 | 1550 | 1294 |
| | arc, inches: | | +2.8 | +3.5 | 0 | -8.4 |

## .25-20 Winchester

| cartridge bullet | | 0 | 100 | 200 | 300 | 400 |
|---|---|---|---|---|---|---|
| Rem. 86 Soft Point | velocity, fps: | 1460 | 1194 | 1030 | 931 | 858 |
| | energy, ft-lb: | 407 | 272 | 203 | 165 | 141 |
| | arc, inches: | | 0 | -22.9 | -78.9 | -173.0 |

| cartridge bullet | range, yards: | 0 | 100 | 200 | 300 | 400 |
|---|---|---|---|---|---|---|
| Win. 86 Soft Point | velocity, fps: | 1460 | 1194 | 1030 | 931 | 858. |
| | energy, ft-lb: | 407 | 272 | 203 | 165 | 141 |
| | arc, inches: | | 0 | -23.5 | -79.6 | -175.9 |

## .25-35 Winchester

| cartridge bullet | | 0 | 100 | 200 | 300 | 400 |
|---|---|---|---|---|---|---|
| Win. 117 Soft Point | velocity, fps: | 2230 | 1866 | 1545 | 1282 | 1097 |
| | energy, ft-lb: | 1292 | 904 | 620 | 427 | 313 |
| | arc, inches: | | +2.1 | -5.1 | -27.0 | -70.1 |

## .250 Savage

| cartridge bullet | | 0 | 100 | 200 | 300 | 400 |
|---|---|---|---|---|---|---|
| Rem. 100 Pointed SP | velocity, fps: | 2820 | 2504 | 2210 | 1936 | 1684. |
| | energy, ft-lb: | 1765 | 1392 | 1084 | 832 | 630 |
| | arc, inches: | | +2.0 | 0 | -9.2 | -27.7 |
| Win. 100 Silvertip | velocity, fps: | 2820 | 2467 | 2140 | 1839 | 1569 |
| | energy, ft-lb: | 1765 | 1351 | 1017 | 751 | 547 |
| | arc, inches: | | +2.4 | 0 | -10.1 | -30.5 |

## .257 Roberts

| cartridge bullet | | 0 | 100 | 200 | 300 | 400 |
|---|---|---|---|---|---|---|
| Federal 120 Nosler Partition | velocity, fps: | 2780 | 2560 | 2360 | 2160 | 1970 |
| | energy, ft-lb: | 2060 | 1750 | 1480 | 1240 | 1030 |
| | arc, inches: | | +1.9 | 0 | -8.2 | -24.0 |
| Hornady 117 SP boat-tail | velocity, fps: | 2780 | 2550 | 2331 | 2122 | 1925 |
| | energy, ft-lb: | 2007 | 1689 | 1411 | 1170 | 963 |
| | arc, inches: | | +1.9 | 0 | -8.3 | -24.4 |
| Hornady 117 SP boat-tail LM | velocity, fps: | 2940 | 2694 | 2460 | 2240 | 2031 |
| | energy, ft-lb: | 2245 | 1885 | 1572 | 1303 | 1071 |
| | arc, inches: | | +1.7 | 0 | -7.6 | -21.8 |
| Rem. 117 SP Core-Lokt | velocity, fps: | 2650 | 2291 | 1961 | 1663 | 1404 |
| | energy, ft-lb: | 1824 | 1363 | 999 | 718 | 512 |
| | arc, inches: | | +2.6 | 0 | -11.7 | -36.1 |
| Win. 117 Power-Point | velocity, fps: | 2780 | 2411 | 2071 | 1761 | 1488 |
| | energy, ft-lb: | 2009 | 1511 | 1115 | 806 | 576. |
| | arc, inches: | | +2.6 | 0 | -10.8 | -33.0 |

## .25-06 Remington

| cartridge bullet | | 0 | 100 | 200 | 300 | 400 |
|---|---|---|---|---|---|---|
| Black Hills 100 Nos. Bal. Tip | velocity, fps: | 3200 | | | | |
| | energy, ft-lb: | 2273 | | | | |
| | arc, inches: | | | | | |
| Black Hills 100 Barnes XLC | velocity, fps: | 3200 | | | | |
| | energy, ft-lb: | 2273 | | | | |
| | arc, inches: | | | | | |
| Black Hills 115 Barnes X | velocity, fps: | 2975 | | | | |
| | energy, ft-lb: | 2259 | | | | |
| | arc, inches: | | | | | |
| Federal 90 Sierra Varminter | velocity, fps: | 3440 | 3040 | 2680 | 2340 | 2030 |
| | energy, ft-lb: | 2365 | 1850 | 1435 | 1100 | 825 |
| | arc, inches: | | +1.1 | 0 | -6.0 | -18.3 |
| Federal 100 Barnes XLC | velocity, fps: | 3210 | 2970 | 2750 | 2540 | 2330 |
| | energy, ft-lb: | 2290 | 1965 | 1680 | 1430 | 1205 |
| | arc, inches: | | +1.2 | 0 | -5.8 | -17.0 |
| Federal 100 Nosler Bal. Tip | velocity, fps: | 3210 | 2960 | 2720 | 2490 | 2280 |
| | energy, ft-lb: | 2290 | 1940 | 1640 | 1380 | 1150. |
| | arc, inches: | | +1.2 | 0 | -6.0 | -17.5 |
| Federal 115 Nosler Partition | velocity, fps: | 2990 | 2750 | 2520 | 2300 | 2100 |
| | energy, ft-lb: | 2285 | 1930 | 1620 | 1350 | 1120 |
| | arc, inches: | | +1.6 | 0 | -7.0 | -20.8 |
| Federal 115 Trophy Bonded | velocity, fps: | 2990 | 2740 | 2500 | 2270 | 2050 |
| | energy, ft-lb: | 2285 | 1910 | 1590 | 1310 | 1075 |
| | arc, inches: | | +1.6 | 0 | -7.2 | -21.1 |
| Federal 117 Sierra Pro Hunt. | velocity, fps: | 2990 | 2730 | 2480 | 2250 | 2030 |
| | energy, ft-lb: | 2320 | 1985 | 1645 | 1350 | 1100 |
| | arc, inches: | | +1.6 | 0 | -7.2 | -21.4 |
| Federal 117 Sierra GameKing BTSP | velocity, fps: | 2990 | 2770 | 2570 | 2370 | 2190 |
| | energy, ft-lb: | 2320 | 2000 | 1715 | 1465 | 1240 |
| | arc, inches: | | +1.5 | 0 | -6.8 | -19.9 |

# Centerfire Rifle Ballistics

## .25-06 REMINGTON TO 6.5X55 SWEDISH

| cartridge bullet | range, yards: | 0 | 100 | 200 | 300 | 400 |
|---|---|---|---|---|---|---|
| Hornady 117 SP boat-tail | velocity, fps: | 2990 | 2749 | 2520 | 2302 | 2096 |
| | energy, ft-lb: | 2322 | 1962 | 1649 | 1377 | 1141 |
| | arc, inches: | | +1.6 | 0 | -7.0 | -20.7 |
| Hornady 117 SP boat-tail LM | velocity, fps: | 3110 | 2855 | 2613 | 2384 | 2168 |
| | energy, ft-lb: | 2512 | 2117 | 1774 | 1476 | 1220 |
| | arc, inches: | | +1.8 | 0 | -7.1 | -20.3 |
| PMC 100 SPBT | velocity, fps: | 3200 | 2925 | 2650 | 2395 | 2145 |
| | energy, ft-lb: | 2273 | 1895 | 1561 | 1268 | 1019 |
| | arc, inches: | | +1.3 | 0 | -6.3 | -18.6 |
| PMC 117 PSP | velocity, fps: | 2950 | 2706 | 2472 | 2253 | 2047 |
| | energy, ft-lb: | 2261 | 1900 | 1588 | 1319 | 1088 |
| | arc, inches: | | +1.6 | 0 | -7.3 | -21.5 |
| Rem. 100 PSP Core-Lokt | velocity, fps: | 3230 | 2893 | 2580 | 2287 | 2014 |
| | energy, ft-lb: | 2316 | 1858 | 1478 | 1161 | 901 |
| | arc, inches: | | +1.3 | 0 | -6.6 | -19.8 |
| Rem. 115 Core-Lokt Ultra | velocity, fps: | 3000 | 2751 | 2516 | 2293 | 2081 |
| | energy, ft-lb: | 2298 | 1933 | 1616 | 1342 | 1106 |
| | arc, inches: | | +1.6 | 0 | -7.1 | -20.7 |
| Rem. 120 PSP Core-Lokt | velocity, fps: | 2990 | 2730 | 2484 | 2252 | 2032 |
| | energy, ft-lb: | 2382 | 1985 | 1644 | 1351 | 1100 |
| | arc, inches: | | +1.6 | 0 | -7.2 | -21.4 |
| Speer 120 Grand Slam | velocity, fps: | 3130 | 2835 | 2558 | 2298 | |
| | energy, ft-lb: | 2610 | 2141 | 1743 | 1407 | |
| | arc, inches: | | +1.4 | 0 | -6.8 | -20.1 |
| Win. 85 Ballistic Silvertip | velocity, fps | 3470 | 3156 | 2863 | 2589 | 2331 |
| | energy, ft-lb: | 2273 | 1880 | 1548 | 1266 | 1026 |
| | arc, inches: | | +1.0 | 0 | -5.2 | -15.7 |
| Win. 90 Pos. Exp. Point | velocity, fps: | 3440 | 3043 | 2680 | 2344 | 2034 |
| | energy, ft-lb: | 2364 | 1850 | 1435 | 1098 | 827 |
| | arc, inches: | | +2.4 | +2.0 | -3.4 | -15.0 |
| Win. 110 AccuBond CT | velocity, fps: | 3100 | 2870 | 2651 | 2442 | 2243 |
| | energy, ft-lb: | 2347 | 2011 | 1716 | 1456 | 1228 |
| | arc, inches: | | +1.4 | 0 | -6.3 | -18.5 |
| Win. 115 Ballistic Silvertip | velocity, fps: | 3060 | 2825 | 2603 | 2390 | 2188 |
| | energy, ft-lb: | 2391 | 2038 | 1729 | 1459 | 1223 |
| | arc, inches: | | +1.4 | 0 | -6.6 | -19.2 |
| Win. 120 Pos. Pt. Exp. | velocity, fps: | 2990 | 2717 | 2459 | 2216 | 1987 |
| | energy, ft-lb: | 2382 | 1967 | 1612 | 1309 | 1053 |
| | arc, inches: | | +1.6 | 0 | -7.4 | -21.8 |

## .25 Winchester Super Short Magnum

| cartridge bullet | range, yards: | 0 | 100 | 200 | 300 | 400 |
|---|---|---|---|---|---|---|
| Win. 85 Ballistic Silvertip | velocity, fps: | 3470 | 3156 | 2863 | 2589 | 2331 |
| | energy, ft-lb: | 2273 | 1880 | 1548 | 1266 | 1026 |
| | arc, inches: | | +1.0 | 0 | -5.2 | -15.7 |
| Win. 110 AccuBond CT | velocity, fps: | 3100 | 2870 | 2651 | 2442 | 2243. |
| | energy, ft-lb: | 2347 | 2011 | 1716 | 1456 | 1228 |
| | arc, inches: | | +1.4 | 0 | -6.3 | -18.5 |
| Win. 115 Ballistic Silvertip | velocity, fps: | 3060 | 2844 | 2639 | 2442 | 2254 |
| | energy, ft-lb: | 2392 | 2066 | 1778 | 1523 | 1298 |
| | arc, inches: | | +1.4 | 0 | -6.4 | -18.6 |
| Win. 120 Pos. Pt. Exp. | velocity, fps: | 2990 | 2717 | 2459 | 2216 | 1987 |
| | energy, ft-lb: | 2383 | 1967 | 1612 | 1309 | 1053 |
| | arc, inches: | | +1.6 | 0 | -7.4 | -21.8 |

## .257 Weatherby Magnum

| cartridge bullet | range, yards: | 0 | 100 | 200 | 300 | 400 |
|---|---|---|---|---|---|---|
| Federal 115 Nosler Partition | velocity, fps: | 3150 | 2900 | 2660 | 2440 | 2220. |
| | energy, ft-lb: | 2535 | 2145 | 1810 | 1515 | 1260 |
| | arc, inches: | | +1.3 | 0 | -6.2 | -18.4 |
| Federal 115 Trophy Bonded | velocity, fps: | 3150 | 2890 | 2640 | 2400 | 2180 |
| | energy, ft-lb: | 2535 | 2125 | 1775 | 1470 | 1210 |
| | arc, inches: | | +1.4 | 0 | -6.3 | -18.8 |
| Wby. 87 Pointed Expanding | velocity, fps: | 3825 | 3472 | 3147 | 2845 | 2563 |
| | energy, ft-lb: | 2826 | 2328 | 1913 | 1563 | 1269 |
| | arc, inches: | | +2.1 | +2.8 | 0 | -7.1 |

| cartridge bullet | range, yards: | 0 | 100 | 200 | 300 | 400 |
|---|---|---|---|---|---|---|
| Wby. 100 Pointed Expanding | velocity, fps: | 3602 | 3298 | 3016 | 2750 | 2500 |
| | energy, ft-lb: | 2881 | 2416 | 2019 | 1680 | 1388 |
| | arc, inches: | | +2.4 | +3.1 | 0 | -7.7 |
| Wby. 115 Nosler Bal. Tip | velocity, fps: | 3400 | 3170 | 2952 | 2745 | 2547 |
| | energy, ft-lb: | 2952 | 2566 | 2226 | 1924 | 1656. |
| | arc, inches: | | +3.0 | +3.5 | 0 | -7.9 |
| Wby. 115 Barnes X | velocity, fps: | 3400 | 3158 | 2929 | 2711 | 2504 |
| | energy, ft-lb: | 2952 | 2546 | 2190 | 1877 | 1601 |
| | arc, inches: | | +2.7 | +3.4 | 0 | -8.1 |
| Wby. 117 RN Expanding | velocity, fps: | 3402 | 2984 | 2595 | 2240 | 1921 |
| | energy, ft-lb: | 3007 | 2320 | 1742 | 1302 | 956 |
| | arc, inches: | | +3.4 | +4.31 | 0 | -11.1 |
| Wby. 120 Nosler Partition | velocity, fps: | 3305 | 3046 | 2801 | 2570 | 2350 |
| | energy, ft-lb: | 2910 | 2472 | 2091 | 1760 | 1471 |
| | arc, inches: | | +3.0 | +3.7 | 0 | -8.9 |

## 6.53 (.257) Scramjet

| cartridge bullet | range, yards: | 0 | 100 | 200 | 300 | 400 |
|---|---|---|---|---|---|---|
| Lazzeroni 85 Nosler Bal. Tip | velocity, fps: | 3960 | 3652 | 3365 | 3096 | 2844 |
| | energy, ft-lb: | 2961 | 2517 | 2137 | 1810 | 1526 |
| | arc, inches: | | +1.7 | +2.4 | 0 | -6.0 |
| Lazzeroni 100 Nosler Part. | velocity, fps: | 3740 | 3465 | 3208 | 2965 | 2735 |
| | energy, ft-lb: | 3106 | 2667 | 2285 | 1953 | 1661. |
| | arc, inches: | | +2.1 | +2.7 | 0 | -6.7 |

## 6.5x50 Japanese

| cartridge bullet | range, yards: | 0 | 100 | 200 | 300 | 400 |
|---|---|---|---|---|---|---|
| Norma 156 Alaska | velocity, fps: | 2067 | 1832 | 1615 | 1423 | |
| | energy, ft-lb: | 1480 | 1162 | 904 | 701 | |
| | arc, inches: | | +4.4 | 0 | -17.8 | |

## 6.5x52 Carcano

| cartridge bullet | range, yards: | 0 | 100 | 200 | 300 | 400 |
|---|---|---|---|---|---|---|
| Norma 156 Alaska | velocity, fps: | 2428 | 2169 | 1926 | 1702 | |
| | energy, ft-lb: | 2043 | 1630 | 1286 | 1004 | |
| | arc, inches: | | +2.9 | 0 | -12.3 | |

## 6.5x55 Swedish

| cartridge bullet | range, yards: | 0 | 100 | 200 | 300 | 400 |
|---|---|---|---|---|---|---|
| Federal 140 Hi-Shok | velocity, fps: | 2600 | 2400 | 2220 | 2040 | 1860 |
| | energy, ft-lb: | 2100 | 1795 | 1525 | 1285 | 1080 |
| | arc, inches: | | +2.3 | 0 | -9.4 | -27.2 |
| Federal 140 Trophy Bonded | velocity, fps: | 2550 | 2350 | 2160 | 1980 | 1810 |
| | energy, ft-lb: | 2020 | 1720 | 1450 | 1220 | 1015 |
| | arc, inches: | | +2.4 | 0 | -9.8 | -28.4 |
| Federal 140 Sierra MatchKg. BTHP | velocity, fps: | 2630 | 2460 | 2300 | 2140 | 2000 |
| | energy, ft-lb: | 2140 | 1880 | 1640 | 1430 | 1235 |
| | arc, inches: | | +16.4 | +28.8 | +33.9 | +31.8 |
| Hornady 129 SP LM | velocity, fps: | 2770 | 2561 | 2361 | 2171 | 1994 |
| | energy, ft-lb: | 2197 | 1878 | 1597 | 1350 | 1138 |
| | arc, inches: | | +2.0 | 0 | -8.2 | -23.2 |
| Hornady 140 SP Interlock | velocity, fps | 2525 | 2341 | 2165 | 1996 | 1836 |
| | energy, ft-lb: | 1982 | 1704 | 1457 | 1239 | 1048 |
| | arc, inches: | | +2.4 | 0 | -9.9 | -28.5 |
| Hornady140 SP LM | velocity, fps: | 2740 | 2541 | 2351 | 2169 | 1999 |
| | energy, ft-lb: | 2333 | 2006 | 1717 | 1463 | 1242 |
| | arc, inches: | | +2.4 | 0 | -8.7 | -24.0 |
| Norma 120 Nosler Bal. Tip | velocity, fps: | 2822 | 2609 | 2407 | 2213 | |
| | energy, ft-lb: | 2123 | 1815 | 1544 | 1305 | |
| | arc, inches: | | +1.8 | 0 | -7.8 | |
| Norma 139 Vulkan | velocity, fps: | 2854 | 2569 | 2302 | 2051 | |
| | energy, ft-lb: | 2515 | 2038 | 1636 | 1298 | |
| | arc, inches: | | +1.8 | 0 | -8.4 | |
| Norma 140 Nosler Partition | velocity, fps: | 2789 | 2592 | 2403 | 2223 | |
| | energy, ft-lb: | 2419 | 2089 | 1796 | 1536 | |
| | arc, inches: | | +1.8 | 0 | -7.8 | |
| Norma 156 TXP Swift A-Fr. | velocity, fps: | 2526 | 2276 | 2040 | 1818 | |
| | energy, ft-lb: | 2196 | 1782 | 1432 | 1138 | |

BALLISTICS

| cartridge bullet | range, yards: | 0 | 100 | 200 | 300 | 400 |
|---|---|---|---|---|---|---|
| Norma 156 Alaska | arc, inches: | | +2.6 | 0 | -10.9 | |
| | velocity, fps: | 2559 | 2245 | 1953 | 1687 | |
| | energy, ft-lb: | 2269 | 1746 | 1322 | 986 | |
| Norma 156 Vulkan | arc, inches: | | +2.7 | 0 | -11.9 | |
| | velocity, fps: | 2644 | 2395 | 2159 | 1937 | |
| | energy, ft-lb: | 2422 | 1987 | 1616 | 1301 | |
| Norma 156 Oryx | arc, inches: | | +2.2 | 0 | -9.7 | |
| | velocity, fps: | 2559 | 2308 | 2070 | 1848 | |
| | energy, ft-lb: | 2269 | 1845 | 1485 | 1183 | |
| PMC 139 Pointed Soft Point | arc, inches: | | +2.5 | 0 | -10.6 | |
| | velocity, fps: | 2850 | 2560 | 2290 | 2030 | 1790 |
| | energy, ft-lb: | 2515 | 2025 | 1615 | 1270 | 985 |
| PMC 140 HP boat-tail | arc, inches: | | +2.2 | 0 | -8.9 | -26.3 |
| | velocity, fps: | 2560 | 2398 | 2243 | 2093 | 1949 |
| | energy, ft-lb: | 2037 | 1788 | 1563 | 1361 | 1181 |
| PMC 140 SP boat-tail | arc, inches: | | +2.3 | 0 | -9.2 | -26.4 |
| | velocity, fps: | 2560 | 2386 | 2218 | 2057 | 1903 |
| | energy, ft-lb: | 2037 | 1769 | 1529 | 1315 | 1126 |
| PMC 144 FMJ | arc, inches: | | +2.3 | 0 | -9.4 | -27.1 |
| | velocity, fps: | 2650 | 2370 | 2110 | 1870 | 1650 |
| | energy, ft-lb: | 2425 | 1950 | 1550 | 1215 | 945 |
| Rem. 140 PSP Core-Lokt | arc, inches: | | +2.7 | 0 | -10.5 | -30.9 |
| | velocity, fps: | 2550 | 2353 | 2164 | 1984 | 1814 |
| | energy, ft-lb: | 2021 | 1720 | 1456 | 1224 | 1023 |
| Speer 140 Grand Slam | arc, inches: | | +2.4 | 0 | -9.8 | -27.0 |
| | velocity, fps: | 2550 | 2318 | 2099 | 1892 | |
| | energy, ft-lb: | 2021 | 1670 | 1369 | 1112 | |
| Win. 140 Soft Point | arc, inches: | | +2.5 | 0 | -10.4 | -30.6 |
| | velocity, fps: | 2550 | 2359 | 2176 | 2002 | 1836 |
| | energy, ft-lb: | 2022 | 1731 | 1473 | 1246 | 1048. |
| | arc, inches: | | +2.4 | 0 | -9.7 | -28.1 |

## .260 Remington

| cartridge bullet | range, yards: | 0 | 100 | 200 | 300 | 400 |
|---|---|---|---|---|---|---|
| Federal 140 Sierra GameKing BTSP | velocity, fps: | 2750 | 2570 | 2390 | 2220 | 2060 |
| | energy, ft-lb: | 2350 | 2045 | 1775 | 1535 | 1315 |
| | arc, inches: | | +1.9 | 0 | -8.0 | -23.1 |
| Federal 140 Trophy Bonded | velocity, fps: | 2750 | 2540 | 2340 | 2150 | 1970 |
| | energy, ft-lb: | 2350 | 2010 | 1705 | 1440 | 1210 |
| | arc, inches: | | +1.9 | 0 | -8.4 | -24.1 |
| Rem. 120 Nosler Bal. Tip | velocity, fps: | 2890 | 2688 | 2494 | 2309 | 2131 |
| | energy, ft-lb: | 2226 | 1924 | 1657 | 1420 | 1210 |
| | arc, inches: | | +1.7 | 0 | -7.3 | -21.1 |
| Rem. 120 AccuTip | velocity, fps: | 2890 | 2697 | 2512 | 2334 | 2163 |
| | energy, ft-lb: | 2392 | 2083 | 1807 | 1560 | 1340 |
| | arc, inches: | | +1.6 | 0 | -7.2 | -20.7 |
| Rem. 125 Nosler Partition | velocity, fps: | 2875 | 2669 | 2473 | 2285 | 2105. |
| | energy, ft-lb: | 2294 | 1977 | 1697 | 1449 | 1230 |
| | arc, inches: | | +1.71 | 0 | -7.4 | -21.4 |
| Rem. 140 PSP Core-Lokt (and C-L Ultra) | velocity, fps: | 2750 | 2544 | 2347 | 2158 | 1979 |
| | energy, ft-lb: | 2351 | 2011 | 1712 | 1448 | 1217 |
| | arc, inches: | | +1.9 | 0 | -8.3 | -24.0 |
| Speer 140 Grand Slam | velocity, fps: | 2750 | 2518 | 2297 | 2087 | |
| | energy, ft-lb: | 2351 | 1970 | 1640 | 1354 | |
| | arc, inches: | | +2.3 | 0 | -8.9 | -25.8 |

## 6.5/284

| cartridge bullet | range, yards: | 0 | 100 | 200 | 300 | 400 |
|---|---|---|---|---|---|---|
| Norma 120 Nosler Bal. Tip | velocity, fps: | 3117 | 2890 | 2674 | 2469 | |
| | energy, ft-lb: | 2589 | 2226 | 1906 | 1624 | |
| | arc, inches: | | +1.3 | 0 | -6.2 | |
| Norma 140 Nosler Part. | velocity, fps: | 2953 | 2750 | 2557 | 2371 | |
| | energy, ft-lb: | 2712 | 2352 | 2032 | 1748 | |

| cartridge bullet | range, yards: | 0 | 100 | 200 | 300 | 400 |
|---|---|---|---|---|---|---|
| | arc, inches: | | +1.5 | 0 | -6.8 | |

## 6.5 Remington Magnum

| cartridge bullet | range, yards: | 0 | 100 | 200 | 300 | 400 |
|---|---|---|---|---|---|---|
| Rem. 120 Core-Lokt PSP | velocity, fps: | 3210 | 2905 | 2621 | 2353 | 2102 |
| | energy, ft-lb: | 2745 | 2248 | 1830 | 1475 | 1177 |
| | arc, inches: | | +2.7 | +2.1 | -3.5 | -15.5 |

## .264 Winchester Magnum

| cartridge bullet | range, yards: | 0 | 100 | 200 | 300 | 400 |
|---|---|---|---|---|---|---|
| Rem. 140 PSP Core-Lokt | velocity, fps: | 3030 | 2782 | 2548 | 2326 | 2114 |
| | energy, ft-lb: | 2854 | 2406 | 2018 | 1682 | 1389 |
| | arc, inches: | | +1.5 | 0 | -6.9 | -20.2 |
| Win. 140 Power-Point | velocity, fps: | 3030 | 2782 | 2548 | 2326 | 2114. |
| | energy, ft-lb: | 2854 | 2406 | 2018 | 1682 | 1389 |
| | arc, inches: | | +1.8 | 0 | -7.2 | -20.8 |

## 6.8mm Remington SPC

| cartridge bullet | range, yards: | 0 | 100 | 200 | 300 | 400 |
|---|---|---|---|---|---|---|
| Rem. 115 Open Tip Match (and HPBT Match) | velocity, fps: | 2800 | 2535 | 2285 | 2049 | 1828 |
| | energy, ft-lb: | 2002 | 1641 | 1333 | 1072 | 853 |
| | arc, inches: | | +2.0 | 0 | -8.8 | -26.2 |
| Rem. 115 Metal Case | velocity, fps: | 2800 | 2523 | 2262 | 2017 | 1789 |
| | energy, ft-lb: | 2002 | 1625 | 1307 | 1039 | 817 |
| | arc, inches: | | +2.0 | 0 | -8.8 | -26.2 |
| Rem. 115 Sierra HPBT (2005; all vel. @ 2775) | velocity, fps: | 2775 | 2511 | 2263 | 2028 | 1809 |
| | energy, ft-lb: | 1966 | 1610 | 1307 | 1050 | 835 |
| | arc, inches: | | +2.0 | 0 | -8.8 | -26.2. |
| Rem. 115 CL Ultra | velocity, fps: | 2775 | 2472 | 2190 | 1926 | 1683 |
| | energy, ft-lb: | 1966 | 1561 | 1224 | 947 | 723 |
| | arc, inches: | | +2.1 | 0 | -9.4 | -28.2 |

## .270 Winchester

| cartridge bullet | range, yards: | 0 | 100 | 200 | 300 | 400 |
|---|---|---|---|---|---|---|
| Black Hills 130 Nos. Bal. T. | velocity, fps: | 2950 | | | | |
| | energy, ft-lb: | 2512 | | | | |
| | arc, inches: | | | | | |
| Black Hills 130 Barnes XLC | velocity, ft-lb: | 2950 | | | | |
| | energy, ft-lb: | 2512 | | | | |
| | arc, inches: | | | | | |
| Federal 130 Hi-Shok | velocity, fps: | 3060 | 2800 | 2560 | 2330 | 2110 |
| | energy, ft-lb: | 2700 | 2265 | 1890 | 1565 | 1285 |
| | arc, inches: | | +1.5 | 0 | -6.8 | -20.0 |
| Federal 130 Sierra Pro-Hunt. | velocity, fps: | 3060 | 2830 | 2600 | 2390 | 2190 |
| | energy, ft-lb: | 2705 | 2305 | 1960 | 1655 | 1390 |
| | arc, inches: | | +1.4 | 0 | -6.4 | -19.0 |
| Federal 130 Sierra GameKing | velocity, fps: | 3060 | 2830 | 2620 | 2410 | 2220. |
| | energy, ft-lb: | 2700 | 2320 | 1980 | 1680 | 1420 |
| | arc, inches: | | +1.4 | 0 | -6.5 | -19.0 |
| Federal 130 Nosler Bal. Tip | velocity, fps: | 3060 | 2840 | 2630 | 2430 | 2230 |
| | energy, ft-lb: | 2700 | 2325 | 1990 | 1700 | 1440 |
| | arc, inches: | | +1.4 | 0 | -6.5 | -18.8 |
| Federal 130 Nos. Partition And Solid Base | velocity, fps: | 3060 | 2830 | 2610 | 2400 | 2200 |
| | energy, ft-lb: | 2705 | 2310 | 1965 | 1665 | 1400 |
| | arc, inches: | | +1.4 | 0 | -6.5 | -19.1. |
| Federal 130 Barnes XLC And Triple Shock | velocity, fps: | 3060 | 2840 | 2620 | 2420 | 2220 |
| | energy, ft-lb: | 2705 | 2320 | 1985 | 1690 | 1425 |
| | arc, inches: | | +1.4 | 0 | -6.4 | -18.9 |
| Federal 130 Trophy Bonded | velocity, fps: | 3060 | 2810 | 2570 | 2340 | 2130 |
| | energy, ft-lb: | 2705 | 2275 | 1905 | 1585 | 1310 |
| | arc, inches: | | +1.5 | 0 | -6.7 | -19.8 |
| Federal 140 Trophy Bonded | velocity, fps: | 2940 | 2700 | 2480 | 2260 | 2060 |
| | energy, ft-lb: | 2685 | 2270 | 1905 | 1590 | 1315 |
| | arc, inches: | | +1.6 | 0 | -7.3 | -21.5 |
| Federal 140 Tr. Bonded HE | velocity, fps: | 3100 | 2860 | 2620 | 2400 | 2200. |
| | energy, ft-lb: | 2990 | 2535 | 2140 | 1795 | 1500 |

**BALLISTICS**

# Centerfire Rifle Ballistics

## .270 WINCHESTER TO .270 WINCHESTER

| cartridge bullet | range, yards: | 0 | 100 | 200 | 300 | 400 |
|---|---|---|---|---|---|---|
| Federal 140 Nos. AccuBond | arc, inches: | | +1.4 | 0 | -6.4 | -18.9 |
| | velocity, fps: | 2950 | 2760 | 2580 | 2400 | 2230. |
| | energy, ft-lb: | 2705 | 2365 | 2060 | 1790 | 1545 |
| Federal 150 Hi-Shok RN | arc, inches: | | +1.5 | 0 | -6.7 | -19.6 |
| | velocity, fps: | 2850 | 2500 | 2180 | 1890 | 1620 |
| | energy, ft-lb: | 2705 | 2085 | 1585 | 1185 | 870 |
| Federal 150 Sierra GameKing | arc, inches: | | +2.0 | 0 | -9.4 | -28.6 |
| | velocity, fps: | 2850 | 2660 | 2480 | 2300 | 2130 |
| | energy, ft-lb: | 2705 | 2355 | 2040 | 1760 | 1510 |
| Federal 150 Sierra GameKing HE | arc, inches: | | +1.7 | 0 | -7.4 | -21.4 |
| | velocity, fps: | 3000 | 2800 | 2620 | 2430 | 2260 |
| | energy, ft-lb: | 2995 | 2615 | 2275 | 1975 | 1700 |
| Federal 150 Nosler Partition | arc, inches: | | +1.5 | 0 | -6.5 | -18.9 |
| | velocity, fps: | 2850 | 2590 | 2340 | 2100 | 1880. |
| | energy, ft-lb: | 2705 | 2225 | 1815 | 1470 | 1175 |
| Hornady 130 SST (or Interbond) | arc, inches: | | +1.9 | 0 | -8.3 | -24.4 |
| | velocity, fps: | 3060 | 2845 | 2639 | 2442 | 2254 |
| | energy, ft-lb: | 2700 | 2335 | 2009 | 1721 | 1467 |
| Hornady 130 SST LM (or Interbond) | arc, inches: | | +1.4 | 0 | -6.6 | -19.1 |
| | velocity, fps: | 3215 | 2998 | 2790 | 2590 | 2400 |
| | energy, ft-lb: | 2983 | 2594 | 2246 | 1936 | 1662 |
| Hornady 140 SP boat-tail | arc, inches: | | +1.2 | 0 | -5.8 | -17.0 |
| | velocity, fps: | 2940 | 2747 | 2562 | 2385 | 2214 |
| | energy, ft-lb: | 2688 | 2346 | 2041 | 1769 | 1524 |
| Hornady 140 SP boat-tail LM | arc, inches: | | +1.6 | 0 | -7.0 | -20.2 |
| | velocity, fps: | 3100 | 2894 | 2697 | 2508 | 2327. |
| | energy, ft-lb: | 2987 | 2604 | 2261 | 1955 | 1684 |
| Hornady 150 SP | arc, inches: | | +1.4 | 0 | 6.3 | -18.3 |
| | velocity, fps: | 2800 | 2684 | 2478 | 2284 | 2100 |
| | energy, ft-lb: | 2802 | 2400 | 2046 | 1737 | 1469 |
| Norma 130 SP | arc, inches: | | +1.7 | 0 | -7.4 | -21.6 |
| | velocity, fps: | 3140 | 2862 | 2601 | 2354 | |
| | energy, ft-lb: | 2847 | 2365 | 1953 | 1600 | |
| Norma 130 FMJ | arc, inches: | | +1.3 | 0 | -6.5 | |
| | velocity, fps: | 2887 | 2634 | 2395 | 2169 | |
| | energy, ft-lb: | | | | | |
| Norma 150 SP | arc, inches: | | +1.8 | 0 | -7.8 | |
| | velocity, fps: | 2799 | 2555 | 2323 | 2104 | |
| | energy, ft-lb: | 2610 | 2175 | 1798 | 1475 | |
| Norma 150 Oryx | arc, inches: | | +1.9 | 0 | -8.3 | |
| | velocity, fps: | 2854 | 2608 | 2376 | 2155 | |
| | energy, ft-lb: | 2714 | 2267 | 1880 | 1547 | |
| PMC 130 Barnes X | arc, inches: | | +1.8 | 0 | -8.0 | |
| | velocity, fps: | 2910 | 2717 | 2533 | 2356 | 2186 |
| | energy, ft-lb: | 2444 | 2131 | 1852 | 1602 | 1379 |
| PMC 130 SP boat-tail | arc, inches: | | +1.6 | 0 | -7.1 | -20.4 |
| | velocity, fps: | 3050 | 2830 | 2620 | 2421 | 2229 |
| | energy, ft-lb: | 2685 | 2312 | 1982 | 1691 | 1435 |
| PMC 130 Pointed Soft Point | arc, inches: | | +1.5 | 0 | -6.5 | -19.0 |
| | velocity, fps: | 2950 | 2691 | 2447 | 2217 | 2001 |
| | energy, ft-lb: | 2512 | 2090 | 1728 | 1419 | 1156 |
| PMC 150 Barnes X | arc, inches: | | +1.6 | 0 | -7.5 | -22.1 |
| | velocity, fps: | 2700 | 2541 | 2387 | 2238 | 2095 |
| | energy, ft-lb: | 2428 | 2150 | 1897 | 1668 | 1461 |
| PMC 150 SP boat-tail | arc, inches: | | +2.0 | 0 | -8.1 | -23.1 |
| | velocity, fps: | 2850 | 2660 | 2477 | 2302 | 2134 |
| | energy, ft-lb: | 2705 | 2355 | 2043 | 1765 | 1516. |
| PMC 150 Pointed Soft Point | arc, inches: | | +1.7 | 0 | -7.4 | -21.4 |
| | velocity, fps: | 2750 | 2530 | 2321 | 2123 | 1936 |
| | energy, ft-lb: | 2519 | 2131 | 1794 | 1501 | 1248 |
| Rem. 100 Pointed Soft Point | arc, inches: | | +2.0 | 0 | -8.4 | -24.6 |
| | velocity, fps: | 3320 | 2924 | 2561 | 2225 | 1916 |
| | energy, ft-lb: | 2448 | 1898 | 1456 | 1099 | 815 |

| cartridge bullet | range, yards: | 0 | 100 | 200 | 300 | 400 |
|---|---|---|---|---|---|---|
| Rem. 115 PSP Core-Lokt mr | arc, inches: | | +2.3 | +2.0 | -3.6 | -16.2 |
| | velocity, fps: | 2710 | 2412 | 2133 | 1873 | 1636 |
| | energy, ft-lb: | 1875 | 1485 | 1161 | 896 | 683 |
| Rem. 130 PSP Core-Lokt | arc, inches: | | +1.0 | -2.7 | -14.2 | -35.6 |
| | velocity, fps: | 3060 | 2776 | 2510 | 2259 | 2022 |
| | energy, ft-lb: | 2702 | 2225 | 1818 | 1472 | 1180 |
| Rem. 130 Bronze Point | arc, inches: | | +1.5 | 0 | -7.0 | -20.9 |
| | velocity, fps: | 3060 | 2802 | 2559 | 2329 | 2110 |
| | energy, ft-lb: | 2702 | 2267 | 1890 | 1565 | 1285 |
| Rem. 130 Swift Scirocco | arc, inches: | | +1.5 | 0 | -6.8 | -20.0 |
| | velocity, fps: | 3060 | 2838 | 2677 | 2425 | 2232 |
| | energy, ft-lb: | 2702 | 2325 | 1991 | 1697 | 1438 |
| Rem. 130 AccuTip BT | arc, inches: | | +1.4 | 0 | -6.5 | -18.8 |
| | velocity, fps: | 3060 | 2845 | 2639 | 2442 | 2254 |
| | energy, ft-lb: | 2702 | 2336 | 2009 | 1721 | 1467 |
| Rem. 140 Swift A-Frame | arc, inches: | | +1.4 | 0 | -6.4 | -18.6 |
| | velocity, fps: | 2925 | 2652 | 2394 | 2152 | 1923 |
| | energy, ft-lb: | 2659 | 2186 | 1782 | 1439 | 1150 |
| Rem. 140 PSP boat-tail | arc, inches: | | +1.7 | 0 | -7.8 | -23.2 |
| | velocity, fps: | 2960 | 2749 | 2548 | 2355 | 2171 |
| | energy, ft-lb: | 2723 | 2349 | 2018 | 1724 | 1465 |
| Rem. 140 Nosler Bal. Tip | arc, inches: | | +1.6 | 0 | -6.9 | -20.1 |
| | velocity, fps: | 2960 | 2754 | 2557 | 2366 | 2187 |
| | energy, ft-lb: | 2724 | 2358 | 2032 | 1743 | 1487 |
| Rem. 140 PSP C-L Ultra | arc, inches: | | +1.6 | 0 | -6.9 | -20.0 |
| | velocity, fps: | 2925 | 2667 | 2424 | 2193 | 1975 |
| | energy, ft-lb: | 2659 | 2211 | 1826 | 1495 | 1212 |
| Rem. 150 SP Core-Lokt | arc, inches: | | +1.7 | 0 | -7.6 | -22.5 |
| | velocity, fps: | 2850 | 2504 | 2183 | 1886 | 1618 |
| | energy, ft-lb: | 2705 | 2087 | 1587 | 1185 | 872 |
| Rem. 150 Nosler Partition | arc, inches: | | +2.0 | 0 | -9.4 | -28.6 |
| | velocity, fps: | 2850 | 2652 | 2463 | 2282 | 2108 |
| | energy, ft-lb: | 2705 | 2343 | 2021 | 1734 | 1480 |
| Speer 130 Grand Slam | arc, inches: | | +1.7 | 0 | -7.5 | -21.6 |
| | velocity, fps: | 3050 | 2774 | 2514 | 2269 | |
| | energy, ft-lb: | 2685 | 2221 | 1824 | 1485 | |
| Speer 150 Grand Slam | arc, inches: | | +1.5 | 0 | -7.0 | -20.9 |
| | velocity, fps: | 2830 | 2594 | 2369 | 2156 | |
| | energy, ft-lb: | 2667 | 2240 | 1869 | 1548 | |
| Win. 130 Power-Point | arc, inches: | | +1.8 | 0 | -8.1 | -23.6 |
| | velocity, fps: | 3060 | 2802 | 2559 | 2329 | 2110 |
| | energy, ft-lb: | 2702 | 2267 | 1890 | 1565 | 1285. |
| Win. 130 Power-Point Plus | arc, inches: | | +1.8 | 0 | -7.1 | -20.6 |
| | velocity, fps: | 3150 | 2881 | 2628 | 2388 | 2161 |
| | energy, ft-lb: | 2865 | 2396 | 1993 | 1646 | 1348 |
| Win. 130 Silvertip | arc, inches: | | +1.3 | 0 | -6.4 | -18.9 |
| | velocity, fps: | 3060 | 2776 | 2510 | 2259 | 2022. |
| | energy, ft-lb: | 2702 | 2225 | 1818 | 1472 | 1180 |
| Win. 130 Ballistic Silvertip | arc, inches: | | +1.8 | 0 | -7.4 | -21.6 |
| | velocity, fps: | 3050 | 2828 | 2618 | 2416 | 2224 |
| | energy, ft-lb: | 2685 | 2309 | 1978 | 1685 | 1428 |
| Win. 140 AccuBond | arc, inches: | | +1.4 | 0 | -6.5 | -18.9 |
| | velocity, fps: | 2950 | 2751 | 2560 | 2378 | 2203 |
| | energy, ft-lb: | 2705 | 2352 | 2038 | 1757 | 1508 |
| Win. 140 Fail Safe | arc, inches: | | +1.6 | 0 | -6.9 | -19.9 |
| | velocity, fps: | 2920 | 2671 | 2435 | 2211 | 1999 |
| | energy, ft-lb: | 2651 | 2218 | 1843 | 1519 | 1242 |
| Win. 150 Power-Point | arc, inches: | | +1.7 | 0 | -7.6 | -22.3 |
| | velocity, fps: | 2850 | 2585 | 2336 | 2100 | 1879 |
| | energy, ft-lb: | 2705 | 2226 | 1817 | 1468 | 1175 |
| Win. 150 Power-Point Plus | arc, inches: | | +2.2 | 0 | -8.6 | -25.0 |
| | velocity, fps: | 2950 | 2679 | 2425 | 2184 | 1957 |
| | energy, ft-lb: | 2900 | 2391 | 1959 | 1589 | 1276 |

BALLISTICS

| cartridge bullet | range, yards: | 0 | 100 | 200 | 300 | 400 |
|---|---|---|---|---|---|---|
| | arc, inches: | | +1.7 | 0 | -7.6 | -22.6 |
| Win. 150 Partition Gold | velocity, fps: | 2930 | 2693 | 2468 | 2254 | 2051 |
| | energy, ft-lb: | 2860 | 2416 | 2030 | 1693 | 1402 |
| | arc, inches: | | +1.7 | 0 | -7.4 | -21.6 |
| Win. 150 Supreme Elite XP3 | velocity, fps: | 2950 | 2763 | 2583 | 2411 | 2245 |
| | energy, ft-lb: | 2898 | 2542 | 2223 | 1936 | 1679 |
| | arc, inches: | | +1.5 | 0 | -6.9 | -15.5 |

## .270 Winchester Short Magnum

| cartridge bullet | range, yards: | 0 | 100 | 200 | 300 | 400 |
|---|---|---|---|---|---|---|
| Black Hills 140 AccuBond | velocity, fps: | 3100 | | | | |
| | energy, ft-lb: | 2987 | | | | |
| | arc, inches: | | | | | |
| Federal 130 Nos. Bal. Tip | velocity, fps: | 3300 | 3070 | 2840 | 2630 | 2430 |
| | energy, ft-lb: | 3145 | 2710 | 2335 | 2000 | 1705 |
| | arc, inches: | | +1.1 | 0 | -5.4 | -15.8 |
| Federal 130 Nos. Partition And Nos. Solid Base And Barnes TS | velocity, fps: | 3280 | 3040 | 2810 | 2590 | 2380 |
| | energy, ft-lb: | 3105 | 2665 | 2275 | 1935 | 1635 |
| | arc, inches: | | +1.1 | 0 | -5.6 | -16.3 |
| Federal 140 Nos. AccuBond | velocity, fps | 3200 | 3000 | 2810 | 2630 | 2450 |
| | energy, ft-lb: | 3185 | 2795 | 2455 | 2145 | 1865 |
| | arc, inches: | | +1.2 | 0 | -5.6 | -16.2 |
| Federal 140 Trophy Bonded | velocity, fps: | 3130 | 2870 | 2640 | 2410 | 2200 |
| | energy, ft-lb: | 3035 | 2570 | 2160 | 1810 | 1500 |
| | arc, inches: | | +1.4 | 0 | -6.3 | 18.7 |
| Federal 150 Nos. Partition | velocity, fps: | 3160 | 2950 | 2750 | 2550 | 2370 |
| | energy, ft-lb: | 3325 | 2895 | 2515 | 2175 | 1870 |
| | arc, inches: | | +1.3 | 0 | -5.9 | -17.0 |
| Norma 130 FMJ | velocity, fps: | 3150 | 2882 | 2630 | 2391 | |
| | energy, ft-lb: | | | | | |
| | arc, inches: | | +1.5 | 0 | -6.4 | |
| Norma 130 Ballistic ST | velocity, fps: | 3281 | 3047 | 2825 | 2614 | |
| | energy, ft-lb: | 3108 | 2681 | 2305 | 1973 | |
| | arc, inches: | | +1.1 | 0 | -5.5 | |
| Norma 140 Barnes X TS | velocity, fps: | 3150 | 2952 | 2762 | 2580 | |
| | energy, ft-lb: | 3085 | 2709 | 2372 | 2070 | |
| | arc, inches: | | +1.3 | 0 | -5.8 | |
| Norma 150 Nosler Bal. Tip | velocity, fps: | 3280 | 3046 | 2824 | 2613 | |
| | energy, ft-lb: | 3106 | 2679 | 2303 | 1972 | |
| | arc, inches: | | +1.1 | 0 | -5.4 | |
| Norma 150 Oryx | velocity, fps: | 3117 | 2856 | 2611 | 2378 | |
| | energy, ft-lb: | 3237 | 2718 | 2271 | 1884 | |
| | arc, inches: | | +1.4 | 0 | -6.5 | |
| Win. 130 Bal. Silvertip | velocity, fps: | 3275 | 3041 | 2820 | 2609 | 2408 |
| | energy, ft-lb: | 3096 | 2669 | 2295 | 1964 | 1673 |
| | arc, inches: | | +1.1 | 0 | -5.5 | -16.1 |
| Win. 140 AccuBond | velocity, fps: | 3200 | 2989 | 2789 | 2597 | 2413 |
| | energy, ft-lb: | 3184 | 2779 | 2418 | 2097 | 1810 |
| | arc, inches: | | +1.2 | 0 | -5.7 | -16.5 |
| Win. 140 Fail Safe | velocity, fps: | 3125 | 2865 | 2619 | 2386 | 2165 |
| | energy, ft-lb: | 3035 | 2550 | 2132 | 1769 | 1457 |
| | arc, inches: | | +1.4 | 0 | -6.5 | -19.0 |
| Win. 150 Ballistic Silvertip | velocity, fps: | 3120 | 2923 | 2734 | 2554 | 2380. |
| | energy, ft-lb: | 3242 | 2845 | 2490 | 2172 | 1886. |
| | arc, inches: | | +1.3 | 0 | -5.9 | -17.2 |
| Win. 150 Power Point | velocity, fps: | 3150 | 2867 | 2601 | 2350 | 2113 |
| | energy, ft-lb: | 3304 | 2737 | 2252 | 1839 | 1487 |
| | arc, inches: | | +1.4 | 0 | -6.5 | -19.4 |
| Win. 150 Supreme Elite XP3 | velocity, fps: | 3120 | 2926 | 2740 | 2561 | 2389 |
| | energy, ft-lb: | 3242 | 2850 | 2499 | 2184 | 1901 |
| | arc, inches: | | +1.3 | 0 | -5.9 | -17.1 |

## .270 Weatherby Magnum

| cartridge bullet | range, yards: | 0 | 100 | 200 | 300 | 400 |
|---|---|---|---|---|---|---|
| Federal 130 Nosler Partition | velocity, fps: | 3200 | 2960 | 2740 | 2520 | 2320 |
| | energy, ft-lb: | 2955 | 2530 | 2160 | 1835 | 1550 |

| cartridge bullet | range, yards: | 0 | 100 | 200 | 300 | 400 |
|---|---|---|---|---|---|---|
| | arc, inches: | | +1.2 | 0 | -5.9 | -17.3 |
| Federal 130 Sierra GameKing BTSP | velocity, fps: | 3200 | 2980 | 2780 | 2580 | 2400 |
| | energy, ft-lb: | 2955 | 2570 | 2230 | 1925 | 1655 |
| | arc, inches: | | +1.2 | 0 | -5.7 | -16.6 |
| Federal 140 Trophy Bonded | velocity, fps: | 3100 | 2840 | 2600 | 2370 | 2150. |
| | energy, ft-lb: | 2990 | 2510 | 2100 | 1745 | 1440 |
| | arc, inches: | | +1.4 | 0 | -6.6 | -19.3 |
| Wby. 100 Pointed Expanding | velocity, fps: | 3760 | 3396 | 3061 | 2751 | 2462 |
| | energy, ft-lb: | 3139 | 2560 | 2081 | 1681 | 1346 |
| | arc, inches: | | +2.3 | +3.0 | 0 | -7.6 |
| Wby. 130 Pointed Expanding | velocity, fps: | 3375 | 3123 | 2885 | 2659 | 2444 |
| | energy, ft-lb: | 3288 | 2815 | 2402 | 2041 | 1724 |
| | arc, inches: | | +2.8 | +3.5 | 0 | -8.4 |
| Wby. 130 Nosler Partition | velocity, fps: | 3375 | 3127 | 2892 | 2670 | 2458. |
| | energy, ft-lb: | 3288 | 2822 | 2415 | 2058 | 1744 |
| | arc, inches: | | +2.8 | +3.5 | 0 | -8.3 |
| Wby. 140 Nosler Bal. Tip | velocity, fps: | 3300 | 3077 | 2865 | 2663 | 2470. |
| | energy, ft-lb: | 3385 | 2943 | 2551 | 2204 | 1896 |
| | arc, inches: | | +2.9 | +3.6 | 0 | -8.4 |
| Wby. 140 Barnes X | velocity, fps: | 3250 | 3032 | 2825 | 2628 | 2438 |
| | energy, ft-lb: | 3283 | 2858 | 2481 | 2146 | 1848 |
| | arc, inches: | | +3.0 | +3.7 | 0 | -8.7 |
| Wby. 150 Pointed Expanding | velocity, fps: | 3245 | 3028 | 2821 | 2623 | 2434 |
| | energy, ft-lb: | 3507 | 3053 | 2650 | 2292 | 1973 |
| | arc, inches: | | +3.0 | +3.7 | 0 | -8.7 |
| Wby. 150 Nosler Partition | velocity, fps: | 3245 | 3029 | 2823 | 2627 | 2439. |
| | energy, ft-lb: | 3507 | 3055 | 2655 | 2298 | 1981 |
| | arc, inches: | | +3.0 | +3.7 | 0 | -8. |

## 7-30 Waters

| cartridge bullet | range, yards: | 0 | 100 | 200 | 300 | 400 |
|---|---|---|---|---|---|---|
| Federal 120 Sierra GameKing BTSP | velocity, fps: | 2700 | 2300 | 1930 | 1600 | 1330. |
| | energy, ft-lb: | 1940 | 1405 | 990 | 685 | 470 |
| | arc, inches: | | +2.6 | 0 | -12.0 | -37.6 |

## 7mm Mauser (7x57)

| cartridge bullet | range, yards: | 0 | 100 | 200 | 300 | 400 |
|---|---|---|---|---|---|---|
| Federal 140 Sierra Pro-Hunt. | velocity, fps: | 2660 | 2450 | 2260 | 2070 | 1890. |
| | energy, ft-lb: | 2200 | 1865 | 1585 | 1330 | 1110 |
| | arc, inches: | | +2.1 | 0 | -9.0 | -26.1 |
| Federal 140 Nosler Partition | velocity, fps: | 2660 | 2450 | 2260 | 2070 | 1890. |
| | energy, ft-lb: | 2200 | 1865 | 1585 | 1330 | 1110 |
| | arc, inches: | | +2.1 | 0 | -9.0 | -26.1 |
| Federal 175 Hi-Shok RN | velocity, fps: | 2440 | 2140 | 1860 | 1600 | 1380 |
| | energy, ft-lb: | 2315 | 1775 | 1340 | 1000 | 740 |
| | arc, inches: | | +3.1 | 0 | -13.3 | -40.1 |
| Hornady 139 SP boat-tail | velocity, fps: | 2700 | 2504 | 2316 | 2137 | 1965 |
| | energy, ft-lb: | 2251 | 1936 | 1656 | 1410 | 1192 |
| | arc, inches: | | +2.0 | | -8.5 | -24.9 |
| Hornady 139 SP Interlock | velocity, fps: | 2680 | 2455 | 2241 | 2038 | 1846 |
| | energy, ft-lb: | 2216 | 1860 | 1550 | 1282 | 1052 |
| | arc, inches: | | +2.1 | 0 | -9.1 | -26.6 |
| Hornady 139 SP boat-tail LM | velocity, fps: | 2830 | 2620 | 2450 | 2250 | 2070 |
| | energy, ft-lb: | 2475 | 2135 | 1835 | 1565 | 1330 |
| | arc, inches: | | +1.8 | 0 | -7.6 | -22.1 |
| Hornady 139 SP LM | velocity, fps: | 2950 | 2736 | 2532 | 2337 | 2152. |
| | energy, ft-lb: | 2686 | 2310 | 1978 | 1686 | 1429 |
| | arc, inches: | | +2.0 | 0 | -7.6 | -21.5 |
| Norma 150 Soft Point | velocity, fps: | 2690 | 2479 | 2278 | 2087 | |
| | energy, ft-lb: | 2411 | 2048 | 1729 | 1450 | |
| | arc, inches: | | +2.0 | 0 | -8.8 | |
| PMC 140 Pointed Soft Point | velocity, fps: | 2660 | 2450 | 2260 | 2070 | 1890 |
| | energy, ft-lb: | 2200 | 1865 | 1585 | 1330 | 1110. |
| | arc, inches: | | +2.4 | 0 | -9.6 | -27.3 |
| PMC 175 Soft Point | velocity, fps: | 2440 | 2140 | 1860 | 1600 | 1380 |
| | energy, ft-lb: | 2315 | 1775 | 1340 | 1000 | 740 |

# Centerfire Rifle Ballistics

## 7MM MAUSER TO 7X65 R

| cartridge bullet | range, yards: | 0 | 100 | 200 | 300 | 400 |
|---|---|---|---|---|---|---|
| | arc, inches: | | +1.5 | -3.6 | -18.6 | -46.8 |
| Rem. 140 PSP Core-Lokt | velocity, fps: | 2660 | 2435 | 2221 | 2018 | 1827 |
| | energy, ft-lb: | 2199 | 1843 | 1533 | 1266 | 1037 |
| | arc, inches: | | +2.2 | 0 | -9.2 | -27.4 |
| Win. 145 Power-Point | velocity, fps: | 2660 | 2413 | 2180 | 1959 | 1754 |
| | energy, ft-lb: | 2279 | 1875 | 1530 | 1236 | 990 |
| | arc, inches: | | +1.1 | -2.8 | -14.1 | -34.4 |

### 7x57 R

| cartridge bullet | range, yards: | 0 | 100 | 200 | 300 | 400 |
|---|---|---|---|---|---|---|
| Norma 150 FMJ | velocity, fps: | 2690 | 2489 | 2296 | 2112 | |
| | energy, ft-lb: | 2411 | 2063 | 1756 | 1486 | |
| | arc, inches: | | +2.0 | 0 | -8.6 | |
| Norma 154 Soft Point | velocity, fps: | 2625 | 2417 | 2219 | 2030 | |
| | energy, ft-lb: | 2357 | 1999 | 1684 | 1410 | |
| | arc, inches: | | +2.2 | 0 | -9.3 | |
| Norma 156 Oryx | velocity, fps: | 2608 | 2346 | 2099 | 1867 | |
| | energy, ft-lb: | 2357 | 1906 | 1526 | 1208 | |
| | arc, inches: | | +2.4 | 0 | -10.3 | |

### 7mm-08 Remington

| cartridge bullet | range, yards: | 0 | 100 | 200 | 300 | 400 |
|---|---|---|---|---|---|---|
| Black Hills 140 AccuBond | velocity, fps: | 2700 | | | | |
| | energy, ft-lb: | | | | | |
| | arc, inches: | | | | | |
| Federal 140 Nosler Partition | velocity, fps: | 2800 | 2590 | 2390 | 2200 | 2020 |
| | energy, ft-lb: | 2435 | 2085 | 1775 | 1500 | 1265 |
| | arc, inches: | | +1.8 | 0 | -8.0 | -23.1 |
| Federal 140 Nosler Bal. Tip And AccuBond | velocity, fps: | 2800 | 2610 | 2430 | 2260 | 2100 |
| | energy, ft-lb: | 2440 | 2135 | 1840 | 1590 | 1360. |
| | arc, inches: | | +1.8 | 0 | -7.7 | -22.3 |
| Federal 140 Tr. Bonded HE | velocity, fps: | 2950 | 2660 | 2390 | 2140 | 1900 |
| | energy, ft-lb: | 2705 | 2205 | 1780 | 1420 | 1120 |
| | arc, inches: | | +1.7 | 0 | -7.9 | -23.2 |
| Federal 150 Sierra Pro-Hunt. | velocity, fps: | 2650 | 2440 | 2230 | 2040 | 1860 |
| | energy, ft-lb: | 2340 | 1980 | 1660 | 1390 | 1150 |
| | arc, inches: | | +2.2 | 0 | -9.2 | -26.7 |
| Hornady 139 SP boat-tail LM | velocity, fps: | 3000 | 2790 | 2590 | 2399 | 2216 |
| | energy, ft-lb: | 2777 | 2403 | 2071 | 1776 | 1515 |
| | arc, inches: | | +1.5 | 0 | -6.7 | -19.4 |
| Norma 140 Ballistic ST | velocity, fps: | 2822 | 2633 | 2452 | 2278 | |
| | energy, ft-lb: | 2476 | 2156 | 1870 | 1614 | |
| | arc, inches: | | +1.8 | 0 | -7.6 | |
| PMC 139 PSP | velocity, fps: | 2850 | 2610 | 2384 | 2170 | 1969 |
| | energy, ft-lb: | 2507 | 2103 | 1754 | 1454 | 1197 |
| | arc, inches: | | +1.8 | 0 | -7.9 | -23.3 |
| Rem. 120 Hollow Point | velocity, fps: | 3000 | 2725 | 2467 | 2223 | 1992 |
| | energy, ft-lb: | 2398 | 1979 | 1621 | 1316 | 1058 |
| | arc, inches: | | +1.6 | 0 | -7.3 | -21.7 |
| Rem. 140 PSP Core-Lokt | velocity, fps: | 2860 | 2625 | 2402 | 2189 | 1988 |
| | energy, ft-lb: | 2542 | 2142 | 1793 | 1490 | 1228 |
| | arc, inches: | | +1.8 | 0 | -7.8 | -22.9 |
| Rem. 140 PSP boat-tail | velocity, fps: | 2860 | 2656 | 2460 | 2273 | 2094 |
| | energy, ft-lb: | 2542 | 2192 | 1881 | 1606 | 1363 |
| | arc, inches: | | +1.7 | 0 | -7.5 | -21.7 |
| Rem. 140 AccuTip BT | velocity, fps: | 2860 | 2670 | 2488 | 2313 | 2145 |
| | energy, ft-lb: | 2543 | 2217 | 1925 | 1663 | 1431 |
| | arc, inches: | | +1.7 | 0 | -7.3 | -21.2 |
| Rem. 140 Nosler Partition | velocity, fps: | 2860 | 2648 | 2446 | 2253 | 2068 |
| | energy, ft-lb: | 2542 | 2180 | 1860 | 1577 | 1330 |
| | arc, inches: | | +1.7 | 0 | -7.6 | -22.0 |
| Speer 145 Grand Slam | velocity, fps: | 2845 | 2567 | 2305 | 2059 | |
| | energy, ft-lb: | 2606 | 2121 | 1711 | 1365 | |
| | arc, inches: | | +1.9 | 0 | -8.4 | -25.5 |
| Win. 140 Power-Point | velocity, fps: | 2800 | 2523 | 2268 | 2027 | 1802. |
| | energy, ft-lb: | 2429 | 1980 | 1599 | 1277 | 1010 |

| cartridge bullet | range, yards: | 0 | 100 | 200 | 300 | 400 |
|---|---|---|---|---|---|---|
| | arc, inches: | | +2.0 | 0 | -8.8 | -26.0 |
| Win. 140 Power-Point Plus | velocity, fps: | 2875 | 2597 | 2336 | 2090 | 1859 |
| | energy, ft-lb: | 2570 | 1997 | 1697 | 1358 | 1075 |
| | arc, inches: | | +2.0 | 0 | -8.8 | 26.0 |
| Win. 140 Fail Safe | velocity, fps: | 2760 | 2506 | 2271 | 2048 | 1839 |
| | energy, ft-lb: | 2360 | 1953 | 1603 | 1304 | 1051 |
| | arc, inches: | | +2.0 | 0 | -8.8 | -25.9 |
| Win. 140 Ballistic Silvertip | velocity, fps: | 2770 | 2572 | 2382 | 2200 | 2026 |
| | energy, ft-lb: | 2386 | 2056 | 1764 | 1504 | 1276 |
| | arc, inches: | | +1.9 | 0 | -8.0 | -23.8 |

### 7x64 Brenneke

| cartridge bullet | range, yards: | 0 | 100 | 200 | 300 | 400 |
|---|---|---|---|---|---|---|
| Federal 160 Nosler Partition | velocity, fps: | 2650 | 2480 | 2310 | 2150 | 2000 |
| | energy, ft-lb: | 2495 | 2180 | 1895 | 1640 | 1415 |
| | arc, inches: | | +2.1 | 0 | -8.7 | -24.9 |
| Norma 140 AccuBond | velocity, fps: | 2953 | 2759 | 2572 | 2394 | |
| | energy, ft-lb: | 2712 | 2366 | 2058 | 1782 | |
| | arc, inches: | | +1.5 | 0 | -6.8 | |
| Norma 154 Soft Point | velocity, fps: | 2821 | 2605 | 2399 | 2203 | |
| | energy, ft-lb: | 2722 | 2321 | 1969 | 1660 | |
| | arc, inches: | | +1.8 | 0 | -7.8 | |
| Norma 156 Oryx | velocity, fps: | 2789 | 2516 | 2259 | 2017 | |
| | energy, ft-lb: | 2695 | 2193 | 1768 | 1410 | |
| | arc, inches: | | +2.0 | 0 | -8.8 | |
| Norma 170 Vulkan | velocity, fps: | 2756 | 2501 | 2259 | 2031 | |
| | energy, ft-lb: | 2868 | 2361 | 1927 | 1558 | |
| | arc, inches: | | +2.0 | 0 | -8.8 | |
| Norma 170 Oryx | velocity, fps: | 2756 | 2481 | 2222 | 1979 | |
| | energy, ft-lb: | 2868 | 2324 | 1864 | 1478 | |
| | arc, inches: | | +2.1 | 0 | -9.2 | |
| Norma 170 Plastic Point | velocity, fps: | 2756 | 2519 | 2294 | 2081 | |
| | energy, ft-lb: | 2868 | 2396 | 1987 | 1635 | |
| | arc, inches: | | +2.0 | 0 | -8.6 | |
| PMC 170 Pointed Soft Point | velocity, fps: | 2625 | 2401 | 2189 | 1989 | 1801 |
| | energy, ft lb: | 2601 | 2175 | 1808 | 1493 | 1224 |
| | arc, inches: | | +2.3 | 0 | -9.6 | -27.9 |
| Rem. 175 PSP Core-Lokt | velocity, fps: | 2650 | 2445 | 2248 | 2061 | 1883 |
| | energy, ft-lb: | 2728 | 2322 | 1964 | 1650 | 1378 |
| | arc, inches: | | +2.2 | 0 | -9.1 | -26.4 |
| Speer 160 Grand Slam | velocity, fps: | 2600 | 2376 | 2164 | 1962 | |
| | energy, ft-lb: | 2401 | 2006 | 1663 | 1368 | |
| | arc, inches: | | +2.3 | 0 | -9.8 | -28.6 |
| Speer 175 Grand Slam | velocity, fps: | 2650 | 2461 | 2280 | 2106 | |
| | energy, ft-lb: | 2728 | 2353 | 2019 | 1723 | |
| | arc, inches: | | +2.4 | 0 | -9.2 | -26.2 |

### 7x65 R

| cartridge bullet | range, yards: | 0 | 100 | 200 | 300 | 400 |
|---|---|---|---|---|---|---|
| Norma 150 FMJ | velocity, fps: | 2756 | 2552 | 2357 | 2170 | |
| | energy, ft-lb: | 2530 | 2169 | 1850 | 1569 | |
| | arc, inches: | | +1.9 | 0 | -8.2 | |
| Norma 156 Oryx | velocity, fps: | 2723 | 2454 | 2200 | 1962 | |
| | energy, ft-lb: | 2569 | 2086 | 1678 | 1334 | |
| | arc, inches: | | +2.1 | 0 | -9.3 | |
| Norma 170 Plastic Point | velocity, fps: | 2625 | 2390 | 2167 | 1956 | |
| | energy, ft-lb: | 2602 | 2157 | 1773 | 1445 | |
| | arc, inches: | | +2.3 | 0 | -9.7 | |
| Norma 170 Vulkan | velocity, fps: | 2657 | 2392 | 2143 | 1909 | |
| | energy, ft-lb: | 2666 | 2161 | 1734 | 1377 | |
| | arc, inches: | | +2.3 | 0 | -9.9 | |
| Norma 170 Oryx | velocity, fps: | 2657 | 2378 | 2115 | 1871 | |
| | energy, ft-lb: | 2666 | 2135 | 1690 | 1321 | |
| | arc, inches: | | +2.3 | 0 | -10.1 | |

| cartridge bullet | range, yards: | 0 | 100 | 200 | 300 | 400 |
|---|---|---|---|---|---|---|

## .284 Winchester

| cartridge bullet | | 0 | 100 | 200 | 300 | 400 |
|---|---|---|---|---|---|---|
| Win. 150 Power-Point | velocity, fps: | 2860 | 2595 | 2344 | 2108 | 1886 |
| | energy, ft-lb: | 2724 | 2243 | 1830 | 1480 | 1185 |
| | arc, inches: | | +2.1 | 0 | -8.5 | -24.8 |

## .280 Remington

| cartridge bullet | | 0 | 100 | 200 | 300 | 400 |
|---|---|---|---|---|---|---|
| Federal 140 Sierra Pro-Hunt. | velocity, fps: | 2990 | 2740 | 2500 | 2270 | 2060 |
| | energy, ft-lb: | 2770 | 2325 | 1940 | 1605 | 1320 |
| | arc, inches: | | +1.6 | 0 | -7.0 | -20.8 |
| Federal 140 Trophy Bonded | velocity, fps: | 2990 | 2630 | 2310 | 2040 | 1730 |
| | energy, ft-lb: | 2770 | 2155 | 1655 | 1250 | 925 |
| | arc, inches: | | +1.6 | 0 | -8.4 | -25.4 |
| Federal 140 Tr. Bonded HE | velocity, fps: | 3150 | 2850 | 2570 | 2300 | 2050 |
| | energy, ft-lb: | 3085 | 2520 | 2050 | 1650 | 1310 |
| | arc, inches: | | +1.4 | 0 | -6.7 | -20.0 |
| Federal 140 Nos. AccuBond And Bal. Tip And Solid Base | velocity, fps: | 3000 | 2800 | 2620 | 2440 | 2260 |
| | energy, ft-lb: | 2800 | 2445 | 2130 | 1845 | 1590 |
| | arc, inches: | | +1.5 | 0 | -6.5 | -18.9 |
| Federal 150 Hi-Shok | velocity, fps: | 2890 | 2670 | 2460 | 2260 | 2060 |
| | energy, ft-lb: | 2780 | 2370 | 2015 | 1695 | 1420 |
| | arc, inches: | | +1.7 | 0 | -7.5 | -21.8 |
| Federal 150 Nosler Partition | velocity, fps: | 2890 | 2690 | 2490 | 2310 | 2130 |
| | energy, ft-lb: | 2780 | 2405 | 2070 | 1770 | 1510. |
| | arc, inches: | | +1.7 | 0 | -7.2 | -21.1 |
| Federal 150 Nos. AccuBond | velocity, fps | 2800 | 2630 | 2460 | 2300 | 2150 |
| | energy, ft-lb: | 2785 | 2455 | 2155 | 1885 | 1645 |
| | arc, inches: | | +1.8 | 0 | -7.5 | -21.5 |
| Federal 160 Trophy Bonded | velocity, fps: | 2800 | 2570 | 2350 | 2140 | 1940 |
| | energy, ft-lb: | 2785 | 2345 | 1960 | 1625 | 1340 |
| | arc, inches: | | +1.9 | 0 | -8.3 | -24.0 |
| Hornady 139 SPBT LMmoly | velocity, fps: | 3110 | 2888 | 2675 | 2473 | 2280. |
| | energy, ft-lb: | 2985 | 2573 | 2209 | 1887 | 1604 |
| | arc, inches: | | +1.4 | 0 | -6.5 | -18.6 |
| Norma 156 Oryx | velocity, fps: | 2789 | 2516 | 2259 | 2017 | |
| | energy, ft-lb: | 2695 | 2193 | 1768 | 1410 | |
| | arc, inches: | | +2.0 | 0 | -8.8 | |
| Norma 170 Plastic Point | velocity, fps: | 2707 | 2468 | 2241 | 2026 | |
| | energy, ft-lb: | 2767 | 2299 | 1896 | 1550 | |
| | arc, inches: | | +2.1 | 0 | -9.1 | |
| Norma 170 Vulkan | velocity, fps: | 2592 | 2346 | 2113 | 1894 | |
| | energy, ft-lb: | 2537 | 2078 | 1686 | 1354 | |
| | arc, inches: | | +2.4 | 0 | -10.2 | |
| Norma 170 Oryx | velocity, fps: | 2690 | 2416 | 2159 | 1918 | |
| | energy, ft-lb: | 2732 | 2204 | 1760 | 1389 | |
| | arc, inches: | | +2.2 | 0 | -9.7 | |
| Rem. 140 PSP Core-Lokt | velocity, fps: | 3000 | 2758 | 2528 | 2309 | 2102 |
| | energy, ft-lb: | 2797 | 2363 | 1986 | 1657 | 1373 |
| | arc, inches: | | +1.5 | 0 | -7.0 | -20.5 |
| Rem. 140 PSP boat-tail | velocity, fps: | 2860 | 2656 | 2460 | 2273 | 2094 |
| | energy, ft-lb: | 2542 | 2192 | 1881 | 1606 | 1363 |
| | arc, inches: | | +1.7 | 0 | -7.5 | -21.7 |
| Rem. 140 Nosler Bal. Tip | velocity, fps: | 3000 | 2804 | 2616 | 2436 | 2263 |
| | energy, ft-lb: | 2799 | 2445 | 2128 | 1848 | 1593 |
| | arc, inches: | | +1.5 | 0 | -6.8 | -19.0 |
| Rem. 140 AccuTip | velocity, fps: | 3000 | 2804 | 2617 | 2437 | 2265 |
| | energy, ft-lb: | 2797 | 2444 | 2129 | 1846 | 1594 |
| | arc, inches: | | +1.5 | 0 | -6.8 | -19.0 |
| Rem. 150 PSP Core-Lokt | velocity, fps: | 2890 | 2624 | 2373 | 2135 | 1912 |
| | energy, ft-lb: | 2781 | 2293 | 1875 | 1518 | 1217 |
| | arc, inches: | | +1.8 | 0 | -8.0 | -23.6 |
| Rem. 165 SP Core-Lokt | velocity, fps: | 2820 | 2510 | 2220 | 1950 | 1701 |
| | energy, ft-lb: | 2913 | 2308 | 1805 | 1393 | 1060. |

| cartridge bullet | | 0 | 100 | 200 | 300 | 400 |
|---|---|---|---|---|---|---|
| | arc, inches: | | +2.0 | 0 | -9.1 | -27.4 |
| Speer 145 Grand Slam | velocity, fps: | 2900 | 2619 | 2354 | 2105 | |
| | energy, ft-lb: | 2707 | 2207 | 1784 | 1426 | |
| | arc, inches: | | +2.1 | 0 | -8.4 | -24.7 |
| Speer 160 Grand Slam | velocity, fps: | 2890 | 2652 | 2425 | 2210 | |
| | energy, ft-lb: | 2967 | 2497 | 2089 | 1735 | |
| | arc, inches: | | +1.7 | 0 | -7.7 | -22.4 |
| Win. 140 Fail Safe | velocity, fps: | 3050 | 2756 | 2480 | 2221 | 1977 |
| | energy, ft-lb: | 2893 | 2362 | 1913 | 1533 | 1216 |
| | arc, inches: | | +1.5 | 0 | -7.2 | -21.5 |
| Win. 140 Ballistic Silvertip | velocity, fps: | 3040 | 2842 | 2653 | 2471 | 2297 |
| | energy, ft-lb: | 2872 | 2511 | 2187 | 1898 | 1640 |
| | arc, inches: | | +1.4 | 0 | -6.3 | -18.4 |

## 7mm Remington Magnum

| cartridge bullet | | 0 | 100 | 200 | 300 | 400 |
|---|---|---|---|---|---|---|
| A-Square 175 Monolithic Solid | velocity, fps: | 2860 | 2557 | 2273 | 2008 | 1771 |
| | energy, ft-lb: | 3178 | 2540 | 2008 | 1567 | 1219 |
| | arc, inches: | | +1.92 | 0 | -8.7 | -25.9 |
| Black Hills 140 Nos. Bal. Tip | velocity, fps: | 3150 | | | | |
| | energy, ft-lb: | 3084 | | | | |
| | arc, inches: | | | | | |
| Black Hills 140 Barnes XLC | velocity, fps: | 3150 | | | | |
| | energy, ft-lb: | 3084 | | | | |
| | arc, inches: | | | | | |
| Black Hills 140 Nos. Partition | velocity, fps: | 3150 | | | | |
| | energy, ft-lb: | 3084 | | | | |
| | arc, inches: | | | | | |
| Federal 140 Nosler Bal. Tip And AccuBond | velocity, fps: | 3110 | 2910 | 2720 | 2530 | 2360. |
| | energy, ft-lb: | 3005 | 2630 | 2295 | 1995 | 1725 |
| | arc, inches: | | +1.3 | 0 | -6.0 | -17.4 |
| Federal 140 Nosler Partition | velocity, fps: | 3150 | 2930 | 2710 | 2510 | 2320 |
| | energy, ft-lb: | 3085 | 2660 | 2290 | 1960 | 1670 |
| | arc, inches: | | +1.3 | 0 | -6.0 | -17.5 |
| Federal 140 Trophy Bonded | velocity, fps: | 3150 | 2910 | 2680 | 2460 | 2250. |
| | energy, ft-lb: | 3085 | 2630 | 2230 | 1880 | 1575 |
| | arc, inches: | | +1.3 | 0 | -6.1 | -18.1 |
| Federal 150 Hi-Shok | velocity, fps: | 3110 | 2830 | 2570 | 2320 | 2090 |
| | energy, ft-lb: | 3220 | 2670 | 2200 | 1790 | 1450 |
| | arc, inches: | | +1.4 | 0 | -6.7 | -19.9 |
| Federal 150 Sierra GameKing BTSP | velocity, fps: | 3110 | 2920 | 2750 | 2580 | 2410 |
| | energy, ft-lb: | 3220 | 2850 | 2510 | 2210 | 1930 |
| | arc, inches: | | +1.3 | 0 | -5.9 | -17.0 |
| Federal 150 Nosler Bal. Tip | velocity, fps: | 3110 | 2910 | 2720 | 2540 | 2370 |
| | energy, ft-lb: | 3220 | 2825 | 2470 | 2150 | 1865 |
| | arc, inches: | | +1.3 | 0 | -6.0 | -17.4 |
| Federal 150 Nos. Solid Base | velocity, fps: | 3100 | 2890 | 2690 | 2500 | 2310 |
| | energy, ft-lb: | 3200 | 2780 | 2405 | 2075 | 1775 |
| | arc, inches: | | +1.3 | 0 | -6.2 | -17.8 |
| Federal 160 Barnes XLC | velocity, fps: | 2940 | 2760 | 2580 | 2410 | 2240 |
| | energy, ft-lb: | 3070 | 2695 | 2360 | 2060 | 1785 |
| | arc, inches: | | +1.5 | 0 | -6.8 | -19.6 |
| Federal 160 Sierra Pro-Hunt. | velocity, fps: | 2940 | 2730 | 2520 | 2320 | 2140 |
| | energy, ft-lb: | 3070 | 2640 | 2260 | 1920 | 1620 |
| | arc, inches: | | +1.6 | 0 | -7.1 | -20.6 |
| Federal 160 Nosler Partition | velocity, fps: | 2950 | 2770 | 2590 | 2420 | 2250. |
| | energy, ft-lb: | 3090 | 2715 | 2375 | 2075 | 1800 |
| | arc, inches: | | +1.5 | 0 | -6.7 | -19.4 |
| Federal 160 Nos. AccuBond | velocity, fps: | 2950 | 2770 | 2600 | 2440 | 2280 |
| | energy, ft-lb: | 3090 | 2730 | 2405 | 2110 | 1845 |
| | arc, inches: | | +1.5 | 0 | -6.6 | -19.1 |
| Federal 160 Trophy Bonded | velocity, fps: | 2940 | 2660 | 2390 | 2140 | 1900 |
| | energy, ft-lb: | 3070 | 2505 | 2025 | 1620 | 1280. |
| | arc, inches: | | +1.7 | 0 | -7.9 | -23.3 |

BALLISTICS

# Centerfire Rifle Ballistics

## 7MM REMINGTON MAGNUM TO 7MM REMINGTON MAGNUM

| cartridge bullet | range, yards: | 0 | 100 | 200 | 300 | 400 | cartridge bullet | range, yards: | 0 | 100 | 200 | 300 | 400 |
|---|---|---|---|---|---|---|---|---|---|---|---|---|---|
| Federal 165 Sierra GameKing BTSP | velocity, fps: | 2950 | 2800 | 2650 | 2510 | 2370. | PMC 160 Barnes X | velocity, fps: | 2800 | 2639 | 2484 | 2334 | 2189 |
| | energy, ft-lb: | 3190 | 2865 | 2570 | 2300 | 2050 | | energy, ft-lb: | 2785 | 2474 | 2192 | 1935 | 1703 |
| | arc, inches: | | +1.5 | 0 | -6.4 | -18.4 | | arc, inches: | | +1.8 | 0 | -7.4 | -21.2 |
| Federal 175 Hi-Shok | velocity, fps: | 2860 | 2650 | 2440 | 2240 | 2060 | PMC 160 Pointed Soft Point | velocity, fps: | 2914 | 2748 | 2586 | 2428 | 2276 |
| | energy, ft-lb: | 3180 | 2720 | 2310 | 1960 | 1640 | | energy, ft-lb: | 3016 | 2682 | 2375 | 2095 | 1840 |
| | arc, inches: | | +1.7 | 0 | -7.6 | -22.1 | | arc, inches: | | +1.6 | 0 | -6.7 | -19.4 |
| Federal 175 Trophy Bonded | velocity, fps: | 2860 | 2600 | 2350 | 2120 | 1900 | PMC 160 SP boat-tail | velocity, fps: | 2900 | 2696 | 2501 | 2314 | 2135 |
| | energy, ft-lb: | 3180 | 2625 | 2150 | 1745 | 1400 | | energy, ft-lb: | 2987 | 2582 | 2222 | 1903 | 1620 |
| | arc, inches: | | +1.8 | 0 | -8.2 | -24.0 | | arc, inches: | | +1.7 | 0 | -7.2 | -21.0 |
| Hornady 139 SPBT | velocity, fps: | 3150 | 2933 | 2727 | 2530 | 2341 | PMC 175 Pointed Soft Point | velocity, fps: | 2860 | 2645 | 2442 | 2244 | 2957 |
| | energy, ft-lb: | 3063 | 2656 | 2296 | 1976 | 1692 | | energy, ft-lb: | 3178 | 2718 | 2313 | 1956 | 1644 |
| | arc, inches: | | +1.2 | 0 | -6.1 | -17.7 | | arc, inches: | | +2.0 | 0 | -7.9 | -22.7 |
| Hornady 139 SST (or Interbond) | velocity, fps: | 3150 | 2948 | 2754 | 2569 | 2391 | Rem. 140 PSP Core-Lokt mr | velocity, fps: | 2710 | 2482 | 2265 | 2059 | 1865 |
| | energy, ft-lb: | 3062 | 2681 | 2341 | 2037 | 1764 | | energy, ft-lb: | 2283 | 1915 | 1595 | 1318 | 1081 |
| | arc, inches: | | +1.1 | 0 | -5.7 | -16.7 | | arc, inches: | | +1.0 | -2.5 | -12.8 | -31.3 |
| Hornady 139 SST LM (or Interbond) | velocity, fps: | 3250 | 3044 | 2847 | 2657 | 2475 | Rem. 140 PSP Core-Lokt | velocity, fps: | 3175 | 2923 | 2684 | 2458 | 2243 |
| | energy, ft-lb: | 3259 | 2860 | 2501 | 2178 | 1890 | | energy, ft-lb: | 3133 | 2655 | 2240 | 1878 | 1564 |
| | arc, inches: | | +1.1 | 0 | -5.5 | -16.2 | | arc, inches: | | +2.2 | +1.9 | -3.2 | -14.2 |
| Hornady 139 SPBT HMmoly | velocity, fps: | 3250 | 3041 | 2822 | 2613 | 2413 | Rem. 140 PSP boat-tail | velocity, fps: | 3175 | 2956 | 2747 | 2547 | 2356 |
| | energy, ft-lb: | 3300 | 2854 | 2458 | 2106 | 1797. | | energy, ft-lb: | 3133 | 2715 | 2345 | 2017 | 1726 |
| | arc, inches: | | +1.1 | 0 | -5.7 | -16.6 | | arc, inches: | | +2.2 | +1.6 | -3.1 | -13.4 |
| Hornady 154 Soft Point | velocity, fps: | 3035 | 2814 | 2604 | 2404 | 2212 | Rem. 150 AccuTip | velocity, fps: | 3110 | 2926 | 2749 | 2579 | 2415 |
| | energy, ft-lb: | 3151 | 2708 | 2319 | 1977 | 1674 | | energy, ft-lb: | 3221 | 2850 | 2516 | 2215 | 1943 |
| | arc, inches: | | +1.3 | 0 | -6.7 | -19.3 | | arc, inches: | | +1.3 | 0 | -5.9 | -17.0 |
| Hornady 154 SST (or Interbond) | velocity, fps: | 3035 | 2850 | 2672 | 2501 | 2337 | Rem. 150 PSP Core-Lokt | velocity, fps: | 3110 | 2830 | 2568 | 2320 | 2085 |
| | energy, ft-lb: | 3149 | 2777 | 2441 | 2139 | 1867 | | energy, ft-lb: | 3221 | 2667 | 2196 | 1792 | 1448 |
| | arc, inches: | | +1.4 | 0 | -6.5 | -18.7 | | arc, inches: | | +1.3 | 0 | -6.6 | -20.2 |
| Hornady 162 SP boat-tail | velocity, fps: | 2940 | 2757 | 2582 | 2413 | 2251 | Rem. 150 Nosler Bal. Tip | velocity, fps: | 3110 | 2912 | 2723 | 2542 | 2367 |
| | energy, ft-lb: | 3110 | 2735 | 2399 | 2095 | 1823 | | energy, ft-lb: | 3222 | 2825 | 2470 | 2152 | 1867 |
| | arc, inches: | | +1.6 | 0 | -6.7 | -19.7 | | arc, inches: | | +1.2 | 0 | -5.9 | -17.3 |
| Hornady 175 SP | velocity, fps: | 2860 | 2650 | 2440 | 2240 | 2060. | Rem. 150 Swift Scirocco | velocity, fps: | 3110 | 2927 | 2751 | 2582 | 2419 |
| | energy, ft-lb: | 3180 | 2720 | 2310 | 1960 | 1640 | | energy, ft-lb: | 3221 | 2852 | 2520 | 2220 | 1948 |
| | arc, inches: | | +2.0 | 0 | -7.9 | -22.7 | | arc, inches: | | +1.3 | 0 | -5.9 | -17.0 |
| Norma 140 Nosler Bal. Tip | velocity, fps: | 3150 | 2936 | 2732 | 2537 | | Rem. 160 Swift A-Frame | velocity, fps: | 2900 | 2659 | 2430 | 2212 | 2006 |
| | energy, ft-lb: | 3085 | 2680 | 2320 | 2001 | | | energy, ft-lb: | 2987 | 2511 | 2097 | 1739 | 1430 |
| | arc, inches: | | +1.2 | 0 | -5.9 | | | arc, inches: | | +1.7 | 0 | -7.6 | -22.4 |
| Norma 140 Barnes X TS | velocity, fps: | 3117 | 2912 | 2716 | 2529 | | Rem. 160 Nosler Partition | velocity, fps: | 2950 | 2752 | 2563 | 2381 | 2207 |
| | energy, ft-lb: | 3021 | 2637 | 2294 | 1988 | | | energy, ft-lb: | 3091 | 2690 | 2333 | 2014 | 1730 |
| | arch, inches: | | +1.3 | 0 | -6.0 | | | arc, inches: | | +0.6 | -1.9 | -9.6 | -23.6 |
| Norma 150 Scirocco | velocity, fps: | 3117 | 2934 | 2758 | 2589 | | Rem. 175 PSP Core-Lokt | velocity, fps: | 2860 | 2645 | 2440 | 2244 | 2057 |
| | energy, ft-lb: | 3237 | 2869 | 2535 | 2234 | | | energy, ft-lb: | 3178 | 2718 | 2313 | 1956 | 1644 |
| | arc, inches: | | +1.2 | 0 | -5.8 | | | arc, inches: | | +1.7 | 0 | -7.6 | -22.1 |
| Norma 156 Oryx | velocity, fps: | 2953 | 2670 | 2404 | 2153 | | Speer 145 Grand Slam | velocity, fps: | 3140 | 2843 | 2565 | 2304 | |
| | energy, ft-lb: | 3021 | 2470 | 2002 | 1607 | | | energy, ft-lb: | 3174 | 2602 | 2118 | 1708 | |
| | arc, inches: | | +1.7 | 0 | -7.7 | | | arc, inches: | | +1.4 | 0 | -6.7 | |
| Norma 170 Vulkan | velocity, fps: | 3018 | 2747 | 2493 | 2252 | | Speer 175 Grand Slam | velocity, fps: | 2850 | 2653 | 2463 | 2282 | |
| | energy, ft-lb: | 3439 | 2850 | 2346 | 1914 | | | energy, ft-lb: | 3156 | 2734 | 2358 | 2023 | |
| | arc, inches: | | +1.5 | 0 | -2.8 | | | arc, inches: | | +1.7 | 0 | -7.5 | -21.7 |
| Norma 170 Oryx | velocity, fps: | 2887 | 2601 | 2333 | 2080 | | Win. 140 Fail Safe | velocity, fps: | 3150 | 2861 | 2589 | 2333 | 2092 |
| | energy, ft-lb: | 3147 | 2555 | 2055 | 1634 | | | energy, ft-lb: | 3085 | 2544 | 2085 | 1693 | 1361 |
| | arc, inches: | | +1.8 | 0 | -8.2 | | | arc, inches: | | +1.4 | 0 | -6.6 | -19.5 |
| Norma 170 Plastic Point | velocity, fps: | 3018 | 2762 | 2519 | 2290 | | Win. 140 Ballistic Silvertip | velocity, fps: | 3100 | 2889 | 2687 | 2494 | 2310 |
| | energy, ft-lb: | 3439 | 2880 | 2394 | 1980 | | | energy, ft-lb: | 2988 | 2595 | 2245 | 1934 | 1659. |
| | arc, inches: | | +1.5 | 0 | -7.0 | | | arc, inches: | | +1.3 | 0 | -6.2 | -17.9 |
| PMC 140 Barnes X | velocity, fps: | 3000 | 2808 | 2624 | 2448 | 2279 | Win. 140 AccuBond CT | velocity, fps: | 3180 | 2965 | 2760 | 2565 | 2377 |
| | energy, ft-lb: | 2797 | 2451 | 2141 | 1863 | 1614 | | energy, ft-lb: | 3143 | 2733 | 2368 | 2044 | 1756 |
| | arc, inches: | | +1.5 | 0 | -6.6 | 18.9 | | arc, inches: | | +1.2 | 0 | -5.8 | -16.9 |
| PMC 140 Pointed Soft Point | velocity, fps: | 3099 | 2878 | 2668 | 2469 | 2279 | Win. 150 Power-Point | velocity, fps: | 3090 | 2812 | 2551 | 2304 | 2071 |
| | energy, ft-lb: | 2984 | 2574 | 2212 | 1895 | 1614 | | energy, ft-lb: | 3181 | 2634 | 2167 | 1768 | 1429 |
| | arc, inches: | | +1.4 | 0 | -6.2 | -18.1 | | arc, inches: | | +1.5 | 0 | -6.8 | -20.2 |
| PMC 140 SP boat-tail | velocity, fps: | 3125 | 2891 | 2669 | 2457 | 2255 | Win. 150 Power-Point Plus | velocity, fps: | 3130 | 2849 | 2586 | 2337 | 2102 |
| | energy, ft-lb: | 3035 | 2597 | 2213 | 1877 | 1580 | | energy, ft-lb: | 3264 | 2705 | 2227 | 1819 | 1472 |
| | arc, inches: | | +1.4 | 0 | -6.3 | -18.4 | | arc, inches: | | +1.4 | 0 | -6.6 | -19.6 |

BALLISTICS

| cartridge bullet | range, yards: | 0 | 100 | 200 | 300 | 400 |
|---|---|---|---|---|---|---|
| Win. 150 Ballistic Silvertip | velocity, fps: | 3100 | 2903 | 2714 | 2533 | 2359 |
| | energy, ft-lb: | 3200 | 2806 | 2453 | 2136 | 1853 |
| | arc, inches: | | +1.3 | 0 | -6.0 | -17.5 |
| Win. 160 AccuBond | velocity, fps: | 2950 | 2766 | 2590 | 2420 | 2257 |
| | energy, ft-lb: | 3091 | 2718 | 2382 | 2080 | 1809 |
| | arc, inches: | | +1.5 | 0 | -6.7 | -19.4 |
| Win. 160 Partition Gold | velocity, fps: | 2950 | 2743 | 2546 | 2357 | 2176 |
| | energy, ft-lb: | 3093 | 2674 | 2303 | 1974 | 1682 |
| | arc, inches: | | +1.6 | 0 | -6.9 | -20.1 |
| Win. 160 Fail Safe | velocity, fps: | 2920 | 2678 | 2449 | 2331 | 2025 |
| | energy, ft-lb: | 3030 | 2549 | 2131 | 1769 | 1457 |
| | arc, inches: | | +1.7 | 0 | -7.5 | -22.0 |
| Win. 175 Power-Point | velocity, fps: | 2860 | 2645 | 2440 | 2244 | 2057 |
| | energy, ft-lb: | 3178 | 2718 | 2313 | 1956 | 1644 |
| | arc, inches: | | +2.0 | 0 | -7.9 | -22.7 |

## 7mm Remington Short Ultra Magnum

| cartridge bullet | range, yards: | 0 | 100 | 200 | 300 | 400 |
|---|---|---|---|---|---|---|
| Rem. 140 PSP C-L Ultra | velocity, fps: | 3175 | 2934 | 2707 | 2490 | 2283 |
| | energy, ft-lb: | 3133 | 2676 | 2277 | 1927 | 1620. |
| | arc, inches: | | +1.3 | 0 | -6.0 | -17.7 |
| Rem. 150 PSP Core-Lokt | velocity, fps: | 3110 | 2828 | 2563 | 2313 | 2077 |
| | energy, ft-lb: | 3221 | 2663 | 2188 | 1782 | 1437 |
| | arc, inches: | | +2.5 | +2.1 | -3.6 | -15.8 |
| Rem. 160 Partition | velocity, fps: | 2960 | 2762 | 2572 | 2390 | 2215 |
| | energy, ft-lb: | 3112 | 2709 | 2350 | 2029 | 1744 |
| | arc, inches: | | +2.6 | +2.2 | -3.6 | -15.4 |
| Rem. 160 PSP C-L Ultra | velocity, fps: | 2960 | 2733 | 2518 | 2313 | 2117 |
| | energy, ft-lb: | 3112 | 2654 | 2252 | 1900 | 1592 |
| | arc, inches: | | +2.7 | +2.2 | -3.7 | -16.2 |

## 7mm Winchester Short Magnum

| cartridge bullet | range, yards: | 0 | 100 | 200 | 300 | 400 |
|---|---|---|---|---|---|---|
| Federal 140 Nos. AccuBond | velocity, fps: | 3250 | 3040 | 2840 | 2660 | 2470 |
| | energy, ft-lb: | 3285 | 2875 | 2515 | 2190 | 1900 |
| | arc, inches: | | +1.1 | 0 | -5.5 | -15.8 |
| Federal 140 Nos. Bal. Tip | velocity, fps: | 3310 | 3100 | 2900 | 2700 | 2520 |
| | energy, ft-lb: | 3405 | 2985 | 2610 | 2270 | 1975 |
| | arc, inches: | | +1.1 | 0 | -5.2 | 15.2 |
| Federal 150 Nos. Solid Base | velocity, fps: | 3230 | 3010 | 2800 | 2600 | 2410 |
| | energy, ft-lb: | 3475 | 3015 | 2615 | 2255 | 1935 |
| | arc, inches: | | +1.3 | 0 | -5.6 | -16.3 |
| Federal 160 Nos. AccuBond | velocity, fps: | 3120 | 2940 | 2760 | 2590 | 2430 |
| | energy, ft-lb: | 3460 | 3065 | 2710 | 2390 | 2095 |
| | arc, inches: | | +1.3 | 0 | -5.9 | -16.8 |
| Federal 160 Nos. Partition | velocity, fps: | 3160 | 2950 | 2750 | 2560 | 2380. |
| | energy, ft-lb: | 3545 | 3095 | 2690 | 2335 | 2015. |
| | arc, inches: | | +1.2 | 0 | -5.9 | -16.9 |
| Federal 160 Barnes TS | velocity, fps: | 2990 | 2780 | 2590 | 2400 | 2220 |
| | energy, ft-lb: | 3175 | 2755 | 2380 | 2045 | 1750 |
| | arc, inches: | | +1.5 | 0 | -6.6 | -19.4 |
| Federal 160 Trophy Bonded | velocity, fps: | 3120 | 2880 | 2650 | 2440 | 2230 |
| | energy, ft-lb: | 3460 | 2945 | 2500 | 2105 | 1765 |
| | arc, inches: | | +1.4 | 0 | -6.3 | -18.5 |
| Win. 140 Bal. Silvertip | velocity, fps: | 3225 | 3008 | 2801 | 2603 | 2414 |
| | energy, ft-lb: | 3233 | 2812 | 2438 | 2106 | 1812 |
| | arc, inches: | | +1.2 | 0 | -5.6 | -16.4 |
| Win. 140 AccuBond CT | velocity, fps: | 3225 | 3008 | 2801 | 2604 | 2415 |
| | energy, ft-lb: | 3233 | 2812 | 2439 | 2107 | 1812 |
| | arc, inches: | | +1.2 | 0 | -5.6 | -16.4 |
| Win. 150 Power Point | velocity, fps: | 3200 | 2915 | 2648 | 2396 | 2157 |
| | energy, ft-lb: | 3410 | 2830 | 2335 1911 | | 1550 |
| | arc, inches: | | +1.3 | 0 | -6.3 | -18.6 |
| Win. 160 AccuBond | velocity, fps: | 3050 | 2862 | 2682 | 2509 | 2342 |
| | energy, ft-lb: | 3306 | 2911 | 2556 | 2237 | 1950 |
| | arc, inches: | | 1.4 | 0 | -6.2 | -17.9 |

| cartridge bullet | range, yards: | 0 | 100 | 200 | 300 | 400 |
|---|---|---|---|---|---|---|
| Win. 160 Fail Safe | velocity, fps: | 2990 | 2744 | 2512 | 2291 | 2081 |
| | energy, ft-lb: | 3176 | 2675 | 2241 | 1864 | 1538 |
| | arc, inches: | | +1.6 | 0 | -7.1 | -20.8 |

## 7mm Weatherby Magnum

| cartridge bullet | range, yards: | 0 | 100 | 200 | 300 | 400 |
|---|---|---|---|---|---|---|
| Federal 160 Nosler Partition | velocity, fps: | 3050 | 2850 | 2650 | 2470 | 2290 |
| | energy, ft-lb: | 3305 | 2880 | 2505 | 2165 | 1865 |
| | arc, inches: | | +1.4 | 0 | -6.3 | -18.4 |
| Federal 160 Sierra GameKing BTSP | velocity, fps: | 3050 | 2880 | 2710 | 2560 | 2400 |
| | energy, ft-lb: | 3305 | 2945 | 2615 | 2320 | 2050 |
| | arc, inches: | | +1.4 | 0 | -6.1 | -17.4 |
| Federal 160 Trophy Bonded | velocity, fps: | 3050 | 2730 | 2420 | 2140 | 1880. |
| | energy, ft-lb: | 3305 | 2640 | 2085 | 1630 | 1255 |
| | arc, inches: | | +1.6 | 0 | -7.6 | -22.7 |
| Hornady 154 Soft Point | velocity, fps: | 3200 | 2971 | 2753 | 2546 | 2348. |
| | energy, ft-lb: | 3501 | 3017 | 2592 | 2216 | 1885 |
| | arc, inches: | | +1.2 | 0 | -5.8 | -17.0 |
| Hornady 154 SST (or Interbond) | velocity, fps: | 3200 | 3009 | 2825 | 2648 | 2478 |
| | energy, ft-lb: | 3501 | 3096 | 2729 | 2398 | 2100 |
| | arc, inches: | | +1.2 | 0 | -5.7 | -16.5 |
| Hornady 175 Soft Point | velocity, fps: | 2910 | 2709 | 2516 | 2331 | 2154 |
| | energy, ft-lb: | 3290 | 2850 | 2459 | 2111 | 1803 |
| | arc, inches: | | +1.6 | 0 | -7.1 | -20.6 |
| Wby. 139 Pointed Expanding | velocity, fps: | 3340 | 3079 | 2834 | 2601 | 2380. |
| | energy, ft-lb: | 3443 | 2926 | 2478 | 2088 | 1748 |
| | arc, inches: | | +2.9 | +3.6 | 0 | -8.7 |
| Wby. 140 Nosler Partition | velocity, fps: | 3303 | 3069 | 2847 | 2636 | 2434 |
| | energy, ft-lb: | 3391 | 2927 | 2519 | 2159 | 1841 |
| | arc, inches: | | +2.9 | +3.6 | 0 | -8.5 |
| Wby. 150 Nosler Bal. Tip | velocity, fps: | 3300 | 3093 | 2896 | 2708 | 2527 |
| | energy, ft-lb: | 3627 | 3187 | 2793 | 2442 | 2127 |
| | arc, inches: | | +2.8 | +3.5 | 0 | -8.2 |
| Wby. 150 Barnes X | velocitiy, fps: | 3100 | 2901 | 2710 | 2527 | 2352 |
| | energy, ft-lb: | 3200 | 2802 | 2446 | 2127 | 1842 |
| | arc, inches: | | +3.3 | +4.0 | 0 | -9.4 |
| Wby. 154 Pointed Expanding | velocity, fps: | 3260 | 3028 | 2807 | 2597 | 2397 |
| | energy, ft-lb: | 3634 | 3134 | 2694 | 2307 | 1964 |
| | arc, inches: | | +3.0 | +3.7 | 0 | -8.8 |
| Wby. 160 Nosler Partition | velocity, fps: | 3200 | 2991 | 2791 | 2600 | 2417 |
| | energy, ft-lb: | 3638 | 3177 | 2767 | 2401 | 2075. |
| | arc, inches: | | +3.1 | +3.8 | 0 | -8.9 |
| Wby. 175 Pointed Expanding | velocity, fps: | 3070 | 2861 | 2662 | 2471 | 2288 |
| | energy, ft-lb: | 3662 | 3181 | 2753 | 2373 | 2034 |
| | arc, inches: | | +3.5 | +4.2 | 0 | -9.9 |

## 7mm Dakota

| cartridge bullet | range, yards: | 0 | 100 | 200 | 300 | 400 |
|---|---|---|---|---|---|---|
| Dakota 140 Barnes X | velocity, fps: | 3500 | 3253 | 3019 | 2798 | 2587 |
| | energy, ft-lb: | 3807 | 3288 | 2833 | 2433 | 2081 |
| | arc, inches: | | +2.0 | +2.1 | -1.5 | -9.6 |
| Dakota 160 Barnes X | velocity, fps: | 3200 | 3001 | 2811 | 2630 | 2455 |
| | energy, ft-lb: | 3637 | 3200 | 2808 | 2456 | 2140 |
| | arc, inches: | | +2.1 | +1.9 | -2.8 | -12.5 |

## 7mm STW

| cartridge bullet | range, yards: | 0 | 100 | 200 | 300 | 400 |
|---|---|---|---|---|---|---|
| A-Square 140 Nos. Bal. Tip | velocity, fps: | 3450 | 3254 | 3067 | 2888 | 2715 |
| | energy, ft-lb: | 3700 | 3291 | 2924 | 2592 | 2292 |
| | arc, inches: | | +2.2 | +3.0 | 0 | -7.3 |
| A-Square 160 Nosler Part. | velocity, fps: | 3250 | 3071 | 2900 | 2735 | 2576. |
| | energy, ft-lb: | 3752 | 3351 | 2987 | 2657 | 2357 |
| | arc, inches: | | +2.8 | +3.5 | 0 | -8.2 |
| A-Square 160 SP boat-tail | velocity, fps: | 3250 | 3087 | 2930 | 2778 | 2631 |
| | energy, ft-lb: | 3752 | 3385 | 3049 | 2741 | 2460 |
| | arc, inches: | | +2.8 | +3.4 | 0 | -8.0 |

**BALLISTICS**

# Centerfire Rifle Ballistics

## 7MM STW TO .30-30 WINCHESTER

| cartridge bullet | range, yards: | 0 | 100 | 200 | 300 | 400 |
|---|---|---|---|---|---|---|
| Federal 140 Trophy Bonded | velocity, fps: | 3330 | 3080 | 2850 | 2630 | 2420 |
| | energy, ft-lb: | 3435 | 2950 | 2520 | 2145 | 1815 |
| | arc, inches: | | +1.1 | 0 | -5.4 | -15.8 |
| Federal 150 Trophy Bonded | velocity, fps: | 3250 | 3010 | 2770 | 2560 | 2350. |
| | energy, ft-lb: | 3520 | 3010 | 2565 | 2175 | 1830 |
| | arc, inches: | | +1.2 | 0 | -5.7 | -16.7 |
| Federal 160 Sierra GameKing BTSP | velocity, fps: | 3200 | 3020 | 2850 | 2670 | 2530. |
| | energy, ft-lb: | 3640 | 3245 | 2890 | 2570 | 2275 |
| | arc, inches: | | +1.1 | 0 | -5.5 | -15.7 |
| Rem. 140 PSP Core-Lokt | velocity, fps: | 3325 | 3064 | 2818 | 2585 | 2364 |
| | energy, ft-lb: | 3436 | 2918 | 2468 | 2077 | 1737 |
| | arc, inches: | | +2.0 | +1.7 | -2.9 | -12.8 |
| Rem. 140 Swift A-Frame | velocity, fps: | 3325 | 3020 | 2735 | 2467 | 2215 |
| | energy, ft-lb: | 3436 | 2834 | 2324 | 1892 | 1525 |
| | arc, inches: | | +2.1 | +1.8 | -3.1 | -13.8 |
| Speer 145 Grand Slam | velocity, fps: | 3300 | 2992 | 2075 | 2435 | |
| | energy, ft-lb: | 3506 | 2882 | 2355 | 1909 | |
| | arc, inches: | | +1.2 | 0 | -6.0 | -17.8 |
| Win. 140 Ballistic Silvertip | velocity, fps: | 3320 | 3100 | 2890 | 2690 | 2499 |
| | energy, ft-lb: | 3427 | 2982 | 2597 | 2250 | 1941 |
| | arc, inches: | | +1.1 | 0 | -5.2 | -15.2 |
| Win. 150 Power-Point | velocity, fps: | 3250 | 2957 | 2683 | 2424 | 2181 |
| | energy, ft-lb: | 3519 | 2913 | 2398 | 1958 | 1584 |
| | arc, inches: | | +1.2 | 0 | -6.1 | -18.1 |
| Win. 160 Fail Safe | velocity, fps: | 3150 | 2894 | 2652 | 2422 | 2204 |
| | energy, ft-lb: | 3526 | 2976 | 2499 | 2085 | 1727 |
| | arc, inches: | | +1.3 | 0 | -6.3 | -18.5 |

## 7mm Remington Ultra Magnum

| cartridge bullet | range, yards: | 0 | 100 | 200 | 300 | 400 |
|---|---|---|---|---|---|---|
| Rem. 140 PSP Core-Lokt | velocity, fps: | 3425 | 3158 | 2907 | 2669 | 2444 |
| | energy, ft-lb: | 3646 | 3099 | 2626 | 2214 | 1856 |
| | arc, inches: | | +1.8 | +1.6 | -2.7 | -11.9 |
| Rem. 140 Nosler Partition | velocity, fps: | 3425 | 3184 | 2956 | 2740 | 2534 |
| | energy, ft-lb: | 3646 | 3151 | 2715 | 2333 | 1995 |
| | arc, inches: | | +1.7 | +1.6 | -2.6 | -11.4 |
| Rem. 160 Nosler Partition | velocity, fps: | 3200 | 2991 | 2791 | 2600 | 2417 |
| | energy, ft-lb: | 3637 | 3177 | 2767 | 2401 | 2075 |
| | arc, inches: | | +2.1 | +1.8 | -3.0 | -12.9 |

## 7.21 (.284) Firehawk

| cartridge bullet | range, yards: | 0 | 100 | 200 | 300 | 400 |
|---|---|---|---|---|---|---|
| Lazzeroni 140 Nosler Part. | velocity, fps: | 3580 | 3349 | 3130 | 2923 | 2724 |
| | energy, ft-lb: | 3985 | 3488 | 3048 | 2656 | 2308 |
| | arc, inches: | | +2.2 | +2.9 | 0 | -7.0 |
| Lazzeroni 160 Swift A-Fr. | velocity, fps: | 3385 | 3167 | 2961 | 2763 | 2574 |
| | energy, ft-lb: | 4072 | 3565 | 3115 | 2713 | 2354 |
| | arc, inches: | | +2.6 | +3.3 | 0 | -7.8 |

## 7.5x55 Swiss

| cartridge bullet | range, yards: | 0 | 100 | 200 | 300 | 400 |
|---|---|---|---|---|---|---|
| Norma 180 Soft Point | velocity, fps: | 2651 | 2432 | 2223 | 2025 | |
| | energy, ft-lb: | 2810 | 2364 | 1976 | 1639 | |
| | arc, inches: | | +2.2 | 0 | -9.3 | |
| Norma 180 Oryx | velocity, fps: | 2493 | 2222 | 1968 | 1734 | |
| | energy, ft-lb: | 2485 | 1974 | 1549 | 1201 | |
| | arc, inches: | | +2.7 | 0 | -11.8 | |

## 7.62x39 Russian

| cartridge bullet | range, yards: | 0 | 100 | 200 | 300 | 400 |
|---|---|---|---|---|---|---|
| Federal 123 Hi-Shok | velocity, fps: | 2300 | 2030 | 1780 | 1550 | 1350 |
| | energy, ft-lb: | 1445 | 1125 | 860 | 655 | 500. |
| | arc, inches: | | 0 | -7.0 | -25.1 | |
| Federal 124 FMJ | velocity, fps: | 2300 | 2030 | 1780 | 1560 | 1360 |
| | energy, ft-lb: | 1455 | 1135 | 875 | 670 | 510 |
| | arc, inches: | | +3.5 | 0 | -14.6 | -43.5 |
| PMC 123 FMJ | velocity, fps: | 2350 | 2072 | 1817 | 1583 | 1368 |
| | energy, ft-lb: | 1495 | 1162 | 894 | 678 | 507 |
| | arc, inches: | | 0 | -5.0 | -26.4 | -67.8 |

| cartridge bullet | range, yards: | 0 | 100 | 200 | 300 | 400 |
|---|---|---|---|---|---|---|
| PMC 125 Pointed Soft Point | velocity, fps: | 2320 | 2046 | 1794 | 1563 | 1350 |
| | energy, ft-lb: | 1493 | 1161 | 893 | 678 | 505. |
| | arc, inches: | | 0 | -5.2 | -27.5 | -70.6 |
| Rem. 125 Pointed Soft Point | velocity, fps: | 2365 | 2062 | 1783 | 1533 | 1320 |
| | energy, ft-lb: | 1552 | 1180 | 882 | 652 | 483 |
| | arc, inches: | | 0 | -6.7 | -24.5 | |
| Win. 123 Soft Point | velocity, fps: | 2365 | 2033 | 1731 | 1465 | 1248 |
| | energy, ft-lb: | 1527 | 1129 | 818 | 586 | 425 |
| | arc, inches: | | +3.8 | 0 | -15.4 | -46.3 |

## .30 Carbine

| cartridge bullet | range, yards: | 0 | 100 | 200 | 300 | 400 |
|---|---|---|---|---|---|---|
| Federal 110 Hi-Shok RN | velocity, fps: | 1990 | 1570 | 1240 | 1040 | 920 |
| | energy, ft-lb: | 965 | 600 | 375 | 260 | 210 |
| | arc, inches: | | 0 | -12.8 | -46.9 | |
| Federal 110 FMJ | velocity, fps: | 1990 | 1570 | 1240 | 1040 | 920 |
| | energy, ft-lb: | 965 | 600 | 375 | 260 | 210 |
| | arc, inches: | | 0 | -12.8 | -46.9 | |
| Magtech 110 FMC | velocity, fps: | 1990 | 1654 | | | |
| | energy, ft-lb: | 965 | 668 | | | |
| | arc, inches: | | 0 | | | |
| PMC 110 FMJ | (and RNSP)velocity, fps: | 1927 | 1548 | 1248 | | |
| | energy, ft-lb: | 906 | 585 | 380 | | |
| | arc, inches: | | 0 | -14.2 | | |
| Rem. 110 Soft Point | velocity, fps: | 1990 | 1567 | 1236 | 1035 | 923 |
| | energy, ft-lb: | 967 | 600 | 373 | 262 | 208 |
| | arc, inches: | | 0 | -12.9 | -48.6 | |
| Win. 110 Hollow Soft Point | velocity, fps: | 1990 | 1567 | 1236 | 1035 | 923 |
| | energy, ft-lb: | 967 | 600 | 373 | 262 | 208 |
| | arc, inches: | | 0 | -13.5 | -49.9 | |

## .30 T/C Hornaday

| cartridge bullet | range, yards: | 0 | 100 | 200 | 300 | 400 |
|---|---|---|---|---|---|---|
| Hornady 150 | velocity, fps | 3000 | 2772 | 2555 | 2348 | |
| | energy, ft-lb | 2997 | 2558 | 2176 | 1836 | |
| | arc, inches | -1.5 | +1.5 | 0 | -6.9 | |
| Hornady 165 | velocity, fps | 2850 | 2644 | 2447 | 2258 | |
| | energy, ft-lb | 2975 | 2560 | 2193 | 1868 | |
| | arc, inches | -1.5 | +1.7 | 0 | -7.6 | |

## .30-30 Winchester

| cartridge bullet | range, yards: | 0 | 100 | 200 | 300 | 400 |
|---|---|---|---|---|---|---|
| Federal 125 Hi-Shok HP | velocity, fps: | 2570 | 2090 | 1660 | 1320 | 1080 |
| | energy, ft-lb: | 1830 | 1210 | 770 | 480 | 320 |
| | arc, inches: | | +3.3 | 0 | -16.0 | -50.9 |
| Federal 150 Hi-Shok FN | velocity, fps: | 2390 | 2020 | 1680 | 1400 | 1180 |
| | energy, ft-lb: | 1900 | 1355 | 945 | 650 | 460 |
| | arc, inches: | | +3.6 | 0 | -15.9 | -49.1 |
| Federal 170 Hi-Shok RN | velocity, fps: | 2200 | 1900 | 1620 | 1380 | 1190 |
| | energy, ft-lb: | 1830 | 1355 | 990 | 720 | 535 |
| | arc, inches: | | +4.1 | 0 | -17.4 | -52.4 |
| Federal 170 Sierra Pro-Hunt. | velocity, fps: | 2200 | 1820 | 1500 | 1240 | 1060 |
| | energy, ft-lb: | 1830 | 1255 | 845 | 575 | 425 |
| | arc, inches: | | +4.5 | 0 | -20.0 | -63.5 |
| Federal 170 Nosler Partition | velocity, fps: | 2200 | 1900 | 1620 | 1380 | 1190 |
| | energy, ft-lb: | 1830 | 1355 | 990 | 720 | 535 |
| | arc, inches: | | +4.1 | 0 | -17.4 | -52.4 |
| Hornady 150 Round Nose | velocity, fps: | 2390 | 1973 | 1605 | 1303 | 1095 |
| | energy, ft-lb: | 1902 | 1296 | 858 | 565 | 399 |
| | arc, inches: | | 0 | -8.2 | -30.0 | |
| Hornady 160 Evolution | velocity, fps: | 2400 | 2150 | 1916 | 1699 | |
| | energy, ft-lb: | 2046 | 1643 | 1304 | 1025 | |
| | arc, inches: | | +3.0 | 0.2 | -12.1 | |
| Hornady 170 Flat Point | velocity, fps: | 2200 | 1895 | 1619 | 1381 | 1191 |
| | energy, ft-lb: | 1827 | 1355 | 989 | 720 | 535 |
| | arc, inches: | | 0 | -8.9 | -31.1 | |

BALLISTICS

| cartridge bullet | range, yards: | 0 | 100 | 200 | 300 | 400 |
|---|---|---|---|---|---|---|
| Norma 150 Soft Point | velocity, fps: | 2329 | 2008 | 1716 | 1459 | |
| | energy, ft-lb: | 1807 | 1344 | 981 | 709 | |
| | arc, inches: | | | +3.6 | 0 | -15.5 |
| PMC 150 Starfire HP | velocity, fps: | 2100 | 1769 | 1478 | | |
| | energy, ft-lb: | 1469 | 1042 | 728 | | |
| | arc, inches: | | | 0 | -10.8 | |
| PMC 150 Flat Nose | velocity, fps: | 2300 | 1943 | 1627 | | |
| | energy, ft-lb: | 1762 | 1257 | 881 | | |
| | arc, inches: | | | 0 | -7.8 | |
| PMC 170 Flat Nose | velocity, fps: | 2150 | 1840 | 1566 | | |
| | energy, ft-lb: | 1745 | 1277 | 926 | | |
| | arc, inches: | | | 0 | -8.9 | |
| Rem. 55 PSP (sabot) "Accelerator" | velocity, fps: | 3400 | 2693 | 2085 | 1570 | 1187 |
| | energy, ft-lb: | 1412 | 886 | 521 | 301 | 172 |
| | arc, inches: | | +1.7 | 0 | -9.9 | -34.3 |
| Rem. 150 SP Core-Lokt | velocity, fps: | 2390 | 1973 | 1605 | 1303 | 1095 |
| | energy, ft-lb: | 1902 | 1296 | 858 | 565 | 399 |
| | arc, inches: | | | 0 | -7.6 | -28.8 |
| Rem. 170 SP Core-Lokt | velocity, fps: | 2200 | 1895 | 1619 | 1381 | 1191 |
| | energy, ft-lb: | 1827 | 1355 | 989 | 720 | 535 |
| | arc, inches: | | | 0 | -8.3 | -29.9 |
| Rem. 170 HP Core-Lokt | velocity, fps: | 2200 | 1895 | 1619 | 1381 | 1191. |
| | energy, ft-lb: | 1827 | 1355 | 989 | 720 | 535 |
| | arc, inches: | | | 0 | -8.3 | -29.9 |
| Speer 150 Flat Nose | velocity, fps: | 2370 | 2067 | 1788 | 1538 | |
| | energy, ft-lb: | 1870 | 1423 | 1065 | 788 | |
| | arc, inches: | | +3.3 | 0 | -14.4 | -43.7 |
| Win. 150 Hollow Point | velocity, fps: | 2390 | 2018 | 1684 | 1398 | 1177 |
| | energy, ft-lb: | 1902 | 1356 | 944 | 651 | 461 |
| | arc, inches: | | | 0 | -7.7 | -27.9 |
| Win. 150 Power-Point | velocity, fps: | 2390 | 2018 | 1684 | 1398 | 1177 |
| | energy, ft-lb: | 1902 | 1356 | 944 | 651 | 461 |
| | arc, inches: | | | 0 | -7.7 | -27.9 |
| Win. 150 Silvertip | velocity,fps: | 2390 | 2018 | 1684 | 1398 | 1177 |
| | energy, ft-lb: | 1902 | 1356 | 944 | 651 | 461 |
| | arc, inches: | | | 0 | -7.7 | -27.9 |
| Win. 150 Power-Point Plus | velocity, fps: | 2480 | 2095 | 1747 | 1446 | 1209 |
| | energy, ft-lb: | 2049 | 1462 | 1017 | 697 | 487 |
| | arc, inches: | | | 0 | -6.5 | -24.5 |
| Win. 170 Power-Point | velocity, fps: | 2200 | 1895 | 1619 | 1381 | 1191 |
| | energy, ft-lb: | 1827 | 1355 | 989 | 720 | 535. |
| | arc, inches: | | | 0 | -8.9 | -31.1 |
| Win. 170 Silvertip | velocity, fps: | 2200 | 1895 | 1619 | 1381 | 1191 |
| | energy, ft-lb: | 1827 | 1355 | 989 | 720 | 535 |
| | arc, inches: | | | 0 | -8.9 | -31.1 |

## .300 Savage

| cartridge bullet | range, yards: | 0 | 100 | 200 | 300 | 400 |
|---|---|---|---|---|---|---|
| Federal 150 Hi-Shok | velocity, fps: | 2630 | 2350 | 2100 | 1850 | 1630 |
| | energy, ft-lb: | 2305 | 1845 | 1460 | 1145 | 885 |
| | arc, inches: | | +2.4 | 0 | -10.4 | -30.9 |
| Federal 180 Hi-Shok | velocity, fps: | 2350 | 2140 | 1940 | 1750 | 1570 |
| | energy, ft-lb: | 2205 | 1825 | 1495 | 1215 | 985 |
| | arc, inches: | | +3.1 | 0 | -12.4 | -36.1 |
| Rem. 150 PSP Core-Lokt | velocity, fps: | 2630 | 2354 | 2095 | 1853 | 1631 |
| | energy, ft-lb: | 2303 | 1845 | 1462 | 1143 | 806. |
| | arc, inches: | | +2.4 | 0 | -10.4 | -30.9 |
| Rem. 180 SP Core-Lokt | velocity, fps: | 2350 | 2025 | 1728 | 1467 | 1252 |
| | energy, ft-lb: | 2207 | 1639 | 1193 | 860 | 626 |
| | arc, inches: | | | 0 | -7.1 | -25.9 |
| Win. 150 Power-Point | velocity, fps: | 2630 | 2311 | 2015 | 1743 | 1500 |
| | energy, ft-lb: | 2303 | 1779 | 1352 | 1012 | 749 |
| | arc, inches: | | +2.8 | 0 | -11.5 | -34.4 |

## .307 Winchester

| cartridge bullet | range, yards: | 0 | 100 | 200 | 300 | 400 |
|---|---|---|---|---|---|---|
| Win. 180 Power-Point | velocity, fps: | 2510 | 2179 | 1874 | 1599 | 1362 |
| | energy, ft-lb: | 2519 | 1898 | 1404 | 1022 | 742 |
| | arc, inches: | | +1.5 | -3.6 | -18.6 | -47.1 |

## .30-40 Krag

| cartridge bullet | range, yards: | 0 | 100 | 200 | 300 | 400 |
|---|---|---|---|---|---|---|
| Rem. 180 PSP Core-Lokt | velocity, fps: | 2430 | 2213 | 2007 | 1813 | 1632. |
| | energy, ft-lb: | 2360 | 1957 | 1610 | 1314 | 1064 |
| | arc, inches, s: | | | 0 | -5.6 | -18.6 |
| Win. 180 Power-Point | velocity, fps: | 2430 | 2099 | 1795 | 1525 | 1298 |
| | energy, ft-lb: | 2360 | 1761 | 1288 | 929 | 673 |
| | arc, inches, s: | | | 0 | -7.1 | -25.0 |

## 7.62x54R Russian

| cartridge bullet | range, yards: | 0 | 100 | 200 | 300 | 400 |
|---|---|---|---|---|---|---|
| Norma 150 Soft Point | velocity, fps: | 2953 | 2622 | 2314 | 2028 | |
| | energy, ft-lb: | 2905 | 2291 | 1784 | 1370 | |
| | arc, inches: | | +1.8 | 0 | -8.3 | |
| Norma 180 Alaska | velocity, fps: | 2575 | 2362 | 2159 | 1967 | |
| | energy, ft-lb: | 2651 | 2231 | 1864 | 1546 | |
| | arc, inches: | | +2.9 | 0 | -12.9 | |

## .308 Marlin Express

| cartridge bullet | range, yards: | 0 | 100 | 200 | 300 | 400 |
|---|---|---|---|---|---|---|
| Hornady 160 | velocity, fps | 2660 | 2438 | 2226 | 2026 | 1836 |
| | energy, ft-lb | 2513 | 2111 | 1761 | 1457 | 1197 |
| | arc, inches | -1.5 | +3.0 | +1.7 | -6.7 | -23.5 |

## .308 Winchester

| cartridge bullet | range, yards: | 0 | 100 | 200 | 300 | 400 |
|---|---|---|---|---|---|---|
| Black Hills 150 Nosler B. Tip | velocity, fps: | 2800 | | | | |
| | energy, ft-lb: | 2611 | | | | |
| | arc, inches: | | | | | |
| Black Hills 165 Nosler B. Tip (and SP) | velocity, fps: | 2650 | | | | |
| | energy, ft-lb: | 2573 | | | | |
| | arc, inches: | | | | | |
| Black Hills 168 Barnes X (and Match) | velocity, fps: | 2650 | | | | |
| | energy, ft-lb: | 2620 | | | | |
| | arc, inches: | | | | | |
| Black Hills 175 Match | velocity, fps: | 2600 | | | | |
| | energy, ft-lb: | 2657 | | | | |
| | arc, inches: | | | | | |
| Black Hills 180 AccuBond | velocity, fps: | 2600 | | | | |
| | energy, ft-lb: | 2701 | | | | |
| | arc, inches: | | | | | |
| Federal 150 Hi-Shok | velocity, fps: | 2820 | 2530 | 2260 | 2010 | 1770 |
| | energy, ft-lb: | 2650 | 2140 | 1705 | 1345 | 1050 |
| | arc, inches: | | +2.0 | 0 | -8.8 | -26.3 |
| Federal 150 Nosler Bal. Tip. | velocity, fps: | 2820 | 2610 | 2410 | 2220 | 2040 |
| | energy, ft-lb: | 2650 | 2270 | 1935 | 1640 | 1380 |
| | arc, inches: | | +1.8 | 0 | -7.8 | -22.7 |
| Federal 150 FMJ boat-tail | velocity, fps: | 2820 | 2620 | 2430 | 2250 | 2070 |
| | energy, ft-lb: | 2650 | 2285 | 1965 | 1680 | 1430 |
| | arc, inches: | | +1.8 | 0 | -7.7 | -22.4 |
| Federal 150 Barnes XLC | velocity, fps: | 2820 | 2610 | 2400 | 2210 | 2030 |
| | energy, ft-lb: | 2650 | 2265 | 1925 | 1630 | 1370 |
| | arc, inches: | | +1.8 | 0 | -7.8 | -22.9 |
| Federal 155 Sierra MatchKg. BTHP | velocity, fps: | 2950 | 2740 | 2540 | 2350 | 2170 |
| | energy, ft-lb: | 2995 | 2585 | 2225 | 1905 | 1620 |
| | arc, inches: | | +1.9 | 0 | -8.9 | -22.6 |
| Federal 165 Sierra GameKing BTSP | velocity, fps: | 2700 | 2520 | 2330 | 2160 | 1990 |
| | energy, ft-lb: | 2670 | 2310 | 1990 | 1700 | 1450 |
| | arc, inches: | | +2.0 | 0 | -8.4 | -24.3 |
| Federal 165 Trophy Bonded | velocity, fps: | 2700 | 2440 | 2200 | 1970 | 1760 |
| | energy, ft-lb: | 2670 | 2185 | 1775 | 1425 | 1135 |
| | arc, inches: | | +2.2 | 0 | -9.4 | -27.7 |

BALLISTICS

# Centerfire Rifle Ballistics

## .308 WINCHESTER TO .308 WINCHESTER

| cartridge bullet | range, yards: | 0 | 100 | 200 | 300 | 400 | cartridge bullet | range, yards: | 0 | 100 | 200 | 300 | 400 |
|---|---|---|---|---|---|---|---|---|---|---|---|---|---|
| Federal 165 Tr. Bonded HE | velocity, fps: | 2870 | 2600 | 2350 | 2120 | 1890 | Hornady 168 TAP-FPD | velocity, fps: | 2700 | 2513 | 2333 | 2161 | 1996 |
| | energy, ft-lb: | 3020 | 2485 | 2030 | 1640 | 1310 | | energy, ft-lb: | 2719 | 2355 | 2030 | 1742 | 1486 |
| | arc, inches: | | +1.8 | 0 | -8.2 | -24.0 | | arc, inches: | | +2.0 | 0 | -8.4 | -24.3 |
| Federal 168 Sierra MatchKg. BTHP | velocity, fps: | 2600 | 2410 | 2230 | 2060 | 1890 | Hornady 178 A-Max | velocity, fps: | 2965 | 2778 | 2598 | 2425 | 2259 |
| | energy, ft-lb: | 2520 | 2170 | 1855 | 1580 | 1340. | | energy, ft-lb: | 3474 | 3049 | 2666 | 2323 | 2017 |
| | arc, inches: | | +2.1 | 0 | +8.9 | +25.9 | | arc, inches: | | +1.6 | 0 | -6.9 | -19.8 |
| Federal 180 Hi-Shok | velocity, fps: | 2620 | 2390 | 2180 | 1970 | 1780 | Hornady 180 A-Max Match | velocity, fps: | 2550 | 2397 | 2249 | 2106 | 1974 |
| | energy, ft-lb: | 2745 | 2290 | 1895 | 1555 | 1270 | | energy, ft-lb: | 2598 | 2295 | 2021 | 1773 | 1557 |
| | arc, inches: | | +2.3 | 0 | -9.7 | -28.3 | | arc, inches: | | +2.7 | 0 | -9.5 | -26.2 |
| Federal 180 Sierra Pro-Hunt. | velocity, fps: | 2620 | 2410 | 2200 | 2010 | 1820 | Norma 150 Nosler Bal. Tip | velocity, fps: | 2822 | 2588 | 2365 | 2154 | |
| | energy, ft-lb: | 2745 | 2315 | 1940 | 1610 | 1330 | | energy, ft-lb: | 2653 | 2231 | 1864 | 1545 | |
| | arc, inches: | | +2.3 | 0 | -9.3 | -27.1 | | arc, inches: | | +1.6 | 0 | -7.1 | |
| Federal 180 Nosler Partition | velocity, fps: | 2620 | 2430 | 2240 | 2060 | 1890 | Norma 150 Soft Point | velocity, fps: | 2861 | 2537 | 2235 | 1954 | |
| | energy, ft-lb: | 2745 | 2355 | 2005 | 1700 | 1430. | | energy, ft-lb: | 2727 | 2144 | 1664 | 1272 | |
| | arc, inches: | | +2.2 | 0 | -9.2 | -26.5 | | arc, inches: | | +2.0 | 0 | -9.0 | |
| Federal 180 Nosler Part. HE | velocity, fps: | 2740 | 2550 | 2370 | 2200 | 2030 | Norma 165 TXP Swift A-Fr. | velocity, fps: | 2700 | 2459 | 2231 | 2015 | |
| | energy, ft-lb: | 3000 | 2600 | 2245 | 1925 | 1645 | | energy, ft-lb: | 2672 | 2216 | 1824 | 1488 | |
| | arc, inches: | | +1.9 | 0 | -8.2 | -23.5 | | arc, inches: | | +2.1 | 0 | -9.1 | |
| Hornady 110 TAP-FPD | velocity, fps: | 3165 | 2830 | 2519 | 2228 | 1957 | Norma 180 Plastic Point | velocity, fps: | 2612 | 2365 | 2131 | 1911 | |
| | energy, ft-lb: | 2446 | 1956 | 1649 | 1212 | 935 | | energy, ft-lb: | 2728 | 2235 | 1815 | 1460 | |
| | arc, inches: | | +1.4 | 0 | -6.9 | -20.9 | | arc, inches: | | +2.4 | 0 | -10.1 | |
| Hornady 110 Urban Tactical | velocity, fps: | 3170 | 2825 | 2504 | 2206 | 1937 | Norma 180 Nosler Partition | velocity, fps: | 2612 | 2414 | 2225 | 2044 | |
| | energy, ft-lb: | 2454 | 1950 | 1532 | 1189 | 916 | | energy, ft-lb: | 2728 | 2330 | 1979 | 1670 | |
| | arc, inches: | | +1.5 | 0 | -7.2 | -21.2 | | arc, inches: | | +2.2 | 0 | -9.3 | |
| Hornady 150 SP boat-tail | velocity, fps: | 2820 | 2560 | 2315 | 2084 | 1866 | Norma 180 Alaska | velocity, fps: | 2612 | 2269 | 1953 | 1667 | |
| | energy, ft-lb: | 2648 | 2183 | 1785 | 1447 | 1160 | | energy, ft-lb: | 2728 | 2059 | 1526 | 1111 | |
| | arc, inches: | | +2.0 | 0 | -8.5 | -25.2 | | arc, inches: | | +2.7 | 0 | -11.9 | |
| Hornady 150 SST (or Interbond) | velocity, fps: | 2820 | 2593 | 2378 | 2174 | 1984 | Norma 180 Vulkan | velocity, fps: | 2612 | 2325 | 2056 | 1806 | |
| | energy, ft-lb: | 2648 | 2240 | 1884 | 1574 | 1311 | | energy, ft-lb: | 2728 | 2161 | 1690 | 1304 | |
| | arc, inches: | | +1.9 | 0 | -8.1 | -22.9 | | arc, inches: | | +2.5 | 0 | -10.8 | |
| Hornady 150 SST LM (or Interbond) | velocity, fps: | 3000 | 2765 | 2541 | 2328 | 2127 | Norma 180 Oryx | velocity, fps: | 2612 | 2305 | 2019 | 1755 | |
| | energy, ft-lb: | 2997 | 2545 | 2150 | 1805 | 1506. | | energy, ft-lb: | 2728 | 2124 | 1629 | 1232 | |
| | arc, inches: | | +1.5 | 0 | -7.1 | -20.6 | | arc, inches: | | +2.5 | 0 | -11.1 | |
| Hornady 150 SP LM | velocity, fps: | 2980 | 2703 | 2442 | 2195 | 1964 | Norma 200 Vulkan | velocity, fps: | 2461 | 2215 | 1983 | 1767 | |
| | energy, ft-lb: | 2959 | 2433 | 1986 | 1606 | 1285 | | energy, ft-lb: | 2690 | 2179 | 1747 | 1387 | |
| | arc, inches: | | +1.6 | 0 | -7.5 | -22.2 | | arc, inches: | | +2.8 | 0 | -11.7 | |
| Hornady 155 A-Max | velocity, fps: | 2815 | 2610 | 2415 | 2229 | 2051 | PMC 147 FMJ boat-tail | velocity, fps: | 2751 | 2473 | 2257 | 2052 | 1859 |
| | energy, ft-lb: | 2727 | 2345 | 2007 | 1709 | 1448 | | energy, ft-lb: | 2428 | 2037 | 1697 | 1403 | 1150 |
| | arc, inches: | | +1.9 | 0 | -7.9 | -22.6 | | arc, inches: | | +2.3 | 0 | -9.3 | -27.3 |
| Hornady 155 TAP-FPD | velocity, fps: | 2785 | 2577 | 2379 | 2189 | 2008 | PMC 150 Barnes X | velocity, fps: | 2700 | 2504 | 2316 | 2135 | 1964 |
| | energy, ft-lb: | 2669 | 2285 | 1947 | 1649 | 1387 | | energy, ft-lb: | 2428 | 2087 | 1786 | 1518 | 1284 |
| | arc, inches: | | +1.9 | 0 | -8.0 | -23.3 | | arc, inches: | | +2.0 | 0 | -8.6 | -24.7 |
| Hornady 165 SP boat-tail | velocity, fps: | 2700 | 2496 | 2301 | 2115 | 1937 | PMC 150 Pointed Soft Point | velocity, fps: | 2750 | 2478 | 2224 | 1987 | 1766 |
| | energy, ft-lb: | 2670 | 2283 | 1940 | 1639 | 1375 | | energy, ft-lb: | 2519 | 2045 | 1647 | 1315 | 1039 |
| | arc, inches: | | +2.0 | 0 | -8.7 | -25.2 | | arc, inches: | | +2.1 | 0 | -9.2 | -27.1 |
| Hornady 165 SPBT LM | velocity, fps: | 2870 | 2658 | 2456 | 2283 | 2078 | PMC 150 SP boat-tail | velocity, fps: | 2820 | 2581 | 2354 | 2139 | 1935 |
| | energy, ft-lb: | 3019 | 2589 | 2211 | 1877 | 1583 | | energy, ft-lb: | 2648 | 2218 | 1846 | 1523 | 1247. |
| | arc, inches: | | +1.7 | 0 | -7.5 | -21.8 | | arc, inches: | | +1.9 | 0 | -8.2 | -24.0 |
| Hornady 165 SST LM (or Interbond) | velocity, fps: | 2880 | 2672 | 2474 | 2284 | 2103 | PMC 168 Barnes X | velocity, fps: | 2600 | 2425 | 2256 | 2095 | 1940 |
| | energy, ft-lb: | 3038 | 2616 | 2242 | 1911 | 1620 | | energy, ft-lb: | 2476 | 2154 | 1865 | 1608 | 1379 |
| | arc, inches: | | +1.6 | 0 | -7.3 | -21.2 | | arc, inches: | | +2.2 | 0 | -9.0 | -26.0 |
| Hornady 168 BTHP Match | velocity, fps: | 2700 | 2524 | 2354 | 2191 | 2035. | PMC 168 HP boat-tail | velocity, fps: | 2650 | 2460 | 2278 | 2103 | 1936 |
| | energy, ft-lb: | 2720 | 2377 | 2068 | 1791 | 1545 | | energy, ft-lb: | 2619 | 2257 | 1935 | 1649 | 1399 |
| | arc, inches: | | +2.0 | 0 | -8.4 | -23.9 | | arc, inches: | | +2.1 | 0 | -8.8 | -25.6 |
| Hornady 168 BTHP Match LM | velocity, fps: | 2640 | 2630 | 2429 | 2238 | 2056 | PMC 168 Pointed Soft Point | velocity, fps: | 2559 | 2354 | 2160 | 1976 | 1803 |
| | energy, ft-lb: | 3008 | 2579 | 2201 | 1868 | 1577 | | energy, ft-lb: | 2443 | 2067 | 1740 | 1457 | 1212 |
| | arc, inches: | | +1.8 | 0 | -7.8 | -22.4 | | arc, inches: | | +2.4 | 0 | -9.9 | -28.7 |
| Hornady 168 A-Max Match | velocity, fps: | 2620 | 2446 | 2280 | 2120 | 1972 | PMC 168 Pointed Soft Point | velocity, fps: | 2600 | 2404 | 2216 | 2037 | 1866 |
| | energy, ft-lb: | 2560 | 2232 | 1939 | 1677 | 1450 | | energy, ft-lb: | 2476 | 2064 | 1709 | 1403 | 1142 |
| | arc, inches: | | +2.6 | 0 | -9.2 | -25.6 | | arc, inches: | | +2.3 | 0 | -9.8 | -28.7 |
| Hornady 168 A-Max | velocity, fps: | 2700 | 2491 | 2292 | 2102 | 1921 | PMC 180 Pointed Soft Point | velocity, fps: | 2550 | 2335 | 2132 | 1940 | 1760 |
| | energy, ft-lb: | 2719 | 2315 | 1959 | 1648 | 1377 | | energy, ft-lb: | 2599 | 2179 | 1816 | 1504 | 1238. |
| | arc, inches: | | +2.4 | 0 | -9.0 | -25.9 | | arc, inches: | | +2.5 | 0 | -10.1 | -29.5 |

BALLISTICS

| cartridge bullet | range, yards: | 0 | 100 | 200 | 300 | 400 |
|---|---|---|---|---|---|---|
| PMC 180 SP boat-tail | velocity, fps: | 2620 | 2446 | 2278 | 2117 | 1962 |
| | energy, ft-lb: | 2743 | 2391 | 2074 | 1790 | 1538 |
| | arc, inches: | | +2.2 | 0 | -8.9 | -25.4 |
| Rem. 125 PSP C-L MR | velocity, fps: | 2660 | 2348 | 2057 | 1788 | 1546 |
| | energy, ft-lb: | 1964 | 1529 | 1174 | 887 | 663 |
| | arc, inches: | | +1.1 | -2.7 | -14.3 | -35.8 |
| Rem. 150 PSP Core-Lokt | velocity, fps: | 2820 | 2533 | 2263 | 2009 | 1774 |
| | energy, ft-lb: | 2648 | 2137 | 1705 | 1344 | 1048 |
| | arc, inches: | | +2.0 | 0 | -8.8 | -26.2 |
| Rem. 150 PSP C-L Ultra | velocity, fps: | 2620 | 2404 | 2198 | 2002 | 1818 |
| | energy, ft-lb: | 2743 | 2309 | 1930 | 1601 | 1320 |
| | arc, inches: | | +2.3 | 0 | -9.5 | -26.4 |
| Rem. 150 Swift Scirocco | velocity, fps: | 2820 | 2611 | 2410 | 2219 | 2037 |
| | energy, ft-lb: | 2648 | 2269 | 1935 | 1640 | 1381 |
| | arc, inches: | | +1.8 | 0 | -7.8 | -22.7 |
| Rem. 165 AccuTip | velocity, fps: | 2700 | 2501 | 2311 | 2129 | 1958. |
| | energy, ft-lb: | 2670 | 2292 | 1957 | 1861 | 1401. |
| | arc, inches: | | +2.0 | 0 | -8.6 | -24.8 |
| Rem. 165 PSP boat-tail | velocity, fps: | 2700 | 2497 | 2303 | 2117 | 1941. |
| | energy, ft-lb: | 2670 | 2284 | 1942 | 1642 | 1379 |
| | arc, inches: | | +2.0 | 0 | -8.6 | -25.0 |
| Rem. 165 Nosler Bal. Tip | velocity, fps: | 2700 | 2613 | 2333 | 2161 | 1996 |
| | energy, ft-lb: | 2672 | 2314 | 1995 | 1711 | 1460 |
| | arc, inches: | | +2.0 | 0 | -8.4 | -24.3 |
| Rem. 165 Swift Scirocco | velocity, fps: | 2700 | 2513 | 2233 | 2161 | 1996 |
| | energy, fps: | 2670 | 2313 | 1994 | 1711 | 1459 |
| | arc, inches: | | +2.0 | 0 | -8.4 | -24.3 |
| Rem. 168 HPBT Match | velocity, fps: | 2680 | 2493 | 2314 | 2143 | 1979 |
| | energy, ft-lb: | 2678 | 2318 | 1998 | 1713 | 1460 |
| | arc, inches: | | +2.1 | 0 | -8.6 | -24.7 |
| Rem. 180 SP Core-Lokt | velocity, fps: | 2620 | 2274 | 1955 | 1666 | 1414 |
| | energy, ft-lb: | 2743 | 2066 | 1527 | 1109 | 799 |
| | arc, inches: | | +2.6 | 0 | -11.8 | -36.3 |
| Rem. 180 PSP Core-Lokt | velocity, fps: | 2620 | 2393 | 2178 | 1974 | 1782 |
| | energy, ft-lb: | 2743 | 2288 | 1896 | 1557 | 1269 |
| | arc, inches: | | +2.3 | 0 | -9.7 | -28.3 |
| Rem. 180 Nosler Partition | velocity, fps: | 2620 | 2436 | 2259 | 2089 | 1927. |
| | energy, ft-lb: | 2743 | 2371 | 2039 | 1774 | 1485 |
| | arc, inches: | | +2.2 | 0 | -9.0 | -26.0 |
| Speer 150 Grand Slam | velocity, fps: | 2900 | 2599 | 2317 | 2053 | |
| | energy, ft-lb: | 2800 | 2249 | 1788 | 1404 | |
| | arc, inches: | | +2.1 | 0 | -8.6 | -24.8 |
| Speer 165 Grand Slam | velocity, fps: | 2700 | 2475 | 2261 | 2057 | |
| | energy, ft-lb: | 2670 | 2243 | 1872 | 1550 | |
| | arc, inches: | | +2.1 | 0 | -8.9 | -25.9 |
| Speer 180 Grand Slam | velocity, fps: | 2620 | 2420 | 2229 | 2046 | |
| | energy, ft-lb: | 2743 | 2340 | 1985 | 1674 | |
| | arc, inches: | | +2.2 | 0 | -9.2 | -26.6 |
| Win. 150 Power-Point | velocity, fps: | 2820 | 2488 | 2179 | 1893 | 1633 |
| | energy, ft-lb: | 2648 | 2061 | 1581 | 1193 | 888 |
| | arc, inches: | | +2.4 | 0 | -9.8 | -29.3 |
| Win. 150 Power-Point Plus | velocity, fps: | 2900 | 2558 | 2241 | 1946 | 1678 |
| | energy, ft-lb: | 2802 | 2180 | 1672 | 1262 | 938 |
| | arc, inches: | | +1.9 | 0 | -8.9 | -27.0 |
| Win. 150 Partition Gold | velocity, fps: | 2900 | 2645 | 2405 | 2177 | 1962 |
| | energy, ft-lb: | 2802 | 2332 | 1927 | 1579 | 1282. |
| | arc, inches: | | +1.7 | 0 | -7.8 | -22.9 |
| Win. 150 Ballistic Silvertip | velocity, fps: | 2810 | 2601 | 2401 | 2211 | 2028 |
| | energy, ft-lb: | 2629 | 2253 | 1920 | 1627 | 1370. |
| | arc, inches: | | +1.8 | 0 | -7.8 | -22.8 |
| Win. 150 Fail Safe | velocity, fps: | 2820 | 2533 | 2263 | 2010 | 1775 |
| | energy, ft-lb: | 2649 | 2137 | 1706 | 1346 | 1049 |
| | arc, inches: | | +2.0 | 0 | -8.8 | -26.2 |

| cartridge bullet | range, yards: | 0 | 100 | 200 | 300 | 400 |
|---|---|---|---|---|---|---|
| Win. 150 Supreme Elite XP3 | velocity, fps: | 2825 | 2616 | 2417 | 2226 | 2044 |
| | energy, ft-lb: | 2658 | 2279 | 1945 | 1650 | 1392 |
| | arc, inches: | | +1.8 | 0 | -7.8 | -22.6 |
| Win. 168 Ballistic Silvertip | velocity, fps: | 2670 | 2484 | 2306 | 2134 | 1971 |
| | energy, ft-lb: | 2659 | 2301 | 1983 | 1699 | 1449 |
| | arc, inches: | | +2.1 | 0 | -8.6 | -24.8 |
| Win. 168 HP boat-tail Match | velocity, fps: | 2680 | 2485 | 2297 | 2118 | 1948 |
| | energy, ft-lb: | 2680 | 2303 | 1970 | 1674 | 1415 |
| | arc, inches: | | +2.1 | 0 | -8.7 | -25.1 |
| Win. 180 Power-Point | velocity, fps: | 2620 | 2274 | 1955 | 1666 | 1414 |
| | energy, ft-lb: | 2743 | 2066 | 1527 | 1109 | 799 |
| | arc, inches: | | +2.9 | 0 | -12.1 | -36.9 |
| Win. 180 Silvertip | velocity, fps: | 2620 | 2393 | 2178 | 1974 | 1782 |
| | energy, ft-lb: | 2743 | 2288 | 1896 | 1557 | 1269 |
| | arc, inches: | | +2.6 | 0 | -9.9 | -28.9 |

## .30-06 Springfield

| cartridge bullet | range, yards: | 0 | 100 | 200 | 300 | 400 |
|---|---|---|---|---|---|---|
| A-Square 180 M & D-T | velocity, fps: | 2700 | 2365 | 2054 | 1769 | 1524 |
| | energy, ft-lb: | 2913 | 2235 | 1687 | 1251 | 928 |
| | arc, inches: | | +2.4 | 0 | -10.6 | -32.4 |
| A-Square 220 Monolythic Solid | velocity, fps: | 2380 | 2108 | 1854 | 1623 | 1424 |
| | energy, ft-lb: | 2767 | 2171 | 1679 | 1287 | 990 |
| | arc, inches: | | +3.1 | 0 | -13.6 | -39.9 |
| Black Hills 150 Nosler B. Tip | velocity, fps: | 2900 | | | | |
| | energy, ft-lb: | 2770 | | | | |
| | arc, inches: | | | | | |
| Black Hills 165 Nosler B. Tip | velocity, fps: | 2750 | | | | |
| | energy, ft-lb: | 2770 | | | | |
| | arc, inches: | | | | | |
| Black Hills 168 Hor. Match | velocity, fps: | 2700 | | | | |
| | energy, ft-lb: | 2718 | | | | |
| | arc, inches: | | | | | |
| Black Hills 180 Barnes X | velocity, fps: | 2650 | | | | |
| | energy, ft-lb: | 2806 | | | | |
| | arc, inches: | | | | | |
| Black Hills 180 AccuBond | velocity, ft-lb: | 2700 | | | | |
| | energy, ft-lb: | | | | | |
| | arc, inches: | | | | | |
| Federal 125 Sierra Pro-Hunt. | velocity, fps: | 3140 | 2780 | 2450 | 2140 | 1850 |
| | energy, ft-lb: | 2735 | 2145 | 1660 | 1270 | 955 |
| | arc, inches: | | +1.5 | 0 | -7.3 | -22.3 |
| Federal 150 Hi-Shok | velocity, fps: | 2910 | 2620 | 2340 | 2080 | 1840 |
| | energy, ft-lb: | 2820 | 2280 | 1825 | 1445 | 1130 |
| | arc, inches: | | +1.8 | 0 | -8.2 | -24.4 |
| Federal 150 Sierra Pro-Hunt. | velocity, fps: | 2910 | 2640 | 2380 | 2130 | 1900 |
| | energy, ft-lb: | 2820 | 2315 | 1880 | 1515 | 1205 |
| | arc, inches: | | +1.7 | 0 | -7.9 | -23.3 |
| Federal 150 Sierra GameKing BTSP | velocity, fps: | 2910 | 2690 | 2480 | 2270 | 2070 |
| | energy, ft-lb: | 2820 | 2420 | 2040 | 1710 | 1430 |
| | arc, inches: | | +1.7 | 0 | -7.4 | -21.5 |
| Federal 150 Nosler Bal. Tip | velocity, fps: | 2910 | 2700 | 2490 | 2300 | 2110 |
| | energy, ft-lb: | 2820 | 2420 | 2070 | 1760 | 1485 |
| | arc, inches: | | +1.6 | 0 | -7.3 | -21.1 |
| Federal 150 FMJ boat-tail | velocity, fps: | 2910 | 2710 | 2510 | 2320 | 2150 |
| | energy, ft-lb: | 2820 | 2440 | 2100 | 1800 | 1535 |
| | arc, inches: | | +1.6 | 0 | -7.1 | -20.8 |
| Federal 165 Sierra Pro-Hunt. | velocity, fps: | 2800 | 2560 | 2340 | 2130 | 1920 |
| | energy, ft-lb: | 2875 | 2410 | 2005 | 1655 | 1360 |
| | arc, inches: | | +1.9 | 0 | -8.3 | -24.3 |
| Federal 165 Sierra GameKing BTSP | velocity, fps: | 2800 | 2610 | 2420 | 2240 | 2070. |
| | energy, ft-lb: | 2870 | 2490 | 2150 | 1840 | 1580 |
| | arc, inches: | | +1.8 | 0 | -7.8 | -22.4 |

# Centerfire Rifle Ballistics

## .30-06 SPRINGFIELD TO .30-06 SPRINGFIELD

| cartridge bullet | range, yards: | 0 | 100 | 200 | 300 | 400 | cartridge bullet | range, yards: | 0 | 100 | 200 | 300 | 400 |
|---|---|---|---|---|---|---|---|---|---|---|---|---|---|
| Federal 165 Sierra GameKing | velocity, fps: | 3140 | 2900 | 2670 | 2450 | 2240. | Hornady 165 SST | velocity, fps: | 2800 | 2598 | 2405 | 2221 | 2046 |
| HE | energy, ft-lb: | 3610 | 3075 | 2610 | 2200 | 1845 | (or Interbond) | energy, ft-lb: | 2872 | 2473 | 2119 | 1808 | 1534 |
| | arc, inches: | | +1.5 | 0 | -6.9 | -20.4 | | arc, inches: | | +1.9 | 0 | -8.0 | -22.8 |
| Federal 165 Nosler Bal. Tip | velocity, fps: | 2800 | 2610 | 2430 | 2250 | 2080 | Hornady 165 SST LM | velocity, fps: | 3015 | 2802 | 2599 | 2405 | 2219 |
| | energy, ft-lb: | 2870 | 2495 | 2155 | 1855 | 1585 | | energy, ft-lb: | 3330 | 2878 | 2474 | 2118 | 1803. |
| | arc, inches: | | +1.8 | 0 | -7.7 | -22.3 | | arc, inches: | | +1.5 | 0 | -6.5 | -19.3 |
| Federal 165 Trophy Bonded | velocity, fps: | 2800 | 2540 | 2290 | 2050 | 1830. | Hornady 168 HPBT Match | velocity, fps: | 2790 | 2620 | 2447 | 2280 | 2120. |
| | energy, ft-lb: | 2870 | 2360 | 1915 | 1545 | 1230 | | energy, ft-lb: | 2925 | 2561 | 2234 | 1940 | 1677. |
| | arc, inches: | | +2.0 | 0 | -8.7 | -25.4 | | arc, inches: | | +1.7 | 0 | -7.7 | -22.2 |
| Federal 165 Tr. Bonded HE | velocity, fps: | 3140 | 2860 | 2590 | 2340 | 2100 | Hornady 180 SP | velocity, fps: | 2700 | 2469 | 2258 | 2042 | 1846 |
| | energy, ft-lb: | 3610 | 2990 | 2460 | 2010 | 1625. | | energy, ft-lb: | 2913 | 2436 | 2023 | 1666 | 1362 |
| | arc, inches: | | +1.6 | 0 | -7.4 | -21.9 | | arc, inches: | | +2.4 | 0 | -9.3 | -27.0 |
| Federal 168 Sierra MatchKg. | velocity, fps: | 2700 | 2510 | 2320 | 2150 | 1980 | Hornady 180 SPBT LM | velocity, fps: | 2880 | 2676 | 2480 | 2293 | 2114 |
| BTHP | energy, ft-lb: | 2720 | 2350 | 2010 | 1720 | 1460 | | energy, ft-lb: | 3316 | 2862 | 2459 | 2102 | 1786 |
| | arc, inches: | | +16.2 | +28.4 | +34.1 | +32.3 | | arc, inches: | | +1.7 | 0 | -7.3 | -21.3 |
| Federal 180 Hi-Shok | velocity, fps: | 2700 | 2470 | 2250 | 2040 | 1850 | Norma 150 Nosler Bal. Tip | velocity, fps: | 2936 | 2713 | 2502 | 2300 | |
| | energy, ft-lb: | 2915 | 2435 | 2025 | 1665 | 1360 | | energy, ft-lb: | 2872 | 2453 | 2085 | 1762 | |
| | arc, inches: | | +2.1 | 0 | -9.0 | -26.4 | | arc, inches: | | +1.6 | 0 | -7.1 | |
| Federal 180 Sierra Pro-Hunt. | velocity, fps: | 2700 | 2350 | 2020 | 1730 | 1470 | Norma 150 Soft Point | velocity, fps: | 2972 | 2640 | 2331 | 2043 | |
| RN | energy, ft-lb: | 2915 | 2200 | 1630 | 1190 | 860 | | energy, ft-lb: | 2943 | 2321 | 1810 | 1390 | |
| | arc, inches: | | +2.4 | 0 | -11.0 | -33.6 | | arc, inches: | | +1.8 | 0 | -8.2 | |
| Federal 180 Nosler Partition | velocity, fps: | 2700 | 2500 | 2320 | 2140 | 1970 | Norma 180 Alaska | velocity, fps: | 2700 | 2351 | 2028 | 1734 | |
| | energy, ft-lb: | 2915 | 2510 | 2150 | 1830 | 1550 | | energy, ft-lb: | 2914 | 2209 | 1645 | 1202 | |
| | arc, inches: | | +2.0 | 0 | -8.6 | -24.6 | | arc, inches: | | +2.4 | 0 | -11.0 | |
| Federal 180 Nosler Part. HE | velocity, fps: | 2880 | 2690 | 2500 | 2320 | 2150 | Norma 180 Nosler Partition | velocity, fps: | 2700 | 2494 | 2297 | 2108 | |
| | energy, ft-lb: | 3315 | 2880 | 2495 | 2150 | 1845 | | energy, ft-lb: | 2914 | 2486 | 2108 | 1777 | |
| | arc, inches: | | +1.7 | 0 | -7.2 | -21.0 | | arc, inches: | | +2.1 | 0 | -8.7 | |
| Federal 180 Sierra GameKing | velocity, fps: | 2700 | 2540 | 2380 | 2220 | 2080 | Norma 180 Plastic Point | velocity, fps: | 2700 | 2455 | 2222 | 2003 | |
| BTSP | energy, ft-lb: | 2915 | 2570 | 2260 | 1975 | 1720 | | energy, ft-lb: | 2914 | 2409 | 1974 | 1603 | |
| | arc, inches: | | +1.9 | 0 | -8.1 | -23.1 | | arc, inches: | | +2.1 | 0 | -9.2 | |
| Federal 180 Barnes XLC | velocity, fps: | 2700 | 2530 | 2360 | 2200 | 2040. | Norma 180 Vulkan | velocity, fps: | 2700 | 2416 | 2150 | 1901 | |
| | energy, ft-lb: | 2915 | 2550 | 2220 | 1930 | 1670 | | energy, ft-lb: | 2914 | 2334 | 1848 | 1445 | |
| | arc, inches: | | +2.0 | 0 | -8.3 | -23.8 | | arc, inches: | | +2.2 | 0 | -9.8 | |
| Federal 180 Trophy Bonded | velocity, fps: | 2700 | 2460 | 2220 | 2000 | 1800 | Norma 180 Oryx | velocity, fps: | 2700 | 2387 | 2095 | 1825 | |
| | energy, ft-lb: | 2915 | 2410 | 1975 | 1605 | 1290 | | energy, ft-lb: | 2914 | 2278 | 1755 | 1332 | |
| | arc, inches: | | +2.2 | 0 | -9.2 | -27.0 | | arc, inches: | | +2.3 | 0 | -10.2 | |
| Federal 180 Tr. Bonded HE | velocity, fps: | 2880 | 2630 | 2380 | 2160 | 1940 | Norma 180 TXP Swift A-Fr. | velocity, fps: | 2700 | 2479 | 2268 | 2067 | |
| | energy, ft-lb: | 3315 | 2755 | 2270 | 1855 | 1505 | | energy, ft-lb: | 2914 | 2456 | 2056 | 1708 | |
| | arc, inches: | | +1.8 | 0 | -8.0 | -23.3 | | arc, inches: | | +2.0 | 0 | -8.8 | |
| Federal 220 Sierra Pro-Hunt. | velocity, fps: | 2410 | 2130 | 1870 | 1630 | 1420 | Norma 180 AccuBond | velocity, fps: | 2674 | 2499 | 2331 | 2169 | |
| RN | energy, ft-lb: | 2835 | 2215 | 1705 | 1300 | 985 | | energy, ft-lb: | 2859 | 2497 | 2172 | 1881 | |
| | arc, inches: | | +3.1 | 0 | -13.1 | -39.3 | | arc, inches: | | +2.0 | 0 | -8.5 | |
| Hornady 150 SP | velocity, fps: | 2910 | 2617 | 2342 | 2083 | 1843 | Norma 200 Vulkan | velocity, fps: | 2641 | 2385 | 2143 | 1916 | |
| | energy, ft-lb: | 2820 | 2281 | 1827 | 1445 | 1131 | | energy, ft-lb: | 3098 | 2527 | 2040 | 1631 | |
| | arc, inches: | | +2.1 | 0 | -8.5 | -25.0 | | arc, inches: | | +2.3 | 0 | -9.9 | |
| Hornady 150 SP LM | velocity, fps: | 3100 | 2815 | 2548 | 2295 | 2058 | Norma 200 Oryx | velocity, fps: | 2625 | 2362 | 2115 | 1883 | |
| | energy, ft-lb: | 3200 | 2639 | 2161 | 1755 | 1410 | | energy, ft-lb: | 3061 | 2479 | 1987 | 1575 | |
| | arc, inches: | | +1.4 | 0 | -6.8 | -20.3 | | arc, inches: | | +2.3 | 0 | -10.1 | |
| Hornady 150 SP boat-tail | velocity, fps: | 2910 | 2683 | 2467 | 2262 | 2066. | PMC 150 X-Bullet | velocity, fps: | 2750 | 2552 | 2361 | 2179 | 2005 |
| | energy, ft-lb: | 2820 | 2397 | 2027 | 1706 | 1421 | | energy, ft-lb: | 2518 | 2168 | 1857 | 1582 | 1339 |
| | arc, inches: | | +2.0 | 0 | -7.7 | -22.2 | | arc, inches: | | +2.0 | 0 | -8.2 | -23.7 |
| Hornady 150 SST | velocity, fps: | 2910 | 2802 | 2599 | 2405 | 2219 | PMC 150 Pointed Soft Point | velocity, fps: | 2773 | 2542 | 2322 | 2113 | 1916 |
| (or Interbond) | energy, ft-lb: | 3330 | 2876 | 2474 | 2118 | 1803 | | energy, ft-lb: | 2560 | 2152 | 1796 | 1487 | 1222. |
| | arc, inches: | | +1.5 | 0 | -6.6 | -19.3 | | arc, inches: | | +1.9 | 0 | -8.4 | -24.6 |
| Hornady 150 SST LM | velocity, fps: | 3100 | 2860 | 2631 | 2414 | 2208 | PMC 150 SP boat-tail | velocity, fps: | 2900 | 2657 | 2427 | 2208 | 2000 |
| | energy, ft-lb: | 3200 | 2724 | 2306 | 1941 | 1624 | | energy, ft-lb: | 2801 | 2351 | 1961 | 1623 | 1332 |
| | arc, inches: | | +1.4 | 0 | -6.6 | -19.2 | | arc, inches: | | +1.7 | 0 | -7.7 | -22.5 |
| Hornady 165 SP boat-tail | velocity, fps: | 2800 | 2591 | 2392 | 2202 | 2020 | PMC 150 FMJ | velocity, fps: | 2773 | 2542 | 2322 | 2113 | 1916 |
| | energy, ft-lb: | 2873 | 2460 | 2097 | 1777 | 1495 | | energy, ft-lb: | 2560 | 2152 | 1796 | 1487 | 1222 |
| | arc, inches: | | +1.8 | 0 | -8.0 | -23.3 | | arc, inches: | | +1.9 | 0 | -8.4 | -24.6 |
| Hornady 165 SPBT LM | velocity, fps: | 3015 | 2790 | 2575 | 2370 | 2176 | PMC 168 Barnes X | velocity, fps: | 2750 | 2569 | 2395 | 2228 | 2067 |
| | energy, ft-lb: | 3330 | 2850 | 2428 | 2058 | 1734 | | energy, ft-lb: | 2770 | 2418 | 2101 | 1818 | 1565 |
| | arc, inches: | | +1.6 | 0 | -7.0 | -20.1 | | arc, inches: | | +1.9 | 0 | -8.0 | -23.0 |

**BALLISTICS**

# Centerfire Rifle Ballistics

| cartridge bullet | range, yards: | 0 | 100 | 200 | 300 | 400 |
|---|---|---|---|---|---|---|
| PMC 180 Barnes X | velocity, fps: | 2650 | 2487 | 2331 | 2179 | 2034 |
| | energy, ft-lb: | 2806 | 2472 | 2171 | 1898 | 1652 |
| | arc, inches: | | +2.1 | 0 | -8.5 | -24.3 |
| PMC 180 Pointed Soft Point | velocity, fps: | 2650 | 2430 | 2221 | 2024 | 1839 |
| | energy, ft-lb: | 2807 | 2359 | 1972 | 1638 | 1351 |
| | arc, inches: | | +2.2 | 0 | -9.3 | -27.0 |
| PMC 180 SP boat-tail | velocity, fps: | 2700 | 2523 | 2352 | 2188 | 2030 |
| | energy, ft-lb: | 2913 | 2543 | 2210 | 1913 | 1646 |
| | arc, inches: | | +2.0 | 0 | -8.3 | -23.9 |
| PMC 180 HPBT Match | velocity, fps: | 2800 | 2622 | 2456 | 2302 | 2158 |
| | energy, ft-lb: | 3133 | 2747 | 2411 | 2118 | 1861 |
| | arc, inches: | | +1.8 | 0 | -7.6 | -21.7 |
| Rem. 55 PSP (sabot) "Accelerator" | velocity, fps: | 4080 | 3484 | 2964 | 2499 | 2080 |
| | energy, ft-lb: | 2033 | 1482 | 1073 | 763 | 528. |
| | arc, inches: | | +1.4 | +1.4 | -2.6 | -12.2 |
| Rem. 125 PSP C-L MR | velocity, fps: | 2660 | 2335 | 2034 | 1757 | 1509 |
| | energy, ft-lb: | 1964 | 1513 | 1148 | 856 | 632 |
| | arc, inches: | | +1.1 | -3.0 | -15.5 | -37.4 |
| Rem. 125 Pointed Soft Point | velocity, fps: | 3140 | 2780 | 2447 | 2138 | 1853 |
| | energy, ft-lb: | 2736 | 2145 | 1662 | 1269 | 953. |
| | arc, inches: | | +1.5 | 0 | -7.4 | -22.4 |
| Rem. 150 AccuTip | velocity, fps: | 2910 | 2686 | 2473 | 2270 | 2077 |
| | energy, ft-lb: | 2820 | 2403 | 2037 | 1716 | 1436 |
| | arc, inches: | | +1.8 | 0 | -7.4 | -21.5 |
| Rem. 150 PSP Core-Lokt | velocity, fps: | 2910 | 2617 | 2342 | 2083 | 1843 |
| | energy, ft-lb: | 2820 | 2281 | 1827 | 1445 | 1131 |
| | arc, inches: | | +1.8 | 0 | -8.2 | -24.4 |
| Rem. 150 Bronze Point | velocity, fps: | 2910 | 2656 | 2416 | 2189 | 1974 |
| | energy, ft-lb: | 2820 | 2349 | 1944 | 1596 | 1298 |
| | arc, inches: | | +1.7 | 0 | -7.7 | -22.7 |
| Rem. 150 Nosler Bal. Tip | velocity, fps: | 2910 | 2696 | 2492 | 2298 | 2112. |
| | energy, ft-lb: | 2821 | 2422 | 2070 | 1769 | 1485 |
| | arc, inches: | | +1.6 | 0 | -7.3 | -21.1 |
| Rem. 150 Swift Scirocco | velocity, fps: | 2910 | 2696 | 2492 | 2298 | 2111 |
| | energy, ft-lb: | 2820 | 2421 | 2069 | 1758 | 1485 |
| | arc, inches: | | +1.6 | 0 | -7.3 | -21.1 |
| Rem. 165 AccuTip | velocity, fps: | 2800 | 2597 | 2403 | 2217 | 2039 |
| | energy, ft-lb: | 2872 | 2470 | 2115 | 1800 | 1523 |
| | arc, inches: | | +1.8 | 0 | -7.9 | -22.8 |
| Rem. 165 PSP Core-Lokt | velocity, fps: | 2800 | 2534 | 2283 | 2047 | 1825. |
| | energy, ft-lb: | 2872 | 2352 | 1909 | 1534 | 1220 |
| | arc, inches: | | +2.0 | 0 | -8.7 | -25.9 |
| Rem. 165 PSP boat-tail | velocity, fps: | 2800 | 2592 | 2394 | 2204 | 2023 |
| | energy, ft-lb: | 2872 | 2462 | 2100 | 1780 | 1500 |
| | arc, inches: | | +1.8 | 0 | -7.9 | -23.0 |
| Rem. 165 Nosler Bal. Tip | velocity, fps: | 2800 | 2609 | 2426 | 2249 | 2080. |
| | energy, ft-lb: | 2873 | 2494 | 2155 | 1854 | 1588 |
| | arc, inches: | | +1.8 | 0 | -7.7 | -22.3 |
| Rem. 168 PSP C-L Ultra | velocity, fps: | 2800 | 2546 | 2306 | 2079 | 1866 |
| | energy, ft-lb: | 2924 | 2418 | 1984 | 1613 | 1299 |
| | arc, inches: | | +1.9 | 0 | -8.5 | -25.1 |
| Rem. 180 SP Core-Lokt | velocity, fps: | 2700 | 2348 | 2023 | 1727 | 1466 |
| | energy, ft-lb: | 2913 | 2203 | 1635 | 1192 | 859 |
| | arc, inches: | | +2.4 | 0 | -11.0 | -33.8 |
| Rem. 180 PSP Core-Lokt | velocity, fps: | 2700 | 2469 | 2250 | 2042 | 1846 |
| | energy, ft-lb: | 2913 | 2436 | 2023 | 1666 | 1362 |
| | arc, inches: | | +2.1 | 0 | -9.0 | -26.3 |
| Rem. 180 PSP C-L Ultra | velocity, fps: | 2700 | 2480 | 2270 | 2070 | 1882 |
| | energy, ft-lb: | 2913 | 2457 | 2059 | 1713 | 1415 |
| | arc, inches: | | +2.1 | 0 | -8.9 | -25.8 |
| Rem. 180 Bronze Point | velocity, fps: | 2700 | 2485 | 2280 | 2084 | 1899. |
| | energy, ft-lb: | 2913 | 2468 | 2077 | 1736 | 1441 |
| | arc, inches: | | +2.1 | 0 | -8.8 | -25.5 |

| cartridge bullet | range, yards: | 0 | 100 | 200 | 300 | 400 |
|---|---|---|---|---|---|---|
| Rem. 180 Swift A-Frame | velocity, fps: | 2700 | 2465 | 2243 | 2032 | 1833 |
| | energy, ft-lb: | 2913 | 2429 | 2010 | 1650 | 1343 |
| | arc, inches: | | +2.1 | 0 | -9.1 | -26.6 |
| Rem. 180 Nosler Partition | velocity, fps: | 2700 | 2512 | 2332 | 2160 | 1995 |
| | energy, ft-lb: | 2913 | 2522 | 2174 | 1864 | 1590 |
| | arc, inches: | | +2.0 | 0 | -8.4 | -24.3 |
| Rem. 220 SP Core-Lokt | velocity, fps: | 2410 | 2130 | 1870 | 1632 | 1422 |
| | energy, ft-lb: | 2837 | 2216 | 1708 | 1301 | 988 |
| | arc, inches, s: | | 0 | -6.2 | -22.4 | |
| Speer 150 Grand Slam | velocity, fps: | 2975 | 2669 | 2383 | 2114 | |
| | energy, ft-lb: | 2947 | 2372 | 1891 | 1489 | |
| | arc, inches: | | +2.0 | 0 | -8.1 | -24.1 |
| Speer 165 Grand Slam | velocity, fps: | 2790 | 2560 | 2342 | 2134 | |
| | energy, ft-lb: | 2851 | 2401 | 2009 | 1669 | |
| | arc, inches: | | +1.9 | 0 | -8.3 | -24.1 |
| Speer 180 Grand Slam | velocity, fps: | 2690 | 2487 | 2293 | 2108 | |
| | energy, ft-lb: | 2892 | 2472 | 2101 | 1775 | |
| | arc, inches: | | +2.1 | 0 | -8.8 | -25.1 |
| Win. 125 Pointed Soft Point | velocity, fps: | 3140 | 2780 | 2447 | 2138 | 1853 |
| | energy, ft-lb: | 2736 | 2145 | 1662 | 1269 | 953 |
| | arc, inches: | | +1.8 | 0 | -7.7 | -23.0 |
| Win. 150 Power-Point | velocity, fps: | 2920 | 2580 | 2265 | 1972 | 1704 |
| | energy, ft-lb: | 2839 | 2217 | 1708 | 1295 | 967 |
| | arc, inches: | | +2.2 | 0 | -9.0 | -27.0 |
| Win. 150 Power-Point Plus | velocity, fps: | 3050 | 2685 | 2352 | 2043 | 1760 |
| | energy, ft-lb: | 3089 | 2402 | 1843 | 1391 | 1032 |
| | arc, inches: | | +1.7 | 0 | -8.0 | -24.3 |
| Win. 150 Silvertip | velocity, fps: | 2910 | 2617 | 2342 | 2083 | 1843 |
| | energy, ft-lb: | 2820 | 2281 | 1827 | 1445 | 1131 |
| | arc, inches: | | +2.1 | 0 | -8.5 | -25.0 |
| Win. 150 Partition Gold | velocity, fps: | 2960 | 2705 | 2464 | 2235 | 2019 |
| | energy, ft-lb: | 2919 | 2437 | 2022 | 1664 | 1358. |
| | arc, inches: | | +1.6 | 0 | -7.4 | -21.7 |
| Win. 150 Ballistic Silvertip | velocity, fps: | 2900 | 2687 | 2483 | 2289 | 2103 |
| | energy, ft-lb: | 2801 | 2404 | 2054 | 1745 | 1473 |
| | arc, inches: | | +1.7 | 0 | -7.3 | -21.2 |
| Win. 150 Fail Safe | velocity, fps: | 2920 | 2625 | 2349 | 2089 | 1848 |
| | energy, ft-lb: | 2841 | 2296 | 1838 | 1455 | 1137 |
| | arc, inches: | | +1.8 | 0 | -8.1 | -24.3 |
| Win. 165 Pointed Soft Point | velocity, fps: | 2800 | 2573 | 2357 | 2151 | 1956 |
| | energy, ft-lb: | 2873 | 2426 | 2036 | 1696 | 1402 |
| | arc, inches: | | +2.2 | 0 | -8.4 | -24.4 |
| Win. 165 Fail Safe | velocity, fps: | 2800 | 2540 | 2295 | 2063 | 1846 |
| | energy, ft-lb: | 2873 | 2365 | 1930 | 1560 | 1249 |
| | arc, inches: | | +2.0 | 0 | -8.6 | -25.3 |
| Win. 168 Ballistic Silvertip | velocity, fps: | 2790 | 2599 | 2416 | 2240 | 2072 |
| | energy, ft-lb: | 2903 | 2520 | 2177 | 1872 | 1601 |
| | arc, inches: | | +1.8 | 0 | -7.8 | -22.5 |
| Win. 180 Ballistic Silvertip | velocity, fps: | 2750 | 2572 | 2402 | 2237 | 2080 |
| | energy, ft-lb: | 3022 | 2644 | 2305 | 2001 | 1728 |
| | arc, inches: | | +1.9 | 0 | -7.9 | -22.8 |
| Win. 180 Power-Point | velocity, fps: | 2700 | 2348 | 2023 | 1727 | 1466 |
| | energy, ft-lb: | 2913 | 2203 | 1635 | 1192 | 859 |
| | arc, inches: | | +2.7 | 0 | -11.3 | -34.4 |
| Win. 180 Power-Point Plus | velocity, fps: | 2770 | 2563 | 2366 | 2177 | 1997 |
| | energy, ft-lb: | 3068 | 2627 | 2237 | 1894 | 1594 |
| | arc, inches: | | +1.9 | 0 | -8.1 | -23.6 |
| Win. 180 Silvertip | velocity, fps: | 2700 | 2469 | 2250 | 2042 | 1846 |
| | energy, ft-lb: | 2913 | 2436 | 2023 | 1666 | 1362 |
| | arc, inches: | | +2.4 | 0 | -9.3 | -27.0 |
| Win. 180 AccuBond | velocity, fps: | 2750 | 2573 | 2403 | 2239 | 2082 |
| | energy, ft-lb: | 3022 | 2646 | 2308 | 2004 | 1732 |
| | arc, inches: | | +1.9 | 0 | -7.9 | -22.8 |

**BALLISTICS**

# Centerfire Rifle Ballistics

## .30-06 SPRINGFIELD TO .300 WINCHESTER MAGNUM

| cartridge bullet | range, yards: | 0 | 100 | 200 | 300 | 400 | cartridge bullet | range, yards: | 0 | 100 | 200 | 300 | 400 |
|---|---|---|---|---|---|---|---|---|---|---|---|---|---|
| Win. 180 Partition Gold | velocity, fps: | 2790 | 2581 | 2382 | 2192 | 2010 | Federal 180 Tr. Bonded HE | velocity, fps: | 3100 | 2830 | 2580 | 2340 | 2110 |
| | energy, ft-lb: | 3112 | 2664 | 2269 | 1920 | 1615 | | energy, ft-lb: | 3840 | 3205 | 2660 | 2190 | 1790 |
| | arc, inches: | | +1.9 | 0 | -8.0 | -23.2 | | arc, inches: | | +1.4 | 0 | -6.6 | -19.7 |
| Win. 180 Fail Safe | velocity, fps: | 2700 | 2486 | 2283 | 2089 | 1904 | Federal 180 Nosler Partition | velocity, fps: | 2960 | 2700 | 2450 | 2210 | 1990 |
| | energy, ft-lb: | 2914 | 2472 | 2083 | 1744 | 1450 | | energy, ft-lb: | 3500 | 2905 | 2395 | 1955 | 1585 |
| | arc, inches: | | +2.1 | 0 | -8.7 | -25.5 | | arc, inches: | | +1.6 | 0 | -7.5 | -22.1 |
| Win. 150 Supreme Elite XP3 | velocity, fps: | 2925 | 2712 | 2508 | 2313 | 2127 | Federal 190 Sierra MatchKg. | velocity, fps: | 2900 | 2730 | 2560 | 2400 | 2240 |
| | energy, ft-lb: | 2849 | 2448 | 2095 | 1782 | 1507 | BTHP | energy, ft-lb: | 3550 | 3135 | 2760 | 2420 | 2115 |
| | arc, inches: | | +1.6 | 0 | -7.2 | -20.8 | | arc, inches: | | +12.9 | +22.5 | +26.9 | +25.1 |
| Win. 180 Supreme Elite XP3 | velocity, fps: | 2750 | 2579 | 2414 | 2256 | 2103 | Federal 200 Sierra GameKing | velocity, fps: | 2830 | 2680 | 2530 | 2380 | 2240 |
| | energy, ft-lb: | 3022 | 2658 | 2330 | 2034 | 1768 | BTSP | energy, ft-lb: | 3560 | 3180 | 2830 | 2520 | 2230 |
| | arc, inches: | | +1.9 | 0 | -7.8 | -22.5 | | arc, inches: | | +1.7 | 0 | -7.1 | -20.4 |

## .300 H&H Magnum

| cartridge bullet | range, yards: | 0 | 100 | 200 | 300 | 400 | cartridge bullet | range, yards: | 0 | 100 | 200 | 300 | 400 |
|---|---|---|---|---|---|---|---|---|---|---|---|---|---|
| Federal 180 Nosler Partition | velocity, fps: | 2880 | 2620 | 2380 | 2150 | 1930 | Federal 200 Nosler Part. HE | velocity, fps: | 2930 | 2740 | 2550 | 2370 | 2200 |
| | energy, ft-lb: | 3315 | 2750 | 2260 | 1840 | 1480 | | energy, ft-lb: | 3810 | 3325 | 2885 | 2495 | 2145 |
| | arc, inches: | | +1.8 | 0 | -8.0 | -23.4 | | arc, inches: | | +1.6 | 0 | -6.9 | -20.1 |
| Win. 180 Fail Safe | velocity, fps: | 2880 | 2628 | 2390 | 2165 | 1952 | Federal 200 Trophy Bonded | velocity, fps: | 2800 | 2570 | 2350 | 2150 | 1950 |
| | energy, ft-lb: | 3316 | 2762 | 2284 | 1873 | 1523 | | energy, ft-lb: | 3480 | 2935 | 2460 | 2050 | 1690 |
| | arc, inches: | | +1.8 | 0 | -7.9 | -23.2 | | arc, inches: | | +1.9 | 0 | -8.2 | -23.9 |

## .308 Norma Magnum

| cartridge bullet | range, yards: | 0 | 100 | 200 | 300 | 400 | cartridge bullet | range, yards: | 0 | 100 | 200 | 300 | 400 |
|---|---|---|---|---|---|---|---|---|---|---|---|---|---|
| Norma 180 TXP Swift A-Fr. | velocity, fps: | 2953 | 2704 | 2469 | 2245 | | Hornady 150 SP boat-tail | velocity, fps: | 3275 | 2988 | 2718 | 2464 | 2224 |
| | energy, ft-lb: | 3486 | 2924 | 2437 | 2016 | | | energy, ft-lb: | 3573 | 2974 | 2461 | 2023 | 1648 |
| | arc, inches: | | +1.6 | 0 | -7.3 | | | arc, inches: | | +1.2 | 0 | -6.0 | -17.8 |
| Norma 180 Oryx | velocity, fps: | 2953 | 2630 | 2330 | 2049 | | Hornady 150 SST | velocity, fps: | 3275 | 3027 | 2791 | 2565 | 2352 |
| | energy, ft-lb: | 3486 | 2766 | 2170 | 1679 | | (and Interbond) | energy, ft-lb: | 3572 | 3052 | 2593 | 2192 | 1842 |
| | arc, inches: | | +1.8 | 0 | -8.2 | | | arc, inches: | | +1.2 | 0 | -5.8 | -17.0 |
| Norma 200 Vulkan | velocity, fps: | 2903 | 2624 | 2361 | 2114 | | Hornady 165 SP boat-tail | velocity, fps: | 3100 | 2877 | 2665 | 2462 | 2269. |
| | energy, ft-lb: | 3744 | 3058 | 2476 | 1985 | | | energy, ft-lb: | 3522 | 3033 | 2603 | 2221 | 1887 |
| | arc, inches: | 0 | +1.8 | 0 | -8.0 | | | arc, inches: | | +1.3 | 0 | -6.5 | -18.5 |

## .300 Winchester Magnum

| cartridge bullet | range, yards: | 0 | 100 | 200 | 300 | 400 | cartridge bullet | range, yards: | 0 | 100 | 200 | 300 | 400 |
|---|---|---|---|---|---|---|---|---|---|---|---|---|---|
| A-Square 180 Dead Tough | velocity, fps: | 3120 | 2756 | 2420 | 2108 | 1820 | Hornady 165 SST | velocity, fps: | 3100 | 2885 | 2680 | 2483 | 2296 |
| | energy, ft-lb: | 3890 | 3035 | 2340 | 1776 | 1324 | | energy, ft-lb: | 3520 | 3049 | 2630 | 2259 | 1930 |
| | arc, inches: | | +1.6 | 0 | -7.6 | -22.9 | | arc, inches: | | +1.4 | 0 | -6.4 | -18.6 |
| Black Hills 180 Nos. Bal. Tip | velocity, fps: | 3100 | | | | | Hornady 180 SP boat-tail | velocity, fps: | 2960 | 2745 | 2540 | 2344 | 2157 |
| | energy, ft-lb: | 3498 | | | | | | energy, ft-lb: | 3501 | 3011 | 2578 | 2196 | 1859 |
| | arc, inches: | | | | | | | arc, inches: | | +1.9 | 0 | -7.3 | -20.9 |
| Black Hills 180 Barnes X | velocity, fps: | 2950 | | | | | Hornady 180 SST | velocity, fps: | 2960 | 2764 | 2575 | 2395 | 2222 |
| | energy, ft-lb: | 3498 | | | | | | energy, ft-lb: | 3501 | 3052 | 2650 | 2292 | 1974 |
| | arc, inches: | | | | | | | arc, inches: | | +1.6 | 0 | -7.0 | -20.1. |
| Black Hills 180 AccuBond | velocity, fps: | 3000 | | | | | Hornady 180 SPBT HM | velocity, fps: | 3100 | 2879 | 2668 | 2467 | 2275 |
| | energy, ft-lb: | 3597 | | | | | | energy, ft-lb: | 3840 | 3313 | 2845 | 2431 | 2068 |
| | arc, inches: | | | | | | | arc, inches: | | +1.4 | 0 | -6.4 | -18.7 |
| Black Hills 190 Match | velocity, fps: | 2950 | | | | | Hornady 190 SP boat-tail | velocity, fps: | 2900 | 2711 | 2529 | 2355 | 2187 |
| | energy, ft-lb: | 3672 | | | | | | energy, ft-lb: | 3549 | 3101 | 2699 | 2340 | 2018 |
| | arc, inches: | | | | | | | arc, inches: | | +1.6 | 0 | -7.1 | -20.4 |
| Federal 150 Sierra Pro Hunt. | velocity, fps: | 3280 | 3030 | 2800 | 2570 | 2360. | Norma 150 Nosler Bal. Tip | velocity, fps: | 3250 | 3014 | 2791 | 2578 | |
| | energy, ft-lb: | 3570 | 3055 | 2600 | 2205 | 1860 | | energy, ft-lb: | 3519 | 3027 | 2595 | 2215 | |
| | arc, inches: | | +1.1 | 0 | -5.6 | -16.4 | | arc, inches: | | +1.1 | 0 | -5.6 | |
| Federal 150 Trophy Bonded | velocity, fps: | 3280 | 2980 | 2700 | 2430 | 2190 | Norma 150 Barnes TS | velocity, fps: | 3215 | 2982 | 2761 | 2550 | |
| | energy, ft-lb: | 3570 | 2450 | 2420 | 1970 | 1590 | | energy, ft-lb: | 3444 | 2962 | 2539 | 2167 | |
| | arc, inches: | | +1.2 | 0 | -6.0 | -17.9 | | arc, inches: | | +1.2 | 0 | -5.8 | |
| Federal 180 Sierra Pro Hunt. | velocity, fps: | 2960 | 2750 | 2540 | 2340 | 2160 | Norma 165 Scirocco | velocity, fps: | 3117 | 2921 | 2734 | 2554 | |
| | energy, ft-lb: | 3500 | 3010 | 2580 | 2195 | 1860 | | energy, ft-lb: | 3561 | 3127 | 2738 | 2390 | |
| | arc, inches: | | +1.6 | 0 | -7.0 | -20.3 | | arc, inches: | | +1.2 | 0 | -5.9 | |
| Federal 180 Barnes XLC | velocity, fps: | 2960 | 2780 | 2600 | 2430 | 2260 | Norma 180 Soft Point | velocity, fps: | 3018 | 2780 | 2555 | 2341 | |
| | energy, ft-lb: | 3500 | 3080 | 2700 | 2355 | 2050 | | energy, ft-lb: | 3641 | 3091 | 2610 | 2190 | |
| | arc, inches: | | +1.5 | 0 | -6.6 | -19.2 | | arc, inches: | | +1.5 | 0 | -7.0 | |
| Federal 180 Trophy Bonded | velocity, fps: | 2960 | 2700 | 2460 | 2220 | 2000 | Norma 180 Plastic Point | velocity, fps: | 3018 | 2755 | 2506 | 2271 | |
| | energy, ft-lb: | 3500 | 2915 | 2410 | 1975 | 1605 | | energy, ft-lb: | 3641 | 3034 | 2512 | 2062 | |
| | arc, inches: | | +1.6 | 0 | -7.4 | -21.9 | | arc, inches: | | +1.6 | 0 | -7.1 | |
| | | | | | | | Norma 180 TXP Swift A-Fr. | velocity, fps: | 2920 | 2688 | 2467 | 2256 | |
| | | | | | | | | energy, ft-lb: | 3409 | 2888 | 2432 | 2035 | |
| | | | | | | | | arc, inches: | | +1.7 | 0 | -7.4 | |
| | | | | | | | Norma 180 AccuBond | velocity, fps: | 2953 | 2767 | 2588 | 2417 | |
| | | | | | | | | energy, ft-lb: | 3486 | 3061 | 2678 | 2335 | |
| | | | | | | | | arc, inches: | | +1.5 | 0 | -6.7 | |

BALLISTICS

# Centerfire Rifle Ballistics
## .300 WINCHESTER MAGNUM TO .300 WINCHESTER SHORT MAGNUM

| cartridge bullet | range, yards: | 0 | 100 | 200 | 300 | 400 |
|---|---|---|---|---|---|---|
| Norma 180 Oryx | velocity, fps: | 2920 | 2600 | 2301 | 2023 | |
| | energy, ft-lb: | 3409 | 2702 | 2117 | 1636 | |
| | arc, inches: | | +1.8 | 0 | -8.4 | |
| Norma 200 Vulkan | velocity, fps: | 2887 | 2609 | 2347 | 2100 | |
| | energy, ft-lb: | 3702 | 3023 | 2447 | 1960 | |
| | arc, inches: | | +1.8 | 0 | -8.2 | |
| Norma 200 Oryx | velocity, fps: | 2789 | 2510 | 2248 | 2002 | |
| | energy, ft-lb: | 3455 | 2799 | 2245 | 1780 | |
| | arc, inches: | | +2.0 | 0 | -8.9 | |
| PMC 150 Barnes X | velocity, fps: | 3135 | 2918 | 2712 | 2515 | 2327 |
| | energy, ft-lb: | 3273 | 2836 | 2449 | 2107 | 1803 |
| | arc, inches: | | +1.3 | 0 | -6.1 | -17.7 |
| PMC 150 Pointed Soft Point | velocity, fps: | 3150 | 2902 | 2665 | 2438 | 2222 |
| | energy, ft-lb: | 3304 | 2804 | 2364 | 1979 | 1644. |
| | arc, inches: | | +1.3 | 0 | -6.2 | -18.3 |
| PMC 150 SP boat-tail | velocity, fps: | 3250 | 2987 | 2739 | 2504 | 2281 |
| | energy, ft-lb: | 3517 | 2970 | 2498 | 2088 | 1733 |
| | arc, inches: | | +1.2 | 0 | -6.0 | -17.4 |
| PMC 180 Barnes X | velocity, fps: | 2910 | 2738 | 2572 | 2412 | 2258 |
| | energy, ft-lb: | 3384 | 2995 | 2644 | 2325 | 2037 |
| | arc, inches: | | +1.6 | 0 | -6.9 | -19.8 |
| PMC 180 Pointed Soft Point | velocity, fps: | 2853 | 2643 | 2446 | 2258 | 2077 |
| | energy, ft-lb: | 3252 | 2792 | 2391 | 2037 | 1724 |
| | arc, inches: | | +1.7 | 0 | -7.5 | -21.9 |
| PMC 180 SP boat-tail | velocity, fps: | 2900 | 2714 | 2536 | 2365 | 2200 |
| | energy, ft-lb: | 3361 | 2944 | 2571 | 2235 | 1935 |
| | arc, inches: | | +1.6 | 0 | -7.1 | -20.3 |
| PMC 180 HPBT Match | velocity, fps: | 2950 | 2755 | 2568 | 2390 | 2219 |
| | energy, ft-lb: | 3478 | 3033 | 2636 | 2283 | 1968 |
| | arc, inches: | | +1.5 | 0 | -6.8 | -19.7 |
| Rem. 150 PSP Core-Lokt | velocity, fps: | 3290 | 2951 | 2636 | 2342 | 2068 |
| | energy, ft-lb: | 3605 | 2900 | 2314 | 1827 | 1859 |
| | arc, inches: | | +1.6 | 0 | -7.0 | -20.2 |
| Rem. 150 PSP C-L MR | velocity, fps: | 2650 | 2373 | 2113 | 1870 | 1646 |
| | energy, ft-lb: | 2339 | 1875 | 1486 | 1164 | 902 |
| | arc, inches: | | +1.0 | -2.7 | -14.3 | -35.8 |
| Rem. 150 PSP C-L Ultra | velocity, fps: | 3290 | 2967 | 2666 | 2384 | 2120 |
| | energy, ft-lb: | 3065 | 2931 | 2366 | 1893 | 1496 |
| | arc, inches: | | +1.2 | 0 | -6.1 | -18.4 |
| Rem. 180 AccuTip | velocity, fps: | 2960 | 2764 | 2577 | 2397 | 2224 |
| | energy, ft-lb: | 3501 | 3053 | 2653 | 2295 | 1976 |
| | arc, inches: | | +1.5 | 0 | -6.8 | -19.6 |
| Rem. 180 PSP Core-Lokt | velocity, fps: | 2960 | 2745 | 2540 | 2344 | 2157 |
| | energy, ft-lb: | 3501 | 3011 | 2578 | 2196 | 1424 |
| | arc, inches: | | +2.2 | +1.9 | -3.4 | -15.0 |
| Rem. 180 PSP C-L Ultra | velocity, fps: | 2960 | 2727 | 2505 | 2294 | 2093 |
| | energy, ft-lb: | 3501 | 2971 | 2508 | 2103 | 1751 |
| | arc, inches: | | +2.7 | +2.2 | -3.8 | -16.4 |
| Rem. 180 Nosler Partition | velocity, fps: | 2960 | 2725 | 2503 | 2291 | 2089 |
| | energy, ft-lb: | 3501 | 2968 | 2503 | 2087 | 1744 |
| | arc, inches: | | +1.6 | 0 | -7.2 | -20.9 |
| Rem. 180 Nosler Bal. Tip | velocity, fps: | 2960 | 2774 | 2595 | 2424 | 2259. |
| | energy, ft-lb: | 3501 | 3075 | 2692 | 2348 | 2039 |
| | arc, inches: | | +1.5 | 0 | -6.7 | -19.3 |
| Rem. 180 Swift Scirocco | velocity, fps: | 2960 | 2774 | 2595 | 2424 | 2259 |
| | energy, ft-lb: | 3501 | 3075 | 2692 | 2348 | 2039 |
| | arc, inches: | | +1.5 | 0 | -6.7 | -19.3 |
| Rem. 190 PSP boat-tail | velocity, fps: | 2885 | 2691 | 2506 | 2327 | 2156 |
| | energy, ft-lb: | 3511 | 3055 | 2648 | 2285 | 1961 |
| | arc, inches: | | +1.6 | 0 | -7.2 | -20.8 |
| Rem. 190 HPBT Match | velocity, fps: | 2900 | 2725 | 2557 | 2395 | 2239 |
| | energy, ft-lb: | 3547 | 3133 | 2758 | 2420 | 2115 |
| | arc, inches: | | +1.6 | 0 | -6.9 | -19.9 |

| cartridge bullet | range, yards: | 0 | 100 | 200 | 300 | 400 |
|---|---|---|---|---|---|---|
| Rem. 200 Swift A-Frame | velocity, fps: | 2825 | 2595 | 2376 | 2167 | 1970 |
| | energy, ft-lb: | 3544 | 2989 | 2506 | 2086 | 1722 |
| | arc, inches: | | +1.8 | 0 | -8.0 | -23.5 |
| Speer 180 Grand Slam | velocity, fps: | 2950 | 2735 | 2530 | 2334 | |
| | energy, ft-lb: | 3478 | 2989 | 2558 | 2176 | |
| | arc, inches: | | +1.6 | 0 | -7.0 | -20.5 |
| Speer 200 Grand Slam | velocity, fps: | 2800 | 2597 | 2404 | 2218 | |
| | energy, ft-lb: | 3481 | 2996 | 2565 | 2185 | |
| | arc, inches: | | +1.8 | 0 | -7.9 | -22.9 |
| Win. 150 Power-Point | velocity, fps: | 3290 | 2951 | 2636 | 2342 | 2068. |
| | energy, ft-lb: | 3605 | 2900 | 2314 | 1827 | 1424 |
| | arc, inches: | | +2.6 | +2.1 | -3.5 | -15.4 |
| Win. 150 Fail Safe | velocity, fps: | 3260 | 2943 | 2647 | 2370 | 2110 |
| | energy, ft-lb: | 3539 | 2884 | 2334 | 1871 | 1483 |
| | arc, inches: | | +1.3 | 0 | -6.2 | -18.7 |
| Win. 165 Fail Safe | velocity, fps: | 3120 | 2807 | 2515 | 2242 | 1985 |
| | energy, ft-lb: | 3567 | 2888 | 2319 | 1842 | 1445 |
| | arc, inches: | | +1.5 | 0 | -7.0 | -20.0 |
| Win. 180 Power-Point | velocity, fps: | 2960 | 2745 | 2540 | 2344 | 2157 |
| | energy, ft-lb: | 3501 | 3011 | 2578 | 2196 | 1859 |
| | arc, inches: | | +1.9 | 0 | -7.3 | -20.9 |
| Win. 180 Power-Point Plus | velocity, fps: | 3070 | 2846 | 2633 | 2430 | 2236 |
| | energy, ft-lb: | 3768 | 3239 | 2772 | 2361 | 1999 |
| | arc, inches: | | +1.4 | 0 | -6.4 | -18.7 |
| Win. 180 Ballistic Silvertip | velocity, fps: | 2950 | 2764 | 2586 | 2415 | 2250 |
| | energy, ft-lb: | 3478 | 3054 | 2673 | 2331 | 2023 |
| | arc, inches: | | +1.5 | 0 | -6.7 | -19.4 |
| Win. 180 AccuBond | velocity, fps: | 2950 | 2765 | 2588 | 2417 | 2253 |
| | energy, ft-lb: | 3478 | 3055 | 2676 | 2334 | 2028 |
| | arc, inches: | | +1.5 | 0 | -6.7 | -19.4 |
| Win. 180 Fail Safe | velocity, fps: | 2960 | 2732 | 2514 | 2307 | 2110 |
| | energy, ft-lb: | 3503 | 2983 | 2528 | 2129 | 1780 |
| | arc, inches: | | +1.6 | 0 | -7.1 | -20.7 |
| Win. 180 Partition Gold | velocity, fps: | 3070 | 2859 | 2657 | 2464 | 2280 |
| | energy, ft-lb: | 3768 | 3267 | 2823 | 2428 | 2078 |
| | arc, inches: | | +1.4 | 0 | -6.3 | -18.3 |
| Win. 150 Supreme Elite XP3 | velocity, fps: | 3260 | 3030 | 2811 | 2603 | 2404 |
| | energy, ft-lb: | 3539 | 3057 | 2632 | 2256 | 1925 |
| | arc, inches: | | +1.1 | 0 | -5.6 | -16.2 |
| Win. 180 Supreme Elite XP3 | velocity, fps: | 3000 | 2819 | 2646 | 2479 | 2318 |
| | energy, ft-lb: | 3597 | 3176 | 2797 | 2455 | 2147 |
| | arc, inches: | | +1.4 | 0 | -6.4 | -18.5 |

## .300 Remington Short Ultra Magnum

| cartridge bullet | range, yards: | 0 | 100 | 200 | 300 | 400 |
|---|---|---|---|---|---|---|
| Rem. 150 PSP C-L Ultra | velocity, fps: | 3200 | 2901 | 2672 | 2359 | 2112 |
| | energy, ft-lb: | 3410 | 2803 | 2290 | 1854 | 1485 |
| | arc, inches: | | +1.3 | 0 | -6.4 | -19.l |
| Rem. 165 PSP Core-Lokt | velocity, fps: | 3075 | 2792 | 2527 | 2276 | 2040 |
| | energy, ft-lb: | 3464 | 2856 | 2339 | 1828 | 1525 |
| | arc, inches: | | +1.5 | 0 | -7.0 | -20.7 |
| Rem. 180 Partition | velocity, fps: | 2960 | 2761 | 2571 | 2389 | 2214 |
| | energy, ft-lb: | 3501 | 3047 | 2642 | 2280 | 1959 |
| | arc, inches: | | +1.5 | 0 | -6.8 | -19.7 |
| Rem. 180 PSP C-L Ultra | velocity, fps: | 2960 | 2727 | 2506 | 2295 | 2094 |
| | energy, ft-lb: | 3501 | 2972 | 2509 | 2105 | 1753 |
| | arc, inches: | | +1.6 | 0 | -7.1 | -20.9 |
| Rem. 190 HPBT Match | velocity, fps: | 2900 | 2725 | 2557 | 2395 | 2239 |
| | energy, ft-lb: | 3547 | 3133 | 2758 | 2420 | 2115 |
| | arc, inches: | | +1.6 | 0 | -6.9 | -19.9 |

## .300 Winchester Short Magnum

| cartridge bullet | range, yards: | 0 | 100 | 200 | 300 | 400 |
|---|---|---|---|---|---|---|
| Black Hills 175 Sierra MKing | velocity, fps: | 2950 | | | | |
| | energy, ft-lb: | 3381 | | | | |
| | arc, inches: | | | | | |

# Centerfire Rifle Ballistics

## .300 WINCHESTER SHORT MAGNUM TO .300 WEATHERBY MAGNUM

| cartridge bullet | range, yards: | 0 | 100 | 200 | 300 | 400 |
|---|---|---|---|---|---|---|
| Black Hills 180 AccuBond | velocity, fps: | 2950 | | | | |
| | energy, ft-lb: | 3478 | | | | |
| | arc, inches: | | | | | |
| Federal 150 Nosler Bal. Tip | velocity, fps: | 3200 | 2970 | 2755 | 2545 | 2345 |
| | energy, ft-lb: | 3410 | 2940 | 2520 | 2155 | 1830. |
| | arc, inches: | | +1.2 | 0 | -5.8 | -17.0 |
| Federal 165 Nos. Partition | velocity, fps: | 3130 | 2890 | 2670 | 2450 | 2250 |
| | energy, ft-lb: | 3590 | 3065 | 2605 | 2205 | 1855. |
| | arc, inches: | | +1.3 | 0 | -6.2 | -18.2 |
| Federal 165 Nos. Solid Base | velocity, fps: | 3130 | 2900 | 2690 | 2490 | 2290 |
| | energy, ft-lb: | 3590 | 3090 | 2650 | 2265 | 1920 |
| | arc, inches: | | +1.3 | 0 | -6.1 | -17.8 |
| Federal 180 Barnes TS | velocity, fps: | 2980 | 2780 | 2580 | 2400 | 2220 |
| And Nos. Solid Base | energy, ft-lbs: | 3550 | 3085 | 2670 | 2300 | 1970 |
| | arc, inches: | | +1.5 | 0 | -6.7 | -19.5 |
| Federal 180 Grand Slam | velocity, fps: | 2970 | 2740 | 2530 | 2320 | 2130 |
| | energy, ft-lb: | 3525 | 3010 | 2555 | 2155 | 1810 |
| | arc, inches: | | +1.5 | 0 | -7.0 | -20.5 |
| Federal 180 Trophy Bonded | velocity, fps: | 2970 | 2730 | 2500 | 2280 | 2080 |
| | energy, ft-lb: | 3525 | 2975 | 2500 | 2085 | 1725 |
| | arc, inches: | | +1.5 | 0 | -7.2 | -21.0 |
| Federal 180 Nosler Partition | velocity, fps: | 2975 | 2750 | 2535 | 2290 | 2126 |
| | energy, ft-lb: | 3540 | 3025 | 2570 | 2175 | 1825 |
| | arc, inches: | | +1.5 | 0 | -7.0 | -20.3 |
| Federal 180 Nos. AccuBond | velocity, fps: | 2960 | 2780 | 2610 | 2440 | 2280 |
| | energy, ft-lb: | 3500 | 3090 | 2715 | 2380 | 2075 |
| | arc, inches: | | +1.5 | 0 | -6.6 | -19.0 |
| Federal 180 Hi-Shok SP | velocity, fps: | 2970 | 2520 | 2115 | 1750 | 1430 |
| | energy, ft-lb: | 3525 | 2540 | 1785 | 1220 | 820 |
| | arc, inches: | | +2.2 | 0 | -9.9 | -31.4 |
| Norma 150 FMJ | velocity, fps: | 2953 | 2731 | 2519 | 2318 | |
| | energy, ft-lb: | | | | | |
| | arc, inches: | | +1.6 | 0 | -7.1 | |
| Norma 150 Barnes X TS | velocity, fps: | 3215 | 2982 | 2761 | 2550 | |
| | energy, ft-lb: | 3444 | 2962 | 2539 | 2167 | |
| | arc, inches: | | +1.2 | 0 | -5.7 | |
| Norma 180 Nosler Bal. Tip | velocity, fps: | 3215 | 2985 | 2767 | 2560 | |
| | energy, ft-lb: | 3437 | 2963 | 2547 | 2179 | |
| | arc, inches: | | +1.2 | 0 | -5.7 | |
| Norma 180 Oryx | velocity, fps: | 2936 | 2542 | 2180 | 1849 | |
| | energy, ft-lb: | 3446 | 2583 | 1900 | 1368 | |
| | arc, inches: | | +1.9 | 0 | -8.9 | |
| Win. 150 Power-Point | velocity, fps: | 3270 | 2903 | 2565 | 2250 | 1958 |
| | energy, ft-lb: | 3561 | 2807 | 2190 | 1686 | 1277 |
| | arc, inches: | | +1.3 | 0 | -6.6 | -20.2 |
| Win. 150 Ballistic Silvertip | velocity, fps: | 3300 | 3061 | 2834 | 2619 | 2414 |
| | energy, ft-lb: | 3628 | 3121 | 2676 | 2285 | 1941 |
| | arc, inches: | | +1.1 | 0 | -5.4 | -15.9 |
| Win. 165 Fail Safe | velocity, fps: | 3125 | 2846 | 2584 | 2336 | 2102 |
| | energy, ft-lb: | 3577 | 2967 | 2446 | 1999 | 1619 |
| | arc, inches: | | +1.4 | 0 | -6.6 | -19.6 |
| Win. 180 Ballistic Silvertip | velocity, fps: | 3010 | 2822 | 2641 | 2468 | 2301 |
| | energy, ft-lb: | 3621 | 3182 | 2788 | 2434 | 2116 |
| | arc, inches: | | +1.4 | 0 | -6.4 | -18.6 |
| Win. 180 AccuBond | velocity, fps: | 3010 | 2822 | 2643 | 2470 | 2304 |
| | energy, ft-lb: | 3622 | 3185 | 2792 | 2439 | 2121 |
| | arc, inches: | | +1.4 | 0 | -6.4 | -18.5 |
| Win. 180 Fail Safe | velocity, fps: | 2970 | 2741 | 2524 | 2317 | 2120 |
| | energy, ft-lb: | 3526 | 3005 | 2547 | 2147 | 1797 |
| | arc, inches: | | +1.6 | 0 | -7.0 | -20.5 |
| Win. 180 Power Point | velocity, fps: | 2970 | 2755 | 2549 | 2353 | 2166 |
| | energy, ft-lb: | 3526 | 3034 | 2598 | 2214 | 1875 |
| | arc, inches: | | +1.5 | 0 | -6.9 | -20.1 |

| cartridge bullet | range, yards: | 0 | 100 | 200 | 300 | 400 |
|---|---|---|---|---|---|---|
| Win. 150 Supreme Elite XP3 | velocity, fps: | 3300 | 3068 | 2847 | 2637 | 2437 |
| | energy, ft-lb: | 3626 | 3134 | 2699 | 2316 | 1978 |
| | arc, inches: | | +1.1 | 0 | -5.4 | -15.8 |
| Win. 180 Supreme Elite XP3 | velocity, fps: | 3010 | 2829 | 2655 | 2488 | 2326 |
| | energy, ft-lb: | 3621 | 3198 | 2817 | 2473 | 2162 |
| | arc, inches: | | +1.4 | 0 | -6.4 | -18.3 |

## .300 Weatherby Magnum

| cartridge bullet | range, yards: | 0 | 100 | 200 | 300 | 400 |
|---|---|---|---|---|---|---|
| A-Square 180 Dead Tough | velocity, fps: | 3180 | 2811 | 2471 | 2155 | 1863. |
| | energy, ft-lb: | 4041 | 3158 | 2440 | 1856 | 1387 |
| | arc, inches: | | +1.5 | 0 | -7.2 | -21.8 |
| A-Square 220 Monolythic Solid | velocity, fps: | 2700 | 2407 | 2133 | 1877 | 1653 |
| | energy, ft-lb: | 3561 | 2830 | 2223 | 1721 | 1334 |
| | arc, inches: | | +2.3 | 0 | -9.8 | -29.7 |
| Federal 180 Sierra GameKing BTSP | velocity, fps: | 3190 | 3010 | 2830 | 2660 | 2490 |
| | energy, ft-lb: | 4065 | 3610 | 3195 | 2820 | 2480 |
| | arc, inches: | | +1.2 | 0 | -5.6 | -16.0 |
| Federal 180 Trophy Bonded | velocity, fps: | 3190 | 2950 | 2720 | 2500 | 2290 |
| | energy, ft-lb: | 4065 | 3475 | 2955 | 2500 | 2105 |
| | arc, inches: | | +1.3 | 0 | -5.9 | -17.5 |
| Federal 180 Tr. Bonded HE | velocity, fps: | 3330 | 3080 | 2850 | 2750 | 2410 |
| | energy, ft-lb: | 4430 | 3795 | 3235 | 2750 | 2320 |
| | arc, inches: | | +1.1 | 0 | -5.4 | -15.8 |
| Federal 180 Nosler Partition | velocity, fps: | 3190 | 2980 | 2780 | 2590 | 2400 |
| | energy, ft-lb: | 4055 | 3540 | 3080 | 2670 | 2305 |
| | arc, inches: | | +1.2 | 0 | -5.7 | -16.7 |
| Federal 180 Nosler Part. HE | velocity, fps: | 3330 | 3110 | 2810 | 2710 | 2520 |
| | energy, ft-lb: | 4430 | 3875 | 3375 | 2935 | 2540 |
| | arc, inches: | | +1.0 | 0 | -5.2 | -15.1 |
| Federal 200 Trophy Bonded | velocity, fps: | 2900 | 2670 | 2440 | 2230 | 2030 |
| | energy, ft-lb: | 3735 | 3150 | 2645 | 2200 | 1820 |
| | arc, inches: | | +1.7 | 0 | -7.6 | -22.2 |
| Hornady 150 SST (or Interbond) | velocity, fps: | 3375 | 3123 | 2882 | 2652 | 2434 |
| | energy, ft-lb: | 3793 | 3248 | 2766 | 2343 | 1973 |
| | arc, inches: | | +1.0 | 0 | -5.4 | -15.8 |
| Hornady 180 SP | velocity, fps: | 3120 | 2891 | 2673 | 2466 | 2268. |
| | energy, ft-lb: | 3890 | 3340 | 2856 | 2430 | 2055 |
| | arc, inches: | | +1.3 | 0 | -6.2 | -18.1 |
| Hornady 180 SST | velocity, fps: | 3120 | 2911 | 2711 | 2519 | 2335 |
| | energy, ft-lb: | 3890 | 3386 | 2936 | 2535 | 2180 |
| | arc, inches: | | +1.3 | 0 | -6.2 | -18.1 |
| Rem. 180 PSP Core-Lokt | velocity, fps: | 3120 | 2866 | 2627 | 2400 | 2184 |
| | energy, ft-lb: | 3890 | 3284 | 2758 | 2301 | 1905 |
| | arc, inches: | | +2.4 | +2.0 | -3.4 | -14.9 |
| Rem. 190 PSP boat-tail | velocity, fps: | 3030 | 2830 | 2638 | 2455 | 2279 |
| | energy, ft-lb: | 3873 | 3378 | 2936 | 2542 | 2190. |
| | arc, inches: | | +1.4 | 0 | -6.4 | -18.6 |
| Rem. 200 Swift A-Frame | velocity, fps: | 2925 | 2690 | 2467 | 2254 | 2052 |
| | energy, ft-lb: | 3799 | 3213 | 2701 | 2256 | 1870 |
| | arc, inches: | | +2.8 | +2.3 | -3.9 | -17.0 |
| Speer 180 Grand Slam | velocity, fps: | 3185 | 2948 | 2722 | 2508 | |
| | energy, ft-lb: | 4054 | 3472 | 2962 | 2514 | |
| | arc, inches: | | +1.3 | 0 | -5.9 | -17.4 |
| Wby. 150 Pointed Expanding | velocity, fps: | 3540 | 3225 | 2932 | 2657 | 2399 |
| | energy, ft-lb: | 4173 | 3462 | 2862 | 2351 | 1916 |
| | arc, inches: | | +2.6 | +3.3 | 0 | -8.2 |
| Wby. 150 Nosler Partition | velocity, fps: | 3540 | 3263 | 3004 | 2759 | 2528 |
| | energy, ft-lb: | 4173 | 3547 | 3005 | 2536 | 2128 |
| | arc, inches: | | +2.5 | +3.2 | 0 | -7.7 |
| Wby. 165 Pointed Expanding | velocity, fps: | 3390 | 3123 | 2872 | 2634 | 2409 |
| | energy, ft-lb: | 4210 | 3573 | 3021 | 2542 | 2126 |
| | arc, inches: | | +2.8 | +3.5 | 0 | -8.5 |

BALLISTICS

# Centerfire Rifle Ballistics

## .300 WEATHERBY MAGNUM TO 7.7X58 JAPANESE ARISAKA

| cartridge bullet | range, yards: | 0 | 100 | 200 | 300 | 400 |
|---|---|---|---|---|---|---|
| Wby. 165 Nosler Bal. Tip | velocity, fps: | 3350 | 3133 | 2927 | 2730 | 2542 |
| | energy, ft-lb: | 4111 | 3596 | 3138 | 2730 | 2367 |
| | arc, inches: | | +2.7 | +3.4 | 0 | -8.1 |
| Wby. 180 Pointed Expanding | velocity, fps: | 3240 | 3004 | 2781 | 2569 | 2366 |
| | energy, ft-lb: | 4195 | 3607 | 3091 | 2637 | 2237 |
| | arc, inches: | | +3.1 | +3.8 | 0 | -9.0 |
| Wby. 180 Barnes X | velocity, fps: | 3190 | 2995 | 2809 | 2631 | 2459 |
| | energy, ft-lb: | 4067 | 3586 | 3154 | 2766 | 2417 |
| | arc, inches: | | +3.1 | +3.8 | 0 | -8.7 |
| Wby. 180 Bal. Tip | velocity, fps: | 3250 | 3051 | 2806 | 2676 | 2503 |
| | energy, ft-lb: | 4223 | 3721 | 3271 | 2867 | 2504 |
| | arc, inches: | | +2.8 | +3.6 | 0 | -8.4 |
| Wby. 180 Nosler Partition | velocity, fps: | 3240 | 3028 | 2826 | 2634 | 2449 |
| | energy, ft-lb: | 4195 | 3665 | 3193 | 2772 | 2396 |
| | arc, inches: | | +3.0 | +3.7 | 0 | -8.6 |
| Wby. 200 Nosler Partition | velocity, fps: | 3060 | 2860 | 2668 | 2485 | 2308 |
| | energy, ft-lb: | 4158 | 3631 | 3161 | 2741 | 2366 |
| | arc, inches: | | +3.5 | +4.2 | 0 | -9.8 |
| Wby. 220 RN Expanding | velocity, fps: | 2845 | 2543 | 2260 | 1996 | 1751. |
| | energy, ft-lb: | 3954 | 3158 | 2495 | 1946 | 1497 |
| | arc, inches: | | +4.9 | +5.9 | 0 | -14.6 |

## .300 Dakota

| cartridge bullet | range, yards: | 0 | 100 | 200 | 300 | 400 |
|---|---|---|---|---|---|---|
| Dakota 165 Barnes X | velocity, fps: | 3200 | 2979 | 2769 | 2569 | 2377 |
| | energy, ft-lb: | 3751 | 3251 | 2809 | 2417 | 2070 |
| | arc, inches: | | +2.1 | +1.8 | -3.0 | -13.2 |
| Dakota 200 Barnes X | velocity, fps: | 3000 | 2824 | 2656 | 2493 | 2336 |
| | energy, ft-lb: | 3996 | 3542 | 3131 | 2760 | 2423 |
| | arc, inches: | | +2.2 | +1.5 | -4.0 | -15.2 |

## .300 Pegasus

| cartridge bullet | range, yards: | 0 | 100 | 200 | 300 | 400 |
|---|---|---|---|---|---|---|
| A-Square 180 SP boat-tail | velocity, fps: | 3500 | 3319 | 3145 | 2978 | 2817 |
| | energy, ft-lb: | 4896 | 4401 | 3953 | 3544 | 3172 |
| | arc, inches: | | +2.3 | +2.9 | 0 | -6.8 |
| A-Square 180 Nosler Part. | velocity, fps: | 3500 | 3295 | 3100 | 2913 | 2734 |
| | energy, ft-lb: | 4896 | 4339 | 3840 | 3392 | 2988 |
| | arc, inches: | | +2.3 | +3.0 | 0 | -7.1 |
| A-Square 180 Dead Tough | velocity, fps: | 3500 | 3103 | 2740 | 2405 | 2095 |
| | energy, ft-lb: | 4896 | 3848 | 3001 | 2312 | 1753 |
| | arc, inches: | | +1.1 | 0 | -5.7 | -17.5 |

## .300 Remington Ultra Magnum

| cartridge bullet | range, yards: | 0 | 100 | 200 | 300 | 400 |
|---|---|---|---|---|---|---|
| Federal 180 Trophy Bonded | velocity, fps: | 3250 | 3000 | 2770 | 2550 | 2340 |
| | energy, ft-lb: | 4220 | 3605 | 3065 | 2590 | 2180 |
| | arc, inches: | | +1.2 | 0 | -5.7 | -16.8 |
| Rem. 150 Swift Scirocco | velocity, fps: | 3450 | 3208 | 2980 | 2762 | 2556 |
| | energy, ft-lb: | 3964 | 3427 | 2956 | 2541 | 2175 |
| | arc, inches: | | +1.7 | +1.5 | -2.6 | -11.2 |
| Rem. 180 Nosler Partition | velocity, fps: | 3250 | 3037 | 2834 | 2640 | 2454 |
| | energy, ft-lb: | 4221 | 3686 | 3201 | 2786 | 2407 |
| | arc, inches: | | +2.4 | +1.8 | -3.0 | -12.7 |
| Rem. 180 Swift Scirocco | velocity, fps: | 3250 | 3048 | 2856 | 2672 | 2495 |
| | energy, ft-lb: | 4221 | 3714 | 3260 | 2853 | 2487 |
| | arc, inches: | | +2.0 | +1.7 | -2.8 | -12.3 |
| Rem. 180 PSP Core-Lokt | velocity, fps: | 3250 | 2988 | 2742 | 2508 | 2287 |
| | energy, ft-lb: | 3517 | 2974 | 2503 | 2095 | 1741 |
| | arc, inches: | | +2.1 | +1.8 | -3.1 | -13.6 |
| Rem. 200 Nosler Partition | velocity, fps: | 3025 | 2826 | 2636 | 2454 | 2279 |
| | energy, ft-lb: | 4063 | 3547 | 3086 | 2673 | 2308 |
| | arc, inches: | | +2.4 | +2.0 | -3.4 | -14.6 |

## .30-378 Weatherby Magnum

| cartridge bullet | range, yards: | 0 | 100 | 200 | 300 | 400 |
|---|---|---|---|---|---|---|
| Wby. 165 Nosler Bal. Tip | velocity, fps: | 3500 | 3275 | 3062 | 2859 | 2665 |
| | energy, ft-lb: | 4488 | 3930 | 3435 | 2995 | 2603 |
| | arc, inches: | | +2.4 | +3.0 | 0 | -7.4 |

| cartridge bullet | range, yards: | 0 | 100 | 200 | 300 | 400 |
|---|---|---|---|---|---|---|
| Wby. 180 Nosler Bal. Tip | velocity, fps: | 3420 | 3213 | 3015 | 2826 | 2645 |
| | energy, ft-lb: | 4676 | 4126 | 3634 | 3193 | 2797 |
| | arc, inches: | | +2.5 | +3.1 | 0 | -7.5 |
| Wby. 180 Barnes X | velocity, fps: | 3450 | 3243 | 3046 | 2858 | 2678. |
| | energy, ft-lb: | 4757 | 4204 | 3709 | 3264 | 2865 |
| | arc, inches: | | +2.4 | +3.1 | 0 | -7.4 |
| Wby. 200 Nosler Partition | velocity, fps: | 3160 | 2955 | 2759 | 2572 | 2392. |
| | energy, ft-lb: | 4434 | 3877 | 3381 | 2938 | 2541 |
| | arc, inches: | | +3.2 | +3.9 | 0 | -9.1 |

## 7.82 (.308) Warbird

| cartridge bullet | range, yards: | 0 | 100 | 200 | 300 | 400 |
|---|---|---|---|---|---|---|
| Lazzeroni 150 Nosler Part. | velocity, fps: | 3680 | 3432 | 3197 | 2975 | 2764 |
| | energy, ft-lb: | 4512 | 3923 | 3406 | 2949 | 2546. |
| | arc, inches: | | +2.1 | +2.7 | 0 | -6.6 |
| Lazzeroni 180 Nosler Part. | velocity, fps: | 3425 | 3220 | 3026 | 2839 | 2661 |
| | energy, ft-lb: | 4689 | 4147 | 3661 | 3224 | 2831 |
| | arc, inches: | | +2.5 | +3.2 | 0 | -7.5 |
| Lazzeroni 200 Swift A-Fr. | velocity, fps: | 3290 | 3105 | 2928 | 2758 | 2594. |
| | energy, ft-lb: | 4808 | 4283 | 3808 | 3378 | 2988 |
| | arc, inches: | | +2.7 | +3.4 | 0 | -7.9 |

## 7.65x53 Argentine

| cartridge bullet | range, yards: | 0 | 100 | 200 | 300 | 400 |
|---|---|---|---|---|---|---|
| Norma 174 Soft Point | velocity, fps: | 2493 | 2173 | 1878 | 1611 | |
| | energy, ft-lb: | 2402 | 1825 | 1363 | 1003 | |
| | arc, inches: | | +2.0 | 0 | -9.5 | |
| Norma 180 Soft Point | velocity, fps: | 2592 | 2386 | 2189 | 2002 | |
| | energy, ft-lb: | 2686 | 2276 | 1916 | 1602 | |
| | arc, inches: | | +2.3 | 0 | -9.6 | |

## .303 British

| cartridge bullet | range, yards: | 0 | 100 | 200 | 300 | 400 |
|---|---|---|---|---|---|---|
| Federal 150 Hi-Shok | velocity, fps: | 2690 | 2440 | 2210 | 1980 | 1780 |
| | energy, ft-lb: | 2400 | 1980 | 1620 | 1310 | 1055 |
| | arc, inches: | | +2.2 | 0 | -9.4 | -27.6 |
| Federal 180 Sierra Pro-Hunt. | velocity, fps: | 2460 | 2230 | 2020 | 1820 | 1630 |
| | energy, ft-lb: | 2420 | 1995 | 1625 | 1315 | 1060 |
| | arc, inches: | | +2.8 | 0 | -11.3 | -33.2 |
| Federal 180 Tr. Bonded HE | velocity, fps: | 2590 | 2350 | 2120 | 1900 | 1700 |
| | energy, ft-lb: | 2680 | 2205 | 1795 | 1445 | 1160 |
| | arc, inches: | | +2.4 | 0 | -10.0 | -30.0 |
| Hornady 150 Soft Point | velocity, fps: | 2685 | 2441 | 2210 | 1992 | 1787 |
| | energy, ft-lb: | 2401 | 1984 | 1627 | 1321 | 1064 |
| | arc, inches: | | +2.2 | 0 | -9.3 | -27.4 |
| Hornady 150 SP LM | velocity, fps: | 2830 | 2570 | 2325 | 2094 | 1884. |
| | energy, ft-lb: | 2667 | 2199 | 1800 | 1461 | 1185 |
| | arc, inches: | | +2.0 | 0 | -8.4 | -24.6 |
| Norma 150 Soft Point | velocity, fps: | 2723 | 2438 | 2170 | 1920 | |
| | energy, ft-lb: | 2470 | 1980 | 1569 | 1228 | |
| | arc, inches: | | +2.2 | 0 | -9.6 | |
| PMC 174 FMJ (and HPBT) | velocity, fps: | 2400 | 2216 | 2042 | 1876 | 1720 |
| | energy, ft-lb: | 2225 | 1898 | 1611 | 1360 | 1143 |
| | arc, inches: | | +2.8 | 0 | -11.2 | -32.2 |
| PMC 180 SP boat-tail | velocity, fps: | 2450 | 2276 | 2110 | 1951 | 1799 |
| | energy, ft-lb: | 2399 | 2071 | 1779 | 1521 | 1294 |
| | arc, inches: | | +2.6 | 0 | -10.4 | -30.1 |
| Rem. 180 SP Core-Lokt | velocity, fps: | 2460 | 2124 | 1817 | 1542 | 1311 |
| | energy, ft-lb: | 2418 | 1803 | 1319 | 950 | 687 |
| | arc, inches, s: | | 0 | -5.8 | -23.3 | |
| Win. 180 Power-Point | velocity, fps: | 2460 | 2233 | 2018 | 1816 | 1629 |
| | energy, ft-lb: | 2418 | 1993 | 1627 | 1318 | 1060 |
| | arc, inches, s: | | 0 | -6.1 | -20.8 | |

## 7.7x58 Japanese Arisaka

| cartridge bullet | range, yards: | 0 | 100 | 200 | 300 | 400 |
|---|---|---|---|---|---|---|
| Norma 174 Soft Point | velocity, fps: | 2493 | 2173 | 1878 | 1611 | |
| | energy, ft-lb: | 2402 | 1825 | 1363 | 1003 | |
| | arc, inches: | | +2.0 | 0 | -9.5 | |

# Centerfire Rifle Ballistics

## 7.7X58 JAPANESE ARISAKA TO .338 WINCHESTER MAGNUM

| cartridge bullet | range, yards: | 0 | 100 | 200 | 300 | 400 |
|---|---|---|---|---|---|---|
| Norma 180 Soft Point | velocity, fps: | 2493 | 2291 | 2099 | 1916 | |
| | energy, ft-lb: | 2485 | 2099 | 1761 | 1468 | |
| | arc, inches: | | +2.6 | 0 | -10.5 | |

### .32-20 Winchester

| cartridge bullet | range, yards: | 0 | 100 | 200 | 300 | 400 |
|---|---|---|---|---|---|---|
| Rem. 100 Lead | velocity, fps: | 1210 | 1021 | 913 | 834 | 769 |
| | energy, ft-lb: | 325 | 231 | 185 | 154 | 131 |
| | arc, inches: | | 0 | -31.6 | -104.7 | |
| Win. 100 Lead | velocity, fps: | 1210 | 1021 | 913 | 834 | 769 |
| | energy, ft-lb: | 325 | 231 | 185 | 154 | 131 |
| | arc, inches: | | 0 | -32.3 | -106.3 | |

### .32 Winchester Special

| cartridge bullet | range, yards: | 0 | 100 | 200 | 300 | 400 |
|---|---|---|---|---|---|---|
| Federal 170 Hi-Shok | velocity, fps: | 2250 | 1920 | 1630 | 1370 | 1180 |
| | energy, ft-lb: | 1910 | 1395 | 1000 | 710 | 520 |
| | arc, inches: | | 0 | -8.0 | -29.2 | |
| Rem. 170 SP Core-Lokt | velocity, fps: | 2250 | 1921 | 1626 | 1372 | 1175 |
| | energy, ft-lb: | 1911 | 1393 | 998 | 710 | 521 |
| | arc, inches: | | 0 | -8.0 | -29.3 | |
| Win. 170 Power-Point | velocity, fps: | 2250 | 1870 | 1537 | 1267 | 1082 |
| | energy, ft-lb: | 1911 | 1320 | 892 | 606 | 442 |
| | arc, inches: | | 0 | -9.2 | -33.2 | |

### 8mm Mauser (8x57)

| cartridge bullet | range, yards: | 0 | 100 | 200 | 300 | 400 |
|---|---|---|---|---|---|---|
| Federal 170 Hi-Shok | velocity, fps: | 2360 | 1970 | 1620 | 1330 | 1120 |
| | energy, ft-lb: | 2100 | 1465 | 995 | 670 | 475 |
| | arc, inches: | | 0 | -7.6 | -28.5 | |
| Hornady 195 SP | velocity, fps: | 2550 | 2343 | 2146 | 1959 | 1782 |
| | energy, ft-lb: | 2815 | 2377 | 1994 | 1861 | 1375 |
| | arc, inches: | | +2.3 | 0 | -9.9 | -28.8. |
| Hornady 195 SP (2005) | velocity, fps: | 2475 | 2269 | 2074 | 1888 | 1714 |
| | energy, ft-lb: | 2652 | 2230 | 1861 | 1543 | 1271 |
| | arc, inches: | | +2.6 | 0 | -10.7 | -31.3 |
| Norma 123 FMJ | velocity, fps: | 2559 | 2121 | 1729 | 1398 | |
| | energy, ft-lb: | 1789 | 1228 | 817 | 534 | |
| | arc, inches: | | +3.2 | 0 | -15.0 | |
| Norma 196 Oryx | velocity, fps: | 2395 | 2146 | 1912 | 1695 | |
| | energy, ft-lb: | 2497 | 2004 | 1591 | 1251 | |
| | arc, inches: | | +3 | 0 | -12.6 | |
| Norma 196 Vulkan | velocity, fps: | 2395 | 2156 | 1930 | 1720 | |
| | energy, ft-lb: | 2497 | 2023 | 1622 | 1289 | |
| | arc, inches: | | 3.0 | 0 | -12.3 | |
| Norma 196 Alaska | velocity, fps: | 2395 | 2112 | 1850 | 1611 | |
| | energy, ft-lb: | 2714 | 2190 | 1754 | 1399 | |
| | arc, inches: | | 0 | -6.3 | -22.9 | |
| Norma 196 Soft Point (JS) | velocity, fps: | 2526 | 2244 | 1981 | 1737 | |
| | energy, ft-lb: | 2778 | 2192 | 1708 | 1314 | |
| | arc, inches: | | +2.7 | 0 | -11.6 | |
| Norma 196 Alaska (JS) | velocity, fps: | 2526 | 2248 | 1988 | 1747 | |
| | energy, ft-lb: | 2778 | 2200 | 1720 | 1328 | |
| | arc, inches: | | +2.7 | 0 | -11.5 | |
| Norma 196 Vulkan (JS) | velocity, fps: | 2526 | 2276 | 2041 | 1821 | |
| | energy, ft-lb: | 2778 | 2256 | 1813 | 1443 | |
| | arc, inches: | | +2.6 | 0 | -11.0 | |
| Norma 196 Oryx (JS) | velocity, fps: | 2526 | 2269 | 2027 | 1802 | |
| | energy, ft-lb: | 2778 | 2241 | 1789 | 1413 | |
| | arc, inches: | | +2.6 | 0 | -11.1 | |
| PMC 170 Pointed Soft Point | velocity, fps: | 2360 | 1969 | 1622 | 1333 | 1123 |
| | energy, ft-lb: | 2102 | 1463 | 993 | 671 | 476 |
| | arc, inches: | | +1.8 | -4.5 | -24.3 | -63.8 |
| Rem. 170 SP Core-Lokt | velocity, fps: | 2360 | 1969 | 1622 | 1333 | 1123 |
| | energy, ft-lb: | 2102 | 1463 | 993 | 671 | 476 |
| | arc, inches: | | +1.8 | -4.5 | -24.3 | -63.8. |

| cartridge bullet | range, yards: | 0 | 100 | 200 | 300 | 400 |
|---|---|---|---|---|---|---|
| Win. 170 Power-Point | velocity, fps: | 2360 | 1969 | 1622 | 1333 | 1123 |
| | energy, ft-lb: | 2102 | 1463 | 993 | 671 | 476 |
| | arc, inches: | | +1.8 | -4.5 | -24.3 | -63.8 |

### .325 WSM

| cartridge bullet | range, yards: | 0 | 100 | 200 | 300 | 400 |
|---|---|---|---|---|---|---|
| Win. 180 Ballistic ST | velocity, fps: | 3060 | 2841 | 2632 | 2432 | 2242 |
| | energy, ft-lb: | 3743 | 3226 | 2769 | 2365 | 2009 |
| | arc, inches: | | +1.4 | 0 | -6.4 | -18.7 |
| Win. 200 AccuBond CT | velocity, fps: | 2950 | 2753 | 2565 | 2384 | 2210 |
| | energy, ft-lb: | 3866 | 3367 | 2922 | 2524 | 2170 |
| | arc, inches: | | +1.5 | 0 | -6.8 | -19.8 |
| Win. 220 Power-Point | velocity, fps: | 2840 | 2605 | 2382 | 2169 | 1968 |
| | energy, ft-lb: | 3941 | 3316 | 2772 | 2300 | 1893 |
| | arc, inches: | | +1.8 | 0 | -8.0 | -23.3 |

### 8mm Remington Magnum

| cartridge bullet | range, yards: | 0 | 100 | 200 | 300 | 400 |
|---|---|---|---|---|---|---|
| A-Square 220 Monolythic Solid | velocity, fps: | 2800 | 2501 | 2221 | 1959 | 1718 |
| | energy, ft-lb: | 3829 | 3055 | 2409 | 1875 | 1442 |
| | arc, inches: | | +2.1 | 0 | -9.1 | -27.6 |
| Rem. 200 Swift A-Frame | velocity, fps: | 2900 | 2623 | 2361 | 2115 | 1885 |
| | energy, ft-lb: | 3734 | 3054 | 2476 | 1987 | 1577 |
| | arc, inches: | | +1.8 | 0 | -8.0 | -23.9 |

### .338-06

| cartridge bullet | range, yards: | 0 | 100 | 200 | 300 | 400 |
|---|---|---|---|---|---|---|
| A-Square 200 Nos. Bal. Tip | velocity, fps: | 2750 | 2553 | 2364 | 2184 | 2011 |
| | energy, ft-lb: | 3358 | 2894 | 2482 | 2118 | 1796 |
| | arc, inches: | | +1.9 | 0 | -8.2 | -23.6 |
| A-Square 250 SP boat-tail | velocity, fps: | 2500 | 2374 | 2252 | 2134 | 2019 |
| | energy, ft-lb: | 3496 | 3129 | 2816 | 2528 | 2263 |
| | arc, inches: | | +2.4 | 0 | -9.3 | -26.0 |
| A-Square 250 Dead Tough | velocity, fps: | 2500 | 2222 | 1963 | 1724 | 1507 |
| | energy, ft-lb: | 3496 | 2742 | 2139 | 1649 | 1261 |
| | arc, inches: | | +2.8 | 0 | -11.9 | -35.5 |
| Wby. 210 Nosler Part. | velocity, fps: | 2750 | 2526 | 2312 | 2109 | 1916 |
| | energy, ft-lb: | 3527 | 2975 | 2403 | 2074 | 1712 |
| | arc, inches: | | +4.8 | +5.7 | 0 | -13.5 |

### .338 Winchester Magnum

| cartridge bullet | range, yards: | 0 | 100 | 200 | 300 | 400 |
|---|---|---|---|---|---|---|
| A-Square 250 SP boat-tail | velocity, fps: | 2700 | 2568 | 2439 | 2314 | 2193 |
| | energy, ft-lb: | 4046 | 3659 | 3302 | 2972 | 2669 |
| | arc, inches: | | +4.4 | +5.2 | 0 | -11.7 |
| A-Square 250 Triad | velocity, fps: | 2700 | 2407 | 2133 | 1877 | 1653 |
| | energy, ft-lb: | 4046 | 3216 | 2526 | 1956 | 1516 |
| | arc, inches: | | +2.3 | 0 | -9.8 | -29.8 |
| Federal 210 Nosler Partition | velocity, fps: | 2830 | 2600 | 2390 | 2180 | 1980 |
| | energy, ft-lb: | 3735 | 3160 | 2655 | 2215 | 1835 |
| | arc, inches: | | +1.8 | 0 | -8.0 | -23.3 |
| Federal 225 Sierra Pro-Hunt. | velocity, fps: | 2780 | 2570 | 2360 | 2170 | 1980 |
| | energy, ft-lb: | 3860 | 3290 | 2780 | 2340 | 1960 |
| | arc, inches: | | +1.9 | 0 | -8.2 | -23.7 |
| Federal 225 Trophy Bonded | velocity, fps: | 2800 | 2560 | 2330 | 2110 | 1900 |
| | energy, ft-lb: | 3915 | 3265 | 2700 | 2220 | 1800 |
| | arc, inches: | | +1.9 | 0 | -8.4 | -24.5 |
| Federal 225 Tr. Bonded HE | velocity, fps: | 2940 | 2690 | 2450 | 2230 | 2010 |
| | energy, ft-lb: | 4320 | 3610 | 3000 | 2475 | 2025 |
| | arc, inches: | | +1.7 | 0 | -7.5 | -22.0 |
| Federal 225 Barnes XLC | velocity, fps: | 2800 | 2610 | 2430 | 2260 | 2090 |
| | energy, ft-lb: | 3915 | 3405 | 2950 | 2545 | 2190 |
| | arc, inches: | | +1.8 | 0 | -7.7 | -22.2 |
| Federal 250 Nosler Partition | velocity, fps: | 2660 | 2470 | 2300 | 2120 | 1960 |
| | energy, ft-lb: | 3925 | 3395 | 2925 | 2505 | 2130. |
| | arc, inches: | | +2.1 | 0 | -8.8 | -25.1 |

| cartridge bullet | range, yards: | 0 | 100 | 200 | 300 | 400 |
|---|---|---|---|---|---|---|
| Federal 250 Nosler Part HE | velocity, fps: | 2800 | 2610 | 2420 | 2250 | 2080 |
| | energy, ft-lb: | 4350 | 3775 | 3260 | 2805 | 2395 |
| | arc, inches: | | +1.8 | 0 | -7.8 | -22.5 |
| Hornady 225 Soft Point HM | velocity, fps: | 2920 | 2678 | 2449 | 2232 | 2027 |
| | energy, ft-lb: | 4259 | 3583 | 2996 | 2489 | 2053 |
| | arc, inches: | | +1.8 | 0 | -7.6 | -22.0 |
| Norma 225 TXP Swift A-Fr. | velocity, fps: | 2740 | 2507 | 2286 | 2075 | |
| | energy, ft-lb: | 3752 | 3141 | 2611 | 2153 | |
| | arc, inches: | | +2.0 | 0 | -8.7 | |
| Norma 230 Oryx | velocity, fps: | 2756 | 2514 | 2284 | 2066 | |
| | energy, ft-lb: | 3880 | 3228 | 2665 | 2181 | |
| | arc, inches: | | +2.0 | 0 | -8.7 | |
| Norma 250 Nosler Partition | velocity, fps: | 2657 | 2470 | 2290 | 2118 | |
| | energy, ft-lb: | 3920 | 3387 | 2912 | 2490 | |
| | arc, inches: | | +2.1 | 0 | -8.7 | |
| PMC 225 Barnes X | velocity, fps: | 2780 | 2619 | 2464 | 2313 | 2168 |
| | energy, ft-lb: | 3860 | 3426 | 3032 | 2673 | 2348. |
| | arc, inches: | | +1.8 | 0 | -7.6 | -21.6 |
| Rem. 200 Nosler Bal. Tip | velocity, fps: | 2950 | 2724 | 2509 | 2303 | 2108 |
| | energy, ft-lb: | 3866 | 3295 | 2795 | 2357 | 1973 |
| | arc, inches: | | +1.6 | 0 | -7.1 | -20.8 |
| Rem. 210 Nosler Partition | velocity, fps: | 2830 | 2602 | 2385 | 2179 | 1983 |
| | energy, ft-lb: | 3734 | 3157 | 2653 | 2214 | 1834 |
| | arc, inches: | | +1.8 | 0 | -7.9 | -23.2 |
| Rem. 225 PSP Core-Lokt | velocity, fps: | 2780 | 2572 | 2374 | 2184 | 2003 |
| | energy, ft-lb: | 3860 | 3305 | 2815 | 2383 | 2004 |
| | arc, inches: | | +1.9 | 0 | -8.1 | -23.4 |
| Rem. 225 PSP C-L Ultra | velocity, fps: | 2780 | 2582 | 2392 | 2210 | 2036 |
| | energy, ft-lb: | 3860 | 3329 | 2858 | 2440 | 2071 |
| | arc, inches: | | +1.9 | 0 | -7.9 | -23.0 |
| Rem. 225 Swift A-Frame | velocity, fps: | 2785 | 2517 | 2266 | 2029 | 1808 |
| | energy, ft-lb: | 3871 | 3165 | 2565 | 2057 | 1633 |
| | arc, inches: | | +2.0 | 0 | -8.8 | -25.2 |
| Rem. 250 PSP Core-Lokt | velocity, fps: | 2660 | 2456 | 2261 | 2075 | 1898 |
| | energy, ft-lb: | 3927 | 3348 | 2837 | 2389 | 1999 |
| | arc, inches: | | +2.1 | 0 | -8.9 | -26.0 |
| Speer 250 Grand Slam | velocity, fps: | 2645 | 2442 | 2247 | 2062 | |
| | energy, ft-lb: | 3883 | 3309 | 2803 | 2360 | |
| | arc, inches: | | +2.2 | 0 | -9.1 | -26.2 |
| Win. 200 Power-Point | velocity, fps: | 2960 | 2658 | 2375 | 2110 | 1862 |
| | energy, ft-lb: | 3890 | 3137 | 2505 | 1977 | 1539 |
| | arc, inches: | | +2.0 | 0 | -8.2 | -24.3 |
| Win. 200 Ballistic Silvertip | velocity, fps: | 2950 | 2724 | 2509 | 2303 | 2108 |
| | energy, ft-lb: | 3864 | 3294 | 2794 | 2355 | 1972 |
| | arc, inches: | | +1.6 | 0 | -7.1 | -20.8 |
| Win. 225 AccuBond | velocity, fps: | 2800 | 2634 | 2474 | 2319 | 2170 |
| | energy, ft-lb: | 3918 | 3467 | 3058 | 2688 | 2353 |
| | arc, inches: | | +1.8 | 0 | -7.4 | -21.3 |
| Win. 230 Fail Safe | velocity, fps: | 2780 | 2573 | 2375 | 2186 | 2005 |
| | energy, ft-lb: | 3948 | 3382 | 2881 | 2441 | 2054 |
| | arc, inches: | | +1.9 | 0 | -8.1 | -23.4 |
| Win. 250 Partition Gold | velocity, fps: | 2650 | 2467 | 2291 | 2122 | 1960 |
| | energy, ft-lb: | 3899 | 3378 | 2914 | 2520 | 2134 |
| | arc, inches: | | +2.1 | 0 | -8.7 | -25.2 |

## .340 Weatherby Magnum

| cartridge bullet | range, yards: | 0 | 100 | 200 | 300 | 400 |
|---|---|---|---|---|---|---|
| A-Square 250 SP boat-tail | velocity, fps: | 2820 | 2684 | 2552 | 2424 | 2299 |
| | energy, ft-lb: | 4414 | 3999 | 3615 | 3261 | 2935 |
| | arc, inches: | | +4.0 | +4.6 | 0 | -10.6 |
| A-Square 250 Triad | velocity, fps: | 2820 | 2520 | 2238 | 1976 | 1741 |
| | energy, ft-lb: | 4414 | 3524 | 2781 | 2166 | 1683 |
| | arc, inches: | | +2.0 | 0 | -9.0 | -26.8 |

| cartridge bullet | range, yards: | 0 | 100 | 200 | 300 | 400 |
|---|---|---|---|---|---|---|
| Federal 225 Trophy Bonded | velocity, fps: | 3100 | 2840 | 2600 | 2370 | 2150 |
| | energy, ft-lb: | 4800 | 4035 | 3375 | 2800 | 2310 |
| | arc, inches: | | +1.4 | 0 | -6.5 | -19.4 |
| Wby. 200 Pointed Expanding | velocity, fps: | 3221 | 2946 | 2688 | 2444 | 2213 |
| | energy, ft-lb: | 4607 | 3854 | 3208 | 2652 | 2174 |
| | arc, inches: | | +3.3 | +4.0 | 0 | -9.9 |
| Wby. 200 Nosler Bal. Tip | velocity, fps: | 3221 | 2980 | 2753 | 2536 | 2329 |
| | energy, ft-lb: | 4607 | 3944 | 3364 | 2856 | 2409 |
| | arc, inches: | | +3.1 | +3.9 | 0 | -9.2 |
| Wby. 210 Nosler Partition | velocity, fps: | 3211 | 2963 | 2728 | 2505 | 2293 |
| | energy, ft-lb: | 4807 | 4093 | 3470 | 2927 | 2452 |
| | arc, inches: | | +3.2 | +3.9 | 0 | -9.5 |
| Wby. 225 Pointed Expanding | velocity, fps: | 3066 | 2824 | 2595 | 2377 | 2170 |
| | energy, ft-lb: | 4696 | 3984 | 3364 | 2822 | 2352 |
| | arc, inches: | | +3.6 | +4.4 | 0 | -10.7 |
| Wby. 225 Barnes X | velocity, fps: | 3001 | 2804 | 2615 | 2434 | 2260 |
| | energy, ft-lb: | 4499 | 3927 | 3416 | 2959 | 2551 |
| | arc, inches: | | +3.6 | +4.3 | 0 | -10.3 |
| Wby. 250 Pointed Expanding | velocity, fps: | 2963 | 2745 | 2537 | 2338 | 2149 |
| | energy, ft-lb: | 4873 | 4182 | 3572 | 3035 | 2563 |
| | arc, inches: | | +3.9 | +4.6 | 0 | -11.1 |
| Wby. 250 Nosler Partition | velocity, fps: | 2941 | 2743 | 2553 | 2371 | 2197 |
| | energy, ft-lb: | 4801 | 4176 | 3618 | 3120 | 2678 |
| | arc, inches: | | +3.9 | +4.6 | 0 | -10.9 |

## .330 Dakota

| cartridge bullet | range, yards: | 0 | 100 | 200 | 300 | 400 |
|---|---|---|---|---|---|---|
| Dakota 200 Barnes X | velocity, fps: | 3200 | 2971 | 2754 | 2548 | 2350 |
| | energy, ft-lb: | 4547 | 3920 | 3369 | 2882 | 2452 |
| | arc, inches: | | +2.1 | +1.8 | -3.1 | -13.4 |
| Dakota 250 Barnes X | velocity, fps: | 2900 | 2719 | 2545 | 2378 | 2217 |
| | energy, ft-lb: | 4668 | 4103 | 3595 | 3138 | 2727 |
| | arc, inches: | | +2.3 | +1.3 | -5.0 | -17.5 |

## .338 Remington Ultra Magnum

| cartridge bullet | range, yards: | 0 | 100 | 200 | 300 | 400 |
|---|---|---|---|---|---|---|
| Federal 210 Nosler Partition | velocity, fps: | 3025 | 2800 | 2585 | 2385 | 2190 |
| | energy, ft-lb: | 4270 | 3655 | 3120 | 2645 | 2230 |
| | arc, inches: | | +1.5 | 0 | -6.7 | -19.5 |
| Federal 250 Trophy Bonded | velocity, fps: | 2860 | 2630 | 2420 | 2210 | 2020 |
| | energy, ft-lb: | 4540 | 3850 | 3245 | 2715 | 2260. |
| | arc, inches: | | +0.8 | 0 | -7.7 | -22.6 |
| Rem. 250 Swift A-Frame | velocity, fps: | 2860 | 2645 | 2440 | 2244 | 2057 |
| | energy, ft-lb: | 4540 | 3882 | 3303 | 2794 | 2347 |
| | arc, inches: | | +1.7 | 0 | -7.6 | -22.1 |
| Rem. 250 PSP Core-Lokt | velocity, fps: | 2860 | 2647 | 2443 | 2249 | 2064 |
| | energy, ft-lb: | 4540 | 3888 | 3314 | 2807 | 2363 |
| | arc, inches: | | +1.7 | 0 | -7.6 | -22.0 |

## .338 Lapua

| cartridge bullet | range, yards: | 0 | 100 | 200 | 300 | 400 |
|---|---|---|---|---|---|---|
| Black Hills 250 Sierra MKing | velocity, fps: | 2950 | | | | |
| | energy, ft-lb: | 4831 | | | | |
| | arc, inches: | | | | | |
| Black Hills 300 Sierra MKing | velocity, fps: | 2800 | | | | |
| | energy, ft-lb: | 5223 | | | | |
| | arc, inches: | | | | | |

## .338-378 Weatherby Magnum

| cartridge bullet | range, yards: | 0 | 100 | 200 | 300 | 400 |
|---|---|---|---|---|---|---|
| Wby. 200 Nosler Bal. Tip | velocity, fps: | 3350 | 3102 | 2868 | 2646 | 2434 |
| | energy, ft-lb: | 4983 | 4273 | 3652 | 3109 | 2631 |
| | arc, inches: | 0 | +2.8 | +3.5 | 0 | -8.4 |
| Wby. 225 Barnes X | velocity, fps: | 3180 | 2974 | 2778 | 2591 | 2410. |
| | energy, ft-lb: | 5052 | 4420 | 3856 | 3353 | 2902 |
| | arc, inches: | 0 | +3.1 | +3.8 | 0 | -8.9 |

BALLISTICS

## .338-378 WEATHERBY MAGNUM TO 9.3X62

| cartridge bullet | range, yards: | 0 | 100 | 200 | 300 | 400 |
|---|---|---|---|---|---|---|
| Wby. 250 Nosler Partition | velocity, fps: | 3060 | 2856 | 2662 | 2475 | 2297 |
| | energy, ft-lb: | 5197 | 4528 | 3933 | 3401 | 2927 |
| | arc, inches: | 0 | +3.5 | +4.2 | 0 | -9.8 |

### 8.59 (.338) Titan

| cartridge bullet | range, yards: | 0 | 100 | 200 | 300 | 400 |
|---|---|---|---|---|---|---|
| Lazzeroni 200 Nos. Bal. Tip | velocity, fps: | 3430 | 3211 | 3002 | 2803 | 2613 |
| | energy, ft-lb: | 5226 | 4579 | 4004 | 3491 | 3033 |
| | arc, inches: | | +2.5 | +3.2 | 0 | -7.6 |
| Lazzeroni 225 Nos. Partition | velocity, fps: | 3235 | 3031 | 2836 | 2650 | 2471 |
| | energy, ft-lb: | 5229 | 4591 | 4021 | 3510 | 3052 |
| | arc, inches: | | +3.0 | +3.6 | 0 | -8.6 |
| Lazzeroni 250 Swift A-Fr. | velocity, fps: | 3100 | 2908 | 2725 | 2549 | 2379 |
| | energy, ft-lb: | 5336 | 4697 | 4123 | 3607 | 3143 |
| | arc, inches: | | +3.3 | +4.0 | 0 | -9.3 |

### .338 A-Square

| cartridge bullet | range, yards: | 0 | 100 | 200 | 300 | 400 |
|---|---|---|---|---|---|---|
| A-Square 200 Nos. Bal. Tip | velocity, fps: | 3500 | 3266 | 3045 | 2835 | 2634 |
| | energy, ft-lb: | 5440 | 4737 | 4117 | 3568 | 3081 |
| | arc, inches: | | +2.4 | +3.1 | 0 | -7.5 |
| A-Square 250 SP boat-tail | velocity, fps: | 3120 | 2974 | 2834 | 2697 | 2565. |
| | energy, ft-lb: | 5403 | 4911 | 4457 | 4038 | 3652 |
| | arc, inches: | | +3.1 | +3.7 | 0 | -8.5 |
| A-Square 250 Triad | velocity, fps: | 3120 | 2799 | 2500 | 2220 | 1958 |
| | energy, ft-lb: | 5403 | 4348 | 3469 | 2736 | 2128 |
| | arc, inches: | | +1.5 | 0 | -7.1 | -20.4. |

### .338 Excaliber

| cartridge bullet | range, yards: | 0 | 100 | 200 | 300 | 400 |
|---|---|---|---|---|---|---|
| A-Square 200 Nos. Bal. Tip | velocity, fps: | 3600 | 3361 | 3134 | 2920 | 2715 |
| | energy, ft-lb: | 5755 | 5015 | 4363 | 3785 | 3274 |
| | arc, inches: | | +2.2 | +2.9 | 0 | -6.7 |
| A-Square 250 SP boat-tail | velocity, fps: | 3250 | 3101 | 2958 | 2684 | 2553 |
| | energy, ft-lb: | 5863 | 5339 | 4855 | 4410 | 3998 |
| | arc, inches: | | +2.7 | +3.4 | 0 | -7.8 |
| A-Square 250 Triad | velocity, fps: | 3250 | 2922 | 2618 | 2333 | 2066 |
| | energy, ft-lb: | 5863 | 4740 | 3804 | 3021 | 2370 |
| | arc, inches: | | +1.3 | 0 | -6.4 | -19.2 |

### .348 Winchester

| cartridge bullet | range, yards: | 0 | 100 | 200 | 300 | 400 |
|---|---|---|---|---|---|---|
| Win. 200 Silvertip | velocity, fps: | 2520 | 2215 | 1931 | 1672 | 1443. |
| | energy, ft-lb: | 2820 | 2178 | 1656 | 1241 | 925 |
| | arc, inches: | | 0 | -6.2 | -21.9 | |

### .357 Magnum

| cartridge bullet | range, yards: | 0 | 100 | 200 | 300 | 400 |
|---|---|---|---|---|---|---|
| Federal 180 Hi-Shok HP Hollow Point | velocity, fps: | 1550 | 1160 | 980 | 860 | 770 |
| | energy, ft-lb: | 960 | 535 | 385 | 295 | 235 |
| | arc, inches: | | 0 | -22.8 | -77.9 | -173.8 |
| Win. 158 Jacketed SP | velocity, fps: | 1830 | 1427 | 1138 | 980 | 883 |
| | energy, ft-lb: | 1175 | 715 | 454 | 337 | 274 |
| | arc, inches: | | 0 | -16.2 | -57.0 | -128.3 |

### .35 Remington

| cartridge bullet | range, yards: | 0 | 100 | 200 | 300 | 400 |
|---|---|---|---|---|---|---|
| Federal 200 Hi-Shok | velocity, fps: | 2080 | 1700 | 1380 | 1140 | 1000 |
| | energy, ft-lb: | 1920 | 1280 | 840 | 575 | 445 |
| | arc, inches: | | 0 | -10.7 | -39.3 | |
| Hornady 200 Evolution | velocity, fps: | 2225 | 1963 | 1721 | 1503 | |
| | energy, ft-lb: | 2198 | 1711 | 1315 | 1003 | |
| | arc, inches: | | +3.0 | -1.3 | -17.5 | |
| Rem. 150 PSP Core-Lokt | velocity, fps: | 2300 | 1874 | 1506 | 1218 | 1039 |
| | energy, ft-lb: | 1762 | 1169 | 755 | 494 | 359 |
| | arc, inches: | | 0 | -8.6 | -32.6 | |
| Rem. 200 SP Core-Lokt | velocity, fps: | 2080 | 1698 | 1376 | 1140 | 1001 |
| | energy, ft-lb: | 1921 | 1280 | 841 | 577 | 445 |
| | arc, inches: | | 0 | -10.7 | -40.1 | |
| Win. 200 Power-Point | velocity, fps: | 2020 | 1646 | 1335 | 1114 | 985 |
| | energy, ft-lb: | 1812 | 1203 | 791 | 551 | 431 |
| | arc, inches: | | 0 | -12.1 | -43.9 | |

### .356 Winchester

| cartridge bullet | range, yards: | 0 | 100 | 200 | 300 | 400 |
|---|---|---|---|---|---|---|
| Win. 200 Power-Point | velocity, fps: | 2460 | 2114 | 1797 | 1517 | 1284 |
| | energy, ft-lb: | 2688 | 1985 | 1434 | 1022 | 732 |
| | arc, inches: | | +1.6 | -3.8 | -20.1 | -51.2 |

### .358 Winchester

| cartridge bullet | range, yards: | 0 | 100 | 200 | 300 | 400 |
|---|---|---|---|---|---|---|
| Win. 200 Silvertip | velocity, fps: | 2490 | 2171 | 1876 | 1610 | 1379 |
| | energy, ft-lb: | 2753 | 2093 | 1563 | 1151 | 844 |
| | arc, inches: | | +1.5 | -3.6 | -18.6 | -47.2 |

### .35 Whelen

| cartridge bullet | range, yards: | 0 | 100 | 200 | 300 | 400 |
|---|---|---|---|---|---|---|
| Federal 225 Trophy Bonded | velocity, fps: | 2600 | 2400 | 2200 | 2020 | 1840 |
| | energy, ft-lb: | 3375 | 2865 | 2520 | 2030 | 1690. |
| | arc, inches: | | +2.3 | 0 | -9.4 | -27.3 |
| Rem. 200 Pointed Soft Point | velocity, fps: | 2675 | 2378 | 2100 | 1842 | 1606 |
| | energy, ft-lb: | 3177 | 2510 | 1958 | 1506 | 1145 |
| | arc, inches: | | +2.3 | 0 | -10.3 | -30.8 |
| Rem. 250 Pointed Soft Point | velocity, fps: | 2400 | 2197 | 2005 | 1823 | 1652 |
| | energy, ft-lb: | 3197 | 2680 | 2230 | 1844 | 1515 |
| | arc, inches: | | +1.3 | -3.2 | -16.6 | -40.0 |

### .358 Norma Magnum

| cartridge bullet | range, yards: | 0 | 100 | 200 | 300 | 400 |
|---|---|---|---|---|---|---|
| A-Square 275 Triad | velocity, fps: | 2700 | 2394 | 2108 | 1842 | 1653 |
| | energy, ft-lb: | 4451 | 3498 | 2713 | 2072 | 1668 |
| | arc, inches: | | +2.3 | 0 | -10.1 | -29.8 |
| Norma 250 TXP Swift A-Fr. | velocity, fps: | 2723 | 2467 | 2225 | 1996 | |
| | energy, ft-lb: | 4117 | 3379 | 2748 | 2213 | |
| | arc, inches: | | +2.1 | 0 | -9.1 | |
| Norma 250 Woodleigh | velocity, fps: | 2799 | 2442 | 2112 | 1810 | |
| | energy, ft-lb: | 4350 | 3312 | 2478 | 1819 | |
| | arc, inches: | | +2.2 | 0 | -10.0 | |
| Norma 250 Oryx | velocity, fps: | 2756 | 2493 | 2245 | 2011 | |
| | energy, ft-lb: | 4217 | 3451 | 2798 | 2245 | |
| | arc, inches: | | +2.1 | 0 | -9.0 | |

### .358 STA

| cartridge bullet | range, yards: | 0 | 100 | 200 | 300 | 400 |
|---|---|---|---|---|---|---|
| A-Square 275 Triad | velocity, fps: | 2850 | 2562 | 2292 | 2039 | 1764 |
| | energy, ft-lb: | 4959 | 4009 | 3208 | 2539 | 1899. |
| | arc, inches: | | +1.9 | 0 | -8.6 | -26.1 |

### 9.3x57

| cartridge bullet | range, yards: | 0 | 100 | 200 | 300 | 400 |
|---|---|---|---|---|---|---|
| Norma 232 Vulkan | velocity, fps: | 2329 | 2031 | 1757 | 1512 | |
| | energy, ft-lb: | 2795 | 2126 | 1591 | 1178 | |
| | arc, inches: | | +3.5 | 0 | -14.9 | |
| Norma 232 Oryx | velocity, fps: | 2362 | 2058 | 1778 | 1528 | |
| | energy, ft-lb: | 2875 | 2182 | 1630 | 1203 | |
| | arc, inches: | | +3.4 | 0 | -14.5 | |
| Norma 285 Oryx | velocity, fps: | 2067 | 1859 | 1666 | 1490 | |
| | energy, ft-lb: | 2704 | 2188 | 1756 | 1404 | |
| | arc, inches: | | +4.3 | 0 | -16.8 | |
| Norma 286 Alaska | velocity, fps: | 2067 | 1857 | 1662 | 1484 | |
| | energy, ft-lb: | 2714 | 2190 | 1754 | 1399 | |
| | arc, inches: | | +4.3 | 0 | -17.0 | |

### 9.3x62

| cartridge bullet | range, yards: | 0 | 100 | 200 | 300 | 400 |
|---|---|---|---|---|---|---|
| A-Square 286 Triad | velocity, fps: | 2360 | 2089 | 1844 | 1623 | 1369 |
| | energy, ft-lb: | 3538 | 2771 | 2157 | 1670 | 1189 |
| | arc, inches: | | +3.0 | 0 | -13.1 | -42.2 |
| Norma 232 Vulkan | velocity, fps: | 2625 | 2327 | 2049 | 1792 | |
| | energy, ft-lb: | 3551 | 2791 | 2164 | 1655 | |
| | arc, inches: | | +2.5 | 0 | -10.8 | |

| cartridge bullet | range, yards: | 0 | 100 | 200 | 300 | 400 |
|---|---|---|---|---|---|---|
| Norma 232 Oryx | velocity, fps: | 2625 | 2294 | 1988 | 1708 | |
| | energy, ft-lb: | 3535 | 2700 | 2028 | 1497 | |
| | arc, inches: | | +2.5 | 0 | -11.4 | |
| Norma 250 A-Frame | velocity, fps: | 2625 | 2322 | 2039 | 1778 | |
| | energy, ft-lb: | 3826 | 2993 | 2309 | 1755 | |
| | arc, inches: | | +2.5 | 0 | -10.9 | |
| Norma 286 Plastic Point | velocity, fps: | 2362 | 2141 | 1931 | 1736 | |
| | energy, ft-lb: | 3544 | 2911 | 2370 | 1914 | |
| | arc, inches: | | +3.1 | 0 | -12.4 | |
| Norma 286 Alaska | velocity, fps: | 2362 | 2135 | 1920 | 1720 | |
| | energy, ft-lb: | 3544 | 2894 | 2342 | 1879 | |
| | arc, inches: | | +3.1 | 0 | -12.5 | |

## 9.3x64

| | | | | | | |
|---|---|---|---|---|---|---|
| A-Square 286 Triad | velocity, fps: | 2700 | 2391 | 2103 | 1835 | 1602 |
| | energy, ft-lb: | 4629 | 3630 | 2808 | 2139 | 1631 |
| | arc, inches: | | +2.3 | 0 | -10.1 | -30.8 |

## 9.3x74 R

| | | | | | | |
|---|---|---|---|---|---|---|
| A-Square 286 Triad | velocity, fps: | 2360 | 2089 | 1844 | 1623 | |
| | energy, ft-lb: | 3538 | 2771 | 2157 | 1670 | |
| | arc, inches: | | +3.6 | 0 | -14.0 | |
| Hornady 286 | velocity, fps | 2360 | 2136 | 1924 | 1727 | 1545 |
| | energy, ft-lb | 3536 | 2896 | 2351 | 1893 | 1516 |
| | arc, inches | -1.5 | 0 | -6.1 | -21.7 | -49.0 |
| Norma 232 Vulkan | velocity, fps: | 2625 | 2327 | 2049 | 1792 | |
| | energy, ft-lb: | 3551 | 2791 | 2164 | 1655 | |
| | arc, inches: | | +2.5 | 0 | -10.8 | |
| Norma 232 Oryx | velocity, fps: | 2526 | 2191 | 1883 | 1605 | |
| | energy, ft-lb: | 3274 | 2463 | 1819 | 1322 | |
| | arc, inches: | | +2.9 | 0 | -12.8 | |
| Norma 285 Oryx | velocity, fps: | 2362 | 2114 | 1881 | 1667 | |
| | energy, ft-lb: | 3532 | 2829 | 2241 | 1758 | |
| | arc, inches: | | +3.1 | 0 | -13.0 | |
| Norma 286 Alaska | velocity, fps: | 2362 | 2135 | 1920 | 1720 | |
| | energy, ft-lb: | 3544 | 2894 | 2342 | 1879 | |
| | arc, inches: | | +3.1 | 0 | -12.5 | |
| Norma 286 Plastic Point | velocity, fps: | 2362 | 2135 | 1920 | 1720 | |
| | energy, ft-lb: | 3544 | 2894 | 2342 | 1879 | |
| | arc, inches: | | +3.1 | 0 | -12.5 | |

## .375 Winchester

| | | | | | | |
|---|---|---|---|---|---|---|
| Win. 200 Power-Point | velocity, fps: | 2200 | 1841 | 1526 | 1268 | 1089 |
| | energy, ft-lb: | 2150 | 1506 | 1034 | 714 | |
| | arc, inches: | | 0 | -9.5 | -33.8 | |

## .375 H&H Magnum

| | | | | | | |
|---|---|---|---|---|---|---|
| A-Square 300 SP boat-tail | velocity, fps: | 2550 | 2415 | 2284 | 2157 | 2034 |
| | energy, ft-lb: | 4331 | 3884 | 3474 | 3098 | 2755 |
| | arc, inches: | | +5.2 | +6.0 | 0 | -13.3 |
| A-Square 300 Triad | velocity, fps: | 2550 | 2251 | 1973 | 1717 | 1496 |
| | energy, ft-lb: | 4331 | 3375 | 2592 | 1964 | 1491 |
| | arc, inches: | | +2.7 | 0 | -11.7 | -35.1 |
| Federal 250 Trophy Bonded | velocity, fps: | 2670 | 2360 | 2080 | 1820 | 1580 |
| | energy, ft-lb: | 3955 | 3100 | 2400 | 1830 | 1380 |
| | arc, inches: | | +2.4 | 0 | -10.4 | -31.7 |
| Federal 270 Hi-Shok | velocity, fps: | 2690 | 2420 | 2170 | 1920 | 1700 |
| | energy, ft-lb: | 4340 | 3510 | 2810 | 2220 | 1740 |
| | arc, inches: | | +2.4 | 0 | -10.9 | -33.3 |
| Federal 300 Hi-Shok | velocity, fps: | 2530 | 2270 | 2020 | 1790 | 1580 |
| | energy, ft-lb: | 4265 | 3425 | 2720 | 2135 | 1665 |
| | arc, inches: | | +2.6 | 0 | -11.2 | -33.3 |

| cartridge bullet | range, yards: | 0 | 100 | 200 | 300 | 400 |
|---|---|---|---|---|---|---|
| Federal 300 Nosler Partition | velocity, fps: | 2530 | 2320 | 2120 | 1930 | 1750 |
| | energy, ft-lb: | 4265 | 3585 | 2995 | 2475 | 2040 |
| | arc, inches: | | +2.5 | 0 | -10.3 | -29.9 |
| Federal 300 Trophy Bonded | velocity, fps: | 2530 | 2280 | 2040 | 1810 | 1610 |
| | energy, ft-lb: | 4265 | 3450 | 2765 | 2190 | 1725 |
| | arc, inches: | | +2.6 | 0 | -10.9 | -32.8 |
| Federal 300 Tr. Bonded HE | velocity, fps: | 2700 | 2440 | 2190 | 1960 | 1740 |
| | energy, ft-lb: | 4855 | 3960 | 3195 | 2550 | 2020 |
| | arc, inches: | | +2.2 | 0 | -9.4 | -28.0 |
| Federal 300 Trophy Bonded Sledgehammer Solid | velocity, fps: | 2530 | 2160 | 1820 | 1520 | 1280. |
| | energy, ft-lb: | 4265 | 3105 | 2210 | 1550 | 1090 |
| | arc, inches, s: | | 0 | -6.0 | -22.7 | -54.6 |
| Hornady 270 SP HM | velocity, fps: | 2870 | 2620 | 2385 | 2162 | 1957 |
| | energy, ft-lb: | 4937 | 4116 | 3408 | 2802 | 2296 |
| | arc, inches: | | +2.2 | 0 | -8.4 | -23.9 |
| Hornady 300 FMJ RN HM | velocity, fps: | 2705 | 2376 | 2072 | 1804 | 1560 |
| | energy, ft-lb: | 4873 | 3760 | 2861 | 2167 | 1621 |
| | arc, inches: | | +2.7 | 0 | -10.8 | -32.1 |
| Norma 300 Soft Point | velocity, fps: | 2549 | 2211 | 1900 | 1619 | |
| | energy, ft-lb: | 4329 | 3258 | 2406 | 1747 | |
| | arc, inches: | | +2.8 | 0 | -12.6 | |
| Norma 300 TXP Swift A-Fr. | velocity, fps: | 2559 | 2296 | 2049 | 1818 | |
| | energy, ft-lb: | 4363 | 3513 | 2798 | 2203 | |
| | arc, inches: | | +2.6 | 0 | -10.9 | |
| Norma 300 Oryx | velocity, fps: | 2559 | 2292 | 2041 | 1807 | |
| | energy, ft-lb: | 4363 | 3500 | 2775 | 2176 | |
| | arc, inches: | | +2.6 | 0 | -11.0 | |
| Norma 300 Barnes Solid | velocity, fps: | 2493 | 2061 | 1677 | 1356 | |
| | energy, ft-lb: | 4141 | 2829 | 1873 | 1234 | |
| | arc, inches: | | +3.4 | 0 | -16.0 | |
| PMC 270 PSP | velocity, fps: | | | | | |
| | energy, ft-lb: | | | | | |
| | arc, inches: | | | | | |
| PMC 270 Barnes X | velocity, fps: | 2690 | 2528 | 2372 | 2221 | 2076 |
| | energy, ft-lb: | 4337 | 3831 | 3371 | 2957 | 2582 |
| | arc, inches: | | +2.0 | 0 | -8.2 | -23.4 |
| PMC 300 Barnes X | velocity, fps: | 2530 | 2389 | 2252 | 2120 | 1993 |
| | energy, ft-lb: | 4263 | 3801 | 3378 | 2994 | 2644 |
| | arc, inches: | | +2.3 | 0 | -9.2 | -26.1 |
| Rem. 270 Soft Point | velocity, fps: | 2690 | 2420 | 2166 | 1928 | 1707 |
| | energy, ft-lb: | 4337 | 3510 | 2812 | 2228 | 1747 |
| | arc, inches: | | +2.2 | 0 | -9.7 | -28.7 |
| Rem. 300 Swift A-Frame | velocity, fps: | 2530 | 2245 | 1979 | 1733 | 1512 |
| | energy, ft-lb: | 4262 | 3357 | 2608 | 2001 | 1523 |
| | arc, inches: | | +2.7 | 0 | -11.7 | -35.0 |
| Speer 285 Grand Slam | velocity, fps: | 2610 | 2365 | 2134 | 1916 | |
| | energy, ft-lb: | 4310 | 3540 | 2883 | 2323 | |
| | arc, inches: | | +2.4 | 0 | -9.9 | |
| Speer 300 African GS Tungsten Solid | velocity, fps: | 2609 | 2277 | 1970 | 1690 | |
| | energy, ft-lb: | 4534 | 3453 | 2585 | 1903 | |
| | arc, inches: | | +2.6 | 0 | -11.7 | -35.6 |
| Win. 270 Fail Safe | velocity, fps: | 2670 | 2447 | 2234 | 2033 | 1842 |
| | energy, ft-lb: | 4275 | 3590 | 2994 | 2478 | 2035 |
| | arc, inches: | | +2.2 | 0 | -9.1 | -28.7 |
| Win. 300 Fail Safe | velocity, fps: | 2530 | 2336 | 2151 | 1974 | 1806 |
| | energy, ft-lb: | 4265 | 3636 | 3082 | 2596 | 2173 |
| | arc, inches: | | +2.4 | 0 | -10.0 | -26.9 |

## .375 Dakota

| | | | | | | |
|---|---|---|---|---|---|---|
| Dakota 270 Barnes X | velocity, fps: | 2800 | 2617 | 2441 | 2272 | 2109 |
| | energy, ft-lb: | 4699 | 4104 | 3571 | 3093 | 2666 |
| | arc, inches: | | +2.3 | +1.0 | -6.1 | -19.9 |

## .375 DAKOTA TO .416 HOFFMAN

| cartridge bullet | range, yards: | 0 | 100 | 200 | 300 | 400 |
|---|---|---|---|---|---|---|
| Dakota 300 Barnes X | velocity, fps: | 2600 | 2316 | 2051 | 1804 | 1579 |
| | energy, ft-lb: | 4502 | 3573 | 2800 | 2167 | 1661 |
| | arc, inches: | | +2.4 | -0.1 | -11.0 | -32.7 |

### .375 Ruger

| | | 0 | 100 | 200 | 300 | 400 |
|---|---|---|---|---|---|---|
| Hornady 300 Solid | velocity, fps: | 2660 | 2344 | 2050 | 1780 | 1536 |
| | energy, ft-lb: | 4713 | 3660 | 2800 | 2110 | 1572 |
| | arc, inches | -1.5 | +2.4 | 0 | -10.8 | -32.6 |

### .375 Weatherby Magnum

| | | 0 | 100 | 200 | 300 | 400 |
|---|---|---|---|---|---|---|
| A-Square 300 SP boat-tail | velocity, fps: | 2700 | 2560 | 2425 | 2293 | 2166 |
| | energy, ft-lb: | 4856 | 4366 | 3916 | 3503 | 3125 |
| | arc, inches: | | +4.5 | +5.2 | 0 | -11.9 |
| A-Square 300 Triad | velocity, fps: | 2700 | 2391 | 2103 | 1835 | 1602 |
| | energy, ft-lb: | 4856 | 3808 | 2946 | 2243 | 1710 |
| | arc, inches: | | +2.3 | 0 | -10.1 | -30.8 |
| Wby. 300 Nosler Part. | velocity, fps: | 2800 | 2572 | 2366 | 2140 | 1963 |
| | energy, ft-lb: | 5224 | 4408 | 3696 | 3076 | 2541 |
| | arc, inches: | | +1.9 | 0 | -8.2 | -23.9 |

### .375 JRS

| | | 0 | 100 | 200 | 300 | 400 |
|---|---|---|---|---|---|---|
| A-Square 300 SP boat-tail | velocity, fps: | 2700 | 2560 | 2425 | 2293 | 2166. |
| | energy, ft-lb: | 4856 | 4366 | 3916 | 3503 | 3125 |
| | arc, inches: | | +4.5 | +5.2 | 0 | -11.9 |
| A-Square 300 Triad | velocity, fps: | 2700 | 2391 | 2103 | 1835 | 1602 |
| | energy, ft-lb: | 4856 | 3808 | 2946 | 2243 | 1710 |
| | arc, inches: | | +2.3 | 0 | -10.1 | -30.8 |

### .375 Remington Ultra Magnum

| | | 0 | 100 | 200 | 300 | 400 |
|---|---|---|---|---|---|---|
| Rem. 270 Soft Point | velocity, fps: | 2900 | 2558 | 2241 | 1947 | 1678 |
| | energy, fps: | 5041 | 3922 | 3010 | 2272 | 1689 |
| | arc, inches: | | +1.9 | 0 | -9.2 | -27.8 |
| Rem. 300 Swift A-Frame | velocity, fps: | 2760 | 2505 | 2263 | 2035 | 1822 |
| | energy, fps: | 5073 | 4178 | 3412 | 2759 | 2210 |
| | arc, inches: | | +2.0 | 0 | -8.8 | -26.1 |

### .375 A-Square

| | | 0 | 100 | 200 | 300 | 400 |
|---|---|---|---|---|---|---|
| A-Square 300 SP boat-tail | velocity, fps: | 2920 | 2773 | 2631 | 2494 | 2360 |
| | energy, ft-lb: | 5679 | 5123 | 4611 | 4142 | 3710 |
| | arc, inches: | | +3.7 | +4.4 | 0 | -9.8 |
| A-Square 300 Triad | velocity, fps: | 2920 | 2596 | 2294 | 2012 | 1762 |
| | energy, ft-lb: | 5679 | 4488 | 3505 | 2698 | 2068 |
| | arc, inches: | | +1.8 | 0 | -8.5 | -25.5 |

### .376 Steyr

| | | 0 | 100 | 200 | 300 | 400 |
|---|---|---|---|---|---|---|
| Hornady 225 SP | velocity, fps: | 2600 | 2331 | 2078 | 1842 | 1625 |
| | energy, ft-lb: | 3377 | 2714 | 2157 | 1694 | 1319 |
| | arc, inches: | | +2.5 | 0 | -10.6 | -31.4 |
| Hornady 270 SP | velocity, fps: | 2600 | 2372 | 2156 | 1951 | 1759 |
| | energy, ft-lb: | 4052 | 3373 | 2787 | 2283 | 1855 |
| | arc, inches: | | +2.3 | 0 | -9.9 | -28.9 |

### .378 Weatherby Magnum

| | | 0 | 100 | 200 | 300 | 400 |
|---|---|---|---|---|---|---|
| A-Square 300 SP boat-tail | velocity, fps: | 2900 | 2754 | 2612 | 2475 | 2342 |
| | energy, ft-lb: | 5602 | 5051 | 4546 | 4081 | 3655 |
| | arc, inches: | | +3.8 | +4.4 | 0 | -10.0 |
| A-Square 300 Triad | velocity, fps: | 2900 | 2577 | 2276 | 1997 | 1747 |
| | energy, ft-lb: | 5602 | 4424 | 3452 | 2656 | 2034 |
| | arc, inches: | | +1.9 | 0 | -8.7 | -25.9 |
| Wby. 270 Pointed Expanding | velocity, fps: | 3180 | 2921 | 2677 | 2445 | 2225 |
| | energy, ft-lb: | 6062 | 5115 | 4295 | 3583 | 2968 |
| | arc, inches: | | +1.3 | 0 | -6.1 | -18.1 |

| cartridge bullet | range, yards: | 0 | 100 | 200 | 300 | 400 |
|---|---|---|---|---|---|---|
| Wby. 270 Barnes X | velocity, fps: | 3150 | 2954 | 2767 | 2587 | 2415 |
| | energy, ft-lb: | 5948 | 5232 | 4589 | 4013 | 3495 |
| | arc, inches: | | +1.2 | 0 | -5.8 | -16.7 |
| Wby. 300 RN Expanding | velocity, fps: | 2925 | 2558 | 2220 | 1908 | 1627. |
| | energy, ft-lb: | 5699 | 4360 | 3283 | 2424 | 1764 |
| | arc, inches: | | +1.9 | 0 | -9.0 | -27.8 |
| Wby. 300 FMJ | velocity, fps: | 2925 | 2591 | 2280 | 1991 | 1725 |
| | energy, ft-lb: | 5699 | 4470 | 3461 | 2640 | 1983 |
| | arc, inches: | | +1.8 | 0 | -8.6 | -26.1 |

### .38-40 Winchester

| | | 0 | 100 | 200 | 300 | 400 |
|---|---|---|---|---|---|---|
| Win. 180 Soft Point | velocity, fps: | 1160 | 999 | 901 | 827 | |
| | energy, ft-lb: | 538 | 399 | 324 | 273 | |
| | arc, inches: | | 0 | -23.4 | -75.2 | |

### .38-55 Winchester

| | | 0 | 100 | 200 | 300 | 400 |
|---|---|---|---|---|---|---|
| Black Hills 255 FN Lead | velocity, fps: | 1250 | | | | |
| | energy, ft-lb: | 925 | | | | |
| | arc, inches: | | | | | |
| Win. 255 Soft Point | velocity, fps: | 1320 | 1190 | 1091 | 1018 | |
| | energy, ft-lb: | 987 | 802 | 674 | 587 | |
| | arc, inches: | | 0 | -33.9 | -110.6 | |

### .41 Magnum

| | | 0 | 100 | 200 | 300 | 400 |
|---|---|---|---|---|---|---|
| Win. 240 Platinum Tip | velocity, fps: | 1830 | 1488 | 1220 | 1048 | |
| | energy, ft-lb: | 1784 | 1180 | 792 | 585 | |
| | arc inches: | | 0 | -15.0 | -53.4 | |

### .450/.400 (3")

| | | 0 | 100 | 200 | 300 | 400 |
|---|---|---|---|---|---|---|
| A-Square 400 Triad | velocity, fps: | 2150 | 1910 | 1690 | 1490 | |
| | energy, ft-lb: | 4105 | 3241 | 2537 | 1972 | |
| | arc, inches: | | +4.4 | 0 | -16.5 | |

### .450/.400 (3 1/4")

| | | 0 | 100 | 200 | 300 | 400 |
|---|---|---|---|---|---|---|
| A-Square 400 Triad | velocity, fps: | 2150 | 1910 | 1690 | 1490 | |
| | energy, ft-lb: | 4105 | 3241 | 2537 | 1972 | |
| | arc, inches: | | +4.4 | 0 | -16.5 | |

### .450/.400 Nitro Express

| | | 0 | 100 | 200 | 300 | 400 |
|---|---|---|---|---|---|---|
| Hornady 400 RN | velocity, fps | 2050 | 1815 | 1595 | 1402 | |
| | energy, ft-lb | 3732 | 2924 | 2259 | 1746 | |
| | arc, inches | -1.5 | 0 | -10.0 | -33.4 | |

### .404 Jeffery

| | | 0 | 100 | 200 | 300 | 400 |
|---|---|---|---|---|---|---|
| A-Square 400 Triad | velocity, fps: | 2150 | 1901 | 1674 | 1468 | 1299 |
| | energy, ft-lb: | 4105 | 3211 | 2489 | 1915 | 1499 |
| | arc, inches: | | +4.1 | 0 | -16.4 | -49.1 |

### .405 Winchester

| | | 0 | 100 | 200 | 300 | 400 |
|---|---|---|---|---|---|---|
| Hornady 300 Flatpoint | velocity, fps: | 2200 | 1851 | 1545 | 1296 | |
| | energy, ft-lb: | 3224 | 2282 | 1589 | 1119 | |
| | arc, inches: | | 0 | -8.7 | -31.9 | |
| Hornady 300 SP Interlock | velocity, fps: | 2200 | 1890 | 1610 | 1370 | |
| | energy, ft-lb: | 3224 | 2379 | 1727 | 1250 | |
| | arc, inches: | | 0 | -8.3 | -30.2 | |

### .416 Taylor

| | | 0 | 100 | 200 | 300 | 400 |
|---|---|---|---|---|---|---|
| A-Square 400 Triad | velocity, fps: | 2350 | 2093 | 1853 | 1634 | 1443 |
| | energy, ft-lb: | 4905 | 3892 | 3049 | 2371 | 1849 |
| | arc, inches: | | +3.2 | 0 | -13.6 | -39.8 |

### .416 Hoffman

| | | 0 | 100 | 200 | 300 | 400 |
|---|---|---|---|---|---|---|
| A-Square 400 Triad | velocity, fps: | 2380 | 2122 | 1879 | 1658 | 1464 |
| | energy, ft-lb: | 5031 | 3998 | 3136 | 2440 | 1903 |
| | arc, inches: | | +3.1 | 0 | -13.1 | -38.7 |

BALLISTICS

# Centerfire Rifle Ballistics

## .416 REMINGTON MAGNUM TO .45-70 GOVERNMENT

| cartridge bullet | range, yards: | 0 | 100 | 200 | 300 | 400 |
|---|---|---|---|---|---|---|
| **.416 Remington Magnum** | | | | | | |
| A-Square 400 Triad | velocity, fps: | 2380 | 2122 | 1879 | 1658 | 1464 |
| | energy, ft-lb: | 5031 | 3998 | 3136 | 2440 | 1903 |
| | arc, inches: | | +3.1 | 0 | -13.2 | -38.7 |
| Federal 400 Trophy Bonded | velocity, fps: | 2400 | 2150 | 1920 | 1700 | 1500 |
| Sledgehammer Solid | energy, ft-lb: | 5115 | 4110 | 3260 | 2565 | 2005 |
| | arc, inches: | | 0 | -6.0 | -21.6 | -49.2 |
| Federal 400 Trophy Bonded | velocity, fps: | 2400 | 2180 | 1970 | 1770 | 1590 |
| | energy, ft-lb: | 5115 | 4215 | 3440 | 2785 | 2245 |
| | arc, inches: | | 0 | -5.8 | -20.6 | -46.9 |
| Rem. 400 Swift A-Frame | velocity, fps: | 2400 | 2175 | 1962 | 1763 | 1579 |
| | energy, ft-lb: | 5115 | 4201 | 3419 | 2760 | 2214 |
| | arc, inches: | | 0 | -5.9 | -20.8 | |
| **.416 Rigby** | | | | | | |
| A-Square 400 Triad | velocity, fps: | 2400 | 2140 | 1897 | 1673 | 1478 |
| | energy, ft-lb: | 5115 | 4069 | 3194 | 2487 | 1940 |
| | arc, inches: | | +3.0 | 0 | -12.9 | -38.0 |
| Federal 400 Trophy Bonded | velocity, fps: | 2370 | 2150 | 1940 | 1750 | 1570 |
| | energy, ft-lb: | 4990 | 4110 | 3350 | 2715 | 2190 |
| | arc, inches: | | 0 | -6.0 | -21.3 | -48.1 |
| Federal 400 Trophy Bonded | velocity, fps: | 2370 | 2120 | 1890 | 1660 | 1460 |
| Sledgehammer Solid | energy, ft-lb: | 4990 | 3975 | 3130 | 2440 | 1895 |
| | arc, inches: | | 0 | -6.3 | -22.5 | -51.5 |
| Federal 410 Woodleigh | velocity, fps: | 2370 | 2110 | 1870 | 1640 | 1440 |
| Weldcore | energy, ft-lb: | 5115 | 4050 | 3165 | 2455 | 1895 |
| | arc, inches: | | 0 | -7.4 | -24.8 | -55.0 |
| Federal 410 Solid | velocity, fps: | 2370 | 2110 | 2870 | 1640 | 1440 |
| | energy, ft-lb: | 5115 | 4050 | 3165 | 2455 | 1895 |
| | arc, inches: | | 0 | -7.4 | -24.8 | -55.0 |
| Norma 400 TXP Swift A-Fr. | velocity, fps: | 2350 | 2127 | 1917 | 1721 | |
| | energy, ft-lb: | 4906 | 4021 | 3266 | 2632 | |
| | arc, inches: | | +3.1 | 0 | -12.5 | |
| Norma 400 Barnes Solid | velocity, fps: | 2297 | 1930 | 1604 | 1330 | |
| | energy, ft-lb: | 4687 | 3310 | 2284 | 1571 | |
| | arc, inches: | | +3.9 | 0 | -17.7 | |
| **.416 Rimmed** | | | | | | |
| A-Square 400 Triad | velocity, fps: | 2400 | 2140 | 1897 | 1673 | |
| | energy, ft-lb: | 5115 | 4069 | 3194 | 2487 | |
| | arc, inches: | | +3.3 | 0 | -13.2 | |
| **.416 Dakota** | | | | | | |
| Dakota 400 Barnes X | velocity, fps: | 2450 | 2294 | 2143 | 1998 | 1859 |
| | energy, ft-lb: | 5330 | 4671 | 4077 | 3544 | 3068 |
| | arc, inches: | | +2.5 | -0.2 | -10.5 | -29.4 |
| **.416 Weatherby** | | | | | | |
| A-Square 400 Triad | velocity, fps: | 2600 | 2328 | 2073 | 1834 | 1624 |
| | energy, ft-lb: | 6004 | 4813 | 3816 | 2986 | 2343 |
| | arc, inches: | | +2.5 | 0 | -10.5 | -31.6 |
| Wby. 350 Barnes X | velocity, fps: | 2850 | 2673 | 2503 | 2340 | 2182 |
| | energy, ft-lb: | 6312 | 5553 | 4870 | 4253 | 3700 |
| | arc, inches: | | +1.7 | 0 | -7.2 | -20.9 |
| Wby. 400 Swift A-Fr. | velocity, fps: | 2650 | 2426 | 2213 | 2011 | 1820 |
| | energy, ft-lb: | 6237 | 5227 | 4350 | 3592 | 2941 |
| | arc, inches: | | +2.2 | 0 | -9.3 | -27.1 |
| Wby. 400 RN Expanding | velocity, fps: | 2700 | 2417 | 2152 | 1903 | 1676 |
| | energy, ft-lb: | 6474 | 5189 | 4113 | 3216 | 2493 |
| | arc, inches: | | +2.3 | 0 | -9.7 | -29.3 |
| Wby. 400 Monolithic Solid | velocity, fps: | 2700 | 2411 | 2140 | 1887 | 1656 |
| | energy, ft-lb: | 6474 | 5162 | 4068 | 3161 | 2435 |
| | arc, inches: | | +2.3 | 0 | -9.8 | -29.7 |

| cartridge bullet | range, yards: | 0 | 100 | 200 | 300 | 400 |
|---|---|---|---|---|---|---|
| **10.57 (.416) Meteor** | | | | | | |
| Lazzeroni 400 Swift A-Fr. | velocity, fps: | 2730 | 2532 | 2342 | 2161 | 1987 |
| | energy, ft-lb: | 6621 | 5695 | 4874 | 4147 | 3508 |
| | arc, inches: | | +1.9 | 0 | -8.3 | -24.0 |
| **.425 Express** | | | | | | |
| A-Square 400 Triad | velocity, fps: | 2400 | 2136 | 1888 | 1662 | 1465 |
| | energy, ft-lb: | 5115 | 4052 | 3167 | 2454 | 1906 |
| | arc, inches: | | +3.0 | 0 | -13.1 | -38.3 |
| **.44-40 Winchester** | | | | | | |
| Rem. 200 Soft Point | velocity, fps: | 1190 | 1006 | 900 | 822 | 756 |
| | energy, ft-lb: | 629 | 449 | 360 | 300 | 254 |
| | arc, inches: | | 0 | -33.1 | -108.7 | -235.2 |
| Win. 200 Soft Point | velocity, fps: | 1190 | 1006 | 900 | 822 | 756 |
| | energy, ft-lb: | 629 | 449 | 360 | 300 | 254 |
| | arc, inches: | | 0 | -33.3 | -109.5 | -237.4 |
| **.44 Remington Magnum** | | | | | | |
| Federal 240 Hi-Shok HP | velocity, fps: | 1760 | 1380 | 1090 | 950 | 860 |
| | energy, ft-lb: | 1650 | 1015 | 640 | 485 | 395 |
| | arc, inches: | | 0 | -17.4 | -60.7 | -136.0 |
| Rem. 210 Semi-Jacketed HP | velocity, fps: | 1920 | 1477 | 1155 | 982 | 880 |
| | energy, ft-lb: | 1719 | 1017 | 622 | 450 | 361 |
| | arc, inches: | | 0 | -14.7 | -55.5 | -131.3 |
| Rem. 240 Soft Point | velocity, fps: | 1760 | 1380 | 1114 | 970 | 878 |
| | energy, ft-lb: | 1650 | 1015 | 661 | 501 | 411 |
| | arc, inches: | | 0 | -17.0 | -61.4 | -143.0 |
| Rem. 240 Semi-Jacketed | velocity, fps: | 1760 | 1380 | 1114 | 970 | 878 |
| Hollow Point | energy, ft-lb: | 1650 | 1015 | 661 | 501 | 411 |
| | arc, inches: | | 0 | -17.0 | -61.4 | -143.0 |
| Rem. 275 JHP Core-Lokt | velocity, fps: | 1580 | 1293 | 1093 | 976 | 896 |
| | energy, ft-lb: | 1524 | 1020 | 730 | 582 | 490 |
| | arc, inches: | | 0 | -19.4 | -67.5 | -210.8 |
| Win. 210 Silvertip HP | velocity, fps: | 1580 | 1198 | 993 | 879 | 795 |
| | energy, ft-lb: | 1164 | 670 | 460 | 361 | 295 |
| | arc, inches: | | 0 | -22.4 | -76.1 | -168.0 |
| Win. 240 Hollow Soft Point | velocity, fps: | 1760 | 1362 | 1094 | 953 | 861 |
| | energy, ft-lb: | 1650 | 988 | 638 | 484 | 395 |
| | arc, inches: | | 0 | -18.1 | -65.1 | -150.3 |
| Win. 250 Platinum Tip | velocity, fps: | 1830 | 1475 | 1201 | 1032 | 931 |
| | energy, ft-lb: | 1859 | 1208 | 801 | 591 | 481 |
| | arc, inches: | | 0 | -15.3 | -54.7 | -126.6. |
| **.444 Marlin** | | | | | | |
| Rem. 240 Soft Point | velocity, fps: | 2350 | 1815 | 1377 | 1087 | 941 |
| | energy, ft-lb: | 2942 | 1755 | 1010 | 630 | 472 |
| | arc, inches: | | +2.2 | -5.4 | -31.4 | -86.7 |
| Hornady 265 Evolution | velocity, fps: | 2325 | 1971 | 1652 | 1380 | |
| | energy, ft-lb: | 3180 | 2285 | 1606 | 1120 | |
| | arc, inches: | | +3.0 | -1.4 | -18.6 | |
| Hornady 265 FP LM | velocity, fps: | 2335 | 1913 | 1551 | 1266 | |
| | energy, ft-lb: | 3208 | 2153 | 1415 | 943 | |
| | arc, inches: | | + 2.0 | -4.9 | -26.5 | |
| **.45-70 Government** | | | | | | |
| Black Hills 405 FPL | velocity, fps: | 1250 | | | | |
| | energy, ft-lb: | | | | | |
| | arc, inches: | | | | | |
| Federal 300 Sierra Pro-Hunt. | velocity, fps: | 1880 | 1650 | 1430 | 1240 | 1110 |
| HP FN | energy, ft-lb: | 2355 | 1815 | 1355 | 1015 | 810 |
| | arc, inches: | | 0 | -11.5 | -39.7 | -89.1 |
| PMC 350 FNSP | velocity, fps: | | | | | |
| | energy, ft-lb: | | | | | |
| | arc, inches: | | | | | |

**BALLISTICS**

# Centerfire Rifle Ballistics

## .45-70 GOVERNMENT TO .500/.465

| cartridge bullet | range, yards: | 0 | 100 | 200 | 300 | 400 |
|---|---|---|---|---|---|---|
| Rem. 300 Jacketed HP | velocity, fps | 1810 | 1497 | 1244 | 1073 | 969 |
| | energy, ft-lb | 2182 | 1492 | 1031 | 767 | 625 |
| | arc, inches | | 0 | -13.8 | -50.1 | -115.7 |
| Rem. 405 Soft Point | velocity, fps | 1330 | 1168 | 1055 | 977 | 918 |
| | energy, ft-lb | 1590 | 1227 | 1001 | 858 | 758 |
| | arc, inches | | 0 | -24.0 | -78.6 | -169.4 |
| Win. 300 Jacketed HP | velocity, fps | 1880 | 1650 | 1425 | 1235 | 1105 |
| | energy, ft-lb | 2355 | 1815 | 1355 | 1015 | 810 |
| | arc, inches | | 0 | -12.8 | -44.3 | -95.5 |
| Win. 300 Partition Gold | velocity, fps | 1880 | 1558 | 1292 | 1103 | 988 |
| | energy, ft-lb | 2355 | 1616 | 1112 | 811 | 651 |
| | arc, inches | | 0 | -12.9 | -46.0 | -104.9. |

### .450 Bushmaster

| cartridge bullet | range, yards: | 0 | 100 | 200 | 300 | 400 |
|---|---|---|---|---|---|---|
| Hornady 250 SST-ML | velocity, fps | 2200 | 1840 | 1524 | 1268 | |
| | energy, ft-lb | 2686 | 1879 | 1289 | 893 | |
| | arc, inches | -2.0 | +2.5 | -3.5 | -24.5 | |

### .450 Marlin

| cartridge bullet | range, yards: | 0 | 100 | 200 | 300 | 400 |
|---|---|---|---|---|---|---|
| Hornady 350 FP | velocity, fps | 2100 | 1720 | 1397 | 1156 | |
| | energy, ft-lb | 3427 | 2298 | 1516 | 1039 | |
| | arc, inches | | 0 | -10.4 | -38.9 | |

### .450 Nitro Express (3¼")

| cartridge bullet | range, yards: | 0 | 100 | 200 | 300 | 400 |
|---|---|---|---|---|---|---|
| A-Square 465 Triad | velocity, fps | 2190 | 1970 | 1765 | 1577 | |
| | energy, ft-lb | 4952 | 4009 | 3216 | 2567 | |
| | arc, inches | | +4.3 | 0 | -15.4 | |

### .450 #2

| cartridge bullet | range, yards: | 0 | 100 | 200 | 300 | 400 |
|---|---|---|---|---|---|---|
| A-Square 465 Triad | velocity, fps | 2190 | 1970 | 1765 | 1577 | |
| | energy, ft-lb | 4952 | 4009 | 3216 | 2567 | |
| | arc, inches | | +4.3 | 0 | -15.4 | |

### .458 Winchester Magnum

| cartridge bullet | range, yards: | 0 | 100 | 200 | 300 | 400 |
|---|---|---|---|---|---|---|
| A-Square 465 Triad | velocity, fps | 2220 | 1999 | 1791 | 1601 | 1433 |
| | energy, ft-lb | 5088 | 4127 | 3312 | 2646 | 2121 |
| | arc, inches | | +3.6 | 0 | -14.7 | -42.5 |
| Federal 350 Soft Point | velocity, fps | 2470 | 1990 | 1570 | 1250 | 1060 |
| | energy, ft-lb | 4740 | 3065 | 1915 | 1205 | 870 |
| | arc, inches | | 0 | -7.5 | -29.1 | -71.1 |
| Federal 400 Trophy Bonded | velocity, fps | 2380 | 2170 | 1960 | 1770 | 1590 |
| | energy, ft-lb | 5030 | 4165 | 3415 | 2785 | 2255 |
| | arc, inches | | 0 | -5.9 | -20.9 | -47.1 |
| Federal 500 Solid | velocity, fps | 2090 | 1870 | 1670 | 1480 | 1320 |
| | energy, ft-lb | 4850 | 3880 | 3085 | 2440 | 1945 |
| | arc, inches | | 0 | -8.5 | -29.5 | -66.2 |
| Federal 500 Trophy Bonded | velocity, fps | 2090 | 1870 | 1660 | 1480 | 1310 |
| | energy, ft-lb | 4850 | 3870 | 3065 | 2420 | 1915 |
| | arc, inches | | 0 | -8.5 | -29.7 | -66.8 |
| Federal 500 Trophy Bonded Sledgehammer Solid | velocity, fps | 2090 | 1860 | 1650 | 1460 | 1300 |
| | energy, ft-lb | 4850 | 3845 | 3025 | 2365 | 1865 |
| | arc, inches | | 0 | -8.6 | -30.0 | -67.8 |
| Federal 510 Soft Point | velocity, fps | 2090 | 1820 | 1570 | 1360 | 1190 |
| | energy, ft-lb | 4945 | 3730 | 2790 | 2080 | 1605 |
| | arc, inches | | 0 | -9.1 | -32.3 | -73.9 |
| Hornady 500 FMJ-RN HM | velocity, fps | 2260 | 1984 | 1735 | 1512 | |
| | energy, ft-lb | 5670 | 4368 | 3341 | 2538 | |
| | arc, inches | | 0 | -7.4 | -26.4 | |
| Norma 500 TXP Swift A-Fr. | velocity, fps | 2116 | 1903 | 1705 | 1524 | |
| | energy, ft-lb | 4972 | 4023 | 3228 | 2578 | |
| | arc, inches | | +4.1 | 0 | -16.1 | |
| Norma 500 Barnes Solid | velocity, fps | 2067 | 1750 | 1472 | 1245 | |
| | energy, ft-lb | 4745 | 3401 | 2405 | 1721 | |
| | arc, inches | | +4.9 | 0 | -21.2 | |

| cartridge bullet | range, yards: | 0 | 100 | 200 | 300 | 400 |
|---|---|---|---|---|---|---|
| Rem. 450 Swift A-Frame PSP | velocity, fps | 2150 | 1901 | 1671 | 1465 | 1289 |
| | energy, ft-lb | 4618 | 3609 | 2789 | 2144 | 1659 |
| | arc, inches | | 0 | -8.2 | -28.9 | |
| Speer 500 African GS Tungsten Solid | velocity, fps | 2120 | 1845 | 1596 | 1379 | |
| | energy, ft-lb | 4989 | 3780 | 2828 | 2111 | |
| | arc, inches | | 0 | -8.8 | -31.3 | |
| Speer African Grand Slam | velocity, fps | 2120 | 1853 | 1609 | 1396 | |
| | energy, ft-lb | 4989 | 3810 | 2875 | 2163 | |
| | arc, inches | | 0 | -8.7 | -30.8 | |
| Win. 510 Soft Point | velocity, fps | 2040 | 1770 | 1527 | 1319 | 1157 |
| | energy, ft-lb | 4712 | 3547 | 2640 | 1970 | 1516 |
| | arc, inches | | 0 | -10.3 | -35.6 | |

### .458 Lott

| cartridge bullet | range, yards: | 0 | 100 | 200 | 300 | 400 |
|---|---|---|---|---|---|---|
| A-Square 465 Triad | velocity, fps | 2380 | 2150 | 1932 | 1730 | 1551 |
| | energy, ft-lb | 5848 | 4773 | 3855 | 3091 | 2485 |
| | arc, inches | | +3.0 | 0 | -12.5 | -36.4 |
| Hornady 500 RNSP or solid | velocity, fps | 2300 | 2022 | 1776 | 1551 | |
| | energy, ft-lb | 5872 | 4537 | 3502 | 2671 | |
| | arc, inches | | +3.4 | 0 | -14.3 | |
| Hornady 500 InterBond | velocity, fps | 2300 | 2028 | 1777 | 1549 | |
| | energy, ft-lb | 5872 | 4535 | 3453 | 2604 | |
| | arc, inches | | 0 | -7.0 | -25.1 | |

### .450 Ackley

| cartridge bullet | range, yards: | 0 | 100 | 200 | 300 | 400 |
|---|---|---|---|---|---|---|
| A-Square 465 Triad | velocity, fps | 2400 | 2169 | 1950 | 1747 | 1567 |
| | energy, ft-lb | 5947 | 4857 | 3927 | 3150 | 2534 |
| | arc, inches | | +2.9 | 0 | -12.2 | -35.8 |

### .460 Short A-Square

| cartridge bullet | range, yards: | 0 | 100 | 200 | 300 | 400 |
|---|---|---|---|---|---|---|
| A-Square 500 Triad | velocity, fps | 2420 | 2198 | 1987 | 1789 | 1613 |
| | energy, ft-lb | 6501 | 5362 | 4385 | 3553 | 2890 |
| | arc, inches | | +2.9 | 0 | -11.6 | -34.2 |

### .450 Dakota

| cartridge bullet | range, yards: | 0 | 100 | 200 | 300 | 400 |
|---|---|---|---|---|---|---|
| Dakota 500 Barnes Solid | velocity, fps | 2450 | 2235 | 2030 | 1838 | 1658 |
| | energy, ft-lb | 6663 | 5544 | 4576 | 3748 | 3051 |
| | arc, inches | | +2.5 | -0.6 | -12.0 | -33.8 |

### .460 Weatherby Magnum

| cartridge bullet | range, yards: | 0 | 100 | 200 | 300 | 400 |
|---|---|---|---|---|---|---|
| A-Square 500 Triad | velocity, fps | 2580 | 2349 | 2131 | 1923 | 1737 |
| | energy, ft-lb | 7389 | 6126 | 5040 | 4107 | 3351 |
| | arc, inches | | +2.4 | 0 | -10.0 | -29.4 |
| Wby. 450 Barnes X | velocity, fps | 2700 | 2518 | 2343 | 2175 | 2013 |
| | energy, ft-lb | 7284 | 6333 | 5482 | 4725 | 4050 |
| | arc, inches | | +2.0 | 0 | -8.4 | -24.1 |
| Wby. 500 RN Expanding | velocity, fps | 2600 | 2301 | 2022 | 1764 | 1533. |
| | energy, ft-lb | 7504 | 5877 | 4539 | 3456 | 2608 |
| | arc, inches | | +2.6 | 0 | -11.1 | -33.5 |
| Wby. 500 FMJ | velocity, fps | 2600 | 2309 | 2037 | 1784 | 1557 |
| | energy, ft-lb | 7504 | 5917 | 4605 | 3534 | 2690 |
| | arc, inches | | +2.5 | 0 | -10.9 | -33.0 |

### .500/.465

| cartridge bullet | range, yards: | 0 | 100 | 200 | 300 | 400 |
|---|---|---|---|---|---|---|
| A-Square 480 Triad | velocity, fps | 2150 | 1928 | 1722 | 1533 | |
| | energy, ft-lb | 4926 | 3960 | 3160 | 2505 | |
| | arc, inches | | +4.3 | 0 | -16.0 | |

**BALLISTICS**

| cartridge bullet | range, yards: | 0 | 100 | 200 | 300 | 400 |
|---|---|---|---|---|---|---|
| **.470 Nitro Express** | | | | | | |
| A-Square 500 Triad | velocity, fps: | 2150 | 1912 | 1693 | 1494 | |
| | energy, ft-lb: | 5132 | 4058 | 3182 | 2478 | |
| | arc, inches: | | +4.4 | 0 | -16.5 | |
| Federal 500 Woodleigh | velocity, fps: | 2150 | 1890 | 1650 | 1440 | 1270 |
| Weldcore | energy, ft-lb: | 5130 | 3965 | 3040 | 2310 | 1790 |
| | arc, inches: | | 0 | -9.3 | -31.3 | -69.7 |
| Federal 500 Woodleigh | velocity, fps: | 2150 | 1890 | 1650 | 1440 | 1270. |
| Weldcore Solid | energy, ft-lb: | 5130 | 3965 | 3040 | 2310 | 1790 |
| | arc, inches: | | 0 | -9.3 | -31.3 | -69.7 |
| Federal 500 Trophy Bonded | velocity, fps: | 2150 | 1940 | 1740 | 1560 | 1400 |
| | energy, ft-lb: | 5130 | 4170 | 3360 | 2695 | 2160 |
| | arc, inches: | | 0 | -7.8 | -27.1 | -60.8 |
| Federal 500 Trophy Bonded | velocity, fps: | 2150 | 1940 | 1740 | 1560 | 1400 |
| Sledgehammer Solid | energy, ft-lb: | 5130 | 4170 | 3360 | 2695 | 2160 |
| | arc, inches: | | 0 | -7.8 | -27.1 | -60.8 |
| Norma 500 Woodleigh SP | velocity, fps: | 2165 | 1975 | 1795 | 1627 | |
| | energy, ft-lb: | 5205 | 4330 | 3577 | 2940 | |
| | arc, inches: | | 0 | -7.4 | -25.7 | |
| Norma 500 Woodleigh FJ | velocity, fps: | 2165 | 1974 | 1794 | 1626 | |
| | energy, ft-lb: | 5205 | 4328 | 3574 | 2936 | |
| | arc, inches: | | 0 | -7.5 | -25.7 | |
| **.470 Capstick** | | | | | | |
| A-Square 500 Triad | velocity, fps: | 2400 | 2172 | 1958 | 1761 | 1553 |
| | energy, ft-lb: | 6394 | 5236 | 4255 | 3445 | 2678 |
| | arc, inches: | | +2.9 | 0 | -11.9 | -36.1 |
| **.475 #2** | | | | | | |
| A-Square 480 Triad | velocity, fps: | 2200 | 1964 | 1744 | 1544 | |
| | energy, ft-lb: | 5158 | 4109 | 3240 | 2539 | |
| | arc, inches: | | +4.1 | 0 | -15.6 | |
| **.475 #2 Jeffery** | | | | | | |
| A-Square 500 Triad | velocity, fps: | 2200 | 1966 | 1748 | 1550 | |
| | energy, ft-lb: | 5373 | 4291 | 3392 | 2666 | |
| | arc, inches: | | +4.1 | 0 | -15.6 | |

| cartridge bullet | range, yards: | 0 | 100 | 200 | 300 | 400 |
|---|---|---|---|---|---|---|
| **.495 A-Square** | | | | | | |
| A-Square 570 Triad | velocity, fps: | 2350 | 2117 | 1896 | 1693 | 1513 |
| | energy, ft-lb: | 6989 | 5671 | 4552 | 3629 | 2899 |
| | arc, inches: | | +3.1 | 0 | -13.0 | -37.8 |
| **.500 Nitro Express (3")** | | | | | | |
| A-Square 570 Triad | velocity, fps: | 2150 | 1928 | 1722 | 1533 | |
| | energy, ft-lb: | 5850 | 4703 | 3752 | 2975 | |
| | arc, inches: | | +4.3 | 0 | -16.1 | |
| **.500 A-Square** | | | | | | |
| A-Square 600 Triad | velocity, fps: | 2470 | 2235 | 2013 | 1804 | 1620 |
| | energy, ft-lb: | 8127 | 6654 | 5397 | 4336 | 3495 |
| | arc, inches: | | +2.7 | 0 | -11.3 | -33.5 |
| **.505 Gibbs** | | | | | | |
| A-Square 525 Triad | velocity, fps: | 2300 | 2063 | 1840 | 1637 | |
| | energy, ft-lb: | 6166 | 4962 | 3948 | 3122 | |
| | arc, inches: | | +3.6 | 0 | -14.2 | |
| **.577 Nitro Express** | | | | | | |
| A-Square 750 Triad | velocity, fps: | 2050 | 1811 | 1595 | 1401 | |
| | energy, ft-lb: | 6998 | 5463 | 4234 | 3267 | |
| | arc, inches: | | +4.9 | 0 | -18.5 | |
| **.577 Tyrannosaur** | | | | | | |
| A-Square 750 Triad | velocity, fps: | 2460 | 2197 | 1950 | 1723 | 1516 |
| | energy, ft-lb: | 10077 | 8039 | 6335 | 4941 | 3825 |
| | arc, inches: | | +2.8 | 0 | -12.1 | -36.0 |
| **.600 Nitro Express** | | | | | | |
| A-Square 900 Triad | velocity, fps: | 1950 | 1680 | 1452 | 1336 | |
| | energy, ft-lb: | 7596 | 5634 | 4212 | 3564 | |
| | arc, inches: | | +5.6 | 0 | -20.7 | |
| **.700 Nitro Express** | | | | | | |
| A-Square 1000 Monolithic | velocity, fps: | 1900 | 1669 | 1461 | 1288 | |
| Solid | energy, ft-lb: | 8015 | 6188 | 4740 | 3685 | |
| | arc, inches: | | +5.8 | 0 | -22.2 | |

BALLISTICS

# Centerfire Handgun Ballistics

Data shown here is taken from manufacturers' charts; your chronograph readings may vary. Barrel lengths for pistol data vary, and depend in part on which pistols are typically chambered in a given cartridge. Velocity variations due to barrel length depend on the baseline bullet speed and the load. Velocity for the .30 Carbine, normally a rifle cartridge, was determined in a pistol barrel.

Listings are current as of February the year *Shooter's Bible* appears (not the cover year). Listings are not intended as recommendations. For example, the data for the .25 Auto gives velocity and energy readings to 100 yards. Few handgunners would call the little .25 a 100-yard cartridge.

Abbreviations: Bullets are designated by loading company, weight (in grains) and type, with these abbreviations for shape and construction: BJHP=brass-jacketed hollowpoint; FN=Flat Nose; FMC=Full Metal Case; FMJ=Full Metal Jacket; HP=Hollowpoint; L=Lead; LF=Lead-Free; +P=a more powerful load than traditionally manufactured for that round; RN=Round Nose; SFHP=Starfire (PMC) Hollowpoint; SP=Softpoint; SWC=Semi Wadcutter; TMJ=Total Metal Jacket; WC=Wadcutter; CEPP, SXT and XTP are trademarked designations of Lapua, Winchester and Hornady, respectively.

## .25 AUTO TO .32 S&W LONG

| cartridge bullet | range, yards: | 0 | 25 | 50 | 75 | 100 |
|---|---|---|---|---|---|---|
| **.25 Auto** | | | | | | |
| Federal 50 FMJ | velocity, fps: | 760 | 750 | 730 | 720 | 700 |
| | energy, ft-lb: | 65 | 60 | 60 | 55 | 55 |
| Hornady 35 JHP/XTP | velocity, fps: | 900 | | 813 | | 742 |
| | energy, ft-lb: | 63 | | 51 | | 43 |
| Magtech 50 FMC | velocity, fps: | 760 | | 707 | | 659 |
| | energy, ft-lb: | 64 | | 56 | | 48 |
| PMC 50 FMJ | velocity, fps: | 754 | 730 | 707 | 685 | 663 |
| | energy, ft-lb: | 62 | | | | |
| Rem. 50 Metal Case | velocity, fps: | 760 | | 707 | | 659 |
| | energy, ft-lb: | 64 | | 56 | | 48 |
| Speer 35 Gold Dot | velocity, fps: | 900 | | 816 | | 747 |
| | energy, ft-lb: | 63 | | 52 | | 43 |
| Speer 50 TMJ (and Blazer) | velocity, fps: | 760 | | 717 | | 677 |
| | energy, ft-lb: | 64 | | 57 | | 51 |
| Win. 45 Expanding Point | velocity, fps: | 815 | | 729 | | 655 |
| | energy, ft-lb | 66 | | 53 | | 42 |
| Win. 50 FMJ | velocity, fps: | 760 | | 707 | | |
| | energy, ft-lb: | 64 | | 56 | | |
| **.30 Luger** | | | | | | |
| Win. 93 FMJ | velocity, fps: | 1220 | | 1110 | | 1040 |
| | energy, ft-lb | 305 | | 255 | | 225 |
| **7.62x25 Tokarev** | | | | | | |
| PMC 93 FMJ | velocity and energy figures not available | | | | | |
| **.30 Carbine** | | | | | | |
| Win. 110 Hollow SP | velocity, fps: | 1790 | | 1601 | | 1430 |
| | energy, ft-lb | 783 | | 626 | | 500 |
| **.32 Auto** | | | | | | |
| Federal 65 Hydra-Shok JHP | velocity, fps: | 950 | 920 | 890 | 860 | 830 |
| | energy, ft-lb: | 130 | 120 | 115 | 105 | 100 |
| Federal 71 FMJ | velocity, fps: | 910 | 880 | 860 | 830 | 810 |
| | energy, ft-lb: | 130 | 120 | 115 | 110 | 105 |
| Hornady 60 JHP/XTP | velocity, fps: | 1000 | | 917 | | 849 |
| | energy, ft-lb: | 133 | | 112 | | 96 |
| Hornady 71 FMJ-RN | velocity, fps: | 900 | | 845 | | 797 |
| | energy, ft-lb: | 128 | | 112 | | 100 |

| cartridge bullet | range, yards: | 0 | 25 | 50 | 75 | 100 |
|---|---|---|---|---|---|---|
| Magtech 71 FMC | velocity, fps: | 905 | | 855 | | 810 |
| | energy, ft-lb: | 129 | | 115 | | 103 |
| Magtech 71 JHP | velocity, fps: | 905 | | 855 | | 810 |
| | energy, ft-lb: | 129 | | 115 | | 103 |
| PMC 60 JHP | velocity, fps: | 980 | 849 | 820 | 791 | 763 |
| | energy, ft-lb: | 117 | | | | |
| PMC 70 SFHP | velocity, fps: | velocity and energy figures not available | | | | |
| PMC 71 FMJ | velocity, fps: | 870 | 841 | 814 | 791 | 763 |
| | energy, ft-lb: | 119 | | | | |
| Rem. 71 Metal Case | velocity, fps: | 905 | | 855 | | 810 |
| | energy, ft-lb: | 129 | | 115 | | 97 |
| Speer 60 Gold Dot | velocity, fps: | 960 | | 868 | | 796 |
| | energy, ft-lb: | 123 | | 100 | | 84 |
| Speer 71 TMJ (and Blazer) | velocity, fps: | 900 | | 855 | | 810 |
| | energy, ft-lb: | 129 | | 115 | | 97 |
| Win. 60 Silvertip HP | velocity, fps: | 970 | | 895 | | 835 |
| | energy, ft-lb | 125 | | 107 | | 93 |
| Win. 71 FMJ | velocity, fps: | 905 | | 855 | | |
| | energy, ft-lb | 129 | | 115 | | |
| **.32 S&W** | | | | | | |
| Rem. 88 LRN | velocity, fps: | 680 | | 645 | | 610 |
| | energy, ft-lb: | 90 | | 81 | | 73 |
| Win. 85 LRN | velocity, fps: | 680 | | 645 | | 610 |
| | energy, ft-lb: | 90 | | 81 | | 73 |
| **.32 S&W Long** | | | | | | |
| Federal 98 LWC | velocity, fps: | 780 | 700 | 630 | 560 | 500 |
| | energy, ft-lb: | 130 | 105 | 85 | 70 | 55 |
| Federal 98 LRN | velocity, fps: | 710 | 690 | 670 | 650 | 640 |
| | energy, ft-lb: | 115 | 105 | 100 | 95 | 90 |
| Lapua 83 LWC | velocity, fps: | 240 | | 189* | | 149* |
| | energy, ft-lb: | 154 | | 95* | | 59* |
| Lapua 98 LWC | velocity, fps: | 240 | | 202* | | 171* |
| | energy, ft-lb: | 183 | | 130* | | 93* |
| Magtech 98 LRN | velocity, fps: | 705 | | 670 | | 635 |
| | energy, ft-lb: | 108 | | 98 | | 88 |
| Magtech 98 LWC | velocity, fps: | 682 | | 579 | | 491 |
| | energy, ft-lb: | 102 | | 73 | | 52 |
| Norma 98 LWC | velocity, fps: | 787 | 759 | 732 | | 683 |
| | energy, ft-lb: | 136 | 126 | 118 | | 102 |

| cartridge bullet | range, yards: | 0 | 25 | 50 | 75 | 100 |
|---|---|---|---|---|---|---|
| PMC 98 LRN | velocity, fps: | 789 | 770 | 751 | 733 | 716 |
| | energy, ft-lb: | 135 | | | | |
| PMC 100 LWC | velocity, fps: | 683 | 652 | 623 | 595 | 569 |
| | energy, ft-lb: | 102 | | | | |
| Rem. 98 LRN | velocity, fps: | 705 | | 670 | | 635 |
| | energy, ft-lb: | 115 | | 98 | | 88 |
| Win. 98 LRN | velocity, fps: | 705 | | 670 | | 635 |
| | energy, ft-lb: | 115 | | 98 | | 88 |

## .32 Short Colt

| cartridge bullet | range, yards: | 0 | 25 | 50 | 75 | 100 |
|---|---|---|---|---|---|---|
| Win. 80 LRN | velocity, fps: | 745 | | 665 | | 590 |
| | energy, ft-lb: | 100 | | 79 | | 62 |

## .32-20

| cartridge bullet | range, yards: | 0 | 25 | 50 | 75 | 100 |
|---|---|---|---|---|---|---|
| Black Hills 115 FPL | velocity, fps: | 800 | | | | |
| | energy, ft-lb: | | | | | |

## .32 H&R Mag

| cartridge bullet | range, yards: | 0 | 25 | 50 | 75 | 100 |
|---|---|---|---|---|---|---|
| Black Hills 85 JHP | velocity, fps | 1100 | | | | |
| | energy, ft-lb | 228 | | | | |
| Black Hills 90 FPL | velocity, fps | 750 | | | | |
| | energy, ft-lb | | | | | |
| Black Hills 115 FPL | velocity, fps | 800 | | | | |
| | energy, ft-lb | | | | | |
| Federal 85 Hi-Shok JHP | velocity, fps: | 1100 | 1050 | 1020 | 970 | 930 |
| | energy, ft-lb: | 230 | 210 | 195 | 175 | 165 |
| Federal 95 LSWC | velocity, fps: | 1030 | 1000 | 940 | 930 | 900 |
| | energy, ft-lb: | 225 | 210 | 195 | 185 | 170 |

## 9mm Makarov

| cartridge bullet | range, yards: | 0 | 25 | 50 | 75 | 100 |
|---|---|---|---|---|---|---|
| Federal 90 Hi-Shok JHP | velocity, fps: | 990 | 950 | 910 | 880 | 850 |
| | energy, ft-lb: | 195 | 180 | 165 | 155 | 145 |
| Federal 90 FMJ | velocity, fps: | 990 | 960 | 920 | 900 | 870 |
| | energy, ft-lb: | 205 | 190 | 180 | 170 | 160 |
| Hornady 95 JHP/XTP | velocity, fps: | 1000 | | 930 | | 874 |
| | energy, ft-lb: | 211 | | 182 | | 161 |
| PMC 100 FMJ-TC | velocity, fps: | velocity and energy figures not available | | | | |
| Speer 95 TMJ Blazer | velocity, fps: | 1000 | | 928 | | 872 |
| | energy, ft-lb: | 211 | | 182 | | 161 |

## 9x21 IMI

| cartridge bullet | range, yards: | 0 | 25 | 50 | 75 | 100 |
|---|---|---|---|---|---|---|
| PMC 123 FMJ | velocity, fps: | 1150 | 1093 | 1046 | 1007 | 973 |
| | energy, ft-lb: | 364 | | | | |

## 9mm Luger

| cartridge bullet | range, yards: | 0 | 25 | 50 | 75 | 100 |
|---|---|---|---|---|---|---|
| Black Hills 115 JHP | velocity, fps: | 1150 | | | | |
| | energy, ft-lb: | 336 | | | | |
| Black Hills 115 FMJ | velocity, fps: | 1150 | | | | |
| | energy, ft-lb: | 336 | | | | |
| Black Hills 115 JHP +P | velocity, fps: | 1300 | | | | |
| | energy, ft-lb: | 431 | | | | |
| Black Hills 115 EXP JHP | velocity, fps: | 1250 | | | | |
| | energy, ft-lb: | 400 | | | | |
| Black Hills 124 JHP +P | velocity, fps: | 1250 | | | | |
| | energy, ft-lb: | 430 | | | | |
| Black Hills 124 JHP | velocity, fps: | 1150 | | | | |
| | energy, ft-lb: | 363 | | | | |
| Black Hills 124 FMJ | velocity, fps: | 1150 | | | | |
| | energy, ft-lb: | 363 | | | | |
| Black Hills 147 JHP subsonic | velocity, fps: | 975 | | | | |
| | energy, ft-lb: | 309 | | | | |
| Black Hills 147 FMJ subsonic | velocity, fps: | 975 | | | | |
| | energy, ft-lb: | 309 | | | | |
| Federal 105 EFMJ | velocity, fps: | 1225 | 1160 | 1105 | 1060 | 1025 |
| | energy, ft-lb: | 350 | 315 | 285 | 265 | 245 |

| cartridge bullet | range, yards: | 0 | 25 | 50 | 75 | 100 |
|---|---|---|---|---|---|---|
| Federal 115 Hi-Shok JHP | velocity, fps: | 1160 | 1100 | 1060 | 1020 | 990 |
| | energy, ft-lb: | 345 | 310 | 285 | 270 | 250 |
| Federal 115 FMJ | velocity, fps: | 1160 | 1100 | 1060 | 1020 | 990 |
| | energy, ft-lb: | 345 | 310 | 285 | 270 | 250 |
| Federal 124 FMJ | velocity, fps: | 1120 | 1070 | 1030 | 990 | 960 |
| | energy, ft-lb: | 345 | 315 | 290 | 270 | 255 |
| Federal 124 Hydra-Shok JHP | velocity, fps: | 1120 | 1070 | 1030 | 990 | 960 |
| | energy, ft-lb: | 345 | 315 | 290 | 270 | 255 |
| Federal 124 TMJ TMF Primer | velocity, fps: | 1120 | 1070 | 1030 | 990 | 960 |
| | energy, ft-lb: | 345 | 315 | 290 | 270 | 255 |
| Federal 124 Truncated FMJ Match | velocity, fps: | 1120 | 1070 | 1030 | 990 | 960 |
| | energy, ft-lb: | 345 | 315 | 290 | 270 | 255 |
| Federal 124 Nyclad HP | velocity, fps: | 1120 | 1070 | 1030 | 990 | 960 |
| | energy, ft-lb: | 345 | 315 | 290 | 270 | 255 |
| Federal 124 FMJ +P | velocity, fps: | 1120 | 1070 | 1030 | 990 | 960 |
| | energy, ft-lb: | 345 | 315 | 290 | 270 | 255 |
| Federal 135 Hydra-Shok JHP | velocity, fps: | 1050 | 1030 | 1010 | 980 | 970 |
| | energy, ft-lb: | 330 | 315 | 300 | 290 | 280 |
| Federal 147 Hydra-Shok JHP | velocity, fps: | 1000 | 960 | 920 | 890 | 860 |
| | energy, ft-lb: | 325 | 300 | 275 | 260 | 240 |
| Federal 147 Hi-Shok JHP | velocity, fps: | 980 | 950 | 930 | 900 | 880 |
| | energy, ft-lb: | 310 | 295 | 285 | 265 | 255 |
| Federal 147 FMJ FN | velocity, fps: | 960 | 930 | 910 | 890 | 870 |
| | energy, ft-lb: | 295 | 280 | 270 | 260 | 250 |
| Federal 147 TMJ TMF Primer | velocity, fps: | 960 | 940 | 910 | 890 | 870 |
| | energy, ft-lb: | 300 | 285 | 270 | 260 | 245 |
| Hornady 115 JHP/XTP | velocity, fps: | 1155 | | 1047 | | 971 |
| | energy, ft-lb: | 341 | | 280 | | 241 |
| Hornady 124 JHP/XTP | velocity, fps: | 1110 | | 1030 | | 971 |
| | energy, ft-lb: | 339 | | 292 | | 259 |
| Hornady 124 TAP-FPD | velocity, fps: | 1100 | | 1028 | | 967 |
| | energy, ft-lb: | 339 | | 291 | | 257 |
| Hornady 147 JHP/XTP | velocity, fps: | 975 | | 935 | | 899 |
| | energy, ft-lb: | 310 | | 285 | | 264 |
| Hornady 147 TAP-FPD | velocity, fps: | 975 | | 935 | | 899 |
| | energy, ft-lb: | 310 | | 285 | | 264 |
| Lapua 116 FMJ | velocity, fps: | 365 | | 319* | | 290* |
| | energy, ft-lb: | 500 | | 381* | | 315* |
| Lapua 120 FMJ CEPP Super | velocity, fps: | 360 | | 316* | | 288* |
| | energy, ft-lb: | 505 | | 390* | | 324* |
| Lapua 120 FMJ CEPP Extra | velocity, fps: | 360 | | 316* | | 288* |
| | energy, ft-lb: | 505 | | 390* | | 324* |
| Lapua 123 HP Megashock | velocity, fps: | 355 | | 311* | | 284* |
| | energy, ft-lb: | 504 | | 388* | | 322* |
| Lapua 123 FMJ | velocity, fps: | 320 | | 292* | | 272* |
| | energy, ft-lb: | 410 | | 342* | | 295* |
| Lapua 123 FMJ Combat | velocity, fps: | 355 | | 315* | | 289* |
| | energy, ft-lb: | 504 | | 397* | | 333* |
| Magtech 115 JHP +P | velocity, fps: | 1246 | | 1137 | | 1056 |
| | energy, ft-lb: | 397 | | 330 | | 285 |
| Magtech 115 FMC | velocity, fps: | 1135 | | 1027 | | 961 |
| | energy, ft-lb: | 330 | | 270 | | 235 |
| Magtech 115 JHP | velocity, fps: | 1155 | | 1047 | | 971 |
| | energy, ft-lb: | 340 | | 280 | | 240 |
| Magtech 124 FMC | velocity, fps: | 1109 | | 1030 | | 971 |
| | energy, ft-lb: | 339 | | 292 | | 259 |
| Norma 84 Lead Free Frangible (Geco brand) | velocity, fps: | 1411 | | | | |
| | energy, ft-lb: | 371 | | | | |
| Norma 124 FMJ (Geco brand) | velocity, fps: | 1120 | | | | |
| | energy, fps: | 341 | | | | |
| Norma 123 FMJ | velocity, fps: | 1099 | 1032 | 980 | | 899 |
| | energy, ft-lb: | 331 | 292 | 263 | | 221 |

# Centerfire Handgun Ballistics

## 9MM LUGER TO .380 AUTO

| cartridge bullet | range, yards: | 0 | 25 | 50 | 75 | 100 |
|---|---|---|---|---|---|---|
| Norma 123 FMJ | velocity, fps: | 1280 | 1170 | 1086 | | 972 |
| | energy, ft-lb: | 449 | 375 | 323 | | 259 |
| PMC 75 Non-Toxic Frangible | velocity, fps: | 1350 | 1240 | 1154 | 1088 | 1035 |
| | energy, ft-lb: | 303 | | | | |
| PMC 95 SFHP | velocity, fps: | 1250 | 1239 | 1228 | 1217 | 1207 |
| | energy, ft-lb: | 330 | | | | |
| PMC 115 FMJ | velocity, fps: | 1157 | 1100 | 1053 | 1013 | 979 |
| | energy, ft-lb: | 344 | | | | |
| PMC 115 JHP | velocity, fps: | 1167 | 1098 | 1044 | 999 | 961 |
| | energy, ft-lb: | 350 | | | | |
| PMC 124 SFHP | velocity, fps: | 1090 | 1043 | 1003 | 969 | 939 |
| | energy, ft-lb: | 327 | | | | |
| PMC 124 FMJ | velocity, fps: | 1110 | 1059 | 1017 | 980 | 949 |
| | energy, ft-lb: | 339 | | | | |
| PMC 124 LRN | velocity, fps: | 1050 | 1006 | 969 | 937 | 908 |
| | energy, ft-lb: | 304 | | | | |
| PMC 147 FMJ | velocity, fps: | 980 | 965 | 941 | 919 | 900 |
| | enerby, ft-lb: | 310 | | | | |
| PMC 147 SFHP | velocity, fps: | velocity and energy figures not available | | | | |
| Rem. 101 Lead Free Frangible | velocity, fps: | 1220 | | 1092 | | 1004 |
| | energy, ft-lb: | 334 | | 267 | | 226 |
| Rem. 115 FN Enclosed Base | velocity, fps: | 1135 | | 1041 | | 973 |
| | energy, ft-lb: | 329 | | 277 | | 242 |
| Rem. 115 Metal Case | velocity, fps: | 1135 | | 1041 | | 973 |
| | energy, ft-lb: | 329 | | 277 | | 242 |
| Rem. 115 JHP | velocity, fps: | 1155 | | 1047 | | 971 |
| | energy, ft-lb: | 341 | | 280 | | 241 |
| Rem. 115 JHP +P | velocity, fps: | 1250 | | 1113 | | 1019 |
| | energy, ft-lb: | 399 | | 316 | | 265 |
| Rem. 124 JHP | velocity, fps: | 1120 | | 1028 | | 960 |
| | energy, ft-lb: | 346 | | 291 | | 254 |
| Rem. 124 FNEB | velocity, fps: | 1100 | | 1030 | | 971 |
| | energy, ft-lb: | 339 | | 292 | | 252 |
| Rem. 124 BJHP | velocity, fps: | 1125 | | 1031 | | 963 |
| | energy, ft-lb: | 349 | | 293 | | 255 |
| Rem. 124 BJHP +P | velocity, fps: | 1180 | | 1089 | | 1021 |
| | energy, ft-lb: | 384 | | 327 | | 287 |
| Rem. 124 Metal Case | velocity, fps: | 1110 | | 1030 | | 971 |
| | energy, ft-lb: | 339 | | 292 | | 259 |
| Rem. 147 JHP subsonic | velocity, fps: | 990 | | 941 | | 900 |
| | energy, ft-lb: | 320 | | 289 | | 264 |
| Rem. 147 BJHP | velocity, fps: | 990 | | 941 | | 900 |
| | energy, ft-lb: | 320 | | 289 | | 264 |
| Speer 90 Frangible | velocity, yards: | 1350 | | 1132 | | 1001 |
| | energy, ft-lb: | 364 | | 256 | | 200 |
| Speer 115 JHP Blazer | velocity, fps: | 1145 | | 1024 | | 943 |
| | energy, ft-lb: | 335 | | 268 | | 227 |
| Speer 115 FMJ Blazer | velocity, fps: | 1145 | | 1047 | | 971 |
| | energy, ft-lb: | 341 | | 280 | | 241 |
| Speer 115 FMJ | velocity, fps: | 1200 | | 1060 | | 970 |
| | energy, ft-lb: | 368 | | 287 | | 240 |
| Speer 115 Gold Dot HP | velocity, fps: | 1200 | | 1047 | | 971 |
| | energy, ft-lb: | 341 | | 280 | | 241 |
| Speer 124 FMJ Blazer | velocity, fps: | 1090 | | 989 | | 917 |
| | energy, ft-lb: | 327 | | 269 | | 231 |
| Speer 124 FMJ | velocity, fps: | 1090 | | 987 | | 913 |
| | energy, ft-lb: | 327 | | 268 | | 230 |
| Speer 124 TMJ-CF (and Blazer) | velocity, fps: | 1090 | | 989 | | 917 |
| | energy, ft-lb: | 327 | | 269 | | 231 |
| Speer 124 Gold Dot HP | velocity, fps: | 1150 | | 1030 | | 948 |
| | energy, ft-lb: | 367 | | 292 | | 247 |
| Speer 124 Gold Dot HP+P | velocity, ft-lb: | 1220 | | 1085 | | 996 |
| | energy, ft-lb: | 410 | | 324 | | 273 |

| cartridge bullet | range, yards: | 0 | 25 | 50 | 75 | 100 |
|---|---|---|---|---|---|---|
| Speer 147 TMJ Blazer | velocity, fps: | 950 | | 912 | | 879 |
| | energy, ft-lb: | 295 | | 272 | | 252 |
| Speer 147 TMJ | velocity, fps: | 985 | | 943 | | 906 |
| | energy, ft-lb: | 317 | | 290 | | 268 |
| Speer 147 TMJ-CF (and Blazer) | velocity, fps: | 985 | | 960 | | 924 |
| | energy, ft-lb: | 326 | | 300 | | 279 |
| Speer 147 Gold Dot | velocity, fps: | 985 | | 960 | | 924 |
| | energy, ft-lb: | 326 | | 300 | | 279 |
| Win. 105 Jacketed FP | velocity, fps: | 1200 | | 1074 | | 989 |
| | energy, ft-lb: | 336 | | 269 | | 228 |
| Win. 115 Silvertip HP | velocity, fps: | 1225 | | 1095 | | 1007 |
| | energy, ft-lb: | 383 | | 306 | | 259 |
| Win. 115 Jacketed HP | velocity, fps: | 1225 | | 1095 | | |
| | energy, ft-lb: | 383 | | 306 | | |
| Win. 115 FMJ | velocity, fps: | 1190 | | 1071 | | |
| | energy, ft-lb: | 362 | | 293 | | |
| Win. 115 EB WinClean | velocity, fps: | 1190 | | 1088 | | |
| | energy, ft-lb: | 362 | | 302 | | |
| Win. 124 FMJ | velocity, fps: | 1140 | | 1050 | | |
| | energy, ft-lb: | 358 | | 303 | | |
| Win. 124 EB WinClean | velocity, fps: | 1130 | | 1049 | | |
| | energy, ft-lb: | 352 | | 303 | | |
| Win. 147 FMJ FN | velocity, fps: | 990 | | 945 | | |
| | energy, ft-lb: | 320 | | 292 | | |
| Win. 147 SXT | velocity, fps: | 990 | | 947 | | 909 |
| | energy, ft-lb: | 320 | | 293 | | 270 |
| Win. 147 Silvertip HP | velocity, fps: | 1010 | | 962 | | 921 |
| | energy, ft-lb: | 333 | | 302 | | 277 |
| Win. 147 JHP | velocity, fps: | 990 | | 945 | | |
| | energy, ft-lb: | 320 | | 291 | | |
| Win. 147 EB WinClean | velocity, fps: | 990 | | 945 | | |
| | energy, ft-lb: | 320 | | 291 | | |

## 9 x 23 Winchester

| | range, yards: | 0 | 25 | 50 | 75 | 100 |
|---|---|---|---|---|---|---|
| Win. 124 Jacketed FP | velocity, fps: | 1460 | | 1308 | | |
| | energy, ft-lb: | 587 | | 471 | | |
| Win. 125 Silvertip HP | velocity, fps: | 1450 | | 1249 | | 1103 |
| | energy, ft-lb: | 583 | | 433 | | 338 |

## .38 S&W

| | range, yards: | 0 | 25 | 50 | 75 | 100 |
|---|---|---|---|---|---|---|
| Rem. 146 LRN | velocity, fps: | 685 | | 650 | | 620 |
| | energy, ft-lb: | 150 | | 135 | | 125 |
| Win. 145 LRN | velocity, fps: | 685 | | 650 | | 620 |
| | energy, ft-lb: | 150 | | 135 | | 125 |

## .38 Short Colt

| | range, yards: | 0 | 25 | 50 | 75 | 100 |
|---|---|---|---|---|---|---|
| Rem. 125 LRN | velocity, fps: | 730 | | 685 | | 645 |
| | energy, ft-lb: | 150 | | 130 | | 115 |

## .38 Long Colt

| | range, yards: | 0 | 25 | 50 | 75 | 100 |
|---|---|---|---|---|---|---|
| Black Hills 158 RNL | velocity, fps: | 650 | | | | |
| | energy, ft-lb: | | | | | |

## .380 Auto

| | range, yards: | 0 | 25 | 50 | 75 | 100 |
|---|---|---|---|---|---|---|
| Black Hills 90 JHP | velocity, fps: | 1000 | | | | |
| | energy, ft-lb: | 200 | | | | |
| Black Hills 95 FMJ | velocity, fps: | 950 | | | | |
| | energy, ft-lb: | 190 | | | | |
| Federal 90 Hi-Shok JHP | velocity, fps: | 1000 | 940 | 890 | 840 | 800 |
| | energy, ft-lb: | 200 | 175 | 160 | 140 | 130 |
| Federal 90 Hydra-Shok JHP | velocity, fps: | 1000 | 940 | 890 | 840 | 800 |
| | energy, ft-lb: | 200 | 175 | 160 | 140 | 130 |
| Federal 95 FMJ | velocity, fps: | 960 | 910 | 870 | 830 | 790 |
| | energy, ft-lb: | 190 | 175 | 160 | 145 | 130 |

BALLISTICS

| cartridge bullet | range, yards: | 0 | 25 | 50 | 75 | 100 |
|---|---|---|---|---|---|---|
| Hornady 90 JHP/XTP | velocity, fps: | 1000 | | 902 | | 823 |
| | energy, ft-lb: | 200 | | 163 | | 135 |
| Magtech 85 JHP + P | velocity, fps: | 1082 | | 999 | | 936 |
| | energy, ft-lb: | 221 | | 188 | | 166 |
| Magtech 95 FMC | velocity, fps: | 951 | | 861 | | 781 |
| | energy, ft-lb: | 190 | | 156 | | 128 |
| Magtech 95 JHP | velocity, fps: | 951 | | 861 | | 781 |
| | energy, ft-lb: | 190 | | 156 | | 128 |
| PMC 77 NT/FR | velocity, fps: | 1200 | 1095 | 1012 | 932 | 874 |
| | energy, ft-lb: | 223 | | | | |
| PMC 90 FMJ | velocity, fps: | 910 | 872 | 838 | 807 | 778 |
| | energy, ft-lb: | 165 | | | | |
| PMC 90 JHP | velocity, fps: | 917 | 878 | 844 | 812 | 782 |
| | energy, ft-lb: | 168 | | | | |
| PMC 95 SFHP | velocity, fps: | 925 | 884 | 847 | 813 | 783 |
| | energy, ft-lb: | 180 | | | | |
| Rem. 88 JHP | velocity, fps: | 990 | | 920 | | 868 |
| | energy, ft-lb: | 191 | | 165 | | 146 |
| Rem. 95 FNEB | velocity, fps: | 955 | | 865 | | 785 |
| | energy, ft-lb: | 190 | | 160 | | 130 |
| Rem. 95 Metal Case | velocity, fps: | 955 | | 865 | | 785 |
| | energy, ft-lb: | 190 | | 160 | | 130 |
| Rem. 102 BJHP | velocity, fps: | 940 | | 901 | | 866 |
| | energy, ft-lb: | 200 | | 184 | | 170 |
| Speer 88 JHP Blazer | velocity, fps: | 950 | | 920 | | 870 |
| | energy, ft-lb: | 195 | | 164 | | 148 |
| Speer 90 Gold Dot | velocity, fps: | 990 | | 907 | | 842 |
| | energy, ft-lb: | 196 | | 164 | | 142 |
| Speer 95 TMJ Blazer | velocity, fps: | 945 | | 865 | | 785 |
| | energy, ft-lb: | 190 | | 160 | | 130 |
| Speer 95 TMJ | velocity, fps: | 950 | | 877 | | 817 |
| | energy, ft-lb: | 180 | | 154 | | 133 |
| Win. 85 Silvertip HP | velocity, fps: | 1000 | | 921 | | 860 |
| | energy, ft-lb: | 189 | | 160 | | 140 |
| Win. 95 SXT | velocity, fps: | 955 | | 889 | | 835 |
| | energy, ft-lb: | 192 | | 167 | | 147 |
| Win. 95 FMJ | velocity, fps: | 955 | | 865 | | |
| | energy, ft-lb: | 190 | | 160 | | |
| Win. 95 EB WinClean | velocity, fps: | 955 | | 881 | | |
| | energy, ft-lb: | 192 | | 164 | | |

## .38 Special

| cartridge bullet | range, yards: | 0 | 25 | 50 | 75 | 100 |
|---|---|---|---|---|---|---|
| Black Hills 125 JHP +P | velocity, fps: | 1050 | | | | |
| | energy, ft-lb: | 306 | | | | |
| Black Hills 148 HBWC | velocity, fps: | 700 | | | | |
| | energy, ft-lb: | | | | | |
| Black Hills 158 SWC | velocity, fps: | 850 | | | | |
| | energy, ft-lb: | | | | | |
| Black Hills 158 CNL | velocity, fps: | 800 | | | | |
| | energy, ft-lb: | | | | | |
| Federal 110 Hydra-Shok JHP | velocity, fps: | 1000 | 970 | 930 | 910 | 880 |
| | energy, ft-lb: | 245 | 225 | 215 | 200 | 190 |
| Federal 110 Hi-Shok JHP +P | velocity, fps: | 1000 | 960 | 930 | 900 | 870 |
| | energy, ft-lb: | 240 | 225 | 210 | 195 | 185 |
| Federal 125 Nyclad HP | velocity, fps: | 830 | 780 | 730 | 690 | 650 |
| | energy, ft-lb: | 190 | 170 | 150 | 130 | 115 |
| Federal 125 Hi-Shok JSP +P | velocity, fps: | 950 | 920 | 900 | 880 | 860 |
| | energy, ft-lb: | 250 | 235 | 225 | 215 | 205 |
| Federal 125 Hi-Shok JHP +P | velocity, fps: | 950 | 920 | 900 | 880 | 860 |
| | energy, ft-lb: | 250 | 235 | 225 | 215 | 205 |
| Federal 125 Nyclad HP +P | velocity, fps: | 950 | 920 | 900 | 880 | 860 |
| | energy, ft-lb: | 250 | 235 | 225 | 215 | 205 |
| Federal 129 Hydra-Shok JHP+P | velocity, fps: | 950 | 930 | 910 | 890 | 870 |
| | energy, ft-lb: | 255 | 245 | 235 | 225 | 215 |

| cartridge bullet | range, yards: | 0 | 25 | 50 | 75 | 100 |
|---|---|---|---|---|---|---|
| Federal 130 FMJ | velocity, fps: | 950 | 920 | 890 | 870 | 840 |
| | energy, ft-lb: | 260 | 245 | 230 | 215 | 205 |
| Federal 148 LWC Match | velocity, fps: | 710 | 670 | 630 | 600 | 560 |
| | energy, ft-lb: | 165 | 150 | 130 | 115 | 105 |
| Federal 158 LRN | velocity, fps: | 760 | 740 | 720 | 710 | 690 |
| | energy, ft-lb: | 200 | 190 | 185 | 175 | 170 |
| Federal 158 LSWC | velocity, fps: | 760 | 740 | 720 | 710 | 690 |
| | energy, ft-lb: | 200 | 190 | 185 | 175 | 170 |
| Federal 158 Nyclad RN | velocity, fps: | 760 | 740 | 720 | 710 | 690 |
| | energy, ft-lb: | 200 | 190 | 185 | 175 | 170 |
| Federal 158 SWC HP +P | velocity, fps: | 890 | 870 | 860 | 840 | 820 |
| | energy, ft-lb: | 280 | 265 | 260 | 245 | 235 |
| Federal 158 LSWC +P | velocity, fps: | 890 | 870 | 860 | 840 | 820 |
| | energy, ft-lb: | 270 | 265 | 260 | 245 | 235 |
| Federal 158 Nyclad SWC-HP+P | velocity, fps: | 890 | 870 | 860 | 840 | 820 |
| | energy, ft-lb: | 270 | 265 | 260 | 245 | 235 |
| Hornady 125 JHP/XTP | velocity, fps: | 900 | | 856 | | 817 |
| | energy, ft-lb: | 225 | | 203 | | 185 |
| Hornady 140 JHP/XTP | velocity, fps: | 825 | | 790 | | 757 |
| | energy, ft-lb: | 212 | | 194 | | 178 |
| Hornady 140 Cowboy | velocity, fps: | 800 | | 767 | | 735 |
| | energy, ft-lb: | 199 | | 183 | | 168 |
| Hornady 148 HBWC | velocity, fps: | 800 | | 697 | | 610 |
| | energy, ft-lb: | 210 | | 160 | | 122 |
| Hornady 158 JHP/XPT | velocity, fps: | 800 | | 765 | | 731 |
| | energy, ft-lb: | 225 | | 205 | | 188 |
| Lapua 123 HP Megashock | velocity, fps: | 355 | | 311* | | 284* |
| | energy, ft-lb: | 504 | | 388* | | 322* |
| Lapua 148 LWC | velocity, fps: | 230 | | 203* | | 181* |
| | energy, ft-lb: | 254 | | 199* | | 157* |
| Lapua 150 SJFN | velocity, fps: | 325 | | 301* | | 283* |
| | energy, ft-lb: | 512 | | 439* | | 388* |
| Lapua 158 FMJLF | velocity, fps: | 255 | | 243* | | 232* |
| | energy, ft-lb: | 332 | | 301* | | 275* |
| Lapua 158 LRN | velocity, fps: | 255 | | 243* | | 232* |
| | energy, ft-lb: | 332 | | 301* | | 275* |
| Magtech 125 JHP +P | velocity, fps: | 1017 | | 971 | | 931 |
| | energy, ft-lb: | 287 | | 262 | | 241 |
| Magtech 148 LWC | velocity, fps: | 710 | | 634 | | 566 |
| | energy, ft-lb: | 166 | | 132 | | 105 |
| Magtech 158 LRN | velocity, fps: | 755 | | 728 | | 693 |
| | energy, ft-lb: | 200 | | 183 | | 168 |
| Magtech 158 LFN | velocity, fps: | 800 | | 776 | | 753 |
| | energy, ft-lb: | 225 | | 211 | | 199 |
| Magtech 158 SJHP | velocity, fps: | 807 | | 779 | | 753 |
| | energy, ft-lb: | 230 | | 213 | | 199 |
| Magtech 158 LSWC | velocity, fps: | 755 | | 721 | | 689 |
| | energy, ft-lb: | 200 | | 182 | | 167 |
| Magtech 158 FMC-Flat | velocity, fps: | 807 | | 779 | | 753 |
| | energy, ft-lb: | 230 | | 213 | | 199 |
| PMC 85 Non-Toxic Frangible | velocity, fps: | 1275 | 1181 | 1109 | 1052 | 1006 |
| | energy, ft-lb: | 307 | | | | |
| PMC 110 SFHP +P | velocity, fps: | velocity and energy figures not available | | | | |
| PMC 125 SFHP +P | velocity, fps: | 950 | 918 | 889 | 863 | 838 |
| | energy, ft-lb: | 251 | | | | |
| PMC 125 JHP +P | velocity, fps: | 974 | 938 | 906 | 878 | 851 |
| | energy, ft-lb: | 266 | | | | |
| PMC 132 FMJ | velocity, fps: | 841 | 820 | 799 | 780 | 761 |
| | energy, ft-lb: | 206 | | | | |
| PMC 148 LWC | velocity, fps: | 728 | 694 | 662 | 631 | 602 |
| | energy, ft-lb: | 175 | | | | |
| PMC 158 LRN | velocity, fps: | 820 | 801 | 783 | 765 | 749 |
| | energy, ft-lb: | 235 | | | | |

# Centerfire Handgun Ballistics

## .38 SPECIAL TO .357 MAGNUM

| cartridge bullet | range, yards: | 0 | 25 | 50 | 75 | 100 |
|---|---|---|---|---|---|---|
| PMC 158 JSP | velocity, fps: | 835 | 816 | 797 | 779 | 762 |
| | energy, ft-lb: | 245 | | | | |
| PMC 158 LFP | velocity, fps: | 800 | | 761 | | 725 |
| | energy, ft-lb: | 225 | | 203 | | 185 |
| Rem. 101 Lead Free Frangible | velocity, fps: | 950 | | 896 | | 850 |
| | energy, ft-lb: | 202 | | 180 | | 162 |
| Rem. 110 SJHP | velocity, fps: | 950 | | 890 | | 840 |
| | energy, ft-lb: | 220 | | 194 | | 172 |
| Rem. 110 SJHP +P | velocity, fps: | 995 | | 926 | | 871 |
| | energy, ft-lb: | 242 | | 210 | | 185 |
| Rem. 125 SJHP +P | velocity, ft-lb: | 945 | | 898 | | 858 |
| | energy, ft-lb: | 248 | | 224 | | 204 |
| Rem. 125 BJHP | velocity, fps: | 975 | | 929 | | 885 |
| | energy, ft-lb: | 264 | | 238 | | 218 |
| Rem. 125 FNEB | velocity, fps: | 850 | | 822 | | 796 |
| | energy, ft-lb: | 201 | | 188 | | 176 |
| Rem. 125 FNEB +P | velocity, fps: | 975 | | 935 | | 899 |
| | energy, ft-lb: | 264 | | 242 | | 224 |
| Rem. 130 Metal Case | velocity, fps: | 950 | | 913 | | 879 |
| | energy, ft-lb: | 261 | | 240 | | 223 |
| Rem. 148 LWC Match | velocity, fps: | 710 | | 634 | | 566 |
| | energy, ft-lb: | 166 | | 132 | | 105 |
| Rem. 158 LRN | velocity, fps: | 755 | | 723 | | 692 |
| | energy, ft-lb: | 200 | | 183 | | 168 |
| Rem. 158 SWC +P | velocity, fps: | 890 | | 855 | | 823 |
| | energy, ft-lb: | 278 | | 257 | | 238 |
| Rem. 158 SWC | velocity, fps: | 755 | | 723 | | 692 |
| | energy, ft-lb: | 200 | | 183 | | 168 |
| Rem. 158 LHP +P | velocity, fps: | 890 | | 855 | | 823 |
| | energy, ft-lb: | 278 | | 257 | | 238 |
| Speer 125 JHP +P Blazer | velocity, fps: | 945 | | 898 | | 858 |
| | energy, ft-lb: | 248 | | 224 | | 204 |
| Speer 125 Gold Dot +P | velocity, fps: | 945 | | 898 | | 858 |
| | energy, ft-lb: | 248 | | 224 | | 204 |
| Speer 158 TMJ +P (and Blazer) | velocity, fps: | 900 | | 852 | | 818 |
| | energy, ft-lb: | 278 | | 255 | | 235 |
| Speer 158 LRN Blazer | velocity, fps: | 755 | | 723 | | 692 |
| | energy, ft-lb: | 200 | | 183 | | 168 |
| Speer 158 Trail Blazer LFN | velocity, fps: | 800 | | 761 | | 725 |
| | energy, ft-lb: | 225 | | 203 | | 184 |
| Speer 158 TMJ-CF +P (and Blazer) | velocity, fps: | 900 | | 852 | | 818 |
| | energy, ft-lb: | 278 | | 255 | | 235 |
| Win. 110 Silvertip HP | velocity, fps: | 945 | | 894 | | 850 |
| | energy, ft-lb: | 218 | | 195 | | 176 |
| Win. 110 Jacketed FP | velocity, fps: | 975 | | 906 | | 849 |
| | energy, ft-lb: | 232 | | 201 | | 176 |
| Win. 125 Jacketed HP | velocity, fps: | 945 | | 898 | | |
| | energy, ft-lb: | 248 | | 224 | | |
| Win. 125 Jacketed HP +P | velocity, fps: | 945 | | 898 | | 858 |
| | energy, ft-lb: | 248 | | 224 | | 204 |
| Win. 125 Jacketed FP | velocity, fps: | 850 | | 804 | | |
| | energy, ft-lb: | 201 | | 179 | | |
| Win. 125 Silvertip HP + P | velocity, fps: | 945 | | 898 | | 858 |
| | energy, ft-lb: | 248 | | 224 | | 204 |
| Win. 125 JFP WinClean | velocity, fps: | 775 | | 742 | | |
| | energy, ft-lb: | 167 | | 153 | | |
| Win. 130 FMJ | velocity, fps: | 800 | | 765 | | |
| | energy, ft-lb: | 185 | | 169 | | |
| Win. 130 SXT +P | velocity, fps: | 925 | | 887 | | 852 |
| | energy, ft-lb: | 247 | | 227 | | 210 |
| Win. 148 LWC Super Match | velocity, fps: | 710 | | 634 | | 566 |
| | energy, ft-lb: | 166 | | 132 | | 105 |
| Win. 150 Lead | velocity, fps: | 845 | | 812 | | |
| | energy, ft-lb: | 238 | | 219 | | |

| cartridge bullet | range, yards: | 0 | 25 | 50 | 75 | 100 |
|---|---|---|---|---|---|---|
| Win. 158 Lead | velocity, fps: | 800 | | 761 | | 725 |
| | energy, ft-lb: | 225 | | 203 | | 185 |
| Win. 158 LRN | velocity, fps: | 755 | | 723 | | 693 |
| | energy, ft-lb: | 200 | | 183 | | 168 |
| Win. 158 LSWC | velocity, fps: | 755 | | 721 | | 689 |
| | energy, ft-lb: | 200 | | 182 | | 167 |
| Win. 158 LSWC HP +P | velocity, fps: | 890 | | 855 | | 823 |
| | energy, ft-lb: | 278 | | 257 | | 238 |

### .38-40

| | | | | | | |
|---|---|---|---|---|---|---|
| Black Hills 180 FPL | velocity, fps: | 800 | | | | |
| | energy, ft-lb: | | | | | |

### .38 Super

| cartridge bullet | range, yards: | 0 | 25 | 50 | 75 | 100 |
|---|---|---|---|---|---|---|
| Federal 130 FMJ +P | velocity, fps: | 1200 | 1140 | 1100 | 1050 | 1020 |
| | energy, ft-lb: | 415 | 380 | 350 | 320 | 300 |
| PMC 115 JHP | velocity, fps: | 1116 | 1052 | 1001 | 959 | 923 |
| | energy, ft-lb: | 318 | | | | |
| PMC 130 FMJ | velocity, fps: | 1092 | 1038 | 994 | 957 | 924 |
| | energy, ft-lb: | 348 | | | | |
| Rem. 130 Metal Case | velocity, fps: | 1215 | | 1099 | | 1017 |
| | energy, ft-lb: | 426 | | 348 | | 298 |
| Win. 125 Silvertip HP +P | velocity, fps: | 1240 | | 1130 | | 1050 |
| | energy, ft-lb: | 427 | | 354 | | 306 |
| Win. 130 FMJ +P | velocity, fps: | 1215 | | 1099 | | |
| | energy, ft-lb: | 426 | | 348 | | |

### .357 Sig

| cartridge bullet | range, yards: | 0 | 25 | 50 | 75 | 100 |
|---|---|---|---|---|---|---|
| Federal 125 FMJ | velocity, fps: | 1350 | 1270 | 1190 | 1130 | 1080 |
| | energy, ft-lb: | 510 | 445 | 395 | 355 | 325 |
| Federal 125 JHP | velocity, fps: | 1350 | 1270 | 1190 | 1130 | 1080 |
| | energy, ft-lb: | 510 | 445 | 395 | 355 | 325 |
| Federal 150 JHP | velocity, fps: | 1130 | 1080 | 1030 | 1000 | 970 |
| | energy, ft-lb: | 420 | 385 | 355 | 330 | 310 |
| Hornady 124 JHP/XTP | velocity, fps: | 1350 | | 1208 | | 1108 |
| | energy, ft-lb: | 502 | | 405 | | 338 |
| Hornady 147 JHP/XTP | velocity, fps: | 1225 | | 1138 | | 1072 |
| | energy, ft-lb: | 490 | | 422 | | 375 |
| PMC 85 Non-Toxic Frangible | velocity, fps: | 1480 | 1356 | 1245 | 1158 | 1092 |
| | energy, ft-lb: | 413 | | | | |
| PMC 124 SFHP | velocity, fps: | 1350 | 1263 | 1190 | 1132 | 1083 |
| | energy, ft-lb: | 502 | | | | |
| PMC 124 FMJ/FP | velocity, fps: | 1350 | 1242 | 1158 | 1093 | 1040 |
| | energy, ft-lb: | 512 | | | | |
| Rem. 104 Lead Free Frangible | velocity, fps: | 1400 | | 1223 | | 1094 |
| | energy, ft-lb: | 453 | | 345 | | 276 |
| Rem. 125 Metal Case | velocity, fps: | 1350 | | 1146 | | 1018 |
| | energy, ft-lb: | 506 | | 422 | | 359 |
| Rem. 125 JHP | velocity, fps: | 1350 | | 1157 | | 1032 |
| | energy, ft-lb: | 506 | | 372 | | 296 |
| Speer 125 TMJ (and Blazer) | velocity, fps: | 1350 | | 1177 | | 1057 |
| | energy, ft-lb: | 502 | | 381 | | 307 |
| Speer 125 TMJ-CF | velocity, fps: | 1350 | | 1177 | | 1057 |
| | energy, ft-lb: | 502 | | 381 | | 307 |
| Speer 125 Gold Dot | velocity, fps: | 1375 | | 1203 | | 1079 |
| | energy, ft-lb: | 525 | | 402 | | 323 |
| Win. 105 JFP | velocity, fps: | 1370 | | 1179 | | 1050 |
| | energy, ft-lb | 438 | | 324 | | 257 |
| Win. 125 FMJ FN | velocity, fps: | 1350 | | 1185 | | |
| | energy, ft-lb | 506 | | 390 | | |

### .357 Magnum

| | | | | | | |
|---|---|---|---|---|---|---|
| Black Hills 125 JHP | velocity, fps: | 1500 | | | | |
| | energy, ft-lb: | 625 | | | | |
| Black Hills 158 CNL | velocity, fps: | 800 | | | | |

BALLISTICS

### .357 Magnum

| cartridge bullet | range, yards: | 0 | 25 | 50 | 75 | 100 |
|---|---|---|---|---|---|---|
| Black Hills 158 SWC | velocity, fps: | 1050 | | | | |
| | energy, ft-lb: | | | | | |
| Black Hills 158 JHP | velocity, fps: | 1250 | | | | |
| | energy, ft-lb: | | | | | |
| Federal 110 Hi-Shok JHP | velocity, fps: | 1300 | 1180 | 1090 | 1040 | 990 |
| | energy, ft-lb: | 410 | 340 | 290 | 260 | 235 |
| Federal 125 Hi-Shok JHP | velocity, fps: | 1450 | 1350 | 1240 | 1160 | 1100 |
| | energy, ft-lb: | 580 | 495 | 430 | 370 | 335 |
| Federal 130 Hydra-Shok JHP | velocity, fps: | 1300 | 1210 | 1130 | 1070 | 1020 |
| | energy, ft-lb: | 490 | 420 | 370 | 330 | 300 |
| Federal 158 Hi-Shok JSP | velocity, fps: | 1240 | 1160 | 1100 | 1060 | 1020 |
| | energy, ft-lb: | 535 | 475 | 430 | 395 | 365 |
| Federal 158 JSP | velocity, fps: | 1240 | 1160 | 1100 | 1060 | 1020 |
| | energy, ft-lb: | 535 | 475 | 430 | 395 | 365 |
| Federal 158 LSWC | velocity, fps: | 1240 | 1160 | 1100 | 1060 | 1020 |
| | energy, ft-lb: | 535 | 475 | 430 | 395 | 365 |
| Federal 158 Hi-Shok JHP | velocity, fps: | 1240 | 1160 | 1100 | 1060 | 1020 |
| | energy, ft-lb: | 535 | 475 | 430 | 395 | 365 |
| Federal 158 Hydra-Shok JHP | velocity, fps: | 1240 | 1160 | 1100 | 1060 | 1020 |
| | energy, ft-lb: | 535 | 475 | 430 | 395 | 365 |
| Federal 180 Hi-Shok JHP | velocity, fps: | 1090 | 1030 | 980 | 930 | 890 |
| | energy, ft-lb: | 475 | 425 | 385 | 350 | 320 |
| Federal 180 Castcore | velocity, fps: | 1250 | 1200 | 1160 | 1120 | 1080 |
| | energy, ft-lb: | 625 | 575 | 535 | 495 | 465 |
| Hornady 125 JHP/XTP | velocity, fps: | 1500 | | 1314 | | 1166 |
| | energy, ft-lb: | 624 | | 479 | | 377 |
| Hornady 125 JFP/XTP | velocity, fps: | 1500 | | 1311 | | 1161 |
| | energy, ft-lb: | 624 | | 477 | | 374 |
| Hornady 140 Cowboy | velocity, fps: | 800 | | 767 | | 735 |
| | energy, ft-lb: | 199 | | 183 | | 168 |
| Hornady 140 JHP/XTP | velocity, fps: | 1400 | | 1249 | | 1130 |
| | energy, ft-lb: | 609 | | 485 | | 397 |
| Hornady 158 JHP/XTP | velocity, fps: | 1250 | | 1150 | | 1073 |
| | energy, ft-lb: | 548 | | 464 | | 404 |
| Hornady 158 JFP/XTP | velocity, fps: | 1250 | | 1147 | | 1068 |
| | energy, ft-lb: | 548 | | 461 | | 400 |
| Lapua 150 FMJ CEPP Super | velocity, fps: | 370 | | 527* | | 303* |
| | energy, ft-lb: | 664 | | 527* | | 445* |
| Lapua 150 SJFN | velocity, fps: | 385 | | 342* | | 313* |
| | energy, ft-lb: | 719 | | 569* | | 476* |
| Lapua 158 SJHP | velocity, fps: | 470 | | 408* | | 359* |
| | energy, ft-lb: | 1127 | | 850* | | 657* |
| Magtech 158 SJSP | velocity, fps: | 1235 | | 1104 | | 1015 |
| | energy, ft-lb: | 535 | | 428 | | 361 |
| Magtech 158 SJHP | velocity, fps: | 1235 | | 1104 | | 1015 |
| | energy, ft-lb: | 535 | | 428 | | 361 |
| PMC 85 Non-Toxic Frangible | velocity, fps: | 1325 | 1219 | 1139 | 1076 | 1025 |
| | energy, ft-lb: | 331 | | | | |
| PMC 125 JHP | velocity, fps: | 1194 | 1117 | 1057 | 1008 | 967 |
| | energy, ft-lb: | 399 | | | | |
| PMC 150 JHP | velocity, fps: | 1234 | 1156 | 1093 | 1042 | 1000 |
| | energy, ft-lb: | 512 | | | | |
| PMC 150 SFHP | velocity, fps: | 1205 | 1129 | 1069 | 1020 | 980 |
| | energy, ft-lb: | 484 | | | | |
| PMC 158 JSP | velocity, fps: | 1194 | 1122 | 1063 | 1016 | 977 |
| | energy, ft-lb: | 504 | | | | |
| PMC 158 LFP | velocity, fps: | 800 | | 761 | | 725 |
| | energy, ft-lb: | 225 | | 203 | | 185 |
| Rem. 110 SJHP | velocity, fps: | 1295 | | 1094 | | 975 |
| | energy, ft-lb: | 410 | | 292 | | 232 |
| Rem. 125 SJHP | velocity, fps: | 1450 | | 1240 | | 1090 |
| | energy, ft-lb: | 583 | | 427 | | 330 |
| Rem. 125 BJHP | velocity, fps: | 1220 | | 1095 | | 1009 |
| | energy, ft-lb: | 413 | | 333 | | 283 |
| Rem. 125 FNEB | velocity, fps: | 1450 | | 1240 | | 1090 |
| | energy, ft-lb: | 583 | | 427 | | 330 |
| Rem. 158 SJHP | velocity, fps: | 1235 | | 1104 | | 1015 |
| | energy, ft-lb: | 535 | | 428 | | 361 |
| Rem. 158 SP | velocity, fps: | 1235 | | 1104 | | 1015 |
| | energy, ft-lb: | 535 | | 428 | | 361 |
| Rem. 158 SWC | velocity, fps: | 1235 | | 1104 | | 1015 |
| | energy, ft-lb: | 535 | | 428 | | 361 |
| Rem. 165 JHP Core-Lokt | velocity, fps: | 1290 | | 1189 | | 1108 |
| | energy, ft-lb: | 610 | | 518 | | 450 |
| Rem. 180 SJHP | velocity, fps: | 1145 | | 1053 | | 985 |
| | energy, ft-lb: | 542 | | 443 | | 388 |
| Speer 125 Gold Dot | velocity, fps: | 1450 | | 1240 | | 1090 |
| | energy, ft-lb: | 583 | | 427 | | 330 |
| Speer 158 JHP Blazer | velocity, fps: | 1150 | | 1104 | | 1015 |
| | energy, ft-lb: | 535 | | 428 | | 361 |
| Speer 158 Gold Dot | velocity, fps: | 1235 | | 1104 | | 1015 |
| | energy, ft-lb: | 535 | | 428 | | 361 |
| Speer 170 Gold Dot SP | velocity, fps: | 1180 | | 1089 | | 1019 |
| | energy, ft-lb: | 525 | | 447 | | 392 |
| Win. 110 JFP | velocity, fps: | 1275 | | 1105 | | 998 |
| | energy, ft-lb: | 397 | | 298 | | 243 |
| Win. 110 JHP | velocity, fps: | 1295 | | 1095 | | |
| | energy, ft-lb: | 410 | | 292 | | |
| Win. 125 JFP WinClean | velocity, fps: | 1370 | | 1183 | | |
| | energy, ft-lb: | 521 | | 389 | | |
| Win. 145 Silvertip HP | velocity, fps: | 1290 | | 1155 | | 1060 |
| | energy, ft-lb: | 535 | | 428 | | 361 |
| Win. 158 JHP | velocity, fps: | 1235 | | 1104 | | 1015 |
| | energy, ft-lb: | 535 | | 428 | | 361 |
| Win. 158 JSP | velocity, fps: | 1235 | | 1104 | | 1015 |
| | energy, ft-lb: | 535 | | 428 | | 361 |
| Win. 180 Partition Gold | velocity, fps: | 1180 | | 1088 | | 1020 |
| | energy, ft-lb: | 557 | | 473 | | 416 |

### .40 S&W

| cartridge bullet | range, yards: | 0 | 25 | 50 | 75 | 100 |
|---|---|---|---|---|---|---|
| Black Hills 155 JHP | velocity, fps: | 1150 | | | | |
| | energy, ft-lb: | 450 | | | | |
| Black Hills 165 EXP JHP | velocity, fps: | 1150 (2005: 1100) | | | | |
| | energy, ft-lb: | 483 | | | | |
| Black Hills 180 JHP | velocity, fps: | 1000 | | | | |
| | energy, ft-lb: | 400 | | | | |
| Black Hills 180 JHP | velocity, fps: | 1000 | | | | |
| | energy, ft-lb: | 400 | | | | |
| Federal 135 Hydra-Shok JHP | velocity, fps: | 1190 | 1050 | 970 | 900 | 850 |
| | energy, ft-lb: | 420 | 330 | 280 | 245 | 215 |
| Federal 155 FMJ Ball | velocity, fps: | 1140 | 1080 | 1030 | 990 | 960 |
| | energy, ft-lb: | 445 | 400 | 365 | 335 | 315 |
| Federal 155 Hi-Shok JHP | velocity, fps: | 1140 | 1080 | 1030 | 990 | 950 |
| | energy, ft-lb: | 445 | 400 | 365 | 335 | 315 |
| Federal 155 Hydra-Shok JHP | velocity, fps: | 1140 | 1080 | 1030 | 990 | 950 |
| | energy, ft-lb: | 445 | 400 | 365 | 335 | 315 |
| Federal 165 EFMJ | velocity, fps: | 1190 | 1060 | 970 | 905 | 850 |
| | energy, ft-lb: | 520 | 410 | 345 | 300 | 265 |
| Federal 165 FMJ | velocity, fps: | 1050 | 1020 | 990 | 960 | 935 |
| | energy, ft-lb: | 405 | 380 | 355 | 335 | 320 |
| Federal 165 FMJ Ball | velocity, fps: | 980 | 950 | 920 | 900 | 880 |
| | energy, ft-lb: | 350 | 330 | 310 | 295 | 280 |
| Federal 165 Hydra-Shok JHP | velocity, fps: | 980 | 950 | 930 | 910 | 890 |
| | energy, ft-lb: | 350 | 330 | 315 | 300 | 290 |
| Federal 180 High Antim. Lead | velocity, fps: | 990 | 960 | 930 | 910 | 890 |
| | energy, ft-lb: | 390 | 365 | 345 | 330 | 315 |

# Centerfire Handgun Ballistics

## .40 S&W TO .41 REMINGTON MAGNUM

| cartridge bullet | range, yards: | 0 | 25 | 50 | 75 | 100 |
|---|---|---|---|---|---|---|
| Federal 180 TMJ TMF Primer | velocity, fps: | 990 | 960 | 940 | 910 | 890 |
| | energy, ft-lb: | 390 | 370 | 350 | 330 | 315 |
| Federal 180 FMJ Ball | velocity, fps: | 990 | 960 | 940 | 910 | 890 |
| | energy, ft-lb: | 390 | 370 | 350 | 330 | 315 |
| Federal 180 Hi-Shok JHP | velocity, fps: | 990 | 960 | 930 | 910 | 890 |
| | energy, ft-lb: | 390 | 365 | 345 | 330 | 315 |
| Federal 180 Hydra-Shok JHP | velocity, fps: | 990 | 960 | 930 | 910 | 890 |
| | energy, ft-lb: | 390 | 365 | 345 | 330 | 315 |
| Hornady 155 JHP/XTP | velocity, fps: | 1180 | | 1061 | | 980 |
| | energy, ft-lb: | 479 | | 387 | | 331 |
| Hornady 155 TAP-FPD | velocity, fps: | 1180 | | 1061 | | 980 |
| | energy, ft-lb: | 470 | | 387 | | 331 |
| Hornady 180 JHP/XTP | velocity, fps: | 950 | | 903 | | 862 |
| | energy, ft-lb: | 361 | | 326 | | 297 |
| Hornady 180 TAP-FPD | velocity, fps: | 950 | | 903 | | 862 |
| | energy, ft-lb: | 361 | | 326 | | 297 |
| Magtech 155 JHP | velocity, fps: | 1025 | | 1118 | | 1052 |
| | energy, ft-lb: | 500 | | 430 | | 381 |
| Magtech 180 JHP | velocity, fps: | 990 | | 933 | | 886 |
| | energy, ft-lb: | 390 | | 348 | | 314 |
| Magtech 180 FMC | velocity, fps: | 990 | | 933 | | 886 |
| | energy, ft-lb: | 390 | | 348 | | 314 |
| PMC 115 Non-Toxic Frangible | velocity, fps: | 1350 | 1240 | 1154 | 1088 | 1035 |
| | energy, ft-lb: | 465 | | | | |
| PMC 155 SFHP | velocity, fps: | 1160 | 1092 | 1039 | 994 | 957 |
| | energy, ft-lb: | 463 | | | | |
| PMC 165 JHP | velocity, fps: | 1040 | 1002 | 970 | 941 | 915 |
| | energy, ft-lb: | 396 | | | | |
| PMC 165 FMJ | velocity, fps: | 1010 | 977 | 948 | 922 | 899 |
| | energy, ft-lb: | 374 | | | | |
| PMC 180 FMJ/FP | velocity, fps: | 985 | 957 | 931 | 908 | 885 |
| | energy, ft-lb: | 388 | | | | |
| PMC 180 SFHP | velocity, fps: | 985 | 958 | 933 | 910 | 889 |
| | energy, ft-lb: | 388 | | | | |
| Rem. 141 Lead Free Frangible | velocity, fps: | 1135 | | 1056 | | 996 |
| | energy, ft-lb: | 403 | | 349 | | 311 |
| Rem. 155 JHP | velocity, fps: | 1205 | | 1095 | | 1017 |
| | energy, ft-lb: | 499 | | 413 | | 356 |
| Rem. 165 BJHP | velocity, fps: | 1150 | | 1040 | | 964 |
| | energy, ft-lb: | 485 | | 396 | | 340 |
| Rem. 180 JHP | velocity, fps: | 1015 | | 960 | | 914 |
| | energy, ft-lb: | 412 | | 368 | | 334 |
| Rem. 180 FN Enclosed Base | velocity, fps: | 985 | | 936 | | 893 |
| | energy, ft-lb: | 388 | | 350 | | 319 |
| Rem. 180 Metal Case | velocity, fps: | 985 | | 936 | | 893 |
| | energy, ft-lb: | 388 | | 350 | | 319 |
| Rem. 180 BJHP | velocity, fps: | 1015 | | 960 | | 914 |
| | energy, ft-lb: | 412 | | 368 | | 334 |
| Speer 105 Frangible | velocity, fps: | 1380 | | 1128 | | 985 |
| | energy, ft-lb: | 444 | | 297 | | 226 |
| Speer 155 TMJ Blazer | velocity, fps: | 1175 | | 1047 | | 963 |
| | energy, ft-lb: | 475 | | 377 | | 319 |
| Speer 155 TMJ | velocity, fps: | 1200 | | 1065 | | 976 |
| | energy, ft-lb: | 496 | | 390 | | 328 |
| Speer 155 Gold Dot | velocity, fps: | 1200 | | 1063 | | 974 |
| | energy, ft-lb: | 496 | | 389 | | 326 |
| Speer 165 TMJ Blazer | velocity, fps: | 1100 | | 1006 | | 938 |
| | energy, ft-lb: | 443 | | 371 | | 321 |
| Speer 165 TMJ | velocity, fps: | 1150 | | 1040 | | 964 |
| | energy, ft-lb: | 484 | | 396 | | 340 |
| Speer 165 Gold Dot | velocity, fps: | 1150 | | 1043 | | 966 |
| | energy, ft-lb: | 485 | | 399 | | 342 |
| Speer 180 HP Blazer | velocity, fps: | 985 | | 951 | | 909 |
| | energy, ft-lb: | 400 | | 361 | | 330 |

| cartridge bullet | range, yards: | 0 | 25 | 50 | 75 | 100 |
|---|---|---|---|---|---|---|
| Speer 180 FMJ Blazer | velocity, fps: | 1000 | | 937 | | 886 |
| | energy, ft-lb: | 400 | | 351 | | 313 |
| Speer 180 FMJ | velocity, fps: | 1000 | | 951 | | 909 |
| | energy, ft-lb: | 400 | | 361 | | 330 |
| Speer 180 TMJ-CF (and Blazer) | velocity, fps: | 1000 | | 951 | | 909 |
| | energy, ft-lb: | 400 | | 361 | | 330 |
| Speer 180 Gold Dot | velocity, fps: | 1025 | | 957 | | 902 |
| | energy, ft-lb: | 420 | | 366 | | 325 |
| Win. 140 JFP | velocity, fps: | 1155 | | 1039 | | 960 |
| | energy, ft-lb: | 415 | | 336 | | 286 |
| Win. 155 Silvertip HP | velocity, fps: | 1205 | | 1096 | | 1018 |
| | energy, ft-lb | 500 | | 414 | | 357 |
| Win. 165 SXT | velocity, fps: | 1130 | | 1041 | | 977 |
| | energy, ft-lb: | 468 | | 397 | | 349 |
| Win. 165 FMJ FN | velocity, fps: | 1060 | | 1001 | | |
| | energy, ft-lb: | 412 | | 367 | | |
| Win. 165 EB WinClean | velocity, fps: | 1130 | | 1054 | | |
| | energy, ft-lb: | 468 | | 407 | | |
| Win. 180 JHP | velocity, fps: | 1010 | | 954 | | |
| | energy, ft-lb: | 408 | | 364 | | |
| Win. 180 FMJ | velocity, fps: | 990 | | 936 | | |
| | energy, ft-lb: | 390 | | 350 | | |
| Win. 180 SXT | velocity, fps: | 1010 | | 954 | | 909 |
| | energy, ft-lb: | 408 | | 364 | | 330 |
| Win. 180 EB WinClean | velocity, fps: | 990 | | 943 | | |
| | energy, ft-lb: | 392 | | 356 | | |

## 10 mm Auto

| cartridge bullet | range, yards: | 0 | 25 | 50 | 75 | 100 |
|---|---|---|---|---|---|---|
| Federal 155 Hi-Shok JHP | velocity, fps: | 1330 | 1230 | 1140 | 1080 | 1030 |
| | energy, ft-lb: | 605 | 515 | 450 | 400 | 360 |
| Federal 180 Hi-Shok JHP | velocity, fps: | 1030 | 1000 | 970 | 950 | 920 |
| | energy, ft-lb: | 425 | 400 | 375 | 355 | 340 |
| Federal 180 Hydra-Shok JHP | velocity, fps: | 1030 | 1000 | 970 | 950 | 920 |
| | energy, ft-lb: | 425 | 400 | 375 | 355 | 340 |
| Federal 180 High Antim. Lead | velocity, fps: | 1030 | 1000 | 970 | 950 | 920 |
| | energy, ft-lb: | 425 | 400 | 375 | 355 | 340 |
| Federal 180 FMJ | velocity, fps: | 1060 | 1025 | 990 | 965 | 940 |
| | energy, ft-lb: | 400 | 370 | 350 | 330 | 310 |
| Hornady 155 JHP/XTP | velocity, fps: | 1265 | | 1119 | | 1020 |
| | energy, ft-lb: | 551 | | 431 | | 358 |
| Hornady 180 JHP/XTP | velocity, fps: | 1180 | | 1077 | | 1004 |
| | energy, ft-lb: | 556 | | 464 | | 403 |
| Hornady 200 JHP/XTP | velocity, fps: | 1050 | | 994 | | 948 |
| | energy, ft-lb: | 490 | | 439 | | 399 |
| PMC 115 Non-Toxic Frangible | velocity, fps: | 1350 | 1240 | 1154 | 1088 | 1035 |
| | energy, ft-lb: | 465 | | | | |
| PMC 170 JHP | velocity, fps: | 1200 | 1117 | 1052 | 1000 | 958 |
| | energy, ft-lb: | 543 | | | | |
| PMC 180 SFHP | velocity, fps: | 950 | 926 | 903 | 882 | 862 |
| | energy, ft-lb: | 361 | | | | |
| PMC 200 TC-FMJ | velocity, fps: | 1050 | 1008 | 972 | 941 | 912 |
| | energy, ft-lb: | 490 | | | | |
| Rem. 180 Metal Case | velocity, fps: | 1150 | | 1063 | | 998 |
| | energy, ft-lb: | 529 | | 452 | | 398 |
| Speer 200 TMJ Blazer | velocity, fps: | 1050 | | 966 | | 952 |
| | energy, ft-lb: | 490 | | 440 | | 402 |
| Win. 175 Silvertip HP | velocity, fps: | 1290 | | 1141 | | 1037 |
| | energy, ft-lb: | 649 | | 506 | | 418 |

## .41 Remington Magnum

| cartridge bullet | range, yards: | 0 | 25 | 50 | 75 | 100 |
|---|---|---|---|---|---|---|
| Federal 210 Hi-Shok JHP | velocity, fps: | 1300 | 1210 | 1130 | 1070 | 1030 |
| | energy, ft-lb: | 790 | 680 | 595 | 540 | 495 |
| PMC 210 TCSP | velocity, fps: | 1290 | 1201 | 1128 | 1069 | 1021 |
| | energy, ft-lb: | 774 | | | | |

BALLISTICS

# Directory of Manufacturers & Suppliers

**Lazzeroni**
Tuscon, AZ
www.lazzeroni.com

**Leatherwood/Hi-Lux Optics**
Torrance, CA
www.hi-luxoptics.com
www.leatherwoodoptics.com

**Legacy Sports International**
Reno, NV
www.legacysports.com

**Les Baer**
LeClaire, IA
www.lesbaer.com

**Leupold**
Beaverton, OR
www.leupold.com

**Ljutic LLC**
Yakima, Washington
www.Ljuticgun.com

**Lone Star Rifle Co.**
Conroe, TX
wwww.lonestarrifle.com

**LUCID**
www.mylucidgear.com

**Lyman Products**
Middletown , CT
www.lymanproducts.com

**M.O.A. Corporation**
Sundance, WY
www.moaguns.com/moa_max.html

**Magnum Research**
Pillager, MN
www.magnumresearch.com

**Magtech**
Lino Lakes, MN
www.magtechammunition.com

**Marlin**
Madison, NC
www.marlinfirearms.com

**Marocchi Arms**
Sarezzo, Italy
www.marocchiarms.com

**McMillian**
Phoenix, AZ
www.mcmfamily.com

**MDM Muzzleloaders**
Maidstone, VT
www.mdm-muzzleloaders.com

**Minox**
Germany
www.minox.com

**MEC Reloading**
Mayville, Wisconsin
www.mecreloaders.com

**Merkel**
Trussville, AL
www.merkel-usa.com

**Millet Sights**
Overland Park, KS
www.millettsights.com

**Mossberg**
North Haven, CT
www.mossberg.com

**MTM Molded Products Co.**
Dayton, Ohio
www.mtmcase-gard.com

**Navy Arms**
Martinsburg, WV
www.navyarms.com

**New England Firearms**
Green Bay, WI
www.nefguns.com

**New Ultra Light Arms**
Granville , WV
www.newultralight.com

**Nightforce Optics, Inc.**
Orofino, ID
www.nightforceoptics.com

**Nighthawk Custom**
Berryville, Arkansas
www.nighthawkcustom.com

**Nikon Sport Optics**
Melville, NY
www.nikonsportoptics.com

**Norma**
Amotfors, Sweden
www.norma.cc

**North American Arms**
Provo, UT
www.naaminis.com

**Nosler**
Bend, OR
www.nosler.com

**Olympic Arms**
Olympia, WA
www.olyarms.com

**P.M.C. Ammunition**
Conroe, TX
www.pmcammo.com

**Para Ordinance/Para USA**
Pineville, NC
www.paraord.com

**Pentax Imaging Co.**
Shelton, CT
www.pentaxsportoptics.com

**Perazzi**
Azusa, CA
www.perazzi.it

**Puma**
Reno, NV
www.legacysports.com

**Purdey**
London, England
www.purdey.com

**Ramshot Powders**
Miles City, MT
www.ramshot.com/powders

**RCBS**
Oroville, CA
www.rcbs.com

**Redding Reloading Equipment**
Cortland, NY
www.redding-reloading.com

**Remington Arms**
Madison, NC
www.remington.com

**Renato Gamba**
Italy
www.renatogamba.it

**Rifles, Inc.**
Pleasanton, TX
www.riflesinc.com

**Rock River Arms**
Colona, IL
www.rockriverarms.com

**Rossi**
Miami, FL
www.Roussiusa.com

**Rogue River Rifle Works**
Paso Robles, CA
Phone: (805) 227-4706

**Ruger**
Newport, NH
www.ruger.com

**RWS**
Draper, UT
www.rws-munition.de/en

**Sako**
Riihimaki, Finland
www.sako.fi.com

**Savage Arms**
Westfield, MA
www.Savagearms.com

**Schmidt & Bender**
Claremont, NH
www.schmidtbender.com

**Shiloh**
Big Timber, MT
www.shilohrifle.com

**Sierra Bullets**
Sedalia, MO
www.sierrabullets.com

**Sig Sauer**
Exeter, NH
www.sigsauer.com

**Simmons Optics**
Overland Park, KS
www.simmonsoptics.com

**SKB Shotguns**
Omaha, NE
www.skbshotguns.com

**Smith & Wesson**
Springfield, MA
www.smith-wesson.com

**Speer Bullets**
Lewiston, ID
www.speer-bullets.com

**Springfield Armory**
Geneso, IL
www.springfield-armory.com

**Stag Arms**
New Britain, CT
www.stagarms.com

**Steiner Division**
Greeley, CO
www.steiner-binoculars.com

**Steyr Arms**
Trussville, AL
www.steyrarms.com

**STI International, Inc.**
Georgetown, TX
www.stiguns.com

**Stoeger Industries**
Pocomoke, MD
www.stoegerindustries.com

**Swarovski Optik**
Cranston, RI
www.swarovskioptik.us

**Swift Bullets**
Quinter, KS
www.swiftbullets.com

**Swiss Arms**
Exeter, NH
www.sigsauer.com

**Szecsei & Fuchs**
Windsor, Ontario, Canada
www.fuchs-fine-guns.com or
www.szceseidoubleboltrepeater.ca

**Tactical Rifles**
Zephyrhills, FL
www.tacticalrifles.net

**Taurus**
Miami, FL
www.taurususa.com

**Taylor's & Co.**
Winchester , VA
www.taylorsfirearms.com

**Thompson/Center**
Rochester, NH
www.tcarms.com

**Traditions Firearms**
Old Saybrook, CT
www.traditionsfirearms.com

**Trijicon**
Wixom, Michigan
www.trijicon.com

**Tristar Sporting Arms**
North Kansas City, MO
www.tristarsportingarms.com

**Uberti**
Pocomoke, MD
www.uberti.com

**VihtaVuori**
Bensenville, IL
www.vihtavuori-lapua.com

**Walther**
Springfield, MA
www.smith-wesson.com

**Weatherby**
Paso Robles, CA
www.weatherby.com

**Weaver Optics**
Onalaska, WI
www.weaveroptics.com

**Western Powders, Inc.**
Miles City, MT
www.accuratepowder.com

**Wild West Guns**
Anchorage, AK
www.wildwestguns.com

**Wildey Guns**
Warren, CT
www.wildeyguns.com

**Wilson Combat**
Berryville, AR
www.wilsoncombat.com

**Winchester Repeating Arms & Ammunition**
East Alton, IL
www.winchester.com

**Woodleigh Bullets**
Australia
www.woodleighbullets.com.au

# Gunfinder Index

# Gunfinder Index

# Gunfinder Index